MW01154502

"John Feinberg has written a splendid work that brilliantly expounds and winsomely defends a classical evangelical doctrine of Scripture. Readers will discover an engaging and comprehensive exploration of topics such as revelation, inspiration, inerrancy, authority, and canonicity, among others. This thoughtful and clearly written volume will certainly be welcomed by students, scholars, pastors, and church leaders alike. It is a genuine joy and privilege to recommend this most recent addition to the outstanding Foundations of Evangelical Theology series."

**David S. Dockery,** President, Trinity International University

"Building on a lifetime of scholarship, John Feinberg provides us with a superb exploration of the 'perfections' of Scripture for a new generation. This is a wise, well-informed, and very important summary of the normative source of faith and practice. What a gift!"

**Michael Horton,** J. Gresham Machen Professor of Systematic Theology and Apologetics, Westminster Seminary California

"In 1978, a young theologian, John Feinberg, signed the Chicago Statement on Biblical Inerrancy, a watershed document for contemporary evangelicalism. Forty years later, as a veteran scholar, he makes another significant contribution to the evangelical doctrine of Scripture, extending his treatment beyond its inerrancy to include inspiration, authority, canonicity, clarity, power, sufficiency, preservation, and intersection with the work of the Holy Spirit. *Light in a Dark Place* is a must-read for scholars, pastors, believers, and skeptics alike!"

**Gregg Allison,** Professor of Christian Theology, The Southern Baptist Theological Seminary; Elder, Sojourn Community Church; author, *Sojourners and Strangers*; *Roman Catholic Theology and Practice*; and *Historical Theology*

"The doctrine of Scripture serves as the foundational doctrine of Christian theology. Apart from God's triune self-disclosure in Scripture, which results in a fully authoritative and reliable Word, everything we say about God, ourselves, and the world is ultimately left unwarranted. For this reason, every generation needs a robust and faithful exposition and defense of Scripture as God's Word written in light of current challenges and debates. From a seasoned theologian who leaves no stone unturned, *Light in a Dark Place* wonderfully meets this need. In this volume, John Feinberg discusses the most significant points of the doctrine of Scripture and tackles some of the toughest issues the doctrine faces today with precision and care. This book will serve as a superb resource for today's church, and it demands a careful reading and embrace of its faithful elucidation of Scripture as God's most holy Word. I highly commend this work."

**Stephen Wellum,** Professor, The Southern Baptist Theological Seminary

# LIGHT IN A DARK PLACE

# LIGHT IN A DARK PLACE

THE DOCTRINE OF SCRIPTURE

# JOHN S. FEINBERG

CROSSWAY®

WHEATON, ILLINOIS

Light in a Dark Place: The Doctrine of Scripture

Copyright © 2018 by John S. Feinberg

Published by Crossway
        1300 Crescent Street
        Wheaton, Illinois 60187

First printing 2018

Printed in the United States of America

Unless otherwise indicated, Scripture quotations are from The New American Standard Bible®. Copyright © The Lockman Foundation 1960, 1962, 1963, 1968, 1971, 1972, 1973, 1975, 1977. Used by permission.

Scripture quotations marked ESV are from the ESV® Bible (The Holy Bible, English Standard Version®), copyright © 2001 by Crossway, a publishing ministry of Good News Publishers. Used by permission. All rights reserved.

Scripture references marked NIV 1984 are taken from The Holy Bible, New International Version®, NIV®. Copyright © 1973, 1978, 1984 by Biblica, Inc.™ Used by permission. All rights reserved worldwide.

Scripture quotations marked KJV are from the King James Version of the Bible.

Scripture quotations marked AT are the author's translation.

All emphases in Scripture quotations have been added by the author.

Hardcover ISBN: 978-1-4335-3927-5
ePub ISBN: 978-1-4335-3930-5
PDF ISBN: 978-1-4335-3928-2
Mobipocket ISBN: 978-1-4335-3929-9

---

**Library of Congress Cataloging-in-Publication Data**

Names: Feinberg, John S., 1946- author.
Title: Light in a dark place : the doctrine of scripture / John S. Feinberg.
Description: Wheaton : Crossway, 2018. | Series: Foundations of evangelical theology series | Includes
    bibliographical references and index.
Identifiers: LCCN 2017038729 (print) | LCCN 2018000857 (ebook) | ISBN 9781433539282 (pdf) | ISBN
    9781433539299 (mobi) | ISBN 9781433539305 (epub) | ISBN 9781433539275 (hc)
Subjects: LCSH: Bible—Evidences, authority, etc. | Reformed Church—Doctrines.
Classification: LCC BS480 (ebook) | LCC BS480 .F45 2018 (print) | DDC 220.1—dc23
LC record available at https://lccn.loc.gov/2017038729

---

Crossway is a publishing ministry of Good News Publishers.

| SH | | 27 | 26 | 25 | 24 | 23 | 22 | 21 | 20 | 19 | 18 |
|----|----|----|----|----|----|----|----|----|----|----|----|
| 15 | 14 | 13 | 12 | 11 | 10 | 9 | 8 | 7 | 6 | 5 | 4 | 3 | 2 | 1 |

*To*
*Colleagues, Past and Present,*
*in the*
*Department of Biblical and Systematic Theology*
*At Trinity Evangelical Divinity School,*
*This Volume Is Dedicated*
*with Undying Love, Respect,*
*and Appreciation*

# CONTENTS

## PART FOUR:
## THE USEFULNESS OF SCRIPTURE

## CONCLUSION

# TABLES

Why another series of works on evangelical systematic theology? This is an especially appropriate question in light of the fact that evangelicals are fully committed to an inspired and inerrant Bible as their final authority for faith and practice. But since neither God nor the Bible change, why is there a need to redo evangelical systematic theology?

Systematic theology is not divine revelation. Theologizing of any sort is a human conceptual enterprise. Thinking that it is equal to biblical revelation misunderstands the nature of both Scripture and theology! Insofar as our theology contains propositions that accurately reflect Scripture or match the world and are consistent with the Bible (in cases where the propositions do not come per se from Scripture), our theology is biblically based and correct. But even if all the propositions of a systematic theology are true, that theology would still not be equivalent to biblical revelation! It is still a human conceptualization of God and his relation to the world.

Although this may disturb some who see theology as nothing more than doing careful exegesis over a series of passages, and others who see it as nothing more than biblical theology, those methods of doing theology do not somehow produce a theology that is equivalent to biblical revelation either. Exegesis is a human conceptual enterprise, and so is biblical theology. All the theological disciplines involve human intellectual participation. But human intellect is finite, and hence there is always room for revision of systematic theology as knowledge increases. Though God and his word do not change, human understanding of his revelation can grow, and our theologies should be reworked to reflect those advances in understanding.

Another reason for evangelicals to rework their theology is the nature of systematic theology as opposed to other theological disciplines. For example, whereas the task of biblical theology is more to describe biblical teaching on whatever topics Scripture addresses, systematics should make a special point to relate its conclusions to the issues of one's day. This does not mean that the systematician ignores the topics biblical writers address. Nor does it mean that theologians should warp Scripture to address issues it never intended to address. Rather it suggests that in addition to expounding what biblical writers teach, the theologian should attempt to take those biblical teachings (along with the biblical mind-set) and apply them to issues that are especially confronting the church in the theologian's own day. For example, 150 years ago, an evangelical theologian doing work on the doctrine of man would likely have discussed issues such as the creation of man and the constituent parts of man's being. Such a theology might even have included a discussion about human institutions such as marriage, noting in general the respective roles of husbands and wives in marriage. However, it is dubious that there would have been any lengthy discussion with various viewpoints about the respective roles of men and women in marriage, in society, and in the church. But at our point in history and in light of the feminist movement and the issues it has raised even among many conservative Christians, it would be foolish to write a theology of man (or, should we say, a "theology of humanity") without a thorough discussion of the issue of the roles of men and women in society, the home, and the church.

Because systematic theology attempts to address itself not only to the timeless issues presented in Scripture but also to the current issues of one's day and culture, each theology will to some extent need to be redone in each generation. Biblical truth does not change from generation to generation, but the issues that confront the church do. A theology that was adequate for a different era and different culture may simply not speak to key issues in a given culture at a given time. Hence, in this series we are reworking evangelical systematic theology, though we do so with the understanding that in future generations there will be room for a revision of theology again.

How, then, do the contributors to this series understand the nature of systematic theology? Systematic theology as done from an evangelical Christian perspective involves study of the person, works, and relationships of God. As evangelicals committed to the full inspiration, inerrancy, and final authority of Scripture, we demand that whatever appears in a systematic theology correspond to the way things are and must not contradict any claim taught in Scripture. Holy Writ is the touchstone of our theology, but we do not limit the source material for systematics to Scripture alone. Hence, whatever information from history, science, philosophy, and the like is relevant to our understanding of God and his relation to our world is fair game for systematics. Depending on the specific interests and expertise of the contributors to this series, their respective volumes will reflect interaction with one or more of these disciplines.

What is the rationale for appealing to other sources than Scripture and other disciplines than the biblical ones? Since God created the universe, there is revelation of God not only in Scripture but in the created order as well. There are many disciplines that study our world, just as does theology. But since the world studied by the nontheological disciplines is the world created by God, any data and conclusions in the so-called secular disciplines that accurately reflect the real world are also relevant to our understanding of the God who made that world. Hence, in a general sense, since all of creation is God's work, nothing is outside the realm of theology. The so-called secular disciplines need to be thought of in a theological context, because they are reflecting on the universe God created, just as is the theologian. And, of course, there are many claims in the nontheological disciplines that are generally accepted as true (although this does not mean that every claim in nontheological disciplines is true, or that we are in a position with respect to every proposition to know whether it is true or false). Since this is so, and since all disciplines are in one way or another reflecting on our universe, a universe made by God, any true statement in any discipline should in some way be informative for our understanding of God and his relation to our world. Hence, we have felt it appropriate to incorporate data from outside the Bible in our theological formulations.

As to the specific design of this series, our intention is to address all areas of evangelical theology with a special emphasis on key issues in each area. While other series may be more like a history of doctrine, this series purposes to incorporate insights from Scripture, historical theology, philosophy, etc., in order to produce an up-to-date work in systematic theology. Though all contributors to the series are thoroughly evangelical in their theology, embracing the historical orthodox doctrines of the church, the series as a whole is not meant to be slanted in the direction of one form of evangelical theology. Nonetheless, most of the writers come from a Reformed perspective. Alternate evangelical and nonevangelical options, however, are discussed.

As to style and intended audience, this series is meant to rest on the very best of scholarship while at the same time being understandable to the beginner in theology as well as to the academic theologian. With that in mind, contributors are writing in a clear style, taking care to define whatever technical terms they use.

Finally, we believe that systematic theology is not just for the understanding. It must apply to life, and it must be lived. As Paul wrote to Timothy, God has given divine revelation for many purposes, including ones that necessitate doing theology, but the ultimate reason for giving revelation and for theologians doing theology is that the people of God may be fitted for every good work (2 Tim. 3:16–17). In light of the need for theology to connect to life, each of the contributors not only formulates doctrines but also explains how those doctrines practically apply to everyday living.

It is our sincerest hope that the work we have done in this series will first glorify and please God, and, secondly, instruct and edify the people of God. May God be pleased to use this series to those ends, and may he richly bless you as you read the fruits of our labors.

*John S. Feinberg*
*General Editor*

Scripture is both the hallmark and foundation of evangelical theology. This is so because evangelicals believe that it is the word of God. Since the subject matter of theology is God's person, works, and relationships, any theologian needs to consult sources as he or she prepares to write a theology. For evangelical theologians, the primary and governing source is Scripture. This is so because it presents God's views on the subject matter of theology. As omniscient, God knows more about any and every subject than does anyone else, and since the subject matter of theology is God himself, of course he knows more about that topic than anyone.

It would be, therefore, wise for any theologian to take Scripture seriously, if he or she wants to know what to say about the various doctrines of systematic theology. Such is at least part of the rationale for Scripture being so foundational to evangelical theology. Of course, this mind-set also means that evangelical theologians turn to Scripture as their governing source, because they actually believe that it is what God himself has said about the topics it covers. And if it is, then it must tell us the truth about whatever it addresses. Of course, as the word of the supreme ruler in the universe and as true, it also possesses supreme authority over all of life.

What, then, does Scripture tell us about its own nature? Suppose, for example, Scripture says that it offers some general religious ideas, words expressing how much various writers have loved and appreciated God, a few *suggestions* about human behavior, and some history about God's interaction with various people (because such stories are interesting, even if they teach us nothing about what God expects of us). That kind of Bible might offer stimulating reading, but it wouldn't help us in addressing life's most pressing and significant issues.

On the other hand, suppose Scripture tells us that it is God's inerrant word and that it has supreme and binding authority on all people. Yes, it offers descriptions of God's character and actions, and explains how humans can establish a saving relationship with God, and tells us what sort of behavior is acceptable in God's eyes, but none of this is simply information that we can merely be aware of intellectually and then push aside as we go on with our lives on our own terms. It has binding authority on every human. We can reject it, ignore it, or obey only the parts of it that we like, but nonetheless, we are accountable to what it teaches, and will be judged by what we have done with what it commands.

In the previous two paragraphs I have described two very different views of what Scripture is and of how we should relate to it. Which description fits what Scripture actually says about itself? That is the subject of the doctrine of Scripture and therefore of this book. As we shall see, the second vision of Scripture's nature is the one it affirms. But, then, it should be clear as to why evangelicals take Scripture so seriously, and why it must be the basis of evangelical systematic theology. If evangelicals are right in their assessment of Scripture's nature, then of course it must be the primary source material and final authority on what anyone should believe about any and every area of systematic theology. Hence, the volumes in this theology series are unapologetically grounded in Scripture and take as their main task the articulation of what Scripture teaches about the particular doctrinal locus under consideration.

Clearly, the doctrine of Scripture is a most important subject. A book on this doctrine certainly needs to "get it right" about what we should believe about this book. Given the importance of the task at hand and the need to reflect accurately what Scripture teaches about itself, lest we misrepresent God and what he has said about this book, it would be easy to pass on the chance to write a volume on Scripture. But I welcome the challenge, in part because it is such an important topic, and so basic to anything else one might do in systematic theology. And, I embrace this task, because I love Scripture, and I know from firsthand experience how powerful and transforming this book can be in individual lives. I am hoping that as you read the chapters of this book and come to see better what a treasure Scripture is and also understand everything God has done to give it to us, your love and appreciation to God will also grow, and that you will commit, or recommit, yourself to reading and obeying what Scripture teaches and requires!

A book of this nature and length does not, of course, get written with little thought and effort. And it certainly cannot be done without the help of many people. Some people have been especially significant in helping me to produce this volume. First, I must thank Crossway for its support of the whole Foundations of Evangelical Theology Series and of my doing this volume on Scripture. We began this series many years ago. A lesser publisher would have "pulled the plug" on the series long ago, assuming that they would have ever agreed to contract it in the first place—I have doubts about whether any other publisher would have done so. As to this volume on Scripture, Crossway has been enthusiastic, patient, and encouraging to me all along the way as I have worked on it! And a special word of thanks is due to Bill Deckard, the very best academic editor I've ever known and worked with! His knowledge of grammar, proper style, and everything else that goes along with academic books is unmatched. And his care in attending to everything—big issues or small—gives authors like me the assurance that what we want to say will be presented as accurately and clearly as possible.

Next, I want to thank the administration and board of Trinity Evangelical Divinity School for granting me sabbaticals and leaves of absence to work on this volume. In fact, the whole book was produced during a series of sabbaticals approved by Trinity, so this volume is indeed a result of Trinity's generous sabbatical policy, and I am extremely grateful for Trinity's generous support and encouragement.

Then, a very special word of appreciation goes to my friend and colleague Graham A. Cole. He read and commented on an earlier version of the whole book, and those comments have been extremely helpful in bringing the book into its present form. This volume is definitely better because of his interaction and advice! Errors that still remain are, of course, mine and not his.

I am also extremely grateful to many graduate student assistants who helped me tremendously in gathering articles and books that I needed to read. Without their efforts, it would have taken much longer to complete this work. Most of them were doctoral students in systematic theology at Trinity Evangelical Divinity School, and they are already doing significant work in the discipline of systematic theology. They have great potential as teachers and scholars, and I find that very encouraging!

Then, I have a special appreciation and thanks for colleagues, past and present, in the Department of Biblical and Systematic Theology at Trinity. All of them are fully devoted to Scripture as God's inspired and inerrant word, and they are most able defenders of an evangelical understanding of Scripture. Having them as friends, colleagues, and dialogue partners has always been extremely helpful to me and my work. And, their interest and many first-rate publications on the doctrine of Scripture are not only instructive about the doctrine, but have also inspired me as I have worked on this volume. As every academic knows, whom you have to talk with about what you are thinking and writing makes a huge difference in what you can produce. Being in this environment for more than three decades has made a huge contribution to me in every way. So it is only fitting and proper that I dedicate this volume to all of my department colleagues, past and present, at Trinity!

As you read this volume, may your appreciation of God grow, and may you be strongly encouraged not only to study Scripture more earnestly and consistently, but also to obey what it teaches! And may your heart be warmed and your life guided by Scripture so that you become the prosperous/happy/blessed person described in Psalm 1! That is possible if your life is firmly rooted and grounded in Scripture, a light in a dark place!

John S. Feinberg
August 2017

| | |
|---|---|
| ANF | *Ante-Nicene Fathers* |
| BSac | *Bibliotheca Sacra* |
| BBR | *Bulletin for Biblical Research* |
| CSR | *Christian Scholar's Review* |
| CTJ | *Calvin Theological Journal* |
| CTQ | *Concordia Theological Quarterly* |
| EvQ | *Evangelical Quarterly* |
| EBC | *The Expositor's Bible Commentary* |
| GTJ | *Grace Theological Journal* |
| ICC | International Critical Commentary |
| JSNTSup | Journal for the Study of the New Testament Supplement Series |
| JSOTSup | Journal for the Study of the Old Testament Supplement Series |
| JETS | *Journal of the Evangelical Theological Society* |
| JTI | *Journal of Theological Interpretation* |
| LCC | Library of Christian Classics |
| MAJT | *Mid-America Journal of Theology* |
| MSJ | *Master's Seminary Journal* |
| NPNF[2] | *Nicene and Post-Nicene Fathers*, Series 2 |
| RelS | *Religious Studies* |
| RevExp | *Review and Expositor* |
| ThTo | *Theology Today* |
| TJ | *Trinity Journal* |
| WTJ | *Westminster Theological Journal* |

# INTRODUCTION

Life without light is unthinkable, impossible! "God is light, and in Him there is no darkness at all" (1 John 1:5). And God "lives in unapproachable light, whom no one has seen or can see" (1 Tim. 6:16 NIV 1984). So to try to live without God and to embrace moral and spiritual blindness instead would be as foolish as if someone with perfect natural vision deliberately blinded himself, choosing instead to live the rest of his natural life in absolute darkness.

Of course, some people through no fault of their own are physically blind. We admire their courage and tenacity as they struggle each day to handle this infirmity and try to live anything like a normal life. It is hard to believe, however, that anyone who can see would choose a life of blindness, or that any blind person wouldn't gladly choose to see, if merely willing it could make it so.

As debilitating as natural blindness is, spiritual blindness is even worse. For it seeks to defeat us during our natural life on earth, and ruin our eternity. Darkness challenges every aspect of our existence.

God, of course, fully knows this; we would expect nothing else. Moreover, our beneficent creator knows exactly what we need in each area of life, and he has provided it. In particular, God gave three special expressions of light to meet life's most pressing needs.

The first is *creation light*. In Genesis 1, we read that "in the beginning God created the heavens and the earth" (v. 1). But the earth as initially created was formless and void, and darkness was everywhere (v. 2). So what did God do next? Divide the land from the water? Create any of the creatures that would inhabit this new world? No, God first spoke physical light into existence (v. 3). On the fourth day of creation, he created the sun, moon and stars, and "placed them in the expanse of the heavens to give light on the earth" (v. 17). God knew that no natural life could exist without these lights, and so he created them.

God later created the first man and woman to live in the paradise he had made. As created, they were morally and spiritually right with God, for they had never sinned. But sadly, they bowed to temptation and chose to disobey the one rule God gave them, plunging themselves and the whole human race into moral and spiritual darkness (Gen. 3:6; Rom. 5:12ff.).

This was and is a problem no mere human can possibly solve. But without a solution the race would be condemned to live forever apart from fellowship with its creator. That would lead only to endless suffering and separation from the blessing and presence of the God who desperately wants a loving relation with us.

Again, God had the solution. The human race needed another infusion of divine light! This time it was *redemption light*. God sent his Son Jesus to pay the penalty that sin had incurred, so that fellowship between God and humans could be reestablished. Jesus said, "I am the light of the world; he who follows Me shall not walk in the darkness, but shall have the light of life" (John 8:12). The darkness of which Jesus spoke is moral and spiritual darkness. Those who have followed Christ by faith can well attest that he is the light of their lives, both now and for eternity.

There is a third form of divine light, *revelation light*, given again to meet humans' needs. In his second epistle, the apostle Peter wrote about it. Peter wrote this letter toward the end of his life, and he wanted to remind his readers of things he had told them many times before. He began chapter 1 with a reminder that God has given believers everything they need for life and godliness, and he has promised great blessing to those who follow him (2 Pet. 1:3–4). In light of that, they should reject the moral corruption of this world and make every effort to develop Christian virtues. If they do, they will make their "calling and election sure," and they will be warmly welcomed into Jesus Christ's "everlasting kingdom" (vv. 5–11 KJV).

Undoubtedly, Peter had encouraged his readers to godly living on many other occasions, but it was right for him to refresh their memories, especially because he knew that before long his mortal life on earth would end and he would go to be with the Lord (vv. 12–14). In verses 16–21 Peter rehearsed for his readers one more time the basis of the hope that he and they had for eternal life and blessing. He knew that salvation with all of its blessings is a marvelously wonderful hope for followers of Christ. But Peter also knew that some things sound much better than they actually are. So, how did Peter know that the gospel and its blessings were true? Perhaps all of that is just a "cleverly devised" story to make people feel secure (v. 16), but has no basis in fact. In the rest of chapter 1, Peter explained why the blessings of which he wrote are not just wishful thinking. They aren't because there are two guarantees that the gospel is absolutely true.

Peter and the other apostles proclaimed many amazing things about Jesus. How could they be sure that what they said about him was true? Peter says that he knew that Jesus is all he claimed to be, first, because of the experience that he, James, and John had at the Mount of Transfiguration (vv. 16–18). During most of Jesus's earthly life, there was little outward, physical evidence that he was the glorious and all-powerful Lord of glory. But Peter, James, and John caught a glimpse of his true majesty when they saw him transfigured, and heard the voice from heaven saying, "This is My beloved Son, with whom I am well-pleased" (Matt. 17:5).

We often say that seeing is believing. Peter says, in effect, "I was there, and I saw and heard, and I believed." Clearly, this event was irrefutable proof for Peter that Jesus was everything he ever claimed to be (2 Pet. 1:17). But Peter knew that only three mere humans witnessed the Mount of Transfiguration event. Peter, James, and John were convinced, and many of their followers believed because they knew these men to be honest and reliable witnesses. But how could others be sure, especially those living at other times and places than in first-century-AD Israel?

In verses 19–21 Peter adds a second reason that anyone can be sure that Jesus is everything he claimed to be. In fact, Peter says that this second evidence is even more certain than his eyewitness testimony (v. 19). That is truly remarkable, for we usually think that there is no better proof of a claim than tangible, empirical evidence, especially eyewitness testimony. What could be stronger proof than that?

Peter's answer? Scripture! Why? Because Scripture, though penned by mere humans, was inspired by God, who supervised the writers and their writing at every step along the way (vv. 20–21). Peter had no doubts about what he saw and heard as he followed Jesus, but he knew that even eyewitness testimony can sometimes be mistaken. Peter and the other apostles weren't wrong about what they saw and heard Jesus do and say. But even so, Peter says that Scripture is even more certainly true than their eyewitness testimony! Whatever Scripture says is unassailably true, and hence, totally reliable—something all can stake their very life on!

Because Scripture is even more certainly true than the most reliable eyewitness testimony, Peter advised his readers (v. 19), "you will do well to pay attention" to it, "as to a light shining in a dark place, until the day dawns and the morning star arises in your hearts." There you have it—the third form of light God gave to guide and protect humans as we live in this world of moral and spiritual darkness: Scripture is a light in a dark place.

From the earliest days of my life, through my childhood and adolescence, and throughout my adult life, Scripture has been the foundation of my life. My parents taught my siblings and me that no one is more important than God, and so if God says anything, we must give it our undivided attention, and obey it. Like others, my life has been blessed with many "light places," but there have been "dark places" as well. What has always remained the same, regardless of circumstance, is the light that Scripture casts upon my way.

And so, I have always loved Scripture, especially as I grew and studied it more. In my preaching and teaching ministries, Scripture has always been and continues to be the foundation and content of whatever I say. In addition, as a teacher of theology, I have the extremely great privilege of teaching others about Scripture.

Scripture is a ray of divine light in a dark place, but we can and should say much more about it. How did Scripture ever come into existence? Why is it so important that we learn and live its content? Can Scripture be trusted in what it says, regardless of the topic?

All of these questions and more demarcate the issues that must be addressed in a book on the doctrine of Scripture. I write unapologetically from a firmly embraced evangelical stance. That means, in part, that as a theologian, I assume that apologists and philosophers of religion have made the case that Scripture is trustworthy in whatever it says about any topic. Given that belief, what does Scripture teach about itself? That is the subject of this volume. I contend that Scripture claims to be the inspired, inerrant, and powerful revealed word of God. Moreover, Scripture also affirms that its basic message of how to establish and grow a positive relationship with God is understandable, and that the Holy Spirit stands ever ready to move and enable each person to apply Scripture's teachings to his or her life so as to grow in the grace and knowledge of our Lord and Savior Jesus Christ. I believe all of these things about Scripture, and more, because, as I shall show in this book, they are what Scripture teaches about itself. I also know it to be true from personal experience, and from seeing Scripture's transforming power in the lives of people who obey it.

Evangelicals are people of the book—the Bible. The hallmark of evangelical theology is its contention that Scripture is God's inspired and inerrant word. Given that belief, evangelical theology strives to be consistent with whatever Scripture claims. And there is very good reason for this understanding of and approach to theology. Systematic theology covers the person, works, and relationships of God. Of course, a crucial question then becomes, what is theology's source material? Nonevangelical theology typically is based on tradition, human reason, and/or some current worldview or philosophy. Scripture may also be a source, but it isn't the touchstone of nonevangelical thinking. If Scripture disagrees with the prevailing philosophy and mind-set of the nonevangelical thinker, Scripture is adjusted to match the theologian's vision of reality and God's place in it.

Evangelical theology is different. While it may use as source material data from various disciplines of study, its primary and governing source is Scripture. Moreover, scriptural teaching, properly interpreted, is the touchstone for anything that goes into an evangelical theology. If the data one proposes to include in theology disagree with Scripture, the data must be either rejected or revised to fit the vision of reality that Scripture presents.

Why does evangelical theology take this approach? The answer is rather simple. The subject matter of theology is God and his relationships with all creation. Who would know the most about what should go into a conceptual scheme that aims to articulate an accurate picture of God? No one knows as much as God does! So, then, if God tells us something about himself, his deeds, his relationships, and anything else he cares to communicate, that information should be the most complete and accurate information available, and hence, it should be the foundation of our theology.

Where can one find such information? That's where Scripture enters the picture. Though Scripture is not the only place God has revealed himself, it is a marvelously thorough, accurate, and clear deposit of the things God most wants us to know about himself, ourselves, and our relation to him. Evangelicals believe that Scripture is God's word, and since no one knows more than God, we would do well to base our thinking on God's word, the Bible. This is why Scripture must be the foundation of evangelical theology, provide its main contents, and be the touchstone against which any and every theological claim is judged.

And so, in this volume I intend to present the various concepts involved in the doctrine of Scripture. I have divided my presentation into four parts. The first deals with how Scripture first came into existence. That is, it covers the creation of Scripture. The concepts of revelation and inspiration explain how Scripture came into existence. The second section treats various attributes or characteristics that are true of Scripture. The discussion will focus on the inerrancy and authority of God's word.

Of course, a discussion of Scripture invariably addresses how it was decided which books would be part of Scripture. Thus, the third portion of our study investigates the boundaries of Scripture. The issue in view is, of course, canonicity. The key question is, what criteria were used to decide which books should be part of the Bible and which should not be?

The final section of this book covers the usefulness of Scripture. In this section I shall discuss various reasons why Scripture can accomplish so many things in people's lives. Some chapters in this section will focus on qualities of Scripture, so they could easily be placed in the second section of the book. But I have placed chapters such as the ones on Scripture's clarity, power, and sufficiency in this fourth section because all of these attributes of Scripture are so crucial to understanding and applying Scripture in individual lives. Of course, without the ministry of the Holy Spirit, Scripture is a "dead letter" to its recipients. Thus, this portion of the book also includes a chapter on the Holy Spirit's illumination of the minds and hearts of Scripture's readers to Scripture's message.

Clearly, in the doctrine of Scripture much more is at stake than merely "filling in" the details of this doctrinal locus in an overall system of theology. What is at stake is what one thinks Scripture to be, how one understands the person of God, and whether one is required to live as Scripture prescribes. If Scripture is merely a compendium of religiously pious thoughts of religiously sensitive people and nothing more, then we may find it inspirational and instructive, but we shouldn't feel any urgency to live in accord with its teachings. But if Scripture is, as evangelicals and their theology have affirmed throughout history, the very word of our almighty, omniscient, and all-loving God, then the only sane choice is to let it enlighten our thinking and our actions each and every day.

As you read this book, I hope you will be thrilled and overwhelmed with appreciation to God for everything he has done to give us Scripture! Just as the giving of his word over so many years to so many writers in a variety of circumstances is truly remarkable, so is God's preservation of his word, despite attempts to silence and even eradicate it altogether! Because God has done that, Scripture can be light in the various dark (and light) places of our lives. May God grant that as you read, you will be thankful that God has not left us to wander and stumble through life without knowing the way to him, and may you be even more determined than before to follow the precepts for the God-pleasing life that Peter exhorted his readers to pursue. Christianity and the Christian way of life are not some cleverly constructed myths and legends. They are truth and they give abundant life and eternal life, because they follow God's light, Scripture!

I

CREATING SCRIPTURE

# TWO

# LIGHT UNVEILED

## The Doctrine of Revelation

Before there was Scripture there was divine revelation. And without divine revelation there could be no Scripture. These are two of the most fundamental tenets in the evangelical doctrine of Scripture. As for God, in 1 Timothy 6:16, Paul wrote that he lives in "unapproachable [*aprositon*] light." His truth provides both light and life for all of humanity.

Physical light warms and it also uncovers things hidden in our way. If we attend to it, light can keep us from stumbling and falling over obstacles in our path. On the other hand, darkness is a problem. The blind must find their way in life by some means other than following where their vision leads them. Of course, those who can see and who yet live in darkness can misstep, stumble, and fall just as a blind person or someone blinded by too much light. Life's challenges are easier to handle in the light of day, unless there is so much light that it blinds us.

While this is true of our physical sight, it also applies to our moral and spiritual perception. Scripture contrasts those who live according to God's will and plan with those who choose to go their own way and ignore or disobey the light of God's truth. The apostle John contrasts these two groups as people of light and people of darkness (1 John 2:8–11).[1] Clearly, the light and darkness that John speaks of are moral, for he says that whether or not one loves his brother determines whether he walks in darkness or in light. In his Gospel, John also says that Jesus is the light who shone in the darkness; sadly, the darkness neither understood nor embraced him (John 1:4–5). Jesus emphatically

---

[1] Even more vividly, in 1 John 3:8–10, these two groups of people are distinguished as children of God and children of the Devil.

proclaimed that he is the light of the world and that whoever follows him will have the light of life (John 8:12).

People need both physical and spiritual light in order to survive, and both come from God. The same God who spoke physical light into existence is also the source and giver of spiritual light for our souls. The transmitting of that light is what theologians call *revelation*. The doctrine of revelation is not only foundational to the doctrine of Scripture, but to all of theology. Of course, logically speaking, the existence of God is more fundamental, for if there is no God, there would be nothing else. But humans would know nothing about God's character, acts, and relationships if he had remained completely silent. Humans might speculate about God and his demands, but theology would be nothing but speculation. So, the questions of whether God has given revelation, and of how, when, and in what form(s) are of utmost import. At stake is not just whether academic theologians will have grist for their theological mills. Of far greater import is whether God exists, what he is like, and what he expects of us. If God exists but has remained silent, or if he has spoken but his revelation is mere gibberish, the human race would be hopelessly lost in moral and spiritual darkness.

Putting aside the question of whether the members of the Trinity have been revealing themselves to each other for all eternity, we can say that the first act of divine revelation manifested "outside" the Godhead was creation. If nothing else, God unveiled the fact that he can make something out of nothing. Creation also makes it possible for God's human creatures to discover that God exists and has certain attributes (see Psalm 19 and Rom. 1:19–20). Of course, until God created angels and humans there were no creatures who could receive and understand the truth God had uncovered about himself by creating.

Genesis 1–3 shows that, after God created Adam and Eve, there were occasions when he spoke to them. Why, before Adam and Eve fell into sin and were blinded to truth (spiritual and otherwise), did they need revelation? Revelation was necessary because, even before the fall, Adam and Eve were finite intellectually, morally, and spiritually. Their finitude was not sinful, but because of it there were many things about their world and themselves that they did not know. And, there must have been gaps in their knowledge about the God who had created them, especially about what he expected of them. How could it make sense for a creature accountable to its creator to remain ignorant of that creator? And, why would a God who fashioned a creature whom he could love and with whom he could have fellowship remain aloof and silent? It makes abundant sense that God and humans would seek each other out to establish and grow a relationship. As that relationship would grow, surely God would uncover and divulge more about who he is and who they are.

Once Adam and Eve (and the human race through them) broke God's law and stood condemned before him, they understood that they deserved punishment, but they did not know how to solve their precarious situation. A loving and merciful God knew the answer. To give them that answer required that, in the words of the writer of Hebrews, God would speak in many ways to the human race (Heb. 1:1). And so God began to unveil himself and his truth to a lost and dying race of sinners.

## DEFINING DIVINE REVELATION

Though the doctrine of revelation is foundational to all of theology, unfortunately it is a concept that is somewhat ambiguous as used in Christian parlance and in evangelical theology. Let me illustrate this point.

### Searching for a Clear Definition

The ambiguity of this concept surfaces when one looks for a clear and concise definition of what evangelicals mean by revelation. Consider the following definitions from various evangelical theologians.

W. G. T. Shedd writes that "revelation in its general and wide signification is any species of knowledge of which God is the ultimate source and cause."[2] Millard Erickson states that because of human finitude, the only way to know God is for God to reveal himself to us. He adds that "by this we mean God's manifestation of himself to man in such a way that man can know and fellowship with him."[3] Interestingly, in a second edition of his *Christian Theology*, Erickson more tersely wrote, "Because humans are finite and God is infinite, if they are to know God it must come about by God's manifestation of himself."[4] Louis Berkhof writes that "when we speak of revelation, we use the term in the strict sense of the word. It is not something in which God is passive, a mere 'becoming manifest,' but something in which He is actively making Himself known. It is not, as many moderns would have it, a deepened spiritual insight which leads to an ever-increasing discovery of God on the part of man; but a supernatural act of self-communication, a purposeful act on the part of the Living God."[5] And, Lewis S. Chafer affirms that in its theological sense, revelation refers to "the divine act of communicating to man what otherwise man would not know."[6]

While each definition has something to commend it, each is also somewhat ambiguous, reflecting the ambiguity of the concept itself. Shedd says that

[2] W. G. T. Shedd, *Dogmatic Theology*, vol. 1 (1888; repr., Grand Rapids, MI: Zondervan, 1969), 62.
[3] Millard Erickson, *Christian Theology*, 3 vols. (Grand Rapids, MI: Baker, 1983), 1:153.
[4] Millard Erickson, *Christian Theology*, 2nd ed. (Grand Rapids, MI: Baker, 1998), 178.
[5] Louis Berkhof, *Systematic Theology*, 4th ed. (Grand Rapids, MI: Eerdmans, 1968), 34.
[6] Lewis S. Chafer, *Systematic Theology*, vol. 1 (1947; repr., Dallas: Dallas Seminary Press, 1974), 48. For a similar definition see Henry C. Thiessen, *Introductory Lectures in Systematic Theology* (1949; repr., Grand Rapids, MI: Eerdmans, 1974), 31.

revelation is any kind of knowledge of which God is the ultimate source. But since God created everything *ex nihilo*, he must, then, be the ultimate source of the fact that I am now looking at my computer monitor, that $2 + 2 = 4$, and that yesterday I went to the health club for a workout. Certainly, such information is not what theologians mean when they speak of divine revelation.

Erickson's two versions of a definition say that revelation is God's *manifestation* of himself to us. The earlier version says that God does this in such a way that we can know and fellowship with him. But what does it mean for anyone, God included, to manifest himself or herself to others? Is this done in actions, speech, dreams, etc.? And how can a God who is pure Spirit do any of these things? As pure Spirit, he is immaterial, and thus doesn't have a voice box and so apparently can't speak in ways humans can hear with their physical ears.[7] Moreover, both versions of Erickson's definition make it difficult to see how there can be any revelation of God in nature. In what sense does the natural world "manifest" God, and if it somehow does, how does it do so in a way that allows humans to have fellowship with him? Theologians of various stripes have denied that natural revelation presents a way to establish a saving relationship with God, so how can that kind of revelation manifest God clearly enough for us to both know and have fellowship with him?

Berkhof's definition seems a bit more specific, but it too is ambiguous. Berkhof calls revelation God's actively making himself known by a supernatural act of self-communication. But what is the content of revelation, according to this definition? Is it God himself, God's actions in history, information about God, or what? And how does a God without a material voice box and mouth communicate, if "communication" here refers to speech? We should also add that Berkhof's definition is one that Søren Kierkegaard, Karl Barth, and others of their ilk could heartily endorse. Barth especially might be pleased, for one way of reading this definition seems to rule out any kind of natural revelation, a point that Barth emphatically made to Emil Brunner in Barth's *Nein!* Berkhof actually does believe in natural revelation, but his definition of revelation gives reason to wonder.[8]

What about Chafer's definition? Here the problem is that it seems too restrictive. It covers only things that we would otherwise not know. This definition fits such biblical information as revelation of end-time events in advance of their occurrence, information about heaven and hell, and biblical narratives about people like Jonah, Job, Rahab, the centurion at Christ's cross, and Ananias and Sapphira, to name a few. But outside of Scripture and natural

---

[7] This must not be misunderstood. Passages like Genesis 3:9ff. show that God can communicate with us, despite lacking a voice box. In addition, a passage like Exodus 4:11 shows that God can manifest his presence in physical ways and speak so as to be heard by physical human ears.

[8] Berkhof, *Systematic Theology*, 36–37ff.

revelation it is possible to collect some, even if meager, information about the history of Israel and her kings, about some general events in Christ's life, and about Paul's various missionary trips to evangelize the lost and start churches. Since there is some information about these matters that is neither in Scripture nor in nature, does Chafer's definition mean that when we read of such things in Scripture, those portions can't be revelation since there are other ways than divine revelation for us to know about them? Surely, Chafer would reject such a notion, but even so, his definition is ambiguous enough to allow that interpretation of various portions of Scripture.

Perhaps readers may think I'm just being too picayune, but that would miss my point. All of the theologians cited are wonderful men of God and outstanding theologians who understand the concept of revelation. I am not critiquing their theologies. My point is that the concept of revelation is difficult to define. Even when one thinks it is precisely defined, one soon sees that the definition needs to be qualified further either to avoid the ambiguities explained above, or to accommodate something else that is true of revelation.

*Uses of the Term "Revelation"*

A second indication of the ambiguity surrounding the notion of revelation is the many ways it is used both in common parlance and in Scripture itself. Consider the following:

1. "Then the glory of the LORD will be revealed, and all flesh will see it together; for the mouth of the LORD has spoken." (Isa. 40:5)
2. "As I've been praying and reading God's word, the Lord has been revealing that he wants me to become a missionary in a foreign country."
3. "Blessed are you, Simon Barjona, because flesh and blood did not reveal this to you, but My Father who is in heaven." (Matt. 16:17)
4. "Let us therefore, as many as are perfect, have this attitude; and if in anything you have a different attitude, God will reveal that also to you." (Phil. 3:15)
5. "God has shown me through my relationship with Jesus that Jesus is more than just a great moral teacher; he is also God."
6. "The heavens are telling of the glory of God; and their expanse is declaring the work of His hands. Day to day pours forth speech, and night to night reveals knowledge." (Ps. 19:1–2)
7. The man who murdered his two children explained, "Just like God told Abraham to sacrifice Isaac, he told me to take my children's lives, and that's why I did it. You always have to obey whatever God tells you to do."
8. "And I saw an angel standing in the sun; and he cried out with a loud voice, saying to all the birds which fly in mid-heaven, 'Come, assemble for the great supper of God. . . .'" (Rev. 19:17)
9. "First Peter 3:18–22 is very hard to understand, but after asking God for wisdom, I looked again, and God answered my prayer; I finally got it."

10. "Boasting is necessary, though it is not profitable; but I will go on to visions and revelations of the Lord. I know a man in Christ who fourteen years ago—was caught up into Paradise, and heard inexpressible words, which a man is not permitted to speak." (2 Cor. 12:1–4)

Even short reflection on the sentences above shows them to be a mixture of many things. If asked to define the concept of divine revelation based on these ten examples, it is hard to see how we could do it. And yet, the list contains Scriptures and samples of conversations that many readers have heard or engaged in themselves. Surely, not all of the ten sentences teach the biblical concept of divine revelation. Or do they?

Let us briefly consider each of the ten sentences. Isaiah 40:5 speaks of God's glory being revealed and all flesh seeing it. What sort of thing is glory and how might it be revealed? And to guarantee that this will happen, the verse ends by saying that the mouth of the Lord has spoken. But God as incorporeal doesn't have a mouth, and anyway, is divine speech revelation? If it is, how can it be *in this instance*, since the verse speaks of doing something (revealing God's glory) that is hard to understand? What does this verse teach that helps us articulate a precise definition of the concept?

How about sentence 2? Christians often make this claim, especially when they want to announce that they have made a decision. But is the sort of thing mentioned in sentence 2 an instance of the theological concept of divine revelation? If it is, it is dubious that it should be included in Scripture. So, then, does it qualify at all as revelation?

Sentence 3 is Jesus's declaration after Peter affirms that Jesus is the Messiah, the Son of God. Jesus says that God revealed this truth to Peter. Most evangelical theologians would say this is an example of divine revelation, but if asked to explain how it differs from "revelation" in sentences 2, 6, and 10, there is no easy answer.

Sentence 4 is a Scripture verse that speaks of God directly revealing something to individuals. Perhaps God might reveal someone's disagreeable attitude through a comment made by another believer, but not necessarily. But when God shows someone that he has an attitude that needs changing, is that revelation? One might respond that it must be because sentence 4 is a Scripture verse and all of Scripture is divine revelation. Indeed, Philippians 3:15 is divine revelation, but that doesn't mean that what it talks about qualifies in itself as revelation. Nor does it certify that whenever God shows someone that he or she has a disagreeable attitude, that qualifies as divine revelation.

Sentence 5 speaks of a great doctrinal truth of the Christian faith. Without Scripture teaching this truth, most wouldn't conclude this about Jesus. A new Christian might, as she experiences life in Christ, come to this realization; even a more mature Christian can learn spiritual truth by living with the Lord. But is the situation imagined in sentence 5 what theologians mean when they speak of divine revelation?

The verses from Psalm 19 (sentence 6) are again about revealing God's glory. However, this time it is not God who reveals, but the heavens, night, and day. Of course, this is beautiful poetic language, but it does mean something literal. What should we make of it? It is hard to imagine how impersonal objects (sun, moon, stars, etc.) that don't possess minds can disclose anything. To say they do personifies them. But what does all of this mean about how we should understand the theological concept of divine revelation?

Sentence 7 is frighteningly close to what we sometimes hear when a mass murderer explains his motive for killing many people. It is easy to say he is insane, for God, we think, would never reveal such a thing. Whatever went on in the killer's mind had nothing to do with God or divine revelation, or so we think.

But God did command Abraham to offer up Isaac as a sacrifice. And God did tell the Israelites to go into the Promised Land and utterly wipe out the Canaanites. So, perhaps the lunatic murderer wasn't so crazy after all? If God gave such revelations in biblical times, why not today as well? Our minds recoil at such thoughts, but explaining how an incident today is not revelation while God's commands to Abraham and to Israel were is not so easy.

Then, the Revelation 19 passage (sentence 8) relays a vision John saw. But so far, most if not all of our examples, have spoken of revealing information—words. Though John records words he heard an angel say, all of what he describes happened in a vision. Does that mean a vision can be revelation? Revelation 19 is part of Scripture, so it must, evangelicals would say, qualify as revelation, but this isn't the sort of thing one thinks of when one thinks of God's words of revelation.

To be sure, many of us can identify with sentence 9, especially if we have ever studied a difficult passage. But is this an instance of revelation? If the reader can't understand the passage, then is it divine *revelation*? If, as a result of divine aid, the imaginary person comes to understand the passage, does that mean that a Scripture passage at one time can be revelation and not so at another?

And finally, in sentence 10 Paul recounts an experience he had fourteen years before writing about it. He says that he has had revelations from the Lord (2 Cor. 12:1). Surely, then, he considers what he relates in verses 2–4 to be a revelation. Paul does not tell what he saw in paradise, but he does tell what he heard. However, he says that he heard inexpressible (*arrēta*) words. The Greek term *arrētos* can have at least two meanings. Something may be inexpressible because it is beyond human powers to speak it. Or it can be inexpressible because, even though it could be put into human words, one isn't allowed to do so. Given what Paul says in verse 4, the latter meaning is preferred. But what does all of this teach about divine revelation? Paul affirms that he was transferred into God's presence and received a verbal revelation. Since Paul wasn't allowed to say what he heard, how can what he heard be revelation to anyone but him? What good does this information do for the rest of us? Some may respond that at least it tells us that Paul isn't boasting groundlessly when he says he has had revelations. But since Paul won't, because he isn't allowed, say what he heard, how can we be sure that this experience ever happened? And what does this passage teach about the concept of revelation?

## Divine Revelation: The Basic Concept

Despite the ambiguity surrounding this doctrine, we can still define it clearly as theologians use it. The basic idea of any kind of revelation is to unveil, uncover, bring to light, disclose, and/or make known that which was previously hidden, veiled, and/or unknown. The object revealed can be a person, information, feelings, thoughts, an action, or any other thing that can be known through reason, intuition, and/or sense perception. For someone or something to be revealed, the one(s) to whom the revelation is given must have been previously either totally or partially unaware of whatever is made known.

This concept of revelation can also be applied specifically to God. Divine revelation is a disclosure made by God or by one of his creatures for him. Its content may be God's very person, disclosed by transmitting information about God or by an act of God whereby he makes his presence known to his creatures. Or the content of divine revelation may be an action performed by God (though his presence may not be sensed as involved in what happens). This action discloses to those who observe or experience it that God was acting in what otherwise seemed to be a totally natural turn of events.

The definitions offered above somewhat explain what divine revelation is, but much is still unspecified. In short, we need to clarify the source(s), content(s), and method/form(s) of divine revelation. Various models of revelation respond differently to each of these issues, and we should briefly mention how each model understands revelation.[9]

---

[9] In composing this section and its definitions of revelation and divine revelation, I found helpful the following: Gerald O'Collins, "Revelation Past and Present," in *Vatican II: Assessment and Perspectives*, vol. 1, ed. Rene Latourelle (New York: Paulist, 1988), 130–132; Carl R. Trueman, "Admiring the Sistine Chapel: Reflections on Carl F. H. Henry's *God, Revelation, and Authority*," *Themelios* 25 (2000); F. Gerald Downing, "Revelation, Disagreement, and Obscurity," *RelS* 21 (1985): 220ff.; Owen Barfield, "The Concept of Revelation," *Anglican Theological Review* 63 (1981); Emmert F. Bittinger, "The Idea of Revelation in Christian Theology and Philosophy of Religion," *Brethren Life and Thought* 5 (Spring 1960): 50; Herbert C. Brichto, "On Faith and Revelation in the Bible," *Hebrew Union College Annual* 39 (1968); Daniel K. Calloway, "An Analysis of the Doctrine of Revelation with Emphasis

*Models of Revelation*

In *Models of Revelation* Avery Dulles presents the main understandings of the nature of revelation throughout church history, with a special emphasis on models that best represent the major approaches to revelation on the contemporary scene. His approach explains what is at the heart of each model, and shows both the similarities and differences between the models.

Dulles speaks of *models* of revelation in the way scientists often talk about models of explanation of phenomena. Following Ian Barbour's notion of a theoretical model, Dulles says that a model is "an 'organizing image' which gives particular emphasis, enabling one to notice and interpret certain aspects of experience."[10] Thus, a theological model, including one about revelation, "explains, and in some degree conditions, the characteristic theses of the theologians who rely on it."[11]

But specifically, what is a model of *revelation* about? Dulles says that a model of revelation has "a central vision of how and where revelation occurs."[12] While this seems correct, it also seems incomplete. A model of revelation will answer a number of different questions. First, it will identify the source of revelation—from whom and/or what does revelation come? Second, a model will explain the content(s) of revelation, and so it will help us identify and distinguish the truly revelatory from the nonrevelatory. Answers about content will also show how (and whether) theologians distinguish between what is revealed and the vehicle or means by which revelation is conveyed. Hence, a model will, third, explain how revelation is transmitted from the "sender" to the intended recipient(s). Fourth, models of revelation usually explain how we can know that a divine revelation has been sent and how revelation should be received by God's human recipients. In fact, many models of revelation insist that reception, *both* in the sense of intellectually understanding the message sent *and* also in the sense of appropriating it into one's life and behavior, is a prerequisite for saying that revelation has actually occurred. Models that require appropriation for there even to be an instance of revelation explain how revelation is to be

on the Perspectives of Karl Barth and Paul Tillich," *Brethren Life and Thought* 37 (Fall 1992); Stephen Williams, "Keith Ward on *Religion and Revelation*," *Scottish Journal of Theology* 48 (1995); Ronald Graham, "Revelation and Atonement," *Lexington Theological Quarterly* 35 (2000); Stewart R. Sutherland, "The Concept of Revelation," in *Religion, Reason, and the Self*, ed. Stewart R. Sutherland and T. A. Roberts (Cardiff: University of Wales Press, 1989); Dewey M. Beegle, "The Biblical Concept of Revelation," in *The Authoritative Word: Essays on the Nature of Scripture*, ed. Donald K. McKim (Grand Rapids, MI: Eerdmans, 1983), 90ff.; Christopher R. J. Holmes, "Disclosure without Reservation: Re-evaluating Divine Hiddenness," *Neue Zeitschrift für Systematische Theologie und Religionsphilosophie* 48 (2006); Glen E. Harris Jr., "Revelation in Christian Theology," *Churchman* 120 (2006); David C. Ratke, "Preaching Christ Crucified: Luther and the Revelation of God," *Dialog* 43 (Winter 2004); and Daniel J. Peterson, "Speaking of God after the Death of God," *Dialog* 44 (Fall 2005). See also standard systematic theologies: Gordon R. Lewis and Bruce A. Demarest, *Integrative Theology* (Grand Rapids, MI: Zondervan, 1996); Erickson, *Christian Theology*; Berkhof, *Systematic Theology*, e.g.

[10] Avery Dulles, *Models of Revelation* (Garden City, NY: Image, 1985), 31, discussing Ian G. Barbour, *Myths, Models, and Paradigms* (New York: Harper & Row, 1974).

[11] Dulles, *Models of Revelation*, 31.

[12] Ibid., 27.

appropriated and how to know that it actually occurred. Finally, a model of revelation at least implicitly answers whether divine revelation (of whatever sort) has ceased or whether more is to be expected. In so doing, the model will also imply some criterion (or criteria) for deciding whether a new claim of divine revelation should be believed.

Given these introductory remarks, what model(s) of revelation best represent Scripture's teaching on revelation? Before offering his own approach, Dulles considers five other models: (1) revelation as propositions/doctrines, (2) revelation as history, (3) revelation as inner experience, (4) revelation as dialectical presence, and (5) revelation as new awareness. The first four have been most widely held among Christians in recent centuries. It is safe to say that no evangelical would espouse the fifth model, which claims that revelation is a heightened form of human consciousness that allows those who have it to experience participation in the divine life.[13]

Though it would, no doubt, be helpful to include a detailed description of the various models Dulles presents, our purpose in this volume is to articulate the evangelical and biblical understanding of revelation. As we present what Scripture says about revelation, it will become clear that God reveals information about a variety of things, and he also reveals himself in acts. There are other forms of revelation, as we shall see, but the two just mentioned coincide most with the first two models of revelation Dulles mentions: revelation as propositions and revelation as history.

## Key Questions about Revelation

Before turning to biblical data about revelation, I want to raise several issues that surround this doctrine. An initial question is whether revelation should be understood as a once-for-all, static deposit of truth that never changes. Or is revelation dynamic, ongoing, and changing? Some thinkers call the former notion a deistic conception of revelation.[14] That is, just as deists believe that God "wound the clock of the universe" and then stepped out of history and

---

[13] Dulles's brief introductory remarks about this model should convince readers that I am right in saying that this isn't a model of revelation that any evangelical would find at all palatable. Dulles explains that while most models of revelation portray revelation coming from above and outside humans to a basically passive recipient, the new awareness approach is different. "According to this approach revelation is a transcendent fulfillment of the inner drive of the human spirit toward fuller consciousness. Far from reducing the subject to passivity, revelation occurs when human powers are raised to their highest pitch of activity. Rather than going beyond experience, revelation is itself an experience of participation in divine life" (Dulles, *Models of Revelation*, 98).

[14] See Richard Swinburne, "Revelation," in Kelly J. Clark, *Our Knowledge of God: Essays on Natural and Philosophical Theology* (Dordrecht: Reidel, 1992), 115–129. For a longer version see Richard Swinburne, *Revelation: From Metaphor to Analogy* (Oxford: Clarendon, 1992). See also Eleonore Stump's reply in "Revelation and Biblical Exegesis: Augustine, Aquinas, and Swinburne," in *Reason and the Christian Religion: Essays in Honour of Richard Swinburne*, ed. Alan G. Padgett (Oxford: Clarendon, 1994). See also Swinburne's response to Peter Byrne's critique of his book on revelation in Richard Swinburne, "Reply: A Further Defence of Christian Revelation," *RelS* 29 (1993). For more on Swinburne's views see Brian Hebblethwaite, "The Communication of Divine Revelation," in *Reason and the Christian Religion*; and John Lamont, "Stump and Swinburne on Revelation," *RelS* 32 (1996).

left it to run on its own, some theologians think that on one or more occasions God delivered his revelation, and then withdrew, never again (or at least very seldom) to reveal himself.

Those committed to the Bible as propositional revelation and to the idea that the canon of Scripture is closed might assume that revelation is not ongoing, but they should not be hasty in adopting such a view. Many theologians, including evangelical ones, believe in progressive revelation. Progressive revelation means that God does not tell us everything he wants to say about a given topic all at once, but gives us information incrementally as time passes. If theologians are right about progressive revelation, can they be sure that revelation has ceased? Evangelical theologians in particular should be very wary as they address this issue, for if they take an overly *static* view of revelation, they may in effect "lock God out of the world."

Next, throughout church history theologians have distinguished between natural and special revelation. They believe that Scripture teaches that both exist. However, in recent centuries many have seen revelation occurring as man tries to reach beyond himself to something transcendent. These theorists believe there is revelation, but, given how it occurs and the impetus to seek it, all revelation is natural in kind. That is, revelation in no way results from a supernatural being breaking into our natural world run by natural laws.

On the other hand, neoorthodox theologians like Karl Barth and many of his followers insist that there is no such thing as natural revelation. Nature does not even in the slightest present a point of contact with the divine. Hence if there is any revelation at all, it must stem totally from God's initiative. Humans don't possess the truth, and they can never, on their own, through reason or anything else arrive at the truth. God possesses the truth, and we have access to it only when God graciously brings it to us.[15]

Then, theologians also discuss the medium/media of revelation. How does divine revelation come to us? Does it come in words, visual images, feelings, actions (divine and/or human), events, or even in a personal encounter with God which may or may not include the transmission of language? Typically, models of revelation have opted for one or (at most) two of these forms of revelation, but can revelation rightly be limited to only one or two forms?

Then, there are questions about the content of revelation. Some say it is words (even speech acts) or doctrinal propositions; others say it comes in

---

[15] Here Barth and Kierkegaard are fully in agreement. However, their insistence that only God possesses the truth and must bring it to mankind stems from different concerns. Kierkegaard fights Hegelian idealism, according to which the truth is already within us. All we need to do, using the Hegelian dialectical method, is unfold the truth we already possess. See Søren Kierkegaard, *Philosophical Fragments: Or a Fragment of Philosophy* (1852; repr., Princeton, NJ: Princeton University Press, 1971). Barth's rejection of anything but divine revelation stems from different concerns. See Karl Barth, "The Doctrine of the Word of God," *Church Dogmatics*, vol. 1, part 1 (New York: Scribner's, 1955), chapter 1; and vol. 1, part 2 (New York: Scribner's, 1956), chapter 3.

great divine acts that are part of salvation history; and others say the content is God himself in personal communion and encounter. Still others speak of the content of revelation as an experience (perhaps mystical) of being one with a supreme being (or even with "the universe"), while others talk of it as a heightened insight about the human condition and a better way to live one's life. So, what should we say about the content of revelation?

Other questions about divine revelation are equally perplexing. Some theologians begin their coverage of revelation by affirming that God is ultimately ineffable and unknowable; he is a complete mystery to us. To use Luther's terminology, he is the *deus absconditus* (the hidden God), about whom we can know little or nothing. The only God we can know anything about is the *deus revelatus* (the revealed God), Jesus Christ. But, of course, Jesus was also a man, and his deity, for all we know, was seldom on display. So, how exactly does he reveal the hidden God?

Even more fundamentally, if God is totally unknowable, how can there be any divine revelation at all? Or, if there is divine revelation, how would we identify it as such since, according to this view, God is totally mysterious? Moreover, the question of how Jesus reveals God becomes even more unanswerable. That is so because Jesus's divine nature was typically hidden, but also because, if we know nothing about God, how can we be sure that things Jesus said and did actually reveal anything about God?

Next, it is common when speaking of divine revelation to hold that, given the difference between God's intellect and ours, God must accommodate his revelation to our finite minds with their limited ability to understand what an infinite intelligence reveals. This seems almost self-evidently true, but what exactly stems from this accommodation? If God must "sufficiently change" what he reveals so that we can understand it, might it no longer be true as God knows the truth? If so, then, what does it mean to say that God has actually revealed anything to us? On the other hand, if what God communicates is true as God actually knows it, then perhaps there isn't much, if any, accommodation at all. As some theologians have argued, an omniscient God must have some way to communicate information that is both true and understandable to his creatures. So, do we fully know what we are saying when we claim that divine revelation is accommodated to our level of understanding?

To illustrate the questions that talk of accommodated language raise, consider the following. Scripture reveals that humans have broken God's law, can't pay for their sins, must pay for their sins by death, and that Jesus paid our debt by his own death and resurrection. But is this information just accommodated to our level of understanding so that it isn't actually true as God knows what is true? If so, then are we really sinners in need of atonement, and did Jesus's death and resurrection actually pay for our sins?

Many may think such questions are absurd because Scripture "clearly" teaches these things. But the questions are not absurd if one says divine revelation is accommodated to human understanding. The questions seem even more cogent if one never articulates exactly what accommodating information does to its truthfulness. And, whether accommodated language is or isn't exactly what God knows, then how should we interpret it—literally, figuratively, or how? Do such questions about interpreting accommodated language even make sense?

This must not be misunderstood. I am not suggesting that, for humans to grasp revelation, they must know what God knows or that their minds must work as his does. I am just asking what a long-held "doctrine" actually means about whether there is revelation, what the revelation is, and whether the revelation as stated is true in the sense of corresponding to reality. There are obvious instances of accommodated language in Scripture. Perhaps most obvious are anthropomorphisms like "the hand of God," "the eyes of the Lord," etc. Without these phrases, biblical authors could speak of God's power and knowledge, but readers would likely wonder how a noncorporeal being could actually know things and act.[16]

So, on the one hand, I affirm accommodation, because to deny it seems to be the apex of intellectual arrogance; but on the other hand, to hold accommodation presents the many conundrums raised above. If divine accommodation of truth to finite minds is to make sense, we must explain the concept in a way that avoids the difficult problems raised.

A further issue raises a different question about human understanding. Evangelical theologians affirm that sin has, to one extent or another, damaged the human mind's ability to grasp either natural or special revelation. Some speak so strongly of sin's devastating effects on the mind that one wonders whether God has actually *revealed* anything at all to nonbelievers. Let me explain. In Romans 1:18–19 Paul says that nonbelievers suppress in unrighteousness the truth available in natural revelation. The same apostle says in 1 Corinthians 2:14 that the natural man (the unbeliever) cannot understand spiritual truth.

Do these verses mean that there actually is no revelation for nonbelievers because of sin's effects on their minds? If so, does that mean they can't even read any Scripture and grasp intellectually what it says? Is Scripture like a foreign language (or even gibberish) to them, and if so, what does it mean to say that God has revealed anything to them?

---

[16] I am indebted to my colleague Graham Cole for this point about anthropomorphisms in Scripture being instances of genuine accommodation of God's thoughts to our level of understanding.

And what about sin's effect on the ability of *believers* to grasp revelation? Is divine revelation rendered useless or inoperative for believers living with unconfessed sin in their lives?[17]

With all of these problems, how should we proceed? Our next step should be to consult Scripture to see what it teaches about this doctrine. As an evangelical, I believe Scripture helps answer the issues raised in the previous paragraphs.

## BIBLICAL AND THEOLOGICAL TEACHING ABOUT DIVINE REVELATION

What is the basic concept of revelation as taught in Scripture? Scripture teaches that something of God is revealed in the natural universe, so our model of revelation must accommodate that insight. Moreover, Scripture is not written in the form of a systematic theology or a doctrinal treatise with propositions laid out in a list, but as we shall see, God does reveal information about himself, us, and a host of other things. And, God reveals more than information. He reveals himself in actions. Some of this he does unilaterally without his creatures as mediators of the revelation in any way, but he does other actions through the

---

[17] In addition to questions evangelicals raise about revelation, non-Christians and Christians who hold a liberal theology also raise serious questions about revelation. I note several key ones. A first stems from Kantian epistemology. Kant argued that all knowledge begins with experience, by which he meant sense experience (see Immanuel Kant, *Critique of Pure Reason*, trans. Norman Kemp Smith [New York: St Martin's Press, 1965]). If so, then things that aren't objects of sense experience can't be objects of knowledge. Into this group Kant placed God. If so, it is quite hard to see how someone who can't be known can reveal himself at all in our world. Prior to Kant, it was assumed that God, though immaterial and invisible, could reveal himself (here see Avery Dulles, *Models of Revelation* [Maryknoll, NY: Orbis, 1996], 6; and Wayne A. Brouwer, review of *Revelation and History: An Analysis of Approaches to the Relationship between Revelation and History in Recent Theological Systems*, in "Thesis Abstracts," *CTJ* 20 [November 1985]: 357. Since Kant, many theologians and philosophers have rejected the idea of divine revelation altogether, while others have revised the concept so that revelation stems from something human faculties can perceive. (For an extremely helpful explanation of how Kantian epistemology has impacted discussions about the nature of revelation, see Johannes Zachhuber, "Religion vs. Revelation? A Deceptive Alternative in Twentieth-Century German Protestant Theology," in *Religious Experience and Contemporary Theological Epistemology*, ed. L. Boeve, Y. De Maeseneer, and S. Van Den Bossche [Leuven: Leuven University Press, 2005], 305–309). A second question about the possibility of revelation stems from Newtonian science. Newton's view of "the system of nature" as a closed system seems to negate the possibility of God "intervening" in our world to reveal himself (see Frans Jozef van Beeck, "Divine Revelation: Intervention or Self-Communication," *Theological Studies* 52 [1991]: 201; see also his footnote 5 on page 201 for other sources discussing this issue). Of course, the prevailing scientific paradigm today isn't Newtonian, but as van Beeck explains, we now live "if not in a closed natural order, then at least in an autonomous one. This predisposes us to regard grace and revelation as purely alternative, elective, not strictly demonstrable interpretations of a world order that is essentially stable. . . . Such a world order spontaneously suggests one single, consistent, *natural* divine plan" (201). Third, anyone acquainted with the history of biblical criticism understands the difficulty of formulating a credible concept of divine biblical revelation. Many biblical scholars and theologians think biblical critical methodologies raise impossible problems for that view. Many contemporary Bible scholars believe that "the prophets and apostles formulated and expressed their own thoughts with the help of the conceptual and linguistic tools available in the place and time. The oracular form of certain statements ("God says . . . ") is attributed in some cases to expanded states of consciousness and in other cases to literary convention (the so-called messenger-form). Attempted proofs of revelation from biblical miracles and prophecies have been abandoned by many scholars, who regard the accounts of such divine interventions as historically unreliable" (Dulles, *Models of Revelation*, 7). Dulles also notes how empirical psychology and critical sociology have undermined the idea that God reveals himself in our world (see ibid., 6–8). These and other assorted complaints move many to question whether revelation is even possible. Others want to believe, but because of the problems mentioned, as van Beeck explains, they sometimes wind up holding "what really amounts to a form of Deism" (van Beeck, "Divine Revelation," 201). Some have even asked whether it might be possible and advisable to hold a theology which completely rejects the idea of divine revelation (see, e.g., a discussion of this option in Mark I. Wallace, "Theology without Revelation?," *ThTo* 45 [1988]).

agency of his creatures. Of course, without explaining the significance of the events and acts, it would be difficult to know what they reveal.

Then, according to Scripture, sometimes what is revealed is a person. In particular, the most complete revelation of God is Jesus Christ. He is that in his very person, and he also revealed many things through his teachings. He taught about God, humanity, etc., but he also made many claims about his own identity as the Son of God. So, while dialectical theologians are right that God reveals himself, revelation comes in other forms as well, and revelation of God in Christ usually comes with words that can accurately be repeated, not in a nonverbal encounter. In addition, the content of revelation in many biblical passages focuses on a divine attribute. And, finally, a biblically adequate model of revelation will also explain how Scripture relates to divine revelation.

From even this brief description, we can say that a biblical model of revelation should include many different things as the content of revelation, and it will likely propose that revelation comes in various forms. It should also distinguish different forms in which revelation comes.

So, how should we start to unpack biblical teaching on divine revelation? I begin with two preliminary points. The first is that revelation is *progressive*. Evangelical and nonevangelical theologians have generally agreed that God didn't "speak his whole mind" on a topic all at once. Certainly, those who believe Scripture is revelation would say that God didn't say everything he wanted to communicate about a topic in just one biblical book or in one passage. Rather, God addressed topics on various occasions, each time revealing more about them.

This does not mean that revelation somehow follows an "evolutionary" path, i.e., that revelation that comes later is truer than what is revealed earlier. Nor does it mean that until recipients had God's fuller explanation of a topic, they couldn't understand any earlier revelation on that subject. While those with more revelation knew more than those with less, those who had only earlier revelation did know something about the topics God addressed, and what they knew was true, even if incomplete. Neither of these rejected ideas is at all the concept of progressive revelation, or even an implication of it.

Instead, revelation as progressive means that even though what God reveals at any time is true, as time goes by, God amplifies and explains in more detail and clarity what he has previously said.[18] God's revelation about salvation and having a right relationship with God illustrates this point well. According to Genesis 1–2, God gave Adam and Eve instructions about appropriate behavior,

---

[18] J. I. Packer, *Revelations of the Cross* (Peabody, MA: Hendrickson, 2013), prefers the term "cumulative" to "progressive." Actually, both ideas have merit. New revelation doesn't void prior revelation, but amplifies it. Hence, as time passes the total amount of divine revelation given accumulates. On the other hand, later revelation doesn't merely elaborate points already revealed but can add new content never before revealed. In this respect, revelation also progresses.

and he told them what would happen if they disobeyed. But he said nothing about how to handle the consequences of disobedience if they should disobey. In Genesis 3 we read of their disobedience and of God's response. Commentators generally agree that Genesis 3:15 is the first hint of a remedy for the human predicament, though it is stated briefly and in rather opaque terms. In Genesis 3 we learn of animal death, because Adam and Eve are clothed with animal skins, and by chapter 4 we read about animal sacrifices and offerings, although very little is explained about their purpose. Later in the Mosaic law, God elaborated a whole sacrificial system, explaining the various kinds of sacrifices and their purposes. He also clarified the relation of sacrifice to sin and showed how sacrifices brought in faith would help to maintain a sinner's right relation with God.

As the storyline of Scripture continues, there are various hints of a coming Messiah, God's anointed one, who would somehow pay for the sins of his people and ultimately lead them to an unparalleled time of blessing and intimacy with God. By the end of the OT, the facts that the Messiah would be born of a virgin (Isa. 7:14), born in Bethlehem (Mic. 5:2), would be despised, rejected, and eventually killed by his own people (Isaiah 53), but then would be brought back to life (resurrected; Isa. 53:10) were all revealed. But the OT didn't identify the exact person who would fulfill this role. Though it also teaches that his death would be a sacrifice for sin (Isa. 53:10–11), it does not say that his death would end the Mosaic system of sacrifice.

In the NT God revealed all of these important pieces of information. Moreover, in the NT epistles God added many details about the salvation worked out by Jesus Christ. Soteriological concepts like justification, sanctification, union with Christ, reconciliation, and more are introduced and explained so that readers can grasp the full nature of human sinners' predicament and can see that God's plan of salvation provides everything needed to establish and maintain a right relationship with God.

More details could be added, but the point should be clear: God did not say everything about sin and salvation on just one occasion or in one place. As time passed, God progressively revealed more and more about our wretched estate because of sin and about God's glorious and gracious remedy. What is true about God progressively revealing details about his plan of salvation is also true of other topics God addresses in Scripture. The fact that revelation is progressive should warn us against isolating a passage or two from the whole of Scripture and thinking that, from them alone, we can know "the biblical teaching of . . . x," where "x" stands for any topic that God has addressed.

The other preliminary point is that we must distinguish (1) *revelation that is available through the created universe* from (2) *revelation that does not occur as part of the natural operation of the universe.* Theologians call these two broad kinds of revelation natural or general revelation, on the one hand, and supernatural or special revelation, on the other. Sometimes the former is labeled original revelation and the latter soteriological revelation. As traditionally is the case in evangelical theology, I think it also best to organize our discussion around these two general foci—natural and special revelation. Though natural revelation is available through sources other than Scripture, Scripture also speaks of this kind of revelation. Natural revelation does not for the most part contain the content of special revelation,[19] but Scripture does. However, that does not mean that Scripture is the only kind of special revelation there is; special revelation comes in various forms.

### Natural, General, or Original Revelation

Though each of the terms in the above subhead underscores a slightly different point, the purpose of this category is to distinguish this kind of revelation from special revelation. The term *natural* intends to note that this kind of revelation is available through the natural order of created and preserved things in our universe. Anyone who can experience the world through their senses can, using reason, grasp that the facts of the universe reveal something about God.

The term *general* underscores the fact that this sort of revelation is available to people living at any time, place, and culture in human history. Of course, some people with limited capacity to reason, and others deprived of normally functioning senses (some are blind, others are deaf, e.g.) may have little or no contact with this revelatory material, or they may access it but be unable to process rationally what it reveals about God. Hence, this revelation is not called universal, but general. It is available to all, but not necessarily accessible by everyone.

The term *original* emphasizes two things. First, it deals with the universe as originally created from God's hand. God's creating the universe is itself an act of special revelation, so original revelation as a divine act is a form of special revelation. So, why include it in a discussion of natural revelation? The reason is that, once created, the universe as created and preserved does reveal God. Of course, when first created, no creatures other than angelic beings and a pre-fallen Adam and Eve were present to observe this world.

Scripture teaches that sin changed the world from its pristine original state

---

[19] I say "for the most part" to accommodate those who believe that from the natural order, without any explanation from Scripture, one can deduce the notion that the universe was created by a superior being. And, indeed, creation, as with God's other miraculous deeds, is special revelation. But, of course, many look at the natural order and don't believe it gives evidence of or suggests creation. Those who think the universe's origins can be explained naturalistically think natural revelation wouldn't at all speak of special revelation. Since there is a debate about whether the natural universe speaks of a divine miracle of creation (and since some think it does), I used the phrase "for the most part." Beyond the issue of the miracle of creation, however, evangelicals would agree that the natural universe doesn't point to any form of special revelation.

(Gen. 3:14–19). Because original revelation was given before humans fell into sin, it did not include information about how to remedy our sinful, lost estate. That is the second point about the term *original*. Once the race fell into sin, humans needed information about how to restore their lost relationship with God. We needed revelation that is *soteriological* (related to salvation) in nature. God did give this kind of revelation, but not as part of natural or general revelation.

For our purposes, I shall use either "natural" or "general" to designate this broad category of revelation. Most of what follows makes no further distinction between "natural" and "general." I think the best way to address natural revelation is to examine the key biblical passages that teach about it. There are five passages that are the most important and most frequently cited when theologians discuss this topic. They are Psalm 19:1–6; Acts 14:15–17; Acts 17:16–29 (esp. vv. 22–29); Romans 1:16–32; and Romans 2:11–16. The Acts passages are narratives, but Luke records some of what Paul preached on two occasions, and his words are relevant to natural revelation. Psalm 19 is a poetic way of extolling God, claiming that even the natural world gives evidence of his existence and attributes. But undoubtedly the richest and most direct theological discussion of natural revelation appears in the first two chapters of Romans, so we start there.

### Romans 1:16–32

This passage, especially verses 19–21, is arguably the most foundational biblical statement about natural revelation. However, it isn't per se intended to teach something about divine revelation, but rather, is part of Paul's overall indictment of both Gentiles and Jews as guilty before God for having rejected truth about God. As a result, chapter 3 concludes that none are righteous, because all have sinned and fall short of God's glory. All are guilty before God, and are helpless to rectify the situation (3:9–12). Lest any doubt this, Paul affirms that no one by keeping the law will be justified (declared righteous) by God (3:20). The only hope for sinful, lost humans is the righteousness that is by faith in Jesus Christ (3:22, 24), whose death paid for our sins (3:25).

The conclusion that there is hope only through faith in Christ is in a sense the same point with which Paul begins in 1:16ff. Paul was eager to preach the gospel in Rome (v. 15), because it is the power of God unto salvation for both Jews and Gentiles (v. 16). The gospel reveals God's righteousness, a righteousness available only by faith (v. 17) in Christ's atoning work (Romans 3).

Romans 1:18 focuses on God's wrath that has repeatedly been expressed to punish sin. Paul says this wrath has been revealed, but he uses the present passive indicative tense for "reveal" (*apokalyptetai*). I agree with Douglas Moo that it is better to understand this not as suggesting that God discloses some idea to people's minds (such as warning them of judgment), but as saying that God's wrath is actually being poured out.[20] This fits the durative sense of the present tense (hence, God's wrath can be constantly poured out throughout history on sinful people), and it suggests that even now, before the eschaton, people actually experience just recompense for their sins.

Verse 18 says that God's wrath is manifested against all ungodliness of men, and Paul adds the participial phrase "who suppress the truth in unrighteousness." The subject of the participial phrase is *anthrōpōn*, "men," which in this sentence also identifies whose ungodliness and unrighteousness is recompensed with God's wrath. So Paul's point is that those who do ungodly deeds are also those who suppress the truth in unrighteousness.

In verse 19 Paul turns to the truth that has been suppressed and explains how all people know that truth. The ungodly have suppressed truth about God, but what truth? In verse 20, Paul names the specific things humans can know from a very specific source. How do they know it? Some suggest that verse 19 proposes one way of knowing (an effable intuition, known *a priori*), while verse 20 presents another way (an inference, *a posteriori*, made from rational reflection on the world around us).[21] However, it is dubious that verse 19 says anything about *how* this information is known. Instead, the point is the source of the knowledge ("God made it evident to them"), a general comment about what is known (knowledge that God exists), and a clear affirmation (stated twice—"is evident within them" and "God made it evident to them") that they do know this information.

Some may object that if God has revealed this knowledge about himself to humankind, the passage speaks about special revelation, not natural revelation. That is possible, but verse 19 *does not* explain how humans acquire this knowledge or how God reveals it to them (through words, visions, dreams, Scripture, the natural world, conscience, etc.). Verse 19 *alone* only says that humans know information about God because God has revealed it to them. But that doesn't tell us whether this verse (and passage) is about natural revelation, special revelation, or both.

Thankfully, verse 20 clarifies verse 19. Verse 20 begins with an explanatory *gar* that links verse 20 to 19 and cues us that verse 20 will more fully explain the points made in verse 19. In verse 20, Paul writes that all people know about God (literally) "his invisible things," but to what could that refer? It might refer to his plans and purposes, but that doesn't fit what the verse says about how "his invisible things" are known. It might also refer to his basic substantiality,

[20] Douglas J. Moo, *Romans 1–8* (Chicago: Moody, 1991), 95–97. As Moo explains, this is the same sense in which *apokalyptetai* is used in relation to God's righteousness in verse 17.
[21] Bruce A. Demarest, "General and Special Revelation: Epistemological Foundations of Religious Pluralism," in *One God, One Lord in a World of Religious Pluralism*, ed. Andrew D. Clark and Bruce W. Winter, (Cambridge: Tyndale House, 1991), 140–141.

which is pure spirit, but how would that be known through things that are made? What Paul has in mind is what most commentators say, namely, God's divine attributes. That this is correct is confirmed by the next phrase, which tells what is known about God: "His eternal power and divine nature." Since power per se does not contain the notion of eternity (e.g., humans also are powerful, but our power doesn't last forever), the phrase *hē . . . aidios autou dynamis* ("His eternal power") is best understood as referring to two divine attributes, God's eternity and his power.

Paul completes his comment about what is known about God with "and divine nature" (*kai theiotēs*). This term may tempt some to construct a precise list of God's other attributes, but it is highly dubious that Paul intends such exactitude. It is better to understand this as a general term referring to qualities one would normally associate with deity.

Implicit in these phrases in verse 20 is another fact about God, the fact that he *exists*. Nonexistent things have no attributes, so to know that various divine attributes exist is also to know that God exists.

In verse 20 Paul answers several other questions about knowledge of God. One is how long this information has been available and known. Paul says, "since the creation of the world," and undoubtedly, "since" should be understood in a temporal sense. Thus, this information has been present ever since the creation of the world. God created the world before he created humans, so this information has "existed" longer than humans have existed. It has been present during the lives of everyone who has ever lived!

What exactly is the source of this information? First, this knowledge comes *tois poiēmasin*, "through things that are made" (v. 20 AT). Surely Paul doesn't mean "manufactured" goods, or even "human-made" goods. How could God's existence and attributes be known through those things? Paul's point is that this information comes from the created universe. And, Paul would think God made creation, so he is the ultimate source of this information, just as verse 19 says. God made himself knowable by creating a universe.

One question remains: how do humans come to know these truths from God's created world? Paul says that this information has been clearly seen (*kathoratai*) and understood (*nooumena*) through things that have been made. The phrase "through things that have been made" occurs only once in the verse, but it clearly refers to both "seen" and "understood" (the exact Greek phrase is *tois poiēmasin nooumena kathoratai*). But how does this occur, and are the two verbs (*nooumena*, the participle; and *kathoratai*, the verb in the present indicative) redundant? The two verbs are not redundant, and their distinct meanings answer how this information about God's invisible attributes becomes known to all people.

As various commentators note, *kathoratai* can refer to sense perception or to intellectual understanding, whereas *noeō* connotes an inner recognition. This inner understanding often comes without any reference to physical sensing, and as Moo notes, "none of the 14 NT occurrences includes physical seeing."[22] Since *nooumena* refers to inner understanding, it is unlikely that *kathoratai* also does (if it does, then the two verbs are redundant). It is more likely that *kathoratai* in this verse emphasizes more physical sense perception. That makes sense, since what sense perception perceives is "the things that are made," i.e., the physical universe which can be perceived through the senses. So, Paul is saying that the invisible things of God are known in a, so to speak, two-step process. First, there is the sense perception of the visible world, and then second, the understanding realizes that what has been sensed must have had a maker. Of course, since no mere human, no angelic being, and no inanimate force could make the created universe, someone (or something) far greater must be its maker. Only God as creator makes sense.

Thus, this knowledge of God comes through the use of human sense perception and human reason. And, no one needs advanced degrees (or even far less education) to make the logical connection from what is made to a maker. Anyone with normal intelligence can make this rational maneuver. Another rational move is also required by what Paul says: Since no one by human sense perception can physically see God's omniscience, power, eternity, etc., reason must move from the fact of a creator to the creator's nature/attributes. That is, having concluded that a creator God made this world, one should see that he must have boundless intelligence, power, etc. Hence, Paul is emphatic that everyone does know these things.[23]

Now that Paul has clarified what everyone knows about God, we see what truth everyone hinders or suppresses (v. 18). Verse 21 offers a decisive clue about *how* unrighteousness hinders this information. Knowing that God exists and has various attributes should lead people to reverence him. Moreover, it should also lead to the conclusion that this creator probably has desires about his creatures' behavior. So, when God's creatures do ungodly and unrighteous things, they show that they have nullified the effect that knowledge of a creator should have on their thinking and resultant behavior.

Paul adds in verse 20 a crushing blow that explains why God's wrath is directed toward ungodly sin and sinners. He says they are without excuse. To whom does "they" refer? Clearly, to all people, for everyone knows what Paul

---

[22] Moo, *Romans 1–8*, 100.

[23] The line of interpretation I have taken in this and the preceding paragraphs is consistent with that taken by Moo, ibid., 99–101; Bruce A. Baker, "Romans 1:18–21 and Presuppositional Apologetics," *BSac* 155 (July–September 1998): 291–292; and Thomas C. Oden, "Without Excuse: Classic Christian Exegesis of General Revelation," *JETS* 41 (March 1998): 59–61.

says in verse 20 about God, and everyone suppresses truth about him in ungodliness, as Paul says in verse 18.

Why are they without excuse? Though Paul doesn't explicitly say in verse 20, how can it be anything but their rejecting the truth about God that they all know? Verse 21 confirms this, for Paul details what they should have done with this knowledge of God, and he also specifies in verses 21–32 what they did instead. The assumption behind all of this is that no one defies God and his rules in ignorance of his existence or of his requirements. As Moo rightly explains, these verses teach that God is revealed in nature, and the result is negative. It doesn't lead people to salvation; it leads to their condemnation, with no acceptable excuse for what they have done![24]

From verse 21 to the end of the chapter, Paul presents further evidence that those who had revelation rejected it and turned to evil. In verse 21 Paul affirms again that they actually know there is a God, but he adds that they refused to worship and honor him as God, and turned to worship idols instead (vv. 21–23).

Before leaving this text, I note several concluding points about the whole passage. First, one might conclude that Paul is saying that whoever rejects God's revelation will eventually commit all of the sins detailed in verses 21–32. Of course, that would be false, and Paul doesn't say that. His point is that those who commit these sins do so ultimately because they have rejected truth about God.

Second, the specific focus of Paul's indictment in chapter 1 is the Gentiles. Though some commentators disagree, most see chapter 2 as Paul's critique of the Jews for failing to reverence God properly and to keep his law as revealed in Scripture. I agree with the majority view, but this should not be misunderstood. It might be tempting to think that Gentiles had only natural revelation while Jews had only special revelation (specifically Scripture). However, the revelation in nature that Paul describes in chapter 1 is available to everyone at all times, Jews and Gentiles alike. Given the source of this revelation (the created universe) and the means of acquiring it—sense perception and reasoning—it is clear that Jews also had this revelation. As for the special revelation of Scripture, in the OT era it was possible for a Gentile to be informed about this and even to become a proselyte to Judaism, but most Gentiles had no contact with such further revelation. Still, Paul's ultimate point is that everybody has had some revelation, and all have rejected it. Thus, by the end of Romans 3 Paul says that all have sinned and need the only kind of righteousness that matters, the righteousness of God through faith in Jesus Christ.

---

[24] Moo, *Romans 1–8*, 101. See also Oden, "Without Excuse," 61–62; and Baker, "Romans 1:18–21 and Presuppositional Apologetics," 292. Also, for a further discussion of Romans 1:18–20 and natural revelation, see John J. O'Rourke, "Romans 1,20 and Natural Revelation," *Miscellanea Biblica* 23 (July 1961).

Third, God's revelation sheds light on who he is and who we are; this is true of both general and special revelation. Of course, the thrust of Romans 1:18–32 is that humans rejected natural revelation and went their own way. One might suspect that, as just recompense, God would "turn off the light." But there is no evidence of that in chapter 1 or elsewhere in Romans. The effectiveness of the light of natural revelation was nullified, but that is our fault, not God's. Though humans repeatedly sin in the face of the truth, God has never turned off the light.

Fourth, some have thought that while Romans 1 teaches divine revelation through nature, human sin is so great that it renders this revelation useless.[25] Some historical theologians have debated whether various Reformers' views on the noetic effects of the fall and of sin in general don't render natural and even special revelation useless. Hence, they believe that the only hope for humanity is for God's Spirit to illumine unregenerate hearts and minds so that they grasp revelation and apply its truth to their own lives.

We need not settle the historical debate, but the issue in question is important theologically. Has human sinfulness, including that detailed in Romans 1:18–32, made even natural revelation altogether useless? Do the unregenerate know and understand nothing from it? In verse 32 Paul answers. He writes, of sinful humanity, that though "*they know the ordinance of God, that those who practice such things are worthy of death*, they not only do the same, but also give hearty approval to those who practice them."

The material I have italicized in verse 32 is truly astounding in light of all the sins Paul details in verses 21–31. You would think that people engaged in so many forms of sin and given over to a reprobate mind because they refuse to acknowledge God at all (v. 28) would no longer believe God exists and might not even have a concept of God, but Paul disagrees. But Paul says that the reprobate not only know God exists but they also know he has various laws, and that those who break those laws must be punished. This claim, coming after a long list of specific sins, means that people not only know in general that God has ethical rules; they know the specific acts forbidden by those rules.

This is very important in answering whether sin so darkens the mind that sinful humans cannot *intellectually* grasp even the least bit of information about God from revelation (natural or otherwise). Verse 32 shows that, despite sin, unrepentant sinners still know there is a God; they know that he has specific rules of conduct for humans; and they know that whoever disobeys those rules deserves to be punished. That hardly supports the view that natural revelation is useless or ineffective because our sin turns it into gibberish.

---

[25] Karl Barth's antipathy to natural revelation is well known. He believed that there is such a difference between the infinite and the finite that nature could never reveal anything about God. But he also believed that, even if revelation was available in nature, human sinfulness is so intellectually destructive that no mere human could grasp it anyway.

According to verse 32, sinners commit even the most horrendous sins not in ignorance of duty, but in defiance of it!

One final point prepares the way for the next passage on natural revelation. In verse 32 Paul says that evildoers know God's ordinance. How do they know this? Where would they get such knowledge? In part, by knowing that there is a God and by reflecting on divine attributes such as moral holiness and justice, it is possible for sinful humans to conclude by reason that a morally holy God would not be pleased with sin, and that a just and righteous God would reward those who do right and punish wrongdoers (sinners). But reasoning is not the only source of such moral knowledge, for in Romans 2 Paul writes about what humans know through their conscience. Hence, Romans 1:32 looks backward (to some extent) to what Paul wrote in verses 19–20, but it also prepares the way for explaining how people without any written form of divine law can still know rules of that law, and are, hence, without excuse if they disobey those rules.

### Romans 2:11–16

In Romans 2, Paul continues his indictment of humankind for sinning against God. Both Gentiles and Jews are guilty (vv. 9–10), because (v. 11) there is no partiality with God. Paul then says that all who sin without the law will perish without it, and those who sin with the Mosaic law (which the Jews possessed) will perish with it (v. 12). In verse 13 Paul argues that those who will be justified are not people who merely hear the law (but don't also do it), but those who obey it. Of course, no one obeys the law, so no one is justified by law keeping. The only way to be justified in God's eyes is to have the righteousness gained by faith in Christ's atoning work.

In 2:14, Paul further explains something he has already said: Jews and Gentiles who do evil can expect punishment (v. 9), and Jews and Gentiles who do good can expect blessing (v. 10). This is fair to the Jews, because they possessed the Mosaic law, but how is it fair to the Gentiles who didn't have any written form of God's law and apparently broke it in ignorance?

Verses 14–15 answer this question. Paul explains that it is fair to judge Gentiles for disobeying God's law, because they do know what he requires. How?

What is that other source of knowledge? In 2:14 Paul says that sometimes Gentiles obey what the law requires *physei*, "by nature," but what does that mean? Is Paul referring to the fact that those who are Gentiles by birth don't possess the Mosaic law (in contrast to the Jews), or is he saying that they do the things of the law by nature, i.e., instinctively? Either option is possible (the location of *physei* in the Greek sentence in 2:14 allows either), but the latter is preferred, because verse 15 explains how people without the Mosaic law can do things in it seemingly instinctively. If "by nature" is taken instead with the Gentiles' state at birth as different from Jews, then the points made in verse 15 don't make quite so much sense.[26]

At the end of verse 14, Paul says that Gentiles who don't have the Mosaic law, but who follow some of its precepts anyway, are a "law to themselves." This doesn't mean that they have a separate set of rules, have the right to make their own rules, or even that no rules apply to them at all. Paul's point is that they are a special case, but why? For two reasons. First, although they don't have a written form of divine law like the Mosaic code, their life occasionally conforms to the moral commands of the Mosaic law.

They are a "special case," secondly, because they do in fact have a sense of right and wrong along with many ethical rules that express right and wrong (v. 15). Those rules are "written in their hearts." But how, when, and under what circumstances? One answer is that all humans are born with this moral knowledge; it is, so to speak, innate knowledge.

It is safe to say that one need not have read John Locke's decisive critique of innate knowledge or Immanuel Kant's explanation that all knowledge is ultimately grounded in experience (which means sense experience of the world outside the mind) to see that Romans 2:15 doesn't teach that. It should be abundantly clear that Paul isn't making some precise epistemological point about the source of this knowledge or about a "triggering mechanism" in people that gives rise to ethical rules. Likewise, those who think they can answer these questions by doing a word study of Pauline usage of *kardia*, "heart," to see to which part of the human immaterial mind it refers and then propose an epistemological explanation of how and when these things arise in someone's mind, are also deluding themselves. The reason is that neither Paul nor any other NT writers use "heart" as part of a precise ontology of human nature, nor do they use it to offer or defend some theory about how humans come to know things. Biblical writers just aren't writing a treatise in religious epistemology.

Another reason that innate knowledge isn't how the Gentiles know right and wrong is that both the basic sense of right and wrong and specific rules of right and wrong are all expressed in language. Thus, believing in innate knowledge requires newborn babies to understand these concepts and at birth to be language users. How anyone thinks that can be affirmed of newborns is hard to fathom! Babies have the abilities to become language users, but language use develops as children interact with the world and learn their "mother tongue."

If this is so, then most likely the law "gets written in a person's heart" as he or she lives and learns that when you do some things, good things result,

---

[26] Moo, *Romans 1–8*, 145–146. Moo notes that Cranfield takes the phrase with what precedes, but Moo agrees that it should go with what follows "do the things of the law." See C. E. B. Cranfield, *A Critical and Exegetical Commentary on the Epistle to the Romans*, vol. 1, ICC (Edinburgh: T&T Clark, 2004).

and when you do other things, hurt or punishment follows. Thus, humans have an inborn *capacity to understand*, by which, upon experiencing life, including hearing their parents tell them to do certain things and avoid others, the law becomes ingrained in them. While I am tempted to opt for this explanation, I fear that even this explanation makes Paul say something he doesn't intend to address. Paul's point isn't so much to explain exactly *how* the law becomes written on our hearts as it is to say that even people without a formal written code of law just naturally know what is right and wrong. Hence, God is just in punishing them when they do wrong.

Some equate conscience (in verse 15) with the law written on people's hearts. But in this verse it is clear that the conscience is a distinct human faculty and our sense of "dos and don'ts" is distinct from our conscience. While we might wish to know where conscience comes from, Paul doesn't say. Nor does he claim that only Gentiles have a conscience. Jews do too, though that isn't Paul's point in verse 15. Is the human conscience part of natural revelation? Paul doesn't make that point, and since it would be hard to show that moral *equipment* is moral *information*, we can't say that the conscience *is* divine revelation, even if it is somehow connected to revelation, which seems to be the case.

So, what does this passage teach about natural or general revelation? It says that a basic sense of right and wrong and certain fundamental ethical rules are commonly known by all people at all times and places. The sticking point is knowing whether the source of this knowledge should be labeled natural revelation. This is hard to decide because Paul doesn't say *who* writes the law on our hearts or *how* it becomes written. It makes sense to say that God writes it, but does he do it (1) unilaterally or (2) through human agency as we live and interact with other people? If the former, then perhaps we should call it special revelation since it isn't rooted in the natural order per se. If he writes it through human agency as we live in the world, then it probably should be labeled natural revelation.

It is hard to decide between these two options. But there is a third possibility that hearkens back to Romans 1:18–32. Perhaps as we perceive the world around us and reason to a creator with various attributes, we also conclude that a creator with so much power probably has expectations for our behavior. As we think on these things, it isn't hard to imagine first generating a basic sense of right and wrong, and secondly, coming up with some "dos and don'ts." Perhaps we generate that list in the way I suggested in discussing Romans 2:15, i.e., by living in the world and hearing people set forth rules and observing what happens when rules are obeyed and what happens when rules are disobeyed.

Of the three options just detailed, I suspect that a combination of the second and third is most likely the case. But because Paul doesn't explain precisely how we acquire this knowledge, we should not be overly dogmatic. While having a conscience and having the law written on everyone's heart might be instances of special revelation, it is quite reasonable to think that Romans 2:14–15 is relevant instead to natural revelation, even if we cannot entirely explain the details of how the law gets written on people's hearts.[27]

### Acts 14:15–17

In Acts 14 Luke recounts some of the missionary ventures of Paul and Barnabas. At Lystra, in the region of Lycaonia, Paul healed a man who had been lame from birth and had never walked (vv. 6–10). Luke says that when the multitudes saw this, they thought Paul and Barnabas must be gods who had become like men. The priest of the pagan god Zeus made preparations to offer sacrifices to Paul and Barnabas (vv. 11–13). When Paul and Barnabas saw what was happening, they were quite dismayed, and they spoke to the crowds (vv. 15–17).

First, they told the crowd to stop preparing sacrifices, for Paul and Barnabas were mere humans just like the people in the crowd (v. 15). They explained that they had come to preach the gospel in Lystra, and that they hoped the people would reject their pagan gods and worship the living God.

This was a most interesting way for Paul and Barnabas to present their message. They didn't argue for God's existence, because many in their audience already believed in God. Paul and Barnabas preached the gospel to them. Verse 15 shows that Paul and Barnabas made it clear that they were preaching so that their listeners would turn from "these vain things to a living God." While the "vain" or useless things might refer to the sacrifices the people were planning to make in honor of mere mortals, given that Paul and Barnabas urged them to turn *to* a living God, it is more likely that "vain things" refers to the gods of the Greco-Roman pantheon, who were mere idols. But there is more here that we must not miss. By saying that the people of Lystra should turn to a *living* God, Paul and Barnabas showed that they knew their listeners believed in god(s). The problem was that they believed in *dead* deities, and that's the nature of an idol. One can pretend that an idol is alive and a help in times of trouble, but pretending won't make it so.

So, Paul and Barnabas offered a living God, one who had created everything (v. 15). About the only argument in verse 15 is the implicit one that the God the apostles presented is alive; that is so because dead gods create nothing,

[27] For further helpful discussions of this passage, see Oden, "Without Excuse," 67–68; Demarest, "General and Special Revelation," 135–136; Mark A. Seifrid, "Natural Revelation and the Purpose of the Law in Romans," *Tyndale Bulletin* 49 (1998); Ronald Ziegler, "Natural Knowledge of God and the Trinity," *CTQ* 69 (April 2005): 146–147; and Robert L. Thomas, "General Revelation and Biblical Hermeneutics," *MSJ* 9 (Spring 1998).

and it is abundantly clear that the world didn't just happen to come into existence. No mere mortal or team of mortals could have made it, either. A divine being must have done it, and no dead god can create anything. So, the implicit argument, if there is one, is that whoever created this world must be alive, but the gods of the people of Lystra are imaginary, not alive.

But where did the people of Lystra (and Gentiles in the Greco-Roman world) get the idea of a creator God, for there is no evidence that they had access to the OT (Genesis 1–2 in particular)? The idea came from popular mythology, but how did that originate? Most likely from natural revelation of the sort Paul detailed in Romans 1:19–20. But Paul also said that, rather than acknowledging and worshiping God properly, humans had turned to idols—the Greco-Roman gods were all idols.

Verse 15 shows that the idea of a creator god who created everything was common ground between the apostles and their listeners. Paul and Barnabas appealed to that common ground, and used it to turn their listeners' attention to the true and living God. In verse 16 the apostles say that, for many generations, God allowed "the nations to go their own ways." As opposed to what, and of whom were Paul and Barnabas speaking? Letting the nations go their own way is opposed to interceding by giving them revelation of a special sort, as God did with the people of Israel. Verse 17 confirms this by recounting that the apostles said that, even though God let the nations go their own ways, he didn't leave them without any witness (*amartyron*) about himself at all. Hence, when Paul and Barnabas spoke about the nations, they referred specifically to the Gentiles.

So, what was the witness of God left among the nations? Verse 15 shows that it was the common knowledge from natural revelation that God exists and that he created the universe. Romans 1 and 2 also show that God gave the nations a sense of right and wrong, plus some basic knowledge of specific "dos and don'ts." But Paul and Barnabas pointed to none of these things (Acts 14:17). As commentators suggest, their listeners had been raised and were living in a largely agrarian culture, so it would be natural to appeal to something very familiar to them.[28] The apostles pointed to God's goodness as seen in sending rain to grow their crops and in granting them ample harvests to supply food to keep them alive and thereby give them joy.

In other words, God's testimony of himself to all people is his providential preservation of life by sending rain and allowing crops to grow and yield a harvest. Anyone who understands how we get our food to keep us alive can know this. No one needs special revelation like Scripture to know this, nor does she or he need even the most basic education to grasp the point.

---

[28] Richard N. Longenecker, *The Acts of the Apostles*, in *EBC*, ed. Frank E. Gaebelein, vol. 9 (Grand Rapids, MI: Zondervan, 1981), 436. See also Bruce A. Demarest, *General Revelation: Historical Views and Contemporary Issues* (Grand Rapids, MI: Zondervan, 1982), 242.

As evidence that these things were common knowledge, notice that Paul and Barnabas offered no argument or evidence that God is the source and preserver of life. Their audience already believed that their gods were responsible for such things. They believed in Ceres, the goddess of grain, and in Bacchus, the god of wine. These farmers knew that they could plant and sow seed, but they believed that "the gods" prospered their efforts and gave them ample harvests. Paul and Barnabas didn't present a revolutionary message. They merely urged their hearers to adjust their thinking from "the gods" to the one living God who sustained life by giving food.

In sum, this passage shows that, through natural revelation (in the ways explained), one can learn that God exists and created everything. Moreover, everyone can also see that, after creating, this deity didn't die or sit idly by and watch his universe without participating in it all. Instead, the creator God sustains life by sending rain to grow crops to harvest and food to eat.[29]

### Acts 17:16–29

Acts 17 recounts Paul's ministry in Thessalonica and Berea. Paul then went to Athens and waited for Silas and Timothy to join him. In Athens, he noticed the enormous number of idols. This troubled him greatly. Verses 17–18 say that he was reasoning with the Jews in the synagogue and with God-fearing Gentiles. He did the same with anyone in the marketplace who would listen. Among his listeners were some Epicurean and Stoic philosophers. Paul's teaching about Christ, and especially about the resurrection, intrigued his audience, so they brought him to the Areopagus to ask him about what he was teaching.

Verses 22–31 contain what Paul said. Many have thought that his words (esp. vv. 22–29) affirm several different sources of natural revelation. Of course, the verses in question are Luke's narrative of Paul's speech, rather than a theological exposition like we find in Romans 1 and 2. But does Paul here actually teach that there is natural revelation? If not, does his speech say something, anyway, that may help in understanding natural revelation?

While some have thought that Paul teaches here that God reveals himself in the natural world and even in the march of history with the rise and fall of nations, we must be careful not to make Paul say more than he intends. Paul wanted to preach the gospel to the Athenians, not to expound a theological treatise on natural revelation. And, given his audience's ethnicity and culture, he wouldn't likely have gotten very far if he had started quoting Scripture or

---

[29] Helpful in constructing this discussion of Acts 14, in addition to Longenecker's commentary on Acts and Demarest's book on general revelation, were Demarest, "General and Special Revelation," 137; Bruce A. Demarest and Richard J. Harpel, "Don Richardson's 'Redemptive Analogies' and the Biblical Idea of Revelation," *BSac* 146 (January–September 1989): 332; Daniel Howard, "A Critical Analysis of General Revelation," *Criswell Theological Review* 8 (Fall 2010): 63; and Henry Stob, "The Doctrine of Revelation in St. Paul," *CTJ* 1 (1966): 183.

talking about Israel's history. Paul wisely found common ground with his listeners, and moved from things they believed, to the gospel, which they probably hadn't heard before.

Is Paul's speech at all relevant to the subject of revelation? I think so, but not so much by explicit teaching as by what we may infer from the common ground between him and the Athenians. Of course, inferential reasoning can be risky. From exactly the same data, one may be able to infer a number of different things, some that contradict other possible inferences. So, we must be careful to see what this passage actually teaches about natural revelation.

According to verse 22, Paul noted that the Athenians were very religious. In fact (v. 23), they had many gods and were so concerned not to overlook any others that they even had an altar dedicated to "an unknown God." Paul said that this God whom they worshiped in ignorance is the one he proclaimed.

Here we must not misinterpret Paul's claim. Some who heard him might have thought he was urging them to remove all the idols and altars except the one to the unknown god, and then worship that idol alone. But that surely wasn't what Paul wanted; he wasn't recommending any kind of idol worship. Instead, he saw that they rightly sensed that, in spite of all their statues and altars in honor of various Greco-Roman gods, they still might have missed another god. The God they did miss, however, is not like any they worshiped; he doesn't live in temples and doesn't need humans to serve him (vv. 24–25).

Their altar to the unknown God contained some truth and some error. The truth is that there is one true God who wasn't represented by all their statues and altars. They erred, however, in thinking this unknown god was just another mythological deity. They didn't need to knock down all statues and altars except the one To The Unknown God. They needed to get rid of all of them, recognize that the true God is not like any of their idols, and worship him alone.

What does this teach about natural revelation? The key point is that these Athenians were very religious. But we aren't explicitly told how they came to believe in *any* gods, let alone in *many*. So, where did they get the idea of God, since from what we know, God didn't give them special revelation? They likely adopted the common belief in the Greco-Roman pantheon, but where did that come from? Probably, as they thought about the natural world around them, they reasoned that there must be a creator (just as Paul says in Romans 1). But, like many pagan people, they misread or deliberately distorted the truth of God available in creation. Rather than seeing just one creator with the attributes of Scripture's God, they distorted the concept of God, turning it into belief in a whole series of gods, each only a bit more powerful than mere humans, and each personifying some aspect of the world and life around them (e.g., a god of war, a goddess of love).

In verses 24 and 25, Paul says that there is one God, creator of everything. He doesn't dwell in temples and isn't served by anyone (as the Greeks sought to serve their idols), because he needs nothing. Moreover, this one God gives to every existing thing life and breath and everything else that they need (most likely a reference to all things needed to sustain life). But Paul does *not* say that they should know this from natural revelation! After reading Romans 1:19–20 and Acts 14:15–17, we may be inclined to say that all these things are knowable from the creation and preservation of the universe. But Paul didn't say that the Athenians already knew these things. If they did know them, they suppressed these truths by turning their concept of God into a concept of many slightly-more-than-human gods.

So, if Acts 17:24–25 is relevant to natural revelation, it isn't because Paul says the Athenians should have known these things from the natural world. Rather, it is relevant because of what other passages teach about natural revelation. Assuming the truth of those other passages (all of which Paul had either spoken or would write), and assuming that his listeners should resonate with what he was saying, because they really should know these things, Paul "revealed" these truths to his audience. But verses 24–25 are not per se an affirmation of natural revelation. They seem to imply that there is such a thing as natural revelation, and we are probably right in inferring that from these verses, but inference and implication are not explicit statements of an idea.

Verses 26–28 continue the sentence that began in verse 24. From our perspective, verse 26 may seem to be a mere statement of the origins of the human race, and so verse 27 may seem a bit strange, because it suggests that the human race and various cultures developed and thrived for a time and then passed off the scene of world history. And it suggests that all of this should move people to seek God in order to find him (v. 27). On the other hand, the facts stated in verse 26 may not seem to point to God, so verse 27 may not strike us as an appropriate envisioned result of the things mentioned in verse 26. After all, even a totally atheistic naturalist could affirm verse 26 without saying that God orchestrated the things Paul mentions. However, there is more here than may at first meet the eye, as Richard Longenecker explains:

> Contrary to the Athenians' boast that they had originated from the soil of their Attic homeland and therefore were not like other men, Paul affirms the oneness of mankind in their creation by the one God and their descent from a common ancestor. And contrary to the "deism" that permeated the philosophies of the day, he proclaimed that this God has determined specific times (*prostetagmenous kairous*) for men and "the exact places where they

should live" (*tas orothesias tes katoikias auton;* lit., "the boundaries of their habitation") so that men would seek him and find him.[30]

In other words, these facts about the origin of humanity and the rise and fall of nations should move people to seek God and find him. Paul does not *explicitly* say that the facts mentioned in verse 26 *reveal* that there is a God who controls history, but that seems to be the implication of what he says. If not, why would Paul think these facts should move anyone to seek God? So, it may seem that Paul is saying that one form of natural revelation is the origin and development of countries, their rise and fall. But clearly, the Athenians hadn't thought so, for as Longenecker says, they thought of themselves as being different from other humans. Hence, while Paul seems to suggest a form of natural revelation, we must ask ourselves whether, from the development of the human race and the rise and fall of societies, anyone would conclude that all of this came from God and showed his hand in history. Perhaps so, but perhaps not—the Athenians didn't think so, and many people think that history is going nowhere, so the rise and fall of nations, etc., is hard to see as a form of natural revelation.

However, before we reject the development of the human race and the rise and fall of nations as natural revelation, we should at least consider what Paul said in verse 28. As he finished his point, Paul quoted from two Greek poets. The first quote, "for 'in him we live and move and have our being'" (ESV), was written by the Cretan poet Epimenides (who lived around 600 BC), and it "appeared first in his poem *Cretica* and is put on the lips of Minos, Zeus's son, in honor of his father."[31] It was part of the following quatrain:

> They fashioned a tomb for thee, O holy and high one—
> The Cretans, always liars, evil beasts, idle bellies!
> But thou art not dead; thou livest and abidest for ever,
> *For in thee we live and move and have our being.*[32]

The second quote, "for we also are his offspring," comes from Aratus, a Cilician poet who lived roughly from 315–240 BC. His poem says, "It is with Zeus that every one of us in every way has to do, for we are also his offspring."[33]

Paul used these quotes to support the points he made in verses 25–26. What do they teach about natural revelation? Perhaps something, but perhaps not. We cannot know what these two poets had in mind when they wrote their

[30] Longenecker, *Acts of the Apostles*, 476.
[31] Ibid.
[32] Ibid. Longenecker quotes this, and italicizes the final line, since it is the one Paul quotes.
[33] Ibid. Longenecker italicizes the part Paul says in his sermon. The poem comes from *Phaenomena* 5. Longenecker adds that the line is also found in Cleanthes's earlier *Hymns to Zeus*, line 4. Cleanthes is thought to have lived sometime between 331 and 233 BC.

poems. It is possible that, from looking at mankind and the growth and decline of civilizations, they drew the conclusion that there is a God (or gods) who controls such things and maintains people in being.[34]

On the other hand, it is also possible that the poets Paul quoted had adopted the mythology of their day, and hadn't really thought about whether those myths arose from reflecting on the rise and fall of civilizations, or whether they believed such things because others in their society did, without questioning the source of those beliefs. Regardless of how these Greek poets came to their beliefs, Paul knew that his Athenian listeners would likely know these poems, and so he used lines from each poet as a point of contact with his audience. Of course, Paul didn't affirm the mythology of these poems; he simply used what they said to confirm his points about God. He used them, so to speak, as common ground between himself and his listeners—as a way to begin a conversation that he would shortly use to make a statement about the coming judgment through the Man God has raised from the dead (vv. 30–31).

In verse 29, Paul made another point based on the idea of humans as God's offspring. Everyone should know from understanding the basics of reproduction that children are the same kinds of creatures as their parents. So, if humans are God's offspring, then God should be like us in some key ways. Human children aren't made of gold, silver, or stone, nor are they mere images crafted by artisans. Hence, those who gave them life, their human parents and their ultimate creator, cannot be correctly represented by images made of gold, silver, or stone.

So, Paul's point rested on common knowledge about how natural reproduction works. But then Paul reasoned with the Athenians that if, as the poets say, we are God's offspring, then, since we aren't made of gold, silver, and stone, our creator cannot be made of such things either. But where would his hearers have gotten the idea that humans are God's offspring? Perhaps from natural revelation, in the way suggested in Romans 1; but they might have gotten the idea, instead, from the pagan Greek poets, and who knows where those poets got the idea?

So, what exactly does this passage teach about natural revelation? It is tempting to say that, from the natural order and from history, we can know that God created all things and controls the rise and fall of nations. And, that, if God is our creator and we are his offspring, the father can't be made of gold, silver, and stone if the children aren't. But other than this very last point being common knowledge to anyone who knows a little about reproduction (or just

---

[34] One thinks of King Nebuchadnezzar, who boasted of his great power, was driven out from human society to live as a wild beast, and then, upon regaining sanity, affirmed that there is a God in heaven who rules forever and does whatever he chooses with no one to challenge or stop him (Dan. 4:29–37). But that wasn't an instance of natural revelation, for that whole incident began with God giving Nebuchadnezzar a dream and Daniel interpreting it, an instance of special revelation.

knows that members of a family aren't made of completely different things), would the other items Paul appeals to also be something that we can know through natural revelation? If Paul had not said such things, and if Luke had not recorded them in Acts 17, is it clear that, just from the world around us, we would know such things?

Some may think we would know them without special revelation, and that's why Paul appealed to them. But think again: The fact that Paul appealed to these things as he did shows that he started from things that were common knowledge. But Paul used very few things that were common knowledge— namely (a) God exists; (b) he made everything, so we are his offspring; and (c) offspring are like their parents—to make the points that (1) the rise and fall of nations shows God's providential hand; (2) God is not made of gold, silver, or stone; (3) God does not live in temples made of stone by human hands; and (4) God is not far from us.

Now, it is not clear that (1)–(4) actually fit the concept of natural revelation—even though (a)–(c) do. That is, (a)–(c) can be known from natural revelation alone, *but* if Paul hadn't made points (1)–(4), would we draw such conclusions just from what we know through natural revelation? If not, then (1)–(4) probably are not items of natural or general revelation. If so, then perhaps they are. My point is this: Paul specifically mentions (1)–(4), and Luke records what Paul said, so they are part of *special* revelation. It at least also *seems* possible that (1)–(4) could be known without special revelation, *but we are not likely to know that from this passage alone.* We know (1)–(4) because they are part of Scripture. Could we know them from only natural revelation? The question seems impossible to answer, since we do know Acts 17, and so we just aren't in a position to say whether we would know (1)–(4) from natural revelation alone if we didn't know the contents of Acts 17. The Athenians had natural revelation, but still didn't seem to grasp (1)–(4); hence it made sense for Paul to make those points.

In sum, this passage is often used to teach about natural revelation, especially as coming from thinking about God's providential control of history. My contention is that what Paul said to the Athenians presupposed items (a)–(c) as common knowledge, and those items can be known from natural revelation. But that doesn't mean that (1)–(4) can be known from natural revelation. In fact, Paul stressed (1)–(4) *because the Athenians had not drawn those conclusions from (a)–(c)!* So, we may be inclined to think that (1)–(4) are knowable through natural revelation. But if they are, why does Paul preface these points by saying in verse 23 that "what therefore you worship *in ignorance*, this I proclaim to you"? Acts 17:23–28 is relevant to the doctrine of natural revelation, but that is so because it presupposes (a)–(c), which *are* knowable from natural revelation. We know (1)–(4) because we have read Luke's account of Paul's encounter with the Athenians. And, because we know this passage, we probably look at day-to-day events and the ebb and flow of history as giving evidence of God. But that means we know (1)–(4) by special revelation, specifically from Acts 17:23–28, part of Scripture which is itself special revelation![35]

*Psalm 19:1–6*

Psalm 19 contains the psalmist's praise for two forms of divine revelation. On the one hand, there is the revelation of God in nature (vv. 1–6). On the other, there is the revelation of God in his word. As to the former, the psalmist says that the heavens declare God's glory (v. 1). While some see this verse as saying that what is also revealed are things that God has made,[36] we must remember that this psalm is Hebrew poetry, and often the second line of a sentence basically repeats the thought of the first, though, of course, in other words. As John Byl explains, "but surely this text merely states the divine authorship of the firmament? Is not the key word here not 'handiwork' but '*his* handiwork'?"[37]

Franz Delitzsch nicely summarizes the verse's thought when he writes that "the doxa, which God has conferred upon the creature as the reflection of His own, is reflected back from it, and given back to God as it were in acknowledgment of its origin."[38] How exactly do the heavens declare God's glory, and what is revealed in revealing his glory? David doesn't explain, but it isn't difficult to understand what he means. The beauty of the sky with its deep blue color during the day, the beauty of a sunrise and sunset, and the beauty of the stars and moon at night all reflect a creator who is glorious. In addition, verses 4–6 mention the sun. The orderliness of its movement and the necessity of its warmth to sustain life all reflect a wise, powerful, and benevolent creator. Moreover, the very expanse of the heavens seems limitless; as far as the eye can see, they don't end. Surely, whoever made this universe, sustains it, and keeps it functioning in an orderly way must have great power! In Romans 1 Paul points to every existing thing as pointing to its creator. In Psalm 19 David focuses on just a portion of what God has made. But the results are the same; by seeing these majestic phenomena of nature, one can with little reasoning conclude that there must be a God who made it all.

---

[35] Helpful in writing this section on Acts 17 were Robert K. Johnston, "Discerning the Spirit in Culture: Observations Arising from Reflections on General Revelation," *Ex Auditu* 23 (2007): 64–65; Ziegler, "Natural Knowledge of God and the Trinity," 147–149; Ed Marks, "The Revelation and Experience of the 'Journeying' Triune God," *Affirmations and Critique* 10 (April 2005): 16; Demarest, "General and Special Revelation," 137–140.

[36] David Diehl, "Evangelicalism and General Revelation: An Unfinished Agenda," *JETS* 30 (December 1987): 448.

[37] John Byl, "General Revelation and Evangelicalism," *MAJT* 5 (1989): 4. See also Howard, "Critical Analysis of General Revelation," 59. Also James Hoffmeier concludes that the phrase "the glory of God" is parallel to and should be equated to "the work of his hands"; see James K. Hoffmeier, "'The Heavens Declare the Glory of God': The Limits of General Revelation," *TJ* 21 (2000): 20.

[38] Franz Delitzsch, *Biblical Commentary on the Psalms*, vol. 1 (repr., Grand Rapids, MI: Eerdmans, 1968), 281.

David's point about the natural order displaying God's glory is not unusual in the Psalms. As Demarest notes, in other Psalms, "the heavens are said to attest God's majesty (Ps. 8:1,9), 'righteousness' (Pss. 50:6; 97:6), 'faithfulness' (Psa. 89:5), 'wisdom' (Psa. 104:24), and 'power' (Pss. 29:4; 89:8)."[39] In verse 2, David adds that this revelation in nature is ongoing. Even as day moves to night and night into day in a seemingly endless cycle, so the revelation of God's glory through these means is ongoing. At every moment of their existence they reveal God's glory.

The thought in verse 3 is debated, and its relation to what precedes and follows is part of that debate. The verse's point, however, is both explicit and implicit. The implicit point is that the existence of the heavens and the alternation of day and night do reveal God's glory. However, they do so—and this is the explicit point—without uttering a single word. As some suggest, they make their point (that God is glorious) not so much by speaking (in human language) but just by existing, by being.[40] How so? In the way already described; i.e., we observe these phenomena and rapidly conclude that this must have been put in place by a powerful, wise, and beneficent creator. No mere mortal (or even a team of them) could produce such phenomena, regardless of their efforts.

Verse 4 teaches that this revelation is universal. Wherever there is sky, sun, and stars, these phenomena are observed. But since that is true of everywhere in the world, this revelation is available to all people everywhere at all times. Even as the sun rises from one end of the heavens and moves to the other, and even as everything on earth feels its warmth as it passes (the writer here is, of course, speaking phenomenologically, not making a precise scientific statement of which planetary and celestial bodies actually move), so it is true that no one escapes the testimony of these phenomena (vv. 4, 6).[41]

### Summary of Biblical Teaching on Natural Revelation

From our study of biblical passages about natural revelation we can crystalize some concluding thoughts about it. And once we clarify those points we can define it.

*Sources of Natural Revelation*—Scripture teaches several sources of natural revelation. The most obvious is the created universe, and this includes several things. From Romans 1, Psalm 19, and to some extent Acts 17, we learn that the mere existence of everything in the universe (as opposed to nothing at all)

---

[39] Demarest, "General and Special Revelation," 136.
[40] This seems to be Delitzsch's interpretation, though he discusses many options and isn't entirely clear, nor does he offer much explanation about the option he prefers. See Delitzsch, *Biblical Commentary on the Psalms*, vol. 1, 281–283.
[41] For further discussion of this passage see Demarest, "General and Special Revelation," 136; and Johnston, "Discerning the Spirit in Culture," 59–60.

reveals something about God. In addition, the universe's continued preservation is evidence of God's providential care. This is evident in Paul's sermon
at Lystra (Acts 14), and also part of the psalmist's point (Psalm 19) when he
speaks of the sun's orderly movement and of its role in sustaining life. And, as
both Paul and the Athenians seemed to believe, humans as God's offspring are
relevant to what we can know about God's nature.

Another source of natural revelation is human sensitivity to morality. All
people seem to have a basic sense of right and wrong, and many specific moral
rules about behavior seem to be commonly accepted. In addition, humans have
a conscience. These facts aren't hard to discern, and they should lead us to ask
how all of this came to be. Romans 1 and 2 give the distinct impression that
this has happened as a result of God's action. Hence, these facts about human
morality seem to point to God.

Various thinkers have also thought that history is a form of natural revelation that points to God. They argue that God's hand is evident in history, and
they believe that Paul made this point as he spoke to the Athenians (Acts 17).
Here, however, we should be cautious, for Acts 17 is a narrative passage about
Paul's experience in Athens. In his sermon at the Areopagus, he said that God
sets the times and boundaries of nations. That is, divine providence governs
the rise and fall of nations. However, nowhere in the passage do we hear Paul
suggesting that everyone knows this just by attending to the events of human
history. In fact, given the Athenians' beliefs that they were not like other people,
Paul's words about the origin and development of the human race and God's
control over the times and boundaries of nations were likely a new thought for
them. As we read Luke's account of Paul's sermon, *we also* learn this, if we
didn't know it from other Scriptures or other doctrines. But then, the source of
this information for us isn't natural revelation but special revelation.

In addition, if natural revelation is something that is available to all people
at all times, we must note that that is not true of most historical events. In our
modern age of television and the Internet, it is easy to think that everyone everywhere knows every major event (and many minor ones, too) that happens
to nations around the world, but that certainly wasn't so for most of history.

And, then, if major historical events are sources of divine revelation, as
Mark Lindsay persuasively argues, this must include all of history. But how,
Lindsay asks, are we to see God's hand at work in such horrific events as the
Holocaust or major natural disasters?[42] Likewise, when some natural disaster
(or even a man-made catastrophe like the carnage and destruction wreaked
upon America in the September 11, 2001, terrorist attacks) befalls a country
and some religious leader says this is God's judgment for the nation's evil,

---

[42] Mark Lindsay, "History, Holocaust, and Revelation," *ThTo* 61 (2005): 455–470.

even many committed Christians are repulsed by such thoughts. Nonbelievers hardly resonate with such sentiments, so it is hard to think that most people see God's providential hand in such terrible events.[43]

If history should be seen at all as a source for natural revelation, perhaps that might make the most sense as we reflect on our own lives. Maintaining good health, having a steady job that provides money for food and clothing, and being privileged to live in a free society, plus other major events in one's life may suggest divine beneficence to the one so blessed. However, while some see their station in life as evidence of God's existence and blessing, others see no such thing. They attribute their good fortune to hard work, good luck, or whatever. So, it is not clear that even the "history" of one's own life is a source of natural revelation. Remember as well that many people's lives are quite unpleasant—often through no fault of their own. Those sad personal histories lead some people to conclude that there is no God, or that if he does exist, either he isn't much involved in the world, or he is, but how he can be considered just and loving is a mystery.

In sum, it is best to see the natural created order and humans' moral nature as sources of natural revelation. While it is possible to see God's hand in the history of nations and in our own personal histories, if we do, that more likely stems from special revelation's teaching of divine providence than from natural revelation. The former two sources are available to all people at all times; the latter is not.

*Contents of Natural Revelation*—Some have suggested that knowledge of various sciences and the humanities is part of what can be known through natural revelation,[44] but Scripture nowhere teaches that. In addition, thinking these academic disciplines are to some extent natural revelation seems to confuse natural revelation with common grace as evidenced through human reason remaining in place despite sin's negative impact on all parts of human nature. Let me explain.

Many theologians, following thinkers like Calvin, argue that, as a result of the fall, without God's intervention humans are utterly blind on moral and spiritual matters, and unable to do what God requires. Still, sin didn't remove the image of God, and so reason, for example, was not ripped from human nature. Human reason can function well in many of the so-called secular disci-

---

[43] Howard, "Critical Analysis of General Revelation," 65–68, makes some of these points as he questions whether history is actually a source of natural revelation.

[44] Here see Diehl in favor of this broadening of the content of natural revelation. Howard cites various theologians who do the same. In contrast, Howard and Thomas rightly note that Scripture limits the content of what can be known to just a few things, and all of them relate in some way to the existence and nature of God. See Diehl, "Evangelicalism and General Revelation," 448–450; Howard, "Critical Analysis of General Revelation," 54–68; and Thomas, "General Revelation and Biblical Hermeneutics," 7–10.

plines of study, and also in various activities such as human government and the general running of society. This is so because God graciously did not destroy the human race when it fell into sin, and he didn't leave us alive but totally unable to do even practical everyday things that are necessary for individuals to function and for societies to run in an orderly manner. This is true for both believers and nonbelievers.

But it is a major mistake to confuse common grace with revelation common to all people. Because of God's grace the fallen world still reveals some things to God's human creatures. Graciously, God also gave us special revelation. But just because the same people who get general revelation also receive common grace, that does not mean that common grace is natural revelation. The truth is that, though we are sinners and deserve punishment and death, God graciously has not struck us dead nor removed our abilities to reason and function at all. Perhaps these are things we can infer from natural revelation. But that is not at all the same thing as saying that *the very content of the sciences and humanities* is natural revelation. Just because common grace and general revelation each extend to the same people, that does not mean that grace and revelation are identical. Hence, the very content of natural revelation does not include the contents of the sciences and humanities.

What, then, can we actually know from natural revelation? Not a lot, but we *can* know some things that are significant. First, God's existence can be known from natural revelation (Rom. 1:19–20, Psalm 19, and Acts 17:17ff.). However, the concept of God that is knowable from natural revelation is not identical to everything the Bible teaches about God. For example, natural revelation does not reveal God to be triune. Nor does it reveal that Jesus is God, is God incarnate, or is our redeemer. It may also be possible to know from natural revelation that there is only one God. But this conclusion would be inferentially made, if made at all. Let me explain.

In Romans 1:20 Paul says that, from the created world, humans can clearly see that there is a God and can know something about his attributes. In verses 21–23, Paul explains that, despite this revelation, humans suppressed this truth and perverted it so that, rather than worshiping the true and living God, they worshiped idols made to represent humans and various animals. Of course, religions that believe idols are (or represent) gods seldom worship just one. So, we can infer from these verses that, when the truth of God's existence and nature are suppressed, people typically turn to idolatry, but they don't just worship one idol. In contrast, if, by God's enablement, the truth about him available in the natural order is rightly read, those who grasp it will likely be *monotheists*, not just theists.

Should we make this inference from Romans 1? It is tempting to do so, but inferential reasoning can be slippery. Having admitted that the idea of God available in natural revelation doesn't include everything we learn about God through special revelation, and granting that Paul doesn't explicitly say that the existence of *only one* God can be known through natural revelation, we cannot be absolutely certain that Paul is teaching that from natural revelation we should infer only one God, not several. And if we do infer that only one God exists, we can't say for sure that the God inferred will be the God of Christianity. After all, there are other monotheistic religions besides Christianity. So, Romans 1 may warrant the idea that natural revelation reveals only one God, but we should not be dogmatic about this. The clearest evidence for monotheism comes from special revelation.[45]

Second, from natural revelation we can also know something of the divine attributes (Psalm 19; Rom. 1:20). Paul specifically names God's power, but then adds "divine nature." From observing creation one can know that its creator is extremely intelligent, benevolent, loving, etc. Whether nonmoral attributes like omnipresence and immutability are knowable by reflecting on the natural world isn't clear, but Paul's statement is general enough so that the inerrancy of his claim is in no way jeopardized. To be sure, natural revelation doesn't reveal the full-blown concept of the Judeo-Christian God, but because of natural revelation, God's existence and nature are not totally unknown.

Third, it also follows that God is understood to be the universe's creator. If creation seemed to be the result of natural forces, then it wouldn't necessarily suggest anything about God. But because God's existence is known *through creation*, then to know of God at all is to understand that he created all things.

---

[45] No doubt, some may wonder whether this basic concept of God is equal to what Calvin called the *sensus divinitatis*. And, Calvin aside, does Scripture teach that there *is* such a thing? That Calvin believed that every human has a *sensus divinitatis* (an "awareness of divinity") is easy to establish from the *Institutes*. See John Calvin, *Institutes of the Christian Religion*, ed. John T. McNeill, trans. Ford Lewis Battles (Philadelphia: Westminster, 1960), 43–44 (1.3.1). What isn't so clear is exactly what Calvin means by the *sensus* and how he thinks it relates to scriptural teaching on knowing God through natural revelation. Calvin answers both questions in book 1 of his *Institutes*. As to the former, Calvin believed that knowledge of God's existence is inborn in every individual; i.e., it is innate knowledge. Calvin explains: "Men of sound judgment will always be sure that a sense of divinity which can never be effaced is engraved upon men's minds. Indeed, the perversity of the impious, who though they struggle furiously are unable to extricate themselves from the fear of God, is abundant testimony that this conviction, namely, that there is some God, is naturally inborn in all, and is fixed deep within, as it were in the very marrow" (see *Institutes*, 45–46 (1.3.3). See also ibid., 43–47 passim (1.3.1–3). Calvin lived before John Locke's withering attack on innate ideas, so belief in innate ideas was common in his day (see Edward Adams, "Calvin's View of Natural Knowledge of God," *International Journal of Systematic Theology* 3 [November 2001]: 284–286). Adams argues that Calvin drew his theory of the *sensus divinitatis* from the Hellenistic philosophical notion of the preconception of God. That aside, Adams clearly confirms that Calvin believed that everyone innately knows that God exists. Did Calvin base this teaching on Scriptures such as Romans 1:19–21? Calvin helps answer this question in book 1 of the *Institutes*. He says that there are actually two distinct aspects of natural knowledge of God. One is the *sensus*, and the other source is the works of God (see Calvin, *Institutes*, 51–52 [1.5.1]). Calvin rightly supports this second avenue of natural knowledge from various Scriptures, including Psalm 19 and Romans 1:19–20. Interestingly, in *Institutes*, 1.3.1–3, where Calvin speaks of the *sensus divinitatis*, he doesn't support the notion with any Scriptures, including Romans 1:19–20. However, in book 1, chapter 4, Calvin says that knowledge of God known via the *sensus* is smothered or corrupted, and he supports that idea by appeal to Romans 1:22. From the preceding, what conclusions should we draw? As we saw in analyzing Romans 1:18ff., Paul doesn't talk of innate knowledge of God, but affirms that God's existence and attributes can be known through the created order. I leave it to readers to decide whether this passage teaches what Calvin means by the *sensus divinitatis*.

Fourth, natural revelation also makes it is possible to recognize God as the preserver of all things. This is evident from the fact that rain makes crops grow, and hence, there is food to sustain life (Acts 14). In line with Jesus's teaching that his disciples should not worry about the bare necessities of life, humans should see that, just as birds and animals have their needs met, and even as God "clothes" the flowers and grass of the fields with beauty, God will meet our most basic needs (cf. Matt. 6:25–30). The preservation of the universe is also knowable from the facts that night follows day, and then day returns—the sun doesn't burn out—and our world doesn't bang into the stars or moon and explode. What power is so great and benevolent that it can preserve all things in being? It must be a supreme being, not just a team of humans or some inanimate force.

Fifth, as noted from Acts 17, if humans are made by God—if we are his offspring—the cause should be equal to or greater than the effect. Humans aren't made of gold, silver, stone, or wood, so our maker cannot correctly be thought of as being made of those materials. Hence, by reflecting on ourselves and our creator, we should know that idols are not really gods at all. In fact, everyone should understand that no mere artifact represents or is a god.

The next few items knowable from natural revelation relate to morality and moral accountability to God. As we saw from Romans 2, everyone, Jew and Gentile, has a sense of moral right and wrong. This is true even if they have never read a Bible or heard a sermon. Moreover, certain "dos and don'ts" seem universal. Even those who claim to have no sense of morality would most certainly protest if their possessions were stolen, if they were misled by someone's lies, or if they were bodily injured by someone for no apparent reason. It is fair to say that just by living in the world, observing people interact with one another, and being given rules to follow and noting consequences for obeying and disobeying, all humans have this moral sense.

In addition, humans have a conscience. When a person obeys what she understands to be the rules, conscience doesn't accuse her of wrongdoing, and she has no sense of guilt. When she breaks the rules, her conscience accuses her and makes her feel guilty. All of these things stem from what Paul teaches in Romans 2, but there is more. We saw from Romans 1 that, just as creation reveals that God exists, humans also sense that this creator makes demands about their behavior, and that if they don't meet these requirements, they are guilty before God and deserve punishment (Rom. 1:32).

So, from natural revelation we can know that we are guilty before God because we have disobeyed him. And, we should know that we are guilty in another sense. If we dismiss God from our lives altogether, or remake him in our own image or to our own liking, we should know that these thoughts are wrong. Hence, we should also understand that, on judgment day, God won't excuse us if we say we would have worshiped and served him if we had known he existed and had certain expectations about our behavior. Even if only through natural revelation, we did know these things! So, we disobeyed in defiance of duty, not in ignorance of it.

One further thing is knowable through natural revelation, although it isn't clear that everyone grasps it. In light of our culpability for rejecting truth about God, and our moral guilt for disobeying God's laws, we can know without any special revelation that we deserve God's punishment and that the punishment is death (Rom. 1:32). We also know that punishment usually follows soon after wrongdoing. But we are still alive and in many cases we escape any punishment for a very long time. How can this be so? We can conclude that God is very longsuffering and gracious to us. We don't deserve his withholding of punishment, and yet that often happens. Thus, our moral judge must be gracious and patient with us.

The point about God's grace to sinners can be known without special revelation. Admittedly, it takes some thought to put together all the items just mentioned so as to conclude that God is gracious. Undoubtedly, many don't reach that conclusion, but that doesn't mean that none do, nor that such information isn't available through natural revelation.

In sum, some significant things can be known through natural revelation, but many things are not knowable through it. We can know that we are guilty sinners who deserve God's punishment, but natural revelation offers no clue about how to solve our predicament. Thankfully, in special revelation God has supplemented natural revelation and has told us how to start and maintain a right relationship with him.

*Usefulness of Natural Revelation*—Some are very skeptical about the usefulness of natural revelation, because human sin gets in the way of an unbeliever's ability to understand and appropriate its truth. Here several things are noteworthy. First, all the passages studied about natural revelation are written from the perspective of people living in a fallen world. For example, Romans 1–2 contains the most detailed discussion of natural revelation, but one of Paul's main points is that none of us on our own lives in accord with natural revelation. However, Paul nowhere says that, because of man's sinfulness and suppressing of truth, there actually is no natural revelation. In addition, in Romans 8:20–23, Paul wrote that the whole creation was subjected to futility because of sin. But Paul adds that it groans as it awaits the revelation of the sons of God, and those who are God's people also groan as they await the full realization of their salvation.

Now, if creation was subjected to futility by sin, one might conclude that it must, then, be useless to reveal God. But Paul wrote both Romans 8 and also Romans 1–2. In chapters 1–2, Paul shows that everyone really knows that God exists. Moreover, despite being steeped in sin, people who do horrendous evil still have enough of a sense of right and wrong and of moral accountability to God that they know they deserve to be punished (Rom. 1:32). And, in Romans 2 Paul does not say that, because of sin, neither the law written in people's hearts nor their consciences work anymore. Paul thinks sin is devastating, but nowhere in Romans 1–2 does he say that because of sin God turned out the "light" of natural revelation. Nor does he say that sin rendered natural revelation nonexistent.

Even so, we should not be overly optimistic about what can be accomplished through natural revelation. In Romans 1–3 Paul explains that no one, whether they have only natural revelation or both natural and special revelation, will on his or her own live in accord with it. This point is illustrated in narrative passages like Acts 14 and 17. Despite the apostles' claims and despite their appeal to natural revelation and other items of common ground, most people who heard them did not turn to Christ. And, Psalm 19 beautifully extols the glory of God revealed in the natural world, but it does not guarantee that anyone will respond to that revelation so as to establish a relationship with God and follow him.

And, as noted in the previous section, natural revelation doesn't contain a gospel message. If someone is led by natural revelation to seek more information about God, he or she won't learn from natural revelation how to be saved. So, though we might be rather excited about the information available in natural revelation, we must not be overly enthusiastic. Everyone, on their own, rejects natural revelation, and no biblical passage suggests that people will be led to Christ through natural revelation alone.

*Natural Revelation and Truth in Other Religions?*—Finally, we should address an issue sometimes raised in relation to Acts 17 and the altar to the unknown God. Paul mentioned that altar as a point of contact from which he began to share the gospel. Paul said that what the Athenians "worship[ed] in ignorance," he proclaimed to them. Some have thought this means that Paul actually approved of their altar, and that he was saying that there is truth in their pagan religion. Hence, some might think this means there is truth in non-Christian religions, perhaps even enough so that those who follow those religions can establish a relationship with God, and be saved without embracing Jesus as Savior.

This, however, is an unfortunate and, I believe, incorrect conclusion. Paul also references the writings of pagan Greek poets, but that does not mean that the Greco-Roman pantheon the poets celebrate is, after all, a valid religion.

Nor does it mean that Paul used the words of these poets in exactly the same sense they meant when they wrote their poems in praise of pagan gods. As Peter said about Jesus, when he stood before the elders, scribes, Annas the high priest, and Caiaphas, John, and Alexander—all of high priestly descent—"there is salvation in no one else; for there is no other name under heaven that has been given among men, by which we must be saved" (Acts 4:12).

In a similar way, Paul used the altar to the unknown God as a point of contact, but he said only that the Athenians were very religious, not that their religion was right (Acts 17:22)! In verse 23 Paul added that the one they worshiped in ignorance is the God he was proclaiming to them. But Paul didn't at all mean that if they would just get rid of all the statues, altars, and temples to the other gods and worship at the altar to the unknown god, they would then be saved.

What Paul said in 17:24–27 about the God he commended to them wasn't true of any of the gods of Greco-Roman mythology, nor did all of them collectively have the qualities Paul described. Hence, the unknown God whom Paul described was nothing like any of the gods the Athenians worshiped. In verses 28–29 Paul again appealed to something that was common knowledge among his listeners, but not to affirm belief in the gods of mythology. Rather, Paul's point was that if God is truly our Father, and if in him we live and move and have our being, then he is nothing like the gods of Greco-Roman mythology. Those gods can be represented by gold, silver, or stone images. In verses 28–29 Paul rejected such things as being mere idols—not true gods.

Lest some think Paul still allowed the Athenians' gods some legitimacy, the clinching argument against this is recorded in verses 30–31. Paul didn't point to a deity of Greco-Roman mythology of whom the Athenians knew very little and whom they celebrated by their altar to the unknown god. No, Paul pointed to Jesus Christ, the crucified and risen Savior! He has no place whatsoever in the Greco-Roman pantheon of gods, nor can he be "synthesized" with the god or gods of any other religion. No mythological deity ever died and rose from the dead. And, even if some religion made such a claim, where is the evidence that it ever happened? No, the God whom Paul proclaimed to the Athenians has no place in their pantheon of gods. Adding Jesus to any other religion's beliefs won't in any way legitimize that other religion!

In sum, we cannot use Acts 17 as evidence that other religions are in some way true paths to eternal life. People who do not know of and trust Jesus are not somehow saved by following faithfully the path of their own culture's religion. Paul used pagan religion and pagan poets as points of contact to start a conversation, but that does not mean he granted some legitimacy to the polytheism of the Greeks. A point of contact is a common idea, but the fact that from this common ground a conversation can begin does not mean the nonbeliever actually possesses the truth. Paul says nothing that would allow us to find "truth" in other religions so that we needn't tell nonbelievers about Jesus. Paul says that the true God is entirely different from anything the Athenians worshiped, including their unknown god of Greek mythology.

*Defining Natural Revelation*—In light of our discussion of natural revelation, it is possible to define it. Natural revelation unveils to all humans, regardless of time and place in history, the truth that a supreme being, God, exists, and it demonstrates something of his divine attributes such as power, wisdom, and goodness. These truths are known through the use of reason applied to the created and preserved (in existence) universe. In addition, apart from any form of special revelation, each human has a basic moral sense of right and wrong, an understanding of some basic rules of moral conduct, and a conscience that accuses those who disobey the rules and exonerates those who obey. Each person, by the light of human reason reflecting on these moral rules and in conjunction with the workings of conscience, knows that she or he has broken the rules and deserves to be punished for doing so. However, natural revelation does not tell how to remove the guilt and punishment for wrongdoing so as to satisfy the demands of a God who demands moral perfection. While what can be known through natural revelation can be stated in language, most of the forms in which natural revelation comes do not themselves contain language.[46]

---

[46] Other helpful works I used about natural revelation are Kenneth S. Kantzer, "Revelation and Inspiration in Neo-Orthodox Theology," *BSac* 115 (October 1958); Millard Erickson, "Revelation," in *Foundations for Biblical Interpretation*, ed. David Dockery, Kenneth Mathews, and Robert Sloan (Nashville: Broadman & Holman, 1993); N. H. Gootjes, "General Revelation in Its Relation to Special Revelation," *WTJ* 51 (1989); Dennis E. Johnson, "Between Two Wor(l)ds: Worldview and Observation in the Use of General Revelation to Interpret Scripture, and Vice Versa," *JETS* 41 (March 1998); and Paul J. Visser, "Religion in Biblical and Reformed Perspective," *CTJ* 44 (2009).

# THREE

# LIGHT UNVEILED (II)

## Special Revelation

Though natural revelation is available to everyone at all times in history, its content, though important, is somewhat limited. As for special revelation, it is at once broader, deeper, and narrower than natural revelation. It is *broader* in that its content *covers many more subjects* than does natural revelation, and its content *comes in more forms or ways* than does natural revelation. For example, scriptural special revelation covers not only spiritual truth; it also covers in both broad strokes (at times) and in specific details (at times) the history of Israel, the life of Christ, and the beginnings of the church. In addition, special revelation comes in words, visions, dreams, and acts, as well in the person Jesus Christ and in Scripture, whereas natural revelation is rooted in the created universe, including human nature.

Special revelation is broader than natural revelation, but there is some overlap in the contents of both. However, special revelation invariably goes *deeper* than does natural. For example, from natural revelation one can know that God exists and has certain attributes, but only from special revelation can we construct a detailed list of divine attributes, and define and distinguish them with precision. Moreover, from Scripture we can learn that God is triune, but no such information is available through natural revelation. And some topics are not covered at all in natural revelation, but in special revelation God has shown us much of his thinking. For example, from natural revelation one can discern one's guilt for disobeying moral rules, but nothing about how to satisfy the wrath and justice of God. In contrast, a major theme of special revelation is the message of salvation, including what God has done to purchase it, and what humans must do to receive forgiveness of sin and eternal life. In part because special revelation goes so deeply into key themes, like the plan of salvation, and in part because God did not give all of special revelation at once, it is *special* revelation that is *progressive* in nature. This is true not only of Scripture but also of other forms of special revelation, such as divine acts. God's release of Abraham from the command to sacrifice Isaac, God's removal of Israel from Egyptian bondage, and God's potential salvation of all people from sin through the death and resurrection of Jesus Christ are all in some way related to personal or corporate salvation. But, surely, God's saving act in Christ is the most intensive and extensive form of a saving act that God has done. In contrast, the content of natural revelation is, has been, and always will be essentially the same.

In spite of special revelation being broader and deeper, there is a sense in which it is *narrower* than natural revelation. Natural revelation is for everyone and accessible to everyone. It covers such broad topics as God's existence and attributes as well as a general sense of right and wrong, and some basic moral norms. Of course, special revelation also covers these themes, but not in such a general way as does natural revelation.

In what sense, then, can special revelation be *narrower* than natural revelation? It is narrower because it isn't accessible to all people at all times and places. Even more, some things God said to one group of people at a given time were never intended to apply to everyone. For example, the Mosaic law with all of its elements was never given to all humanity. Even if one believes that during the OT era, non-Jewish peoples should have been "evangelized" and brought under the rule of the Mosaic code, it is hard to see this as being so during the NT era. The book of Hebrews, for example, should convince anyone that the OT sacrificial system is no longer in force. Moreover, Israel in the OT was a theocracy, but NT injunctions to submit to the powers in authority—at a time when the Roman Empire was the ruler—make it unthinkable that the early church (or the church at any time after that) should have tried to impose a theocracy wherever Christians lived.

It isn't just verbal revelation that is narrower than natural revelation. As we shall see, much special revelation came in specific divine actions. Some of them were miracles, like the parting of the waters of the Red Sea, but some were not, like God's use of Assyria and Egypt to judge Judah (as promised in Isa. 7:17–25). But the revelation contained in many of those divine acts wasn't meant for everyone, only for a limited few. For example, when Jesus healed someone of a disease, only that person was healed, not every sick person, and the healing of one person was not a promise that others would also be healed.

There is another significant difference between natural and special revelation. No form of natural revelation includes language, whereas language is part of various forms of special revelation.[1] Of course, special revelation is not just divine speech, but as we shall see, even nonverbal forms of special revelation come with language to explain the significance of what is revealed. Because special revelation includes language, it can cover more topics in greater depth, and it allows God to disclose specific things to particular persons that are not relevant to others. Without natural revelation it would be hard to understand such basic concepts as God as creator and sustainer of the universe, nor would it be so evident as to what sin is and why humans need to be saved. So, natural revelation "supports" special revelation, but special revelation explains everything contained in natural revelation, and special revelation addresses many more topics and themes than natural revelation could ever communicate.

From the preceding, it would be easy simply to equate special revelation with language and to think only of Scripture. Scripture is one form of divine revelation, but it is not the only kind of special revelation God has given. In what follows, I shall present the various forms of special revelation, according to Scripture.

## FORMS OF SPECIAL REVELATION

Some might approach a biblical study of special revelation by noting that the main Hebrew word for "reveal" is *gālāh*, and the main Greek word is *apokalyptō*, and then by looking up each passage where these words occur and "reading off" the results. However, that approach would be wrong in two respects. First, if one decides to do a word study, many other Hebrew and Greek words are used to mean "to disclose, unveil, uncover" that which was hidden. For example, we could point to the Hebrew words *qārā'*, *'āmar*, and *dābar*. Those terms all refer to the transmitter of revelation. There are Hebrew terms that focus on the recipient and mean such things as "to perceive, behold or see, discern, or look on." The Hebrew words in these cases are *shama'*, *hāzāh*, and *rā'āh*.[2] In Greek, the NT also uses terms like *phaneroō*, *phainomai*, *epiphainō*, and *optomai*. These terms can mean "to manifest" and "to appear."

The second and more fundamental reason for not relying on a simple word study is that we are investigating the meaning of a concept, not the different ways a word can be used in various settings. A conceptual investigation seeks to understand what sort of thing the notion, in this case divine revelation, is. Theology involves conceptual articulation and clarification, so in our case the

---

[1] Some may contest this in light of Psalm 19:1–4. But that would misunderstand how nature "declares" God's glory. It doesn't literally speak, but "declares" *by being* magnificent, beautiful, etc. Those with sense perception and reason who view nature conclude that it is amazing and couldn't have occurred just by chance; it must have been made by a being with supreme power, intelligence, wisdom, and goodness. But that doesn't mean that nature literally speaks to say that God is glorious. Its grandeur leads *us,* however, to think and say such things.

[2] Herbert Brichto, "On Faith and Revelation in the Bible," *Hebrew Union College Annual* 39 (1968): 35, is very helpful in detailing these terms.

task is to consult any passage that incorporates the concept of divine revelation, regardless of what words the verse uses to convey that something was revealed. To illustrate this point, Klyne Snodgrass has written a most stimulating essay on the concept of revelation in relation to the gospel in the book of Romans. He details some thirty different expressions used throughout Romans in contexts where Paul clearly talks about something being revealed to someone.[3] I shall use some of his material in what follows, but readers would find his article a very potent illustration of the need to define concepts, not just words, when doing theology.

So, rather than simply looking for passages that use a term(s) for revelation, we will look for passages that speak about instances of revelation from God to someone or some group. Using that strategy, what stands out is the many different forms in which divine special revelation came.

### Divine Acts or Deeds

God has revealed himself in various actions. Acts alone might be ambiguous as to what they show about God or anyone else, but Scripture normally interprets or explains their significance. Divine acts can be divided into two categories, although theologies of revelation tend only to focus on the former. The first sort of revelatory divine act is miracles done either by God alone or through the agency of his creatures. The second kind of divine action is nowhere near as evident as a miracle, but God's hand is still at work in the normal flow of events which otherwise give little or no evidence of divine involvement.

As for miracles, their supernatural character discloses the divine power of the one by whom they are wrought. Creating our universe was an act of divine revelation, and the apostle Paul affirms in Romans 1:19–20 that, from creation, God's existence and many of his attributes can be clearly seen. But creating the world isn't all that reveals God. As we read in Acts 14:15–17 and 17:22–28 (Paul's speech on Mars Hill in Athens), it is also God's preserving the universe that reveals him. In addition to showing that a powerful God exists, it also shows his kindness and mercy on his creatures, and his patience with those who disobey him and deserve judgment immediately but don't receive it!

Miracles were often used to authenticate a new phase in God's program (e.g., the miracles on the day of Pentecost as the Holy Spirit was poured out on those who believed), or to authenticate a specific message or messenger (e.g., Ex. 4:2–5, to authenticate Moses as God's spokesman and to show that Pharaoh and the Egyptians had better listen to him). In particular, the life

---

[3] Klyne Snodgrass, "The Gospel in Romans: A Theology of Revelation," in *Gospel in Paul: Studies on Corinthians, Galatians, and Romans for Richard N. Longenecker*, ed. L. Ann Jervis and Peter Richardson, JSNTSup 108 (1994): 291–292.

of Jesus was filled with various miracles which showed that he was who he claimed to be. Even so, the Scribes and Pharisees always wanted more signs. Jesus said that the only further sign he would give was the sign of Jonah. Jesus used the swallowing of Jonah by the great fish and then Jonah's expulsion as a sign of Jesus's forthcoming death and resurrection (Matt. 12:38–40). Jesus was saying that when he would rise from the dead, that would be the clinching miracle to authenticate everything he had said, done, and claimed to be. Sadly, when Christ died and rose again, rather than believe, his critics and opponents concocted stories, like the one that the disciples stole his body, to "prove" that a miracle hadn't occurred. Clearly, the resurrection reveals much about Jesus, even though many who were witnesses rejected it. As Jesus said in Matthew 12:41, even the citizens of Nineveh on judgment day will condemn Jesus's opponents, for when Jonah preached to Nineveh, they believed. Many of Jesus's contemporaries saw the risen Christ and still refused to believe!

One final note on miracles authenticating a messenger as from God relates to Jesus himself. In John 5:30ff., Jesus says that there is John's testimony that Jesus is truly from God, but there is an even greater proof. In verse 36, Jesus says, "But the witness which I have is greater than that of John; for the works which the Father has given Me to accomplish, the very works that I do, bear witness of Me, that the Father has sent Me." Many of Jesus's works were miracles, and his acts of redemption and resurrection also involved miracles. All of these works showed that he was sent by the Father!

In addition, miracles often displayed the superior power of Israel's God to that of the various idols Israel's enemies worshiped. Think of Elijah and the prophets of Baal at Mount Carmel (1 Kings 18), and the ten plagues God rained down on Egypt. Moses told Pharaoh that Israel's God wanted Pharaoh to let Israel go. Pharaoh refused, saying that he knew no such God. He probably thought that if the God of the Jews was so mighty and powerful, why would he leave his people in slavery to Pharaoh for over four hundred years? So a contest, so to speak, was set up between Pharaoh and the gods of Egypt, and Yahweh and the people of Israel. God told Pharaoh that Israel was his "firstborn," and that Pharaoh must let "him" go. Pharaoh refused, so God decided to teach Pharaoh a lesson. Before this contest would end, God would kill Pharaoh's firstborn son and liberate Israel, God's firstborn. In fact, each of the ten plagues God miraculously rained down on Egypt was a stroke of judgment against something worshiped as god in Egypt. That included the tenth and climactic plague, the killing of the firstborn. In Egyptian religion, not only the Pharaoh but his firstborn son was thought to be divine and were worshiped as gods. What was at stake in this contest with Pharaoh was not just liberation of God's people; the question of whose God was the true and living

God was most fundamentally at stake. By miraculous intervention, including the parting of the Red Sea and drowning Pharaoh's armies in it, the God of Israel won every "round" in that match!

While it might be possible to detail the physical conditions necessary to produce a miracle, that could never explain why the miracle occurred when it did, nor could we simply explain the miracle as happening by natural means. For example, Moses parted the waters of the Red Sea. Someone versed in the science of wind velocities, etc., might be able to explain the amount of force and the exact direction of the winds needed in order to part the waters of the Red Sea. However, those natural conditions might never occur in the normal course of nature. Or, if they did, it would be impossible to explain in purely naturalistic terms why the waters parted just when they did, why all the Israelites passed over the riverbed before the waters came back to drown some, and why, since the waters were parted and would have provided a pathway for the Egyptian soldiers to follow the Jews, the waters receded at just the right time to drown the Egyptian soldiers, instead of staying parted. These details are explainable only by appeal to divine miracle.

Likewise, it might be possible to explain the natural conditions necessary to produce at least some of the ten plagues that God brought upon Egypt. Plagues of darkness, infestation of locusts, murrain on the cattle, and even turning the Nile to blood might occur in some naturalistic course of events. But why those events happened when they did and then ceased when Pharaoh relented is explainable only by divine miracles.

On the other hand, some miracles are inexplicable by any naturalistic means. This is true for the resurrection of Jesus, restoring sight to a man blind from birth (John 9), creating the world out of nothing (Genesis 1 and 2), sending fire on Mount Carmel to consume not only Elijah's sacrifice but the altar, the animal, and everything else (1 Kings 18:20–39), and multiplying five loaves of bread and two fishes to produce enough food to feed five thousand people (Matt. 14:13–21).[4]

In the OT, especially in Psalms, many passages praise God for his deeds. For example, some psalms extol God's name for punishing the writer's enemies and protecting God's people (Pss. 46:8; 64:9). In another, the psalmist prayed for God's help and God acts to set him free (Ps. 118:5). Then, there are other psalms written to praise and thank God for his love and wonderful deeds (the psalmist refers to all of God's acts in general). Invariably, the psalm-

---

[4]For more on God's miracles, see Millard J. Erickson, "Revelation," in *Foundations for Biblical Interpretation*, ed. David Dockery, Kenneth Mathews, and Robert Sloan (Nashville: Broadman & Holman, 1993), 12; Richard C. Gamble, "The Relationship between Biblical Theology and Systematic Theology," in *Always Reforming: Explorations in Systematic Theology*, ed. A. T. B. McGowan (Downers Grove, IL: InterVarsity Press, 2004), 216; and C. P. Price, "Revelation as Our Knowledge of God: An Essay in Biblical Theology," in *Faith and History*, ed. John T. Carroll, Charles H. Cosgrove, and E. Elizabeth Johnson (Atlanta: Scholars Press, 1990), 317.

ist urges his readers to do the same (Psalm 66; Ps. 75:1; 107:21). And in Job, Elihu exhorts all to praise God for his wondrous works (all in general), and he adds that all humans have seen them (Job 36:24–25; see also Amos 4:13). Undoubtedly, Elihu was thinking most specifically of God's works in creating and preserving the universe and in controlling the various forces of nature, but this passage can also reasonably apply to other works of God which only a few people have seen.

Another kind of divine action also reveals God, though not in such a spectacular, noticeable way. Think of the many times God is at work in history to bring about his will through the seemingly ordinary events of people's lives. Such actions are, so to speak, done by dual agency. The obvious agent, who makes the deed not seem supernatural at all, is a human who does the deed. The not-so-obvious participant, however, is God himself working through the actions of his creatures to accomplish what he wants to do. In these cases, if Scripture didn't teach that divine providence superintends the world's affairs, and if in specific instances Scripture didn't say that God's hand was involved in otherwise ordinary events, we might never suspect it. But Scripture does teach these things, and a few examples show that to be so.

Consider the story of Joseph. He was badly abused by his brothers, who sold him into slavery. Eventually, Joseph wound up in Egypt in prison. Joseph later came to the Pharaoh's attention by interpreting his dream. Pharaoh gave Joseph a position of prominence over all of Egypt, and during seven years of plenty, Joseph's administrative skills were wisely put to use in preparing the country for seven years of famine. In fact, Joseph did so well in this job that there was enough food for Egypt and for other neighboring countries. During the famine, Joseph's brothers traveled to Egypt for food to keep their families alive.

The details of what happened next are well known and are in no way miraculous. Eventually, Joseph revealed his true identity to his brothers. He assured them that he had no desire for revenge, and he encouraged them to bring their whole families into Egypt so that they could survive the famine and be safe.

If the details were all you knew about the story of Joseph and his brothers, you might think, "What a happy series of coincidences!" "Wow! That is one lucky family!" and, "How's that for being at the right place at the right time!" But no such explanation is given, because a different understanding of what happened came from Joseph's lips. He told his brothers, "Do not be afraid, for am I in God's place? And as for you, you meant evil against me, but God meant it for good in order to bring about this present result, to preserve many people alive" (Gen. 50:19–20). This is the hidden story behind the story. In this seemingly all-too-human set of events, God was at work all along behind the scenes, orchestrating events to achieve his goals for his people. So somehow God was also working in what Joseph's brothers, Pharaoh, and Joseph did. No spectacular miracles occurred, but God was still at work. See also Isaiah 7–10 and God's judgment both on the northern kingdom of Israel at the hands of the Assyrians and on the Assyrians themselves.

And then there is the capture, trial, crucifixion, and burial of Jesus Christ. On the surface, none of these events seems miraculous. Had we visited Jerusalem when these things were happening, we might have thought Jesus was wrongly convicted and sentenced to die, but his death might have seemed nothing more than another case of an innocent person being murdered at the hands of the state. If we heard a few days later that his tomb was empty, we might have believed the story that his disciples had stolen his body. These events could be seen (and probably were seen by many) as just part of the normal flow of events under the Roman rule of Palestine.

But much more was going on! We don't need to read the Gospels to convince ourselves of that. In Peter's sermon on the day of Pentecost, we get "the rest of the story." Speaking of Jesus and the miracles he did to show that he was sent from God—miracles of which his listeners were fully aware (Acts 2:22)—Peter proclaimed, "this Man, delivered up by the predetermined plan and foreknowledge of God, you nailed to a cross by the hands of godless men and put Him to death" (2:23). What a remarkable statement! In this one act of a grossly unjust murder, there were two "doers." Both God and man were at work, for Peter says that what happened was as God had planned. What plan? Before Peter completed the rest of his message (as recorded in verses 24–39) it became clear that the plan was God's plan of salvation. The rest of the NT confirms this. So here was a sequence of events that at first glance seemed to evidence nothing of God's work—indeed what happened to Jesus seems to speak of abandonment by God. But that act of unjust murder done by humans was also God's act of paying for the sins of the world!

### Direct Communication of Information

The largest group of things revealed are unveiled by direct communication of information (words). God revealed information in many different ways. Each form of direct communication will be illustrated with some examples.

*"And God Spoke," "God Said"*—The first set of instances where God directly communicated information relates to a common practice in the OT. Often a writer claimed, "And God spoke" or "God said," and then added what-

ever the Lord said on that occasion.[5] Exactly how God sent the message isn't always stated, but we can often see what God said, because the writer repeated it.[6]

*Direct Speech*—On various occasions God spoke directly to one person or a group. In some cases what he said was audible, whereas in others it was likely inaudible. Examples of times when God could be audibly heard are Genesis 1:28–30 and 3:9–19. In both instances, God spoke to Adam and Eve. There is no reason to think that God spoke inaudibly (especially because, for example, in Gen. 3:8–10 we read that Adam and Eve heard the sound of God walking in the garden and that God called to Adam and Adam told God he had heard God in the garden), and what God said was written down.

In Genesis 4:9ff. we read that God spoke to Cain after he killed his brother, and what God said was written down. And, as recorded in Exodus 3:2–4:17, God spoke directly to Moses from the burning bush. In fact, God and Moses had a conversation, and what each said is written down. It is most likely that Moses heard God's voice, because all he saw was a burning bush, and the way the passage connects the words God spoke with the burning bush suggests that Moses audibly heard God speaking. See also the incident of the call of Samuel, when Samuel thought Eli was calling to him (1 Sam. 3:1ff.).

Then, Numbers 12:6–8 records what the Lord said to Aaron and Miriam. They had complained about Moses, and the Lord defended Moses. God said that he spoke with Moses differently from how he communicated with any other prophet. With others God spoke in a dream or a vision, but with Moses, God spoke "mouth to mouth, even openly, and not in dark sayings, and he beholds the form of the LORD" (12:8). While Moses didn't always write down what God said, in many cases he did. Given what God said in Numbers 12:8, many of God's communications with Moses quite likely came "mouth to mouth." Though we cannot be absolutely certain, it is reasonable to think that on those occasions God spoke audibly to Moses. See also Exodus 33:11. It is also worth noting Exodus 31:18, which says that the tablets with the Ten Commandments were "written by the finger of God." Though this isn't audible speech, it is definitely direct speech, and we know what God "said," because Scripture records the Ten Commandments (e.g., Ex. 20:1–17).

---

[5] There are so many of these that they can't all be listed here. For a complete list see *Young's Analytic Concordance*, 839–841.

[6] Here two subsidiary points will avoid confusion. First, in English translations of Scripture, the Lord's words are often set off from the rest of the text by using quotation marks. But modern conventions about quotations shouldn't be read back into the original Hebrew text. In other words—and this is the second point—when we see quotation marks in a text, we assume that whatever appears within quotation marks is a verbatim quote of what someone said. But we do not need always to assume that such quotations are verbatim. For example, so long as a prophet accurately offers the substance of what the Lord said, we know what God revealed to his prophet for his people. None of this undermines Scripture as divine revelation. It just warns us not to impose on Scripture our modern conventions about quotation marks.

In the NT there were also instances when God spoke audibly to someone. At Jesus's baptism, a voice from heaven said, "This is My beloved Son, in whom I am well-pleased" (Matt. 3:17). It isn't clear how many people heard this, but what is the point of saying that a voice from heaven spoke if no one could hear it? And, at the Mount of Transfiguration, the same thing happened (Matt. 17:5). In that case we know that Peter, James, and John were present, and we also know that they heard the voice, because verse 6 says that when they heard the voice, they fell on their faces and were much afraid.

Then, the confrontation of Saul (Paul) on the Damascus Road is very well known. We know what Christ said to him, because it was written down (Acts 9:4–6). We also know that Jesus's words were audible, because Luke says that the men traveling with Saul were speechless, because they heard the voice from heaven, but saw no one.

Of course, many OT and NT passages say that the word of the Lord came to someone, but it isn't always clear that it came in an audible form. For example, Numbers 24:3–9 says that the Lord spoke to Balaam, and then Balaam spoke for the Lord. Whether Balaam spoke words God spoke to him, we aren't told. It is reasonable to assume that what Balaam said bore some relation to what God said to him, but we are in no position to confirm the degree to which Balaam repeated exactly what God spoke to him. Then, in the NT, Acts says that the Spirit spoke to Philip (Acts 8:29) and to Peter (Acts 10:19–20). It is possible that the Spirit spoke audibly, but nothing in the text confirms this. He might just as well have spoken inaudibly.

One final passage is noteworthy. The book of Hebrews begins by saying that God in times past spoke through the prophets "in many ways." The author then added that in these last days of revelation, God has spoken through his Son, Jesus Christ (Heb. 1:1–2). Hence, when we read in the Gospels what Jesus said to his disciples, to the multitudes, and to his opponents, we are reading God's very words. Those who heard Jesus speak, of course, heard the audible words of God, and thanks to the Gospel writers, in many cases we know what Jesus said, because they wrote it down. For further biblical claims that God spoke some information to someone or some group, see Leviticus 1:1; Jeremiah 1:8 (God told Jeremiah that he put his words in Jeremiah's mouth, so when Jeremiah says he speaks the word of the Lord, it is the Lord speaking audibly to Jeremiah's audience, big or small); 7:1; 11:1; and 18:1 ("the word that came to Jeremiah on behalf of YHWH" AT); Hosea 1:1; Joel 1:1; and Amos 3:1.[7]

---

[7] For further discussion of divine revelation by direct speech, see Erickson, "Revelation," 12–13; Dewey Beegle, "The Biblical Concept of Revelation," in *The Authoritative Word: Essays on the Nature of Scripture*, ed. Donald K. McKim (Grand Rapids, MI: Eerdmans, 1983), 95–97; and Bob Becking, "Means of Revelation in the Book of Jeremiah," in *Prophecy in the Book of Jeremiah*, ed. Hans M. Barstad and Reinhard G. Kratz (Berlin: Walter de Gruyter, 2009), 34.

*Answers to Questions*—God also revealed information by answering questions asked of him. The way he answered wasn't always the same. In some cases God answered a prayer. For example, in 1 Samuel 10:22 the Lord was asked where Saul was. The Lord answered so that the people could find him—their intent was to make him king. In 1 Samuel 23:4, David asked God if on that occasion he should fight the Philistines, and God told him to do so. In 1 Samuel 30:8, David asked the Lord if he should pursue a band of Amalekites who had made a raid on the south country. The Lord said yes, because David would overtake them and rescue those taken captive. See also 2 Kings 8:13, 2 Chronicles 34:23, and 2 Samuel 21:1.

In addition, Job searched for God. He wanted to present his case to God but also wanted to hear God's explanation of what had happened to him. Though God delayed his answer, Job 38–41 records God's extended reply to Job. Having heard from God, in chapter 42 we see a Job who was satisfied, not because God told him what happened (as recorded in chapters 1–2) but because he received a new picture of God's power and majesty.

Moreover, sometimes God invited his people to call upon him. In the days of Jeremiah, God said that if his people would call to him, "I will answer you, and I will tell you great and mighty things, which you do not know" (Jer. 33:3). On another occasion, it was clear that questioning God and getting an answer was commonplace. Hence, Jeremiah told his people (42:4) that he would ask God for what they wanted, the Lord would answer, and Jeremiah would give them the Lord's response. Later (v. 21) he scolded them because he prayed to God, gave them God's answer, and they disobeyed what God said, even though they had promised to obey.

This phenomenon of calling on God and getting a response also appears in many psalms. The contexts differ, however, from the ones already noted, for the psalmists say that they prayed to God—usually for help in time of need or danger—and he answered their prayer. See, for example, such Psalms as 81:7; 91:15; 99:8; and 138:3. Though the psalmists don't exactly say how God answered, in each case *divine* action was so evident that the petitioner knew God had answered the prayer. These passages in Psalms also show us to pray to God in times of need, for he often answers those prayers.

*Speaking and Appearing*—A number of passages show that sometimes God appeared to people while speaking to them. On other occasions, God sent an angel to deliver a message. Of course, God is immaterial and invisible, so when he appeared, he did so in some physical way, but of course without adding a physical component to his divine nature. Sometimes the writers tell us the physical form God took, but often, they only say God appeared.

This phenomenon is especially prevalent in the Pentateuch, Genesis in particular. For example, Genesis 12:7 and 17:1 say that God appeared to Abraham and spoke to him. We are told what God said to him. Then, Genesis 26:2, 24 says that God appeared to Isaac and spoke to him. Again, we are told what God said. Genesis 35:1 explains that the God who appeared to Jacob after he fled from Esau told Jacob to go to Bethel, live there, and make an altar there to God. In 35:9–12, God appeared again to Jacob, blessed him, changed his name to Israel, promised him many descendants, and gave him the land given to Abraham and Isaac. See also Genesis 48:3–4.

None of these Genesis passages tells what physical form God took when he appeared. In contrast, we know that God appeared to Moses in the burning bush (Ex. 3:2, 16). These verses say that God appeared and spoke to Moses, and Exodus 3 records what God said. This incident was well known in Christ's time and in the early days of the church, for Stephen referred specifically to it (see Acts 7:30–35). For other OT times when God appeared to someone and spoke to him, see 2 Chronicles 1:7; 7:12; 1 Samuel 3:21; and Jeremiah 31:3. The physical form God took is not mentioned.

In the NT, Matthew's birth narrative records several times when an angel of the Lord appeared to Joseph in a dream (Matt. 1:20; 2:13, 19).[8] Then, Luke 1:11–17 relates that an angel of the Lord appeared to Zacharias in the temple and announced that his wife would give birth to John the Baptist, the forerunner of the Messiah. And of course, there are Acts 9:3–6, 10–16, Paul's Damascus road experience and its aftermath. Paul heard the Lord speak to him, and what Jesus said is recorded in verses 4–6. Luke adds that the men with Paul were speechless, because they heard the voice but saw no one. Verses 10–16 add that the Lord spoke to Ananias about Paul, and Luke records what God said. Since Luke also says that God spoke to Ananias in a vision (v. 10), Ananias definitely saw something physical—perhaps an angel. We aren't told just what.

From the preceding list of occasions when God both appeared and spoke to someone, it might seem that this sort of thing happened much more frequently in the OT era than in NT times. But that isn't so. In the Gospels (and elsewhere in the NT) there are many instances when God spoke directly to any number of individuals. We know what he said, because the Gospel writers tell us in detail. Perhaps you are thinking, "I don't remember that, and I've read the Gospels many times!" But think again. The Gospels record Jesus Christ's teachings. Whenever he spoke to someone during his earthly pilgrimage, it was an instance of God appearing and speaking to that person!

So, about two thousand years ago, for the better part of thirty-three and-a-half years, God, in the person of the God-man Jesus Christ, appeared and spoke to many people. Some heard, believed, and followed him. Most rejected

---

[8] These will be covered in more detail when I discuss dreams.

him even to the point of agreeing to crucify him. But their stubborn, sinful rejection couldn't overturn the fact that God was with us and had spoken!

*Information about the Future*—On many occasions and in various ways God revealed what would happen in the future. Some prophecies were fulfilled soon after the news came. Other prophecies were about the Messiah, and weren't fulfilled until his first advent. And, other prophecies predict events surrounding Christ's second coming.

There are too many prophecies of the first and second advent to survey them all, but I offer samples of each type of prediction. As an introduction to these predictions, we should note what the Lord said in Isaiah 42:9; 46:10; and 48:3, 5–7. In each passage, before God revealed what he would do, he reminded his people that he is a God who proclaims what will happen and then brings it to pass. In fact, his ability to know and predict the future long before it comes to pass is a sign that only he is God. No idol can do this, nor can any mere human. To make the point that his knowledge of and disclosure of the future even extends to specific events and actions, in Amos 3:7 God told Israel that he does nothing without revealing his secret counsel to his servants the prophets.

More specifically, God predicted things that would happen soon after the prediction, and then the prophecy came to pass. For example, in 1 Samuel 2:27ff. God, through "a man of God," predicted the destruction of Eli's house. In 1 Samuel 3:11–14 it was predicted again. In other cases, the prediction was not just about one man and his family. For example, in Jeremiah 4:5–9 God predicted through Jeremiah that an invasion would come upon his people. Later, in 11:6–17 and again in 19:2–13, the Lord revealed through Jeremiah that disaster would fall on Judah, because she had disobeyed her covenant with God.

God's revelation about Israel's near future wasn't always bad news. For example, in Jeremiah 50 (esp. vv. 2 and 28–32), God told captive Judah that he would destroy its captor, Babylon. In fact, in Isaiah, the Lord even revealed that the liberator would be Cyrus (Isa. 44:28–45:1). Again, in chapter 46 God refers to what he would do through Cyrus (v. 11). Cyrus isn't specifically named this time, but there is no need to do so since this is part of the same prophecy (stated in Isa. 44:28ff.) of deliverance from Babylon. And, things said in 46:11 about the liberator also clearly point to Cyrus. See also Isaiah 23:1–18 with its oracle against Tyre.

In each of the abovementioned cases, God used words to unveil information about the future. In one instance, God used a very different way. Ezekiel was informed that God would take his wife, i.e., she would die. This would be difficult, but Ezekiel shouldn't mourn. Ezekiel did what he was told, and his people asked why he acted this way. Ezekiel replied that the Lord was using Ezekiel's wife's death as an "object lesson" to let them know that God would profane his sanctuary, "the pride of your power, the desire of your eyes, and the delight of your soul; and your sons and your daughters whom you have left behind will fall by the sword" (Ezek. 24:21). Just as Ezekiel didn't mourn the loss of his wife, Judah shouldn't mourn this predicted destruction (Ezek. 24:15–20). As the Lord said, "Ezekiel will be a sign to you; according to all that he has done you will do; when it comes, then you will know that I am the Lord GOD" (Ezek. 24:24).

As to predictions about the coming Messiah, there is ample revelation. In Isaiah 7 God predicted that he would perform the miracle of the virgin birth (v. 14) as a sign of his willingness and ability to protect Judah. Though many think this prophecy must have been fulfilled in Ahaz's day or it couldn't serve as a sign to him, there is no doubt that it was also fulfilled with the birth of Jesus (Matt. 1:22–23).

Through Isaiah, more was revealed about this coming child (Isa. 9:2–7). In fact, God even revealed through Micah (5:2) the place of the Messiah's birth. Moreover, the NT has predictions related in one way or another to the Messiah's first coming. For example, the Holy Spirit revealed to Simeon that he wouldn't die until he saw the Lord's Messiah, who would bring consolation to Israel (Luke 2:26). In addition, Peter says (1 Pet. 1:10–12) that OT prophets who wrote of the coming Messiah sought to learn from the Lord when the Messiah would come. Peter says that God revealed that it wouldn't happen in their lifetimes, but during the times when Peter lived and wrote his epistles.

Hebrews 9 also has a very interesting statement about the OT sacrificial system and its relation to Christ. In verses 6 and 7 the writer says that the OT high priest would enter the Holy of Holies once a year to make atonement for the sins of the people. The author then explains (v. 8) that by this practice, the Holy Spirit signified that the way into the Most Holy Place had not yet been disclosed. In contrast (v. 11), when Christ appeared as high priest, entrance into God's presence was fully opened. In essence, Hebrews is saying that the OT sacrificial system and the high priest's actions once a year were the Holy Spirit's "prediction" of a greater sacrifice and high priest to come, namely, Jesus!

*End-Time Prophecies*—Prophecies about the end times and Christ's second advent are legion. A few examples will suffice. In Jeremiah 3:12ff., the Lord called his people to repentance and promised that if they would repent, he would someday regather them to Jerusalem, which would become the very throne of the Lord (vv. 16–17). In Ezekiel 36, God promised to give Israel a "new heart," cleansed from sin, and that they would then in the fullest sense be his people, and he would be their God. Isaiah 62:11–12 also predicts a time when God's salvation will come to Zion. And then, in a vision of a valley of dry bones (Ezek. 37:1–14), God told Israel his plans to reconstitute and save her.

Many Bible scholars would say that conditions described in these passages can be true only after the Lord returns to set up his kingdom. Of course, the book of Revelation, though seen by some as predicting events fulfilled in very early church history, is understood by many evangelical scholars to speak of the end times. Many of its chapters contain prophecies given to John in visions. In some of the visions the apostle wasn't just shown things but was also told what would happen and what the vision meant.[9]

*Information about Various Things*—In addition to the passages already mentioned, there are many more in which God reveals information. The information involved is rather diverse, and we can only be selective. For example, according to Deuteronomy 4:5, 13, Moses told Israel that he had taught them the covenant and commands, especially the Ten Commandments, which God spoke and ordered them to obey. In Deuteronomy 29:29 Moses wrote that Israel was to obey not just the Ten Commandments but all the words of God's law.

Then, many times a verse begins or ends with the words, "declares the Lord," and it includes whatever God actually said. This formulaic saying is especially prevalent in Isaiah (e.g., 1:24; 3:15; 14:22, 23; 17:3, 6; 30:1; 31:9), but any full concordance shows that it also appears repeatedly in Jeremiah, Ezekiel, and the Minor Prophets.

In addition, in 2 Samuel 7:27, David says that God revealed that he would build David a house. This was a promise about the Davidic dynasty, namely, that there would never lack a man to sit on the throne of David (7:9–17). In Psalm 50, the psalmist wrote that God has summoned the earth, the heavens, and his godly ones to judge God's people Israel. In the rest of the psalm (vv. 7–23) God presents his complaints against his people. A different psalm (147) praises the Lord for restoring Jerusalem and prospering it.

In the prophets, the Lord addressed his people on various occasions. On one occasion (Isa. 44:6–8), he told Judah that there is no God but himself; none can compare with him. In Isaiah 45:18–19, God said that he created the heavens and the earth, and has also spoken righteousness to his people and declared things that are upright. In Jeremiah 5:20 God tells Jeremiah to speak for him to his people, and then in verses 21–31 says that his people foolishly refuse to seek and obey him. He details specific complaints, and ends the chapter (vv. 30–31) by summarizing his indictment with a critique and condemnation. See also Amos 4 and Daniel 10:1.

In the NT, the Lord also reveals all sorts of information. For example,

---

[9] The OT book of Daniel also contains many visions (e.g., chapters 7 and 9:24–27). Some predict things that happened shortly after Daniel wrote, and others make predictions that were fulfilled at Christ's first advent. Of course, some things can be true only of the end times. Evangelicals don't unanimously agree on the meaning of these end-time prophecies. Even if one disagrees with my interpretation of these prophecies, my point in raising them still stands.

before his crucifixion Christ promised to send the Holy Spirit to his disciples. The Holy Spirit would lead them into all truth. He would take of the things that are Christ's and reveal them to the disciples (John 16:13, 14, 15). As we shall see when discussing inspiration, this promise in effect guaranteed the Holy Spirit's ministry to the apostles when they preached about Christ, and also when they would pen the books that became the NT.

More generally, on one occasion Jesus warned his disciples to be on guard against the hypocrisy of the Pharisees. He added that nothing hidden would not be revealed (Luke 12:2; par. Matt. 10:26). On another occasion, Jesus gave instructions to seventy-two disciples before sending them out (Luke 10). In the midst of giving instructions, he praised his Father for hiding these things from the wise and learned and revealing them to "little children" (Luke 10:21 ESV; par. Matt. 11:25).

Then, Paul's letters present many different things that God revealed. Perhaps the classic passage on major aspects of the doctrine of Scripture is 1 Corinthians 2. Paul speaks of revelation (vv. 6–11), inspiration (vv. 12–13), and illumination (vv. 14–16). He writes that there are things that neither eyes have seen nor ears have heard. God has prepared them for those who love him, and the Holy Spirit has revealed them.

Speaking again of Scripture and the privileges God gave the Jewish people, in Romans 3:2 Paul says that God gave Israel the very "oracles of God." Undoubtedly, Paul's most famous and significant comments about Scripture are found in 2 Timothy 3:16. This passage will be discussed in detail in relation to inspiration, but for now it is enough to say that Paul calls Scripture the very product of God's breath. That is, as God's word, it is divine revelation.

In two passages in Romans Paul writes more specifically of matters related to the gospel. He says in Romans 3:21 that a righteousness apart from the Mosaic law has been revealed, and even the OT Law and Prophets testify to this truth. Later, Paul ends Romans with a doxology. He says that the gospel of Jesus Christ was a mystery hidden for long ages, but now it is revealed (Rom. 16:25–26). In Ephesians 3:3–5 Paul speaks of another mystery now revealed, the mystery that during the current age both Jew and Gentile would be united to Christ and to one another on equal footing before God in the church.

Then, in Galatians 1:12, Paul emphatically affirms that his gospel didn't come from any man, nor was it learned from some teacher. He received it by revelation from Jesus Christ himself. See also 2 Corinthians 12:1ff., where Paul says that he was caught up to paradise and given a vision. He saw and heard things that he wasn't allowed to tell (v. 4). Other Pauline passages that speak about various kinds of information revealed by God are Romans 8:16 (the

Holy Spirit's assurance that believers are saved); 1 Corinthians 14:6, 26, 30 (instructions about orderly church worship); Galatians 2:2; and Philippians 3:15 (revelation of an improper attitude).

One final passage from Peter and one from John complete our discussion of information that God reveals. In 2 Peter 1:21, to be discussed in detail when discussing inspiration, Peter says that OT writers were "carried along" (ESV) by the Holy Spirit. As a result, what they wrote was God's word. Since the OT covers many different things, it shows how vast and diverse are the things God revealed to the writers.

As for the apostle John, he begins 1 John by writing that he and the other apostles proclaim what they have seen and heard, and what their hands have touched in relation to Christ. In 1:5, John adds that the message Christ gave the apostles is that "God is light, and in Him there is no darkness at all." John argues that sin is spiritual darkness, so you can't live in God's light if you live in sin.

*Dreams*—During both OT and NT times, God sometimes used dreams to reveal information. As already noted, Numbers 12:6 says that God revealed himself to most prophets through dreams and visions. And, as Diana Edelman observes about an occasion when King Saul wanted to ask the Lord a question, the Lord didn't answer him by dreams, Urim, or prophets.[10] These, according to Edelman, are three legitimate ways of receiving a divine communication. Since Saul didn't get an answer in any of these ways, he decided to consult a spirit medium, which was not acceptable in the OT for finding God's will.

God disclosing information through dreams involved, at least in the OT era, two things. Often dreams came without interpretation. The butler and baker to the king of Egypt (Gen. 40:5ff.) each had a dream, but had no one to interpret it. Genesis 41 recounts that Pharaoh had a troubling dream about two groups of seven cows (41:1–4), and shortly thereafter another dream about two groups of seven ears of grain (41:5–7). Pharaoh initially couldn't find anyone to interpret the dreams. Finally, Joseph affirmed that God would give the answer (Genesis 41, esp. v. 16). He did, and Joseph interpreted the dreams.

Then, think of Daniel 2 and King Nebuchadnezzar's very troubling dream. He forgot it, but wanted to recover it and learn its meaning. No one but Daniel could reveal the mystery. The Lord revealed the dream to Daniel (vv. 19–23), and later gave its interpretation (vv. 28–30). Daniel was careful to note (v. 30) that he was able to do this not because of his own special wisdom but because God revealed it to him. Nebuchadnezzar was overwhelmed by the dream's meaning and exclaimed to Daniel (v. 47), "Surely your God is a God of gods

---

[10] Diana Edelman, "From Prophets to Prophetic Books: The Fixing of the Divine Word," in *The Production of Prophecy*, ed. Diana V. Edelman and Ehud Ben Zvi (London: Equinox, 2009), 39. See also Becking, "Means of Revelation in the Book of Jeremiah," 40–42, on dreams.

and a Lord of kings and a revealer of mysteries, since you have been able to reveal this mystery."

Of course, sometimes the person receiving the dream didn't need an interpreter. This was true of Jacob's dream of a ladder that reached from earth to heaven, with angels ascending and descending on it. In the dream, the Lord promised Jacob great blessings to him and his descendants (Gen. 28:12–16). And, at the start of the Joseph story, Joseph had two dreams, which he willingly shared with his father and brothers. Though Joseph did not present the dreams' interpretations, their meaning was transparent to both his brothers and his father. His brothers were not pleased, and they became jealous of him, although, of course, Joseph had no control over his dreams' contents (Gen. 37:5–11).

The NT speaks less of dreams that are divine revelation, but Matthew mentions several related to Jesus's birth. In each instance an angel spoke to someone in a dream. The first, recorded in Matthew 1:20ff., relates to Mary's pregnancy. In the eyes of Jewish law, Joseph and Mary were married, but they hadn't lived together as husband and wife. When Joseph learned of Mary's pregnancy, he decided to divorce her but didn't want to disgrace her publicly. An angel of the Lord appeared to Joseph and explained how Mary had become pregnant. He said that the baby would be a boy, and told Joseph to name the child Jesus. Joseph put away all thoughts of divorce and obeyed the angel's instructions (Matt. 1:20–21, 24–25).

Matthew 2 says that wise men came from the east to Jerusalem seeking to find and worship the baby Jesus. When they arrived in Jerusalem, they asked King Herod where they might find Jesus. Herod truthfully told them that he didn't know where to find Jesus. Herod then consulted the chief priests and scribes, who, quoting from Micah, said that the child was to be born in Bethlehem. Herod then told the wise men to find the child, return, and tell him where he could find him. Lying, Herod said he wanted to know so that he also could go and worship the child. The wise men found Jesus, Joseph, and Mary, and planned to return to give Herod the news. However, in a dream, God told them not to return to Herod, so they went home a different way (Matt. 2:12).

After the wise men departed, Joseph had another dream. An angel appeared and told him to take Jesus and Mary and flee to Egypt, because Herod would search for Jesus to destroy him (Matt. 2:13). (Indeed, in his efforts to kill the infant Jesus, Herod ordered every male child in Bethlehem and its vicinity who was two years old and younger killed.) Eventually, Herod died, and an angel appeared to Joseph in another dream and told him to return to Israel, because those who wanted to harm Jesus were dead. Joseph obeyed, and with his family returned to Israel (Matt. 2:19–21). When they returned,

Joseph learned that Herod's son, Archelaus, was reigning in Judea. Joseph's fears of Archelaus were confirmed by God in another dream, and he departed for Galilee and settled in Nazareth (Matt. 2:22–23).

One further passage worth mention is Job 33:14–18. These verses are part of one of Elihu's speeches to Job. Job, claiming innocence, said that God counted him as his enemy, watched his paths, and constructed reasons to torment him (vv. 8–11). Elihu said Job was wrong (v. 12), and he asked why Job complained that God hadn't explained what he was doing (v. 13). Elihu then affirmed that

> Indeed God speaks once,
> Or twice, yet no one notices it.
> In a dream, a vision of the night,
> When sound sleep falls on men,
> While they slumber in their beds,
> Then he opens the ears of men,
> And seals their instruction,
> That he may turn man aside from his conduct,
> And keep man from pride;
> He keeps back his soul from the pit,
> And his life from passing over into Sheol. (vv. 14–18)

Several things about this passage are noteworthy. Job's friends were wrong about him, and they said many untrue things. Thus, we could dismiss this passage as totally false. But that would be wrong, for while Elihu was wrong about Job being guilty and needing to repent, he wasn't wrong about God revealing information in dreams. Job was certain that God wasn't punishing him for some terrible sin, but he never denied that God reveals things in dreams. Elihu was right about that.

This passage has another significance. Sometimes Christians and non-Christians alike wonder how God can get revelation to people who never saw a Bible and never talked with a Christian missionary. Job 33:14–18 explains how God can do that. This is very important, for if God can give people with only natural revelation more information through dreams, it is reasonable to think he can do so in other ways than getting them a Bible or sending a missionary to tell them about Jesus.

*Visions*—Visions also directly reveal a message to a recipient. Visions occur when the recipient is awake, and sometimes a recipient is even transported beyond his material environment. For example, Ezekiel (37:1–14) received a vision of a valley of dry bones, but verse 1 says that the Lord brought Ezekiel out by the Holy Spirit and set him in the midst of a valley strewn with dry bones. Since there is no such valley at some geographical location that any tourist or traveler could visit, when Ezekiel says he was brought out by the Spirit, this likely means that his physical body remained exactly where it was, while his immaterial part was transported out of his body to see this vision. Similarly, Paul speaks of being lifted into the third heaven, but he didn't know whether he was in his body or out of his body as this happened (2 Cor. 12:2–3). See also John's testimony in Revelation 17:1–3.

On the other hand, many accounts of visions say nothing about the recipient being transported to another place. The recipient just tells us what he saw. Examples of this are Revelation 19:17; 20:1–10, 11–15; and Daniel 8. Though the Revelation passages cited don't call what John relates visions, since he tells us what he saw, and gives no indication that he was asleep, what he details likely came as visions.

There are many visions recorded in Scripture, but I offer just a sample. The book of Daniel records many end-time prophecies, and many were given in visions. One of the most significant is the vision of the seventy weeks (Dan. 9:24–27). The angel Gabriel gave Daniel this vision while Daniel was praying for his people Israel and for Jerusalem (vv. 20–23). In addition, the book of Zechariah is filled with many prophetic visions. In fact, it begins with a series of eight visions that are recorded in chapters 1–6. What is astonishing, in part, is that Zechariah received all eight of the visions in the same night! See also Genesis 15, which says that in a vision the Lord told Abraham that though he was childless, he would have descendants as innumerable as the stars in the sky.

In the NT, fewer visions are recorded in nonprophetic passages. However, in 2 Corinthians 12:1 Paul speaks of having visions and revelations from the Lord. He writes about one vision in which he was caught up into "the third heaven." In addition, at various points in his writings Paul notes that he preaches the same gospel other apostles preach, a gospel he received through a revelation of Jesus Christ (e.g., Gal. 1:11–17). In another passage Paul states clearly that he had seen the Lord (1 Cor. 9:1; 15:8). It is not certain whether he is talking about the Damascus Road experience, or some other vision of the Lord. And 2 Corinthians 12:1–4 doesn't sound like the Damascus Road experience, but Paul recounts definitely having a vision.

The book of Revelation contains more visions than any other NT book. It is possible, though uncertain, that the messages to the seven churches (Revelation 1–3) were given in visions. Chapter 4 begins with a vision, and the rest of the book contains individual prophetic visions about the end times.

In sum, visions contained imaginary things, as did many dreams, but the messages conveyed were not imaginary. The visions predicted actual events that either have happened (e.g., the first 69 weeks of Daniel's vision of 70 weeks), or that are yet to come (e.g., Ezek. 37:1–14; the book of Revelation). Visions like the one in Revelation 13 contain imaginary beasts and a dragon, etc., but the beasts and dragon stand for real people and real demonic beings (or Satan himself, the dragon of Revelation 13) whose end-time exploits against God and his people will actually occur in the future.[11]

*Angels and Theophanies*—Two other ways God revealed information directly involve angelic messengers and theophanies. As for angels, sometimes they delivered messages in dreams, and in other cases they were involved in visions. In Revelation 19:17 John saw an angel standing in the sun. This angel summoned all the birds to assemble for the great supper of God; as the passage predicts, they won't be coming to be eaten, but to feast on the flesh of men and horses that will be slain at the battle of Armageddon (19:18, 21).

In some passages, angels are involved in visions, but as interpreters, not as actors in the vision. The prophet or apostle receiving the vision or dream does not understand it, and asks an interpreting angel to explain it. For example, an interpreting angel explained the meaning of the vision Daniel recounted in Daniel 7 (vv. 15–16, 23). In addition, in the first of eight visions Zechariah received in one night, two angels were participants. One, called the "angel of the LORD," was an actor in the vision (e.g., Zech. 1:11–12). The other, referred to as "the angel who was speaking with me," several times explained to Zechariah the meaning of what he was seeing (Zech. 1:9, 13, 14, 19).

Then, sometimes an angel appeared (but neither in a dream or vision) and had a conversation with some human. Perhaps the most famous example of this is the angel who visited Mary and told her that she would give birth to the Messiah (Luke 1:26ff.). Another well-known instance of an angel encountering humans relates to Christ's resurrection (Matt. 28:2–7). An angel also talked to the women who came to the tomb on Sunday morning, informing them of Jesus's resurrection (28:5–7). See also Acts 1:10–11, where the angels appeared at Jesus's ascension; and in Acts 7:38, 53 and Galatians 3:19, note the comments that angels were in some way involved in the giving of the Mosaic law.

In addition to angels delivering information, God also revealed himself through theophanies, appearances of God in some physical form. For example, on one occasion Moses, Aaron, Nadab, Abihu, and seventy elders of Israel saw "the God of Israel" (Ex. 24:9–10). The physical thing they saw isn't described, but only that they had seen God. In Deuteronomy 5:4–5, Moses tells the people of Israel that at Horeb the Lord spoke to him face-to-face from the midst of fire[12] (see also Ex. 3:16). In addition, the Lord led the people of Israel through their wilderness wanderings both day and night with a cloud and a pillar of smoke and fire.

---

[11] For more on visions, see Henry Stob, "The Doctrine of Revelation in St. Paul," *CTJ* 1 (1966): 189; and Brichto, "On Faith and Revelation in the Bible," 44.
[12] Brichto, "On Faith and Revelation in the Bible," 47.

Most theophanies, however, were appearances of one called the Angel of the Lord. This angel seems to be no ordinary angel but rather a way in which God himself took on a visible form and spoke to various individuals. Some scholars have argued that the Angel of the Lord was the second member of the Godhead. While we can't be absolutely certain, it is significant that once Jesus was born, we never again in the NT hear of the Angel of the Lord. See also various OT passages in which the Angel of the Lord appears, and from what the verses say, this is no ordinary angel (Ex. 3:2, 14). See also Genesis 16:7–13—Hagar and the Angel of the Lord. And, it was the Angel of the Lord who stopped Abraham from plunging the knife into his son Isaac to offer him in sacrifice to the Lord (Gen. 22:11, 12). See also Genesis 31:11–13; Joshua 5:13–15; Judges 6:12; and 13:3.

*Indirect Communication through Symbolic Acts and Events in People's Lives*

God at times revealed himself through a prophet's symbolic act. God used the prophet's act to make a moral or spiritual point. In addition, there were times when events occurred or situations arose in a prophet's life, and God used those situations to illustrate his relationship to his people, and as an occasion for the prophet to deliver God's message to the people.

I have labeled these instances of divine revelation *indirect*, because in themselves, apart from their divine interpretation or from the point God used the situation to make, the acts, events, and circumstances wouldn't suggest any divine revelation. Indeed, the symbolic acts were real acts, and the situations used as illustrations actually happened, but they don't in themselves reveal anything about God. What is revelatory is how God used them. Let me illustrate.

Becking offers two examples from Jeremiah of what he calls "sign acts." The first is the use of an iron yoke to convey how hopeless Jerusalem was in the face of the Babylonians. In Jeremiah 27–28, Jeremiah encountered the prophet Hananiah. Jeremiah was wearing a wooden yoke around his neck. Hananiah broke it (28:10), and used that act to say that in two years God would break the yoke of Nebuchadnezzar, king of Babylon, from the necks of all the nations. This was actually a false prophecy, and so God told Jeremiah to tell Hananiah that, though he had broken a yoke of wood, he had made instead yokes of iron. In verse 14, the Lord explained the meaning thus: "I have put a yoke of iron on the neck of all these nations, that they may serve Nebuchadnezzar king of Babylon; and they shall serve him."[13]

A second symbolic act involved a message for Jeremiah. In Jeremiah 1, God instructed him to be a prophet to the nations. Jeremiah protested that he was too young and inexperienced. In response, the Lord put forth his hand, touched

---

[13] Becking, "Means of Revelation in the Book of Jeremiah," 35–36.

Jeremiah's mouth, and said, "Behold, I have put My words in your mouth" (Jer. 1:9).[14] Another example appears in Ezekiel 37. Ezekiel was told (vv. 15ff.) to take two sticks and to write on one, "For Judah," and on the other, "For Joseph, the stick of Ephraim." Then, Ezekiel was to take the two sticks and join them to one another so that they became one stick in his hand. In the verses that follow, the Lord explained that this symbolic act meant that even though Judah and Israel at that time were separate kingdoms, God would reunite them into one kingdom. David (actually, David's greater son, Jesus) would be their king, and the people would obey God's law (Ezek. 37:18–28). See also God's use of Hosea's marriage to an unfaithful wife as an example of his relationship to Israel (see esp. Hosea 3).

These examples show why this form of revelation is indirect, as opposed to direct speech, visions, and dreams. The mere acts and situations mentioned would reveal little or nothing without the words that accompany them and explain their meaning.

### Revelation of a Person, Usually God

On many occasions the form and content of revelation was a person. Usually that person was God himself, but the exact way that he revealed himself differed from time to time.

On some occasions God appeared in the physical form of a cloud (Ex. 34:5–7). On one occasion (Lev. 16:1–2) God told Moses to tell Aaron not to come into the Most Holy Place just whenever he wanted, because God dwells in a cloud over the atonement cover of the ark, and if it wasn't the appropriate time for Aaron to enter, but he did anyway, he would die. And in Deuteronomy 31:15, we learn that God appeared in a pillar of cloud at the Tent of Meeting.

In many other OT passages, we read that God appeared to some human, but we aren't told what physical form he took. For example, God appeared to Jacob at Bethel when he was fleeing from Esau (Gen. 35:7). On another occasion, God made his presence known to Samuel, although from what the text says he seems to have done so through his words (1 Sam. 3:21). On several occasions, God appeared to Solomon (1 Kings 3:5 [in a dream]; 9:2–3; 2 Chron. 1:7; 7:12). These passages also show that God also spoke to Solomon when he appeared, but the author's point is that God actually somehow appeared to Solomon. See also Exodus 6:3; Leviticus 9:4; and Acts 7:2 about God appearing to Abraham while he lived in Mesopotamia. In a prophetic portion of a psalm (102:16), the writer prophecies that the Lord will rebuild Zion and appear in his glory. Isaiah 65 begins with the Lord saying (v. 1) that he revealed himself to people who didn't ask for him, and was found by people who didn't seek him or

---

[14] Ibid., 36.

call on his name. And Jeremiah speaks of a day when the people of Israel will recount the fact that God appeared to them and told them that he had loved them with an everlasting love (Jer. 31:3).

The NT is also filled with passages that show the content of revelation to be a person. In most cases the person revealed is Christ, but not just him alone. For example, in John 1:14, John says that the second member of the Godhead became flesh and dwelt among us. We beheld his glory, but not just that. It was the glory of one who is the only begotten of the Father. So, the incarnation not only revealed the second member of the Godhead but disclosed something about the first member as well. To confirm this, four verses later (v. 18) John says that no one has ever seen God, but the only begotten Son has revealed him. In John 17:6, Jesus says that he revealed the Father to those whom the Father gave him. And in Matthew 11:27 (par. Luke 10:22) Jesus says that no one knows the Father except those to whom the Son has chosen to reveal him. See also John 14:21 and 1 John 1:2.

### The Incarnate Word, Jesus Christ

God reveals himself most clearly in Jesus Christ, the incarnate Word. Hebrews 1:1 says that in more recent days of revelation, God has revealed himself in his Son. This doesn't mean that God's revealing activity ended with the life, death, resurrection, and ascension of Christ. Christ promised his disciples to send his Spirit after he left, to continue to teach them and to remind them of things they had seen and heard from Jesus. If divine revelation ended with the life of Jesus, then the NT, written after his ascension, couldn't be revelation—but of course, it is.

In interpreting Hebrews 1, many fixate on verses 1–2, which compare God's way of revealing himself during OT times and his revelation in and through Christ. It would be a mistake, however, to omit verse 3, because in it we see why Jesus Christ is such a powerful and complete revelation of God. He is the fullest revelation of God ever given to humankind. Hebrews 1:3 says,

> And He is the radiance of His glory and the exact representation of His nature, and upholds all things by the word of His power. When He had made purification of sins, He sat down at the right hand of the Majesty on high.

In the prologue to John's Gospel, John explains that Christ is the eternal Word, coequally divine with the Father. Later in the chapter John explains that the Word became flesh and dwelt among us. Those who lived then beheld his glory "as of the only begotten from the Father, full of grace and truth" (1:14). These verses contain the paradox that dialectical theologians find so enticing, namely, that in one and the same person was united the finite and the infinite,

God who is pure spirit and man who is both spirit and flesh. These truths point to another paradox, namely, that Jesus Christ is the fullest revelation of God, but in Jesus God is also hidden, for more often than we might think, Jesus seemed to be a mere man.[15] Indeed, there were times recorded in the Gospels when Jesus performed miracles, and on the Mount of Transfiguration Jesus fully displayed his glory, but the Gospels also present a very human Jesus. At times he was tired and he slept, at other times he was hungry, and he was capable of dying and did die.

As argued elsewhere, these human features of Jesus's life on earth didn't mean that he lost his divine attributes. Rather, they meant that during his earthly pilgrimage he set aside the full and constant use of his attributes and the display of the glory that was his (Phil. 2:5–8).[16] In what sense, then, is Jesus divine revelation? He is divine revelation most fundamentally in his person. As the God-man, the apostle Paul wrote of him that "He is the image of the invisible God" (Col. 1:15) and that "in Him all the fullness of Deity dwells in bodily form" (Col. 2:9). In 1 Timothy 3:16 Paul says that God was manifest or revealed in the flesh, and this can only refer to Jesus.

Because Jesus, in his very being, is divine, John wrote (John 1:18) that, while no one has at any time seen God, the "one of a kind God" (*monogenēs theos*), a reference that could only point to Jesus, has *exēgēsato* God (literally, has "led out" God). The verb *exēgēsato* is the Greek word from which we derive the English term "exegesis." To give an exegesis of something is to interpret it, to explain its meaning, or more literally, to "lead out" its meaning. How did Jesus do this? By his interpretation of Scripture, or by his teachings about God? Certainly those things were revelatory, but in the context of John 1:1, 14, and 18, John most likely means that in his very person Jesus revealed God. He helped us to understand God just by being himself.

As a result, on one occasion (John 14:9), when Philip asked Jesus to show the disciples the Father, Jesus replied that "He who has seen Me has seen the Father; how do you say, 'Show us the Father'?" At the very least, by the time John wrote 1 John, he had gotten the message that in his very person, Jesus is God. John begins 1 John by saying that Jesus existed from the beginning with the Father and that he was manifested to humanity (through the incarnation—remember John 1:14). Because of that, John and the other apostles saw and heard him and touched him. It is that Jesus, who is both fully divine and

[15] Phee-Seng Kang, "The Christ of History and the Christ of Revelation," *The Greek Orthodox Theological Review* 43 (1998): 407–408. Though Kang uses the notion of being veiled in Christ's unveiling, he cites Calvin as holding such views. Hence, though dialectical theologians at times overemphasize these points, that doesn't mean that Reformers like Calvin and Luther didn't grasp the point at all. Of course, the Reformers didn't believe Christ as revelation negates Scripture as revelation (as dialectical theologians do).

[16] See my "The Incarnation of Jesus," in *In Defense of Miracles*, ed. Gary Habermas and Douglas Geivett (Downers Grove, IL: InterVarsity Press, 1997).

fully human, of whom John and the other apostles preached and wrote (1 John 1:1–3). See also Matthew 11:27, which records Jesus's claim that only he, and anyone to whom he reveals the Father, knows the Father.

Jesus also revealed divine truth in his teachings. This is true not only in that he often used the OT in his teaching (and the OT is divine revelation), but also in that at times he explained the proper interpretation and application of OT themes (as in the Sermon on the Mount, with its formulaic "You have heard it said . . . but I say to you"). Jesus's teachings also included things that had never been said in the OT, and because of his deity, we must affirm that those "new" things are also divine revelation.

Jesus also revealed God through his deeds. Here the point isn't just to focus on his miracles and their role in confirming his deity and/or in teaching some moral or theological point. Even many of his nonmiraculous deeds were things that only God could do. For example, without ever having met the woman at the well, Jesus knew everything about her (John 4); he knew that Judas would betray him (John 13:21–30); and on various occasions he forgave sins (e.g., Mark 2:1–12). Of course, anyone can "say" they forgive sins, but only God can do so. In order to show that he had power to forgive sins, Jesus healed the paralytic (a deed that on the surface would seem harder to do than to forgive sins).

Then, think of how Jesus conducted himself during his trial and crucifixion. He submitted to all the abuse and mocking of the soldiers and the crowds that yelled for his crucifixion. His patience and longsuffering are beautiful illustrations of attributes that only God could have in such measure. As he hung on the cross in agony, he didn't speak words of rebuke, anger, or judgment to those who were doing this. Rather, he asked his Father to forgive them, because, he said, they didn't know what they were doing (Luke 23:34). That was an incredibly generous and forgiving interpretation of what his enemies were doing; surely he had told many of them on many occasions that he was the Messiah and the Son of God, so they should have known what they were doing when they put him to death. No mere human being could show such forgiveness and concern for those persecuting him! Jesus's actions and words of forgiveness reveal just how far God is willing to go to forgive even the worst of sinners!

For anyone who cares to look closely, in those last few days of his earthly life (and all the years before), what Jesus said and did—and what he refused to abandon—provide a beautiful character sketch of many divine attributes. Words used to describe God's character come alive as we watch and listen to how Jesus conducted himself under those most difficult circumstances. Surely, all of these things show why Jesus fully deserves the exaltation and glory he received upon his resurrection and ascension, and the praise and power that are his as reigning King of the universe forever![17]

Of course, as expected, there is great emphasis on Christ's atoning sacrifice for our sins. In addition to the obvious fact that this deed paid for our sins so that we don't have to do so ourselves, in dying for us, all members of the Godhead revealed a number of their divine attributes. As Paul writes in various places (Eph. 2:8–9; 2 Tim. 1:9–10), this is a gift of God's grace (as is all of salvation), and it also shows God's love for lost and hopeless sinners (Rom. 5:8). John echoes this theme when he writes in 1 John 4:10 that we see what love is when we look at Christ's sacrifice. Love is not defined by our love for God, but by the fact that he loves us and sent his Son to be the atoning sacrifice for our sins. As Paul adds in Romans 3:25–26, Christ's sacrifice allows God to handle salvation in a way that upholds the demands of his justice but also demonstrates gloriously his mercy and grace.

To be sure, the incarnation and sacrifice on Calvary alone would have been extraordinary displays of God's humility and of his desire to meet our needs and teach us how to live, but if the story ended at Calvary, our lost condition would still be hopeless. Thus, the purchase of our salvation cannot rightly be described without pointing to another of God's miraculous acts, the resurrection of Jesus Christ! As Paul says in 1 Corinthians 15:17, if Christ has not been raised, our faith is vain and we are still dead in our sins. Hence, the resurrection not only displays God's amazing power (Rom. 1:4), but as Paul adds in Romans 1:4, it is the act that declares that Jesus is the Son of God. And, it shows that God through Christ has conquered sin and its penalty of death so that, when he offers us eternal life (e.g., John 3:16), he really has something to offer!

Then, there are three other passages that speak of Christ being revealed, but that do so in a different way than any so far discussed. The first is the account of Paul's conversion on the road to Damascus. A great light appeared, and Christ spoke words that Paul heard (Acts 9:1–18). In 2 Corinthians 4:10 and 11, Paul wrote of his ministry as an apostle of Jesus Christ. He noted that there was often hardship and suffering, and that his mortal body was also wearing out. He "carried about in his body the dying of Jesus Christ, so that the life of Jesus might be revealed or manifested in his body" (see v. 10). Speaking of death again in verse 11, he said that this was happening so that Christ's life might be "manifested in our mortal flesh."

---

[17] For more on Jesus Christ as revelation, see Avery Dulles, *Models of Revelation* (Garden City, NY: Image, 1985), chapter 10; Mark D. Thompson, "The Uniqueness of Christ as the Revealer of God," in *Christ the One and Only*, ed. Sung Wook Chung (Grand Rapids, MI: Baker, 2005), 96–102; Ben Quash, "Revelation," in *The Oxford Handbook of Systematic Theology*, ed. John Webster, Kathryn Tanner, and Iain Torrance (Oxford: Oxford University Press, 2007), 341–342; Dirkie Smit, "The Self-Disclosure of God," in *Doing Theology in Context: South African Perspectives*, ed. John W. De Gruchy and Charles Villa-Vicencio (Maryknoll, NY: Orbis, 1994), 42–47; Gabriel Moran, "What Is Revelation?," *Theological Studies* 25 (June 1964): 226–228; and C. Price, 332–334.

In another passage (Gal. 1:15–16) Paul wrote about his divine call to preach the gospel. He said that the Lord was pleased to reveal Christ in him so that he could preach the gospel to the Gentiles. Whether this means that information about Christ was given to Paul, or whether the point is that, along with giving Paul the gospel to preach, God also made it the case that people could see in Paul a Christlike character, isn't entirely clear. In either case, 1:16 is clear that Christ was revealed in and through Paul and his ministry.

A final group of passages about God's revelation of himself in Christ are prophetic in nature. Either, as in one case, they speak of God's revealing to OT prophets that Christ would come and work out salvation in the time when the apostles lived (1 Pet. 1:10–12), or the writer says that Christ's first coming revealed God's incredibly generous grace. The grace to save us was always planned by God, but in Christ's life and death it became blatantly evident.

Scripture speaks not only of Christ's revelation at the first advent, but also of his revelation at the second. The NT especially promises Jesus's return for his church, destruction of his enemies, and his kingdom rule in power and justice. But our focus now is just the fact that Christ will return. Jesus spoke of it as recorded in various places (e.g., John 14:1–3; Matt. 24:30–31),[18] and so did his apostles. Some passages involved simply mention his return in glory and power, while others note that his return will involve punishment of the wicked and reward for faithful servants. Examples of passages that mention Christ's return are Romans 2:5; Colossians 3:4; 2 Thessalonians 1:7; 1 Timothy 6:14; 2 Timothy 4:1, 8; Titus 2:13; 1 Peter 1:7; 5:4; 1 John 3:2; Revelation 19:11–21, but this list is by no means exhaustive.

While such verses may comfort us as the godly suffer and the unrighteous seem to prosper no matter what they do, most of the passages about the eschatological revelation of Christ contain "good news" for believers. Paul told Timothy (2 Tim. 4:1–2) that in view of Christ's appearance and coming kingdom, he must preach the word of God. Later in the chapter (v. 8) Paul wrote that when Christ appears, he will award to Paul and to all who long for his appearing a crown of righteousness. The writer of Hebrews says that when Christ appears a second time it will be, not to be a sin offering, but to bring salvation to all those waiting for him (Heb. 9:28). Peter also says that there will be rewards for faithfulness in suffering when Christ comes in a future day (1 Pet. 1:7). Paul affirms that when Christ, who is our life, appears (eschatologically), we his people will also appear with him in glory (see Col. 3:4). And John wrote

---

[18] Actually, the two passages aren't identical. John 14, I believe, speaks of the rapture, when the Lord returns for his church. Matthew 24 speaks of Christ's return at the end of the tribulation to destroy his enemies and set up his literal, physical kingdom on earth. Theologians debate the timing of the rapture in relation to the second advent at the end of the tribulation. I believe the rapture will occur before the tribulation, but other evangelicals believe it happens in the middle or at the end of the tribulation. These interesting issues are covered in the Foundations of Evangelical Theology volume on eschatology.

(1 John 3:2) that, when Christ appears for his church (at the rapture), we shall be like him! That doesn't mean we will be deified, but that we will be glorified. That is, sin will no longer have any power over us. Even more, John writes, we shall have firsthand experiential knowledge of Christ, for we shall see him just as he is. As a result of these wonderful blessings that will come to God's people, Paul (Titus 2:13) refers to the coming/the future revelation of Christ (whom he calls our "great God and Savior") as believers' blessed hope! How interesting this is! The blessed hope of the church is not a bigger budget, more programs, better facilities, or even droves of new converts; it is the eschatological return and revelation of our great God and Savior, Jesus Christ!

*Scripture, God's Written Word*

A final form of special revelation is Scripture. Scripture presents a record of many instances when revelation came to someone by direct communication, miracles, symbolic acts, and by the life and ministry of Jesus Christ. But many nonevangelical theologians refuse to see Scripture as anything more than a human, flawed book that points, albeit imperfectly at times, to whatever these theologians believe is genuine divine revelation.

In contrast, evangelicals believe that all Scripture, regardless of its content, is divine revelation. Paul says that all of it is "the product of God's breath" (2 Tim. 3:16).[19] Peter says that, as biblical writers wrote, they were so superintended ("carried along") by the Holy Spirit that they wrote God's very words (2 Pet. 1:21 ESV). These and many other Scriptures mean that the Bible is God's inspired word. It reveals many different topics that God wants us to know. Since later chapters cover in detail the doctrine of inspiration, I offer no further explanation now. Suffice it to say that Scripture is a form of divine revelation.

## DOES REVELATION OCCUR TODAY?

Evangelicals don't agree on the answer to this question, and I begin by explaining why. I think the disagreement about the answer to this question stems from a desire to avoid two extremes. On the one hand, if one answers that there will be no further divine revelation, that seems to "lock" God out of the world. No evangelical wants to say that God cannot and does not still act in history.

On the other hand, if we think God can reveal himself today, some fear that well-meaning Christians may believe that just about anything that happens

---

[19] This is true of even personal and incidental instructions like those in 2 Timothy 4:13. Whatever is in Scripture, regardless of its content, is God's word, not just the human author's. It may be hard to see why God inspired Paul to write 2 Timothy 4:13 and to grasp what it reveals about God. But if it is part of Scripture, it is God's word. In 2 Timothy 3:16, "all Scripture" either refers to "all" or it doesn't. If it does, but some Scripture isn't divine revelation, then 2 Timothy 3:16 is false, inerrancy is compromised, and we should reconsider what Scripture teaches about inspiration.

or any new thought they have qualifies as divine revelation. That also seems excessive. No doubt, some conservative evangelicals fear that if we grant that revelation can occur today, that opens the door to many things being revelation that charismatics might call revelation. That possibility troubles those conservative evangelicals quite a bit.

Are such fears unfounded? Apparently not, for some charismatics believe they have the gift of prophecy or of a "word of knowledge," and that when they exercise those gifts, they are receiving revelation. Even more, those who think speaking in tongues is for today may also think that, when they speak in tongues and someone interprets, the result is new revelation from God. If these present-day phenomena are deemed divine revelation, some might think these "revelations" have authority on a par with Scripture. That thought should disturb any evangelical!

So, can we answer this question about ongoing revelation so as to avoid the excesses of both extremes mentioned? I think we can, but the answer isn't a simple yes or no. Actually, the answer is yes *and* no, but everything depends on the type of revelation in view, the form of revelation under consideration, and whether certain phenomena that appear in popular Christian conversation are actually about revelation or are not. So, how should we begin to answer the question of this section?

My answer begins with the distinction between natural and special revelation. From what I presented about natural revelation, it is certain that God reveals himself today through it. In fact, I think some form of natural revelation will always exist. Even when God destroys the current heaven and earth and creates a new heaven and earth, God's existence as creator and sustainer of everything will shine forth to everyone. To be sure, it is dubious that anyone in the eternal state will need such "natural" revelation to know of God's existence, etc., but still, it will be there. So, the answer to whether God reveals himself today is yes, if the revelation in view is natural revelation.

What about special revelation? Here the answer is both no and yes, depending on the form of revelation in view. If the form is Scripture, the answer is no. Proof of this claim will be established in the chapters on canonicity, but even now we can say that no new divine revelation should be added to Scripture.

What about other forms of special revelation? Can God still perform a miracle today? I can't think of any evangelical who would deny this, and even some nonevangelical Christians would agree that divine miracles can happen today. No one expects a huge number to occur, but to deny that God can perform, for example, a miracle of healing would seem indefensible biblically and would be rejected by anyone who has experienced things that can only be explained by saying that God performed a miracle. Of course, divine miracles are revelation, so, yes, this form of special revelation can happen today.

What about various kinds of direct communication God used in the past? Some might say that because Hebrews 1:1ff. says that God is now speaking to us through Christ, other forms of special revelation aren't available. But that makes the writer of Hebrews say something he doesn't want to say. His point is that Christ is the fullest form of divine revelation we have; that differs from how God revealed himself during the OT era. But the writer does not say that other means of revelation are now impossible. If someone lives in a remote part of the world where there is no Bible and no missionary has ever come, can he or she get revelation from God? Can't God give revelation in a dream or a vision? Can't he even send an angel to convey a message? There seems to be no biblical reason to think this couldn't happen. After Christ's first advent, the NT teaches that revelation still came to people in some of these forms, so why not again today?

As to "new revelation" through various charismatic sign gifts, here I refer readers to the volume in this series on the Holy Spirit.[20] Though I think it hard to verify that most of what is labeled revelation actually qualifies as such, unless one is an absolute cessationist on miraculous sign gifts, some divine revelation could be given through these avenues. But if the canon of Scripture is closed, then none of these charismatic phenomena, even if genuine, can be considered part of Scripture.

What about Scripture? Is it just a set of static data that one can form into even more static propositions, or does Scripture serve today as revelation? I am not asking whether there is more Scripture forthcoming; I've already said no. I'm asking whether the Bible is divine revelation to anyone *today*. This is somewhat of a trick question, because it involves the question of whether or not revelation can occur only when the recipient accepts and obeys it. And that question also raises the issue of what counts as revelation and what counts as illumination, instead. All of this requires explanation.

Throughout this chapter I have argued on biblical and rational grounds that revelation can and does occur even if the recipient rejects it and lives in a different way than the revelation requires. This is true for natural revelation, true of Christ, the apex of divine revelation, and also true of Scripture. In 2 Timothy 3:16 Paul doesn't say that all Scripture is the product of God's breath (revelation) if you obey it. God spoke all of it and it is his word—period! Some people have read Scripture many times, others a relatively few times, and yet others have never read it at all. Anyone who reads any part of Scripture can

---

[20] Graham A. Cole, *He Who Gives Life: The Doctrine of the Holy Spirit*, Foundations of Evangelical Theology (Wheaton, IL: Crossway, 2007).

intellectually learn things they didn't know. When that happens, the Bible is not only divine revelation in general, but also revelation to that reader.

Some will say that, unless we obey what we read, no revelation occurs, but this is wrong, because it demands appropriation of what God said in order for there even to be revelation. That is false for other forms of revelation, and false for Scripture, too. It is also wrong because, if the reader grasps and obeys Scripture, that is not *revelation* but *illumination*. This comment about illumination may disturb some readers, but it is correct, because, as I'll argue in the chapter on illumination, for far too long in evangelical circles we have been working with an incorrect notion of illumination. For now, let me just say that, when one reads Scripture, there is content to grasp intellectually, and then the reader must decide whether to yield his or her will to obey what is now known. Grasping intellectually what is written relates to revelation; bending the heart, mind, and will to obey relates more to illumination.

So, does Scripture today reveal anything from God? Yes, and not just for those who have never before read it. Even the most avid Bible student can read it again and learn something she or he never saw before. He might learn things about Israel's history, the life of Christ, and Scripture's rules for conduct—all things he never knew before. Wouldn't that count as an instance of divine revelation through Scripture? Certainly it would, even if the reader didn't change his behavior and/or wasn't interested in establishing a relationship with the Lord. Similarly, those who have read Scripture before can find it to reveal something they didn't already know.

So, yes, the Bible today reveals truth about God and many other things. Worries about propositional revelation and Scripture being static revelation are unfounded. To be dynamic doesn't mean that new Scripture must be written. Nor must Scripture be appropriated to qualify as revelation. Scripture is dynamic revelation when its content is read and intellectually understood. That happens even today.

What about Christians' claims that God is revealing to them something about the future course of their life? Is that revelation? Scripture offers no such specific information for a given individual about whom she should marry, where she should attend school, and what sort of career she should pursue. But that doesn't mean that, as one reads Scripture and sees what God has done in others' lives, or that as one reads various doctrinal passages and grasps, for example, the hopelessly lost condition of sinners without Christ, that God the Holy Spirit can't give the reader direction for the next step(s) in her life. God may impress on her mind that what a biblical character did in her situation is what a modern-day reader should do in her current circumstances. Or the Holy Spirit may use the truth of the lost condition of the ungodly to show her that God wants her to pursue a full-time evangelistic ministry.

Would "learning" that direction for her life be an instance of revelation? Probably not. It would probably be better understood as God illumining Scripture to show her how the text applies to her life (and then urging her to obey). This kind of occurrence is better understood as a form of divine illumination called divine guidance. It isn't actually what theologians mean when they speak of revelation.

Similarly, when someone says that the Lord has been revealing to him through prayer, paying attention to what is happening in his life, etc., things about the future course of his life, this is most likely again divine guidance. It isn't normally what theologians mean when they speak of divine revelation.

This doesn't mean that God doesn't lead individuals as they make specific decisions in their life. It only means that what they may call revelation is likely a different work of God in their life. But in spite of this caveat, God still reveals truth to humans in various ways! Holding a traditional conservative evangelical account of revelation doesn't lock God out of the world. Nor does it view every act, event, and word spoken by anyone as divine revelation.

Jesus is the highest form of divine revelation we have. But probably *Scripture* is the largest *amount* of divine revelation available. How God transferred revelation into the written form of Scripture is the subject of the next chapters.

# LIGHT WRITTEN

## The Inspiration of Scripture

God has revealed himself to humans in many different ways. This should be no surprise, for a God who loved us enough to create us and put us in a world where we could flourish, would most certainly want to communicate with us. Sometimes Scripture seems to show God giving dreams and visions or speaking directly to many people. But relatively few people who have ever lived have actually received revelation in those ways.

So, how are the rest of us, who never had a revelatory dream or vision and to whom God never spoke directly, supposed to know what God wants us to know? Thankfully, God spoke to many people at various times and in different ways, and they left accounts of what he said. For example, many saw and heard what Christ said and did, and the apostles wrote about it so that people in their day and thereafter would know about Jesus, the early church, the apostles, etc. And in the OT era, God spoke to prophets in Israel, and moved many of them to write down what he said and did.

The transfer of divine revelation into writing, namely, the inspiration of Scripture, is this chapter's topic. Scripture is God's inspired word, but what exactly does that mean? Does Scripture define inspiration and teach its own inspiration? If so, which passages do that?

The biblical word for inspiration is the Greek word *theopneustos*, but it appears only once in Scripture (2 Tim. 3:16). There is no OT word for "inspiration"; one will search the Septuagint in vain for *theopneustos* or any word like it. Even so, in this chapter I shall argue that Scripture teaches its own verbal plenary inspiration. What that means is best explained and defended after analyzing Scripture's teaching about its own nature. But before turning directly to that, I must address a key question about the proper method for formulating a doctrine of Scripture.

## A QUESTION OF METHOD

Evangelical theologians use Scripture as their primary source book. That is true for what Scripture teaches about its own nature. Undoubtedly, some skeptics will question why we should believe what Scripture teaches about anything, including itself. Theologians should want to know that Scripture is true and reliable before trusting what it says about itself. Defending its reliability, however, is a task for apologists and philosophers of religion. Elsewhere I have written a defense of the Gospels' reliability,[1] and it shows how one might build a case for the reliability of all of Scripture.

Theologians must assume that apologists have done well their job of defending Scripture's right to be trusted on any topic. Given that assumption, theologians must articulate what Scripture teaches on any given subject.

Granted that it is acceptable to hear Scripture's testimony about itself, which passages are relevant to the doctrine of inspiration? Many will reply that we should use the same strategy we use in formulating any other doctrine: use the passages that teach something about the doctrine! But which passages teach, for example, the doctrine of reconciliation, or the doctrine of the imputation of Adam's sin, or the doctrine of Scripture? Let me illustrate.

Consider the doctrine of reconciliation. What biblical passages are relevant to it? Should the *governing passages* be ones, for example, in Pauline epistles, where Paul talks about God in Christ reconciling us to himself (e.g., 2 Cor. 5:18–20; Eph. 2:12–18; Rom. 5:10)? Or are the crucial passages ones like Genesis 45, which describes the scene as Joseph reveals himself to his brothers, weeps over them, and blesses them? In other words, are the crucial passages for understanding the concept of reconciliation ones which Millard Erickson refers to as the *didactic passages* (passages which address and explain the concept of reconciliation), or are the key Scriptures ones that *describe* various people settling their differences and fostering good relationships with their enemies/opponents? Hopefully, readers understand that *if you want to learn what Scripture teaches about a concept, you find and analyze the passages that address that concept. Hence, passages like 2 Corinthians 5:18–20, etc., are the governing passages for understanding reconciliation, not passages like Genesis 45 which describe people reconciling with one another.*

How does all of this apply to Scripture? What passages teach Scripture's concept of its own inspiration, inerrancy, etc.? Are they didactic passages like

---

[1] John S. Feinberg, *Can You Believe It's True? Christian Apologetics in a Modern and Postmodern Era* (Wheaton, IL: Crossway, 2013), chapter 11 on the reliability of the Gospels.

2 Timothy 3:16; 2 Peter 1:21; John 10:35; 17:17? Or are they ones containing what are often called the phenomena of Scripture? As Erickson explains, "the phenomena . . . concern what the Scriptures are actually like rather than what the authors thought about their own or other biblical writers' writing."[2] Those who cite the phenomena to determine Scripture's character refuse to grant passages like 2 Timothy 3:16; 2 Peter 1:21; John 10:35, etc., the definitive say on what we should think about the nature of Scripture. They claim that in Scripture there are apparent factual inaccuracies (e.g., the mustard seed is not the smallest known seed to botanists, contrary to what Jesus says in the parable of the mustard seed), apparent contradictions (e.g., the Gospel writers seem to disagree on the number of times the cock crowed after Peter denied Christ), and the like. Those who appeal to the phenomena of Scripture for their understanding of inspiration and inerrancy claim that their method is inductive, while the method that makes the so-called "didactic" passages central is deductive. Of course, their assumption is that only an inductive method can be objective and fair with the data, whereas a deductive method assumes without proof a view as true and then interprets phenomena to square with one's presuppositions about Scripture. A deductive method is said to be unfair with the data and unwilling to see Scripture as anything other than what evangelicals have allegedly always taken it to be. Those who make this complaint typically add that a deductive method focuses too much on the divine aspect of Scripture to the exclusion of its true human element. Only an inductive method, which emphasizes Scripture's phenomena, can see Scripture's true humanity.[3]

How should we respond? What is the proper way to do theology? Should we focus on passages that address the nature of Scripture or on the phenomena of Scripture?[4] Even to ask this question is in essence to answer it. *It should be patently clear that if one wants to formulate a particular doctrine using Scripture, the governing passages should be those that address the topic in question.*

This doesn't mean that the phenomena of Scripture are irrelevant to the doctrine of Scripture. Since the doctrine of Scripture is about the nature of Scripture, what we find in Scripture itself is certainly relevant to our study. My point is that proper theological method demands that the *normative, governing*

---

[2] Millard Erickson, *Christian Theology*, 2nd ed. (Grand Rapids, MI: Baker, 2000 printing), 234.
[3] One who presents this complaint against those who hold a more traditional evangelical view of inspiration and inerrancy is Peter Enns. See his *Inspiration and Incarnation* (Grand Rapids, MI: Baker, 2005), and also his remarks, e.g., to Bruce Waltke in, "Interaction with Bruce Waltke," *WTJ* 71 (2009): 98–100. See also Don Carson's discussion of this issue in "Recent Developments in the Doctrine of Scripture," in *Hermeneutics, Authority, and Canon*, ed. Donald Carson and John Woodbridge (Grand Rapids, MI: Zondervan, 1986), 23–25. See also Fernando Canale, "The Revelation and Inspiration of Scripture in Adventist Theology, Part 1," *Andrews University Seminary Studies* 45 (2007): 201.
[4] Actually a similar debate besets the doctrine of God. Open theists say that God doesn't know the future. They base their claims not on Scriptures that tell us what God knows, but on narrative passages that describe a situation where God changed his mind or claimed to have learned something he apparently didn't know (e.g., Gen. 22:12). For details see my *No One Like Him: The Doctrine of God*, Foundations of Evangelical Theology (Wheaton, IL: Crossway, 2001), 761–770, esp. 764–765.

passages for a doctrine are those that actually address it. Hence, in formulating our doctrine of Scripture, we must first see what Scripture teaches about itself. Then we look at whether the phenomena of Scripture support what the didactic passages affirm or whether they contradict them. So passages like 2 Timothy 3:16; 2 Peter 1:21; and John 10:35; 17:17 are normative for understanding the nature of Scripture, because they are the ones that address the topic under study, the nature of Scripture. These passages must be allowed to say whatever their authors intended to say. When theologians turn to the phenomena of Scripture, they must not ignore apparent contradictions and apparent factual errors. However, rather than assuming that the passages actually do contain errors, and rather than investing little or no effort to find solutions to the problems raised by the texts in question, theologians should invest great effort to find solutions to the apparent problems. Why? Because the passages that govern what we should think about Scripture teach that it is God's word and is fully true. So, there must be answers and explanations to why apparent errors are not actual ones.

Still, some will object that this approach is deductive when an inductive method is needed. Their complaint is that by beginning with what I have called the didactic passages, one assumes certain things a priori, and then skews the exegesis of the phenomena of Scripture to fit the theologian's presuppositions about Scripture. Of course, this can occur, but so can assuming that apparent errors are real and then "reinterpreting" passages like 2 Timothy 3:16, 2 Peter 1:21, John 10:35 and 17:17 so that they *don't* teach verbal plenary inspiration and the full inerrancy of Scripture. The truth is that, regardless of whether one begins with the didactic passages and then goes to the phenomena of Scripture, or whether one treats first the phenomena of Scripture, proper theological method involves a combination of both inductive and deductive investigation. Let me explain.

Those who begin with didactic passages about Scripture don't assume without evidence that it is God's word and inerrant, and then *impose* those ideas on the didactic passages and the phenomena. Rather, they begin with inductive exegesis of passages like 2 Timothy 3:16; 2 Peter 1:21; John 10:35 and 17:17, and they allow those passages to teach whatever their authors intended to say. After handling the didactic passages inductively, the theologian draws together the strands of teaching from the various passages and formulates a statement about what Scripture says about itself. Then, the next step is to turn to the phenomena of Scripture to see whether they support what the didactic passages teach. If the didactic passages teach that Scripture is God's word and entirely truthful, then when apparent problems show up in the phenomena, the theologian should give Scripture the benefit of the doubt and seek a resolution to the apparent problems. Giving the benefit of the doubt is certainly a deductive move, but it is warranted, given the results of exegesis on the didactic passages. Still, the theologian must inductively interpret the phenomena passages to see what they say and whether there is any way to resolve apparent problems. Theologians and exegetes should not impose just any resolution, including dubious ones, upon problem passages so as to superficially smooth over the difficulties. Rather, solutions that make sense and are probable must be sought. If a solution is hard to find, given what the didactic passages say about Scripture, the theologian has a right to conclude that, when all facts are known, the passage(s) involved, properly interpreted, will be shown not to contain errors. Arriving at such a conclusion is, of course, a deductive move, but it is warranted because an *inductive* analysis of the passages that actually speak to the nature of Scripture show them to teach a fully inspired and inerrant text. Deductive reasoning and methodology is not inherently irrational or illegitimate, not when used along with inductive methodology in the way I have suggested. Deductive methodology is problematic when the theologian adopts a viewpoint without any investigation and then imposes it on every bit of research he does. But that's not the strategy I am proposing, nor is it the way evangelicals have traditionally constructed their views about Scripture.

Still, some may think, we should make the phenomena of Scripture normative for our thinking about Scripture, because only then can we use a purely inductive method. Such attitudes are quite prevalent among many who speak about the doctrine of Scripture, even among some who call themselves evangelical. But the prevalence of views doesn't make them correct. The truth is that those who make the phenomena normative *also* use both induction and deduction. They begin with inductive exegesis of biblical passages that appear to contain an error. After noting the problems and concluding that the passage actually contains an error, they often remind us that Scripture is a very human book. Yes, God was also involved, but not so as to keep the authors from making any mistakes.

But this is not the end of the story. Having concluded that Scripture, though divinely inspired, has some errors, those who begin with the phenomena must still do something with the didactic passages about the nature of Scripture, and they do. What becomes apparent, however, is that the exegesis of those passages in many instances is not purely inductive; rather, conclusions about the nature of Scripture, gleaned from a study of the phenomena of Scripture, govern the exegesis of didactic passages like 2 Timothy 3:16, John 10:35, etc. (this is definitely a *deductive* maneuver). As a result, the theologian or exegete often offers a "reinterpretation" of familiar passages like 2 Timothy 3:16. This reinterpretation makes the passage say things that are consistent with a Bible that is less than fully verbally inspired and isn't necessarily true in everything it affirms.[5]

It should be clear from the preceding that approaches that start with the didactic passages *and* those that begin with the phenomena *both* use induction *and* deduction. To complain that those who start with the didactic passages use only deduction and appeal to presuppositions is to offer a smokescreen in an attempt to obscure the truth, namely, the truth that those who begin with the phenomena *and* those who begin with the didactic passages *both* use induction and deduction.

The important question, then, methodologically speaking, is not which approach is inductive and which deductive. *The crucial issue is which passages are normative for understanding the nature of Scripture.* And here the answer must be that *the normative passages are the ones that actually address the doctrine.* So, if you want to formulate the doctrine of reconciliation, you go to passages that teach that concept. If you want to construct the doctrine of divine omniscience, you appeal to passages that speak of what/how much God knows. *And, if you want to know what Scripture teaches about itself, you consult passages that address the nature of Scripture, not passages that speak about the size of mustard seeds, or passages that recount cocks crowing, or ones that report how many people were killed in a particular war.*

So, while theologians shouldn't ignore the phenomena of Scripture, the passages that teach us about inspiration and inerrancy are the ones the church has historically and traditionally taken to be the governing passages. For the doctrine of inspiration the key ones are 2 Timothy 3:16–17; 2 Peter 1:20–21; 1 Corinthians 2:12–13, but not those alone. As we shall see, there is more than ample evidence that Scripture presents itself as God's inspired word. The key passages enable us to clarify what that means!

## BIBLICAL TEACHING ON THE INSPIRATION OF SCRIPTURE: THE KEY GOVERNING PASSAGES

Biblical attestation to the inspiration of Scripture is both plentiful and diverse. Though few passages directly say that Scripture is God's inspired word, the concept of biblical inspiration is taught in both Testaments in a variety of ways. Some passages speak so clearly of the Bible's inspiration that we must begin with them. In particular, I want to offer first a careful and thorough exegesis of 2 Timothy 3:16–17; 2 Peter 1:19–21; 1 Corinthians 2:12–13; and Romans 3:1, 2. Then the discussion will turn to other biblical passages that

---

[5] A "classic" example of reinterpretation of familiar passages about Scripture so as to allow for errors in the text is found in David Hubbard's call for fresh exegesis of Matthew 5:17–18; John 10:34–36; 2 Timothy 3:14–17; and 2 Peter 1:20–21. See his "The Current Tensions: Is There a Way Out?," in *Biblical Authority*, ed. Jack Rogers (Waco, TX: Word, 1977), 172–175.

in one way or another teach Scripture's inspiration. That evidence includes Jesus's views about Scripture, the OT prophets' views of what they wrote, the NT apostles' views of the OT, and their claims about their own writings and those of other NT apostles. What becomes quite clear as one studies Scripture is that there is an equation between God's word, Scripture, and the words of humans that are recorded in Scripture. Thus, if a passage is part of Scripture, biblical writers treat it as what God said, regardless of whether it is something God actually said, the comments of the human who wrote the biblical book, or something some human said which was referenced in the pages of sacred writ.

### 2 Timothy 3:16–17

*The Context of 2 Timothy*—Paul wrote 2 Timothy shortly before his life ended. He was in prison at Rome and would be put to death under the reign of the Roman Emperor Nero. Nero is thought to have committed suicide in AD 68, and the early church held that Paul was put to death before Nero died.

Most commentators assume that Timothy was ministering in Ephesus when Paul wrote this letter. Paul clearly (4:6) expected to die very soon. Assuming that he died in 67 AD, commentators believe he probably wrote 2 Timothy in 66 or 67.[6]

The tone of the letter is very personal as Paul offered final words of advice and encouragement as he "passed the baton" of ministry to his beloved "spiritual son" Timothy. Chapter 3 begins on a very somber note as Paul describes the last days of the age. Though Paul probably didn't expect to be alive at that time, he seemed to believe that Timothy would be. Paul describes (3:1–5) many evil traits that will characterize people in the last days, and he then speaks of things people will do to lead others into sin (3:6–9). Paul predicts that the false teachers and evil people won't ultimately succeed (3:9), but still, it won't be easy to stand against them. Paul reminds Timothy of the many trials and persecutions Paul endured to serve the Lord, and adds that anyone who serves the Lord should expect the same (3:10–12).

Paul then warns Timothy to resist the evil people who will seduce others into error and godless living. Paul reassures Timothy that he has the safeguards to resist successfully the wickedness of the last days. Timothy has the godly teaching and example of Paul and of Timothy's godly family (1:5), and Timothy also has the Scriptures (3:14–15). But why should anyone think Scripture guards against falling into sin and apostasy? It does so because of Scripture's

---

[6] Ralph Earle, *2 Timothy*, in *EBC*, ed. Frank E. Gaebelein, vol. 11 (Grand Rapids, MI: Zondervan, 1978); J. J. van Oosterzee, *The Two Epistles of Paul to Timothy*, in *Commentary on the Holy Scriptures*, ed. John Peter Lange, vol. 11 (Grand Rapids, MI: Zondervan, 1969); H. D. M. Spence, *The Epistles to Timothy and Titus*, in *Ellicott's Commentary on the Whole Bible*, ed. Charles John Ellicott, vol. 8 (Grand Rapids, MI: Zondervan, n.d.); and Charles J. Ellicott, *The Pastoral Epistles of St. Paul* (London: Longmans, Green, 1883).

*nature* and because of the *uses* to which Scripture can be put (3:16). In fact, anyone who takes seriously what Scripture is and puts it to the uses for which God gave it will be completely prepared for all good works (3:17). Don't miss this point of the final verse of chapter 3, and be sure to compare the life-style it portrays to the lifestyle of the godless, described so vividly in 3:1–5. What a stark contrast between lives based on Satan, evil, and the ways of the world, and lives based on the godly examples of other believers and grounded in Scripture!

If Scripture can do all the things Paul describes (v. 16), then preachers must preach Scripture, God's word! They must do so tirelessly and constantly, in good times and in bad (4:1–4), despite how people will reject it and even turn to false teaching. The only antidote for them and for keeping the faithful on track is God's word! Paul ends this letter by encouraging Timothy again to endure afflictions and to do the work of the ministry (4:5), by speaking of his imminent departure, and by adding final warnings and greetings (4:6–22).

*Exegesis of 2 Timothy 3:14–17*—From the description above, it should be clear that this passage isn't a "doctrinal nugget" that God "dropped from the heavens," that just happened to fall into chapter 3. What Paul says about Scripture is integral to his overall message in chapter 3. Though Timothy didn't live to the end of the age, nor have we so far, that doesn't mean that at other times evil is so "tame" and "domesticated" that Christians can easily fight it. Believers of every era know how hard it is to live godly lives and to stand for the truth of the gospel against encroaching evils. So we, also, must avail ourselves of the safeguards that Paul prescribes for Timothy.

Why, however, is Scripture so valuable a safeguard against falling to the temptations that surround us? Verses 14–17 give the answer. Having just warned (v. 13) of evil men who will "deceive and be deceived," Paul begins verse 14 with a strong contrast indicated by "but you" (*su de*). "They will deceive and be deceived, but you, Timothy, must be different. You must continue to hold the things you have learned and become convinced of" (AT). As some commentators note, the last phrase doesn't repeat the idea of learning the truths of the faith. Paul's point is that Timothy has intellectually understood the essentials of the faith and has also subjectively become convinced of and committed to the truth of what he has learned.[7]

Verses 14–15 offer two reasons for Timothy to remain true to the faith. First, he knows from whom he has learned these truths. Should "from whom" in the Greek text be *para tinos* (singular) or *para tinōn* (plural)? If the former,

[7] Patrick Fairbairn, *Commentary on the Pastoral Epistles* (1874; repr., Grand Rapids, MI: Zondervan, 1956), 376; and van Oosterzee, *Two Epistles of Paul to Timothy*, 108.

then it likely refers just to Paul and the gospel he preached and taught Timothy. If the plural is adopted (this is the reading of the Nestle text and seems to be the better attested reading), then the reference is not only to Paul but likely also to Timothy's mother, Eunice, and his grandmother, Lois. Some commentators argue that, in light of verse 15 and of Timothy's upbringing, which didn't include Paul, verse 14 must refer to Timothy's mother and grandmother.[8] But, given everything Paul has endured and all he has taught—things that Timothy knows (vv. 10–14)—Paul likely has at least himself (if not other apostles also) in view in verse 14.

Verse 15 offers a second reason for Timothy to remain true to the faith. From Timothy's early childhood, he has been taught the holy Scriptures. Scripture can make anyone wise unto salvation, a salvation that comes through faith in Jesus Christ.

The phrase in verse 15 translated "holy Scriptures" (more literally, "sacred writings") appears in the NT only there. However, it also occurs in the writings of Philo (*Life of Moses* 3.39) and Josephus (*Antiquities* x.10.4)[9], where it is used as a technical term "to designate that body of authoritative books which constituted the Jewish 'Law'."[10] Hence, in 2 Timothy 3:15 it undoubtedly refers to the OT.

But why, we might ask, is Scripture such a good safeguard against deception and apostasy? Paul answers (v. 16) that Scripture's nature and its possible uses prepare those who obey it for every good work (v. 17). What quality(ies) of Scripture make(s) it such a powerful defense against evil? Paul answers, "*pasa graphē theopneustos kai ōphelimos*." Comments on each word are in order.

The Greek word *pasa* may be translated either "all" or "every." If the former is used, then what this verse says relates to Scripture taken as a whole. If the latter rendering is chosen, then the verse claims that each or every individual Scripture, taken distributively (i.e., verse by verse, and even sentence by sentence), has the qualities named in the rest of 3:16. Either rendering of *pasa* is possible in this context. Some say it must mean "every" because the next word, *graphē*, appears without the definite article.[11] Others don't find this compelling because *graphē* is so frequently used in the NT to refer to Scripture that there is no need for a definite article to designate which writing is under consideration.[12] Yet others opt for "every" on contextual grounds. Their point is that in verse 15 Paul speaks of the whole of Scripture with the phrase "sacred

---

[8] See Ellicott, *Pastoral Epistles*, 152.

[9] See Earle, *2 Timothy*, 409 for the specific works. They are Philo, *Life of Moses* 3.39; and Josephus, *Antiquities* 10.10.4.

[10] B. B. Warfield, "The Biblical Idea of Inspiration," in *The Inspiration and Authority of the Bible* (repr., Philadelphia: Presbyterian & Reformed, 1970), 133.

[11] Fairbairn, *Commentary on the Pastoral Epistles*, 377.

[12] Van Oosterzee, *Two Epistles of Paul to Timothy*, 109; but interestingly, he thinks *pasa* should be translated "all" to refer to Scripture as a whole or aggregate.

writings," so now in verse 16, as a counterbalance to verse 15, he focuses on each individual passage of Scripture.[13]

In my judgment, there are neither grammatical nor sufficient contextual grounds to favor one rendering over the other. Thankfully, no significant theological point hinges on whether we translate *pasa* as "all" or "every." If we choose the former, it is all-inclusive, so no specific passage need be left out. If the latter, where every passage of Scripture taken individually is the thought, no passage is omitted, so the meaning is the same as "all," anyway.[14]

There is a point, however, that must not be missed. Whether one renders *pasa* as "all" or "every," this word means that the qualities attributed to the thing *pasa* modifies, i.e., *graphē*, are qualities possessed by every single part of the *graphē*. That is, Paul affirms that every single verse of Scripture possesses equally the qualities he will mention. The word *pasa* in this verse is a major reason why evangelicals believe in the *plenary* (full, total) inspiration of Scripture. Of course, 2 Timothy 3:16 isn't the only source of this notion, as we shall see.

The next word in verse 16 is *graphē*, a noun that comes from the verb *graphō*, "to write." While *graphē* can refer to any writing whatsoever, in the context of verses 14–17 Paul is thinking about a very specific written document. The words *graphē* and *graphai* (plural) appear some fifty times in the NT. Each use refers to Scripture or the Scriptures. Though twenty uses are plural, the term is singular in 3:16, because it is qualified by the adjective *pasa*. Thus, Paul refers to the same thing he calls "sacred Scriptures" (*iera grammata*) in verse 15.[15]

But which Scriptures does Paul have in mind? Is he thinking about the OT alone, or also the NT? The most obvious reference is to the OT, for those would have been the "sacred Scriptures" (v. 15) from which Timothy was taught, beginning in his childhood. While it is possible that Paul intended in verse 16 to include the NT, the most natural interpretation is that he refers to the same Scriptures in both verses. Of course, when Paul wrote 2 Timothy, many NT books had been written, but how widely they had been circulated and recognized as Scripture isn't clear. Hence, it is safest to assume that he had in mind first and foremost the OT. But that is an issue distinct from the question of whether 2 Timothy 3:16 can be *applied* to the NT, and also distinct from whether Paul himself, as he wrote 2 Timothy, would have thought some books now in our NT canon (but not yet recognized as canonical in Paul's day) were

---

[13] See, e.g., Ellicott, *Pastoral Epistles*, 154; and John Meier, "Second Biblical Reflection on the Canon: The Inspiration of Scripture: But What Counts as Scripture?," *Mid-Stream* 38 (January–April 1999): 74.

[14] Here I follow the logic and reasoning of Warfield, *Inspiration and Authority of the Bible*, 134.

[15] Edward W. Goodrick, "Let's Put 2 Timothy 3:16 Back in the Bible," *JETS* 25 (1982): 480–481; David S. Dockery, "A People of the Book and the Crisis of Biblical Authority," in *Beyond the Impasse? Scripture, Interpretation, and Theology in Baptist Life*, ed. Robison B. James and David S. Dockery (Nashville: Broadman, 1992), 23; and Fairbairn, *Commentary on the Pastoral Epistles*, 378.

also Scripture. For now, suffice it to say that Paul had in view in 3:16 the books widely held to be the OT in his day.

The third word in 3:16 is *theopneustos*. It is a hapax legomenon in the NT, typically rendered in English as "inspired of God" or, more simply, "inspired." This is an unfortunate rendering, since it has the idea *either* of breathing into someone or something that already exists *or* the notion that some existing thing (in this case *graphē*) breathes out something. The Greek term, however, has a different meaning.

*Theopneustos* is actually an adjective that modifies the noun *graphē*. It is formed by combining a noun (*theos*, "God") with a verb (*pneō*, "to breathe out"), and then adding the adjectival ending *-tos*. Though this particular adjective appears in the NT only in 2 Timothy 3:16, forming an adjective by combining a noun and a verb is not entirely unheard of. For example, in 1 Thessalonians 4:9 Paul says that he doesn't need to teach the Thessalonians about brotherly love, because they already know, having been "taught by God" (*theodidaktoi*, an adjective formed from *theos* and the verb *didaskō*, "to teach") about brotherly love. In addition, though not in Scripture, this type of adjective appears in Ignatius's *Letter to the Smyrnaeans*, chapter 1 (1:2). There Ignatius describes Christ's passion as "divinely blessed" (*theomakaristos*, an adjective formed from *theos* and the verb *makarizō*, "to consider blessed").[16]

*Theopneustos* raises three related yet distinct issues. Though these issues may seem important only for Greek grammarians and academic theologians, they matter to everyone, for they have significant implications for what Paul is teaching about Scripture. The first issue is whether the noun in this adjective is the subject of the verbal part of the adjective or the direct object of it. In answering, we must remember that *theopneustos* modifies the noun *graphē*, the subject (the main noun) of the whole sentence. That is, *theos* is not the main noun and subject of the sentence; it is part of an adjective that modifies the main noun of the sentence, *graphē*. But we do need to know whether the noun *theos* is the subject of the verbal part of this adjective (thus, literally, "God breathes or breathes into") or the direct object of *pneō* (thus, literally, "breathes out God").

A second issue involves the fact that *pasa graphē theopneustos* contains no finite verb. Given the whole verse, the missing verb is *esti* ("is"); the apostle Paul expects readers to supply it as they read. "Is" needs to be added, but where? Should it go between *graphē* and *theopneustos* ("All Scripture is *theopneustos*")? Or should it go after *theopneustos* (or actually after *ōphelimos*, since *kai ōphelimos* is most naturally taken with *theopneustos*)? In that case

[16] See William F. Arndt and F. Wilbur Gingrich, *A Greek-English Lexicon of the New Testament and Other Early Christian Literature* (Chicago: University of Chicago Press, 1957), 357.

the verse would read, "All *theopneustos* and profitable Scripture is for teaching, rebuking . . . " The first option makes *theopneustos* a predicate adjective; the second makes it an attributive adjective.

The third issue is whether *theopneustos* is in the active or passive voice (this question arises because of the verbal part of the adjective—i.e., *pneō*). Though this question may seem insignificant, it is actually quite important. If the adjective is *active*, then, assuming that *theos* is the *subject* of *pneō*, Paul is saying that "All God-breathing [into or out] and profitable Scripture is for . . . " (if the adjectives are attributive). Or Paul is saying, "All Scripture is God-breathing [into or out] and profitable (if the adjectives are predicate adjectives). If the adjective is *active* and *theos* is the *direct object* of *pneō*, then Paul is saying "All breathing out God and profitable Scripture is . . . " (if the adjectives are attributive). If the adjectives are predicate adjectives, then with *theos* as the direct object of *pneō*, Paul is saying that "All Scripture is breathing out God and profitable . . . "

Before turning to the options if *theopneustos* is passive, we should note what Paul would mean if the adjective is in the active voice. If in the adjective *theos* is the subject of *pneō*, that would mean that Scripture already exists and God breathes through it or into it. If *theos* is the direct object of *pneō*, then Paul affirms that Scripture already exists and that it breathes out God. Either of these options yields a phrase that makes sense, though the meaning would be more in tune with illumination than with inspiration.

But what if *theopneustos* is a *passive* adjective? What would it mean and how would it modify *graphē*? If the adjective is passive and *theos* is the *direct object* of *pneō*, then we would have to render the phrase, "All breathed out God Scripture is . . . " if *theopneustos* is an attributive adjective; or it would read, "All Scripture is breathed out God . . . " if *theopneustos* is a predicate adjective. Of course, neither of these two renderings makes sense. That is, what is "breathed out God Scripture," and what does it mean to say, "Scripture is breathed out God"? Since neither rendering quite makes sense, if *theopneustos* is a passive adjective, *theos* must be the subject of *pneō*, not its direct object, assuming that the resultant rendering makes sense.

What, then, would this phrase mean if *theopneustos* is in the *passive* voice and *theos* is the *subject* of the verb *pneō*? Then Paul would be saying, "All God-breathed out Scripture," if the adjective is attributive, or, "All Scripture is God-breathed out," if the adjective is a predicate adjective. Would either rendering make any sense? Absolutely! For example, if *theopneustos* is a passive *predicate* adjective, then Paul is saying that Scripture is the product of or the result of God's breathing out, i.e., the result of his speaking. Thus, before God spoke ("breathed out"), Scripture did not exist, but as a result of his speaking (breathing out), Scripture came into existence. Such a claim makes abundant sense, so if *theopneustos* is passive, the sentence makes sense only if *theos* is the subject of *pneō*, not the direct object.

To *summarize* the three issues about *theopneustos*, we need to know whether it is an attributive or a predicate adjective. We also want to know whether it is active or passive, and third, whether, within the adjective, *theos* is the subject or the direct object of *pneō*. How should we even begin to answer these questions? I propose that, until we know the exact meaning of *theopneustos*, it makes little sense to worry about its placement in the sentence (attributive or predicate). So, we should first handle the other two issues. We have already seen that if the adjective is active, the sentence makes sense, regardless of whether *theos* functions as the subject or direct object of *pneō*. We also saw that if *theopneustos* is passive, it makes no sense of the sentence if *theos* is the direct object of *pneō*, but it does make sense if *theos* is the subject of *pneō*.

Given that the sentence can make sense on some reading of *theopneustos* as active or as passive, we should address first whether *theopneustos* is active or passive. Perhaps the most extensive study of this word is that done by B. B. Warfield. As he shows, there is ample evidence for understanding this adjective as passive.[17]

Since *theopneustos* is passive, we can answer whether *theos* is the subject or direct object of *pneō*. We saw that if it is the direct object, the sentence makes no sense, but it does make sense if *theos* (God) is the one who does the breathing. Since *graphē* (Scripture) is the noun modified by *theopneustos*, Paul is saying, then, that all of Scripture is the result or product of God's breath (or breathing out, i.e., speaking). Since speaking is an action, we can say that Scripture resulted from God's speech acts.[18]

What about the positioning of the implied or understood main verb *esti*? Should it come between *graphē* and *theopneustos* or after *theopneustos kai ōphelimos*? When we see the difference in meaning between the two options, we can say that it actually does matter where the main verb is placed. If the verb comes after the two adjectives, the sentence then reads, "All God-breathed and profitable Scripture is for doctrine . . . " If it comes instead between *graphē* and *theopneustos*, then the sentence reads "All Scripture is God-breathed and profitable for doctrine . . . "

There is a significant difference between these two options. With the second reading, Paul is saying that all or every passage of Scripture has the qualities of being spoken by God and of being useful/profitable. Thus, no biblical passage

---

[17] See Warfield, *Inspiration and Authority of the Bible*, 245–296.
[18] The handling of whether *theos* does the action of *pneō* or is its direct object fits the explanation offered by Goodrick, "Let's Put 2 Timothy 3:16 Back in the Bible," 484, of how such adjectives constructed from a noun and verb are to be understood.

fails to have these characteristics. On the other hand, with the first reading, the verse can be taken to say that all passages which are God-breathed and profitable are for doctrine, etc., suggesting that there might be some Scriptures which are neither God-breathed nor profitable. If so, then those passages are not to be used for doctrine, reproof, etc. That is, the first reading distinguishes between Scriptures that are God-breathed and profitable and Scriptures that aren't.

Which of the two readings is more likely Paul's point? Nothing lexicographical about the words Paul uses helps us decide where to place the verb. And no point of Greek grammar is conclusive here. The only grammatical point worth noting is that *theopneustos* and *ōphelimos* are linked together by *kai*. Often when two verbs, two nouns, etc., are linked by the word *kai*, the author intends the two to be taken together as a pair. While it wouldn't be impossible to split the pair, there would need to be clear contextual grounds for doing so. In 3:16, it seems that Paul intends the two adjectives to go together. I say this because if the adjectives are attributive (and then the main verb comes after *pasa graphē theopneustos kai ōphelimos*), then Paul is not only saying that some Scriptures are God-breathed while others are not, but he is also implying that some Scriptures are profitable while others are not. It is hard to believe that Paul would say something that derogatory about any Scripture!

Even so, the grammatical point just made about *kai* doesn't really tell us whether to take the adjectives as predicate or attributive. Nor does the actual word order of the phrase in 2 Timothy 3:16 decide the issue for us. Though it might seem to work best with placing the verb between "Scripture" and "God-breathed," the Greek text's word order could also fit with the rendering "All God-breathed and profitable Scripture is . . . "

If none of these factors tells us where to place the understood *esti*, how should we decide this matter? Our only option is to consult the verse's context to determine what Paul is most likely saying. Thankfully, the context is clear enough to favor decisively one reading over the other. Remember how Paul begins chapter 3—with a warning about the evils of the last days. Many will lead godless lives and teach deceptive doctrine. Paul urges Timothy not to fall into that trap, and he reminds Timothy of two safeguards against falling into apostasy. He has the godly examples of his grandmother, his mother, Paul, and other apostles, and Timothy also knows Scripture. Verse 16 then explains why Scripture is such a potent safeguard against falling into the wicked ways and teachings of the last days. So, wherever we place *esti* in verse 16, it must allow Paul to make his point, and it must not weaken Paul's point about Scripture as a safeguard.

With that context in mind, what is Paul more likely saying? Is he saying that Timothy knows the Scriptures, and some of them are God-breathed and profitable for doctrine, instruction in righteousness, etc., so if Timothy knows those Scriptures he'll be ready for every good work (v. 17)?—and, by the way, Paul doesn't actually identify which Scriptures are God-breathed and profitable and which ones aren't? Or is Paul saying that Timothy's knowledge of the holy Scriptures (v. 15 refers to all of them, not just some) will help him avoid entrapment in false teaching and wicked living because all Scripture, without exception, is God-breathed and profitable for, among other things, instruction in righteousness, so that the one who knows and obeys it will be ready for all good works?

It should be clear that if someone recommends something as protection against a problem, the recommendation will be far more convincing if the protecting qualities apply to the whole of the solution, not just to a part (a part which isn't even identified)! That is, Scripture is a much greater safeguard against the ills of the last days if *all of it* is God's word, not just some unspecified part. So, given the context of chapter 3, it makes the most sense to place *esti* between *graphē* and *theopneustos* so that the passage reads "All Scripture is God-breathed and profitable for doctrine . . . "

The rest of verse 16 lists various uses to which God's inspired word can be put. Each use is preceded in the Greek text by the preposition *pros*. Repeating this preposition suggests that Timothy should think about each use individually, and that each term doesn't simply repeat the others. As Goodrick suggests, "Paul is telling Timothy to look at each one separately to see each use to which he is to put the *graphe*. It is the basis for the doctrine one teaches, it forms the words of rebuke to those who know better and the words of correction to those who do not, it guides people in their ethical living."[19] The second use of Scripture (noted by the term *elegmon*) can also mean refutation of false teaching,[20] and sometimes it will be necessary to do this, regardless of whether those who hear the rebuttal know the truth.

Verse 17 begins with "so that" (*ina*). This may indicate that what follows is the *purpose* of using Scripture for the activities mentioned in verse 16, or that verse 17 tells the *result* of using Scripture as stated in verse 17. Either option is possible grammatically, but it is best to take verse 17 as expressing a purpose clause. The reason is that if verse 17 is a result clause, then Paul guarantees that when Scripture is used for any of the four activities mentioned in verse 16, the result *will be* that those who hear Scripture so used will be/become spiritually mature, completely ready for every good work. That interpretation is problematic, for Paul knows that there are times when Scripture is used in

---

[19] Ibid., 485.
[20] Walter Lock, *A Critical and Exegetical Commentary on the Pastoral Epistles*, ICC (Edinburgh: T&T Clark, 1959), 110.

one of these ways, and people reject it. So, if verse 17 is a result clause, what Paul writes is not true.

However, if verse 17 explains the *purpose* of using Scripture as stated in verse 16, then using Scripture in those ways intends to accomplish the goal of verse 17, but Paul isn't predicting that the goal will always be reached when Scripture is used as verse 16 says. So, if verse 17 is a purpose clause, verses 16b–17 are true, regardless of how hearers of the word respond. I conclude, then, that verse 17 expresses the purpose of using God-breathed Scripture, but guarantees nothing about the results of using it for what verse 16 says.

One issue remains about 2 Timothy 3:14–17. These verses speak specifically about the OT. Can this passage also apply to the NT, and would Paul have thought these things about any writings other than the OT? The answer to the first question is a resounding yes, and that will become clear as we present other evidence for the inspiration of both Testaments. Moreover, even after studying only 2 Timothy 3, we can answer the second question affirmatively. Let me explain.

First, there are passages in Paul's writings where he says that he writes the commands of the Lord (1 Cor. 14:37; see also 1 Cor. 7:10ff.). Paul also speaks approvingly of how the Thessalonians received his preaching as not merely the words of men but as God's word, which Paul says it actually was (1 Thess. 2:13). If Paul thought this about the words he *preached* to the Thessalonians, would he likely think any less of what he *wrote* to them (1 and 2 Thessalonians)? Not at all. I say this because Paul relates some of what he preached at Thessalonica (1 Thess. 2:11–12), and those words are also included in his letter to the Thessalonians. Those words are also consistent with things he wrote in other letters (compare 1 Thess. 2:11–12 with Eph. 4:1, 1 Cor. 1:9, 2 Thess. 2:13–14, and 2 Tim. 1:8–9, e.g.).[21]

---

[21] First Timothy 5:18 is also noteworthy. It says, "For the scripture says, Thou shalt not muzzle the ox that treadeth out the grain; and The laborer is worthy of his reward" (New Scofield Reference Bible). The word translated "scripture" is *graphē*, as in 2 Timothy 3:16. But Paul then quotes from an OT passage and then appears to quote an NT passage. The first is, "Thou shalt not muzzle . . . the grain," a quote of Deuteronomy 25:4. But it is more, because Paul quoted the same verse in 1 Corinthians 9:9, and Paul wrote 1 Corinthians before 1 Timothy, and he would have known that he had quoted Deuteronomy 25:4 in 1 Corinthians 9:9. So, at the very least Paul seems to claim that 1 Corinthians 9:9 is also Scripture and God's word, since it quotes an OT passage and Paul clearly believes the OT is Scripture, according to 2 Timothy 3:16.

The second part of 1 Timothy 5:18 quotes Jesus (Luke 10:7). Paul begins 1 Timothy 5:18 with "For the scripture [*graphē*] says." While that introduction might apply only to his quote of Deuteronomy 25:4, nothing in 1 Timothy 5:18 says it doesn't also apply to the rest of the verse, an apparent quote of Luke 10:7. If so, Paul equates Jesus's words from Luke 10:7 (which verse he calls Scripture) with Scripture, and also shows familiarity with that part of the Gospel of Luke! This seems to be what Paul does in 1 Timothy 5:18, but not all commentators agree. Some think the first phrase, containing *graphē*, refers only to the quote of Deuteronomy 25:4, but not to the second quote. The second quote, it is claimed, was just a common saying of Jesus that Paul likely would have known, and he used it here to support the point he makes by quoting Deuteronomy 25:4. If so, then Paul isn't calling Luke 10:7 and Jesus's words Scripture. This latter approach is supported by van Oosterzee, *Two Epistles of Paul to Timothy*, 63–64; Fairbairn, *Commentary on the Pastoral Epistles*, 218–219; Spence, *Epistles to Timothy and Titus*, 206; and Ellicott, *Pastoral Epistles*, 80.

However, many think 1 Timothy 5:18 doesn't quote Luke 10:7, because they doubt that Paul would have known that portion of Luke, or because they think 1 Timothy wasn't written by Paul but was composed much later than

There are, of course, other evidences (many to be offered later in this chapter) that the NT should be considered Scripture, but, from the Pauline evidence presented so far, it is very likely that Paul would have thought that 2 Timothy 3:16 applies not only to the OT but to the parts of the NT he knew.

In sum, 2 Timothy 3:14–17 teaches that Scripture is the product of God's breath, i.e., it is what he has spoken. Moreover, 3:16 says this quality is true of *all* Scripture, not just some. As such, it is useful for practical purposes such as refuting false teaching, rebuking those who have gone astray, and showing everyone how God wants us to live. Those who obey Scripture will be ready for all good works, rather than being governed by the lies of false teaching and godless living that will typify the last days before Christ returns.

2 Timothy 3:14–17 doesn't explain *how* the words God spoke wound up as written texts. Nor does it tell us *who*, other than God, was involved in transferring God's spoken words into writing. Other passages about Scripture's inspiration provide that information.

*2 Peter 1:19–21*

*The Context of 2 Peter*—Peter is believed to have died around AD 64. In 2 Peter 1:13–14, Peter says that the Lord has revealed to him that his death is not far off. So, it is reasonable to think this letter was written sometime between 60 and 64 AD.

As for the epistle's contents, in the first chapter Peter exhorts his readers to grow in their faith and to develop various Christian virtues (vv. 2–9). Doing so will show the genuineness of their faith (vv. 9–10). They must not become complacent about their spiritual growth, because their faith will be tested. In chapter 2 Peter warns of false teachers who will live godless lives and tempt others to do the same. In chapter 3 he predicts that there will even be people who laugh at the idea of the Lord's return and a day of accountability for what they have done.

So there are ample reasons for Peter to exhort his readers to grow and develop godly lives, even though they already know these things (1:12–13). In 1:15 Peter launches into a defense of what he has told them and is now telling

he could have written it, or because they think it was a common saying of Jesus that Paul could have known by oral tradition, not from Luke 10:7. But such suppositions may just be speculation, as may also be the view that Paul did know Luke 10:7 and intended the reference to *graphē* to refer to both Deuteronomy 25:4 and Luke 10:7. Still, it is *possible* that in 1 Timothy 5:18 Paul referred to Luke 10:7 and was thinking of it as Scripture, God's word. Certainly, nothing in 1 Timothy 5:18 limits *graphē* only to the first part of the verse and not to the second quote (which is found in Luke 10:7). One who supports the view that Paul possibly intended to quote Luke 10:7 and call it Scripture is Lock, *Critical and Exegetical Commentary on the Pastoral Epistles*, 62–63 (Earle, *2 Timothy*, 380, presents the option, but doesn't state his preference). Goodrick seems to see this as even more than just possible. See his "Let's Put 2 Timothy 3:16 Back in the Bible," 481. See also Wayne Grudem's reasoning in support of this view in his footnote 73, 366, and his discussion of 1 Timothy 5:18 in the text of his essay on pages 48–49 of "Scripture's Self-Attestation and the Problem of Formulating a Doctrine of Scripture," in *Scripture and Truth*, ed. D. A. Carson and John D. Woodbridge (Grand Rapids, MI: Zondervan, 1983).

them again. His first proof that what he says about Christ and the life of faith is true is that he was an eyewitness to who Christ truly is. What Peter and the other apostles teach about Christ is not a "cleverly devised" story meant to deceive them (1:16).

Peter's words about Christ should be believed, he says, because he saw Christ in all his majesty. While we might expect Peter to refer to Christ's resurrection, he points instead (1:17–18) to the Mount of Transfiguration experience (Matt. 17:1–13).

Actually, it makes sense for Peter to mention this event rather than the resurrection. For one thing, Peter saw the empty tomb and the risen Christ, but he didn't actually see Christ's dead body resurrect. Moreover, only Peter, James, and John were at the Mount of Transfiguration. They saw Jesus in all his glory, not the Christ of the humiliation of his earthly journey. But even more, Peter also heard the voice out of the cloud saying, "This is My beloved Son with whom I am well-pleased." Thus, he had been an "eyewitness" to the existence of two members of the Godhead; how many other disciples could say that?

In addition, at the Mount of Transfiguration Peter, James, and John also saw Moses and Elijah talking with Jesus. Think of the significance. Moses wrote the first five books of the Bible and had led the people of Israel out of Egyptian bondage. Now Peter had eyewitness proof that Moses actually existed! And Elijah was not only an important prophet in his day, but the OT names him as the Messiah's forerunner (Mal. 4:5–6). The OT repeatedly promised a coming Messiah, and Jesus claimed to be that anointed one. But what if there was no Messiah, and what if Elijah never existed and never would, so he couldn't be the Messiah's forerunner? On the Mount of Transfiguration those doubts were removed for Peter, James, and John when they saw Jesus in all his glory and Elijah talking with him. What other event in Jesus's life which any of the disciples witnessed was so full of confirmation of what Jesus taught about himself and what the OT taught about Israel's history and the coming Messiah? And to prove that Peter wasn't hallucinating, two other eyewitnesses (James and John) saw and heard the same things.

We often say, "I'll believe it when I see it." Well, Peter did see it. But even though seeing is believing, in 2 Peter 1:19–21 Peter says there is something even more believable and trustworthy than his own eyewitness testimony. That something is Scripture!

As with 2 Timothy 3:16–17, 2 Peter 1:19–21 didn't just accidentally wind up where it is. It plays a critical role in the points Peter had already made about Christ and the Christian life, and in the predictions he would make in chapters 2–3 about the future. In chapter 2 Peter confirms that the false teachers will be punished by appealing (vv. 4–9) to three events in OT Scripture that show that God knows when evil is done and will punish it, even if it seems to take a very long time to do so. In chapter 3 Peter answers the mockers who will say that Christ will never return and judge them. He affirms Christ's return, destruction of the current heavens and earth, and creation of a new heaven and earth. These events were predicted in the OT, and they will happen.

When Peter appeals to the OT to make his points in chapters 2 and 3, what he says must be believed. Why? Because of what Peter says in 1:19–21 about the certain truth of Scripture. So, these verses at the end of chapter 1 are not a mere afterthought. They are crucial to believing everything else Peter says in this whole epistle; and they are even more certain than Peter's eyewitness testimony to the majesty and glory of Jesus Christ!

*Exegesis of 2 Peter 1:19–21*—This passage, especially verse 19, is fraught with a number of exegetical questions. Thankfully, we need not solve them all to ascertain what Peter says about Scripture. Verse 19 says that we have "the prophetic word" (more literally) or "the word of prophecy" made more sure or certain. To what does "the prophetic word" refer, and what is "more certain"—the word of prophecy or Peter's eyewitness testimony about the Mount of Transfiguration? Commentators uniformly agree that *ton prophētikon logon* ("the prophetic word") refers to the OT, not to the words of NT prophets and NT prophecy. But that is where unanimity ends. Is Peter referring to all OT prophecies about any subject, only to OT prophecies that speak of Christ's coming (in this case, the reference would likely be to his second coming, since his first coming had already occurred before Peter wrote this letter), or is Peter referring to the whole OT as prophecy in the most fundamental sense of prophecy? If the third option is in view, we must remember that the basic notion of a prophet is someone who speaks for someone else. That person may speak about the past, present, or future, but the key is that he speaks for another.

While a case can be made for each option, I believe that since verse 19 is tied to the transfiguration event (vv. 16–18), which Peter says showed the power and coming of the Lord, in verse 19 he is probably speaking about OT prophecies that predicted Christ's parousia. There are plenty of these passages (e.g., Zechariah 12, esp. v. 10; 14:4). Of course, taking the phrase to refer to all of the OT as prophetic also works, because in 1:19b–21 Peter seems to broaden his reference to the whole OT, not just to OT prophecies about the parousia.

What isn't so clear is the force of Peter's comparison between his eyewitness testimony of Christ's glory (based on the transfiguration) and OT prophecies of Christ's coming. That is, is Peter saying that the transfiguration makes it more certain that prophecies of the second advent will be fulfilled?[22] Or is his point that something even more certain than his eyewitness testimony is available, namely, OT Scriptures about Christ's coming?[23]

A case can be made for either option, but I believe the second is better. If Peter's point is to say that eyewitness testimony of the transfiguration by three disciples makes OT prophecy about Christ's second advent more certain, then why not in verses 19–21 extol the virtues of his, James's, and John's eyewitness testimony? Why talk in verses 20–21 about Scripture and note that it comes from God, if the point is that the eyewitness testimony of three disciples confirms OT prophecies?

This must not be misunderstood. I am not saying that eyewitness testimony of the transfiguration has no value. It confirms that prophecies about the Messiah are fulfilled in Jesus. My point is only that, if that point about eyewitness testimony is the main thing on Peter's mind, we would expect him to elaborate it in verses 19b–21. But it is hard to see verse 19b as saying that Peter's eyewitness testimony is a light in a dark place and that his readers should hold on to it. The end of verse 19 makes more sense if it is about Scripture; and beyond that, verses 20–21 are unquestionably about Scripture. But then, why reflect on Scripture's nature if Peter's point is that his eyewitness testimony makes Scripture more certain?

For these reasons, we should understand Peter as saying that, even though he was an eyewitness of the glory and coming of the Lord, Scripture is an even more certain witness to these truths. It is available to everyone, not just to Peter, James, and John (the witnesses of the transfiguration). Moreover, given Scripture's nature (vv. 19b–21), it is even more certain than the disciples' eyewitness testimony (though of course, their testimony also counts for much).

The rest of verse 19 is even more difficult, though we don't need to answer all the problems to grasp what Peter says about Scripture. Scripture is likened to a light in a dark or murky place. The metaphor of Scripture as a light likely hearkens back to Psalm 119:105. All should heed Scripture "until the day dawns, and the morning star arises in your hearts."[24]

---

[22] This is the view of R. H. Strachan, *The Expositor's Greek Testament*, vol. 5, *The Second Epistle General of Peter* (Grand Rapids, MI: Eerdmans, 1970), 133–134. Edwin A. Blum appears to favor this view in his commentary *2 Peter*, in *EBC*, ed. Frank E. Gaebelein, vol. 12 (Grand Rapids, MI: Zondervan, 1982), 274.

[23] This is the preferred view of Alfred Plummer, *The Second Epistle General of Peter*, in *Ellicott's Commentary on the Whole Bible*, ed. Charles John Ellicott, vol. 8 (Grand Rapids, MI: Zondervan, n.d.), 449; G. F. C. Fronmuller, *The Second Epistle General of Peter*, in *Commentary on the Holy Scriptures*, ed. John Peter Lange, vol. 12 (Grand Rapids, MI: Zondervan, 1968), 19–20; and Michael Green, *The Second Epistle General of Peter*, Tyndale New Testament Commentaries, ed. R. V. G. Tasker, vol. 18 (Grand Rapids, MI: Eerdmans, 1982), 86–87.

[24] Commentators suggest various interpretations of the daystar and the dawning of the day. Some think it refers to accepting Christ (the daystar) as personal Savior, while others think it points to Christ's second advent. Strachan mentions both options, but prefers the second (*Expositor's Greek Testament*, vol. 5, 132). Charles Bigg, *A Critical and Exegetical Commentary on the Epistles of St. Peter and St. Jude*, ICC (Edinburgh: T&T Clark, 1975), 269, also favors the parousia interpretation, as does Blum (*2 Peter*, 274). Fronmuller thinks it refers to growing spiritually in the knowledge of the Lord (*Second Epistle General of Peter*, p. 20, though he mentions many other views). Green (*Second Epistle General of Peter*, 88) favors the parousia interpretation. And Plummer (*Second Epistle General of*

Verses 20–21 again speak of prophecy, but the subject seems to be more than just predictions about the future coming of the Lord. These verses explain further why the prophetic word is even more certain than eyewitness testimony like Peter's. While some still think these verses refer only to predictions of Christ's coming, I believe it is better, given the context of 2 Peter, to see them as referring to the whole OT. Remember, Peter exhorts his readers to grow in their faith, and he later warns them about false teachers and wicked living. Some of what the false teachers and mockers will say is about a future return of Christ and judgment by him (chapter 3). Certainly, the parts of the OT that are predictive alone don't seem to offer reasons to grow spiritually (chapter 1), nor will they necessarily help guard against the doctrinal deception and godless living spoken of in chapter 2. In addition, if what Peter says about the origin of prophecy and the involvement of both the Holy Spirit and biblical authors is true only of the predictive portions of Scripture, what are we to think about the origin and composition of the rest of Scripture? Did it originate merely from humans? Was the Holy Spirit uninvolved when humans wrote those parts of Scripture—or involved in a different way than verse 21 states (it is hard to say what that other way might have been)? Surely, Peter is not trying to make a distinction about the origin and composition of passages about the future and the origin and writing of other parts of Scripture! So, while Peter's reference to prophecy in verses 20–21 could refer only to passages that predict the future, it fits better with the context to see them referring to all of the OT.

One other preliminary item about verses 20–21 is noteworthy. In commenting on verse 21, Walter Vogels says it doesn't apply to Scripture but only to the spoken words of the prophets.[25] Hence, he thinks it tells us nothing about Scripture, despite how evangelicals have traditionally used this passage.

However, this is surely wrong, for it fragments verse 21 from the rest of the text. Verse 21 begins with an explanatory *gar*, which links it to verse 20 as that verse's explanation. But the subject of verse 20 (and hence, the subject of verse 21) is clearly Scripture, not just the prophets' spoken words. Peter writes about *pasa prophēteia graphēs*, and as noted in discussing 2 Timothy 3:16, *graphē* is the NT way to designate Scripture—the OT in particular.

In verse 20, Peter says that he wants to make one point first. It is that no prophecy of Scripture came by private interpretation (*idias epiluseōs*). The key word is *epiluseōs*, which is used only here in the NT. However, its cognate verb occurs in Mark 4:34 and Acts 19:39, where it seems to relate to the "unraveling of a problem."[26] The verb is typically taken to mean "to explain" or "to

*Peter*, 449) offers the options of (1) Christ's return and (2) a reference to the "clearer vision of the purified Christian, whose eye is single and his whole body full of light."

[25] Walter Vogels, "Inspiration in a Linguistic Mode," *Biblical Theology Bulletin* 15 (July 1985): 90.

[26] Green, *Second Epistle General of Peter*, 89.

interpret," and the noun is rendered "interpretation." There are many different views on the meaning of this phrase and on the whole verse. Most commentators seem to take *epiluseōs* in the sense of interpretation. Hence, they see Peter as saying one should not interpret by oneself the meaning of Scripture. The thought here is, according to some, that this is precisely what the false teachers who will come (chapter 2) will do with Scripture. They will twist its meaning to their own advantage, rather than understanding it as the author intended.[27] Other commentators think this means that individuals shouldn't interpret Scripture by themselves, for it should be done by the church. Yet others hold that Peter means that, while the writers did write these prophecies (here taken to mean specifically the predictive parts of the OT), they didn't necessarily understand how the prophecies would be fulfilled (their interpretation). Those who take it this way see a link between this verse and 1 Peter 1:10–12, where Peter says that OT prophets predicted the coming and sufferings of the Messiah but sought help in ascertaining the fulfillment of their prophecies.

In spite of the many commentators who see the phrase as saying something about interpreting Scripture,[28] I disagree. The problem is that this interpretation rests too much on lexicography and not enough on context. Let me explain. I don't deny the meaning of Mark 4:34, nor would I try to rewrite lexicons when they define *epiluō* and *epiluseōs*. Rather, my point is that whatever we take this word (and verse) to mean, it must be relevant to the context of 2 Peter 1:19–21. It is here that the commonly held interpretations seem inadequate. If interpretation is the point of verse 20, how does that assure Peter's readers that Scripture is more certainly true than Peter's eyewitness testimony? Why, for example, would the interpretation of OT prophecies by the believing community be more certainly true than the eyewitness testimony of the Mount of Transfiguration by Peter, James, and John? Put in any other type of interpretation you wish, the problem still remains.

But the problem is not just that the typical interpretation doesn't fit the verses that precede; it doesn't fit with verse 21, the intent of which is to explain verse 20! That is, if verse 20 is about interpreting OT Scripture, how does verse 21 with its comments about the origin of Scripture explain what verse 20 says? Verse 21 seems irrelevant if the point of verse 20 is proper interpretive methodology.

So, we should take *epiluseōs* to mean something other than "interpretation," but what? Evangelical theologians have traditionally understood this verse to refer, as does verse 21, to the origin of Scripture.[29] If that is correct,

---

[27] Wolfram Von Soden interpreted the phrase this way, as cited in Strachan, *Second Epistle General of Peter*, 132.

[28] See the views of Von Soden, Strachan, Blum, Bigg, and Plummer (all cited above), for example.

[29] Michael Green, in his commentary, reasoning much like a theologian, takes this view. As he notes, none of the views that take *epiluseōs* to be about interpretation of Scripture makes sense with verse 21. That is, verse 21 is irrelevant if verse 20 is about interpretation. See Green, *Second Epistle General of Peter*, 90–91.

what does verse 20 mean? We can, I think, do no better than Warfield, who wrote that it talks about the origin of Scripture. Thus, Peter says of Scripture that "it is not the result of human investigation into the nature of things, the product of its writers' own thinking. This is as much as to say it is of Divine gift."[30] Verse 21 confirms the divine origin of what the biblical prophets wrote.

The suggested understanding of verse 20 makes abundant sense in the preceding and following contexts. The reason that OT Scripture (whatever subject it addresses) is even more certain than Peter's eyewitness testimony about Christ's glory is that Peter's testimony originates from him, a mere human. In contrast, Scripture comes from God, and God's testimony is more certainly true than any human's. Moreover, with this interpretation of verse 20, Peter's further explanation in verse 21 makes sense. It is hard to doubt that verse 21 is about Scripture's origin, but then the points Peter makes in verse 21 about that expand on his point in verse 20. And, all of these claims explain why Scripture is even more certainly true than eyewitness testimony.

In verse 21, Peter further amplifies what he has just said. He presents something of the "how" of inspiration, though he certainly doesn't answer every question about that. He first affirms, lest his readers be unclear about what verse 20 means, that no OT prophecy came or was produced by "the will of man" (ESV). Peter does *not* mean that OT writers were passive when inspiration happened, using neither their minds nor their wills but merely writing down what the Holy Spirit said. Rather, his point is that neither Scripture's content nor the impetus to write it originated with its human authors. That is, they did not totally on their own get some religious ideas and then decide to write about them. God gave them the ideas and then moved them to write them down.

But this doesn't mean God produced Scripture on his own. The second half of verse 21 says that Scripture resulted from both divine and human authors. The prophets spoke as they were borne along/carried along by the Holy Spirit. The word order in the Greek text is obliterated in the English translation, but it is striking. Having just said that Scripture didn't come from the will of man, Peter immediately juxtaposes, in antithesis to the first phrase, the following: *alla hupo pneumatos hagiou pheromenoi elalēsan apo theou anthrōpoi* (literally, "but by the Holy Spirit carried along spoke from God men").

The second half of verse 21 teaches several things. First, it shows that humans were involved in writing the OT ("men . . . spoke"). While it is possible to say this about human writers taking dictation, it is a rather awkward way to speak of taking dictation. That is especially so since the text says the prophets "spoke." Did OT prophets preach by dictation? What does that even

---

[30] Warfield, *Inspiration and Authority of the Bible*, 136.

mean? Given the connection of verse 21 with verse 20 ("prophecy of *Scripture*," *graphē*), verse 21 is certainly about Scripture, not just about the preaching of OT prophets. But then, by mentioning the human action involved and by placing emphasis on "men" (by putting the word in the Greek text at the very end of the sentence), Peter emphasizes that the Scriptures had human authors.

So, the OT had human authors, but not just human authors alone. Peter's second point is that it also had a divine author. Specifically, the Holy Spirit was involved in the writing of Scripture (2 Tim. 3:16–17 merely says that Scripture is the product of God's breath, without emphasizing the action of any specific member of the Trinity).

How did the divine and human authors together produce Scripture? Peter says the Holy Spirit *pheromenoi*, "carried along" or "bore along," the human writers. This word comes from the verb *pherō*, "to bear, carry, or bring along." It is often used of ships being carried by the wind (e.g., Acts 27:15, 17). Hence, Peter "connects" the human and divine authors by using a metaphor. Even as a sailing ship must rely on the wind to move it, so the human authors of Scripture depended on the Holy Spirit's action to write the words of Scripture. Just as the ship really moves, carried by the wind, so the human writers actually wrote, but did so under the influence of the Holy Spirit. They were carried along to the Holy Spirit's intended destination, so that what they wrote was from God. That is, they wrote God's word.

We must be careful not to push this nautical metaphor too far. Once a real ship moves under the wind's influence, the ship will still move on apace if the wind stops. In contrast, if the Spirit stopped his inspiring of the human writer, and the writer continued to write a bit, that further writing would come from the human author's mind alone, not from God. Just as the sailor without the wind might start paddling his boat, stop, or turn the boat in another direction, so the biblical writer without the Holy Spirit's influence might write words the Spirit didn't say. In order for all the words written by the human authors to be God's word, when the Holy Spirit stopped "blowing," the human writer stopped writing—"dead in his tracks," so to speak. If the writer continued on his own, how could his words be more certainly true than the eyewitness testimony of Peter, James, and John about which Peter wrote in verse 18?

Many evangelical theologians summarize this point by saying that the Holy Spirit superintended the work of the human writers. I agree, but I note that this doesn't tell us as much as we might think. The Holy Spirit acted upon the human writers, but exactly what he did isn't clarified. My point is that superintending work can mean a number of very different things.

For example, as a teacher I can supervise my students' writing of a paper in various ways. I can assign a general topic, give them a due date, and then let them do the research and writing. Or, I can name specific topics they can work on. Alternately, I can give particular topics and suggest what they should read, and send them off to work. I can withhold interacting with my students until I make comments on their finished paper. Or my supervising might include everything just mentioned, except that I require them to report to me on their progress every few weeks and to discuss with me any problems they are facing. But I might also supervise a paper by standing over a student, watching her write, and stopping her whenever I have a question about or disagree with what she writes. And, I suppose we might also say I supervised a student if, when he took up pen to write, I took hold of his hand and made him form the words I wanted written.

No doubt there are other things I might do which would also qualify as superintending the writing of a paper. But anyone can see that my imagined involvement in each instance differs significantly from my involvement in any of the others. Similarly, the Holy Spirit's superintendence of the biblical writers might involve any number of different things. It is, of course, highly dubious that as the Holy Spirit watched a human author write, he sent an "eraser" of some sort to blot out whatever he didn't like. But while we can rule out certain activities, this verse still doesn't tell us exactly how the Holy Spirit moved the writers. Did he, for example, transmit by mental telepathy the ideas and even the words he wanted the writers to write? This passage doesn't allow us to answer either yes or no.

What we do know from 2 Peter 1:21 is that in writing the OT both the Holy Spirit and the human authors were involved. The Holy Spirit's guidance, regardless of how he did it, produced a book that is God's word. Given the meaning of *pheromenoi*, the Holy Spirit was involved moment by moment as the authors wrote.

Can this verse be applied to all of Scripture, including the NT? The answer is affirmative, and the evidence for this is even more straightforward than for 2 Timothy 3:16. Would Peter think NT writings already finished while he was alive would be more certainly true than his eyewitness testimony, if those writings were not God's word? Not at all. But how do we know he thought existing NT books were God's word? Peter says something toward the end of 2 Peter 3 that lets us know his view of other books that wound up in the NT. In 3:15 Peter says God is longsuffering to give sinners time to come to salvation. He adds (v. 16) that the apostle Paul also makes this point in his writings. Peter then says that there are people who read Paul's words and misunderstand them, as they also do "the other Scriptures" (ESV; *tas loipas graphas*).

Peter's point is quite clear. He equates Paul's epistles (those written by the time Peter wrote 2 Peter; and if we are right about the date of 2 Peter, that means most of Paul's epistles) with Scripture. But Paul's epistles are not part of OT prophetic writings. So, Peter is saying that there are books that are not part of the OT that are also Scripture. In particular, Peter considers the letters of Paul to be Scripture. Now, having established that there are writings that aren't part of the OT but that are written by an apostle and are Scripture, is it likely that Peter would think his own writings are not Scripture? It seems unreasonable to think he would exclude his own writings from this list. It is also unlikely that writings of other apostles, like James and John (Peter's companions at the Mount of transfiguration event), that were completed by the time Peter wrote 2 Peter, would not also be writings that Peter thought of as Scripture.

This point gains further confirmation from 2 Peter 3:2. In verses 1 and 2 Peter says that he wrote this second letter to remind them of "the words spoken before by the holy prophets" (who could this be but OT writers?) and by "the commandment of the Lord and Savior spoken by your apostles." While this doesn't call the writings of Christ's apostles Scripture (3:2 doesn't call the writings of the OT prophets Scripture either, but from 1:20–21, we know that Peter thought of those writings as Scripture), it does seem to equate the words of the apostles with the words of the OT prophets. But in what way? Is Peter thinking only of their spoken preached words? Given our analysis of 2 Peter 1:19–21, we can say that Peter is most likely thinking about their writings, too, when he tells his readers in 3:2 to be mindful both of the words of the OT prophets and of Christ's apostles. Of course, Peter was an apostle, so he very likely included his own preaching and writing when he wrote in 3:2 about the apostles.

So, there are very good reasons to think that 2 Peter 1:19–21 can properly be applied to the NT as well as the OT. Peter's comments (in 3:15–16 and 3:1–2) seem clearly to amount to that.

*In sum, 2 Peter 1:19–21 advances our understanding of inspiration beyond 2 Timothy 3's teaching. It affirms that there are two authors, human and divine, of each book of Scripture. It says that the Holy Spirit was so involved with the human authors that they wrote what he wanted them to say. So Scripture is fully God's word. Though 2 Peter 1:19–21 doesn't tell us exactly what God did and how he worked with the human writers to produce it, the next passage we shall consider sheds some light on that matter, and not on that matter alone!*

*1 Corinthians 2:12–13*

*The Context of 1 Corinthians 2*—What Paul says in 1 Corinthians 2:12–13 underscores a conceptual point he makes about Christian wisdom in contrast to the philosophies that stem solely from human thinking. And his point about Christian wisdom helps him address a problem at the church in Corinth.

Though this particular passage in 1 Corinthians raises significant exegetical conundrums, Paul's reasons for writing this letter to Corinth are certain. First, he had heard from members of Chloe's household about divisions and contention within the Corinthian church (1:11). At the end of the letter (16:17–18), Paul also mentions the visit of several members of the Corinthian church, and they may well have further informed Paul about the situation at Corinth. In addition, according to 1 Corinthians 7:1, the Corinthians had written Paul a letter, asking him about several theological and practical issues. Paul wrote to answer their questions and to address other issues (chs. 5–6) in the Corinthian church.

So, how does 2:12–13 fit into Paul's letter? After his typical salutation (1:1–3), Paul commends and blesses the church (1:4–9). But then he turns to the issue of factions in the Corinthian church (1:10–13). Paul notes the absurdity of those divisions by asking rhetorical questions whose answers are obvious (v. 13). One of those questions is whether Corinthian believers were baptized in Paul's name. The answer is no; nor were they baptized in the name of Apollos or Cephas (other prominent preachers at Corinth around whom Corinthian believers had formed factions). One's relationship to Christ and growth in the faith is about Christ, not about one preacher or another.

Paul then mentions the baptism of Corinthian believers (vv. 13–16) but affirms (v. 17) that Christ sent him to Corinth not to baptize but to preach the gospel. And, God sent him to preach not by using "flowery" words and rhetoric. Sadly, in Paul's day many followed one speaker or another based on how well he reasoned and how effectively he delivered his arguments. But that wasn't Paul's style, for if it had been, the Corinthians would have been convinced by human rhetoric and reasoning, and Christ's cross would have mattered little (1:17). Of course, had that happened, they wouldn't have been saved.

Having raised the distinction between human reasoning and philosophy, as opposed to Christian wisdom with its focus on Christ's cross, Paul begins an extended comparison of the "wisdom"/philosophies of this world and Christian wisdom (1:18–2:16). From 1:18 to 2:5, Paul shows that Christian wisdom and its message have nothing to do with the world's wisdom. In fact, those committed to worldly wisdom find the gospel to be foolishness. But *they* are the fools, for they missed the most important thing, namely, who Christ is and why he died and rose again. They missed these truths so badly that, instead of embracing Christ as Savior, they crucified him.

The rest of chapter 2 (vv. 6–16) illustrates Paul's point that Christian wisdom has nothing to do with the world's ways of thinking. Human philosophies are based on empirical investigation (what eye can see and ear can hear; v. 9) and the processes of reasoning (what has entered into the heart of man; v. 9).

Christian truth isn't accessible to those ways of acquiring knowledge. Christian truth is hidden from ordinary understanding until the Holy Spirit reveals it (vv. 9–10). Lest we wonder why the Holy Spirit must reveal that truth, Paul answers (v. 11) that no one knows better God's mind than God's Spirit, just as a person's own spirit knows better than anyone else what that person is thinking. The good news is that Christians have God's Spirit, so that God can reveal Christian wisdom to them (2:12). Nonbelievers don't have the Spirit of God, so they aren't "tuned in" to the source of Christian wisdom. When they hear or read the gospel or other Christian truth, they can't grasp its full significance and apply it to themselves (vv. 14–15). Only those who know Christ as Savior can understand and apply this truth (2:15–16).

In verses 6–16, Paul also writes that not only do Christians get their wisdom through divine revelation, but the Holy Spirit also helps them express the truth in language for others (2:13). First Corinthians 1:18–2:16 may seem to be a "detour" from Paul's plea to end the factions and divisions in the church at Corinth. But 1:18–2:16 is no detour. Beyond the points already mentioned about the themes of 1:18–2:16, Paul explains why the focus at Corinth can't be on any of the pastors who have served there. To focus on them instead of on Christ and the gospel follows the world's example. It neglects God and the true wisdom of Christianity in favor of the reasoning and rhetoric of mere men. Just as human wisdom misses the truth by focusing on the reasoning and "flowery" speech of mere men, so the Corinthians, by emphasizing the teachings and presentations of one pastor over others, make the same mistake. Stressing an individual preacher's preaching skills has nothing to do with what really matters, namely, God's truth about Christ and the salvation he wants everyone to receive.

*Exegesis of 1 Corinthians 2:12–13*—In 1 Corinthians 2:7–9 Paul says that those who preach Christ speak a mystery which neither natural eyes nor natural ears have seen or heard. Nor can they, for those who speak from only the "spirit of this world" do not speak from God's mind. As Richard Gaffin says, the phrase "spirit of this world" "captures the world, as humanity in rebellion against God . . . , with the attitudes and standards that characterize it as a whole. . . . As we speak of 'the spirit of the times' or 'the spirit' that controls a culture, so here Paul speaks in effect, sweepingly, of 'the spirit of this world-age'."[31]

In contrast, what Paul and others preach comes from God, who revealed it by the Holy Spirit (v. 10). They can know this truth about God, because they have received God's Spirit, and (vv. 11–12) no one knows a person's thoughts better than that person's mind or spirit (here there is a play on the word *pneuma*

[31] Richard B. Gaffin Jr., "Some Epistemological Reflections on 1 Cor 2:6-16," *WTJ* 57 (1995): 113.

in verse 11; its first use refers to the immaterial part of humans, and its second use to the Holy Spirit). This is true of both humans and of God.

In verse 12 Paul affirms that believers have the Spirit of God so that we might know the things God has graciously given us. When Paul speaks of "we" and "us," he probably thinks first of the apostles, including himself, but in the context of the factions at Corinth that grew out of allegiance to one minister/ preacher or another, Paul likely also thinks of those who preached the gospel at Corinth (and by extension, those who preach Christian truth elsewhere).

Having mentioned the things of God (v. 12), Paul next (v. 13) addresses what he and others have done with them. Paul affirms that he and others speak those things. Because of how Paul says he and others speak these words, this verse doesn't likely refer to what happens when ordinary Christians speak (in general) or preach (in particular) about the things of God—though what Paul says may sometimes be true of believers' conversations. Paul's primary reference, however, is to what he and others do with the truth the Spirit revealed to them. As to the others ("we" and "us"), Paul may mean others who pastored at Corinth, or the apostles more generally.

Many exegetes and theologians take "we" as a reference to the apostles, because they think verse 13 teaches the doctrine of inspiration. But verse 13 doesn't mention *writing* words that the Spirit teaches, but *speaking* them. So, even though some take this verse to be only about the inspiration of Scripture, it is probably best to see its primary reference as the message and words Paul and others preached.

This must not be misunderstood. I don't mean that the verse is irrelevant to the doctrine of inspiration. My concern is that many exegetes and theologians "lift" this verse from its context in chapters 1 and 2 and treat it as though Paul is writing a "treatise" (one verse long!) on Scripture's inspiration. Paul writes first of the character of the preaching he (and perhaps others) had done at Corinth. But that doesn't mean that what Paul says is irrelevant to the doctrine of inspiration. When Paul writes of "speaking words taught by the Spirit," it is reasonable to think that he would apply this idea to things he and other apostles *wrote*. This is especially so in light of what we saw when asking if 2 Timothy 3:16 could apply to the NT, which includes Paul's own writings. Paul likely would think of his epistles, including 2 Timothy and 1 Corinthians, as being written under divine inspiration. So, what he says in 1 Corinthians 2:13 about what he *speaks* would also likely be what he thought about the words he wrote to the Corinthians (and about epistles he wrote to other churches and people).

Each of the last two phrases of verse 13 is important for understanding inspiration. Paul has already said that his words are *not* taught by human wisdom, and he adds that they *are* taught by the Holy Spirit. The adjective "taught" comes from the Greek verb *didaskō*, "to teach." I think this is important, though I don't want to overestimate its importance, because Paul's purpose here is not to write a theologically precise treatise on the doctrine of inspiration.

What, then, is my point? My point concerns a theory of inspiration that many believe the evangelical position on Scripture embodies and even requires. That theory is the mechanical dictation theory of inspiration. Throughout the centuries of church history, some evangelicals and many nonevangelical critics of evangelical views about Scripture's inspiration have thought that the traditional evangelical concept of inspiration requires that the Holy Spirit dictated Scripture to "writers" who, in effect, functioned as secretaries writing down verbatim what the Holy Spirit said. Scripture does *not* teach that theory of inspiration, nor is it the concept of inspiration held by evangelicals who correctly understand what Scripture teaches about its origin and character. I mention this aberrant theory of inspiration now, because the last two phrases of verse 13 help to refute it. Let me explain.

As to the apostles speaking words the Holy Spirit *teaches*, I think it is important that Paul used the word "taught." He could have used "gave" or "spoke" ("words which the Holy Spirit gave" or "words which the Holy Spirit spoke"). Either of those wordings would be entirely consistent with a dictation theory. That is, to say that the Holy Spirit gave or spoke the words would be totally consistent with the biblical authors taking down word for word exactly what the Spirit said. That wouldn't rule out the dictation theory. But if the Holy Spirit gave dictation to the biblical authors, why say the words they wrote were "taught" by the Spirit? Someone giving dictation *teaches* nothing! The secretary either understands the language and writes verbatim what is said, or the secretary doesn't know what was said and writes nothing. No *teaching* needs to be or is involved in giving dictation. That the writers of Scripture (and the preachers at Corinth) spoke words the Spirit *taught* suggests (though it doesn't prove beyond a shadow of doubt) that they did something other than take dictation as the Spirit spoke.

No doubt some will reply that this doesn't disprove dictation, because someone may record verbatim what a teacher teaches. That is true, and it is why I said that "taught" doesn't entirely rule out dictation. My point, however, is that if Paul speaks of dictation, other words would more likely be understood to mean dictation than the term "taught." Of course, this is not conclusive disproof of dictation, because to be conclusive we would have to know that Paul in this verse intended to make a conceptually precise statement about inspiration, and that doesn't seem to be what Paul is doing. My point is that Paul's choice of "taught" is more consistent with a different concept of inspiration than mechanical dictation. In the verse Paul's point is that his words (and those of other apostles and of preachers at Corinth) come from the Holy Spirit, not from "the spirit of the world."

The final phrase of 2:13 is rather elliptical, so it is open to many different interpretations. Literally, it says "matching" or "combining" "spiritual" (plural) "with spiritual" (plural). But the first "spiritual" is *pneumatikois*, and the second is *pneumatika*. The verb *sunkrinō* ("matching" or "combining") appears only here and twice in 2 Corinthians 10:12 in the NT. Part of what makes it so difficult to interpret this phrase is that *pneumatikois* may be either neuter or masculine. Hence, Paul may be saying, "matching spiritual things (*pneumatikois*—neuter) with spiritual things" (*pneumatika*), or he could be saying, "matching [or explaining, some commentators say] spiritual things with [or to] spiritual people [*pneumatikois*—masculine]." In fact, if *pneumatikois* is masculine, it could also refer to "words," for *logois* ("words") is masculine plural—in that case, Paul would be saying, "matching spiritual words with spiritual things," and "things" could refer to concepts or ideas.

Given all these possible meanings, there will be evidence for each, and absolute certainty about which meaning to choose isn't likely. Still, we can say some things conclusively. Apart from the meaning of the two uses of "spiritual" in this phrase, I believe it is critical to decide, if possible, who does the combining or matching that this phrase mentions. Given the content of verse 13, there are only two possibilities. Either the Holy Spirit combines "spiritual" with "spiritual" or those who speak do it (*laloumen*, "we speak," is first person plural, and is the sentence's main verb). If the Holy Spirit does the matching (and words are combined with ideas), then the phrase is consistent with the Holy Spirit giving the biblical writers dictation, for the matching goes on in his mind. On the other hand, if the speakers (writers, as this verse applies to Scripture) do the combining, then, assuming that words are matched to ideas, the verse doesn't fit with dictation. For a secretary taking dictation doesn't combine anything with anything else. He or she merely writes exactly what the one giving dictation says. If the ones doing the "combining" are the writers and Paul is thinking of dictation, it is hard to know what he means by using the word "combining," for a secretary combines nothing when taking dictation.

So, who does the combining, the Holy Spirit or the writers ("we")? Thankfully, we can answer, because the verb *sunkrinō* ("combine" or "match") appears as a participle, and participles must agree in number and gender with the noun that does the action indicated by the participle. So, if the Holy Spirit does the combining, since *pneuma* is neuter singular, the participle must be neuter singular. If the writers do the matching, since a reference to them would be masculine plural, the participle must be masculine plural. In verse 13 Paul uses the participle *sunkrinontes*. It is masculine plural, and that settles the matter. Regardless of what is combined with what, the writers do it, not the Holy Spirit.

Think of what this means. The Holy Spirit teaches those who speak, but they do the combining. Whatever the writers are combining, this participle suggests that their minds are not passive like the mind of a secretary taking dictation might be. So, the "combining" spoken of in verse 13 argues heavily against dictation! What, though, is Paul most likely saying that he and others combined with what? I believe we must affirm that it has something to do with the words the Holy Spirit speaks, because the verse is about words the Holy Spirit teaches and Paul and others speak (see vv. 10 and 12).

Archibald Robertson and Alfred Plummer are very helpful by plotting the possible meaning depending on whether *pneumatikois* is masculine or neuter. If it is neuter, there are two basic options (though the second is capable of three possible understandings). The first is that Paul talks of combining spiritual things with spiritual things. Though the spiritual things (perhaps concepts) might be combined with words, the Greek for "words" is masculine whereas this understanding of *pneumatikois* takes it as neuter.[32]

The second option with *pneumatikois* as neuter understands the phrase to mean interpreting or explaining spiritual things by spiritual things. As Robertson and Plummer note, this may mean one of three things. It may mean (1) interpreting OT types by NT doctrines; (2) interpreting spiritual truths by spiritual language; or (3) interpreting spiritual truths by spiritual faculties.[33] Robertson and Plummer rightly note that option (1) is very unlikely, for it is hard to see how that fits the context of what Paul is saying. Option (2) seems equivalent to the first option if *pneumatikois* is neuter, except that *sunkrinontes* is taken to mean interpreting, not combining. Actually, the main problem with all three of these renderings is that while *sunkrinontes* means "to interpret" in the LXX, it is used in that sense only in the cases where dreams are interpreted, and that certainly isn't the point of 1 Corinthians 2:9–12.[34]

What if *pneumatikois* here is masculine, not neuter? Robertson and Plummer see two options. The first takes the phrase to say "suiting" or "matching" spiritual matters to spiritual hearers. The second takes *sunkrinontes* to mean

[32] Archibald Robertson and Alfred Plummer, *A Critical and Exegetical Commentary on the First Epistle of St. Paul to the Corinthians*, ICC (Edinburgh: T&T Clark, 1971), 47. They seem to have this option backwards. They say the things combined might be words, while the things the words are combined with are the subject matter. But the things combined, *pneumatika*, are neuter, while the things they are combined with are the *pneumatikois*. If *pneumatikois* here refers to words, then it is more likely that *pneumatikois* is masculine (because *logois* is), but on the supposition under consideration, *pneumatikois* is neuter. Even so, the option for what this means could be combining spiritual things (the subject matter, *pneumatika*) with spiritual things (*pneumatikois*), which happen to be words.
[33] Ibid.
[34] Ibid.

"interpreting," and renders the phrase "interpret spiritual truths to spiritual hearers."[35] Of these two options, Robertson and Plummer prefer the former, because rendering *sunkrinontes* as "interpreting" uses it in a sense which elsewhere is confined to dreams. Robertson and Plummer believe it is better to understand *pneumatikois* as masculine, not neuter.[36]

The options set forth by Robertson and Plummer show the complexity of the phrase and help to sort the options initially, but the phrase has been understood in a number of different ways, as can be seen by consulting various commentaries.[37] So, how should we interpret it? Here I note several things. First, does the *sunkrinontes* phrase speak of what Paul and others do as they speak, or of what they do as the Spirit teaches them with words not of human wisdom? If the comparing/combining happens as Paul and the others speak (and by extension write), then they are most likely matching the ideas taught by the Spirit with the appropriate words to express them (because their speaking or writing involves presenting words to express concepts). If the comparing/combining happens before Paul and the others speak (and write), the matching still results from the words taught by the Spirit, so the Holy Spirit is teaching them the truth (concepts). Of course, truth comes in words, but the verse says Paul and his associates do the combining of spiritual with spiritual. It still seems most likely that if the combining happens before the preaching or writing, it is spiritual truth combined or expressed in words designating the spiritual concepts that are in view. What else could Paul and his associates be combining before speaking, since the Holy Spirit teaches them what only the Spirit of God could know?

Second, Robertson and Plummer present various possible meanings of this phrase, but they omit one option. They seem to assume that if *pneumatikois* is masculine, it must refer to people, but that is not so. It could just as easily refer to *logois*. The word *logois* is in the masculine gender (and is plural), though

---

[35] Ibid.

[36] Ibid.

[37] For example, Frédéric Godet, *Commentary on the First Epistle of St. Paul to the Corinthians*, vol. 1 (Grand Rapids, MI: Zondervan, 1957), takes the phrase to mean "adapting spiritual teachings to spiritual men" (155–156), in which case the phrase serves as an introduction to verses 14–16. T. Teignmouth Shore, *The First Epistle of Paul the Apostle to the Corinthians*, in *Ellicott's Commentary on the Whole Bible*, ed. Charles John Ellicott, vol. 7 (Grand Rapids, MI: Zondervan, n.d.), 294, rejects this basic option because it uses *sunkrinontes* as "explaining," a use it has in Scripture (LXX) only when the subject is interpreting dreams. Instead, he thinks the phrase means "comparing" (in the sense of expounding or teaching) spiritual things with the spiritual language in which they are stated. Charles Hodge, *Commentary on the First Epistle to the Corinthians* (Grand Rapids, MI: Eerdmans, 1972), 41, takes basically the same interpretation as Shore, but does so because it means "explaining." W. Harold Mare (1 *Corinthians*, in *EBC*, ed. Frank E. Gaebelein, vol. 10 [Grand Rapids, MI: Zondervan, 1977], 202), who says very little about this verse, takes the phrase to mean that Paul and his associates "express spiritual truths in words conveying the real spiritual truth." F. W. Grosheide, *Commentary on the First Epistle to the Corinthians*, New International Commentary on the New Testament (Grand Rapids, MI: Eerdmans, 1968), 72, in an interpretation not far from Shore or Mare, says the phrase talks of "the work of believers through which they in their speaking, in words taught by the Spirit, compare spiritual things with other spiritual things in order to come to a more definite conception and to penetrate more deeply into them. *The comparing precedes the speaking*" (italics mine).

in this verse it wouldn't refer to people. If *pneumatikois*, an adjective, is taken as masculine rather than neuter, it could easily modify an understood (but not stated) *logois*. The phrase would then say "combining" or "matching spiritual things"—*pneumatika*—(probably concepts, ideas, or truths) "with spiritual words"—*logois* (understood, but not in the text) *pneumatikois*.[38] If we take this interpretation, it has the advantage of placing the emphasis on the term "words," which is in fact a major emphasis of this verse. That is, Paul wants to clarify that what he and his associates speak are not words taught by human wisdom, but words taught by the Spirit. If so, it seems quite natural for Paul to say that as he speaks (or before, if one prefers), his words combine the spiritual truths taught by the Spirit with just the right words to express them. This allows us to take *sunkrinō* in a sense consistent with its use in classical Greek; it rejects the meaning of "interpreting," which seems to be used only to refer to interpreting dreams (not the topic in verse 13).

So, what is my view about the options related to *pneumatikois*? It is first that we should take it as masculine rather than neuter.[39] My further point is that if we do that, the only option for its meaning is not "spiritual *people*." Since *logoi* (in this case *logois*) is also masculine, Paul could be talking about combining or matching spiritual concepts with spiritual words.

If one adopts my suggestion, we must still ask what sort of things spiritual concepts and spiritual words are. Paul surely doesn't mean that some concepts and words are made out of immaterial substances rather than material ones. His point is that the concepts are about spiritual matters, and the words are words used to express spiritual truths. Spiritual matters and words are concepts and words about our religious/spiritual relation to God, or, if one prefers, about our relation to religious/spiritual beings and entities.

In verses 14–16 Paul writes about who can and who cannot understand such truths. That discussion moves beyond the doctrine of inspiration and is more relevant to the doctrine of illumination (to be covered in a later chapter).

*In sum, what we learn in this passage about the doctrine of inspiration is that the source of what the apostles taught and wrote was nothing merely human, but rather God himself. This verse doesn't say, as 2 Peter 1:21 does, that as the apostles spoke and wrote, the Holy Spirit carried them along, but noth-*

---

[38] Please do not miss my point in saying that *logois* is understood but is not in the text. Some will turn to the Greek, note that the word *logois* already appears in the sentence between *sophias* and *alla*, and will think I am talking about this *logois*. I am most assuredly *not* talking about that *logois*, for that part of the sentence makes the point that what Paul and his associates preach doesn't stem from words of worldly wisdom, but from words taught by the Spirit. Rather, my point is that our phrase is elliptical—i.e., something has been left out. I am suggesting that we provide the word *logois* between *pneumatos* and *pneumatikois*. Thus, the sentence will have two occurrences of *logois* (the second one understood but not stated in the text), and it is that second *logois* which *pneumatikois*, an adjective, modifies.

[39] Of course, as noted from my discussion in the text, if it is taken as neuter, the phrase can still mean "combining spiritual thoughts with spiritual words"—though that really takes *pneumatikois* as masculine. Or it can mean "interpreting spiritual thoughts with or by spiritual language"—this fits better with *pneumatikois* as neuter, but gives a meaning to *sunkrinō* that it seems to have only when used of interpreting dreams.

*ing in the verse precludes such involvement by the Holy Spirit. Then, the fact that the verse says the Holy Spirit taught (rather than spoke or gave) the writers spiritual truth, and even more, that the text says they took what the Spirit taught and they, not the Spirit, combined thoughts with words, argues strongly against any mechanical dictation theory of inspiration. Clearly, what Paul and the others spoke/wrote involved both divine and human agency. Hence, though dual authorship of Scripture isn't stated in just those words in this passage, what the verse teaches seems to warrant the conclusion that apostolic writing had a divine and human author. The Holy Spirit's teaching/revealing and the writers' combining and writing were distinct actions, but that doesn't mean Paul says that they didn't happen conjointly. If the Spirit and the apostles worked completely independently of one another, then what the apostles wrote might well have been only their own thoughts and words, not God's. But Paul says that he and others spoke and wrote what came from God.*

Two other points about this verse are worth noting. What Paul writes about combining concepts with words (assuming, for reasons presented above, that this is the best understanding of the verse's final phrase) and then speaking/writing, shows that the inspiration of Scripture extends not merely to the thoughts or concepts in Scripture. It extends to the authors' very choice of words. If not, why even mention "matching spiritual with spiritual" and imply that all of that happened under the Spirit's revealing/teaching activity? It is from verses like this that evangelicals conclude that Scripture teaches *verbal* inspiration, i.e., inspiration extends beyond the ideas of Scripture to its very words!

Finally, whereas the 2 Timothy and 2 Peter passages speak most directly about OT Scripture (*graphē* and *prophēteia*), what Paul says in 1 Corinthians 2:13 is clearly about his own speaking and writing (and by extension, that of other apostles). That is, it is about apostolic teaching, and we find that in the NT, not in the OT. As already noted, Paul and the other apostles would have thought of their writings as God's words, Scripture. Moreover, given what Paul later wrote in 2 Timothy 3:16 about *pasa graphē*, it is inconceivable that he would think that what he wrote in 1 Corinthians 2:13 doesn't also apply to the experience of OT writers as they wrote their books. Hence, even if we had only these three foundational verses (2 Tim. 3:16; 2 Pet. 1:21; and 1 Cor. 2:13), we would be warranted in concluding that what they conjointly teach about Scripture applies to the whole Bible, OT and NT alike!

*Romans 3:1, 2*

*The Context of Romans 3:1–2*—Paul begins Romans with a typical salutation. In 1:15 he says he is ready to preach the gospel, and in verses 16–17 he adds that he is not ashamed of the gospel, for it contains the power of God unto salvation for both Jew and Greek.

Some might think it not fully necessary for God to provide salvation, since humans are righteous in their own way. But in 1:18 Paul begins to show how unrighteous (by God's standards) people are and how desperately they need salvation. Everyone has some divine revelation and knows that God exists and has certain attributes. Still, humans refused to worship God for who he really is, and fell into a host of sins that Paul catalogues in the rest of chapter 1.

Many commentators hold that chapter 1 indicts primarily the Gentiles, those without a written form of God's law (like the Bible), but still possessing natural revelation and yet failing to live in accord with it. Perhaps the Jews did better? In chapter 2 Paul demolishes that idea. The Jews received God's written law but fell into sin just as the Gentiles did. And God will judge all who are guilty of breaking his law, Jew and Gentile alike.

In Romans 2:17–29, Paul discusses the Jew's special relation to the law. He emphatically states that being a Jew, being circumcised, etc., offers no escape from punishment if they disobey the law. What matters is not an outward, physical procedure like circumcision, but an inward circumcision of the heart. By the end of chapter 3, Paul clearly shows that both Jews and Gentile have broken God's law and deserve judgment.

Beginning in 3:21ff. Paul explains God's remedy. There is a righteousness apart from the law and law keeping. It is God's righteousness, available to everyone, but it comes only through faith in Jesus Christ as Savior.

In chapter 4 and following Paul elaborates on the necessity of being righteous by faith alone. Even OT saints were justified by faith, not by their ethnicity or their deeds (4:1–8). In light of Romans 1–4ff., a question would quite naturally arise. If being God's chosen people, having both natural and biblical revelation, and being circumcised don't save you (or, if you *have* been saved by faith, if also being God's chosen people doesn't make you more saved than Gentiles who are saved by faith), then what is the advantage of being a Jew? Paul asks this question in Romans 3:1 and answers it (even if cryptically) in verse 2. Paul points to one advantage, and then continues with his argument that all are unrighteous and need the righteousness by faith. Not until Romans 9 does Paul return to the advantages of being a Jew. Though the Jews' privileges are considerable, they don't guarantee salvation.

So, what are the Jews' advantages? Paul mentions the first in Romans 3:1. What does it mean to possess or to be given "the oracles of God"?

*Exegesis of Romans 3:1, 2*—In 3:2 Paul begins a list of advantages (the term *proton*, "first," shows that Paul was thinking of a list), but only offers one advantage. Paul doesn't return to the list until the start of chapter 9. In Romans

3:3, Paul takes the discussion in another direction. But what Paul says about the Jew's first advantage is quite significant for the doctrine of inspiration. God entrusted to the Jews as a people *ta logia tou theou*. This is typically rendered "the oracles of God."

As B. B. Warfield wrote, the phrase appears only four times in the NT (Acts 7:38; Rom. 3:2; Heb. 5:12; and 1 Pet. 4:11).[40] The Acts reference is most likely to the law of Moses, and the one in Hebrews is about the fundamentals of the Christian faith. Peter speaks about use of spiritual gifts in ministering (1 Pet. 4:10–11). In verse 11 he mentions gifts that involve speaking, and encourages those with such gifts to use them. When they do, they should "say what God would say" (speak, as it were, the oracles of God), not offer their own "soap-box" philosophies.

None of these other passages seems to convey the exact meaning of *ta logia* that we find in Romans 3:2. That is so because Paul talks about an advantage shared by all Jews. Certainly, that rules out the thought conveyed in the Hebrews and 1 Peter passages with their focus on Christian truth and Christian service with spiritual gifts. The Acts reference seems more relevant to the topic of Romans 3:2, but it seems focused mainly on the Mosaic law, whereas in Romans 3:2 nothing suggests that Paul's comments are only about that part of the OT.[41]

So, to what does Paul most likely refer in Romans 3:2? As B. B. Warfield has shown in his extensive study of inspiration and of "the oracles of God," the term was quite commonly used in Philo's writings to refer to the OT as the sacred oracles, i.e., the holy words of God. As Warfield says, Philo "very commonly refers to Scripture as 'the sacred oracles' and cites its several passages as each an 'oracle.' Sharing, as they do, Philo's conception of the Scriptures as, in all their parts, a word of God, the New Testament writers naturally also speak of them under this designation."[42]

In addition, *logia* is the typical Greek word used in the LXX to translate words from the *mr* and *dbr* roots in relation to Balaam's "oracle" (Num. 24:4, 16). As Moo notes, *logia* is sometimes used in the LXX to refer to a specific word of God (Ps. 105:19), but more often is used to speak of God's revelation in general (Moo notes twenty-four such occurrences in Psalm 119).[43] In Romans 3:2, since Paul is talking about an advantage the whole nation of

---

[40] B. B. Warfield, "The Oracles of God," in *The Inspiration and Authority of the Bible* (Philadelphia: Presbyterian & Reformed, 1970), 351.

[41] Douglas J. Moo, *Romans 1–8*, Wycliffe Exegetical Commentary, gen. ed. Kenneth Barker (Chicago: Moody, 1991), 182.

[42] Warfield, *Inspiration and Authority of the Bible*, 148. But see also his extensive study of "The Oracles of God" in the same work, 351–407.

[43] Moo, *Romans 1–8*, 182.

Israel has, it is unlikely that, having mentioned *any* of the OT, he would not be referring to all of it.

So, the common understanding among the Jews (given Philo, the LXX, and use in classical Greek, etc. [see Warfield's study]) was that "the oracles of God" refers to the very words of God. Though some might wonder if "the oracles of God" refers to Scripture, it is hard to see what else Paul might mean. When Paul wrote Romans, the only way that the Jews as a whole group would have possessed the oracles of God was in written form. And, the only written form widely available in Paul's time was the OT.

Given Paul's reference in 2 Timothy 3:16 to Scripture as *graphē*, we might have expected him to use that term here (or *iera grammata*, as in 2 Tim. 3:15). But, given common usage of *ta logia tou theou*, Paul's readers would know he meant Scripture, and the OT in particular.

One further point is worth making about the choice of "oracles of God," as opposed to *graphē*. Paul wrote this letter to Roman Christians. Surely, that church had Hebrew Christians, but also many Gentile Christians. Given those Gentile Christians, it would make sense to speak of the "oracles of God" because of the idea of oracles in the Greco-Roman world. In Greco-Roman mythology and pantheism, with which many Gentile Christians would be familiar (perhaps many of them came to the Lord out of that religion), oracles played a key role. In that mythology, it was said that there were places one could go to consult God. Those places were geographical locations where there would be an opening in the earth. Typically, a sybil, a young maiden, would sit next to or over this opening, and the vapors rising out of the earth would have the effect of putting the maiden into a trance (or so it was believed) in which she would utter words that were thought to be of divine origin. One well-known oracle was at Delphi, Greece. So according to Greco-Roman religion, to hear a word from the gods, visit an oracle.

Thus, to talk of the Jews possessing the oracles of God would resonate with Gentiles. Paul, of course, wasn't talking about Greco-Roman mythology or religion. Instead, by choosing "oracles of God" rather than *graphē*, Paul would evoke connections to the very words of God in both Jewish and Gentile Christian minds.

One question remains. How was it an advantage to the Jews to have Scripture? They were just as guilty as the Gentiles for breaking God's law, so what good did having Scripture do them? First, note that Paul's question is "What advantage, then, has the Jew?" Paul begins his answer in verse 2, but to see his complete answer, we must turn to Romans 9:1–6. The valuable things mentioned in chapters 3 and 9 make it quite clear that it is a great advantage to be a Jew. Of course, none of those advantages guarantees spiritual salvation at all.

Why, then, would Paul think it advantageous for the Jews to have the "oracles of God"? The answer becomes clear once one thinks about the alternative. If the Jews didn't have Scripture, they would have had basically the same amount and kind of revelation as the Gentiles. The Gentiles' revelation was natural revelation. As we saw in chapter 2, one can know from natural revelation various helpful information, but natural revelation tells nothing about how to establish a relationship with the creator God, nor does it explain what to do to avoid judgment when one breaks the moral law. Moreover, in light of many misconceptions of God in cultures with only natural revelation, it is easy to see that, while natural revelation is better than nothing, it doesn't give a very full picture of God's nature and how to please him.

Of course, in addition to natural revelation, God could also reveal himself to individuals by some form of special revelation like a dream or a vision, or he could send an angel to speak to a person, or he could speak directly to someone (as he did to Paul on the Damascus Road). But, any of those forms of special revelation would be person-specific. How could the person receiving the revelation prove that it ever happened? Indeed, how could the recipient be sure that he or she wasn't imagining, for example, a vision? If somehow the recipient was certain that revelation had occurred, how could he be sure many years later that he remembered the revelation correctly?

The previous two paragraphs describe the circumstances of someone without Scripture. All the problems mentioned are, in principle, solved if one has the Scriptures. This doesn't mean that every Jew who has lived has possessed a copy of the OT, nor that those who had a copy could even read. But the Jews as a people had "the oracles of God," and at least some people could read it and tell the rest what it said. Of course, having God's written word doesn't guarantee proper interpretation. Indeed, the OT and NT show that many Jews didn't understand the truth revealed in Scripture, especially the truth about the coming Messiah.

Even so, it is hard to see how the Gentiles' circumstances, with little or no access to Scripture, could have led to less misunderstanding about God. Without Scripture at all, one has no clear and certain idea of how to please God. The Jews, in having Scripture, at least knew what God required, and they knew how to repent and gain forgiveness when they disobeyed. Having that information is an advantage, regardless of what you do with it.

# FIVE

# Light Written (II)

## Other Biblical Testimony about
## Scripture's Inspiration

In addition to the four key passages on inspiration studied in chapter 4, there is ample further biblical testimony about Scripture's inspiration. In this chapter I shall first cover Jesus's assessment of Scripture, then turn to OT teaching about inspiration, and end with a section covering further NT testimony about Scripture's inspiration.

### THE TESTIMONY OF JESUS

For most evangelicals, if Jesus said or believed something, it must be so, and we should also believe it. So we should ask about Jesus's attitudes toward Scripture. During his lifetime on earth, the only Scriptures available were the OT. Jesus never called them *theopneustos*, nor did he speak of OT prophets being "carried along" by the Holy Spirit so that they spoke and wrote God's words. Even so, there is plenty of evidence that Jesus thought the OT was the inspired word of God.

The evidence for this begins with noting the general "atmosphere" or "ethos" of the Gospels. In them, the Gospel writers take some things as underlying assumptions, and so do the people whose words and deeds they portray. That "atmosphere" of the Gospels is saturated by a knowledge of, commitment to, and reverence for Scripture. When Jesus cites Scripture to prove a point, his Jewish listeners never ask what he quotes. Nor do they claim that he has misquoted or twisted the Scripture he quotes. Both Jesus and all of his Jewish listeners, regardless of how religious they were, had a thorough knowledge of Scripture. The OT was common ground among all Jews. Gentiles aren't portrayed as having such thorough knowledge, but they aren't always closed-minded to Scripture. And some seem to be aware of some Scripture.

But there is much more, in the Gospels, than an atmosphere saturated by knowledge of Scriptures. Jesus and his Jewish listeners take Scripture as the final authority for every topic under consideration. Quoting Scripture to make a point, refute an argument, correct a misunderstanding is always seen as the "final word." Even more, if the Lord is making a theological point, he may illustrate it by referring to some historical figure or event in the OT. He knows that his listeners will know what he is talking about and will grasp his point. Even in some of Jesus's parables, he cites something from the OT to tell the story and make his point (e.g., Matt. 13:41, 43; Mark 12:10–11). He expects his audience to recognize the allusion or quotation from the OT and to agree.

On occasion there may be disagreement about what Scripture means or how it applies, but whatever the answer, Scripture must be right and it must be obeyed. Even Satan seems to know Scripture and to understand that quoting it ends an argument. For when he tempts Jesus to throw himself off the pinnacle of the temple (Matt. 4:6), he reassures Jesus that doing so won't harm Jesus because Scripture (Ps. 91:11–12, which Satan quotes) says there are angels ready to protect Jesus. Of course, Jesus answers this and Satan's other temptations by quoting Scriptures (Matt. 4:4, 7, 10; Luke 4:4, 8, 12), and the temptations end. Satan never replies that Jesus has misquoted or misinterpreted Scripture. Even Jesus doesn't answer Satan's second temptation by saying that Satan misquoted Psalm 91. Jesus knows the passage well, and he also knows that Satan uses it for his own devious ends (tempting Jesus to sin). Jesus quotes another Scripture which, in effect, says, "Don't use Scripture against the one who gave it, because Scripture also says that no one is to tempt God!" (Matt. 4:7).

This knowledge of and reverence for Scripture are all the more remarkable when we remember that most people of that time probably didn't know how to read, and many who did read didn't have a copy of even a part of the OT. Certainly, copies of various OT books were available, but not in a form that could be easily distributed *en masse*. Still, the Jews who heard Jesus preach knew the Scriptures, and so did others. And, they seemed to take Scripture as the foundation for any teaching about God, morality, or whatever.

But why did Jesus and his listeners make it a point to know and respect Scripture? When we see what Jesus and the Jews of his day thought about Scripture, the answer to this question becomes abundantly clear.

Though there is no specific passage where Jesus calls Scripture the word of God or says that it is divinely inspired, he did say things that warrant concluding that he believed just that. To support this claim, I begin with Jesus's answer to Satan's first temptation. Jesus had been in the wilderness fasting for forty days and forty nights. Understandably, he was hungry. Satan tempted him to prove his deity by turning rocks into bread (Matt. 4:3; Luke 4:3). Jesus responded by quoting Scripture (Matt. 4:4; Luke 4:4), but the contents of the Scripture quoted are significant. In quoting Deuteronomy 8:3, Jesus told Satan that humans are not to live by bread alone. Rather they are to live on "every word that proceeds out of the mouth of God." In Deuteronomy 8, Moses reminded the people of Israel how God provided for them during their wilderness wanderings. God fed them manna, a nourishing but uninteresting food when that is all there is to eat every day. God did this to teach them not to rely solely on manna for sustenance, but rather to rely on the word of God.

Neither Moses nor Jesus commented on where "the words that proceed out of God's mouth" are to be found. From our study of foundational passages on inspiration, however, we can say that Peter (2 Pet. 1:21) and Paul (2 Tim. 3:16; 1 Cor. 2:13; Rom. 3:2) believed that many words from God's mouth are written as Scripture. Moses knew, of course, that God spoke to him and often told him to write what he revealed. So, Moses began many sentences in his books with the formulaic "and the word of the Lord came unto me saying," or simply with, "thus says the Lord," and then he wrote what God had said to him. Of course, when Moses wrote Deuteronomy 8:3, there simply wasn't enough evidence to prove that Moses thought "the words from God's mouth" are found in Scripture. But what about Jesus? Where would he likely have thought one could find words from God's mouth? None of the apostles had written any of their books, so Jesus wasn't referring to any NT book.

Other passages help us answer these questions, especially two in John's Gospel. The first is John 6:45. It is part of Jesus's discourse about himself as the bread of life. Jesus said he is the bread of life who came down from heaven (John 6:38–40). His listeners were skeptical (vv. 41–42), and Jesus told them to stop grumbling. He then added that no one can come to him unless the Father draws him. In 6:45 Jesus quoted from two OT prophets (Isaiah and Jeremiah; Isa. 54:13 and Jer. 31:34). He did so to teach "that God would do his drawing through the Scriptures and that those who were obedient to God's will as revealed in Scriptures would come to Jesus."[1] So, in this passage Jesus connected Scripture (two OT passages) with teaching by God. The verse ends with Jesus saying, "everyone who has heard and learned from the Father, comes to Me." But where would they hear and learn from the Father? Jesus, in effect, says that this would come through the Scriptures. Now, it is possible that this only means that God would use Scripture, though written by someone other than God, to

---

[1]Merrill C. Tenney, *The Gospel of John*, in *EBC*, ed. Frank E. Gaebelein, vol. 9 (Grand Rapids, MI: Zondervan, 1981), 76.

draw people to Christ. But it is more likely that, in speaking of being taught by God by quoting from Scripture itself, Jesus intended his listeners to see that Scripture is God's word and that God's word points to him. At the very least, this passage links God with Scripture and with Jesus.

A second passage from John's Gospel (17:7–8) is of a different sort but also shows what Jesus believed about Scripture. In John 17 Jesus prays to his Father. He has glorified God on earth and asks to be glorified with the glory that he and the Father had before creation (17:4–5). He adds that he has manifested the Father's name to those whom the Father has given him, and they have kept his Father's word. Jesus then says (vv. 7–8), "Now they have come to know that everything Thou hast given Me is from Thee; for the words which Thou gavest Me I have given to them; and they received them, and truly understood that I came forth from Thee, and they believed that Thou didst send Me."

Jesus says that he gave the disciples the words the Father gave him. Thus, Jesus speaks the words of God. But where can we find the words of Jesus? Unless we think the Gospel writers were lying or mistaken when they wrote what Jesus taught, we would have to think that the Gospels contain Jesus's words. But, since Jesus says in John 17:8 that the words the Father gave him, he has given to his disciples, that means the words of Jesus recorded in the Gospels must also be the words of God the Father. But then to say that these words are God's words is to say that, at the very least, Jesus's teachings recorded in the Gospels are God's words. Thus, these portions of the NT are inspired.

From the two passages in John's Gospel, we can say that Jesus would likely, if asked directly, say that anything recording the words of Scripture, or recording words that will wind up as Scripture, is God's word and thus inspired. This intuition is confirmed by further biblical evidence. One piece of evidence relates to how Jesus cited the OT on some occasions. Here we need not offer every example; a passage in Matthew's Gospel will suffice.

Matthew 19:1–12 contains Matthew's account of Jesus's teaching on divorce and remarriage. The Pharisees asked Jesus if it is lawful to divorce one's wife for any reason whatsoever (a reference to Deut. 24:1–4 and the debate in Jesus's day over the meaning of *'erwat dābār*). They wanted to see whether he would allow divorce on seemingly any grounds or only on a few. Rather than fall into their trap, Jesus in verses 4–6 referred them back to God's original intention for marriage. He quoted Genesis 1:27 and Genesis 2:24 as part of his argument that God originally never intended for there to be any divorce at all.

The theological point is clear enough, but *how* Jesus states his point is germane to our topic. The two quotes from Genesis are linked in one sentence that begins in verse 4 and ends in verse 5. Jesus asked his listeners whether they had not read that "*He who created them from the beginning . . . said, 'For this cause . . .*'" "He who created them" is none other than God, but note that this phrase is also the subject of the verb "said" in verse 5. So Jesus is saying that God spoke Genesis 2:24, the verse Jesus quoted in verse 5. But Genesis 2:24 in its context is either part of Adam's comment upon the creation of woman, or it is Moses's commentary on what Adam has just said (Gen. 2:23). In either case, it is not what God himself said. But Jesus (Matt. 19:5) identifies these words of Scripture, spoken or written by a human being, as God's words.

When Jesus attributed the words of Genesis 2 to God, was he mistaken? If he was wrong, the Pharisees would have jumped on such a mistake and ridiculed him for it. In Matthew 19:7, the Pharisees replied, but their answer had nothing to do with attributing Genesis 2:24 to God. Instead, they cited Deuteronomy 24:1–4 to contest Jesus's theological claim about permanence in marriage. They asked why, if God wanted permanence in marriage, Moses commanded divorce (Matt. 19:7). Jesus answered (v. 8) that Moses *permitted* divorce because of the hardness of their hearts; nowhere did Jesus say that Moses or anyone else *commanded* anyone to divorce and remarry. In verse 9, Jesus continued his teaching on divorce and remarriage, and verse 10 records the disciples' comment about remaining single. Jesus replied (v. 12) that not everyone is able to remain unmarried. Nowhere in this passage did anyone say that Jesus was wrong for attributing the words of Moses (or Adam) to God. They knew that Jesus quoted Scripture, but they didn't say that the Scripture in question wasn't spoken by God.

While Jesus's Jewish listeners were wrong about many things, evidently they saw nothing wrong with Jesus referring to Genesis 2:24 as being what God said. Jesus didn't retract this claim about Genesis 2:24, nor did he chide the Pharisees for missing the fact that Genesis 2:24 is actually Moses's (or Adam's) words. Everyone seemed to agree that if a passage comes from an OT book, then it is God's word, regardless of whether God or some human being actually spoke the words recorded in the text. But then, this shows that Jesus thought this text (at the very least) from Moses was God's word, i.e., that it is inspired.

Another noteworthy passage is Mark 7:9–13. Mark 7 begins with comments about Jesus's disciples not following traditions about washing their hands before eating bread. Jesus counters the challenge by saying that the critics honor God outwardly, but their hearts are far from God (7:6–7, quoting Isa. 29:13). In fact they set aside God's commandments and hold people captive to their traditions (v. 9). Jesus supports his accusation by citing various commandments from the Ten Commandments written by Moses. Having criticized them for setting aside these commandments, Jesus says that, by doing so, they have invalidated God's word with their traditions (v. 13). What could be clearer?

Surely, the commands of God are God's word, but then Jesus quotes some of those very commands (v. 10). Note that verse 10 begins with "For Moses said." Hence, words written by Moses are the commands of God, but then they must also be God's word, i.e., they must be inspired. So, it isn't just Moses's record of various events (Gen. 2:24) that are God's word. God's commands written by Moses are also God's word![2]

Here we should pause and assess the evidence amassed so far. Jesus says we must live by the words that come from God's mouth. In the John 6 passage, Jesus says that the prophets speak of him, but he also ties the words of the prophets to God, and does so as he quotes from OT passages written by Isaiah and Jeremiah. In addition, Jesus makes a point about divorce by referring to words of Scripture, said either by Adam or by Moses, as words that God spoke (Matt. 19:4–5, citing Gen. 2:24). And, Jesus also quotes in Mark 7 from commandments written by Moses and refers to them as *the commandments of the Lord*. Finally, Jesus connects the words he speaks with the words of his Father (John 17:7–8). But we know that many of the words Jesus spoke are recorded in the Gospels. It is legitimate then to conclude that at the very least Jesus believed those portions of the Gospels to be God's word.

The picture already beginning to emerge is that Jesus thought of large portions of the OT as God's word, and he said things (e.g., John 17) that would require large portions of the NT Gospels as well to be the word of God. This impression is only heightened as we turn to other evidence of what Jesus thought about Scripture and of how he used it.

One of Jesus's habits was to say the formulaic "it is written" (*gegraptai*) and then quote some passage of Scripture. This happens in Matthew 4:4, 7, 10 (par. Luke 4:4, 12, and 8); in Matthew 11:10; and in Mark 14:27. Since these are examples of Christ quoting from the OT, he could just as easily have said, "it says," or "Scripture says."[3] In all of the Matthew 4 examples, *gegraptai* is followed by a quote from Deuteronomy. In each instance, quoting Scripture is Jesus's answer to Satan's temptation. In other words, Satan says one thing, but Scripture rejects what Satan says. That settles the issue for Jesus! This is also a good example for us: in answer to Satan's temptations, we should quote Scripture to the contrary.

In the Matthew 11 passage, Jesus quoted a prophecy from Malachi about Elijah as the Messiah's forerunner, and applied it to John the Baptist. And in

[2] This point was suggested by Walter R. Roehrs in his "Faith and Holy Scriptures," *Concordia Journal* 17 (April 1991): 156.
[3] In an essay that is truly remarkable for its detail and erudition, B. B. Warfield shows that often in the NT the following three phrases are used interchangeably: "it says," "Scripture says," and "God says." I haven't cited any such texts from Christ's teaching, because not all the examples Warfield notes are in the Gospels and thus are not Christ's very words. However, it isn't unreasonable, in light of evidence already presented, to think that Christ made that equation in his thinking. See B. B. Warfield, "'It Says:' 'Scripture Says:' 'God Says'," in *The Inspiration and Authority of the Bible* (repr., Philadelphia: Presbyterian & Reformed, 1970).

Mark 14:27, after the Last Supper, as Jesus and the disciples departed to the Mount of Olives, Jesus made the startling statement that all of his disciples would fall away or stumble, and he confirmed this by quoting Zechariah 13:7. The Zechariah passage says that the shepherd will be struck down and the sheep will be scattered. In the verses that follow in Mark 14, Peter protested that he wouldn't desert Christ, but Christ answered that Peter would deny him three times before the cock crowed twice.

What we see from this evidence is that, whether answering Satan's temptations, identifying John the Baptist as his forerunner and confirming that by quoting Malachi, or predicting what his disciples will do very soon and confirming it by quoting a prophecy from Zechariah, Jesus quotes Scripture, introducing it with the phrase "it is written." That settles the matter for Jesus, and neither Satan (Matthew 4/Luke 4) nor the multitude Christ addresses about John the Baptist has any reply to the contrary. When Jesus predicts that the disciples will desert him, Peter protests, but he doesn't quote a Scripture to the contrary. Peter just enthusiastically pledges his loyalty to Christ and his willingness to follow Jesus, come what may.

But why should quoting Scripture on these occasions settle the matter? Jesus treated Scripture as conclusive, because he believed it to be God's words. And when Jesus said, "it is written," no one offered a counterargument, except Peter—but his response wasn't a genuine objection but rather unwarranted bravado about his loyalty to Christ. Most likely Jesus's Jewish listeners offered no refutation because, for them, too, if Scripture says something, that settles it. It does so because it is God's word, and no one, including Satan, can refute what God says!

Jesus's comments about his relation to the law also show his respect for Scripture. Some might think that Jesus came to abolish the OT altogether, but in Matthew 5:17–18 Jesus squelches that idea rather convincingly. This passage is part of Jesus's Sermon on the Mount and precedes the part of the sermon where Jesus cites commandments from the Mosaic law and comments on them. Some think Jesus rejects these commandments and puts others in their place, but he actually explains them more fully and shows how the commands apply in specific situations.

Matthew 5:17–18 is a robust statement that Jesus does not cancel what the OT teaches. He affirms that he did not come to abolish the Law or the Prophets. This refers to two of the three major sections of the OT, and is tantamount to saying that he did not come to do away with the Mosaic system in place during the OT era. Rather, Christ's mission was to fulfill (*plēroō*) it, to bring it to its intended goal. As Paul says, Christ is the goal, purpose, fulfillment of the law (Rom. 10:4). The OT points to and anticipates him and his work. While theologians and ethicists debate the extent to which the Mosaic law should be followed in the NT era,[4] a debate that need not concern us here, evangelicals agree that Christ did not abolish the OT. Rather, the OT points to him, and he shows its deeper meaning by explaining how he fulfills it. No evangelical view holds that Christ's first coming falsified the OT or made it irrelevant.

In verse 18, Jesus further showed his concern to uphold the OT by saying that not one "jot [or] tittle" (KJV) (*iōta en e mia keraia*) of it would go unaccomplished. Commentators agree that "jot" refers to the smallest letter of the Hebrew alphabet (*yod*). As for *keraia* ("tittle"), Carson outlines the options: (1) the Hebrew letter (*waw*); (2) the small extended stroke of a pen that distinguishes two Hebrew letters from one another (as examples, the difference between [resh] and [daleth], or the difference between ([beth] and [caph]); or (3) a totally ornamental stroke; or (4) "it forms a hendiadys with 'jot,' referring to the smallest part of the smallest letter."[5] Rather than trying to decide between these options, it seems wisest to follow Carson's suggestion to take *keraia* as a reference to "the least stroke of a pen."[6]

Jesus's point, then, is that heaven and earth will pass away but even the most minute particles of the OT will be fulfilled. As Carson argues, Jesus in verse 18 does not merely refer to the Mosaic law but rather speaks of the whole OT as divine instruction (law). Verse 17 (which verse 18 explains) confirms this and speaks of both the Law *and* the Prophets. "Until everything is accomplished" (v. 18) "simply means the entire divine purpose prophesied in Scripture must take place; not one jot or tittle will fail of its fulfillment."[7]

When taken together, verses 17 and 18 show an extraordinary respect for and concern to uphold OT Scripture. Jesus doesn't explicitly say that he has this degree of concern because Scripture is God's inspired word, but why would Jesus have such respect for Scripture if it were merely an ordinary book? Even an exceptional book, a work of genius, written solely by a mere human, would not garner such a positive reaction. And why would anyone be concerned to ensure that its predictions would come to pass? It would be irrational to take a merely human book with such seriousness, and of course, Jesus evidenced no signs of irrationality!

No doubt, some will say that the most this passage shows is that Jesus considered Scripture as supremely authoritative. Indeed, he did, but why? And

---

[4]For those interested, a good place to start is with Greg Bahnsen's *Theonomy in Christian Ethics* (Phillipsburg, NJ: Presbyterian & Reformed, 1984); John S. Feinberg and Paul D. Feinberg, *Ethics for a Brave New World*, 2nd ed. (Wheaton, IL: Crossway, 2010), chapter 1; Knox Chamblin, "The Law and the Law of Christ," in *Continuity and Discontinuity: Essays in Honor of S. Lewis Johnson*, ed. John S. Feinberg (Westchester, IL: Crossway, 1988); Douglas Moo, "The Law of Moses or the Law of Christ," in Feinberg, *Continuity and Discontinuity*; and Stanley N. Gundry, ed., *Five Views on Law and Gospel* (Grand Rapids, MI: Zondervan, 1996).
[5]D. A. Carson, *Matthew*, in *EBC*, ed. Frank E. Gaebelein, vol. 8 (Grand Rapids, MI: Zondervan, 1984), 145.
[6]Ibid.
[7]Ibid., 146. See 145–146 for other interpretations of this phrase. Carson's assessment seems to best capture what Jesus has in mind.

why did he commit himself in verse 17 to fulfilling it? It is one thing to say that one won't abolish a system already in place, but another to make a point to bring that system to its fullest potential. Why make such claims if this is an exceptional but purely human book?

A further evidence of how seriously Jesus took the OT is his response to OT commands. In several instances, he quoted OT commands and affirmed that they must be obeyed. We see this in Matthew 22:37–40 (par. Mark 12:28–34 and Luke 10:25–28). We also see it in the Sermon on the Mount when Jesus discussed various OT commands (Matt. 5:21–22, 27–28, 31–32, 33–37, 38–42, 43–47). Though some take Jesus's reactions to these commands as rejecting them, I disagree. Others think Jesus's comments correct Jewish misunderstandings of the command. While Jesus does correct some misunderstanding, he seems mostly to expand and elaborate what the commands mean and to explain how they apply in specific situations. For example, Jesus didn't cancel the command against adultery; rather, he applied it to situations where one doesn't commit the act but lusts after a woman (5:27–28). He didn't reject the command against murder, but added that various expressions of anger (short of murder) reveal an evil heart that is culpable before God.

Of course, Jesus corrected mishandlings of commands. For example, he says that some say one must love one's neighbor but hate one's enemies (Matt. 5:43). Jesus affirms the command to love the neighbor but adds that we should love even our enemies. Though some thought it permissible to hate one's enemies, the Mosaic law commands no such thing. So, when Jesus says we must love our enemies, he abolishes nothing written in the law.

Another evidence of Jesus's high regard for the OT is his repeated reference to OT prophecies. This appears in several forms. Jesus's main appeal to OT prophecies relates to himself and things he did. He constantly wanted to connect himself to the OT, and did so by saying that in one way or another he fulfilled OT prophecy about the Messiah. Or, he noted that something had happened so that an OT prediction would be fulfilled. This happens especially in the Synoptic Gospels, but it isn't entirely absent from the Gospel of John. Note a few examples.

In Matthew 11:4–5 (par. Luke 7:22–23) Jesus answers questions sent through John the Baptist's disciples about whether Jesus is the one who was to come or whether they should look for another. Jesus points to his miracles of healing, and he adds, as proof, that the gospel is being preached. However, he makes these points by quoting Isaiah 29:18–19 and 35:4–6. At very least, Isaiah 35 can be seen as referring to kingdom blessings for Israel when her Messiah reigns.

On another occasion, Jesus was in the synagogue and was handed the

Isaiah scroll. In Luke 4:18–19 we hear him read from Isaiah 61:1–2. He finishes reading, returns the scroll to the attendant, and then says, "Today this Scripture has been fulfilled in your hearing" (Luke 4:21). Clearly, he was referring to himself and his mission, but in effect he was also saying that he fulfills OT prophecy.

A rather famous instance of Jesus quoting an OT messianic prophecy and applying it to himself appears in Matthew 21:42 (par. Mark 12:10–12 and Luke 20:17) as part of the parable of the landowner. The parable's point is that those who were supposed to tend the vineyard for its owner had instead looked out for their own interests. Regardless of whom the landowner sent to look after his interests, including his own son, those who tended the vineyard mistreated them (even killing the son). When the landowner returns, Jesus says that he will surely punish the wretches who did this and will rent the vineyard to other tenants. Jesus then connected this parable to himself and how the Jewish religious leaders had treated him. Despite their stumbling over him, he is the Son and the cornerstone of a new people of God that God is building. To confirm his message, Jesus quotes Psalm 118:22–23 as predicting what has happened, and asks his listeners if they have ever read this Scripture (Jesus, of course, knew that they knew it). In effect, the point of the parable is confirmed by how Jesus's own people treated him, and that fulfills Scripture's prediction.

Another well-known passage (Matt. 22:41–45; par. Mark 12:35–37 and Luke 20:41–44) links Jesus with another messianic Psalm (110) but doesn't blatantly say Jesus fulfills it. Jesus questioned the Pharisees about the coming Messiah. He asked whose Son the Messiah would be. They rightly answered, "The son of David." Jesus then asked, "'How is it then that David, speaking by the Spirit, calls him "Lord"? For he says, "The Lord said to my Lord: 'Sit at my right hand until I put your enemies under your feet.'" If then David calls him "Lord," how can he be his son?'" (NIV 1984).

Here note several things. Jesus quoted Psalm 110:1, part of Scripture, and claimed that David is the author. But note that Jesus said David wrote this, "speaking by the Spirit" (Matt. 22:43 NIV 1984). If David wrote the verse and was speaking by the Spirit, isn't that an instance of what 2 Peter 1:21 says? Wasn't Jesus, by making this comment (and knowing that he was quoting Scripture) in effect also saying that what David wrote is God's word, so it must be true? By including this phrase, Jesus removed the chance for the Pharisees to dismiss Jesus's question by saying, "Well, that was just David's opinion, but he didn't know what he was talking about." That response is excluded, because Jesus quoted Scriptures that the Pharisees knew, and attributed the comment to both David and the Holy Spirit. If the Pharisees thought this was just David's wrong opinion, they should have protested that Jesus's question was wrong-headed. Instead, no one could answer the question Jesus asked (Matt. 22:46).

But there is more to say about this verse. Jesus was subtly affirming (though posing a question) that Psalm 110:1 referred to him, David's Lord. He wanted the Pharisees to see that someone living about a thousand years after David would be David's Lord. Thus, when Jesus claimed to be the Messiah, he was telling the truth and wasn't deluded. But Jesus was too clever to state this baldly and blatantly. By posing a question that cited Scripture (and implicitly connecting himself to that Scripture as its refer-ent), Jesus gave the Pharisees an impossible choice: either deny that David, speaking by the Spirit, knew what he was talking about, or agree that some-one born after David could be his Lord—and hence, that Jesus could be the Messiah. Either option would cause the Pharisees trouble, so they remained silent, and Matthew says that, from that day on, no one dared to ask Jesus any more questions.

Other passages in which Jesus quotes an OT prediction and says he or events related to him fulfill it are Matthew 13:14–15, which quotes from Isaiah 6:9–10; Matthew 21:16; 26:31 (par. Mark 14:27), 54, 56, 64 (par. Mark 14:62 and Luke 22:69); 27:46 (par. Mark 15:34); Luke 22:37; John 13:18; and 15:25.

There are also passages where Scripture is not quoted but we are told that a certain saying or event fulfills Scripture. For example, on the cross, Jesus said, "I thirst." This recalls Psalm 69:21, though it doesn't exactly quote it. Even so, John writes that Jesus, in order "to fulfill the Scripture," said "I thirst" (John 19:28 ESV).[8] In John 17:12, Jesus, praying to his Father, says that none that the Father gave him has perished, except the son of perdition (Judas). Jesus says that Judas has been lost so that Scripture might be fulfilled (Jesus is thinking of Ps. 41:9, but he doesn't quote it).

In addition, Jesus sometimes referred to large portions of Scripture (with-out quoting any verse) as being fulfilled in him or as speaking about him. For example, Jesus told his listeners (John 5:45–47) that if they believed Moses, they would believe him, because Moses wrote of him. Earlier in the same chap-ter (v. 39), he instructed his hearers to search the Scriptures, because they think they find in them eternal life. Jesus says that those Scriptures (the OT) bear witness of him.

Luke 24 is also very important on this matter. On the road to Emmaus, Jesus chided his disciples for not believing what OT prophets had predicted about his suffering and entering into glory (vv. 25–26). Luke then adds (v. 27) that, "beginning with Moses and with all the prophets" (two of the three major portions of the OT canon), "He explained to them the things concerning

---

[8] Ibid., 183.

Himself in *all* the Scriptures"—the last phrase broadens the reference to all of the OT. Later in the chapter (v. 44) Luke says that Jesus appeared to the disciples and said, "These are My words which I spoke to you while I was still with you, that all things which are written about Me in the Law of Moses and the Prophets and the Psalms must be fulfilled." This comment refers to all three major portions of the OT canon. Obviously, for these comments in verses 25–27 and 44 to be true, the OT passages referenced, but not quoted, must be prophecies, since all were written many years before the life of Christ.

But it isn't just Jesus who fulfills OT prophecies. Jesus refers to the prophecies in Malachi about Elijah, the Messiah's forerunner, and says that John the Baptist fulfills them (Matt. 11:10, 14; par. Luke 7:27). In Mark 9:11–13, Jesus also mentions the prophecy about Elijah, but doesn't quote it. Nor does he mention John's name, saying only that Elijah has indeed come. Given what Jesus says happened to this "Elijah," we might suspect that he was speaking of John the Baptist, but the Matthew and Luke references remove any doubt, for they identify John as the one who fulfilled the Elijah prophecies.

So, Jesus quotes or alludes to many things in the OT and says that he fulfills them. But readers may ask what this tells us about Jesus's opinion of Scripture. Actually, it says more than we might at first think. Let me explain.

Jesus refers to various OT predictions. Now, Jesus surely knew that Moses spoke of the tests of a true prophet, that is, of one fully accredited as God's spokesman. The passages that speak about this are Deuteronomy 13:1–5 and 18:18–22. Moses sets forth several criteria for whether a prophet speaks for the Lord or tries to lead the people astray. Deuteronomy 18:22 says that if a prophet speaks in the Lord's name and what he says does not come about, then what he says should not be believed. What can this mean but that, if a prophet's prediction goes unfulfilled, you shouldn't believe he speaks for the living God?

It should now be clear why it was so important for Jesus to cite OT Scriptures as being fulfilled by him. If passages that predict the Messiah's life and ministry are not fulfilled, then they were spoken/written by false prophets and cannot be from God. If those prophecies *are* fulfilled, then (assuming that the passages containing them pass the other tests of Deuteronomy 13 and 18 of a true prophet), they come from God and the prophet is an accredited spokesman for God. That also means that these prophecies meet a crucial requirement for being inspired, namely, they were written by people who were accredited spokesmen for God.

If Jesus didn't fulfill the prophecies he quoted or alluded to, there are serious repercussions for him. Specifically, his "case" that he is Israel's long-awaited Messiah is dealt a telling blow. If those prophecies are about Israel's Messiah (and Jews before and during Jesus's day thought they were), but Jesus doesn't fulfill them, then he isn't who he claims to be. The consequences for Israel are devastating, but also for the whole world, for then there is no reason to think Christ's death atoned for anyone's sin, and there is ample reason to think accounts of his post-resurrection appearances are just wishful thinking.

So, much more is at stake in Jesus's claims to fulfill various OT prophecies than just showing that he respected those OT passages and thought they were authoritative. Whether these passages are from God (i.e., inspired), and whether he himself is from God are also at stake!

Jesus also quotes or cites other OT prophecies, but they are end-time prophecies, including predictions about what we now understand to be his second coming. For example, in the Olivet Discourse, as Jesus answers his disciples' questions about signs of his coming and of the end of the age, he quotes or cites OT end-time prophecies. In Matthew 24:15 (par. Mark 13:14), Jesus refers to a prophecy from the book of Daniel. The most likely referent is Daniel 9:27, a prophecy about Daniel's seventieth week and the erecting of the abomination of desolation. In effect, Jesus affirms that this prediction should still be believed. Later (Matt. 24:29–31; par. Mark 13:24–27), he mentions his second coming at the end of the tribulation, but he doesn't just say it will happen. He quotes various OT end-time prophecies (Isa. 13:9–13; 24:23; 27:12–13; 34:1–4; Ezek. 32:7; Dan. 7:13–14; Joel 2:10, 31; 3:15ff.; Zeph. 1:14ff; Deut. 4:32ff.; and Zech. 9:14ff.). Whether or not these passages in their original contexts actually refer to end-time events, I leave to readers' study (I believe most, if not all, do). What is clear is that Jesus quotes these OT passages and uses them to teach about end-time events, including his second coming.

So, the fact that in speaking of the end times Jesus referenced so many OT prophecies shows first that God's plans (assuming the OT is from God) haven't changed. It also assures us, if we need such assurance, that Jesus's predictions rested not only on his own claims and authority but on those of the OT. Quoting OT passages in support of what he taught doesn't mean he had doubts about his own credibility. Rather the quotes add credibility (for any who need it) to his predictions, because, given Jesus's obvious belief (and that of at least his Jewish listeners) that OT Scripture comes from God, the predictions are not just what Jesus thinks but also are what God has already said in his word.

My next point doesn't prove that Jesus thought the OT is inspired, but it is relevant to his overall perception of the trustworthiness of the OT. There is ample evidence in the Gospels that Jesus believed that various OT characters actually existed and that OT events actually occurred. In fact, he often mentioned OT people or events to make a theological point about himself, his listeners, or things that were happening in his life. For example, Jesus's teaching on divorce (Matt. 19:4–6) shows that he believed God instituted marriage between Adam and Eve. On several occasions he referred to the sinfulness of Sodom and Gomorrah and to their destruction, and he also believed to be historical the story of Lot and his departure from Sodom as it was being destroyed. And he believed what the OT said happened when Lot's wife looked back on Sodom as she left and was turned into a pillar of salt (Matt. 10:15; 11:23–24 [par. Luke 10:12ff]; Luke 17:28–29, 32).

In addition, Jesus believed in the historicity of Noah and of the Noahic flood (Matt. 24:37–38 [par. Luke 17:26–27]). He also believed that David ate the showbread in the house of God on the Sabbath. In fact, Jesus appealed to this event as historical to make a point that he (Christ) is Lord of the Sabbath (Matt. 12:2–8 [par. Mark 2:24–28 and Luke 6:3–5]). Jesus also believed in the historical Elijah, and on various occasions referred to events in Elijah's life to prove a point he was making (Luke 4:25–27).[9]

Then, it is crucial that Jesus believed that the OT story about Jonah preaching to Nineveh and the story of Jonah and the fish were historically true. This is quite significant because on so many occasions Jesus appealed to the story of Jonah and the fish as a sign of his forthcoming resurrection. If that story is actually fictitious (or if Jesus believed it was), then appealing to it to "prove" his claims about his own resurrection offers no proof at all! Passages where Jesus appealed to one or another aspect of the Jonah story are Matthew 12:39–41 (par. Luke 11:29–32); and 16:4.

Of course, we also know that Jesus believed that Moses actually lived and wrote the Pentateuch. In fact, I have already cited a number of passages where Jesus referred to what Moses wrote about a subject. In one passage already noted, Jesus even says that Moses wrote about *him*. Moreover, Jesus sometimes appealed to Moses to make a theological point. For example, in Luke 20:37 Jesus expressed his belief in Moses as a historical person and quoted Moses to make a point about resurrections. John's Gospel gives further evidence that Jesus believed that various events in Moses's life actually occurred. In John 3:14 Jesus referred to Moses's lifting up the serpent in the wilderness as prefiguring his own crucifixion. If the event in Moses's day didn't happen, then Jesus's point about his own crucifixion and the redemption it wrought is severely undercut. In Jesus's discourse on himself as the bread of life (John 6), we see that Jesus believed as historical Israel's wilderness wanderings under Moses and God's provision of manna to sustain them. Jesus remarks that the people who ate that bread died. In contrast, Jesus asserts that he is also bread from heaven, and adds that those who eat of him will never die (vv. 48–58). Without mentioning Israel and manna in the wilderness, Jesus still could have made the

---

[9] Readers should note that this is a different point than the one previously made about the fulfillment of *prophecies* about Elijah as the forerunner of the Messiah. My point here refers to the historical prophet Elijah who lived in the OT era. The passage cited in my text from Luke also affirms Jesus's belief in the prophet Elisha.

point that he is the bread of life. But the point of comparing himself to manna (bread which when eaten sustains the eater eternally, not just temporarily) is lost if Jesus doesn't mention the wilderness experience. And, if the story of manna in the wilderness is not historically true, then what does saying that he is the bread of life that sustains life forever prove about himself?

Then, as already noted, Jesus repeatedly referred to and even quoted Scripture to prove or make his point. Interestingly, on various occasions when Jesus told a parable to teach a moral and spiritual lesson or to make a theological point, he even included quotes and allusions to OT passages as part of the parable. A parable is a literary form that doesn't require quotes of other literature to tell the story. But Jesus included such references in some parables (e.g., Matt. 13:41, 43; Mark 12:10–12 [cf. Matt. 21:33–46 and Luke 20:9–19]). On one occasion (Matt. 21:41–42) Jesus even quoted from Psalm 118 to show that the point of his parable about the landowner and the tenant farmers is that the leaders of the Jews had terribly mistreated him, the "landowner's son" (in the words of the parable). That is, the parable makes a point about Jesus, but Jesus makes the point by citing an OT prophecy about the Messiah.

Other instances (but not all) where Jesus quoted or alluded to the OT to make a point are Matthew 9:13; 10:34–36; 15:3–9; Mark 7:6–9; 8:18; 11:17; Luke 8:10 [par. Matt. 13:11, 13]; 18:18–26 [par. Matt. 19:16–26 and Mark 10:17–30]; John 2:16–17 [see Matt. 21:12–13 and Luke 2:49]; 7:22–23, 38; 8:17–18, 39–40. Jesus's mind was so totally saturated with Scripture that it seems he couldn't even tell a story to teach a moral or spiritual lesson or make a theological point without somehow incorporating Scripture into it!

So far, what we have seen about Christ's view of Scripture relates to the OT. But Jesus also says things that are very important to NT inspiration. Unfortunately, evangelicals often take the passages I'll mention to refer to illumination rather than inspiration. Jesus promised, as John's Gospel recounts, that after he went away, he would send the Holy Spirit. Of course, the Holy Spirit hadn't been totally absent from our world, but as Jesus said, he had been with us but in a coming day he would indwell believers. In John 14–16 Jesus mentioned the Holy Spirit's coming three times. In each case, he told his disciples something about the Spirit's ministry when he would come. In 14:26, Jesus says that the Holy Spirit would teach the disciples all things and remind them of all that Christ had said to them. In 15:26, Jesus promises that when the Spirit of truth comes, he will bear witness of Christ. Christ's most extensive comment about the Holy Spirit's ministry is recorded in 16:13–15. Jesus says the Spirit "will guide you into all the truth; for He will not speak on His own initiative, but whatever He hears, He will speak; and He will disclose to you what is to come. He shall glorify me; for He shall take of Mine, and shall disclose it to you. All things that the Father has are Mine; therefore I said, that He takes of Mine, and will disclose it to you."

Taken together, these statements promised that the Holy Spirit would remind the disciples of everything Christ had said to them. He would glorify Christ because he would reveal the things of Christ to them. But even more, Jesus promised that the Holy Spirit would teach them all things, guide them into all truth, and show them what is to come. As one reads especially John 16:13–15, it is hard not to think of the Spirit's relation to God and to the apostles as stated in 1 Corinthians 2:10–13.

These passages in John's Gospel are often taken by evangelicals to promise the Holy Spirit's illumining work as we read Scripture (both OT and NT). However, when Jesus first spoke these words, only the OT had been written. The OT predicted some things about the coming Messiah, but what Christ says in John 14–16 is nowhere to be found in the OT. And Jesus also had taught many things that aren't in the OT in any of the detail and clarity we find in Christ's teachings. Moreover, Jesus says the Spirit would teach the disciples of things to come. Certainly, the OT contains many end-time prophecies, and Jesus had also given the disciples the Olivet Discourse. And yet, one senses that when Jesus spoke about things to come, he was thinking of more detail than we can find in the OT. Hence, it is hard to see how these three passages in John, when Jesus first spoke them, can refer to the Spirit's illumination of the disciples' minds as they read existing Scripture.

What, then, is the point of these three passages? For what purpose would the Holy Spirit be given and do the ministries of which Jesus spoke in the lives of his disciples? There were two goals for this ministry of the Holy Spirit. First, Jesus's life and teachings were very fresh in the minds of the disciples. But Jesus knew they would outlive him—in some cases, by many years. Over time they would likely begin to forget the details of what Jesus had said and done. Even so, Jesus knew that his disciples would go throughout the world testifying of him, and that their ministry would last for the rest of their lives. Obviously, when they would tell the story of Jesus, bring new converts to Christ, establish churches, and help new believers to grow in their faith, it would be crucial for them to "get the message right." So, one of the intended purposes of the Holy Spirit's anticipated ministry was the preaching and teaching the disciples would do as they evangelized the lost and helped ground new believers in the faith.

But to think only of the disciples' oral ministry is to be shortsighted. If the stories of Jesus's teachings and deeds would grow dim in his disciples' memories as they grew older and as time passed after Christ's life on earth, what would happen when these disciples and other eyewitnesses to Christ's life would all have died? Without written records about Christ's life and ministry, firsthand, accurate knowledge about Christ would likely be gone before too long. In fact, over enough time, nothing about Christ might be known other than a few legends with very sketchy details. Obviously, Christ couldn't allow this, nor could the Father or the Holy Spirit. Somehow this information had to be written down and passed on for future generations.

Once Christ's apostles decided to write about what they had seen and heard, how could they be certain that they would remember things correctly? Moreover, undoubtedly, situations would arise in the early church that weren't covered in Jesus's teachings, but he would definitely want to instruct his church on those issues. In light of these considerations, Jesus's intentions regarding the Holy Spirit's ministry, spoken of in John 14, 15, and 16, also included his desire for his disciples to "get it right" when they sat down to write Scripture. And what better way to guarantee their getting it right than to send the Holy Spirit, who would lead them into all truth? Of course, if the Holy Spirit played the role Jesus described in these passages in John, then what the apostles would write would be the very words of God.

*In sum, the best understanding of Jesus's promise of the Spirit and of the Spirit's ministry is that the Spirit would make sure that the disciples would get the message right when they preached and taught about Jesus, and also when they wrote about him and his teachings. In essence, the John 14, 15, and 16 passages guaranteed in advance that the soon-to-be-written NT would also be of divine origin. It also helps to confirm this point that many of the men who first heard Jesus say these words did wind up writing many of the NT books.*[10]

## OLD TESTAMENT TESTIMONY

Many things in the OT itself indicate that it is from God and thus is inspired. First, certain formulaic statements that say the writers wrote the words of God show up repeatedly at the start of a verse or paragraph, followed by what God said. These amount to saying that what comes next is either what God said, the word of God coming to a prophet, or simply, "Thus says the Lord."

For example, a whole book or portion of a book begins with the phrase, "The Word of the Lord that came to . . . saying." But even when the word "saying" isn't added, what follows the declaration that the word came to the prophet is an account of what God said. The OT is replete with such formulaic claims, so the following list is only representative: Deuteronomy 5:22; 1 Samuel 15:10; 2 Samuel 7:4; 1 Kings 16:1; 17:2, 8; 2 Kings 20:4; Isaiah 38:4; Jeremiah

---

[10] Readers may wonder why I haven't mentioned Jesus's teaching in John 10:30–36; 17:17; and Matthew 22:29–30 [par. Mark 12:24–25]. I haven't, because they are actually more relevant to authority and inerrancy than to inspiration, and will be addressed when we turn to those topics.

1:4, 11, 13; 28:12; Ezekiel 3:16; 36:16; 37:15; Hosea 1:1; Joel 1:1; Amos 3:1; Jonah 1:1; Micah 1:1; Zephaniah 1:1; Zechariah 1:1, 7; 8:18; Malachi 1:1.[11]

Another formulaic saying is, "the Lord spoke unto . . . saying." This appears quite often in the Pentateuch, preceding what God said to Moses. But it also appears frequently elsewhere in the OT. Consulting any concordance quickly shows that. Often we also read, "Thus says the Lord," followed by what the Lord said to those addressed. A slight variation of this is the writer recounting the words God spoke, followed by the phrase "says the Lord." As J. I. Packer notes, the formulaic "Thus says the Lord" appears some 359 times in the OT.[12] As Wayne Grudem explains, this sort of formula, or one like it

> would have been used in the Ancient Near East to introduce an edict issued by a king to his subjects. . . . The formula "Thus says the Lord," appearing hundreds of times in the Old Testament, is a royal decree formula used to preface the edict of a king to his subjects, an edict that could not be challenged or questioned but simply had to be obeyed. God is viewed as the sovereign king of Israel, and when the prophets speak, they are seen as bringing the divine king's absolutely authoritative decrees to His subjects.[13]

We must be careful not to miss the import of these locutions for the inspiration of the OT. If the OT writer merely said that the Lord's word came to him, or that God spoke to him, but he never wrote down what God said, we would have reports that God spoke to a prophet, but we wouldn't know what God said. Thankfully, the writers also told us what God said. Of course, in most cases, the prophet, not God, "penned" the words on tablets or parchment, but those are still words God said. All of this means that OT Scriptures qualify as inspired by God.

Another indication of OT inspiration comes from the writers themselves. Often, they preface what they write by saying that God told them to write in a book the words that follow. Examples of this can be found in Joshua 24:26; Isaiah 8:1; 30:8; 34:16; Jeremiah 30:2; 36:1–6, 18, 27–31; Habakkuk 2:2.[14] A corollary of this is that many OT writers claimed to speak the very words of the Lord. It is hard to imagine that they thought that that claim applied to their speech (whether preaching or otherwise) but not to their writing. Given the many passages where they prefaced their account of what God said with,

---

[11] See A. Graeme Auld, "Word of God and Word of Man: Prophets and Canon," in *Ascribe to the Lord: Biblical and Other Studies in Memory of Peter C. Craigie*, ed. Lyle Eslinger and Glen Taylor, JSOTSup 67 (1988), 246; and Cardinal Leo Scheffczyk, "Sacred Scripture: God's Word and the Church's Word," *Communio* 28 (Spring 2001): 29.
[12] J. I. Packer, "Inspiration of the Bible," in *The Origin of the Bible* (Wheaton, IL: Tyndale, 1992), 32.
[13] Wayne Grudem, "Scripture's Self-Attestation and the Problem of Formulating a Doctrine of Scripture," in *Scripture and Truth*, ed. D. A. Carson and John D. Woodbridge (Grand Rapids, MI: Zondervan, 1983), 21–22.
[14] Wayne Grudem, *Systematic Theology: An Introduction to Biblical Doctrine* (Grand Rapids, MI: Zondervan, 1994), 49–50; Gordon R. Lewis and Bruce A. Demarest, *Integrative Theology*, vol. 1 (Grand Rapids, MI: Zondervan, 1987), 140. For a listing and quoting of further passages of the written words of God, see Grudem, "Scripture's Self-Attestation," 25–27; and Lewis and Demarest, *Integrative Theology*, vol. 1, 138.

"Thus says the Lord," their claims about speaking the very words of the Lord also cover what they wrote. Some instances where OT writers said they spoke the words of the Lord are Jeremiah 1:7; Ezekiel 2:7; and Amos 3:7.[15]

Of course, on one occasion, not only did the concepts and words come from God, but the Lord even did the writing himself. Moses says that God, after speaking to him on Mount Sinai, gave him the two tablets of stone on which the Mosaic law was "written by the finger of God" (Ex. 31:18; see also Ex. 24:12; 32:16; 34:1, 28).[16] Obviously, God doesn't have a literal finger, so this is an anthropomorphism. What likely happened was that God miraculously emblazoned or engraved the Ten Commandments on the tablets. None of the passages just cited lists the commandments, but Exodus 20:1–17 details them. Of course, if the Ten Commandments come from God, even to the point of his writing them on the tablets, they are his inspired word.

Another indication of God's inspiring an OT writer appears in the book of Jeremiah. In Jeremiah 1:9, Jeremiah says that the Lord touched his mouth and said to him, "Behold, I have put My words in your mouth."[17] Already in the same chapter Jeremiah wrote (1:4–5) that the word of the Lord came to him saying that, even while he was in his mother's womb, God chose him to be his prophet. From what we read in these verses, plus verses 6–8, it is reasonable to believe that the Lord made the declaration of verse 9 to Jeremiah early in his life. Undoubtedly, this statement encouraged Jeremiah, when speaking for God, not to fear that he wouldn't know what to say, because God would give him words to say. It also makes sense to think this happened when Jeremiah sat down to write what became the book of Jeremiah. This is especially so, for we have already noted times when God told Jeremiah to write in a book the words that God would tell him (Jer. 30:2; 36:1–6, 27–31).

Some may say that this is true of Jeremiah because the passages cited say so, but that it isn't true for any other OT prophet or writer. But that objection is unwarranted, for whether a writer says that God put his words in the writer's mouth or not, there are many instances where the OT writer claimed that the word of the Lord "came unto him, saying," or he wrote, "Thus says the Lord, . . . " Surely, these locutions are tantamount to saying that the Lord put his words in the prophet's mouth. In addition, another passage in Jeremiah talks about something that is *not* true of *false* prophets, and by contrast we can see what *is* true of genuine prophets, including Jeremiah. The passage is Jeremiah 23:16, 22: False prophets speak a vision "of their own heart," not "out of the mouth of the Lord"; they don't "[stand] in [God's] counsel" (KJV), so they don't give God's word to his people. A true

[15] Packer, "Inspiration of the Bible," 33.

[16] Lewis and Demarest, *Integrative Theology*, 138; and Packer, "Inspiration of the Bible," 34.

[17] Charles Hodge, *Systematic Theology*, vol. 1 (London: James Clarke, 1960 ed.), 159.

prophet *does* speak out of the Lord's mouth; he stands in God's counsel and gives God's word to God's people. Surely Jeremiah would affirm this as true not only of OT speaking prophets, but also of those who wrote Scripture. But then, this amounts to saying that what the prophets spoke (and wrote) is God's word; i.e., it is inspired.

There is also a recurrent theme related to the law of Moses, and it also relates to other laws as well. In some instances it likely refers to the whole Pentateuch, or at least to a part of it. That theme is that the law of Moses is the very word of God. For example, in 2 Kings 14 we read about Amaziah's ascension to the throne of Judah. Verse 5 says that, once the kingdom was confirmed, Amaziah killed his servants who had killed his father (the king before Amaziah). However, verse 6 says that he didn't kill the children of these murderers, because he followed *the command of the Lord written in the book of the law of Moses.* That command said that "the fathers shall not be put to death for the sons, nor the sons be put to death for the fathers: but each shall be put to death for his own sin" (14:6). The passage to which Amaziah referred is Deuteronomy 24:16.[18]

Then, there is Psalm 119. Repeatedly the psalmist extols the law of the Lord and its various commands. He is certainly thinking of more than just the moral precepts of God's word, though in many instances the author refers to specific statutes or commands from God's law. While Psalm 119 is generally understood to be about Scripture, many of its references to God's commands, the law of the Lord, etc., refer especially to the law of Moses. Of course, the assumption undergirding the whole psalm and stated repeatedly therein is that the law, Scripture, is from God.

Each of the passages cited equate the law of Moses with God's words. In so doing, they affirm the inspiration of these writings. We also find Joshua reading all the blessings and curses in the book of the law written by Moses (Josh. 8:30–35). Of course, Moses claimed that what he wrote was from God. In effect, Joshua, in following the book of the law of Moses, knew that he was following God's word. And 2 Chronicles 17:9 refers to teaching the people the law of the Lord, but clearly what was in view were the books of the law of Moses. Some other passages that equate the law of Moses with the law of God are 1 Kings 2:3; 2 Kings 21:8; 2 Chronicles 33:8; 34:14; Daniel 9:11, 13; and Malachi 4:4.

Not only are the books of Moses said to be from God, but so are other OT books. A few examples illustrate this point. The book of Ezra opens with a claim that, because of a need to fulfill *the word of the Lord spoken by the*

---

[18] J. Oliver Buswell, *A Systematic Theology of the Christian Religion*, vol. 1 (Grand Rapids, MI: Zondervan, 1963 [1972 printing]), 202.

*mouth of Jeremiah*, the Lord stirred up the Persian king, Cyrus, to build the God of Israel a house at Jerusalem. As a result, Cyrus issued a decree to allow Jews to return to Jerusalem to repair and rebuild the temple (Ezra 1:1–4). In that passage, the writer begins with a reference to the prophecy of Jeremiah about the seventy years of Babylonian captivity, and he clearly asserts that Jeremiah wrote the word of the Lord (v. 1) in writing this prophesy.

Similarly, Daniel knew the prophecy of the seventy-year captivity of Judah in Babylon. Noticing that seventy years had passed, in Daniel 9 we see Daniel begin to pray that God would fulfill the prophecy of the return to Judah. God answered Daniel's prayer by predicting seventy weeks for God to fulfill his purposes with Israel (Dan. 9:24–27). It's as though God was saying, "Daniel, you've been wondering about the prediction of a return after a seventy-year captivity. I'm going to show you what will happen in seventy times seven (490) years to your people." It would be easy to get so wrapped up in the details of this vision that we miss the way this whole incident begins. Daniel 9:2 says, "In the first year of his reign I Daniel understood by books the number of the years, whereof the word of the LORD came to Jeremiah the prophet, that he would accomplish seventy years in the desolations of Jerusalem"(KJV). Here is a clear statement that Jeremiah's prophecy is the word of the Lord. Though Daniel refers specifically to one prediction, surely he would think that more than just that is God's word. In Daniel's mind the whole book of Jeremiah is God's word; hence any specific statement in it, including a prediction of the future, is from God.

One further OT passage, Zechariah 7:12, is noteworthy because of its testimony about the OT. This passage describes several men coming to the Lord's house to speak to the priests and prophets about a day of fasting in commemoration of the destruction of Jerusalem. Though God hadn't instituted the fast, the delegation from Babylon wanted to know whether they should continue it. Through Zechariah, the Lord gave one scathing rebuke after another. One of those critiques (7:8–10) told them that God didn't want fasting when their hearts were far from him. God required, instead, a change of moral and spiritual direction that would yield concern for the oppressed and a desire to treat everyone with justice and compassion. However, the people refused, and had been doing so for a long time. In 7:12 we read, "Yea, they made their hearts as an adamant stone, lest they should hear the law, and the words which the LORD of hosts hath sent in his spirit by the former prophets: therefore came a great wrath from the LORD of hosts" (KJV). In light of the commands referred to in verses 8–10, ones that the people had refused to obey, it is probably best to see the reference to "law" in verse 12 as pointing to the moral commands of the Mosaic law, not a reference to instruction in general.[19] The words sent "by the former prophets" most likely refers to the prophets before the Babylonian captivity, given the overall context of Zechariah 7 and verses 8–14 in particular.[20]

Now it was certainly standard fare by the time Zechariah was written to consider the law of Moses the word of God. Evidence to that effect has already amply been presented. Note, however, the further comments about the words of the "former prophets." They are called the "words which the LORD of hosts hath sent in his spirit by the former prophets." Here we have a clear statement of the divine origin of the former prophets' words (nothing suggests that this comment didn't refer to what they wrote), and it links their words to both the Lord of hosts and the Holy Spirit. In effect, verse 12 certifies that large portions of the OT canon (the law of Moses and the writings of the former prophets) are God's word! Hence, they are inspired.

To say nothing further about this verse, however, would miss a major point. It is easy to think that, because this verse is part of the book of Zechariah, it records only his words and his opinions. But this verse is part of a paragraph that begins by saying that what we next read is the "word of the LORD," . . . saying" (v. 8), and then God's answer (which begins in verse 9) is prefaced with, "Thus speaketh the LORD of hosts, saying" (KJV). What we read in verse 12 is the claim of God himself. We know this, in part, because verses 13–14 are clearly God's words, and nothing in the transition from verse 11 to 12 or from 12 to 13 suggests that anyone other than God is speaking. So, this passage not only attributes the words of the law and the former prophets to the Lord of hosts and the Holy Spirit; God himself testifies that this is so. What an incredible recommendation of these writings! Nothing less than the divine imprimatur!

*In sum, the OT evidence presented affirms that large portions of the OT canon come from God. That is, they are his words, and thus, they are inspired. When we combine this evidence with Jesus's opinion of the OT and that of Paul (2 Tim. 3:16–17; 1 Cor. 2:12–13; Rom. 3:1, 2) and Peter (2 Pet. 1:19–21), we must conclude that the whole OT is God's inspired word!*

## NEW TESTAMENT TESTIMONY

The NT presents two main types of testimony about Scripture. The most prevalent are NT writers' comments about the OT. The other main strand of thought is what NT writers thought of their own words and of those of other NT writers.

---

[19] Carl F. Keil, *The Twelve Minor Prophets*, vol. 2 in C. F. Keil and F. Delitzsch, *Biblical Commentary on the Old Testament* (repr., Grand Rapids, MI: Zondervan, 1967 printing), 309.
[20] Charles L. Feinberg, *God Remembers: A Study of the Book of Zechariah* (New York: American Board of Missions to the Jews, 1965).

### New Testament Writers on the Old Testament

NT writers have many of the same attitudes about the OT that Christ had. For example, they frequently quoted or alluded to OT passages to make a theological, moral, or spiritual point. One of the most frequent ways of doing this introduces the OT quote with the formulaic "it is written." In the Gospels we saw Christ do this to make his point, but in the Gospels others do the same. For example, in Matthew 2:5–6 the chief priests and scribes answer Herod's question about where the Messiah was to be born by saying, "it is written," and then quoting Micah 5:2. Likewise, Mark's Gospel begins (1:2) by introducing Jesus's forerunner, John the Baptist, immediately tying him to Jesus by declaring, "it is written," and then quoting Malachi 3:1. Luke also uses this phrase on two occasions early in his Gospel. He uses it in Luke 2:23 to show that, after Jesus's birth, Joseph and Mary presented him to the Lord at Jerusalem in strict accordance with the regulations of the Mosaic law. And in chapter 3, as Luke introduces John the Baptist and the start of his ministry, in order to confirm that what John was doing was of God, Luke explains that "it is written" (v. 4) and then quotes Isaiah's prediction of the voice in the wilderness, crying out to prepare the way of the Lord. See also, in John 6, Jesus's discourse on the bread of life.

So, it is not just Jesus who uses the "it is written" formula in the Gospels. Luke also uses it in Acts as he records the words of the apostles in their various encounters with believers and nonbelievers (e.g., Acts 7:42; 13:33; 15:15–17; 23:5). And Luke and other NT writers also use "it is written" to quote portions of Scripture to tell a narrative or to make their theological or moral point.[21] There are many examples of this, so the following list is only representative: Acts 1:20; Romans 1:17; 3:4, 10; 4:17; 8:36; 9:13, 33; 15:3, 9, 21; 1 Corinthians 1:19; 2:9; 3:19; 9:9; 10:7; 15:45, 54; 2 Corinthians 8:15; 9:9; Galatians 3:10, 13; 4:22, 27; 1 Peter 1:16.

What I described earlier about the "atmosphere" of the Gospels is definitely true of the rest of the NT. There is an assumed reverence for Scripture. If a point needs to be made, the best way to do so is by appealing to the OT. Doing so is taken to be irrefutable proof and confirmation of what the NT writer says. If a point is made in an OT passage, because that passage is Scripture, no other evidential support is needed. Why? Because the apostles believed that Scripture is God's word, and if God says something, it must be true. No argument could possibly overturn what Scripture says.

A second line of NT testimony about the OT involves two passages that refer to the Holy Spirit working in the minds of various OT prophets. The

---

[21] John Reumann, "The Doctrine of Scripture as a Doctrine about Tradition and the Church," *Journal of Ecumenical Studies* 28 (Summer 1991): 457, makes this point in general.

first comes at the end of Acts (28:25–27). Paul was witnessing to a group of Jews in Rome. He told his audience that the *Holy Spirit* spoke to Jews of an earlier day *by Isaiah the prophet.* In verses 26–27, Paul told them what the Holy Spirit said through Isaiah by quoting Isaiah 6:9–10! How could the point be clearer? Paul is saying that, when Isaiah wrote those words that are part of the book of Isaiah, the Holy Spirit was speaking to the Jews of Isaiah's day by Isaiah's written word! That doesn't say that the book of Isaiah as a whole or the verses from Isaiah 6 in particular are inspired, but it is hard to imagine that Paul's words don't amount to acknowledging the inspiration of those verses.

The second passage that speaks of the Holy Spirit at work in the lives of OT prophets is 1 Peter 1:10–12. Peter begins his first epistle with a discourse on salvation. In verse 10, he writes that the salvation in view is something about which the prophets who prophesied about it had wanted to know more. Verse 11 says they searched for "what, or what manner of time the Spirit of Christ who was in them did signify, when he predicted beforehand the sufferings of Christ, and the glory that should follow" (AT). Peter then says that it was "revealed" to the OT prophets who made the predictions that the events they prophesied would not happen in their lifetime but at a later time—specifically, the lifetime of Peter and his readers (v. 12).

This passage makes several important claims, but it also raises a number of questions. The first is about the identity of these prophets. Were they prophets who prophesied only orally? If so, we have no access to what they spoke (but never wrote down). It is quite possible that OT preaching prophets were given this revelation, but it is also possible that they *didn't* receive it. Not only are *we* in the dark about this; Peter himself would have had no access to the words OT prophets preached (but never wrote down).

Hence, the only prophets Peter could have in mind are OT prophets who wrote the messages the Holy Spirit gave them. Of course, those are the only OT prophets to whom Peter's readers, including us, had any access. OT prophets like Isaiah, Jeremiah, Ezekiel, Daniel, and the twelve minor prophets did predict that a Messiah would come. He would be born of a human woman (Isa. 7:14), but he would also be divine (Isa. 9:6). As to his sufferings and glory, many OT passages speak of this. Perhaps the best known is Isaiah 53, but there are many others, as Bible students well know.

That we should apply 1 Peter 1:10ff. to OT writing prophets, even though Peter only says they "prophesied" (which could refer only to oral speech), is further confirmed by 2 Peter 1:21. That passage speaks of the inspiration of the written OT books (Peter writes, "no prophecy of *Scripture*" [2 Pet. 1:20]), but in 2 Peter 1:19–21, Peter also refers to OT prophets as *speaking.* Similarly, in 1 Peter 1:10ff., even if Peter used the word "prophesied" in verse 10 to refer to oral speech, what he says should also be applied to the words the prophets *wrote*. As noted above, those written prophecies are the only OT prophecies about the sufferings and glory of Christ that Peter and we know.

Does this passage teach the inspiration of the writings of the prophets in question? Some theologians and exegetes definitely think so.[22] I agree, but maintain that because of Peter's difficult syntax, the point is not so blatantly made as some might suspect. Several things, however, are very clear. In verse 10, Peter says that these OT prophets prophesied of the "salvation" (the "grace") to come. Verse 11 says that they wanted to know but did not understand *when* the events that *the Holy Spirit* had predicted beforehand (*promartyromenon*) would happen, and how these events would be fulfilled. Verse 12 says that the Holy Spirit informed them that it would happen later in history, a time Peter identifies as his own era.

Wanting to know when a prophecy would be fulfilled and having the Holy Spirit show them the answer deals more with the *illumination* of God's word than with its *inspiration*. I also note that the verses do not say that as the prophets prophesied, the Holy Spirit carried them along (inspiration), though, of course, they don't reject such a notion either. It is easy to think the passage teaches that this happened, because it speaks of the Holy Spirit in the prophets. But we must be precise. The text says the *Holy Spirit* in them predicted beforehand the sufferings and glory of Christ, and the prophets wanted to know what time the Spirit meant when he made these predictions. Nothing Peter says about the prophets' desires to know the fulfillment of these prophecies requires anything more from the Holy Spirit than illumination. That is, the Spirit's being "in them" does not require his work of inspiration; it could just as easily refer to his presence to illumine them about the fulfillment of the prophecies they reflected upon.

What Peter says in verse 11 about who predicted beforehand Christ's sufferings and glory is also crucial. The participle translated "predicted beforehand" is *promartyromenon*, and it is neuter singular. That means it does not fit with "the prophets" as its subject, because *prophētai* is masculine plural. Thus, it is the Holy Spirit (*pneuma*, "spirit," in Greek is neuter singular) who predicted Christ's sufferings and glory. So while verse 10 says it was the prophets who prophesied of the grace to come, verse 11 says it was the Holy Spirit who made the specific prediction about the sufferings and glory of Christ.

Does this mean that we can't use 1 Peter 1:10–12 at all to teach inspiration? Not at all, but we must see why. Verse 10 says the prophets predicted the

---

[22] Lewis and Demarest, *Integrative Theology*, vol. 1, 146, give this impression. B. H. Carroll, "Our Articles of Faith: Article 1—The Scriptures," *Southwestern Journal of Theology* 44 (Summer 2002): 9; and Edwin A. Blum, *2 Peter*, in *EBC*, ed. Frank E. Gaebelein, vol. 12 (Grand Rapids, MI: Zondervan, 1982), 222, also hold this view.

salvation that was to come. Verse 11 shows they didn't know when the details of such prophecies would be fulfilled. Verse 11 also says it was the Holy Spirit who predicted Christ's sufferings and glories. Despite the difficult syntax of verse 11, do not miss this crucial point: Peter says the prophets sought to know the time the Holy Spirit meant (*edēlou*), *when he predicted beforehand the sufferings of Christ and the glory that should follow*. That is, we must not dismember the subject of the prophets' search from what the Holy Spirit revealed about Christ.

Now comes a key question. How would the OT prophets have known, and where would they have learned, the Holy Spirit's predictions about the suffering and glory of Christ? The Holy Spirit might have revealed them to them in a dream or vision, or in direct speech, none of which was ever written down. If so, that would mean they were asking for illumination of what was revealed but never written down (i.e., there was revelation and a request for illumination, but no inspiration). Or, the Holy Spirit could have revealed these things to ordinary people who never wrote any Scripture. But how likely is it that what the Spirit revealed beforehand about Christ wasn't revealed to OT writing prophets, and if it was revealed to them, how likely is it that they never wrote it down? If no one ever wrote down the Holy Spirit's predictions, then how would the prophets have known anything about them and have had questions about them?

The most reasonable answer is that the prophets knew about the predictions and had questions because someone wrote down what the Holy Spirit predicted. But who? The most likely candidates are the OT prophets themselves, especially since verse 10 says they wrote of the grace of salvation that would come.

So, what does 1 Peter 1:10–12 tell us about OT inspiration? Actually, when you take verse 10 (which says that OT prophets wrote of the salvation to come), link it to the Holy Spirit's predictions about Christ's sufferings and glory (v. 11), and add what I have said about how the OT prophets would have known of those predictions and what they would have done with them, the conclusions seem logically inevitable. OT prophecies about Christ's suffering and glory are God's word. And, since OT prophets wrote those words, we seem required to affirm dual authorship of those passages—both the Holy Spirit and the human writers are said in verses 10–12 to have prophesied about the salvation to come! Hence, at the very least, OT passages about those subjects must be God's inspired word![23]

---

[23] Here I note a corollary point: In Romans 1:1–2 Paul says that the gospel of God that he was called to preach had been promised by God's prophets before in the Holy Scriptures. Hence, Paul links the gospel message with OT Scriptures, and in effect claims that both are from God. But that means such material is inspired. This passage gives fewer details than 1 Peter 1:10–12 does, but it also more directly and succinctly makes the point that, at the very

A final part of NT testimony about the OT is how it cites various OT passages as God's word, and also the way it quotes from the OT. As to the former kind of passages, we have already discussed many examples (e.g., 2 Tim. 3:16; 2 Pet. 1:19–21; Matt. 4:4; Rom. 3:2), but there are other NT passages in which the writer refers to an OT passage as God's word or as one in which the Holy Spirit spoke. Acts 1:16 says that the Holy Spirit spoke beforehand by the mouth of David words about Judas that must be fulfilled and were. In Acts 4:25, as members of the church prayed to God with one accord, they claimed that he had said, "by the mouth of thy servant David," "Why did the heathen rage, and the people imagine vain things?" (KJV) The reference to David's writing is to Psalm 2:1–2. And, in Luke 1:70, Zacharias, in his own prophecy, says that the Lord God "spoke by the mouth of His holy prophets." Of course, for Zacharias to know that and also to know some of the content they spoke (which he obviously did, as can be seen by reading verses 67ff.), these prophets must have put their words in writing. Otherwise Zacharias, living when Christ was born, would have had no basis for making such claims. The only writings in which the prophets would have spoken about the things Zacharias relates are OT Scriptures.[24]

Perhaps even more intriguing is how many NT writers quote the OT, and especially what they say about who wrote or spoke the words they quote. Many years ago B. B. Warfield wrote a masterful work on the equivalence/interchangeability of the biblical phrases "God says," "It says," and "Scripture says." Readers would benefit greatly from studying that essay with its careful attention to detail.[25] For our purposes, the main points can be made by citing several instances of the phenomena in question. Actually, we already saw one example from Matthew 19, when Jesus quoted Genesis 2—written by Moses but spoken either by Adam or Moses—and said that *God* said it. But there are many others examples of this: In Romans 9:17 Paul quotes Exodus 9:16. Paul prefaces the quote by saying it is *Scripture* speaking to Pharaoh, but the Exodus passage shows that it was the word of the Lord through Moses that was spoken to Pharaoh. In effect, Paul is saying that the word of the Lord through the human being Moses is also Scripture. And, of course, this means that Scripture is God's word, even when the Scripture in view contains the words of a mere human like Moses.

Another example is how Hebrews 3:7 quotes Psalm 95:7–8. The psalm quoted is the psalmist's words, but the writer of Hebrews says the Psalms passage is what the Holy Spirit said. And in Acts 13:34–35 Luke quotes from Psalm

---

least, OT passages about the gospel are God's inspired word. For a passing reference to this point see Scheffczyk, "Sacred Scripture," 30.

[24] Grudem, "Scripture's Self-Attestation," 38–40, lists these and many other passages of this nature.

[25] Warfield, "'It Says:' 'Scripture Says:' 'God Says'."

16:10, a psalm written by David. But Luke writes that God said these words. Thus, the human words of a Scripture passage are equated with God's word.

A final example, Romans 15:9–12, is most interesting because it cites or quotes from four different OT passages—Psalm 18:49; Deuteronomy 32:43; Psalm 117:1; and Isaiah 11:1, 10. Paul introduces these quotes in Romans 15:9 with the formulaic "it is written." As we have seen, this can be understood as "Scripture says," and of course, for Paul if Scripture says it, then God does, too (Rom. 3:2–3; 2 Tim. 3:16, etc.). However, the two psalms quoted are the words of the human psalmist, and the Deuteronomy passage is part of Moses's discourse to his people. As for the Isaiah passage, Paul says Isaiah spoke it, but Isaiah 11 clearly contains information that Isaiah would never have written as a result of his own thinking and/or research. The truths of Isaiah 11:1–10 are things that only God knows and that Isaiah could know only because God revealed them to him. So, the Isaiah passage is clearly God's word, but Paul assigns it to Isaiah, whereas the other Scriptures referenced are the words of a human being, and yet they are introduced as Scripture's words, which for Paul means they are God's word.[26]

The most reasonable explanation for these methods of citing and quoting OT passages in the NT is that, in the minds of Jesus, the apostles, and their followers, if Scripture says something, that means God says it, regardless of whether the words quoted are actually God's, the human writer's, or some other human being spoken of in the passage in question. Hence, "it is written," "Scripture says," "it says," "the Holy Spirit says," and "Isaiah (David, the prophets, etc.) says" are all equivalent to "God says," and thus the NT writers making such claims are saying they are quoting God's word. And if it is God's word, then it is inspired!

### New Testament Writers on the New Testament

Here the testimony is of two kinds. First, various NT authors wrote about their own teachings. Those teachings came first as they preached, but it is hard to believe that they would say, for example, that what they preached was from God but what they wrote was not. A good place to begin is the testimony of the apostle Paul, and we should first remember 1 Corinthians 2:12–13, already discussed in detail in chapter 4. Paul is very clear that he and the others who preached and wrote about God received their information from the Holy Spirit (vv. 10–12). He then adds that the Holy Spirit taught them how to match the

---

[26] For more examples of this method of quoting the OT and of passages that refer to some OT passage as God's word, see Lewis and Demarest, *Integrative Theology*, vol. 1, 144; David S. Dockery, "A People of the Book and the Crisis of Biblical Authority," in *Beyond the Impasse? Scripture, Interpretation, and Theology in Baptist Life*, ed. Robison B. James and David S. Dockery (Nashville: Broadman, 1992), 20; and Grudem, "Scripture's Self-Attestation," 38–40.

right spiritual words with the truths revealed (v. 13). They, of course, did the actual combining. This verse claims inspiration not only for Paul's words but also for the words of other apostles. But Paul says much more than this.

In 1 Thessalonians 2 Paul speaks about his ministry at Thessalonica. In verse 9, he says that he preached to them the gospel of God, and in verse 13 Paul writes about how they received his messages. He applauds them because, "when you received from us the word of God's message, you accepted it not as the word of men, but for what it really is, the word of God, which also performs its work in you who believe." If Paul says this of what he preached to the Thessalonians, how could he think that what he wrote them was less than God's word, especially when his letters cover many of the topics he preached to them? That Paul thought of his letters as God's word is confirmed in 2 Thessalonians. In 2 Thessalonians 2:13–14 Paul gives thanks that God chose these people for salvation through what Paul labels "our gospel" (v. 14). Paul then commands them to stand firm and hold the traditions they have been taught "whether by word of mouth or by letter from us" (v. 15). This is quite significant, because Paul's letter professes the same gospel and presents the same doctrinal tenets that he had preached to them. If not, verse 15 is rather odd, since it seems to equate his preaching and his epistle when it comes to the Thessalonians knowing the gospel and the doctrinal traditions from him. In addition, we also already know from 1 Thessalonians 2:13 that Paul believed that what he preached to them was God's word, and they received it as such. If Paul claims that his words and letters both teach the gospel and doctrinal traditions, and we know that he believed that what he preached was God's word, then it is unthinkable that he would believe his epistle to them was less than God's words. These Thessalonians passages, taken together, seem to warrant the conclusion that Paul believed that 1 and 2 Thessalonians were God's word. And if so, they must be inspired.

In other Pauline letters, he also affirms that the gospel he preached came from the Lord. For example, in Galatians 1:11–12 Paul clarifies that he received his gospel by revelation from Jesus Christ. In Galatians, it is quite clear what that gospel is. And, if that gospel came from Christ, then at the very least, the parts of Galatians where Paul clarifies the gospel must be God's words. And, Paul's gospel in Galatians is the same gospel that he presents in his other writings. So those other epistles, at least the parts that present the gospel, must also have been ultimately revealed to Paul by Christ. Thus, they are God's inspired word, not just Paul's correspondence to one group of Christians or another.

Another key passage is Ephesians 3. In its first 12 verses, Paul writes of the mystery that was hidden from people of an earlier era (v. 5) but which God revealed to Paul and which they will understand when they read what he writes (v. 4). The mystery is that, in the NT era, Gentiles would be fellow heirs with Jewish believers (v. 6), and of the same body, and partakers of God's promises in Christ. In 3:5 Paul says that this mystery of Christ which wasn't known in an earlier era is "now revealed unto his holy apostles and prophets by the Spirit" (KJV). The prophets mentioned in verse 5 (after the apostles) are likely NT prophets, and surely, with everything Paul says in 3:1–8, he would include himself as one of the apostles.

But then notice what Paul says in verse 5. He says that the mystery of Christ has been revealed to Christ's holy apostles by the Spirit. Where do we learn of the gospel and the other mysteries of Christ? The specific mysteries in question form much of the content of Ephesians. Is it reasonable to believe that Paul thought he only relied on those mysteries when he preached, but not when he wrote about them in letters such as Ephesians? No, it is not reasonable to exclude Paul's writings on these topics. But then again, here are claims that amount to Paul affirming that at the very least, the parts of Ephesians that explain the mysteries of Christ originated from revelation Paul received from Christ (v. 3) and the Holy Spirit (v. 5). Paul most likely believed that Christ and the Holy Spirit also saw to it that he transmitted it correctly when he preached and when he wrote. Surely, if Paul were asked whether 3:3–8 means that the words he writes about those topics are from God, he would say yes. But, then, even though Paul doesn't use the word here, he would agree that what he writes are truths that are *theopneustos*.[27]

One other passage (2 Pet. 3:1–2) is also noteworthy. As Peter begins chapter 3, in verse 2 he says that he will remind his readers of things spoken "before by the holy prophets, and of the commandment of us, the apostles of the Lord and Savior" (KJV). The reference to holy prophets is clearly to OT prophets, and Peter is quite clear about whom he means when he refers to the apostles: he includes himself. In this verse, Peter places on a par the things spoken by OT prophets and by NT apostles. Each has equal import and authority.

How would Peter's readers know anything about things spoken by the OT prophets and the NT apostles? Their only access to the words of OT prophets would have been through OT Scriptures. As for the apostles' words, readers might have heard some of them preach, but it is unlikely that most of Peter's readers would have heard all of them preach. So, it is much more likely that they would have confronted the words of the apostles through the apostles' writings, including works like 2 Peter. In effect, this passage gives equal authority to the OT and NT writings.

---

[27] Appealing to Ephesians 3 in relation to this point was suggested by Walter Roehrs's article, "Faith and Holy Scriptures," 157. However, Roehrs mentions Ephesians 3:1–5 with very little comment. The development of the point in my text is my own.

Undoubtedly, some will say that, while this is true, it doesn't claim that the apostles' writings (or the prophets') are God's word and thus inspired. This is true of what Peter says in 2 Peter 3:1–2, but Peter has already certified at least the inspiration of the OT (see 2 Pet. 1:19–21). If the NT is not also God's word, how can it have the same credibility as the OT? And yet, in 3:1–2, Peter gives it equal credibility. The only way 3:2 makes sense is if Peter believed that the words of the apostles, especially their written words, are as much a product of divine inspiration as are the words of the OT prophets, recorded in the OT. So, 2 Peter 3:1–2, when linked with what Peter (2 Pet. 1:19–21) and Paul (see the evidence presented above) say elsewhere, asserts the inspiration of the NT.

The second kind of NT testimony about the NT is what NT writers thought of what other NT authors wrote. Second Peter 3:1–2 fits here, but so does 2 Peter 3:15–16, a set of comments about Paul's writings. In 2 Peter 3:9, Peter says that the delay in the Lord's return and the final day of accountability is due in part to the longsuffering of God (v. 9). God is longsuffering because he wants more people to hear the gospel, repent, and be saved. But verse 9 says that God is longsuffering "to you," i.e., to Peter's readers.[28] Why would God be longsuffering to believers, since they are already saved? God wants nonbelievers to repent and believe, but he knows they won't if they don't hear the gospel. Hence, when Peter says that God is longsuffering with believers, he means that God is patiently waiting for the church to put evangelism of the lost at the top of its priority list and to get on with sharing the gospel. The first phrase of verse 15 repeats this basic idea of verse 9, and then Peter adds that what he writes is what Paul had also written to them. In verse 16 Peter says of Paul's writings, "as also in all his letters, speaking in them of these things, in which are some things hard to understand, which the untaught and unstable distort, as they do also the rest of the Scriptures, to their own destruction."

This is a remarkable verse. Peter confirms what he said in verse 15 by noting that it is consistent with what Paul teaches *in all his letters*. It is debatable whether all of Paul's epistles had been composed when Peter wrote these words, but surely many did already exist, given the way Peter refers to "all his epistles." Peter then notes that some things in Paul's writings are hard to understand—and we can certainly agree, though Peter's NT writings are equally challenging! But Peter also says that untaught and unstable people who read Paul's letters misinterpret and misunderstand them, as they also do with

---

[28] There is some question as to whether Peter wrote that God is longsuffering "to us" or "to you." If one takes the former reading, it means that God is longsuffering toward humanity, especially those who are unsaved, and so he doesn't bring judgment quickly, so that unbelievers may still hear the gospel and respond. On the latter reading, Peter says that God is longsuffering to "you," i.e., to his first readers and, by extension, to all believers. While either reading of the original text makes sense, the better text tradition favors "to you", not "to us."

"the other Scriptures" (*tas loipas graphas*). Peter here equates Paul's letters with other Scriptures. We should note that the word translated "Scriptures" is *graphē*, the word used in the NT to designate Scripture. Of course, if Paul's writings are Scripture, then they are, to use Paul's terminology, *theopneustos*, the product of God's breath. This verse, then, ascribes divine inspiration to Paul's writings.[29]

---

[29] Grudem, "Scripture's Self-Attestation," 46, makes this point well.

# LIGHT WRITTEN (III)

## Theological Formulation of the Doctrine of Inspiration

In chapters 4–5, I have presented biblical testimony about Scripture's inspiration, but we can say more. For example, nothing yet has been said about the very "texture" of Scripture. Is it all written in the same literary genre, or are different ones used? When two authors use the same genre, are their works identical in style, content, and vocabulary?

We can also ask whether biblical books show marks of a distinct personality and of personal interests of these authors? Answers to these questions will help us understand better the human nature of Scripture.

In addition, none of the Scriptures studied, either individually or collectively, articulates a "theory of inspiration." Nor is there in the Scriptures studied an *orderly, systematic* explanation of what it means that the Bible is God's inspired word. *The systematician must bring together the strands of biblical teaching and any other relevant data to construct a biblically accurate theory of inspiration,* and that is now our task.

### EIGHT THESES ABOUT THE INSPIRATION OF SCRIPTURE

Biblical writers had great respect for what OT prophets and NT apostles wrote, and made strong claims about the origin of those books. I shall now give in eight major theses a point-by-point statement of what the Bible teaches about Scripture's inspiration. I maintain that these theses, properly explained, accurately portray what Scripture teaches about itself.

*Thesis One: God as the Source of Scripture*

Scripture frequently says that God is its source. This means several things. It means that Scripture originated first in God's mind and in his various revelations to humans. Peter emphatically claims (2 Pet. 1:20–21) that the impetus for writing Scripture, and its content, never originated from any human being. And Paul affirms that what he and others wrote cannot be known by the usual ways humans attain knowledge—through sense perception and reasoning (1 Cor. 2:9–10). Rather, they wrote truths known only to God, and without his decision to reveal them, humans would not on their own ever construct such information or even know of it. We know it only because God revealed it through his Spirit (1 Cor. 2:10–12).

This is so partly because many biblical authors wrote of things (deeds and words) they never saw or heard themselves, and of things no mere human could know by empirical investigation or rational reflection. And, following Peter, we can also say that the writers' motivation for writing Scripture (2 Pet. 1:20–21) came ultimately from God.

In addition, since many NT writers, for example, wrote about some of the same things as others did, but didn't write exactly on the same things and didn't repeat what others said when addressing the same topic, we can also conclude that each author's choice of topics and how to present them also came from God. If not, it is hard to agree with Peter (2 Pet. 1:20–21) that no Scripture originated from the human author's own initiative to research and write what became part of Scripture.

We have also noted that one portion of Scripture was *originally* written with the very "finger of God" (Ex. 31:18; 24:12; 32:16, etc.), not with the "fingers" of any human writer. In Exodus Moses recounts what God himself wrote, and it came from no human mind. Most of Scripture was not emblazoned on tablets or parchment by the "finger of God," but it still originated from him.

God is also Scripture's source because the Holy Spirit superintended the writers as they wrote (2 Pet. 1:21). Since the result was the word of God, the Holy Spirit's "carrying the writers along" must have lasted for as long as they wrote. If the Scriptures we have contain any words that the writers wrote after the Spirit's activity stopped (or before it started), then those words are not the words of God but of mere men. Peter says they wrote God's word, and Paul added that *all* Scripture, not just a part, is the product of God's breath (2 Tim. 3:16), i.e., it is what he spoke.

Exactly how the Holy Spirit superintended the composing of Scripture is not fully explained. In 1 Corinthians 2:13, Paul says that, as he and others spoke (and wrote), they matched spiritual concepts with just the right words to express them. But Paul affirms that the words he and others spoke were taught by the Holy Spirit. From what Peter says about Scripture's origin and from what Paul says about all of Scripture (it is *theopneustos*, the result of divine speech), the Holy Spirit's role as the ultimate originator of Scripture must have begun prior to the writers' actual matching of words with concepts. The Holy Spirit must also have guided (carried along) the matching of words with concepts as the writers thought and wrote. If not, the result wouldn't be entirely God's words; God wouldn't be its ultimate source. But Scripture is the "oracles of God" (Rom. 3:2), God's very words.

*Thesis Two: The Product Is God's Word*

Because Scripture originated in God and because the Holy Spirit superintended the writers, we must secondly affirm with Paul that Scripture is *theopneustos*, the product of God's breath. It resulted from God's speech acts. Scripture presents various evidences for this truth.

First, in the foundational Scripture passages on inspiration, Paul called Scripture the product of God's breath (2 Tim. 3:16). Peter wrote that, because the Holy Spirit guided the writers as they wrote, they wrote God's word (2 Pet. 1:21). They wrote exactly what God wanted, and even though they produced documents in human language, the documents were God's very words.

Second, this was also Jesus's opinion of Scripture. For example, he quoted in Matthew 19:4ff. what either *Moses or Adam* said (recorded in Gen. 2:24), but he claimed that *God* said it. In John 6:45, Jesus connected the words of two OT prophets with the words of God; that is, what they wrote is what God said. And, Mark 7:9–13 shows that Jesus considered OT commands to be the very words of God. In that passage Jesus critiqued the Pharisees for setting aside God's word in favor of their traditions (v. 13). He then quoted from the Ten Commandments and called them the Lord's commands. Since the commands Jesus quoted are in Scripture, if Jesus said they are God's word, then the Scriptures that contain them are also God's word.

In addition, we can explain Jesus's use of Scripture only by his belief that it is God's very word. Jesus supported a moral or spiritual point by quoting from the OT or by appealing to some person or event in OT history as historically true. For example, Jesus cited the story of Jonah and the fish as being a sign of his forthcoming death, burial, and resurrection. He confirmed his teaching that he is Lord of the Sabbath by appealing to the story of David eating the showbread in the temple. Why would Jesus rest such important events in his own life (crucifixion and resurrection) and doctrinal truths (he is Lord of the Sabbath) on fictional stories? If the words alluded to are God's word, then Jesus's points rest ultimately on the testimony of God's word, and are irrefutable.

For Jesus always and for his Jewish audience (at least usually), appeal to

Scripture was the decisive argument. Even the Pharisees thought they could trip Jesus up by quoting, for example, biblical teaching on divorce. They asked Jesus about his understanding of Moses's teaching on divorce and remarriage (Matt. 19:3). They thought that, however he answered, he would offend someone. Jesus initially deflected their question about allowable grounds for divorce by pointing to Scripture's teaching that God originally intended marriage to be permanent (he quoted Gen. 2:24). The Pharisees, however, weren't ready to give up. If God really didn't want divorce, then why, they asked, did Moses command a husband to give his wife a certificate of divorce, and divorce her? Jesus corrected their error: Moses *allowed* divorce because humans stubbornly refused to live in accord with God's no-divorce desire, but Moses never *commanded* anyone to divorce, and Jesus reiterated God's original design of permanence in marriage.

Note that for both the Pharisees and Jesus, whatever Scripture demands is the rule. Their "debate" wasn't about whether Scripture or something else is the final authority. Their disagreement was about what Scripture actually says; whatever it does say is conclusive and irrefutable. Jesus repeatedly showed that he held God to be the highest authority. Jesus confirmed his teachings and refuted his critics by appeal to Scripture because Scripture is God's word. Scripture comes from the person with supreme authority, so it has supreme authority. Jesus's Jewish audience fully agreed.

Then, our biblical study showed Jesus's extreme care to fulfill and show that he fulfilled prophecies about the coming Messiah. If Jesus proved that he fulfilled those prophecies, then no argument could refute his claim to be the Messiah. If he didn't fulfill them, he couldn't possibly be the Messiah, because Scripture, as God's word, is true, and its predictions must be fulfilled. Jesus's credibility rested on his fulfilling the OT's messianic prophecies.

Jesus also often said that what he said and did, and what happened to him, fulfilled prophecy, because the truth of those predictions mattered to him very much. Since those prophecies are part of God's word, they could not be mistaken. God would never lie, and as omniscient, he would never believe a falsehood, and he would know everything, including the future. So, if predictions never came to pass, they couldn't be from God. What was at stake in Jesus's claims to fulfill prophecy was not just his own credibility but also that of Scripture and of the God who Jesus knew had spoken the words of Scripture. And so Jesus said (Matt. 5:17–18), even the least stroke of the pen of Scripture won't pass away, but all of it will be fulfilled. No wonder Jesus made a point of saying that what had happened fulfilled some prophecy of Scripture!

Next, our discussion of OT teaching about Scripture showed that OT writers repeatedly claimed that they were writing God's words. The formulaic "the word of the Lord came unto . . . saying" and "thus said the Lord" are two oft-repeated introductions to so much of the OT. We also noted that in Zechariah 7:12 God himself certified large portions of the OT as his word. And, there is ample evidence that NT writers viewed the OT as God's word. There is less evidence that NT writers viewed other NT books as God's word, but there is still some. As noted when discussing the foundational passages about Scripture's inspiration (all four of them from the NT), it is highly likely that the writers thought that what they wrote about Scripture's inspiration applied to the NT as well as to OT.

Before turning to my third thesis, I must add that what Scripture teaches about the product of inspiration applies to the books the authors originally penned. Scripture teaches nothing per se about copies or translations of these books. Nor is anything said about Scripture used in lectionaries (compilations of Scripture passages for readings in public worship), commentaries, or doctrinal treatises. Manuscript evidence for both OT and NT books shows variant readings of various passages. Thus, some copyists and translators must have introduced error into individual copies of a portion of Scripture. Those errors are not the product of God's breath.

This must not be misunderstood. Despite variant readings in a number of passages, there are enough manuscripts of the books of the Bible to allow textual critics to piece together what the original actually said. The degree of certainty with which we know what the original said is phenomenally high—higher than for most books of the ancient world whose authenticity is not in doubt.[1] So when someone holds in his or her hands an English, French, Japanese, etc., translation of the Bible, to the extent that it is based on the best textual tradition and is an accurate translation, one holds the very words of God. Still, it is most precise to say that inspiration refers to the original documents penned by the biblical authors. Errors of wording or grammar, omissions or inclusions of words, and poor translations are not God's doing.

However, as has been widely attested, such mistakes are minimal, and even though we don't possess the very scrolls, tablets, or pieces of parchment the original authors first used in writing their books, there is an extremely high degree of certainty about what exactly they wrote. For most passages, there is no question of what the author originally wrote. In cases where there is still some debate, textual critics uniformly say that the passages involved don't affect any matters of doctrine or practice that would undermine the central tenets of the faith or instructions on how God wants us to live. The product of inspiration is God's word!

---

[1] By authenticity I mean two things. It refers first to whether we know who wrote the document in question. Second, it is about whether the words in the document are actually the same words the author originally wrote. When there are variant readings of a verse, e.g., not all readings record *exactly* what the author first wrote.

*Thesis Three: All Scripture Is God's Word*

Here the central passage is 2 Timothy 3:16. Paul says that all (*pasa*) Scripture (*graphē*) is the product of God's breath. Whether "all" means Scripture taken collectively or each individual passage taken distributively, the result is the same. Everything in Scripture is God's word.

This thesis, however, doesn't rest solely on one passage. Jesus's testimony shows that he believed all of the OT to be God's word, and his pledge of the Holy Spirit's teaching ministry in effect promised that, when the apostles went to preach and write about Jesus and the things of God, they would "get it right." That is, Jesus, in advance, promised the inspiration of the soon-to-be written NT. We also saw that OT writers claimed to write God's word. NT authors also said they wrote God's words, and they thought other documents written by other apostles also qualified as Scripture.

These affirmations mean that Scripture's inspiration was not done by degrees. Some might think that genealogies in Genesis, chronicles of the lives and reigns of various kings in Kings, Samuel, and Chronicles, and narrative stories that don't even mention God's name (like Esther) are less (or not at all) inspired than Jesus's parables or heavily doctrinal letters like Romans, 1 Peter, and Hebrews. We might also think Daniel's prophetic visions are fully inspired but the narratives about him and his Jewish friends are simply "window dressing" in which resides the "real" word of God predicting the future. Scripture refutes those notions. No biblical writer makes such distinctions when he speaks of Scripture's character as a whole or in part.

Some, of course, object to this point. For example, why, if all Scripture is equally inspired, did Martin Luther famously dismiss the Epistle of James as a "letter of straw"? And why do Roman Catholics include the Apocrypha in the Bible while Protestants don't? Do Roman Catholics think the Apocrypha is equally inspired as, for example, the Pentateuch or the four Gospels? Do Protestants believe these books are less inspired than the rest and so they don't include them in the Bible, or do Protestants think these books aren't inspired at all? And, didn't the apostles write other books which weren't considered Scripture, some written to churches other biblical epistles address?

These questions raise significant issues, but all are about canonicity. That topic will be discussed in later chapters, but I must now give some answer to these questions. As to Luther and James, Luther's complaint wasn't that James was Scripture but was just less inspired than the rest. Instead, he believed the content of James to be so out of harmony with the rest of the NT that it couldn't at all be God's inspired word. But Luther never said that any book which *is* God's word is more or less inspired than other Scriptures, nor did any other Reformers say such a thing. So, this debate was about which books are canonical, not about degrees of inspiration.

As for the Apocrypha, Protestants exclude it from Scripture because they don't think it to be inspired at all. They don't see these books as totally valueless, but they don't believe them to be God's word. As for Catholics, it is hard to say exactly what each Catholic scholar thinks. Most likely some see the apocryphal books as equally inspired as other biblical books. Other Catholics may think they are less inspired than the OT and NT, but still come from God and so should be included as Scripture. Regardless, the issue again isn't about the degree of inspiration of some biblical books as opposed to others. The debate is about whether the Apocrypha is God's word at all. Protestant evangelicals affirm that, if a book is inspired, everything in it is equally God's word.

As for apostolic writings not included in Scripture, they aren't deemed inspired to a lesser degree than canonical books. Rather, they don't have the marks of inspiration, and only books with those marks are God's word and should be included in Scripture. In addition, apostles didn't point to other things they wrote and call them Scripture, God's word. NT authors knew when they wrote under the Spirit's inspiration and when they didn't. How they distinguished the two is beyond our knowledge, but this issue isn't about the degree and extent to which inspired books are inspired. A book either is or isn't God's word. If it is, it is fully inspired.

Others think 1 Corinthians 7 suggests degrees of inspiration. Paul addresses divorce and remarriage, and in verse 10 offers a command for the married. Before stating it, he says that the command comes from "not I, but the Lord." Verse 12 continues the discussion, and Paul writes, "But to the rest I say, not the Lord . . . " What do these two "introductions" in verses 10 and 12 mean? Does Paul mean that verses 10–11 are fully inspired because they come from the Lord, but verses 12–16 are less inspired, or not inspired at all, since they come from him, not the Lord? If so, that suggests that 1 Corinthians 7 contains fully inspired material and also less inspired or uninspired thoughts. If that's Paul's thought, then it is probably true of Paul's other books and of other biblical authors' works.

Alexander Jensen comments on this passage (and on the traditional view that the Bible is God's word). He says that no apostle claims to be writing God's word verbatim. Some say they write with high authority (e.g., 1 Cor. 11:23, where Paul says he writes what he received from the Lord), but "none of them claims that their very words were dictated by God."[2] Jensen then adds,

---

[2] Alexander S. Jensen, "Word of God or Witness? Issues in Christian Biblical Hermeneutics," *Islam and Christian-Muslim Relations* 20 (July 2009): 216.

"in addition, in one place Paul even writes explicitly that he is speaking on his own account, not on God's (1 Corinthians 7:12)."[3]

Jensen's claims (and others also raise questions about 1 Cor. 7:10) suggest that there might be three kinds of Scripture. The first is verbatim dictation of God's very words (though Jensen denies that the apostles claimed to do this). A second type is written with "high authority," because the authors say they write what they received from the Lord. And a third kind of Scripture consists of passages the author explicitly says he writes on his own account, not God's.

Is this what Paul means in 1 Corinthians 7? If so, then it isn't clear that verses 12–16 are *theopneustos*, nor was this material superintended by the Holy Spirit in the way 2 Peter 1:21 suggests. Thankfully, there is a plausible explanation of what Paul means in 1 Corinthians 7, and it removes any apparent contradiction with other things Paul says about Scripture. In 1 Corinthians 7:10 and 12 Paul makes what I would call two "historical" comments. Let me explain.

Paul says that the commands in verses 10–11 are the Lord's commands. Verses 10–11 capture tersely the substance of Jesus's teaching on divorce and remarriage (recorded in the Gospels). Jesus's basic teaching in Mark 10, a passage that excludes the exception clause present in Matthew's Gospel, is that if a man divorces his wife and marries another, he commits adultery. The same rule applies if a woman divorces her husband and marries another man. Since under Mosaic law adultery was punishable by stoning to death, Jesus's basic rule about divorce and remarriage means that no one should do this. That is why Paul in 1 Corinthians 7:10 tells the wife not to divorce, and adds in verse 11 that if she does, she should either remain unmarried or reconcile with her husband. Paul's even briefer comment in verse 11b shows that the same rule applies to husbands divorcing wives. So, verses 10–11 briefly summarize Jesus's teaching on divorce and remarriage; Paul is right that it didn't originate with him.[4]

In verses 12–16, Paul's comment about speaking to this subject himself, not the Lord, is another "historical" remark. From what the Gospels record, Jesus didn't say what verses 12–16 say. In those verses Paul addressed situations that arose in the early church at Corinth and elsewhere. As the gospel spread, especially among the Gentiles, many believed, but many did not. As a result, many marriages had one believing and one nonbelieving spouse. In such cases, what should the believer do? Paul offers instructions if the nonbeliever wants to continue the marriage, and other instructions if the nonbeliever wants to end the marriage just because the believing spouse is now a Christian.

---

[3] Ibid.

[4] For a fuller explanation of Jesus's teaching on divorce and remarriage and why Paul's words are consistent with Jesus's teaching, see my discussion of divorce and remarriage in *Ethics for a Brave New World*, 2nd ed. (Wheaton, IL: Crossway, 2010), chapter 13.

Jesus's teaching on divorce and remarriage, as recorded in the Gospels, doesn't comment on situations like those addressed in 1 Corinthians 7:12–16. So, what Paul says about what he writes is historically accurate.

Some may reply that this is tantamount to saying that 1 Corinthians 7:12–16 isn't God's word at all, and so it isn't Scripture. Several responses are appropriate. First, 1 Corinthians, if inspired, was written under the Holy Spirit's superintendence (2 Pet. 1:21). Things Paul says in 1 Corinthians 2 aren't available through human reasoning or sense perception; God alone knows them and reveals them through his Spirit. The fact that the Holy Spirit didn't move Paul to strike the words in question from 1 Corinthians 7 shows God wanted them written; they are his word. Who first said the words doesn't nullify them as inspired.

1 Corinthians 14:37 further confirms this answer. Paul claimed to write the Lord's commands. This must first refer to the contents of chapter 14, but look at that chapter. Very little, if any, of it can be found in the Gospels. During his earthly life, Jesus may have said some of these things to his disciples, but we have no evidence of that. Paul wasn't among those disciples, so he didn't hear it from Jesus while Jesus was on earth. As far as we know, Paul was historically the first to say what we find in 1 Corinthians 14, and yet he says that what he wrote are the Lord's commands. How can this be true? Because biblical inspiration involved both a divine and a human author.

When I discussed 1 Corinthians 14:37, I also suggested that Paul likely thought that more than just chapter 14 came from the Lord. In fact, I presented evidence from other Pauline books that he thought he wrote God's word. There is, then, no good reason to think Paul's comment in 1 Corinthians 7:12 means he thought he wasn't writing God's word.

One further matter about thesis three requires comment. This thesis affirms that all of Scripture is God's word. However, Scripture contains Satan's lies, Job's friends/comforters' erroneous evaluations of his situation, the mishandlings of Scripture (as in the Pharisees' twisting of Scripture to try to trap Jesus), and immoral reasoning of people like Caiaphas who believed it morally preferable that an innocent man, Jesus, should die instead of many Jews being slaughtered by the Romans as they quelled a rebellion that Jesus's followers might instigate. All of this is in Scripture, and since *all* Scripture is God's word, the incorrect thinking just mentioned must also be God's word. But how can it be, since God has nothing to do with lies and falsehoods?

This is an important question, and the correct way to answer is to ask what the biblical authors say about these lies, errors, and twistings of Scripture. If they say that God agrees with these falsehoods, then there are problems. God would either be immoral or less than omniscient, or both.

But what biblical writer ever says that Satan's lies are true? What author claims that the Pharisees' twisted understanding of Scripture is correct? Does the author of Job say that Job's friends' wrong opinions are correct? Do Gospel writers affirm Caiaphas's "moral reasoning" as correct?

The truth is that all the biblical authors do with Satan's lies is report them. Likewise, they recount what Jesus's opponents said as they twisted Scripture for their own purposes, and they record what Job and his friends said without ever saying that their errors were true. Caiaphas's reasoning is reported, but not affirmed. So, the Holy Spirit moved the biblical writers to report these erroneous ideas, but nothing more. These passages are the word of God, but that just means the Holy Spirit wanted a written account of what these individuals said, not that their false claims are true!

### Thesis Four: Scripture Was Also Written by Human Authors Using Human Language

Theses one through three focus almost entirely on the divine aspect of Scripture. Thesis four is about Scripture's humanness. Before addressing it, I want to reflect briefly on the incredible blessing of a gracious God to allow humans the kind of involvement to be discussed in writing his word.

When a king makes an edict, he may write it himself, but not always. Usually, an assistant who is especially adept at writing and who also knows the king's heart and mind will write it. Whatever the assistant contributes, it is a great honor to be entrusted with publishing abroad the words of a ruling monarch. How much greater the honor of being entrusted to write the royal edict of the King of kings and Lord of lords! This is so in part because the God who spoke the worlds into existence without our help, could have easily produced Scripture without human help. He could have simply spoken his word into existence ("Let there be Scripture . . . "), or assigned a band of good angels to write it. Instead, God chose and prepared human instruments to be the couriers of his royal word!

Of course, not just any human would be fit to convey the King's words, and this brings me to my first point about thesis four. If God needed nothing but a group of relatively passive secretaries to record his dictated words, then probably many people who could read and write could have done the job. But if the human part of Scripture involved more than just taking dictation, and it did, then not just anyone would do. To get the right authors in the right places at the right time to say just what God wanted involved a huge amount of planning and providential guidance on God's part.

Jeremiah wrote that while he was in his mother's womb, God chose him to be a prophet to the nations (Jer. 1:5). This involved much more than just protecting Jeremiah and his mother during pregnancy and delivery. Once born, Jeremiah wasn't ready to write anything, let alone the book that bears his name. It took many years of providential preparing and "growing" of Jeremiah, and of every other biblical author, to prepare them to write the words God would reveal to them.

Think, for example, of the theological depth of the apostle Paul's writings. As Paul was trained in Judaism, he could hardly have envisioned how that knowledge would be used, but God knew that the author of Romans and Galatians, for example, needed profound biblical and theological knowledge and intellectual acumen. What if Paul had been saved before receiving all of that training in Judaism?

Similarly, it took forty years in the wilderness to prepare Moses to get the Israelites ready for the Promised Land and to write the Pentateuch. My point is that in order to produce any part of Scripture, God had to "grow" just the "right" author.

Because the books of Scripture evidence being written by distinct individuals with their own styles, interests, and personalities, not just anyone could have written them. Biblical authors wrote what they did with the passion and intellectual and spiritual savvy they evidence because God uniquely prepared them to do so through their life experiences. God didn't need to do any of this unless he really intended Scripture's human authors to contribute more than their abilities to listen and take dictation.

The preceding suggests a second point in elaborating thesis four. Scripture doesn't evidence its being dictated to the human writers. Of course, we noted the Exodus passage written with the "finger of God." But the rest of Scripture evidences being written by the fingers of human authors. The defense of this claim is manifold, and very significant. Critics of an evangelical view of inspiration invariably think that our view is dictation; otherwise how could God guarantee that what was written was exactly what he wanted? Since critics also believe that Scripture contains errors and that God wouldn't superintend, let alone dictate, error, they conclude that the evangelical view of inspiration as dictation can't be true. There have also been evangelicals who reasoned that for God to get just the words written that he wanted, the only way to do so was by dictation. These evangelicals *don't* find errors in Scripture, so they conclude God used dictation. Unfortunately, some great evangelical thinkers (e.g., some of the Reformers) have also talked about Scripture's inspiration using the term "dictation."

Despite the beliefs among many nonevangelicals and some evangelicals that evangelicals believe that Scripture was dictated to humans who served as mere scribes, I contend that Scripture teaches things that are inconsistent with dictation. Moreover, when one looks at what the writers wrote and how they said it, dictation loses credibility. Of course, my view needs defense.

I begin the defense by referring readers to my discussion, in chapter 4, of 1 Corinthians 2:13. Paul says that he wrote words "taught" by the Holy Spirit, combining spiritual with spiritual. We noted that the teaching/revealing was done by the Holy Spirit and that teaching is a rather strange way to refer to giving a secretary dictation. Even more compelling, however, is Paul's claim that the actual combining of the truths revealed with the appropriate words to express them was done by the writers themselves. No such combining or matching is necessary if one merely takes dictation.

Equally significant is what we find in the various biblical books. There is great diversity, and I don't mean that the books cover different subjects. As a matter of fact, some authors wrote about the same topics. Nor is my point that biblical writers used a variety of literary genres (history, narrative stories, Gospels, epistles, parables, didactic treatises on one topic or another, e.g.), though they surely did. Instead, my point is that there is ample evidence of diverse writing styles, vocabularies, and personal interests in the various biblical books. Let me illustrate.

Paul, John, and Peter all wrote letters. Certain things about any letter written at that time were fairly formulaic, so we don't see diversity at those points. But each apostle's writings are distinct. Peter's sentences contain multiple dependent clauses stacked upon one or more independent clauses. As a result, his sentences often cover several verses, and his syntax is open to a host of possible meanings (and misunderstandings), as is the case in the classically difficult passage 1 Peter 3:18–22. In contrast, John writes rather straightforward prose. That doesn't mean his writings contain no complex sentences, but only that it is quite easy to grasp his points, because his syntax is simple. Often, in doing evangelism, those considering Christianity are given the Gospel of John to read. That is so, I believe, at least in part because the message is clear and easy to understand. As for Paul, the difficulty level of his syntax is somewhere between that of Peter and John. Paul, unlike John and Peter, is also known for beginning a thought and interrupting it as another point captures his attention. He may or may not come back to the first point and complete it. As noted in studying Romans 3:2, Paul began a list there and stated the first item in it, but then left the topic, only to resume it in Romans 9:1–6.

Another example of differences in style, even when authors use the same literary genre, is found in the poetry of various OT books. Psalms contains much poetry, and readers familiar with the book of Isaiah know that portions of it are filled with poetry. But these two books show different styles in writing poetry. Many psalms are written in crisp, terse lines, whereas portions of Isaiah much more elaborately develop an idea so that one might initially think those portions are prose except for all the metaphors and other figures of speech which make the text read like poetry. And, when it comes to wisdom literature, comparing the styles of Job, Ecclesiastes, and Proverbs gives three different experiences. Proverbs is filled with crisp aphorisms that offer sage advice or commentary on the human condition. In contrast, Ecclesiastes seems more like an extended lament on the human condition without God as viewed only from the perspective of those "under the sun." Most of Job is more like a dialogue or play than a treatise. We are not only told that there is pain and joy in life (as we learn also in Ecclesiastes and Proverbs) but we are allowed to feel this man's pain as he tries to cope with the tragedies that befall him—with the friends who judge him for what he must have done to deserve such a fate, and with a God who seems distant and unavailable.

What do these examples show? They show that the diversity in Scripture isn't just that different literary genres are on display. It is rather that different authors using the same genre use it in distinctive ways. In fact, even when they discuss the same topic their vocabularies and writing styles are quite different. Think, for example, of Galatians and Romans on the one hand and 1 Peter on the other. All three books contain extensive material on the nature of salvation. But the style of 1 Peter 1:1–12 is dramatically different both in length and in the complexity of its syntax from the more expansive and elaborate treatments of salvation in Romans and Galatians.

So, Scripture evidences great diversity, and that brings us to the main point related to the dictation theory, namely, the features explained above are inconsistent with dictation and quite consistent with biblical writers adding their own personal touches to their books. If Scripture is the result of divine dictation, then why bother to give the letters of Peter, Paul, and John their distinctive characteristics?

The differences in various books seem explainable in only two ways: either the Holy Spirit dictated the biblical writings using styles, etc., that mirrored each author's own style and approach so that it appears that they wrote these works themselves (which would implicate the Holy Spirit in a massive plan to deceive readers about who wrote these books); or the books were not dictated but were written incorporating the writers' background experiences, personal interests, training, vocabulary, and style of writing so that their books are truly products of human creativity, even as they *also* resulted from divine creativity and supervision.

If the second explanation is incorrect, we are still at a loss to prove that these writings were dictated. They don't seem dictated. If they were, why would the Holy Spirit dictate the books so as to look like they were not dictated? To answer that question, we must, among other things, answer the charge of deception against the Holy Spirit for inspiring the books to look like they weren't dictated. It is far simpler, and much more consistent with what we know about the Holy Spirit's moral integrity and about Scripture's nature, to conclude that these books were not dictated.[5]

Scripture's not being dictated suggests another important point about what I would label the very "texture" of Scripture. If Scripture were written in just one style, using repeatedly only one or two literary genres and a rather meager vocabulary, it would "feel" like basically the same things are being said, and in precisely the same way. That is, using topographical terminology, the landscape of Scripture would appear to be little more than a flat, smooth plain. Though distinct topics might suggest different emotional reactions, the literary style would be monotonous enough to "buffer" the emotional impact of the book.

Let me illustrate this point. The Gospel of Matthew shows Jesus interacting with many people. Some accepted him as Messiah, while others rejected him. By the time the narrative arrives at "Passion Week," it is quite clear that most Jews were happy for Jesus to be the messianic leader who would lead a war against the Roman overlords and defeat them, while relatively few were willing to claim him as Savior from sin and to establish a life-transforming relationship with him. So, by the end of Matthew 23, Matthew shows us a Jesus who was triumphantly welcomed on Palm Sunday and yet was on his way to the cross in less than a week thereafter.

Now, Matthew could have written that despite Palm Sunday, Jesus knew that most people rejected him, and so he was sad and somewhat angry. Instead, Matthew records (23:37–39) Jesus's very words that display an outpouring of these emotions. As we read, "How often I wanted to gather your children together, the way a hen gathers her chicks under her wings, and you were unwilling," we see Jesus's vivid expression of unrequited love. In the next moment we see a flash of Jesus's righteous anger as he pronounced judgment on this city he loved—"Behold, your house is being left to you desolate! For I say to you, from now on you shall not see Me until you say, 'Blessed is He who comes in the name of the LORD!'" By reporting Jesus's very words, Matthew heightens the irony of the situation, for just a day or so before (on Palm Sunday) the

---

[5] Though it isn't a disproof of dictation, there is an unwelcome result for apologists defending Christianity if the dictation theory is correct. Typically, apologists claim that it is credible to believe things like Christ's resurrection, because in the Gospels we have four independent eyewitnesses to it. But if the dictation theory of inspiration is correct, that argument no longer works. If the Holy Spirit dictated the Gospels, we only have the testimony of one person. Of course, that one person is the Holy Spirit, who is totally reliable. But if he engaged in the kind of deception that I have suggested, there is reason to rethink our beliefs about his reliability. Thus, if the dictation theory is correct, a traditional line of defending certain tenets of the faith is nullified.

*crowds* had shouted, "Hosanna; . . . Blessed is He who comes in the name of the LORD . . . !" (Matt. 21:9).

Think of the difference between these two possible ways of telling this story. For Matthew to say, "Jesus knew that despite the events of Palm Sunday, his own people didn't want what he really offered, and so he was sad and angry," would distance us from the situation and from what Jesus was really feeling. For Matthew to write the actual words Jesus said, as he did, gives us an emotional immediacy that the other way of telling the story could not have given. That is, the "texture" of this passage, if written in the first way, would be smooth, unbroken, and monotonous. Matthew's way of writing it just "feels" different. Its texture isn't monotonous. There are the "mountain peaks" on Palm Sunday as the crowd roars its approval (Matthew records the very words that many shouted as Jesus rode by), and deep valleys of sadness and rejection as we hear and feel Jesus's lament over Jerusalem.

Consider a second example, the book of Job. Most of it is written as a dialogue between Job and his friends. Even the prologue, which sets the stage for what follows, incorporates dialogues between God and Satan. And in the epilogue, which presents the denouement of this story, we hear God speak first (Job 38–41) and then Job responds (Job 42). The issue this book addresses is most basically why the righteous suffer. The author of Job could easily have written the book as a philosophical treatise on the problem of suffering. Or, using somewhat emotionally sterile prose, he could have written a brief summary of what happened and then explained what we should learn from Job's experience. It might have looked like the following:

> There once was a righteous man named Job. Satan told God that Job served God only because God blessed him. So God let Satan afflict Job to prove that some people serve God because it is right to do so, not because it pays. Job lost basically everything—his family, his possessions, and ultimately his health. This experience lasted a long time. Job's friends, though at first sympathetic, later accused him of all sorts of evil that had resulted in what happened. God was punishing Job, they claimed. Job professed his innocence, and he sought a hearing with God to plead his case. Eventually, God spoke to Job out of the whirlwind and overwhelmed Job with a sense of his power and knowledge. In response, Job said that he now understood that God and his ways are above us, and that he shouldn't have questioned what God was doing and why. As for Job, God then blessed him beyond anything he previously had experienced, and he lived a long and happy life. Satan lost his "bet" with God, because Job remained true to God in spite of all his pain and suffering. As for Job's friends, they were wrong, and before the story ended, God told them so.

The above is a succinct, rather emotionally distant snapshot of Job. The "texture" of the summary is quite smooth and even—no peaks and valleys are in evidence. That is so in part because the account tells what people thought, said, and did without us hearing any of them speak. From this snapshot we may have some idea of how they felt and of the questions that tormented Job's troubled mind, but we are mainly left to imagine them. Imagined emotions are seldom actually felt.

But Job is written as a dialogue between Job and his friends, between God and Satan, and between God and Job. Through the dialogues, emotions are not described from a distance but are instead "experienced" as we "hear" Job and his friends directly say what they think and feel. In short, we are not told in abstraction from a real case of suffering about the problem of evil. We are "shown" very vividly a man in the midst of a crisis of faith. There is quite a difference between Job and an abstract theological or philosophical treatise on why the righteous suffer.

This point about Scripture's texture raises another significant point. The predominant trend in nonevangelical theology in recent centuries has been to reject the idea that God gives propositional revelation, and to embrace the notion that God himself is the content of revelation. Recently, evangelicals have raised another issue about propositional revelation. It is arguably a more subtle point than the one that deals with the content of revelation, so we must not misunderstand it. This point deals with inspiration and involves my point about the texture of Scripture. Let me explain.

Evangelicals want to safeguard the idea that divine revelation in Scripture involved the transmission of cognitive data. God is revealed in Scripture, but that happens mostly by means of propositional information. This simply means that, in giving us Scripture, God revealed information about himself, us, our world, etc., which can be stated in the form of various propositions. A proposition is a sentence stated in the indicative mood that affirms some state of affairs to be the case. While questions, commands, interjections don't normally affirm some concept (and hence don't take the usual sentential form of a proposition), what those questions, commands, etc., are about can be formulated into a proposition. Hence, even those sentences have propositional content.[6]

So far, this may seem fairly straightforward, but there is more to this discussion. Some have complained that some evangelical writers are so concerned to safeguard the idea of propositional revelation that they have superimposed it

---

[6] There is also a debate among philosophers about whether propositions (or their content) are individual entities or not entities at all. But that isn't the debate over the relation of propositional revelation to inspiration. For examples of those who raise the matter of propositions and relate it to inspiration, see Carl F. H. Henry, "The Priority of Divine Revelation: A Review Article," *JETS* 27 (March 1984); Everett Berry, "Theological Vs. Methodological Postconservatism: Stanley Grenz and Kevin Vanhoozer as Test Cases," *WTJ* 69 (2007); Everett Berry, "Speech-Act Theory as a Corollary for Describing the Communicative Dynamics of Biblical Revelation: Some Recommendations and Reservations," *Criswell Theological Review* 7 (Fall 2009); and Kevin J. Vanhoozer, "Lost in Interpretation? Truth, Scripture, and Hermeneutics," *JETS* 48 (March 2005).

on the way inspiration (verbal, plenary inspiration, in particular) is portrayed. As a result, they give the impression that Scripture's inspiration means that God revealed a series of propositions in Scripture for our enlightenment and edification.[7] Where can one find this "list" of propositions? The answer would typically be "in all of Scripture." If, as 2 Timothy 3:16–17 says, Scripture is profitable for all the uses named in verse 16, it can only be so as a set of propositional sentences.[8]

Various evangelicals have critiqued this portrayal of Scripture's inspiration. One noteworthy critic is Kevin Vanhoozer, but we must understand what he is and isn't saying. Vanhoozer addressed this issue in some detail in a paper delivered at a national meeting of the Evangelical Theological Society. He linked the view in question with both Charles Hodge and Carl F. H. Henry. Vanhoozer described Henry's commitment to propositional revelation, and argued that it impacted Henry's understanding of Scripture's nature and of theology. Vanhoozer explains:

> The Scriptures, says Henry, contain a divinely given body of information actually expressed or capable of being expressed in propositions. Those parts of the Bible that are not already in the form of statements may be paraphrased in propositional form. In Henry's words: "Christian theology is the systematization of the truth-content explicit and implicit in the inspired writings."[9]

Some will undoubtedly wonder why this is problematic, especially if they believe the alternative is the neoorthodox view that the content of divine revelation isn't information about God (propositions), but God himself in nonverbal, personal encounter. To respond this way, however, misses Vanhoozer's real concern about propositional revelation. Vanhoozer's questions about propositional revelation aren't about the debate between neoorthodox and evangelical thinkers over the content of revelation. At various points in Vanhoozer's address, he affirms belief in propositional revelation.

Vanhoozer's concern is with seeing Scripture *as little more than* a set of propositions to be mined through exegesis and strung together as the sum total of what God says about what he has done and what he wants us to do. Instead, we should grasp the whole of Scripture as it was given in various forms (literary genres). To do so is to see Scripture as part of what Vanhoozer calls theodrama. This drama is about God's word and deeds, as recorded in

---

[7] For various objections to revelation as propositional, see Avery Dulles, *Models of Revelation* (Garden City, NY: Image, 1985), 48–52.

[8] This last point about 2 Timothy 3:16–17 (and what Scripture must be for it to be usable as 3:16 describes) is my own comment. That is, I'm not saying that those who hold the position described in the text cite this verse in support. They may do so, though I haven't seen that in print. My point is only to show that one could think that the view being described in my text is necessary because of what 2 Timothy 3:17 teaches.

[9] Vanhoozer, "Lost in Interpretation?," 95.

Scripture, and about what God wants readers of Scripture to know and to do. Viewed this way, God and humans are actors in a drama "written" in God's mind and revealed and directed both in Scripture and in God's ongoing action in history and in individual lives. But, Scripture, Vanhoozer argues, isn't just the script of this theodrama. "It is one of the leading players in the ongoing drama, interrupting our complacency, demanding its reader's response."[10] Hence, to emphasize "propositional content only is to fail to recognize the Bible as divine communicative action, a failure that leads one to *dedramatize* the Scriptures. The result: a faith that seeks only an abbreviated understanding that falls short of performance knowledge."[11]

What should we say about this, and how does it relate to my point about Scripture's texture? I note initially that one doesn't need to agree with Vanhoozer on theodrama to agree that Scripture resulted from divine action (speech acts initially, and then superintending acts as biblical writers penned their books). Nor should we disagree that God in giving Scripture intended to do more than give us information. He certainly wanted Scripture to guide our actions and our thinking. But what about concerns over propositions and a "propositional" view of inspiration, the more basic concern of my discussion? Here several points should be made.

First, in contrast to neoorthodox views on the *content* of revelation, we must affirm that revelation has a variety of contents that come in diverse forms. Those forms include propositions/information, acts, and the very person of God. Of course, Christ is the highest form of divine revelation because he is God. Henry, Hodge, Vanhoozer, and many other evangelicals, including myself, agree on this point. But the point in contention now is the nature of the book that God inspired. Did God produce through human writers a Bible that is little more than a set of propositions about God, humans, etc., or is the Bible something more?

To answer this question we must distinguish the nature of theology from the nature of biblical revelation, and that is my second point. There should be little debate that *systematic theology* should take the form of treatises filled with propositions, including their meaning and applications. This is so because systematic theology is about the articulation and clarification of concepts (and when necessary, the defense of a particular understanding of a concept). Hence, we expect theological writing to be filled with doctrinal propositions.

In contrast, the Bible isn't written in the form of a theological treatise. It is written in many different literary forms, but none of them is a form that strings together propositions like beads in a necklace. Actually, a good piece of

---

[10] Ibid., 101.

[11] Ibid., 102. As Vanhoozer explains, the themes involved with Scripture and theology as theodrama are developed in greater detail in his *The Drama of Doctrine* (Louisville: Westminster John Knox, 2005).

theological prose shouldn't simply string together propositions one by one, or it is likely to strike readers as little more than a "grocery list" of ideas. Scripture teaches many different concepts, but it does so in a variety of literary forms. One value of the concern about a propositional notion of inspiration is that it reminds us that in Scripture God did use a great variety of *literary* ways to present his message. To deny or overlook this misunderstands what I have said about the "texture" of Scripture. It is to see Scripture incorrectly as a set of isolated conceptual nuggets that God dropped from heaven to land in various places, surrounded by words that serve merely as fillers between the nuggets.

But all of Scripture, not just its isolated propositions, is God's word, and it has come to us in a variety of literary forms. The texture of Scripture is not smooth, even, and monotonously the same. As seen from my examples about Scripture's texture, the forms in which Scripture's content is delivered not only help to convey that content but are themselves part of the content God wants us to know.

So, we shouldn't deny that there is propositional revelation, nor should we reject the idea that systematic theology involves taking the data of revelation and synthesizing them in concepts. Rather, we should just be sure to emphasize that part of the way the authors express their individual humanity (and Scripture's humanity), and thereby demonstrate that these books didn't result from divine dictation, is that the texture of these books is not monotonously the same.

*Thesis Five: Scripture Was Written with Dual Authorship but in a Way that Maintained the Integrity of Both Authors*

As we have seen, Scripture was written by both the Holy Spirit and human authors. Normally when two authors cowrite a book, each contributes a portion of the work. When each finishes, he shares what he has written with his coauthor. Each author comments on the other's part, suggesting changes in content and wording where appropriate. As a result, the whole book is justly attributed to both authors, not because each wrote every word, but because each read every word, helped with editing various drafts, and approved the final draft.

The model of coauthoring just described, however, wasn't the approach used in writing Scripture. There is ample evidence that human authors penned the books, using their own styles, vocabularies, and appropriate content for the occasion. On the other hand, the Holy Spirit was involved in every step of the writing process. The impetus to write, the actual subjects for each book, and each book's very wording were all superintended by the Holy Spirit. This was not a remote kind of superintendence but an active, moment-by-moment involvement to "carry along" the biblical writers so as to bring them to the Holy

Spirit's "destination," the concepts and words he wanted written. Hence, even though the Holy Spirit didn't "hold in his hands" the writing instrument and pen the very words on scrolls or parchment, he so guided the writers' thought processes that they wrote exactly what he wanted.

As a result, evangelicals affirm that the Scriptures were written using dual authorship. This kind of inspiration is sometimes called concursive inspiration. This does not mean that what the Holy Spirit did in the process is exactly what the human writer did, or vice versa. Rather, it means that each played his respective role in the process *simultaneously*, and that without the efforts of each, Scripture wouldn't have been written at all, or at the very least, it would have different content than it does. The Holy Spirit's role was to reveal the truths to be written, in some cases remind the authors of things they knew but weren't thinking about, and teach the writers how to match the concepts revealed with just the right words, so that what they wrote said exactly what the Holy Spirit wanted written.

The human writers needed first to be sensitive to the Holy Spirit's leading about topics to discuss. In some instances, the topics required some research before they wrote (see, e.g., Luke 1:1–4). As they sorted through the data they gathered, they had to decide what to include and what to omit, but that wasn't done without seeking the Holy Spirit's guidance. They don't tell us how the Spirit guided them or how he convinced them to include one thing and omit another. The choosing of the actual words, though superintended by the Holy Spirit, was done by the writers themselves, and of course they, or their assistants, put actual pen to actual parchment.

This is as much of an explanation of how the Holy Spirit inspired the writing of Scripture as we can give. Though it might seem strange to say that God did the deed that a human author did, and vice versa, that notion is not without biblical precedent. Think of what Scripture says of Pharaoh's refusal to let the people of Israel go. Scripture says that Pharaoh hardened his heart against the request for freedom, but it also says God hardened Pharaoh's heart (Ex. 7:22; 8:15, 19, 32; 9:12; 10:1–2, 20; 11:10; 14:8). Isaiah says that God "hired the Assyrian juggernaut" to attack and punish the northern kingdom of Israel, but it was also true that Assyria's king led his army into battle and utterly destroyed the kingdom of Israel. We know as well that Judas betrayed Jesus, but Scripture also says that Satan entered Judas to betray Christ. So this deed was both Satan's and Judas's.[12] Jesus said that no one can come to him unless he and the Father draw him, but when individuals asked Jesus or the disciples what they needed to do to be saved, they were told to believe on Christ and

---

[12] Elsewhere I have explained how one act can be attributed to more than one agent. For details see my "Divine Causality and Evil: Is There Anything Which God Does Not Do?," *CSR* 16 (July 1987): 394–402.

they would be saved. So there is a sense in which a decision to accept Christ is both God's act and an act of the one who chooses Christ.

None of these examples explains the exact "mechanics" of how this works. I raise them to show that the idea of dual agency in the writing of Scripture shouldn't seem impossible or even strange. Scripture often attributes an action both to God and to humans.

So, the Holy Spirit and human beings both wrote Scripture. Given the obvious differences between the divine and human authors, I note several implications of this dual authorship. First, one may wonder what the dual authorship of Scripture means for the free will of the agents (human and divine) involved. If the Holy Spirit was limited to the knowledge and acumen of a given writer, was he not free to say what he really wanted to say? And, if the Holy Spirit's superintendence of the human authors is what I have described, how could the human writers write their books freely?

As to the Spirit's freedom, few would deny it. But they would add that, depending on the human writer, there are things he just wouldn't know and likely couldn't understand if the Spirit revealed them. For example, had the Holy Spirit revealed truths about the nature of the universe, using the concepts of quantum physics, it is unlikely that any biblical writer could do much with it. So, wouldn't that limit the Spirit's freedom? Yes, if the Spirit intended to reveal and inspire a treatise on physics. That topic, however, goes beyond Scripture's intended content. So, it is safe to say that the topics handled in Scripture don't go totally beyond what human authors and readers can understand.

Even so, the Holy Spirit couldn't have enlisted just anyone to write Scripture. Some people were more qualified than others in virtue of their training, life experience, and relation to the Lord. The writers of Scripture were not just thought of and chosen a few moments before they began to write. God decided long before they were born who would write what, and he providentially guided the growth and development of each writer so that at the right time, each was ready to write. So, the Spirit's freedom to say what he wanted wasn't abridged, at least in part because God prepared the writers he needed to write exactly what he wanted.

What about the freedom of the human writers? The Holy Spirit's action guaranteed that the books say exactly what he wanted written. But how can there be guarantees, and how can the kind of superintendence explained be involved, if the human writers were truly free as they wrote? Because many believe that the kind of involvement required to guarantee outcomes would remove the writer's free will, they find it hard to believe that the evangelical concept of inspiration is anything but dictation. And yet, evangelicals who don't hold the dictation theory, do embrace concursive inspiration, and also maintain that the human writers wrote freely. I agree and add that, regardless of their beliefs about free will, evangelicals who hold concursive inspiration also believe that both the human and divine authors of Scripture did their part freely.[13]

A second implication of dual authorship is the matter of accommodating divine knowledge to human understanding. If concursive inspiration can at all work, the two authors must be able somehow to communicate with each other. At the very least, they must understand what the other is thinking and saying. However, as theologians through the centuries have rightly noted, God and humans have two qualitatively distinct thinking apparatuses. God's intellectual abilities and knowledge are far beyond ours. Expecting God to have a conversation with us without accommodating his thoughts to our level of understanding is like asking someone with a doctorate in astrophysics to converse about his academic discipline with a three- or four-year-old child. If the expert speaks as he would when presenting an academic paper to others in his field, the child will likely understand nothing. If they are to communicate at all, he must simplify the subject so that the youngster can grasp at least something he is saying. God's communicating understandably with us is said to be analogous to the situation just described. Speaking of God accommodating his thoughts to our human thought forms, Calvin described God as "lisping" in what he says to us.[14]

How should we respond? Some are so convinced of this view and of its implications that they believe it required God to inspire the human writers to write things that God knew included some error. If God didn't accommodate his revelation in this way to our ignorance, it is argued, we couldn't have understood what God was saying. In the chapters on inerrancy, we will return to this objection. For now, we must decide whether the idea of accommodation is correct, and how we should understand it.

From my perspective, there is something obviously correct about accommodation, but there are also reasons for concern. As to the latter, a major concern is that, in order to verify for sure that accommodation has occurred, one would have to have a copy of the Bible written "exactly the way God knows it" in order to compare it with our present Bibles. But no one has such a copy, and it isn't clear how we could get it. The problem, in short, is that a comparison is being made not between the texts we have and texts that say things exactly as

---

[13] Evangelicals disagree on the meaning of free will. Some hold libertarian free will, while others hold compatibilistic free will. This volume isn't the place to discuss which view of free will is preferable. My point here is that evangelical proponents of each view believe that biblical authors wrote their books freely (in their sense of "free"). For more on different views of free will, see my *No One Like Him: The Doctrine of God*, Foundations of Evangelical Theology (Wheaton, IL: Crossway, 2001), chapters 13–16.

[14] John Calvin, *Institutes of the Christian Religion*, ed. John T. McNeill, trans. Ford Lewis Battles (Philadelphia: Westminster, 1960), 121 (1.13.1).

God knows them, but rather between texts we have *and* what we know about God's intellectual abilities and knowledge. Hopefully, readers will see that the comparison we are making is not a matter of comparing "apples with apples" and "oranges with oranges." The result is that the idea usually associated with accommodation may well be right, but we have no way to demonstrate it.

This must not be misunderstood. I'm not at all denying the infinite superiority of the divine mind.[15] In addition, I don't know whether a text of Scripture written to reflect the way God knows things would be impossible to understand and whether it would immediately appear to require knowledge and intellectual powers that exceed what we need to understand the Scriptures we have. Perhaps it would be, but we don't know that, and that is my point, for those who think accommodation requires that what we have in Scripture is little like Scripture would be if God told us things precisely as he knows them, can't say how Scripture would read if God moved writers to write about topics as God alone understands them.

On the other hand, it would be foolish to deny all divine accommodation to human thought forms. Perhaps what accommodation involves is first a choice of subjects that are within the range of human understanding, and then a presenting of those topics in vocabulary and literary forms that are common to human understanding. In other words, perhaps Scripture gives us what God actually thinks, but he has given revelation only on topics that his spokesmen grasp and can articulate in words and styles that they know and use. Everyone agrees that the contents of Scripture aren't everything God knows. Can it not be that God has chosen to speak to us on topics he knows we can understand and to do so in language we understand?

Part of my hesitancy to adopt a usual sort of view of accommodation is that I contend that we should shy away from a notion of accommodation that requires Scripture as a whole and/or in its parts to be wrong in what it says, not just because it is stated differently than God would say it if discussing a topic with other members of the Trinity, but also because for us to understand any of it, God has to include errors in the content; that is, if he were to tell it the way he really sees it, we would see that the contents of Scripture are actually wrong. It is this notion that I most vehemently object to if it is thought to be required by accommodation. If accommodation is thought of more along the lines I suggested in the previous paragraph, I see no reason to think that God has given us half-truths (or two-thirds truths), and that the only way to get a Bible that is fully true is to get a Bible (which we don't have) which says things as God really knows and thinks them. My contention is that what we have in

---

[15] Interested readers will find my discussion of the divine intellect and of omniscience in *No One Like Him*, 299–320.

Scripture is, when properly interpreted, what God really knows is true about the topics Scripture addresses. Accommodation of divine thoughts to human language doesn't require that the texts we have be wrong and that God knows them to be wrong. That takes too dim a view of the powers of the divine intellect to speak the truth in words and ways we can understand. It also raises the question of whether *anything* God wants us to know has truly been revealed—if the texts we have aren't true as God knows the truth!

A third implication of dual authorship concerns what the authors meant and what they understood themselves to have written. This, of course, has significant implications for what we understand them to be saying. Here we can't enter a full-scale discussion of hermeneutics, but some points relevant to interpretation are worth noting. I begin with the distinction between the sense and reference of language. The sense of what someone says or writes is determined by the definition of the words they use, the grammatical construction of those words into a sentence, and the overall context in which the sentence appears. If I want to know the sense of a given word such as "chair' or 'run," I should consult a dictionary for a definition. For "chair" there would be a description of a certain type of object on which people can sit; the description, if I understand it, will help me identify a chair whenever I see one. As to "run," there will be a description of a certain action or activity. If I understand the description, when I observe an instance of running I can identify it as running.

In contrast to sense, the reference of a word or sentence is the specific thing in the world to which the word or sentence points. Words have reference to specific things in the world only when the words are part of a sentence, for sentences assert something about the world. Outside of a sentence, words have meaning, but they refer to a general class of objects or actions, not to specific ones that are actually part of the world we experience.[16]

Because an author understands a literal sense of a word, he also understands when he uses in his writing or speech figures of speech (nonliteral uses of language). And, he knows specifically to what he refers when he uses language either literally or figuratively. To understand the difference between sense and reference, and that between literal and figurative language, the biblical writer need not be taught such things by the Holy Spirit. Anyone who knows how to read and write as more than a novice understands how language works.

Now, the sense of a sentence will be about something past, present, or future; and of course its reference, depending on the specific action, event, or object to which the sentence points, will be about something past, present, or future as well. When a biblical author writes about a past person or event,

---

[16] The distinction between the sense and reference of language is one most typically associated with the German philosopher Gottlob Frege, who introduced it into philosophy of language.

usually, if not always, he will know not only the sense of what he has written but also its reference. So, for example, when Hosea writes in 11:1 about Israel being a child and God loving him and calling him out of Egypt, Hosea understands that the nation is being depicted as a male child whom his father loves greatly. Hosea also understands that this sentence refers to God's bringing Israel out of Egyptian bondage. Hence, he understands that the phrase "calling him out of Egypt" is a figurative way of referring to the removal of Israel from Egypt. Undoubtedly, Hosea also knew of the contest between God and Pharaoh which led to the tenth plague upon Egypt, after which Pharaoh finally told Moses, Aaron, and the people of Israel to leave. Hosea also likely knew that Pharaoh changed his mind and sent his armies after the Israelites as they were departing. Only after the Israelites crossed the Red Sea and the Lord brought the waters of the sea upon the Egyptian army and drowned its soldiers was Israel fully and totally freed from Egypt.

Hosea would understand these things without the Holy Spirit teaching him them. Likewise, other human authors writing about past events would normally understand the sense and reference of what they wrote. The same can be said of sentences with verbs in the present tense.

As to sentences about the future, the situation is different. A writer may well understand the sense of a prediction, but it is unlikely, unless the Holy Spirit reveals it to him, that he will know the sentence's specific reference. For example, Daniel could understand, as he finished writing Daniel 7, that there would be a sequence of four mighty kings who would lead great empires. Because the parallel vision in chapter 2 identifies the first king as Nebuchadnezzar, Daniel could know that the referent of the first beast of Daniel 7 was also Nebuchadnezzar and Babylon. He might also have had a good guess about who would fulfill the prediction of the second beast/world ruler. However, it is unlikely that he could have guessed the referent of the third or fourth beasts, though he certainly could know that those beasts represented great kings and their empires. Of course, the Holy Spirit knew exactly who would fulfill those prophecies, and he knew even before Daniel 7 was written.

Similarly, OT prophets could have understood that they were predicting the coming of a future Messiah. They could have understood that he would die and rise again, as well as do many other things. What they couldn't know, unless the Holy Spirit revealed it to them, is that the person who would fulfill the messianic prophecies would be Jesus of Nazareth.

Readers may agree with what I have written but wonder why I mention it. My response comes in terms of implications of these points about the sense and reference of language. This discussion underscores that the biblical writers didn't always know the referent of every sentence they wrote. But because the Holy Spirit did, he could ensure that the language the writer used to make the prediction was true. That is, the language was precise enough to exclude predictions of things that would never happen. None of this, of course, means that the sense of prophetic passages is perfectly clear and can't be misunderstood. Interpreting prophecy, whether about the first advent or about end times and the second advent, requires the interpreter's careful attention. Just because the Holy Spirit knows the referent of each prophecy doesn't mean the human authors did, too, just because they wrote it. We confirmed this in our study of 1 Peter 1:10–12. Though Peter tells us that the writers of prophecies about Christ's coming and his sacrifice were told when their prophecies would be fulfilled, that doesn't mean they knew that Jesus of Nazareth would fulfill them. Nor does it mean that they ever knew the referents (fulfillments) of many of the other prophecies they wrote which were about either advent of Christ. Even so, because we know that the Holy Spirit, the divine author, knows the sense and reference of every sentence in Scripture, and because he superintended the writing of Scripture, there is ample reason to think that passages about the future (from the human author's perspective) will be fulfilled as predicted.

The upshot of this point is that the human writers of Scripture didn't have to understand the referent of everything they wrote in order to ensure that they wrote what the Holy Spirit wanted. Because of the Holy Spirit's involvement, what the human authors wrote accurately reflects what the Holy Spirit knows and wanted to say.

*Thesis Six: Inspiration Extends to the Very Words*
*of Scripture, Not Just the Ideas*

Some have thought that divine inspiration need not extend to the choice of Scripture's very words. As long as the Holy Spirit told the writers the basic ideas he wanted addressed, they could develop and state their themes however they wanted. Of course, this would mean less active involvement of the Spirit in the actual writing process. Some have thought it necessary to opt for such a view of inspiration because they believe there are errors in Scripture, even though the topics addressed and the basic things said about each topic are deemed to be accurate. If the Spirit didn't superintend the very choice of words but left that to the human writers, then it is clear how God could be involved in producing Scripture and yet Scripture could contain an occasional error on some matter of little consequence.

A further advantage of the view just described is that it seems to uphold the writers' freedom as they wrote, whereas the view of inspiration presented so far as the biblical one undoubtedly makes many wonder how the writers could actually be free—if the Holy Spirit was involved as I have proposed. This doesn't mean that a better fit with human freedom is an *argument* for the view that only the ideas were inspired. Rather it is a consequence (a welcome one for many) of holding such a view.

Regardless of any positive consequences of holding that only Scripture's ideas are inspired, there are significant objections against it. First, 2 Peter 1:21 demands superintendence that requires the Holy Spirit's guidance and governing of the whole process of writing Scripture. If not, there is no guarantee that the author's text is actually what the Holy Spirit intended to say. Some may think this an overreaction, because there is usually more than one way to make a point. I agree about there being more than one way to make a point, but I also note that ordinary human language can be very ambiguous. Such ambiguity need not always make it impossible to say things that represent exactly what the Holy Spirit thinks. But surely there are some subtle points (and other not-so-subtle but complicated points) that need precise stating. Even when stated precisely, such points can be misinterpreted, but if not stated well, a given text may suggest things that are actually contrary or opposite to what the Holy Spirit wanted to say. So, giving a general assignment to write on various topics and include certain ideas won't guarantee that the resultant text actually says what God intended. And since what is at stake in some instances is one's eternal destiny, an accurate view, for example, of God's plan of salvation and the consequences of rejecting it must be presented. No one understands it better than God does, and he wouldn't just leave it to the human writers to "get it right."

Second, 1 Corinthians 2:13 is relevant here. That verse says the Holy Spirit revealed to the apostles the truths they preached and later wrote. Those truths weren't taught or received through human wisdom. Paul also affirms that the Holy Spirit's teaching involved the apostles' choice of the right words to match the concepts the Holy Spirit wanted them to address. We also saw that, in various writings of Paul, like those to the church at Thessalonica, he affirmed that the words he wrote were God's very words. Though Paul was likely talking about the content of his messages, it is hard to conceive of the content without the words used to convey it. Thoughts without language are impossible, so if Paul says his preaching and writing are God's word, that must extend beyond concepts to actual words.

A final line of evidence is relevant to this point, but it is a bit more inferential than the preceding arguments. Millard Erickson has discussed the issue of the *intensiveness* of inspiration (does it include the writers' thoughts only, or does it extend to their very words?) as thoroughly and cogently as any, and he reminds us that, depending on whether one makes didactic passages about Scripture the central focus or the phenomena of Scripture the focus, a different answer may arise. In concert with Erickson, I agree that both types of data must be taken seriously, but that the didactic passages that address the nature of Scripture must be the governing data. Hence, both Erickson and I are moved to argue that inspiration does extend to the very choice of words.[17]

Of course, one still needs to present evidence from didactic passages about Scripture's nature showing that Scripture teaches that inspiration extends to the choosing of Scripture's very words. One line of evidence Erickson presents appeals to the way NT writers use various OT passages. Erickson points to John 10:35; Matthew 22:32; Matthew 22:44; and Galatians 3:16.[18] The points relevant to each of these passages hang on small details of various OT texts. I shall present those points shortly. But first, I think it important to see what Erickson concludes from these examples. He writes that "since the NT writers considered these Old Testament minutiae authoritative (i.e., as what God himself said), they obviously regarded the choice of words and even the form of the words as having been directed by the Holy Spirit."[19]

I have already presented ample evidence to show that both Jesus and NT writers considered the OT God's word. That this means they considered the choice of words and even their form as being directed by the Holy Spirit is, I believe, also correct, but not quite so obvious from the passages Erickson cites as one might expect. So, we should look at the passages and see what we have a right to conclude.

As for John 10:35, Jesus cites Psalm 82:6 to counter the charge of blasphemy. Erickson claims that Jesus's argument rests on the fact that the word "god" is plural in Psalm 82:6. But a quick look at Psalm 82:6 shows that it is about people (plural) who in Israel served as judges (plural). So, since the passage is about more than one person, whatever it would say would be plural—hence, "gods," not "god." Jesus's point would have been made just as easily if the Psalms passage had used the singular for "god." Why? Because his point is that the term "god" is, in Scripture (and you know it can't be wrong about anything—"the Scriptures cannot be broken"), applied to people who are merely human beings, and yet no one thinks that blasphemy. The individuals referred to in Psalm 82 were judges in Israel (a role thought to qualify them to render justice for God), and so it was thought appropriate to call them "gods," even though the judges in view in Psalm 82:6 were evil. Jesus's point was that he, too, serves God (but does only good, not evil), so why should it be blasphemy if he refers to himself as God, when no one is offended by referring to the evil human judges mentioned in Psalm 82:6 as gods?

Jesus's point hinges not on whether the word "god" in Psalm 82:6 is singular or plural, but rather on the fact that Scripture, God's word, calls people

---

[17] Millard Erickson, *Christian Theology*, 2nd ed. (Grand Rapids, MI: Baker, 2000 printing), 238–240.
[18] Ibid., 238.
[19] Ibid.

who are only human "gods," and yet no one thinks that is blasphemy. The question for us is whether this proves that inspiration extends to the very words of Scripture, even in this one instance? Perhaps, but not straightforwardly, and perhaps not at all. Let me explain. If Psalm 82:6 were not in Scripture, Jesus couldn't make his point by appeal to it, and the crucial point in the passage is that "gods" is used to speak of mere humans. But suppose that Psalm 82:6 were written as it is, but no one believed that Psalms is the word of God? Would appeal to this passage prove that inspiration extends to the very words of Scripture? Of course not. But what does this show us? It shows us that inferring that Psalm 82:6 and John 10:35 confirm that inspiration extends to Scripture's very choice of words offers a valid argument only if one has already established that all of Scripture, including its very words, is inspired. And that just means that the argument for inspiration extending to Scripture's very words hinges on passages like 2 Timothy 3:16, 1 Corinthians 2:13, and other testimony that these are God's words. Since we have clearly established that all of Scripture is inspired, I think we have a right to note that the very words God inspired are crucial because of how Jesus uses them, but it is hard to see that this directly proves that John 10:35 *teaches* that inspiration extends to the very words of Scripture.

In Matthew 22:32, Jesus answers the Sadducees' question about the resurrection of the dead. The Sadducees didn't believe in resurrections (as Matthew tells us; v. 23), and so their question was intended to trap Jesus: If in her lifetime a woman was married to seven men (one at a time), and then she died, whose wife would she be in the resurrection? Jesus answered that she would be no one's wife, because in the resurrection there is no marriage. In verse 32 he then made a point about resurrections. He quoted Scripture (Ex. 3:6), which says, "I am the God of Abraham, and the God of Isaac, and the God of Jacob." As Erickson notes, the crucial point is the verb tense of "am." That point leads Jesus to draw the conclusion that God isn't the God of the dead, but of the living.[20]

So, in this case, Jesus's point hinges on the verb tense used in Exodus 3:6, but does that prove that inspiration extends to the very choice of Scripture's words? It is tempting to say that this fact alone makes the case, but I again demur. Jesus could have made his point by appealing to something other than Exodus 3:6. The fact that Exodus 3:6 reads as it does allows him to appeal to it, and it was wise for him to do so because, since Exodus 3 is part of Scripture, he knew the Sadducees would respect it. But, as in the case of John 10:35, the ultimate reason that appealing to Exodus 3:6 makes sense is not that its verb tense proves that inspiration extends to the very words of Scripture. Rather, it is that one has already established that Exodus 3:6 is Scripture and that all Scripture is inspired. Since it is God's word, the words in it are the ones he chose, but that's the point that proves that inspiration extends to the very words of Scripture, not that the verb tense in Exodus 3:6 fits the point Jesus wants to make.

And, the Matthew 22:44 passage suffers the same analysis and fate. In Matthew 22:41–44 Jesus asked the Pharisees questions about the Messiah. Whose son, Jesus asked, is the Messiah? The Pharisees replied that he is David's son. In verses 43–45 we read that Jesus answered, "How then doth David in spirit call him Lord, saying, The LORD said unto my Lord, Sit thou on my right hand, till I make thine enemies thy footstool?' If David then call him Lord, how is he his son?" (KJV).

Jesus here quotes Psalm 110:1 and affirms that David wrote it. In effect, he also certifies that the verse is inspired, because he says that David, in the Spirit (meaning he wrote with the Spirit guiding him), wrote Psalm 110:1. The crux of Jesus's "riddle" hinges on the suffix (in the Hebrew) "my" on the Hebrew word "Lord" (la'donî). If the Messiah will be David's Son, why then does the father (David) call his Son (the Messiah) his (the father's) Lord? No one listening to Jesus could answer this riddle, and Matthew adds (v. 46) that from that day onward, no one dared ask him any further questions.

Now, there is no doubt that Jesus here makes his point by appealing to Scripture, and it is also true that without the suffix "my" on the Hebrew word "Lord," Jesus couldn't make his point by appealing to this passage. But is it the suffix that makes us say inspiration extends to the very words of Scripture, or isn't the point that Jesus uses this verse because he believes the whole thing to be God's word? Put differently, David could have written this verse without divine inspiration and said the same thing. Would Jesus then have appealed to it to make his point? Possibly, but not if he wanted his point to rest on something irrefutable—the word of God. If Psalm 110:1 is merely the words of a human writer, then the Pharisees might simply slough off this passage as mistaken and/ or irrelevant as the words of a mere human. The reason they couldn't give such a response to what Jesus said isn't because of the suffix on "Lord" but because they agreed with him that Psalm 110 is God's word. So what really proves that inspiration extends to the very words of Scripture is not something like the suffix on "Lord" in Psalm 110, but the belief, grounded in Scriptures that teach it, that all Scripture is God's word. Once you grant that God inspired all of Scripture, then, of course, we can agree that David wrote what he did "in the Spirit." So, the fact that Jesus's argument hinges on the suffix on the word "Lord" wouldn't matter without the prior statement that David wrote the whole verse "in the Spirit," and without the belief, proved on other biblical grounds, that if something is written under the Holy Spirit's supervision, it is God's word.

The fourth and perhaps most frequently quoted passage intended to show that inspiration extends to the very words of Scripture is Galatians 3:16. In the verses that precede 3:16 Paul affirms that Christ has redeemed us from the curse of the law so that "the blessing of Abraham might come to the Gentiles" through Jesus Christ (v. 14). But how can this be so, since it means that blessings and promises were to come to and through Abraham's descendants, none of whom were Jews? While it is true that Abraham's descendants were not Gentiles, that doesn't mean Gentiles could not be blessed through Abraham's seed. In fact, God had promised Abraham that in (or, we might say, "by" or "through") his seed all the families of the earth would be blessed (see Gen. 22:18). In Galatians 3:16 Paul plays upon this biblical language, focusing on the singular use of "seed," to make the point about Gentiles being blessed through Abraham's seed. He writes, "Now to Abraham and his seed were the promises made. He saith not, 'And to seeds, as of many; but as of one, And to thy seed, which is Christ'" (KJV).

As James Boice notes, this is a most interesting passage because the term "seed," though singular, often is used in a collective sense to refer to a whole group of people. In Scriptures where God talks to Abraham about his seed (Gen. 12:7; 15:5; 22:17, 18), invariably the word is in the singular, though arguably most, if not all, of the references just cited use this singular term in a collective sense. Paul, in order to avoid such ambiguity, makes a point to show that he is thinking of "seed" not in a collective sense but in a sense that allows it to refer only to one person. And, he names that person: Christ. It is through Abraham's seed, Christ, that the blessing of Abraham (v. 14) can come to the Gentiles who, biologically speaking, are not Abraham's seed.[21]

What is quite interesting here is that Paul could have made his point by saying that "seed" can be used collectively to refer to a lot of people, or in a narrower sense to refer to one person. Rather than make this more technical linguistic point about possible usages of the word "seed," Paul chooses to make the point in a way that all of his readers are more likely to understand, namely, by comparing the singular ("seed") with the plural ("seeds"). But since Paul's point is really about a singular use of the word rather than a collective one, hasn't he really missed the point? Not at all, once we remember what the point is! The point is that Jesus, the seed of Abraham, is the means by whom Gentiles can get the promises made to Abraham and his descendants. That point Paul makes with crystal clarity!

---

[21] James Montgomery Boice, *Galatians*, in *EBC*, ed. Frank E. Gaebelein, vol. 10 (Grand Rapids, MI: Zondervan, 1976), 462–463. Boice makes the basic point about seed being singular but normally having a collective sense and about Paul narrowing the focus of the term to one person. The development of this idea is mine.

But what about Paul's appeal to what the Scripture says and the fact that it says "seed," not "seeds"? Here again, Paul says nothing false. Look up the Genesis passages cited above and you will see that all of them use "seed" in the singular. Of course, the collective notion of "seed" is in view in most, if not all, of the Genesis references, but Paul intends to stay away from that point, because his point is not about word usage. It is about Christ, as the seed of Abraham, being the "door" to Gentiles participating in the blessings promised to Abraham and his seed.

Perhaps readers will agree, but wonder why I am devoting so much space to this Galatians text. The reason is that it is this passage which is often cited as the prime example that proves that inspiration extends to the choice of the very words of Scripture, because Paul's argument hinges on whether a specific word of Scripture is singular rather than plural. It is true that Paul appeals to the fact that "seed" is singular, not plural, to make his theological point about Christ as the seed of Abraham. It is also true that there are Scriptures in Genesis where God speaks to Abraham about his future seed, and those passages use the singular for "seed."

Beyond those two points, however, appeal to this passage to prove that inspiration extends to the very choice of Scripture's words falls apart. It does so for two major reasons. The first is the problem we saw with the John and Matthew passages. The argument in all of these passages appeals to something said in a given OT passage (in the case of Galatians 3, several OT passages) of Scripture. But even if those passages hadn't been written under divine inspiration, they might have read the same way, and then appeal to them wouldn't necessarily seem all that significant. The reason that appeal to those passages makes a difference is that we already know from other biblical teaching that all of Scripture is inspired. But then it is the fact of inspiration alone that makes us take Paul's argument based on these Scriptures seriously, not the fact that they use "seed" in the singular rather than in the plural. Hence, the fact of "seed" being singular in the cited OT passages does not in itself prove that inspiration extends to the very choice of Scripture's words. The broader fact that all of Scripture is inspired is what allows us to claim that inspiration extends to any part of it!

The second reason that appeal in this case to a specific detail about OT Scriptures won't prove the intended point about inspiration is the fact that Paul's argument intends to narrow the focus to one seed, Jesus, but the word Paul uses, *sperma* (singular), is used in a collective sense in the passages of Genesis to which Paul would be referring. And, of course, the collective sense of "seed" is not germane to Paul's point about Christ as *the* seed of Abraham! So, if you really force us to focus on exactly what some OT passages not only say but mean, Paul's theological point about Christ is in trouble, because "seed" in those OT passages, though singular in form, is collective in sense! Hence, to take everything involved with the meaning of "seed" in those OT passages as *proving* that inspiration extends to the very choice of Scripture's words is both wrongheaded and endangers the important theological point Paul makes about Christ (this is so because "seed" in the OT passages is used in a collective sense, and Paul's focus is on one seed, Christ).

What should we say, then, about this third line of argument (the one that appeals to the Gospels and Galatians passages) for inspiration extending to Scripture's very words? Is it useless? While I hope you see that it doesn't prove what it intends to show, I also believe it is not entirely useless. If we believe *on other grounds* that all of Scripture, including the very words used, is inspired (and we should), and if we believe that the divine author always knew how NT writers would use the OT (and we should), then we can see beautiful examples of divine providence at work in OT books to prepare the way for points that NT books would make by appealing for support to things written in the OT. We shouldn't be surprised that an omniscient Holy Spirit would, throughout the history of the writing of the Bible, prepare the way for the content of biblical books to be written later. That tells us something important about the unity of our Bible and about the omniscience and providential action of its divine author. Those are not insignificant truths, but they aren't the points theologians intend to make when they cite these passages as proof that inspiration extends to Scripture's very words.

None of this should be misunderstood. Ample evidence has already been presented (without this third line of argument) that inspiration extends to the very choice of biblical words. In addition, as Erickson rightly affirms, the "words-versus-thoughts" question is a bogus issue.[22] For how can concepts be communicated to biblical writers (or anyone else) without using language? And if a concept requires pristine clarity, then the words used to divulge it to the biblical writer will need to be precise. This idea that anyone could inspire thoughts without the use of actual words goes contrary to the most fundamental intuitions of philosophy of language, and of common sense.

### Thesis Seven: Scripture Contains Many Forms of Revelation, and Is One Form Itself

According to Karl Barth, Scripture is a record of and witness to revelation, but not revelation itself. Rather, the content of revelation is God himself given in personal encounter with individuals. Such a personal encounter is one of God's mighty acts. In an attempt to distance themselves from such a view

---

[22] Erickson, *Christian Theology*, 240.

about Scripture, some evangelicals have emphasized propositional revelation, Scripture, to the point of deemphasizing the many and various forms in which God has revealed himself. They believe in natural and special revelation, but the latter tends to be reduced only to Scripture and to Christ (the highest form of divine revelation).

This is unfortunate, because there are actually many different forms of revelation, natural and special, and that helps us understand the nature of the Scriptures we possess. Scripture, of course, is a form of special revelation. In this chapter, I have offered ample proof of its being God's word, not just a witness or signpost pointing to the word. But there is much more to say about Scripture than just that it is a form of special revelation.

While Scripture is not a form of natural revelation, nor is natural revelation Scripture, Scripture contains passages that speak of various forms of natural revelation (see chapter 2). Scriptures that speak of natural revelation underscore the fact that natural revelation exists, and at the same time those biblical passages are part of a form of special revelation, Scripture.

In addition, Scripture recounts times when God spoke directly to someone, or did so in a dream or a vision. It also tells of times when an angel delivered God's message, and other occasions when revelation was communicated by a theophany. Scripture sometimes says that revelation occurred, but doesn't relate the content revealed. Because records of times when God revealed himself are part of Scripture (which is a form of special revelation), those records are themselves revelation.

Scripture also records miracles performed not only by God but also by various OT and NT humans acting on God's behalf. These miraculous acts, when originally done, were revelation to those who witnessed them. The scriptural accounts of those acts are themselves revelation as well, because they are part of Scripture.

Of course, Christ is the highest form of divine revelation. His whole life, death, and resurrection while on earth revealed God to his contemporaries. Thankfully, Scripture records what he said and did (and what happened to him); otherwise we might have only very skimpy and vague information about him. Biblical passages about Christ are not themselves Christ, nor do they miraculously become Christ. Still, they are more than just witnesses or signposts pointing to Christ, God's highest revelation. Those passages are part of Scripture, and since Scripture is special revelation, *passages* about Christ's deeds and words are themselves also special revelation.

Some may wonder why I am spending so much space on these points, because they seem rather obvious. I do so in part because we should take seriously something the Barthians claim about Scripture. Scripture contains many accounts of times when God revealed himself to people in one way or another. In our haste to distance ourselves from the Barthian notion that the content of revelation cannot be information, propositions about God, I fear that many have also rejected the idea of Scripture as a witness to revelation as well. As Scripture recounts various times when God revealed himself in one way or another, it is in fact a witness to revelation. But—and this is a crucial disagreement with Barthians—Scripture is so much more than just a witness! Scripture itself, and so the evangelical doctrine of inspiration, requires that all of Scripture, regardless of any passage's contents, is revelation! So, Scripture is more than just a witness to revelation, but that doesn't mean that it isn't at all a witness of many times and ways when God revealed himself to people. Hence, we must rid ourselves of this false dichotomy—that Scripture is *either* a witness to revelation *or* revelation itself. Scripture is actually both.

Then, Scripture also contains many passages that don't record revelatory events that others saw and/or heard; rather, in many instances, the Holy Spirit revealed information to the human author available nowhere else and then superintended its transfer into the pages of Scripture. Here one thinks of OT wisdom literature and the didactic contents of many NT epistles, but these are only examples of the kinds of content now in view.

*In sum, Scripture, as God's word, is a major form of God's special revelation. But that doesn't limit the kinds of literature to be found in Scripture. Scripture contains narratives about times when God revealed himself to one person or another. It also records instances when some person, perhaps the human author himself, received a vision or dream from the Lord, and then it tells us the content of the same. Scripture also includes history; texts rich in philosophical implication (Job; Ecclesiastes) and practical wisdom (Proverbs); predictions of the future (prophecies of the first and second advent); accounts of miracles; accounts of the moral and spiritual teachings of Jesus (the Gospels); passages where writers share their feelings of personal sorrow and triumph and their praise for God's hand in their lives (Psalms); information relevant to constructing a biblical worldview (didactic passages of the OT and NT); and so much more. Hence, Scripture's contents give it a variegated texture that is as rich and diverse as the knowledge, interests, and personalities of its various human authors and its divine author. It records information about the many forms in which revelation came, and Scripture itself is a distinct form of revelation.*

*Thesis Eight: Both Old and New Testaments Are the Inspired Word of God*

As we studied biblical teaching on inspiration, we noted that many of the most crucial passages were written either when only the OT existed and was recognized as God's word, or when only part of the NT was written and deemed to be Scripture. Hence, several of the key passages on the nature of Scripture refer specifically to the OT. This is true of OT and much apostolic testimony about Scripture, and true of most of Jesus's comments. Jesus and various OT and NT writers firmly believed the OT to be God's word.

As for NT inspiration, there is less evidence, but it is still convincing. I noted the implications of Jesus's teaching in John 14, 15, and 16 about the Holy Spirit, who would be sent after Jesus's departure. I also mentioned Paul's claims in 1 Corinthians 2:13 about the Spirit's relation to the words he and others spoke. I argued that these passages promised the Holy Spirit's ministry in the apostles' lives, so that when they preached, they would get the message right. And, I explained why this same ministry was also intended to help the apostles when they wrote of Christ and his teachings. All of this amounted to Jesus promising the inspiration of the NT, which hadn't been written during his earthly lifetime. Paul's words in 1 Corinthians 2 affirm the same. And, we saw Pauline and Petrine Scriptures that affirm that the apostles' writings are God's word and equally authoritative as OT Scriptures.

Hebrews 1:1–2, an NT passage not yet considered, is also relevant to the NT's inspiration. It says: "God, who at sundry times and in divers manners spoke in time past unto the fathers by the prophets, hath in these last days spoken unto us by his Son, whom he hath appointed heir of all things, by whom also he made the worlds; . . . " (KJV). Verse 1 refers to special revelation in the OT era through prophets and affirms that God revealed himself in the OT era in a variety of ways (i.e., using various forms of revelation). Verse 2 speaks of how God reveals himself "in these last days." I agree with commentators who say that the "last days" doesn't refer to the very end of all things (though the writer of Hebrews might have thought those days weren't far off), but rather to days of God's revealing himself. The writer says that, as opposed to OT times, God is now revealing himself through his Son.

It is important that the writer of Hebrews does *not* say that God is revealing himself in these last days *only* through his Son. That is, he doesn't say that no other forms of special revelation can occur, nor does he mean that there is no longer any natural revelation. Instead, his point is that Christ is the culmination of divine revelation, and in these last days of revelation, he is the main form thereof.

During his time on earth, Jesus revealed God to his contemporaries in his very person, in his teachings, and in his deeds. His death and resurrection also marvelously revealed God. After Jesus died, rose, and ascended, his contemporaries had memories of his life and teachings, but no longer experienced his physical presence. Still, many eyewitnesses knew and told the stories about Jesus, and in that way Jesus's revelation of God continued even after his ascension.

But before long, eyewitnesses died, one by one. Once all were dead, including Christ's apostles, had divine revelation ended? If no one alive had firsthand knowledge of Christ, and if no one had written anything about his life, teachings, death, and resurrection, God's ability to speak through his Son to future generations would have been significantly limited.[23]

Put simply, how would God speak through Jesus after Jesus's ascension? Jesus answers that it would continue to happen through the Holy Spirit's ministry to his disciples (John 14; 15; 16). But how would they continue to reveal God through Jesus? First by their preaching as eyewitnesses, but also as people who were attuned to the Holy Spirit's teaching ministry. But if they revealed Christ only through their preaching, before long they would die and God's speaking through Christ would seemingly end. Thankfully, God avoided that circumstance. The same Holy Spirit who taught Jesus's disciples as they preached also superintended their writing of the NT. Because the Holy Spirit inspired them to write about Jesus and then ensured that those writings were preserved, God continues to reveal himself through his Son to later generations, including ours.

All the evidences presented in this chapter lead to the conclusion that both the OT and NT are God's inspired word. Jesus's testimony confirms this, and so does the testimony of the OT and NT writers.

### INSPIRATION AND INCARNATION: IS THE LATTER AN APT METAPHOR FOR UNDERSTANDING THE FORMER?

Jesus is the very Word of God, and so is Scripture. Some have thought that these two facts beg us to draw an analogy between the incarnate Christ and the incarnate Scripture.[24] Actually, it need only suggest the ambiguity and polysemy of language, for there are very many differences between the person Jesus Christ and the Scriptures.[25] Still, in Jesus there is a combination of the divine and the human, and the same is true of Scripture. So, many emphasize an analogy between the incarnate Word and the inspired words of God.

In recent centuries some have appealed to this analogy to affirm that if the two Words are analogous, then, since the incarnate Word is sinless, the

---

[23] Here I speak strictly from the perspective of how much information would have been available about Jesus through normal sources a researcher might consult in preparing to write a book, or for merely gaining accurate knowledge of who Jesus was and what he did. Of course, after all eyewitnesses died, God could have revealed by various forms of direct communication any information about Christ needed by later generations.

[24] Nigel M. de S. Cameron, "Incarnation and Inscripturation: The Christological Analogy in the Light of Recent Discussion," *The Scottish Bulletin of Evangelical Theology* 3 (1985): 35.

[25] The key here isn't sameness of phraseology, for depending on the context, the exact same words may mean any number of different things. For example, think of all the different uses of the English word "head," including slang ones. The fact that this word can be applied to a number of different things doesn't mean there is an analogy between all things rightly called head.

inscripturated word must be errorless.[26] In contrast, Peter Enns's recent *Inspiration and Incarnation: Evangelicals and the Problem of the Old Testament* has appealed to the incarnational analogy to demonstrate just the opposite about Scripture. That is, just as Jesus was fully human (and his humanity was not eclipsed by his deity), the dual authorship of Scripture means that there will be genuine marks of its human authors. Rather than sublimating these elements to the divine authorship of Scripture, we should recognize Scripture's human elements, even though they introduce into Scripture items of "diversity" (Enns's favorite term) that we wouldn't expect in a book also authored by God. These palpable evidences of human limitation convince us that this is a genuinely human book, not just a truly divine book.

What are the marks of this humanity? Enns proposes to cover three different topics that relate to the OT. First, in various places the OT looks like other literature from the ancient world. If the Bible is God's word, why does it fit so well with other ancient writings? Second, Enns notes theological diversity in the OT. One might think that a monotheistic faith would tell just one story about its God and his relation to his people. Instead, OT writers say different things about the same topic, some apparently contradictory, or at least proposing a difference of opinion. Finally, Enns discusses the way NT writers use the OT. They use it in different ways, even if they quote the same passage in several instances. Some uses of the OT make it appear that NT writers have taken an OT passage out of context and used it as they wished.[27] Though these features of Scripture might trouble some, Enns argues that they are expected results of a genuinely human book.

But Enns knows that evangelicals have never been satisfied with this alone, for Scripture also has a divine author. So, how should we think of divine and human in Scripture? Enns believes the starting point for this discussion should be *"as Christ is both God and human, so is the Bible."*[28] Why does Enns think this is such an apt analogy? Hear him as he draws some of the most basic comparisons between Christ and Scripture:

> In other words, we are to think of the Bible in the same way that Christians think about Jesus. Christians confess that Jesus is both God and human at the same time. He is not half-God and half-human. He is not sometimes one and other times the other. He is not essentially one and only apparently the other. . . .
>
> This way of thinking of Christ is analogous to thinking about the Bible. In the same way that Jesus is—*must be*—both God and human, the Bible is

---

[26] See Cameron, "Incarnation and Inscripturation," for various evangelical divines who have used this analogy to affirm inerrancy of the biblical text.

[27] Peter Enns, *Inspiration and Incarnation: Evangelicals and the Problem of the Old Testament* (Grand Rapids, MI: Baker, 2005), 15–16.

[28] Ibid., 17.

also a divine and human book. Although Jesus was "*God* with us," he still completely assumed the cultural trappings of the world in which he lived. In fact, this is what is implied in "God *with us*." . . .

So, too, the Bible. It belonged in the ancient worlds that produced it. It was not an abstract, otherworldly book, dropped out of heaven. It was *connected to* and therefore *spoke to* those ancient cultures. The enculturated qualities of the Bible, therefore, are not extra elements that we can discard to get to the real point, the timeless truths. Rather, precisely because Christianity is a historical religion, God's word reflects the various historical moments in which Scripture was written. God acted and spoke in history. As we learn more and more about that history, we must gladly address the implications of that history for how we view the Bible, that is, what we should expect from it.[29]

Elsewhere Enns has presented evidence that some key theologians, including Warfield, A. A. Hodge, and Charles Hodge, wrote of the genuine humanity of Scripture. Though these theologians didn't question Scripture's inerrancy, they pointed to many features of Scripture that show that it was written at distinct times and cultures. These features, of course, reflect different understandings of the world than ours. The Old Princetonians used these characteristics to demonstrate the true human nature of Scripture, not to question its truth. In contrast, Enns proposes that comments from theologians not so warm to the notion of inerrancy suggest that we should grapple with these time-bound, culture-bound elements of Scripture and recognize that God's accommodation to the limitations of any generation of humans means that we won't always find claims in Scripture that square with what we know to be facts today.[30]

Though Enns talks at great length about inspiration, his actual focus is biblical inerrancy. That topic, and Enns's specific critiques of it, will be handled in later chapters. But we shouldn't dismiss him altogether at this point, for his work raises a significant question about inspiration. Many theologians throughout church history have thought it helpful to think of Scripture's nature along the lines of the nature of the incarnate Christ. That is, many have seen an analogy between the incarnation and Scripture's inspiration. My concern is whether that is a good analogy that helps to illumine our understanding of either Christology or Bibliology. Without this analogy, is something significant (about either Christ or Scripture) lost?

In reply, I must first briefly address the nature of analogies.[31] The most

---

[29] Ibid., 17–18.

[30] For discussion of these theologians and Enns's interpretation of what their claims about Scripture's humanity mean, see Peter Enns, "Preliminary Observations on an Incarnational Model of Scripture: Its Viability and Usefulness," *CTJ* 42 (2007): 219–236.

[31] See Cameron, "Incarnation and Inscripturation" (40–42), for further discussion of different types of analogies. For our purposes, the points I make in the text will suffice.

obvious point is universally acknowledged, namely, analogy is not identity. To say that two things are analogous doesn't mean either that they are numerically one or that all characteristics of both items are the same. Hence, it is always possible to point out trivial differences between compared items, but those don't prove the analogy is invalid. In contrast, if there are differences in qualities that are at the heart of why the analogy was drawn in the first place, that is reason to ask if the analogy actually illumines anything worth knowing.

Second, I note that some analogous characteristics are clearly stated while others are only implied, because a quality of one analogue is known (and perhaps stated), while it isn't clear that the other analogue has the same characteristic. An example illustrates this point. In Romans 5, Paul draws a sustained analogy between Adam and Christ. Some general things true of both are analogous. Both Adam and Christ are heads of their race, and their acts have profound influence on all members of their respective races. But there are clearly differences. Adam is natural/biological head of his race, but Jesus had no children and wasn't the first, biologically speaking, member of his race. He is the soteriological head of his race. And, while all members of Adam's and Christ's races are impacted by their deeds, in Adam all *die*, while members of Christ's race are all *made alive* by his deed on Calvary.

Because Christ is no one's biological head (while Adam is biological head of all humans), Christ, as head of his race, must have acted as a representative for his race. In Romans 5 Paul doesn't actually say that Adam served as representative of his race. Still, many theologians have believed that if Adam and Christ are truly analogous heads of their races, Adam must be representative head of his race, not just its natural head. Thus, this characteristic, they claim, is unstated but should still be understood.[32] Those of a different persuasion believe that since Paul didn't say Adam acted as federal head, and since other key things about Adam and Christ aren't analogous, we don't really have a right to interpolate (i.e., fill in) the notion that Adam was also federal head of his race.

Those acquainted with the debate over the imputation of Adam's sin will be familiar with the above arguments. My purpose is not now to solve that issue but to use it as an illustration. Of what? Specifically, it illustrates a distinction between a loose and a strict analogy, a third point about analogies. When dealing with a loose analogy, some characteristics of one of the items being compared match the same characteristics of the other analogue. But with a

---

[32] To be the seminal or natural head of the human race means that one is biologically related to those who are born after the head was created, and that the seminal head is the first person who existed in the long line of all the humans who have ever lived. To be a federal head means that one is chosen to represent everyone else in one's race. It doesn't require the federal head to be the first person who ever lived or that there is any biological relation to those the federal head represents. According to Scripture, Adam was the natural head of the human race. Various theologians, commenting specifically on the imputation of Adam's sin to the human race, say that God also chose him to be federal head of the race. So, whatever Adam did impacted not only himself but the whole human race, for he acted as our representative.

loose analogy, some qualities of both analogues differ from one another. The differences don't mean the two aren't analogous, but only that the analogy is a loose or general one. Often, as well, the characteristics being compared are stated in a rather general way. For example, in a loose analogy it is sufficient to say that the incarnate Christ is both divine and human and so is Scripture, without becoming any more specific about the exact nature of the humanity and divinity of either Christ or Scripture. If the characteristics of such analogues were more precisely stated, some qualities of the analogues might not actually be analogous to one another.

In contrast, a strict analogy involves matching all characteristics crucial to the reason(s) for which the analogy was drawn. That is, each quality of one analogue bears a one-to-one correspondence with the same characteristic of the other analogue. When dealing with a strict analogy, if some comparison between the two analogues isn't stated, but all the other key comparisons are affirmed, interpolating an analogy between the unstated characteristic of the two is deemed to be warranted. For example, suppose there are ten parallel characteristics at the heart of why the analogy was drawn. Suppose also that for nine of those characteristics the attribute is clearly predicated of both analogues. Suppose further that the tenth quality is attributed to one analogue but not to the other. The tenth characteristic isn't denied of the other; it just isn't stated. In such a case, if one assumes that the unstated quality is actually an attribute of the analogue because the quality has been predicated of the first analogue, this sort of interpolation is thought appropriate. There would be little objection to "filling in the blank" when all other "blanks" are stated and parallel.

So, is the analogy between the incarnation and Scripture loose or strict? This is an important question, first, because Scripture nowhere states such an analogy. Hence, the analogy is a deduction that theologians and exegetes have made on the basis of what Scripture actually says about Christ and about Scripture. This shouldn't surprise us, because nowhere does Scripture speak of the hypostatic union of Christ or even explicitly say that he is a fully divine and fully human person. Of course, scriptural teaching about Christ amounts to such claims, but Scripture doesn't explicitly say so. Similarly, as we have seen, the doctrine of Scripture's inspiration is clearly taught in Scripture, but nowhere does one find a formal definition of verbal, plenary inspiration. So, if we don't find these formal statements about Christ's and Scripture's nature, it isn't surprising that there is no clear biblical statement of an analogy between the incarnation and inspiration.

We must also determine whether the analogy is strict or loose because of what Enns thinks the analogy helps us see about Scripture. Enns emphasizes

Scripture's humanity, and he likes to talk about Scripture's diversity, but what he thinks this proves about Scripture isn't actually strictly analogous to what he believes and what we know about the incarnate Christ.

So, is the analogy between Christ and Scripture loose or strict? I maintain that if the analogy should be drawn at all, it is a loose one. Furthermore, some things Enns says about Scripture actually show that it is *not* analogous to the incarnation. If that is so, then Enns's attempt to get us to reject inerrancy on the basis of an alleged analogy between the incarnation and inspiration falls flat! Given the failures in analogy that I shall note, failures apart from those Enns presents, there is reason to be suspicious about the value of this analogy altogether. This is my third and final claim, namely, that if one can use this analogy at all, it is only a very loose analogy whose terms are stated in a very general way. In fact, the analogous characteristics are stated in such general terms that I doubt that this analogy illumines much of anything about either Christ or Scripture.

How can I support these claims? I propose to do so through the three tables below. The first table lists ways in which Jesus and Scripture are analogous. These aren't trivial characteristics, but I note that they are all stated very generally. If we become much more precise, as in the second table, the analogy begins to break down. All of that supports the points I made in the previous paragraph.

The first table below shows six different ways that Jesus and Scripture are analogous. The characteristics chosen are important to the incarnation/inspiration analogy that Enns wants to exploit. The table's meaning should be very clear, but a brief word of explanation is in order. When comparing the "origin" of Jesus and of Scripture, I'm not suggesting that there was some time when Jesus's divine nature didn't exist, and then it later came into being. Rather, my point is about the incarnation's source and Scripture's source. Then, the table refers to an ancient Christological heresy known as docetism. According to docetists, Jesus appeared to have a human nature but didn't actually have a real one. Hence, during his earthly life he seemed to be human, but upon death his human nature, which wasn't, after all, actually real, ceased to exist. The point of the analogy is that Jesus didn't just seem to have a human nature; he actually had a real one which, once created, doesn't stop existing. As for Scripture, it shows evidence of human authorship. If the authors were only taking dictation, then they weren't really contributing anything, and the appearance of a human element in Scripture is just that—apparent, not real.

Then, note the final category of comparison. We know that Jesus was sinless. As fully human, he could be tempted, but he never fell into sin, because his divine nature ensured that his human nature didn't yield to temptation. As to Scripture, the analogy seems to be an errorless Bible, but I have put asterisks by this entry. The reason is that this is the very issue under contention when evaluating Enns's proposal. Despite Jesus's sinless nature, Enns argues that unless the human authors of Scripture are taken seriously, the analogy won't work. What does this mean? Human beings are capable of error—no one disagrees with that. But, even more, Enns believes he sees (and that we, too, should see) reasons in Scripture itself that suggest that human proneness to error was not checked by the divine author. But if Enns is right, the analogy fails, for the parallel to a sinless Christ is an errorless Scripture. And yet, Enns wants us to think of Scripture incarnationally, for only then can we see what is really present in it—diversity, which for Enns equals error.

Clearly, Enns's logic is faulty, for if what he says about Scripture is correct, then on this very important point Christ and Scripture aren't analogous; the analogy fails! And, if it does, that calls into question the foundation of Enns's whole project. What he says about diversity in Scripture may have some merit; it is undercut, however, because the analogy between incarnation and inspiration that he so highly prizes doesn't work at this very important point.

**TABLE 6.1: ANALOGIES**

|  | JESUS | SCRIPTURE |
|---|---|---|
| ORIGIN | Holy Spirit and Human | Holy Spirit and Human Authors |
| NATURE | Fully Human, Fully Divine | Fully Human, Fully Divine |
| REFERRED TO AS | Word of God | Word of God |
| FIT WITH SURROUNDINGS | Lived in and Assumed Culture of His Day to Serve It | Accommodation to Culture of Times when Written |
| RELATION TO DOCETISM | Non-Docetic–Truly Human | Non-Docetic–Truly Human |
| RELATION TO SIN | Sinless–Divine Governs Human Nature | ***Errorless–Divine Author Guides Human Authors |

From the table above, it is clear that there are enough similarities between the incarnate Jesus and inspired Scripture to think there is at least a loose analogy. But the next table disproves a strict analogy. At least two things should be clear from it. One is the obvious point that in significant respects Jesus and Scripture are not analogous. The other is that the comparisons focus on much more specific qualities than was the case when plotting analogies. This tells us, since the qualities aren't analogous, that we don't have a strict analogy. It should also warn us not to make too much of this analogy.

In the table below, "origin" means what it did in the previous table. As to the entry "# of Substances," the point is to note how many distinct things, ontologically speaking, there are in each case, and also to state how the distinct things relate to one another. As for Jesus, the point is that he has both a fully human and a fully divine nature (two natures). Even so, he is one unified person, not a schizophrenic. However, the unity of the natures doesn't mean that attributes of his divine nature get mixed with attributes of his human nature (and vice versa) so that his human nature is somewhat divine and his divine nature is somewhat human. In contrast, Scripture has only one nature—it is words. This one book has both human and a divine author, but it isn't always clear which words come from the Holy Spirit and which from the human author. That is, it isn't as easy to distinguish the divine parts from the human parts of Scripture as it is to distinguish Christ's two natures. Hence, on that item, the analogy breaks down, as it does with the other five items compared in the table below.

## TABLE 6.2: FAILURES OF ANALOGY

|  | JESUS | SCRIPTURE |
|---|---|---|
| ORIGIN | Holy Spirit Active; Mary Passive | Divine and Human Authors Active |
| NATURE | A Person | A Thing—Book/Words |
| REFERRED TO AS | Word of God—Nonlinguistic | Word of God—Only Linguistic |
| HOW LONG TO CREATE | Incarnation at Once | Written over 1,500 Years |
| # OF SUBSTANCES | Two: One Human, One Divine, Both Distinct | One: A Book, Divine and Human Elements Blended Together |
| ACTS, ONCE CREATED | Many, but No Sin | No Acts because Not a Person/Agent |

Enns doesn't mention the failures in analogy noted above. He doesn't go into the detail contained in either of the first two tables. Nor are these analogies and failures of analogy stated in Scripture. I produced the tables comparing Christ and Scripture on the basis of things Scripture teaches about each and that we, as a result, know.

The first two tables confirm the first and third points I made prior to presenting the first table. Christ and Scripture have enough similarities to say they are analogous, but only loosely so. The failures in analogy make it impossible for this to be a strict analogy. And, since the items become so much more precise and specific when we talk about failures of analogy than when we talk about actual analogies, it is truly dubious whether this analogy illumines much at all.

The third table, which follows, suggests a major failure in Enns's logic. In this table I list things that Enns himself claims about Christ and about Scripture. Though he intends to show that there is reason to think of Scripture using an incarnational motif, he fails to see that the things he mentions actually show the incarnate Christ and Scripture not to be analogous. Hence, one wonders why Enns believes this is a helpful way to think of Scripture!

**TABLE 6.3: ENNS'S VIEWS–FAILURES OF ANALOGY**

|  | JESUS | SCRIPTURE |
|---|---|---|
| RELATION TO DOCETISM | Fully Human, but No Sin | Real Marks of Human, So Can and Does Have Errors |
| RELATION OF TWO NATURES | Divine Won't Let Human Nature Fall into Sin | Divine Author Didn't Stop Human Authors from Error |
| FIT WITH CULTURE | Assumed Culture to Serve It, but No Sin | Accommodation to Culture to Be Understood, Allows Errors |
| IMPACT OF CULTURE | Didn't Make Jesus Ordinary, Sinful, or Intellectually Mistaken | Impacts So We Must Expect Errors to Reflect Cultures and Times when Written |

In sum, the three tables above show serious problems with Enns's proposal that we should think of Scripture with an incarnational analogy. But we must not conclude too much from this. It raises questions about the value of the analogy as Enns understands it. In short, he treats the analogy as a strict one, but when we look closely at Jesus and Scripture, it is easy to see failures in analogy. Those failures on key points, ones raised especially in the second table, should show anyone that this isn't a strict analogy. Because it is only a loose one, the way the logic of analogies works means that what Enns includes in the third table about Scripture is *not logically allowable interpolation*! I say this in part also because nothing in table 6.3 about Enns's views of Scripture is taught in Scripture itself. So, what he says about Scripture (as plotted in table 6.3) is *speculation*, not logically legitimate "filling in of the blanks" in comparing Christ and Scripture!

But we must not conclude too much. Table 6.1 shows that there is an analogy between incarnation and inspiration. It is just that tables 6.2 and 6.3 show that the analogy is a loose one. Hence, the only way for Enns to say correctly what table 6.3 says about Scripture is for him to provide concrete evidence that Scripture is guilty of his accusations. The reasons Enns thinks Scripture's humanity has allowed errors in it need to be answered, and they will be in the chapters on inerrancy. My point here is that Enns's argument against inerrancy, *based on an analogy between incarnation and inspiration*, doesn't prove his case. For his argument to have serious weight, the analogy would have to be a strict one, but as shown, there is only a loose analogy between incarnation and inspiration.

## SUMMARY DEFINITION OF VERBAL, PLENARY INSPIRATION

Verbal, plenary inspiration presupposes that God has revealed himself in human thought forms and language. Inspiration refers specifically to the process of transferring that revelation into written texts that we know as Scripture. God wanted many things he revealed to be available to more people than just those who first received it. Verbal, plenary inspiration involves both a divine and human authors of the words of Scripture. The Holy Spirit both revealed truth to the writers, and prompted them to write. He guided them to choose just the topics and words he wanted written. His constant superintendence of their writing guaranteed that what they wrote is what God wanted to say; Scripture is the word of God.

On the other hand, the human authors didn't take dictation from the Holy Spirit. Rather, using their own writing styles, vocabularies, and marks of personal interests, they composed the very words of Scripture that communicate exactly what God wanted them to say. Working under the Spirit's guidance didn't preclude them from doing research on the topics they addressed and even elaborating and explaining more fully the teachings of the OT and of Jesus himself. But all of this was done under the guidance of the Holy Spirit. The influence of the Holy Spirit did not remove the writers' freedom as they wrote. The Holy Spirit knew just what to do and to bring about in their lives in order to move them, without constraining them, to write what he wanted. But they chose the very words to match the concepts they were presenting, albeit under the guidance of the Holy Spirit. The attributes of being inspired and being the very word of God are true of all Scripture, including the very words the human writers chose. No part of Scripture is more or less inspired than any other. All Scripture resulted from God's revealing and inspiring activities, and all of it is profitable unto all good works.

# 11

---

# CHARACTERISTICS
# OF SCRIPTURE

# TRUE LIGHT

## Inerrancy and Infallibility

Revelation is a divine act. Inspiration is a divine act that secures some of what God has revealed in the written form of revelation known as Scripture. Inspiration also involves the work of the humans who, along with God, wrote Scripture. Illumination is also a divine act, but not something God does to the text of Scripture but rather to the mind, heart, and will of the reader.

In contrast, inerrancy and infallibility focus not so much on another divine action. Rather they are characteristics of the product of God's revealing and inspiring the Bible.

You would expect those who believe that God revealed and inspired Scripture also to affirm Scripture's inerrancy, but some in our day who call themselves "evangelical" believe that Scripture affirms some things that are not true. For some this mix of views is rather shocking, for it seems impossible that God would reveal information and superintend its writing as Scripture, and yet it would contain error.

Not so long ago the belief that a fully inspired Bible *has to be* fully inerrant was thoroughly ingrained in evangelical thinking. My seminary theology professor defined verbal plenary inspiration so as to include an inerrant Bible, and he wasn't at all unusual in doing so, as can easily be seen in most evangelical systematic theologies available during the first two-thirds or so of the twentieth century. When I began to teach in 1976, I did the same thing when I taught the doctrine of Scripture.

Before long, however, evangelical theologians no longer incorporated inerrancy in their definition of verbal plenary inspiration, because many thinkers questioned whether a fully inspired Bible had to be fully inerrant. They

232 □ Characteristics of Scripture

concluded that incorporating inerrancy in the very definition of inspiration was question begging. What question was begged? The question of whether a book fully inspired by God must be fully inerrant.

So, what did those who denied inerrancy put in its place? Some were still comfortable with calling Scripture infallible (though not everyone defined that concept in the same way), and all who thought of themselves as evangelical affirmed Scripture's authority—in some sense of authority. In fact, in our day even some nonevangelicals espouse biblical authority, depending on how it is defined.

I affirm inerrancy, infallibility, and authority, but these concepts must first be defined. Infallibility has been defined in so many distinct ways that it is clouded in ambiguity. I'll explain why, but my view is that it isn't a very helpful *term* in this discussion. Thus, my focus will be on inerrancy.

After clarifying the concept of inerrancy, I'll defend it biblically. Though some deny it, I shall argue that Scripture teaches its own inerrancy. After defending biblical inerrancy, the next chapters will address and answer various objections to inerrancy on the contemporary scene. My immediate task, however, is to present a working definition of inerrancy and explain it.

Put simply, *any assertion that matches reality is true or inerrant, and any claim that does not correspond to reality is false or errant.* Thus, inerrancy is about truth, but saying that only begins the discussion. I turn next to some basic definitions and distinctions.

## INITIAL DEFINITIONS AND DISTINCTIONS

Several distinctions will be useful in our discussion. The first was already raised in an earlier chapter, but its significance to this topic makes it worth repeating. It is the difference between *defining a term* and *defining a concept*. Some seem to think that the heart of the debate over inerrancy is the meaning of terms like "inerrancy," "infallibility," and "authority." While we should define these terms precisely, if possible, the inerrancy discussion is about much more than that. It is most fundamentally about (1) what sort of thing inerrancy is, and (2) whether Scripture teaches its own inerrancy and (3) can be shown to be inerrant.

What, then, is the term-concept distinction, and why is it important to this discussion? To define a *term* is to do a word study of its various *uses* in different contexts. Lexicographers turn the results of such study into lexicons or dictionaries. Word studies give us a term's semantic range; that is, they list the possible things a term might mean in any given context. That information can be very helpful if one translates a text from one language to another and wants to know the possible renderings of a given word. For those working within a language, a word study can help in deciding a term's meaning in an ambiguous passage.

A word study of *terms* for truth and error cannot, however, explain what kind of things truth and error are. That is the job of defining a *concept*. Consulting a word study may help in searching for a concept's meaning, but seeing, for example, what the word "true" means in various contexts won't elucidate the *concept* of truth, for different uses of terms for truth may in fact contradict one another, or they might have no relation to one another at all (for example, there is little apparent connection between the concepts of a true sentence and a true friend). Of course, a word study of the term "truth" may point to contexts where the nature of truth is discussed, but there are no guarantees that this will happen. And, one may also find a discussion of the concept of truth even if no term or word for truth appears at all.

So, what are we looking for in our study of inerrancy?[1] Theology is not *word* study but *conceptual* study. Thus, we want to know what the concepts of inerrancy and infallibility are, and whether Scripture predicates those qualities of itself. If so, is biblical inerrancy defensible?

In contemporary discussions about inerrancy, theologians are even divided over which *English* term to use (and how to define it) for this characteristic of Scripture. Should we refer to Scripture's inerrancy, infallibility, or authority, or to combinations of the three? And whichever *term(s)* we choose, how do we define them so as to clarify the *concepts* in view with these *terms*?

Clearly, this discussion can become rather complicated! Even so, our first task is defining the concepts of inerrancy and infallibility. Our second is to choose appropriate English terms to designate these concepts.[2]

Since this discussion is about characteristics of Scripture, and since Scripture is language, I note some distinctions about the nature of language. First, we can distinguish a word's sense and its reference. The sense/reference distinction, of course, also applies to phrases, whole sentences, paragraphs, and documents. A term's sense is its "dictionary meaning." In addition to a word's definition, there is also the object, action, state of affairs in the world to which it points or refers. This doesn't mean that every word in every sentence must refer to something, but only that many words are used frequently to do so. Of course, words in isolation from other words refer to no specific thing in the

---

[1] In recent theological discussions it isn't hard to find instances of confusing the meaning of terms for truth and error with the meaning of the concepts. In fact, a biblical word study of these terms is often taken *to be* a conceptual study. See examples from both sides on the inerrancy debates: David Hubbard says that truth and error must be defined biblically, after which he offers a brief word study of "error" (David Hubbard, "The Current Tensions: Is There a Way Out?," in *Biblical Authority*, ed. Jack Rogers [Waco, TX: Word, 1977], 167–168). For the same kind of method and result, see Roger Nicole, "The Biblical Concept of Truth," in *Scripture and Truth*, ed. D. A. Carson and John Woodbridge (Grand Rapids, MI: Zondervan, 1983), 288–296.

[2] In any language, the task in this chapter is conceptual clarification. Even so, I suspect that in non-English languages there may also be a question about the best terminology for these concepts. Given the nature of this series in theology, our concern is with the concepts but also with the English terms best suited to denote the concepts.

world. Only within the context of a sentence does a word refer to some specific thing or state of affairs in the world.[3]

Second, what does it mean to teach something using language? This is an important question because scholars debate whether Scripture *teaches* its own inerrancy. In a most fundamental sense, to teach something is to assert or deny its truth. But how, for example, does one teach moral commands, since they are not per se assertions? Typically, moral rules are taught by saying, "here are rules to govern behavior." This assertion will be followed by a series of imperatives—"don't steal"; "don't lie"; "don't commit adultery."

Of course, "teaching" also happens by *showing* learners *how to do* something. If I want to teach someone how to tie a knot, I may explain how to do it, but I am more likely to *show* him how to tie the knot.

Teaching something by *showing how* or *modeling* are ways to teach something by our actions, but they aren't the way to teach something by means of language. To teach something using language, I must either assert or deny it. This may seem obvious, but there is a point I must make. Consider the following illustration. Suppose I own a cat, and she is resting on a mat in the family room. A guest who likes cats very much asks, "Where is your cat this morning?" Now, imagine that my guest is hard of hearing, so I write on a piece of paper, "the kat is resting on a mat in my family room."

I have just "taught" my friend something, but what? Have I taught something about my cat's location? Have I taught him how to spell "cat"? Or both? In answer, remember that *only an assertion or denial* of some state of affairs qualifies as *teaching, using language*. Since the sentence I wrote to answer my friend's question only *asserts* something about my cat's location, that is all it teaches.

Some may think I also taught that "k-a-t" is the proper way to spell "cat," although of course it isn't. But it is just false that I have taught anything about *how to spell* "cat" just by writing "kat" on paper. In order for me to teach something about how to spell "cat," my sentence would have to read, "the kat is resting on a mat in the family room, and 'k-a-t' is the proper way to spell 'cat.'" The sentence I just wrote *does* assert something about how to spell "cat." But obviously, the sentence I wrote in answer to my friend's question about my cat's location *contains no assertion about how to spell any word*. Hence, by misspelling a word, I don't teach that the wrong spelling is right, unless I add (in the imagined case) "and 'k-a-t' is the right

---

[3] For the sense/reference distinction see Gottlob Frege, "Sense and Reference," *Philosophical Writings*, trans. T. Geach and M. Black (Oxford: Blackwell, 1952). For the point that only in a sentence does a word refer, see Paul Ricoeur, "Creativity in Language," *Philosophy Today* 17 (Summer 1973): 98; and John Wallace, "Only in the Context of a Sentence Do Words Have Any Meaning," in *Contemporary Perspectives in the Philosophy of Language*, ed. Peter A. French, Theodore E. Uehling Jr., and Howard K. Wettstein (Minneapolis: University of Minnesota Press, 1979), 305–311. For discussion of all of these points see my "Truth: Relationship of Theories of Truth to Hermeneutics," in *Hermeneutics, Inerrancy, and the Bible*, ed. Earl D. Radmacher and Robert D. Preus (Grand Rapids, MI: Zondervan, 1984).

way to spell 'cat'." Since I don't affirm that, I'm not teaching it, despite what may appear to be the case.

It is important to remember this point about what it means to *teach* something using language as we read any book, including Scripture. This is so because we want to be clear and accurate about what an author actually espouses/teaches in his or her writing. Inerrancy and infallibility are about what Scripture actually teaches/asserts. To teach something using language requires asserting or affirming it.

Finally, many evangelicals, myself included, believe that inerrancy is about truth, but what is truth? Below I shall offer an extended discussion of theories of truth, but now I note a basic distinction about truth. I want to distinguish *propositional truth, truth of a person,* and *personal truth. Propositional truth* is a characteristic of language, though as we shall see, many kinds of sentences can be propositionally true or false, whereas other kinds can be neither true nor false. In speaking of propositional truth we want to know what, in general, makes sentences true or false, and whether a particular sentence is true or false.

*Truth of a person* is entirely different. It appeals to qualities of character that humans may possess. To say that someone is a true teacher usually means that she is a prime example of what teaching is about, for she embodies the best characteristics (knowledge, patience, communication skills, etc.) a teacher should have. To say that someone is a true friend means that she has qualities most prized in a friend. Often the point of this locution is to say that someone is dependable and reliable, someone who won't desert you when "the going gets rough."

Two things should be clear about propositional truth and truth of a person. The first is that the one kind of truth has nothing to do with the other kind. Propositional truth doesn't apply to humans, and truth of a person doesn't apply to sentences, as is easily seen in comparing a true friend with a true sentence. Second, our discussion about biblical inerrancy is not about truth of a person, for Scripture isn't a person. It is a book, filled with language, sentences.

*Personal truth,* at least as it is often used in common parlance, is a distinct thing again. Something is a personal truth if it has special significance to the one who holds it. She has tested it out (whatever "it" refers to), and it works for her. Of course, personal truth is person-relative, for what *you* find helpful in life may have little or nothing to do with *my* experiences. While personal truth can usually be articulated in language, personal truth is not per se equivalent to *propositional* truth. Many propositions, if true for anyone, are true for everyone, but not so with personal truth. And, what makes a personal truth true for an individual is not usually what makes a proposition true. For evangelicals, inerrancy, and the inerrancy debate, is about propositional truth, not about other kinds of truth.

## DEFINING THE CONCEPTS

Inerrancy is about truth, but what does it mean to say that the Bible is true? Though it might seem easy to articulate these notions, defining inerrancy and infallibility is no easy task, in part because some use these concepts synonymously, while others distinguish them. Though our main concern is inerrancy, as we clarify that concept, Scripture's infallibility will also become clear.

### Inerrancy

The English word "inerrancy" doesn't appear in Scripture, and it is often seen as a negative term, telling us what *is not* true of something rather than stating positively what the thing is. On both grounds, some reject the term. However, terms and concepts like trinity and hypostatic union are nowhere found in Scripture, but we cannot reject them on that basis, since Scripture teaches the concepts they denote.

As to inerrancy being negative, for the sake of argument let us assume that this is so. Even so, why, in defining a concept that talks about a thing's or a person's attributes, wouldn't it be helpful to know what is *not* true of it? Words like "unfailing," "inaccurate," "indefatigable," "incandescent," and "insincere" are also negative, but that doesn't make them inappropriate when discussing things with those qualities. I suspect that the lack of enthusiasm for "inerrancy," as opposed to these other terms, stems at least in part from the fact that people think they know the positive notion at the heart of "unfailing," "unwavering," "inaccurate," "indefatigable," etc., while they aren't sure what "inerrancy" and "errancy" mean. Moreover, in the list of words just enumerated, most are prefixed with the word "in," but the main part of some of them is a positive concept. Without the "in" in "inerrancy" all that is left is a negative concept, so there is no getting away from negativity if we use this term and concept (in-errancy involves the negation of a negative concept, as some critics complain[4]). I find this objection invalid, however, because "inerrancy" denoting a negative concept is no different in that regard than "unfailing." If you remove "un," what is left is a negative notion, but no one thinks on that basis that we shouldn't use "unfailing" in any conversation or written document. So why should any negative notion at the core of "inerrancy" exclude it from use?

But there is more to say here. Terms like "unfailing" and "unwavering" may seem to be negative, but aren't necessarily so. The same is true with "inerrancy." At the core of "unfailing" (failing) and "unwavering" (wavering) are negative

---

[4]See, e.g., William S. LaSor, "Life under Tension—Fuller Theological Seminary and 'The Battle for the Bible'," *Theology, News and Notes*, Special Issue, Fuller Theological Seminary (1976), 23, quoted in Paul Feinberg, "The Meaning of Inerrancy," in *Inerrancy*, ed. Norman Geisler (Grand Rapids, MI: Zondervan, 1979), 292.

concepts. The "prefix" 'un' negates the main concept, so we may seem to have very negative concepts, but in fact just the opposite is the case. To be unfailing and unwavering can be very positive. For example, someone's unwavering stand for the truth is admirable, even as someone's unfailing memory for details is positive, and in an emergency can be of crucial importance. Similarly, "inerrancy" isn't negative at all, even though it seems to involve the negation of a negative thing. But that's just the point! To negate a negative is to turn it positive. Consider the following sentence: "if you want the best deal on a new car, consult Steve, because his knowledge of cars and their true value is inerrant—at least I've always found that to be so." In the sentence just imagined, how is it negative to say that someone's knowledge is inerrant? That's a very positive thing!

Of course, to be unwaveringly or unfailingly stubborn in your refusal to take wise counsel isn't good. But that just shows that those terms are positive or negative depending on what they are paired with—stubbornness or honesty and courage. As for "inerrant," it is hard to think of pairing this adjective with another adjective (or noun) that is something negative. It makes no sense, for example, to speak of someone's inerrant foolishness or stupidity; nor does it make sense to speak of an inerrant mistake—e.g., the sentence "put Joe in situation x and he will inerrantly do the wrong thing" defies common usage and makes little sense. Actually, that sentence means something like the following: "put Joe in situation x and he will unfailingly do the wrong the thing," which means you can count on him to make a mistake.

In light of what I have just said about the meaning and proper uses of the English terms "unwavering," "unfailing," and "inerrant," it isn't at all clear that to be "inerrant" is a negative thing. In fact, "inerrancy" can be a fine term, if we can decide what it means to err and what kind of error is in view, just as "unfailing" can be either clear or ambiguous, depending on what it means to fail and what kind of failure qualifies as negative (e.g., a student might answer incorrectly two questions on a test containing one hundred questions, but missing only two would result in a high pass on the whole exam, not a failure).

Earlier in this chapter I defined inerrancy in terms of truthfulness. As applied to Scripture, what does this mean? In my judgment, the definition that best captures the various strands of thought under discussion in this chapter is offered by Paul Feinberg in his essay "The Meaning of Inerrancy." He writes,

> Inerrancy means that when all facts are known, the Scriptures in their original autographs and properly interpreted will be shown to be wholly true in everything that they affirm, whether that has to do with doctrine or morality or with the social, physical, or life sciences.[5]

---

[5] Feinberg, "Meaning of Inerrancy," 294.

The Chicago Statement on Biblical Inerrancy (from the first International Council on Biblical Inerrancy [ICBI] summit meeting) stated the matter similarly in its Article XII as follows:

> We affirm that Scripture in its entirety is inerrant, being free from all falsehood, fraud, or deceit.
>
> We deny that Biblical infallibility and inerrancy are limited to spiritual, religious, or redemptive themes, exclusive of assertions in the fields of history and science. We further deny that scientific hypotheses about earth history may properly be used to overturn the teaching of Scripture on creation and the flood.[6]

Several years later there was a second ICBI summit meeting. Out of that meeting came a statement on biblical hermeneutics. It defined biblical inerrancy in a way more akin to the wording of Feinberg's definition. Article VI of the Chicago Statement on Biblical Hermeneutics reads,

> We AFFIRM that the Bible expresses God's truth in propositional statements, and we declare that biblical truth is both objective and absolute. We further affirm that a statement is true if it represents matters as they actually are, but is an error if it misrepresents the facts.
>
> We DENY that, while Scripture is able to make us wise unto salvation, biblical truth should be defined in terms of this function. We further deny that error should be defined as that which willfully deceives.[7]

The statements from the two ICBI summits attempt to exclude various objections and objectionable alternatives to the basic concept of biblical inerrancy. In so doing, their wording may seem strange to those who did not attend those summits or who simply are unfamiliar with discussions of inerrancy in the late 1970s and early 1980s, the time when these meetings were held. Moreover, I note that the Chicago Statement on Biblical Inerrancy links together inerrancy and infallibility, while the statement on hermeneutics and Paul Feinberg's statement do not.

*Explaining the Definition*—First, inerrancy applies only to the original autographs of Scripture—those documents which came from the author's pen as the Holy Spirit moved him to write. This point shows that proponents of inerrancy recognize that transcriptional errors have crept into manuscript copies, and there have also been errors in translations since the documents were

---

[6] "The Chicago Statement on Biblical Inerrancy," in Geisler, *Inerrancy* (Grand Rapids, MI: Zondervan, 1979), 496.
[7] "The Chicago Statement on Biblical Hermeneutics," *JETS* 25/4 (December 1982): 398.

originally written. Still, because of the science of textual criticism, there is little doubt that we can construct the equivalents of the autographs. Even so, inerrancy is a quality affirmed of the originals. Even critics of inerrancy understand this.

Second, Feinberg's definition rightly says that inerrancy is a quality of a correctly interpreted Bible. I note several things about correct interpretation. First, proper interpretation of any text doesn't obliterate figures of speech, so that no language other than literal can be an affirmation and true. Jesus said, "I am the door." For that claim to be true Jesus doesn't need to be made of wood, metal, hinges, etc., for his statement isn't about being made of those elements. Proper interpretation recognizes that Jesus used a metaphor. A metaphor joins things whose characteristics are well known, and yet the two things are not usually connected, because they are mostly dissimilar. The two are connected via metaphor because they have something in common (analogous) that the writer wants to say about one or the other. That analogous thing(s) is(are) the metaphor's point. A metaphor's point can be stated in literal language, and the point is either true or false.

Physical doors both keep out and let in. Jesus is like a physical door in that one's relation to him either opens the way to a relationship with God or precludes it. Claims about Christ's role in our spiritual relation to God are either true or false.

Recognizing figures of speech may sometimes provide an answer to a particular biblical difficulty. For example, hyperbole is exaggerating a point to make it more memorable. A passage often cited as containing an error is Jesus's parable of the mustard seed. Jesus likens the kingdom of heaven to a mustard seed. Though this seed is very small, when it blooms and flourishes it develops into a large and beautiful plant. Similarly, the kingdom of heaven begins with just a few people, but when it grows to its full dimensions, it will cover everything, and will have an immense number of inhabitants. This is a well-known parable, but unfortunately, some miss the spiritual truth about the kingdom and focus on Jesus's claim that a mustard seed is the smallest of all seeds. Science knows of a smaller seed, so, critics complain, Jesus made an error, and since the biblical author didn't "correct" it, we must assume that he affirms it. How, then, can one hold biblical inerrancy as defined by Feinberg?

Let me respond with several points that relate to interpreting Scripture properly. Though I'm not saying that *the* proper way to resolve this apparent factual error is to say it is hyperbole (a kind of figure of speech), that is a *possible* way to explain Jesus's statement. Hyperbole is exaggeration to make a point. Jesus's point is that something very small and insignificant at the outset, when it has fully grown, is a very large and beautiful thing (literally true of the kingdom of heaven). The point of the analogy between the kingdom of heaven and a mustard seed would be lost if Jesus had chosen a larger seed, or if he had been scientifically precise and had named the very smallest seed of all, perhaps one unknown to his audience. His audience evidently knew about mustard seeds, and they knew that those seeds are very small.

Perhaps, then, appealing to the mustard seed to tell this parable is hyperbole to make a point. When someone exaggerates a point, we may not always understand that she is doing so, but if we do, we don't accuse her of error. For example, suppose that one day after work my wife asks me how I'm feeling. To communicate how bad I feel I answer, "I'm so exhausted that I feel like I could die."

Hearing this, what should my wife do? Should she dial 911 for an ambulance and a paramedic? Should she rush me to a doctor and have him run tests on me? And if he does and then assures her that I am nowhere close to death, should she turn to me and say, "You liar! How dare you scare me like this! You aren't dying! If you ever pull this trick again, what I'll do to you may make you wish you *were* dead"?

Would any of these responses be appropriate? Of course not! Would I be guilty of lying? Should I fear that my wife may actually kill me if I don't in the future tell her with absolute precision how I feel? Of course not! Adult humans with properly functioning minds and a basic awareness of how language works will realize, as my wife would, that I was exaggerating to make a point.

Perhaps this is also how we should understand Jesus's comment about the size of a mustard seed. Even if not, he certainly didn't intend that his audience should consult their local botanist or their science textbooks, nor did he expect them to search the gardens and fields around Jerusalem to see if they could find a plant with a smaller seed. Properly interpreting Jesus's parable, they would have understood him to be making a point by analogy, and that point is spiritual, not scientific. If Jesus was using hyperbole, that wouldn't count as an error or a lie any more than would my complaining after a hard day that I'm about to die.

Properly interpreting Scripture also means that we understand that *a writer may write of things as they appear to him.* Hence, he may speak of sunrises and sunsets, or of the universe as appearing to have various levels, etc. In our day, we know that the sun doesn't rotate around the earth, and yet we speak of sunrises and sunsets. Everyone knows this is a phenomenological comment (telling how things appear), not a precise scientific one. Even if biblical writers thought the sun rotates around the earth, etc., that wouldn't mean that in using terms like sunrise and sunset they were trying to make a precise scientific comment. They would be speaking of how things appeared. Hence, properly interpreting any document, including Scripture, recognizes phenomenological language and doesn't accuse the author of falsehood.

Of course, we should also remember the point made early in this chapter about using language to teach something. Just as using an errant word spelling doesn't teach that the misspelling is correct, so using phenomenological language to describe what one sees doesn't *teach* a scientific inaccuracy contained in that language. Of course, a text would contain an error if a writer said something like the following: "On the morning of the next day, after the sun came up, Abraham arose and took Isaac with him to Mount Moriah, and on that morning the sun had actually rotated around Planet Earth so that Abraham and Isaac traveled in the daylight." *That* claim would be wrong, because it would assert as fact something that is factually wrong. But of course, no biblical writer makes such claims about sunrises and sunsets, so they don't in fact teach erroneous science any more than I *teach* that "k-a-t" is the proper spelling of the English word for cat by writing that "my kat is on the mat."

Properly interpreting Scripture also recognizes that, as with other documents and oral speech, authors or speakers sometimes uses approximations. This may be so in passages where data about the number of people assembled or killed may be rounded to an even number. Of course, a rounded number could also be literally true. Only careful exegesis can tell whether the author intended to give an exact number or an approximation. For example, if on one occasion Jesus actually fed 4,963 people, not 5,000, from two loaves of bread and five fishes, we can understand that by reporting that 5,000 were fed, the writer isn't lying or just wrong, and he isn't trying to be absolutely precise. Thus, we shouldn't call his report of feeding 5,000 an error. Of course, Jesus might have fed exactly 5,000, and that is why the writer reported that number.

Similarly, if the millennial kingdom actually lasts 994 years or even 1,006, not 1,000, that wouldn't mean that Revelation 20:1–10 is factually wrong. Of course, the kingdom may last exactly 1,000 years, and that would fit Revelation 20, too.

Please don't misunderstand this. I'm not saying Scripture is never precise about anything it reports or claims. There is evidence that the very choice of words, singulars versus plurals, and the present tense as opposed to the past tense, for example, are made with great care and precision. In one passage (Matt. 22:31–32) Jesus's entire argument for resurrection of the body rests on his appeal to Exodus 3:6 and the fact that God told Abraham, "I am . . . ," not "I was." The verb tense is crucial, and Jesus makes a theological point on the basis of it; precision in Exodus 3:6, in Jesus's citing this passage, and in Matthew's recording of what Jesus says is critical!

Galatians 3:16 is another example. Paul presents an argument about promises made to Abraham, but also to Abraham's seed. Paul cites Genesis 12:7; 13:15; and 24:7 and says that Scripture doesn't say *seeds* (plural), but *seed* (singular). This, Paul says, refers to one person, who is Christ. Hence, the force and accuracy of his argument depends on the noun being singular rather than plural.[8] Clearly, biblical writers were quite precise when their point required it.

Then, proper interpretation also takes seriously each biblical book's and each passage's literary genre. For example, a Gospel is a particular literary genre with affinities to a history text, but it also contains things that are not part of a historical document. Moreover, however one defines the literary genre of Gospel, things appear in it that are not identical to a Gospel. For example, a Gospel isn't the same literary genre as a parable. But the Synoptic Gospels, for example, include many of Jesus's parables. Moreover, a parable is a literary genre distinct from prose, poetry, drama, apocalyptic literature, letter/epistle, etc. Evidently, however, literature that is an instance of some of those genres can also contain a parable. We also know that an allegory is a distinct figure of speech, and that an epistle (itself a distinct literary genre) can contain an allegory (think of Galatians, and Paul's use of Sarah and Hagar as an allegory to make his theological point). Of course, other literary genres can contain allegories as well.

Why is this point important to interpretation and inerrancy? Let me explain. Consider Jesus's parable of the ten virgins (Matt. 25:1–13). It appears in a Gospel. Now, the basic strategy of the four Gospels is to report with accuracy various historical facts about Christ's life. But a Gospel can also recount a parable Jesus used to teach a spiritual truth. The fact that the parable appears in a Gospel doesn't make the parable a *historically factual* story. Normally, as in Matthew 25:1–13, a parable is a fictional story used to make a moral or spiritual point. Hence, the fact that the Matthew 25 parable appears in a Gospel doesn't mean that the ten virgins mentioned in Jesus's story actually existed. Moreover, the *moral and spiritual point* of the parable is not false if the ten virgins Jesus mentioned never existed, if there never was a bridegroom, and if there were no lamps.

Moreover, a parable isn't an allegory. In an allegory, every item is a symbol for something else, whereas this is not so in a parable. That means that, in the parable of the ten virgins, the lamps—those trimmed and those not trimmed—symbolize no hidden meaning. Moreover, though oil is used sometimes in Scripture as a symbol for the Holy Spirit, since this is a parable and not an allegory, the oil in this parable need not *symbolize* anything, and in this

---

[8] See Feinberg, "Meaning of Inerrancy," 286, for all three examples.

case, it isn't a symbol for the Holy Spirit. If we don't understand these features of various literary genres, we may think Jesus teaches things he doesn't, some of which are wrong.[9]

One final point about proper interpretation is noteworthy. The goal in interpretation must be to uncover the author's intended meaning. This is crucial because, while biblical authors wrote under the Holy Spirit's inspiration, no biblical exegete *interprets* Scripture under the "Holy Spirit's inspiration" (whatever such a notion might mean). Our interpretations are not inerrant. A faulty interpretation that introduces error into the text is *the interpreter's error, not Scripture's!* So, before any biblical statement comes under suspicion of error, the accuser must show that *his interpretation* of the passage with the alleged error *is itself inerrant!*

Paul Feinberg's definition of biblical inerrancy talks about affirmations being true. By affirmations he means sentences that assert something about the world. In affirming Alfred Tarski's theory of truth, he also clarifies that the notion of truth in view in his definition is truth as correspondence.[10] I shall explain these points in more detail, but for now I note that I also espouse this.

Feinberg's definition speaks of *what the biblical author asserts as true being true.* This is important, because, for example, Satan's lies are sometimes recorded in Scripture (e.g., Gen. 3:4). Moses writes that the serpent said to the woman, "You surely shall not die." *Moses* isn't asserting, contrary to what God said, that if Eve ate the forbidden fruit, she wouldn't die. Moses only says that *Satan said this*, and it is either true or false that Satan did say it. This example shows that, since inerrancy is about what the *biblical writer* asserts, we must clarify exactly what he *affirms,* on the one hand, and what he merely *reports* someone else saying, on the other hand.

Sometimes critics claim that what several different writers report about an event cannot be true because they don't say exactly the same thing about it. Here consider the apparently varying reports about how many times Peter denied Christ before the cock crowed (Mark 14:30, 66–72; Matt. 26:34, 69–75; Luke 22:34, 56–60; and John 13:38; 18:15–27), or how many men appeared to the women at Jesus's tomb on resurrection morning. And were the men wearing a white robe or a dazzling, shiny robe (Luke 24:4; John 20:12–16; Matt. 28:2–7; and Mark 16:5)? Elsewhere I have shown in detail how these

---

[9] One of the first to make this point about literary genres (and certainly one of the best at expressing it) is Kevin Vanhoozer. Though Vanhoozer covers many things in his "Semantics of Biblical Literature," one of his most fundamental points is that, in deciding what inerrancy means and in testing any text's inerrancy, one must interpret aright, and an interpreter must early on correctly identify a text's literary genre, for Scripture uses many different genres. See Kevin J. Vanhoozer, "The Semantics of Biblical Literature," in *Hermeneutics, Authority, and Canon,* ed. D. A. Carson and John D. Woodbridge (Grand Rapids, MI: Zondervan, 1986).

[10] Feinberg, "Meaning of Inerrancy," 294–295.

apparent discrepancies can be harmonized, and I encourage readers to consult that data.[11] For our purposes now, suffice it to say that, so long as none of the writers reporting the event says something that would make it impossible for the other accounts to be true, there is no reason that all accounts cannot be true. The fact that different writers give different but complementary accounts of an event lends credibility to the story; they aren't likely copying from a common source but, rather, are independent eyewitnesses. All the details they collectively report are more likely correct because their thorough accounts show that they were actually present.

Relatedly, did the Gospel writers report Jesus's exact words (*ipsissima verba*) or only his exact voice (*ipsissimus vox*). If the former, then we have more than the gist of what Jesus said; we have a verbatim quote. The latter may contain some of the words Jesus actually spoke, but not necessarily all of them. The key is that the writer's report conveys the substance of Jesus's message, even if not his exact words. Some say that at most we can only have Jesus's voice, because he likely gave most of his teachings in Aramaic but the NT is written in Greek. Others counter that Greek was sufficiently common in Palestine as the everyday language in the Roman Empire, that many or even most of Jesus's teachings were in Greek. If so, then we may have his exact words in the Greek NT.[12]

From my perspective, this is an issue in part because several Gospel writers record the same teachings of Jesus but with wording that is not always identical. Hence, one wonders whether one of the accounts is wrong, and about what Jesus actually said. As to the former issue, I think it rests on an inappropriate attempt to impose modern conventions about quotation marks and direct quotes on these ancient documents. With or without quotation marks, when someone today relates what someone else said, listeners/readers assume that they are receiving the exact words. But there were no such conventions about written documents or even oral reports in Jesus's day. Undoubtedly when someone reported what someone else said, they did use many of the exact words spoken, but so long as the substance of what was said is reported, no one would think it an error if exact words were not repeated. There just isn't evidence that modern conventions about quotes and quotation marks applied to literature of that time.

As to knowing what Jesus said, as Feinberg argues, "undoubtedly the exact words of Jesus are to be found in the New Testament, but they need not be so in every instance."[13] We are probably not in a position to know

---

[11] See my *Can You Believe It's True? Christian Apologetics in a Modern and Postmodern Era* (Wheaton, IL: Crossway, 2013), chapter 11.

[12] For more on the two positions, proponents of each, and their arguments, see Robert L. Thomas, "The Rationality, Meaningfulness, and Precision of Scripture," *MSJ* 15 (Fall 2004): 198–203.

[13] Feinberg, "Meaning of Inerrancy," 301.

which quotes from Jesus are his exact words. However, that doesn't mean the Gospel accounts of Jesus's teaching are wrong. If they contain the substance of what he said, there is no reason to think they err just because we don't know Jesus's exact words.

Also important is the fact that our definition of biblical inerrancy says that Scripture's truth can be demonstrated "when all facts are known." Of course, many facts are known, and they confirm many things Scripture asserts. However, we are not yet able to confirm everything—but we will be someday. We cannot now empirically prove that end-time prophecies are true, but they will be verified at the eschaton. And, comments about heaven and hell are confirmable by personal experience, but only after one dies, not before.

All of this suggests that, in thinking about any book's inerrancy, it would be wise to distinguish what is *true* from what is *verifiable*, and to see that both of those are distinct from what *has been verified*. A claim can be true, even if no one has verified it. For example, Jesus told his disciples (John 14:2–3) that in his Father's house there are many mansions, that he would go and prepare a place for them, and that he would return for them and take them to his Father's house. There is no good reason to think that Jesus was lying or mistaken about this. Still, no mere human in a natural body can verify or has verified it. However, it is all verifiable, in principle. When those who know Christ as Savior die, they will confirm the truth about heaven. When Jesus returns for his church, church members will confirm the truth of his return and of his bringing his people to his Father's house.

Why emphasize this distinction? If Scripture teaches its truthfulness, then whatever it affirms is true, even if we haven't verified it and if, *in our current circumstances*, we cannot do so. Moreover, it also means that it isn't wrong to include "when all facts are known" in our definition of inerrancy.

Our discussion so far has focused on the concept of biblical inerrancy and on what the term "inerrancy" means. To how much of Scripture does inerrancy apply? This is a crucial question in at least two distinct respects. It is important because not all who call themselves evangelicals agree on how much of Scripture is inerrant. Millard Erickson details seven different positions one might take on biblical inerrancy. Three reject the term and concept entirely. Two claim that inerrancy covers everything that Scripture *affirms about any subject*. Yet another limits inerrancy only to whatever *Scripture asserts about matters of doctrine and practice*. It guarantees nothing about matters of history, science, etc., contained in Scripture. A final position affirms only the *inerrancy of Scripture's purpose*. According to this view, Scripture inerrantly accomplishes its purpose to bring people to a saving relationship with Christ.

Inerrancy on this final view needn't have anything to do with the factuality of propositions affirmed.[14]

Which view should we choose? According to Paul Feinberg's definition, inerrancy extends to everything Scripture teaches/affirms, regardless of the topic. I agree and plan to defend this view before this chapter ends. So, I affirm that inerrancy extends to all sixty-six books of the Bible, and deny that limited inerrancy or a denial of inerrancy altogether are correct views.

There is a second respect in which we should ask how much of Scripture is inerrant. Inerrancy deals with propositional truth, but not all sentences can bear truth. Commands, questions, and interjections that assert nothing about reality are not truth bearers. Only assertions can bear truth. So, inerrancy, defined in terms of propositional truth, can apply only to sentences that affirm something about the world. This is true for all books, including Scripture. Of course, the fact that inerrancy doesn't apply to every sentence of Scripture doesn't mean those sentences are in any way deficient! Though they aren't inerrant, they are *not errant* either!

### What Does It Mean to Say that Scripture Is True?

Readers may be puzzled by what I have written in the last few paragraphs, but the key is a proper understanding of the nature of propositional truth. In this section I want to clarify several points about propositional truth, and that will help us understand more precisely what it means to say that any book, including Scripture, is inerrant.

As I argued in my essay for the second ICBI summit, "Truth: Relationship of Theories of Truth to Hermeneutics," we must address two fundamental questions about propositional truth. First, what kinds of sentences can bear truth? Not all can, and if a sentence cannot bear truth, then inerrancy, defined in terms of truth, can't apply to it. This suggests no inadequacy of sentences that don't bear truth. Rather it helps clarify the Scriptures to which inerrancy extends—this is so not just for the Bible, but for any book. The second key question about truth is which *theory of truth* is in view when we talk about sentences being true. There are several theories of truth, and each identifies something distinct that makes a true sentence true. In what follows, I summarize the findings of my article on truth.

*Truth Bearers*—What are the linguistic bearers of *truth*? To answer this question, we must first address a more fundamental question, namely, what are the linguistic bearers of *meaning*? Words, phrases, sentences, the world as a whole, a state of affairs, or what? Depending on one's theory of truth, truth

---

[14] Millard Erickson, *Christian Theology*, 2nd ed. (Grand Rapids, MI: Baker, 2000 printing), 248–250.

will relate to one or more of these items. How does meaning enter the picture? Any linguistic phenomenon (word, phrase, sentence) can't be true or false if it lacks meaning, so we must ask about linguistic bearers of meaning.

Prima facie, it might seem that anything verbal could bear linguistic meaning. But here we must remember the distinction between a word's sense and reference. Words have a sense, a "dictionary meaning," we might say, and so do phrases. We can identify the sense (or intension) of every individual word and phrase. However, as mere words or phrases unattached to a full sentence, these linguistic "markers" affirm nothing, ask nothing, demand nothing, etc., about the world outside our minds. As philosophers of language would say, they have no semantic meaning. So, words and phrases *alone* don't *refer* to anything specific in the world outside the mind.[15] Hence, they don't have the qualities I'll note that are at the heart of each theory of truth.

In order for words to have semantic meaning and so to *refer* to something, not just have a sense, they must be part of a whole sentence. As Paul Ricoeur explains, "individual words are semiotic entities or signs, and such signs are units within a specific linguistic system, but they do not relate to extralinguistic realities such as things or events."[16] So having semantic meaning requires a whole sentence, and sentences come in a number of varieties. Some are assertions, others are questions, others are commands, and yet others are exclamations. The type of sentence doesn't matter as to whether it has a meaning; the rule is that whatever kind of sentence is in view, it must be a complete sentence, not just a word or phrase, for it to have a meaning.

If only a complete sentence can have semantic meaning, then only a sentence can be a bearer of truth. Individual words or phrases apart from the context of a whole sentence don't have a meaning, so it makes no sense to ask if they are true or not. This must not be misunderstood. In a dialogue, "just one" might serve as an acceptable sentence, though it looks like a phrase. If "just one" is the response to "how many hot dogs do you want for lunch?" then "just one" is shorthand for "I want just one hot dog for lunch." Of course, in this context "just one" has both a sense and refers to something in the world, and it is either true or false.

But I am not here thinking about this kind of brief phrase, when I say that neither individual words nor phrases can have meaning or bear truth. The kind of words and phrases I have in mind are divorced from any context of discourse. Those words and phrases have no semantic meaning and they can't bear truth.

So, only whole sentences have meaning and can be either true or false. But

---

[15] John Feinberg, "Truth: Relationship of Theories of Truth to Hermeneutics," 24–26.

[16] Ibid., 25, and then I quote Ricoeur at length, making this point. See Paul Ricoeur, "Creativity in Language," *Philosophy Today* 17 (Summer 1973): 99.

does every complete sentence also bear truth? Contrary to what one might think, the answer is no. Only sentences that *affirm or assert* something can bear truth. Thus, a promise can bear truth, even though we must wait to find out if the promise is true or false. An "expressive" (i.e., an exclamation) can make an assertion (e.g., "Great is the Lord, and greatly to be praised") or not; those that do, bear truth. Even a declarative (e.g., "I now pronounce you husband and wife"), said by someone with the requisite authority and in a situation where the declaration applies, can affirm something that actually happens by means of the declaration he or she makes. So declaratives can also be bearers of truth or falsity. But questions, commands, and interjections that don't affirm anything are neither true nor false. They have a meaning but aren't the bearers of truth. Thus, they cannot be either inerrant or errant, so they do not in any way effect Scripture's inerrancy. That is, Scripture can still be fully inerrant; we just now understand exactly to which sentences of Scripture inerrancy applies.

*Definitions of and Theories of Truth*—Sentences, then, which affirm something can be true or false, but what do truth and falsity mean? Here there are several options, and there is also some confusion.

As to the confusion, some theologians have argued that we should define truth as Scripture does. Of course, Scripture nowhere presents a philosophical or theological discussion about the nature of truth. Proponents of this approach agree, but they still think it is possible to uncover the biblical understanding of truth and error by seeing how OT and NT writers used the biblical *terms* for truth and error. This strategy is proposed not only by some who reject inerrancy, but also by some of its defenders.

So, what do these thinkers claim that error and truth mean, biblically speaking? According to David Hubbard, "*error* theologically must mean that which leads us astray from the will of God or the knowledge of this truth."[17] Similarly, G. C. Berkouwer writes that, biblically, error should be understood as sin and deception, not divergence from the formal accuracy of Scripture's statements (i.e., not factual inaccuracy).[18]

As for the so-called "biblical" understanding of truth, here the key OT word is *'emet*, and critics of biblical inerrancy often note that it is broadly used in the OT to mean faithfulness.[19] Roger Nicole, a thoroughly committed inerrantist, agrees that "truth" in the OT frequently speaks of faithfulness,

---

[17] Hubbard, "Current Tensions," 167–168, quoted in my "Truth: Relationship of Theories of Truth to Hermeneutics," 14.

[18] G. C. Berkouwer, *Studies in Dogmatics: Holy Scriptures*, trans. Jack Rogers (Grand Rapids, MI: Eerdmans, 1975), 181, cited in my Truth: Relationship of Theories of Truth to Hermeneutics," 14.

[19] Anthony Thiselton, s.v. "Truth," in *The New International Dictionary of New Testament Theology*, 3 vols. (Grand Rapids, MI: Zondervan, 1979), 3:877, shows that some use this claim to dichotomize Old and New Testament concepts of truth. I make this point in my "Truth: Relationship of Theories of Truth to Hermeneutics," 14.

and that means reliability or dependability to perform whatever one has promised.[20] Of course, that has little to do with the truth of an assertion that isn't a promise, but Nicole rightly argues that this OT word for "truth" has another meaning. Often it means "conformity to facts,"[21] and of course, that is relevant to the inerrancy debate.

Nicole pursues this line of argument into the NT and its understanding of truth. He notes that several lines of evidence are relevant. One is to see how translators of the LXX rendered 'emet into Greek. They typically used the Greek alētheia. The NT also uses terms and phrases that have a Semitic tone to them. Picking up on an OT expression, hesed we 'emet ("grace and truth"), there are NT passages that are reminiscent of this combination (e.g., John 1:14, 17). And, the Semitic amen appears at least some 129 times in the NT (typically, it is translated "truly," and we find it most often in the words of Jesus).[22] In addition, the NT itself typically uses the adverb alēthōs to speak of something actually conforming to fact. In fact, Nicole shows that in the NT, the basic uses of "truth" mean either conformity to fact or completeness.[23]

In light of his biblical study of "truth," Nicole offers the following summary:

> The biblical view of truth ('emet-alētheia) is that it is like a rope with several intertwined strands. It will not do to isolate the strands and deal with them separately, although they may be distinguished just as various lines in the telephone cable may be distinguished by color. *The full Bible concept of truth involves factuality, faithfulness, and completeness.* Those who have stressed one of these features in order to downgrade either or both of the others are falling short of the biblical pattern. Notably those who have stressed faithfulness, as if conformity to fact did not matter, are failing grievously to give proper attention to what constitutes probably a majority of the passages in which the word *truth* is used.[24]

What should we say about these attempts to define error and truth "biblically"? First, as to error as being whatever leads us astray from God's will, that idea is as much about those who read Scripture as about Scripture itself. Many people throughout history have misunderstood Scripture and fallen into theological or practical error. But neither Hubbard nor anyone else who proposes this definition would argue that God or the biblical writers intentionally included things to mislead people. If the biblical authors included misleading things unintentionally, that would result because they were not omniscient. But

---

[20] Nicole, "Biblical Concept of Truth," 288.
[21] Ibid., 290–292, in which he presents ample evidence of this use of 'emet. See also Thiselton, "Truth," who also shows that 'emet means more than faithfulness in the OT.
[22] Nicole, "Biblical Concept of Truth," 292–293.
[23] Ibid., 293–296.
[24] Ibid., 296 (italics are Nicole's).

given the Holy Spirit's superintendence, he would surely have caught anything that would unintentionally confuse readers. Even if every sentence of Scripture is crystal clear, that wouldn't make it impossible for readers and interpreters to misunderstand it. But this definition ultimately seems to be more about what readers/interpreters do than about what God or the human author did. Moreover, even if this is the preferred definition of error, Scripture could be free of this kind of error and still contain many factual errors—as long as they didn't lead readers into doctrine or practice that diverges from biblical teaching, factual errors wouldn't matter!

What about error as willful deception? As Paul Feinberg explains, with this notion of error, most books ever written would qualify as inerrant.[25] To be sure, people have written books intending to deceive readers, but that isn't so for most books. Such deception would not in most cases be difficult to expose. I note also that an inerrant book, on this notion of error, might contain all sorts of factual errors. As long as its author didn't intend to deceive anyone by including such errors, the book would qualify as inerrant. Clearly, this notion of truth and error doesn't help much to articulate a positive statement about Scripture's characteristics.

What about the discussions of biblical words for truth? Here the OT word has more than one meaning. The idea of being faithful, or faithfulness, is relevant to truth of *a person*, but biblical inerrancy is about *propositional* truth, *not* truth of a person. In the NT, biblical usage of "true" and "truth" gives two options again, and the same complaint about various OT meanings also applies to attempts to define the NT notion of truth by a word study.

Actually, this method of defining truth and error is fatally flawed. The problem isn't that those who espouse it have failed to uncover "the key use" of terms for truth and error. The problem is that this methodology contains a conceptual error! The flaw relates to a point made early in this chapter about the difference between defining terms and defining concepts. You don't define any *concept* by doing a *word study* of various *terms*. That is, the fatal mistake of this approach to finding a "biblical" idea of truth is that a word study of *terms* for truth and error doesn't uncover the *concepts* of truth and error. Theology is not about word meanings; it is conceptual study, and doing a word study won't uncover the meaning of the concept! Contrary to the sentence Nicole italicized in the passage I quoted from him, what he and other thinkers who adopt the word study strategy have done does *not* uncover *the biblical concept of truth*, assuming that there even is such a thing (debatable, since Scripture isn't a treatise on the theological or philosophical concept of truth). What they have shown, instead, is how biblical *words* for truth and error might be used in

---

[25] Paul Feinberg, "Meaning of Inerrancy," 291.

various biblical passages. Doing that has value, including helping to interpret various texts where these terms appear (even if the texts have nothing to do with the concept of propositional truth). But none of that uncovers the *concept* of truth, or articulates a *theory* of truth.

So, how should we proceed if the methodology just discussed is flawed? We should explain and evaluate various theories about what sort of thing propositional truth is. In my essay on theories of truth and theories of meaning,[26] I argued in favor of what is known as the semantic theory of truth.[27] Several other theories of truth are much better known, and one is a form of the semantic theory. For the sake of clarity, let me expound these theories.

The first theory of propositional truth, a form of the semantic theory, has the longest "pedigree" in Western philosophy. It is the *correspondence theory of truth*. Though Aristotle didn't use the label "correspondence theory," what he said about truth captures the essence of this theory. According to Aristotle, "to say of what is that it is not, or of what is not that it is, is false, while to say of what is that it is, or of what is not that it is not is true."[28]

According to this theory, propositional truth is a relation between word and world. If what we say in language about the world matches what is the case in the world, then our language is true. If what we say doesn't match the world, then what we say is false. This notion of truth is relevant to sentences that assert or affirm something of the world. Such sentences can bear truth (i.e., can be true or false).

The correspondence notion of truth is the most widely held understanding of propositional truth. It is actually the idea of truth that underlies ordinary language. Given these facts, why do we need any other theory of truth? For a long time in philosophy, that was the basic attitude, but over the last few centuries (the most recent one in particular), philosophers became increasingly disenchanted with the correspondence theory and have even argued that it cannot be used. Why? Because they would like to say that something is true in this sense, but they believe we aren't in a position to do so. The reasons for this stem from developments in epistemology, beginning at least as early as Immanuel Kant. Increasingly, epistemologists have argued that the picture of the mind as a passive mirror of the world outside cannot be correct. Kant teaches us that, in the knowing relation, the world works on the mind and the mind interacts with the world. Hence, human subjectivity is always involved in the knowing process, and it guarantees that we cannot with pristine objectivity

---

[26] John Feinberg, "Truth: Relationship of Theories of Truth to Hermeneutics."
[27] See ibid., 11–13, for details of this theory.
[28] Aristotle, "Metaphysics," *The Basic Works of Aristotle*, ed. Richard McKeon (New York: Random House, 1941), book 1, chapter 7 (749).

access the world outside our minds. All of our learning, past experiences, preferences, and prejudices are brought to the task of learning anything. Hence, it is dubious that any human can connect with the world outside the mind with the objectivity needed to confirm conclusively that our words do match the world outside our minds.[29]

Elsewhere I have argued that, despite biases and presuppositions, humans can in fact know correctly what is true of the world. Of course, that doesn't mean we never err. My only point is that truth as correspondence is possible. The defense of this viewpoint goes beyond the purposes of this book, but interested readers can read my defense elsewhere.[30] Suffice it to say that even proponents of the correspondence theory of truth find some correct intuitions at the core of other theories of truth. What are those other theories?

A second well-known theory of propositional truth is the *coherence theory of truth*. According to this theory, truth is still a relation, but one between words and other words. When the coherence theory was first proposed (and for a long time thereafter), it was believed that affirmations could be tested for fit with the world, but it was also thought that something else should characterize a true claim: claims about reality should fit consistently with one another. Sentences do this (i.e., cohere with one another) if they don't contradict one another. In logic, a contradiction is an affirmation and denial of one and the same thing, at the same time, and in the same way. Thus, to say that as I write this sentence, I am both physically present at my home working in my study *and at the same moment also* physically present and swimming at a local beach fifteen miles from home is to utter a contradiction. It is impossible for someone in a natural body to be at both places at once, so a claim to be at both places cannot be true. Actually, the coherence notion of truth follows a correct assumption about the world, namely, in the world we don't find genuinely contradictory states of affairs. Thus, if language is intended to refer to the world, true sentences shouldn't contradict one another.

As philosophers became more skeptical about truth as correspondence, that didn't rattle their confidence in truth as coherence. Even if we can't know whether our views match the world, we can still see whether claims contradict one another or not. Hence, for many in our day, coherence is a useful alternative to correspondence, but they also think it is just about all that we have, since truth as correspondence isn't available. Thus, if someone holds five beliefs that assert something, and four of them are internally consistent (i.e., none contradicts any of the other four), then the set of four is deemed to be true. If the fifth belief contradicts any of the other four, it must be false.

---

[29] For more details about this skepticism about knowing the world and hence testing our statements against it to see if they match, see my *Can You Believe It's True?* chapters 2 and 4 especially.
[30] See my *Can You Believe It's True?* chapters 2–6, but especially chapters 4–6.

While this theory of propositional truth might seem enough, we should look more closely. While our beliefs shouldn't contain contradictions, still, if all we can say about a set of beliefs is that it tells a logically consistent story, that isn't enough. What if this logically consistent set of claims (some or all of them) doesn't match the actual world in which we live? We need to know that our internally consistent story is about the real world.

Could such a thing actually happen? If a belief system didn't match reality, wouldn't it also contain some contradiction(s) somewhere within it? Not necessarily. At the very least, in the history of Western thought there have been a number of philosophers (and no doubt, theologians and ordinary people) who have been good enough at logic to know how to build a set of beliefs that doesn't contradict itself. As a result, they have produced an internally consistent system (hence true in a coherence sense), but that doesn't mean that the beliefs affirm anything that matches the world. Hence, their views, though true in a coherence sense, may be false in a correspondence sense. That's not the kind of truth we should want, especially when what is at stake is one's relation to the creator and preserver of the universe and one's eternal destiny!

Let me illustrate the problem with truth as only coherence. Consider the following propositions: (1) the Bible is fully inspired; (2) the Bible is both a divine and a human book; (3) the Bible is the final authority for matters of doctrine and practice; (4) the Bible tells us without error what God wanted to reveal by giving us Scripture; and (5) the Holy Spirit is able and willing to illumine human minds so that they can appropriate the Bible's message. Now, none of the five propositions contradicts any of the others. Hence, if coherence is our measure of truth, all five must be true. But don't we want to know more than this about the five sentences? Each claim affirms something about the universe in which we live. If what these sentences affirm doesn't match/correspond to states of affairs in our world, then these five propositions may be nothing more than fantasies—perhaps comforting ones, but fantasies nonetheless.

Certainly, we want to know more than just that propositions (1)–(5) cohere. We also want to know if they correspond to reality. If not, why believe them and live as though they are true and binding? The problem with coherence as the criterion of truth is that it can't tell us whether (1)–(5) accurately correspond to the world. So, even though true sentences (in a correspondence sense) should and do cohere with one another, coherence alone won't tell us whether an assertion matches the world or not, and that is what we most want to know.

A third theory of truth, the *pragmatic theory of truth*, has also become quite popular in our day. When first proposed, its advocates believed that truth as correspondence is available. They just thought that if a claim is true, it should say something more. A true claim should also help us live successfully in the world. Thus, if a sentence supposedly corresponds to reality but when people try to live in accord with it, disaster occurs, it may not actually correspond to the real world. A true claim should be useful in guiding people to a prosperous, enjoyable life.

As skepticism grew about objective knowledge of the world outside the mind, many who espoused the pragmatic theory came to believe that truth as correspondence isn't available. So, truth *as useful* seemed the best way to understand truth, and seemed to be about all we could know about truth. Of course, many proponents of the pragmatic theory also hold the coherence theory, but even so, neither theory helps us discover whether our worldviews are fantasies or not. And what proves useful for one person may not help others. In fact, something once useful for someone may be unhelpful for him later.

Of these three theories, which one(s) should we use to assess the truth of any literary work? While it may be interesting to know that a book has helped others, that isn't normally the point of most nonfiction books. Those books intend to present what has happened and what is the case, or at least to reflect the author's beliefs about reality. Given this intent, it would definitely help to know if a book's contents are internally consistent. If a book contains contradictions, then at least some of its claims cannot reflect reality.

Wouldn't we also want to know which claims match our world? No one can live in a fantasy world. So, what we most want to know about nonfiction literature is whether it says anything about the actual world around us. Correspondence is the only notion of truth that can tell us that.

As for the Bible, the situation is no different. Its contents aren't fiction (even a parable makes a moral or spiritual point about reality) but purport to recount what actually has happened, what God expects of us, and how we should understand human nature, sin, salvation, the church, end-time events, etc. In judging Scripture's truthfulness, it is only fair to ask what the biblical writers intended to do when/as they wrote Scripture, and to use that as a measure of whether they succeeded or not. So, what did they intend? To write sentences that don't contradict one another, and nothing more? To offer advice that each author found useful in living his life? Or to recount what really happened and what we need to know about the topics they address, and to explain what God requires of us?

To answer, we need only look at Scripture itself. We don't want a Bible filled with contradictions—how would we know what to believe? We would also like to know that Scripture gives good advice about how to live. But first and foremost, we want to know that what it says matches the world. Thankfully, biblical writers clearly intended to report what they saw, heard, and knew to be true of the life they lived and the events they witnessed. This point can be easily confirmed, and I offer two examples to show this is so.

The first is 2 Peter 1:16, 19a:

> We did not follow cleverly invented stories when we told you about the power and coming of our Lord Jesus Christ, but we were eyewitnesses of his majesty. . . . And we have the word of the prophets made more certain, . . . (NIV 1984)

In verses 16–18, Peter recounts his experience at the Mount of Transfiguration, but verse 16 certainly covers more than just that one experience. Regardless of how much it covers, what is the point of saying that he was an eyewitness of what he reports and isn't making up fables? How can that mean anything but that what he reports actually happened in the world outside the apostles' minds?

But note something more. Even though seeing is believing, Peter says something is even "more certain" (v. 19) and believable than the apostles' eyewitness testimony; that something is Scripture. In my chapters on inspiration I covered this passage in detail, so I won't belabor its details. But I must ask now why it matters that Scripture is even more certainly true than eyewitness testimony, if the point of being true is only to write logically consistent sentences and/ or thoughts that some have found useful— and *nothing* more? It only matters that Scripture is more certainly true than eyewitness testimony if Scripture's authors intended to write exactly what happened and to present accurate information about God, humans, sin, salvation, etc.

Isn't it obvious that the most fundamental thing Peter wanted to do was tell his readers things that match reality? Consider another passage, 1 John 1:1–3a:

> That which was from the beginning, which we have heard, which we have seen with our eyes, which we have looked at and our hands have touched—this we proclaim concerning the Word of life. The life appeared; we have seen it and testify to it, and we proclaim to you the eternal life, which was with the Father and has appeared to us. We proclaim to you what we have seen and heard, so that you also may have fellowship with us. . . . (NIV 1984)

What could John's point be other than that he writes about what he saw, heard, and touched? And that means that what he writes matches the real world in which he lived!

When we put Peter's, John's, and other apostles' statements together, it is easy to see that they intended to write what matched what they had experienced. Thus, the theory of truth they presupposed as they wrote is the correspondence theory. That is no surprise, since that is the theory that undergirds ordinary language, the type everyone uses every day to converse with others. Moreover, when Peter writes that what OT prophets wrote is even more certain than the apostles' eyewitness testimony, that cannot be true unless the OT matches reality.

These examples (and they could be multiplied for both Testaments) show that the human authors of Scripture presupposed the correspondence notion of truth as they wrote. They intended to record things that match reality. If so, shouldn't that notion of truth be the one we use to assess whether their writings tell the truth?

In sum, inerrancy is about the truth of assertions, and truth should be understood as the correspondence of language to reality. Biblical sentences that assert nothing are neither true nor false, but that in no way undermines the inerrancy of biblical sentences that can and do bear truth.[31] This definition of inerrancy applies to Scripture, and to any book that asserts something about reality.

### Testing the Definition of Inerrancy

So far the discussion has been about definitions of terms and concepts. What does inerrancy look like when predicated of individual passages? Let me answer by examining some Scriptures and by noting what about them is inerrant. Consider the following: Matthew 20:1–16; Isaiah 7:14; Matthew 2:15's handling of Hosea 11:1; 1 Timothy 2:12; John 14:1–3; 1 Timothy 1:15; and Revelation 19:17.[32]

*Matthew 20:1–16*—Matthew 20:1–16 is the parable of the landowner and the workers in his vineyard. A parable may be a true story, but it needn't be and usually isn't. So, this parable can be inerrant, even if the people in it are totally fictitious. Jesus tells this story to show how he runs his kingdom. It shows

---

[31] Other works not yet cited that were helpful in my thinking on the definition of inerrancy are Cornelis Venema, "Functional Inerrancy: A Neo-Evangelical View of Biblical Authority," *MAJT* 5 (1989); Michael D. White, "Charles Hodge, Hermeneutics, and the Struggle with Scripture," *JTI* 3 (2009); L. Russ Bush, "Understanding Biblical Inerrancy," *Southwestern Journal of Theology* 50 (Fall 2007); Stephen R. Holmes, "Evangelical Doctrines of Scripture in Transatlantic Perspective," *EvQ* 81 (2009); Harold O. J. Brown, "The Inerrancy and Infallibility of the Bible," in *The Origin of the Bible*, ed. Philip W. Comfort (Wheaton, IL: Tyndale, 1992); William A. Dembski, "The Problem of Error in Scripture," in *Unapologetic Apologetics*, ed. W. A. Dembski and J. W. Richards (Downers Grove, IL: InterVarsity Press, 2001); Robert M. Price, "Inerrant the Wind: The Troubled House of North American Evangelicals," *EvQ* 55 (July 1983); James D. G. Dunn, "The Authority of Scripture according to Scripture," *Churchman* 96 (1982); Donald A. Hagner, "The Battle for Inerrancy," *Reformed Journal* 34 (April 1984); Roy L. Honeycutt, "Biblical Authority: A Treasured Heritage!" *RevExp* 83 (Fall 1986); Tom Finger, "A Life-Giving Authority," *The Other Side* 19 (August 1983); J. Kenneth Grider, "Wesleyanism and the Inerrancy Issue," *Wesleyan Theological Journal* 19 (Fall 1984); Roger Nicole, "Why I Am 'Comfortable' with Inerrancy," *Reformation and Revival* 11 (Summer 2002); John A. Delivuk, "Inerrancy, Infallibility, and Scripture in the *Westminster Confession of Faith*," *WTJ* 54 (1992); David Clark, "Beyond Inerrancy: Speech Acts and an Evangelical View of Scripture," in *For Faith and Clarity*, ed. James K. Beilby (Grand Rapids, MI: Baker, 2006); and E. J. Young, *Thy Word Is Truth* (London: Banner of Truth Trust, 1963), chapters 5–7.

[32] There is also a question about whether 1 Corinthians 7:10, 12 ascribe different levels of inspiration and truthfulness to what Paul writes. Rather than discussing this passage in this chapter, I covered it in detail in my chapter 5 on inspiration.

the difference between grace and justice. When affairs are handled by justice, whatever is earned is owed and must be paid exactly. But when things are done according to grace, as Christ does in his kingdom, people who deserve little or nothing may get much more than they deserve. In giving some more, God isn't being unfair to those who worked more and received less, as long as God gives them what he agreed to "pay," and God does.

For this parable to be inerrant, Jesus must have taught it, and its spiritual lesson must be true. There is no reason to think Matthew lied or was mistaken about Jesus telling this parable. And the parable must accurately distinguish between grace and justice, and it does. It must also be true that the Lord runs his kingdom often on the basis of grace, not justice. And, dispensing grace instead of justice must not be unfair. These things are all true, so the parable is inerrant, even though its story likely never happened.

*Isaiah 7:14*—Isaiah 7:14 is a prophecy. God gave King Ahaz a sign to prove that he would protect Judah if Ahaz would only trust the Lord. The sign/prophecy was that a virgin would conceive and bear a son. For this prophecy to be true, and thus inerrant, several things must be the case. First, God had to perform this miracle. Matthew, of course, applies the prophecy to Jesus Christ and says that his birth fulfills the prophecy (Matt. 1:22–23).

Second, to be inerrant, did Isaiah 7:14 have to be a fulfilled during Ahaz's lifetime? After all, God promised Ahaz a sign to prove his willingness and ability to protect Ahaz and Judah. Our usual intuition is that a prophecy has only one fulfillment. But that isn't always so, for some prophecies apparently have multiple fulfillments. This isn't the place to make the case, but an example is Joel's prophecy in Joel 2:28–32. Peter claimed (Acts 2:16–21) that it was fulfilled on the day of Pentecost, but the prophecy was given specifically to Israel. On the day of Pentecost some Jews surely responded as Peter preached, but there was no national revival within Israel, as Joel 2 seems to predict. Still, Peter said that what happened at Pentecost fulfilled Joel's prophecy ("this is that . . . "), but he didn't say "this, and only this, is that which was spoken by Joel the prophet." Hence, there is reason to think that, in addition to the fulfillment of this prophecy on the day of Pentecost, it still will be fulfilled in national Israel as a whole in a coming day.[33]

Similarly, some argue that Isaiah 7:14 needs multiple fulfillments: one in the NT with Jesus's birth, because Matthew, writing under inspiration, says Jesus's birth fulfilled the prophecy; and another during Ahaz's lifetime, because God promised him a sign to prove his power and willingness to protect

---

[33] For more details see my "Theological Systems of Discontinuity"; and Paul D. Feinberg, "Hermeneutics of Discontinuity," in *Continuity and Discontinuity: Essays in Honor of S. Lewis Johnson*, ed. John S. Feinberg (Westchester, IL: Crossway, 1988).

Ahaz and Judah. Some OT scholars believe this prophecy was fulfilled in Ahaz's lifetime, though of course it wasn't fulfilled by the birth of anyone who could qualify as the God-man. Readers can consult commentaries on Isaiah to see how interpreters have argued that this passage was fulfilled during Ahaz's lifetime.

The key question is whether it had to be fulfilled in Ahaz's lifetime in order for the verse to be inerrant. Here I suspect that we may be misled into thinking God had only one way to give Ahaz a sign, namely, by actually performing the miracle in his lifetime. But isn't it possible that the mere promise of a miracle, without performing it immediately, could serve as a sign? By telling Ahaz what the miracle would be, God did not also say he would perform the deed immediately (or even soon). Of course, nothing in Isaiah 7:14 forbids God from fulfilling this prophecy during Ahaz's lifetime, but the text doesn't clearly limit the fulfillment to Ahaz's lifetime. So, just telling Ahaz that God would do this miracle, regardless of whether the miracle happened, could serve as a sign to Ahaz of God's seriousness about protecting him and Judah. In contrast, if one thinks this prophecy had to be fulfilled in Ahaz's lifetime, it is possible to find fulfillment during Ahaz's lifetime—here, consult the commentaries for the child's identity.

What about the name he was to be called, Immanuel? Saying, "you shall call his name Immanuel, God with us," can be seen as both a prediction and an order. As an order, it can neither be true nor false, only obeyed or disobeyed. As a prediction, it must be fulfilled, but even so, it isn't clear that the one who fulfills the prophecy must actually be named "Immanuel," or whether "Immanuel" is a description that will be true of him. However, from what we know about how Jesus fulfilled this prophecy, it is surely correct to think of him as "Immanuel" ("God with us"), regardless of whether anyone ever called him that.

*Matthew 2:15*—Matthew 2:15 speaks of the return of Joseph, Mary, and Jesus from Egypt after the death of Herod. Herod wanted to kill Jesus, because he had been told Jesus was King of the Jews, and Herod wanted no competition for his throne. Matthew says the return from Egypt fulfilled what the Lord said through Hosea, and then quotes Hosea 11:1.

When we look more closely at Matthew 2:15 and its use of Hosea 11:1, it appears that Matthew made a mistake or two. Matthew appealed to Hosea 11:1 as though it were a prophecy that Jesus fulfilled. But in its own context, Hosea 11:1 is part of a very passionate love story—God's love for his ancient people Israel. In Hosea's day, Israel had gone after strange gods, even as Hosea's wife had gone after strange lovers. Despite Israel's unfaithfulness, Hosea 11 details God's enduring, compassionate love for his wayward people.

It recounts various ways God showed his love for her. Verse 1 refers to Israel's deliverance from Egyptian bondage via the exodus. This happened very early in Israel's history—in God's words, "when Israel was a child." In fact, in Hosea 11 God likens his relation to Israel to that of a father to his son. Often in the OT, Hosea included, Israel is portrayed as God's wife (and an unfaithful one at that), but in this verse Israel is depicted as God's son.[34]

But Hosea 11:1 doesn't prophesy something future to Hosea. It refers to a past (from Hosea's perspective) historical event, and it is a specific reference to Israel, not to a coming Messiah. So, Matthew appears to have made two errors. Hosea 11:1 is not a prophecy, and it isn't about Jesus's return to Israel after Herod died. It's about Israel's departure from Egyptian bondage many centuries before Jesus. How can this verse be inerrant? I believe it is inerrant, but how that is so requires some explanation.

First, what should we do with Matthew's claim that Hosea 11:1 is a prophecy, one that Jesus fulfilled? Actually, the question just asked contains an incorrect assumption. To see this, we must first see the Greek phrase that precedes the quote of Hosea 11:1. Matthew wrote, *hina plērothē to rēthen hupo kuriou dia tou prophētou legontos* ("in order that the saying from the Lord through the prophet might be fulfilled, saying" [AT]). I note first that the word for "the saying" (*rēthen*) does not per se mean "a prediction," though of course, in the appropriate context, it could mean that. A *rēthen* could be about the past, present, or future. We know that in its context, Hosea 11:1 is a saying about Israel's past.

Thus, one can use *rēthen* without having to predict something. So, from that standpoint, it doesn't appear that Matthew has misused Hosea. But that doesn't end the story, because Matthew *does* say that what happened with Jesus occurred so that the saying of the Lord through the prophet *might be fulfilled (plērothē)*. Doesn't using *plērothē* mean that Matthew took the quote to be a prediction, and if so, how can Matthew 2:15 be inerrant?

My contention is that, when we properly interpret the verse, we see that Matthew used typological interpretation. Typological interpretation, as I have argued elsewhere,[35] follows the rules for handling typology. Of course, all of this requires explanation.

In various places Scripture uses typology. Typology is a kind of figure of speech, if one prefers that terminology, but the key is what a type is and how it functions. A type is a person, object, action, or event which, while real in its

---

[34] The use of two different images for God's people Israel (wife and son) shouldn't be surprising. The same kind of thing is done in the NT with members of the church. We are the bride of Christ and also the children of God—God's sons and daughters.

[35] See my "Salvation in the Old Testament," in *Tradition and Testament: Essays in Honor of Charles Lee Feinberg*, ed. John S. Feinberg and Paul D. Feinberg (Chicago: Moody, 1981); and my "Theological Systems of Discontinuity" for these points about typology and typological interpretation.

own right, also points forward to a person, object, action, or event that will exist/happen in the future. That to which the type points is called the antitype, and it is also real, in addition to pointing backward to the type. Scholars also emphasize that the meaning of the antitype "escalates" the meaning of the type. For example, if a person used as a type was a noteworthy individual, the antitype will be an even greater person. As readers undoubtedly sense, there must be a parallel of some kind between type and antitype for typology to work. We can also say that, while a type doesn't per se *predict* a future person, object, event, or action, it is forward-looking and anticipates something future. It foreshadows (and in that sense is a "kind of prediction") what is to come.

Examples illustrate these points. Some types and their antitypes are identified in Scripture, while most are not. When Scripture doesn't say typology is at work, the exegete must ensure that the analogy between the type and antitype is so strong that to call them type and antitype is more than just creative interpretation. With that said, I believe we can see Abraham offering up Isaac as a sacrifice on Mount Moriah as a type of God the Father offering up God the Son as a sacrifice on Calvary. Many have also argued, I believe correctly, that Joseph, in his purity amid temptation and in his suffering at the hands of brothers but living to serve them, is a type of Jesus Christ. Paul says that the rock in the wilderness that gave water to the Israelites was Christ (1 Cor. 10:4). Even these few examples show that the antitype "escalates" in value and significance whatever the type is.

How are these facts about typology relevant to Matthew 2:15? As follows: I believe Matthew used typological interpretation here. Typological interpretation follows the rules of typology: both type and antitype have their own meaning in their respective contexts while also pointing forward or backward to the other. Hence, Matthew sees a real event, the exodus of Israel (God's son) from Egypt, as a type of the exodus of Jesus (God's greater Son) from Egypt after Herod dies, another real event. Since a type foreshadows an antitype, it isn't wrong to say that the antitype "fulfills" the type. Hence, Matthew isn't wrong about the "saying" being fulfilled.

So far so good, but why didn't Matthew just refer to the exodus and cite a passage from the book of Exodus? Because it was much simpler to cite Hosea 11:1, which refers to the exodus and to God calling his son out of Egypt. Is there a single verse in Exodus that does all of that? Perhaps, but perhaps not. In any case, Hosea 11:1 says concisely and completely what Matthew wanted to say about Jesus's return from Egypt, so why not use it? Once we realize that Matthew is using Hosea 11:1 typologically, it isn't a problem that Hosea 11:1 is about a past (from Hosea's perspective) historical event. Matthew knew that, but by applying this passage to Jesus, Matthew says more than just that Jesus and his parents returned home from Egypt. He also asserts that the exodus of Israel, God's son, from Egypt is a type of a later exodus of God's greater Son Jesus from Egypt.

So, what Matthew says is true. The key, of course, is seeing that he used the exodus, and Hosea 11:1's comment about it, as a type of Jesus's return from Egypt. In addition, it is also true that Israel and Jesus are analogously God's son, though the latter in a much more exalted and magnificent way than the former! So, Matthew 2:15 is true, and hence, inerrant.

*1 Timothy 2:12*—1 Timothy 2:12 is a key passage in the debate over male and female roles in ministry, especially in the local church. Egalitarians have offered some rather creative interpretations of what Paul means here. Some have even interpreted this passage as complementarians do, and then added that Paul is wrong or that this passage must be understood in light of passages like Galatians 3:28.

While I understand this passage in effect to prohibit a woman from being pastor of a local church, that is irrelevant to whether it is inerrant. One way to interpret the passage (though, I think, incorrectly) is to say that Paul just gives a report of his practice in churches he had founded or where he had ministered. "I do not permit . . . " would then be nothing more than Paul reporting what he had done. If so, the verse is inerrant if, in fact, Paul followed the practice he described in this verse. Since he adds an explanation and justification of this rule (in vv. 13–15), he must have remembered correctly what he had done. Hence, there is no good reason to think this report is false; the verse, on this interpretation, is true and hence inerrant.

But surely this verse isn't a simple report of Paul's practice in local churches. Paul states a rule, and clearly says that other churches are to obey it. "I do not permit/allow . . . " is just another way of saying, "Do not let . . . " This is a command, and that is in part why this verse is so contentious. If it is a command, it seems to say a woman cannot pastor a local church.

Given that this verse is a command, what should we say about its inerrancy? As already shown, commands are neither true nor false, so they cannot be inerrant, but they can't be errant either, if inerrancy is defined in terms of truth. This must not be misunderstood, however. Just because this verse is neither errant nor inerrant, that doesn't mean obedience is optional. However one interprets it, it is God's command and must be obeyed.

*John 14:1–3*—John 14:1–3 begins with a command, and then moves to a promise. The command is neither true nor false, but should be obeyed. Jesus then talks about heaven, tells his disciples he is going there to prepare a place for them, and assures them that he will return and take them there. What Jesus says about heaven is either true or false. What he promises to do there and his promise to return for his disciples is also either true or false. This is one of those situations, however, where we cannot now verify it. But once our lives in our natural bodies end, we *will* be able to verify what Jesus says about heaven. Of course, if Jesus returns for his church before we die, we will be able to verify it sooner.

This passage is a good example of why the definition of inerrancy includes a proviso about Scripture being shown to be true *when all facts are known*. Of course, as some apologists argue, even now we can show that Jesus is God's divine Son, as evidenced by his resurrection. Since he is, whatever he says must be true; being omniscient, he knows the truth, and being morally perfect, he wouldn't lie or mislead us.[36] Thus, what he says about heaven must be true, and it is verified by his own testimony.

If one takes this second approach, this passage is still inerrant. The basis for that belief, however, will not be evidence we'll know only after we die or are translated into Christ's presence. Rather, by this second approach, belief in this passage's inerrancy would stem from Christ's testimony and who he is.

*1 Timothy 1:15*—1 Timothy 1:15 may seem at first to make a single, rather straightforward assertion. But it actually asserts four different things, and each must be true for the verse to be inerrant. Paul writes,

> Here is a trustworthy saying that deserves full acceptance: Christ Jesus came into the world to save sinners—of whom I am the worst. (NIV 1984)

Paul's four claims are: (1) what he writes is true (*pistos* is the word for "trustworthy," but in this sentence it means "true"); (2) what he writes is worthy of everyone's acceptance; (3) Christ became incarnate to save sinners (and he did so by his death and resurrection, neither of which Paul mentions, but Timothy would understand that); and (4) Paul is the worst of all sinners.

Are (1)–(4) all true? I believe they are, but I must explain why. Clearly, (3) is the key to the whole verse. If it is false, then neither (1) nor (2) can be true. Of course, the NT offers ample evidence that (3) is true, and so (1)–(2) must also be true. What about (4)? Surely there have been much greater sinners than Paul, before, during, and after he lived.

So, is (4) false, and the whole verse errant? Not at all, for Paul uses hyperbole—exaggeration—to make a point. To confirm this, we need only read the next verse, where Paul uses his great sinfulness to say that God's intent in saving such a terrible sinner was that others who are also terrible sinners could see

---

[36] An apologist who uses this line of argument to affirm Scripture's reliability is John W. Montgomery. See his *Where Is History Going?* (Minneapolis: Bethany Fellowship, 1969).

that they aren't beyond God's saving grace. If God could save Paul, those who think they are so sinful that God could never save them should think again.

Is (4), then, true after all? Yes, and even if Paul wasn't the worst sinner ever. As noted earlier in this chapter, we don't call someone a liar who exaggerates to make a point. Paul's point is surely true. Properly interpreted, (1)–(4) are true, and hence 1 Timothy 1:15 is inerrant.

*Revelation 19:17*—Revelation 19:17 is the beginning of an apocalyptic vision— or, if preferred, it is part of the apocalyptic vision that begins at least as early as verse 11. Verse 17 also begins a sentence that goes to the end of verse 18. The key questions are whether this verse asserts something as true (and, *what* it asserts), and if so, whether the vision must be fulfilled in order for the verse to be true. Arguably, what this vision predicts has not come to pass yet on Planet Earth, but *must* it be fulfilled in order for the verse to be true? Let me quote verses 17–18, and then the answer should be clear. John writes,

> And I saw an angel standing in the sun, who cried in a loud voice to all the birds flying in midair, "Come, gather together for the great supper of God, so that you may eat the flesh of kings, generals, and mighty men, of horses and their riders, and the flesh of all people, free and slave, small and great." (NIV 1984)

Now, it is important initially to note that the author of these words is also the one having this vision. John says that he saw an angel standing in the sun, and that the angel stated the command recorded in the rest of verse 17 and in verse 18. Must there have been a real angel standing where John saw the angel standing and saying what John claims the angel said? Must this vision (however it will be fulfilled) come to pass in order for John's assertions in verse 17 to be true?

These questions are perhaps more difficult than they might seem, but their answers depend on our understanding of a particular form of divine revelation: visions. As we saw in the chapter on special revelation, in visions God reveals something directly to a recipient. Typically, the recipient is awake, and often he is transported beyond his physical surroundings. Is he taken to a place that is real, or only imaginary? It depends on the vision. We can say with some degree of confidence that Isaiah (Isaiah 6) actually did see the "throne room of God" in heaven, and that Paul most likely was transported into heaven (2 Corinthians 12). On the other hand, it isn't clear that there ever was an actual valley filled with dry bones (Ezekiel 37) that one could locate on Planet Earth. Certainly, what Ezekiel saw happen there isn't something we would see if we just found the plot of land on earth where it happened.

So, a vision can be of something that actually exists, and the vision prophesies something that will literally come true; or the vision may be of something that doesn't actually exist but it still serves as a prophecy of things to come. Thankfully, we don't have to decide that issue in order to ask whether Revelation 19:17–18 is true. The reason is in how John begins verse 17. He says that he saw (presumably in a vision) an angel and he heard the angel say the words recorded in the rest of verses 17 and 18. For this to be inerrant, it must be true that John saw and heard these things. Since John received a vision, and since we know that visions can include objects, people, and places that are either real or unreal, it isn't necessary that what John saw could be seen and verified by anyone else.

Now, we should add that whatever the vision predicts, when properly interpreted, must come to pass in order for the vision to be true. Even so, for us now to say that verses 17–18 are true and thus inerrant, all that must be true is that John actually had this vision and heard the words he claimed the angel said. John, of course, could be hallucinating—as could be true for all the visions contained in Revelation, but John reports them as actual visions, not as hallucinations. Given the details and content of these visions, there seems to be no good reason to doubt that John actually had these visions. We are still waiting for this vision to come to pass. When it does come to pass, we can *verify* that the vision's predictions are true. For now, we need only to affirm that John told the truth when he relates what he saw and heard. There seems little chance of making a convincing case against those claims.

### The Concept of Infallibility

While many may agree with what I have said about inerrancy, some may want to say something more about biblical sentences that are neither errant nor inerrant. They are also revelation, and as inspired, they are the very words of God.

Prime candidates for describing such sentences are infallible and authoritative. Those are two distinct qualities, and they are also ambiguous. In chapter 10, I shall address authority, but now I want to look at infallibility. Infallibility seems to have a much longer history than inerrancy as a predicate applied to Scripture. As with inerrancy, we must explain both its meaning and its extension (i.e., how much of Scripture it covers).

Even a brief study of infallibility in relation to Scripture will quickly quench any initial optimism about it being a concept supplemental to inerrancy. The meaning and use of infallibility even during the past fifty years don't actually help to clarify our understanding of Scripture. Instead, they often confuse and conflate a number of issues. Hence, I must ask: does this term and concept have a clear, universally agreed upon meaning among those who discuss Scripture's nature, or are they so clouded in ambiguity that, though they once may have been helpful, they now confuse issues, rather than clarifying them?

To clarify the problems, consider the different possible meanings for infallibility. I begin with this term's root meaning and its basic "dictionary meaning," as seen in works like the *Oxford English Dictionary*. My beginning the discussion in this way may surprise some, because normally, evangelical theology begins with Scripture. However, "infallibility" is no more a biblical term than is "inerrancy." As for the concept, there are many different ways to define it, and it is dubious that many of them can be supported by Scripture. But even if one could define infallibility, the plethora of possible meanings makes it unclear how to use the term and concept in relation to Scripture.

The English terms "infallible" and "infallibility" come from the Latin root *fallo*, which means, among other things, "to lead astray" or "to deceive."[37] In the seventeenth-century *Oxford English Dictionary*, "infallibility" is defined as "the quality or fact of being infallible or exempt from liability to err."[38] As for the adjective "infallible," the *Oxford English Dictionary* relates it to people and to things. As to persons and their judgments, it means "not liable to be deceived or mistaken; incapable of erring." In terms of things, it means "not liable to fail, unfailing, not liable to prove false, erroneous, or mistaken; that unfailingly holds good."[39]

In comparing these definitions with the concept of inerrancy, it should be clear that in their most fundamental sense, "infallibility" and "inerrancy" are actually synonymous. The *Oxford English Dictionary* helps to see this. As Delivuk notes, "inerrant" was used only in relation to astronomy in the seventeenth century, while the dictionary says that "inerrancy" wasn't used until the nineteenth century. However, "inerrability" and "inerrable" were used earlier than the nineteenth century. "Inerrability" is defined as "freedom from liability to err; infallibility." "Inerrable" is defined as "incapable of erring; not liable to err; exempt from the possibility of error; infallible, unerring."[40]

As to actual usage in theological discourse, we can also say that for a long time, and even in our day, many understand "inerrancy" and "infallibility" as synonymous.[41] As James D. G. Dunn notes, while there have been others

---

[37] *Cassell's Latin-English and English-Latin Dictionary* (New York: Funk & Wagnalls, n.d.), 217.

[38] Delivuk, "Inerrancy, Infallibility, and Scripture," 350. Delivuk cites *The Oxford English Dictionary*, 13 vols. (Oxford: Clarendon, 1933), 5:249.

[39] Ibid., for both the dictionary and Delivuk. See also Paul Feinberg, "Meaning of Inerrancy," for the same definitions of "infallibility" and "infallible" (287).

[40] Delivuk, "Inerrancy, Infallibility, and Scripture," 350, citing *The Oxford English Dictionary*, 5:242–243.

[41] See, e.g., the following who assess the issue in this way; that is, they note that at one point not long ago, infallibility was defined quite like inerrancy. See Honeycutt, "Biblical Authority: A Treasured Heritage!," 617; Nicole, "Why I Am 'Comfortable' with Inerrancy," 112–113; and Venema, "Functional Inerrancy," who claims (134) that a biblically warranted doctrine of infallibility holds that *the biblical texts are unfailingly and invariably true in all that they teach and affirm about all those matters on which they choose to speak, whether doctrinal, ethical, historical, etc*" (italics are Venema's). In many ways this "mirrors" Paul Feinberg's definition of biblical inerrancy.

who define "infallibility" in a different sense, biblical scholars and theologians within the tradition of the great Princeton theologians, like E. J. Young, have defined it as equivalent to inerrancy. Dunn quotes Young as follows:

> In all parts, in its very entirety, the Bible, if we are to accept its witness to itself, is utterly infallible. It is not only that each book given the name of Scripture is infallible but, more than that, the content of each such book is itself Scripture, the Word of God written and, hence, infallible, free entirely from the errors which adhere to mere human compositions. Not alone to moral and ethical truths, but to all statements of fact does this inspiration extend.[42]

If this were all there is to say about infallibility, we could easily use it interchangeably with inerrancy. The concepts would be indistinguishable. However, things are not so easy, for in recent and current literature one finds at least another *seven* definitions of infallibility. And, as will quickly become clear, these different senses are not synonymous, and most of them have just as much "right" to the term "infallibility" as do the others!

Undoubtedly, the most common modification of infallibility narrows its *extension* from all of Scripture to only a portion of it. Now, this may seem acceptable, since I have argued that inerrancy applies only to Scriptures that are assertions, but the point here is a different one. Even if we take inerrancy to cover all biblical assertions, this first different sense of infallibility says it extends only to some of those assertions. Which specific assertions infallibility extends to is easy to identify, though different authors express it slightly differently. The main idea, though, is that Scripture is infallible in all it asserts about matters of doctrine and practice. Or, as some put it, infallibility applies only to saving knowledge—matters of faith and obedience.[43]

One can hardly say this more clearly than Stephen T. Davis does in his *The Debate about the Bible*. He writes,

> The Bible is *inerrant* if and only if it makes no false or misleading statements on any topic whatsoever. The Bible is *infallible* if and only if it makes no false or misleading statements on any matter of faith and practice. In these senses, I personally hold that the Bible is infallible but not inerrant.[44]

---

[42] Young, *Thy Word Is Truth*, 48, quoted in James D. G. Dunn, "Authority of Scripture," 105–106.
[43] For this sense of "infallibility" see Honeycutt, "Biblical Authority: A Treasured Heritage!," 609, 617; Brown, "Inerrancy and Infallibility of the Bible," 38; Price, "Inerrant the Wind," 136–137; Dunn, "Authority of Scripture," 105; Holmes, "Evangelical Doctrines of Scripture in Transatlantic Perspective," 45; Dembski, "Problem of Error in Scripture," 93; and Ted G. Jelen, Clyde Wilcox, and Corwin E. Smidt, "Biblical Literalism and Inerrancy: A Methodological Investigation," *Sociological Analysis* 51 (1990): 307–308.
[44] Stephen T. Davis, *The Debate about the Bible* (Philadelphia: Westminster, 1977), 23. Though not using the same terminology, Daniel Fuller, by distinguishing between revelational and nonrevelational Scripture, makes the same basic point in a rather famous/notorious article, "Benjamin B. Warfield's View of Faith and History," *Bulletin of the Evangelical Theological Society* 11 (Spring 1968).

Though this distinction between inerrancy and infallibility is quite clear, it is still somewhat odd in two respects. To say that Scripture is infallible if it makes no false or misleading statements on matters of doctrine and practice already implies that there might be errors in other things it says. Even casual readers know the Bible contains much more than doctrinal claims and commands about how one should live, organize and run a church, etc. So it is a bit odd that a claim meant to be positive implies something negative about Scripture.

There is a further oddity worth noting. The Bible is said to be infallible on matters of practice, but what sort of biblical teaching relates to practice? Normally, this refers to imperatives meant to govern behavior, that is, Scripture's commands about the Christian's manner of life and relationships to God and the world. But commands don't bear truth—they are neither true nor false. If so, then it makes no sense to say that Scripture is infallible if it makes no false or misleading claims on matters of practice. This comment is irrelevant to every command about anything in Scripture. I'm not saying that Scripture has no assertions that are relevant to practice, only that most of what Scripture says about matters of practice are commands, not assertions. The result of this point is that infallibility, as this definition conceives it, really applies mostly to matters of doctrine and to little, if anything, else. When I cover objections to inerrancy, more will be said about rejecting Scripture's complete inerrancy and holding only the truth of what the Bible says about matters of faith and practice.

James Denney offers a slightly different notion of infallibility. He focuses on matters of saving knowledge, but his emphasis isn't just on information. Rather, he speaks of a functional infallibility that Scripture possesses. As he puts it,

> The infallibility of the Scriptures is not a mere verbal inerrancy or historical accuracy, but an infallibility of power to save. The Word of God infallibly carries God's power to save men's souls. If a man submits his heart and mind to the Spirit of God speaking in it, he will infallibly become a new creature in Christ Jesus. That is the only kind of infallibility I believe in. For a mere verbal inerrancy I care not one straw. It is worth nothing to me; it would be worth nothing if it were there, and it is not.[45]

Then, inerrancy has been defined in a number of different ways over the last century that are somewhat idiosyncratic. For example, in an attempt to distinguish inerrancy from infallibility, some have argued that infallibility is actually the stronger term. That is, to be inerrant means that Scripture *does not* err. This is meant as a factual claim about Scripture. In contrast, infallibility, as applied to Scripture, means that it is *not capable* of error; i.e., error

---

[45] Quoted by A. B. Bruce, *Inspiration and Inerrancy* (London: James Clarke, 1891), 19–20, quoted in Dunn, "Authority of Scripture," 106.

isn't even possible. Hence, infallibility entails inerrancy, but inerrancy doesn't entail infallibility.[46]

In a somewhat unusual use of infallibility, William E. Hull relates the concept to matters pertaining to the very text of Scripture itself. Reminding readers that no one possesses the autographs from the biblical authors, Hull says that we have texts that are a fairly reliable representation of what was originally written, but certainly not infallible, i.e., not identical to the autographs. Moreover, even if we had perfect *copies* of the originals, the autographs were written primarily in Hebrew and Greek, so they would need to be translated, and with the way modern language continues to change, there can be no such thing as an infallible translation. And, finally, even if we could produce an infallible translation from an infallible text, we still wouldn't have an infallible Bible, because it would have to be interpreted and explained by fallible interpreters.[47] Clearly, these considerations have nothing to do with Scripture and truth, but are more relevant to textual criticism, Bible translation, and hermeneutics.

Yet another distinction between inerrancy and infallibility comes from Gordon Lewis, as described in an article by Stanley Obitts. Obitts notes that it is propositions (here Obitts uses "propositions" as equivalent to what I mean by assertions) that in the primary sense are what can be either true or false. Of course, a given sentence can be either effective or ineffective in stating a proposition. Having made this point, Obitts adds that "this is the reason for Gordon Lewis' suggestion that the term 'infallible' be reserved for the never-failing ability of the words in the autographs to convey the revealed truths, while the term 'inerrant' be reserved for the truth of what is expressed by those symbols—viz., the revealed propositions."[48]

Two more definitions of infallibility are worth noting, though again, they are a bit unusual. Both, however, carefully distinguish between infallibility and inerrancy. The first comes from Carl F. H. Henry and isn't totally unlike that of Gordon Lewis. According to Henry, inerrancy relates only to the oral and written proclamation of the originally inspired prophets and apostles. Henry adds that "not only was their communication of the Word of God efficacious in teaching the truth of revelation, but their transmission of that Word was error-free." Just to clarify this last point, Henry adds that "inerrancy does not extend to copies, translations or versions."[49] So, what was error-free (inerrant)

[46] Venema, "Functional Inerrancy," 133. Roger Nicole makes the same distinction, assuming that one needs to distinguish between the terms "inerrancy" and "infallibility." See Nicole, "James I. Packer's Contribution to the Doctrine of the Inerrancy of Scripture," in *Doing Theology for the People of God: Studies in Honor of J. I. Packer*, ed. Donald Lewis and Alister McGrath (Downers Grove, IL: InterVarsity Press, 1996), 177–178.
[47] William E. Hull, "Shall We Call the Bible Infallible?," *Perspectives in Religious Studies* 37 (Summer 2010): 211–212.
[48] Stanley Obitts, "A Philosophical Analysis of Certain Assumptions of the Doctrine of the Inerrancy of the Bible," *JETS* 26 (June 1983): 129. Obitts refers to an article by Gordon Lewis that appeared in the *Bulletin of the Evangelical Theological Society* 6 (Winter 1963): 18–27. That article is, "What Does Infallibility Mean?"
[49] Carl F. H. Henry, *God, Revelation, and Authority, Volume II: God Who Speaks and Shows* (Waco, TX: Word, 1976), 14.

about Scripture was the author's original transcription into written text of what the Lord had revealed.

At least two things are a bit unusual in Henry's definition. The first is applying it to the oral proclamation of prophets and apostles. The second is that what turns out to be inerrant is the transference of divine revelation into written form, not the resultant document. That is, the content of revelation might have errors, but Scripture is still inerrant because what God revealed to the writers, they accurately recorded. Of course, Henry doesn't think anything God revealed was false (he does speak of the truth of revelation), but his actual definition of inerrancy relates to the accurate transfer of divine revelation from the author's mind to "paper," the autograph.

Greater novelty enters the picture when Henry defines infallibility. He explains that copies of Scripture can be called infallible "in that these extant derivatives of the autographs do not corrupt the original content but convey the truth of revelation in reliable verbal form, and infallibly lead the penitent reader to salvation."[50] This, of course, has nothing to do with whether these documents' contents are true. Rather, it focuses on the derivatives of the autographs' ability to convey reliably the content of the autographs, and upon their salvific function in the lives of repentant sinners. This definition of infallibility sounds a lot like that proposed by Gordon Lewis.

A final definition for consideration appears in Kevin Vanhoozer's "The Semantics of Biblical Literature: Truth and Scripture's Diverse Literary Forms." Vanhoozer rightly notes that Scripture isn't written like a theological treatise. Moreover, it isn't written in just one literary form. The distinction between the various literary genres of Scripture is not just the difference between prose and poetry. Rather, one finds literary forms as diverse as poetry, Gospel, epistles, drama (one way to understand the book of Job), apocalyptic literature, and much more. The content of what any two authors say may be the same, but that doesn't mean they say it in the same way. This is even true for one author who writes several biblical books—think of the apostle John, who wrote a Gospel, epistles, and an apocalypse.

In addition, Vanhoozer proposes that we should think of biblical books as divine discourse, the results of divine speech acts. Here Vanhoozer invokes the speech act analysis of language first proposed by J. L. Austin and later refined and developed by John Searle. According to speech act theory, the utterance of any sentence performs three acts. The first is the locutionary act, the act of saying something. The second is the illocutionary act, the act of saying or doing something *by* uttering the locution. The utterer may intend what he says to warn, inform, command, etc., his or her hearer. So, for example, by telling

---

[50] Ibid.

someone that she is standing within inches of a cliff's edge, my intention isn't just to give her information, but also to warn her of impending danger.

The third act performed when a sentence is uttered is called a perlocutionary act. This refers to the intended (and hoped for) response of the listener to what is said. In the example just used, the intended perlocutionary uptake of the person in danger is that she will move away from the cliff's edge and no longer be in danger of falling over it.[51]

Vanhoozer proposes that speech act theory be applied not only to oral speech but to written discourse as well.[52] In particular, he wants to apply it to Scripture. As Austin and Searle note, a speech act can fail or be defective.[53] However, Vanhoozer argues, God's intended speech acts in Scripture never fail to achieve their goal. Vanhoozer explains this as follows:

> In any divine communication, the four conditions necessary for felicitous or nondefective speech acts are always fulfilled. God's locutions are always meaningful; the performance of the discourse act is always appropriate; the author is always sincere; the propositional content (predication and reference) is true (fitting) for its illocutionary mode.[54]

Having made these points about speech acts, Vanhoozer next offers his definitions of infallibility and inerrancy. The diverse literary forms of biblical books (as a whole, and also diverse literary genres within a given book) suggest that we can't see every biblical sentence as doing only one thing, making an assertion about the world. Of course, many biblical speech acts are assertions, but there are many other types of speech acts such as warnings, commands, and expressives that assert nothing. While Vanhoozer grants that assertive speech acts do, to use my terminology, bear truth or falsity, and so it is proper to speak of them as inerrant, this leaves many biblical sentences entirely out of the picture. We need a descriptor that will apply to all of Scripture with its many different speech acts, not just something like inerrancy that is relevant to only one kind of speech act—assertions. Vanhoozer proposes that the proper concept to cover all of Scripture's many and diverse speech acts is infallibility.

---

[51] For the basics of speech act theory, see J. L. Austin, *How to Do Things with Words* (Cambridge: Harvard University Press, 1975); and John R. Searle, *Speech Acts: An Essay in the Philosophy of Language* (New York: Cambridge University Press, 1969).

[52] It isn't clear that Austin and Searle intended their theory to apply to anything other than oral discourse. There are major differences between an oral speech act and a written one. For example, a written speech act contains no nonverbal behavior that comes with oral speech—e.g., facial expressions, gestures, voice inflections, all of which help listeners to grasp the illocutionary force of the utterance. Nonetheless, since the nature of speech act theory is not our purpose, we can be charitable for the sake of this discussion and grant that it can be applied to written documents as well. Even if so, one thing is certain: as biblical authors wrote, they couldn't have had this theory of language and meaning in mind. Hence, we should be careful not to force them to say or do things they didn't intend to say or do by making them fit this, or any other, theory of meaning that was quite foreign to their thinking as they wrote Scripture.

[53] See, e.g., Austin, "Lecture II," in *How to Do Things with Words*, 12–24.

[54] Vanhoozer, "Semantics of Biblical Literature," 94–95.

But what is it about any given speech act of Scripture that makes it infallible? Vanhoozer explains as follows:

> Scripture is therefore indefatigable in its illocutionary intent. It encourages, warns, asserts, reproves, instructs, commands—all infallibly. Note that this makes inerrancy a *subset* of infallibility. On those occasions when Scripture does affirm something, the affirmation is true. Thus, we may continue to hold to inerrancy while at the same time acknowledging that Scripture does many other things besides assert. Logically, however, infallibility is prior to inerrancy. God's word invariably accomplishes its purpose (infallibility); and when this purpose is assertion, the proposition of the speech act is true (inerrancy). Note too that inerrancy is subject to the intention and context of the assertive speech act.[55]

As for the meaning of inerrancy, Vanhoozer later in his essay quotes Paul Feinberg's definition of biblical inerrancy.

Though this understanding of infallibility gives it a sense that is clearly distinct from inerrancy, and offers a term that can apply to all of Scripture, not just to sentences that can bear truth, there is still some ambiguity inherent in the definition. The ambiguity resides in the claim that "God's word invariably accomplishes its purpose (infallibility)." Vanhoozer correctly says that the purpose in view in this definition is the author's intended illocutionary act. The problem is that whenever someone speaks or writes, there is another intended purpose, namely (in speech act terminology), the perlocutionary uptake one hopes to evoke. In fact, I suspect that most of the time this is the purpose that most concerns the writer or speaker. Thus, if I *warn* you (the illocutionary force of my utterance) without defect (my illocutionary act is successful) of the danger of falling off a cliff, what difference does it make if you ignore my warning, fall off the cliff, and die? Would I say to myself, "well, we didn't get the perlocutionary response I had hoped for, but at least my illocutionary act was without defect, so I can be happy"? Perhaps I might think this, but if that is my only response, it is quite insensitive!

What am I saying about this definition of infallibility, besides the fact that it is rather unusual? My point is that it focuses on the *author's intended purpose*, but *that idea is ambiguous* because there are at least two purposes the author has: the *first* is about successfully performing the illocutionary act he wants, and the *second* focuses on getting the desired result from those who hear/read the illocutionary act. Indeed, infallibility defined in this way does cover all of Scripture, but what are we actually attributing of importance to Scripture when we say, with this meaning in mind, that it is infallible? Since nothing is assured about the response to what is written—and surely we don't

---

[55] Ibid., 95.

merely speak to hear ourselves talk; we want our words to have an impact—what of significance have we said when we say that every sentence of Scripture fulfills its intended illocutionary force? For assertives, that amounts to their being inerrant, and of course, that is important. But for other speech acts like expressives, directives, etc., why does that matter? That is, for example, to say that God's commands are infallible means that they contain the orders God wanted them to contain, and they do command. True, but am I at all bound to follow these commands? Infallibility, defined as Vanhoozer has, doesn't tell me; it only allows me to say that God succeeded in stating clearly what he wants to be done (the complaint here is not that this says nothing about the truth of the command, for as I have argued, commands can't be either true or false). Vanhoozer is not to be faulted for leaving out whether a command is true or false; he could be faulted if he didn't understand that commands can be neither true nor false, but he doesn't make that error. My point is first to ask what one has actually accomplished of importance by saying that all of Scripture's commands fulfilled their intended illocutionary force. And my second point is to note the ambiguity in this definition since the speaker/author has an intention *about his illocution* but *also intends* and hopes *to produce a certain result* (the perlocutionary force of the claim). Surely, there can be no guarantees about how any reader will respond, but getting the intended response seems more significant than being able to say that the author succeeded in making the kind of illocutionary act he intended to make!

Put differently, with Vanhoozer's definition, the focus is on God's intention when he speaks. But when God speaks, he has two intentions. He intends to perform an illocutionary act and he *infallibly* does so. In addition, he intends to evoke a particular result, but that doesn't always happen! So, the perlocutionary act he intends to produce is *not infallibly* produced! In cases where the illocutionary act succeeds but the perlocutionary act fails, are we to say that those Scriptures are infallible, or not? Vanhoozer's definition doesn't help us out here.

Equally important, what is the value of saying that God's word is infallible in that it completes the illocutionary act God wanted to perform? Doesn't that essentially mean that God said what he wanted to say? Even if not, how does this notion of infallibility tell us anything about inerrancy? Perhaps the response is that it isn't intended to do so. But, then, what business does it have in a discussion about biblical inerrancy? Given Vanhoozer's definition of infallibility as achieving the illocutionary act that God intended, perhaps that sense of infallibility would fit better the concept of Scripture's inspiration (or maybe even revelation). As for the second thing God intends with a speech act, the perlocution, since that doesn't always happen, we can't actually say that Scripture is infallible in that it always generates God's desired response. Hence, defining infallibility as Vanhoozer does seems problematic in several ways.

What should we say about all of these different definitions of infallibility? Must we pick one, and dismiss the others? How can such a suggestion be taken seriously, for who is to decide which definition should be used? I do think that it is a bit sad that a term with a long history and that has in the past been put to good use, has now been used in so many different ways, that it is in effect impossible to say how we should define it now. Even more, if one simply stipulates that it be defined in a certain way, how could a case be made that such a definition *is henceforth going to be the definition*? Clearly, we can't use all of these definitions, for some contradict others, and they don't all address the same thing about Scripture.

In light of these considerations, it seems that one is free to define the term as one chooses. But one can't think that such a definition will be "the authoritative definition" henceforth. For me the most significant point in the discussion in this chapter is that Scripture tells the truth, in a correspondence sense of truth. But "inerrancy," as defined in this chapter, suffices to communicate that. If one wants to add "infallibility," for reasons presented above, I think that only muddies the waters needlessly. But if one persists in using "infallibility," so long as one clearly defines how he or she will use it and so long as that definition doesn't contradict inerrancy, I see no problem in using the term. What must be avoided, however, is using infallibility in several of the distinct senses already presented. Even if none of them contradicts inerrancy or other senses of infallibility, using multiple senses of infallibility will only continue the confusion that abounds, as seen in the many different definitions presented. For myself, I prefer to use inerrancy. If infallibility must be used, I prefer to use it synonymously to inerrancy.

## BIBLICAL TEACHING ON INERRANCY

I have devoted many pages to defining precisely the concept of biblical inerrancy. However, that matters little if Scripture doesn't affirm its own inerrancy. Indeed, the Bible never uses the word "inerrancy" in regard to anything, including itself. Of course, that alone isn't decisive, because we aren't doing a word study but a conceptual study. The relevant question is whether Scripture portrays itself as inerrant.

Indeed, there is a case for inerrancy. In fact, two distinct cases can be made. One might argue for biblical inerrancy as an apologist would, citing many extrabiblical evidences that support Scripture's reliability or inerrancy. When dealing with a nonbeliever, it isn't likely that merely quoting Scriptures that say or suggest that Scripture is reliable will be convincing. Hence, we need evidences other than Scripture's testimony about itself to make an apologetic case for Scripture. Elsewhere I have presented a defense of the Gospels' reliability, and the methodology used for that defense is the one to use in defending the reliability of all of Scripture.[56]

In contrast to an apologetic defense of Scripture, there is a defense a theologian should build. The theologian must assume that apologists have made the case that Scripture is reliable, regardless of the topic it addresses. Now the theologian wants to see what Scripture says about itself. Even if Scripture doesn't claim to be inerrant, it could still in fact be inerrant, as defined earlier in this chapter. However, I contend that Scripture asserts its own inerrancy.

Some who would grant that a biblical and/or theological case can be made for inerrancy still complain that it is suspect, because the argument for inerrancy is made by inference alone. Actually, there are two kinds of arguments one can make for inerrancy. One is an inferential argument that begins with inspiration and moves ultimately to inerrancy. But, contrary to what many think, there is even more direct evidence in support of Scripture's inerrancy. This case is built by citing Scriptures that amount to affirming Scripture's inerrancy. To that line of evidence we turn first.

While it is tempting to say that some Scriptures directly say that Scripture is inerrant, that isn't exactly so. As noted a number of times, Scripture never uses the *term* inerrancy of itself (or of anything else), so we might wonder if it actually teaches the *concept*. Even if the term "inerrancy" were used, we would still need to determine what it means, so lacking the term isn't at all a major setback in defending biblical inerrancy.

Perhaps readers are a bit confused, because they know many Scriptures that speak of Scripture as true. Indeed, there are many such Scriptures, but how does one know that inerrancy should be defined in terms of truth? I have argued that it should be, but there are other ways to define it. There are many types of errors that might appear in a document, but many have nothing to do with truth (e.g., grammatical mistakes, spelling errors). I have argued that it is Scripture's truth or falsehood that most concerns us, and therefore, we should define inerrancy in terms of truthfulness. Still, the very idea of truthfulness isn't inherent in the notion of being without error. Hence, when we survey what the Bible says about itself, we should cite all the passages that say that Scripture tells the truth. But we must also add that *if inerrancy is defined in terms of truth*, then *to say* that Scripture is *true means* that *it is inerrant*.

---

[56] See my *Can You Believe It's True?*, chapter 11.

*Old Testament Evidence for Inerrancy*

OT evidence for inerrancy appears predominantly in Psalms, with another reference in Proverbs. Most of the Psalms passages center on one of two main word groups, although other verses in Psalms also teach inerrancy. The first word group stems from the verb *'aman* and includes the noun *'emet* and the adjective *'amunah*. One of these verses appears in Psalm 19. In verse 9 [Hb. 10] the psalmist writes that the Lord's judgments are true. While we are inclined to think of judgments as verdicts or even punishments in a court case, the idea in this passage is much broader. A judgment as mentioned in verse 9 refers to one's thoughts about something. Since the psalmist thinks of more than one judgment, he most likely generalizes to God's judgments about all things. Of course, a key question is where one would find God's judgments or assessments of things. While God might on occasion reveal his thoughts directly to someone, the psalmist is probably thinking that we can find God's judgments in Scripture.

The remaining verses that use *'aman, 'emet*, and *'amunah* about Scripture appear in Psalm 119, the great psalm about Scripture. In verse 86, the psalmist writes that all of God's commandments are faithful (*'amunah*). How could this be true if any are false? Surely, the point is that what God has commanded will lead no one astray—the writer knows by personal experience that this is true. He writes again in verse 138 that God has "commanded [his] testimonies in righteousness and exceeding faithfulness" (*'amunah*). It is hard to imagine that this would be true if the psalmist had found them to be false. Again in verse 151 the psalmist writes that all of God's commandments are truth (*'emet*). If we think the writer thinks this only about Scripture's precepts, that is unlikely, for in verse 142 he writes that God's law is truth (*'emet*).

While we are inclined to think only of rules when we see the term "law," here, as often in the OT, *tôrāh* (law) refers to any teaching from the Lord. Hence, this verse applies to the whole OT. Of course, that assumes that the place to find God's commands, and more broadly, his teaching (his law), is Scripture. It is most reasonable to believe that the psalmist had that in mind when he penned these verses. After all, where would the psalmist find God's law but in Scripture?

Some may protest that earlier in this chapter I explained that commands cannot bear either truth or falsity, so when the psalmist says that all God's commands are true, he actually makes a false claim, which those who know some philosophy of language can detect. However, concluding that would force our precise "metaphysical" jacket upon a psalm that intends to extol the wonders of God's word, not to make a point in philosophy of language. Surely, Jews typically thought that whatever Scripture contains (commands, assertions, etc.) came from God and, hence, they had to know

Scripture and to live in accord not only with its commands but also with anything else it teaches.

A second set of OT passages uses the word *ṣārap* of Scripture. The English translation of this word ("tested" or "tried") might suggest that the writer was unsure about whether what was tested can be trusted to be true. However, when we understand *ṣārap*, those doubts are removed. This Hebrew adjective comes from a verb used of refining or smelting precious metals. Ore that had gone through this process was purified. All imperfections were removed, and pure metal was the result. To use this term of something other than metal, such as a person or a person's words, means that they have been tested and found to be pure, without imperfection.

Psalm 12:6 (Hb. 7) declares that,

> The words of the LORD are pure words;
> As silver tried in a furnace on the earth, refined seven times.

Franz Delitzsch, writing about this verse, explains the psalmist's point (one that appears several times in various psalms) as follows: "God's word is solid silver smelted and leaving all impurity behind, and, as it were, having passed seven times through the smelting furnace, *i.e.*, the purest silver, entirely purged from dross. Silver is the emblem of everything precious and pure . . . ; and seven is the number indicating the completion of any process. . . . "[57] What could it mean to say that God's word is *ṣārap* other than that it has been put to the test and found to contain no impurity? But how could a book with falsehoods be considered pure, passing the test? That would be unthinkable, especially since the words in view are those of almighty God, who knows all truth and, because of his moral perfection, cannot lie. Surely, the psalmist means that God's word has been put to the test repeatedly ("refined seven times") and found to be without flaw; it is therefore totally truthful.

The Hebrew term *ṣārap* appears again in Psalm 18:30 (Hb. 31). The writer says that the word of the Lord is tested (*ṣārap*) and found pure. In Psalm 119:140 the psalmist says to God, "your word is very pure" (*ṣārap*). We find similar sentiments in Proverbs (30:5), where the writer affirms that "every word of God is tested" (*ṣārap*) and found pure. How could the writers make such claims if they thought God's word contains untruth? The writers would certainly think that the purity of God's word includes its truthfulness. If it fails the test of truth, it seems impossible that it has been tested and passed the test. The only other question is where these writers would think one could find God's word, and certainly they would answer that *Scripture* is God's word.

---

[57] Franz Delitzsch, *Biblical Commentary on the Psalms*, vol. 1 (repr., Grand Rapids, MI: Eerdmans, 1968), 197.

Hence, all of the Scriptures cited amount to teaching that Scripture (specifically the OT) is true, and if we add that inerrancy should be defined in terms of truth, then it is not a mishandling of these passages to say that they teach Scripture's inerrancy. But other OT passages are also relevant to our discussion, even though they don't use any of the words from the 'aman word group or ṣārap. Psalm 19:7–8 (Hb. 8–9) says that God's law is blameless and his testimony is sure. Moreover, his precepts are right; his commandments are pure. In Psalm 119 the psalmist writes (v. 128) that he esteems as right all of God's precepts concerning everything. And in verse 137 he adds that all of God's judgments are upright/righteous/just. Of course, the writer of each of these psalms believes that the place to find God's law, his testimony, his commandments and judgments is in his word, i.e., in Scripture. But how could any of these things said of God's word be true if Scripture contains falsehoods? They couldn't be true, and the writers surely knew that. Hence, by attributing these characteristics to God's word, they in effect say that it is what we have defined as inerrant.

### New Testament Evidence for Inerrancy

The NT offers ample evidence of Scripture's truth. While Jesus and the NT authors often spoke of the OT, their teachings also include the NT. NT evidence divides into two main parts. First, there is Jesus's testimony and testimony about him. Second, there is the testimony of NT writers about Scripture.

*Testimony of and about Jesus*—Jesus said many things about Scripture, but I begin with three key passages that teach Scripture's truth. Once those passages are presented, then we can glean further evidence from other things Jesus said about Scripture, and from how the Gospel writers in particular related the OT to Jesus's life, ministry, and death.

First, there is Matthew 22:29. Beginning at verse 23, Matthew says that the Sadducees asked Jesus a question. They didn't believe in resurrection of the dead, but they knew Jesus did. They thought they could prove him wrong by posing a hypothetical situation: Imagine seven brothers. The first was married to a woman, but he died. One by one his brothers married her. Each died after marrying her, and, following the OT law of levirate marriage (cf. Deut. 25:5–10), she was passed on to each successive brother. Eventually, all the brothers died, and the woman also died. The Sadducees asked Jesus whose wife she would be in the resurrection, since all of the brothers had married her. They thought this imaginary case would show the folly of believing in resurrections.

Jesus responded quite differently than expected, and as always, got to the heart of the matter. He said (v. 29), "You are mistaken, not understanding [i.e., knowing] the Scriptures, or the power of God." He then explained that in the resurrection there won't be marriage, so their imaginary scenario proved nothing. Jesus then (vv. 31–32) quoted something Scripture *does* teach about the resurrection, something they had either overlooked or ignored. It's as though Jesus said, "If you want to ask a theological question, it would really help if you had firsthand knowledge of and actually believed the 'textbook' upon which theology is based!"

The key phrase for our purposes is, "You are mistaken, not knowing the Scriptures" (*planasthe me eidotes tas graphas*; v. 29). The main verb *planasthe* comes from *planaō* and means "to be mistaken in judgment" or "to be deceived." Of course, someone could be mistaken for any number of reasons, but Jesus clarifies the heart of the problem. The verb *eidotes* comes from *oida*, "to know." This kind of knowledge isn't reasoned out information but something one knows immediately, almost intuitively. Being Jews, they should have "intuitively" known what Scripture teaches on this matter, but they either didn't know it or rejected it. The error in their hypothetical case was twofold. It shows they lacked knowledge of God's power—he is powerful enough to resolve all dilemmas, including the one they posed. And, despite their disbelief in resurrections, God has power even to raise the dead.

Their most fundamental error, however, was that they didn't know the Scriptures. What should we assume from Jesus's claim? Surely, he meant that if they knew (and believed) the Scriptures, they wouldn't have made this mistake. Why? Because Scripture tells the truth about the issue they raised. It also tells the truth about all other issues it addresses. If they had read Scripture, learned it, and accepted it, they would have known the answer to the scenario they posed, and they wouldn't even have asked the question. Even more, they would have known that Christ is God's Son and Israel's Messiah, and they would follow and obey him, not try to trap him with their silly scenario!

Obviously, Jesus didn't say everything I have just written, but the clear implication of "you are mistaken, not knowing the Scriptures" is that if they knew and believed the Scriptures, they wouldn't believe the error contained in their question, because Scripture tells the truth! So, this passage teaches biblical inerrancy without using the word, assuming that inerrancy is defined in terms of truth.

But something more subtle than anything said so far happens in this passage. Don't miss several facts about this incident. The Sadducees' question is ultimately about what Scripture teaches. Jesus didn't answer by appealing to philosophy or any other discipline. He appealed directly to Scripture, and told them that they were wrong because they didn't know it. Couldn't someone know Scripture, believe it, and still be mistaken? The answer is a resounding no. No such notion is even remotely entertained; whatever Scripture teaches is right, and there is no further authority beyond it to refute it. Jesus, after rebuking the Sadducees, then reminded them that they should know he was right. How did he do this? By quoting more Scripture! Did the Sadducees have a rebuttal? Of course not, and the crowd was amazed and helpless to respond as well.

The picture of Scripture that emerges from this incident is that Scripture is supremely important and authoritative. Whatever it teaches cannot be refuted! Scripture is the final court of appeals on this issue, and once Scripture is heard, the debate is over. Even the Bible-denying Sadducees had to respect Scripture's clear teaching, even if they didn't believe it!

A second major teaching from Jesus about Scripture is found in John 10:31–38, especially verses 34–36. This passage's main point seems to be Scripture's authority, but it is also often used to support inerrancy. During the Feast of Dedication (v. 22), Jesus was walking in the temple, and various Jews asked him whether he was the Messiah (vv. 23–24). Jesus replied that he had already answered this question affirmatively many times before, but they had refused to believe him (vv. 25–26). Jesus added that if they were his "sheep," they would hear and understand, but they were not his sheep (vv. 25–28). In verse 30 Jesus said that he and the Father are one (v. 30). The Jews understood him to mean that he is God, and they took up stones to stone him, as the law required for blasphemy (vv. 31–33).

In verse 34 Jesus began his rebuttal. If they had misunderstood him, he could just have said that he wasn't claiming to be God and could explain what he really meant. Or, if they had understood him correctly, he could confirm his deity by performing miracles. Or maybe a voice from heaven would say, "This is my beloved Son." Or perhaps he would appear to them in all of his glory (as on the Mount of Transfiguration). Jesus did none of these things, and it makes sense that he didn't. He had done and said such things before, and most who had heard or seen these things hadn't believed. Why should Jesus think the same responses would convince these nonbelievers now?

Instead, Jesus responded in a way that wouldn't get them to believe, but that did silence them (vv. 34–37). Jesus commented on their concern that someone they thought was merely a man had called himself God. He first quoted from Psalm 82:6 and asked his listeners if "it is not written" in their law that "I said, 'You are gods'" (v. 34). We should note here several things. First, Jesus quoted a psalm but called it "Law." This wasn't an error but rather fit the typical custom of seeing the whole OT as God's instruction (law). Then, Jesus began his next question with "Is it not written" (*ouk estin gegramme-non*), and this is, as we saw in discussing inspiration, a typical way of referring to Scripture. As Warfield showed, phrases like "it is written," "it says,"

"God says" are all equivalent ways of pointing to Scripture and to calling it God's word.

Third, the psalm Jesus quoted laments the injustice of those who have positions as judges but use their authority to oppress the poor and excluded, rather than doing right. In Psalm 82:6 the psalmist writes, "I said, 'You are gods'," referring to these evil judges, but he then adds (v. 7) that they would die like men, for they were mere men. Jesus only quoted, "I said 'You are gods'," but he knew that his listeners knew this psalm is about mere men. As to why these wicked judges were called "gods," it was because of their position as judges. In Israel, those who made judgments in disputes (or when evil was done to someone) were seen as implementing God's justice among men. Because their role served both God and the people, they were called gods, sons of the most high (cf. Ps. 82:6). Of course, the judges mentioned by the psalmist had used their power for evil, and hence it is ironic that they were called gods, but nonetheless, that's what they were called.

Having quoted Scripture, Jesus was ready to make his point, which utterly refuted the charge of blasphemy. Jesus argued (John 10:35–36) that if it is acceptable to call these mere humans gods (and they weren't even doing good for God), how could Jesus's accusers believe that he was blaspheming when he called himself God and actually *did* the work God sent him into the world to do? If it isn't blasphemy to call these wicked judges gods, then Jesus's accusers have no case against him at all. And if that wasn't enough, Jesus added (v. 37) that, if he wasn't doing his Father's work, then they shouldn't believe him. In other words, even though the judges referred to in the OT psalm didn't do God's work but were called gods anyway, Jesus in effect was saying that, if he didn't do God's work, they should reject him and his claim to be God's Son. But if he did do God's work, then they should believe him and his claim to deity. So, even if they tested him by a tougher standard than the one used for judges in the OT (Psalm 82), he still wouldn't be guilty of blasphemy.

Jesus's further comment (in John 10:35) clinched his case. Jesus began his line of argument based on Psalm 82:6 with an "if" clause. But before he gave the "then" clause, Jesus paused to make a comment about the Scriptures. He said, "and the Scripture cannot be broken." The verb translated "broken" is *luō*, and it is an aorist passive infinitive in this verse. In the passive, when used of statements, laws, and commands, it means "to be repealed," "to be annulled," "to be abolished."[58]

What did Jesus mean? We might paraphrase verse 35 as follows: "if the psalmist called them gods to whom the word of God came—and you know

[58] William F. Arndt and F. Wilbur Gingrich, *A Greek-English Lexicon of the New Testament and Other Early Christian Literature* (Cambridge: Cambridge University Press, 1965), 485.

that if Scripture says this (and it does), it can't be annulled or repealed. That is, whatever Scripture says must be so, because you can't overturn Scripture. So, my argument rests on Scripture, and you can't ignore it, because if Scripture says something, it is so, and can't be annulled."

Notice that John records no attempt by Jesus's opponents to refute him. John says they tried again to seize Jesus, but he eluded them. What does this passage show about Scripture? Beside the obvious point that Jesus answered his attackers by appealing to Scripture, Jesus underscored the point that, in quoting Psalm 82:6, where mere men are called gods, his accusers knew that his argument was on solid ground.

Why, however, should that matter? And why didn't Jesus answer based on another source (reason, their experience of seeing him and the miracles he performed, the opinion of the truly pious in Israel, e.g.)? The reason that Jesus's appeal to Scripture should matter is that whatever Scripture says is the final, authoritative word. Jesus didn't appeal to another source, because there is no higher authority. Yes, part of Jesus's point is that if Scripture says it, it must be true, but the overarching theme here is the clear ring of Scripture's authority.

A final major word from Jesus about Scripture is found in John 17:17. John 17 records Jesus's prayer to his Father, not long before Jesus's death. Jesus "reviewed," broadly speaking, how his life and ministry had fulfilled the Father's will for him. He then spoke on behalf of his disciples; though he would soon leave the world (v. 11), his disciples would remain in it.

Verses 15–16 are important for understanding verse 17, though seldom are they considered when verse 17 is cited. In those verses, Jesus asked his Father not to remove his disciples from this world, even though they were hated for following Jesus. Instead, he asked his Father to protect them from the Evil One (Satan and his followers) while they were in the world. This request was significant because it was based on real danger the disciples had already and would yet experience. Jesus knew how he had been treated and would be treated at the end of his life, and he knew that his disciples lived by the same principles he followed (v. 16).

So, exactly how did Jesus ask his Father to protect his disciples? Jesus said (v. 17), "Sanctify them in the truth; Thy word is truth." The word for "sanctify" (*hagiason*) in its most fundamental sense means "to be separate, distinct." One way to be separate from others is to be morally pure, but the more fundamental sense of the word seems to be in view here. Jesus asked his Father to set the disciples apart from the world by means of the truth. People of the world, before they hear what we think and see what we do, will think we hold the same philosophies, goals, and lifestyles as they do. When they hear us talk and see us live the truth of God, they will know we are different.

But what truth did Jesus have in mind? Jesus answered that God's word is truth. And where would Jesus think his disciples could find God's word? They could find it in Scripture. It is the truth!

We might wonder, however, how God's word would protect them from the world. If they spoke it and lived it, that would show how different they were from the world, but it would also evoke great persecution. The disciples had already experienced that and could expect more. They would also, however, find in God's word comfort and reassurance in times of affliction and persecution. If they focused on their distinctive message (found in Scripture), they would represent God accurately in the world. And, in Scripture they would also find promises that would help them persevere in their mission when the going would get rough.

To say that this verse is a key affirmation of Scripture's truth is an understatement. God's word, wherever it is found (in OT and NT alike), is truth. But then, if inerrancy is defined in terms of truth, Scripture must be inerrant. And if truth is authoritative, by implication Scripture must also be authoritative. But the explicit points of this verse are that Scripture is inerrant, it presents a distinct way of thinking and acting, and it is a safeguard for those who follow Christ but live in a world that doesn't!

In addition to these three key passages (Matt. 22:29; John 10:34–36; and 17:17), how Jesus used Scripture in his life and ministry shows what he thought of it. As Bruce Demarest and Gordon Lewis explain, Jesus believed that the OT is historically accurate and true. They write,

> Jesus treated as factual the accounts of Adam and Eve (Matt. 19:4-5), Cain and Abel (Luke 11:51), Noah and the Flood (Matt. 24:37-39; Luke 17:26-27), the destruction of Sodom and Gomorrah (Matt. 10:15; 11:23-24), the experience of Lot (Luke 17:28-32), Moses the lawgiver (Matt. 19:8; Mark 7:10), David eating the shewbread (Matt. 12:3-4; Luke 6:3-4), the splendor of Solomon (Matt. 6:29; Luke 11:31), Elijah and the widow of Zarephath (Luke 4:25-26), Elisha and Namaan [sic] the Syrian (Luke 4:27), and Jonah and the fish (Matt. 12:39-41; Luke 11:29–32).[59]

In other words, Jesus considered these people and events to be historically true. If inerrancy is defined in terms of truth, then Jesus considered the Scriptures about these things inerrant.

In discussing inspiration, I presented Jesus's thinking about Scripture's inspiration. Much of that material is relevant in this chapter, though I need only summarize some main points without repeating all the details. One very noteworthy point is Jesus's habit of repeatedly telling his listeners that what he

---

[59] Bruce Demarest and Gordon Lewis, *Integrative Theology*, vol. 1 (Grand Rapids, MI: Zondervan, 1987), 141.

was doing or what had happened fulfilled Scripture. A good summary verse of this point records Jesus's words to his disciples after his resurrection. In Luke 24:44, he said, "These are My words which I spoke to you while I was still with you, that all things which are written about Me in the Law of Moses and the Prophets and the Psalms must be fulfilled."

This verse and many others where Jesus informed his listeners that he fulfilled prophecy were, of course, very important to Jesus. But why was Jesus so concerned about this, and should we take it seriously? Indeed, whether prophecies are fulfilled is supremely important. The reasons are found in Deuteronomy 13 and 18, which give the tests of a true prophet. One test is that if a prophet makes a prediction, it must come to pass. Otherwise, he is a false prophet and doesn't speak from God.

So, prophecies about the Messiah must be fulfilled by Jesus, or his claim to be the Messiah has no credibility. And, if neither Jesus nor anyone else fulfills those messianic prophecies, they were spoken by false prophets and cannot be God's word. This issue, then, is of supreme importance to Jesus's credibility and to whether Scripture is actually God's word, and it is critical to Scripture's inerrancy and authority.

I must also remind readers of how Jesus (and even his unbelieving Jewish countrymen) used Scripture. In any dispute about theology or practice, what Scripture says was always the clinching argument. And there was no rebuttal to an argument grounded in Scripture. In addition, when tempted by Satan, Jesus repeatedly quoted Scripture. Satan never had a rebuttal; instead, he moved to another temptation, which Jesus again answered by quoting Scripture without rebuttal. What do these uses of Scripture say about Jesus's, his Jewish brethren's, and even Satan's opinion of Scripture? They show that all of them viewed it as the final word, the final court of appeal. It is supremely authoritative and stops any and all counterarguments. Even Satan gets that right on occasion—though sadly, of course, he doesn't see the futility of warring against Scripture and the God who spoke it!

Jesus also laced his teaching repeatedly with references to Scripture. Something in the OT either illustrated his point, proved it, and/or was the best way to express the point he was making. Why would Jesus appeal to Scripture at all, let alone so much, if he thought its claims were false? Jesus used Scripture so much, because he thoroughly believed it to be true and supremely authoritative. And, he knew that his Jewish listeners, regardless of how they treated him, held Scripture in the same high regard. It wouldn't have made any sense to ground his teaching in anything else!

*Other NT Teaching*—Not only Jesus, but the Gospel writers also made a point to say that what Jesus said or did fulfilled prophecy. Details of some of those passages can be found in the chapters on inspiration. It is safe to say that they had this habit for the same reasons Jesus did. They knew about Deuteronomy 13 and 18.

In addition, various NT writers spoke of their own writings in ways that show they believed them to be true and authoritative. John ended his Gospel (21:24) by saying that he witnessed the things he wrote about, and his witness is true! John began his first epistle by telling his readers that he would write about what his hands had handled, his eyes had seen, and his ears had heard (1 John 1:1, 3). What could his mean but that what he wrote was true because he was an eyewitness?

Peter makes some key points in a passage on inspiration (2 Pet. 1:16–20) that we already covered in detail. He says that he and the other disciples didn't tell fables when they spoke of Christ's glory and majesty. They were eyewitnesses of the Mount of Transfiguration experience. What is the point of saying this but to affirm that what he reported was true, because he witnessed it in person? Undoubtedly, Peter would have said the same about other events of Jesus's life and ministry that he witnessed.

But Peter said more. Though seeing is believing (and Peter did both), something is even more certain than his eyewitness testimony. That something is Scripture (v. 19). What can this mean and what does it affirm other than the truthfulness of Scripture? If your eyewitness testimony is reliable, but Scripture is even more reliable, how could this be so if Scripture is untrue? If inerrancy is defined as truthfulness, this passage also teaches biblical inerrancy.

And what of Paul? He told Timothy to study to be an approved workman before God, "handling accurately the word of truth" (2 Tim. 2:15). What would Paul mean by the "word of truth"? Surely, he would mean Scripture; a chapter later (3:16) he says all Scripture is *theopneustos*, inspired of God! In 2 Corinthians 6 Paul rehearsed specifics of his life and ministry with the Corinthians, all things that justified his claim to be an apostle and validated what he taught. As Paul offered this brief "resume," he reminded them of his labor "by the word of truth" (2 Cor. 6:7 KJV). To what did Paul refer here other than his preaching of the truth that Jesus and the OT taught?

In addition, Paul referred to the gospel he preached as the "word of truth" (Eph. 1:13 [KJV]; Col. 1:5) by which people were saved. In Galatians (1:9) Paul even wrote that if someone preaches another gospel, he should be accursed. Why should Paul say this if his gospel was only partly true and there was truth in other gospels? Clearly, Paul thought that only the gospel he preached was true.

We shouldn't think Paul would limit "the gospel" just to the basics of how to be saved (succinctly summarized in 1 Cor. 15:3–5). It includes that, of course, but it also includes every other truth about life and godliness that grows out of that. And if what Paul *preached* is true, when he *wrote* the same things, his writings must be equally true.

Finally, James speaks of God's many good and perfect gifts. One of them is the gift of new spiritual life. God "brought us forth," he "begat" us (KJV) (*apekuēsen*), "by the word of truth" (James 1:18). What would James likely think qualifies as the "word of truth"? Like Paul, he would undoubtedly think of the gospel as the word of truth involved in our spiritual birth. And, of course, that gospel is found throughout Scripture.

From all the evidence presented, we can affirm with utmost confidence that both Testaments teach that Scripture is God's word and is true.[60] There is, however, one further line of evidence for this, namely, an inferential argument that an inspired Bible must also be inerrant. To that argument we now turn.

*Inference from Inspiration to Inerrancy*

In addition to evidence already presented, there is an inferential argument for inerrancy. Its premises can be supported by inductive exegesis of various Scripture passages, and then the teaching of these Scriptures is used to form a deductive argument that moves from Scripture's inspiration to its inerrancy. I shall first present the argument, and then briefly offer support for each step.

Some critics of biblical inerrancy don't see how one can move from biblical inspiration to inerrancy. In truth, it can't be done, because at least two other steps must be added to the argument. All of this is best illustrated by presenting the six-step argument:

1. All Scripture is the product of God's breath. He has spoken it, and it is his word. (2 Tim. 3:16)
2. The Holy Spirit so superintended the writers of Scripture that what they wrote, while their own words, are God's very words. (2 Pet. 1:21)
3. Scripture teaches that God cannot and does not lie. He speaks only the truth. (Num. 23:19; Titus 1:2; Heb. 6:18)
4. Scripture teaches that God is omniscient. As a result, he knows everything and couldn't be mistaken about anything. (Job 36:4; Pss. 33:13–15; 139:1–4; 147:4–5; Heb. 4:13)
5. Whatever is true is inerrant.
6. Therefore, because Scripture is what God has said, because God speaks only truth and couldn't be mistaken about anything, and because an inerrant document is a true one, the whole Bible as God's inspired word is also inerrant.

[60] Many works already cited in this chapter were helpful in compiling the list of biblical passages and other evidence for biblical inerrancy and authority. Several helpful ones not yet cited are: Eugene H. Merrill, "Ebla and Biblical Historical Inerrancy," *BSac* 140 (October–December 1983); "The Basis for Our Belief in Inerrancy," *Presbyterion* 7 (Spring–Fall 1981), reprinted from the *Bulletin of the Evangelical Theological Society* 9 (Winter 1966); and John MacArthur, "The Sufficiency of Scripture," *MSJ* 15 (Fall 2004).

The first two premises affirm Scripture's inspiration. In our discussion of inspiration, we saw that the passages cited teach Scripture's complete inspiration. Since God has spoken and the result is Scripture, the next question is whether God only speaks truth. Could he in ignorance speak a falsehood or by malice deliberately lie? Neither is possible because of his omniscience and absolute moral holiness. God's inability to lie is confirmed by verses cited above, and his knowledge of all things is confirmed in step 4. Hence, steps 3 and 4 are confirmed.

As for premise 5, its support is offered in the lengthy discussion earlier in this chapter about the meaning of inerrancy. Truth is conceived of as correspondence to reality. The arguments that inerrancy is about truth and that the idea of truth in view is correspondence were offered in this chapter.

When steps 1–5 are taken together, the conclusion follows with logical inevitability. If it doesn't, then either Scripture isn't God's word, or God can make a mistake or lie, or we should define inerrancy in another way. Some will say that this argument doesn't take seriously enough the human factor in producing Scripture. In response, the argument doesn't intend to overlook the human author. The kind of superintendence premise 2 requires is such that human abilities and styles of writing are used to produce Scripture but are guided and guarded by the Holy Spirit so that the authors' words are also God's. So, if the words of a written document are literally God's words, then we must ask whether God knows the truth and is inclined to tell it. The answer to both questions is yes. Hence, the argument doesn't deny dual authorship of Scripture, because that would deny the biblical doctrine of inspiration. But even with dual authorship, God still ensured that what was written is what he wanted said, and the God of truth speaks only the truth and wouldn't want falsehood recorded as his word.

In sum, this argument's premises are true, and the conclusion logically follows. The argument captures what most people would say about anything God speaks. Hence, many evangelical Christians find it quite baffling that people who call themselves evangelicals and believe in Scripture's full inspiration still think that somehow a fully inspired Bible might contain some errors. In the next chapters, we shall look at the most common and significant objections to biblical inerrancy raised by purported evangelicals, and answer them.

CHAPTER

EIGHT

# True Light (II)

## Objections to Inerrancy

Despite the evidence for biblical inerrancy, many still deny it. This is, of course, expected from nonevangelicals and nonbelievers. But biblical inerrancy has also been attacked by some who otherwise fully embrace evangelical theology, including belief in the full inspiration of Scripture.

While those who believe Scripture has errors might not consider Scripture authoritative, this is not true for all. In fact, even nonevangelicals at times espouse the authority of Scripture while denying that it is God's inspired word and affirming their belief that it contains errors. Even Karl Barth's comments about the Bible's authority must not be misread. Barth didn't say that Scripture has no authority at all. Rather, it has authority because it points to what is revelation: God. In fact, with Barth's belief that Scripture isn't God's word or inerrant, we might wonder why he had any use for it at all. The reason was that he believed it is a witness to many instances of revelation.

Barth aside, why, given the evidence for biblical inerrancy, would someone holding Scripture's verbal plenary inspiration believe that it contains false claims? In chapters 8 and 9, I want to identify the main objections and to answer them.[1]

### The Phenomena of Scripture Do Not Support Inerrancy

This objection is foundational to the rest. Convinced by biblical scholarship of the last two centuries or so that Scripture contains factual errors, evangelicals

---

[1] As an example, some complain that proponents of biblical inerrancy tend to revere Scripture, but don't always read and obey it. This is, of course, true, even as it is also true that many proponents do obey it, and that there are also those who reject its inerrancy and also ignore it, and some who reject it but basically follow its demands. So whether you believe in inerrancy or not doesn't seem logically tied to whether or not you submit your life to its demands. More importantly, if this objection counts for anything, it shows that some people who hold right doctrine don't always live what they believe. But that is totally irrelevant to whether the Bible is inerrant. Hence, this kind of argument needn't detain us in this chapter.

who don't want to throw out the Bible altogether try to explain how Scripture can be fully inspired and authoritative and yet have factual errors. They contend that making this concession in no way nullifies the Bible's main intent to tell us how to start and grow a relationship with God. And if one doesn't concede that there are some historical and scientific errors in Scripture, few reputable scholars (evangelical or not), it is claimed, will listen to anything evangelicals might say about Scripture's saving message and its power to transform and guide lives. Besides, biblical scholarship has helped us understand the times and situations in which the writers composed their books, and thus has helped us understand what they wrote. Moreover, no one thinks every factual claim in Scripture is in error, so the Bible's relatively few errors are no reason to throw it out entirely.

This objection actually contains two distinct complaints, but we should begin by explaining what is meant by "the phenomena of Scripture." The term "phenomenon" in its most basic sense refers to that which appears, and that is its sense in this objection. Of course, lots of things appear in Scripture, including verses about inspiration, divine truthfulness, and the truth of God's word—are those the phenomena in view? Not really. Instead, as one reads Scripture, one finds assertions that seem either to contradict other things it says or that don't match the facts of our world. While these phenomena normally don't touch on any matter of doctrine or practice, they still falsify the belief that whatever Scripture affirms is true.[2]

This objection actually is shorthand for two objections. The first is about theological method and the second is about specific alleged errors in Scripture. As to the former, the complaint is that inerrantists use a deductive method while an inductive method is preferred if one hopes to maintain even a semblance of objectivity. What exactly does this mean?

Those who propose that we move inductively claim that such a method makes no prejudgments about what Scripture teaches about its own inerrancy. We simply read Scripture with an open mind and examine what we find. There is no "privileged set" of texts that are decisive for understanding whether Scripture contains errors. To assume that certain passages "govern" the discussion moves deductively, and brings our presuppositions to the table, so to speak, when we study Scripture. Induction comes with no preconceived doctrines to validate; the inductive thinker functions like a careful scientist who confronts the data and observes and examines them. Conclusions are drawn only after all data are examined, even if the conclusions go counter to what the scientist originally

---

[2] I say that these alleged errors *normally* don't touch on matters of doctrine and practice, because some evangelicals have claimed to find an error in doctrine. Perhaps most notorious is Paul Jewett's claim that the apostle Paul presents the case in 1 Corinthians and 1 Timothy against a woman serving as pastor of a church, and Paul is just wrong. See Paul Jewett, *Man as Male and Female* (Grand Rapids, MI: Eerdmans, 1990).

expected to find. The same strategy, we are told, is right for theological study, and it is especially important for the discussion of inerrancy, because only this method allows us to see whether Scripture's affirmations square with the facts. As Paul Feinberg has shown, there are different types of induction and inductive arguments,[3] but the inductive method involved in the critique of inerrancy rests on assumptions just described about the proper handling of the data.

Critics of biblical inerrancy complain that its proponents violate the essentials of inductive study. They privilege certain passages and doctrines already formulated (such as inspiration, and God's character as truthful), and make them the basis for formulating this doctrine. If other Scriptures seem to falsify inerrancy by apparently containing an error, they are either explained away (not always plausibly), or inerrancy is reaffirmed and we are told that, when all facts are known, it will be shown that apparent errors aren't real ones. Clearly, the complaint goes, nothing can shake the belief that Scripture is inerrant. But that just shows that objectivity is thrown to the wind, and a fair examination of the data is impossible and unwanted. When the phenomena of Scripture seem to contain unresolvable errors, inerrantists won't hear of it, because their deductive conclusions from "key" Scriptures and doctrines won't allow it.

Not only is the methodology of inerrantists deductive, but their deductive argument for inerrancy is flawed, according to Michael Bauman, originally an inerrantist. He explains that inerrantists typically argue that, because Scripture is inspired and God doesn't lie, it must also be inerrant. However, Bauman sees two flaws in this argument. The first is the equation of error with lies. That is, we shouldn't assume that errors in Scripture are divine lies. Neither God nor the human author intended to write a falsehood (the requisite mind-set for telling a lie, according to Bauman), and yet the human authors might have included factual error in their books out of ignorance of the truth. The second flaw in the deductive argument, claims Bauman, is that it confuses God's intentions about what he wants to communicate (these do reflect his character) "and the resultant phenomena in space and time (which may not)."[4]

In addition, Joel Stephen Williams complains that part of the problem with this deductive approach is that it leads proponents to adopt an all-or-nothing approach to alleged errors. Appealing to James Barr, Williams argues that while some biblical critics want to destroy Scripture by pointing out its errors, many scholars who love the Bible have no such agenda. They just want an accurate picture of the Bible, and pointing to errors invariably raises matters of fact that aren't actually relevant to what the Bible is really about.[5] Actually,

---

[3] Paul D. Feinberg, "The Meaning of Inerrancy," in *Inerrancy*, ed. Norman L. Geisler (Grand Rapids, MI: Zondervan, 1979), 273.

[4] Michael Bauman, "Why the Noninerrantists Are Not Listening: Six Tactical Errors Evangelicals Commit," *JETS* 29 (September 1986): 320.

[5] Joel Stephen Williams, "The Error of Inerrancy," *Encounter* 57 (Winter 1996): 53–54.

Williams complains, biblical critics don't exacerbate the situation; rather, it is fundamentalistic thinkers, who refuse to allow any sort of error in Scripture, who magnify the relatively few and insignificant errors there are. Williams, espousing an inductive method for studying the nature of Scripture, explains that it is difficult to defend inerrancy using an inductive approach. He writes,

> Attempting to defend inerrancy inductively is a difficult task. One single proven error or contradiction in the most minor details is enough to defeat inerrancy. But when a defender of inerrancy is bombarded with scores of errors and contradictions, a shift in defensive tactics is usually evident. As J. Ramsey Michaels explains: "Though he pays lip service to objectivity and an empirical-rational method, there is in fact no evidence that will ever convince him of an error. . . . He accepts reason when it helps his case, but retreats to a more fideistic stance when the going gets rough." . . .
>
> If a likely explanation is not available, a contrived one may be given. Maybe the autographs do not have the problem, we are told, even if there is no evidence of textual corruption. If no possible explanation is forthcoming, maybe one will be found in the future. Suspension of judgment hoping for a future solution has some legitimacy, but it is not appropriate for most problems. As Gundry explains: "Despite a historical solution now and then, increasingly sophisticated methods of literary analysis, coupled with new discoveries of comparative materials, turn up more and more evidence of editorial liberty in what was naively thought to be purely historical narrative. To try holding such data in suspension amounts to denying the clarity of Scripture; for many of them rest, not on ambiguities or arguments from silence, but on the plain, explicit wording of the text." So against all odds, against strong evidence, ignoring the facts because minds are already made up, most inerrantists simply refuse to examine in a fair way strong evidence for errors in the Bible.[6]

The complaint about Scripture's phenomena contains a second objection. It is the more foundational objection about phenomena. It says that when you look at biblical phenomena, you find that, despite efforts to avoid it, there are errors that have no satisfactory answers.

Now it is important to note that critics are not saying that every factual claim is in error. Nor do they think that every apparent contradiction in Scripture is an actual one. They only claim that there are some errors, and then present what they believe to be irreconcilable mistakes. Such supposed mistakes have led many to reject Scripture altogether as neither inerrant, inspired, nor divine revelation.[7] Scholars who prefer to believe the Bible is revelation, and is

---

[6] Ibid., 55, 56–57. The quote from Michaels is taken from Michaels's "Inerrancy or Verbal Inspiration? An Evangelical Dilemma," in *Inerrancy and Common Sense*, ed. Roger R. Nicole and J. Ramsey Michaels (Grand Rapids, MI: Baker, 1980), 66. The quote from Robert Gundry is taken from *Matthew: A Commentary on His Literary and Theological Art* (Grand Rapids, MI: Eerdmans, 1982), 625.

[7] Here one thinks immediately, though not exclusively, of neoorthodox thinkers for whom the content of revelation is God himself in the person of Jesus Christ, given in personal encounter with human beings. The refusal to equate

inspired and authoritative, cite their list of alleged mistakes and add that none of them has anything to do with doctrine or practice. Thus, whether Scripture is or is not inerrant is actually rather inconsequential.

Alleged mistakes are potentially legion. We can't mention all, but I note some that appear rather frequently. First, there is the problem of harmonizing apparently parallel passages in some OT historical books. For example, 2 Samuel 24:1–2 says that God was angry with Israel and so he incited David to number them. In contrast, 1 Chronicles 21:1–2 says that Satan moved David to number them. And the numbers reported don't match. Second Samuel 24:9 lists 800,000 warriors in Israel and 500,000 in Judah. First Chronicles 21:5 says there were 1,100,000 in Israel and 470,000 in Judah.[8]

Second, in the parable of the mustard seed (Matt. 13:31–32), Jesus said that the mustard seed is the smallest of all seeds. However, botanists know that there are smaller seeds (some orchid seeds, e.g.).[9] Third, parallel passages in the Gospels seem to disagree about whether Jesus told his disciples to take a staff on a preaching mission (Mark 6:8) or told them not to do so (Matt. 10:9–10; Luke 9:3).[10] Then, Gospel accounts seem to disagree about how many times Peter denied Christ and about exactly when, during the events surrounding Jesus's capture and trial, he did so (Matt. 26:34, 74–75; Mark 14:30, 72; Luke 22:34, 60–61; and John 13:38; 18:27).[11]

Fifth, how many men did the women see at the tomb on Easter morning? Were they inside the tomb or outside? Were they men or angels? (Matt. 28:2, 5; Luke 24:4). Sixth, how many years passed between the promise made to Abraham and the giving of the law? "Paul declares it to be a span of 430 years (Gal. 3:17; Ex. 12:40 in the LXX), but a number of 645 years can be derived from the Hebrew Old Testament (Gen. 12:4; 21:5; 25:26; 47:9; Ex. 12:40–41)."[12] And finally, whom was Matthew quoting in Matthew 27:9–10? Matthew attributes it to Jeremiah, but the quote seems to be a loose rendition of Zechariah 11:12–13.[13]

---

Scripture with divine revelation stems in part from the belief that Scripture has errors and that God couldn't lie or be mistaken about anything, so Scripture must not be revelation. If revelation comes in a person (a divine person), then revelation can't contain errors. So, someone adopting a neoorthodox stance on Scripture can believe that divine revelation is inerrant; but that belief has nothing to do with Scripture, because it isn't deemed divine revelation.

[8] Williams, "Error of Inerrancy," 63; and Stephen T. Davis, *The Debate about the Bible* (Philadelphia: Westminster, 1977), 98.

[9] Davis, *Debate about the Bible*, 100.

[10] Ibid., 105–106; Williams, "Error of Inerrancy," 64–65.

[11] Williams, "Error of Inerrancy," 65.

[12] Ibid., 63.

[13] Davis, *Debate about the Bible*, 102. The list of problems is only a small sample of the number of alleged factual errors in Scripture. Perhaps one of the lengthiest lists is Joel Williams's in the essay I have cited ("Error of Inerrancy"). His list covers at least pages 58–72. A. T. B. McGowan, *The Divine Spiration of Scripture: Challenging Evangelical Perspectives* (Nottingham, UK: Apollos, 2007), 112–113 (this book was also released in the United States as *The Divine Authenticity of Scripture* [Downers Grove, IL: InterVarsity Press, 2007]), also discusses this objection briefly. He cites a few other apparent inconsistencies in Scripture, and complains that inerrantists either respond by saying that these are apparent antinomies, but not actual ones, or they claim that if we had the autographs, we would see that there actually is no error. He thinks that the amount of time some inerrantists devote to resolving

What should we say about these and many other alleged problems in the phenomena of Scripture? Since the alleged errors noted seem inconsequential to doctrine and practice, does it truly matter if they *are* actual errors?

### Responses

At its root, this objection is about proper theological method. I agree, but contend that this objection is itself methodologically flawed in several significant respects.

The most fundamental question is about the proper way to do systematic theology. Critics of inerrancy tell us to look at the phenomena of Scripture, because then we will easily see that Scripture is not inerrant. I agree that we must consult the phenomena, but the crucial question is *which are the phenomena that are relevant to this topic*. Should passages that actually speak about Scripture's nature be the basis for our doctrine of Scripture, or should we formulate this doctrine on the basis of passages that say nothing about Scripture's nature but that address things like the size of mustard seeds and how many times the cock crowed when Peter denied Christ?

In reply, if I want to learn about the biblical doctrine of sin, I shouldn't consult passages that deal with officers in the local church. If I want to know what Scripture teaches about divine omniscience, I should consult passages that say something about the extent of God's knowledge and the way his mind functions, not passages that show God doing something unexpected, so that his actions suggest that he has learned something new (see here God's response in Genesis 22 to Abraham after he attempted to sacrifice Isaac).[14] *And, if I want to know what Scripture teaches about its own inspiration and inerrancy, I must first attend to passages that actually address those issues, not to a passage about the nature of the kingdom as explained by a parable whose point is not to present a botanic fact about the size of mustard seeds in comparison to other seeds.* Nor should I make normative passages that discuss whether God or Satan incited David to number the people. *How do any of these passages give a plain statement from the author, human or divine, about whether Scripture's words are God's word and whether those assertions are true?*

This must not be misunderstood. I am not suggesting that a discussion of divine omnipotence should utterly ignore passages like Genesis 22:12 or that a discussion of Scripture's nature should totally bypass passages about cocks

---

such apparent problems is neither justified nor profitable. Since God can do his work through the errant copies we have, why spend so much time and effort defending autographs we don't have?

[14] Here I would refer readers to open theism's views on divine omniscience and immutability on the basis of passages that suggest God changes his mind or learns something, and my discussion of their views in *No One Like Him: The Doctrine of God*, Foundations of Evangelical Theology (Wheaton, IL: Crossway, 2001), 648–649, 759–775. The problem I noted in relation to open theism's handling of the doctrine of God, especially divine omnipotence, etc., is the same methodological problem we see here in the critics' objection to inerrancy on the basis of the phenomena of Scripture.

crowing, people being numbered, the size of mustard seeds, etc. Rather my point is that those kinds of passages cannot be normative or determinative for the doctrines in question, since they don't even address the doctrines under discussion. *Doctrine must first be formulated based on passages which actually address the topic in question.* Of course, if passages that don't address the topic appear in some way to falsify the teaching of passages that do address the doctrine, we cannot simply ignore the "problem" passages. They must be explained so as to be consistent with what passages that directly address the doctrine say. If they can't be, then either the "problem" passages or concepts are wrong, or our understanding of the normative passages for the doctrine is mistaken. But it makes a world of difference as to whether the normative passages' teachings are assumed innocent until proven guilty, or assumed guilty until proven innocent! Whatever the passages that actually address the doctrine teach should be assumed innocent until proven guilty; that is, we should assume that what God says explicitly on a topic is true, because he would know the truth, and wouldn't lie. Thus, when there is other "evidence" that suggests our doctrine is wrong, we should try to harmonize that evidence, assuming innocence of the doctrine. If we can't harmonize the data, then we may just be wrong about the doctrine, but that conclusion should be reached only after consulting all the evidence. Obviously, in this life we aren't in a position even to know all the evidence, let alone consult it. But if Scripture clearly teaches a doctrine, and if we believe Scripture to be God's word, Scripture should be given the benefit of the doubt. It is not special pleading to argue that, when all facts are known, Scripture will be shown to be true in whatever it affirms.

Why does this matter in the inerrancy debate? It matters because critics complain that a method that makes passages like 2 Timothy 3:16, 2 Peter 1:19–21, John 17:17, etc., the foundation and the governing texts for the doctrines of inspiration and inerrancy is methodologically wrong, because it proceeds deductively and because it presupposes inspiration and inerrancy, and as a result, it cannot objectively look at the phenomena of Scripture! Any passage of Scripture, regardless of its topic, should be just as normative for formulating the doctrine of Scripture as those just mentioned above. After all, critics of inerrancy complain, the topic is the inerrancy of *Scripture*! That being so, any biblical passage should be relevant to our understanding of whether Scripture teaches inerrancy or not. So, we should just look at what we find in Scripture and decide whether or not to hold inerrancy. If apparent errors can be resolved, fine, but if we can't find a solution, an objective, inductive method requires us to conclude that the text in question is in error. In essence, a suspect passage should be considered guilty of error until proven innocent.

Though the preceding sounds cogent and contains some truth, in several crucial respects it is flawed. The element of truth is that since the doctrine in question is Scripture's truth, it is relevant to ask if individual passages teach things that are true. Ones that seem wrong shouldn't be ignored altogether. But that is where the element of truth in the objection ends.

How is this objection about methodology flawed? First, it is wrong in the way already explained, namely, *contrary to critics of inerrancy, the normative passages for any doctrine are the ones that actually address the concept in question.* Passages about how long Israel was in Egyptian bondage, the size of a mustard seed, how many men the women saw at Jesus's tomb on Easter morning, etc., *do not* address the issue of Scripture's truthfulness! Hence, passages about these subjects *teach* nothing *about the nature of Scripture.* Thus, they aren't passages in which the author, divine or human, asserts anything about whether Scripture is true. Thinking they do is just as wrong as thinking that a verse with a misspelled word is an instance of the writer *teaching* that the improper spelling is the correct spelling. As we saw in the previous chapter, using a misspelled word or using grammar incorrectly asserts nothing about the proper spelling of a word or about proper grammar. Similarly, passages about numbering people, etc., don't address the truthfulness of Scripture—in fact they *assert* nothing about Scripture's nature.

*This means that such passages cannot be normative for determining whether Scripture does or doesn't teach its own inerrancy. Passages mentioned in my defense of inerrancy in the previous chapter are the normative ones! That doesn't mean we can ignore apparent mistakes in Scripture, but only that we should assume that there is an explanation for the problems, because what God has said about Scripture requires that its affirmations are in fact true.*

Critics will complain that we should conclude that there is an error, because after all, the verses with apparent errors are normative for the doctrine. As we have seen, this is wrong, but it raises another problem. If we conclude that there are errors in Scripture, then passages cited in the previous chapter that assert Scripture's truth must themselves be wrong. But if so, how should we handle them? Should we reinterpret them so that they don't say that Scripture is truthful? Or should we say that they do claim that Scripture is true, but they are just wrong? Neither option is appealing, for it is unwise to use "hermeneutical gymnastics" to make a text say the opposite of what it plainly says. And, if we let it say what it does but then claim that it is wrong, that is even more problematic. If neither the divine nor the human author was correct in passages that say Scripture is true, why should we trust their judgment about any other matter, doctrinal or otherwise? The problem is not just that *we* have a hard time determining what in Scripture is believable. The deeper problem is that even the authors probably didn't know what is believable. If so, what one chooses to believe seems doomed to rest solely on whatever appears comfortable to believe, not on the testimony of the divine or human author!

Still, critics will likely respond that my methodological comments show that I have rejected objectivity and have adopted biblical inerrancy as a presupposition and then moved deductively from that. Actually, while some theologians may have done just that, the objection contains three separate complaints, none of which is true of what I have done. First, neither I nor most evangelicals who espouse inerrancy adopt it as a presupposition without any proof. If you read my preceding chapter on inerrancy, you know that I didn't adopt inerrancy as an assumption without proof. I cited a number of Scriptures and explained how they teach that Scripture is true. I also explained why inerrancy should be defined in terms of truth—I didn't just adopt the definition as a presupposition. When you join passages that teach that Scripture is true with the definition of inerrancy as truthfulness, the passages referenced amount to saying that Scripture is inerrant. Nothing was adopted as a mere unproved presupposition.

Second, there is nothing subjective about the way I defined or defended inerrancy, and that is true of others who hold biblical inerrancy. If the complaint is that my methodology is less than pristinely objective, the critic is confused about whether that sort of objectivity is even possible. That is, if the demand is that the knower's noetic structure with all of its contents be removed from the investigation of Scripture's nature, then regardless of one's position on biblical inerrancy, this requirement cannot be met. Critics of inerrancy don't bring a mind that is a blank slate when they address passages about cocks crowing, the size of mustard seeds, etc., nor can they do so. Elsewhere, I have discussed at length the issue of objectivity and subjectivity, and readers are encouraged to consult that.[15] The key issue in that discussion is whether subjectivity, in the sense that all of us come to any study with our past learning and experiences and bring our preferred ideas to the table, is so overwhelming that it is impossible to treat data in a fair and unbiased way. As explained, it may at times be difficult to remove biases, but it isn't impossible. Also, the facts that the evidence is public and that we should do theology in community mean that I am not the only one addressing the issue. If I am wrong, others can correct me, and they can do so based on the data of Scripture, not just based on their own presuppositions. So, subjectivity, in the sense of unfairly handling data, is not inevitable.

But there is more to this objection about subjectivity. The further complaint is that inerrantists use a deductive method, and a deductive method is always subjective, whereas those who deny inerrancy use an inductive method,

---

[15] See my *Can You Believe It's True? Christian Apologetics in a Modern and Postmodern Era* (Wheaton, IL: Crossway, 2013). Here the whole section on the question of truth is relevant, but more specifically chapter 4, in which the postmodern objection to objectivity is addressed, should be read.

which is objective. In response, this objection is flawed in several important respects. Consider my defense of inerrancy in the previous chapter. Various biblical passages were examined which teach something about Scripture's truthfulness. An inductive method of exegesis was used in that process. It was admitted that those passages alone don't prove inerrancy, because none of them teaches that inerrancy should be defined in terms of truth. But a defense of defining inerrancy in terms of truth was also included in the previous chapter. Again, a basically inductive method was used. I also explained that putting together the definition of inerrancy as truthfulness with passages that teach that Scripture is true involves inferential reasoning. Inferential reasoning is not per se subjective and inappropriate.

Critics of inerrancy, in fact, use the same method. They find passages that they believe contain an untruth. Even if they are right, why should that disprove inerrancy? Because, they too have defined inerrancy in terms of truthfulness, and so they have concluded that Scripture isn't inerrant by using a method that is both inductive and inferential. If it is acceptable for critics of inerrancy to use such a method, why is it unacceptable when inerrantists use the same method? *The real bone of contention is not whose methodology is inductive and objective, but rather which verses are determinative for understanding Scripture's teaching on this issue.* As I have explained, critics of inerrancy are wrong on that matter, and so this objection is fatally flawed.

Critics of inerrancy may reply that what I have said may work for my first line of defense for inerrancy, but it is surely wrong in regard to my inferential argument from inspiration to inerrancy; *that* is a deductive argument. The answer is yes and no. Yes, the form is surely more like a deductive proof than an inductive one. But what the critic really means is that the premises have been adopted as presuppositions without proof, and then the argument has been constructed. This part of the complaint is clearly false. Premises about Scripture's inspiration were fully supported in the chapters on inspiration by inductive exegesis of various biblical passages relevant to that topic. The premise about God's truthfulness was supported with Scripture, and as noted above, defining inerrancy in terms of truth wasn't simply adopted without support but was argued for in some detail in the previous chapter on inerrancy. So, my inferential argument for inerrancy was no more illegitimate methodologically than an inferential argument for the Trinity based on premises about God as one and about each member of the godhead as divine that are derived from inductive exegesis of Scripture. The charge of improper methodology by inerrantists, though perhaps true of some, is not true of the way in which many inerrantists come to their conclusion about this doctrine.

There is another methodological point I must make before turning to the other part of the objection. As one peruses the various alleged errors that critics raise, one sees that they aren't all of one sort. Some deal with what appear to be blatant factual errors (e.g., the mustard seed issue). Many of them, however, deal with apparent contradictions in Scripture.

Since the complaint in many cases is that Scripture contradicts itself, I must say a word about contradictions. Put simply, a contradiction is the affirmation and the denial of one and the same claim. It is the assertion that A (where "A" stands for a proposition) and not A are both true at the same time and in the same way. To charge a contradiction in logic means something very specific and strong. It means that there is no *possible* way for all things affirmed to be true. Hence, no one, not even God, can show that all things affirmed are true. This is so now and forevermore.

This is a very robust complaint. What kind of response would meet the charge of contradiction? Since the complaint is that there is no *possible* way for everything asserted to be true, the defender of the claims as noncontradictory needs only to offer *a possible way* that all things said could be true. Of course, there may be some rather implausible ways for all things claimed to be true, so it would be best if the solution offered was plausible. But as a point of logic, all that is required is a possible way for all things to be true.

I raise this point because often critics of inerrancy say that they can't see how an apparent contradiction can be resolved, so there must be a genuine contradiction in Scripture. At times such claims sound as though no one has ever offered an explanation, when in reality critics know that various explanations have been offered. The truth is that the critic doesn't find the explanations *plausible*, so he reasserts that there is a genuine contradiction. Clearly, in the critic's mind Scripture is guilty of error until proven innocent, and innocence will be the verdict only if the explanation offered satisfies the critic.

Now surely defenders of inerrancy should offer explanations that are as plausible as possible, but plausibility *is not* the requirement to meet the charge of contradiction! If the explanation offered is a *possible* way to resolve the contradiction (that is, if the explanation were added to the other claims made, it would render them internally consistent), then the defender of inerrancy has answered the objection of "no *possible* way" to affirm everything said as true!

When this point about the nature of a contradiction and how to answer it is added to Scripture's clear teaching about its truthfulness (clear in the sense that we appeal to passages that actually address the issue and show by careful exegesis that they affirm that Scripture is true), all should understand why Scripture should be considered innocent of error until proven guilty. It should also be evident why it isn't unreasonable to say that, even if we aren't totally satisfied with the explanations we offer, there is reason to think that, when all facts are known, there will be a satisfactory resolution.

From the preceding discussion, I conclude that the objection, though extremely important, is methodologically flawed in the ways presented. If so, we could legitimately move to the next objection. However, many critics would complain that unless I answer at least some of the alleged errors, I shall have hidden behind a cloud of methodological fine points. So as not to be guilty of that charge, and because we can't ignore the apparent errors altogether (alleged errors are not nonevidence), I shall address some of the problems raised. Elsewhere I have addressed a number of these alleged errors, so I needn't repeat my answer to all of them.

Let me begin with complaints about Peter's denials and the crowing of the cock.[16] Mark records Jesus as telling Peter that, before the cock crowed twice, Peter would deny him three times (Mark 14:30). Later, Peter denied Jesus three times (Mark 14:66–71), and then the cock crowed a second time (14:72). Matthew records Jesus as saying that "before a cock crows, you shall deny Me three times" (Matt. 26:34). Matthew then writes that a cock crowed *after* Peter denied Jesus three times (26:69–75). Luke says (Luke 22:34) that Jesus told Peter that the cock wouldn't crow that day until after Peter had denied Jesus three times. He then shows Peter denying Christ three times, and says that while Peter was denying Christ the third time, a cock crowed (Luke 22:56–60). And finally, John (John 13:38) says Jesus told Peter that a cock wouldn't crow until *after* Peter denied him three times. In John 18:15–27, John records Peter's three denials of Christ, and says that the cock crowed after Peter denied Jesus (given John's account of the times Peter denied Jesus) the third time. How many times did Jesus say the cock would crow, and how many times did it crow? Which Gospel account is correct?

All four Gospel writers record Jesus's telling Peter that he would deny him three times, and each Gospel records Peter denying Jesus three times. In addition, each Gospel says that a cock crowed after Peter's third denial. The "rub" is with Mark's claim that the cock would crow a second time after Peter denied Christ, and Luke's recording of Jesus saying that a cock wouldn't crow that day until Peter had denied Jesus three times. Here I think it is important to note that the prediction in each case is that Peter would first deny Christ three times, and then the cock would crow. Luke's account says the cock wouldn't crow at all on the day Peter denied Christ before Peter did deny him. While in Mark's account Jesus says the cock would crow twice, Mark is very clear that Peter would deny Christ three times before the cock crowed twice. Hence, the

---

[16] I am taking this material from my *Can You Believe It's True?* It comes from chapter 11 on the reliability of the Gospels.

cock wouldn't crow the first time after the first or second denial; he would crow at all only after the third denial. Moreover, it is Luke who says that, while Peter was denying Jesus the third time, the cock crowed. The other Gospel writers suggest that the cock crowed after Peter completed his third denial.

From the preceding, I think it is quite possible to show that there is no contradiction among the Gospel accounts. Here is how: Jesus, according to Mark, told Peter that the cock would crow twice after his denial. Luke tells us that as Peter was speaking the cock crowed. Hence, Peter had already denied Jesus twice, and was in the process of doing so a third time. Luke 22:60 records Peter's third denial as well as the fact that the cock crowed while Peter was denying that he knew Christ. Now, if this had happened in our day, someone might have been keeping track of the exact timing of the cock crowing—perhaps even using a stop watch to determine how far into Peter's third denial it was before the cock crowed. But it would be ridiculous to impose such methods on Scripture or on the situation itself (had we been there to witness it). Since the cock crowed while Peter was speaking, he had begun this third denial before the cock crowed, and surely it is possible to see how this sequence fits with the claim that the cock wouldn't crow until after the third denial.

But there is more, because in Mark's account Jesus says that the cock would crow twice after Peter denied Jesus. Since Luke says the cock started crowing while Peter was denying Christ a third time, it is possible to see that the cock also crowed a second time, but did so completely *after* Peter finished denying Jesus the third time. This would fit with the requirement from Mark's Gospel that the cock crow twice after the third denial. It would also fit with Luke 22:34 that the first crowing of the cock on that day wouldn't happen until Peter denied Jesus three times. Since the cock first crowed while Peter was denying Jesus a third time, and the second crowing was completely after Peter finished, nothing in Luke about the cock not crowing on that day until Peter denied Jesus three times is contradicted. Both crowings could have happened after Peter's third denial, and they surely could have been the first time that day that the cock crowed. Matthew and John record Jesus as saying that a cock would crow after Peter denied Jesus three times, and both Gospels record Peter denying Jesus three times and then the cock crowing. What Jesus says in Matthew, Luke, and John in no way precludes the cock from crowing more than once after Peter's denial. The only stipulation is that the crowing comes after the third denial, but none of the Gospels says that the cock couldn't start crowing while Peter was denying Christ the third time. That being so, I have suggested above how all of what we see in Matthew, Luke, and John can be consistent with Mark's account of Jesus predicting the cock would crow twice after Peter's third denial. Neither Matthew's, Luke's, nor

John's account of Jesus's prediction records him as saying that the cock would crow once and *only* once after Peter's third denial. I should also add that it is quite possible that when Matthew, Luke, and John speak of the cock crowing, they are referring to the second crowing that happened *completely after* Peter finished denying Christ a third time. Or, they may be referring to the crowing that Mark tells us happened while Peter was denying Jesus the third time. We can't be absolutely sure about which of the two crowings Matthew, Luke, and John refer to, but that is really irrelevant to whether the Gospels contradict one another on this matter. My explanation shows how all four Gospel accounts *can* be true at the same time. And, remember, all that is required is a *possible* way for all four to be true.

Second, 2 Samuel 24 and 1 Chronicles 21 raise a set of problems. The first is about who moved David to number the people. Second Samuel 24:1 says it was God, but 1 Chronicles 21:1–2 says Satan incited David to do it. Which is correct? One way not to resolve this issue is to claim that these passages record two different instances. Scholars agree that both passages talk about the same incident.

In my judgment, the best way to explain this apparent inconsistency is that both are true. David only did one action: he moved Joab to number the people. But that doesn't mean that the impetus behind this could only come from one place. It is possible that the various agents in this situation could have different motives. As some have suggested, David increasingly thought of his personal wealth and manpower as king, not his relation to and help from God, as the source of his strength. His motive for wanting the census was very likely a desire to confirm his thoughts of self-pride by showing how truly powerful he was. Of course, this wasn't the ultimate source of his success, and God wanted to teach him a lesson. On the other hand, Satan likely knew that David's motivation was wrong and punishable by God, so Satan would have been quite pleased to incite David to this act of self-congratulation. Perhaps Satan even knew that God would punish David, and Satan wanted that because David had been so successful in extending Israel's kingdom, as God had planned.

The point of the preceding is that one act can have different motivations, and each motive can come from a distinct actor in bringing the event to pass. Anyone who thinks this is impossible should read the first two chapters of Job. Both God and Satan were involved in Job's afflictions, though their roles were not the same, nor were their motivations. Similarly, Jesus's crucifixion was both a sacrifice by the Lord for sin and at the same time a horrible murder done by Christ's sinful enemies. What these evil men wanted to accomplish did happen, but God's work was also done in this same act. So, God can and does use Satan on occasion to accomplish his own ends, even if Satan willingly acts to accomplish his own ends. Hence, there is no contradiction in saying that both God and Satan incited David to number the people, though for different reasons.

What is more difficult is harmonizing the results of the census taking. Second Samuel 24:9 says that in Israel (the northern part of the kingdom) there were 800,000 valiant men who drew the sword, while in Judah (the southern part of the kingdom) there were 500,000 men. In contrast, 1 Chronicles 21:5 says that in all Israel (the northern part of the kingdom) there were 1,100,000 men who drew the sword, while in Judah there were 470,000 men who drew the sword. While the figures for Judah in both passages are not horrendously far off, so that one might say the writer of Samuel rounded the number up by 30,000, the number in 1 Chronicles is a round number, and to "round up" numbers by 30,000 people when one is taking a census seems a bit odd. However, even if one can make a case for "rounding up" the figures for Judah, no such option seems possible for the numbers of men in Israel. The two passages differ by 300,000 men! It also isn't very likely that these inconsistencies can be explained as scribal errors in copying manuscripts of these two books.

Gleason Archer seems to offer a better explanation. As for the figures for Israel, the numbers reported in 1 Chronicles could have included all available men of fighting age, regardless of whether they had ever been battle tested. In contrast, in 2 Samuel 24 Joab's report was of the number of "mighty men" (*'is hayil*), that is, of men tested in battle. That number was only 800,000. Even so, there still could have been another 300,000 men who hadn't been tested in battle. Putting these two totals together, we arrive at 1,100,000, the figure in 1 Chronicles.[17]

As for the figures for Judah, the figures in 2 Samuel are 30,000 more than those in 1 Chronicles. As Archer notes, however, 1 Chronicles 21:6 makes it clear that Joab didn't finish the task of numbering, because David came under conviction about completing the census, and so Joab didn't get to number the tribes of Benjamin or Levi. As Archer explains,

> The procedure for conducting the census had been to start with the Transjordanian tribes (2 Sam. 24:5) and then shift to the northernmost tribe of Dan and work southward back toward Jerusalem (v. 7). This meant that the numbering of Benjamin would have come last. Hence Benjamin was not included with the total for Israel or that for Judah, either. But in the case of 2 Samuel 24, the figure for Judah included the already known figure of 30, 000 troops mustered by Benjamin (which lay immediately adjacent to Jerusalem itself). Hence the total of 500,000 included the Benjamite contingent.[18]

[17] Gleason Archer, *Encyclopedia of Bible Difficulties* (Grand Rapids, MI: Zondervan, 1982), 188–189.
[18] Ibid., 189.

What should we say about this resolution to the difference in numbers? I note first that if it is adopted, the apparent contradiction between the passages is removed. To answer the charge of contradiction, all that is needed is a *possible* way for both passages to be true. There is nothing impossible (i.e., logically self-contradictory) about the solution proposed, and if it is added to the data of both biblical passages, the numbers are the same. The apparent contradiction is resolved.

Though this is enough to answer the charge of contradiction, one would like a solution that is also plausible. Is Archer's plausible? It seems that it clearly is. In relation to the figures for Judah, Archer appeals to the textual evidence that Joab didn't finish the census for Judah. If it was known that there were 30,000 fighting men in Benjamin, that would explain the discrepancy between the Samuel and Chronicles passages. However, one may ask, if Joab didn't complete the census, why did the writer of 2 Samuel include the extra 30,000 men? Evidently, it was known that there were 30,000 fighting men in Benjamin. The author of 2 Samuel included them in the total, whereas the author of 1 Chronicles didn't, because Joab didn't actually number them on that occasion.

As to the number difference for Israel, Archer's explanation may seem less plausible, but I think we shouldn't dismiss it too hastily. Note that nowhere in either passage in question are we given detailed information about the criteria used in counting the number of available men. Note also that in the 2 Samuel passage the numbers for Israel are reported as the number of "valiant men" (or "mighty men," as some translations say). The phrase *'is hayil* is not used of the men of Judah, and in 1 Chronicles the numbers reported for both Israel and Judah are simply of the number of men in each case. No distinction is made between "valiant men" and "unseasoned warriors"; there is just a tally of the total number of men. Is the phrase *'is hayil* purely incidental to the narrative? Perhaps, but perhaps not. It is surely possible that it is intended to make the sort of distinction that Archer raises, and if that is the difference between the two passages, it explains why the numbers for Israel differ.

Again, remember that all that is required to harmonize these passages is a possible resolution, and this solution is possible. Is it plausible? The answer in a way depends on whether one is certain that the phrase *'is hayil* is intended to make the distinction Archer proposes. I don't see how we can be certain that this isn't the phrase's point, and if it is, the reason for the figures in 2 Samuel for Israel being less than those in 1 Chronicles would be exactly what Archer says.

In offering these explanations of the differences between 2 Samuel 24 and 1 Chronicles 21, I am not suggesting that there are no other possible resolutions to these apparent inconsistencies. If others are more plausible, then by all means we should adopt them. However, the solutions proposed do remove the apparent contradictions, and they are not implausible. All that is required is a possible way to resolve the dilemmas; we don't have to withhold judgment about whether these passages contain contradictions until someone proposes a "final solution" (whatever that would look like) that satisfies all.

There are, of course, many other alleged errors in Scripture. We can't address them all in this work. But if my comments about the methodological aspects of this objection are correct, it isn't necessary to suspend belief in inerrancy until all possible errors have been explained. This objection about the phenomena of Scripture is important, but not insuperable.

## INERRANCY OF DOCTRINE AND PRACTICE ONLY

In light of the alleged problems in the phenomena of Scripture, many non-evangelical scholars have abandoned the notion of an inerrant Bible altogether. Some evangelicals agree that there are factual errors, but they won't throw out Scripture as entirely unreliable on everything it affirms. So, they reject what they believe to be an all-or-nothing position. Instead, they note that the alleged errors invariably come in matters of fact, whether historical, scientific, geographical, or whatever. But such items are really of no consequence, for they don't cast doubt on what Scripture's doctrinal teachings or its practical requirements affirm.

Considerations like these have led various evangelicals to postulate that the Bible is inerrant and fully authoritative on all matters of faith and practice, but that when it comes to factual historical and scientific accuracy, there may be some errors in Scripture. After all, many who take this approach remind us, the Bible isn't a book about botany, geology, or history. Its intent is to make us wise unto salvation. It imparts revelation from God about how to establish a relationship with God and maintain it.

This is not a new objection,[19] but let me focus on two recent expressions of it. Roy Honeycutt, writing on Southern Baptist views on Scripture, explains that Southern Baptists have always affirmed that Scripture focuses on the truth of salvation, not on fields of study like the humanities and sciences. Quoting W. A. Criswell, Honeycutt writes, "The Bible is a book of redemption. It is that or nothing at all. *It is not a book of history, science, anthropology, or cosmogony*. It is a book of salvation and deliverance for lost mankind."[20] Honeycutt quotes the Chicago Statement on Biblical Inerrancy, and says that, while on the surface it seems fine, Baptists wouldn't say that Scripture is a reliable

[19] See Daniel Fuller's article on Warfield's view on inspiration: Daniel Fuller, "B. B. Warfield's View of Faith and History," *Bulletin of the Evangelical Theological Society* 10 (1967). See also Davis, *Debate about the Bible*, 23, where he makes this distinction by defining inerrancy and infallibility differently, and opting for infallibility.
[20] Roy L. Honeycutt, "Biblical Authority: A Treasured Heritage!," *RevExp* 83 (Fall 1986): 609.

rule and guide in all matters, but rather that it is such a guide in all matters of faith and practice.[21] Later in his essay, Honeycutt quotes from various Baptist statements of faith which emphasize Scripture's authority and truthfulness on all matters of faith and practice.[22] In fairness to Southern Baptists, this essay was written before the relatively recent move by this denomination, including its seminaries, to a more conservative stance on Scripture, so that the view that Scripture is reliable on all matters is now the norm.

In an article that appeared about the same time as Honeycutt's, Robert Price set forth a "map" of various positions on inerrancy. Not only did he distinguish those who believe that Scripture is inerrant in doctrine and practice only from those who hold inerrancy in all things, but Price also pointed to some who would be even narrower in their understanding of how far inerrancy extends. Some have claimed that not even all doctrinal claims are true. Thus, they would limit infallibility "to a reliable 'central message' of salvation. Now it is the *gospel*, not even all the *theology* of the Bible, that is infallible."[23]

## Responses

This may seem to be a good way to admit what historical critical scholarship has proposed without discarding our Bibles altogether. Certainly, the exact number of fighting men David numbered on the occasion discussed above has little to do with whether NT believers are still required to bring a blood sacrifice each time they sin (as was the case in the OT) in order to obtain divine forgiveness.

Still, I can't see this objection as a compelling reason to abandon inerrancy as defined and defended in the previous chapter. There are several significant reasons why this is so. First, if we want to construct a doctrine of Scripture based on what Scripture actually teaches about itself, then we can't ignore the fact that no biblical writer teaches (i.e., affirms as the case) a distinction between doctrinal and practical claims, on the one hand, and historical, scientific, factual matters on the other. I note also that those who have proposed such distinctions have yet to cite any passage where a biblical author makes that distinction, let alone affirms it as true.

Second, there are just too many passages where this distinction doesn't apply to think we should impose it on Scripture. Consider, for example, the following sentences which either quote or paraphrase biblical texts: (1) In the beginning God created the heavens and the earth. (2) The Word became flesh

---

[21] Ibid.

[22] Ibid., 613–616.

[23] Robert M. Price, "Inerrant the Wind: The Troubled House of North American Evangelicals," *EvQ* 55 (July 1983): 137. The different positions of (1) infallible in all matters of doctrine and practice, as opposed to (2) infallible in regard to the gospel are spelled out by Price on pages 133–138.

and dwelt among us. (3) A virgin shall conceive and bear a son, and you shall call his name Immanuel, God with us. (4) Why do you look for the living among the dead? He is not here; he has risen! (5) For Christ died for sins once for all, the righteous for the unrighteous, to bring us to God. (6) Simon Peter answered, "You are the Christ, the Son of the living God." And finally, (7) Prophecy never had its origin in the will of man, but men spoke from God as they were carried along by the Holy Spirit.

With respect to each of these assertions, I have a question: Is it a statement of doctrine or a statement of history/matter of fact? Sentence (1) encompasses the doctrine of creation, but it also asserts that as a matter of fact, God actually performed this deed. Sentence (2) is about Christ's incarnation, a cardinal Christian doctrine. But, in John 1 it is also a statement of a historical event that actually occurred. If not, then the rest of John's Gospel that records what Jesus said and did is pure fiction. Sentence (3) is the promise of the virgin birth. Christ's virgin birth is another essential doctrine of Christianity, but Isaiah predicts it as a future (to him) historical occurrence. If it is not a historical claim, how could it serve as a sign from God to Ahaz that God was ready, willing, and able to protect the southern kingdom from its enemies? Even more, Matthew tells us that when Mary was pregnant and then gave birth to Jesus, this fulfilled the Isaiah 7:14 prophecy. Matthew affirmed the prophecy as referring to a historical event!

Sentence (4) teaches one of the greatest (for sinners) doctrines of all, the resurrection. But the men at the tomb were not merely reciting a doctrinal statement. The tomb, as the women found it, was empty, and the men told them how it became empty: Jesus had risen from the dead! Sentence (5) is a passage from 1 Peter 3 which succinctly presents the doctrine of the atonement. But it does more than that; Peter explains to his readers not only the fact that Jesus died, but also the meaning of that historical event for the removal of sin from all mere humans.

Sentence (6) may at first appear to be only a doctrinal claim, but we should look more closely. In the verse that precedes it, Jesus didn't ask Peter what it says in some creed. He didn't even ask what the OT said about a coming Messiah. Jesus, a real historical person, living in first-century-AD Palestine, asked another real person (Peter), living at the same time, who, as a matter of fact, he thought Jesus actually was. When Peter responded, he definitely wasn't thinking of a doctrinal statement; he spoke from his knowledge of what the Messiah would be like and from his firsthand experience of the life and teachings of a real person, Jesus. Peter in effect said that, as a matter of historical fact, this real human person Jesus is the Messiah and the Son of God.

Finally, sentence (7), of all seven sentences cited, seems to be purely doctrinal, for it teaches the inspiration of Scripture. But Peter is doing more than just repeating a creed. He is saying that, as a matter of historical fact, there have been specific people who at one time or another in history picked up pen and wrote an actual book, and also as a matter of fact, the Holy Spirit so guided them that what they wrote is also what God said to them and wants all of us to know.

The analysis of these seven sentences shows that they are simultaneously both doctrinal and factual (historical) claims. The doctrine/fact distinction makes no sense when you try to apply it to these claims. But even more, unless the factual element in each of these sentences is true, the doctrine each enunciates cannot possibly be true! If the tomb on Easter morning actually contained Jesus's dead body, then the doctrine of the resurrection is a sham. If Jesus was just a mere human, there is no reason to believe the doctrine of the incarnation. So, we can't divorce the history of these statements from the doctrines they proclaim, and the doctrines can't be true if the history on which they rest is untrue!

A final problem with this objection is that it asks us to believe the absurd. We are reassured that every doctrinal and practical claim in Scripture is fully inerrant, but why should we believe that any doctrinal claim that is neither empirically nor rationally verifiable or falsifiable is totally true, especially when we are told that things we *can* verify or falsify empirically do contain some errors? Who would believe such a thing? Is there anyone who seriously thinks this sort of explanation ("Doctrines of Scripture are totally true though there is no way to prove that—trust us!—but factual matters contain some errors, and you can prove that!") would persuade a nonbeliever?

Let me illustrate the problem. Jesus in John 14 tells his disciples that he goes to prepare a place for them and will come again and receive them unto himself. He adds that in his Father's house there are many mansions. These claims tell us something about the nature of heaven and also predict Christ's return for his church. Both are matters of doctrine, so according to critics of inerrancy who espouse this objection, they are fully true. However, short of dying and going to heaven or seeing Jesus return for his church, there seems to be no possible way empirically to verify such doctrinal claims, and yet we are reassured that these things must be true because they are part of Scripture's doctrine. On the other hand, when we are told that apparently inconsistent things about how many men were at the empty tomb on Easter morning, etc., actually could be factually wrong, and we know that such matters are in principle verifiable (at least they were for people who lived when these events occurred and when the Gospel writers wrote about them), how can we reasonably be expected to believe that things we *can't* verify at all (various doctrines) are most certainly true? If things we can verify or falsify have errors, that gives little confidence that things that are unverifiable and unfalsifiable are certainly true, anyway! Asking us to trust that the doctrines are all true, anyway, is utter nonsense.

## INERRANCY AND THE AUTOGRAPHS OF SCRIPTURE

An objection to inerrancy related to the original autographs of Scripture has been raised at various times, and it is significant. Recently, it appeared in A. T. B. McGowan's *The Divine Spiration of Scripture*. McGowan offers various objections to biblical inerrancy, but emphasizes that this doesn't mean he agrees with those who think Scripture to one degree or another has errors. He proposes a view that he claims takes a mediating path between full inerrancy (as defined and defended in chapter 7) and an errant Bible. Before ending my discussion of objections to inerrancy, we shall address McGowan's "mediating alternative" to inerrancy and errancy. However, we must understand why he rejects inerrancy, and his complaints about the autographs as inerrant are a major reason why he does so.[24]

McGowan says that proponents of biblical inerrancy know there are errors in the texts we possess. He isn't referring specifically to the types of errors detailed in the objection about the phenomena of Scripture, but he wouldn't entirely exclude those kinds of problems.[25] Rather, he specifically refers to errors introduced into Scripture by copyists and translators. In light of such mistakes, it makes no sense to say that the Bibles we possess are inerrant, for inerrantists surely don't want the impossible task of arguing that errors in transcription and translation aren't actually errors at all.

Inerrantists typically say that the original autographs that came "from the pen" of the biblical author are inerrant. Of course, even that claim isn't entirely precise, because, McGowan explains, Deuteronomy, for example, couldn't have been written completely by Moses; a redactor must have finished the book, because its final portion records Moses's death.[26] In addition, some apostles occasionally used an amanuensis in writing their book. Paul often signed his letters in his own hand, because its recipients would know that a secretary actually put the letter on paper as Paul first wrote it; Paul's signature guaranteed that it wasn't a forgery.[27]

To what, then, do the autographs refer? To the first complete document of each book of the Bible, as put down on "paper" either completely by

---

[24] Others who have raised this objection are David Hubbard, "The Current Tensions: Is There a Way Out?," in *Biblical Authority*, ed. Jack Rogers (Waco, TX: Word, 1977); and Honeycutt, "Biblical Authority: A Treasured Heritage!"

[25] See McGowan's question as to whether all the problems of apparent contradictions can be traced to the copying of manuscripts and thus were not present in the autographs—McGowan, *Divine Spiration of Scripture*, 109.

[26] Ibid.

[27] Greg L. Bahnsen, "The Inerrancy of the Autographa," in Geisler, *Inerrancy* (Grand Rapids, MI: Zondervan, 1979), 168.

the author, completely by a secretary, by a combination of author and secretary, or as completed by a final editor (e.g., in the case of Deuteronomy, Moses likely first put most of it into writing, but a final editor added the last content of the book and then it was complete for the first time). This explains the meaning of "autograph," but scholars of any persuasion about inerrancy know that we do not now possess, nor has any generation of believers (OT or NT) ever had, the autographs of all biblical books. While the books were being written, only copies of books written by that time were available.

Since all biblical scholars agree on this point, and also agree that the copies of Scripture we have, have always, including now, had transcriptional and translational errors, what is the value of inerrantists' claims that, "at least the originals were totally free of error"? Since nobody has possessed or will possess the originals, how can such claims ever be tested? And this distinction between inerrant autographs and errant copies is nowhere taught in Scripture itself. We know that the Bibles possessed through the centuries have contained mistakes, and since the distinction between autograph and copy isn't taught in Scripture, how can we be sure that we should make that distinction? Doesn't this show that the idea of inerrancy is unacceptable, especially when one must appeal to nonexistent texts to defend what is falsified by the texts we possess?[28]

One other element to this objection as McGowan presents it should be mentioned. McGowan argues that if inerrancy is so critical to Scripture's value and usefulness, why didn't God preserve copies and translations from error? McGowan writes,

> Those who emphasize the inerrancy of the *autographa* are thus faced with a difficult question: 'What was the point of God acting supernaturally to provide an inerrant text providentially if it ceased to be inerrant as soon as the first or second copy was made?' If God could act with such sovereign overruling providence to ensure that the text was absolutely perfect when it left the hand of the author, why did he not preserve it for us, if an inerrant text is so vital to the life of the church?[29]

McGowan later adds that even Greg Bahnsen and B. B. Warfield, who defend the inerrancy of the autographs, add that the translations and copies we do have, even with their mistakes, are adequate to accomplish God's purposes in giving Scripture. McGowan wishes thinkers like Bahnsen would take more seriously this point about Scripture's adequacy, despite copyists' mistakes.[30]

---

[28] McGowan, *Divine Spiration of Scripture*, 109–112.
[29] Ibid., 109.
[30] Ibid., 110.

*Responses*

This is a significant objection. Many who reject inerrancy are annoyed when inerrantists exhaust all other defenses for a text's inerrancy and appeal to the inerrancy of the autographs. Critics take this defense as proof that committed inerrantists will hold on to inerrancy despite the evidence against it. No possible evidence could falsify this belief, or so it seems, when it is defended by saying that inerrancy belongs to the autographs alone and at least the text in the (inaccessible) original is inerrant. This seems to be a clever ploy to admit the obvious errors the critic notes, but hold the doctrine anyway.

This objection actually encompasses several complaints. A first is that Scripture gives no warrant for this distinction between inerrant autographs and errant copies and translations. A second is that we don't possess in any sense (nor have we ever had) the autographs of all the biblical books at once. Third, the errant copies and translations we possess are adequate to accomplish God's purposes in giving Scripture. Fourth, if inerrancy is so important, why didn't the God who supposedly insured it in the autographs do the same in copies and translations? Finally, there is no biblical proof that the Scriptures available through the centuries are inerrant, but that hasn't kept them from accomplishing the purposes for which God gave them.

Let me address each objection individually. As to the first, Scripture doesn't explicitly distinguish between inerrant originals and errant copies and translations. The crucial question, however, is whether anything Scripture says warrants that distinction. I believe it does. Here I appeal to key Scriptures on inspiration like 2 Timothy 3:16; 2 Peter 1:20–21; and 1 Corinthians 2:13. According to 2 Timothy 3:16, all Scripture is the product of God's breath. Paul refers specifically to the OT, but the passage can also apply to the NT. So, God spoke and the result was the written text of Scripture. Scripture is inspired, not the writer. Surely, Paul must be referring to the original document produced by the writer. He says nothing about copies or translations as the product of God's breath. While the verse doesn't say that God didn't guide copyists and translators, it doesn't affirm that God was involved as they worked. In fact, it is hard to think of a Scripture that teaches God's involvement in those activities through the centuries.

But there is more. Second Peter 1:21 speaks of the Holy Spirit's action in conjunction with the work of the biblical authors. This passage teaches that the divine author carried along the human author to the goal the Holy Spirit envisioned when he moved the human author to write. As a result, the author's words were the very words of God. Again, as with 2 Timothy 3:16, it is the text of Scripture that is God's inspired word. This passage, however, adds that a human author was involved, but it says only that the human writer who received the divine revelation and superintending work of the Holy Spirit was the one whom the Holy Spirit "carried along." Nothing is said about guidance of those who would later copy or translate Scripture into other languages. To say that either this passage or the 2 Timothy 3 passage warrants belief in inspired copyists and translators because neither passage denies it is an argument from silence.

Some might reply that the two verses discussed most specifically refer to the OT, but what about the NT? While I have argued that the 2 Timothy and 2 Peter passages can properly be applied to the NT, let us look at two NT passages that specifically relate to the NT. First, there is John 14, 15, and 16, in which Jesus promised the Holy Spirit's ministry to the apostles. We noted that the ministries described in these verses would be used when the apostles went to preach and when they would write the books that would become the NT. Nothing in John 14, 15, or 16 says anything about any Holy Spirit ministry to copiers or translators of NT books.

A final NT passage relevant to this issue is 1 Corinthians 2:13. Paul says that the Holy Spirit taught him and his fellow apostles how to combine the right words with the thoughts revealed by the Holy Spirit. This relates to the doctrine of inspiration and speaks of both the Holy Spirit's activity and that of the human writer in producing Scripture. The result of this ministry is the biblical book, not a copy or translation of it.

Why have I referenced these verses on inspiration? Because they show that inspiration is a quality of texts written by human authors who were superintended and taught by the Holy Spirit when they first wrote their books. Inspiration applies to the writing of the original documents. Now, many copies of these documents were made. Even during Christ's life, before any NT book was written, many copies of OT books had been made down through the centuries. No one in Jesus's day suggested that the copies of OT books they possessed were originals that the authors wrote. The OT books Jesus and his disciples read were made from a series of copies made after the close of the OT canon (it had closed some 400 years prior to the time of Christ).

As for the NT, once NT books began to be written, they were also copied for circulation. Though we don't possess copies of NT books dated right after the originals were written, we know from copies we do possess that it wasn't very long before copies were made. Early manuscripts we have of various NT books were not likely the very first copies made after the originals (one of the earliest dated manuscripts, p52, contains parts of the Gospel of John and is dated AD 125; John's Gospel was written well before AD 100). Even if the NT autographs still existed today, there would still be many copies of NT books, for the Bible was given for all people, not just a few, and one set of originals wasn't enough for everyone who would want to read these books.

When we put these facts together (i.e., inspiration is attributed only to the books the original authors wrote; there is ample biblical evidence that people in OT and NT times had copies of these books; and we have a large number of manuscripts of the Greek NT, of translations, and of various manuscripts of OT books so that we know the OT and NT were both copied and translated), there seems to be ample warrant to distinguish the autographs from copies and translations of the various biblical books. Even if one rejects inerrancy, refusing to acknowledge that there were originals and there are copies and translations is obscurantist. What is contestable is whether the originals were inerrant, and whether we have any access to what they said. McGowan and others who raise this objection seem to think we have little or no access to the originals, and so it is special pleading to say that at least the originals were inerrant. For reasons explained, it is legitimate to distinguish the originals from later copies and translations.

As just suggested, McGowan's second issue really gets to the nub of this objection. If we have little or no idea of what the originals said, then to say they are inerrant is irrefutable but it is also unconfirmable! Probably McGowan would agree and would add that this is why defense of inerrancy should be dropped.

In response, I note initially that this objection seems to drive a significant wedge between the text of the originals and the text of the copies and translations available at any time in the OT and NT eras. Now, there are really only three options in relation to the originals. Either they are (1) exactly like the copies, or they are (2) totally unlike the copies, or (3) to one degree or another they are similar and dissimilar to the copies. Option (1) cannot be true, for if it were, there would be no textual variants in copies we possess, and we know that isn't so. For McGowan's objection to stand, either option (2) or some form of option (3) must be the case. Option (2) had better not be correct, for then we would have no idea of what the originals said, and how could anyone, McGowan included, claim that the errant copies and translations we have are adequate to fulfill God's purposes? If we don't know what the originals said, then the Bibles we possess may have nothing to do with the actual words God inspired and the human authors of Scripture wrote. If that is so, there is serious trouble for all of us—inerrantists, errantists, and followers of McGowan's mediating position (to be explained later).

So, the relation of copies and translations to the originals must be that suggested by option (3). But that option has room for variation. That is, the originals may be quite similar to the copies, somewhat similar, or basically dissimilar. In order for McGowan's claim to be true—that we don't possess or know what the originals actually said—the copies must be either basically dissimilar or only somewhat similar to the originals. If, on the other hand, from copies and translations we can reconstruct the original so that the best copies are quite similar to the original, then appealing to inerrancy of the originals is a cogent way to defend biblical inerrancy.

Thankfully, we know how close copies and translations are to the originals. In fact, several lines of evidence show that they are quite similar, so appeal to the autographs is not irrelevant. The most fundamental line of evidence comes from the science of textual criticism. Oddly, McGowan never mentions the results of textual criticism when he discusses the autographs. But the evidence is overwhelming! Readers should note here that none of this evidence establishes the inerrancy of anything. Rather, it helps us establish what the originals actually said and allows us to know whether the Bibles we possess are at all like what the Holy Spirit originally inspired the biblical authors to write.

Let me begin with the NT, for there is much more evidence from which to establish that text than there is for the text of the OT. Elsewhere I have set forth this evidence in more detail,[31] so I shall just summarize it here. There are many Greek manuscripts of portions of the NT (over 5,000 such manuscripts exist). In addition, a huge number of manuscripts are translations of all or part of the NT. There are also quotes from the NT in commentaries or theological treatises written by early church fathers, and there are also lectionaries. Obviously, these four groups are not equally distant from the originals. The Greek manuscripts are the nearest, and the lectionaries are the farthest. Still, there are in total more than 8,000 pieces of manuscript evidence from which textual critics can construct the NT text.

Not only is there this amount of evidence (which far exceeds manuscript evidence for any other book from the ancient world), but the dates of the earliest manuscripts we possess are much closer to the originals than is true of other works of the ancient world. For example, the earliest manuscript of part of the NT is dated about AD 125, less than a century from when the original was composed. The works of Homer are the best-attested nonbiblical works of the ancient world. There are some 643 copies of parts of his work (as compared to 5,000-plus Greek manuscripts of parts of the NT), but the dating of manuscripts of Homer's works is unclear—his works were thought to have been composed in the ninth century BC, centuries earlier than the copies we possess. The next best attested works from the ancient world are those of Demosthenes. In his case, however, there are only 200 copies, and the earliest of them is dated AD 1100. Demosthenes is thought to have written these works in

---

[31] See my chapter on the reliability of the Gospels in *Can You Believe It's True?*

the fourth century BC, so there is a time gap of some 1,500 years between their composition and the first copy of any of them that we possess.

The authenticity of these nonbiblical texts of the ancient world is not seriously doubted by scholars; i.e., scholars believe they know what words the authors originally wrote. If that is so in those cases, it should be granted that we know the text of the original NT, especially since we possess so many more manuscripts, and many early ones are dated within a couple of centuries from when the originals were written. But even more, through the science of textual criticism, scholars are able to establish what the original NT books said with 99 percent–plus accuracy, and they add that variant readings that are still uncertain as to which reading is correct in no way impact any matter of doctrine or practice.[32] The message is clear: we know what the autographs of the NT said!

What about OT originals? Here we don't have as much manuscript evidence as for the NT, but there is some. In addition, the discovery of the Dead Sea Scrolls in the early twentieth century was a major find. Though these Scrolls didn't include the whole OT, they did contain substantial parts of major OT books (e.g., Isaiah). One of the most important things about these Scrolls is that they are judged to have been made about a thousand years earlier than other manuscripts of OT books we possess. In comparing those manuscripts with the Dead Sea Scrolls, scholars found very little variation. This helped confirm the thinking that, because of the extreme care the Jews took in copying OT books, it is likely that few transcriptional errors have crept in over time.

In addition to Hebrew manuscripts of parts of the OT, there are translations, the most important of which is the Septuagint (LXX), the Greek OT. Various copies of the LXX help scholars to establish the text of the OT. In addition, commentaries on the OT like the Mishnah, the Gamaras, etc., also help in establishing the text of the OT. As with the NT, the further the copy is from the original text of the OT book (because it is a translation, or because it is a small part of an OT book used for commentary, etc.), the less helpful it is in establishing what the original text actually said. Still, OT scholars, using the tools of textual criticism, believe they know what the original text of the OT said to a degree of 90 to 95 percent certainty. Readings still in doubt do not impact any matter of doctrine or practice.[33]

None of this evidence from textual criticism shows that either the OT or

---

[32] For support of these data, see footnote 32 in chapter 11 of my *Can You Believe It's True?*

[33] Ellis Brotzman and Eric Tully write, "Textual criticism, by its very nature, focuses on the variant readings, but the 90 percent or more of the text that exists without variation must also be kept in view." See Ellis R. Brotzman and Eric J. Tully, *Old Testament Textual Criticism: A Practical Approach* (Grand Rapids, MI: Baker Academic 2016), 3–4. A special word of thanks to my colleague, OT scholar Richard Averbeck, for his help on this point and with pointing me in the direction of the Brotzman and Tully book.

the NT tells the truth about what it records. But that isn't the point of Mc-
Gowan's objection. The point is whether we know what the autographs said.
If not, it means little to talk of errant copies and inerrant autographs. But if
we do know what the autographs said, and we do, then holding inerrancy of
the autographs isn't just a clever debater's ploy. It is a correct claim that reflects
what we know about the Bible.[34]

In addition, there is further evidence beyond textual criticism that we
should believe that we know what God said and the writers wrote. This evidence comes from Scripture itself, though the Bible doesn't directly say we
have the autographs. Think first about Paul's (2 Tim. 3:16) and Peter's (2 Pet.
1:20–21) comments about the inspiration of Scripture. As noted, Paul and Peter
were most specifically commenting on the OT, for when they wrote, the NT
wasn't completed, and the parts that were finished hadn't likely been widely
circulated. When Paul and Peter wrote about inspiration, they didn't have access to actual autographs of OT books. They only had copies of the OT. But
then how could they claim that God inspired the OT if they had no idea of
what the autographs contained? If the copies they had were as distant from
the autographs as McGowan and others suggest, then Paul and Peter had no
business making the comments they made about the OT! And, by the way, Paul
and Peter wrote 2 Timothy 3:16 and 2 Peter 1:20–21 under divine inspiration,
and surely the Holy Spirit knew that neither of them possessed the autographs.
If the copies Paul and Peter possessed weren't essentially equivalent to the autographs, then not only were Paul and Peter presumptuous in their comments,
but also the Holy Spirit misled them when he moved them to write what they
did about the OT! Obviously, such suppositions are absurd, but *why*? Because
Paul and Peter knew what the autographs of the OT said, and the Holy Spirit
knew that they knew!

Further evidence about the OT comes from Jesus. During his earthly life,
Jesus never possessed the OT autographs. And yet we saw in the chapters on inspiration that Jesus sometimes quoted an OT passage that was said or written
by a mere human, and he attributed the passage to God as the spokesman. One
example is Jesus's appeal in Matthew 19:4–5 to Genesis 2:24 as God's words
whereas in Genesis 2, verse 24 was either spoken by Adam or was Moses's
commentary on the creation of Eve and God's institution of marriage. There
are, of course, many other examples of this phenomenon, as noted in our dis-

---

[34] One practical word of advice is in order at this point before I move to other evidence that the Scriptures we have
should be trusted. What I have said about knowing what the autographs said should not be misunderstood. It
doesn't mean that every translation is of equal value, nor that two different copies in the same language are of equal
worth. Some translations are more accurate than others, and some copies of Scripture are based on better textual
traditions than others. The practical point is that one should get the best translation available in one's language,
i.e., one based on the best textual tradition. When one does that, it is right to point to that Bible and claim that it
is God's word. It is right to preach it as God's word and to study and obey it as his word.

cussion of inspiration, but what is my point? My point is first that, when Jesus spoke Matthew 19:4–5, at no time during his earthly life prior to his comment did Jesus ever see the autograph of Genesis. Still, he quoted what he knew from copies of Genesis to be Genesis 2:24 and said that God said those words. If no one really knows what the autographs of Scripture said and so it is senseless to appeal to them to defend inerrancy, then Jesus was wrong to quote from the copy of Genesis 2:24 and say it is God's word. But Jesus did quote the verse and said that God spoke those words. Jesus on many other occasions cited or quoted OT Scriptures to prove a point, but the Scriptures he possessed weren't the autographs. Should we say that all of Jesus's arguments based on the OT and all of his quotes and citations of the OT are suspect, because he didn't possess the autographs? To draw such conclusions would be devastating, for it would undermine many of Jesus's teachings. It would also cast doubts about whether he fulfilled OT messianic passages, because without the autographs, we don't know whether the original prophecy actually said something that his actual life and deeds did or even could fulfill!

In John 17:17 Jesus asked his Father to sanctify his disciples in the truth. He added that the Father's word is truth. As we saw when discussing this passage in relation to inerrancy, Jesus, given what he thought of Scripture, would have believed that the Father's word is present in Scripture, the OT. But Jesus and his disciples possessed only copies of the OT's various books, not the autographs, and Jesus knew that! If there is a gap between the copies Jesus had and the autographs, so that he didn't actually know what the autographs said, Jesus's testimony about his Father's words as truthful are unverifiable and unfalsifiable, because Jesus refers to something no one possesses. If the copies don't accurately reflect the autographs, then no one has access to what God originally said. Jesus, of course, knew all that and still uttered the prayer of John 17:17. What can that mean other than that he knew that, in having the copies, he and his disciples possessed equivalents of the autographs?

These examples from Jesus's teaching show that Jesus believed he and his contemporaries had access to the equivalent of the autographs, and as omniscient, he would know. If he used the OT in his day and deemed it equivalent to what God inspired the OT authors to write, we should do the same. It isn't wrongheaded to appeal to autographs![35]

---

[35] Before leaving Jesus's testimony about Scripture, we must pause long enough to consider Matthew 5:18. This verse relates most specifically to biblical authority and the preservation of Scripture, but it isn't irrelevant to inerrancy. I raise it now because Jesus said it when copies of OT books were the only Scripture. Jesus said that not even the slightest stroke of the pen would disappear from the law until all was accomplished, but if the copies of the OT Jesus possessed weren't equivalent to the autographs, then the slightest and the largest strokes of the OT (and everything in between) had already disappeared! And heaven and earth hadn't yet disappeared, but God's word had, if the copies in Jesus's day weren't equivalent to the autographs! If it is absurd to appeal to the autographs to uphold inerrancy because we only have copies and copies aren't equal to the autographs, then what Jesus said is absurd, because heaven and earth still stood when he made these comments, and yet God's word had passed away! How absurd to think such a thing! What Jesus said wasn't nonsense, nor did he say it because he knew what

Hence, it isn't wrong to distinguish inerrant autographs from errant copies and translations. But what about McGowan's third objection? In light of our answer to the second objection, we can affirm that the Scriptures people have had through the centuries have accomplished God's purposes, because they were essentially equivalent to the autographs, and there is great power in God's word (Heb. 4:12). If we had little idea of what the autographs said, we wouldn't know whether the Bibles available down through history had led people to God or misled them. Thankfully, we know that copies, despite transcriptional and translational mistakes, are essentially the word of God, and accurately record what God has revealed.

As to McGowan's fourth argument, only God knows why he didn't providentially keep all copies and translations absolutely identical to the originals— just as only God knows why he didn't begin our world history with the eternal state with everyone in glorified bodies,[36] since that's where history is eventually going. Thankfully, we don't have to answer such questions to decide whether Scripture is inerrant. If we could answer McGowan's question, I doubt that rejecters of inerrancy would at last embrace biblical inerrancy. Moreover, not having an answer to his question doesn't prove inerrancy wrong. What is crucial *is not* why God *didn't do* something. What matters is understanding what he *did do* when he gave Scripture. The answer is that he gave us an inerrant Bible!

But, even more directly, because of results from textual criticism, it makes sense to say that God has preserved his word through the centuries of transmission! No, there isn't just one copy, repeated numerous times without variation. But because of textual criticism we know what the autographs said. God has preserved them, just as Jesus promised in Matthew 5:18.

As to McGowan's final complaint about the autographs, there is biblical proof that the Scriptures people have possessed are inerrant. It comes from the testimony of Paul, Peter, and Jesus already cited. None of them commented on the autographs, but they considered the texts they had to be God's word. And, they held them to be inerrant (as shown in my defense of inerrancy). What about other evidence from the testimony of Paul, Peter, and Jesus? We have Jesus's promise of the Holy Spirit's ministry (John 15–17) which, in effect, guaranteed the inspiration of the soon-to-be-written NT. Paul says he writes the commands of the Lord (e.g., 1 Cor. 7:10). Peter says people have a hard time

the "real" Scriptures (the autographs) said and he was thinking about them, not the copies everyone possessed in his day! This verse makes sense only if Jesus fully believed that the copies of the OT that were available to him contained what God had revealed and OT authors had written, namely, the equivalent of the autographs! To think otherwise turns Jesus's testimony into nonsense!

[36] As my colleague Graham Cole says, if the autographs had remained, they might have become idols like the bronze serpent in Hezekiah's time. This is not mere conjecture, as anyone can affirm from seeing how various Christian groups have built shrines and churches on the sites of various places in the Holy Land thought to have been where Jesus did one thing or another.

understanding Paul and distort what he writes as they do with *other* Scripture (2 Pet. 3:16)—Paul wrote much of the NT, and many of his works would have been written by the time that Peter wrote these words about Paul's writing. The above claims make little sense, if those who made them didn't know what these authors originally wrote.

In sum, this objection is very significant, and so, I have responded to it at length. Thankfully, we can know what was originally revealed and inspired. It isn't nonsensical to distinguish inerrant autographs from copies and translations with some errors.

## ACCOMMODATION AND INERRANCY

Often in studies on the doctrine of Scripture the author appeals to "accommodation." Sometimes it is invoked in discussing revelation, and at other times it is raised when the subject is inspiration. I have waited to address it in this chapter, because in current debates over biblical inerrancy, an objection to biblical inerrancy is based on accommodation. In fact, this concept raises several issues about inerrancy and Scripture in general. One (to be addressed first) is a historical matter, while the others are more strictly theological in nature.

First, I must clarify what accommodation means. God's knowledge and the powers of his mind are way beyond those of human beings. Still, he wanted to reveal truth to us, anyway. If God revealed things exactly as he knows them (in all their complexity and with exact precision), it is doubtful that humans could understand what he said. Imagine, for sake of argument, that an Einsteinian conception of physics is the correct way to understand our universe. Of course, when the Bible was written, no one had any idea of such a conception. Though Scripture is neither a formal nor an informal treatise on physics, it discusses events and actions against the backdrop of the universe in which we live. If God, as he gave revelation, and the Holy Spirit, as he inspired the writing of Scripture, had included statements about the world in language reflective of Einsteinian physics, neither the biblical authors nor anyone else at the time would have understood what was said. So, God had to accommodate his revelation to its recipients' understanding. He had to present it simply enough for its recipients to understand it.

If this is true of human understanding of science, it is even more so when the topics are matters entirely beyond the empirical world. Imagine how hard it would be to understand God's word if he didn't use terms and analogies we could understand! Hence, for centuries Christian thinkers have held that God, in order for his message to be understandable, had to accommodate his thoughts to language we could understand. In speaking of God's accommodating his thoughts to human thought forms, John Calvin famously wrote of God "lisping," so to speak, in giving us his word so that we could understand it.[37]

Though Christian theologians and Bible scholars have for the most part commonly agreed that God did accommodate his truth to us in language and concepts we can understand, it makes sense to ask whether God's doing so resulted in distorting things a bit so that we could get the basic gist of the message. And so, several issues about accommodation and inerrancy have arisen. The first is a historical question, while the others are about core theological issues.

So, what have Christian theologians said about God's accommodation of truth to human understanding? Some say that the orthodox position has always been that, while it was necessary for God to simplify his revelation, doing so didn't require distorting it so that Scripture would affirm things that are actually false. Others have argued that accommodating truth did require God to include things that he knew were not true. Proponents of the latter view say this is what major Christian thinkers have always held. Which understanding is correct?

In the late 1970s, Jack Rogers and Donald McKim published *The Authority and Interpretation of the Bible: An Historical Approach.* In it they argued that inerrantists have misread the historic position of the church on the doctrine of inerrancy. They have assumed that the majority position has been the inerrancy of Scripture, but that is wrong. In a separate section on history and inerrancy, we shall examine this matter in more detail. For now, the key historical point is that Rogers and McKim claim that the historic position of the church has been that, in accommodating his revelation to human ways of understanding, God included various erroneous ideas that biblical authors and their contemporaries held. Lest we criticize God for this, remember that his goal was to reveal himself. Had he used language that rejected the mistaken ideas of each author's day, neither the biblical writer nor his contemporaries would have understood what he wrote. This accommodation to error extended not only to matters of historical and scientific fact but was also necessary in doctrinal passages.[38]

To support their contention that this has been the historic position of the church, Rogers and McKim quote from Origen, Chrysostom, Augustine, Luther, Calvin, and Berkouwer. In contrast, others maintain that God did accommodate his thoughts to human understanding but without including

[37] John Calvin, *Institutes of the Christian Religion*, ed. John T. McNeill, trans. Ford Lewis Battles (Philadelphia: Westminster, 1960), 121 (1.13.1).
[38] Jack B. Rogers and Donald K. McKim, *The Authority and Interpretation of the Bible: An Historical Approach* (San Francisco: Harper & Row, 1979), 10.

any errors in Scripture. Rogers and McKim and Kenton Sparks[39] have argued that the latter view hasn't been the historic position of the church, so where do they think it came from? They say the "culprit" is Charles Hodge, whose views were grounded in the Protestant Scholasticism that stemmed in part from Francis Turretin. Hodge, the claim goes, wasn't a historical theologian and really wasn't familiar with the church's historic position on the issue of accommodation. As a result, he introduced a more modern notion of it into theology, one that proposes that divine accommodation to human knowledge and thought forms didn't require including errors in the written revelation of Scripture.

Thus, this objection to biblical inerrancy claims that there have actually been two versions of the concept of accommodation in the history of the church. The older one claims that, in accommodating his truth to human thought forms, God adapted his message to human knowledge and understanding in ways that required including errors in Scripture, both in factual matters relating to science and history, and even in Scripture's doctrinal claims. Because it is more recent, and because of who first popularized it and the circumstances that led them to do so, the second view that accommodation doesn't destroy biblical inerrancy departs from the church's historic position and should be rejected.

The historical question about accommodation, then, can be stated as follows: what is actually the historic position of the church on the issue of divine accommodation? Has the church affirmed that accommodation requires including errors in Scripture, or has it held that God accommodated his thoughts to human language without including any errors?

In addition, the historical question raises the theological issue. At least as early as 1972, Daniel Fuller, who held that there could be errors in factual matters of Scripture (but he hadn't found errors in doctrinal matters), attempted to explain the factual problems by appealing to accommodation. He claimed that God enabled the biblical writers to see ways to use various cultural matters, without changing them, to enhance God's communicating what he wanted to say. So, Scripture may have some factual mistakes, but don't blame God, for he was only trying to insure that we would understand his word.[40]

In addition, Kenton Sparks's *God's Word in Human Words* espouses the Rogers and McKim historical point on accommodation. But, apart from the history, Sparks holds that Scripture does contain errors, and he links this with divine accommodation to human finitude. But Sparks makes the point in a

---

[39] Kenton Sparks, *God's Word in Human Words: An Evangelical Appropriation of Critical Biblical Scholarship* (Grand Rapids, MI: Baker, 2008), 230ff.
[40] Daniel Fuller, "The Nature of Biblical Inerrancy," *Journal of the American Scientific Affiliation* (June 1972): 49, quoted and discussed in Davis, *Debate about the Bible*, 42–43. This article was originally given as a paper read at Wheaton College on November 5, 1970.

slightly different way than these other thinkers did. This is even clearer in his more recent book on Scripture entitled *Sacred Word, Broken Word*.

In *Sacred Word, Broken Word* Sparks wants to affirm that Scripture is God's word. He also wants to clarify that Scripture contains various types of errors. After quoting such historical giants as Gregory of Nazianzus, Justin, Calvin, and Wesley as saying that various passages contain one sort of error or another, he argues that his quotes show that such errors were *God's* accommodation to the levels of understanding of those who wrote Scripture and of those who first received it.[41] In general, Sparks agrees, but he prefers to modify a bit this understanding of accommodation.

First, Sparks thinks Scripture's human authors were colluding partners in the act of accommodation. The key, though, is that accommodation didn't happen between the author and his audience, but between God and the human author. As Sparks explains, this means that "God *adopted* the author of Genesis as *his* author and, in doing so, adopted that human author's ancient view of the cosmos; God knew the right cosmology, but neither 'Moses' nor the Israelites did."[42]

This first point leads to Sparks's second amendment about accommodation. Typically, Christian thinkers appeal to accommodation when a biblical passage contains an error or something very difficult to understand. As to passages that seem fine as they are, theologians don't appeal to accommodation. In contrast, the fact that God adopts each biblical author as his spokesman means that *all* of Scripture is accommodated discourse, not just some. This is so, claims Sparks, "for the very reason that, on every page of Scripture, God has *adopted* the words and viewpoints of finite, fallen human authors as the words and viewpoints of his holy book: the entire Bible is accommodated discourse. And this is why God's book includes all things native to human discourse—truth and error, good and bad, righteousness and things unrighteous: one finds all this in the Bible."[43]

Sparks's final amendment involves the term "accommodation" itself. In light of his first two suggestions, Sparks believes we should drop the term "accommodation" and substitute for it "providential adoption." He offers this suggestion, because the former term suggests that God plays an active role in the production of Scripture, whereas Sparks believes God's role was actually more passive. "That is, in inscripturation God allowed his human authors the freedom to be precisely who they were when they wrote Scripture. . . . in the process of reaching a greater end, the humans

---

[41] Kenton Sparks, *Sacred Word, Broken Word: Biblical Authority and the Dark Side of Scripture* (Grand Rapids, MI: Eerdmans, 2012), 50–53.

[42] Ibid., 53.

[43] Ibid., 54. Sparks begins his explanation of his second amendment on 53.

involved in writing Scripture inevitably showed their true colors, including their errors and sins."[44] Lest we think this makes God too passive in the writing of Scripture, Sparks suggests that we include the doctrine of divine providence. According to that doctrine, even when God doesn't seem very involved, he is still providentially involved to accomplish his goals. In light of these things, Sparks prefers the term and concept "providential adoption," rather than "accommodation."[45] Sparks's amendments explain why God cannot be held responsible for Scripture's errors, but just as clearly, they reject biblical inerrancy.

*Responses*

I want first to address the historical question, though the key issue isn't what various people held, but what Scripture teaches about itself. There are several elements to this objection, as follows: (1) Reformers like Calvin understood accommodation to mean that accommodation of God's thoughts to human language required the inclusion of errors in Scripture; (2) Francis Turretin's scholastic methodology was almost the exact opposite of Calvin's, and in his writings the idea of accommodation used by Calvin and the church fathers was absent; (3) Charles Hodge was strongly influenced by Turretin, having studied his theology as a student and having used it as his text when teaching, and Hodge formulated his theology basically in ignorance of the fact that the historic notion of accommodation involved some errors in Scripture; (4) and Hodge's notion of accommodation didn't include the idea that for God to accommodate his word to humans, he had to include in Scripture ideas that were false; (5) hence, those who think accommodation doesn't involve errors are out of step with the church's historic position.

Various historians and historical theologians have interacted with the Rogers and McKim proposals, most notably John Woodbridge and Richard Muller.[46] Their works are worthy of careful study, but let me highlight a few details. First, Woodbridge shows that Rogers and McKim and others who follow them have misread the church fathers and the Reformers on accommodation. Thinkers like Calvin and Luther did speak of divine accommodation, but not in a way that suggested that accommodation resulted in including errors in Scripture.[47]

Second, the idea that Turretin's approach to theology was the exact opposite of Calvin's is unfounded. Even more, it has been shown that Turretin

---

[44] Ibid., 54.
[45] Ibid., 55.
[46] See John D. Woodbridge, *Biblical Authority: A Critique of the Rogers/McKim Proposal* (Grand Rapids, MI: Zondervan, 1982); and Richard Muller, *Post-Reformation Reformed Dogmatics*, vol. 2: *Holy Scripture: The Cognitive Foundation of Theology* (Grand Rapids, MI: Baker, 1993).
[47] For example, see Woodbridge, *Biblical Authority*, 141–148.

didn't discard the notion of accommodation, but instead, it was central to his entire theological system and at the heart of his understanding of God's communication with humanity.[48] In particular, Turretin's belief in divine accommodation appears prominently in his distinction between archetypal and ectypal theology. The former refers to God's knowledge of himself, while the latter was "the wisdom of divine things having been communicated to the creature in proportion to the creature's precise limitations and conditions."[49] According to Turretin, we can have ectypal knowledge of God because of God's revelation in Scripture. Speaking about accommodation in much the same terms as Calvin did, Turretin wrote,

> Conclusions concerning the Word of God must not be drawn from [the nature of] the mind of God, nor is the meaning of the utterances to be measured by the richness of the speaker, which is infinite, but from the fixed and determinate intention, in accordance with which he speaks in a manner *accommodated* to human capacity. When God understands anything he understands it for himself, and as he is infinite, he understands according to infinity, but when he speaks he is not speaking to himself, but to us, that is, in a manner *accommodated* to our capacity, which is finite, and cannot understand several meanings.[50]

Clearly, Turretin knew and used the notion of accommodation in his theology. It is also clear from the passage just cited (and others from Turretin that could be cited) that Turretin didn't think accommodation requires errors in Scripture.

From the preceding, we can also say that the basic notion in (3) above is wrong. Hodge did study Turretin and was greatly influenced by him. However, in doing so, he wasn't ignorant of the issue of accommodation. Mark Rogers has also clearly shown that Hodge knew of this issue from his study of German theology. One evidence of that is seen in the first two volumes of a journal (1825–1826) entitled *Biblical Repertory: A Collection of Tracts in Biblical Literature*, a journal Hodge started and edited. Rogers explains:

> The articles in these volumes contain multiple descriptions and rebuttals of German theology, which Hodge thought was advancing a dangerous form of rationalism. Hodge and the authors of the articles he edited identified

---

[48] See Mark Rogers, "Charles Hodge and the Doctrine of Accommodation," *TJ* 31 (2010): 231. Here Rogers relies on the following essay by Martin Klauber: "Francis Turretin on Biblical Accommodation: Loyal Calvinist or Reformed Scholastic?," *WTJ* 55 (1993); see especially page 86 of Klauber's article on the importance of accommodation to Turretin.

[49] Rogers, "Charles Hodge and the Doctrine of Accommodation," 232, quoting Timothy Phillips, "Francis Turretin's Idea of Theology and Its Bearing upon His Doctrine of Scripture" (PhD diss.; Vanderbilt University, 1986), 135.

[50] Quoted in Rogers, "Charles Hodge and the Doctrine of Accommodation," 233. Rogers italicizes the two instances of the word "accommodated," but I have quoted the passage as it was in Turretin. This quotation comes from Francis Turretin, *The Doctrine of Scripture: Locus 2 of Institutio Theologiae Elencticae*, ed. J. W. Beardslee (Grand Rapids, MI: Baker, 1981), 202–203 (2.19.8).

an innovative form of biblical accommodation as central to the rationalistic biblical scholarship that was common in Germany. These volumes demonstrate that Hodge had a better understanding of the history of the doctrine of accommodation than is sometimes acknowledged. Before he was thirty, Hodge had identified two types of biblical accommodation in the history of Christianity, rejecting one and accepting the other.[51]

The view of accommodation that Hodge adopted was the one Calvin and the church fathers held, not the one that claims that accommodation comes with errors.

As Rogers showed, Hodge actually saw this aberrant view of accommodation stemming from the theology of Germans like Johann Semler. Semler's higher criticism seems to have come from seventeenth-century English Deists and French philosophers who had raised many skeptical attacks against Christianity, including an attack on the notion of Scripture as fixed truth. Hodge relied heavily on the analysis of Hugh James Rose's *The State of the Protestant Church in Germany* and C. F. Staeudlin's *History of Theological Knowledge and Literature, from the Beginning of the Eighteenth Century to the Present Time* for his understanding of the situation in German theology at this time in Hodge's life.[52] Of Semler's views, Rose wrote,

> This was the origin of that famous theory of Accommodation . . . which in the hands of [Semler's] followers became the most formidable weapon ever devised for the destruction of Christianity. Whatever men were disinclined to receive in the New Testament, and yet could not with decency reject while they called themselves Christians, and retained the Scripture, they got rid of by this theory, and quietly maintained that the apostles, and in fact Jesus himself, had adapted himself, not only in his way of teaching, but also in his doctrines to the barbarism, ignorance and prejudices of the Jews, and that it was therefore our duty to reject the whole of this temporary part of Christianity, and retain only what is substantial and eternal.[53]

Rogers further traces this notion of accommodation to thinkers like Socinus, Hugo Grotius, and later Louis Sabatier. This was definitely not the concept of accommodation found in the church fathers or the Reformers. Nor was it Hodge's view, as can easily be seen from his *Systematic Theology*. The *new* and *innovative* notion of accommodation is the one that says errors were included in Scripture so as to adjust Scripture to the level of knowledge and understanding of the people to whom it was first written.

Mark Rogers offers a helpful summary to this part of the discussion about

[51] Rogers, "Charles Hodge and the Doctrine of Accommodation," 234.
[52] Ibid., 235.
[53] Ibid., 235–236. Here Rogers quotes from Hugh James Rose, "The State of the Protestant Church in Germany," *Biblical Repertory* 2 (1826): 436.

the history of the concept of accommodation. It would be helpful to quote him as follows:

> Charles Hodge's view of the history of accommodation is also largely consistent with the interpretations of contemporary historians who have a more thorough knowledge of the history than Hodge ever did. John Woodbridge found that what he calls "Socinian" accommodation first appeared in the writings of men like Fastus [sic]" Socinus and Hugo Grotius, who "began to fashion a doctrine of accommodation different from the one proposed by Augustine and Calvin." This new and different version of accommodation "began to account for 'genuine discrepancies' between what the Bible taught and what 'scientists' believed to be the case." Richard Muller explains that the "traditional" view of accommodation refers "to the manner or mode of revelation . . . not to the quality of the revelation or to the matter revealed." The idea that accommodation includes the use of time-bound and erroneous statements has "no relation to the position of the Reformers," but arose in eighteenth-century thinkers like Semler.[54]

We could go further on the historical issue, but the evidence already produced is sufficient to show that the views of Rogers, McKim, and Sparks, etc., on accommodation don't accurately reflect the understanding of the concept in the history of the Christian church. But that isn't the end of this issue, for apart from the historical question, it raises a theological point in objection to inerrancy. Is it true that for God to communicate his truth at all he had to accommodate his revelation to various erroneous ideas of the authors who wrote Scripture and of the people who first received it?

At first glance, this idea has an air of cogency. It seems to get further support when one examines Scripture's phenomena. There are many apparent discrepancies and contradictions in Scripture, and it is reasonable to think that while many can be resolved, not every one has a convincing solution. It also makes sense that someone who knows everything in all its complexities, would have to simplify what he says. Otherwise, how could his recipients grasp any of it?

It is just at this point, i.e., with the divine attribute of omniscience, however, that the idea that accommodation necessitates error runs aground. Granted that, with our limited knowledge, it may be impossible to explain the most complex things we know without so simplifying them that we distort the truth a bit. Once our listeners or readers understand the basic gist of what we are saying, we then revisit the topic and remove the imprecision we had to include originally if our audience was to grasp anything.

---

[54] Rogers, "Charles Hodge and the Doctrine of Accommodation," 238. Rogers bases his comments about Woodbridge on Woodbridge's *Biblical Authority*, 193, n. 52; see also, 189, n. 1, 49–68, 85–100. The comments from Muller are based on his *Dictionary of Latin and Greek Theological Terms* (Grand Rapids, MI: Baker, 1985), 19.

But how can any of this be true of an omniscient being? Remember, Scripture, though lengthy and at times complicated, isn't everything God knows, even if it is more than any mere human can fully grasp in even a lifetime of study. But then, if Scripture is only *some* of what God knows, and if he knows everything, surely he must have known how to reveal what he wanted us to know in ways that would be both understandable and true. If God's revelation isn't understandable, then there is a sense in which little, if anything, has been revealed. If Scripture isn't true, then God has either been unintentionally misinformed or ignorant of the truth (neither of which could be true of an omniscient being), or he has deliberately told us falsehoods (which contradicts his honesty and absolute moral purity). It won't help to say that God included false information in Scripture, but did so for a worthy cause—he so desperately wanted to communicate with us that he did whatever it took to do so. Lying is still lying, even if it is done for a "worthy" cause. Erring in ignorance of the truth still means that one's knowledge is deficient, but how can that be true of someone who knows everything there is to know?

If the objector's point is that there just is no fully truthful way to explain some concepts without simplifications that necessitate including errors, that is a theory worth considering. The problem is how anyone could possibly prove such a thesis without knowing everything himself or herself! Since we don't know everything, how can we be sure that there is no truthful way to reveal what God wants us to understand? Even more, since God *does* know everything, he must know how to tell us truthfully and understandably whatever he wants to reveal. Even Stephen T. Davis, who rejects inerrancy, in his evaluation of Fuller's claims about accommodational errors in Scripture rightly argues that Fuller's justification of such errors "in the Bible will work only if in each case there was available to the Biblical writer no equally good or better inerrant way to make this point. And this seems dubious."[55]

On this point, it is hard to see how Davis is wrong. I conclude that this objection to inerrancy is unsuccessful. But this whole discussion raises a theological issue that deserves more attention than it has received. I want here at least to start discussing it. The idea of divine accommodation has been in Christian theology for a very long time. Our historical discussion confirms that. The theological question I want to raise is whether the idea of accommodation is itself accurate, and regardless of our answer, how do we know? Let me explain.

Though Christian thinkers have definitely held this doctrine, what is its biblical support? That is, what Scripture or Scriptures actually say that, in inspiring Scripture, the Holy Spirit had to accommodate his thoughts to human language? Please don't misunderstand; the question is not about God's choice

---

[55] Davis, *Debate about the Bible*, 45.

of language to use in revealing himself. By this question I am not even remotely suggesting that Hebrew, Greek, and Aramaic are actually God's "mother-tongue," so he just naturally used those languages. No human language is God's "mother-tongue"; he does, however, know and can speak all languages.

My question is this: theologians always say that if God told us things exactly as he knows them, we couldn't understand what he said. Hence, he had to accommodate his thoughts to human speech. But how do we know this is so? Is there any mere human who has any access to the content of God's knowledge as it is in itself, unaccommodated for us? Of course not! But if not, how do we know that what God has revealed in Scripture is any different from what God knows in his own mind apart from the way he has stated it in revelation? And, why have Christian theologians felt it necessary to hold a doctrine of accommodation at all? Is it a result of a pious belief that God's intellect is so superior to ours that what God knows and how he thinks is too complicated for us to understand? Or is this doctrine the result of Christian thinkers finding things in Scripture they can't quite understand or that even seem to be errors, and then concluding that, since God can't err, this must be accommodated speech so that, if we could see the concept as God *actually* sees it, there would be no error?

There is, of course, at least one passage where Paul tried to make a theological point and yet affirmed that it strains human language to make the point, so he says he speaks anthropomorphically (Rom. 6:19).[56] But that doesn't cover every passage, for most biblical concepts are ones with which we are familiar. We may not fully understand what is being said because it speaks of things that go beyond the empirical and beyond what reason unaided by revelation could even imagine, but that doesn't mean the concept is totally foreign to us. If nothing in Scripture is the way God knows things in his own mind, then how can we be sure what exactly God is thinking and what exactly he wants us to know? Even if what Scripture says isn't literally and univocally what goes through God's mind when he thinks about these topics, must it not at the very least be analogically what he thinks, or how can we be sure of what God was actually thinking when he revealed what we find in Scripture?

Let me illustrate this problem. If Scripture's contents are an accommodation of what God really knows, but not what he actually knows, what, then, do words like justification, sanctification, and even revelation actually mean? As readers know, these words and concepts as we find them in Scripture are hard enough to define, but at least we believe we understand them well enough to make sense of Scripture. But if these terms (and so many others) are accom-

---

[56] Here see Douglas Moo's fine discussion of this verse in *Romans 1–8*, Wycliffe Exegetical Commentary, ed. Kenneth Barker (Chicago: Moody, 1991), 419–420.

modations to finite human minds, then what do these concepts as God thinks them actually mean? If Scripture is accommodated to our ignorance, then what do Gospel accounts of Jesus as virgin born really mean as God understands them? And if talk about Jesus Christ's resurrection is just God's thoughts accommodated to what we can understand, then what was God really thinking when he inspired the writers to write about the resurrection—and even more important, what actually happened that first Easter morning?

I trust that readers see the problem I am raising with the notion of Scripture as God's knowledge accommodated to our human, finite minds and languages. To be sure, some will ask for my proof that Scripture isn't accommodated language. And, of course, I can cite no passage or set of biblical passages that suggest that it isn't accommodated, just as there is no passage that says all or even most of Scripture is accommodated language. If the motivation behind the doctrine of accommodation is to lift high and praise God's infinite intellect, that is unobjectionable. But an infinitely intelligent being surely knows how to say exactly what he is thinking in words that exactly capture his thoughts! So, can we be sure that accommodation is a correct doctrine?

In contrast, if the motivation behind this doctrine is to use it to explain away problem passages and apparent errors in Scripture, I must protest. Whether or not apparent errors are actual errors should first depend on what Scripture teaches about its own nature. Once we understand that—and it had better not be so accommodated that we don't know what God literally and univocally thinks about it—then we should be clear about whether it is even possible for there to be an error in Scripture. If an error in Scripture is possible, that doesn't mean there actually is an error, and so we should search for resolutions. If such an error is impossible, then there can be no error, and so we should all the more commit ourselves to finding a resolution, because we know the passage cannot contain an error. But then, isn't it clear that, if the motivation behind this doctrine is to use it to explain away apparent errors, that motivation is wrongheaded!

So, what should we conclude about the idea of accommodation? From my perspective, I wouldn't claim that any mere human knows enough to be certain that what is stated in Scripture is exactly stated as it is in God's mind. The only certain access we have to what goes on in God's mind is what we read in his word, the Bible. So, perhaps the Bible is accommodated, but perhaps not (or at least perhaps not everything is accommodated—e.g., how can the recounting of historical events and genealogies in Scripture be stated any differently in God's mind than in Scripture?). I don't think we can know the answer for certain until we get to heaven, and even then it isn't clear that we will have access to the internal workings of God's mind. Maybe even God's speech to those in his presence in heaven is accommodated (after all, glorification doesn't make humans omniscient); how can we be sure, even then, unless he tells us?

What I would contend and defend above all is twofold: if one's reason for holding this doctrine is to account for apparent errors in Scripture, that is illegitimate, because it bases one's assessment of biblical inerrancy too much on the phenomena of Scripture, rather than on what Scripture teaches about itself. Second, if one decides to hold on to the doctrine of accommodation, please hold it in such a way that there isn't such a huge gap between concepts "as presented in Scripture" and concepts "as present in God's mind" that it no longer makes sense to speak of Scripture as *revealing* what God wants us to know. If there is such a huge gap between the words and concepts of Scripture and the thoughts in God's mind, then we may not in fact know what God thinks about anything. That would be devastating in terms of how to lead our life now, and we could also be misled by the words of Scripture about what God knows about what we need to do to secure eternal salvation, blessing, and communion with him![57]

## INERRANCY AND CHURCH HISTORY

In addition to the issue of accommodation, there has been a more general challenge to biblical inerrancy raised on the ground that inerrancy isn't the historic position of the church. While what one Christian theologian or another has held isn't the arbiter of whether Scripture teaches its own inerrancy or is inerrant, no one wants to hold a view on a major doctrine that few, if any, in the history of the church have espoused. If a position on a cardinal doctrine is correct, the Holy Spirit has probably taught it to someone else in church history, not just to Christians living today.

So, what do opponents of inerrancy say about the church's historic beliefs about Scripture? A most significant attempt to argue that inerrancy wasn't the focus of the early church or of the Reformation, but entered the theological scene in Post-Reformation Scholasticism and found its fullest development in the theology of Old Princetonian theologians like Hodge and Warfield in the late nineteenth century, came in the aforementioned book by Jack Rogers and Donald McKim. Their book, *The Authority and Interpretation of the Bible: An Historical Approach* (see note 38, above), was not the first time scholars tried to label inerrancy a recent and novel injection into the life of the church.[58]

---

[57] Here please note that I am neither denying nor adopting the doctrine of accommodation. I am merely saying that I don't see that we have definitive biblical teaching on it one way or another. And, I am also saying that if we hold the doctrine, we must be sure not to do so in a way that drives such a huge wedge between God's thoughts and the words of Scripture that we can no longer say with any confidence that Scripture is God's word and does in fact tell us some of what God knows and thinks.

[58] For example, proposals by Bruce Vawter and George Marsden also have questioned the origin of the doctrine of inerrancy. They link it with late-nineteenth- and early-twentieth-century developments in theology, and deny that the contemporary position of inerrancy held by many conservative evangelicals has a pedigree that is much

However, their proposal is extensively argued, and has received a great deal of attention. Though John Woodbridge's *Biblical Authority: A Critique of the Rogers/McKim Proposal* (see footnote 46) offers the definitive refutation of their major and minor theses, their main proposals still persist. We already saw their proposal about accommodation, and needn't address it again. In what follows, I'll present their main thesis, along with one of its corollaries that continues to persist, despite evidence against it.

Rogers and McKim's major theme is that modern inerrantists are out of step with the church's historic position on the doctrine of Scripture. Rogers and McKim distinguish between the form and function of Scripture. According to them, early church fathers and Reformers like Calvin who followed them placed their emphasis on Scripture's authority, especially its authority "in its function of bringing people into a saving relationship with God through Jesus Christ."[59]

In contrast, they say, the focus of contemporary belief in inerrancy emphasizes Scripture's authority resting on "its form of inerrant words."[60] Rogers and McKim explain that, according to this second understanding which focuses on the inerrant form of Scripture's words,

> The Bible was a repository of information about all manner of things, including science and history, which had to be proven accurate by then-current standards. There was no trace of the central Christian tradition of accommodation. Rather, it was assumed that what the Bible told us was what God told us, down to the details. Inspired men thought God's thoughts after him and transmitted them in writing. The historical and cultural context faded in importance for the interpreter. It was assumed that all persons in all places thought alike and that Western logic was the clue to reality. Therefore, statements in the Bible were treated like logical propositions that could be interpreted quite literally according to contemporary standards.[61]

Obviously, if the view described is what contemporary inerrantists hold, there are some problems. However, readers should know from reading my previous chapter on inerrancy, and from the discussion of objections to inerrancy in this chapter, that what Rogers and McKim say in the passage just quoted distorts what contemporary inerrantists believe.

---

older than one to two hundred years. For details, see John Woodbridge, "Does the Bible Teach Science?," *BSac* 142 (July–September 1985) on Vawter; and John Woodbridge, "Is Biblical Inerrancy a Fundamentalist Doctrine?," *BSac* 142 (October–December 1985) on Marsden. See also Donald Carson's discussion of these and other trends in historiography (along with other developments in relation to the doctrine of Scripture) as set forth in his "Recent Developments in the Doctrine of Scripture," in *Hermeneutics, Authority, and Canon*, ed. D. A. Carson and John D. Woodbridge (Grand Rapids, MI: Zondervan, 1986)—also reprinted in D. A. Carson, *Collected Writings on Scripture* (Wheaton, IL: Crossway, 2010).
[59] Rogers and McKim, *Authority and Interpretation of the Bible*, xvii.
[60] Ibid.
[61] Ibid., xvii-xviii.

Nonetheless, don't miss the Rogers-McKim point. Throughout church history, one has either focused on Scripture's authority, as evidenced in its *function* of bringing people to salvation in Christ, or one has grounded Scripture's authority in the *precise accuracy* of whatever it affirms, regardless of the topic. Rogers and McKim say they can prove that the former view has been the emphasis of the church, not the latter view.

If so, when did the church "go astray" and switch its emphasis from Scripture's function to its alleged inerrant form? According to Rogers and McKim, there are a number of culprits, beginning with Protestant Scholasticism after the Reformation. In fact, the views described above in the quoted passage are Rogers and McKim's descriptions of Francis Turretin's views. Turretin is of great importance, among other reasons, because of his highly influential *Institutio Theologiae Elencticae*. It is taken by many to embody many of the methods (and doctrines worked out through those methods) of Protestant Scholasticism.

But Turretin is especially important, say Rogers and McKim, because his *Institutes* was the theology textbook at Princeton University in the late 1800s for students like Charles Hodge. We have already seen the Rogers-McKim thesis that Turretin said nothing about accommodation, and so Hodge knew nothing about it as a result of his theological studies. Even more, Turretin's emphasis on the precise form of biblical statements became the doctrinal emphasis of the Old Princeton theology on Scripture.

The views about Scripture embedded in the above-cited portion from Rogers and McKim also stem from another influence, the Scottish Common Sense Realism of Thomas Reid. Rogers and McKim claim that Princeton theologians uncritically adopted this epistemology, and it impacted their views on Scripture. According to this epistemology, sense perception can be reliable for getting us in touch with the world, and for accurately and basically objectively reading off the results. As applied to the doctrine of Scripture (along with prevailing thinking about scientific method at that time), this meant that interpreters could perceive accurately exactly what Scripture affirmed and they were in a position to confirm its contents. It is this concern about the inerrant form of every claim and a need for certainty of the truth of Scripture's claims that drives the contemporary notion of biblical inerrancy, according to Rogers and McKim.

Of course, as can be expected, B. B. Warfield was also a crucial player in developing the contemporary inerrancy position. In the onslaught of higher criticism against Scripture, Warfield came full force to defend Scripture. This emphasis on the apologetic defense of Scripture required various refinements to the notion of inerrancy so that what it claimed about all of Scripture's affirmations (that they match reality, in particular) could be demonstrated. It is this more modern "invention," this view of inerrancy related to the precise and accurate form of whatever Scripture claims, that has captured the day in twentieth-century battles over Scripture. In fact, this view was adopted into formal statements about Scripture like the International Council on Biblical Inerrancy's Chicago Statement on Biblical Inerrancy.

According to Rogers and McKim, this modern inerrancy doctrine has been so emphasized and publicized by evangelicals that it is usually presented as the historic doctrine of the church, going all the way back through the Reformers to the early church fathers. But Rogers and McKim try to show that this just isn't true. An accurate reading of the sources, they claim, shows that the current inerrancy doctrine is a recent invention, and that the church's true historical position has been to focus on biblical authority that stems from its power to bring people into a saving knowledge of Jesus Christ.

Rogers and McKim offer more than 450 pages of "evidence" to support their theory. As one can imagine, this involves many quotes from various figures in church history, but it also includes their own interpretation both of the portions quoted and of their interpretation of the "story" this tells about the church's position on inerrancy.

What I have described actually contains two distinct, though related, historical claims. The first, and overarching one, is that the church historically hasn't been committed to inerrancy but rather to Scripture's authority to lead people to Christ. As noted below, this major thesis has been roundly refuted by scholars who hold biblical inerrancy, and even by some scholars who reject inerrancy.

If the Rogers and McKim thesis has been fatally destroyed, shouldn't their whole proposal be rejected? Not according to many who reject inerrancy. In their thinking, while Rogers and McKim's main thesis has proved wrong, their secondary thesis still has many supporters. That second thesis is that inerrancy (as currently held) is a recent invention that stems from Protestant Scholasticism's overly rationalistic handling of Scripture, and was refined in the midst of the apologetic battles with liberals that engaged thinkers like Hodge and Warfield in their day. Having shown that something like the contemporary notion of inerrancy has always been the church's position, one would have expected this secondary thesis to be seen as bankrupt. Sadly, many believe that, even if inerrancy in some form has always been the church's view, the current inerrantist views are a recent invention and aren't supported by Scripture.[62]

---

[62] As an example of someone who holds that Rogers and McKim's major proposal has been refuted, but that they are still right about the contemporary inerrancy doctrine and the theology of the Old Princetonians, see McGowan's *Divine Spiration of Scripture*, 97–102, 113–119, 124–125.

*Responses*

Initially, I must reaffirm that whether or not Rogers and McKim are right doesn't make inerrancy correct or incorrect. The key issue is what Scripture says about itself, and as my defense of inerrancy (in chapter 7) shows, various considerations support biblical inerrancy. Still, if a doctrine is true, the verdict of history should confirm that, or at least shouldn't falsify it.

So, what should we say about the Rogers/McKim proposal? Let us look at each of its major theses individually. Are Rogers and McKim correct that the consensus view of the church hasn't been belief in biblical inerrancy, but adherence to Scripture as authoritative because of its role in bringing people to salvation in Christ? The definitive answer is contained in John Woodbridge's *Biblical Authority: A Critique of the Rogers/McKim Proposal*. In this book Woodbridge shows that in fact the consensus view of the church throughout its history has been belief in biblical inerrancy. This doesn't mean that Christian thinkers have always used the term "inerrancy," for that wouldn't be true. It does mean that the concept of biblical inerrancy has been held by key thinkers throughout church history.[63]

While this shouldn't surprise Christians (who would really believe that early church fathers, some of whom either knew apostles or knew people who had known apostles, would think that NT records, for example, about Jesus's life and ministry aren't true?), Woodbridge's analysis does show something that should shock scholars and even nonacademics.

Specifically, Woodbridge shows that, too often, Rogers and McKim have taken quotes out of context and used them to say just the opposite of what their author originally said. In other instances, historical figures are simply misquoted so as to undergird the theory that is imposed on the data. In short, the Rogers/McKim book evidences sloppy scholarship, at the very least, and deliberate mishandling of data at worst. This is not just Woodbridge's conclusion or that of proponents of inerrancy. Even some opponents of inerrancy grant that Woodbridge's work, while not questioning Rogers and McKim's acumen as scholars in general, does show a lack of careful scholarship on this issue on Rogers and McKim's part.[64]

Even so, as already noted, some still persist in supporting Rogers and McKim's theses. At the very least, some think they have made an adequate case about Old Princeton and the alleged "modern invention" of the iner-

---

[63] Detailed proof of this is presented in the chapters of Woodbridge's *Biblical Authority*.

[64] For an example of a recent complaint of this sort, see A. T. B. McGowan's assessment of the scholarship evidenced in Rogers and McKim's proposal (McGowan, *Divine Spiration of Scripture*, 99–100). It is worth noting that McGowan's thesis rejects both biblical inerrancy and biblical errancy. The fact that he rejects biblical inerrancy and yet has to agree with the critique of Rogers and McKim shows that even some scholars who have no axe to grind in favor of inerrancy have come to the same conclusion as inerrantists who reject both Rogers and McKim's conclusions and the scholarship used to support them.

rancy doctrine. And so, in academic literature, one still sees various forays in the debate over the second Rogers and McKim thesis. I contend that those who hold that belief in biblical inerrancy isn't a recent invention have the greater evidence on their side. Actually, Woodbridge made the case in his book, but others have also confirmed that judgment, as can be seen from a study of the literature.[65]

In addition to that historical evidence, let me mention several other problems with the Rogers/McKim view. First, this whole line of argument, even if true, is guilty of committing the genetic fallacy. That error in reasoning claims that because of a view's origin (normally amid questionable circumstances, but even more respectable origins might be considered unacceptable), it can't be true. Or at the very least, we should entertain serious doubts about its truthfulness. Of course, who, where, and how a view originated is actually irrelevant to whether it is true. Ideas that come from thoroughly reputable sources and circumstances may still be false (here, simply consult various scientific dogmas considered "orthodox" at one time by the ablest practitioners, which later in history were proved false as science advanced). Likewise, viewpoints that stem from people with questionable backgrounds, motivations, etc., may be true, anyway. A viewpoint's origin should neither legitimize nor "demonize" it. Only the evidence in its favor and against it can show whether it is true or false. Rogers and McKim's thesis about the origin of the contemporary view of biblical inerrancy is guilty of committing the genetic fallacy.

Second, readers no doubt will notice that the second thesis about the origin of the contemporary notion of inerrancy postulates causal connections between various philosophical and theological doctrines and what thinkers like Charles Hodge and B. B. Warfield came to conclude about Scripture. Unfortunately, causal connections are notoriously difficult to prove, especially when they concern a thinker's intellectual commitments and the intellectual precursors and causes that led him or her to adopt their views. Rogers and

---

[65] As a sampling of the literature on this issue, see D. Clair Davis, "Princeton and Inerrancy: The Nineteenth-Century Philosophical Background of Contemporary Concerns," in *Inerrancy and the Church*, ed. John D. Hannah (Chicago: Moody, 1984); John H. Gerstner, "The Contributions of Charles Hodge, B. B. Warfield, and J. Gresham Machen to the Doctrine of Inspiration," in *Challenges to Inerrancy: A Theological Response*, ed. Gordon R. Lewis and Bruce Demarest (Chicago: Moody, 1984); Moises Silva, "Old Princeton, Westminster, and Inerrancy," *WTJ* 50 (1988); and more recently, Paul Helm, "B. B. Warfield's Path to Inerrancy: An Attempt to Correct Some Serious Misunderstandings," *WTJ* 72 (2010). See also an interesting article by D. G. Hart: "A Reconsideration of Biblical Inerrancy and the Princeton Theology's Alliance with Fundamentalism," *CSR* 20 (1991). For further material on the positions on inerrancy of various historical figures, see as examples, Michael W. Holmes, "Origen and the Inerrancy of Scripture," *JETS* 24 (September 1981); Roger Nicole, "John Calvin and Inerrancy," *JETS* 25 (December 1982); John D. Hannah, "The Doctrine of Scripture in the Early Church," in Hannah, *Inerrancy and the Church*, (Chicago: Moody, 1984); D. Clair Davis, "Inerrancy and Westminster Calvinism," in *Inerrancy and Hermeneutic: A Tradition, a Challenge, a Debate*, ed. Harvie M. Conn (Grand Rapids, MI: Baker, 1988); John A. Delivuk, "Inerrancy, Infallibility, and Scripture in the *Westminster Confession of Faith*," *WTJ* 54 (1992); Robert D. Preus, "The View of the Bible Held by the Church: The Early Church through Luther," in Geisler, *Inerrancy*; John H. Gerstner, "The View of the Bible Held by the Church: Calvin and the Westminster Divines," in Geisler, *Inerrancy*; and Henry Krabbendam, "B. B. Warfield versus G. C. Berkouwer on Scripture," in Geisler, *Inerrancy*.

McKim propose that the reason thinkers like Hodge and Warfield adopted the views they held is that the views of Turretin, Protestant Scholasticism, and Common Sense Realism, and a Baconian approach to intellectual disciplines, caused them, when Scripture was attacked by higher criticism, to adopt the views on biblical inerrancy Rogers and McKim attribute to them. I must object to this line of argument, because in order to prove such causal connections one would have to have privileged access to the mental states of Hodge and Warfield to construct a psychological "history" of how they came to hold the views on Scripture they espoused. Even if Hodge and Warfield told us what led them to those views, as a report on their own psychological history leading up to adopting these views, many psychologists would doubt that Hodge and Warfield could know such things for certain.

In short, this second Rogers and McKim thesis posits causal connections between ideas and what caused Hodge and Warfield to adopt their views on Scripture, but those causal connections are unprovable. So, if this hypothesis were correct, only God would likely know it!

Undoubtedly, some intent on holding the Rogers/McKim thesis about Old Princeton and inerrancy would remind us that the intellectual movements and concepts named above were part of the "intellectual atmosphere" when Hodge and Warfield lived. The problem with this argument, however, as Woodbridge shows, is that it is so reductionistic. That is, Rogers and McKim focus on several things that were part of the intellectual atmosphere (and probably known by Hodge and Warfield), but fail to mention other major events and ideas that were also present when Hodge and Warfield lived. Neither Woodbridge nor I am saying that these other items *caused* Hodge and Warfield to hold the views on Scripture they adopted. Rather, the point is that if one is determined to offer causal connections as an explanation of why certain things happened and why people believed what they did, at the very least one should give a much fuller account of things that were true of nineteenth-century America and that Hodge and Warfield would have known. Consider, for example, the things Rogers and McKim leave out in their analysis of Hodge, Warfield, and the Old Princeton theology. As Woodbridge explains,

> The authors do not set the historical stage well for understanding the nineteenth-century Princetonians. They make a few glancing remarks . . . about the importance of Witherspoon's moral philosophy and Baconianism in the last decades of the eighteenth century, but then turn full bore to the first prominent theologian of Princeton Seminary, Archibald Alexander (1772-1851). By taking this tack, our authors essentially skirt more than one hundred and fifty years of Reformed thinking in the Thirteen Colonies. If they had discussed Reformed traditions in the colonies, they might have noted William Ames's *Marrow of Christian Divinity* (1623, 1627, 1629), which

served as an important textbook at Harvard. We recall that Ames advocated complete biblical infallibility in that volume. They might have discovered that Jonathan Edwards (1703–1758), one of the most brilliant intellects of the eighteenth century, maintained similar belief. They might have observed that some Americans had questions concerning the concept of biblical infallibility in the early eighteenth century, that is, more than one hundred years before the idea of founding Princeton Seminary was more than a twinkle in the eyes of Archibald Alexander or Ashbel Green. They might have encountered the discussions of Timothy Dwight and Samuel Hopkins who in the early national period defended complete biblical infallibility. Although there were important Enlightenment personalities such as Thomas Jefferson, Benjamin Franklin, Elihu Palmer, Thomas Paine, and others who very firmly denied biblical infallibility as well as several cardinal doctrines of the Christian faith, many colonists apparently affirmed complete biblical infallibility years before Witherspoon arrived in this land and before Princeton Seminary was planted in Princeton, New Jersey. Rogers and McKim do not tell the story of these colonists; if recounted, it would not accord well with their recurring theme that the Old Princetonians developed something new (and yet "scholastic") by speaking about the Bible's absolute infallibility.[66]

As noted above, postulating causal conditions to explain other people's mental states is risky business. But if you insist on doing it, at least give a full and accurate account of everything in the academic and intellectual atmosphere of the times, not a selective description that excludes an explanation that is the opposite of the one you propose.

In sum, the evidence presented (and far more evidence than can be presented in a work of this length) shows that the various theses of Rogers and McKim are insupportable. This doesn't prove that biblical inerrancy is correct, but it does show that anyone who wants to reject it on grounds that it doesn't reflect what the church has held on Scripture throughout its history is on extremely shaky grounds. Church history supports biblical inerrancy as the church's view on biblical truthfulness, not the Rogers and McKim proposal to the contrary.

---

[66] Woodbridge, *Biblical Authority*, 121–122.

# NINE

# TRUE LIGHT (III)

## More Objections to Inerrancy

The objections to inerrancy covered in chapter 8 are substantial. But they are not the only ones often raised against the doctrine. In this chapter, I turn to five more of the most significant and most frequently heard objections.

### INERRANCY IS AN INFERENCE, AND NOT A WARRANTED ONE

Those who have doubts about inerrancy sometimes object to how it is supported. They think that the doctrine of Scripture should be supportable by biblical teaching. However, some critics of inerrancy believe that it isn't taught in Scripture. Instead, it is an inference from certain things Scripture does teach, but of course, inferential reasoning can be very slippery. From the same set of data, one can infer several different things, each of which contradicts the others.

Some years ago, Clark Pinnock raised this objection. He claimed that it is not clear whether inerrancy is actually taught in Scripture or whether it is just an inference made by godly people with pious minds. He believed the latter was more accurate. Even more, Pinnock added that when one takes the phenomena of Scripture seriously, inferring from biblical data that Scripture is inerrant is not the only inference possible. You might just as easily, and more accurately, infer an errant Bible.[1]

More recently, A. T. B. McGowan has offered a similar critique of inerrancy, though he frames the point a bit differently. According to McGowan, the

---

[1] Clark Pinnock, "Three Views of the Bible in Contemporary Theology," in *Biblical Authority*, ed. Jack Rogers (Waco, TX: Word, 1977), 63–64, 67–68.

most basic mistake inerrantists make is to claim that inerrant autographs are the direct implication one must draw from the doctrine (which Scripture does teach) of biblical inspiration. Why do inerrantists think an inspired Scripture must yield inerrant autographs? McGowan answers that it is because inerrantists make an unwarranted assumption about God: "The assumption is that, given the nature and character of God, the only kind of Scripture he could 'breathe out' was Scripture that is textually inerrant. If there was even one mistake in the *autographa*, then God cannot have been the author, because he is incapable of error."[2]

McGowan quickly adds that the problem isn't whether God *can* do such a thing. The problem, according to McGowan, is that inerrantists think that God's character requires that "God is *unable* to produce anything other than an inerrant autographic text."[3] McGowan adds that this assumption, which moves the argument from inspiration to inerrancy in light of God's character, has a number of flaws. The first flaw is that inerrancy is not a biblical doctrine. To set the record straight, McGowan presents the inerrantists' inferential argument so that no one can imagine that he misunderstands what they are arguing. McGowan writes,

> Let me begin by noting the core argument of the inerrantists: God chose to give us the Scriptures through the writers he chose. They spoke directly from him, being under the direct influence of the Holy Spirit. This ensured that the resultant text could be said to be 'God-breathed'. Since God is perfect and does not mislead us and since God is all-powerful and able to do all things, it is inconceivable that he would allow mistakes in this process of Scripture-production. In short, since God is God, we must assume that the Scriptures he gave us are inerrant in every respect.[4]

Essentially, this is an accurate description of the inerrantist's argument, though readers will note differences with the inferential argument I presented in chapter 7. Even so, the argument as stated by McGowan seems acceptable, so what is the problem? McGowan explains:

> Nevertheless, this inerrantist conviction that the doctrine of the divine spiration of Scripture implies inerrancy is the weak point in their argument. The divine spiration of the Scriptures is undoubtedly a biblical doctrine. The apostles clearly teach that God 'breathed out' the Scriptures and that their authors wrote as they were 'carried along by the Holy Spirit', but nowhere in Scripture itself is there a claim to the kind of *autographic* inerrancy Warfield taught. Those who advocate inerrancy might well (and do) argue that it is a

---

[2] A. T. B. McGowan, *The Divine Spiration of Scripture: Challenging Evangelical Perspectives* (Nottingham, UK: Apollos, 2007), 112.
[3] Ibid.
[4] Ibid., 114.

legitimate and natural implication of the doctrine of divine spiration, but they cannot argue that inerrancy is itself taught in Scripture.[5]

It would be easy to think McGowan is saying nothing more than that you won't find the term "inerrancy" in Scripture, so the doctrine is not taught either, but that wouldn't grasp his objection adequately. Surely, McGowan knows that the doctrines of the Trinity and the hypostatic union of Christ are not taught in Scripture as theologians formulate them, and that doesn't keep him from holding those doctrines. No, the problem must be deeper, and it is. McGowan's fundamental complaint is not just that the doctrine is formed as an inference from what Scripture teaches about inspiration and the character of God. Rather, it is that inferring inerrancy, which isn't taught per se in Scripture, from these other doctrines that Scripture does teach is unwarranted.

But why is this inference unwarranted? At this point McGowan's discussion begins to wander to various things which in truth have little to do with whether or not the inference is warranted. For example, he claims that the thinking behind such an argument is rationalist, and he takes us through his reconstruction of the events that led thinkers like Hodge and Warfield to propose inerrancy as we have come to know it. It should be clear that whatever McGowan means by rationalism (he never precisely—or even in general—defines it; all of us are just supposed to see that what he describes is correct), it has nothing to do with whether the inferential argument from inspiration to inerrancy that McGowan attacks is warranted or not. Actually, McGowan's arguments here border on being guilty of (perhaps they *are* guilty of) committing the genetic fallacy. As noted in the previous chapter, that is the logical error of believing that if a position's origin is a bit suspect, or if the person who first espoused it is at all suspect, then the ideas proposed must be dismissed. Hopefully, readers understand that who first held an idea and how it originated is irrelevant to its truth or falsity.

Eventually, McGowan offers a reason for thinking the inference from inspiration to inerrancy is unwarranted. It amounts to saying that when you look at what the biblical authors actually wrote (and thus, what God let them put into Scripture), you find various discrepancies and inconsistencies (the sorts of things addressed in the discussion of the phenomena of Scripture) that suggest the inference to inerrancy is unwarranted. Well, then, most of us would conclude, McGowan espouses an errant Bible! But, as we shall see in another objection from McGowan, he doesn't espouse errancy, though he can't believe inerrancy is correct either.

For our present purposes, let me quote McGowan to show that I have not

---

[5] Ibid.

misrepresented his reason for thinking the inference to inerrancy is unwarranted. Rejecting what he calls the inerrantist assumptions that require inerrancy, McGowan explains,

> In opposition to these inerrantist assumptions, we must surely argue that God is free to act according to his will. With this in mind, we might suggest an alternative view: God the Holy Spirit breathed out the Scriptures. The instruments of this divine spiration were certain human beings. The resulting Scriptures are as God intended them to be. Having chosen, however, to use human beings rather than a more direct approach (e.g. writing the words supernaturally on stone without human involvement, as with the Ten Commandments), God did not overrule their humanity. This explains, for example, the discrepancies between the Gospels. Nevertheless, this is not a problem because God, by his Holy Spirit, has ensured that the Scriptures in their final canonical form are as he intended them to be and hence is able to use them to achieve his purpose.[6]

Though this quote raises other objections to inerrancy that I'll handle below, the comment about Gospel discrepancies being what God intended and allowed is actually the point made by those who claim that the phenomena of Scripture don't support inerrancy. This is also why thinking that inspiration, plus God's character, requires an inerrant Bible is an unwarranted inference.

To confirm my interpretation of McGowan, I must explain further what he adds in support of this view. McGowan claims that inerrantists argue that God's divine nature and involvement could not have allowed the human authors' mistaken ideas to creep into Scripture. However, answers McGowan, thinking this is so is as wrong as thinking that just because a preacher is not sinlessly perfect, God can't use his preaching to accomplish wonderful spiritual growth in the lives of those who hear his sermons. What does using the preaching of fallible preachers to accomplish God's work have to do with inerrancy? McGowan answers: "If God can effectively communicate and act savingly through the imperfect human beings who are called to preach his gospel, why is it necessary to argue that the authors of Scripture were supernaturally kept from even the slightest discrepancy?"[7] Though McGowan is loath to use the term "error" or "falsehood," the analogy he draws with God using sinful preachers despite their sin actually works as an analogy only if the "discrepancies" are actual errors.

Doesn't this clearly reject the inference from inspiration to inerrancy on the grounds that the phenomena of Scripture must be evidence considered, and that when you do take them seriously, the more natural inference to draw from the data is an errant Bible, not an inerrant one?[8]

---

[6] Ibid., 118.
[7] Ibid.
[8] Pinnock makes these points in "Three Views of the Bible in Contemporary Theology," 63–64, 67–68.

*Responses*

McGowan's objection actually raises several issues, and I shall address each. The first is whether the sort of inference McGowan envisions is the only kind of evidence available to support biblical inerrancy. The answer is clearly no. Of course, one must add to any argument for or against inerrancy how inerrancy is to be defined. Most thinkers (for or against inerrancy) would understand inerrancy to be about truth, and they would be thinking of truth in a correspondence sense. Undoubtedly, those who adopt the conclusions of biblical-critical scholarship believe that such evidence makes it impossible for various biblical claims to be true in a correspondence sense. Those who are more evangelical in their approach but believe Scripture contains errors are also thinking in terms of truth and falsehood (if you have doubts about this, just reread my earlier section and note what the phenomena that supposedly invalidate inerrancy are about—they are about truth and falsity of various biblical claims and the truth in view is linguistic truth in a correspondence sense), and certainly defenders of inerrancy are thinking in terms of truth in a correspondence sense.

But once inerrancy is defined in terms of truth, it just isn't true that inerrancy can be supported only by an inferential argument from inspiration and God's character. In chapter 7, in my defense of inerrancy, I presented a number of passages that directly speak of Scripture as true. If truth has anything to do with inerrancy, and it does, then those passages affirm biblical inerrancy. It is just false that the only support for biblical inerrancy is the inferential argument from inspiration, etc., to inerrancy. And, it is also wrong to say that inerrancy is not a biblical doctrine. The term appears nowhere in Scripture, but theology/doctrinal study is not word study, but concept study, and the concept of inerrancy is clearly taught in Scripture, as demonstrated in my defense of the doctrine.

A second aspect to this objection (though not explicitly stated) is that the doctrine of inerrancy is suspect because it is based on inference. Now we certainly would prefer each doctrine to be plainly stated in Scripture, but God didn't inspire biblical writers to pen a work of systematic theology that named and explained each doctrine we should believe. But that is no reason for thinking a doctrine formed by inference is suspect or is a "second-class" doctrine. As noted above, nowhere does Scripture set forth the doctrines of the Trinity or of the hypostatic union of Christ; both must be formulated by inference. The critical question is not whether a doctrine is formed by inference, but whether, in cases where it is, the inference is warranted by the data that suggest it. If the inference is warranted (as in the case of the Trinity and the hypostatic union), the doctrine has just as firm a standing as doctrines directly stated in Scripture.

So, even if inerrancy were only formulated by an inferential argument (which, as we have seen, is not the case), the only relevant question would be whether the data warrant the inference. But here is where we come to the "rub" again in this issue. What are the relevant data that must be accounted for in judging whether this inference is warranted? Those who reject inerrancy insist that passages about cocks crowing, the size of mustard seeds, etc., are the relevant data. But this violates proper theological method, because the passages relevant to constructing the doctrine of inerrancy are ones that address Scripture's truthfulness (or concepts relevant to it—like the character of the God who revealed and inspired it), not passages about the size of mustard seeds, etc. If the data relevant to Scripture's character warrant the inference that Scripture is inerrant, we should hold biblical inerrancy and also seek answers to the alleged errors and inconsistencies. But the alleged errors and inconsistencies do not *assert* anything about *the nature of Scripture*, and so they cannot be the passages on which the various bibliological doctrines are grounded.

Well, then, if one follows the methodological rules just stated and also stated in answer to the phenomena objection, is the inference as McGowan presents it one that warrants inerrancy? As explained in my defense of inerrancy (chapter 7), you cannot simply appeal to inspiration and God's character in general as warrant for inerrancy. The inferential argument must include a definition of inerrancy (one that is supportable as a legitimate definition—hence the lengthy discussion in chapter 7 just to clarify the meaning of inerrancy and to show that it is neither question begging in regard to our assessment of Scripture nor an ad hoc definition that is irrelevant to any other written document). Moreover, appeal to God's character needs to be specific. In particular, the relevant attributes are God's truthfulness and omniscience. These attributes guarantee that he cannot be mistaken about anything, since he knows everything that is knowable, and they also guarantee that he wouldn't speak a falsehood deliberately (lie) since as the God of all truth, he cannot lie. Some would also add omnipotence, to show that God has the power to reveal and inspire Scripture, but that point is already made in the argument in the steps that show that he inspired the writing of Scripture.

Reviewing my inferential argument from chapter 6, then, it was argued that if Scripture is what God has spoken, if God knows everything and therefore he cannot be mistaken about anything, and if he won't lie because he is truthful, and if inerrancy is truthfulness, then a book that is inspired by such a God must be inerrant. Some will complain that this leaves out the human aspect of Scripture, but the first two premises about inspiration clarify that human authors were also involved in writing this book. No inerrantist who grasps clearly what his or her belief means thinks that Scripture doesn't show marks of its human authors. Differences in literary genre, style, and even grammatical and spelling anomalies that don't change the meaning of assertions are marks of the human authors. Since none of these things jeopardizes the truth of what the authors wrote, God had no reason to obliterate those marks of humanness—they implicate no one in ignorance or in the immoral telling of lies. But, if something a biblical writer wrote contained a factual mistake, that would implicate the divine author either in lying or in being ignorant of the facts, if the divine author let such errors stand in Scripture. So, it is reasonable to expect that God would take steps to ensure that the human author would include nothing in Scripture that would implicate either himself or the divine author in either deliberate or unintentional falsehood.

Why have I just offered this detailed explanation? Because we must explain the thinking that lies behind the inferential argument. That is, we must understand what each premise means and why the premises about inspiration, God's character traits, and the definition of inerrancy do logically entail the conclusion that Scripture must also be inerrant. Why is that inference any less warranted than the inference from biblical data to the doctrine of the Trinity? Critics will reply, because no biblical phenomena refute the inference to the Trinity and many biblical passages support it, but there are biblical phenomena that should at least cause us to pause, if not reject altogether the inferential argument for inerrancy. My response is the same as my reply to the objection about biblical phenomena and inerrancy.

So, this objection to inerrancy is helpful in that it forces us to clarify the nature of the evidence in support of inerrancy, and it also forces us to be clear about how and why the inferential argument for inerrancy works and is warranted. But, for the reasons stated, it does not succeed in refuting biblical inerrancy!

## Divine Freedom, Scripture's Humanness, and Inerrancy

The "nub" of this objection focuses on human nature and, accordingly, on what we can expect the human authors of Scripture to do in any given circumstance. However, various critics of inerrancy nuance this objection in slightly different ways, and we should address all of those complaints. As with other objections, A. T. B. McGowan brings his unique perspective to this objection.

Those who use this objection often begin by claiming that evangelicals have focused too much on the divine side of Scripture and have overlooked the fact that humans were involved in its writing. We should pay more attention to that aspect of it, and when we do, we should see that it is unrealistic to think that a book covering so many different topics and written in such diverse places, times, and circumstances would contain no error. Humans are not omniscient, and in addition to their finitude, every human biblical author was a sinner, even though each was saved. Being saved doesn't make one omni-scient, nor does it make it impossible to be confused or wrong because of the sins that beset all of us.

It is also unrealistic to think Scripture's human authors made no mistakes, because each lived at a particular time in history and had to reflect the times and cultures of their day. Of course, no culture and no particular era of history knows or could know all truth. So, very naturally, biblical authors reflected the prevailing ideas of their own day, but they couldn't completely know which ideas were wrong and avoid them altogether. Here we must understand that this is not a critique of the times when Scripture was written as being too pre-scientific and primitive to understand the universe around them correctly. Even if the whole Bible were composed today, the authors would be just as time- and culture-bound as were those who composed the Old and New Testaments. Though we believe our knowledge is far more accurate than that of those who lived in biblical times, there are still likely things we take as common knowledge which science will someday show to be wrong.[9]

Though the above is sufficient to make this point, thinkers like A. T. B. McGowan add further elements to the mix. For one thing, McGowan says that regardless of how much we think the biblical authors knew, when you look at the various discrepancies and inconsistencies Scripture contains, it is evident that God didn't override the authors' humanity. While McGowan agrees that God could have done that, evidently he didn't. Still, McGowan reminds us, the result is not a useless book, for God has used and does use Scripture to accomplish his purposes. We can certainly affirm this in light of all the people throughout history whose lives have been transformed by this book.[10]

There is another problem with refusing to take seriously Scripture's human-ness. The inferential argument from inspiration and God's character to inerrant autographs is problematic, McGowan claims, because it sets limitations on how God had to "do" revelation and inspiration. Just because it seems logical to us that a God with the character ascribed to him in Scripture would have to inspire the biblical authors to produce an inerrant text, that doesn't mean that God can do it no other way. This inferential argument, which McGowan calls rationalis-tic, "assumes that God can only act in a way that conforms to our expectations, based on our human assessment of his character. It assumes that whatever God does must conform to the canons of human reason. It also assumes that our desire for epistemological certainty must be satisfied and that it can be satisfied only through the receiving from God of inerrant autographic texts."[11]

---

[9] Daniel Fuller, "The Nature of Biblical Inerrancy," *Journal of the American Scientific Affiliation* (June 1972): 9–12. This reference is to this article as it was given as a paper at Wheaton College in 1970.
[10] McGowan, *Divine Spiration of Scripture*, 118–119.
[11] Ibid., 118.

Despite our expectations, God is free to do whatever he wants. That means he is free to give us his word and use it as he pleases. Thinking that God must produce inerrant texts if he chooses to reveal himself in written form limits God's freedom. It also fails to square with the Bibles we have with all of their discrepancies and apparent inconsistencies.[12] If we avoid prejudging how God must give Scripture, and we see what he has actually done, we can see that he didn't transgress the human writers' freedom to reflect their own times and ways.

*Responses*

This objection contains elements of truth, but is essentially misguided. It is surely true that Scripture evidences being written by various authors with their own styles and personalities, and what the authors wrote gives us windows into the times in which they lived. It is also true that no mere human, even though an author of Scripture, knew all things, nor could he escape the time, culture, and place in history in which he lived. God alone has a "God's-eye" view of all times, cultures, and historical events. Being chosen by God to write a book of Scripture made none of the writers omniscient. We surely can't expect Moses, Matthew, or Malachi to reflect our scientific understanding of the universe, and of course, our time and culture don't have a "God's-eye" view of everything either.

It is also true that we shouldn't overlook the humanity of the biblical authors. Sometimes in doing biblical and theological studies we are so eager to state in precise propositions the substance of what God's word teaches that we can be guilty of "flattening out" Scripture in ways that seem to treat it like a treatise in systematic theology, written by a cold, detached, rational scholar who puts together into a neatly ordered system the various strands of thought he or she has crystallized from Scripture. Some critics of inerrancy complain that this is what inerrantists want to do with Scripture itself, and that seems to deny Scripture's humanity.

Despite these helpful reminders to take seriously the human side of Scripture, this objection still fails to overturn biblical inerrancy. First, as already argued, to be human means that one is a sinner and finite, and so is capable of error. It does not require that everything one thinks, says, or does must be filled with error. If that were so, how could anyone ever get anything correct on any subject? So, being human, the biblical authors were capable of error, and if they had been left on their own to write Scripture without any divine guidance and intervention, they likely would have made some mistakes.

But—and this is the second point—every word of Scripture has two authors, one human and one divine. As 2 Peter 1:21 says, the Holy Spirit so

---

[12] Ibid.

superintended the writers that what they wrote were the very words of God himself. The ultimate problem with this objection is that, while it wants us to take Scripture's humanness seriously, it underestimates the divine authorship of these books. Of course, when a biblical writer expresses his interests and uses his own style to convey a message, so long as nothing he writes is false, God doesn't need to expunge those elements of the human author's humanity, and he doesn't. It is not a sin to write a parable instead of a poem, a letter instead of a history text. Of course, if the human writer includes something in his text that is false or mistaken, that has moral implications for the divine writer since, as the God of all truth who omnisciently knows all truth, he would then knowingly be guilty of contributing to a work which makes claims that he knows to be false. So while the human author with his limitations can be expected to be wrong about many things, writing under the supervision of the Holy Spirit who knows everything, the result should be an inerrant Bible.

McGowan, of course, complains that this view limits God's freedom, but this is simply theological confusion. Who is it who limits God's freedom, and why? It isn't we humans who limit it; it is God's very nature that causes him to limit what he believes and does. When the limitation is self-imposed by God's nature, that isn't a limitation that removes God's freedom altogether! Free will for anyone does not include the ability to do the impossible, and inability to do the impossible is not a limitation that makes any significant difference.[13] For God to be involved in producing Scripture to the extent that he was, so that it is his word, and yet for Scripture to contain error, would be to contradict God's very nature. God cannot deliberately lie, and he cannot even unintentionally be ignorant of anything that is knowable so as to utter a falsehood accidently or allow his written word to contain untruth. So, it is the divine author who limits the content and character of Scripture so that it contains no error, and he does so not merely because inerrantists rationally conclude that he had better do so. He keeps Scripture free from error, because his own all-knowing, perfectly holy character would not allow him to do anything else!

Fourth, while humans are time- and culture-bound, the Holy Spirit is not. He knows what is true for all times, and he also knows what only seems true at certain times and cultures in history but will be refuted as human knowledge increases. Given the kind of superintendence by the Holy Spirit demanded

---

[13] Of course, one can so define divine omnipotence that God is free to do the logically impossible and that which contradicts his nature as God, and some theologians have held just that view. But most evangelical theologians hold that divine omnipotence allows God to do whatever is doable for a being of his nature. Given that he is the supremely rational being (and contradictions are irrational) and a morally perfect being, he cannot actualize contradictions, and he cannot act contrary to his holy nature. For a discussion of different forms of theism and their implications for understanding divine omnipotence and freedom, see my *No One Like Him: The Doctrine of God*, Foundations of Evangelical Theology (Wheaton, IL: Crossway, 2001), chapters 6–8 on divine attributes, and chapter 2, pages 62–75 on different forms of theism. See also my *The Many Faces of Evil* (Wheaton, IL: Crossway, 2004), chapters 1–6, which describe in even greater detail different forms of Christian theism.

by what Scripture says about inspiration (2 Pet. 1:21), it is right to expect the Holy Spirit to so guide the biblical authors that none of them will assert as true something which, from a "God's-eye" view, everyone would know is false. If God didn't do so, then he, as one of the authors of every word of Scripture, is guilty of falsehood. But an omniscient, wholly truthful God could never participate in propagating error.

Of course, critics will retort that this sounds good in theory but it just doesn't square with the nature of Scripture as we have it. The phenomena of Scripture suggest that God didn't exercise the kind of superintendence inerrancy requires. But this assumes, of course, that all of the alleged problems in Scripture are actual errors and that there is no possible way that everything Scripture affirms could be true. I shall not repeat what I have already said about the phenomena of Scripture, but will only make two comments. I ask that readers reread my responses (in chapter 8) to that objection. I also ask that everyone understand that the appeal to the phenomena of Scripture actually shifts the objection from the complaint that the humanness of Scripture means it can't be inerrant to a different objection, one about the phenomena of Scripture. If the humanness of Scripture objection is to work at all, it must do so on its own terms, not on the basis of another objection!

One final comment about the idea that holding inerrancy tends to flatten out Scripture into a mere set of propositions, and hence it runs roughshod over the very human nature of Scripture. If true, this would be a significant objection, for we want to portray Scripture as accurately as we can. The problem with this objection is that it confuses Scripture with a theology of Scripture. Systematic theology, whether it includes a commitment to errancy or to inerrancy, can be written in the form of a set of propositions, and usually is (sometimes in a very boring way!). But a treatise in systematic theology is not Scripture, nor does it turn Scripture into something that it is not. We should expect our theological reflections on any topic, including Scripture, to take the form and style of a coherent, well-ordered treatise. But our theological reflections on any doctrine do nothing to change the nature of Scripture itself. So, this objection amounts to nothing, because it confuses the nature of a treatise in systematic theology with the nature of Scripture itself. Even those who reject inerrancy write about it in the form of an academic treatise that contains various propositions about Scripture's nature. By writing such treatises, those scholars don't change the nature of Scripture itself into a sterile set of propositions. Similarly, it is hard to understand why errantists think that writing a theological treatise espousing inerrancy turns *Scripture* into nothing but a "lifeless" set of propositions! Don't confuse the object under discussion (the Bible) with the discussion (theology, done orally or in writing) of it!

## A. T. B. McGowan's Infallibility as an Alternative to Errancy and Inerrancy

A number of the preceding objections have been raised by A. T. B. McGowan, so it seems that he must adopt an errantist position on Scripture. However, relatively early in his book, McGowan warns us not to reach that conclusion, because he disagrees with both an errantist and an inerrantist approach to Scripture. McGowan believes that the issue has wrongly been portrayed as a choice between the full inerrancy of Scripture and some sort of limited inerrancy view. In fact, at one point McGowan describes three forms of an inerrancy position, and though he is most sympathetic to the one he labels the "Chicago inerrantists," those whose views are most fully expressed by the Chicago Statement on Biblical Inerrancy that came from the first ICBI Summit meeting in 1978, he still prefers to hold no form of biblical inerrancy.[14]

Since McGowan rejects any kind of inerrancy view, one would think he believes that Scripture has errors. But that supposition is wrong. McGowan describes several anti-inerrancy positions, and rejects them all. One approach accepts the results of higher criticism, and so cannot see how Scripture could be inerrant in any sense. McGowan rejects it because it is founded on Enlightenment presuppositions, which he rejects. Then, a second group of thinkers holds that the Bible is inerrant in matters of doctrine and practice, but contains errors of fact in some of its historical, scientific, etc., claims. McGowan rejects this position because he thinks it is hard to maintain a distinction between the parts of Scripture that have errors and those that don't. There is, however, a third group of scholars who are uncomfortable with the term "inerrancy" but who reject the notion of errancy as well. These thinkers believe that errancy and inerrancy aren't the only options; hence those two approaches present a false dichotomy of views one might hold on Scripture. McGowan holds this third position.[15]

If there is a mediating position between inerrancy and errancy, what is it, and why is it better than the alternatives? McGowan explains that a mediating position, a path taken more typically by European evangelicals than by Americans (Americans either hold some form of inerrancy or of errancy, according to McGowan), espouses biblical infallibility. What exactly does this mean, and how might one defend it? It is here that McGowan's project flounders, largely because he nowhere offers a precise definition of infallibility, nor does he defend it as biblically correct, nor does he actually distinguish it from inerrancy or errancy.

So, what exactly is this view? McGowan assures us that he isn't the first

---

[14] McGowan, *Divine Spiration of Scripture*, 101–105, in which he discusses three forms of an inerrancy position. In the following pages, he offers several reasons for rejecting inerrancy of any sort. As for the Chicago Statement on Biblical Inerrancy, it is contained in *Inerrancy*, ed. Norman Geisler (Grand Rapids, MI: Zondervan, 1979).
[15] McGowan, *Divine Spiration of Scripture*, 105–106.

to espouse this position. He appeals to Charles Briggs, Herman Bavinck, and G. C. Berkouwer (in his later work). On the surface, this seems a bit ambiguous, because many scholars would say that Briggs believed there were actual errors in Scripture and so rejected inerrancy. Similarly, Berkouwer's later work on Scripture clearly rejects inerrancy, and does so in a way that seems clearly to hold that Scripture has errors. The evidence from Bavinck is more ambiguous because, at least in the material McGowan cites, Bavinck doesn't seem to discuss the topic.[16]

Most of McGowan's discussion centers around Bavinck, and I leave to Bavinck scholars the question of whether McGowan accurately presents his views.[17] Still, what does McGowan mean by infallibility? It is easiest to discern this by quoting several passages where he offers as clear a definition as we get from him. He writes,

> My argument is that Scripture, having been divinely spirated, is as God intended it to be. Having freely chosen to use human beings, God knew what he was doing. He did not give us an inerrant autographical text, because he did not intend to do so. He gave us a text that reflects the humanity of its authors but that, at the same time, clearly evidences its origin in the divine speaking. Through the instrumentality of the Holy Spirit, God is perfectly able to use these Scriptures to accomplish his purposes.[18]

McGowan vehemently denies that the view just quoted is an errancy position, but then adds that it isn't an inerrantist view either. Those two options are the way the discussion is handled in the debate in the United States, but they aren't the only two options. He holds a third position, about which he says,

> Instead, I am arguing for a high view of Scripture, based on a verbal spiration of the text but one which accepts that God chose to use human authors, with all the implications of that decision. In other words, I am arguing that Scripture is as God intended it to be, in his gracious providential overruling, but reject the implication that thereby the *autographa* must be inerrant.[19]

On the next page, McGowan attempts to link his position to Calvin and Luther. Of them he writes,

> These Reformers had a very high view of Scripture as the voice of God speaking by his Spirit through his servants, and they resisted any suggestion that it

---

[16] McGowan discusses all of these thinkers in his chapter 5 as supportive of his main ideas, and offers what he labels an "evangelical alternative" to the two main views on inerrancy held by evangelicals, namely, the position of Rogers and McKim, on the one hand, and that of B. B. Warfield on the other.

[17] See, e.g., Peter Barnes's critique of McGowan's handling of Bavinck in Peter Barnes, "Review Article: The Divine Spiration of Scripture," *Reformed Theological Review* 67 (December 2008): 152–153. The evidence seems clear that McGowan has taken out of context things Bavinck said and applied them to support McGowan's views when Bavinck was talking about entirely different topics.

[18] McGowan, *Divine Spiration of Scripture*, 124.

[19] Ibid.

was unreliable or lacking in authority. On the other hand, however, they were quite dismissive of minor textual discrepancies or varying accounts or whatever. As far as they were concerned, the Scriptures had come from God and could therefore be trusted, but having used human authors one must expect these minor textual difficulties. Certainly, these textual matters should not be regarded as undermining the supreme authority of God's Word.

Thus to speak of the Scriptures as inerrant or errant is to apply an inappropriate classification to them. We must simply accept the Scriptures as they are and trust that what they teach is for our good (and above all for our salvation) because they have come from God.[20]

I could add a number of other quotes, but I offer just one more. In this passage, McGowan discusses Bavinck's views. McGowan notes that Bavinck held an organic view of Scripture's inspiration, not a mechanical one (such as a dictation theory). He quotes Bavinck to the effect that an organic view allows both God and man to play their respective parts in the writing of Scripture. This means that God causes the human writers to function in accord with their own nature, and guarantees to these authors not to disrupt their own personalities, rationality, and freedom. God doesn't coerce anyone. Rather, he treats the human authors as intelligent and moral beings, not as blocks of wood.[21] McGowan, on the basis of Bavinck's organic view, writes,

This enables Bavinck faithfully and clearly to emphasize both sides of any orthodox doctrine of Scripture, namely that God is the author but yet human beings are the authors. This concursive understanding of authorship is the key to understanding his position. How is this dual authorship possible? It is possible because of the work of the Holy Spirit: 'The Spirit of the Lord entered into the prophets and apostles themselves and so employed and led them that they themselves examined and reflected, spoke and wrote as they did. It is God who speaks through them; at the same time it is they themselves who speak and write.' These writers 'also retain their own character, language, and style'. In taking this position, Bavinck can emphasize and maintain the genuine humanity of the authors of Scripture. This stands in marked contrast to many inerrantist writers who pay lip service to the humanity of the authors but often descend almost into a 'dictation theory', so anxious are they to safeguard God's authorship of Scripture. One gets the impression that some of these writers are almost embarrassed by the humanity of the writers of Scripture and want to play it down as much as possible. On the other hand, we must note that Bavinck's view is not that of Rogers and McKim and their supporters, who, in affirming the humanity of Scripture, so stress the mistakes and inadequacies of the human authors that one is sometimes left wondering about the nature and extent of God's involvement in the process.[22]

---

[20] Ibid., 125.
[21] Ibid., 147–148. I have summarized a quote from Bavinck that McGowan uses.
[22] Ibid., 148.

Let me summarize the view that McGowan presents as biblical infallibility:

1. The Scriptures have come from God and are as he wanted them. They accomplish his purposes through the ministry of the Holy Spirit.
2. God used humans to write Scripture, and he didn't overrule their personality, rationality, or freedom. The texts they wrote evidence their humanness.
3. There are textual discrepancies and inconsistencies in Scripture, but these are insignificant signs of the humanness of the authors. This does mean, of course, that there are no inerrant autographs.
4. Despite the textual discrepancies, etc., we should trust Scripture because it comes from God and is authoritative. The textual matters don't undermine the authority of Scripture.
5. Those who hold biblical inerrancy tend to hold a dictation theory of inspiration, which is wrong. Hence, it is not wise to hold inerrancy.
6. Those who hold biblical errancy tend to see Scripture's text as so corrupt that it is hard to see God's hand in Scripture's production at all. Hence, it is unwise to hold errancy.
7. It is preferable to hold biblical infallibility, and this is defined as set forth in items 1–4 above.

*Responses*

The substance of McGowan's view is contained in items 1–4, but these are significantly unclear and ambiguous. In fact, they are so ambiguous as to suggest that the author does not himself know what he holds. McGowan clearly wants to uphold concursive inspiration, and Scripture's authority and usefulness to accomplish God's purposes. By concursive inspiration, he means that both God and the human authors *freely* participated in the process of producing Scripture. He also affirms that while there are textual discrepancies and inconsistences, none are errors or falsehood. Still, that doesn't mean we should hold biblical inerrancy, because that tends toward a dictation theory. In our chapters on inspiration and in the first one on inerrancy, I explained why holding inerrancy doesn't require a dictation theory. The reason McGowan thinks it does stems from his confusion about the meaning of free will and what it requires. In what follows, I want to explain the ambiguities and incoherence in McGowan's views.

First, McGowan says there are textual discrepancies and inconsistencies, but like the Reformers, he dismisses them as insignificant. Now to what does McGowan actually refer? If he is talking about transcriptional errors, then indeed, those aren't problems. They wouldn't have appeared in the autographs (those mysterious documents McGowan claims never existed), and can easily be explained away. They don't affect the truthfulness of what Scripture affirms. Or is McGowan talking about apparent contradictions in Scripture? When he sets forth some of the textual phenomena that lead him to reject inerrancy,[23] these cannot be mere scribal errors. If these apparent contradictions cannot be resolved, then there are falsehoods that biblical authors actually affirm. Such problems can't be simply dismissed as inconsequential, and if they can't be resolved, we should not trust Scripture, anyway, just because it comes from God! If Scripture is what God has actually spoken and it has genuine errors, then God is responsible (as one of the two authors) for falsehood. If there is one such error in Scripture, there *might be* others, and given that *possibility*, how can we trust that what we read is actually from God and authoritative?

McGowan's unwillingness to specify exactly the kind of textual problems he has in mind when he defines biblical infallibility makes it unclear whether he actually holds that Scripture is inerrant (if the only problems are transcriptional ones, then no genuine errors are part of Scripture) or errant (if the problems are contradictions or factual errors, then there are genuine errors in Scripture). McGowan thinks inerrancy/errancy is a false dichotomy, and opts for biblical infallibility. The problem is that the question, *does Scripture contain any falsehoods*, is a legitimate question. McGowan's decision to reject the question and opt for a view that supposedly avoids that issue doesn't help. It doesn't help because his biblical infallibility view at some points seems to espouse errors in Scripture and at other points seems to require no genuine errors in Scripture. This is incredibly ambiguous and unhelpful, but McGowan shows no sign of even being aware of the confusion he is propagating! Even if McGowan doesn't want to address the question of errancy or inerrancy, it is still a legitimate question. Espousal of biblical infallibility is not a *possible* answer to the question of whether Scripture contains errors. It is a refusal to address that question and an attempt to change the subject, but such a maneuver can't erase the question about inerrancy. And, it is very clear that McGowan's discussion of inerrancy is *very unclear* about whether he accepts or rejects it! That's not conceptual clarification; it's conceptual confusion.

What McGowan says about taking seriously the fact that Scripture was written by humans is important. But when he says that Scripture shows signs of the authors' humanity, it is unclear what this means. I agree that the books of Scripture show us the distinctive interests of each author, and they also show us distinctive writing styles. In no way does any of that require errors (falsehoods) in Scripture. To what, then, does McGowan refer when he talks of Scripture's humanness and says this makes it impossible to embrace inerrancy? Is he thinking of the old adage that "to err is human"? McGowan never says this, but perhaps he thinks it. If so, the adage is incorrect. To be *capable* of error is to be human, but being human does not *guarantee* error on every occasion and in

---

[23] See McGowan's discussion in ibid., 112–113.

every instance. If it did, how could anyone ever get one hundred percent correct answers on an exam? Without God's involvement in the writing of Scripture, there likely would have been errors, but God was involved! The humanness of the authors, plus divine involvement, does not require errors!

Perhaps, then, when McGowan refers to evidence of the authors' humanness, he is thinking of those textual discrepancies and apparent inconsistencies. If so, he needs to clarify that, but even clarifying that won't help, because McGowan refuses to say that any of those textual matters are actual errors. So how does his view differ from biblical inerrancy? More to the point, if these items are not what McGowan means when he talks of "signs of humanness," then to what does McGowan refer? This isn't an insignificant question, because it is these matters, at least in part, that make it impossible for McGowan to espouse inerrancy. No clear answer from McGowan to these questions is forthcoming, and so his views collapse in ambiguity and incoherence.

More can be said about McGowan's proposal, of course, but the preceding suggests its major flaws. Though he wants to rehabilitate infallibility as a key idea in this discussion of Scripture, his book only adds another layer of ambiguity to a term and concept that are too unclear and too diffusely used to be at all helpful.

### Peter Enns's *Inspiration and Incarnation*

The objection to inerrancy that Peter Enns raises in his book *Inspiration and Incarnation* is sufficiently complicated that it isn't easily stated concisely in a few paragraphs. Hence, my strategy in dealing with it will be to state an aspect of the objection and respond to it, rather than separating my responses completely from the whole set of objections stated all at once.

At first glance, one might think the issues Enns raises are just another example of the objection about the phenomena of Scripture. This is so because an initial reading of his book gives the impression that he has doubts about inerrancy (and even rejects it outright) and that topics he discusses offer reasons why he questions inerrancy. The issues he raises don't address what Scripture says about itself. Rather they focus on passages that seem to create tension either with other biblical passages or because they have parallels in ancient Near Eastern (ANE) literature (and thus raise questions about Scripture's uniqueness, e.g.).

Especially because Enns claims to be an evangelical, his book has generated a lot of heat from reviewers. Thankfully, Enns has responded to some of those reviews. In doing so, he has clarified that he does believe in inerrancy and doesn't think his book casts doubts on it.[24] His book still raises questions

---

[24] Peter Enns, "Response to G. K. Beale's Review Article of *Inspiration and Incarnation*," *JETS* 49 (June 2006): 323.

of concern, but once we know that he holds inerrancy and that his lengthy discussion of the diversity one finds in Scripture, for example, isn't intended to assert that the apparent incongruity of various passages shows Scripture to be an errant book, his book doesn't seem to pose quite the "threat" some have seen it to be.

Even so, Enns chides some reviewers for not taking seriously what he explicitly says about his intended audience and the goals of the book. Early on, he says that he writes for nonacademic evangelicals, i.e., basically for Christian laypersons. Such people have heard of various developments in OT studies, and nonbelievers have used those findings to discredit Scripture as just another ancient Near Eastern document, nothing that we should see as divine revelation any more than the pagan *Epic of Gilgamesh*. Enns believes he can write a popular level book that admits the evidence nonevangelical scholars point to, but still show Scripture to be God's inspired word. So, his purpose in part is also apologetic.[25] Enns also makes it very clear that he intends neither to solve all apparent biblical difficulties nor to capitulate to the prevalent view in nonevangelical biblical scholarship that the difficulties in Scripture show it to be nothing but an ordinary book. Enns intends to show a better way for handling biblical problems than the other two approaches take.[26]

Because this book is a nonacademic work for laypeople, we shouldn't complain that there are few, if any, footnotes to back up his claims, and many technical details that academics would understand are omitted in order to communicate with a more popular audience.[27] Fair enough, but then Enns should know that, when teachers address students with little background in the subject, they need to explain as much as possible the points they are making. In particular, they shouldn't only present material that makes a given point, but they should also tell their audience what they want to say (in this case, about Scripture) by what they say. If a teacher doesn't do this, what's a layperson to conclude about what his or her teacher is trying to teach by what he or she presents?

So, let's be fair to Enns's book, but let's also ask whether he clarifies his points, and beyond that, whether he explains what he intends to say about how we should view Scripture. Even granting that Enns writes for a popular audience, there are some serious problems with this book. Let me mention a series of issues that are troublesome.

First, at the heart of Enns's book is his thesis that our understanding of Scripture's human elements is analogous to our understanding of Christ's in-

[25] Ibid., 314. See also his preface and introductory chapter in *Inspiration and Incarnation: Evangelicals and the Problem of the Old Testament* (Grand Rapids, MI: Baker, 2005), 9, 13.
[26] Enns, *Inspiration and Incarnation*, 14–15.
[27] Enns, "Response to G. K. Beale," 314–315.

carnate humanness and of the implications of living in the world as a fully human being. Hence, the title of his book is *Inspiration and Incarnation*. Enns doesn't deny the divine side either of Scripture or of Christ's person, but he wants us to see the similarities, despite differences, between the human part of Christ's being and the human aspects of Scripture. This is fine, but then it would have helped to explain the biblical doctrine of Scripture's inspiration and to explain the two natures in Christ.

Here, I am not asking that Enns give an exegesis of Philippians 2:5–11 and explain Chalcedonian Christology, nor that he explain the meaning of *theopneustos* in 2 Timothy 3:16 or of *pheromenoi* in 2 Peter 1:21. That would likely be a bit technical for a popular audience. Instead, I am asking for a clear (in English) explanation of the concept of inspiration, including the fact that it means dual authorship of Scripture and doesn't include dictation. I am asking that he explain that 2 Peter 1:21 means that as the human authors wrote, using their personal styles, interests, vocabulary, etc., the Holy Spirit superintended (without dictating) their writing so that their books are both their words and God's. Nowhere in Enns's book does he even come close to such explanations, but if you address laypersons, you can't just assume that they know what inspiration means. Similarly, it would help to explain that Jesus had two complete natures in his one person. One was fully divine and wasn't subject to the limitations of humans living in a finite world, while the other nature was fully human and was subject to all human limitations.

Why would those explanations help? Because only then would readers be ready to grasp how the humanity of Scripture is analogous to Christ's incarnate humanity. And, by the way, Enns never quite explains the focus of his analogy, though he probably thinks he did. Let me explain. Enns is quite clear that, though Jesus was fully human, he committed no sin, and he didn't inherit any sin (Enns, I'm sure, believes this, though he doesn't say it) from Adam and Eve. Though unstated, Enns also agrees that, if during his earthly pilgrimage Jesus had committed sin, that would have disqualified him from being a substitutionary atonement for our sin and would have implicated the whole person Jesus Christ (divine and human natures included) in sin. So, the point of using Jesus's humanity as an analogue to the human part of Scripture cannot be to say that Jesus's sin is analogous to something about Scripture, because Jesus had no sin.

Though Jesus was sinless, as fully human he still had human limitations. Sometimes he was hungry and at other times he was tired and needed sleep. Though Scripture doesn't discuss such matters, it is unrealistic to think that Jesus never got the flu, nor a head cold, and never got the typical cuts and bruises that come with any child growing up. Perhaps when these things happened, Jesus miraculously and immediately healed himself, but we have no data to support that either. Now nothing mentioned so far (flu, head cold, cuts and bruises, hunger, thirst, tiredness) is in any way sinful, so Christ could be subject to such things without compromising his moral perfection.

If Christ in his humanity is supposed to be analogous to Scripture in its humanness, what things about Scripture are analogous to Christ's humanity? Well, just as a sinful act would ruin the moral perfection of Christ, a false claim (either in ignorance or as a lie) would seem to be the parallel defect in Scripture—if Scripture contained a false claim, whoever wrote it would be guilty of sin if they deliberately lied, and at least of saying something untrue, if they did so in ignorance. So, for Scripture's humanness to be parallel to Christ's humanity, neither should contain anything that would bring either any moral stain.

But now comes the hard part. What about Scripture is analogous to Christ's suffering human limitations (hunger, thirst, tiredness, illness)? Sadly, Enns never informs us. He says that the analogy is real and that it works, but doesn't explain what human but nonsinful things about Scripture are analogous to the human but nonsinful things about Christ's humanity. Enns's book is filled with various "issues" that the OT raises, and he assures us that these features show us Scripture's "humanity," but he never quite explains how those things actually are analogous to Christ's human limitations. He only says that they are and that is why, he thinks, the analogy works. But, when you don't explain how the analogy works, and you don't say that in raising an issue like Scripture's "diversity" you don't intend to say that Scripture contains contradictions—though many of the instances of diversity you raise appear to be contradictions—what's a layperson to conclude? If your point is that the elements of diversity are part of Scripture's humanity, and yet they seem to be contradictions (and you don't say they aren't)—even laypeople know this much about logic and contradictions—then wouldn't it seem that if Scripture's "diversity" is analogous to Christ's humanity, that would require that Christ sin? What's a layperson to think? Indeed, what's an academic to think?

Please do not misunderstand this! I am not denying that there can be any analogy between Christ's humanity and that of Scripture, nor am I saying that Enns even indirectly, by presenting "errors" in Scripture, analogously predicates sin of Jesus. What I am saying is that in his book Enns never says that the tensions created by Scripture's "diversity" are not contradictions. And since that "diversity" seems to suggest errors in Scripture (and yet that "diversity" supposedly points to an analogy between Jesus's humanity and Scripture's humanity), what's a layperson to think?

Put simply, how do the issues Enns raises serve as actual analogues to Christ's limitations as a human without those scriptural items being errors/falsehoods? What is it about there being other ANE texts that have similarities to Genesis 1–11, what is it about theological diversity in the OT, and what is it about the way NT writers use the OT that is *analogous* to the limitations of Christ's humanity like his hunger, exhaustion, susceptibility to illness, etc.? Please explain, so that we can see how the proposed analogy works! If you don't, might not a layperson conclude that at least some issues you (Enns) raise assert that there are errors in Scripture, and that *by analogy* you are also postulating some sin in Jesus?

Enns might reply that to think what I've just said is to misunderstand him. Hopefully he would, but Enns needs to remember that he is addressing laypeople who don't automatically know how *he* understands analogies to work, and they also can't on the face of it see how the features of Scripture *he* raises are analogous to Christ's humanity. Wouldn't it have helped to explain more clearly his understanding of both inspiration and incarnation and of how the two are analogous without either being implicated in moral defect? I don't think Enns intended to imply any immorality in Christ or Scripture by drawing this analogy. But then, he should have made that clear so that laypeople wouldn't misunderstand him to be saying something unintended! Even academics could be enlightened on how the features of Scripture he raises are analogous to Christ's limitations as a human without either Christ or Scripture being implicated in any wrongdoing! The main problem here is that the analogy between incarnation and inspiration is at the heart of Enns's book, but nowhere does he explain either doctrine or the points of similarity he wants to emphasize. He merely affirms that both are analogous, and that recognizing this helps us understand what Scripture is. Really? At the very least, laypeople need more explanation in order to get the point!

A second problem is that nowhere in *Inspiration and Incarnation* does Enns talk about progressive revelation. What is this, and why would it help laypeople to understand him better? Progressive revelation means that God didn't reveal everything he had to say on a topic all at once. As time passed, he increasingly gave more information. Sometimes the new information included new requirements, and sometimes it didn't. Thus, the fact that Scripture teaches one thing on a topic at one time and another on the same topic later is no deficiency for Scripture; it only reflects the progress of revelation, which in turn may also reflect the progress in God's plan of redemption. For example, under the Mosaic code, animal sacrifice was required as payment for sin. However, in the NT era after Christ's death and resurrection, no longer are any sacrifices required to pay for sin. If that isn't diversity, I don't know what is! Does that diversity mean that God might be contradicting himself, or more to the point, that OT and NT authors are at odds with one another on this matter? Not at all! It shows that God's redemptive plan has moved on from where it was in the OT era. God revealed through NT writers that the sacrificial system is no longer in force!

Would Enns say that this diversity is at all problematic? I doubt it. Rather, he would say that, in the progress of revelation, God showed in the NT era that his plan of redemption had moved forward. Christ's sacrifice changes everything having to do with sin and atonement. In no way does this mean that the Mosaic law was wrong in its day. Rather it shows that what the Mosaic law anticipated has come to pass in Christ, and hence, its sacrificial system is outmoded.

Isn't the concept of progressive revelation something a popular audience could understand? And, wouldn't mentioning it be a way to show that some of the theological diversity Enns raises in no way suggests that Scripture contradicts itself, but is rather a signal of the progress of revelation? Wouldn't that help laypeople to see that what he is *not* saying by pointing to such diversity is that the diversity suggests contradictions? The sad thing about all of this is that Enns actually does espouse progressive revelation, even if only briefly, in a response to one of his reviewers.[28] Part of good teaching and preaching is anticipating how your words might be misunderstood and then mentioning the possible misunderstandings and defusing them by explaining why you aren't proposing the error you might appear to be saying. Mentioning progressive revelation would also have helped to forestall the idea that Enns is offering an evolutionary picture of the development of religions, including Israel's.

Before surveying some of the actual things Enns says about the OT, I must comment on his methodology. This is a point already made in response to the objection that the phenomena of Scripture don't support inerrancy. One of the problems with that objection and with Enns's methodology is that he seems to think that the way to learn about Scripture's nature is to look at things that appear in Scripture, regardless of whether or not they affirm anything about Scripture's nature. As already argued, the way to form any doctrine is to interpret carefully the biblical passages that actually address the topic. Enns's decision not to explain inspiration means that he does none of that. Rather his strategy is to point to similarities in ANE documents to Genesis 1–11, to note theological diversity, and to focus on how NT writers use the OT.

By using this strategy, what is Enns saying about how to formulate the doctrine of Scripture, including the doctrine of inspiration? More pointedly, what's a layperson to think, especially when he or she starts reading the passages Enns cites and finds that they make no comments about Scripture's nature? Wouldn't many think that the way to formulate a doctrine of inspiration

---

[28] Ibid., 318. Enns introduces this notion in response to a complaint that what he is presenting is an "evolutionary" concept of the development of religion. Had he just talked about progressive revelation in his book, he could have saved himself from some critique and readers from misunderstanding.

is by looking at the phenomena of Scripture, even if they don't say a thing about Scripture's nature? Maybe Enns actually thinks this is the correct way to do systematic theology, but it isn't. Evangelical systematic theology should focus on what God affirms about any given doctrine. None of the passages Enns cites says a thing about inspiration or any other bibliological doctrine.

This must not be misunderstood. As already noted, we can't simply ignore the phenomena. But we must formulate our doctrine of Scripture from careful exegesis of passages that actually talk about revelation, inspiration, and inerrancy. Once we clarify those notions, then we should turn to passages like the ones Enns discusses to see how these doctrines actually apply to specific passages. This in part is why in chapter 7, after defining inerrancy, I discussed many different Scriptures to see what inerrancy means about them. Similarly, it is biblical teaching about inspiration and inerrancy that should govern how we handle the phenomena Enns presents, not the other way around. Sadly, the impression Enns gives is that the phenomena determine how we should understand at least the humanness of inspired Scripture. However, 2 Peter 1:21 and 1 Corinthians 2:13, which actually say things about inspiration, are the places to begin. From understanding those passages (and also passages that affirm Scripture's truthfulness) we then address the phenomena Enns presents. By saying nothing about the passages just mentioned (or any other passages relevant to inerrancy) but instead by focusing on passages that, taken together, create "tension," and by not denying that the tension is a genuine contradiction, what should a layperson conclude about those passages? Even more, what should a layperson think about the doctrine of Scripture's inspiration? If even academics aren't sure what Enns wants to convey by presenting the data he does, shouldn't he have taken steps in a book written for nonacademics to clarify what he isn't saying, let alone what he wants them to understand?

I have spent many words on these preliminary matters, because they are very important, and they are flaws in the book. From Enns's responses to some reviews, I can tell that he isn't guilty of some of the most serious charges hurled at him. What he says in those responses is not particularly technical, and it could have easily been said clearly and briefly in a book written for nonacademics. By not doing so, what's a layperson to think Enns is saying about Scripture by what he does say about it?

Turning more directly to issues Enns raises, there are far too many to cover in this chapter, but some require response, especially when Enns doesn't satisfactorily deal with them. The first is about Genesis 1–11 and myth. As Enns rightly notes, between the last half of the nineteenth century and the early part of the twentieth century, archaeological discoveries have shed light on the ancient Near Eastern context and culture that Bible scholars didn't have before.

We once thought, for example, the Genesis 1–11 accounts of creation and of the Noahic flood were unique. Discoveries of "literature" from Israel's ancient Near Eastern neighbors show that, despite differences between Genesis 1–11 and other peoples' creation and flood stories, there are many similarities. Genesis 1–11 doesn't seem as unique as Christians used to think.

As to other cultures' creation stories, the Babylonian *Enuma Elish* bears strong similarities, despite differences, to the Genesis account of creation. As for the Noahic flood, parallels to the Akkadian *Atrahasis* and the Sumerian *Epic of Gilgamesh* are even more striking.[29] All of these works are believed to predate the writing of Genesis, so they certainly would have been "in the intellectual air" when the writer of Genesis 1–11 wrote these chapters. Enns seems to deny causal dependency of Genesis on these other works, but then he asserts that it is likely there anyway. He writes,

> Reading these stories side by side with Genesis 6-8 makes clear the extent of the similarities between *Atrahasis/Gilgamesh* and Genesis. As with *Enuma Elish*, one should not conclude that the biblical account is directly dependent on these flood stories. Still, the obvious similarities between them indicates a connection on some level. Perhaps one borrowed from the other, or perhaps all of these stories have older precursors. The second option is quite possible, since, as mentioned above, there exists a Sumerian flood story that is considered older than either the Akkadian or biblical versions. In either case, the question remains how the Akkadian evidence influences our understanding of the historical nature of the biblical story.[30]

This is truly remarkable. In the second sentence of the quote Enns says that we shouldn't conclude that the biblical account is *directly dependent* on these flood stories. Two sentences later he proposes that perhaps one borrowed from the other or that all of them have older precursors. What counts as *direct dependence*? What should anyone conclude when you deny direct dependence but two sentences later postulate that material was borrowed from an older source? How can borrowing content not be direct dependence?

This is hardly a clear way to inform laypeople about what they should think about Scripture. But don't miss the crucial move in this quote, the conceptual move made in the final sentence of the quote. Enns introduces the possibility—though he doesn't affirm it actually to be so—that this apparent borrowing should lead us to ask what the borrowing says about the historicity of the biblical stories. Depending on what and how much is borrowed (and the portions Enns quotes from these ancient Near Eastern texts show substantial content overlap), and depending on whether you think these other texts are at

---

[29] Enns, *Inspiration and Incarnation*, 25–29.
[30] Ibid., 29.

all historical (laypersons know of some of them and know that scholars of all stripes consider them myths), the "table is set," so to speak, to say that perhaps Genesis 1–11 is also myth. Again, what would a layperson conclude from Enns's quote? Indeed, how should an academic react to it?

Now, in fairness, what these documents show, as Enns says, is that the Genesis accounts are not so unique as many Christians for many centuries have thought. This, of course, makes sense, since even nonbelievers had access to general revelation in the created order. Romans 1 says that from the created order everyone knows that there is a creator. Of course, Romans 1 also says that natural men suppress and distort revelation. Surely, nonbiblical creation stories show this to be so. As to the flood, multiple stories suggest that there really was a cataclysmic event—why else would stories written before Scripture create a flood story? Some humans survived the flood. Wouldn't they tell others about it? Over the centuries after the flood, as the story was passed on orally, various mythological elements could have been added, and that could explain why the nonbiblical accounts don't match Genesis 6–8.

Sadly, Enns doesn't seem to consider such things as a possible explanation of why these stories exist. In addition, neither the quote above nor anything else Enns says about Genesis 1–11 suggests that the differences between Genesis and these other stories may stem from the fact that God revealed the content of Genesis 1–11 to the biblical writer. No, Enns's answer is that one must have borrowed from the other, or both borrowed from even older stories.

Equally sad is that in postulating the connection between Genesis 1–11 and older stories, Enns doesn't seem to realize that he either has committed the *post hoc* fallacy so typical of this biblical studies approach, or is at least very close to doing so. For those unfamiliar, the fallacy I mentioned is *post hoc, ergo propter hoc*, which means, "after this, therefore because of this." It is the error of thinking that because two things have similarities, the one created after the other must have been caused to be what it is by the earlier item. That certainly seems to be the reasoning ensconced in what Enns proposes about the relation of Genesis 1–11 to these other ancient Near Eastern documents. But this reasoning is fallacious because the item produced later in time may have stemmed from the creativity of its creator, not from borrowing anything from anyone else—the creator of the latter may not even have known that the former existed, but even if he did, that proves nothing about a causal connection between the two. Or it could be that the Genesis accounts were divinely revealed to the writer, and that Genesis is so similar to earlier works because all of the documents in question are based on actual events—even if the nonbiblical accounts have mythological elements that attached to them as the stories were told and retold.

What is somewhat "tacked on" at the end of the quote above becomes explicit later in the chapter. In addition to saying that the Genesis accounts aren't as unique as many might think, Enns also introduces the supposition that Genesis 1–11 might be more myth than history. Enns knows that evangelicals are very sensitive about attributing myth to Scripture, because myth is usually understood to be untrue. However, Enns says that we should think of myth differently. It is important to see exactly what Enns says about this, so I quote him:

> Christians recoil from any suggestion that Genesis is in any way embedded in the mythologies of the ancient world. On one level this is understandable. After all, if the Bible and the gospel are true, and if that truth is bound up with historical events, you can't have the beginning of the Bible get it so wrong. It is important to understand, however, that not all historians of the ancient Near East use the word *myth* simply as shorthand for "untrue," "made-up," "storybook." It may include these ideas for some, but many who use the term are trying to get at something deeper: A more generous way of defining myth is that it is *an ancient, premodern, prescientific way of addressing questions of ultimate origins and meaning in the form of stories: Who are we? Where do we come from?*[31]

Enns adds that ancient peoples just didn't describe the universe in terms associated with modern science—they couldn't because the science was unknown and unavailable.[32] Still, they wanted to know something about questions of ultimate origins, and so they invented various mythological stories about beginnings that have come to light in recent centuries. And Genesis 1–11 surely seems to be written in a literary genre similar to that of these other creation and flood stories.

What, then, should we conclude about the genre of Genesis 1–11? Again, we should hear Enns's own words:

> If the ancient Near Eastern stories are myth (defined in this way as prescientific stories of origin), and since the biblical stories are similar enough to these stories to invite comparison, does this indicate that myth is the proper category for understanding Genesis? Before the discovery of the Akkadian stories, one could quite safely steer clear of such a question, but this is no longer the case. We live in a modern world where we have certain expectations of how the world works. We neither understand the ancient ways—nor feel that we need to.
>
> To give a hint of where this discussion is going, it is worth asking what standards we can reasonably expect of the Bible, seeing that it is an ancient Near Eastern document and not a modern one. Are the early stories in the Old Testament to be judged on the basis of standards of modern historical inquiry and scientific precision, things that ancient peoples were not at all

---

[31] Ibid., 40 (italics are Enns's).
[32] Ibid.

aware of? Is it not likely that God would have allowed his word to come to the ancient Israelites according to standards *they* understood, or are modern standards of truth and error so universal that we should expect premodern cultures to have understood them? The former position is, I feel, better suited for solving the problem. The latter is often an implicit assumption of modern thinkers, *both conservative and liberal Christians*, but it is somewhat myopic and should be called into question. What the Bible is must be understood in light of the cultural context in which it was given.[33]

I have quoted Enns at some length, so that readers can see that the quote is not taken out of context. Note that in the first paragraph of the quote Enns asks a crucial question. Note also that in the rest of that paragraph, he doesn't answer it. By the end of the second paragraph, we have Enns's answer, though by no means is it clearly stated. I suppose that Enns could say that he didn't explicitly say "yes, Genesis 1–11 is myth," but he certainly says nothing to deny that. Moreover, the option he chooses (of the two mentioned in the second paragraph) about which standards we should use in evaluating ancient literature surely sounds consistent with claiming that Genesis 1–11 is myth. Again, what do you think laypeople, Enns's audience, would conclude from the two paragraphs quoted? Indeed, what's an academic to conclude?

Of course, Enns believes this is fine, because he thinks his definition of myth is innocuous and in no way a threat to a high view of Scripture. In this assumption, Enns is fatally wrong! Though I grant that his definition of myth does "sanitize" it a bit, it still avoids, and so does Enns's discussion, addressing the question of whether a myth (in Enns's sense of myth) can contain any truth at all. If it can at all be true, which parts and how much of it are likely to be true? And, true in what sense, everyone should ask. True because the story matches what actually occurred in our universe and on Planet Earth?!

Sadly, Enns never answers these questions anywhere in this book, and I haven't seen him even address them in any clear way in his responses to reviews of his book. But these are crucial questions, and without clear answers—or more to the point, with answers that basically equate Genesis 1–11 with other ancient Near Eastern stories that Enns seems rightly to believe are not true (in a correspondence sense of truth)—what are laypeople to think Enns is saying about their Bible?

Why is this such a major issue? Because two key things are at stake. The first is the inerrancy of Scripture, something which in later journal articles Enns clearly espouses. How is inerrancy at stake here? As follows: Genesis 1–3 and 6–9, as examples, seem to give a factual (even if not a historical, in the sense of modern notions of written history) account of the origins of the

---

[33] Ibid., 41 (italics are Enns's).

universe, including the creation of the first man and woman, the fall of those first humans into sin, and the results for the rest of the race and for Planet Earth, and a cataclysmic flood in the days of Noah. That is, these chapters assert that the events just mentioned actually occurred. If these stories are myths, even in Enns's sense of myth, then what the passages assert did not actually happen—at least, not all of it happened, and all that is needed to dethrone Scripture's inerrancy is even one factual error. I don't mean that one error would make everything else in Scripture false, but only that the concept of inerrancy could not cover as much of Scripture as the concepts of biblical revelation and inspiration do. And once that happens, then who knows what else might be factually wrong? That is the significance of this to inerrancy.

But, you may reply, Enns doesn't reject biblical inerrancy! Let's assume charitably that he even believes inerrancy is a predicate of all of Scripture. How do his views about Genesis 1–11 and myth defend inerrancy? Enns could easily explain that what these chapters teach is inerrant; it's just that they don't intend to teach precise history or science—that once you properly interpret these chapters, there is no error in what they affirm. Indeed, one might make those claims, even as one might also call the resurrection of Christ a mythological way of proclaiming that "the spirit of Christ" (encapsulated in his teachings) lives on, and the substance of that "spirit" of his teachings is true.

Indeed, one might make just such a claim, and one could make similar claims about every other biblical account of a miracle. But the result would be that we really know very little about what actually happened in the history of Israel and in the lives of Christ and his apostles. All the accounts of these things seem to be factual but are actually mythology. What the myths intend to teach (their moral and/or spiritual "message") is true, so inerrancy is upheld.

But is this the way to uphold the full inerrancy of Scripture? Hardly! This sounds like any significant sense of biblical inerrancy has died the death of a thousand exegetical qualifications! In other words, this sort of strategy is not just bad hermeneutics and exegesis. It is also a way to claim to hold inerrancy while denying that many of Scripture's most significant factual claims are even remotely true in a correspondence sense. That isn't the way to defend biblical inerrancy! And Enns's presentation is not the way to instruct lay evangelicals about their Bible so that they will be informed and their trust in Scripture will be enhanced!

In addition, a second issue is at stake in this discussion, and it is just as important as the first. It involves maintaining a high Christology. How so? Enns never discusses what Jesus thought about Genesis 1–11. But we know the answer: In chapter 7, in my defense of inerrancy, I noted that Jesus affirmed the factuality of Genesis 1–3, he seems to have believed in the historicity of

Cain and Abel, and he definitely believed in the Noahic flood. In fact, various of his doctrinal teachings rest on the historicity of these events. If these events never happened and the people involved were nothing more than mythological characters created by the writers to make some moral, spiritual (or other) point, then Jesus's teachings that rest upon the historicity of these people and events are in deep trouble. And so are we, for now the question is not simply what we should believe about origins, the entrance of sin into the human race, etc., but also which of Jesus's theological teachings we can believe.

If Jesus's theology could be that badly askew, perhaps he was also deluded about his mission in life. Perhaps it wasn't necessary after all to go to the cross. If Genesis 3 is myth, and so the curses God doled out could also be myths, then perhaps there is no problem for which a perfect victim needs to be sacrificed as payment. The possible implications of Genesis 1–11 being myth, even in Enns's sense of myth, are devastating to Christology. Now, holding some wrong ideas about historical events is not a sin—even for Jesus. But it is totally inconsistent with the fact that Jesus, as the God-man, must be omniscient!

Please do not misread what I am saying. I am not saying that Enns rejects the hypostatic union of Christ, or his omniscience, or the need for substitutionary atonement! I doubt that Enns would deny such truths. My point is that if Enns is right about Genesis 1–11, and if that means that the events described therein are only in part (who knows which parts) factual, then that undercuts the aspects of Christology mentioned. If Enns does think that myth can contain some truth (in a correspondence sense), he should have said so, and he should have said which parts of the stories in Genesis 1–11 are factually true. Otherwise, what's a layperson, and even an academic, to conclude about Jesus's opinions of these chapters and the events in his life and the teachings he expounded that are based on his belief in the historical factuality of the people and events described in these chapters?

Enns's book also has a lengthy chapter about the unusual ways many NT writers use the OT. As he notes, in many cases they use an OT passage in ways quite unexpected, if one just looks at the passage in its OT context. Enns doesn't call such usage errors—indeed, he had better not, since by the end of the chapter he encourages readers to follow apostolic hermeneutical strategies—but what should a lay reader conclude? No doubt, many would think that by showing these uses of the OT Enns is saying that the NT writers who quote an OT passage and say that it is fulfilled in what happened in the NT author's era got it wrong, because what the NT writer does with it isn't what the OT author had in mind when he wrote the words. But then, after giving that distinct impression (at the very least), to end the chapter by applauding the NT writers' hermeneutics and suggesting that we should handle the OT in similar ways can only leave laypeople (and a lot of academics) confused about whether this method of interpretation contains errors, and if so, confused about why Enns recommends it to his readers. Such a message does not help a popular audience to respect Scripture more, and it is hard to see how the chapter on NT usage of the OT will drive laypeople to a deeper study of Scripture. Enns seems to be sending multiple and conflicting messages in that chapter. How can such lack of clarity help anyone better understand the Bible?

In sum, the value of Enns's book is that it shows that Scripture has greater depth and richness than may at first meet the eye. I believe that by making this point Enns wanted to whet his readers' appetites for digging into Scripture more deeply so as to mine its many treasures. But if that is the point, why write a book that relentlessly seems to assert that there are errors at various points in Scripture? Just a brief word assuring readers that he isn't claiming errors in Scripture and a brief word in each chapter about how the points he makes actually fit with an inerrant Bible would have removed much lack of clarity. I think it would also have allowed readers to learn from Enns's book without raising significant doubts about whether what he is subtly trying to do is undermine readers' confidence in Scripture's truthfulness. For many, both laypeople and academics, the book as written seems to undermine inerrancy, and that message comes through so loudly that it drowns out the various helpful things Enns wants to teach about the nature of the OT and how to understand it better.

## "TEXTS OF TERROR" AND INERRANCY

It has recently become the "complaint *du jour*" to take God to task over his allegedly defective morals, as supposedly evidenced in the pages of Scripture. God made such morally outrageous commands (especially in the OT), we are told, that he is either morally reprehensible, or the writers of Scripture aren't telling the truth about what God actually commanded on various notorious occasions.

Though this complaint is nuanced differently by various critics, I want to interact with two presentations of it. Wesley Morriston, in the journal article "Did God Command Genocide?," and Kenton Sparks, in a recent book entitled *Sacred Word, Broken Word: Biblical Authority and the Dark Side of Scripture*, both question the morality of God's commanding the Israelites to destroy utterly and entirely the Canaanites. Believing it immoral to demand genocide, Morriston concludes that the biblical author was simply wrong when he wrote that God commanded the Israelites to possess the Promised Land, and to destroy completely its occupants, leaving no vestige whatsoever of their culture and especially of their religion.[34]

---

[34] Wesley Morriston, "Did God Command Genocide? A Challenge to the Biblical Inerrantist," *Philosophia Christi* 11 (Summer 2009): 26.

Kenton Sparks pays significant attention to what he calls Scripture's ethical and moral diversity. By this he means that on the one hand, Jesus summed up the law and gospel with the command to love God and one's neighbor, which Sparks thinks entails loving our enemies, turning the other cheek, and praying for our persecutors. On the other hand, in "glaring contrast" Scripture contains passages which "list women as property, that praise God for smashing infants against rocks, that allow slave owners to beat their slaves, and that present God as commanding the extermination of ethnic and religious groups."[35] To support his complaints, Sparks cites Exodus 20:17; Psalm 137:9; Exodus 21:20–21; and Deuteronomy 7.

These are serious objections, not just to inerrancy but also, assuming Scripture is God's word, to the very moral rectitude of God himself. Let me, therefore, describe in more detail each author's exact complaint. I begin with Morriston, who claims that any Christian who believes in biblical inerrancy must explain how their view of Scripture fits the OT God's behavior, which is sometimes harsh and shocking. Specifically, one must explain how the writer of Scripture can likely be correct when he says that God commanded the people of Israel to exterminate entire nations. Lest we doubt this, Morriston offers as an example Deuteronomy 7:1–2. Just in case we are unsure about the meaning of "utterly destroy" and "show no mercy," Morriston offers Deuteronomy 20:16 as an explanation: " . . . in the cities of these peoples that the LORD your God gives you for an inheritance, you shall save alive nothing that breathes. . . . [36]

This is a problem because "a genocidal attack on another nation is a moral outrage, and God is generally assumed to be perfectly good in a sense that is incompatible with commanding moral outrages."[37] Morriston quickly adds that, undoubtedly, those who wrote Deuteronomy believed that God had given that order, but a perfectly good God would never make such a demand. Hence, if we believe that God is morally perfect and good, we must also believe that the writers of Deuteronomy were mistaken. Morriston formulates his objection as follows:

(1) God exists and is morally perfect.
(2) So God would not command one nation to exterminate the people of another *unless He had a morally sufficient reason for doing so.*
(3) According to various OT texts, God sometimes commanded the Israelites to exterminate the people of other nations.
(4) It is highly *unlikely* that God had a morally sufficient reason for issuing these alleged commands.
(5) So it is highly *unlikely* that everything every book of the OT says about God is true.[38]

---

[35] Kenton L. Sparks, *Sacred Word, Broken Word: Biblical Authority and the Dark Side of Scripture* (Grand Rapids, MI: Eerdmans, 2012), 20.
[36] Morriston, "Did God Command Genocide?," 8, in which he quotes from Deuteronomy 20:16.
[37] Ibid.
[38] Ibid.

Morriston believes this argument offers a strong prima facie case against inerrancy. Surely, no evangelical Christians (nor many of a less conservative stripe) would doubt premise (1), and (2) seems to follow logically from (1). If God is perfectly good, and that is nonnegotiable for most Christians, then, premise (4) is the controversial one. Morriston adds that his point (and the argument's) is not that it is logically impossible in any circumstance for God to have a morally sufficient reason for commanding genocide, but rather to deny that "*in the circumstances that actually obtained* at the time that the genocidal commands described in the OT texts were supposedly given—it is at all likely that God had satisfactory reasons [sic] issuing *those* commands."[39] If this is right, then, Morriston claims, there is a strong prima facie reason for rejecting the OT's inerrancy.

To shore up his argument, Morriston next explains that it won't do for inerrantists to reply that God's transcendence and our cognitive limitations make it impossible for us to discern what God's morally adequate reason for such a command might be. This is so because, in the passages in question, God's reasons for issuing the commands are stated, and they are not very complicated or mysterious. So, in defending the inerrancy of these texts, inerrantists will have to show that, relevant to everything else we know, the reasons for commanding the Israelites to kill their enemies are plausible and not morally suspect.[40] In the rest of his article, Morriston interacts with Paul Copan's and then William Lane Craig's attempts to justify God's commands. Of course, Morriston believes that neither succeeds in exonerating God, but what they say and why Morriston disagrees are of interest, especially as we try to answer this objection.

Morriston first addresses Paul Copan's handling of this issue. Copan offers several reasons to justify God's command to destroy the Canaanites. First, the Canaanites were incorrigibly wicked, so God had every right to punish them. Second, the language of Deuteronomy 7:2–5 assumes that even though the Canaanites were to be punished, they wouldn't be completely destroyed, because Israel is warned not to intermarry or make political alliances with them. God was more concerned to get rid of Canaanite religion than to obliterate this people group. Third, the language of Joshua (e.g., Josh. 10:40) about the destruction is clearly hyperbole, because the book of Joshua assumes that Canaanites still inhabit the land. Finally, the crux of the issue, as Copan sees it, is that God is the author of life and isn't obligated to let each person live seventy or eighty years; he has a right to take and give life as he chooses. Some will complain, however, that the women and children were innocent, but Copan replies

---

[39] Ibid., 9.
[40] Ibid.

that the Canaanites were sufficiently morally depraved that their women were far from innocent. An example of this is the seduction of Israelite males by Midianite women, as recorded in Numbers 25.[41] But what about the innocent children who were also destroyed? Copan says that in a just war against an evil power, sadly, there will be "collateral damage." In addition, though it might seem cruel to kill the children, it is actually merciful because they would be saved from a morally corrupt and corrupting society, ushered into God's presence, and would recognize the justness of what had happened. The assumption here is that children who die before the age of accountability go to heaven and spend eternity in God's presence with his blessings.[42]

None of these answers impresses Morriston. Though the whole Canaanite society wasn't actually destroyed, that was still God's command. Morriston's moral assessment is made on the basis of the morality of the command, not on whether Israel succeeded or failed in carrying it out. But, Morriston adds, Israel did not fully destroy the Canaanites, and Israel repeatedly fell to the temptations of Canaanite society and were punished for it. So, if God was really interested in destroying Canaanite religion by destroying the society, his chosen means was quite unsuccessful.

The key issue, however, according to Morriston, is whether God had a morally sufficient reason to order genocide. Morriston thinks not. Leviticus 18:19–25 outlaws various practices and seems to imply that the Canaanites engaged in them. Specifically, it outlaws having sexual intercourse with a woman during her menstrual period, incest, child sacrifice (in this case, to the pagan god Molech), homosexual behavior, and bestiality. In response, Morriston argues that either these things are not so bad, or that even in Jewish thinking, some of these things were done. For example, Morriston cites Exodus 22:29c–30 as a prescription for sacrificing one's firstborn son. He grants that Exodus 13:2 says that the firstborn should be "consecrated," but it doesn't say how. In contrast, Exodus 34:20 says the firstborn is to be redeemed, and Morriston claims that this is apparently to be done by an animal sacrifice, so the "redemption" must be from having to be sacrificed in the manner in which oxen and sheep were sacrificed (as mentioned in Ex. 22:30). None of this, according to Morriston, suggests that the people of Israel saw child sacrifice as an abomination, even though that was one reason God gave for destroying the Canaanites. Morriston also thinks that Jephthah's vow to sacrifice the first thing that came from his house if the Lord granted Israel a military victory (which wound up meaning the death of Jephthah's daughter) again shows that child sacrifice was not particularly foreign to Israel, nor was it something that God had clarified as

---

[41] Ibid., 10–11. Morriston quotes from a lengthy passage in Paul Copan's "Is Yahweh a Moral Monster? The New Atheists and Old Testament Ethics," *Philosophia Christi* 10 (Summer 2008).
[42] Morriston, "Did God Command Genocide?," 12; quotes are from Copan, "Is Yahweh a Moral Monster?," 26.

an abomination. Jephthah was one of Israel's judges, so whatever "rules" God had given, Jephthah would surely have known them, and would not have taken such a chance with his daughter's life.[43]

In turning to the sexual offenses mentioned in Leviticus 18, Morriston argues that "there is nothing uniquely 'Canaanite' about them. All, or nearly all, of these practices—from sexual intercourse during a woman's menstrual period to homosexual behavior to bestiality—are still common. Is there any real reason to believe that these things were *more* common among the Canaanites in the ancient world?"[44]

Perhaps, then, the complaint is actually about cultic temple prostitution. There are OT passages which outlaw such practices, including Deuteronomy 23:17–18 and Hosea 4:14. The Deuteronomy passage doesn't mention the Canaanites, but Morriston admits that one might argue that there was no need for such a command in the Mosaic law unless the peoples surrounding the Israelites engaged in it. On the other hand, Hosea 4:14b implies that temple prostitution existed among some Israelite men long after the conquest of Canaan, so the commanded genocide in Deuteronomy and Joshua didn't succeed in removing this. Morriston ends his critique on this point by saying that we really don't have much evidence about how widespread temple prostitution was, and we must remember that the fullest historical account of the conquest of Canaan we have is the one in Scripture, and that was written by the victors. It should surprise no one that they thought their actions were fully justified and sanctioned by God. Morriston adds that the Ras Shamra tablets, which come from the Canaanite city of Ugarit, are an archaeological find that helps us understand the culture. Ugarit seems to have been at its cultural and economic height around 1200 BC, the time at which Morriston claims that Israel settled in Canaan. In looking at the Ras Shamra tablets' contents, one doesn't find evidence "of a particularly 'debauched' or 'cruel' culture—unless you count animal sacrifice as 'cruel'! The texts do make it clear that the people of Ugarit worshiped numerous gods— . . . What the Ugaritic texts do *not* contain is any mention of child sacrifice or ritual prostitution, or, for that matter, any of the abominations mentioned in Leviticus 18."[45]

As to the claim that the Canaanites were incorrigibly wicked, Morriston argues that there just isn't enough biblical evidence about them to reach such a conclusion. He then ends by addressing what Copan sees as the crux of the issue: God's right to do with human life as he chooses and when he chooses. Morriston answers that, while this may be so, "by itself it does nothing to demonstrate that God had a morally sufficient reason for *commanding the Israelites*

[43] Morriston, "Did God Command Genocide?," 14–15.
[44] Ibid., 16.
[45] Ibid., 18.

*to practice genocide.* And *that*, surely, is the 'crux' of the issue. On the face of it, there is quite a lot to be said *against* commanding the Israelites to engage in such brutal behavior. Slaughtering countless women and children would surely be bad for their moral development. By commanding them to practice genocide God would, in one very important respect, be encouraging them to stay on the same moral level as their 'brutal' neighbors in the ANE."[46]

Morriston next turns to William Lane Craig's handling of this issue. He quotes Craig to the effect that, by ordering the extermination of the Canaanites, God forced the Israelite soldiers, among other things, to break into houses and kill terrified women and children. This would undoubtedly have a brutalizing effect on the soldiers who did it. However, Craig responds that life in the ANE was already brutal, and no one involved seemed to be wringing his hands over having to kill the Canaanites. As a result, evidently the Israelites weren't harmed by participating in this act of genocide.

In responding to Craig, Morriston agrees that life in the ANE was brutal and that genocide was not uncommon. Hence, in their own culture and time, the Israelites were not any more brutal than their neighbors. Women and children were part of a nation and hence were implicated in its guilt, and this was a "normal" way to punish the enemies of God and his people. Though he agrees with Craig on all of these matters, Morriston in effect replies that it is irrelevant. He believes that Craig has missed the key point about moral sensibilities, for he doesn't seem to grasp that "the point about the moral sensibility of the ANE (and of ancient Israel) does not speak to the principal issue, which concerns *God's* behavior. God is not stuck with an ANE moral sensibility. *He* is supposed to be *perfectly* good. As such, he must surely be opposed to the 'brutality' that Craig openly acknowledges. A just and loving God could hardly want His Chosen People to be cruel or to be indifferent to the sufferings of other peoples."[47]

Morriston also addresses Craig's claims that God wanted his people to learn that their God "is not to be trifled with" and that Israel is to be "set apart" to serve God and him alone. Morriston thinks this doesn't warrant God to command genocide. For one thing, using Israelites to obliterate an idolatrous nation would tend to reinforce a brutal approach to warfare and make it harder for them to learn that killing noncombatants in warfare is morally wrong. Second, giving Israel such an order would likely give them the wrong reason for obeying God, namely, fear, rather than obeying him out of gratitude and love. And, even if God intended to teach Israel the lessons Craig proposes, it isn't clear that commanding genocide is the only way, let alone the best way,

---

[46] Ibid., 19.
[47] Ibid., 20–21. Morriston responds to the following by Craig: William Lane Craig, "Slaughter of the Canaanites," Reasonable Faith with William Lane Craig, http://reasonablefaith.org/site/news2?page=NewsArticlesid=5767.

to teach these lessons. God could have, instead, just written the message on every Israelite's heart (as Jer. 31:33 says).[48]

Morriston turns next to the slaughter of innocent Canaanite children. He believes that we can't claim that their killing was merely collateral damage from the killing of their wicked parents. This is so because the Israelites were explicitly commanded to exterminate the children *along with* their parents. Morriston quotes Craig to the effect that, had the children been allowed to live, they would have perpetuated the wicked Canaanite culture, and that would have been a great temptation to Israel. Morriston disagrees, because if the young children had been spared and raised by the Israelites, they might have adopted the Israelites' culture and religion. In addition, the extermination plan did not in fact succeed in removing the temptations of intermarriage and apostasy. There were always foreigners in the neighborhood, and Israel was always tempted by their religion and culture, and she repeatedly fell to the temptation. So, if exterminating the Canaanites was intended to protect Israel's devotion to God and moral purity, it didn't work.[49]

Morriston then cites Craig's explanation that slaughtering the Canaanite children was a tangible illustration of what it means for Israel to be "set apart for God." Morriston asks exactly what this means. If slaughtering innocent children is what it means, Morriston doubts that being "set apart" in this way has any value. "A better way to distinguish the Israelites from their neighbors would have been to encourage them to be less brutal, more compassionate, and more loving."[50] Any way, even if killing the innocent children was an effective way to accomplish the goals Craig sets forth, the means used to accomplish these ends is morally objectionable. Morriston rejects Craig's answer that at least the children killed would have a glorious afterlife; i.e., they would have been saved from their parents' debauchery by being killed and transported to a better world.

Morriston answers that this suggestion has no biblical support. The texts that give reasons for killing the Canaanites say nothing about a glorious afterlife for anyone. Of course, Morriston adds, we shouldn't be surprised that little is said about the afterlife, for the OT didn't have a very "lively notion of the afterlife."[51] But he is still unconvinced, because certainly God knew about the afterlife, and it is *God's* actions that need to be justified. There is no reason, however, to think, from the Scriptures that record God's command and its carrying out, that God planned to give the children a gloriously blessed eternity. Even if we construct such an argument, it is more likely that God knew that

---

[48] Ibid., 21.
[49] Ibid., 22–23.
[50] Ibid., 23.
[51] Ibid.

brutally killing the Canaanite children would be very bad for both the children and their attackers. So, it is more likely that God would not have commanded anyone to kill them.[52]

Morriston also wonders whether the children would know of their parents' eternal punishment. If so, then how can Copan be right that they would side with God and see the justness of their parents' punishment? Even more, granted that Canaanite practices were morally repugnant to God, "they may have adopted those practices simply *because they did not know any better.*"[53] Craig claims that if the children had lived, they likely would have continued their parents' religion, but Morriston believes that this should remove the children's moral culpability, because they would have no way of knowing about Yahweh, the true and living God. Morriston then adds what he believes is the clincher: "But if this is true of the Canaanite children, surely it is also true of their parents. They, too, were once children. They were taught to worship the wrong gods by *their* parents. I simply cannot see any reason to assume that practicing the religion of their parents makes them morally culpable, or that they deserve to be punished for this. What they do deserve, I would say, is enlightenment about the true nature of God and about His requirements for human beings. Once that is granted, we can begin talking about moral culpability. But it is far from sufficient merely to point to odious religious practices (temple prostitution or human sacrifice, for instance)."[54]

This is truly a remarkable claim. It means that if one simply follows the practices of one's parents and doesn't know anything different, then one isn't worthy of being punished. So, neither the Canaanite children nor their parents actually deserved this punishment, for they were simply following the practices of their parents and didn't know any better! The proper conclusion, then, is that God did not in fact demand the killing that the biblical writers claim he demanded. God's moral perfection can be upheld, but only at the expense of the inerrancy of biblical texts that say he commanded the Israelites to exterminate the Canaanites![55]

In turning to Kenton Sparks, we can be briefer, because he doesn't present lengthy argumentation like Morriston does. The heart of Sparks's complaints is found in chapters 4 and 5 of his *Sacred Word, Broken Word*. In chapter 4 he introduces three basic kinds of problems that he finds in Scripture. The first kind stems from what he labels the problem of human finiteness. Roughly, this involves the sort of apparent inconsistencies and discrepancies already treated in dealing with the phenomena of Scripture issue. While Sparks thinks some

---

[52] Ibid., 24.
[53] Ibid., 25.
[54] Ibid.
[55] Ibid., 25–26.

inconsistencies can be harmonized, it is not so for all, especially when some stem from outmoded ways of looking at the universe. For example, Genesis says that there are "waters above the heavens," but even John Calvin knew this was wrong. Of course, it is to be expected of the writer of Genesis, given the then current scientific understanding of the universe.[56]

Sparks claims that a second set of biblical problems stems from the problem of culture. As examples, Sparks notes that one Scripture requires roasting the Passover lamb, while another demands boiling it (Ex. 12:9; Deut. 16:7), a difference, he claims, that stems from diverse social conditions that produce different understandings of acceptable ritual practice. But some differences of culture stem from what was practiced in biblical times as opposed to our day. Sparks offers as an example the rule in Deuteronomy 22:28–29 that if a man raped a woman, he was required to marry her and could not under any circumstances divorce her. While this seems outrageous from our perspective, it was actually a way of protecting the raped woman's rights. In Israelite culture of the time, virginity was highly valued, so a raped woman's chances of being married were limited. But, of course, in those societies there weren't many ways a woman could provide for her needs and those of her children. The only respectable way was by marriage. So, the Deuteronomy 22 law was intended actually to help raped women and to warn any potential rapist that if he raped someone, he would have to support her for the rest of their lives.[57]

Sparks presents a third problem with Scripture, and it is the most serious, even though it typically gets the least attention. It is the problem of human fallenness. Sparks believes this problem is associated with the traditional philosophical and theological problem of evil. Several things should be noted about Sparks's understanding of this problem, but before we do, we must identify the kind of biblical texts that illustrate this problem.

Sparks turns first to Gregory of Nyssa's troubled response to the story of Israel's exodus from Egypt. In particular, it was the tenth and climactic plague, the killing of the firstborn, which included the king's firstborn son, that troubled Gregory. In a passage quoted from Gregory, he wonders how it can be just to make the innocent son pay for the sin of his father, the king. Pharaoh's son was not even at an age where he could discern right from wrong, but he was punished for his father's sin. Ezekiel said that the soul that sins, it shall surely die, meaning that each person dies for his or her own sins, not for the sins of their parents. Believing that what happened to Pharaoh's son was unjust, Sparks says, Gregory considered the Passover story to be allegory, not literal history. Moreover, Sparks adds that this is only one of many examples

[56] Sparks, *Sacred Word, Broken Word*, 38–39. See also the many sorts of apparent problems in Scripture he details earlier in his chapter on pages 30–38.
[57] Ibid., 39–40.

where church fathers handled such problem texts either by ignoring them or by treating them as allegories.[58]

Of course, earlier in the chapter, Sparks added the further example of the killing of the Canaanites that Morriston discusses in such detail. Sparks sums up these kinds of problems with the following assessment:

> . . . my main point is that the ethical problems I speak of are very obvious to thoughtful readers of Scripture in any era of church history. This is because the problems are not the inventions of arrogant human readers who stand in judgment over Scripture. Rather, the problems are engendered by the fact that Scripture sometimes renders judgment on itself.[59]

Sparks says that these ethical problems in Scripture are, in his judgment, just a form of the philosophical problem of evil. Stated in its simplest form, this is the atheistic complaint that if an all-loving, all-powerful God exists, then surely he would remove the evil in our world. Since evil in many forms surrounds us, God must not exist. Similarly, the ethical problems in Scripture are evidence that Scripture is not God's word. As Sparks explains, some would say that "'if a good God truly existed . . . and if Scripture were truly his word, then Scripture would present a consistent and beautiful ethical vision, wholly consistent in matters of love and morality.' But this does not appear to be what Scripture offers. So Scripture is not the word of God. This is the logic."[60]

While one might conclude from these ethical problems that Scripture is not God's word, Sparks thinks there are other ways to handle this problem. A second way in which many conservative Christians would respond is one that Sparks labels fundamentalist biblicism. Sparks believes that these people would handle the ethical problems roughly as Christian Science would. That is, rather than admitting the horrendous nature of these evils, they would try to relativize (my term) "evils" so that what at first appears evil, upon further reflection shows itself actually to be good. The result is that the genocide by Israel is deemed "just fine and probably not as bad as it sounds."[61]

Having rejected other solutions to what he calls the problem of Scripture, how would Sparks solve it? In chapter 5 he offers his resolution. Here again we must remember that Sparks sees this problem as parallel to the problem of evil. Accordingly, even though he in no formal or informal way states clearly what he is doing, his answer parallels the free will defense against the problem

---

[58] Ibid., 41.
[59] Ibid., 42.
[60] Ibid., 43.
[61] Ibid. Sparks then adds (43–44) that some have used "speech act" theory to handle these problems. According to that approach, God's demand of genocide wasn't about ordering genocide against the Canaanites. Rather, the author intended to use the act of ordering genocide as a way to construct a distinct Israelite identity. So, God didn't actually order genocide. In fairness to all sides, while there may be some who use speech act analysis in this way, Sparks doesn't show that key evangelicals who use such approaches to written texts would analyze this command in this way.

of moral evil. Just as we can defend God against the evils in our world by arguing that the world as created contained no evil in it, but moral evil was introduced into it by abuse of human free will, so also if the production of Scripture were totally left to God, it would have been error-free, but fallen human authors wrote of their own free will what we find in Scripture. Just as fallen humanity needs redemption—God is not to be blamed for moral evil in our world—so also "fallen" Scripture also needs redemption. But, rest assured, the ethical problems (as well as the problems of finitude and culture) are not God's responsibility, but resulted from human authors expressing their fallen, finite, culture-bound nature as they wrote Scripture.[62]

Now, at first glance, we must say that if we are considering the problem of Scripture as one of the many problems of evil,[63] and if we are handling it in its logical form (as Sparks seems to do, though he seems unaware of the different forms in which the problem of evil can be posed), where the accusation is that evil (in this case, errors in Scripture) contradicts the existence of an all-loving, all-powerful, morally perfect God as Scripture's source, Sparks's response shows a possible way for God to have the attributes we attribute to him while we could still see Scripture somehow as his word, despite the evil it records. Hence, Sparks's proposal meets the *logical demands* of showing how all things one might believe about God and Scripture could be true. There is, however, a major reason to reject altogether Sparks's theology and its defense against the problem of Scripture. That reason is the doctrine of inspiration. That is, if we understand Scripture's inspiration as presented in my chapters on inspiration, God was just as involved in producing Scripture as were the human authors, though, of course, their roles differed.

Sparks doesn't cover this issue in chapter 5, but he still knows it needs to be addressed, so he raises it in chapter 6 where he considers various theological questions about his proposal. What he says about inspiration is most revealing. To his credit, Sparks appeals to 2 Timothy 3:16 and 2 Peter 1:20–21, but what he says isn't particularly enlightening. As to the former verse, Sparks rightly notes that *theopneustos* is the key word, but says that "the Greek word itself does not really imply anything in particular about *how* the transaction between God and the human authors took place. It is possible that the author's understanding of inspiration (whether Paul or someone else) went no deeper than this, but even if he knew more, he has left it unsaid."[64]

---

[62] I have summarized Sparks's argument in his chapter 5. Actually, I have given it more explanation than he does in order to clarify what he is saying. The key passage in the chapter appears on page 47, where he writes two parallel sentences that describe his answer to the problem of moral evil (humans introduced it into the perfect world God created) as analogous to his answer to the problem of Scripture (Scripture is God's good written word, but its fallen human authors introduced the "evil things" we find in it, so it is their fault, not God's).
[63] See my *The Many Faces of Evil*, chapter 1 especially, for an explanation of why there are *many* problems of evil.
[64] Sparks, *Sacred Word, Broken Word*, 56.

As for 2 Peter 1, Sparks argues that the key point is that the writers were carried along by the Holy Spirit. Thus, this verse emphasizes the writers, not their writings. Sparks adds that the passage says little about what the Holy Spirit did, but he thinks the most natural way to interpret "carried along" is in terms of dictation. While that view was prevalent among many earlier Christian thinkers, modern Christians reject the dictation theory. Hence, 2 Peter 1 really doesn't say much about the nature of inspiration.[65]

Sparks offers some further thoughts, including the fact that Scripture contains a number of diverse types of literature, but this only adds mystery about what was actually involved in inspiration. Summing up his thoughts, Sparks writes,

> the whole matter becomes quite fascinating and puzzling if one thinks much about it. I believe that Stephen Chapman is right when he describes *inspiration* as "a cipher for a mysterious process of divine-human co-writing." In the end, we simply do not understand how it worked. Inspiration affirms that the Bible is God's authoritative word and that we should read it with seriousness, but conceptually speaking this does not tell us with precision either *what* we should expect from the Bible or *how* we should read it.[66]

Astute readers will recognize that this really says very little about what Sparks means by "inspiration," and that he is rather unclear in his own mind about its meaning. Thankfully, two paragraphs later he adds further explanation which reveals more than anything else he has said. Because of this matter's significance, I quote exactly what he wrote:

> In Scripture, God speaks to us through the finite and fallen perspectives of human authors and, thereby, through the limited and fallen horizons of human cultures and audiences. And the process whereby he accomplished this was and is very human, both in the production of the individual biblical books themselves and in the lengthy historical process—both Jewish and Christian—that finally produced our respective canons of Scripture (Jewish, Catholic, Orthodox, and Protestant). Just as God's providential and creative hand was in the long and convoluted evolutionary processes that produced human lives and souls, so his hand was in the complex historical process that produced Holy Scripture. It is difficult to go much beyond this in explicating the theological details of inspiration and inscripturation. We see the matter "through a mirror dimly" (1 Cor 13:12). And in the end, I think that our grasping after a metaphor for inspiration turns out to be mainly academic. For regardless of the manner in which God gave us Scripture, the end result is the text that we have before us. And our interpretation of that text and its message is not deeply affected by the divine activity that created Scripture, whatever this may have been.[67]

---

[65] Ibid., 57.
[66] Ibid., 58.
[67] Ibid., 59–60.

Those who have read my chapters on inspiration know that what Sparks describes is nothing like what the Bible teaches about inspiration! But even if you haven't read those chapters, it should be clear that Sparks thinks the Bible was produced by human beings alone, and that somehow God speaks through it and was involved along the way, but we can't say how. The analogy with evolution is most revealing, because evolution, as many scientists describe it, can proceed without God's involvement. For theistic evolutionists, it is quite important to note what they think God actually *did* in the evolutionary process so as to warrant the description "theistic." I don't mean that theistic evolutionists have no explanation. I only mean that the ways they typically explain it make it very hard to know exactly what God did either to start the process or to keep it going.

Please do not miss my main point: what Sparks defines as inspiration basically leaves God out of the process of the actual writing of Scripture. What he says about inspiration matches what many would correctly say when they hear a moving sermon and affirm that God was speaking through the pastor and his message to them. That isn't inspiration, nor does Sparks's notion of inspiration match Scripture's concept. It is now quite clear why he can be so certain that Scripture has all sorts of errors. He can easily affirm this because doing so says nothing whatsoever negative about God! God wasn't really involved at all in writing any of this book—only finite, sinful humans were. Hence, we shouldn't be surprised to find the writers attempting to sanction various and sundry atrocities against their enemies while claiming that God commanded his people to carry out such horrors!

In sum, Morriston and Sparks offer two different versions of the same objection to biblical inerrancy. Morriston is outraged by the alleged immorality of ordering genocide, and is certain that a good God wouldn't actually order any nation or person to commit such atrocities. Therefore, the biblical author isn't telling the truth when he claims that God ordered the slaughter of the Canaanites. Either he was inaccurately told that God ordered genocide, or he claimed this himself to justify what Israel did. In neither case did God actually command it, so Scripture can't be inerrant.

While Morriston doesn't present his understanding of inspiration, Sparks does. What Sparks says, however, makes it clear that only humans actually wrote Scripture. God was "somehow" mysteriously involved, but not in any way that actually involved genuine dual authorship of Scripture. Scripture was written by finite, fallible humans, and that is why it has errors of various sorts, including passages that erroneously say that God commanded morally reprehensible actions. The way to defend God's moral perfection is to argue that there are real errors in Scripture, not just apparent ones, but the human authors, not God, are entirely responsible for them. This, according to Sparks, parallels the way we should solve the traditional problem of evil: God is all-loving and omnipotent, despite evil in the world, because God created the world without evil. Evil was not introduced into the world by God, but by the abuse of human free will. Thus, God is exonerated in the face of both of these problems by arguing that there is real evil in the world and there are actual errors in Scripture, but none of that produces any stain on God, because humans exercising their free will are totally responsible for both of these unhappy results (evil in the world and errors in Scripture)!

*Responses*

These complaints are so problematic that it is hard to know where to begin. Since Sparks's version is more compact and has less argumentation, I begin with him. Sparks's first problem, hinted at above, is that his view of inspiration doesn't match biblical teaching on this doctrine. There is mystery about the "how" of inspiration, but we can certainly say more than Sparks does. We definitely shouldn't describe inspiration as a process actually generated by the human authors. Moreover, I should remind readers that I have already addressed how inadequate Sparks's account of divine accommodation in inspiration is, and I needn't repeat it again.

Second, as shown in chapter 7 of this book, Scripture does teach its own inerrancy. Not only does Sparks say nothing about scriptural teaching on this issue, but he offers a view that demands biblical errancy. It requires biblical errancy because, when coupled with Sparks's view of inspiration, it appears to justify God in the face of such errors and in the face of the atrocities biblical writers wrongly claim God approved and ordered. I agree that God needs to be defended on these matters (because critics do point an accusing finger at God), but this isn't the way to do it. The way to defend God can't be one that rejects what his own word says about inspiration and inerrancy!

Third, Sparks thinks what he calls the problem of Scripture parallels the problem of evil that attacks traditional forms of Christian theism, but in one very important way it does not. The different problems of evil that are used to attack Christian theism all assume that the world in which we live was created by God. Some theologies claim that God created the world morally perfect and then his creatures introduced sin into it. Others say that the world as created contained evil, but God isn't morally deficient for creating such a world, for he will eventually use evil to maximize good.[68] All of these theologies agree that God created the world and did so unilaterally. Because he created and sustains our universe, critics claim that he should have the power to remove evil (or to

---

[68] See my *The Many Faces of Evil* for details on these different theologies and their distinct defenses.

create a world without evil in the first place), and so theists need to explain God's morally sufficient reason for not doing so. If they can't offer such a reason, then evil's existence shows that the God who made the world either isn't powerful enough or isn't loving enough to do anything about it. In either case, this means that the God of traditional Christian theism doesn't exist.

In contrast, once one understands Sparks's concept of inspiration and what he says about Scripture's origin, it is clear that Sparks thinks God isn't responsible for creating/producing Scripture at all. Such a view is *not* analogous to God's relation to the world, because he did create the world. In fact, on Sparks's view, the "divine side" of Scripture amounts to nothing more than what we might say about God's relation to a pastor's sermon. God can use both, but just as we don't need to defend God against any errors in the preacher's sermon because God didn't write the sermon, so there is no need to defend God against any errors in Scripture, since on Sparks's account, God didn't actually have anything to do with writing it.

Hopefully, it is clear that the two cases (God's relation to the universe and his relation to Scripture) are not analogous. But even more, because God was actively (not to mention solely) involved in producing and preserving the universe, it makes sense to think that he is in some way accountable for the evil in it, and that he needs to be defended in the face of it. On the other hand, since God, to use Sparks's terminology, merely adopted the biblical writers and their writings but didn't himself participate in the actual production of Scripture, he can't be held accountable for its contents. This is Sparks's defense, but he fails to see that his views on God's relation to the actual writing of Scripture are such that there is nothing to defend! The only way "the problem of Scripture" can be at all analogous to the problem of evil—in fact the only way there can even be a problem of Scripture—is if God actually actively participated in the writing of Scripture. Sparks's understanding of inspiration shows that he thinks God wasn't involved. But, then, there is no "problem of Scripture," and so there is no need to defend God against the charge that he either lied in Scripture or said things that show he is mistaken. On Sparks's view, God is not Scripture's author in any meaningful way that could hold him responsible for its contents. So, the problem of evil isn't analogous to Sparks's "problem of Scripture."

Let us turn to Morriston. Some will likely protest, because I didn't address the issue of genocide as Sparks presents it. However, Morriston presents that matter in more detail, so I can handle it once as it relates to both of them. I note at the outset, however, that Morriston doesn't appeal to the problem of evil, so we can't critique him on those grounds. Moreover, Morriston never actually discusses inspiration, so we don't know how his views on that would fit into what he argues. Even so, what he does say gives ample reason for comment.

Both Morriston and Sparks are confident that God would not order genocide, because it is grossly immoral. But what ethical standard leads them to that conclusion? Morriston, at least, thinks Scripture is on his side, because Jesus summed up the law by saying that we are to love God and our neighbor. Jesus also commanded us to love our enemies and to do good to those who persecute us. Fulfilling those commands, claims Morriston, rules out genocide.

While Jesus certainly did say these things, I think Morriston has to some extent misunderstood them, and to a greater extent has misapplied them. Jesus's comments about loving the enemy and doing good to persecutors refer, in their biblical contexts, to interpersonal relationship, not to the way governments relate to their people or nations relate to one another. What Morriston offers is actually at the heart of what drives pacifists to their views on war. If carried out consistently by governments, these rules would forbid any form of penal system in societies, for anyone who committed a crime should be set free as an act of love. Obviously, this is nonsense, and anyone who holds a form of just war theory also knows that appealing to these rules of interpersonal conduct is unconvincing as an argument against a Christian going to war to protect and defend his country.[69] Moreover, these rules surely don't require a whole nation to remain passive in the face of a moral, spiritual, and military foe that threatens its very existence!

But then, if these Scriptures don't actually justify Morriston's and Sparks's claims about God acting immorally, what does? Neither author ever shares his ethical theory (or its justification), so the most we can say is that God's orders offend their moral sensibilities, and they think readers of Scripture are ethically deficient if they don't agree with such moral assessments. This sounds like "ethical imperialism," that is, without any justification, they present their "proper" ethical assessment, and if we disagree, that shows how morally insensitive we are! Why should anyone agree with such nonsense?

Let's be honest. What is the source of Morriston's and Sparks's complaint? Do they think there shouldn't be rules against idolatry, child sacrifice, temple prostitution, homosexuality, bestiality, and the like? If they reject these moral rules, they never say so. They appear to think such acts are evil, and they don't say that there should be no moral rules forbidding those practices. So what is so offensive, if not the rules? What they find so offensive is the *punishment* that God attached to this notorious incident when a nation was guilty of disobeying a number of these commands. In other words, it is all right to say certain

---

[69] For more details on these positions and the arguments that support them, see John S. Feinberg and Paul D. Feinberg, *Ethics for a Brave New World*, 2nd ed. (Wheaton, IL: Crossway, 2010), the chapter on war.

practices are immoral, as long as you punish those who do them only to the extent that people like Morriston and Sparks think is acceptable.

But when did they become judges of acceptable punishments for breaking God's laws? They appointed themselves to this position, in part because they think that any "moral" person would agree that they are right! But this just isn't the way to determine moral rules and punishments, and certainly not the way to justify them. Morriston complains that Copan tries to wriggle out of the problem by minimizing the extent of the atrocities done to the Canaanites, but by the end of his article Morriston argues that the Canaanites weren't really all that immoral. In fact, since they all just followed what their parents taught them, they really shouldn't be held morally accountable at all! Morriston's claims don't rest on tangible evidence but on inferences he makes from lack of extrabiblical evidence that the Canaanites were all that bad. But this is an inference based on silence, and arguments from silence are rationally bankrupt.

Morriston also tries to minimize the moral evil resident among the Canaanites by arguing that even the Israelites showed a fondness at times for child sacrifice. Anyone who knows logic should recognize this as the fallacy of *tu quoque* (literally, "you, too," i.e., "I may be guilty of something, but that is all right, because you're guilty of the same thing").

Moreover, anyone who knows Scripture knows that Morriston grossly misinterprets passages in Deuteronomy, for example, about being redeemed from being sacrificed. Even more, it is totally wrongheaded to think that the case of Jephthah's daughter in any way shows that Israel was sympathetic to child sacrifice, let alone practiced it. Sadly, when Jephthah made his vow, he wasn't thinking that the first thing out of his house might be a family member. Surely, he was foolish to make the vow, but it is one thing to be guilty of foolishly failing to think of how your vow might be fulfilled (Jephthah's error), and totally another to insinuate that Jephthah must have realized a family member might be the first thing out of his house but wasn't bothered by that since he was fine with human sacrifice. Only on the latter understanding can this incident support Morriston's claim that child sacrifice wasn't completely unheard of among the Israelites, but how can that interpretation possibly be right, given what the text actually says about this incident?

Returning to Morriston and Sparks being bothered by the punishment, not by the moral rules, let us be clear about what Morriston is doing. If Sparks actually believed God was involved in writing Scripture or in preserving it in its current form, I would include Sparks in the following description. Perhaps Sparks does agree with the viewpoint I'll describe, but that isn't clear. Morriston definitely holds what I shall describe.

Morriston believes God can't have the morals required to demand wiping out the Canaanites, so passages that say God commanded it must be wrong. On what grounds does he base this judgment? On his own judgment about what would be appropriate punishment for these immoralities. But he never *justifies* his claim that genocide isn't a proper punishment—I've explained why his appeal to Jesus's teaching won't work, and he offers no other justification of his views. He assumes that he is right and that all will agree, imposes on Scripture his evaluation of the punishment, and concludes that accounts of God commanding genocide are wrong. Please note that if Morriston gets away with this, then anyone should be allowed to dismiss any biblical rule and punishment as immoral and conclude that the biblical writer was wrong in setting forth the rule and/or the punishment and in saying that he records God's command. Hence, we can in effect ignore anything in Scripture we don't like by saying the writer is wrong when he says God told him to say it.

Not only is it incredibly arrogant for creatures to sit in judgment of their creator's morals. It also allows us to ignore whatever we don't like in Scripture, just as many nonbelievers do. I suspect that, in light of Morriston's reaction to this punishment, he would also likely think that sending people to eternal damnation is too harsh a punishment for a finite amount of sin, especially if they never heard the gospel. So, then, only Satan may wind up inhabiting the lake of fire, unless that punishment is deemed too harsh for even him!

Of course, Morriston makes no such claims about eternal punishment for not accepting Christ, etc., but if Morriston is permitted to handle Scripture on this one matter as he does, how can others be prevented from doing the same thing with passages in Scripture that they find offensive? I repeat, neither Morriston nor Sparks ever say that the moral rules involved are wrong—on what grounds could they make that case? Their complaint is that the punishment is too harsh. Even if the Canaanites were not merely benignly immoral, as Morriston argues by the end of his article, he would still think this punishment for sin was too much!

So, how would I justify God in this case, and how would I uphold inerrancy? As to the latter, one doesn't have to agree with what God ordered, to say that the Deuteronomy, etc., passages are inerrant. The author merely reports what God said. We don't have to like the report to say that the writer affirms that God made this command, and that the author is right about God commanding it. Of course, Morriston is so self-assured about his moral judgments that he thinks the author must not be reporting the truth. But what evidence does he offer? Nothing but his own assessment of the morality of the punishment. But why should we agree, especially when it is reported that God decided on the punishment (do we know better than God what is a just punishment?), and especially when the only support offered for Morriston's assessment is his own sense of justice? While Morriston could be right about the author being mistaken about what God ordered, the text gives no evidence of that, and we can't agree with Morriston's assessment just because he thinks he's right and that everyone should see as self-evident that he is right. Backed by no ethical theory or theory of retributive justice, he hasn't made his case!

Some will still think Morriston and Sparks have made the case for their ethical judgment, because everyone should see that genocide is unjust punishment. Are they right, or can God be justified? I think God can be justified, but my approach is not that of either Copan or Craig (though what they say is helpful). The major problem with both Morriston and Sparks is that they underestimate the enormity and heinousness of the sins the Canaanites committed! Here my point is not about the *amount* of their sins, but about God's evaluation of the sins they committed. Neither Morriston nor Sparks seems to notice, but many of the sins they catalogue as present among the Canaanites (idolatry, incest, homosexuality, bestiality, e.g.) are not just forbidden in the Pentateuch. They are called an abomination in God's eyes. The Hebrew word *toebah* for abomination is an extremely strong word, indicating that in God's eyes these are exceptionally heinous and repugnant sins. We, of course, are so used to sin of all kinds, that while any sin seems bad, none of the Canaanite sins probably strikes us as extraordinarily horrid.

But this just shows how comfortable we are with sin around us and how far we are from God's absolute moral perfection! Morriston and Sparks think they know what God should think about these sins and their punishments. How arrogant and ludicrous to think that mere humans know what God's perspective should be unless he has told it to us! This seems to assume that, if we were God, we would see this punishment as outrageous, and since God is more moral than we are, of course he would think it excessive. In truth, we have no idea of what we would think and how we would evaluate these sins if we were God! The only one who knows that is God himself, and if Scripture is God's word (Morriston, at least, doesn't deny that, and Sparks sort of affirms it), then we also know God's evaluation. Mentally and morally finite creatures have no right to assume that they know better than God the proper punishment for anything.

There is one further problem with what Morriston and Sparks say about this punishment. In essence, they claim that it is immoral because it doesn't meet the demands of grace and mercy. That is, God shouldn't have been pleased with the Canaanites' sins, but he should have given them a more gracious punishment. God owed it to them to extend them more grace and mercy than he did—they received none. Neither Morriston nor Sparks makes this point as pointedly as I just have, but they certainly agree with it, for they complain that God's punishment was cruel and unmerciful!

My response is threefold. First, by not punishing each infraction of the moral law immediately, God had already extended them plenty of mercy! Second, remember what Romans 1 and 2 say about natural revelation. Paul says that, from the created universe, everyone knows God exists and knows something about what he is like. Moreover, all have an inborn sense of the moral law written on their hearts. The problem with the unsaved, Paul says, is that they know the truth but suppress it in unrighteousness. No one can say that God is unjust in condemning them because they didn't know the truth about God or his laws. Everyone knows, and we are all without excuse (Rom. 1:20). While some might argue that God would have been unmerciful and unjust to the Canaanites if they had no revelation of his existence and moral rules, that argument is irrelevant, because they did have revelation that renders them guilty.

Finally, this complaint about God not extending enough mercy or grace is totally wrongheaded. Grace is unmerited favor. That means one gets something good that one didn't earn, doesn't deserve, and cannot merit. Since grace and mercy cannot be earned, they also cannot be owed. Hence it is totally wrongheaded to suggest that the Canaanites (or any other sinners) *deserved* more mercy or grace. What we *deserve* is justice, and justice requires that when we break the rules, we must pay. If God chooses graciously to exempt us from paying, that is his right to do. But God owes no one any mercy or grace, so when he doesn't extend it, but gives them justice instead, no one can rightly complain that God failed to give grace that he owed. Grace is never owed to anyone!

So, the only serious complaint is the one with which we started; the punishment (not the rules) was unjust. But, as argued, that proves nothing about whether the punishment was actually unjust. Rather it shows how we as humans minimize the significance of sin, and in so doing we show how far we are both from God's absolute moral perfection and from his evaluation of the heinousness of sin. To sit in judgment of our creator about his morals in effect indicts ourselves for not thinking of sin as God does. But once we realize that, how can we possibly think that Morriston's, Sparks's, or any other human's evaluation of this punishment's justness is correct, unless it accepts God's evaluation? They haven't shown that God has done anything wrong in ordering the destruction of the Canaanites. Hence, they haven't demonstrated that Scripture is in error on this matter of morality. That doesn't mean that these aren't "hard" passages of Scripture, but it does mean that these critics haven't made their case.[70]

---

[70] Readers may still wonder how I would justify God against the charge of unjust genocide. In fact, they may think that unless I can justify God, Scriptures that say God ordered destroying the Canaanites must be wrong. However, just because someone disagrees with how we can understand God's orders as just, that no more proves that

CONCLUSION

In chapters 8 and 9 I have considered what I believe to be the most significant objections to biblical inerrancy. Some are biblical/textual; others are more doctrinal/theological in nature. Yet others are historical, and still others are more conceptual/philosophical. I have tried to represent each objection accurately, in some cases quoting its proponent at length. I don't intend to suggest that there are no other possible objections to inerrancy, nor that there won't be future challenges to it. Rather, my contention is that the most significant current objections to inerrancy can be answered and that I have done so. Moreover, my explanation of the concept of inerrancy and its defense, presented in chapter 7, when taken together with answers to the most significant objections against it, lead me to conclude that the Bible is the inspired and inerrant word of God!

---

Scriptures about God giving the order are wrong than it would be correct to say that Scriptures which claim that God created the universe in seven days are wrong because we must then interpret the days as literal twenty-four hour days but we think science proves that it took much longer than a literal week to produce Planet Earth and its inhabitants. What is my point? It is that, in both cases mentioned, the question is how to interpret a given Scripture, and there is supposedly a problem with the "traditional" interpretation because of something extrabiblical that allegedly falsifies the traditional understanding. But the proper interpretation of a text must be grounded in the text itself, not in some extrabiblical claim that is allegedly true which, if adapted, seems to contradict what Scripture says. What does this mean about the complaint that God ordering the destruction of the Canaanites must not be factual? It means either that the *objector's assessment* of what is morally right for God to order is incorrect—and in that case, this objection amounts to nothing. Or the objector's assessment is correct, and then the defender of inerrancy does need to explain how (in this case) God's command can be morally right. If so, I note first that this actually raises the problem of evil, but not every problem of evil. Specifically, it raises the problem of apparently gratuitous evil. And, I would argue, this objection also bears a likeness to the problem of hell, for that problem claims that the punishment (everlasting) far exceeds the crime (disobeying God and not accepting his salvation, it is argued, does not merit eternal, unending punishment).

The answers to these problems of evil can't be stated simply in a few sentences. However, I have handled the problem of apparently gratuitous evil, the problem of hell, and many other problems of evil in an extensive work based on my doctoral dissertation. That work is *The Many Faces of Evil* (Wheaton, IL: Crossway, 2004), and I encourage readers to read it. In that work you will find extensive defenses, for example, of how it can be just (and logically consistent) for an all-powerful, all-loving God to allow/impose a never-ending punishment.

# DIVINE COMMANDING LIGHT

## The Authority of Scripture

Ours is not a time of great respect for authority. Of course, those who possess authority expect compliance from those under their power. But for most people, including many evangelical Christians, personal freedom and liberty are avidly pursued virtues. So it is difficult for many in our day to comply with the demands of those in authority.

If submitting to an individual is deemed a marginal virtue (if a virtue at all), the idea of a religious authority one must obey is even harder to swallow for many of our contemporaries. This is especially so when the religious authority is a religion's book. If one believes, for example, that the Bible is merely a human book written long ago, then it is easy to dismiss it as a book of little relevance and value in our day. The Bible presents a worldview, and it addresses matters that each person must think about, but how can it have a right to prescribe what we should think and do when it was written in times and situations so different from ours?

Still, those committed to Scripture's divine inspiration and inerrancy understand that if the Bible actually is God's word, then it must be the guidebook for living in relation to God and others. Throughout the centuries of church history, at least the Christian church has said that Scripture is God's authoritative word, even if attending to its teachings and obeying them haven't always accompanied affirming Scripture's authority. In fact, the Reformers' disagreement with Roman Catholicism, at least in part, was about who and what should be the final authority for Christians in matters pertaining to God and our relation to him individually and collectively (as the church).

Somewhere in discussing the evangelical doctrine of Scripture one will likely hear the phrase *sola Scriptura*! This is not a mere slogan, but rather a precise summary of one of the main issues of the Protestant Reformation. Prior to the Reformation, it was an age of authority. There were political authorities to whose whims most of the populace was subject. There were also ecclesiastical authorities, especially the Roman Catholic Church, its clergy, and its hierarchy, culminating in the pope. Church tradition was also held to be an authority, and of course, Scripture was believed to have some authority in matters of faith and practice.

Unfortunately, all too often clerical and papal authority, plus church tradition, trumped Scripture's authority. When Martin Luther realized that his interpretation of key Scriptures and doctrines didn't match those of the church, trouble was brewing. It is likely that other Catholic priests disagreed with the church on some matter of doctrine, but most dissidents kept silent. Luther's temperament was different, but his revolt wasn't simply a matter of having an aggressive personality. Luther's study of Scripture convinced him that the church was wrong about some of the most important doctrines, like how to establish and maintain a right relation with God. In addition, by elevating church tradition and clergy, including the pope, above Scripture's authority, the church all but guaranteed that there was little hope of correcting theological error.

Luther felt compelled to protest. His posting of the Ninety-five Theses was not in itself unusual; academics often posted theses for debate with other academics, just as Luther had done. But the content of Luther's Theses, the debates that ensued, and what was at stake were not the usual matters of an ordinary medieval *disputatio*. Eventually, Luther was brought before the Diet of Worms in April, 1521, and was ordered to recant his doctrinal views about justification and about ecclesial and biblical authority. His reply left no doubt about the source of authority for him:

> Since then Your Majesty and your lordships desire a simple reply, I will answer without horns and without teeth. Unless I am convicted by Scripture and plain reason—I do not accept the authority of popes and councils, for they have contradicted each other—my conscience is captive to the Word of God. I cannot and I will not recant anything, for to go against conscience is neither right nor safe. God help me. Amen.[1]

As you can see, for the Reformers *sola Scriptura* was not just a slogan. And that has been true of evangelical Christians thereafter.

Not all Protestants, however, have taken that tack. In light of the withering critique of Scripture via historical criticism, many have rejected Scripture as inspired and inerrant, let alone authoritative. During the twentieth century

---

[1] Roland H. Bainton, *Here I Stand: A Life of Martin Luther* (New York: Mentor, 1955), 144, quoted in Richard L. Mayhue, "The Authority of Scripture," *MSJ* 15 (Fall 2004): 227.

neoorthodoxy arose. Having digested biblical criticism's handling of Scripture, but also recognizing the bankruptcy of liberalism, Karl Barth and his followers took a different view of Scripture. In his *Church Dogmatics* Barth wrote about biblical authority:

> Why and wherein does the Biblical witness possess authority? Precisely in this, that it claims no authority at all for itself, that its witness consists in allowing that Other Thing to be itself and through itself the authority. Hence we do the Bible a misdirected honour, and one unwelcome to itself, if we directly identify it with this Other Thing, the revelation itself. This can happen . . . in the form of a doctrine of the general and uniform inspiration of the Bible.[2]

For Barth, the Bible's authority is purely derived from its function, and that function is to point to God himself, that "Other Thing" by which Barth meant revelation (for Barth, God in personal encounter with us through Jesus Christ is revelation), who is the real authority. In and of itself, Scripture has no authority, and it is easy to see why Barth held that view. If Scripture has authority in itself, there must be a reason, and the reason evangelicals have always given is that it is God's word. But if biblical and historical criticism are right about all the errors in Scripture, how could the words of Scripture be divine revelation? God wouldn't lie, nor could he be mistaken about anything. So, for the neoorthodox, Scripture cannot be God's word and so it can't be authoritative in itself. Even so, Barth didn't abandon Scripture altogether, for he believed it was an able witness or signpost to revelation, despite its errors and humanness.

As the twentieth century moved on, at least Western cultures increasingly imbibed the spirit of postmodernism. Postmoderns typically reject any sort of foundationalism, i.e., the view that some set of ideas, some person(s), some organization(s) are the ultimate reference point against which the truth, power, and authority of all else must be judged. As a result, we live at a time increasingly characterized by rejection of all authority. Hence, for many it is unthinkable that any religious belief or book should be the ultimate arbiter in disputes about anything. The mood of our times is one of rampant individualism, emphasizing what is true "for me," and that usually means whatever approach to life increases my enjoyment and reduces my pain, suffering, and inconvenience.

Even so, evangelical Christians still care about divine authority, and they cannot overturn the commonsense conclusion that if God, the highest authority, has given us his word, it must have authority over us. So, how should we address the topic of biblical authority? Scripture assumes its own authority, and there is a biblical and theological case to be made for it, but Scripture

---

[2] Karl Barth, *Die kirchliche Dogmatik* (München, 1932), 115, quoted in John Baillie, *The Idea of Revelation in Recent Thought* (New York: Columbia University Press, 1964), 34–35.

defines neither authority in general nor biblical authority in particular. Hence we should begin by clarifying those notions.

## The Concept of Authority

In addressing biblical authority, we must not adopt a notion of it that is ad hoc, created solely to fit Scripture, but irrelevant to anything and anyone else possessing authority. I propose that we begin by identifying the bases upon which authority of various sorts is founded. In short, I believe that authority depends in part on the person or thing that possesses authority. A person, an institution, an idea, etc., may each possess authority. But the basis of each's authority is not necessarily the same. Let me explain.

First, consider the authority of an idea or concept. There is a relationship between the idea's truth and its authority. Specifically, whatever is true, in a correspondence sense of "true," is authoritative, just because it is true. Something is true in this sense, because it matches the world in which we live. Now, undoubtedly at times we wish the world "worked" differently so that we could do things we fantasize about. But, like it or not, we must live in the real world as it is, not in a fantasy world.

This point has nothing to do with the person who has the idea or makes a claim that uses the concept. What makes someone an authority is at the very least that he or she can back up his or her views with evidence that shows their views to be true. So, ideas have authority if they are true. We may resist truth, but we must live in the real world, and in the real world truth matters.

Readers will immediately see the relevance of this to Scripture's authority. Every Scripture capable of bearing truth has authority in virtue of its being true. But what about the rest of Scripture? Do biblical sentences that are neither true nor false have no authority? Does only truth have authority?

Though we might think so, it is not so. Sometimes documents, laws, practices, etc., that are false, or based on falsehoods, still have authority for other reasons. For example, many believe that the US Supreme Court's decision to legalize abortion on demand is morally wrong and based on false ideas. Still, the Supreme Court used its authority to legitimize this immoral practice. Sadly, as individual citizens acting alone we have no authority to change the laws. Even if some who reject abortion are elected to governmental office, the majority of elected officials may be proabortion, and so officials who are antiabortion cannot overturn the laws and court decisions that legalized abortion.

So, the authority of an idea can't be reduced just to its truth. Moreover, the authority of an institution and of a person are seldom based solely on whether it tells the truth or not. Having authority also stems in part from having or holding a position which by its nature imbues the thing or the person who holds it with power to tell people how and what to think and how to act. Thus, an authority figure's commands, though neither true nor false, have authority in virtue of the power granted him or her by holding a position of power/authority. An idea's authority may stem also from its being held by someone in a position to choose the idea to be believed, even if the idea is false. Coordinately, a true idea may have and exercise little authority if the idea is rejected by those with power to ban or enforce the idea.

The above suggests a third element that can be a basis of authority. Someone in authority has authority if he or she has power to *enforce* whatever he or she demands. Authority to make binding laws without the power to enforce them is merely a "paper" authority. Genuine authority stems from being able to enforce whatever ideas and rules are binding on those under authority.

Let us "test" these second and third elements of authority by seeing if and how they apply to people in positions of authority. Think initially of a parent. A parent commands her children to obey certain rules and to perform certain chores around the home. The child must obey not because the rules and requirements are true (commands are neither true nor false), but because a parent's position in the family gives her the right to make demands and expect obedience from her children.

Likewise, a teacher has authority over her pupils, regardless of their age and the course subject, because her position as teacher comes with the power to present course content, without interruptions by students that would make doing so impossible, and to require students to write papers, do reading, take tests, etc. Moreover, being the teacher comes with authority to decide on a grading scale for course work. Students may dislike a teacher's grading scale, but in virtue of her rights as teacher, she can resist making changes.

Similar comments are true of the authority of a CEO of a corporation, a president of a university, a state congress member, or an official of the federal government. In addition, we should apply these concepts to the position of a divine being. Some religions' deities are little more than projections of human characteristics. Their authority is minimal, so each has only so much power to enforce his or her will and wishes on other gods (think here of the Greco-Roman pantheon of gods) or humans. Even if there is a supreme god, that doesn't mean the other gods can't or won't try to defy the supreme one. And, sometimes a lesser deity may even win "the contest" with a higher one.

The God of Scripture is different in many respects. The fact that he is the only God is only part of the story. Were he weak in will and/or in power, the fact that he has no other divine competitors wouldn't amount to much. But the God of Scripture is accountable to no one above him (there is no such being) or below him. He knows all truth, so he knows what is best (and worst) for every existing thing, and he has power to enforce his wishes. When he chooses not to enforce what he knows is correct, that decision comes solely from his own will. He has the power to decide the rules, enforce them, and punish those who disobey. He also knows what is right, and he has the right to expect us to conform our thinking and behavior to his standards.

All of these points suggest something further. Specifically, if this God speaks to us, we must listen. We must take his words seriously, and we must adjust our thinking and behavior to match his wishes. Hence, Scripture, as God's word, has authority not just because its statements are true. Even sentences that affirm or assert nothing still have authority, because they are the words of the highest power there is. As such, God has the right to be heard and obeyed, and he has power to enforce his word and will.

In sum, there are three sources of/elements in someone's or something's authority. The first is its truth, in cases where it makes sense to speak of truth or falsity. The second is, in virtue of the position she/he/it holds (a position which in its very nature is authoritative), the right and power to tell us whatever she/he/it wants to say and to expect us to learn it and to obey whatever it commands. The third element of authority is the right and power to enforce punishment when we disobey the requirement(s) and to dispense reward when we obey. Of course, people defy authority figures all the time, and sometimes in a dispute, the "rebel" can win. But this cannot be so with God and his authority. Those who blaspheme him can do so only because he holds their wits together from one end of a blasphemous sentence to the other. Those who defy him may not be punished immediately, but God is longsuffering, not "forever suffering"! Judgment will come eventually, if disobedience does not end.

Before defining biblical authority, let me add two further points about authority in general. First, we can distinguish between an *ontological* and a *functional* sense of authority. By the former, I mean that authority is possessed by someone or something, regardless of whether it is ever used. Functional authority refers to whether someone or something functions in a situation as something/someone that has authority (as defined ontologically). Sometimes a person, idea, etc., functions as if it possessed authority, even though it doesn't actually have it. It is also possible to have authority or be authoritative (in the ontological sense), and never use it, so that you don't function as one in authority. Of course, often a person or thing with authority also functions authoritatively.

Second, there is a difference between *intrinsic* and *extrinsic* authority. To illustrate, if you accept a suggestion because the person offering it is an authority on such matters or because she has power to make you follow the suggestion (e.g., a teacher might have power to require students to use a certain style of writing for their current assignment), then you obey in virtue of authority extrinsic to the suggestion itself. On the other hand, you may follow the suggestion because it is inherently the appropriate thing to do, as anyone who understands the suggestion can easily see. As to biblical authority, the Bible might possess authority intrinsically because what it says is self-evidently true, wise, etc. Or, some might think the Bible authoritative because they believe it to be God's word, and they believe God has supreme authority. What the Bible says may also be true and wise, but it is the person who "spoke" it that makes us obey it.[3]

## DEFINING BIBLICAL AUTHORITY

Scripture uses various words for authority (*toqeph* in Hebrew and *exousia* in Greek), but none of the passages that use these terms define them or relate them to the authority of the Bible itself. While this does not mean that Scripture doesn't and can't teach anything about biblical authority, it does mean that we can't define biblical authority simply by appealing to a Scripture or two.

It is tempting just to say that the Bible is authoritative because it is true, and truth is always authoritative. But that would cover only sentences that can bear truth. As we have seen, some sentences (e.g., commands, questions, and many interjections) cannot bear truth. However, we want to say that all of Scripture is authoritative, not just its affirmations. So, Scripture's truth plus something more must be the keys to its authority. Consider the following:

> As the word of the supreme authority in the universe, the Bible's authority is consequently its right or entitlement over all creatures, including humans, to command action or compliance, or to determine belief or custom, expecting assent and obedience from those under authority, so they conform to what Scripture intends them to know and do. As the word of the supreme authority in the universe, what it teaches and demands will be enforced by the one who revealed it. As true, it has this authority because it accurately says what is true in the universe all living beings inhabit. Everything Scripture says possesses this authority.

Scripture is authoritative, then, because, as the word of the supreme authority in the universe, God, it has the right to command thought and behavior, and its divine author has the right and power to enforce compliance. It is also authoritative in that its truth cannot be successfully resisted, for we must all live in the real world, not a fantasy world. Hence, to say that Scripture is inerrant is not to say the same thing as attributing to it authority. Moreover, authority covers all of Scripture, while inerrancy covers only those Scriptures that can bear truth. It is in no way a defect, however, that authority extends

---

[3] See Richard Bauckham's especially helpful discussion of the difference between intrinsic and extrinsic authority in "Scripture and Authority," *Transformation* 15 (April 1998): 5–6.

to more of Scripture than does inerrancy. It only shows that we recognize that, while not every kind of sentence can be true or false, every sentence can have authority.[4]

## CLARIFYING THE DEFINITION

While this definition is a good start in clarifying biblical authority, it leaves some important issues unclear. First, does it mean that Scripture actually possesses authority as defined, or does Scripture's authority reside in the way(s) it is used to accomplish the various things mentioned in the definition? That is, is biblical authority ontological or purely functional? If biblical authority is part of Scripture's very nature (ontological), we would expect it to function authoritatively on many occasions, even if it is not always allowed to do so. Second, is the Bible's authority intrinsic to it, extrinsic, or both? Third, does the Bible's authority cover any and every subject, or is its authority limited to only certain topics? Fourth, how much of Scripture is authoritative today, or at any time since it began to exist?

I also note that neither the definition of biblical authority nor the questions just raised suggest how the Bible might be used authoritatively in the church (and also outside it). But this is an important question, for it would help to know what things we should want to do with Scripture, given its authority. Let me further explain the concept of biblical authority by answering the questions raised above, and by addressing the proper use of Scripture in light of its authority.

### Ontological or Functional Authority?

Is the authority of Scripture ontological or functional? This question logically precedes the others. Theologians disagree about the answer. Historically, the more theologically conservative wings of the church have held that authority is inherent in Scripture. Of course, given its inherent authority, proponents

---

[4] Kevin J. Vanhoozer, "The Semantics of Biblical Literature: Truth and Scripture's Diverse Literary Forms," in *Hermeneutics, Authority, and Canon*, ed. D. A. Carson and John D. Woodbridge (Grand Rapids, MI: Zondervan, 1986), 94, takes matters a bit further. Applying speech act theory, he explains how the different kinds of speech acts express authority, and the kind of response each type of act expects. Also, in defining both authority in general and biblical authority in particular, I found extremely helpful the following: Richard L. Mayhue, "The Authority of Scripture," *MSJ* 15 (Fall 2004): 227–229, 232, 234–236. Also noteworthy are J. Christiaan Beker, "The Authority of Scripture: Normative or Incidental?," *ThTo* 49 (1992): 376–377, 381–382; Douglas Blount, "The Authority of Scripture," in *Reason for the Hope Within*, ed. Michael J. Murray (Grand Rapids, MI: Eerdmans, 1999), 403–404; David Dockery, "Biblical Inerrancy: Pro or Con?," *The Theological Educator* 37 (Spring 1988): 15, 25–27; Francis S. Fiorenza, "The Crisis of Scriptural Authority," *Interpretation* 44 (April 1990): 359, 361ff.; Stephen R. Holmes, "Evangelical Doctrines of Scripture in Transatlantic Perspective," *EvQ* 81 (2009): 45, 47–48, 51–52, 57–58, 62; Theresa F. Koernke, "The Authority and Function of Scripture in Catholic Tradition," in *Ancient Faith and American-Born Churches*, ed. Ted A. Campbell, Ann K. Riggs, and Gilbert W. Stafford (New York: Paulist, 2006), 249; Eugene Ulrich, "From Literature to Scripture: Reflections on the Growth of a Text's Authoritativeness," *Dead Sea Discoveries* 10 (2003): 7–8; and Jonathan R. Wilson, "Toward a New Evangelical Paradigm of Biblical Authority," in *The Nature of Confession: Evangelicals and Postliberals in Conversation*, ed. Timothy R. Phillips and Dennis L. Okholm (Downers Grove, IL: InterVarsity Press, 1996).

believe that it should *function* authoritatively in the lives of all people, but that even if Scripture is ignored entirely, it still has authority.

On the other hand, others have believed that Scripture's authority is best understood in terms of how people (believers and unbelievers) let it function in their lives. Since many in our world either ignore or thoroughly reject Scripture's teachings, for them Scripture has no authority at all. It can't function authoritatively in their lives, so of course, there can be no question of whether it inherently possesses any authority whatsoever.

David Scott is someone who sees Scripture's authority as functional. Speaking about authority in general in contemporary culture, Scott admits that he starts with certain assumptions. As is quite clear, those assumptions rule out the possibility that anyone's or anything's authority might reside in its possessing some inherent quality or characteristic. He writes,

> Authority is a way people are willing to regard institutions, texts, other people, namely to let them guide their believing and acting. I assume, but cannot argue here, that the phenomenon of authority changes through time. Authority is not a substance or an object. Whatever else it may be, authority is a subjective disposition in people to regard something else as a reliable guide in thinking and doing. Because all authority has this relational character, the authority of the Bible is subject to social, historical and cultural change. What, why and how people regard anything, including the Bible, as authoritative changes through time.[5]

The crucial point in Scott's view is that authority is a *subjective disposition* to regard something (or someone) as a reliable guide to thought and action (I would add that in many cases, the perspective Scott describes is that something or someone is a mandatory guide, regardless of how reliable it/he/she is deemed to be). I don't deny that for anyone or anything, including Scripture, to play an authoritative role in someone's life, what Scott describes is necessary. But that is beside the point of whether the thing or person in question has any authority apart from the subjective attitude of those who obey it/him/her. In essence, Scott's view means that Scripture would have little or no authority if people didn't consider it a reliable guide (and a mandatory one) to govern thought and action. This is probably true of how humans have regarded and treated Scripture, but it doesn't answer whether Scripture, apart from how people esteem, reject, or ignore it, actually does possess the quality of authority.

At issue here is whether authority is *only* a relational concept, and can't govern a person or thing in itself/herself/himself apart from any relations they (or it) may have. In a way, this discussion is similar to the discussion about the concept of revelation. Some believe that nothing has been revealed until

---

[5] David A. Scott, "Teaching the Authority of the Bible," *Anglican Theological Review* 84 (Winter 2002): 13.

someone receives what has been transmitted. Here the claim is that nothing has authority unless those thought to be under authority recognize the person or thing as having authority and hence recognize an obligation to think and/ or act in a certain way. As to revelation, we saw that although God's revelation has been ignored and/or rejected, that doesn't mean God has not spoken. Revelation has been given, even if everyone ignores it. Of course, for revelation to help anyone, they must attend to it, making sure they understand it, and then act accordingly.

Similarly, authority is a relational concept. It makes no sense to claim that someone has, for example, political and governmental authority, but possesses neither a realm nor a people to rule. Having authority over that kind of "kingdom" amounts to very little. Similarly, Scripture's right to govern how we think and behave changes little if humans are either ignorant of its contents or know what it says but refuse to follow it.

Does this mean that Scripture's authority is *exclusively* a function of whether people assent to its teaching and live their lives accordingly? Views like Scott's answer affirmatively. But then, on this view, nothing about the book *in itself* suggests that it has any authority.

So, is Scripture's authority ontological or functional? Evangelicals have historically held that Scripture possesses authority intrinsically, and thus, ontologically, this book is authoritative. Of course, Scripture also functions authoritatively in the lives of those who embrace it, but allowing Scripture to play this role is not at all why Scripture *in itself* possesses authority. Scripture is authoritative because of what it is—the true word of an absolutely sovereign God. In holding that view, I believe that evangelicals are right.

Why do I (and, I believe, many other evangelicals) see authority as an ontological quality of Scripture? There are two main reasons for thinking this. First, Scripture has God as its divine author. That is, Scripture's inspiration leads evangelicals to believe in its authority. This is so because God, as supreme lawgiver and judge, possesses supreme authority. Thus, what he thinks and says possesses authority.

So, the first reason that evangelicals believe Scripture is ontologically authoritative is its divine author. His authority imbues his words with authority both to command and to enforce whatever he requires and teaches. This first reason for Scripture's ontological authority covers all of Scripture, regardless of whether a text is an assertion, a question, a command, an exclamation, or anything else.

Second, Scripture's authority is ontological because of Scripture's inerrancy. We defined inerrancy in terms of truth. Not every kind of sentence can bear truth, but assertions can, and Scripture contains many assertions. In the chapters on inerrancy, I offered evidence for biblical inerrancy. As already explained in this chapter, whatever is true possesses authority. We may resist and reject the truth, but we cannot indefinitely ignore it, and we certainly can't overturn it.

In sum, Scripture's authority is ontological. This is so because of two of its characteristics: (1) it is the word of the supremely authoritative being in the universe; and (2) its affirmations are totally true. Neither quality depends on any creature's subjective dispositions, opinions, or anything else!

*Intrinsic versus Extrinsic Authority*

Is Scripture's authority intrinsic or extrinsic? This is a corollary point to Scripture's authority as ontological and not merely functional. As can be understood, it is often liberals who refuse to see Scripture as God's inspired and/or inerrant word who espouse an extrinsic view of biblical authority. As already presented, David Scott understands authority as extrinsic, stemming from people's willingness to regard it as authoritative. What makes them see Scripture as authoritative is, according to Scott, historically conditioned.[6] Scott doesn't mention things that move people in this direction, but it isn't hard to construct such a list. For one thing, a decision by a religious leader (e.g., a pope) or even by a whole church (e.g., the Roman Catholic Church) to regard this book as authoritative can result in its being authoritative, not only for members of that church, but also for everyone, believers and nonbelievers alike, if the church is dominant in a society.

A culture's mores and mind-set may also be extrinsic factors that move people to view Scripture authoritatively. In its colonial period and for much of its first two centuries as a nation, a Judeo-Christian worldview rooted in Scripture has been a common presupposition of American society and life. This doesn't mean every American was saved or that they always obeyed Scripture. Rather, a worldview based on Scripture's teachings was the assumed mind-set of American society, and out of that mind-set citizens passed laws and also decided what kinds of behavior would be acceptable and what kinds unacceptable. By the end of the twentieth century that mind-set was not only under attack but was rejected by many Americans. Hence, to say that abortion, for example, is wrong because Scripture teaches that human life at any stage of development qualifies as a person and deserves respect and protection no longer resonates with many in our culture. Even many who are antiabortion wouldn't build a case against it by appealing to Scripture.

What I have just said about American attitudes toward abortion is also true of homosexual and lesbian sexual relations and marriages. A recent US

---

[6] Ibid., 15.

Supreme Court decision legalized gay marriage. Needless to say, the biblical perspective on these matters, even if carrying some authority, was rejected in the Court's ultimate decision. Whether the Court was most influenced by pressure from the gay and lesbian community, alleged scientific evidence that this alternate form of sexual expression is inborn and neither learned nor based on a decision, a commitment to personal liberty in all activities that don't limit the liberty of others, or by some or even all of these matters wasn't clarified publicly when the Court announced its decision.

I raise these examples to show how considerations extrinsic to Scripture can be why people consider it authoritative, not authoritative, or an authority but not the supreme one. Another extrinsic factor that may give something authority is its function or use. As for Scripture, some people consider it authoritative because in following its teachings, they have found joy, happiness, and success in life in general or in a particular venture. Others esteem it because in times of tragedy, only in Scripture have they found comfort and strength to go on.

What about characteristics intrinsic to Scripture that have caused people to consider it authoritative? Here one can point to many things, some already raised in our broader discussion. For example, many believe Scripture is authoritative because of its divine author. Since they consider God to have authority more than anyone or anything else, Scripture is for them supremely authoritative.[7] Others point to Scripture's truthfulness as the ground of its authority.

Yet others identify specific contents of Scripture as the reason for its authority. For example, John Stott mentions Scripture's inspiration, but he also notes its role in making Christ known to us, i.e., it is a witness to Jesus's life and teachings.[8] As a result, it is authoritative. And, then, some view Scripture as authoritative because Jesus himself did. They reason that whatever Christ favors, we must favor as well.

As to this last reason, it isn't entirely clear whether it is an extrinsic or intrinsic factor, or both. We learn of Jesus's life and teachings in Scripture, but he is not Scripture himself. Hence, his affirmation of Scripture's authority seems to be extrinsic. On the other hand, he is one of Scripture's authors, and his life and teachings take up extensive and important parts of Scripture. And in Scripture we learn of his view that Scripture is supremely authoritative. As God, he couldn't be wrong about anything, including Scripture's worth, accuracy, and authority.

[7] For example, J. I. Packer sees the Christian's authority to be God through Christ. Christ exercises authority through Scripture by revealing to us "God's mind and will." See Gatiss's description of Packer's book, in Lee Gatiss, "Biblical Authority in Recent Evangelical Books," *Churchman* 120 (2006): 328. Packer's book is *Truth and Power: The Place of Scripture in the Christian Life* (Wheaton, IL: Harold Shaw, 1996).
[8] Gatiss, "Biblical Authority in Recent Evangelical Books," 322. Gatiss discusses John Stott's *Evangelic Truth: A Personal Plea for Unity* (Leicester: InterVarsity Press, 1999).

What, then, should we say? Is Scripture's authority intrinsic, extrinsic, or both? As for extrinsic grounds of authority, I certainly wouldn't deny the extrabiblical factors detailed above that grant Scripture authority. However, careful consideration of those factors shows them to be, so to speak, sociological factors that explain how authoritative Scripture is considered to be, and to a certain extent why individuals and groups of people think it so. If Scripture's authority rests only or even mainly on extrinsic factors, then its authority isn't a result of any quality inherent in it.

However, as demonstrated in earlier chapters, Scripture is God's inspired word, and it is entirely truthful. Those two characteristics are intrinsic to this book. It is hard to see how any book with either or both of those qualities would not possess authority. Hence, Scripture's divine author and its truth are the grounds of its authority.

In sum, Scripture's authority stems ultimately from factors internal to it. Because of these qualities, there are also extrinsic grounds for the authority it has and exercises in individual lives, in churches, and in societies in general.

## The Scope of Biblical Authority

What about the scope of biblical authority? That is, how much of Scripture is authoritative, which of its subjects are authoritative, and during which era(s) have its contents possessed that authority?

In reply, I offer three basic points about the scope of biblical authority. First, since Scripture possesses authority inherently because of its divine author and its truthfulness, all of Scripture is authoritative. Individual words, apart from a linguistic context, do not refer to *specific objects or states of affairs in our universe*, but sentences do. God is the divine author of every sentence in Scripture. God's position as creator, sustainer, and moral governor of the universe is by itself enough to grant every sentence of Scripture authority. In addition, many of Scripture's sentences can bear truth or falsity.[9] All the biblical sentences that have that capacity are true, and since truth has authority, those biblical sentences possess authority *both* because of their divine author *and* because of their truth. As for biblical sentences that cannot bear truth (e.g., commands, exclamations, questions), they have authority, too. Since God is the supreme authority, whatever he says has full authority. Hence, even sentences that can't bear truth are *equally* authoritative as the rest of Scripture.

Even so, is Scripture authoritative on every topic whatsoever? This is my second point. The answer is negative, but that is no reason for worry or concern.

---

[9] For a more complete explanation about which types of sentences can and which can't bear truth, see my "Truth: Relationship of Theories of Truth to Hermeneutics," in *Hermeneutics, Inerrancy, and the Bible*, ed. Earl Radmacher and Robert Preus (Grand Rapids, MI: Zondervan, 1984).

That Scripture isn't authoritative for topics like astrophysics, algebra or geometry, or home decorating in no way denigrates Scripture's importance and value. Nor is Scripture a treatise about the most compelling and powerful writing styles. And it doesn't say much of anything about how to play and win a particular sport.

While Scripture covers many subjects, it doesn't cover all. In fact, Scripture doesn't even say everything that could be said about topics it does address. The Gospels, for example, recount many events in Jesus's life, but they don't offer a moment-by-moment account of everything that happened to him and everything he did. We might be interested to know certain things about Jesus (e.g., what was his favorite color, what was his favorite food and his favorite way to relax?), but Scripture says nothing about those things. The same is true of other people mentioned in Scripture. Nor does Scripture record every event in the history of whole nations like Israel.

This point may seem self-evident or of little significance to anyone at all familiar with Scripture. But I think it is significant, because it means that Scripture doesn't have to cover all possible topics, nor exhaustively cover the topics it does address, in order to be authoritative. God certainly knows more than the contents of Scripture, but for Scripture to be authoritative it doesn't have to contain everything God knows. Its divine author and its truthfulness make it supremely authoritative.

A third point about biblical authority's scope relies on an insight from Brian Walsh. Any book with God as one of its authors (or even its only author) would possess authority, just as a book whose contents are true has authority. Even so, the book might be of little interest and significance if it addressed subjects of little import to key questions about life, death, and eternity. Hence, a book about how to make sturdy shoes would have some significance for one's health, well-being, and comfort, but few would consider it a must-read if they wanted to know how to decide whom to marry, what life career to pursue, etc. Advice on any of those things is important, but knowing how to make sturdy shoes won't help on those decisions. But discussions about marriage, career, etc. (and many other matters) are significant, and so are Scripture's main themes and teachings. As Walsh puts it, Scripture is a worldview text of ultimacy. This means that

> Like the divine authority it mediates, the Bible doesn't address only one dimension of life; it addresses all of life. What kind of text can do such a thing? Only a text, I submit, that addresses questions of ultimacy. James Olthuis describes texts of ultimacy as 'certitudinal' in character. Such texts "have one overriding kind of preoccupation: calling to commitment, engendering faith, promoting hope, encouraging and exhorting certitude."[10]

---

[10] Brian J. Walsh, "Reimaging Biblical Authority," *CSR* 26 (Winter 1996): 211. Walsh cites J. H. Olthuis, *A Hermeneutics of Ultimacy* (Lanham, MD: University Press of America, 1986), 24.

One need not agree with everything Walsh says (nor with everything in Olthuis's book) to see that his point is very important. Scripture's subject matter is not just of marginal or negligible import. Its topics are extremely important to life on earth and life thereafter. Why does anything exist, why was *I* born, how should we conduct ourselves while on earth, and what happens after we die? Everyone has a vested interest in answers to such questions. Scripture's authority over everyone stems in part from its teachings about these topics. It has a certain *gravitas* that a book about lesser issues can't have.

Unfortunately, many overlook and/or reject what Scripture teaches, but they cannot do so forever. When they finally realize that this is no ordinary book and that its contents matter supremely, the time and circumstance to accept the Lord and Savior Scripture so vividly and magnificently presents may be gone forever. But because Scripture offers God's answers to ultimate issues, it is supremely authoritative.

## Applicability of Scripture's Authority

Fourth, to say that all of Scripture has ultimate authority doesn't mean that all of Scripture always has applied, does apply, or even always will apply. For example, the OT system of blood sacrifices as offerings for the various purposes required during the OT era no longer applies to us. The NT clearly teaches that Jesus's death was the final sacrifice for sin, so no further blood sacrifices are or will be required to be right with God.

Despite some changes in God's rules and expectations for us, one thing remains constant: at various times in history God gave new revelation about what we need to know and do to have a right relationship with him. Whatever God reveals, we must believe and obey. Otherwise, there will be divine judgment.

Even so, Christians must ask whether a given Scripture passage applies today, and if it does, how it applies. This is true even for some texts Christians assume always apply. Consider, for example, the Great Commission to preach the gospel to everyone. Though you won't find it or its exact equivalent in the OT, it is wrong to think that during the OT era there was no "gospel," no "good news" of how to have a proper relationship with God. In the OT era, despite her failure to do so, God intended Israel to be a light, a witness, to the Gentiles (e.g., Isa. 42:6; 49:6).

Since Christ's first advent, the need to evangelize the lost has been clearly known by those who heard Jesus's teaching and by any who were told of or read Jesus's command to spread the gospel. As history moves toward the end of this age, people will still need to hear about Christ. Even during Christ's millennial reign, people will be born, and they will need to hear and believe the gospel to be saved.[11]

Will the Great Commission still be in force for all eternity? We might think so, but we should think again. Life on this earth as we know it will eventually end. Revelation 19:11ff. speaks of Christ's return to earth at the end of the tribulation. After he returns, Jesus will establish his millennial kingdom. Revelation 20:1–10 says Christ will reign for one thousand years. The godly dead will be raised to reign with him, and any believer alive at Christ's return will also enter the kingdom he sets up. Verses 7–10 say that at the end of the kingdom Satan will be loosed one last time, will deceive many people living at the time, and will lead them in one last rebellion. The rebellion will fail, and Satan will be cast into the lake of fire, where he will remain forevermore.

In verse 11, after the events just recounted, John says he saw a great white throne. Heaven and earth had fled from the face of the one who sat on the throne. Second Peter 3 also speaks of end-time events, and Peter mentions the destruction of the current heavens and earth. Evidently, that happens between the events mentioned in Revelation 20:7–10 and the Great White Throne Judgment mentioned in 20:11–15. But if the current heavens and earth are destroyed between the events of Revelation 20:7–10 and 11–15, no one in a natural body could survive! According to Revelation 20:11–15, the ungodly dead of all ages will have been judged and cast into the lake of fire. After the Great White Throne Judgment, Revelation 21–22 speaks of life in the new heaven and the new earth. Second Peter 3:13 confirms that God will create a new heaven and earth. Nonbelievers won't be present in the new heaven and new earth, because they will be thrown into the lake of fire, as just noted. Believers will inhabit the new heavens and earth, but since no one could survive there in a natural body, they will all have glorified bodies.

Why do I mention these things? To show that evangelism won't be needed in the new heavens and new earth. People in glorified bodies are totally exempt from sin and its consequences. They can't get sick, decay, or die! And people in glorified bodies can't give birth. So those who populate the new heavens and earth will do so in glorified bodies. They won't need to be evangelized, because they will already be saved, and can't lose their salvation.

Does this mean the gospel will no longer be true? Not at all! It only means that the Great Commission won't apply to that situation, because everyone will be irrevocably saved. And those in the lake of fire won't get another chance to hear the gospel and accept it.

---

[11] Examples of passages that show that there will be birth and death during the millennium are Isaiah 65:20–23 and Revelation 20:7–9. People in glorified bodies can't be deceived or rebel against God at the end of the millennium, so those mentioned in Revelation 20:7–9 must be born during the millennial kingdom and don't die before its end. The exact proof of this is one of the subjects that is covered in the Foundations of Evangelical Theology volume on eschatology.

Will the gospel no longer have the authority it does today (or perhaps any authority)? Not at all! The difference will be that during the eternal state the gospel will be the authoritative explanation of why those who inhabit the new heavens and earth are there and why those in the lake of fire didn't get saved and will endure a horrible eternity. At the Great White Throne Judgment, when the Lord pronounces you guilty and sentences you to eternity in the lake of fire (Rev. 20:11–15), there will not then be an invitation to accept Christ!

In this section, I have offered two examples (OT blood sacrifices, and the Great Commission) relevant to the applicability of Scripture's authority. My point is that, though all Scripture is authoritative, it doesn't all apply in exactly the same way at all times and places. Parts that no longer apply or that do not yet apply still have authority, now, because they are the words of an absolutely sovereign God and they tell the truth. This point about the scope of the Bible's authority should help us interpret and apply Scripture, but it does not even slightly nullify Scripture's authority!

Another question arises when asking how much of Scripture is authoritative today. Specifically, which parts *apply* today, and why? Are we, for example, bound by rules in the law of Moses, the NT Law of Christ, or a combination of both?

These questions raise important hermeneutical issues. Elsewhere[12] others and I have addressed these issues, and readers are encouraged to consult those works. For our purposes now, suffice it to say that all of Scripture's rules and regulations are authoritative, but careful interpretation is required to discern which ones must be obeyed today. Those that apply to contemporary circumstances are supremely authoritative for our thinking and action.

## Uses of Authoritative Scripture

In light of Scripture's intrinsic authority, how might it be used authoritatively? The church has traditionally replied that Scripture should be seen as both source and norm for Christians. But, source and norm for what purpose(s)? The most frequent answer is that Scripture should be the source and norm for both life and doctrine. As Graham Cole explains in his fine discussion of the concept of *Sola Scriptura*, for Luther *Sola Scriptura* meant that Scripture is the source and norm of the Christian gospel and of Christian doctrine. Other Reformers also claimed that Scripture is the source and norm of the church's preaching.[13]

---

[12] On the questions of how the OT and NT relate to one another and how this impacts various doctrines such as the nature of the kingdom and who are the people of God, see John S. Feinberg, ed., *Continuity and Discontinuity: Essays in Honor of S. Lewis Johnson* (Westchester, IL: Crossway, 1988). On the issue of how the Mosaic law (and the OT more generally) relates to NT individuals, see John S. Feinberg and Paul D. Feinberg, *Ethics for a Brave New World*, 2nd ed. (Wheaton, IL: Crossway, 2010).

[13] Graham A. Cole, "Sola Scriptura: Some Historical and Contemporary Perspectives," *Churchman* 104 (1990): 21–22.

What does it mean to say that Scripture as authoritative is the source of doctrine (including the gospel) and of life? As to doctrine, it does *not* mean that, in constructing a system of theology or even a doctrinal treatment of one area of theology like the doctrine of Scripture, one must use only Scripture as source material. Some evangelicals do theology (and insist that it be done) based on Scripture alone, but that isn't what it means for Scripture to be the source of doctrine. Rather, it means first that Scripture provides most of the content for evangelical theological reflection, even though data outside of Scripture can also be useful in constructing a full understanding of a doctrine. Scripture as doctrine's source also means that whether data internal or external to Scripture should be used to construct doctrine is determined by the data's "fit" with biblical teaching. If proposed data contradict scriptural teachings, the proposed materials should not be used in doctrinal formulation or explanation.

Scripture as ultimate authority is also the source for life, but this needs explanation. It doesn't mean that Scripture will answer questions about how to plant and cultivate a garden, how to fix a damaged automobile, or how to play a sport. Rather, Scripture is the authoritative source about how we should relate to God, others, our world, and ourselves. It details the kind of behavior required to please God and maintain fellowship with him, and it articulates the actions God calls sinful and the punishments for doing such deeds. Calling Scripture the source for life also means that it reveals what God expects about how his followers will treat other members of his church. And, it also means that Scripture gives instructions on how to set up and run a church. What I have just said about Scripture as the source of life doesn't mean that no other sources can help us on these matters, but only that Scripture is our primary source, and that the usefulness of other data depends on their fit with Scripture.

What about Scripture as the *norm* for doctrine and life? Here what I hinted at in discussing Scripture as source comes into full focus. To say that Scripture is the norm for doctrine means that what Scripture teaches is the final judge of whether any doctrinal claim is true or false, and hence of what to include or remove from one's theology. There can also be other norms or rules for judging doctrine; throughout church history, whatever the church has traditionally held on a given doctrine has also mattered, and it should matter to us as we construct our system. But if Scripture and tradition conflict, Scripture as norm means that Scripture's teaching is correct and tradition is wrong. Even if Scripture and tradition agree, one should hold the doctrine in question because Scripture teaches it. Tradition can reassure us that our understanding of Scripture is likely accurate, but it is still the fit with

Scripture that decides which doctrines to include in theology and how to state and defend those doctrines.

Scripture as the norm for life means that if you want to judge whether your current or proposed behavior pleases God, test it by what Scripture teaches. If it matches Scripture's demands, it is acceptable. If not, it is sinful and must not be done. As with Scripture as doctrinal norm, Scripture as the norm for living doesn't mean we can't get any help from anywhere else in making a decision. For example, if I am deciding which house to buy, Scripture may offer some help, but other information may be more helpful and determinative. Scripture as the norm for living means that, in regard to actions and activities Scripture addresses, scriptural teaching decides what is right and wrong. If an action doesn't measure up to Scripture's requirements, we must not do it.[14]

What I have set forth above is, I contend, what evangelical churches have meant and still mean when they say that Scripture is the source and norm for doctrine and life/practice. Because Scripture is God's word and totally truthful, it is completely understandable that it should function that way. That its divine author is all-wise should assure us that its advice and counsel, not to mention its requirements, are the sanest way to a life that pleases God and is the most enjoyable and fulfilling for us. Hence, living under Scripture's authority isn't odious or cumbersome. It is liberating, and it leads to a fulfilling, prosperous, and joyous life!

## Church History and Biblical Authority

Throughout the history of the church, many Christians have attributed supreme authority to Scripture. As we shall see later in this chapter, biblical authors considered Scripture to be God's word. And, of course, they wouldn't think it inspired and then reject its authority. A simple reading of the Gospels, noting how the authors appealed to the OT to support their points, and that the people they describe, including Jesus, did the same thing to make a point or refute the claims of Jesus's enemies shows that for them the OT was the final word on any matter of doctrine or practice.

Hence, it is quite evident that God's people in OT times, during Christ's life on earth, and in the early NT church assumed the absolute authority of the OT. Jesus predicted and promised the Holy Spirit's revelation of more truth and guidance of the apostles as they would record that truth in the books that became the NT. And as one reads the NT, one finds no hint that any NT authors believed their books or those of other apostles had any less authority than the OT.

---

[14] For further discussion of Scripture as both source and norm, see Cole's article. For further discussion of the concept of biblical authority, see Maarten Wisse, "The Meaning of the Authority of the Bible," *RelS* 36 (2000).

Of course, many people living when the first NT books were penned were eyewitness to various events in Jesus's life. Moreover, many of them also knew various apostles and could verify by eyewitness testimony the truth of things written in the book of Acts and in other NT books that mention factual matters. In addition, these people could see the impact of the apostles' ministry, and could verify by experience that God's blessing was on all aspects of it.

So, it is not unexpected that these very early Christians granted authority to the OT and to the various NT books, especially the Gospels and Acts, as they were penned by their authors. But what would happen later as apostles and other early Christian eyewitnesses died? In early church history, what would people think of books written toward the end of the first century AD? In what follows I want to sketch briefly the views of the church at various points in its history toward the authority of Scripture. Though there have been times when biblical authority has been attacked and other times when something else like church tradition has rivaled Scripture's authority, the consensus of what might be called evangelical Christians has been and still is that Scripture is supremely authoritative.

It might be tempting to think that throughout church history there has been some struggle over the authority of Scripture, tradition, and the church. But that frames the discussion far too simplistically. In fact, at various times, especially in early church history, this was not what Christians were thinking. The first centuries after the life and ministry of Christ and his apostles were times marked by various doctrinal disagreements. Initially, there were Trinitarian controversies, and then Christological debates arose. In many of these debates, the problem was not that heretics ignored Scripture, but rather that they interpreted Scripture so as to formulate views not espoused by other Christians who read and interpreted the same Scriptures.

In part at least, to safeguard apostolic teaching, there arose in the early church what was known as the *regula fidei* (rule of faith). James Merrick explains that it "was a formalized summary of the essential core of early Christian belief assumed to be of apostolic origin and to possess . . . hermeneutical and apologetic authority."[15] Merrick adds that this rule of faith was likely "an oral tradition, either preached directly by the apostles or formulated from their preaching, which spread among the early churches through preaching and catechesis."[16] The rule of faith not only defined the key doctrines but also

---

[15] James R. A. Merrick, "*Sola Scriptura* and the *Regula Fidei*: The Reformation Scripture Principle and Early Oral Tradition in Martin Chemnitz' Examination of the Council of Trent," *Scottish Journal of Theology* 63 (2010): 258.

[16] Ibid. For more on the rule of faith see Andrew Sandlin, "Two Paradigms for Adherents of *Sola Scriptura*," *Reformation and Revival* 9 (Fall 2000): 39–40.

legitimized a particular way of interpreting Scripture, especially those passages abused by heretics for their own ends.

As Merrick explains, in the early church both Tertullian and Irenaeus were strong proponents of the rule of faith. Interestingly, in his *On Prescription of Heretics*, in which he defends against Gnostic oral tradition, Tertullian relied heavily on the rule of faith. In fact, rather than turning first to Scripture to refute heretics, Tertullian argued that the proper way to determine correct doctrine was to turn first to the church's rule of faith. That was necessary because it showed how Scripture should be interpreted in regard to the doctrine(s) in question. Without doing so, Scripture would likely be abused, as various heretics had done. According to Tertullian,

> The rule was first declared by Christ, then disseminated by his apostles and, finally, deposited in the apostolic churches. This apostolic faith ensures the global unity of the church: 'Therefore the churches, although they are so many and so great, comprise but the one primitive church, founded by the apostles, from which they all spring. . . . We hold communion with the apostolic churches because our doctrine is in no respect different from theirs'.[17]

In a similar way, Irenaeus claimed that the unity of the church everywhere was based on its one apostolic faith. The problem with the Gnostics was that their interpretations departed from the rule of faith and foisted on Scripture "an alien scheme of their own creation."[18] As some have explained, "the rule was considered to be 'the "plot" which actually informs the Scriptures'. . . . Hence, the rule as the hypothesis or 'plot' of scripture is the hermeneutical key for interpreting it."[19]

Also important is how Irenaeus saw the presence of the apostolic faith in the churches of his own time. Arguing that his views were similar to Tertullian's, Merrick explains that in Irenaeus's thinking

> the faith is present through a succession of church leaders. Irenaeus spoke of a 'tradition which originates from the apostles and which is preserved by means of the successions of presbyters in the Churches'. After recounting the succession of the bishops of Rome from the apostles on, he concluded that 'by this succession, the ecclesiastical tradition from the apostles, and the preaching of the truth, have came [sic] down to us'. Hence, this rule of faith which was for him apostolic was present in the church ultimately through the bishops of the church. The faith is thus found ostensibly in the apostolic churches where the rule is present.[20]

---

[17] Merrick, "*Sola Scriptura* and the *Regula Fidei*," 258–259. Merrick is quoting from Tertullian's *Prescription against Heretics* 20–21, ANF 3:252.

[18] Irenaeus, *Against Heresies* 1.9.1–5, in, ANF 3:329–330, cited and discussed in Merrick, "*Sola Scriptura* and the *Regula Fidei*," 259.

[19] Merrick, "*Sola Scriptura* and the *Regula Fidei*," 260.

[20] Ibid.

Both Tertullian and Irenaeus, then, appealed to the rule of faith as their strategy for refuting Gnostic thinking. It had both hermeneutical and apologetic roles, and seems to have functioned that way throughout the church fathers.[21] So, was there a distinction between this apostolic teaching and Scripture? In the minds of the church fathers, the answer seems to be both no and yes. On the one hand, they didn't say the rule of faith was God's word. But on the other hand, at this time in church history thinkers like Tertullian never seemed to see a distinction in *content* between Scripture and the rule of faith. As Merrick explains, to have posited such a distinction would have undercut his argument against Gnostics, whom he accused of interpreting Scripture in ways that did not match the content of the rule.[22]

So, during this early period of church history, Scripture, tradition (the rule of faith), and the church were allies in fighting heresies that arose. And that worked well as long as the three were in agreement. Of course, what Scripture teaches is more important than tradition and was considered to be so. But what would happen if one or more of these were used against the other? As has been argued, some have simplistically thought that this is exactly what happened prior to and during the Reformation. That is, the church claimed to have sole authority over how to interpret Scripture, and did so in accord with tradition. Now, if the church, appealing to the rule of faith (doctrine traditionally held since the church's inception), pronounced how anyone should understand Scripture and biblical doctrine, that wouldn't necessarily have caused the theological, etc., problems that led people like Luther to break from the church. But it should also be clear that it would be possible to interpret Scripture in ways that supported the authority of the church and its leaders, even though such interpretations didn't match what Scripture actually taught. In fact, it is often thought and stated simplistically that the Reformation happened because the church claimed the exclusive right to interpret Scripture, and did so according to its understanding of theology as informed by various traditions, while people like Luther argued that anyone could interpret Scripture on his or her own and had the right to do so, and should opt for Scripture rather than the tradition to which the Roman Catholic Church appealed in order to legitimize its control over believers.

The situation as just described is not entirely incorrect, but things seem to have been a bit more complicated. Indeed, the Roman Catholic Church contended that the right to interpret the Bible belonged to the clergy, and that the authoritative interpretation of Scripture came from the clerical hierarchy. Luther and other Reformers insisted that anyone had the right to interpret

---

[21] Ibid., 261. Merrick offers Athanasius as a prime example.
[22] Ibid., 259.

Scripture, and that on various matters the Roman Catholic Church's interpretation was wrong. Often it is thought that the Church was wrong because it appealed to tradition rather than Scripture for doctrinal formulation. So, with such a view it is easy to see how the view makes sense that says that the Roman Catholic Church opted for tradition over Scripture, while the Reformers chose Scripture alone as the source of doctrine and as the authority in all matters of doctrine and practice.

But various scholars have argued that, on this matter of tradition, matters were a bit more complicated. Scripture versus tradition is typically seen as God's word versus man's. D. H. Williams is helpful, however, in explaining that, though evangelicals have been taught to see Scripture and tradition as enemies,

> In truth, however, "tradition" in the patristic and early medieval period was concerned first with *doctrina*, that is, the church's essential teaching, which was always understood in concert with scripture and was handed down in the course of history (*tradere*). Tradition was secondarily defined as the accepted practices of the church (e.g., discipline and liturgy). In other words, tradition is not always ancillary, and therefore a later addition to the essential beliefs of Christianity. The definition of Tradition in the primary sense—for clarity, often rendered with a capital "T"—points to the central expressions of Christian faith, usually distinguished from the various "traditions" that pertain to church or sacramental polity. It is this second sense of tradition that became the chief battleground during the Reformation. The conflict between the early Reformers and Rome was not one of scripture versus Tradition, but rather a clash over what the traditions had become, or between divergent concepts of tradition. This is what Luther inherited as he developed his own views on the authority of Scripture.[23]

This basic analysis seems to be supported even by some events that are often interpreted as showing that for Luther it was either tradition or Scripture. One such event was the famous Diet of Worms in 1521. At that meeting, Luther was ordered to recant his teachings on such views as justification by faith. Luther famously replied that unless he could be convinced by Scripture and plain reason, he would not recant. He added that he did not "accept the authority of popes and councils, for they have contradicted each other."[24] Luther wasn't

---

[23] D. H. Williams, "The Search for *Sola Scriptura* in the Early Church," *Interpretation* 52 (October 1998): 356–357. See also Craig D. Allert, "What Are We Trying to Conserve?: Evangelicalism and *Sola Scriptura*," *EvQ* 76 (2004): 332–334, for a similar analysis of the issue of tradition in the Reformers' thinking. Moreover, in various Protestant camps, the sources and arbiters of theology and practice are even more complicated than just Scripture and tradition. For example, Wesleyan thinking espouses what is known as the Wesleyan Quadrilateral. The four sources here are Scripture, tradition, reason, and experience. Even so, in all of these different conceptions, evangelicals have held that Scripture is the most important source of Christian faith and life and the final arbiter in disputed matters of doctrine and practice. For a helpful discussion of biblical authority and how it relates to tradition, reason, etc., see Peter Jensen, "The Authority of Scripture," in his *The Revelation of God* (Downers Grove, IL: InterVarsity Press, 2002).

[24] Roland Bainton, *Here I Stand: A Life of Martin Luther* (New York: Mentor, 1955), 144.

rejecting all teachings of earlier church councils, but rather those (along with recent and current [to him] popes) that had wandered far from Scripture and the historic positions of the church. In further support of this, Craig Allert cites Luther's *On the Councils and the Church*, which was written in 1539. As Allert explains, this treatise shows that "the argument was not about the acceptance of the early church's creeds and doctrines, but about who has the right to claim them as authorities. The papacy was singled out in this document because Luther believed it was playing off the councils and fathers against scripture in order to legitimize decisions founded on the claim of tradition."[25] The councils of which Allert writes are the early church councils, which Luther held in high esteem.

As Luther wrote on this issue in *On the Councils and the Church*,

> But they would like to rule the church, not with trustworthy wisdom, but with arbitrary opinions, and again confuse and perplex all the souls in the world, as they have done before. But just as they reject all the fathers and theologians in their petty canons, so do we, in turn, reject them in the church and in Scripture. They shall neither teach us Scripture nor rule in the church; they are not entitled to it, nor do they have the competence for it. . . . They have cast us poor theologians, together with the fathers, from their books; for this we thank them most kindly. Now they propose to throw us out of the church and out of Scripture; and they themselves are not worthy to be in them. That is too much, . . . we shall not put up with it.[26]

Calvin agreed that authority is in Scripture, not elsewhere. But he added that Scripture's authority is self-convincing or self-attesting (*autopistos*) to those whom the Holy Spirit has inwardly taught. As Henk van den Belt explains, according to Calvin, the church doesn't determine Scripture's authority. The church receives and recognizes its authenticity and authority.[27] In addressing the relation of the church to Scripture's authority, Calvin wrote,

> As to their question—how we can be assured that this has sprung from God unless we have recourse to the decree of the church?—it is as if someone asked: how shall we learn to distinguish light from darkness, white from black, sweet from bitter? Scripture does not give an obscurer sense of its own truth than white and black things do of their color or sweet and bitter things do of their taste. If we desire to take care for our consciences in the best way, so that they may not waver by continual doubt, we must derive the authority of Scripture from something higher than human reasons, indications or conjectures. That is from the inner testifying of the Holy Spirit, for although it

---

[25] Allert, "What Are We Trying to Conserve?," 339.

[26] Martin Luther, *On the Councils and the Church*, in *Martin Luther's Basic Theological Writings*, ed. Timothy F. Lull (Minneapolis: Fortress, 1989), 559–560.

[27] Henk van den Belt, "Heinrich Bullinger and Jean Calvin on the Authority of Scripture (1538-1571)," *Journal of Reformed Theology* 5 (2011): 314.

gains reverence for itself by its own majesty, still it only then really impresses us seriously when it is sealed by the Spirit to our hearts.[28]

Though other key Reformation figures say similar things, the point is clear enough. Likewise, after the Reformation, despite the onslaught of attacks on Scripture by reason and Enlightenment thinking, and later by use of the historical critical method, evangelical theology has continued to maintain Scripture's supreme authority. Of course, along with such views came Luther's claim that Scripture interprets Scripture, rather than having to look to popes and church councils for proper interpretation, and a belief that anyone, regardless of education and tradition, could read and understand Scripture's basic message.

While we want to affirm Scripture's authority and applaud the desire to study Scripture on one's own, there is still good reason for any reader of Scripture to learn some basic tools of interpreting any text, including Scripture. All readers, however, must submit to Scripture's authority, even when it says things we don't wish to hear. Either one assents merely intellectually to Scripture's authority or one actually lets its teachings govern one's life. The difference is substantial, for often those who give mere assent to Scripture but live on their own terms have lives that don't look much different from the lives of those who reject biblical authority altogether. A key question, however, is whether Scripture teaches its own authority and what other supports there are for this doctrine. To those issues we turn next.[29]

## A Biblical and Theological Case for Scripture's Authority

Though evangelicals throughout church history have held to the authority of Scripture, it is not always easy to find a biblical and theological defense of the doctrine. This is likely so because it is taken for granted that God is supremely authoritative, and given his authority, whatever he says must have paramount authority. If one adds to this the belief that Scripture is God's word, then it is easy to see that Scripture must also be authoritative. Of course, since Scripture covers only certain topics, it must be authoritative for only those topics it addresses.

Though Scripture's authority is often assumed, especially once Scripture is affirmed to be God's inspired and inerrant word, its authority can also be defended on other biblical and theological grounds. No verse explicitly says,

---

[28] Ibid., 314, quoting from Jean Calvin, *Opera Selecta*, 3rd ed., ed. Peter Barth and Wilhelm Niesel (Munich: Christian Kaiser, 1967), 3, 67, 69, 70—these quotes are from Calvin's *Institutes*.
[29] Some other helpful articles on the history of views on biblical authority are Ian Christopher Levy, "Holy Scripture and the Quest for Authority among Three Late Medieval Masters," *Journal of Ecclesiastical History* 61 (January 2010); Stephen E. Lahey, "Reginald Pecock on the Authority of Reason, Scripture and Tradition," *Journal of Ecclesiastical History* 56 (April 2005); David W. Lotz, "*Sola Scriptura*: Luther on Biblical Authority," *Interpretation* 35 (July 1981); and Vitor Westhelle, "Luther on the Authority of Scripture," *Lutheran Quarterly* 19 (2005).

"Scripture is authoritative in whatever it teaches." Rather, there are verses whose teaching amounts to ascribing authority to either some or all of Scripture. In addition, there are other biblical truths that affirm or clearly imply Scripture's authority. In what follows, I shall begin with several verses that are about as close to ascribing authority to all of Scripture as can be found in the Bible. Then I shall turn to biblical and theological truths that require either part or all of Scripture to be authoritative.

### General Statements about Scripture's Authority

Two passages, Matthew 5:17–18 and John 10:35, are frequently referenced in support of various doctrines about Scripture. In addition to teaching inspiration and inerrancy, they are also relevant to Scripture's authority. Both come from Jesus during his earthly life and ministry. In addition, we also have the example of Jesus as he responded to Satan's temptations (Matt. 4:1–11) and as he interacted with the Sadducees (Matt. 22:23–33, as discussed in my chapter 6 on inerrancy).

Matthew 5:17–18 (parallel to v. 18 are Mark 13:31 and Luke 16:17) comes from Jesus's Sermon on the Mount. As recorded in Matthew's Gospel, Jesus begins with the Beatitudes (5:1–12). He then likens believers to salt and light in our world (5:13–16). Though we might expect Jesus next to present his teaching about divine expectations for human behavior in various areas of life, he does something else first. Jesus knows that what he will say in the rest of the Sermon has some continuity with OT teaching, but it will also contain things that can't be found in OT law. Undoubtedly, some in his audience would wonder whether Jesus's Sermon nullifies and abolishes all, or even some, OT teaching. If that was Jesus's intent, that would seem quite strange to some of his audience, because they had always been taught that OT books are God's word.

Knowing full well that his listeners might have such reactions, Jesus prefaced his Sermon with the words of verses 17–20. These verses clearly teach Scripture's preservation. It is also likely that Jesus says Scripture would last because truth cannot be cancelled. But the major focus of this teaching is Scripture's authority. Verses 17–18 are especially relevant to the OT's authority.

Jesus says that he doesn't intend to abolish the Law or the Prophets, two of the three major parts of the OT canon. Though he didn't mention the Writings, what he says in verses 17–18 about Scripture/the OT means that he intended to confirm it, not cancel it. Specifically, he will fulfill (from the verb *plēroō*) it all. Why would Jesus be so concerned to inform his disciples that he had no disrespect for or intention to abolish Scripture? We know from our discussion of inspiration that Jesus thought the OT is God's word. But then surely that answers our question. If God says anything, one doesn't reject it, ignore it, twist it to one's own use, or do anything else disrespectful. When a king issues a decree, his subjects may not like what it says but they dare not trifle with it or ignore it. The King of the universe has issued his decree—the Bible—and his subjects, all of humanity, dare not treat it lightly or with disdain.

Just in case Jesus's listeners thought his intention to fulfill Scripture wasn't enough to keep it from passing away and becoming irrelevant, Jesus added verse 18. The overall message is that Scripture will last longer than even heaven and earth. It is more stable and certain to exist than the universe in which we live. Jesus said the law wouldn't pass away, but certainly he was thinking of more than just the Pentateuch. Here, as often, the whole OT is seen as God's law, his instruction for all people. To refer to it as law bespeaks its binding nature on everyone and everything.

Jesus said that heaven and earth will pass away. The verb comes from *parerchomai* and means "to pass away," "to come to an end," and "to disappear." One could read this verse as saying that Scripture will pass away after heaven and earth are gone. But that would miss verse 18's point about Scripture. Jesus says that none of it will pass away until all of it is fulfilled; his point is that all of it will be fulfilled.

Jesus makes this point, I believe, by using hyperbole. He says that not one jot or tittle (*iōta*, *keraia*) of Scripture will pass away before all of it is fulfilled. Clearly, Jesus was thinking of the OT, written in Hebrew. The Greek word *iōta* stands for the Hebrew letter *y*, *yôdh*. As to the amount of physical space this Hebrew letter takes up on a page, it is the smallest of all Hebrew consonants. As for a tittle, some Hebrew consonants have no physical part of the letter that extends beyond the rest of the letter. Other Hebrew consonants do. For example, a *daledth* is written by joining a horizontal line and a vertical line (the horizontal line is written above the vertical one). The two lines meet in the northeast corner, but they do not meet and end. Rather, the horizontal line extends "eastward" beyond where it intersects the vertical line. That extension, small though it is, is a tittle (other Hebrew consonants also have a tittle, but not all do).

In contrast to these smallest strokes of a pen, Jesus mentions the heavens and the earth. In effect, Jesus compares the minutest parts of the Hebrew language with the largest parts of reality—in essence, the whole universe. One would probably think that the bigger of the two would last longer than the smaller. But Jesus says just the opposite. The biggest thing you can think of will cease to exist before even the very smallest part of Scripture will pass away. In fact, the bigger will pass away, but Scripture can't pass away without being completely fulfilled. Jesus exaggerates by comparing the biggest thing to the smallest part of Scripture in order to make his point about the importance and permanence of Scripture.

What, then, does this passage teach about biblical inerrancy and authority? One might argue that the reason Scripture will last longer than the universe is that truth is always truth; it cannot be cancelled, even if we would like it to be. While this is true, I don't think it is Jesus's main point. Rather, his point is Scripture's authority, and also that he hasn't come to abolish its authority but to uphold it by fulfilling it. Why such concern to be sure that even the smallest portion will be fulfilled? Why emphasize so clearly that he didn't intend to abolish it but to fulfill it? Because it is God's word, and God's word cannot be twisted to meet our wishes, ignored, or rejected. The word of the king is law; it must be obeyed to the letter. This shows Jesus's reverence for God's word, but even more, it shows that he recognized its authority. Everything else in the universe can fall apart, but not Scripture. It must stand and must be obeyed![30]

Does Matthew 5:18 imply that someday Scripture will be abolished, namely, in the eternal state? I think this question is wrongheaded, for it takes Jesus to be making a *precise* statement about how long Scripture will be in force, when Jesus, as noted, is exaggerating to make the point that he did not come to cancel Scripture but to uphold it. In the rest of the passage Jesus makes no metaphysically precise comment about how long Scripture will be in force. To think he does misses the fact that Jesus is showing his reverence for Scripture and doing so by using hyperbole. Everyone who knows how language works understands that what is exaggerated to make a point is not to be taken as literally true. And hence we should understand that neither Jesus nor Matthew makes a comment about the precise amount of time during which Scripture will be authoritative.[31] Jesus's point is that Scripture is supremely authoritative and will always continue to be so.

John 10:35 is a second passage relevant to Scripture's authority. I have discussed it in several chapters, including the ones on inerrancy. While it is definitely relevant to inerrancy, it also affirms Scripture's authority. In this passage Jesus defends himself against the charge of blasphemy that stems from his referring to himself as divine. His Jewish listeners had complained that, although he was just a man, he made himself equal to God (10:33).

Jesus could have answered their complaint in a number of ways. He could have performed a miracle that only God could do. Or he could have asked his

---

[30] See D. A. Carson, *Matthew*, in *EBC*, ed. Frank E. Gaebelein, vol. 8 (Grand Rapids, MI: Zondervan, 1984), 141–147, for his handling of this passage. Carson discusses various exegetical options related to the different parts of these verses. The interpretation I have given is consistent with that which he suggests as most likely.

[31] Here perhaps we should add that even if Scripture is cancelled in the eternal state, believers in glorified bodies won't transgress its teachings. We won't be able to do so; that is part of what comes with being glorified! Nor will the nonbelieving in the lake of fire be able to overturn Scripture so as to escape God's judgment.

Father in heaven to say or do something very public that all of his critics could hear and see that would affirm his deity. Jesus responded differently.

OT Scripture is very clear that for a mere mortal to claim deity and equality with God is blasphemy, punishable by death. So, Jesus's enemies believed that he had violated biblical law, and deserved punishment. Since their complaint appealed to Scripture (the OT), Jesus chose to refute it with Scripture. Scripture says that a mere human isn't equal to God. But Jesus reminded his critics that there is a passage in the OT where mere mortals are referred to as gods. Jesus cited Psalm 82:6, which refers to mere humans as gods because they were judges, performing a service for God. Despite their role in society, they were still mere men, and Psalm 82 shows that they were evil judges. Still, Psalm 82:6 refers to them as gods.

In essence, Jesus used this OT passage as follows: "if mere humans who did evil, though they were supposed to be serving God, are referred to as gods, how can you complain when I come doing good things in obedience to God's will, and refer to myself as God?" Jesus then added that, if he didn't do the works of God, his Father, they should reject him, but if he did God's work, they should realize that Jesus is indeed in the Father and the Father is in him. Jesus's enemies had no rebuttal or refutation of what he said; rather, they tried to seize him, but he escaped.

Don't miss the fact that Jesus's defense appealed to something clearly stated in Scripture, and that none of his accusers replied by saying that Scripture nowhere calls mere mortals divine. Nor did they accuse him of misinterpreting Psalm 82. And none of them suggested that, although Jesus quoted and interpreted the verse correctly, the verse is just false and/or irrelevant.

None of his opponents disagreed with or dismissed what Jesus said about Psalm 82:6. But Jesus did more than just quote this verse from Psalm 82; he added, after quoting it, "and the Scripture cannot be broken." As we saw in discussing inerrancy, this means that what Scripture affirms can't be overturned, annulled, or proved wrong! But surely there is more in this verse than just an affirmation of Scripture's truth. For something could be true and people could know that it is true, but decide to defy and reject it, anyway.

When Jesus said, "and the Scripture cannot be broken" (John 10:35), he was affirming its authority. It's as if Jesus was saying that his defense rested on what Scripture says, and whether they liked it or not, if Scripture says something, no one can get around it. How could that not be Jesus's way of attributing authority to Scripture?

Jesus's enemies couldn't refute what he said (they didn't even try), and that shows that even they knew that, when a point of debate is supported by appeal to Scripture, that ends the debate. Though this verse doesn't *explicitly* affirm Scripture as the final authority in this situation, it is hard to understand Jesus's defense and his enemies' silence as anything but an acknowledgement that what Scripture says settles the matter. All his opponents could do was resort to physical violence by attempting to seize Jesus, but that response failed as well (v. 39).

The preceding discussion supports the belief that this passage teaches Scripture's authority. But the case becomes even stronger when we note another fact. Jesus cited Psalm 82:6 in his defense. He could have added that the passage is certainly true, and then offered arguments for the veracity of the Psalms in general or of this psalm in particular. But Jesus said something even more significant. Rather than refer only to this one psalm and/or one verse, Jesus made a comment about *all* of Scripture. He said that it cannot be broken.

This is quite interesting, because it actually says more than Jesus needed to say to defend himself. By referring to the whole OT as true and authoritative, he opened himself to an even greater attack by his enemies. Now, they might not only complain about his referring to this one verse in one psalm; they could also claim that he was too "generous" in his evaluation of Scripture in general. In fact, they might have even said that, while Psalm 82:6 does call mere humans gods, Jesus was just wrong in his deference to whatever Scripture says.

Of course, their response to Jesus included nothing of the sort. In fact, they had no answer to his intellectual argument. All they could do was resort to physical violence. They knew that if they responded to Jesus by rejecting Scripture's truth and authority, they would be in trouble with their own people. The most likely explanation of why they responded to Jesus as they did is that they agreed with his comments about Scripture and had no other answer to refute him, but were so determined to destroy him that all they could do was resort to violence.

It is also important to see how Jesus used Scripture in various situations. For example, in response to Satan's temptations (Matt. 4:1–11), Jesus repeatedly quoted Scripture. Satan didn't try to rebut the Scripture Jesus quoted. Rather, Satan moved on to another temptation, for he knew that no argument he could offer could refute and have greater authority than Scripture. In fact, in his second temptation, Satan even cited a Scripture himself (v. 6). Either Satan deluded himself into thinking his request was appropriate (because he could quote a Scripture to "support" it), or he knew his use of Scripture was wrong but thought by quoting Scripture he could get Jesus to agree to his request. In either case, Satan's appeal to Scripture showed that he recognized Scripture's authority at least for some people, even if not for himself.

Jesus's answering Satan by quoting Scripture showed his respect for and belief in Scripture as supremely authoritative. Similarly, the Matthew 22 incident with the Sadducees about the woman married seven times is also instructive. The Sadducees posed a problem that they thought would refute the idea of resurrection of the dead, and therefore would embarrass Jesus, who held that belief. Remember Jesus's response to their question: "You are mistaken, not understanding the Scriptures, or the power of God." As noted in discussing inerrancy, this affirms Scripture's truth. But it also shows Scripture's authority. Jesus quoted Scripture that refuted the Sadducees, and they had no reply. In part, that is likely because they weren't ready to rebut what Jesus said. Regardless, the fact that for Jesus Scripture settled the matter, and the fact that the Sadducees neither then nor later raised the issue again shows that Jesus certainly believed (and so did the Sadducees) that Scripture settled the matter. Scripture is God's word, and there is no higher authority than that. Jesus knew that, and so did they!

### Other Biblical and Theological Evidences for Scripture's Authority

Though the passages just discussed offer strong support for Scripture's authority, there is other biblical and theological evidence for it as well. In this section, I want to present that evidence, but I note that many of the evidences and arguments to be offered are more inferential than the evidence already presented. That doesn't mean they are of less value. If they are true and relevant, they offer substantial support, and I believe readers will agree that the evidences and arguments to be offered are both relevant to the topic and true.

Let us begin with an argument that links several different concepts together in support of Scripture's authority. The argument is deductive, and its premises yield the conclusion that Scripture is authoritative. I shall first state the argument, and then offer support for each premise.

1. The God of the Bible is the one and only God.
2. The God of Scripture is omniscient, omnipotent, absolutely sovereign, and truthful.
3. As omniscient, God knows everything that can be known, including every proposition, and he knows which are true and which are false.
4. As a God of truth, God speaks only what is true; he cannot lie.
5. As omnipotent and absolutely sovereign, God has power to accomplish whatever he chooses, including every power needed to reveal information in language and guarantee that what he reveals is transferred accurately into writing.
6. Scripture, containing sixty-six books, was composed under the superintendence of the Holy Spirit, guaranteeing that what the human authors wrote is exactly what God moved them to write. So, Scripture is God's inspired word.
7. Scripture is totally true in everything it affirms; i.e., it is inerrant.

8. Authority is the right/power to command both thought and behavior and to enforce whatever rules are deemed necessary to gain compliance. Authority is the right/power to bring about intended goals.
9. Whatever is true possesses authority.
10. Whatever someone with authority demands/requires/says is the case or must happen bears the authority of the one making the demands.
11. Therefore, Scripture as God's inspired word (and thus true, and the speech of a being who knows the truth and has power to guarantee that what he speaks is accurately transferred into writing, and has the right and power to demand that those under his authority obey what he demands) possesses the authority of God.

The starting point of this argument, its first two premises, focuses on God's nature. Scripture affirms that there exists only one God (Deut. 6:4; Isa. 44:6, 8; 46:9; Mark 12:32; and 1 Cor. 8:4). In addition, God is omniscient, omnipotent, absolutely sovereign, and his nature also possesses the attribute of truth. Elsewhere I have defined and supported biblically these divine attributes. Let me briefly summarize the main point in regard to each.

As omniscient, God knows everything that a being with God's attributes can know, and thus he knows the informational content of every proposition, as well as whether every assertion is true or false.[32] God as omnipotent possesses every logically possible power that a being with his nature can possess.[33] God is also absolutely sovereign, and thus has the ability to deliberate and make choices, and to carry out those choices. His choices and actions are based solely on his own nature and purposes, and his choices and control cover all things.[34] And, finally, God has the attribute of truth. This means that in contrast to other things that people worship, the God of Scripture is genuinely deity. It also means that he knows what is true and always speaks the truth.[35]

There is ample biblical support for each of these divine attributes. Let me offer just a sampling. As for divine omniscience, some key passages are Psalm 147:4–5; Job 36:4; and Hebrews 4:13.[36] Scriptures teaching God's omnipotence are Job 42:2; Psalm 62:11; Genesis 17:1; Ezekiel 10:5; and 2 Corinthians 6:18.[37] In support of divine sovereignty, there are Ephesians 1:11; Psalm 115:3; and Job 42:2.[38] And there are many verses that speak of God as a genuine deity (e.g., 2 Chron. 15:3; Jer. 10:10; and 1 John 5:20), and many others that affirm that he speaks only truth (e.g., Ps. 119:142, 160; John 3:33;

[32] John S. Feinberg, No One Like Him: The Doctrine of God, Foundations of Evangelical Theology (Wheaton, IL: Crossway, 2001), 315.
[33] Ibid., 288.
[34] Ibid., 294.
[35] Ibid. 372.
[36] For further biblical support, see ibid., 299–304.
[37] For further biblical support, see ibid., 279–283.
[38] For further biblical support see ibid., 295–298.

17:17—a reference specifically to Scripture but an affirmation that it is true—Heb. 6:18; and Titus 1:2).[39]

The data presented above support the first and second premises of the argument. Premises 3 and 4 are basically definitional. That is, premise 2 predicates four attributes of God, and steps 3 and 4 explain what those attributes as applied to God mean about his knowledge and actions. Were those attributes predicated of any other being, they would affirm the same characteristics as are affirmed of God in premises 3 and 4. Of course, this doesn't mean that any other being is omniscient, omnipotent, and truthful, but only that these attributes mean the same thing, regardless of who they are predicated of.

Support for premise 5 involves several things. On the one hand, it affirms God's omnipotence and absolute sovereignty. Evidence in support of those divine attributes was offered in regard to premise 2 above. But premise 5 asserts something further, for it singles out power to do two things in particular. Divine omnipotence means that God has every power to do whatever a being of his nature can do, and absolute sovereignty means that he decides and carries out whatever he chooses to happen. Of course, that sovereignty can be exercised only in terms of things that a being of God's nature can in fact do. Despite God's absolute sovereignty and omnipotence, given his divine nature, he cannot sin, catch a cold, kick a football, or fail a test.

Because God cannot do certain things, we must ask if he can reveal information and ensure that it is accurately transferred into writing. In my chapters on revelation, I presented biblical evidence that God reveals a variety of things, and does so in different forms. One thing God can disclose is information. He can do it, for example, by direct speech addressed to human beings, and in dreams and visions given to various humans. Specific biblical support for these claims is presented in my chapter on special revelation.

What about guaranteeing that his revelation is transferred into writing accurately? Actually, this involves two things. The first invokes Scripture's inspiration. Scripture as God's inspired word means that the Bible is what God revealed to individuals and then guided them to write in the words of the sixty-six books we know as the Bible. In my chapters on inspiration I presented plenty of evidence that God inspired the Bible. I needn't repeat it here, but only refer readers to those chapters.

Premise 5 asserts more than Scripture's inspiration. It also affirms that the biblical writers recorded correctly what God revealed. This might seem to affirm inerrancy, but it doesn't. Inerrancy refers to the truthfulness of what is revealed. Premise 5 refers to whether or not the biblical books we have are what God actually said. Of course, we aren't in a position to ask either the

---

[39] For further biblical evidence affirming the truthfulness of God see ibid., 372–374.

biblical authors or God whether the biblical authors wrote *accurately* what God said. Various biblical books are replete with phrases like "Thus saith the Lord" and "The word of the Lord came unto me saying." If Scripture's content affirms things that are wrong or incorrect, then, given God's omniscience and truthfulness, it is unlikely that God actually revealed what the biblical author wrote. But, as argued in the chapters on inerrancy, there is ample evidence that Scripture is inerrant. Still, we might wonder whether these true sentences of Scripture and sentences that are not assertions are accurate records of exactly what God said. Might there not be a slightly different wording of a sentence that would say the exact same thing the sentence affirms? That seems at least possible. So, if "accurately" means a verbatim recording of what God revealed, maybe we can't say that of Scripture.

In response, none of us was present when God revealed and inspired Scripture. Even so, biblical authors claim that they wrote what God revealed and instructed them to write. If the content of their books contains errors, then there is reason to believe they are lying about writing what God told them to write. But if their books don't contain errors, why should we doubt that they wrote what God revealed? If any book's content is something inappropriate for God to reveal, then we might be inclined to think the authors misunderstood what God wanted them to write. Of course, some people do think some of Scripture's content (such as passages which speak about God as vengeful and as ordering genocide) is unbefitting of God. But that likely is little more than the critic's belief that if he were God, he wouldn't say anything like that, so what is written must not be what God said. Of course, no such critic is God, so it is ludicrous to speculate about what one would think, do, or say if one were God.

I have raised several points in the previous two paragraphs in order to say that, while there are reasons to wonder whether some Scripture passages accurately record what God revealed, there is far from conclusive evidence that this complaint is correct. Moreover, critics don't raise such a complaint about the vast majority of biblical texts. When has a critic argued, for example, that passages which say God loves us or is compassionate, wise, and just must not actually be what God revealed to the biblical author? Surely, there have been and are critics who think God doesn't possess one or more of those attributes, but what critic rejects those divine attributes because she or he thinks that passages about those divine attributes aren't actually what God moved a biblical author to write?

Even so, a critic might reply, while the things I've said make it likely (assuming that one believes God can inspire a book) that the biblical authors wrote what God actually revealed, my arguments aren't absolutely conclusive. I would agree, but this is not an issue that this side of heaven we can likely affirm or reject with absolute certainty. But what evidence is there that biblical writers did not record exactly what God revealed? The content of biblical books is consistent with what we might expect God to say, and, given inerrancy, we know that no writer could deviate from what God revealed to the point of introducing error into the text. Moreover, we also saw in our study of inspiration that inspiration extends to the very words of Scripture. Hence, it is abundantly reasonable to believe that the biblical books contain exactly the wording God wanted. As a result of these considerations, I believe that this part of premise 5 has been adequately confirmed so as to be accepted as true.

Perhaps I should mention one further point in support of premise 5. One might grant that God is omnipotent and absolutely sovereign, but claim that a being with those characteristics cannot do things like reveal information and superintend its transference into a written document that accurately records what was revealed. The problem with this supposition is that it is hard to imagine any sort of conclusive evidence to support it. This must not be misunderstood. Critics of theism in general might deny that God, even if he exists, can act in such ways in the world. But it is hard to give thoroughly meaningful content to the notion of a divine being who is omnipotent and absolutely sovereign but incapable of acting in the world. If he can't act in the world, how can he have these attributes?

If the critic replies that God can do some things in the world, but not reveal information and inspire a book, what evidence supports such a claim? It isn't clear that revealing information and inspiring a book are miraculous deeds (like turning water into wine, creating the universe out of nothing, and resurrecting someone from the dead). Human beings can transfer their thoughts into writing, and that requires no miracle. Why should we think that for God to do such things requires miracles? Of course, critics may reply that all of this misses the point. The point is that God is a disembodied spirit, and it is unclear how such a being can act as needed to produce a book like the Bible (or any other book). But, in response, the fact that we don't know exactly how a disembodied being does various deeds isn't evidence that the being can't and/or doesn't do those acts.

In sum, the majority of what premise 5 affirms has been supported with conclusive evidence. Some of what it proposes cannot be proved with absolute certainty, but the evidence offered shows that it is highly probable that those parts of the premise are true. As for premise 6, it affirms Scripture's inspiration. Clearly, Scripture teaches its own inspiration, and that can easily be confirmed by consulting the evidence offered in my chapters on inspiration.

Premise 7 affirms biblical inerrancy. The evidence in support of that is contained in my chapters on inerrancy. Premise 8 is purely definitional, and it reflects my discussion in an earlier section of this chapter. One might quibble with some of the wording, but any alternate wording that still affirms the same notion of authority would be granted as an appropriate definition of the concept. Premise 9 may appear to be another definition, but it isn't. It is an important premise that links inerrancy with authority. Is truth authoritative? Earlier in this chapter I explained why it is, and by authority I mean what premise 8 affirms. Premise 8 is written from the perspective of an agent, but that isn't intended to suggest that only agents can have authority. An institution (like a government), a written document (e.g., a constitution of a country), and a spoken edict (a law announced by a king, for example) can also possess authority. While we don't normally speak of the truth of an institution, it is appropriate to speak of the truth of a spoken or written text. Premise 9 asserts that a true oral or written text also possesses authority.

Premise 10 isn't hard to support. It amounts to saying that if someone has authority, that authority applies not only to their very being, but also to whatever they say. This is especially true if they speak truth. If what they say is false, they may still have power to enforce it. But eventually, even the person enforcing untruth will have to face the consequences of rejecting truth. Of course, premise 10 isn't about speaking truth or error; it is about issuing commands. If the person issuing a command has authority over the activity involved and over people who must obey his demands, then what he says has authority. The point of this premise, then, is to distinguish the person who speaks from the words spoken. Lest one think a person could have authority over an activity and yet his demands related to that activity have no power to require obedience, premise 10 denies that this is so.

Finally, premise 11 is the conclusion. It asserts what one may conclude about the Bible in light of each of the premises of the argument. In simplest form it asserts that whatever has the characteristic of being the word of God also has the quality of being authoritative. The parenthetical remark in the premise attempts to detail the basis of linking Scripture's inspiration with its authority. Of course, readers must decide whether they think the premises are true and whether the conclusion follows from the premises. I have presented evidence for the truth of the premises, and it is hard to see why the conclusion is unacceptable if the premises are correct.

Hence, I believe that the argument presented is successful. Some may doubt the truth of one premise or another, so I have offered what seems to me the most direct support (though not necessarily exhaustive support) for each step in the argument. I am also open to entertaining an explanation of why the conclusion does not follow from the premises, if someone thinks it doesn't.

But such comments speak to some of the formal aspects of argument and evidence presentation and evaluation. What I want to affirm, however, is that even if one doesn't agree (for example, on some formal grounds or on grounds that the wording of a premise needs adjustment) that this particular structured argument succeeds, that doesn't mean that the argument's basic strategy fails. That is, what I have done in this argument is bring together the various diverse elements that evangelicals have in mind when they argue that a fully inspired and inerrant Bible must also be authoritative. My contention is that this basic argument is correct and that it can be successfully supported by the meaning of the concepts of inspiration, inerrancy, and authority, and by biblical teaching relevant to these topics.

Let me turn to other arguments for biblical authority. Some of them adopt or adapt one or more points made in the previous argument. For example, that argument makes the point that whatever is God's word possesses his authority. Hence, all Scriptures—and the number is legion—that begin with "Thus says the Lord," "The word of the Lord came unto me saying," "Scripture says," "It says," and "It is written" in effect say that what comes next is what God said.[40] And, if something in Scripture claims to be God's word, it also possesses his authority. Hence, verses with that formulaic beginning have the authority of being God's word.

Another implication of Scripture as God's word is also relevant to biblical authority. As the lengthy argument above notes, God is absolutely sovereign. As such, he is King of the universe, and Scripture often refers to him as King. While many refuse to acknowledge him as King, Scripture clearly teaches that history is headed toward a kingdom with God as supreme ruler, not just in principle but in fact. Of course, certain prerogatives come with being a king. One is that your word is law, and your subjects must obey. If they disobey, the king can punish them as he chooses. Of course, Scripture is God's word, and so, its every word is the word of the King. As the word of the supreme King, its authority exceeds the word of any other ruler, for all rulers other than God have limits to their authority. God's kingship is unlimited, and accordingly, his word has unlimited authority.

Then, a further argument relates specifically to the OT. Both OT and NT authors refer to OT books as law. In addition, there are places in the OT and NT where the whole OT is referred to as prophecy. This is not inaccurate, for the basic idea of a prophet is that he is a forthteller, someone who speaks a message from someone else. The message may be about the past, the present, or the future, but since the messenger speaks for another, it is a prophecy. All OT books present what God moved their authors to write. So, in that sense, they are all divine prophecy.

---

[40] This point is made brilliantly and exhaustively by B. B. Warfield in "'Scripture says,' 'It Says,' 'God Says',," in *The Inspiration and Authority of Scripture* (repr., Philadelphia: Presbyterian & Reformed, 1970).

Similarly, while *tôrāh*/law is used in the OT to speak of precepts, commands, and requirements—hence, we tend to think of law as a list of "dos" and "don'ts"—the term is also used generally in the basic sense of instruction. Instruction may offer commands, but it may also present a narrative of what has happened, predict future events, express worship, and many other things. Because *tôrāh* can refer to so many things, we might think it is just a general way to refer to anything the writer (and God) wanted to say. But if so, there are other words and ways in Hebrew to present instruction from God without using the term "law." And many of them are used in the OT—e.g., "thus says the Lord," "the word of the Lord came to me, saying," "the Lord revealed that," etc. And many verses begin by saying that what comes next is the law of the Lord. Is the word "law" merely a "filler word" with no use other than to serve as a formulaic way to introduce a sentence's theme? If so, then surely the writer could have used another word to introduce the main thought of the sentence.

But the writer refers to what he will say (or to what other OT books say) as law. Maybe he uses the word in the sense of instruction, but then, is what follows just information, and those who read it can do with it as they please? Though they might reject or ignore it, the people of Israel knew there were consequences for how they responded to *tôrāh*. God's reactions to their responses to his *tôrāh* show that he didn't give it just for information's sake, optional but not binding.

Why do I make these comments about OT law? My point is that by calling the OT law, God revealed that what he was saying had binding authority on those who received it. Some of it is commands, while other parts are narratives, etc., but Israel needed to know that everything in these inspired books is law. OT law not only communicated information; it also revealed obligations, and I am not just referring to passages that contain commands. Passages that describe God's nature, human nature, etc., state from God's perspective how he understands things. One might reject God's vision of things, but the world conceived of differently from how God sees things isn't the real world. Sooner or later everyone will realize that, and they will either reap the benefits of living life as God envisioned it or pay the price of rejecting God's vision of things. So, both the contents of the OT and the fact that all of it is called law imply that the OT has authority over human beings, like it or not.

Finally, critics might complain that most of the biblical evidence presented for Scripture's authority refers to the OT. What about the authority of the NT? Here I remind readers that in my chapters on inspiration, we saw that various NT writers saw their writing, and books by other apostles that became part of the NT, as God's word. But perhaps the most significant argument for NT inspiration came from Jesus's lips. In John 14, 15, and 16 he predicted the inspiration of the soon-to-be-written NT.

Perhaps readers are puzzled, because inspiration alone does not prove authority. True, but appeal to evidences of NT inspiration is only part of this final argument. I also refer readers to the lengthy argument (presented in this chapter) that whatever is inspired and inerrant is also authoritative. Jesus affirmed on many occasions his belief in the inspiration and inerrancy of the OT. He also promised (John 14; 15; 16) the Holy Spirit's ministry, and we noted that it would result in his disciples' powerful preaching ministries, and also in the production of the soon-to-be-written NT. All of these passages about the inspiration of the OT *and* NT, and all the evidence in support of the whole Bible's inerrancy are significant for biblical authority as well. That is so because, as shown in the argument from inspiration and inerrancy to authority, an inspired and inerrant Bible is also authoritative.

In this chapter I have discussed the concept of biblical authority and evidence in support of it. Because Scripture is the word of the King of kings, we should be surprised only if Scripture were not authoritative. Of course, many people reject its authority and go their own way, but they do so to their own peril. Just as eventually every knee will bow and every tongue confess that Jesus Christ is Lord, even so all people will someday recognize the authority of God's word! Sadly, those who spurn Scripture's authority in life will have no chance to relive life in full accord with its demands. The time to acknowledge and submit to the authority of God's word is now! What better guide through the vagaries of life could there be than the word of our beneficent King who knows everything and wants us to experience all of the best that he designed life to be! Scripture is God's manual for life. Ignore it at your own peril. Sooner or later everyone will submit to its authority! Why not now?

# III

---

SETTING THE BOUNDARIES

# ELEVEN

# Light Canonized

## The Doctrine of Canonicity

Since God can and still does reveal himself today, might someone write a new inspired book that would be Scripture? If not, how do we know that, and how do we know when the last biblical book was written? These are not fanciful questions, because other books written during the OT era, and before and after the life of Christ until the second century AD, were thought to be Scripture by some among God's people. Why aren't some of those books in our Bibles today? Who excluded them, and why? In addition, we know that some apostles whose books are part of the NT wrote other religious books, but those other books weren't considered God's word, and weren't included in Scripture when decisions were made about the exact contents of the NT. What is it about the books of the Bible that caused God's people to consider them Scripture while rejecting other apostolic works as not Scripture?

And, in the twentieth century, archaeologists discovered ancient texts like the Dead Sea Scrolls and materials at Nag Hamadi. These documents increased our knowledge of the OT immensely, and even changed some prevailing theories about the nature of intertestamental Judaism (including Judaism at the time of Christ) and about whether during that era there was in Judaism a consensus about what books belonged in the OT. What if, during the twenty-first century, researchers find a heretofore unknown book written by, for example, the apostle Peter or Paul? Would we be compelled to add it to the NT and call it Scripture? On what grounds would we decide whether that work should be part of our Bible?

These questions raise the topic of canonicity. In current literature one finds a veritable explosion of information about this issue. Though we might expect that nearly two thousand years after Christ's earthly life, the church would have long ago answered questions like those already raised, most of those questions are still debated in our day. In fact, there are different theories about when the various parts of the OT canon were closed and about when the NT canon was formalized. In fact, some scholars claim that the canon of Scripture has never been closed, not because there exist new claimants to a place in the canon, but because different parts of Christendom have distinct biblical canons, and because a general church council representing *all* Christians has never met and formally decided which books are Scripture and which are not.

Today, some even debate the purpose of canons in general, and of a biblical canon in particular. For example, William Abraham has argued that the purpose of canons, including the canon of Scripture, is to help people grow and mature in the Christian faith. However, Abraham claims, early in church history, the canon of Scripture became an epistemological criterion. That is, it was turned into a standard of doctrinal truth, and any views that disagreed with biblical teaching were deemed heretical. Moreover, this also meant that whatever is in Scripture must be true. That is so, regardless of what it affirms, whether it is consistent with the rest of Scripture, and whether it matches the facts of our world. Handling Scripture as an epistemological criterion has stayed with the church throughout its history. The net result, Abraham argues, is that we have missed Scripture's purpose, and instead have used it for things it was never intended to do.[1] Regardless of one's evaluation of Abraham's major thesis (to which we shall return in this chapter), what he argues shows that there is even disagreement over what the concept of canonicity is or should be.

These issues (and more) are difficult, but we can't ignore them, for too much is at stake. At various points in this book, I have explained that my understanding of the doctrine being considered (revelation, inerrancy, authority, etc.) assumes that the canon of Scripture is closed. But what if there is other Scripture (already in existence, but hidden, or yet to be revealed and written)? Since we don't know the contents of such imagined books, are we certain that we can defend biblical inerrancy if it includes those other works? Clearly, what the canon is and whether or not it is still open make a huge difference to other doctrines discussed in this volume.

Canonicity is also important to theological reflection in every area of systematic theology. Evangelical theology is based on Scripture, and that assumes very specific things about what counts as Scripture. If we are wrong about which books are canonical, then what our theology looks like may be anyone's guess. Suppose, for example, that the many scholars who have doubts about books like 2 Peter, Jude, or Esther are right in thinking that these books should

---

[1] William J. Abraham, *Canon and Criterion in Christian Theology* (Oxford: Clarendon, 1998).

not be considered Scripture. The loss of 2 Peter, for example, would not only significantly impact our understanding of end-time prophecy; it would also significantly damage our doctrine of Scripture. Second Peter 1:19–21 is a biblically and theologically foundational passage for the whole concept of inspiration. And 2 Peter 3:15–16 is a key passage in establishing the apostle Paul's writings as divinely inspired Scripture. If 2 Peter were not part of the canon, important texts that teach inspiration would be lost.

Then, canonicity is also crucial to biblical interpretation. Increasingly, biblical and theological scholars are calling for interpretation to consider the many contexts of each biblical passage. One of those contexts is the whole canon of Scripture. But even for those who don't emphasize considering the whole canon in interpreting any particular Scripture, canonicity still has implications for interpretation. Typical among exegetes (evangelical ones, especially) is the belief that Scripture interprets Scripture. As a result, we may find help in understanding a difficult passage by consulting a clearer passage on the same topic. Moreover, given a commitment to biblical inerrancy, an exegete must not propose an interpretation for one passage that contradicts what other passages teach. But all of these interpretive "rules of thumb" assume a stable, known canon. What if the canon is actually in a state of flux? What if a given interpretation contradicts the clear teaching of another passage in a different book, but it is determined that that other book should not be considered part of the canon? That would be catastrophic to our understanding of what Scripture actually teaches.

Perhaps the greatest practical implication of canonicity is its impact on our understanding of what God wants us to believe and of how he wants us to live. Even the staunchest Christian probably wishes that some biblical commands about behavior were not there. What if the biblical books that contain them aren't actually part of the canon? Wouldn't it be tempting to make a case against the canonicity of any book that contains commands we would like to ignore?

In short, what is ultimately at stake in debates about the canon is the matter of authority. Evangelicals believe that Scripture is the final authority for all matters of faith and practice. Committed Christians, scholars and laypeople alike, are willing to believe whatever Scripture teaches and obey whatever it requires; they just want to know exactly what God's word demands. But all of this assumes that we know what writings count as Scripture. Most of us, in thinking about our doctrinal beliefs and in deciding what is right and wrong to do, don't often, if at all, ask about whether the biblical books we consult on these matters are actually God's word and should be in the canon. But perhaps we should, since so much is debated today about biblical canonicity.

Because canonicity is so important, it is a bit puzzling that this topic receives so little coverage in most standard evangelical systematic theologies of the last few centuries, including many written during the last hundred years. Perhaps some systematicians prefer to leave issues of canon to biblical scholars, and indeed, OT and NT scholars offer much help on these matters. But, given this doctrine's implications for theology, it is indeed strange that systematic theologians haven't given it more attention.[2] Hopefully, we can do better in these chapters; a thorough discussion of issues related to canonicity is my goal.

## ISSUES FOR DISCUSSION

In my treatment of canonicity I shall focus on six questions. First, what is the concept of canonicity? While this may seem to be a very easy question, appearances are deceiving. That is so, not only because scholars don't define it identically, but because the concept itself is rather ambiguous.

But, assuming that we can adequately define canonicity, a second question is whether Scripture *directly* teaches this concept. I shall argue that Scripture does not, but even so, Scripture does teach things that imply and warrant this doctrine. But I must produce evidence to support such claims. If there is no biblical basis for this doctrine, then what is its warrant?

Third, a discussion of biblical canonicity should present the historical process of the canon's formation. But here we must distinguish two issues. One is the story of how the books were written, edited (if they were), and transcribed into various copies and translations and then disseminated. The other story is the history of the *recognition* of the books of the Bible as canonical. As for the latter, the story is multifaceted, for we must understand not only the story of each Testament's contents being recognized and formalized as canon, but we must also distinguish the process of OT canonization among the Jews from the same process in the Christian church. The first of these stories, the one about how the books were written, edited, etc., is not the subject for a theological discussion of canonicity, as noted above. The stories of how the different books came to be *recognized* as part of the OT or NT canon *are* part of the theological discussion of canonicity. At least part of the reason why this latter issue must be part of a doctrinal discussion of canonicity is that it involves who decided, when, and on what bases, that a given book should be in the canon.

In rehearsing these stories for various OT and NT books, we need an explanation not only of why certain books "made it" into the canon, but also an understanding of why others were not included. These matters are significant

---

[2] Here I confess that, in teaching the required course that includes the doctrine of Scripture, there is so much material to cover that canonicity seldom gets much attention. In a course that also covers prolegomena to theology and the doctrine of God, it is dubious that one can cover all areas related to the doctrine of Scripture. Even so, canonicity is just too important to pass over it entirely.

in themselves, but they also raise a fourth issue, the matter of criteria. The question of criteria is actually multifaceted. One facet is historical. Specifically, what criteria did the people of Israel and the church actually use in deciding whether a book had a right to a place in the canon of Scripture? Were those criteria ever explicitly stated in discussions of whether books qualified as canonical, or was it just assumed without any discussion that everyone knew the qualities that would convince most people that a book should be part of the canon? Regardless of the answers to those questions, does Scripture itself present criteria for determining canonicity? If so, does Scripture plainly assert those criteria, or must they be inferred from other scriptural teachings?

In discussing the issue of criteria, there are two extreme positions, both of which amount to there being no set criteria for canonicity. One extreme focuses on decisions made by the Jews and their general understanding of which books are canonical without articulating the criteria used to make the decisions. This extreme also focuses on the church councils that met and declared various OT and NT books canonical. According to this first approach, various criteria may have been used, but we don't know them. We do know the consensus view among the Jews and in the church councils, and that is the most we can say about how decisions were made. Proponents of this approach usually tell the story of which books were chosen, when, and by whom, and say no more. Thinkers who take this approach seem to speculate about what must have led the decision makers to choose as they did. This position amounts to the view that we can't state with any certainty clear criteria used to decide which books are in the canon.

At the other extreme are scholars who propose that genuinely canonical books have the quality of *autopistia*. That is, they are self-authenticating. This view often comes with the position that the Holy Spirit internally witnesses to believers that what they are reading is indeed God's word, and that therefore it should be in the canon. Of course, the obvious question is, what are the grounds for such self-authentication? That is, what exactly does the Holy Spirit say or do to convince believers that they are reading God's canonical word? Typically, proponents of this view reply that this is a request for objective criteria of canonicity, but the Holy Spirit's witness and Scripture as self-authenticating are things known subjectively. Just as the Holy Spirit witnesses internally to believers that they are saved (even though they can't articulate specifically what the Spirit did or said to give them that assurance), similarly he witnesses internally to us as we read Scripture that it is God's word. In that sense, Scripture is self-authenticating. While this view may seem to presuppose a criterion for canonicity, it actually doesn't, for most scholars who discuss criteria present characteristics of a book that anyone can objectively confirm or disconfirm.

Fifth, a discussion of biblical canonicity should show its relation to other doctrines in the doctrine of Scripture. For example, we should ask whether there is a legitimate distinction (as key thinkers like Albert Sundberg and his followers think) between what counts as Scripture and what counts as canonical. Scholars who press this distinction note that a given writing can be treated as Scripture (authoritative, and even thought to be of divine origin) and yet not be canonical (part of an authoritative list of books recognized as belonging in the canon). This distinction may seem odd, but it needn't be judged so. After all, there is a difference between a list of authoritative books and an authoritative list of books, and only the latter is what some mean by canonicity. Even more to the point, as various OT books were being written and read, they may have generally been viewed as from God and hence as Scripture, even though they were never formally recognized as such at a meeting of Jewish leaders (history suggests there never was such a meeting that would have been like a church council). Some scholars have argued that this was precisely the situation in Jesus's day, for even by his time the OT canon wasn't closed. While a consensus in Jesus's day saw the Torah as Scripture, and it was commonly held that the Prophets was another part of OT Scripture (even if there was disagreement over which books exactly fit into that section of the OT and which fell into a third category), it is argued that, though there is evidence that Jews saw a third part to the OT, in Jesus's day its exact contents hadn't yet been clearly decided. Some hold that, in light of the findings at Qumran (the Dead Sea Scrolls), it is likely that there were variant readings in manuscripts of various biblical books, but also that other books, not now seen as part of the OT canon, were collected along with biblical books and apparently treated as Scripture.[3]

There was a somewhat similar situation in regard to the NT canon. Before the twenty-seventh book of the NT was written, many other NT-era books were in circulation, and there is evidence that many of them were considered to be Scripture. In addition, there were also works like *The Shepherd of Hermas* that were widely circulated and seemed to have been treated as Scripture. In fact, such books even show up in lists of certain church fathers as though they were Scripture. And yet it wasn't until Athanasius's *Festal Easter Letter*

---

[3] For a discussion of this issue see, e.g., Lee Martin McDonald, *The Biblical Canon: Its Origin, Transmission, and Authority* (Peabody, MA: Hendrickson, 2007); McDonald, "The Integrity of the Biblical Canon in Light of Its Historical Development," *BBR* 6 (1996); Hans Peter Ruger, "The Extent of the Old Testament Canon," *The Bible Translator* 40 (July 1989); Sidnie White Crawford, "The Fluid Bible: The Blurry Line between Biblical and Nonbiblical Texts," *Bible Review* 15 (1999); and Timothy J. Stone, "The Biblical Canon according to Lee McDonald: An Evaluation," *European Journal of Theology* 18 (2009). See also Paul R. House, "Canon of the Old Testament," in *Foundations for Biblical Interpretation*, ed. David S. Dockery, Kenneth A. Mathews, and Robert B. Sloan (Nashville: Broadman & Holman, 1994). Especially helpful on this matter is a chart on 137 of House's chapter which compares the lists of OT books in the Rabbinic canon, the Septuagint, the Roman Catholic OT, and the Protestant OT canon.

(AD 367) that we have anything like a complete list of the NT, and it included our current twenty-seven books. And then, it wasn't until the synod of Carthage in 397 that a group of church leaders ruled on which NT books were part of the canon.

None of the above per se covers the Christian understanding of the canon of the *whole* Bible, and not all Christians agree on that matter, anyway. It isn't just that the Protestant and Roman Catholic canons differ. There are also differences in the canon of the Eastern churches, and others as well. I shall add more details later, but what I have already presented should convince readers that we must discuss exactly how the concept of Scripture should relate to the concept of canon.

Finally, a discussion of canonicity should address whether the canon of Scripture is closed. It is interesting to see how few authors even broach this issue, let alone state an argument for or against closure. Some who do handle it seem to think that a thorough historical reconstruction of the process of canon-building by books being recognized as canonical, plus a statement that the church hasn't deemed other books canonical, is all that can and should be said about the matter of closure. But that doesn't tell us whether from *God's* perspective the canon is closed. A proper understanding of the doctrine of revelation shows that God can today still reveal himself in our world. Shouldn't evangelicals want to know whether any of that revelation could become Scripture? If it can't, can any biblical or extrabiblical case be made to prove that this couldn't happen because the canon of Scripture is closed?

The issue of the closure of the canon actually raises two questions. The first is easier to answer, and often is the one addressed if canon closure is addressed at all. It is the question of how we might, on biblical grounds, disqualify any past, current, or future claimant to a rightful place in the canon. In fact, I contend that most arguments evangelicals offer to prove that the canon is closed are actually ways to discredit potential "contenders" for a place in the canon. Such arguments need to be stated, and when necessary used to evaluate claims of other religious books (past, present, and future) to a place in the canon. However, no argument of that kind can tell us unequivocally that the canon is closed. Such arguments still leave open the door to the *possibility* that a "successful" candidate for a position in the canon might come along in the future, and that as a result, it would be necessary to expand Scripture beyond its current sixty-six books.

In light of these considerations, we should address a second (and more difficult) issue. Put simply, is there an argument (or a set of arguments) that decisively requires that the canon be closed? If so, that argument would preclude even the possibility that God would inspire (in the biblical sense of inspiration) someone to write a sixty-seventh book that we would be compelled to add to the canon of Scripture.

## The Concept of Canonicity

Our discussion begins with defining canonicity. The English word for canon and canonicity comes from the Greek word *kanon*, which in turn is derived from the Hebrew word *qāneh*, which means "reed" or "measuring rod."[4] In its most fundamental sense, *kanon* means a reed or a rod used for measuring things. Derivatively it came to mean a criterion for judging whether a particular thing met the standard(s) for qualifying as an instance of some thing or concept. As an example of this notion, think of the discussion in our times over the concept of human personhood. Depending on how one defines personhood, various characteristics or qualities must be true of a purported person in order for him or her to qualify as a human person. Those characteristics or qualities are the "canons," the measuring qualities, that must inhere in an unborn fetus, a five-year-old child, an adult, and a comatose individual fighting a terminal disease, in order for those individuals to qualify as specific instances of the more general concept of human persons. Of course, if there are "canons" of this sort, there must be a way to test individual purported instances of the phenomenon in question to determine whether it possesses the qualities (and thus, meets the requirements) needed to be an instance of the thing in question.

What I shall say next is *not* a definition of the concept of biblical canonicity, but I offer it as an example of how the meaning of the *word* "canon" (in the sense articulated above) might apply to Scripture. If someone asked whether a religious document, such as Esther, 1 Samuel, Luke, or Jude possesses the quality of canonicity, that question would assume that there are qualities of religious books, that is, various "canons," that must be true of a book for it to be part of the OT or NT of the Bible. Whatever those qualities/measuring standards are, we could then examine each purported instance of a biblical book to see whether it meets the measuring standards (i.e., possesses the "canons"). On that basis, we could decide whether it should be considered part of the Bible.

Both examples (the one about personhood and the other about qualifying as a member of the Bible) illustrate the sense that the Greek word *kanon* came to have, but they don't per se define the *concept* of canonicity. Nor is the Greek word *kanon* used in either the OT (LXX) or the NT in a discussion of the *concept* of biblical canonicity. In the NT, the Greek word *kanon* appears in 2 Corinthians 10:13, 15, 16; and Galatians 6:16. Some manuscripts also include

---

[4] Ronald Youngblood, "The Process: How We Got Our Bible," *Christianity Today* 32 (February 5, 1988): 24; and James H. Charlesworth, "Writings Ostensibly outside the Canon," in *Exploring the Origins of the Bible*, ed. Craig A. Evans and Emanuel Tov (Grand Rapids, MI: Baker, 2008), 58.

it in Philippians 3:16. In the Septuagint (the Greek OT), *kanon* only occurs in Micah 7:4.[5] Even a brief survey of these NT and LXX instances of *kanon* should convince readers that none of these passages are about the concept of Scripture as a canon or of what makes a biblical book canonical.

These facts alone about *kanon* don't show that Scripture doesn't define the concept of canon and canonicity, for the concept can be discussed without using the words *qāneh* or *kanon*.[6] However, one will look in vain for any passage or combination of passages in Scripture that define this concept. This doesn't mean that Scripture offers no help in determining what books should be included in either Testament. It does mean, however, that Scripture doesn't address directly the concept of canonicity or in any way define it. Still, the concept has been present in Christian thinking about both the OT and NT for more than 1,600 years. Moreover, the idea of an OT canon has been present in Jewish thinking for considerably longer, even though one would be hard pressed to identify anything in Jewish writings about Scripture that would approximate how we might define canon and canonicity today.

Though the concept of canonicity has certainly been held in Christian theology throughout much of church history, not every thinker defined the concept in the same way. And contemporary discussions about canonicity use a seeming myriad of different definitions.

An initial definition of canonicity focuses on the relation between canon and Scripture. For most evangelicals there is no difference between the content of these two. Whatever is part of the canon is Scripture and whatever is part of Scripture is canonical. Since this is self-evident for many, undoubtedly, while recognizing that each concept has a distinct definition, they would think that the referent of these two concepts (Scripture and canon) is identical. Hence, they would wonder why I am making a distinction between canon and Scripture. The answer is that, as students of the canonicity issue know, in our times, various biblical and theological scholars have argued that these concepts are not the same. Not only do Scripture and canon have different definitions (a point on which all agree), but the *referent* of each is also distinct. Let me explain.

We can begin to understand this distinction if we focus on times during the OT era and then the first century AD when there were religious books that the people of Israel and the church, respectively, viewed as sacred writings of divine origin. During these times nothing like an OT or NT canon (a specific collection) had been formed. In fact, when these books were being written,

---

[5] The LXX also contains the Apocrypha, and *kanon* appears in *Judith* 13:6 and 4 *Maccabees* 7:21. Neither of these passages uses it in the sense of the concept of biblical canonicity.
[6] Implicit in my discussion so far is the distinction between defining a term/word and defining a concept. I have used that distinction elsewhere in this book already, and will explicitly apply it to canonicity later in this chapter.

it is dubious that anything like the concept of a canon was on the minds of God's people.

Much of the emphasis to distinguish between Scripture and canon stems from the work of Albert C. Sundberg Jr. and Theodore Swanson.[7] According to Sundberg, the term "Scripture" refers to writings that are considered holy and function in some sense authoritatively for a religious community. In contrast, "canon" refers to a defined collection of these books that is held to be exclusively authoritative as opposed to other writings. As some have noted, to the notion of canon also attaches the idea that once a canon is defined, nothing can be added to it or removed.[8]

Given this distinction, there could be Scripture without there being a canon, but there couldn't be a canon without the existence of biblical books. So canon logically presupposes Scripture, but not the opposite.[9] While there were biblical books at certain times in history that functioned authoritatively in the Jewish or Christian community even before there was any sense of an OT or NT canon, some thinkers have used implications of this distinction for purposes that evangelicals would not necessarily sanction. For example, some have said that Scripture, as defined in the sense stated, is a rather fluid and inclusive concept. At least, it can be and has been used this way by thinkers who would say that, at one time in history, various apocryphal books were treated as Scripture by the Jewish community, and that at another time, the very early church era, other books like the *Shepherd Of Hermas*, the *Gospel of Thomas*, and the *Apocalypse of Peter* were read and used in churches as Scripture. While such things probably happened, to designate these works as Scripture seems only to cast doubts on the reasoning behind the processes, whatever they were, of eventually recognizing certain books and not others as canonical. Perhaps there were many Christians in the early church, for example, who were confused about which new religious writings should be considered from God and which ones should not be. That alone doesn't seem to be a good reason for us, with twenty centuries of hindsight, to be as puzzled as some early Christians might have been about why some books became canonical and others didn't. The puzzlement only escalates, it seems, when one persists in calling books Scripture that would not and did not make it into the canon. In other words,

---

[7] The distinction to be explained seems to have originated with Sundberg's *The Old Testament of the Early Church* (Cambridge, MA: Harvard University Press, 1964). Also of importance was Theodore N. Swanson's doctoral dissertation at Vanderbilt University (completed in 1970) entitled *The Closing of the Collection of Holy Scripture*.

[8] For this distinction see Stephen B. Chapman, "The Canon Debate: What It Is and Why It Matters," *JTI* (2010): 277–278; Michael W. Holmes, "The Biblical Canon," in *The Oxford Handbook of Early Christian Studies*, ed. Susan A. Harvey and David G. Hunter (Oxford: Oxford University Press, 2010), 406–407; Craig D. Allert, "The State of the New Testament Canon in the Second Century: Putting Tatian's *Diatessaron* in Perspective," *BBR* 9 (1999): 12; and Nancy L. deClaisse-Walford, "The Dromedary Saga: The Formation of the Canon of the Old Testament," *RevExp* 95 (1998): 495. Each of these authors states the distinction slightly differently, but each statement amounts to that of the others.

[9] Allert, "State of the New Testament Canon in the Second Century," 15.

while I think the distinction between Scripture and canon articulates a genuine distinction, it only confuses things to call *any* literary text Scripture that functioned in a religiously authoritative way.

A further consequence of this distinction is that it allows theologians and Bible scholars to postulate any of a variety of dates (and procedures) for the actual closing of the canon. Since there can be Scripture while there is no canon, scholars can espouse any dates they want for the writing of biblical books and for the close of each canon, while not denying that various religious writings (including all that made up the canon) were treated as divinely inspired and authoritative for the Jewish and/or Christian community. My point here is that matters such as the dating and authorship of biblical books and the dates for the close of the OT and NT canons (and parts of each) shouldn't be manipulated just because they can be made to seem innocuous by claiming that, while there was no canon, there was still Scripture. Historical questions shouldn't be solved by introducing conceptual distinctions that allow historians to choose whatever answers to historical questions please them.

Despite these possible consequences of the distinction between Scripture and canon, I think the basic differences noted between the two concepts are sound. In particular, it is undeniable that, at times when believing communities were not at all thinking about canon, they still had religious writings to guide their lives.

A second set of definitions distinguishes between what proponents call a broad versus a strict or narrow definition of canon. David Carr explains that the narrow usage of the term "canon" refers "to the recognition of a closed, clearly defined body of Scriptures." In contrast, the broad sense of "canon" refers "to the process leading up to this recognition, a process which might be more precisely termed 'proto-canonical'."[10] In explaining "proto-canonical," Carr adds,

> The two halves of this latter term recognize both truths about the process leading to canonization: 'proto' indicates the distinction of such preliminary recognition of authority from the later official codification of a clearly defined, exclusive canon in church or synagogue decisions; 'canonical' indicates the extent to which such preliminary recognition is not only an indispensable precondition for later inclusion of such writings in an official 'canon', but is also already implicitly exclusive, implying that the recognized writings enjoy a certain noteworthy authority beyond that of others.[11]

Eugene Ulrich also offers a distinction between a "broad" and a "strict" definition of canonicity, but his distinction sounds quite like the distinction

---

[10] David M. Carr, "Canonization in the Context of Community: An Outline of the Formation of the Tanakh and the Christian Bible," in *A Gift of God in Due Season: Essays on Scripture and Community in Honor of James A. Sanders*, ed. Richard D. Weis and David M. Carr, JSOTSup 225 (1996), 24.

[11] Ibid.

between Scripture and canon already presented. For Ulrich, a broad definition of "canon" includes sacred texts traditionally considered authoritative,
but it doesn't necessarily include the ideas of a "reflexive articulated decision
that specific texts and not others belong to a special category and are binding
for all believers for all time." In contrast, a strict definition does include the
elements of "conscious decision, unique status, necessarily binding."[12] Ulrich
further thinks it best to use the stricter definition and to do so consistently
when speaking of the canon of Scripture. He believes the key items involved
in that definition are a reflexive judgment, one "that is made in retrospect,
self-consciously looking backward and recognizing and explicitly affirming
that which has already come to be," a closed list, and a concern with biblical
books, not the specific textual form of the books. Ulrich explains that "text"
can be used to refer either to a literary opus or to the particular wording of
that work. He argues that in Judaism and Christianity it is the literary works,
not the precise textual wording thereof, that is considered canonical.[13]

Stephen Chapman is concerned about Ulrich's narrowing and limiting
of the notion of canonicity, because by limiting the meaning as Ulrich does,
Ulrich winds up defining canonicity in a sense that can't be applied to any
actual list of biblical books. This is so because "an officially complete and
absolute listing of the canon *never really took place at all* in either Jewish
or Christian tradition."[14] Chapman thinks it would be better to find another
definition of canon, rather than using one that refers to something that never
actually existed.

In a later journal article, Chapman commented at length on all of these
distinctions. He proposed that there are basically two positions on how canon
should be used. He calls them an *exclusivist* and an *inclusivist* view of canon.
According to the former, the rigid distinction between Scripture and canon (in
the senses explained above) is affirmed, and the term "canon" is used only in
the sense of a set of sacred books consciously chosen as the definitively authoritative books for the religion in view. It includes the idea that the corpus is
closed, so that no book in the canon can be removed and no book can be added.
As Chapman explains in evaluating Ulrich's preferred definition of canon, the
problem with the exclusivist view is that there never was such a list decisively
selected by either the Jews or Christians.[15]

In contrast to the exclusivist view, Chapman explains that the inclusivist

---

[12] Eugene Ulrich, "The Canonical Process, Textual Criticism, and Latter Stages in the Composition of the Bible,"
in *"Sha'arei Talmon": Studies in the Bible, Qumran, and the Ancient Near East Presented to Semaryahu Talmon*,
ed. Michael Fishbane and Emanuel Tov (Winona Lake, IN: Eisenbrauns, 1992), 270.

[13] Ibid., 272–273. See also Stephen B. Chapman, "The Old Testament Canon and Its Authority for the Christian
Church," *Ex Auditu* 19 (2003): 135–136, who presents Ulrich's distinction and comments on it.

[14] Chapman, "Old Testament Canon," 136.

[15] Chapman, "Canon Debate," 277–278, 280–281.

view doesn't make such a rigid distinction between Scripture and canon as defined above. Rather, the two overlap, and "canon" can be rightly used to designate one or the other, or both. As Chapman explains, this position is most closely associated with Brevard Childs and James Sanders. As to what leads them to this inclusivist view, Chapman says they contend that,

> . . . historically, the term *canon* has designated a norm as well as a list, that a canon is likely to function as a norm before being formalized, and that this for-malization is better understood as the recognition of an already-authoritative literary collection than as the conferral of authority. It is possible to use the term *Scripture* to describe a functional but informal canon, these scholars concede, yet the term *canon* goes farther to establish the normativity of the tradition this collection represents and makes a claim about the continuity of that normative tradition over time. Hence, the concern is not only to distin-guish the idea of a normative Scripture from merely "inspirational" writings but also to describe how normative Scripture both generates and influences subsequent tradition.
>
> Scholars with this second approach therefore emphasize the *inclusive* sense of canon and tend to take early indications of a work's authority and influence as evidence suggestive of its canonicity. Even though the boundaries of Israel's literary collection still may have been porous or open, application of the term *canon* is justified according to these scholars because the essential contours of the later formalized canon and a certain characteristic dynamic between the community and its Scripture were already palpably in place.[16]

So that these definitions won't overwhelm us with conceptual confusion, let me explain how they relate to one another. What some thinkers define as Scripture fits basically what Ulrich labels a *broad* definition of canon and what Chapman labels an *inclusivist* definition of canon. In addition, what those who distinguish Scripture and canon mean by canon fits best with what Ulrich calls a *strict* definition of canon and what Chapman means by an *exclusivist* definition of canon. There are, of course, depending on the scholar who holds the definitions, various nuances for each of these concepts, but in general they connect with one another as just explained.

To complicate matters a bit further, Gerald Sheppard has proposed a dis-tinction to which many scholars appeal. He distinguishes two different senses of "canon" which he labels "canon 1" and "canon 2." Canon 1 is essentially a norm, rule, guide, or standard that functions authoritatively in a community. Such a religious work has not been officially recognized as part of a closed list, but nonetheless it functions as though it is. Hence, the canon as canon 1 can be fluid and flexible; that is, further works can become authoritative in a com-munity at a particular time, and works already having that status can later lose

---

[16] Ibid., 278–279.

their normative sense and no longer be viewed as canonical in any sense. In contrast, canon 2 refers to a situation where the authority of various religious books becomes so fixed in a faith community that thereafter there is very little doubt about their authority. Hence, a given book becomes part of a fixed list of authoritative books. Once a community ascribes such authority to a large number of books, for all intents and purposes canon 2 becomes a closed list. So the basic distinction between canon 1 and canon 2 is between books that *function* as a norm or authority but may cease to do so in a religious community, and a *closed, fixed list of books* with religious authority for a community.[17]

Somewhat parallel to the distinction between canon 1 and canon 2 is a distinction posited by James Sanders. He differentiates between canon as "*norma normans*, where focus is on the function of a community's authoritative or canonical literature . . . and *norma normata*, where focus is on the structure of canons effected by the phenomenon of canonical 'closure'."[18] *Norma normans* means "norming norm." As applied to Scripture, it means that it is the authoritative rule that makes binding whatever it affirms as mandatory. This is roughly the idea of Sheppard's canon 1. *Norma normata* means "normed norm." As related to Scripture it means that Scripture, by being recognized in a formal, fixed list as the normative standard is thereby the normed (or formally recognized) norm (rule, standard) for faith and practice. This is substantially what canon 2 points to.

From the definitions offered so far, it should be clear that canon 1 is roughly equivalent to the inclusive notion of canon defined by Chapman and to the broad sense of canon defined by Ulrich. Canon 2 is closest to Chapman's exclusivist and Ulrich's strict definitions of canon. The distinction detailed between Scripture and canon is also relevant; the former fits best with canon 1, the inclusivist notion, while the latter is more akin to canon 2 and the exclusivist concept of canon.

While these various distinctions and definitions may appear to say basically the same thing, canon has been defined in other senses. For example, a number of scholars define canon as the normative ethical and doctrinal guide according to which a member of the religious community was to live his or her life. In relating this sense to the OT, Sid Leiman writes, "A canonical book is a book accepted by Jews as authoritative for religious practice and/or doctrine,

---

[17] The distinction originates with Gerald T. Sheppard and is to be found in his essay "Canon," in *The Encyclopedia of Religion*, 10 vols., ed. Mircea Eliade (New York: MacMillan, 1987), 3:62–69. The following articles cite and discuss this distinction: Stephen Dempster, "Canons on the Right and Canons on the Left: Finding a Resolution in the Canon Debate," *JETS* 52 (March 2009): 50; Allert, "State of the New Testament Canon in the Second Century," 13; Chapman, "Old Testament Canon," 135; John C. Peckham, "The Canon and Biblical Authority: A Critical Comparison of Two Models of Canonicity," *TJ* 28 (2007): 232; and McDonald, "Integrity of the Biblical Canon," 101–102.

[18] James A. Sanders, "Intertextuality and Canon," in *On the Way to Nineveh: Studies in Honor of George M. Landes*, ed. Stephen Cook and S. C. Winter (Atlanta: Scholars Press, 1999), 317.

and whose authority is binding upon the Jewish people for all generations."[19] Though this definition may seem identical to canon 1, it is not. For example, this definition does not include the notion of fluidity that is part of canon 1; clearly, Leiman's definition requires that a canon is authoritative and binding on all Jews of all generations. So, it gives a more fixed sense to the canon without absolutely requiring a closed canon, and in that sense it differs from canon 2.

Yet another definition of canon basically seems to combine the notions contained in canon 1 and canon 2. After noting several different senses in which "canon" had been applied to the NT, Linda Belleville explains that in the fourth century AD the term "*kanon* came to be applied to a list of books whose content was viewed as authoritative for matters of faith and practice." As she notes, Athanasius seems to be the first church father who used the notion of canon in that sense, when he claimed that *Shepherd of Hermas* doesn't belong in the canon.[20] The first clear use of "canon" in this way is found in Athanasius's *Thirty-Ninth Festal Easter Letter*, written in AD 367.[21] As some have noted, with this kind of definition it is worth asking whether we have an authoritative list of books or a list of authoritative books. In the latter case, authority is inherent in the books, whereas in the former the emphasis is on the authority ascribed to the books included in the list.[22] In the case of the notion of canon now under consideration, both seem to be the case, for the books' contents are what is authoritative for faith and practice, but formalizing a list of such books also gives them a further sense of authority.

In addition to the preceding definitions, others have defined canon as a closed, fixed collection of documents regarded as Scripture. This definition clearly has affinities with elements in previous definitions, including canon 1 and canon 2. The key element in this definition is its emphasis on *closure* of the canon. In fact, for some the idea of closure is even more significant than the notion of a particular list. This idea of a fixed or closed canon is central to

---

[19] Sid Z. Leiman, *The Canonization of Hebrew Scripture: The Talmudic and Midrashic Evidence* (Hamden, CT: Archon, 1976), 103. Leiman's quote appears in Paul R. House, "Canon of the Old Testament," 136. For the same basic notion of canon see also Holmes, "Biblical Canon," 407; Chapman, "Old Testament Canon," 135; and David Dunbar, "The Biblical Canon," in *Hermeneutics, Authority, and Canon*, ed. D. A. Carson and John Woodbridge (Grand Rapids, MI: Zondervan, 1986), 300.

[20] Linda L. Belleville, "Canon of the New Testament," in *Foundations for Biblical Interpretation*, ed. David Dockery, Kenneth Matthews, and Robert Sloan (Nashville: Broadman & Holman, 1994), 375. This notion of canon also seems to be present in Elmer Dyck, "What Do We Mean by Canon?," *Crux* 25 (March 1989): 18; Bruce Metzger, "The Context and Development of the Christian Canon," in *Living Traditions of the Bible*, ed. James Bowley (St. Louis: Chalice, 1999), 85; and M. James Sawyer, "Evangelicals and the Canon of the New Testament," *GTJ* 11 (1991): 39.

[21] This particular point finds wide agreement among scholars. See, e.g., Dempster, "Canons on the Right and Canons on the Left," 50; Ulrich, "Canonical Process," 271; House, "Canon of the Old Testament," 136; and deClaisse-Walford, "Dromedary Saga," 495.

[22] Several scholars who make this distinction between an authoritative list of books and a list of authoritative books are Bruce M. Metzger, *The Canon of the New Testament: Its Origin, Development, and Significance* (Oxford: Clarendon, 1987), 282; Holmes, "Biblical Canon," 407; and Sawyer, "Evangelicals and the Canon of the New Testament," 39.

Lee McDonald's understanding of canon, and is also a key point in one of the many senses in which Brevard Childs speaks of canon.[23]

Another definition of a canonical book is one that many evangelicals would begin with, in part because it seems inherent in what Scripture teaches about itself. According to this definition, a book is canonical if it is considered to be inspired by God.[24] Of course, if a book was considered inspired, it was deemed orthodox and whatever disagreed with it was regarded as heretical.[25] Though it is likely that the Jews held the OT to be inspired and the early church held the OT and the various NT books (as they were written) inspired, given the negative effects of the historical-critical method as applied to Scripture, it is easy to see why inspiration is seldom mentioned among nonevangelical biblical scholars and theologians.

As we search for other characteristics or criteria of a canonical book, we must be careful not to confuse criteria with tests for canonicity. The criteria explain the characteristics in virtue of which a book is canonical. However, those criteria don't test any purported canonical book to see if it is in fact canonical. One must construct a way of testing candidates to see if they have the characteristics inherent in a canonical book. Of course, the kind of test involved (empirical, historical, rational, e.g.) will depend on the characteristics of canonicity, but even so, these qualities are not themselves the tests. In fact, before one can devise tests and apply them to purported canonical books, one must first define what canonicity is.

There is a final noteworthy definition of canon. During the second century AD, before many NT books had gained much circulation and before there was much of a sense of an NT canon (in the previous senses of canon already defined), the concept of canon came to refer to the rule or essentials of the faith. This rule of faith contained the substance of apostolic teaching about Christ. As D. H. Williams explains, "Although there is no one structure or content in the earliest stages of the apostolic message, one does find a set of reoccurring themes which are based on the revelation of God in Christ as seen through his incarnate life, servanthood through his crucifixion, death, burial, and the

---

[23] See McDonald, Biblical Canon. His definition and understanding of the biblical canon are discussed at length in Stone, "Biblical Canon according to Lee McDonald." On 57–58, Stone specifically discusses McDonald's definition. Childs's definitions can be found in his The New Testament as Canon (Philadelphia: Fortress, 1983), 41. All of this is discussed in Richard R. Topping, "The Canon and the Truth: Brevard Childs and James Barr on the Canon and the Historical-Critical Method," Toronto Journal of Theology 8 (1992): 243ff. For others who discuss this definition, see Holmes, "Biblical Canon," 407; Charlesworth, "Writings Ostensibly outside the Canon," 58; Allert, "State of the New Testament Canon in the Second Century," 13 (in relation to Harry Gamble's "Canon—New Testament," in The Anchor Bible Dictionary, ed. David N. Freedman, 6 vols. [New York: Doubleday, 1992], 1:852–861).

[24] See here House, "Canon of the Old Testament," 136; Sawyer, "Evangelicals and the Canon of the New Testament," 39; and Thomas Finley's quote of Andrew Steinmann's definition of canon: Steinmann's definition is taken from his work The Oracles of God: The Old Testament Canon (St. Louis: Concordia Academic, 1999), 18; his definition is quoted in Thomas J. Finley, "The Book of Daniel in the Canon of Scripture," BSac 165 (April–June 2008): 195.

[25] For this point, along with his critique of it, see Robert W. Funk, "The Incredible Canon," in Christianity in the 21st Century, ed. Deborah A. Brown (New York: Crossroad, 2000), 37.

remaking of creation from his resurrection and realized lordship. There was indeed some sense of a 'canon' of teaching as the above passages show, having to do with standard features of the apostles' preaching."[26]

As G. A. Robbins has shown, Eusebius definitely used *kanon* in this sense in his *Ecclesiastical History*. That is, he used it to refer to the church's rule of faith or standard of orthodoxy in his discussion in 4.23.4, 6.13.3, 6.33.1, and 7.30.6. In these passages it is used to refer to the "Canon of Faith."[27] Craig Allert shows that church fathers in both the second and third century AD used "canon" in this sense. As he says, the church fathers Irenaeus and Tertullian answered Marcion, Gnosticism, and Montanism by appealing not to a closed canon of Scripture but rather to a canon of truth that matched apostolic writings but didn't match the teachings of Marcion, Gnostics, or Montanists. In fact, even in the early third century Serapion did a similar thing. As Allert explains,

> In writing to his church, Serapion wished to settle the question of whether the *Gospel of Peter* could be read in that church. He had previously allowed it to be read in the church but later reversed this decision on the basis that it denied the humanity of Jesus. The point here is that Serapion did not revoke his permission to allow the *Gospel of Peter* to be read in the church on the basis of an appeal to a closed collection of scripture but on the basis of the canon of truth, on the basis that certain doctrines contained in that Gospel were at variance with what was handed down through the Apostles to the Bishops of the churches. The issue was dealt with on the basis of orthodoxy, not canonicity.[28]

There are definitely other definitions of canon and canonicity,[29] but the ones provided seem to be the main ones relevant to our discussion. Obviously, those presented offer a wide variety of senses of canon and canonicity, and

[26] D. H. Williams, "The Patristic Tradition as Canon," *Perspectives in Religious Studies* 32 (2005): 360.
[27] Gregory Allen Robbins, "Eusebius' Lexicon of 'Canonicity'," *Studia Patristica* (Berlin: Akademie-Verlag, 1957), 137–138.
[28] Allert, "State of the New Testament Canon in the Second Century," 15. See also Belleville on this point that during the second century, canon came to refer to the rule or essentials of the faith to which Christian life and teaching was to conform. See Belleville, "Canon of the New Testament," 375.
[29] For example, Christine Helmer, "Trust and the Spirit: The Canon's Anticipated Unity," *JTI* 1 (2007): 62–63, 73, argues that the key theological notion related to canon is unity. Then, several senses in which Brevard Childs uses "canon" and "canonical" (many of them in relation to interpretive concepts) are discussed in Topping, "Canon and the Truth," 243–245; Dyck, "What Do We Mean by Canon?," 18–19; and Jeffrey Kloha, "The Problem of Paul's Letters: Loss of Authority and Meaning in the 'Canonical Approach' of Brevard Childs," *Concordia Journal* 35 (Spring 2009): 157–159. Funk, "Incredible Canon," 33, and William W. Hallo ("The Concept of Canonicity in Cuneiform and Biblical Literature: A Comparative Appraisal," in *The Biblical Canon in Comparative Perspective: Scripture in Context IV*, ed. K. Lawson Younger Jr., William W. Hallo, and Bernard F. Batto [Lewiston, NY: Edwin Mellen Press, 1991], 3) discuss various secular senses of canon. Finally, Jonathan R. Wilson discusses three other notions of canonicity that he takes from John Howard Yoder's terminology ("high Protestant scholasticism," "high Tridentine Catholicism," and "high modernism"). Wilson shortens these labels to "Protestant," "Catholic," and "Modernist," and discusses them in "Canon and Theology: What Is at Stake?," in Evans and Tov, *Exploring the Origins of the Bible*. In addition, Bruce Metzger says that a canon may be drawn up as a list of titles of different texts, or refer to the assembled texts themselves. "So the term canon has both these connotations: It is a list as well as the contents of what is comprised in that list." See Metzger's "The Context and Development of the Christian Canon," 85.

many of them seem to capture something that is true about Scripture. And yet many speak of things distinct from other definitions. Thus, if we tried to combine all of the definitions into a huge one, I don't think that would likely clear up all the confusion surrounding this concept. It would probably only add to it. So how should we proceed? In the next section I shall briefly summarize the definitions proposed, extracting from each whatever we might want to emphasize in a definition, add whatever concepts seem appropriate, and then propose a definition of canon and canonicity in general and a definition of biblical canon and canonicity in particular.

## DEFINING BIBLICAL CANONICITY

### A Summary of the Definitions with Brief Commentary

The definitions presented in the preceding section cover a variety of things. I think it would be helpful to summarize them by setting forth as distinct points the foci of the various definitions studied so far. Hence, the major themes of the definitions already presented can be organized as follows:

1. Some definitions focus on a formalized list of books deemed canonical, whereas others emphasize a *functional* authority that attaches to various books, regardless of whether or not they are part of a formal list.
2. Inherent in the notion of canon as possessing functional authority and as being part of a formalized list is the idea that whatever is canon or canonical is normative or the standard for faith and practice.
3. An early used notion of canon focused not so much on a book or list of books, but rather on specific doctrinal truths held to be the standard for faith and practice; this is canon in the sense of the rule of faith or the essentials of the faith. Books that are deemed canonical are seen, at least in part, to be normative or the standard, because they either incorporate beliefs that are part of the rule of faith, or they at the very least don't contradict anything in the essentials of the faith.
4. At least one definition links canonicity with the concept of divine inspiration.
5. Central to some definitions is the idea that the canon is closed, while for other definitions, the notion of closure is not only absent but those definitions emphasize the canon as open and fluid.

What should we say to such emphases? I find many things helpful in attempting to formulate a definition of canon and canonicity, but some things are in my judgment a bit dubious. For one thing, thinkers who place emphasis on the canon functioning authoritatively in a community often make it sound as though the community of believers made a decision to make that happen. Hence, on that assessment, canonicity isn't a quality God put in Scripture but rather focuses on how human beings have received and used Scripture. While it isn't a problem to think of canon as being authoritative and as functioning authoritatively, the key question is why that is so. If some think the answer is that this was how the believing community decided to treat these works, I find that both odd and objectionable. I say this because, for every other bibliological doctrine we have studied, the doctrine speaks of a quality Scripture has either because God made Scripture that way or because God acted in a certain way in relation to existing Scripture. None of these other acts (revelation, inspiration, etc.) was initiated by humans. Hence, if we define canonicity in such a way that Scripture doesn't inherently possess authority but rather acquires it by human decisions to use it in an authoritative way, that seems to leave God out of the picture far too much. If we are to have a doctrine of canonicity at all, it should be one that, like the other doctrines, places the emphasis on what God has done, not on whether humans have received or perceived it in a certain way. This means that canonicity, whatever it is, should be understood as a quality inherent in Scripture, not a characteristic imposed on it from outside, based on human assessment alone.

As to the second point, I agree entirely that whatever is canonical is normative and is the standard for faith and practice. The key, however, is why this should be true. It is not true because someone or some group decided to put it in a formalized list of canonical books, nor is the key that it functioned authoritatively in a given community. The reason, instead, is the intrinsic nature of Scripture itself. If Scripture is indeed God's word, and is inerrant and authoritative at least in part because God is its divine author and God wouldn't speak error, then of course, Scripture should be the standard for both faith and practice. Here again, note that Scripture possesses these qualities because of what God has done in producing Scripture, not because of what humans have done to create Scripture and not because they decided to treat it as canonical.

The point I have just been making also fits the third main point in our summary. That the early church used "canon" in the sense of a rule of faith is more than an interesting historical fact. They used it that way before there was an NT canon, but we are not in that same historical position. Even so, the intuitions of the early church were on target. Whatever is considered canonical, whether it be oral tradition or written texts, must be consistent with the rule of faith. As defined in my previous section, the rule of faith focused on the key doctrines about Jesus and the gospel. It is not hard to prove (though this is a point for historians to attest) that the gospel Jesus lived and preached is consistent with what the apostles preached and converts to Christianity accepted as true. We find the same contents in NT books deemed to be Scripture and hence part of the canon. So, while we live in a different situation than did the early church, however we define canonicity, our definition should presuppose the basic contents of the rule of faith, and shouldn't include anything inconsistent with it.

Of course, one may respond that this works fine for NT canonicity, but if it is a requirement for the whole Bible, then apparently the OT can't be canonical. On the contrary, the OT speaks of God, humans, sin, and salvation, and not just in general terms. It looks forward prophetically to God's provision of a Savior who would give himself as the payment for sin. But, of course, the OT never names this person, nor does it describe many of the details of his life. The NT teaches much more about Christ and his sacrifice, and about God's intent that humans who accept him as their Savior would have forgiveness of sin and assurance of eternal life. The NT doesn't contradict the OT's message about God, humans, sin, and salvation; it just gives more details. Given the consistency of the OT with the NT, I think that the OT does fit with what came to be the rule of faith for the NT church, even if the OT gives far fewer details than the NT does. Hence, if we in some way include in our understanding of canonicity the basic truths contained in the rule of faith, we don't rule out the OT as part of the biblical canon.

As to the final two items in the summary points above, I believe that inspiration is relevant to a concept of biblical canonicity. In the next section, I shall explain in more detail why I think so, but the concept of inspiration was clearly in the minds of Jews as they thought of their Scripture, and it was in the minds of at least early Christians as they reflected on both OT and NT Scripture. As to the close of the biblical canon, including the independent closure of each Testament's canon, I shall argue in a later section that the biblical canon is closed. However, I don't think that whether the canon is closed or open should be part of a definition of canon and canonicity. Certainly, while the OT and NT books were being written, books that made it into the canon did not do so because the canon was open (and everyone agreed about that), nor did any of the sixty-six books in our Bibles get into the canon because it was closed (that would make no sense as counterintuitive, but more fundamentally because the openness or closure of the canon was not and is not a defining characteristic of what makes a book canonical). Put differently, we must distinguish two issues as follows: (1) what sort of thing is canonicity and what makes something canonical? and (2) given one's answer to (1), is the canon of Scripture closed or open?

It should be clear that these are two *logically* distinct issues, but let me illustrate why this is so. It is possible to answer question (1) without having any answer to question (2). That is, I should be able to tell you what makes a biblical book canonical, even if I don't know whether more Scripture (and how much) is forthcoming. On the other hand, I might not know what makes a book canonical or even whether a given book has those characteristics, but I might know how closure of the canon is decided (perhaps just by knowing who decided that it is closed and/or on what bases), and as a result, know whether the canon is open or closed. Or I might simply know that Christians and Jews think their respective biblical canons are closed without knowing who decided that, and when they did so or on what bases. I might know this, of course, without having any answer to question (1). My points here are not intended to underscore human (or even believers') ignorance of such things. Rather they are intended to show that *logically* questions (1) and (2) are distinct. And, that just means you don't have to know the answer to one in order to know the answer to the other.

## Elements of a Suitable Definition

In this section, I want to identify things that should help us define the concepts of canon, canonicity, and the canonical. This incorporates items from the previous section but adds other things that need to be said. I begin by noting that what we are defining relates to texts, books, literary products. While this may seem obvious, it is not necessarily so, because it is possible to refer to the canon of various objects and the canon of various actions. For example, in thinking of an artist's work, it makes sense to refer to all of his pictures as the canon of his paintings, or to say that a particular art museum has the canonical collection of a given artist's paintings. In addition, if someone presented a newly found painting allegedly done by the artist in question, after examining its characteristics, experts might say it could not be part of the "canon" of the artist's works, because it lacks qualities that are typical of the artist's main body of work.

As an example of a canon of actions, it is possible to speak of the canon of a professional baseball player's work as a pitcher. Here, one would cite various statistics about games won and lost, strikeouts, and base on balls issued, but one could also include descriptions of the pitcher's pitching motion, of how many different types of pitches he can throw, and any commentary about which sort of pitch he is most likely to throw in each at bat of opposing hitters.

Obviously, we don't normally use "canon" and "canonical" in the ways just illustrated. But, were conventions about language usage different, we not only could but likely would apply these concepts to nonliterary objects and to various actions. My point is that we are looking for a definition of canon and canonicity that relates to texts, books, literary products, not to something else. So whatever canonicity is, for the sake of this chapter's discussion it is a quality of individual books and collections of them.

Second, we should distinguish canonicity of literary works in general from biblical canonicity. It is meaningful to speak of the canon of Shakespeare's writings or of Homer's. We can even apply this notion to a group of literary works done by someone who isn't a professional writer. We could speak of a canon of someone's correspondence to one or more persons. None of these senses of canonicity matches biblical canonicity, but lest a definition of biblical canonicity seem entirely strained and ad hoc, at least some characteristics of a biblical canon and of biblical canonicity should apply to these other forms of literature. Of course, a definition of *biblical* canonicity must include more than these common attributes, because the Bible has characteristics that are not true of any other book or books. This also means that our definition of biblical canonicity may not entirely match a definition of canonicity related to another religion's holy book(s).

Third, we must not define biblical canonicity in a way that begs the question, but this needs explanation. In logic, to beg the question is to assume as true what you are trying to prove is true but haven't yet proved. As to biblical canonicity, what questions must a definition avoid begging? There are at least three. We ultimately want to know which specific books are and which are not canonical, but we must not so define canonicity that the definition includes a list of the books in the canon. The definition should tell us what sort of thing canonicity is, but it should leave open to testing whether individual books qualify as canonical.

Then, our definition should not say whether the canon is open or closed. As noted above, what canonicity is and whether the biblical canon is open are two distinct issues. We need a definition of canonicity that leaves open for further investigation whether the canon of either Testament is closed. For the definition to tell us the answer before we consider any evidence for or against the canon's closure begs the question.

In addition, if either the OT or NT canon is closed, we would like to know when its closure happened. However, our definition of canonicity shouldn't include that information. Giving a date for closure would tell us the answer before we could investigate evidence for and against the date—that is question begging. Or, if the definition states that a closure date can't be given because the canon is still open, that begs the previous question (is the canon open or closed?) for which we haven't yet consulted the evidence. To avoid begging the question either about closure or about a specific date of closure, our definition should say nothing about whether the canon is closed, and nothing about when it closed if it is thought to be closed.

Fourth, as we define canonicity, it is essential to distinguish between what makes a book canonical and what makes a book *become considered* canonical. The former deals with characteristics intrinsic to the book itself, and may also include a word about who gave the book those qualities. The latter deals with a book's recognition as canonical and emphasizes not only who recognized the book as canonical but also when and why they did so—all of which are *historical* issues about a community's perception of a book as canonical or not. Strictly speaking, the canonicity of any book should depend on the qualities of the book itself. Unfortunately, what often happens in attempts to define canonicity is that qualities of the book itself get mixed in with matters related to a community's recognition of a book as canonical. This results in a definition that is both about the nature of the book and about the community's reception of it as canonical. As an example, some of the definitions of canonicity include the idea that the book functions authoritatively for a given community. The problem with those definitions is that they don't necessarily say anything about a quality inherent in the book itself, but instead emphasize something about the community that considers it canonical. Of course, if such matters about the community are part of the very definition of canonicity, then canonicity depends at least in some substantial way on qualities of the communities that either accept or reject its canonicity. Because discussions of canonicity often do include information about how a book is perceived and functions for a community, I must emphatically affirm that those matters do not define a book's canonicity. That is, what is at stake is not how people perceive a book, but what qualities intrinsic to a book make it canonical!

This point must not be misunderstood. Given what I have said about functioning in an authoritative way, some might suspect that I am saying that a book's authority has nothing to do with its canonicity. I am in fact *not* saying that, because I believe, and shall soon explain, that a canonical book *is* authoritative. It is just that a canonical book's authority doesn't depend on how people perceive it or how it functions in a community. Rather it is authoritative in itself, even if no one recognizes it as such. How could a book—a particular biblical book or even the whole Bible—be authoritative in itself if no one recognizes its authority? The answer goes back to my definition of biblical authority presented in my chapter on authority. Shortly, I shall reintroduce that point and relate it to canonicity. For now, I want to be sure that readers understand that I am not rejecting a book's intrinsic authority as irrelevant to canonicity. I am rejecting a community's *perception of* or *recognition of* a book as authoritative (and hence allowing the book to *function* authoritatively in the community) as having anything to do with what makes a book in and of itself canonical.

Fifth, in defining a concept, one seeks to identify qualities at the core or the essence of what the thing being defined is. In other words, one searches for characteristics that a particular instance of the thing being defined must possess for it to be an instance of the thing at all. That is, to define a concept, one must set forth the sufficient and necessary conditions a person, object, action must possess for him or her or it to be an example of the thing in question. Of the two (sufficient and necessary conditions), *necessary* conditions are the more significant, for these are qualities a thing could not lack and yet still be an instance of the item in question. As this relates to canonicity in general and biblical canonicity in particular, our definition of these concepts must identify the characteristic(s) that must be present in a book (or set of books) if it is to be canonical. Even if the book has other qualities that canonical books possess, if it doesn't have as part of its very essence those necessary attributes required for a book to be canonical, it cannot be a canonical book.

In relation to biblical canonicity, what is the quality/are the qualities without which a given book couldn't be canonical or part of Scripture's canon? In answering that question—and this is my final point about what to include in a definition of biblical canonicity—the best way to proceed is to remind ourselves of things we already know Scripture teaches about itself. For one thing, anything that qualifies as OT or NT Scripture is revelation from God. Of course, there are many forms of divine revelation; we enumerated them in chapters 2 and 3. Special revelation comes in divine acts, divine communication through direct speech, dreams, or visions, and it comes in the incarnate Son of God, Jesus Christ. But none of these forms of special revelation are written texts, and we said that the sort of canonicity in view in this discussion is a characteristic of literary texts. Thankfully, one form of special revelation, the Bible, is literature.

So, if canonicity has anything to do with revelation (and it does), it pertains to written revelation, Scripture. To invoke this form of revelation also invokes the doctrine of Scripture's inspiration. As we saw in discussing inspiration, Scripture has both human authors and a divine author. The Holy Spirit so superintended the human authors' writing of their books that what they wrote was also actually the word of God. Whatever is genuine OT or NT Scripture is what God has said. Hence, inspiration is a quality inherent in Scripture.

Scripture also has two other characteristics, discussed in earlier chapters of this book. Since Scripture is God's word and God cannot be mistaken about anything and would not lie, then whatever Scripture affirms is in fact true. Hence, inerrancy is a quality intrinsic to Scripture. Scripture is also inherently authoritative. Thus, what it says must be believed, and what it commands must be obeyed. Scripture's authority stems primarily from three things. On the one hand, its assertions are true. In addition, Scripture's authority also stems from the authority of its divine author. God is the sovereign creator who has the right to rule the universe as he pleases. As omniscient, morally perfect, and the supreme authority in the universe, whatever God says must be true, and whatever he demands must be obeyed. And God has the power and authority to enforce his word. In addition, whatever he does has supreme authority over any and all creatures affected by his deeds. Scripture is what God has spoken; therefore, as his word, it is supremely authoritative over any other word. In producing Scripture, God also used human authors, but not as passive secretaries taking dictation. Rather, working in and through them as they wrote, he ensured that they wrote in their own words and style what he wanted written. In essence, what these human authors wrote was "elevated" to supreme authority because they were writing God's words, which are supremely authoritative.

In sum, Scripture is a written form of divine revelation, written with dual authorship so that the words penned by the human authors are also God's words. As such, Scripture is both inerrant and supremely authoritative for whatever topics it addresses. These characteristics of Scripture, along with it being revelation and the result of inspiration, are, I contend, all necessary conditions of it being Scripture. That is, if any of these concepts (revelation, inspiration, inerrancy, and authority) don't belong to the very essence or nature of a written document, then it cannot be Scripture.

Wherein lies the canonicity of Scripture? Is it canonical because it is revelation, and/or, inspired, and/or inerrant, and/or authoritative, or is it canonical in virtue of some other quality? My contention is that the key to biblical canonicity is the four characteristics of Scripture already enumerated. If that is right, then canonicity is, given the nature of biblical revelation, inspiration, inerrancy, and authority, something that only God could give to Scripture. If canonicity depends on some other or further quality that Scripture has, it is hard to know what that characteristic might be. In light of the preceding discussion, we are now ready to define canonicity in general and biblical canonicity in particular.

### Proposed Definitions of Canonicity and Biblical Canonicity

Though Scripture says things relevant to canonicity, no passage or set of texts defines it. This is in part why I think it is important to talk about canonicity of nonbiblical writings. If that notion is drastically different from biblical canonicity, then our definition of biblical canonicity will likely be rather dubious.

Let me first define canonicity in general. To speak of the *canon* of some literary artist's work is *to refer to all the literary texts that give evidence of having been produced by the writer in question*. A literary text may be a novel, a short story, a poem, or a letter, for example, but all works written by the author in question compose his canon. Hence, we can speak of William Shakespeare's canon, which refers most specifically to all the plays and poems written by the named writer who lived in Elizabethan England. To say, further, of Shakespeare's work that a given literary work is *canonical* means that *it has a right to be included in the group (canon) of texts that give evidence of having been produced by Shakespeare.* The *canonicity* of a given text, or of all Shakespearean texts taken together, refers to its possessing characteristics which serve as evidence that it/they were composed by William Shakespeare.

This definition, by being general, as applied to any nonbiblical literary piece purported to be written by a given author, doesn't beg the question about whether the work under consideration is or isn't canonical. That is, if I want to know whether a given literary work is part of Shakespeare's canon, nothing in the definition of canonicity answers that question before I examine the work in question to see if its qualities make it likely that Shakespeare wrote it. Of course, nothing in the definition guarantees that I will properly identify every literary work that actually is part of Shakespeare's canon. But that is a good thing, for if the definition so specifically presented the qualities a literary piece must have to be part of Shakespeare's canon, I might never err in assigning a work to Shakespeare, but that would be so because the definition of canonicity would beg the question in favor of or against a given literary work before much, if any, analysis of it had been done. If that happened, everyone might call the work canonical, but that wouldn't necessarily mean we would be right about who wrote it. Even a non–question-begging definition won't guarantee that, but it does allow for a more objective evaluation of the evidence for and against the work's canonicity.

In moving to *biblical* canonicity, I think we should take a similar route. Of course, matters are more complicated, because we now have multiple authors (divine and human) for each book that purports to be canonical. While scholars should be interested in the identity of a biblical book's human author(s), the crucial issue is whether it is possible to detect evidence of the divine author as well. This is so because Scripture is supposed to be *divine* revelation in written form. If the literary piece in question gives evidence of a human author but none of a divine author, then it isn't likely part of the canon of Scripture.

In light of the above, I propose that we define the biblical canon (and canonicity) as follows: to speak of the biblical canon is *to refer to all the literary texts which give evidence of having been produced by both a human and a divine author, i.e., the biblical canon refers to all texts that give evidence of divine inspiration.*[30] To say, further, that a literary work is *canonical* means that *it has a right to be included in the group/canon of texts that give evidence of being divinely inspired.* The *canonicity* of a

---

[30] Some may think this rules out a book like Luke from being canonical, because Luke says that he carefully investigated "everything from the beginning" in order to write his Gospel (Luke 1:1–4). However, the fact that he did research doesn't preclude God superintending his choice of the material to use and also superintending the actual writing of the Gospel. For a book to be inspired (and hence canonical) doesn't require that none of its contents come from any source other than the mind and speech of God.

given text or of all biblical texts taken together refers to *its/their possessing characteristics which serve as evidence that it/they were composed under divine inspiration.*

To be sure, many scholars, nonevangelicals in particular, will reject these definitions. Given their adoption of the historical-critical method (and perhaps possessing a healthy dose of anti-supernaturalism), there is no way that they could see God involved in composing biblical books so as to qualify as one of their authors. This, however, should not in the least deter us. If the notions of canon and canonicity in general teach us anything, they show that at the heart of the concept of the canonicity of literary texts is the point that a canonical book gives evidence of its authorship. If it doesn't, it won't be considered part of that author's canon. All I am proposing is that the same basic concept of literary canonicity should apply to Scripture. What is different is that books that qualify as Scripture have a divine author, not just a human one. Though such definitions won't appeal to nonevangelical scholars, these have been, I believe, fairly standard definitions for evangelical theology throughout church history. Moreover, the OT people of God also saw their Scriptures as more than just ordinary books, because in those texts they heard what seemed to be words produced by a divine author, not just the writings of mere humans.

Other scholars may reject my definitions because they don't name specific characteristics that would indicate divine authorship. It is fine to say that a canonical book is divinely inspired, but that only raises the question of how we can know that a book is divinely inspired. Indeed, this is true, but I see it as little different, if at all, from our definition of canonicity in general. We defined that notion as a work's having characteristics that are evidence that it was written by its purported author. We didn't get more specific *in our definition*, because doing so would require every literary work to have the qualities enumerated in order to be canonical, even if on some other ground we knew it was written by the author in question. Depending on the author in question, characteristics that are typical of his or her work may vary; we need to study that author's presumed corpus of work to see if it has the defining characteristics of his or her works. In advance of such study, no one can predict the exact qualities that will be necessary conditions to convince us that the work in question is part of the author's canon.

In a similar way, our definition of biblical canonicity shouldn't identify any set of characteristics (beyond inspiration and inerrancy) that each work must have to qualify as part of the biblical canon. Rather, we should examine each book's contents to see what qualities it has that evidence it as divinely inspired. Given the sheer number and diversity of purported biblical books, to try to capture in a simple definition all the qualities a book must have to be canonical might be a futile task. I say this, because biblical books are so diverse that each may have distinctive qualities that few, if any, other biblical books possess. Think, for example, of characteristics of books like the Song of Solomon or Job that are unique to them. To make those qualities part of the list of attributes a book must have for it to be part of the biblical canon would likely mean that only the Song of Solomon and Job would qualify as canonical. So it is preferable that our list of qualities a book must possess to be canonical not be too detailed.

This must not be misunderstood. We should identify other conditions that would support a claim that a given book is canonical. My point here is twofold. The first is that, for the sake of *defining* canonicity, we don't need to produce a list of qualities that point to inspiration. A more general definition like the one I have offered will suffice. Even so, before we can decide which specific books do or do not belong to the canon, we should identify some features of books that we can use to identify specific books as inspired by God and hence canonical. My second point is that we dare not generate a lengthy list of qualities (that suggest inspiration) that will likely include things that could be true of only a few books. Rather, we should identify qualities that cover as many books as possible, and we should be able to show that those attributes actually have something to do with inspiration. If not, then, even if a book possesses those attributes, that won't prove that it is divinely inspired, and hence, its qualities won't prove that it should be part of the canon of Scripture.

In later sections of this discussion, I plan to identify further qualities that a book might have which would be a sign of divine inspiration. Before ending this section, however, we can identify some things, given what we already know about Scripture, that would have to be true of a book for it to be part of the canon. First, a book that is divinely inspired revelation would have to tell the truth. If things it affirms are false, or if things it rejects are true, that would be a sign that the book couldn't be God's word, and hence couldn't be canonical.

Of course, inerrancy cannot be the only criterion of inspiration. A book on any topic could be factually true, in a correspondence sense, and not be divine revelation or inspired by God. Still, if a book is divine revelation in written form, it must also be inerrant. As to other evidences of inerrancy, Scripture itself can help us, because it teaches some things that are relevant to canonicity, and we should see what they are.

## WILLIAM J. ABRAHAM AND THE CONCEPT OF CANON

However, before going any further, we should consider William J. Abraham's proposal about the nature of canon and canonicity. In his *Canon and Criterion in Christian Theology*, Abraham offers both an unusual definition of canonicity (though he argues that the one adopted by Christians and Christian theology is unusual and incorrect and has misled the church throughout its history) and a theory that Christian theology has gone wrong in its understanding of canonicity. This also means that Abraham thinks Christian theology has erred in the way it uses Scripture.

How has Christian theology erred in its understanding of canonicity? Abraham explains that there is a major problem when ecclesial canons are misinterpreted as epistemic criteria. To clarify this point, Abraham explains what he means by ecclesial canons and epistemic criteria:

> . . . ecclesial canons, comprise materials, persons, and practices officially or semi-officially identified and set apart as a means of grace and salvation by the Christian community. They are represented by such entities as creed, Scripture, liturgy, iconography, the Fathers, and sacraments. The latter, epistemic criteria, are constituted by norms of justification, rationality, and knowledge. They are represented by such entities as reason, experience, memory, intuition, and inference.
>
> . . . means of grace refer to various materials, persons, and practices which function to reconnect human agents with their divine source and origin. They are akin to medicine designed to heal and restore human flourishing; they are akin to various exercises appointed to reorient the whole of human existence to its proper goal. Their natural home is the Church. In fact they are brought into existence by the Church, as she is guided in her pilgrimage into the kingdom of God.
>
> Epistemic criteria belong to a very different arena. Norms or criteria generally arise out of puzzlement about gaining rationality, justified beliefs, and knowledge. Historically they have often arisen out of intellectual curiosity and out of conflict concerning what to believe as true. At their best they are carefully crafted means of articulating the justification of one's beliefs. They are means of demarcating truth from falsehood, . . . .
>
> Over a long period of time and due to a great variety of pressures, ecclesial canons, which served in very diverse ways to initiate one into the life of God, were transformed into epistemological categories. The simplest way to record this change is to say that the term 'canon' ceased to be seen as a list of concrete items, such as a list of books to be read in worship, and came to be seen as a criterion of justification in theology. More broadly, Scripture and the tradition of the Church were interpreted as sources of authority. Thus the creeds, a list of doctrines, were treated as a source and warrant of theological claims. Or the canon of Fathers, a list of teachers and theologians, was taken as a graded system of warrant and probability in theological theory building. Most dramatically, the bishop of Rome, one person in a delicate system of oversight adopted by the Church as a whole, was seen as having privileged access to the truth about God. In general, the diverse and complex canonical heritage of the Church was quietly divided up into Scripture and tradition; in the process of abstraction and reduction, these were refashioned as epistemically privileged criteria of truth in theology. This transition had devastating

consequences for both sets of concepts. As the canonical materials, persons, and practices of the Church were transformed into norms of epistemology, they were forced into molds which warped their original use and purpose. At the same time, discussions about epistemology were forced into channels which pictured the justification of theological claims in terms of offering sure and certain foundations upon which everything else could be constructed.[31]

In essence, Abraham is saying that canons (and there are more than just one) were intended to play a role in the spiritual growth of believers, but instead, Scripture in particular was turned into, so to speak, a test for truth on any topic it addressed. Whatever disagreed with scriptural teaching shouldn't be believed, for it was deemed false, and whoever disagreed with Scripture was deemed a heretic. To treat Scripture this way is to misunderstand its nature and canonicity. It is also to be captivated by a foundationalist epistemology and, relatedly, by a belief that there must be some ultimate justification (ultimate foundation) for whatever one believes. Since Scripture was deemed to be divine revelation, Christians reasoned that there could be no higher authority than God and his word, and so it is understandable that Scripture came to be viewed as an epistemic norm for determining what is true and false about any topic Scripture addresses.

Unfortunately, Abraham argues, the church, early on and throughout its history, has made that perilous move from treating Scripture as a means of grace to treating it as a source of truth, the appeal to which was thought to render epistemically certain whatever Scripture teaches. One further quote from Abraham helps to underscore the error of confusing canon and criterion. Abraham illustrates the problem by showing what happens when one uses Scripture as the final word about moral right and wrong. He explains,

> For the moment it is sufficient to make a simple distinction. It is one thing to say that Scripture is a canon; it is another thing entirely to advance a very particular interpretation of Scripture as canon by insisting that the canon-icity of Scripture is constituted by its being a criterion of moral judgment. We cannot automatically assume that because scripture [sic] is described as canon or because it functions at times as a criterion in moral theology this means that its canonical status and significance are constituted by its being a criterion or norm.
>
> We might expand on this initial distinction graphically in this way. In appealing to Scripture in moral or theological argument, it is one thing to argue from Scripture, assuming that scripture [sic] is a sure and certain foun-dation of knowledge; it is quite another to argue from Scripture, assuming that Scripture gives us access to special revelation. It is one thing to construe Scripture as a sure and certain foundation of knowledge; it is another to see it as a contingent medium of divine revelation. In turn, both of these need to

---

[31] Abraham, *Canon and Criterion in Christian Theology*, 1–2.

be distinguished from the idea of Scripture as canonical. We cannot automatically assume that claiming Scripture to be a sure and certain foundation, or declaring that Scripture is a contingent medium of divine revelation, or saying that Scripture is canonical, are all one and the same assertion.[32]

Abraham explains that one of the factors in moving from canon as a means of grace to canon as an epistemic criterion is the fact that the term "canon" can be used in varied ways. Abraham appeals to Floyd Filson's explanation of the matter. Filson explains that the word "canon" may mean either a list of the books of the Bible or the "*rule* or *standard* of faith and life which they contained."[33] Though Abraham is willing to grant the use of "canon" as a rule or standard, and hence as an epistemic standard or norm, he contends that canon as a list of the Bible's books is the preferred understanding of the concept. But he grants that it is very easy to slide from canon as a list to canon as a norm. Even so, that does not make it correct to treat Scripture as a final arbiter of truth in any dispute about theology, morality, or anything else.

Though his main thesis may have some plausibility, one wonders how Abraham arrived at such conclusions. Actually, his thesis involves at least two nonbiblical supports and one appeal to Scripture. First, Abraham argues that regardless of how one construes the canon of Scripture, it is a mistake to think that the notion of canon applies just to Scripture. In fact, there are at least six other kinds of canonical tradition that came to function in the church. Abraham names them as follows: (1) there are practices, experiences, and rites related to baptism and the Lord's Supper; (2) there are liturgical traditions about how worship is to be conducted; (3) there is a rather sophisticated tradition of icons; (4) there are ecclesiastical regulations about the internal regulation of the life of the church and its members; (5) as time passed, certain teachers and leaders in the church were designated as fathers, saints, and teachers, and this gave them a special status as intellectual and spiritual leaders in the church that far exceeds the status of regular teachers and members of the church; and (6) the final canonical tradition relates to the internal structures and ordering of the community, i.e., the development of the episcopate as a way of internally supervising the church as a whole.[34] These canons clearly have little to do with epistemology or epistemic norms, but they are the canons that developed in the early church, along with Scripture. Within this context, it is hard to show that any of these canons was intended to provide a test for truth.

Even granting that these other six items became canons in the church, one wonders what legitimized them as canons. Abraham's emphatic answer is that

---

[32] Ibid., 5.
[33] Floyd Filson, quoted in ibid., 13–14.
[34] Abraham, *Canon and Criterion in Christian Theology*, 37–38.

the different canons were constituted as such by the community. In his second chapter, Abraham rehearses the development of the canon of Scripture as well as other canons of the church. Throughout his description, he repeatedly explains that what came to be part of the canon of Scripture and what came to count as other canons of the church was determined entirely by the believing community. He says little about why the various canons were developed; instead Abraham merely repeats that the community decided to honor certain practices and beliefs as canons. Unfortunately, this can give the impression that there likely weren't biblical and theological reasons for such decisions, but rather the decisions were based on the "tastes" of the believing community as the church developed. Abraham doesn't say this, but by offering community choice as the reason for adopting various practices, etc., as canons, he gives the impression that the personal, subjective tastes of the believing church during the first centuries of Christianity made the practices, beliefs, etc., canons.[35]

Through all of this, one wonders how Abraham's notion of canons might be supported biblically. Abraham believes that Scripture affirms his belief about the proper use of canons, including the canon of Scripture. Here Abraham appeals to 2 Timothy 3:14–17, with special emphasis on verse 17. This passage not only says that Scripture is a gift from God, but it also presents the intended purposes for which Scripture should be used. Clearly referring to verses 15 and 17, Abraham explains that "the fundamental purposes of the material are soteriological, pedagogical, and pastoral. In broad terms, the Scriptures are designed for use in the Church to bring people to salvation, to make people holy, to make believers proficient disciples of Jesus Christ, and the like."[36] Abraham later adds that, while it might seem correct to claim that the church's canonical heritage is not just a means of grace, but of grace and of truth, the temptation to do so should be resisted, because it is very hard to see how most of the canons enumerated can tell us anything about what is true or false. They serve a different function. The biblical canon, given its nature as opposed to the nature of other canons, can be seen as a means of grace and of truth, but unfortunately, too often the only emphasis has been on the latter to the exclusion of the former. The result, according to Abraham, is that Scripture is made to function as an arbiter of disputes about what is true, and in the process an epistemology alien to Scripture's point and purpose is forced upon it and upon those who use it as an epistemic norm rather than as a means of grace.

Having articulated his thesis in his first chapter, and having shown how in

---

[35] Ibid., 30. Here Abraham firmly claims that the community constitutes its canons, and then, reciprocally, the canons form the community along the lines indicated by the canons. In the rest of the chapter, Abraham offers his construction of the events that created the various canons, including the canon of Scripture. Throughout the description, it is always the decision made by the community that is critical in determining what will and won't become canonical.

[36] Ibid., 51.

the early church various canons (ones that are clearly means of grace and have nothing to do with epistemic norms) arose, Abraham then offers his reconstruction of each period of church history and shows how identifying Scripture as an epistemic criterion rather than as a true canon (among other canons) happened in every era of church history to the extreme detriment of the church and of those in it, as well as of those outside the church. By the end of his book, what Abraham thinks about the wrong way to view and use Scripture is very clear. His remedy for this alleged malady, however, is not entirely clear, but the main issue for our consideration is whether Abraham's understanding of the nature of canonicity is correct and whether he is right about the implications of his thesis for the emphasis in Christian theology on Scripture as divine revelation, inspired by God, and thus inerrant and authoritative for faith and practice (and anything else Scripture affirms).[37]

In assessing Abraham's proposal, I can't cover every aspect of his book. Others have addressed the accuracy of his historical reconstruction of church history, and I leave interested readers to read those reviews as they deem appropriate. Also, though my reaction to Abraham's book is basically critical, I don't want to suggest that it makes no contributions whatsoever. I think that Abraham is right, for example, that there is a difference between a means of grace meant to aid in spiritual growth and a final arbiter of truth for deciding which theological concepts are true and false. Moreover, I wouldn't deny that throughout church history, Scripture has been used in this way. In fact, though he didn't intend to do so, Abraham's construction of church history and his handling of various theologians, if at all right, seem to buttress the evangelical case that at all times, not just in the late nineteenth century and throughout the twentieth century, evangelicals have held that Scripture is inerrant and hence supremely authoritative for faith and practice and anything else it discusses. If the Rogers and McKim proposal, for example, is correct, it is unlikely that Scripture would have been used throughout much of church history as the inerrant authority which articulates what is right and wrong to believe and do, as Abraham painstakingly attempts to demonstrate through his version of how Scripture has been used throughout church history.

This positive comment doesn't "baptize" as correct everything Abraham

---

[37] To interact with the details of Abraham's reconstruction of the history of the theology of canon, while of some value, goes beyond the focus of this chapter. As this book is intended to be a piece of evangelical theology, it would be wrong to spend undue time and space on an alternate conception of canonicity, especially if that means that what Scripture and believers (during the centuries when Scripture was being written and received) actually believed about the canon of Scripture receives short shrift. For those who wish to pursue in more detail critical interaction with Abraham's book, I suggest the following: David H. Johnson, "Canon and Criterion Synopsis and Critique," *Didaskalia* 14 (Winter 2003): 1–12; Kenneth J. Stewart, "William J. Abraham's *Canon and Criterion in Christian Theology*: An Historical-Theological Evaluation," *Didaskalia* 14 (Winter 2003): 13–28; Vernon J. Steiner, "*Canon and Criterion in Christian Theology*: A Critical Response," *Didaskalia* 14 (Winter 2003): 29–50; and Bernie Van De Walle, "William J. Abraham's *Canon and Criterion*: A Systematic-Theological Response," *Didaskalia* 14 (Winter 2003): 51–61.

says in his presentation of how the church has handled Scripture throughout its history, but only means that Abraham probably isn't entirely wrong about Scripture being used as an epistemic norm to decide questions of doctrinal and practical truth and error. The question, of course, is whether Christians have been wrong in using Scripture this way, and that is where I must disagree with Abraham. There are many items I find problematic with his thesis and its development.

First, I take issue with his understanding of canon, but even more so with his method of determining what it should mean. As noted, Abraham, citing Filson favorably, appeals essentially to two ways that the term "canon" has been used in church history. I can agree on those two uses ("list" and "norm"), but our study of the different senses in which canon has been defined suggests that there are more senses than just those two. In addition, he proposes that a canon is a means of grace, but it isn't clear how he came to that conclusion. Certainly, nothing etymological about the term suggests such a use. Basically, one gets the impression that the six items he lists as additional canons were things that developed in the Christian tradition as significant to believers as they interacted with the church. Because at least some of the six items, like baptism and the Lord's Supper, can be seen as means of grace, Abraham seems to think that the other canons, including Scripture, are also means of grace. Hence, Abraham's preferred meaning of "canon" is neither "list" nor "norm" but "means of grace."

In response, this part of Abraham's proposal seems flawed on several grounds. The first is to think that what constitutes the canonicity of one canon is what constitutes the canonicity of another. As I noted at some length in defining canonicity in general and biblical canonicity in particular, we are talking about the canonicity of literary texts. It isn't at all clear how baptism and the Lord's Supper, rules for organizing and running a church, and traditions about liturgy for worship, for example, qualify as literary texts. Hence, it isn't clear that whatever constitutes the canonicity of those canons has anything to do with the canonicity of literary texts, including Scripture. And, as a result, it isn't clear that what constitutes biblical canonicity should not have anything at all to do with truth (or at least that Scripture shouldn't be used as an arbiter of truth).

The most fundamental problem with Abraham's understanding of canonicity, however, is that he seems to confuse defining a term with defining a concept. To define a term means to present the different ways in which the word can be and has been used in various contexts. Both Abraham's appeal to Filson and his own application of the term "canon" to the six other canons of the early church show different ways the term came to be used in the early church. However, defining this *term* says nothing about the *concept* of canonicity. That is, it does not explain what sort of thing canonicity is. Fundamentally, Abraham has noted different uses of the term "canon" and then has decided that one of them (means of grace) actually tells what sort of thing a canon and canonicity are. This is conceptually flawed, for explaining what canonicity is says nothing about how the word can be used in various contexts to communicate one thing or another. Nor does a *conceptual* definition need to give the semantic range of a term; that isn't its purpose. As a philosopher, Abraham should know this, and probably does. Unfortunately, it doesn't seem that he used this distinction when articulating his concept of canonicity.

Of course, none of that may matter if theology is about word studies. But theology *is not* word study; it is a study of concepts. A *theological* discussion of canonicity is not about how various terms have been and can be used. Unfortunately, Abraham offers a *word study* as the key to the meaning of the *concept* of canonicity. Given the methodological flaw this incorporates, there is little reason to think that Abraham is right about the *concept* of canonicity. I should add here that, in light of the difference between defining a term and defining a concept, it is also hard to see how the *concept* of canonicity per se involves anything about epistemic norms. But that doesn't mean that what the concept of canon is, especially that of the biblical canon (as defined earlier in this chapter), has no implications at all about whether Scripture can or should be used as an arbiter of truth.

Third, I am concerned about Abraham's emphatic claims that whatever serves as canonical is determined by the community. Now, I certainly wouldn't say that something deemed canonical can serve as such in a given community without the reception and approval of the canon as a canon. But that is far different from whatever it is about a canon that recommended it to the church to serve a canonical function. Put simply, Abraham gives the impression that there is nothing inherent in the items chosen as canons that moved the church to adopt them as canons. Hence, the decision to receive certain things as canonical almost seems arbitrary; had the community been in a different mood or of a different mind-set, perhaps it would have chosen different things as canons. While Abraham doesn't explicitly make such claims, what he does say about how canons are constituted leaves the reader with this impression.

Readers may wonder why this matters; it certainly doesn't seem to refute anything about Abraham's major thesis that canon should be viewed as a means of grace, not as an epistemic criterion. It matters, because if the church at all decided on its canons in virtue of characteristics or qualities inherent in the canonical item, that puts things in a very different light. This is especially important in regard to Scripture, if, as I have proposed, a biblical text is canonical because it shows evidences of being the very word of God. If Scripture's being perceived to be God's word has anything to do with why it was chosen as a canon—and I intend to show in later chapters that it does—readers will see that the books chosen to be part of Scripture's canon were chosen because they were deemed (rightly) to be God's word.

But think of what that means and of its implications! Does anyone have more authority than God? Does anyone know more than God? Does God know, for every proposition, whether it is true or false? If Scripture is God's word, then should we expect it to tell the truth about anything it addresses? The answers are obvious. No one has more authority or knows more than God. Indeed, God, in knowing everything, knows which claims are true and which are false. And if the Bible is God's word, then surely it speaks truth about anything it affirms or asserts. Doesn't that mean that, if there is a dispute about what is true, and Scripture addresses the issue(s) involved in the conflict, Scripture should be seen as giving the definitive word on which view is right and which is wrong? Surely we are not the first to recognize these implications; they follow very naturally from God's nature and from Scripture being God's word.

Abraham, by not seriously considering why Christians might have chosen certain things to be canons but instead by only emphasizing that canons are chosen by the community (which is then further constituted by the canons), leaves out a very important piece of the story of how and why canons became canons. When you include those parts of the story, the results for the community's view of the inherent nature of Scripture can't also be dismissed. And then it becomes much harder to claim that there is no basis for using Scripture for any epistemic function at all. In saying that canons are constituted by choices of the community, Abraham is not giving us the whole story.

Fourth, Vernon Steiner raises a very significant point in relation to Abraham's narrative of how canons were established and what was done with them. Abraham begins his narrative with the early church, but as Steiner rightly argues, this doesn't start the story early enough. The place to start the story is with Scripture itself. When you see how various OT authors use other OT books, how the NT invokes the OT, and how some NT writers appeal to other NT books, the story becomes more complete. To what is Steiner referring? He is referring to the fact that often in Scripture, a writer supports his teaching by an appeal to Scripture. This is abundantly clear when NT Gospel writers appeal to the OT to prove something, for example, about the truth of Jesus's claims to be Israel's Messiah. In the chapters on inspiration, we also saw that when Jesus had a theological or moral dispute with his contemporaries, he quoted OT Scripture, and that settled the matter. Jesus's Jewish listeners at least knew that Scripture said what Jesus claimed it said, and they knew and agreed with what his argument strategy of citing Scripture to support one's views implies. It implies that whatever Scripture says settles the debate, because Scripture is true and supremely authoritative! It is also true that often, as recorded in the book of Acts, when the apostles defended Christianity, if their audience was Jewish, they typically made their case by appealing to Scripture.

These kinds of inner- and intertestamental uses of Scripture are part of the story of how the canon of Scripture came to be a canon. And, what do they show? The uses of Scripture cited above (and many others could be cited) show that the believing community, including Jesus and his disciples, did consider Scripture as, among other things, an epistemic norm for determining what was right and wrong in theological and practical disputes. By failing to start his narrative with Scripture's use of Scripture, Abraham leaves out a significant part of the story, one that undercuts his claim that Scripture wasn't at all intended to be and shouldn't be used as an arbiter of truth![38]

Fifth, Abraham believes that 2 Timothy 3:14–17 gives biblical warrant for his understanding of canonicity as a means of grace. While it is encouraging that Abraham thinks Scripture is relevant to deciding this theological issue (namely, what is the nature of canonicity?), his interpretation of the passage is inadequate. Abraham focuses on verse 15's claim that Scripture is able to make one wise unto salvation, and also on verse 17, which states that the various uses of Scripture are intended to make the child of God thoroughly equipped for every good work. No one should deny that Scripture was given to accomplish such things, or that it does. What is troublesome is that Abraham seems to overlook *how* Scripture can make one wise unto salvation, and he also overlooks the last half of verse 16. As for the former issue, Scripture can't make anyone wise unto salvation if it doesn't present a path to salvation. If it presents many paths without specifying which one will save, or if it presents no specific path as the way to salvation, how are people to learn from the Bible how to be saved? The sad truth is that many do not realize, or refuse to accept, the fact that Scripture presents one and only one specific way of salvation. That means that it asserts that there is no other way. How could such claims not serve as the arbiter of truth about how to become right with God?

As I also noted, Abraham's appeal to this passage overlooks the latter half of verse 16. That tells the various things for which Scripture can be profitably used so that (v. 17) the child of God who uses Scripture for those purposes will be fully ready for every good work. Specifically, according to verse 16, Scripture is profitable for "teaching, for reproof, for correcting, for training in righteousness" [AT]. But how can it serve these functions if it does not say what we should think about the issues it addresses? If Scripture "teaches" that

---

[38] Steiner, "*Canon and Criterion in Christian Theology*: A Critical Response," 42–45.

466    □   SETTING THE BOUNDARIES

every understanding of each concept discussed is equally valid, so that one must decide on nonbiblical grounds which to believe, it is hard to see that from Scripture anyone would know what to think as the basis of being prepared for every good work.

What about reproof? If Scripture does not teach that certain things are true and others are not, how can it be used to correct (for reproof) any wrong idea? And, if Scripture presents no path of life as correct, implying that others are incorrect (as well as stating that others are wrong—cf. Psalm 1's comparison of the life of the wicked to that of the righteous), how can it be used to call any lifestyle incorrect and then to correct it? And, finally, if Scripture presents no actions as morally superior and right and none as immoral, how can it possibly give anyone a clue about which actions are righteous in God's estimation (and hence encouraged) and which are sinful (and hence forbidden)? Unless Scripture takes a stand on what is right to think and do, it is hard to see how it can perform the various functions verse 16 says it profitably does. And, if coming under the influence of such biblical functions, and learning and agreeing with them, is necessary for the child of God to be fully prepared for all good works, then it is not clear how Scripture can serve the purpose it claims to fulfill, and which Abraham sees as its only purpose. In short, the very passage Abraham chooses as support for his notion of canonicity, when properly understood, actually refutes it.

Sixth, Abraham has erroneously chosen to cast his thesis in terms of a dichotomy about the uses of Scripture: either Scripture is a means of grace *or* it is an epistemic norm. The whole of Abraham's book assumes as a presupposition that Scripture can be used as one or the other, but not as both. I am certainly not the first (nor the last) to say that this is a false dichotomy. Scripture can be and is both. As just shown above, the very biblical passage that Abraham believes proves that only the first disjunct (Scripture is a means of grace) is Scripture's proper use actually shows that *both* are appropriate uses of Scripture. And so does the rest of Scripture. Scripture teaches us what to believe, and it also shows us what difference our beliefs should make in the way we live. If Scripture's teaching is followed, it will likely serve both uses in a person's life, not just one or the other. Abraham has not convincingly shown that these two possible uses of Scripture are mutually exclusive—though the thrust of his book is that they are. Indeed, we can agree that it is wrong to use Scripture *only* as an epistemic norm, but that doesn't prove that it is wrong to use Scripture *at all* as an arbiter of truth when there is a dispute about which religious belief(s) one should hold. Hence, it seems that Abraham's whole project is flawed from the very outset because it rests on the means of grace/epistemic norm dichotomy, but that either/or is a false dichotomy!

Finally, for those who still don't think that Scripture defines spiritual, religious, and theological truth, or that such truth has nothing to do with spiritual growth and maturity, I would only say that if that is correct, then Jesus got things all wrong when he prayed for his disciples' spiritual health and well-being! In John 17:17 Jesus prays for his disciples, "Sanctify them in the truth; Thy word is truth." And we know, from our study of inspiration, *where* Jesus thinks one can find God's word! Apparently, Jesus thinks that Scripture can serve both an epistemic and a soteriological function at the same time. In fact, it is Scripture's nature as truth to which Jesus appeals as the basis for it to play a soteriological role. Sadly, Abraham did not seem to grasp this point. We would do well to side with Jesus; on this point he is surely one greater than Abraham!

# TWELVE

# LIGHT CANONIZED (II)

## Scripture on Canonicity

In chapter 11, I discussed various notions of canonicity and biblical canonicity and settled on a definition of these concepts. That discussion focused very little on Scripture itself, because Scripture doesn't offer much help in defining this concept. However, that does not mean Scripture has nothing of value to say on this topic. In this chapter I turn to things Scripture does teach that are relevant to our subject.

As we begin, we should remember several things from the chapter on inspiration. We noted not only that various NT passages teach the inspiration of all of God's word, but also that, especially in the OT, writers have certain formulaic ways of saying that what they write comes from God (and is, thus, inspired). In addition, NT writers also use various ways of referring to or of introducing a quote from the OT. These formulaic phrases are ways of saying that what is quoted or recorded is God's word. Hence, it is inspired.

As a result of these phenomena related to inspiration, we argued that the different phrases are equivalent and interchangeable ways of referring to some verse or portion of written text as Scripture. Those phrases are: "it is written," "God says," and "Scripture says." By using such phrases, biblical writers intended readers to equate (as the authors evidently did) Scripture with God's word.

Why do I raise these points? Because we defined biblical canonicity as a document's having characteristics that evidence its being composed under divine inspiration. But then, all of the evidence offered in my chapter on inspiration for Scripture's complete inspiration also supports its canonicity. Of course, some may say that all of this is circular reasoning. It seems that I am defining canonicity in terms of inspiration and vice versa. Unless we know what characteristics are typical of an inspired book, we can't be sure a given book is inspired and thereby canonical. Put differently, before any books were recognized as inspired, how did anyone know which to identify as God's word, and hence, as canonical?

These are legitimate questions, but they don't destroy what I am claiming about scriptural teaching about either inspiration or canonicity. Rather, they underscore the need to delineate criteria for determining whether a document written in the OT era is inspired and criteria for deciding whether documents written in the NT era are inspired. Once that is explained, I believe the air of circularity will dissipate to a large extent. I say "to a large extent," rather than entirely, for a specific reason. Undoubtedly, criteria for OT and NT inspiration will be taken from Scripture itself. Skeptics will, of course, ask why we should rely on Scripture for these criteria when we aren't yet clear that the books cited are at all correct and have anything reliable to say about the topic in question. If we answer that we rely on these books because they are God's inspired word, we beg the question. That is, the question is whether any of the books of the Bible are inspired and hence, are to be used as God's word. If we say they all are because they say so, that begs the question. If we just assume that they are because the church has thought so for a long time, that also begs the question.

Is there a way, independent of Scripture's testimony about itself, to confirm that Scripture should be believed when it speaks on any topic, including its own inspiration? Indeed, there is a case to be made for Scripture's reliability, but it is one that apologists and philosophers of religion, not theologians, make. Systematicians must assume, in order to do evangelical theology using the Bible, that apologists and philosophers have made the case for Scripture's reliability on any topic.[1] Once that has been done, systematicians can use Scripture to formulate theology. Hence, it is acceptable to say that Scripture teaches its own inspiration, and that this testimony is also relevant to the issue of canonicity.

But this isn't the end of the story, because Scripture doesn't define canonicity, nor does it discuss it per se, as a theological essay might. That being so, I argued in chapter 11 that apart from Scripture we must construct a non–question-begging definition of biblical canonicity, and I have also done that. However, I noted that since we are defining canonicity in terms of inspiration, we need to know how to detect a book's being inspired. To do so we must set forth criteria of inspiration, and in later sections of our discussion I shall do so. Some criteria will come from Scripture itself, while others may come from data external to Scripture.

---

[1] As to how one might do this, see my chapters 9 on "Christian Evidentialism" and 11 on "The Reliability of the Gospels" in *Can You Believe It's True? Christian Apologetics in a Modern and Postmodern Era* (Wheaton, IL: Crossway, 2013).

## THE OLD TESTAMENT AND CANONICITY

For now, my point in appealing to inspiration is just to note that any biblical information that suggests that Scripture is inspired is relevant to canonicity. In addition to evidence for inspiration presented in my chapters on that topic, there are some Scriptures worth noting as examples of a writer referring to a book of the Bible as Scripture and then quoting it with the introductory formula "it is written," or some other equivalent phraseology. Here I am specifically thinking of OT texts that use such language. As an example, Exodus 31:18 (see also Deut. 9:10) says that the Ten Commandments were written on two stone tablets by the finger of God. Clearly, they are his word, so once the tablets were written, as God's inspired word, they were also canonical. Of course, this is a rather small number of canonical verses, but as is well known, much more of Scripture is also inspired, even if not written by the finger of God.

Further examples of this phenomenon are found in Leviticus 1:1; 4:1; 5:14; and 6:1. Each passage essentially begins with the phrase, "The Lord said to Moses." In each case, Moses tells us what God said by writing it down. In the Leviticus 4 passage, Moses also says that God told him to speak to the people of Israel. He told them what God wanted to say to them, but he also recorded it in chapter 4. Since these passages contain words God actually spoke, and they are written for us in Scripture, they are, as inspired, also canonical. A further example is found in Jeremiah 29:1, 4. In verse 1 we learn that Jeremiah wrote a letter to the captives from Judah who were held in Babylon. By verse 4 Jeremiah begins to record the words he wrote in that letter. He writes that the letter began with "Thus says the LORD," so what he writes is not only Jeremiah's letter but also is from God. And all of this is preserved in the book of Jeremiah. Since the words of the letter are clearly God's words, they are also canonical.

Daniel 9:2 is also relevant to this point. Daniel had been reading the prophet Jeremiah's book, and he noticed that it predicted Judah's captivity in Babylon for seventy years. He also knew that the captivity had lasted seventy years, and so he wondered why it continued. The rest of the chapter presents Daniel interceding in prayer for his people in light of the fact that the prophecy had not been fulfilled. For our purposes, it is important to note that Daniel refers to this prophecy about the seventy-year captivity as "the word of the LORD to Jeremiah." In other words, Daniel considered the book of Jeremiah to be God's word—at the very least the part about the seventy-year captivity, but it is likely that Daniel thought of the rest of Jeremiah as God's word as well. So, this verse evidences that, at Daniel's time, there was a written prophecy by Jeremiah, and that Daniel considered it to be God's word. Hence, Daniel believed things about Jeremiah that were equivalent to its being part of the canon of Scripture—though I am not suggesting that Daniel had a full-blown concept of canonicity at that time. He clearly knew that some writings were God's word, and if it is right to define canonicity in terms of inspiration, then there was a sense in which some writings were canonical while others were not (though Daniel and his contemporaries likely wouldn't have used the term "canon," nor would they have been thinking of the concept).

This group of verses also includes Jesus's answers to Satan's temptations, as recorded in Matthew 4:1–11. In response to each temptation, Jesus quoted OT Scripture, always beginning with "it is written." Since this way of introducing a statement is equivalent to "Scripture says" and "God says," Jesus's answers to Satan's temptations are that, despite what Satan says, God says something that refutes Satan. But since Jesus is quoting Scripture, and since those Scriptures are God's word in written form, they are also canonical texts.

None of the texts cited says exactly how extensive Scripture's canon is, but they do show that there is a canon of some extent, because the written words recorded in Scripture are identified as what God says; that is, they are inspired. A second set of biblical texts relevant to biblical canonicity say that the human author was told to write in a book what God said, and the author did so. In some cases, the writer and the people of Israel were told to pass along/teach this information to their offspring so that they could know this information and live in accord with what it prescribes. Some of this information can, of course, be passed to children orally, but if there is a lot of information, even a first generation of offspring would benefit from having it in written form. Even for those who first received this information, as time passed by, these revelatory data would recede further into the community's collective memory. The only safe way to ensure that the instructions and information wouldn't be lost would be to record them in writing and to pass the writings from generation to generation.

Though many OT passages make this point, a good place to begin is Deuteronomy 6:6–7. After setting forth the commandments, statutes, and judgments that the Lord commanded Moses to teach the people of Israel, in verses 6–7 Moses tells the people that the words he is teaching should be on their hearts, and they are to teach these things to their children. If God's laws were few in number, it might be possible to remember them and pass them on from generation to generation. But God's laws, statutes, and judgments are far more extensive than just a few rules. If the people of Israel were to obey these laws and teach them to their children, that could happen only if they were written down and passed to each new generation. But since what would be written down and taught to future generations is God's word, the books that contain them must be part of Scripture's canon.

The next two verses of Deuteronomy 6 (vv. 8–9) even instruct the people to bind these words as a sign on their hands and as "frontals" on their foreheads. They were even to write them on the doorposts of their houses and on their gates. If they were to obey, the commands would have to be preserved originally in some written form. That form is the Bible, and since it is God's words and commands, it is canonical. So, for the people of Israel to obey what verses 6–9 require, there had to be some enduring written texts that are canonical.

Many other passages fit this category of texts: Exodus 13:9–10, 16; 17:14; 20:1–24:3, 4, 7; Numbers 33:2; Deuteronomy 4:1, 2; 31:9–29 (esp. 13, 19, 21–22, 24, and 26); Joshua 24:26; Jeremiah 2:1, 4; and 30:2. The Exodus 13 verses instruct the people of Israel to tell their children about the exodus from Egypt and to celebrate this event from year to year. That information, plus instructions for preparing and celebrating the Passover, would have to be written down so that it wouldn't be lost. Since this information is from God, the written text containing it is Scripture, God's word, and also part of the canon. The command to teach one's children these things seems to assume that there would have to be texts that record this information so that it wouldn't get lost as time passed.

The Exodus 17 passage tells Moses to write about the destruction of Amalek. Since we have that story, it is certain that Moses obeyed the command. In Exodus 20:1–24:3 Moses wrote down all of the ordinances God gave Israel to keep, and Moses says that he told them to the people. Exodus 24:4 and 7 repeat that Moses did write down in a book all the ordinances God gave him and in verse 7 he refers to it as the book of the covenant. Exodus 34:27 says that Moses was to write down the commands God gave him; they would be the basis of God's covenant with Israel. None of these verses directly teaches the concept of canonicity, but if Moses obeyed what he was told to do (and he did), the result would be written records of what God said. But then, if canonicity is defined in terms of inspiration, then those verses mean that there would be a lasting deposit of written texts of God's word—in short, a canon of Scripture.

Then, Numbers 33:2 says that Moses recorded the journeys of Israel once they left Egypt. Specifically, the rest of chapter 33 contains that record. Since Moses did this at God's command, Numbers 33 is God's word. In Deuteronomy 4:1 and 2, we learn that Moses told Israel to listen to the statutes and judgments he was telling them and to obey them. In fact, verse 2 says that the people must neither add to nor detract from any of them. Of course, those commands were given by God and are contained in the Pentateuch. The people who first heard them probably heard them orally, but as time would pass, they would need reminders, and so the commands needed to be put into writing. If that was so for those who first received the commands, it was even more the case for later generations. If they were to keep the commands, they would have to know of them, but the laws would likely be lost if not preserved in written form. These laws are God's word, so the texts that contain them must be part of the biblical canon.

Deuteronomy 31 is also relevant to this point. Verse 9 says that Moses wrote down the law of the Lord and gave it to the elders and priests to teach to the people. In verse 13, Moses explained that this was to be done so that their children would hear it and learn to fear the Lord. Verse 19 says that there was a song to be written and taught to the children of Israel so that they could know what God commands. Moreover, they were to sing this song (vv. 21–22), and it would testify against them if they disobeyed God's commands. Then in verse 24 we learn that Moses wrote the words of God's law in a book, and (v. 26) told them to put the book in the ark of the covenant. It would serve as a witness against them after Moses died. Obviously, the song and the words of God's law are all God's word. Clearly, God wanted a lasting record of his commands to Israel, and Moses acted to ensure that there would be such a written record. Though the word "canon" doesn't appear in this chapter, what Moses said and did required creating and keeping texts that are canonical, because they are God's word. For this to be read and obeyed not only by the generation alive when Moses first wrote these words but also by future generations, there would have to be a written record of these things; otherwise how would the children know what God required?

Joshua 24:26 says that Joshua wrote down in the book of God's law the fact that the people of Israel said that they would follow the Lord. He also put a stone under an oak tree as a reminder of this fact. Verse 26 shows at least two things. One is that there was a book of God's law (undoubtedly written by Moses, containing God's commands and instruction) that had been kept. The fact that Joshua wrote that the people would follow the Lord would mean little if the book wasn't preserved as a reminder. Since the book of the law is from God, then, using our terminology, it must have been part of the canon. We aren't told how extensive the book was, but it likely included many of God's commands.

Finally, we come to several passages in Jeremiah. Chapter 2 says that Jeremiah was told to hear the word of the Lord, and we learn that the word came to him and he wrote it down. Since the words came from God, what he wrote down was canonical. And Jeremiah 30:2 says God told Jeremiah to write in a book all the words God had spoken to him. In obedience, Jeremiah wrote the prophecy of Israel's deliverance that we have in chapter 30–31.[2] Since this is

---

[2] C. F. Keil, *The Prophecies of Jeremiah*, vol. 2, in C. F. Keil and F. Delitzsch, *Biblical Commentary on the Old Testament* (repr., Grand Rapids, MI: Eerdmans, 1967), 4.

clearly called what God had spoken (i.e., his word), and if what is God's word is canonical, then these chapters in Jeremiah are canonical.[3]

A third group of texts is similar to the previous group, but slightly different. In these texts the people of Israel were told to obey God's commands, and then the commands were written down. The main difference between this group of texts and the preceding one is that in these texts the emphasis is more on the need for the people to obey God's commands, whereas in the former group the focus is on God's command to write in a book whatever God revealed and to teach these things to future generations. What God revealed might be commands, but it might also recount some deed(s) God did on behalf of the people of Israel. Obviously, these texts somewhat overlap the previous group, as some things that are to be written in a book are commands God wants obeyed. (Passages that fit in both categories are Deuteronomy 6:6–7; 31:21–22, 26.)

Two passages that fit this third category best are Deuteronomy 5:22–33 and 8:1–4. According to Deuteronomy 5:22–33, God told Moses that the people should do all his commands. He also reminded Moses of giving him the law at Mount Sinai. Moses then gave it to the people of Israel and they promised to obey. Again, for these commands not to be lost, they must be recorded and passed down from generation to generation (there are too many to recall them all from memory). That requires written texts of God's commands—in short, canonical writings.

As for Deuteronomy 8, in it the Lord told Moses and the people of Israel to obey all the commands he was giving them. In addition, they were to remember everything God did for them and taught them in leading them through the wilderness to the Promised Land. Of course, no one could simply remember all of this information. Moreover, future generations would need to know of God's commands and about their forefathers' wilderness wanderings. Some of this might be passed on from memory, but the most likely way to preserve it would be to write it down and pass the written record from generation to generation. So, if Moses and the people of Israel were to do what this text commanded, the best way to ensure that they and future generations would know of it was to have it in writing. The texts that resulted are God's word (since they include what God told Moses to write), and they should also be seen as part of the biblical canon.

In another group of texts, the people are commanded to obey things written specifically in the law of Moses or in some other part of the OT. In some

---

[3] In no way do these limited references in Jeremiah mean that only these few verses and chapters are canonical. Rather, my point is to identify specific Scriptures that explicitly say they are God's word, because then they must be canonical. But focusing only on these limited passages doesn't mean the rest of Jeremiah, for example, isn't canonical. Other evidences show that it is also God's word, and so is canonical.

of those passages, God complained that Israel had disobeyed the law of Moses or some other OT teaching. For those commands to make any sense, Scripture that records the law of Moses (or some other part of the OT) would have to exist. In cases where Israel disobeyed, if there weren't texts containing God's law, it would be easy for Jews to say they would have obeyed if only they had known. But texts that speak of Israel's disobedience don't give even the slightest hint that they disobeyed in ignorance of God's commands. So there must be written texts containing God's law, and those texts must be canonical. Passages that fit in this category are Joshua 1:1–18 (esp. verse 8); 8:30–31, 34–35; 13:8; 1 Kings 2:3; 8:56; 2 Kings 14:6; 22:1–23:25 (esp. 22:11–13 and 23:3); 2 Chronicles 8:13; 23:18; 24:9; 25:4; 30:15, 16, 18; Ezra 3:2, 4; 6:18; 7:6; Nehemiah 8:1, 8–9, 14–17, 18; 10:28–39; 13:1–3; Proverbs 28:4, 7, 9; Isaiah 24:5; Jeremiah 11:10; Hosea 6:7; Malachi 3:7; and 4:4.

As the book of Joshua opens, Moses had died and God addressed Joshua, Israel's new leader. He gave instructions about what the people should do next—they must go in and possess the Promised Land. God also told Joshua to be courageous, and encouraged him by saying that no one would be able to defeat him; God would be with him for the rest of his life, just as he was with Moses. In verse 8, God added that the book of the law must not depart from his mouth. He was to meditate on it and obey it; only then would he have success. Undoubtedly, this refers to the law of Moses, but that is more than just a few verses of commands. For Joshua and Israel to obey God seems to require a written form of the books of the law. Since we can be sure that these are the words God revealed to Moses, for Joshua and his people not to forget the laws there must be a canon of writings containing the books of the law.

In Joshua 8 we learn two things that required Joshua to possess in some form (most likely written) the law of Moses. In 8:30–31, after the battle of Ai, Joshua built an altar to worship God. He built it "as Moses . . . had commanded . . . in the book of the law." Then verses 34–35 say that Joshua read all the words of the law to Israel. Both passages require that the law of Moses was written in a book, because Moses was dead and thus couldn't remind Joshua or the people of his instructions. Since we also know that the book of the law is revelation received from God, clearly these are special books that Israel possessed even at this early stage of its history. Given what is said about these books (and our definition of canonicity), we can conclude from Joshua 8 that there was already a book (or more) of canonical writings. This sense is heightened when we read in Joshua 13:8 that, after the people conquered the Promised Land, the land was divided as Moses had apportioned it. Since Moses had been dead for some time before these events, to know how he had divided up the land would have required Israel to have a written record of Moses's instructions on that matter. Since those instructions were revealed by God, the texts containing them would be, by our definition of canonicity, canonical.

In moving to Kings and Chronicles, we find a similar circumstance. In 1 Kings 2:3, we learn that David told Solomon to obey God's commands as written in the law of Moses, and in 8:56 Solomon said that God had done what he promised through Moses. For these things to make sense and be true, somewhere there had to be written copies of the law of Moses, and they are referenced in a way that shows they were considered God's word. Even though canonicity is never mentioned in these texts, they amount to saying that certain texts existed which, to use our terminology, are canonical.

Then, a significant event happened during King Josiah's reign (recorded in 2 Kings 22:1–23:25). A lost book of the law was found in the Lord's house and read to King Josiah (22:11–13). Later Josiah went to the Lord's house, along with the people of Judah, and he read to them the book of the law that had been found (23:2). Verse 3 says that Josiah made a covenant with the Lord to keep all the commands, testimonies, and statutes contained in this book. All the people entered into this covenant as well. For these things to happen there must have been a written form of the law of Moses that was God's word. Hence, these incidents require there to be texts that, using our terminology, are canonical.

In Ezra and Nehemiah, there are also many references to the regulations in the law of Moses. We read that various people built an altar for burnt offerings, according to the regulations in the law of Moses, and they also celebrated the Feast of Booths as prescribed in the law of Moses (Ezra 3:2, 4). Chapter 6 tells of the completion of repairs to the temple and of its rededication. Ezra also says that priests and Levites were appointed to serve in the temple, according to regulations set forth in the law of Moses (6:18). And then, in Ezra 7:6 we read that Ezra left Babylon, and the text says that he was skilled in the law of Moses that God had given. All of these texts require that the law of Moses be available in written form, and of course it was, as it forms much of the Pentateuch. But the 7:6 reference also says that this law was given by God. Hence, it must be his word, and that means that the books that record it must also be his word. But if a canonical book is a divinely inspired one, then the law of Moses (and the books that contain it) must be canonical.

A number of passages in Ezra–Nehemiah make a similar point. Nehemiah 8:1–2, 8–9, 14–17; and 10:28–39 are examples. Obviously, there had to be a written copy of the law for any of these passages to report accurately what happened. Many of them clarify that Moses's law was given by God, so the books containing them are inspired and hence canonical.

There are also similar references in Proverbs 28:4, 7, 9, and in various of the prophets. Relevant passages in the prophets are Isaiah 24:5; Jeremiah 11:10; Daniel 9:11, 13; Hosea 6:7; and Malachi 3:7; and 4:4. Daniel 9 is an especially revealing passage. It records Daniel's praying about Jeremiah's prophecy of seventy years for the Babylonian captivity. In verses 11 and 13, Daniel confessed that the people had indeed broken the law as written in the law of Moses, and they had suffered the punishments the law required, because they disobeyed God's demands recorded in that law. Clearly, Daniel (and his people, as well) had access to the book of Jeremiah and to books that contained the law of Moses. Verses 11–13 make it abundantly clear that Daniel knew that the commands in the law are God's word. Hence, as Daniel prayed for his people, books existed that were deemed the word of God. Those books are also canonical.

A fifth group of passages refer to various historical figures. Though the author may have written much about the person in his book, he added that more is written in some other works. Some of the works cited seem to be other OT books. Others may be references to books in the OT canon as well. Passages involved in this category are 2 Kings 18:17–20:11; 1 Chronicles 29:29; 2 Chronicles 9:29; 20:34; 26:22; 32:32; and Isaiah 36:1–38:8. Let me begin with 2 Chronicles 32:32. In this chapter the author writes about Hezekiah. He says that further acts of Hezekiah are written in visions of Isaiah and in the book of the Kings of Judah and Israel. It seems likely that 2 Chronicles 32:32 refers to Isaiah 36:1–38:8. As to the other reference, it may be to 2 Kings 18:17–20:11.

Similarly, 1 Chronicles 29:29 says that the rest of David's acts are written in the chronicles of Samuel the Seer. Does this refer to 1 and 2 Samuel? Even more nebulous, 2 Chronicles 9:29 says that the rest of Solomon's acts are written in a variety of documents. None of them name an OT book, but is it possible that they are part of existing OT books, written by the people mentioned in 2 Chronicles 9:29? Second Chronicles 20:34 speaks of the acts of Jehoshaphat written in the annals of Jehu, recorded in the book of the Kings of Israel. Is this part of 1 or 2 Kings written by Jehu, or is the author of 2 Chronicles referring to another document? Finally, 2 Chronicles 26:22 refers to the acts of Uzziah written by Isaiah. This likely refers to the book of Isaiah.

What do these passages show? None of them calls itself the word of God, nor does it *label* writings it refers to "the word of God." In fact, we don't know that each book mentioned is even part of our OT. So, why mention these texts? The reason is to show that it wasn't unusual at those times in history for the deeds of various rulers to be written about and for the written records to be preserved. Hence, what Samuel, Kings, and Chronicles, for example, say about the lives and deeds of various prominent figures in Israel's history isn't unusual. Of course, keeping annals of these things doesn't make them God's word or part of the biblical canon. But it does show that if God moved various writers to use any of these existing documents (or to write their own annals about a particular set of kings), that wouldn't be unusual. Hence, the idea that at that time in history there could be a group of literary documents that could serve as a model for books that became Scripture (or that even contained material used by biblical authors) is not unthinkable. This shows that it is possible that one of the requirements for a canon of Scripture, a group of written documents about prominent rulers, preserved over a period of time, would have existed.

A sixth group of OT texts focuses on God's law and the blessings that come from following it. Relevant passages here are Psalm 1:2; 19:7; 40:8; 119:1; and Proverbs 29:18. Psalm 1 says that the righteous man delights in the law of the Lord. Psalm 19:7 says that the law of the Lord is perfect. In Psalm 40:8 the psalmist writes that he delights to do God's will and that God's law is within his heart. Psalm 119:1 says that those who walk in the law of the Lord are blessed. And Proverbs 29:18 says that the one who keeps the law is happy. All of these Scriptures likely refer to the Mosaic law, but they also refer to much more. The psalmists and the writer of Proverbs often use "law" in the broader sense of any instruction from God, and that is likely its meaning in these passages.

How would these psalmists know God's law? Surely, by oral tradition various rules and regulations would have been passed down. But the amount of instruction in view is much larger than just a few (or even many) moral norms. Undoubtedly, these writers referred to teachings they knew because those instructions were in written form. Though no specific OT book is mentioned in any of these passages, it is safe to say that the books of our OT canon would qualify as the law of the Lord. Undoubtedly, when the psalmists and writer of Proverbs wrote, there was more Scripture to come, but at the very least, books they could have known in their own day would be included. So, evidently, there was some sense of an OT "canon," even if the term wasn't used and the concept wasn't on the mind of most Jews.

## THE NEW TESTAMENT AND CANONICITY

The rest of the passages relevant to canonicity are all from the NT. In several different ways, NT writers do things with Scripture that already exists and speak about works written or to be written in the NT era. What they do shows that these works were considered God's word, and if so, they must be part of the canon. The first group of NT passages, our seventh group of biblical passages relevant to canonicity, speaks of OT books as God's word or his law. Passages in this category are Matthew 4:1–11; 5:17, 21–26, 27–30, 31–32, 33–37, 38–42; 7:12; 11:13; 22:29, 40; 23:35; Luke 4:1–13; 16:16, 29, 31; 24:25, 27, 44, 45; John 6:45; 7:51–52; 10:34–36; 12:34, 38, 40; 20:9; Acts 13:15, 39;

18:24; 24:14; 26:22; 28:23; Romans 1:2; 3:21; 14:21; 2 Timothy 3:15; 1 Peter 2:6; and 2 Peter 1:20; 3:2.

This is a large and diverse set of texts, and we can divide it into groups that make the same basic point. However, it is clear that during Christ's life and the early NT era when these NT books were written, there was no doubt among God's people that the OT was Scripture, and as such, it was God's authoritative word. Also clear is that by this time certain typical ways of referring to large portions of the OT were used. The most frequent references were to two large sections of the OT known as the Law and the Prophets. The former referred to the books of Moses, while the latter pointed to a second section of OT books penned by writers who held a prophetic office in Israel. Examples of references to these portions of the OT are plentiful. In Matthew 5:17, Jesus says that he didn't come to abolish either the Law or the Prophets, but to fulfill them. In Matthew 7:12 Jesus states the command commonly known as the "Golden Rule," and adds that "this is the Law and the Prophets." In other words, this command summarizes the substance of what those large portions of the OT teach. Similarly, in Matthew 22:37–39 Jesus responded to the Pharisees' question that the greatest commands in the law are those that require love of God and of one's neighbor. In verse 40 Jesus adds that on these two commands depend everything else in the Law and the Prophets, those two large sections of the OT.

In other Gospel texts Jesus also speaks of the Law and the Prophets, but not to make a point about specific commands. For example, in Matthew 11:13 (par. Luke 16:16) Jesus says that "the prophets and the Law prophesied until John." The reference to the prophets need not be taken as referring to a large block of OT books, but that was likely Jesus's thinking. In the parallel passage in Luke 16:16 there is no doubt that Jesus refers to two large groups of OT books, for the verse begins with a reference to "the Law and the Prophets" prophesying until John.

Later in Luke 16 Jesus tells the story of the rich man and Lazarus. The rich man, in torment after death, asks father Abraham to send Lazarus to warn his five brothers not to continue to reject the truth and wind up with his fate. Abraham replies that there is no need to warn them, because they have Moses and the Prophets (v. 29), and they should heed them. The rich man responds that this isn't enough to convince his brothers. Abraham answers (v. 31) that if they won't believe Moses and the Prophets, they wouldn't believe even if someone rose from the dead. In the context of this story the references to Moses and the Prophets are not just general references to individual people. They point to two major sections of OT books, the books of Moses and those of the Prophets.

This is further evidence that the Jewish mind-set in Jesus's day was that certain OT books were God's word and were divided into large groups of books.

Luke 24 is a further example. There we read of Jesus's encounter with several disciples on the road to Emmaus. Verse 27 says that, "beginning with Moses and with all the prophets, He explained to them the things concerning Himself in all the Scriptures." "Moses and . . . the prophets" refers to the same thing as "the Law and the Prophets." In a preceding verse (v. 25), Jesus chides the disciples for being so slow to understand what Scripture teaches about him, but in this verse he refers only to what the prophets wrote. Later that evening Jesus appeared to a group of disciples, giving evidence that he was truly risen. Jesus then reminded them that while he was still with them, he taught that everything written about him "in the Law of Moses and the Prophets and the Psalms must be fulfilled" (v. 44), and then verse 45 says that Jesus opened their minds to understand the Scriptures. Jesus was, at the very least, referring to two parts of the OT (the Law and the Prophets). Some think the reference to the Psalms (which is in neither the Law nor Prophets portions of the OT) referred just to that book and the fact that there are various messianic psalms in it. On the other hand, it is just as likely, especially given what verse 45 adds, that the reference to the Psalms is a reference to the third major portion of the OT canon, the Writings, of which Psalms was a major part. So, by the time of Jesus not only were certain OT books viewed as Scripture and God's word, but the Jews had divided the various OT books into several major sections.

In various other ways Jesus also referred to the OT as a whole or in part, or to specific OT books. What he said shows that he considered those books God's word and authoritative. Hence, on our definition, they must also be canonical. For example, in response to Satan's temptations, Jesus answered repeatedly by saying, "it is written," and by quoting from the OT (Matt. 4:1–11; Luke 4:1–13). As noted already, "it is written" is a formulaic way of saying that something is God's word or what God says. There would be no point in quoting Scripture if Jesus thought it was just an ordinary writing, one among many. On the other hand, if Jesus thought it was God's word, and he did, there was every reason to respond to Satan's challenges by answering with God's word. If there wasn't during Jesus's lifetime a sense of what is Scripture and what is an ordinary book, it would be hard to explain why Jesus responded to Satan's temptations as he did.

The Sermon on the Mount also contains some interesting uses of OT Scriptures. In a series of comments on various laws in the Decalogue, Jesus quoted a command, and then offered his "escalation" of it. Here I am referring to the "you have heard it said . . . but I say unto you" comments in Matthew 5 (vv. 21–26, 27–30, 31–32, 33–37, 38–42). While some might think that in these verses Jesus rejected the Mosaic commandment, that is surely not so, as it would be totally inconsistent with what he says about the law in Matthew 5:17. A better understanding is that Jesus was getting at the very essence of what these commands were all about. Mere external conformity to the law's demands isn't enough; a heart attitude that signifies genuine obedience to the command is needed.

Then, various Gospel passages show Jesus quoting from part of the OT and calling it God's word. Sometimes, he began the quote with "it is written." For example, in John 6:45 Jesus says, "it is written in the prophets" and then quotes from Isaiah and Jeremiah. In previous chapters I have discussed in detail John 10:34–36, so I mention it only briefly. Jesus quoted from a psalm and called it the word of God. He also claimed that Scripture cannot be broken (annulled, overturned, be found wrong). In John 15:25, on another occasion, Jesus quoted from a psalm but called it law. His purpose was to show that the passage predicted something that was fulfilled in Jesus's life.

A final Gospel text is John 20:9. In chapter 20 John recounts details of the resurrection. After the women went to Jesus's tomb and found it empty, they ran to tell the disciples. They told Peter and John, and these two ran to the tomb. They were amazed when they found the tomb empty except for the grave clothes that had been left. John explains in verse 9 that the disciples were amazed because they did not yet understand the Scripture, that Christ must rise from the dead. Though this doesn't refer to any specific book, it clearly refers to the OT in general, which was at that time the only Scripture that existed. Of course, to refer to Scripture, as we have seen, is to refer to what was considered God's word. That being so, they were referring to what we would label the OT canon.

In the rest of the NT, we find much the same thing. In Acts, as the apostles preached, they referred to what was written in the Law and the Prophets (see Acts 24:14; 26:22; 28:23). In Acts 13 we learn that Paul and his companions came to Pisidian Antioch, and went to the synagogue on the Sabbath. Verse 15 says there was reading from the Law and the Prophets, and then Paul and his friends were asked to speak any word of exhortation they wanted. Paul did speak, and his speech is recorded. Near its end, Paul said that everyone who believes in Jesus is freed, through him, from all things from which the law of Moses could free no one. Of course, since the Pentateuch sets forth the Mosaic law in detail, in referring to the Mosaic law Paul also referred to a part of the OT and called it the law of Moses. See also Romans 3:12–22, especially verse 21.

Other NT passages also refer to the OT (sometimes quoting a passage). Though they do not specifically call it God's word, they refer to the OT in general or to a specific passage and speak of it in ways that clearly say that it is Scripture or God's word. Examples of this are Acts 18:24; Romans 1:1–2; 2 Timothy 3:15; 2 Peter 1:20; and 3:2. In Romans 1:1–2 Paul speaks of himself as an apostle "set apart for the gospel of God, which He promised before-hand through His prophets in the holy Scriptures, concerning His Son," Jesus Christ. This can only refer to the OT, for Paul would know of no other texts written by prophets that predicted the Messiah's coming and that could be said to be about God's Son, Jesus Christ. In 2 Timothy 3:15 Paul says that Timothy had from his childhood known the sacred writings. In the chapters on inspiration we noted that this must refer to the OT. In 2 Peter 1:20 Peter writes of the prophecies of Scripture. Again we saw that this must refer to the OT. And in 2 Peter 3:2 Peter puts on a par the commandments of the Lord spoken by the apostles and the words spoken in the OT era by the holy prophets. The reference to the words spoken by the holy prophets can refer to nothing other than to OT books. How could Peter grant to either the words of the prophets or those of the apostles such authority unless he considered them to be Scripture, God's word?

And, there are also some NT passages where the writer makes a point about the Law or Scripture and then quotes from an OT passage. In 1 Corinthians 14:21 Paul tells the Corinthians that in the Law, the first section of the OT, it is written (the typical way to say that something is Scripture), but then quotes from Isaiah. In Galatians 3:8 Paul writes that Scripture preached the gospel to Abraham, but then quotes from Genesis, so he must think that Genesis is Scripture. And finally, in 1 Peter 2:6, as Peter speaks about the nature of the church, he supports his claims by referring to "Scripture" and then quotes from Isaiah. In verse 7 he adds another point and supports it in verses 7–8 with quotes from Psalm 118 and then from Isaiah 8. As with the many other references in this group of NT passages, these OT books are called God's word, his law, or Scripture, and if so, they must also be canonical, given our definition of canon.

The next group of texts refers to NT writings as Scripture and God's word. If so, then the NT must also be canonical. Here there are fewer verses, but still clear enough: John 3:11–12, 32; chs. 14–16; 1 Corinthians 7:10–11; 11:23; and 2 Peter 3:2, 16. John 3:11–12 is part of Jesus's answer to Nicodemus's question about Jesus's claim that one must be born of the Spirit. Jesus said that he spoke things that he knew and bore witness of, and yet his witness was rejected. Jesus asked how, if Nicodemus couldn't believe the earthly things Jesus taught, he could believe if Jesus spoke of heavenly things? To what was Jesus referring? He was referring to his teachings as recorded in the Gospels. But if the Gospels are deemed Scripture, then things Jesus taught which were recorded in the Gospels are also Scripture. In effect, this means that the Gospels are Scripture.

But what Scripture teaches that the Gospels should be considered Scripture? As noted in my chapters on inspiration, in John 14–16 Jesus promised the Holy Spirit's ministry to the disciples after Jesus's departure. As we saw, these promises in effect guaranteed the soon-to-be-written NT to be God's word, Scripture, since it would be written under the Holy Spirit's guidance. Since the apostles certainly would have considered the four Gospels to be some of those books, they most certainly would have considered those books, once written, to be Scripture. Along similar lines, the way Luke begins his Gospel is significant. In 1:1–4 he says that even as others have written accounts of Jesus's life and ministry, he wanted to do the same. At least some of those other accounts to which Luke referred are others of the four Gospels. Hence, he undoubtedly saw himself as doing what the other Gospel writers had done. If so, then he must have considered his book to be Scripture. Thus, his Gospel must also be canonical.

Then, there are NT passages where the writer refers to his own writings or to those of other NT authors and calls them Scripture, or says that what is written came from the Lord. If so, they must be God's word, and hence, canonical. For example, in 1 Corinthians 7:10–11, as Paul began to discuss divorce and remarriage, he said that what he wrote first is the Lord's command. What Paul then wrote does indeed match the basic substance of Jesus's teaching on this subject, as recorded in the Gospels. But if Paul wrote what Jesus taught, he must be writing God's word, and that means he wrote Scripture. In 1 Corinthians 11:23ff. Paul addressed the Lord's Supper. He began by saying that he received what he was writing from the Lord. But then, what Paul wrote must be God's word, Scripture. As also noted previously, in 2 Peter 3:2 Peter put on a par the commands of the NT apostles and those of the OT prophets. That means both qualify as Scripture. But where are the NT apostles' commands? In the books of the NT. In the same chapter (3:16) Peter also referred to Paul's writings as Scripture. He wrote that wicked men distort what Paul wrote, as they do with *the rest of Scripture*. The number of passages in this group of texts is far fewer than that of texts that call the OT (or individual books in it) Scripture, but the ones cited clearly enough make the same point about all of the NT. And, if they are Scripture, they are God's word, and if they are God's word, they are canonical!

A final set of NT texts is relevant to the canonicity of NT books. In these texts Jesus said that what he was saying came from God. Thus, whether or not one believes Jesus is God, he spoke God's word. But then, NT books that record Jesus's words also record God's word, since Jesus spoke what the Father gave to him. All the verses in this group are found in the Gospel of John: John

3:34; 8:26, 28, 38; 12:49; 17:6–8, 14. In John 3:34, referring to himself, Jesus said that he spoke God's words, for God gives the Spirit without measure. So, any words of Jesus recorded in the Gospels, including John 3:34, are God's words. If so, that part of the book (at the very least) must be canonical.

John 8 records various conversations with Jesus's opponents. During one of them, Jesus said three times (vv. 26, 28, 38) that he spoke things that he heard from or saw with the Father or that the Father taught him. On another occasion, recorded in John 12, Jesus summed up his message by saying that he didn't speak of his own initiative, but spoke what the Father had given him. Since things that the Father gave him to say (and that he taught) are recorded in the Gospels, those parts (at the very least) of the Gospels are God's word. But then they must also be canonical. And finally, in John 17 Jesus prayed to his Father. He said that the words he had spoken to the men the Father gave him are his Father's words. Thus, they are God's word, and to the extent that Jesus's teachings are recorded in the Gospels, for example, we have the word of God. But if so, then those teachings, as God's word, mean that the books that contain them (or at the very least the parts of the books with Jesus's teachings) are part of the canon.

What should we conclude from these OT and NT teachings about Scripture? Let me summarize it: *biblical data discussed in this chapter don't use the terms "canon" or "canonicity." However, if the concepts are defined as we have done, then Scripture itself contains many passages relevant to canonicity. While the concept of canonicity is a theological construct, it is not without warrant. Given the special nature of various religious writings, it is evident why God's people in any era would want to have a way of singling out certain writings as distinctive in that they are God's very words. If one adopts a definition of canonicity at all like the one I have proposed, it is also clear as to why, for as long as there have been religious writings by OT prophets and NT apostles, there has been reason enough to want a way to identify which ones qualify as the word of God, and hence as canonical, and which ones do not.*

# THIRTEEN

# LIGHT CANONIZED (III)

## Old Testament Canonicity

While our discussion in chapter 12 of biblical teaching relevant to canonicity is a good start in understanding why some books are considered canonical and others are not, it isn't the whole story. For the rest of the story, we must look at the actual processes which the people of God used to consider certain books canonical and others not. The story of how this happened is both complex and distinctive for each Testament. In this chapter we will discuss different theories of when the OT canon was closed, who made that decision, and why.

### THE OLD TESTAMENT CANON

Composition of OT books took place over a long period of time, and that is one reason why scholars disagree on the exact timing of canonizing the various OT books and on the date of the OT canon's closure. Matters are complicated further because the OT is typically divided into three groups of books, and there is debate about the "closure" of each group. Of course, determining dates for all of this is complicated even more by one's theory about when, by whom, and how each book was composed. The point isn't that those committed to higher critical methodologies and to some form of the documentary hypothesis about the origin of the Pentateuch have one theory about the forming and closing of the different segments of the OT canon, while those who reject such methods and theories have another. Rather, there are many theories about the closure of each part of the canon even among those committed to higher criticism and some form of documentary hypothesis.

For evangelicals, this might matter little if those who hold traditional views about the dates and authorship of OT books agreed about closure of the parts of the OT canon. Unfortunately, it is even hard to find in more current literature what might be called *an* evangelical theory, let alone *the* evangelical theory, of OT canon formation and closure. It is beyond the scope and purpose of this book to present arguments for dates and authorship of each OT book. Let me just say that I hold traditional evangelical views on dates and authorship so that, for example, I believe that Moses authored the Pentateuch (even if not the very end of Deuteronomy); that there was only one Isaiah, who penned the whole book that bears his name; and that Daniel was the author of the book named for him, and it was written in the sixth century BC, not during the time of the Maccabees. Thus, it contains genuine predictions about things future to Daniel (and some even future to us), rather than merely recounting past historical events "cleverly" disguised as prophecies of future events.

Given these assumptions about the dating and authorship of OT books, I propose to proceed as follows: I shall describe some of the major current theories on OT canon formation and closure, including some suggestions from an evangelical or two. Then, in attempting to judge which of these theories is most likely accurate (if such a judgment can be made), I want first to present evidence internal to Scripture relevant to this discussion, and then evidence external to Scripture.

## Theories of Old Testament Canon Formation and Closure

Let me begin this section with what many scholars label the standard theory about the formation and closure of the OT canon. This theory was fairly well entrenched among biblical scholars, at least nonevangelicals, by the end of the nineteenth century. According to this theory, the first part of the OT to be recognized as distinct and to be canonized was the Torah or the books of Moses. The key event for canonizing this part of the OT was finding the book of the law in the temple during the reign of King Josiah, after the Jews returned from Babylonian exile (see 2 Kings 22:11–13). These events are thought to have happened about the middle of the fifth century BC, and the key figure in this "canonizing" of the books of Moses was Ezra.

Next, the standard theory says that two centuries later a second section of the OT, known as the Prophets, was finished and joined to the Pentateuch as also "canonical." This part of the OT is largely composed of works by both major prophets (e.g., Isaiah, Jeremiah, and Ezekiel) and minor prophets (the twelve—Hosea through Malachi), but it also included books like Joshua, Judges, 1 and 2 Samuel, and 1 and 2 Kings. Of course, if this view is correct, it is unlikely that any of the authors traditionally held to have written these books could have done so, for even the postexilic prophets whose names are on these books likely would have been dead by 450–400 BC. As for the third section of the OT canon, known as the Writings (the Kethubim or the Hagiographa), the standard theory holds that they were basically completed by the end of the first century BC. However, this part of the canon wasn't finalized until the end of the first century AD at the Council of Jamnia (AD 90).[1]

The standard view has fallen on hard times, especially its views about the closure of the third part of the canon. While some still accept roughly the story about the closing of the first two sections (even on this there are diverse theories), almost no scholar agrees that the Kethubim was closed at Jamnia. This is so for at least a two reasons. On the one hand, available evidence about the Council suggests that several disputed books like Esther were discussed at the Council, but no decisions were made about all the books that should comprise the third part of the canon nor about those explicitly excluded. In addition, some scholars have argued that there actually never was a Council of Jamnia, or that it was held at a later date. Thus, something happened at Jamnia, but not anything like a council meeting of many authorities, and certainly not to discuss the shape of the whole canon or even part of it.

If the standard view is untenable, what has taken its place? In two recent articles, Stephen Dempster has offered a helpful survey of the field of theories. In the current canon debate, Dempster identifies two major positions. The first is held by a minority of scholars, and Dempster labels it the maximalist view. It says that the Hebrew Bible/OT was formed before the time of the early church. Views vary on just when, but some have argued that the tripartite canon emerged at the latest during the time of the Maccabees. If this is so, then the early church was, to use Dempster's language, "born with the canon in its hands." As time passed, the church grew away from its roots in Judaism, and eventually it engaged in a debate to determine its canon. Even so, the maximalist view says the canon was closed even before the church began.[2]

---

[1] For further description of and arguments favoring and against this theory see Stephen B. Chapman, "The Canon Debate: What It Is and Why It Matters," *JTI* 4 (2010): 274–277; Stephen Dempster, "Canons on the Right and Canons on the Left: Finding a Resolution in the Canon Debate," *JETS* 52 (March 2009): 55–58; Dempster, "Torah, Torah, Torah: The Emergence of the Tripartite Canon," in *Exploring the Origins of the Bible*, ed. Craig A. Evans and Emanuel Tov (Grand Rapids, MI: Baker, 2008), 88–91; Dempster, "From Many Texts to One: The Formation of the Hebrew Bible," in *The World of the Aramaeans I*, ed. P. M. Michèle Daviau, John W. Wevers, and Michael Weigl, JSOTSup 324 (2001): 19; Michael W. Holmes, "The Biblical Canon," in *The Oxford Handbook of Early Christian Studies*, ed. Susan A. Harvey and David G. Hunter (Oxford: Oxford University Press, 2008), 408–409; S. A. Nigosian, "Formation of Jewish and Christian Scriptures," *Theological Review* 24 (2003): 128–137; Stephen B. Chapman, "The Old Testament Canon and Its Authority for the Christian Church," *Ex Auditu* 19 (2003): 127–128; Chapman, "What Are We Reading? Canonicity and the Old Testament," *Word and World* 29 (Fall 2009): 335–341; David Dunbar, "The Biblical Canon," in *Hermeneutics, Authority, and Canon*, ed. D. A. Carson and John Woodbridge (Grand Rapids, MI: Zondervan, 1986), 301–303; R. T. Beckwith, "The Canon of the Old Testament," in *The Origin of the Bible*, ed. Philip W. Comfort (Wheaton, IL: Tyndale, 1992), 55–61; David Kraemer, "The Formation of Rabbinic Canon: Authority and Boundaries," *Journal of Biblical Literature* 110 (1991): 614–614; and David M. Carr, "Canonization in the Context of Community: An Outline of the Formation of the Tanakh and the Christian Bible," in *A Gift of God in Due Season: Essays on Scripture and Community in Honor of James A. Sanders*, ed. Richard D. Weis and David M. Carr, JSOTSup 225 (1996): 25–26.

[2] Dempster, "Canons on the Right and Canons on the Left," 48–49; and Dempster, "Torah," 89–90. For evidence that the third section of the OT canon was closed during the time of the Maccabees, see Beckwith, "Canon of the Old Testament," 59–63. For a rejection of one line of evidence sometimes used to support the closing of the canon

In contrast, Dempster labels the majority view among canon scholars the minimalist view. This view says the OT canon wasn't finalized before the founding of the church. In fact, the OT canon hadn't even been completed during the early part of the second century AD. Over time, however, it became clearer as to which books should be deemed canonical; but even so, this view claims that the contours of the canon weren't settled in Judaism until later in the second century or in the third century AD. In the church, the OT canon wasn't settled until the fourth or fifth century AD.[3]

As Dempster explains, each camp has a major complaint with the other. Minimalists believe that maximalists come to study the canon with the preconceived notion of the completed canon and impose it on the data. In particular, they tend to maximize the later understanding of the rabbinic canon and read it back into the pre-Christian evidence. As one might suspect, maximalists are often accused of anachronism in their assessment of testimony related to the OT canon. On the other hand, maximilists who believe in an early canon closure complain that minimalists don't take seriously enough the importance of tradition (like Josephus's clear statements about the OT canon) and other earlier evidence such as the prologue to the apocryphal book *Ben Sira* (the date and contents of this work are explained below).[4]

James Charlesworth is a proponent of a minimalist theory. He grants that the Hebrew Bible is divided into three sections, and also holds that each section was closed separately from the others. As for the Torah, he believes it was most likely closed during the third century BC. Next came the Prophets, most likely before the defeat of Bar Kokhba (135/136 BC). However, he argues that the exact contents of the books of Samuel and Jeremiah were not clarified until

---

in the time of the Maccabees, see Armin Lange, "2 Maccabees 2:13–15: Library or Canon?," in *The Books of the Maccabees: History, Theology, Ideology*, ed. Geza G. Xeravits and Jozsef Zsengeller (Leiden: Brill, 2007). Also, in footnote 7 of Dempster's "Canons on the Right and Canons on the Left," he lists as proponents of the maximalist view S. Liemann, *The Canonization of the Hebrew Scripture: The Talmudic and Midrashic Evidence* (Hamden: Archon, 1976); R. T. Beckwith, *The Old Testament Canon of the New Testament Church* (Grand Rapids, MI: Eerdmans, 1985); Earle Ellis, *The Old Testament in Early Christianity: Canon and Interpretation in the Light of Modern Research* (Grand Rapids, MI: Baker, 1992); Philip R. Davies, *Scribes and Schools: The Canonization of the Hebrew Scriptures* (Louisville: Westminster John Knox, 1998); and Andrew Steinmann, *The Oracles of God: The Old Testament Canon* (St. Louis: Concordia, 1999).

[3] Dempster, "Canons on the Right and Canons on the Left," 49; and Dempster, "Torah," 90. In Dempster's "Canons on the Right and Canons on the Left," his footnote 8 lists, among others, the following as proponents of the minimalist view: John Barton, *Oracles of God: Perceptions of Ancient Prophecy in Israel after the Exile* (Oxford: Oxford University Press, 1985); Peter R. Ackroyd, "The Open Canon," in *Studies in the Religious Tradition of the Old Testament* (London: SCM, 1987); James A. Sanders, "Canon: Hebrew Bible," in *The Anchor Bible Dictionary*, ed. David N. Freedman, 6 vols. (New York: Doubleday, 1992), 1:837–852; Lee Martin McDonald, *The Formation of the Christian Biblical Canon*, 2nd ed. (Peabody, MA: Hendrickson, 1995); McDonald, *The Biblical Canon* (Peabody, MA: Hendrickson, 2007); Carr, "Canonization in the Context of Community; James VanderKam, *From Revelation to Canon" Studies in the Hebrew Bible and Second Temple Judaism* (Journal for the Study of Judaism, Supplement 62, Leiden: Brill, 2000); and Eugene Ulrich, *The Dead Sea Scrolls and the Origins of the Bible*, Studies in the Dead Sea Scrolls and Related Literature (Grand Rapids, MI: Eerdmans, 1999).

[4] Dempster, "Canons on the Right and Canons on the Left," 49; and Dempster, "Torah," 90–91.

at least AD 70. As for the Writings, some of them were debated until the sixth century AD.[5]

Another minimalist approach is presented by Lee Martin McDonald. McDonald's chief complaints with the maximalist approach are that it is guilty of anachronism, and that this is evident when one looks at the alleged evidence for an earlier understanding of the canon. That evidence just doesn't support the claim that, for example, the five books of Moses were recognized as Scripture in the days of Ezra–Nehemiah (see Ezra 9–10 and Nehemiah 8–9). What is clear from the event of the finding of the book of the law is that in the days of Ezra and Nehemiah, the law of Moses was normative, but McDonald explains that it isn't clear that this is equal to the whole of the Pentateuch. In addition, while there is some reference to some of the earlier prophets in passages like Jeremiah 26:18, there is no mention of any normative status of the Former Prophets.[6]

As another example, McDonald references the *Prologue to Sirach*, dated around 130 BC. In it, three groupings of writings are mentioned, the Law and the Prophets, and the "others that followed them" or the "other books of our ancestors" or "the rest of the books." As McDonald says, it is tempting to read back into this third category all the books we think of as making up the Writings, but there is no list in the Prologue, so we can't say that the third group referred to contains the same books that we understand to be in the Writings.[7] McDonald even argues that the OT canon we think of wasn't necessarily the one understood in Jesus's day. While many appeal to Luke 24:44 with its reference to the law of Moses, the prophets, and the psalms as evidence of a tripartite canon, McDonald disagrees. While it is common to think the third part referred to what was considered (as early as the second century BC) the Hagiographa or Kethubim, McDonald argues that there is nothing in the first century or before that would lead to that conclusion. In fact, even in the first century AD, it isn't possible to show that such a notion existed. While the Luke 24 passage shows a growing sense of a third part of the OT canon, there simply is no reference in the first century AD, McDonald claims, to terms like Hagiographa or Kethubim. Even more, it is unlikely that in Jesus's time the portion of the OT he references as the Psalms would have included books like Chronicles and Ezra–Nehemiah.[8]

After dismissing further alleged evidence to the effect that the canon was recognized by Christ's time,[9] McDonald concludes that the OT canon wasn't complete in Jesus's time, and the only surviving forms of Judaism (represented

---

[5] James H. Charlesworth, "Writings Ostensibly outside the Canon," in Evans and Tov, *Exploring the Origins of the Bible*, 59.

[6] Lee Martin McDonald, "The Integrity of the Biblical Canon in Light of Its Historical Development," *BBR* 6 (1996): 105.

[7] Ibid., 106.

[8] Ibid., 107–108.

[9] See ibid., 109–111.

by the Pharisees, Sadducees, Essenes, and earliest Christians) didn't hold a unified picture on the contents and extent of the canon. While some groups of Jews and Christians may have finalized in their thinking the extent of the OT canon by the second century AD, this simply isn't true for many. Into the fourth and fifth centuries AD Jews were still arguing about whether books like Ecclesiastes, Song of Songs, Proverbs, Esther, and Ruth should be in the canon. Moreover, there are examples in the works of the early church fathers of references to noncanonical apocryphal literature which are referred to as Scripture. So, clearly, the extent of the OT canon wasn't finalized during the time of Christ or even relatively soon after his time.[10]

In all of this it is important to note that at least part of what drives Mc-Donald's theory is his commitment to a concept of canon as a fixed list of authoritative books. If that is the working definition, then the finalizing of the OT canon must surely be dated later than if one works with a notion of canon as books that function authoritatively in a community of believers, even if those books haven't been recognized as canonical in some formal way like at a council that represents large numbers of groups that hold the religion represented by the books.

There are surely other theories of interest among nonevangelicals, but what might an evangelical conception of the formation and closure of the OT canon look like? Here I offer examples from two evangelical thinkers. Bruce Waltke, noted evangelical OT scholar, offers one approach to the canon's formation. He sees it as involving four stages. Connecting canonicity with inspiration, Waltke explains that the process began when godly people recognized that various things spoken to people like Moses and different prophets were inspired utterances. Such revelations, according to Waltke, were given at various times between about 1400 and 400 BC. Waltke explains that the Ten Commandments were the first piece of canonical literature received. To this, God added/revealed material which later became known as the Book of the Covenant (Ex. 24:3ff.). In addition to materials revealed to Moses, the prophets also began as "isolated oracles that the elect recognized as from God."[11]

A second stage in canon formation involved gathering the various revelations into inspired books. This not only involved an original form of each book, but also various expansions that were added to each along the way. Waltke, affirming Sid Leiman's view, explains that we really know very little about the literary history of each book that makes up the OT. But, Waltke adds, what we do know is that the books themselves and the canon of the OT were fixed by about 164 BC.[12]

---

[10] Ibid., 111–112.

[11] Bruce Waltke, "How We Got the Old Testament," *Crux* 30 (1994): 13–14.

[12] Ibid., 14. On pages 15–16, Waltke offers a further description of various ways in which different OT books were expanded.

The third stage of canon formation was the collection of books. That is, individual books were collected to form new unities. For example, the books of Moses were collected to form a unit. Waltke adds that many OT scholars have concluded that Deuteronomy, Joshua, Judges, Samuel, and Kings form a closed, or at least shaped, unity. The reference in Daniel 9:2 to Jeremiah's prophecy about the seventy years of captivity as part of "the books" is, according to Waltke, "the earliest reference to a collection of books recognized as Scripture."[13] Waltke then adds that the book of Psalms consists of five hymn books added to one another during the preexilic, exilic, and postexilic periods.[14]

The fourth and final stage of canon formation involved reaching a fixed canon. Waltke explains that, though we don't know for certain when the canon was fixed, he believes that Roger Beckwith has made a plausible case for 164 BC. Regardless, it is clear that by the time of the NT there was a fixed OT canon. As Waltke further explains, there is plenty of evidence that this OT canon was conceived of as consisting of three distinct parts. Waltke grants that there were, of course, books like Ezekiel, Proverbs, Ecclesiastes, Song of Solomon, and Esther that were disputed by some rabbis, but he adds that the key point to remember is that these books, even though disputed by some, were assumed to be canonical.[15]

While some might think Waltke's dating of the OT canon's closure at 164 BC is too late to fit an evangelical understanding of the OT, that is not necessarily so. What must be remembered is that Waltke isn't talking about when the books were *composed*, but when they were formally *recognized* as canonical, and when the OT canon was deemed closed. What evangelicals have traditionally believed about when OT books were composed, and who wrote them, isn't negatively impacted by Waltke's proposal about *recognition* of books as canonical and the canon *as closed*.

Writing at about the same time as Waltke, Paul House offers another approach to OT canon formation. Actually, the main lines of his theory are consistent with Waltke, but he takes a bit more traditional view on when the books were likely composed, and he gives dates for the closing of the three different parts of the OT canon. As for the Pentateuch, House explains that as early as 622 or 550 BC, and no later than 450 BC, these books were quoted as authoritative and binding for Israel. In fact, even from the time of Moses onward, Israel "had a concept of a binding, law-based covenant" with God.[16]

---

[13] Ibid., 17. On pages 16–17, Waltke describes various ways in which books of the OT were gathered into groups.
[14] Ibid., 17.
[15] Ibid., 18–19.
[16] Paul R. House, "Canon of the Old Testament," in *Foundations for Biblical Interpretation*, ed. David S. Dockery, Kenneth A. Mathews, and Robert B. Sloan (Nashville: Broadman & Holman, 1994), 154.

House adds that all of the Prophets were written by 400 BC, and they were considered canonical no later than 200 BC. Even with this late date, however, the various writings were considered authoritative among the Jews long before 200 BC.[17] I should also add that, saying that all of the Prophets were written by 400 BC doesn't mean they were all written close to 400 BC. Isaiah and Jeremiah, for example, still could have been written before the Babylonian captivity (and at least parts of Isaiah before the Assyrian invasion). All that House proposes is that no book in this portion of the canon was written later than 400 BC. As for the Writings, though some have argued that they weren't set as canonical until AD 90 or later, House disagrees. Evidence from sources such as Josephus, the Qumran community, and rabbinical writings suggest a much earlier sense of a completed canon than AD 90. Thus, House concludes, the Writings portion of the OT was considered canonical between 180 and 114 BC, and that just means that the whole OT canon was fixed by 150 BC, if not sooner.[18]

House offers a quote from Sid Leiman that sums up this basic conclusion about the fixing of the OT canon. It is worth repeating here:

> Jewish sources such as the Apocrypha, Philo, and Josephus, as well as Christian sources reflecting Jewish practice, such as the NT and the church fathers, support the notion of a closed biblical canon in most Jewish circles throughout the first centuries before and after the Christian era. . . . Critical analysis of the book of Daniel, evidence from the Apocrypha, and newly discovered biblical texts in Hebrew and Greek (from Qumran, Nahal Hever, and elsewhere) suggest the possibility and likelihood that the biblical canon was closed in the Maccabean period. The talmudic and midrashic evidence is entirely consistent with a second century B.C. dating for the closing of the biblical canon.[19]

What I have presented in this section is only a sampling of the many different theories about the formation and closure of the OT canon. There is little unanimity. Also, how one defines canon make a difference. If one uses a definition like McDonald's that there is only canon when there is a fixed list of canonical books, then of course, one will opt for a late date for canon closure. On the other hand, if one uses a different notion (such as the definition I proposed), it is surely likely that individual books were deemed canonical well before there was a definitive collection and a fixed list of all the books we know today as the OT canon. Put simply, there is no need to think that no book was considered canonical until all thirty-nine were jointly recognized.

---

[17] Ibid.
[18] Ibid.
[19] Ibid., quoting Sid Z. Leiman, *Canonization of Hebrew Scripture: The Talmudic and Midrashic Evidence* (Hamden, CT: Archon, 1976), 135.

Regardless of which theory of canon closure readers hold, so far very little has been said about evidence, especially outside of Scripture, for the canonicity of the various OT books. Actually, I think it best to put aside specific theories and to examine available evidence relevant to canon recognition. Once we see that evidence, we should be in a better position to judge which overall theory is most likely to be correct. To that evidence we now turn.

## TESTIMONY RELATED TO THE OLD TESTAMENT CANON

In compiling testimony about OT books that were considered canonical, we can't expect to find the terminology of canon and canonicity, for those terms were introduced well after the OT canon was written. Even so, biblical and extrabiblical testimony are relevant to which books were and which were not considered canonical, in part because we are defining canonicity in terms of inspiration, and there is much Scripture and extrabiblical testimony that speaks of OT writings as God's word and hence Scripture. So, if Bible passages refer to OT books as God's word or Scripture, then the writer believed, in regard to the book(s) in question, that it/they had the quality we have used to denote canonicity.

### Old Testament Testimony

The starting point for our testimony about OT canonicity is Scripture itself. Here I refer readers to the detailed handling of biblical materials earlier, in chapter 12, but I want to highlight at least some of the findings. Many passages in the OT refer to some OT book or books as God's word. Hence, the writer appeals to it as authoritative and binding, and the people of Israel also recognized these features about these books. Regardless of whether Scripture was always obeyed, it was still perceived to be God's word. As is clearly evident from the data presented in chapter 12, most of the OT references to other parts of the OT as God's word refer to the Pentateuch. Whether the emphasis is on the Mosaic law or some other part of the books of Moses, the Pentateuch was uniformly deemed to be of divine origin. So, whatever one chooses as dates for the composition of these books, this testimony from other OT books seems to be the earliest testimony about the Pentateuch.

We also noted in chapter 12 that the OT has many references to the law of God. This includes the Mosaic law but is broader, as many passages speak of law in the sense of instruction from God. Law in this broader sense is applied to more than just the Pentateuch. There are also various references to the prophets (former, mainly, but some refer to later prophets) as speaking the word of the Lord, and often the prophet himself begins a section of his book by saying that the Lord told him to write what he then wrote, or that "the word of the Lord came unto him, saying," and then he recounts the substance of God's revelation. In effect, this means that the various prophetic books claim to be God's word. If so, that means (though the author never uses such terminology) they qualify as canonical.

When it comes to books contained in the Writings, there are few, if any, OT references to these books as a whole or individually as God's word or Scripture. Moreover, in books like Job, Proverbs, Ecclesiastes, Psalms, and even some of the more historical books that make up this section of the canon, one won't find the author saying that he writes what God told him to write, or that God revealed himself to the author and now the author is writing up the results of that revelatory disclosure. Even so, while some books in this part of the canon were contested even into the first century AD and beyond, they were still generally seen as Scripture.

### New Testament Testimony

*Biblical* testimony about the OT also appears in the NT. Here again the details are contained in chapter 12, so I can summarize. From the Gospels, it is clear that by Jesus's time both the Law and Prophets were well established as two major parts of OT Scripture (and hence canon). Depending on what one thinks of Luke 24:44, this can be seen as certifying a tripartite structure to the OT.[20]

When we move beyond the Gospels per se, as we saw in the chapter on inspiration, Paul in 2 Timothy 3:14–17 calls the whole OT Scripture, the product of God's breath. In addition, Peter refers to OT prophecy (2 Pet. 1:20–21), and he most likely had in mind the whole of the OT as prophecy. What he says about the origin and nature of those books teaches their inspiration. So this first-century-AD testimony shows that the whole OT was deemed Scripture. It also shows rather clearly that, during Jesus's day, the OT writings available were considered to be God's word, and not just by Jesus alone but also by his Jewish contemporaries. If so, then on our definition, it was also canon.

Of course, this testimony from the NT is rather general, because it doesn't name the specific books included in each OT section or in the OT as a whole. But part of the evidence for individual OT books as God's word is the fact that so many are quoted or alluded to in the NT. These references to specific books aren't simple quotes of a few words from OT books or a reference to an incident recorded in an OT book. Rather, many of these quotations and allusions are introduced by the author saying, "as Scripture says," "God said," "it is written," the typical introductory formulas used to denote that what comes next is God's word. Moreover, as we saw in discussing inspiration, the identity

---

[20] For more on the canon in Jesus's day see Craig A. Evans, "The Scriptures of Jesus and His Earliest Followers," in *The Canon Debate*, ed. Lee M. McDonald and James A. Sanders (Peabody, MA: Hendrickson, 2002).

between the written words of Scripture and the words of God is so close in the minds of NT writers that sometimes there will be a quote of an OT passage that records the words of a human being, and yet the NT author will attribute the words of the OT passage to God as the one speaking in that passage (see, e.g., Matt. 19:4–5).

But even more specifically, every OT book is quoted in the NT except Esther, Ecclesiastes, Song of Solomon, Ezra, Nehemiah, Obadiah, Nahum, and Zephaniah.[21] Usually the quote refers to the OT passage as God's word or Scripture. As to the books not quoted, the last three are part of the Minor Prophets, known as "the twelve," and these were presented as a continuous unit, rather than being divided into separate individual books. As for the others, they come from a section of the canon that is well represented by NT quotes, and the fact that they aren't explicitly quoted doesn't mean the NT authors deemed them noninspired. The lack of quotes from these books likely has more to do with their contents not coinciding with the topics in view in NT books. Nonetheless, the overwhelming message from the NT is that the OT is Scripture and God's word. If so, then on our definition of canonicity, the OT books must be canonical.

### General Extrabiblical Testimony

Roger T. Beckwith has noted another fact, confirmed by both the OT and some secular literature, that relates to canonicity. It was common practice to keep and use books considered holy in holy places, and Israel was no exception to this rule. The earliest example of this is the laying up of the tables of the Ten Commandments and the book of Deuteronomy, respectively, in and beside the ark of the covenant as it sat in the tabernacle (Ex. 25:16, 21; 40:20; Deut. 10:1–5; 31:24–26). This was also done with the record of Joshua's covenant with the people, written in the copy of the

> Book of the Law at the sanctuary of Shechem (Josh 24:26); and Samuel's account of the manner of the kingdom, laid up before the Lord, apparently at the sanctuary of Mizpah (1 Sam 10:25). The transference of the ark, still containing its tables, to Solomon's Temple, when the building was dedicated (1 Kgs 8:6-9; 2 Chr 5:7-10), and the finding of the Book of the Law in the Temple in the reign of Josiah (2 Kgs 22:8; 23:2, 24; 2 Chr 34:15, 30), indicate that the custom of keeping sacred writings in the sanctuary continued in the First Temple; and the Second Temple would have been the natural location for the library of the nation's religious records said to have been gathered together after the Exile by Nehemiah, and for that more certainly assembled after the Antiochene persecution by Judas Maccabaeus (2 Macc 2:13–15).[22]

---

[21] See, e.g., House, "Canon of the Old Testament," 143.

[22] Roger T. Beckwith, "Formation of the Hebrew Bible," in *Mikra: Text, Translation, Reading and Interpretation of the Hebrew Bible in Ancient Judaism and Early Christianity*, ed. Martin J. Mulder and Harry Sysling (Philadelphia: Fortress, 1988), 41.

As Beckwith explains, writings laid up in earlier Israelite sanctuaries and then later in the temple were considered holy because of either their origin, their subject matter, or both. Moreover, by laying up something in the temple, one in effect dedicated it to the Lord, and that gave it even more sanctity.[23]

Beckwith also quotes portions from the *Antiquities*, the Mishna (*Moed Katan* 3:4) and the Tosefta (*Kelim Bava Metsia* 5:8) which show that the temple Scriptures included the whole Pentateuch, Joshua, and other books in the Hebrew Bible that were part of the Prophets portion. For example, from the Tosefta we read,

> The Book of Ezra, if it comes out (viz. of the Temple), makes the hands unclean; and not the Book of Ezra alone, but the Prophets and the Fifths. But another book makes the hands unclean if it is brought in there. (*T. Kelim Bava Metsia* 5:8)

In Jewish thinking, books that make the hands unclean do so because they are sacred, considered God's word. Of course, if one uses a scriptural book in the temple, it won't make the hands ceremonially unclean, because everything, including people, to be in the temple at all must be ceremonially clean. On the other hand, an ordinary book will make the hands unclean, if handled *in* the temple. As Beckwith also shows, the Mishna and Tosefta speak of a copy of the Pentateuch in the temple that was called the book of Ezra, referred to in the quote above. And, the "Fifths" most likely refers to the book of Psalms which was contained in five books. But the reference to the Psalms was, in Beckwith's estimation, "shorthand" for the whole of the third section of the OT, the Writings. From this line of evidence, Beckwith concludes, with good reason in my judgment, that books laid up in the temple were considered sacred Scripture, God's word, and that is why they would make the hands unclean, unless one read them in the temple itself.

Both the Biblical and extrabiblical data noted suggest that these OT books were considered God's word, Scripture, and if so, then, using our definition, they must also be canonical. This practice suggests also that the beginning of revering the various documents in our OT as Scripture must have been well before the time when Ezra found the lost book of the law in the temple.

## Other Extrabiblical Testimony

There is much extrabiblical testimony about the OT in general, and about specific books in particular. I want to present a good portion of it, and will do so using a chronological ordering of the materials.

---

[23] Ibid., 42.

*The Septuagint (LXX)*—As Jews moved away from Palestine, they gradually lost facility with Hebrew and Aramaic and began to speak the Greek that was common in the Greco-Roman world. These Greek-speaking Jews wanted a copy of their Bible in a language they could read. Though the exact impetus for doing it is a bit clouded in mystery, such a translation, the *Septuagint* (LXX), was made. The translation was done in stages, but there is reason to think that at least some of the OT may have been translated into Greek by the third century BC. As House notes, *Sirach* spoke as if all three sections of the canon had been translated by 132 BC, and even Esther, a contested book and one absent from Dead Sea Scroll manuscripts, was translated by 114 BC.[24]

One notable characteristic of the LXX is that it contains a number of books not included in Hebrew versions of the OT. It includes 53 books, and those not included in the Hebrew OT are: *1 Esdras*; apocryphal *Additions to Esther*; *Judith*; *Tobit*; *1–4 Maccabees*; *Odes*; *Wisdom of Solomon*; *Sirach* (also known as *Ecclesiasticus* or *The Wisdom of Jesus the Son of Sirach*); *Psalms of Solomon*; *Baruch*; *Letter of Jeremiah*; and apocryphal additions to Daniel such as the *Prayer of Azariah and the Song of the Three Children*, *Susanna*, and *Bel and the Dragon*.[25] At one time it was thought that the LXX showed that there were two canons in Judaism, one of Palestinian origin (in Hebrew and Aramaic) and the other one likely of Alexandrian origin (a Greek version done by Jews in Egypt) which included all of these extra books. However, scholars today have rejected that hypothesis, arguing that by including the extra books, the translators were not saying those books were Scripture, but only that they were informative and spiritually valuable to read along with the OT.[26]

The significance of the LXX for our purposes is that it was likely translated at a time when the Law and Prophets and at least some of the Writings were already believed to be canonical. Moreover, the contents of the Hebrew OT and the LXX, despite the extra books, otherwise match quite closely. Because of the extra books, we can't say for certain that those who translated the LXX saw all the books that were contained in the Hebrew OT as canonical. However, biblical evidence already presented, along with the fact of the various books being laid up in the temple, indicates that the books in the LXX that match the Hebrew OT probably were considered Scripture. If so, then, given our definition, they were also canonical. At the very least, all the books in the LXX clearly had a very positive status in Jewish thinking.

---

[24] House, "Canon of the Old Testament," 147.
[25] Ibid., 137. On this page House includes a helpful chart that compares the contents of the Rabbinic canon, the LXX, the Roman Catholic OT, and the Protestant OT.
[26] Ibid., 147–148.

*The Apocrypha*—Next, we should turn to several books of the Apocrypha, in particular *Tobit* (dated between 200 and 170 BC), *Sirach* (dated about 180 BC), and *Baruch* (whose first part can be dated 116 BC at the latest). As for *Tobit*, it explicitly mentions the law of Moses, for example, in such passages as 1:8; 6:12; and 7:12, 13. In addition, several prophets are cited by name: Amos (*Tobit* 2:6); Nahum (14:4) and Jonah (*Tobit* 14:4).[27] And, in 14:5 the author expresses his hope that the Lord will restore his people and Jerusalem, and that the temple will be rebuilt "just as the prophets spoke." Dempster sees this as a reference to the prophets speaking collectively.[28] In contrast, Beckwith explains that in *Tobit* 14:4–7 we have a general reference to the prediction of the prophets of Israel, but also probably a specific reference to Isaiah, Jeremiah, Ezekiel, and Daniel. Predictions of the exile (*Tobit* 14:4) suggest Jeremiah, prediction of the return (14:5) sounds like Isaiah, judgment on Babylon (14:4) evokes either Jeremiah or Isaiah, the prophecy of the rebuilding of the temple (14:5) evokes Ezekiel, and the fulfilling of times and seasons (14:5) sounds like Daniel.[29]

Regardless of whether one agrees with Beckwith, what do these references in *Tobit* show? As Dempster explains, neither the Law nor the Prophets is spoken of collectively as Scripture in this book. Even so, "the *Torah* has clearly functioned as a guide to ethics in the present situation; and now at the end of the book where the stress is on the future, 'the prophets' are mentioned. This implies that the author was aware of two divisions of sacred authority: the Torah for present ethics and the Prophets for future hope."[30]

The book of *Sirach* (*Ben Sira* or *Ecclesiasticus*) is especially significant, because in chapters 44–49 it includes a list of heroes that are ordered chronologically and drawn from a collection of sacred writings. Dempster calls these chapters "one long meditation on the Scriptures from Enoch to Nehemiah before Simon the high priest is praised. In fact, the heroes are not really introduced formally, as Ben Sira assumes they are virtually household names to his audience."[31] The overall significance of this list is that it includes a reference to many of the books that comprise the Hebrew OT and our current OT. This doesn't mean that *Sirach* calls them canonical or even Scripture, but it is interesting that the various heroes' stories all appear in biblical OT books.

Two ways to see this can be presented. The first, based on a chart that Stephen Dempster presents, is a list of the heroes *Sirach* names with a corresponding list of the OT books in which the stories of the heroes are found. The list of heroes (with corresponding OT books) is: Enoch, Noah, Abraham, Isaac, Jacob (Genesis); Moses (Exodus); Aaron (Exodus; Leviticus; Numbers);

[27] Dempster, "Torah," 105; Dempster, "From Many Texts to One," 23.
[28] Dempster, "Torah," 105; Dempster, "From Many Texts to One," 23.
[29] Beckwith, "Formation of the Hebrew Bible," 46.
[30] Dempster, "From Many Texts to One," 23. See also, Dempster, "Torah," 105.
[31] Dempster, "Canons on the Right and Canons on the Left," 59.

Dathan, Abiram, Korah, Phinehas (Numbers); Joshua (Deuteronomy; Joshua); Caleb (Numbers; Joshua); Judges (Judges); Samuel, Nathan (Samuel); David (Chronicles is used as source material for David as musician); Solomon, Rehoboam, Jeroboam, Elijah, Elisha, Hezekiah, Isaiah (Kings); Isaiah (Isaiah); Josiah (Kings); Jeremiah (Jeremiah); Ezekiel (Ezekiel); Job (Ezekiel); The Twelve (*The Twelve*); Zerubbabel (Ezra–Nehemiah); Joshua, Nehemiah (Haggai; Zechariah); Enoch, Joseph (Genesis); Shem, Seth, Enosh, Adam (Chronicles).[32]

Another way to look at this list is to note the OT books alluded to for the information about the various heroes, along with the passages in *Sirach* that refer to the OT book. Roger Beckwith helps us on this matter, having already made such a list as follows: Genesis (*Sir.* 44:16–23; 49:14–16); Exodus and Leviticus (*Sir.* 45:1–15); Numbers (*Sir.* 45:15–24; 46:7); Joshua (*Sir.* 46:1–10); Judges (*Sir.* 46:11–12); Samuel (*Sir.* 45:25; 46:13–47:8; 47:11); Kings (*Sir.* 47:12–48:9; 48:11–23; 49:1–6); Isaiah (*Sir.* 48:24–25); Jeremiah (*Sir.* 49:6–7); Ezekiel (*Sir.* 49:8–9); the Twelve Minor Prophets (*Sir.* 49:10); Haggai (*Sir.* 49:11); Malachi (*Sir.* 48:10), Psalms and Proverbs (*Sir.* 44:4–5 Hb.; cf. 47:8, 14–17); Ezra–Nehemiah (*Sir.* 49:11–13); and Chronicles (*Sir.* 47:9–10).[33]

In addition to these references in *Sirach* itself, the grandson of Sirach translated the original Hebrew of the book into Greek. Once completed, he also offered a brief preface or prologue. Scholars date that prologue anywhere from about 132 to 112 BC. In the prologue the grandson not only refers to his grandfather's work, but of special import is the fact that he mentions that Israel had three categories of writings which can be read and which give encouragement and benefit. Those three groups are referred to as "the law, the prophets, and the other books which followed them,"[34] or the "other books of our ancestors," or the "rest of the books."[35] They are clearly distinguished from the writings of the grandfather, Ben Sirach.

If this is in fact a reference to three distinct parts of the OT canon, as some have argued, it is one of the earliest (if not the earliest) such reference. However, that isn't the only way scholars have understood the prologue. Some have argued that there is only a reference to a bipartite canon, with the third section referring to all other books in general. Others have suggested that, given the early date of the prologue, it is more likely that it refers only to a bipartite canon. On this assumption, the author may be doing nothing more than attempting to collect books into groups, as a modern bookstore might have two

---

[32] Dempster, "From Many Texts to One," 25–26. On page 26, Dempster adds that "Although there are no canonical divisions mentioned, it is interesting that the sequence of names of the heroes largely corresponds to the sequencing of scrolls in the first two divisions of virtually all attested canonical orders in the Jewish tradition." In the following pages, Dempster mentions various proposals to the effect that the list of heroes does or does not reflect a tripartite canon (see 27–29).

[33] Beckwith, "Formation of the Hebrew Bible," 46.

[34] Dempster, "From Many Texts to One," 29.

[35] McDonald, "Integrity of the Biblical Canon," 106.

sections of books—one on the Bible and the other on Theology. In this case, the law and the prophets would refer to the Bible, and the remainder of the books would refer to highly esteemed theological works.[36]

Though the ultimate intent of the prologue (to mention a bipartite or a tripartite canon) may be beyond our ability to determine, the reference to the three groups of books is significant. The first two groups are named, and we know the sections of the OT canon to which they refer. As to the third group, the initial reference, at the very least, seems to equate it with the other two groups. Whether this is because all three are deemed Scripture or just because they are all "esteemed books" because of their spiritual value is not clear. It might also be the case that since some books in the third section were still disputed (like Esther and Ecclesiastes?), the author of the prologue didn't want to become any more specific than to refer to them as he has. What is clear, however, is that the grandson surely knew the work of his grandfather, and as shown above, that book definitely refers to a number of books that are part of neither the law nor the prophets. Hence, it isn't at all unthinkable that the grandson was thinking about books in what we know to be the third division of the canon. At the very least, these references in the prologue refer to three distinct groups of books, and the grandson surely would have known of three groups of esteemed holy books that Israel possessed (books that we know as parts of the OT). And, he would also have known that chapters 44–49 of his grandfather's work referred to events and people recorded in books belonging to what we know as all three parts of the OT canon.

The first part of the book of *Baruch* was written by 116 BC at the latest. This book says that the people of Israel have failed to heed various sacred books in the OT. For one thing, the people "did not listen to the voice of the Lord our God to walk in the statutes of the Lord" (*Bar.* 1:18), and as a result, they "incurred the curses 'written in the law of Moses'" (2:2). Similarly, they did not obey the Lord's voice "according to all the words of the prophets" (1:21). As a result, there are predictions of judgment (made by Jeremiah) that will befall them, and these predictions are cited as coming from "thy servants, the prophets" (2:20–24). While these quotes from *Baruch* don't refer to Scripture as a whole with the phrase "the Law and the Prophets," they do show that there were two broad groups of sacred writings that the people had failed to heed. The reference to all the words of the prophets suggests that the author knew of a group of writings from prophets that were part of an authoritative collection of sacred works.[37]

Then, we should note some other citations from other apocryphal books.

---

[36] Dempster, "Canons on the Right and Canons on the Left," 60–61. See also, Dempster, "From Many Texts to One," 29–30.

[37] Dempster, "From Many Texts to One," 24. See also Dempster, "Torah," 105–106.

Beckwith gives a helpful summary, and then we can look more closely at specific books. Beckwith says that in the Apocrypha we find evidence that,

> 1 Maccabees quotes Psalms as predictive (1 Macc 7:16-17); that 4 Maccabees explicitly includes among 'the Law and the Prophets' Isaiah, Ezekiel, Psalms, Proverbs and Daniel (4 Macc 18:10-18); and that 2 Esdras (4 Ezra) refers to the twenty-four inspired books which Ezra published openly, i.e. the books of the canon (2 Esdr 14:23-6, 38-47).[38]

More specifically, we can say that *1 Maccabees* is dated about 110 BC, and it constantly refers to the law scrolls which Antiochus Epiphanes burned. In addition, the book contains many allusions to and a citation of a psalm, all of which show that Scripture was seen as extending to more books than just the Torah. This is so, despite the fact that terminology used to describe Scripture "refers to the books of the law or covenant."[39]

*Second Maccabees*, written shortly after *1 Maccabees*, has a "preface" of two short letters attached to it. The purpose of the first letter is to encourage celebration of the purification of the temple (1:1–9; 1:10–2:18), while that of the second is to mention texts that recount two events in the nation's past and the responses to them which resulted in preserving of sacred texts (2:1–15). As for the first text, Dempster writes that it states that "after the destruction of the temple, Jeremiah gave to the departing exiles a copy of the law and urged them not to let it depart from their hearts (2.1-3)." As for the second situation,

> it is stated in a group of records as well as memoirs of Nehemiah, who had returned to Judah after the return of the exiles, that he had founded a library consisting of 'the acts of the kings and prophets, and the things of David and the letters of the kings concerning holy gifts' (2.13). The writer then brings the reader up to date by continuing with the information that Judas Maccabaeus has had to gather together the writings that have been lost as a result of the recent war and has made them available for use if any require them (2.14).[40]

As Dempster explains, the verses cited give evidence for three different divisions of OT Scripture as follows:

> . . . 'the law'—during Jeremiah's time, 'the acts of kings and prophets' and 'the things of David and letters of kings regarding holy gifts'. The first division is self-evident, and the second division would correspond to the Prophets (the former prophets—Joshua, Judges, Samuel, Kings—mainly concerned with the rise of kingship and the exploits of kings, and the latter prophets—

---

[38] Beckwith, "Formation of the Hebrew Bible," 47.
[39] Dempster, "From Many Texts to One," 30.
[40] Ibid., 30–31.

Jeremiah, Ezekiel, Isaiah, the Twelve—the actual collections of prophetic oracles). Finally, a third division may be indicated by the things regarding David—perhaps Ruth with a Davidic genealogy, the Psalter which is by far the largest book of the third division and also stands at the beginning or near the beginning of many orders of the Writings, and books viewed as written by David's son Solomon (Proverbs, Ecclesiastes, Song). The 'letters regarding holy gifts' could be another way of describing the content of a significant work at the end of this division, Ezra-Nehemiah, since in this work there are many references to letters and written edicts back and forth between Judah and the Persian empire regarding the rebuilding of the temple and the walls of Jerusalem and the bringing of gifts and sacrifices for the temple.[41]

Dempster adds that this second letter, which contains the division of OT biblical materials into three parts, predates the book of *2 Maccabees*. It was once thought to be a forgery, but has been shown to be authentic. A key point, though, is that it is dated at about 160 BC, not long after the conflict with Antiochus Epiphanes.[42]

*The Dead Sea Scrolls*—The Dead Sea Scrolls found at Qumran were discovered only in the twentieth century, but they shed a great deal of light on the text of the OT, and also help in determining when a sense of an OT canon (and its contents) was in place among the Jews. The documents found date approximately from 200 BC to AD 70. Among the scrolls, archaeologists found copies of every OT book except Esther. In addition, they found copies of a number of noncanonical (from our perspective) books such as *Tobit, Ecclesiasticus*, and some pseudepigraphical works.[43] Some of the noncanonical books found claim to be inspired, and in various of the books found there are references to authoritative Scripture. One such apparent reference is to the book of *Jubilees*, not part of the canon. In addition, several scholars note that the scrolls found contained both canonical and noncanonical books next to one another with no way to determine which ones the community considered canonical and which they did not.[44]

Besides the fact that, with the discovery of the Dead Sea Scrolls, the number and early dates of manuscripts of OT books greatly increased, specific facts about the Dead Sea Scrolls are noteworthy in relation to canonicity. First, while there was only one copy found of Ezra, Nehemiah,

---

[41] Ibid., 31.

[42] Ibid. For further discussion of the Apocrypha, see also Daniel R. Schwartz, "Special People or Special Books? On Qumran and New Testament Notions of Canon," in *Text, Thought, and Practice in Qumran and Early Christianity*, ed. Ruth A. Clements and Daniel R. Schwartz (Boston: Brill, 2009), 49; McDonald, "Integrity of the Biblical Canon," 106; and Beckwith, "Canon of the Old Testament," 60–61. For a discussion of the Apocrypha's canonicity see Henri Blocher, "Helpful or Harmful? The 'Apocrypha' and Evangelical Theology," *European Journal of Theology* 13 (2004): 82–87.

[43] House, "Canon of the Old Testament," 146.

[44] Dempster, "Canons on the Right and Canons on the Left," 61. See also McDonald, "Integrity of the Biblical Canon," 107.

and Chronicles, there were multiple copies of other biblical books. Some scholars working through different copies of some books have noted that readings in various copies of a given book weren't identical. This has led some scholars, including some who believe in a very late date for OT canon closure, to argue that these variant readings show that the very text of a number of OT books wasn't even set at this time, so it is unlikely that any notion of a distinct set of canonical OT books was recognized or that it was held that the OT canon was closed. However, such conclusions seem to be unwarranted extrapolations from the data possessed. For one thing, variant readings don't relate to every verse in every book (or even to most verses). Moreover, there are enough extant manuscripts so that textual critics are hardly in doubt about what the majority of the text of each OT book actually says. And, it is unlikely that, at Qumran, there was a lot of doubt about the majority of what each OT book actually said. As we shall see, the Essenes wrote extensive commentaries on books that are part of our OT. For such commentaries to have been of any value, there must have been a sense of the content of the books commented on.

In addition, if one defines canon as a strict, fixed list of books deemed to be inspired, then, of course, the Qumran findings suggest an open and even fluid canon. But we have already seen that such a notion of canon is unwarranted. To say that some books were present at Qumran which are not now part of our OT canon doesn't mean that the community at Qumran (let alone Jews more generally) had little idea of the canonicity of most of the books that we recognize as canonical. The exact boundaries of the canon may not have been clear, but that doesn't mean there was no sense of which books were holy and inspired. So, it seems that those who have concluded from variant readings of different texts that there was no clear sense even of the text of the OT, let alone a sense of which books are canonical, have concluded more than the data warrant.

Second, Roger Beckwith summarizes some of the findings from the Dead Sea Scrolls. He notes that a number of OT books were referred to as divine writings or were quoted, using the typical introductory formulas used when quoting Scripture. Beckwith writes,

> In the Dead Sea Scrolls, conventional formulas for quoting Scripture are used in the cases of the books Samuel, Isaiah, Hosea, Amos, Micah, Nahum and Proverbs (*IQS* 5:17; 8:14; *CD* 1:13-14; 4:20; 7:14-16; 8:3; 20:16; 16:15; 9:5, 8-9; 11:20-21; 13:23-14:1; *4QFlor* 1:7, 12; *IIQMelch* 23). In addition, Isaiah, Ezekiel, Zechariah, Malachi and Daniel are quoted as divine or prophetic writings (*CD* 3:20-4:4; 4:13-14; 6:13-14; 7:10-12; 7:20-21, MS. B; *4QFlor* 1:14-17; 2:3-4). The Qumran Pesharim are often continuous commentaries on books

(Isaiah, Hosea, Micah, Nahum, Habakkuk, Zephaniah and Psalms), and such books were, more likely than not, already canonical.[45]

Beckwith's conclusion in the last sentence of the quote may be a bit overzealous, because it is dubious that anyone at Qumran had in mind what we think about when we invoke the concept of canonicity. Still, it is significant that the books listed were evidently deemed of divine origin and valued as Scripture.

Third, in scrolls found at Qumran that contained commentaries on OT documents, a bipartite reference to the law and the prophets was quite common. Two examples suffice to show this point. In the *Damascus Document* (CD) and the *Community Rule* (1QS), documents that likely go back to the early years of the community's existence (125–75 BC), there are various citations of this nature. CD 7.15–17 contains an allegory in which "the hut of David refers to the books of the law and Kiyyun, an image, is the words of the Prophets." And in 1QS 1.2–3 the Qumran community "is ordered to 'do that which is good and upright before God just as He commanded by the hand of Moses and by the hand of all His servants the prophets'."[46] Neither of these is the simple phrase "the Law and the Prophets," but in both examples, that is clearly in view.

The citation from the Dead Sea Scrolls that seems to have gotten as much comment as any comes from the document *Miqsat Ma'ase Ha-Torah* (4QMMT). The passage in view, likely from the late second century or early first century BC, has a reference to a bipartite canon and what appears to be a reference to a tripartite canon. The passage seems to be addressed to a leader in an attempt to impress on him "the fact that the Scriptures were being fulfilled. As a result of recognizing this fact the leader, the letter says, will be able to understand 'the Book of Moses and the Words of the Prophets and David'. Later the fulfillment of the prophecies predicted 'in the Book of Moses and the words of the Prophets' are regarded as coming true."[47]

It would be easy to see in the reference to David a reference to the third part of the OT canon, the Writings. However, various scholars have suggested other possibilities. For example, even though neither of the phrases offers a list of books, for some time it was assumed that at the very least the reference to David is a reference to some books. However, in 2001 Timothy Lim proposed a different understanding. He noted in regard to the references to Moses and the Prophets, that each phrase clearly includes a reference to books, but the reference to David has no word that suggests books. Hence, Lim proposed that the phrase actually refers to David's deeds. As Daniel Schwartz explains, this is a

---

[45] Beckwith, "Formation of the Hebrew Bible," 47.
[46] Dempster, "From Many Texts to One," 32–33.
[47] Ibid., 33.

reasonable proposal, given that in the context of the remark in question (in the MMT), the writer urges the addressee to consider the events of the past, things that happened in every generation. On the other hand, Schwartz notes that in the phrase in question, "David" seems to be parallel to the "Book of Moses" and "the Words of the Prophets." Hence, it is likely that the reference to David is also to books, but not a book like Psalms which doesn't actually record much about David's deeds. The reference to David is probably to books like Samuel and Kings which do record the deeds of David.[48] Of course, if this is so, then it isn't at all clear that "David" refers to a third section of the OT canon.

Dempster explains some of the other suggestions about this reference's meaning. He writes,

> Ulrich . . . suggests that an original two-part canon's second division has been 'stretched too far', 'so the Book of Psalms . . . began to establish a new category which eventually would be called the Ketubim or the Hagiographa'. Others suggest a variation of this by stating that the second division was simply extended since David was regarded as a prophet . . . or the term 'David' was regarded as 'the biblical accounts of the Davidic monarchy' . . . A more economical explanation, however, is that the canon is already tripartite and two designations can be used to describe it, a short form ('Moses and the words of the prophets') and a long form ('Moses, the words of the prophets and David'). In short, a bipartite designation does not imply a bipartite canon, but can also be a shorthand term for a tripartite one. Both designations are interchangeable for the same body of literature. It should also be noted that designations for canonical books vary at Qumran. The fact that 'Moses' and 'the books of the *Torah*' can be used to refer to the same body of literature does not imply anything about the incomplete state of these writings.[49]

Given all of these possible options, it is hard to be dogmatic about the meaning of this phrase in 4 QMMT. In evaluating the data from the Qumran finds, we are clearly better off by having them. However, it is difficult to draw huge conclusions with certainty. This is so because both canonical and noncanonical books were found together, and yet nothing found seems to designate which books the community considered Scripture and which it didn't. Thus, even though, for example, noncanonical books were found at Qumran, nowhere in the finds does anything say that they were deemed canonical, nor is there any comment to the effect that they were not considered Scripture. In

---

[48] Schwartz, "Special People or Special Books?," 51–52.
[49] Dempster, "From Many Texts to One," 33–34. Dempster's mention of Ulrich refers to Eugene Ulrich, "The Bible in the Making: The Scriptures at Qumran," in *The Community of the Renewed Covenant*, ed. Eugene Ulrich and James VanderKam (Notre Dame: University of Notre Dame Press, 1993), 82. The suggestion about David being a prophet comes from J. J. Collins, *The Scepter and the Star: The Messiahs of the Dead Sea Scrolls and Other Ancient Literature* (New York: Doubleday, 1995), 21. And the view that "David" refers to biblical accounts of the Davidic monarchy comes from L. H. Schiffman, *Reclaiming the Dead Sea Scrolls* (Philadelphia: Jewish Publication Society, 1994), 84.

addition, though phrases that amount to "the Law and the Prophets" appear frequently in Qumran literature, nowhere is there a list of which books were thought to comprise each group. Of course, we can have some idea about this because all OT books except Esther were found at Qumran. But deciding which books *the community* considered to be in each group probably would involve imposing on the books found what we know from other sources about Jewish conceptions at that time, and what we know from later sources that referred to OT books.[50]

*Philo of Alexandria*—Roger Beckwith has noted in Philo's works a series of brief references to various OT books, some of which introduce a quote from OT books like Judges or Samuel with the conventional formula for introducing a quote of Scripture.[51] However, Philo's *On the Contemplative Life* has received the most attention. This work was written sometime in the first century AD (Dempster suggests approximately 20–50 AD). It is about an ascetic group called the Therapeutae, who seemed to love meditation and didn't focus on bodily comforts. There is a passage in it where Philo describes their practice of meditation as follows:

> In each house there is a consecrated room which is called a sanctuary or closet and closeted in this the members of the sect are initiated into the mysteries of the sanctified life. They take nothing into it, either drink or food, or any of the things necessary for the needs of the body, but laws and oracles delivered through the mouths of the prophets, and psalms and anything else which fosters perfection and knowledge and piety (*De vit. cont.* 1.25).[52]

On the surface, this may seem to support a tripartite canon. In fact, four types of literature are actually mentioned: law, prophets, psalms, and "anything else." This fourth set of writings might refer to other books that we know are part of the third division of the OT canon, or it could refer to nonbiblical books that are helpful in promoting spiritual growth and health. When the last phrase of the final sentence in the quote is taken in the context of the whole quote, it doesn't seem that Philo wants to make anything like a definitive statement on the contents of the OT. Instead, his point is about the practices of this religious sect. As with the Qumran reference (4QMMT) to "David," so the reference here to "psalms" may refer to a third section of the OT, the Writings, or it may refer only to one book. Even if it does refer to a third sec-

---

[50] Some of these concluding remarks about the Dead Sea Scrolls are based on comments by House, "Canon of the Old Testament," 146–147, and some are my own assessment of the evidence found at Qumran.

[51] Beckwith, "Formation of the Hebrew Bible," 47–48. In these pages Beckwith cites a number of different works from Philo and notes one way or another that they refer to biblical books as sacred, inspired, etc.

[52] This quote from Philo is presented and discussed in Dempster, "From Many Texts to One," 34. It is also discussed in Dempster, "Torah," 117–118, and McDonald, "Integrity of the Biblical Canon," 106–107.

tion of the OT, that wouldn't mean that at that point in history, there was a settled opinion among the Jews as to the exact number and identity of the books in the third portion. It is interesting to note, however, that Jesus in Luke 24:44 refers apparently to the three divisions of the OT, using the same basic formula—law, prophets, and psalms. Depending on the exact date of Philo's work, Jesus might have uttered these words recorded in Luke 24 at about the time Philo was writing his piece. These references, plus others we have seen, at the very least suggest that by this time it was not unusual in references apparently to the OT to speak of the law, the prophets, and the psalms (or, as at Qumran, David). An exact accounting of specific books to be included in each segment, however, doesn't seem to have appeared yet in references to these three OT sections.

*Josephus*—In a work entitled *Against Apion* (likely written about AD 90), Josephus engages in a bit of apologetics. Judaism and its writings were being attacked as inferior to the writings of the Greeks, who have numerous religious treatises of various sorts. In response, Josephus replied that there is an enormous amount of Greek literature, and various pieces of it contradict each other. In contrast, the writings of the Jews are of divine origin and number only twenty-two. In contrast to the Greeks, Josephus writes that the Jews

> do not possess myriads of inconsistent books, conflicting with each other. Our books, those which are justly accredited, are but two and twenty, and contain the record of all time. Of these, five are the books of Moses, comprising the laws and the traditional history from the birth of man down to the death of the law-giver. This period falls only short of three thousand years. From the death of Moses until Artaxerxes who succeeded Xerxes as King of Persia, the prophets subsequent to Moses wrote the history of the events of their own times in thirteen books. The remaining four books contain hymns to God and precepts for the conduct of human life. . . .
>
> From Artaxerxes to our own time the complete history has been written, but has not been deemed worthy of equal credit with the earlier records, because of the failure of the exact succession of the prophets.[53]

A few lines later, Josephus adds the following about the Jews' attitude toward their sacred writings:

> We have given practical proof of our reverence for our own Scriptures. For although such long ages have now passed, no one has ventured either to add, or to remove, or to alter a syllable; and it is an instinct with every Jew, from

---

[53] Josephus, *Against Apion*, 1.37–40. This portion of the treatise is quoted in Dempster, "From Many Texts to One," 35; House, "Canon of the Old Testament," 151; McDonald, "Integrity of the Biblical Canon," 109; and Sid Z. Leiman, "Josephus and the Canon of the Bible," in *Josephus, the Bible, and History*, ed. Louis H. Feldman and Gohei Hata (Detroit: Wayne State University Press, 1989), 50–51.

the day of his birth, to regard them as the decrees of God, to abide by them, and, if need be, cheerfully to die for them. . . .

Already, frequently many of the prisoners have been seen enduring tortures and every form of death in the theatres rather than utter a single word against the laws and the allied documents.[54]

From these quotes, several things become clear. First, Josephus says that the Jewish writings are twenty-two in number, not the twenty-four of the talmudic canon, or the thirty-nine of our Old Testament. Actually, there isn't a huge discrepancy among the three, though it may appear that there is. For one thing, the Jews commonly counted the twelve Minor Prophets as one book, not as twelve. Then the difference between Josephus's number and that of twenty-four is easily accounted for. If Lamentations is counted together with Jeremiah as one book, and if Judges and Ruth are counted as one book, there is really no discrepancy between Josephus and the twenty-four book canon. Even so, if one counts the Minor Prophets as one book, there seem to be more books in our OT than twenty-four.

Second, in the first quote above from Josephus, he divides the books into three distinct sections. While he doesn't name them, he does say how many are in each section and tells something of their contents. It is hard to imagine that the five books of Moses wouldn't include the five we attribute to the Pentateuch. The second section, consisting of thirteen books, likely includes both the former and latter prophets. As to the third (containing four books), because of what is said about their contents (hymns and precepts for life), Josephus is probably thinking at least that Psalms and Proverbs are two of the four. What he would consider as the other two is not clear. But this does seem to suggest a tripartite canon.

Third, some have argued that the portion quoted last (above) is a bipartite reference to the OT—"the laws and the allied documents." While this may be so, it doesn't necessarily indicate only two parts to the OT canon. Though Josephus doesn't mention it, he may be thinking that the allied documents can be further divided into two sections, as he did earlier in the passage. Even if he isn't thinking that, what he says earlier shows that he has divided the OT into three sections. Part of his point in this latter quote may be just to emphasize the centrality of the Torah in all of Jewish life and thinking. At any rate, given what I have said about the possibility of dividing the second section further, there is no need to see this latter statement and the earlier one (about three parts) as contradictory.

Fourth, in the materials quoted above, Josephus says that no one has sought to add or remove anything from these books, "although such long ages

---

[54] *Against Apion*, 1.43. This portion is quoted in House, "Canon of the Old Testament," 151.

have now passed." In other words, the tripartite apportioning of the OT sacred writings isn't something new with Josephus, nor was it even recent. Evidently, for some time in Judaism this was the fixed mind-set, even if there were still some debates over a few books. Though Josephus's words about "long ages . . . passed" are likely a bit of hyperbole ("long ages . . . passed" could be understood to mean thousands and thousands of years), at the very least it suggests that his understanding of the sacred Scriptures, both their number and the three divisions, wasn't unusual in Judaism. Such an understanding had probably been in place for a long time; exactly how long is hard to say, but we do have some hint from materials cited earlier from the second century BC.

Josephus's comment about nothing being added to or removed from these texts could indicate that he (and others like him) saw the OT canon as closed. However, while some have suggested this,[55] I am not sure that this is the only possible inference to draw from Josephus's words. Surely, Josephus wouldn't think that no scribe ever made any changes to what he was copying. Likewise, Josephus wouldn't have to be a "higher critic" way before his time to think that somewhere along the way various books probably received some editing, even if only by their original author. So, it is possible to take this statement as a bit of hyperbole in order to make the apologetic point that the writings of the Jews have been stable, while the writings of the Greeks continue to increase, even though the new writings don't remove ambiguities and contradictions present in earlier literature. If that is Josephus's point, and such a point would make sense in a work of apologetics, it can hardly be seen as an emphatic endorsement of the notion that the OT writings were closed.

Also relevant to the completion of the writing of the OT canon (even if not to the recognition of it as closed), the references to Xerxes, Artaxerxes, and the failure of the exact succession of the prophets are significant. Below I shall explain their significance, but let me just say now that these comments actually fit the notion that, after 400 BC, prophecy in Israel had ceased. How that is so will be explained below.

While some thinkers like McDonald have largely dismissed these passages from Josephus on the grounds that Josephus was notorious for exaggerating and that in a work on apologetics the point is not exact precision,[56] this assessment seems overly harsh. What Josephus claims is hardly even close to being outrageously different than common notions among Jews in his day about the number of OT books. Nor is his division of the books into three sections (with the amounts he lists in each of the three) out of step with what we saw in testimony that is much earlier than the first century AD. While various

---

[55] For example, House, "Canon of the Old Testament," 151.
[56] See McDonald, "Integrity of the Biblical Canon," 109–111, for details.

scholars have affirmed that at times Josephus did exaggerate,[57] there seems to be little evidence that he was doing that in his main points in this passage. Surely, if one is writing an apologetic treatise, if one's arguments are not at all grounded in fact, the defense will have little force. It is also worth noting that McDonald's theory of the closure and shape of the OT canon requires that at Josephus's time in history things would be nowhere near as settled on the contents and shape of the canon as Josephus's comments suggest. Hence, his evaluation of Josephus's views comes with a theory about canon that McDonald wants to uphold.[58]

*Jamnia*—A final testimony from within Judaism about the OT comes from the discussions at Jamnia in AD 90. As already noted, the traditional theory that there was such a council has been rejected, but that doesn't mean that nothing at all happened there relevant to the OT canon. As House explains, there are at least three major flaws in thinking that a council at Jamnia declared the canon closed. First, the group of rabbis who met and discussed the Scriptures were not functioning as an "official" council which was to make decisions for Jews about the contents of their sacred books. Whatever the outcome of the discussions, it had no binding authority, and that can easily be seen because debates about individual books continued after these meetings. Another problem with the hypothesis of a council closing the canon is that at Jamnia only Ecclesiastes and the Song of Solomon were discussed, and there were no debates of any significance on the whole OT canon. And, the books these scholars accepted aren't really different from the ones Josephus and NT books already included. Thus, it is hard to see that the meetings at Jamnia resulted in any binding decisions that covered all of the OT. So, it seems that a sense of an OT set of authoritative books already existed; the meetings at Jamnia merely affirmed what was already held.[59]

## Conclusions about Old Testament Canonicity

From the data presented above, what should we conclude about the shape and closure of the OT canon? I must initially insist again that we distinguish between the completion of the *writing of the books* that comprise the OT canon and the *process of recognition* of the various books as inspired and hence, using my definition, canonical. What is not at issue in this chapter is the former, the dating of when OT books were composed. As already stated, I believe that all OT books were written before 400 BC, most of them well before that time. And, I adopt the broadly conservative consensus on the date of each of these

---

[57] Again, see the evidence presented in ibid., 109–111.
[58] For more on Josephus, see Sid Z. Leiman, "Josephus and the Canon of the Bible."
[59] House, "Canon of the Old Testament," 152–153.

books. This means that, unlike those who espouse higher critical theories, I believe that OT books were written when those whose names are on the books and who have been traditionally deemed to be the authors could have written them. Nonevangelical scholarship, at the very least, sees the composition of these books as so late that there is little possibility that the people whose names the books take and whose deeds they describe could have been alive, let alone could have authored of any of them. I leave to readers the consultation of commentaries and other literature by various evangelical scholars to affirm my assessment of the dates of the various OT books.

As for the process of recognizing OT books as God's inspired word (and hence, canonical), we should draw some conclusions from the evidence presented so far. It would be desirable if we could pinpoint the exact dates for recognition of various OT books, OT sections of the canon, and closure of the canon. Unfortunately, the evidence presented doesn't allow us to be dogmatic or precise about such matters. Part of the reason is that nowhere in any of the evidence produced is there even one reference that uses the term "canon." Hence, it is conjecture as to whether the authors of the various sources presented even had a concept like canonicity in mind when they commented on various OT books.

So, what can we say about the OT? I think we can conclude some things, but they are less precise and thorough than we might wish. First, from biblical teaching relevant to canonicity, it should be clear that within the OT itself, there is ample recognition of the books of Moses as God's word—as inspired Scripture. Thus, even during much of the time when the OT was being written, OT writers (using my definition of canonicity) considered the Pentateuch canonical (though they never used such language). We learn this not only from the fact that Moses prefaced many things he wrote by saying that "the word of the Lord came unto him, saying . . . " We also learn it from the many OT references to the law of Moses and the books of Moses as God's word. In addition, we noted a few references to some books in the Prophets section of the OT that were deemed to be God's word (see here Dan. 9:2, for example). But also, in the chapters on inspiration we saw many other examples in OT prophetic books where the author says that the word of the Lord came to him, and that he was instructed to write what God then revealed. Probably, though we can't survey people during the OT era to confirm this, those who read such claims by the prophets considered their books to be Scripture, God's word to Israel. This doesn't happen with any frequency in the books that make up the Writings section of the OT canon.

In addition, I think the evidence about books being laid up in the temple (or other religious sites before the temple was built), whether mentioned in

Scripture or in nonbiblical documents, is significant testimony to the view among the Jews that many of the books from (at least) the Law and the Prophets sections of the OT were deemed sacred and of divine origin. Given our definition of canonicity, this would mean they were considered canonical.

Moving beyond the OT itself, we noted various evidences, in second-century-BC literature especially, that a bipartite understanding of the OT (Law and the Prophets) was quite common by that time. This was true of the various apocryphal books like *Tobit*, *Sirach*, and *Baruch*, but it was also common in writings found at Qumran that commented on various OT books. As noted in that discussion, books from all three parts of the OT were referred to as Scripture and/or were cited or quoted using the typical formulas for quoting Scripture. It is also noteworthy that the Dead Sea Scrolls contained copies of every OT book except Esther. Of course, we must not conclude too much from this, because the scrolls also contained noncanonical books, and nowhere in the documents found at Qumran was there a comment about what was considered Scripture and what wasn't. However, as noted, it is significant that in works found at Qumran that were commentaries, no commentaries seem to have been written on books other than those in our OT. Evidently, the community must have seen something special about those books that it didn't think applied to the other religious books found there.

We also saw instances (in second-century literature) of references to OT books which can reasonably be interpreted as dividing the OT into three sections (though many of them could refer to a bipartite canon, as explained when discussing the evidence). And, that is also true of Philo's testimony. Even more definitive is Josephus's testimony, which not only mentions three distinct parts, but even gives the number of books in each. What these works from the second century BC through the first century AD present is consistent with what we found in the way the NT refers to the OT. There are bipartite references to the OT and also likely at least one tripartite reference (Luke 24:44) from Jesus. In addition, we noted that all but five OT books are alluded to or quoted in the NT. Such references are often introduced with "Scripture says," "it is written," or other similar phrases which attribute divine origin (inspiration) to these books. If we put together these data from the second century BC through the first century AD and add to it our definition of canonicity, it is warranted to conclude that during this time (and certainly by the end of this period), it was likely that Jews believed that most of the books in our OT were the word of God and thus were canonical. At the very least, it seems rather clear that in the minds of the Jews (as evidenced from the sources cited) both the Law and Prophets were thought of during this period as God's word. Perhaps prior to 200 BC it was the settled opinion of many Jews that both parts were God's word, but I don't think we have enough evidence to say conclusively that this was so for most Jews.

As to a tripartite canon, from the evidence presented it is safe to say that the prevailing perception was also likely that at least by the *end* of the period from 200 BC to AD 100, if not sooner, it was common to divide OT books into three sections. To make such comments as those made in the previous paragraph about a bipartite canon and in this paragraph about a tripartite canon must not be misunderstood. It would be easy to think that either the bipartite or the tripartite canon contained (in Jewish thinking) exactly the books we have in our OT, so that the Prophets and Writings sections are no different than we would conceive of them today. But we must not be too hasty in making such a judgment. This is so in part because we know that some books that are in our OT were contested during that period, and we can also tell from the findings at Qumran, for example, that noncanonical books were held in esteem. Perhaps some at Qumran thought some of those noncanonical books were the inspired word of God. What makes it hard to be dogmatic about these things is that, as we have seen, until the NT documents were written, and until the testimony of Josephus, it isn't clear exactly which books would, in common opinion between 200 BC and AD 100, have been placed in the categories of "the Prophets" and "the Writings." This doesn't mean that evidence presented tells us nothing about such matters, but only that whatever we conclude about which books would have been esteemed as of divine origin must be inferred from the data available, and there are more possible conclusions from that data than just that people of that time conceived of the OT as containing just the books we hold as canonical today.

We should mention one further item before turning to when it was concluded that the OT canon was closed. It was the opinion among the Jews at a certain point in history that prophecy and prophets, at least those which were written and became viewed as Scripture, had ceased. It would, of course, be tempting to say that whenever the Jews held that prophecy had ceased, they also thought that meant the OT canon was closed. However, drawing that conclusion likely imposes our understanding of canonicity (and of closure of the canon) on people whom we can't be sure were thinking in such terms. What we can say on more solid ground is something about when it was held that prophecy had ceased.

Evangelicals have widely held that the consensus opinion among the Jews was that by 400 BC prophecy had ceased. Some have contested this conclusion, because even in Josephus, there are passages where he affirms that after 400 BC and throughout the Second Temple period the phenomenon of prophecy was still present in Israel.[60] Indeed, having offered examples of people living in the second century BC and the first century AD whom Josephus described as prophets or as having the gift of prophecy, one wonders why Josephus said in passages in *Against Apion* that literary prophecy had ceased during the period of Artaxerxes. I think Sid Leiman's explanation and conclusions on this matter are quite helpful, so I quote him at some length:

> It would appear that a careful reading of the *Against Apion* passage, and an analysis of Josephan terminology for prophetic phenomena, provide some insight into Josephus' position on the matter. Josephus is quite clear in formulating a qualitative difference between prophecy prior to the period of Artaxerxes and prophecy following the period of Artaxerxes. So long as there was an exact succession of prophets, from Moses on, literary prophecy was possible. Once there was a break in the exact succession of the prophets, after the period of Artaxerxes, isolated instances of prophecy were possible but not literary prophecy. Perhaps, for Josephus prophecy and history were integrally bound up with each other and linked to Moses, the greatest prophet and historian. The stress may well have been on the "historical" aspect of literary prophecy. Only a continuous history could be deemed inspired. Interrupted or sporadic histories are by definition incomplete and therefore inferior. Once the chain was broken, nothing new could be added to the biblical canon. This qualitative difference between pre- and post-Artaxerxes prophecy is also reflected in Josephan terminology. The term προφήτης is almost exclusively reserved for pre-Artaxerxes prophets. A post-Artaxerxes prophet is almost always called μάντις, or a related Greek term, but not προφήτης.[61]

In light of the evidence offered to this point, I think it safe to conclude that the succession of writing prophets did end around 400 BC. However, that only suggests something about the latest possible date for composition of a book in our OT. It says nothing about the process of recognizing writings as Scripture. When you take account of the evidence from the second and first century BC, it seems reasonable to think there was general recognition of the books that form the Prophets section of the OT. Surely, by the time of Jesus (as evidenced from Gospel accounts of Jesus's use of and opinion of the OT), both the Law and the Prophets sections were recognized as God's word (and hence, on my definition, canonical). Even if there was some disagreement about whether certain books belonged in one of these two groups, that doesn't mean there was no settled opinion among the Jews about any or even most of the books in the Law and Prophets.

As to the third section of the OT canon, it is harder to say what Jews thought about its contents and closure, and exactly when they concluded that

---

[60] Leiman, "Josephus and the Canon of the Bible," 56.
[61] Ibid. Leiman notes that this view of the cessation of writing prophets is confirmed by *4 Esdras (Ezra)* 14:44ff. (written in about AD 100), and also in rabbinic thinking. For evidence that this was true of rabbinic thinking see works cited in Leiman's footnote 44.

it was closed. Josephus's dividing of the OT sacred books into three distinct groups shows that certainly by his time a tripartite canon was known, and probably most of the books, if not all, in each section were agreed upon. In fact, his claim that for a long time those books had been considered special suggests that such a conception of the OT was prevalent before his time. Certainly, if most of the NT books were written in the first century AD (as evangelical scholars have traditionally held), that is the consensus view, given that all OT books except five are quoted in the NT, and that a bipartite, and even a tripartite conception of the OT canon was prevalent at the time the NT was written. Given the evidence from the second century BC and Qumran, it is likely that many, if not all, the books in the section known as the Writings were deemed to be Scripture. And, as we saw in analyzing evidence from that time period, it is possible that at least some in Judaism saw the OT as tripartite. More precise dating of the consensus about books that belonged in this part of the OT (and about a tripartite, rather than a bipartite canon) may not be possible.

In sum, there seems to be sufficient evidence to say that the books in the Pentateuch were in the days of the prophets (former and latter)—perhaps even earlier—deemed to be divinely inspired. Moreover, it is not unlikely that most books from the Prophets section of the OT were deemed to be Scripture well before the end of prophecy in 400 BC, and that is likely also true of books in the Writings section like Psalms. From the evidence offered it also seems reasonable to conclude that most of the books that comprise our OT were deemed to be Scripture, divinely inspired, by at least 100 BC, and probably earlier. In Jesus's time this seems to be even more evidently so. By the time of Josephus, at the very latest, there seemed to be a clear conception of the OT as tripartite, and that is also reflected in the NT. Moreover, even before Josephus (given his testimony that the Jewish sacred writings numbered twenty-two, and that this had been held for a long time), the three divisions of the OT canon and most, if not all, of the books that comprised the OT were recognized as from God and thus Scripture. If so, then given our definition of canonicity, these works were viewed in ways that we would call canonical.

This summary, while not attempting to tie down exact dates for the recognition of parts or all of the OT being closed, is not so noncommittal as to say nothing concrete. The data with regard to NT canonicity becomes more explicit about the OT as well, and it confirms the basic approach summarized in the paragraph above.

## THE QUESTION OF CRITERIA

Though much has been said in our discussion about books considered to be divinely inspired and, hence, canonical, nothing has been said about the basis for judging any book as deserving a place in the canon. Though few would contest that the books of Moses are divinely inspired and should be included in the OT canon, that doesn't mean we know exactly why those books were viewed that way. Some may reply that they were judged to be Scripture because they were divinely inspired, but that won't suffice. For we still can reasonably and meaningfully ask what it was about them that made the people of Israel believe they came from God when Moses said so.

Put simply, what characteristic(s) did an OT book have to have in order to qualify as being from God? This is actually the question of criteria for inclusion in the canon of sacred Scripture. Unfortunately, we can't interview any OT-era Jews, or Jews in Christ's time and the centuries after, to ascertain what criteria they used to decide which books were from God and hence belonged in the OT. Still, we should at least try to ascertain some grounds upon which we can rest our belief that the books included in the OT should be there.

What, then, might be reasons for considering an OT book inspired and hence canonical? At least two things are of significance. The first appeals to OT teaching about the tests for a true prophet. In OT thinking, a prophet is a spokesperson for another. He delivers a message to someone or some group on behalf of the person who wants to send the message. The message could be about the past, present, future, or a combination of these. While a prophet might deliver his own message, more often than not, OT prophets spoke for someone else. Even more, many OT prophets claimed to speak a message from God. If they were in fact doing so, then the message is divine revelation. If the message was committed to writing, then the writing is the inspired word of God, written by the hand of a human prophet. And, if the written words of the prophet are God's word, then, given my definition of canonicity, the written word should be part of the canon of Scripture.

Readers may follow this logic but still wonder how it helps us decide which books are canonical. The reason is that anyone might claim to be a genuine prophet of the living God and yet not be an actual prophet. How would one distinguish a genuine prophet from a fraud? This question evidently arose in Israel of old, because Moses answered it in the book of Deuteronomy. In two separate passages—Deuteronomy 18:18–22 and Deuteronomy 13:1–3—Moses offered the tests of a true prophet. Though chapter 18 comes after 13, the tests mentioned in chapter 18 logically precede those detailed in chapter 13.

Deuteronomy 18 presents three tests of a true prophet. First, he must speak in the Lord's name (vv. 18–20). This means that he must speak on behalf of the God of Israel, i.e., what he says must be what Yahweh wants him to say. If he speaks only for himself, or worse yet, in the name of another god, he can't be a true prophet of Yahweh.

But if the prophet does claim to speak in God's name, would that make him a genuine prophet? Not at all. Verse 22 teaches that if the prophet makes a prediction in God's name, and the prediction doesn't come to pass, he isn't a true prophet of Yahweh. What if the prophet merely delivers a message he claims comes from God, but it doesn't include a prediction? Verse 22 states that if what the prophet says is not in fact true, then his message can't be from the true and living God.

So, to be an accredited spokesperson for the God of Israel, (1) the prophet must speak in God's name, (2) any predictions he makes must come to pass, and (3) any nonpredictive message he brings must be true.

What if a given prophet claims to be speaking for Yahweh, and passes all three tests, but actually speaks for a different god? Deuteronomy 13 gives the answer. In verses 1–2 Moses imagines someone who speaks of a miraculous sign, and the sign or wonder takes place/happens. But that doesn't end the matter, for Moses supposes that this alleged prophet of Yahweh uses the miracle predicted and performed as a basis for encouraging the people of Israel to follow some god other than Yahweh. Moses says that in that case, the people of Israel should not listen to the supposed prophet of Yahweh. He is a fraudulent prophet and is being used by Yahweh to test the people of Israel to see if they are truly determined to follow Yahweh alone. In verses 4–5 Moses says that the people must follow Yahweh and obey his commands; the "imposter" must be put to death. But how would Israel know what Yahweh's commands are? By listening to or reading the words of a prophet who genuinely speaks for Yahweh.

From these two passages and the tests of a true and false prophet, we have a criterion for determining whether a book written during the OT era is genuinely inspired. That criterion is that the book must be written by someone who is an accredited spokesperson for God or an associate of a true prophet who wrote the book under the genuine prophet's supervision and command. How do we know whether a given book meets this requirement? Its author should write in God's name—or at the very least he should not write on his own authority or on that of some god other than Yahweh. If the book contains predictions, they must come to pass. If the predictions haven't come to pass, we must discern whether that is so because the time for their fulfillment has come and gone, or whether it isn't yet time for the prediction to come to pass. Moreover, the rest of the book must be true in whatever it affirms. And, finally, the intent of the book must be to lead its readers to worship the true and living God. If that isn't entirely clear in regard to a given book, at the very least there should be nothing in the book that would lead any reader to worship a god other than Yahweh.

There is a second criterion for OT canonicity. It is whether the NT cites or quotes an OT book, and if it does, does the NT writer do this in a way that affirms that the book alluded to or quoted is God's word? And, if the NT book records *Jesus* referring to an OT book as God's word, that should lend even greater weight to the OT book being canonical.

Of course, the previous paragraph should leave readers a bit puzzled. Why should the NT be given such weight, even if it does quote an OT book? The answer has to be that we at some point have shown that the NT is the inspired word of God. Readers know from reading earlier chapters of this book that I am assuming in this chapter that this is true of the NT, but that doesn't mean we have provided the evidence and made the case for the canonicity of the twenty-seven books that make up most editions of the NT. That will be covered in the next chapter. Thus, our second criterion for OT canonicity can be of value only if we succeed in demonstrating the canonicity of the NT. Of course, even if we do, I must remind readers that we have already noted that five OT books are not quoted or alluded to in the NT. Hence, this second criterion is helpful confirmation of the canonicity of the OT books that are quoted or otherwise referenced. But it can't be an absolute criterion that must be met for an OT-era book to qualify as canonical. Otherwise our OTs should contain only thirty-four books, and we surely don't want to reach that conclusion, especially if the books not quoted in the NT pass the tests involved in the first criterion.[62]

---

[62] Here I should probably add a further proviso. Just because an NT book alludes to an OT era book, that alone isn't reason enough to include it in the OT canon. That book must still pass the tests involved in meeting the first criterion of OT canonicity. I add this because NT books like Jude and 2 Peter refer to events spoken of in apocryphal books. That fact isn't enough to add those books to the OT canon.

# FOURTEEN

# LIGHT CANONIZED (IV)

## New Testament Canonicity

The timing of the formation and closure of the NT canon is far less controversial than that of the OT canon. That isn't because everything is clear-cut as to when and why books were included in the NT and when it was closed. It is because there is not a plethora of theories about such issues.

Of course, not long ago, given their commitment to higher critical methodologies, many liberals believed that none of the NT was written in the first or second centuries AD. Instead, they were written much later as propaganda to bolster and publicize a movement struggling for its very existence. So traditional views about who wrote various NT books and when they were first considered canonical couldn't be right. But the discovery of manuscript copies of parts of various NT books (dated to the early part of the second century AD) shows that the NT certainly could have been composed in the first and early second century AD. There are still attacks, like those posed in the recent *Da Vinci Code*, that claim that the Gospels were written by the early church (but not too early) as propaganda meant to portray Christ and Christianity in a positive light.[1]

Though there is overall less controversy about the general path to canonicity NT books took, there are still some questions. There is what Michael Holmes calls a traditional view of the rise of the NT canon, consisting of three main stages. During the first stage (between the mid-first century and mid-second century AD), various Christian writings rose to the status of Scripture.

---

[1] For a discussion of the *Da Vinci Code* and other such theories about NT documents and Christianity being steeped in some form of gnosticism, see Ben Witherington III, "Why the 'Lost Gospels' Lost Out," *Christianity Today* 48 (June 1, 2004).

As Holmes explains, by the middle of the second century, there seemed to be a "core" of about twenty books that Christians esteemed as Scripture. This included the four Gospels in our current NT, the book of Acts, thirteen letters by Paul, and 1 John and 1 Peter. In addition, there was a much larger group of books whose status as Scripture (or not) was under consideration, but nothing definitive had been decided about these books.[2]

According to the traditional view, the second stage of NT canon formation went from about the middle of the second to the middle of the third century AD. At the outset of this period, Marcion presented his understanding of the canon of Scripture. In addition to omitting the OT entirely, Marcion proposed an NT canon of edited versions of ten of Paul's letters and of the Gospel of Luke. The church responded informally by acknowledging a core group of about twenty books (enumerated above) around which there were many other books whose status as Scripture (or not) was debated.[3]

The third stage of NT canon formation occurred in the late third and the fourth centuries AD. During this time the church more formally affirmed the contents of the NT canon, as authoritative decisions were made about which books should be included and which excluded. As Holmes notes, John Barton agrees that the basic three-stage process is the proper way to understand the formation of the NT canon. However, Barton explains that there is disagreement over which of the three stages was the most important, and the various views on this are both right and wrong to a certain extent. As Holmes reports, Barton's claims are as follows:

(1) Some early Christian writings 'did have considerable authority' early on (as Zahn thought), but no one was yet thinking of anything like a 'New Testament'; (2) while other books were raised to this same authoritative status during what Harnack considered the key second-century 'formative period', a central core was already well established by then; and (3) authoritative rulings appear only in the fourth century, but they essentially codify what was already a matter of widespread practice.[4]

As Holmes explains, Barton's proposal is that the history of the NT canon involved two simultaneous and interacting processes. One process involved growth, and the other involved limitation of the books in the canon. Holmes's main concern, and wise counsel as we study the various data that offer testimony to the recognition of NT books as canonical, is that we shouldn't view the process from the end (the fourth century), because that conceptualizes the story of the formation of the NT canon from the viewpoint of its outcome.

[2] Michael W. Holmes, "The Biblical Canon," in *The Oxford Handbook of Early Christian Studies*, ed. Susan A. Harvey and David G. Hunter (Oxford: Oxford University Press, 2010), 416.
[3] Ibid.
[4] Ibid., 416–417.

To do so tends to trace a single line of development as though the direction it took was to be expected and inevitable. Hence, Holmes thinks it is better to start the discussion from the middle of the second century and move forward, rather than starting at the end and looking backward.[5] This is a helpful suggestion, for we don't want to impose on the data (looking at them from the perspective of knowing how the canonizing process ended) interpretations that may lead us to conclude that those who wrote about the developing canon were ascribing credibility to various writings before such writings were actually even considered Scripture.

Heeding these caveats, we can say that a proper view of the timing of recognition of various books as canonical is nowhere near as complicated as for the OT.[6] But before presenting early church testimony about the NT canon, I want to present some basic dates about key events and persons involved in forming and closing the NT canon. I am constructing the following data from charts presented by Ben Witherington and Patricia Shelly.[7]

Jesus's death and resurrection occurred around AD 33. During approximately the years 49–90 AD, various documents that would become part of the NT were composed. Then, in AD 110 Papias presented some anecdotal information about the four Gospels. In addition, a manuscript fragment of part of the Gospel of John was found that dates to around 120. By about AD 130, the four Gospels and thirteen of Paul's letters were deemed authoritative in some parts of the church. Around 125–150 AD the Gnostics Valentinus and Basilides were active in Rome and Alexandria. Somewhere around 140–150, Marcion proposed his version of the NT canon, and around 150, the *Gospel of Thomas* was also composed. Then, around 175 Tatian in Syria presented the *Diatessaron*, which combined the four Gospels and some other traditions into one narrative. About AD 180, Irenaeus was the first to mention the four Gospels in the order in which we have them, and around AD 200 the Muratorian Canon was published. It contains a nearly complete list of the current NT; of course, there are, as we shall see, some who dispute this date, claiming that the Muratorian Canon was significantly later.

Next, we should mention Clement of Alexandria from Egypt. Around AD 220 he offered his understanding of the NT canon. While it included many books in our NT canon, it also included books like the *Epistle of Barnabas*, the *Shepherd of Hermas*, the *Revelation of Peter*, the *Didache*, and *1 Clement*,

---

[5] Ibid., 417.

[6] Of course, there are always factors that can complicate the matter. For example, various pseudepigraphical books were written during the early centuries of church history. Typically, both evangelical and nonevangelical scholars have held that such works were excluded from the NT canon. But what if some of the books that became part of the NT are actually pseudepigraphical works? For a discussion of such issues, see Eduard Verhoef, "Pseudepigraphy and Canon," *Biblische Notizen* 106 (2001).

[7] Witherington, "Why the 'Lost Gospels' Lost Out," 28–29; and Patricia Shelly, "The Bible as Canon: God's Word and the Community's Book," *Mennonite Life* 44 (1989): 8.

none of which was later deemed canonical. Next, between about 250 and 450 AD, the Gnostic Nag Hammadi manuscripts were published. In 303–306, Emperor Diocletian unleashed widespread persecution of Christians, destroying various copies of the NT Scriptures. But soon thereafter, Emperor Constantine legalized Christianity in the Roman Empire. In 325 the Council of Nicea met, and Eusebius published a list of a nearly complete NT. In AD 332, Emperor Constantine ordered the production of 50 vellum Bibles; and around 350, Codex Vaticanus and Codex Sinaiticus were published. These two codices were early complete Bibles (i.e., they included both Testaments). In 367 AD Bishop Athanasius of Alexandria issued the first list of NT books that matches our current list. And finally, in AD 382 Pope Damasus called a council, and out of that council came a complete list of NT books as we know them in our day.

Of course, this isn't the whole story, but it gives a basic outline of key people and events of the first few centuries of church history, and that should help us as we present the various people and events that helped shape the NT canon.

## TESTIMONY RELATED TO THE NEW TESTAMENT CANON

Unlike those who first received and wrote OT revelation, the newborn early church already had a Bible. And most, if not all, who would write the NT were alive during Christ's lifetime or at least during the lifetime of most of his twelve disciples and later apostles like Paul. That Bible, for these early NT-era believers, was the OT. While it was God's word to Israel and to all other people, it anticipated something hidden in the OT era. It looked forward to a Messiah who would be Israel's Savior and King, and ultimately Savior and King of the whole world.

### Jesus's Testimony

During Jesus's life on earth, most Jews and Gentiles didn't understand fully, and in some cases not at all, who he actually was. Even his closest disciples didn't fully understand when he spoke of needing to go away and of sending the Holy Spirit. Jesus's followers during his life were mainly Jews, and the OT was their Bible as well. Jesus expounded and explained the OT, including how he fulfilled what the OT foreshadowed. Having the OT and Jesus, why was there need for anything more?

In addition, Jesus's teachings, as seen in the Gospels, expanded on OT themes, and he added things that would be hard, if not impossible, to find in the OT. And, Jesus stressed the importance of his teaching by "placing his words not merely above scribal interpretation (Matt. 5:33–37, 43–48) but on a par with OT law itself (Matt. 5:21–26, 27–30, 38–42)—a move that was reinforced by the crowd, which on more than one occasion observed that Jesus taught with an authority the scribes lacked (Matt. 7:29; Mark 1:22; cf. Luke 4:32)."[8] While Jesus was alive, there was no need to write down what he said, because one could always hear him again. What few of even Jesus's closest followers seemed to grasp was that he wouldn't be with them for the rest of their lives, and that he would depart sooner than they could imagine. After all, if Jesus was the long-awaited Messiah, how could he possibly die? That would seem to quash any hope of a messianic kingdom of the sort predicted in the OT.

When Jesus was arrested, tried, convicted, and crucified, that must have been an incredible shock to his disciples. Among other things, the worldview they had inherited from OT teaching about the Messiah and his kingdom must have been utterly shattered. Had they completely misunderstood the OT? Or had they just been totally confused about who Jesus claimed to be and who he was? Or both?

And then, everything changed again when, several days after the crucifixion, Jesus appeared to them, alive and resurrected. Overwhelmed and overjoyed by his reappearance, perhaps his disciples thought he would remain on earth indefinitely and begin his kingdom rule. But then, Jesus had more shocking news: He was going away, but not this time to the grave. He would ascend into heaven and sit down at the right hand of his Father. And, what would happen to his disciples, and what were they to do?

Jesus clarified their assignment, and this time they understood. Jesus would continue to teach about God and having a relationship with him, but after the ascension, he would do it through the witness of the disciples. The Holy Spirit would come upon them and minister through them (John 14; 15; 16). And so, the disciples went out and preached the gospel. While the apostles who had been with Jesus (and followers who had encountered Jesus otherwise, or who heard the apostles and believed) were alive, there was little need to write down Jesus's life story and teachings. All of it was so vividly impressed upon the disciples' minds.

### Early Church Testimony

As the apostles preached the gospel, people far from Palestine believed, and churches were founded. After a while, Christianity had spread to many places in the Roman world. Occasionally, problems arose in a church the apostles had founded, and needed to be addressed. The apostles couldn't drop everything and travel quickly to churches in need, churches with questions. The most

---

[8] Linda Belleville, "Canon of the New Testament," in *Foundations for Biblical Interpretation*, ed. David S. Dockery, Kenneth A. Mathews, and Robert B. Sloan (Nashville: Broadman & Holman, 1994).

efficient way to communicate with those churches was to write them a letter. Apostles like Paul, Peter, John, and James did just that.

In addition, the early verses of Luke's Gospel show that many people had written an account of what eyewitnesses to Jesus's life and teachings said had happened. Since Luke had actually done a good bit of research about the story of Jesus, he decided to write an account as well (Luke 1:1–4). Of course, Luke was right about others doing the same, not only because of three other Gospels in the NT canon, but also because of other "Gospels" that never made it into the canon. With so many stories circulating about Christ, it was a good thing that eyewitnesses, or at least people who had talked with eyewitnesses, wrote an account of Jesus's life and teachings while the eyewitnesses were still alive.

From their experiences with Christ during his life, from the sermons of the apostles in Acts, and from other confessional material contained in other NT books, Robert Sloan rightly says it is quite clear as to what early Christian preachers (and writers of the NT books) believed about Jesus. Sloan identifies six different things of which these preachers and teachers were convinced. First, they believed that, in the events of Jesus's life, especially at its end, God was fulfilling ancient Jewish Scriptures. Second, they believed that Jesus's death, though a traumatic shock when it happened, was ordained by God and actually conquered sin and death, and provided deliverance from bondage to sin. His resurrection confirmed this. Third, they believed that even further vindication came when the risen Lord ascended to heaven and was exalted as he sat at his Father's right hand and received all the powers and privileges of being Messiah and Lord and ruler of God's kingdom. Fourth, they believed, because of the events of Pentecost (at the very least) that Jesus had sent his Holy Spirit and was now ministering to them through the Holy Spirit as the living Lord. These teachers also proclaimed that Jesus would return to earth to vindicate his people and judge all the earth. And finally, they preached that to be saved through Christ's sacrifice and to be part of God's people, individuals must turn from their sin and believe in the risen Christ as Lord, Messiah, and Savior. That confession of faith was to be followed by baptism in his name.[9] As Sloan notes, this was a pattern of theology that developed even before the NT was written, and was evident in NT books once they were written.

As the apostles and other eyewitnesses began to grow old, the early church saw that all of the eyewitnesses to Christ's life would soon die out. It was time to write down the stories of Jesus's life so that they wouldn't become mythologically embellished, incorrectly remembered, or just plain forgotten. And, as

---

[9] Robert B. Sloan, "Unity in Diversity: A Clue to the Emergence of the New Testament as Sacred Literature," in *New Testament Criticism and Interpretation*, ed. David A. Black and David S. Dockery (Grand Rapids, MI: Zondervan, 1991), 442.

noted, various churches faced problems, and one apostle or another wrote a letter or two to address those issues.

Would these kinds of documents be inventions of mere human research and creativity? Not at all, for we already saw, when discussing inspiration, that various NT writers claimed to write the Lord's command, and they passed on to their readers what they received from the Lord himself (e.g., 1 Cor. 7:10; 11:23; Gal. 1:12).

It is also extremely important to note, as thinkers like Robert Sloan do, that NT writers often spoke of their readers as holding on to the "tradition" or "traditions" regarding Christ (e.g., Col. 2:6, 8; 1 Cor. 11:2; 2 Thess. 2:15; 3:6; cf. Rom. 6:17; 1 Cor. 11:23; 15:1, 3; Gal. 1:9, 12; Phil. 4:9; 1 Tim. 1:18; 2 Tim. 2:2; Jude 3). Some NT texts even refer to the gospel itself as tradition (1 Cor. 15:1, 3; Gal. 1:9, 12). Undoubtedly, the tradition of Christ referred not to something negative (as is often the case when Protestants think of tradition), but to something quite positive. It seems to refer to the stories and teachings of Christ and his apostles as proclaimed and passed on orally from one group of people to another. All of the passages cited just above show that the apostles commended their readers for holding the traditional beliefs about Jesus, no doubt initially conveyed orally.[10] Given these phenomena, as Sloan suggests, the NT didn't so much create a theology for the early church (though indeed, it does contain much theology that would have been present in preaching, and adds even more), as it records in writing the basic beliefs and deeds of Jesus's life passed along initially orally by the apostles.[11] In other words, the church came to the NT, once it was written, with a theology already in place, taken from the OT and apostolic preaching.

By the time many NT books were written, there was also biblical testimony like that of Peter to the effect that Paul's writings (however many had been written when Peter wrote 2 Peter 2) were Scripture.[12] If so, then Paul's writings must also be canonical, given our definition of canonicity. And, if Jesus is God and speaks the words of his Father who is also God, then those Gospel books that record Jesus's teachings also record the words of God, and hence qualify as canonical. Whether this exact line of reasoning moved early Christians to view works like the Gospels and the Epistles as inspired and canonical, we aren't in a position to say. My point is that, if one adds my definition of canonicity to what we know Jesus promised about the Holy Spirit's ministry, about what the NT writers said about their own writings, and about what they said about other NT books, etc., then all of those works qualify as canonical.

---

[10] Sloan, "Unity in Diversity," 446. See also David Dunbar, "The Biblical Canon," in *Hermeneutics, Authority and Canon*, ed. D. A. Carson and John Woodbridge (Grand Rapids, MI: Zondervan, 1986), 319–321, on the authority of Jesus's teaching and that of the apostles in the early church.
[11] Sloan, "Unity in Diversity," 441–442.
[12] Here see Linda Belleville's helpful discussion in "Canon of the New Testament," 376–377.

## Apostolic Fathers

The next stage in recognition of books as Scripture and hence canon is the period of the Apostolic Fathers. This designation refers to "the earliest post-biblical literature up to about the year A.D. 120 . . . "[13] Four names stick out from this group: Clement of Rome, Polycarp of Smyrna, Ignatius (bishop of Antioch, who died either 108 or 116 AD), and Papias, bishop of Hierapolis (c. 130–140 AD).

*Clement of Rome*—Clement of Rome, traditionally thought to be the third bishop of Rome, wrote a letter, *1 Clement*, to the church at Corinth in approximately 95 or 96 AD. In it he urged them to read Paul's first letter to the Corinthian church. He also quoted (*1 Clement* 13:1–2) the words of Jesus (parts of his Sermon on the Mount) in parallel with OT passages and gave both equal authority. In addition, Clement alluded to portions of a fairly large Pauline collection, and used them authoritatively, as he did with Matthew's Gospel. Michael Holmes also surmises that Clement likely knew Romans and Hebrews. Milton Fisher adds that in this letter there are also some reflections of 1 Timothy, Titus, 1 Peter, and Ephesians. Even Eusebius commented that *1 Clement* was read aloud to worshipers in the early days, just as in Eusebius's day. These comments hint that, at a rather early stage in church history, some NT books had been copied and disseminated to some extent, and that practice suggests that some were beginning to think of collections of early Christian writings.[14]

*Polycarp*—The key work of Polycarp, an acquaintance of the apostle John, is his *Epistle to the Philippians*, written in AD 107. In it Polycarp used quotes or direct allusions to Matthew, Luke, 1 and 2 Corinthians, Galatians, Ephesians, 1 Thessalonians, 1 and 2 Timothy, 1 Peter, and 1 and 2 John as authoritative writings. In fact, as Fisher notes, Polycarp even used a quote which combined Psalm 4:4 and Paul's warning in Ephesians 4:26. Polycarp introduced this quote by saying, "as it is said in *these Scriptures* (12:4)."[15]

*Ignatius*—Around AD 115, Ignatius wrote letters to seven churches while he was traveling to Rome. These letters have correspondences with several pas-

---

[13] Sloan, "Unity in Diversity," 454.

[14] For these details about Clement of Rome see Milton Fisher, "The Canon of the New Testament," in Comfort, *Origin of the Bible*, 69–70; Belleville, "Canon of the New Testament," 380–381; Holmes, "Biblical Canon," 415; James B. Joseph, "Second-Century Heresy Did Not Force the Church into Early Canonization," *Faith and Mission* 18 (2001): 44–45; Ronald Youngblood, "The Process: How We Got Our Bible," *Christianity Today* 32 (February 5, 1988): 26; Bruce Metzger, "The Context and Development of the Christian Canon," in *Living Traditions of the Bible*, ed. James E. Bowley (St. Louis: Chalice Press, 1999), 95; and Roy W. Hoover, "How the Books of the New Testament Were Chosen," *Bible Review* 9 (1993): 44.

[15] Fisher, "Canon of the New Testament," 71, quoting Polycarp (italics are Fisher's). For other details in the paragraph about Polycarp see Joseph, "Second-Century Heresy," 44–45; and Holmes, "Biblical Canon," 415. Also, for more on Polycarp and Ephesians and Philippians see Paul Hartog, "Historical and Theological Studies: Polycarp, Ephesians, and 'Scripture'," *WTJ* 70 (2008).

sages in the Gospels, and they also incorporate language from various Pauline epistles. Sloan says that in spite of these letters, Ignatius seemed to prefer the living prophetic voice (as evidenced in his *Letter to the Philadelphians* 6:1; 8:2; 9:2; *Letter to the Smyrnaeans* 5:1; 7:2).

Regardless of whether Sloan's assessment is accurate, he adds that "Ignatius never referred to any of the New Testament materials as Scripture nor did he associate what appear to us to be New Testament literary traditions with the traditional categories and/or formulas suggestive of the use of Scripture."[16] Hoover adds that Ignatius often tried to elaborate in his letter to these churches points that Paul had made. He also told the Ephesian church that Paul mentions them "in every letter" (see Ignatius's *Letter to the Ephesians*). If Ignatius wasn't exaggerating, he seemed, as Hoover says, to know of at least several of Paul's letters.[17]

*Papias*—Papias lived from 60–130 AD. We only know of his works thanks to Eusebius's preserving some of them. In one of his works, Papias mentions by name the Gospels of Matthew and Mark. Sloan claims that in this work, Papias clearly stated his preference "for the 'living voice' of tradition (*Ecclesiastical History* 3.39.4), but it is not clear that such a preference has to do with the oral sayings of Jesus over against their written form."[18] Nonetheless, Fisher claims that the way Papias used both Matthew and Mark as the basis of his exposition indicates that, for Papias, these Gospels were canonical.[19]

## Other Testimony

At about this same time, there were several other significant religious writings in the early church. One was a Gnostic-oriented work from about AD 140 called the *Gospel of Truth*. It used a number of canonical NT sources, and treated them as authoritative. Fisher claims that its use of NT sources is "comprehensive enough to warrant the conclusion that in Rome (at this period) there was a New Testament compilation in existence corresponding very closely to our own. Citations are made from the Gospels, Acts, letters of Paul, Hebrews, and the book of Revelation."[20]

Five other works were of special significance. One was the *Epistle of Barnabas*. The Barnabas in question wasn't Paul's companion, but another

---

[16] Sloan, "Unity in Diversity," 451. See also Hoover, "How the Books of the New Testament Were Chosen," 44; and Fisher, "Canon of the New Testament," 70–71.

[17] Hoover, "How the Books of the New Testament Were Chosen," 44.

[18] Sloan, "Unity in Diversity," 451.

[19] Fisher, "Canon of the New Testament," 71. Though the comments by Sloan and Fisher seem contradictory, that need not be so. Sloan could be right that Papias preferred something oral to the written works, but even so, thought that Matthew and Mark were Scripture and should be in the canon. I leave to Patristics scholars the resolution of these brief but apparently contradictory comments by Sloan and Fisher.

[20] Fisher, "Canon of the New Testament," 71.

Barnabas, and this letter was written about AD 125 from Alexandria, Egypt. Its focus is how Christians should interpret the OT. Of special import for the NT is that Barnabas used various parts of the NT, even though he didn't refer to any particular book. This work seems to have been a favorite especially in the Eastern churches.[21]

A second widely read and positively received work in the second and third centuries is the *Shepherd of Hermas*. It is an apocalypse, filled with a rambling narrative of parables and visions. It was written in the mid-second century. The book contained various allusions to several NT books and some references to the OT. As Bruce Metzger explains, both the *Shepherd* and the *Epistle of Barnabas* "were so highly regarded that the famous codex Sinaiticus, a fourth-century copy of the Greek Bible and one of the earliest parchment manuscripts of the Bible, contains both of these writings following the end of the New Testament."[22] Linda Belleville adds that the *Shepherd* was accepted by early church fathers like Irenaeus (*Against Heresies* 4.20.2), Clement of Alexandria (*Stromata* 1.17.29), and Tertullian (*De Oratione* 16).[23] Despite its popularity, neither it nor the *Epistle of Barnabas* was ultimately included in the NT canon.

Then, three other works were also well received among early Christians. One was *1 Clement* (already discussed), and the others were the *Apocalypse of Peter* and the *Didache*. As to the *Apocalypse*, it appeared in one of the earliest canonical lists, the Muratorian Canon, but it came with the proviso that "some do not want it to be read in the church."[24] As for the *Didache*, or the *Teaching of the Twelve Apostles*, it purports to have been written by the twelve apostles, but dates proposed for its composition make it impossible for them to have written it. Some like Metzger date it to the early part of the second century, around AD 125, while Belleville claims that it is commonly thought to have been written in the latter part of the second century AD.[25] With either date, it could at most reflect apostolic doctrine, but surely couldn't have been written by all twelve apostles. The work contains echoes and allusions from the Synoptic Gospels. According to Eusebius, the work was rejected by some, but "included 'among the recognized books' by others" (*Ecclesiastical History* 3.25).[26] As Belleville notes, it is interesting that the five books (the *Epistle*, *Shepherd*, *1 Clement*, *Apocalypse*, and *Didache*) were widely used and valued in the early centuries of church history, while

---

[21] Metzger, "Context and Development," 95; and Belleville, "Canon of the New Testament," 380.
[22] Metzger, "Context and Development," 95.
[23] Belleville, "Canon of the New Testament," 380.
[24] Ibid., 381.
[25] Metzger, "Context and Development," 95; and Belleville, "Canon of the New Testament," 381.
[26] Belleville, "Canon of the New Testament," 381. See also Metzger, "Context and Development," 95, for discussion of this work.

James, Hebrews, 2 Peter, 2 and 3 John, and Revelation, books later included in the canon, were disputed in some quarters of the church during the same time period.[27]

## Marcion

The next key figure in the recognition of the NT canon is Marcion (85–160 AD). He has the dubious distinction of being the first to draw up a "list" of "canonical" books. I call it a dubious distinction, because his motivation was his succumbing to heretical teachings. Marcion was a wealthy ship owner from Sinope on the Black Sea, and also the son of a bishop of the church in Asia Minor. Some have suggested that his views were gnostic, or at least gnostic-like, but his primary concern was that he couldn't see how the God of the OT is consistent with the God of the NT. The God of the OT promoted pillaging, killing, and even genocide, and he was also guilty of favoritism to one nation, despite its checkered history of on-again/off-again obedience to his commands. In addition, Marcion regarded matter as basically evil, so the God who created it (and the OT God is surely portrayed as its creator) couldn't be a good God. Rejecting matter as evil, Marcion also rejected Jesus's virgin birth, along with his true humanity (Jesus only appeared to be human), arguing that Jesus had just suddenly appeared full grown in AD 29 at a synagogue in Capernaum. God, as presented in the NT, wasn't the same as the OT God, and Jesus came to oppose him, according to Marcion. In fact, Marcion believed that Jesus had come to destroy OT law, not to fulfill it. The God of the NT was a merciful and forgiving God with a passion and care for all humans.

Marcion claimed to have come to this understanding by reading about Jesus in some of Paul's epistles and in what he thought was the Gospel of Paul—actually it was Luke, but Marcion thought it was wrongly assigned to Luke. During Paul's lifetime, he was opposed by Judaizers, and Marcion held that after Paul died, Paul's opponents added pro-Jewish elements to his letters and to Luke, and produced what Marcion thought were spurious Gospels, namely, Matthew, Mark, and John. As a result, Marcion proposed that the only true canon of Scripture completely omitted the OT, and contained a very truncated NT. It consisted of only the Gospel of Luke, with pro-Jewish references and quotes/allusions to the OT edited out. Marcion's NT also included a second section, a group of ten Pauline letters, significantly edited to match Marcion's beliefs. These beliefs, along with Marcion's proposal about the canon, appeared around AD 140, about the time he came to the church in Rome, presenting himself for membership. Despite the fact that Marcion gave the church a rather generous financial gift, the Roman church declared him a

---

[27] Belleville, "Canon of the New Testament," 381.

heretic, returned his gift, and rejected his views about the OT and the canon of Scripture in general. After these events, Marcion became a traveling preacher, spread his views, and established Marcionite churches throughout the Eastern part of the Roman Empire where Christianity had already spread.[28]

Scholars vary over how important the Marcionite controversy was in prodding the church to designate a list of books as Scripture and to define in a more intentional way an OT and NT canon. If nothing else, the church definitely confirmed its commitment to the OT as Scripture, and before too long, various Christian scholars began to make deliberate pronouncements about the contents of the NT. Still, some scholars, like James B. Joseph, have argued somewhat convincingly that neither Marcionism nor other second-century heresies spurred the church to produce its own list of authoritative writings. The reason, according to Joseph, is that there is evidence (much of it already presented above) that by early to mid-second century, many churches already had their own collections of inspired writings, books that functioned with canonical authority among those Christians. Joseph adds that these various collections among the different churches were similar to each other, and the books that comprised them were viewed as distinct from all other religious writings.[29]

## Justin Martyr

Justin Martyr (c. 100–165 AD) lived during the time of the Marcionite heresy. According to Irenaeus, Justin wrote a treatise against both Marcionism and various forms of gnosticism, and he was the first to respond to Marcion. Unfortunately, Justin's treatise is lost, and his three treatises that we do have say nothing about Marcion.[30] However, the works of Justin that we do possess give us insight into his understanding of the number and significance of the Gospels. Justin referred to these books as "the memoirs of the apostles," and it is agreed that he cited Matthew and Luke frequently (*Dialogue with Trypho* 103, passim). He is also known to have cited Mark on at least one occasion (*Dialogue with Trypho* 106, in which he quotes directly from the Gospel of Mark as the memoirs of the apostle Peter). While there is some doubt that Justin cited or alluded to John's Gospel, in a recent article, Jordan May has

[28] My description of Marcion and his views reflects a compilation of material from various sources. Among them are Charles E. White, "Marcion," *Christianity Today* 32 (February 5, 1988): 27; Dunbar, "Biblical Canon," 331–333; Youngblood, "Process: How We Got Our Bible," 26; Belleville, "Canon of the New Testament," 381; Fisher, "Canon of the New Testament," 71; Shelly, "Bible as Canon," 8; Hoover, "How the Books of the New Testament Were Chosen," 44–45; Holmes, "Biblical Canon," 417; Richard B. Gaffin Jr., "The New Testament as Canon," in *Inerrancy and Hermeneutic: A Tradition, a Challenge, a Debate*, ed. Harvie M. Conn (Grand Rapids, MI: Baker, 1988), 166; and Steven M. Sheeley, "From 'Scripture' to 'Canon': The Development of the New Testament Canon," *RevExp* 95 (1998): 516, 520.
[29] Joseph, "Second-Century Heresy," 40. In the rest of his article Joseph presents the evidence that supports his main thesis.
[30] Dunbar, "Biblical Canon," 333.

shown conclusively that Justin's works contain, if not direct quotes of John's Gospel, clear allusions to his teaching in wording similar to what John used.[31]

Having said the above, it should be remembered that at Justin's time various religious writings claimed to be Gospels, and Justin referred to the memoirs of the apostles. He never explained how many of these "memoirs" he had in mind, so he might have been thinking of a number of the documents circulating at that time as Gospels. What we do know from the evidence presented above, however, is that he believed that there were at the very least four Gospels—Matthew, Mark, Luke, and John.

This evidence alone, however, doesn't tell whether Justin thought of these books as Scripture. In answer, we can say that he clearly regarded the OT as Christian Scripture (see his *1 Apology* 31–35). In addition, scholars agree that the way Justin spoke of the use of the apostolic memoirs in Christian liturgical worship shows that he thought of them as Scripture. For example, in his *1 Apology* 67, Justin wrote about the order of worship within liturgical assemblies as follows:

> And on the day called Sunday, all who live in cities or in the country gather together to one place, and the memoirs of the apostles or the writings of the prophets are read, as long as time permits.[32]

As David Dunbar also notes, in Justin's *Dialogue with Trypho* 81.4, he mentions the book of Revelation by name and cites the apostle John as its author. His works also show awareness of Acts, various Pauline epistles, Hebrews, 1 John, and possibly 1 Peter, though none of these books is directly cited.[33]

### Tatian

Tatian was a contemporary of both Marcion and Justin Martyr. In fact, Tatian was a Syrian Christian who had been Justin's student in Rome. Somewhere between AD 170 and 185 Tatian produced the *Diatessaron* (literally, "one through four" or "by means of four"). This was the first attempt to produce a harmony of the Gospels. There is some scholarly debate about the sources of this work, but all agree that it included material from each of Matthew, Mark, Luke, and John. Some material may have been taken from some other Gospel or other source (this is debated by scholars), but the *Diatessaron* doesn't evidence any

---

[31] Jordan D. May, "The Four Pillars: The Fourfold Gospel before the Time of Irenaeus," *TJ* 30 (2009): 72–74.

[32] Ibid., 75, quoting Justin Martyr's *1 Apology* 67. On these points, see also Belleville, "Canon of the New Testament," 384; Joseph, "Second-Century Heresy," 44; Fisher, "Canon of the New Testament," 71–72; Lee M. McDonald, "The Integrity of the Biblical Canon in Light of Its Historical Development," *BBR* 6 (1996): 117; D. Moody Smith, "When Did the Gospels Become Scripture?," *Journal of Biblical Literature* 119 (2000): 5; and Darrell D. Hannah, "The Four-Gospel 'Canon' in the *Epistula Apostolorum*," *Journal of Theological Studies* 59 (October 2008): 605–606.

[33] Dunbar, "Biblical Canon," 334.

major change in content from our four Gospels in what it reports about Jesus's life and ministry. As many scholars suggest, at the very least Tatian's reliance on Matthew, Mark, Luke, and John for the majority of his material shows that by his time the four were likely thought of as equal in status, even if other Gospels were of interest to various people in the early church.

Though the *Diatessaron* was used in Syrian churches for several centuries, in general the church rejected it and opted for the four independent accounts of the life and teachings of Christ that we know as Matthew, Mark, Luke, and John.[34]

### Irenaeus

One of the most significant second-century-AD figures was Irenaeus (AD 130–200), Bishop of Lyons in France. Irenaeus was a disciple of Polycarp, who was himself a disciple of the apostle John. Irenaeus is significant to the process of NT canon recognition for a number of reasons. First, around AD 180 Irenaeus wrote a very important work called *Against Heresies*. It is divided into five books and is a resounding critique of and answer to various forms of Gnosticism at his time. One Gnostic who gets lots of attention in this work is Marcion. While Irenaeus complained that most forms of Gnosticism erred by misinterpreting Scripture, Marcion was guilty of mutilating Scripture by removing the OT altogether, by refusing to acknowledge most of the NT, and by shortening the Gospel according to Luke and Paul's letters (*Against Heresies* 3.12.12)[35] so as to remove things that didn't fit his heretical beliefs.

Irenaeus is important, secondly, because he was the first church father to affirm explicitly that there are four and only four Gospels, Matthew, Mark, Luke, and John (*Against Heresies* 3.1.1). While others before him had recognized these four Gospels, Irenaeus was the first to limit the number to exactly four. Not only did Irenaeus argue for only four Gospels, but he also produced a somewhat elaborate argument that there couldn't possibly be any more. The argument is exegetically unsustainable and conceptually defective, but it shows how committed he was to the four Gospels as the only Gospels that are Scripture. Irenaeus stated his case as follows:

> It is not possible that the gospels can be either more or fewer in number than they are. For, since there are four zones of the world in which we live, and four principal winds, while the church is scattered throughout all the world,

---

[34] For this information and more on Tatian and the *Diatessaron*, see Shelly, "Bible as Canon," 8; Hoover, "How the Books of the New Testament Were Chosen," 46; Metzger, "Context and Development," 96; Youngblood, "Process: How We Got Our Bible," 26; Fisher, "Canon of the New Testament," 71–72; and May, "Four Pillars," 75–77. For a more detailed study of the *Diatessaron* see Craig D. Allert, "The State of the New Testament Canon in the Second Century: Putting Tatian's *Diatessaron* in Perspective," *BBR* 9 (1999).

[35] Joseph, "Second-Century Heresy," 45.

and the pillar and ground [of the Church is] the gospel and the spirit of life; it is fitting that she should have four pillars, breathing out immortality on every side, and vivifying men afresh. From which fact, it is evident that the Word . . . he that sits upon the cherubim, and contains all things, he who was manifested to [people], has given us the gospel under four aspects, but bound together by one Spirit. (*Haer.* 3.11.8)[36]

In addition to these examples of things that are fourfold, Irenaeus also marshalled as proof the four figures of the Apocalypse (Rev. 4:7), the four revelatory activities of Christ (the Word of God in John, the priest in Luke, the son of David in Matthew, and the prophet in Mark), and the four covenants, namely, those made with Adam, Noah, and Moses, and the gospel.[37] Interestingly, he didn't mention the covenants with Abraham and David, or the New Covenant, but my point isn't to judge the cogency of his argument but only to note the passion and conviction behind it. Despite the weakness of this argument, given Irenaeus's importance in the church of his time, this emphatic endorsement of Matthew, Mark, Luke, and John as Scripture and the only Gospels was persuasive to many.

Irenaeus is also important for a third reason. In his writings he also recognized a number of other books as Scripture. In addition to acknowledging the OT as Scripture (it points to Christ, he of whom the NT speaks and about whom the apostles preached), Irenaeus in various works written around AD 185 quoted from twenty-two books as authoritative: "the four gospels, Acts, Paul's letters (excluding Hebrews), 1 John and 1 Peter, Revelation and the *Shepherd of Hermas*."[38] Coming from such an influential person as Irenaeus, this is significant, even though the final book in his list never made it into the NT canon.

In addition, Irenaeus is quite important for his emphasis on what is known as "the rule of faith." God sent Christ to live among us and teach us the truth, and to die and rise again for the forgiveness of our sins. Christ commissioned the apostles to preach this good news, and the apostles passed to the church what they received from Christ. This rule of faith is normative for faith, and Tertullian and Irenaeus held that the "rule of faith is the indispensable key to the scriptures."[39] Robert Sloan explains it as follows:

> . . . about the middle of the second century, a series of labels and/or categories *emerged to refer to the correct interpretation of the apostolic tradition itself*. Iranaeus [sic] and Tertullian refer to such things variously as "the rule

---

[36] Quoted in May, "Four Pillars," 70. May misquotes Irenaeus, omitting "of the Church is."
[37] Ibid.
[38] Hoover, "How the Books of the New Testament Were Chosen," 45.
[39] Kilian McDonnell, "The Formation of the Canon and the Recognition of Scriptural Authority as an Ecclesiological Process," *Mid-Stream* 38 (January–April 1999): 23.

of faith" (*regula fidei*), "the truth" (*aletheias/veritatis*), or "the canon/rule of truth" (*kanon tes aletheias/regula veritatis*). These labels do not refer so much to any given confession per se but to interpretive material that, while sounding like creedal material, had not yet been formalized as a creed. However, the "rule of faith" seems on a historical trajectory that began with what I have called the apostolic theology, was itself expressed early on in various confessional forms, and ended in some of the more classical creeds, for example, the Apostles' Creed. To be sure, the sociological function of the rule of faith was not unlike that of later, more formalized creeds, i.e., it served as an interpretive guideline to distinguish acceptable from unacceptable theology and thus to reveal those who are truly within the church and those who are heretics. But, more specifically, for Irenaeus the rule of faith served, among other things, as the standard for judging whether or not one had correctly interpreted *Scripture*, especially the apostolic Scriptures that, as both written and indispensable, were themselves now the object of both focus and abuse (*Against Heresies*, 1.8.1, 9.1, 9.4).[40]

In light of Irenaeus's connection through Polycarp to John and the other apostles, and through them ultimately to Christ, it isn't at all surprising to see that the "rule of faith" was such a key emphasis for Irenaeus. It is also easy to see that conformity to the "rule of faith" (or to some doctrinal standard like it) would be a key ingredient in deciding if an NT-era writing should or should not be part of the NT canon.[41]

## Muratorian Fragment

The next item of significance is known as the Muratorian Fragment. It consists of eighty-five lines of Latin text that list the books considered authoritative by the church. It also includes historical and theological comments. The copy of the document that was found is dated to the eighth century, so the original was constructed earlier.[42] This eighth-century copy was found in 1740 by Ludovico Muratori. It is referred to as a fragment, because the document isn't complete; its beginning is missing. What remains begins by naming Luke and John the third and fourth Gospels, so it is assumed that the document originally also listed Matthew and Mark. The list also includes Acts, thirteen of Paul's letters, two (or possibly three) letters of John, Jude, and Revelation. Some have attributed the omission of the rest of the NT epistles to a copyist's error, while others have suggested that the fragmentary nature of the document may explain the omission. Either is possible, but we cannot, of course, be certain.

---

[40] Sloan, "Unity in Diversity," 455–456.

[41] For more on Irenaeus and Scripture see Holmes, "Biblical Canon," 419; Fisher, "Canon of the New Testament," 72; Metzger, "Context and Development," 96; Hannah, "Context and Development," 598–606; Dunbar, "Biblical Canon," 334–337; M. C. Steenberg, "Irenaeus on Scripture, *Graphe*, and the Status of *Hermas*," *St. Vladimer's Theological Quarterly* 53 (2009); and T. C. Skeat, "Irenaeus and the Four-Gospel Canon," *Novum Testamentum* 34 (1992).

[42] McDonnell, "Formation of the Canon," 518.

In addition to listing or describing these books, the Muratorian Fragment also says that the church accepts the *Wisdom of Solomon*, but excludes the *Shepherd of Hermas*.[43]

In short, the document is divided into four categories of Christian books. The first contains books universally accepted as Scripture. It includes the four Gospels, Acts, thirteen letters of Paul, Jude, two (or three) letters of John, the *Wisdom of Solomon*, and the book of Revelation by John. The second category contains one disputed book, the *Apocalypse of Peter*. The Muratorian Fragment also includes the following statement: "We accept only the Apocalypse of John and Peter, although some of us do not want it [Apocalypse of Peter is 2 Peter?] to be read in the Church."[44] The third group lists books that were not to be used for public reading and worship but were acceptable for reading in private, like the *Shepherd of Hermas*. The *Shepherd of Hermas* was excluded from the list of Scripture, according to the Fragment, because it was written "very recently in our times in the city of Rome . . . and therefore ought indeed to be read, but not publicly to the people in church either among the prophets nor among the apostles, for it is after [their] time" (lines 73–80).[45] Finally, the Muratorian Fragment lists various books which should be rejected completely by the church.

The key question debated about the Muratorian Fragment is when the original document was constructed. Traditionally, scholars have dated its composition in the late second century AD, around 200. However, scholarly opinion about this is divided. The other main theory is that it wasn't written until the fourth century. Generally, those who tend to push for a picture of the canon as open and fluid for a longer time in early church history opt for the later date, while those who see the process as more fixed seem to hold an earlier date for the Muratorian Fragment. Key proponents of the later date are Geoffrey M. Hahneman and Lee M. McDonald, but many others hold the traditional second-century date.[46] Thankfully, we need not resolve this debate, as its answer decides neither the exact contents of the NT canon nor the date of its closure.[47]

---

[43] C. E. Hill, "The Debate over the Muratorian Fragment and the Development of the Canon," *WTJ* 57 (1995): 437. For the view that the Fragment omits various Catholic Epistles because it is fragmentary, see Youngblood, "Process: How We Got Our Bible," 26.

[44] This quote is taken from Fisher, "Canon of the New Testament," 72–73.

[45] This quote is taken from Belleville, "Canon of the New Testament," 384.

[46] Those who want to pursue the details of this debate should read Geoffrey M. Hahneman, *The Muratorian Fragment and the Development of the Canon*, Oxford Theological Monographs (Oxford: Clarendon, 1992); and Lee M. McDonald, *The Formation of the Christian Biblical Canon*, rev. and expanded ed. (Peabody, MA: Hendrickson, 1995) for supports for the fourth-century dates. For arguments for an earlier date, see, for example, Hill, "Debate Over the Muratorian Fragment," who gives a lengthy review of Hahneman's book. See also Michael W. Holmes's review of Hahneman's book in a 1992 article in the *Catholic Biblical Quarterly* 56.

[47] For further discussion of the Muratorian Fragment see Dunbar, "Biblical Canon," 339–340; Holmes, "Biblical Canon," 419; M. James Sawyer, "Evangelicals and the Canon of the New Testament," *GTJ* 11 (1991): 42; Shelly, "Bible as Canon," 8; Hannah, "Context and Development," 600; and Verhoef, "Pseudepigraphy and Canon," 90.

## Tertullian

Before leaving second-century-AD testimony, we should note three more items. The first is Tertullian's testimony. Tertullian lived in the North African city of Carthage. He was trained as a lawyer, but was converted to Christianity in midlife and became a powerful proponent of the faith. He was also a prolific writer. One of his topics was to write against heresy, and he wrote a lengthy and rigorous attack on Marcion. Metzger reports that in about the year AD 200 Tertullian "wrote several treatises in which he quoted from eighteen of the twenty-seven books of the New Testament."[48] In comparing Tertullian to his contemporaries—Irenaeus, Clement of Alexandria (see below), and the Muratorian Canon—James Brooks notes that Tertullian accepted Philemon. He also accepted Hebrews, but attributed it to Barnabas. Both Tertullian and Clement accepted Jude and Revelation, though Tertullian used Revelation even less than Clement did. Tertullian made no reference to James, 2 Peter, and 2 and 3 John. Brooks adds that Tertullian bested his contemporaries by accepting no book into the NT that didn't ultimately become canonical.[49] Dunbar also notes that Tertullian rejected the *Shepherd of Hermas* as an "apocryphal" book, one not recognized in the churches in earlier times.[50]

## Montanism

Into this late second-century mix, beginning in Asia Minor by AD 170, came Montanism. As Dunbar explains,

> The Montanist movement . . . was an attempt to repristinate the church by stressing a fervent eschatological hope, a vigorous asceticism, and a renewal of the prophetic gift. "Montanus himself seems to have made the claim that the promise of Jesus concerning the Paraclete had been uniquely fulfilled in him." It was this claim to the inspiration of the Holy Spirit, made not only by Montanus but also by some of his disciples, that challenged the church's understanding of authority."[51]

The exact impact of Montanism on canon formation is debated. Belleville claims that it was a factor that pushed the early church "to consider once and for all which writings would serve as the definitive yardstick for the church's faith and practice."[52] If so, a definitive list was not soon forthcoming, as is evident from studying such late-second- and early-third-century thinkers as Clement of Alexandria, and from studying Origen (third century) on the canon.

---

[48] Metzger, "Context and Development," 96.
[49] James A. Brooks, "Clement of Alexandria as a Witness to the Development of the New Testament Canon," *Second Century* 9 (1992): 55.
[50] Dunbar, "Biblical Canon," 340.
[51] Ibid., 338.
[52] Belleville, "Canon of the New Testament," 390.

Hence, it is probably safer to follow Dunbar's conclusion that the significance of Montanism on canon formation is simply a matter of debate. However, the church responded to Montanism by rejecting the so-called "inspired" writings of the Montanists. It also questioned the authority of long-accepted writings like Revelation, the Johannine emphases on the filling and anointing activities of the Holy Spirit, and the book of Hebrews, because the Montanists used these works to support their views.[53]

## Clement of Alexandria

At the end of the second century and the start of the third century AD, we come to Clement of Alexandria. In about AD 180 he came to Alexandria and worked to convert the pagans and educate the Christians. He became head of a catechetical school in Alexandria, where he lectured to his students and wrote many books. Most of the books have disappeared, but three major works did survive. They are *Protrepticus* ("Exhortation to the Greeks"), which was addressed to pagan readers; *Paedagogos* (on Christian life and morality); and his *Miscellanies*.[54]

In his works, Clement referred to and/or quoted many different works, including OT books and books that would become part of the NT canon. As for the OT, he referred to every book in the Hebrew canon except Ruth, Song of Solomon, and Obadiah. Of course, he also referred to books that never made it into the OT canon, like *1* and *2 Esdras*, *Tobit*, *Judith*, the *Additions to Esther*, the *Wisdom of Solomon*, *Sirach*, *1 Baruch*, *Susanna*, *Bel and the Dragon*, *2 Maccabees*, *1 Enoch*, the *Assumption of Moses*, and the *Sibylline Oracles*.[55]

As for the NT, Clement knew and used twenty-three of the twenty-seven books of our NT. The only ones not mentioned are Philemon, James, 2 Peter, and 3 John, and Brooks says it is uncertain that Clement even knew of the latter three.[56] In his works, Clement cited a number of books. Citing Otto Stahlin's index as his source, Brooks reports that Clement has 3,279 references to the NT, "71 to New Testament apocrypha, 258 to patristic writings, 126 to other Christian sources including heretics, and 3,162 to classical and other non-Christian writings—a total of 8,612. The New Testament can be broken down into Gospels—1,579, Acts—57, Pauline Epistles (including Hebrews)—1,372, General Epistles—237, and Revelation—34."[57]

---

[53] Ibid.
[54] Metzger, "Context and Development," 96.
[55] Brooks, "Clement of Alexandria," 41–42.
[56] Ibid., 44.
[57] Ibid., 47. These statistics are taken from the index in Otto Stahlin, ed., *Clemens Alexandrinus*, 4 vols. (12, 15, 17, and 39) of Die griechischen christlichen Schriftsteller der ersten drei Jahrhunderte (Leipzig: J. C. Hinrichs'sche Buchhandlung, 1905–1936). Metzger's statistics are slightly different but consistent with Brooks's. Metzger claims there are 1,575 quotations from the four Gospels and about 1,375 from the Pauline epistles (see Metzger, "Context and Development," 97).

Lest we think Clement's citing of twenty-three NT books specifies a definite NT canon, we must remember that he also cited various noncanonical books. For example, he quoted the *Gospel of the Hebrews* with the formulaic "it is written," but lest we assume that this means he viewed it as Scripture, Brooks reminds us that Clement used the phrase rather loosely, and even used it to refer to secular writings.[58] Clement also referred to the *Epistle of Barnabas*, the *Shepherd of Hermas*, the *Didache*, *1 Clement*, and the *Apocalypse of Peter*. As to Clement's opinion of these writings, Brooks explains,

> It is difficult to decide how much authority Clement attached to the above writings. Only the *Apocalypse of Peter* is certainly called scripture. The fact that Clement included the *Epistle of Barnabas* and the *Apocalypse of Peter* in a biblical commentary may indicate that he regarded them as scripture. The description of the *Shepherd* as having been given to Hermas "by revelation" may indicate the same status for it. The number and nature of the quotations from the *Preaching of Peter* indicates a very high regard for it. Therefore it is possible—even probable—that Clement recognized as scripture four or five early Christian writings which ultimately failed to find a place in the canon.[59]

One further point about Clement is noteworthy. Relying on Stahlin's statistics, Brooks notes that Clement used the word *kanon* some twenty-one times. However, as Brooks explains,

> invariably the word means *a standard or rule by which something is measured or judged*. He speaks of the "canon of the church" and an "ecclesiastical canon," by which he means the inner principle of authority which the church possesses in the areas of doctrine and conduct. Likewise he speaks of a "canon of truth" and a "canon of faith." None of these, however, has anything to do with books. That use of the word did not emerge for another century.[60]

Even so, as Brooks and other scholars note, Clement seemed to have a concept of what we have defined as a canon of Scripture. Most books in our NT were in his list, even if it also included books that didn't finally make it into the NT canon.[61]

From the preceding data, it seems clear that by the end of the second century, the basic idea of a collection of writings to which nothing could be added and from which nothing could be removed was circulating, even if the exact contents were debated.[62] But as Richard Gaffin explains, contemporary scholarship for the most part agrees that by the end of the second century "the four Gospels, Acts, the thirteen letters of Paul, 1 Peter and 1 John were widely

---

[58] Brooks, "Clement of Alexandria," 44.
[59] Ibid., 47.
[60] Ibid., 53–54.
[61] For more on Clement, see Shelly, "Bible as Canon," 8; McDonald, "Integrity of the Biblical Canon," 124; and Dunbar, "Biblical Canon," 340–341.
[62] Holmes, "Biblical Canon," 419.

accepted throughout the church as canonical, that is, as constituent parts of a 'New Testament,' on a par in revelatory character and authority with what by that acceptance became its 'Old Testament'."[63] Brooks adds Revelation to this list, but admits that it came under attack later in the East. Still, Irenaeus, the Muratorian Canon, Clement, and Tertullian didn't reject any book that ultimately became part of the NT canon.[64]

### Origen

In the third century AD, undoubtedly, the key figure is Origen (AD 185–254). He is important as a serious Bible scholar and theologian, having produced many writings of both a scholarly and a more "popular" (homilies) variety. He is also significant because of his many travels. Though he was born in Egypt and spent most of his life in Alexandria, he traveled extensively in the Roman world. His travels led him to Antioch, Athens, Arabia, Ephesus, and Rome, and he lived for a long time in Caesarea in Palestine. These travels allowed him to see how various churches and individuals in the wider church used and accepted the various books that became our NT.[65]

In his writings, Origen clearly distinguished between accepted books which all Christians viewed as Scripture and disputed books which some didn't accept. As to the former, he listed the four Gospels, fourteen letters of Paul (interestingly, including Hebrews, though it was Origen who said only God knows its author), Acts, 1 Peter, 1 John, and the Revelation of John. Disputed books were James, 2 and 3 John, Jude, and 2 Peter, but Origen personally accepted each of them.[66]

William Oliver has argued that in his later, more mature work, Origen essentially accepted all twenty-seven books of our NT. A passage from his *Homilies on Joshua* 7.1 shows both his allegorical method of interpretation and what he thought about the contents of the NT. In the following he allegorized the meaning of the destruction of the walls of Jericho:

> Our Lord, whose advent was typified by the son of Nun, when He came, sent His Apostles as priests bearing well-wrought trumpets. Matthew first sounded the priestly trumpet in his Gospel. Mark also, Luke and John, each gave forth a strain on their priestly trumpets. Peter moreover sounds loudly on the twofold trumpet of his Epistles; and also James and Jude. Still the number is incomplete, and John gives forth the trumpet-sound in his Epistles and Apocalypse; and Luke while describing the Acts of the Apostles. Lastly however came he who said: "I think that God has set forth us Apostles last

---

[63] Gaffin, "New Testament as Canon," 166.
[64] Brooks, "Clement of Alexandria," 55.
[65] Metzger, "Context and Development," 97.
[66] Ibid. See, for more details on which books were accepted and which weren't, and on Origen's comments on various books, Belleville, "Canon of the New Testament," 390–391.

of all," and thundering on the fourteen trumpets of his Epistles, threw down even to the ground the walls of Jericho, that is to say all the instruments of idolatry and the doctrines of the philosophers.[67]

Of import is that only authors whose works were later included in the NT are mentioned. Origen not only affirmed twenty-seven books but explained what type of literature each is. What makes this a bit uncertain is that much of what we know about Origen's works comes in Eusebius's descriptions of them. As for the *Homilies on Joshua*, it is likely that Rufinus translated it into Latin (the original Greek of the passage is lost), and Rufinus was known to take liberties in his translation. Hence, Everett R. Kalin sides with those who doubt that Origen ever made a list of the books of the NT canon; rather Eusebius and Rufinus present him as doing so in various passages, because they want it to appear that way. I leave to Origen scholars the resolution of this debate, but note that those who seem most skeptical about the legitimacy of the passages where Origen is said to offer specifics about the NT canon seem also to believe in an open and fluid NT canon—much later than those who believe its contents were set basically by the end of the second century.[68] From our perspective, there are no huge differences between Origen's basic views and those of thinkers at the end of the second century AD.

## Eusebius

Eusebius (AD 280–340) was a crucial figure in early church history in general. He became Bishop of Caesarea about 315, and he did a great service to the Christian church by writing a comprehensive history of its first several hundred years. He grouped his material according to the reigns of the Roman emperors, and

> tells the story of the succession of the bishops in the most important churches, recounts the development of Christian doctrine through the biographies of theologians, and calls the church to remember its heroes by recounting the triumphs of the martyrs. Eusebius quoted from his sources extensively, often providing the only record of otherwise unknown works. His passion for including everything makes his work a gold mine for those seeking to understand the church's first 300 years.[69]

Eusebius also attended the council of Nicea in 325. His own creed was vague on Jesus's relationship to God the Father, the point at issue at Nicea.

---

[67] William G. Oliver, "Origen and the New Testament Canon," *Restoration Quarterly* 31 (1989): 24–25, includes this quote from Origen's *Homilies on Joshua*.
[68] For more details on Origen's views on the NT canon, see Oliver's article. For a contrary view on what Origen actually believed and said about the NT canon, see Everett R. Kalin, "Re-examining New Testament Canon History: 1. The Canon of Origen," *Currents in Theology and Mission* 17 (August 1990).
[69] Richard Gaffin Jr., "Eusebius, Bishop of Caesarea," *Christianity Today* 32 (February 5, 1988): 31.

Some suspected him of heresy, and after the Council in the struggle between Arius and Athanasius, Eusebius was in the middle. He seemed to think Athanasius the more dangerous and so used his influence against him. Of course, Athanasius's views were adopted by the church, but the church forgave Eusebius for his opposition to Athanasius. He seems to have been more of a compiler than an original thinker or theologian, and of course, the doctrine of the Trinity is no easy doctrine.[70]

Of special import for our study is Eusebius's *Ecclesiastical History*, which traces the history of the Christian Bible. At the time of the work's publication in about AD 325, Eusebius in book 3, chapter 25, stated the views of the church at that time on various writings held to be Scripture (or at least debated as to whether they were scriptural books). The list indicated his own opinions, but its main purpose was to, so to speak, give an update on how various churches and Christians saw the matter. Eusebius divided the list into three sections. The first included writings that were accepted (*homologoumena*); these books were universally recognized by all the churches as authoritative and authentic. That list included the four Gospels, Acts, the Pauline Epistles (including Hebrews), 1 Peter, and 1 John. In addition, Eusebius wrote that to these "may be added, if it is thought proper, the Apocalypse of John." Eusebius himself included it, but noted that some wouldn't include Revelation in the list of accepted books. Hence, Eusebius later listed it again among the group of rejected books.[71]

Eusebius labeled the second group of writings disputed books. These books were familiar to the church and were widely received and used, and yet some in the church disputed whether they qualified as Scripture. The books involved were James, Jude, 2 Peter, and 2 and 3 John. The third group of works Eusebius labeled "spurious," and they were to be rejected as nonscriptural. However, this group included some works that various Christians found profitable, even if not on the same level as Scripture. Into this group, Eusebius put Revelation, adding again, "if it is thought proper." This part of the list also included the *Epistle of Barnabas*, the *Shepherd of Hermas*, the *Acts of Paul*, the *Apocalypse of Peter*, the *Teachings of the Apostles*, and the *Gospel of the Hebrews*. And it included various books that heretics put forward under the name of various apostles, such as Gospels of Peter, Thomas, and Matthias, and the Acts of Andrew and John.[72]

Eusebius added some commentary to the group of works deemed spurious. He explained that they were excluded for several reasons. One was that they hadn't been mentioned by earlier generations of church leaders (a historical

---

[70] Ibid.

[71] Belleville, "Canon of the New Testament," 391. See also Metzger, "Context and Development," 97; and Shelly, "Bible as Canon," 518–519.

[72] Belleville, "Canon of the New Testament," 391; Shelly, "Bible as Canon," 519; and Metzger, "Context and Development," 97–98.

criterion). Another was that their character and style didn't mesh with works known to have been written early in the church's history (a literary criterion). And, their thought and content was inconsistent with established orthodoxy (a doctrinal criterion).[73]

In summarizing Eusebius's list, Michael Holmes takes a slightly different stance on the accepted books. He puts Hebrews in the category of disputed books, where he also places Revelation. These two books, plus James, 2 Peter, 2–3 John, and Jude make seven disputed books. That leaves a core of twenty accepted books, and Holmes notes that this means that the shape of the core group had remained stable since the time of Irenaeus.[74]

Regardless of whether one accepts Holmes's reckoning or also lists Hebrews and Revelation as "accepted" in Eusebius's list, Holmes's basic point is correct. From the time of Irenaeus to Eusebius there was a common core of works agreed on as Scripture, even while other works were debated. What must be recognized, however, is that while we may say that this reckoning is consistent with *our* understanding of the concept of an NT *canon*, Eusebius didn't use such language. In a very careful study of Eusebius's writings, Gregory Robbins has shown that throughout his *Ecclesiastical History*, Eusebius didn't refer to his list of books as a "canon" (*kanon*). Rather, he called books the church accepted as Scripture *endiathekos*—"covenantal" or "encovenanted" writings. They are not called "canonical."[75] Moreover, while Eusebius used the term *kanon* some twelve times in the *Ecclesiastical History*, Robbins discusses each instance and shows that all but two clearly have nothing to do with a list of books.[76] Of the two ambiguous ones, one may refer to such a list, but it is dubious that Eusebius meant anything like what we mean when we speak of a canon of Scripture.[77]

But this is not the end of the story, for Robbins also discusses how Eusebius typically referred to a list of sacred writings, or of anything else. In such cases Eusebius used the Greek word *katalogos*, "catalogue." He used it to refer to Origen's list of Old Testament Scriptures.[78] Robbins explains further, about Eusebius's use of this term, that

> He uses 'catalogue' to describe Melito's list of Jewish scriptures in 4.26.12. The group of Paul's letters in 3.25.2 is a 'catalogue'. The entire list of Christian writings categorized in 3.25 is referred to as a 'catalogue'. In 1.12.1, Eusebius catalogues apostles; in 3.4.4, Paul's fellow workers; in 3.38.1, the writings of Ignatius; in 5.17.2, Christian prophets; in 6.32.3, Origen's corpus.

---

[73] Hoover, "How the Books of the New Testament Were Chosen," 46–47; and Belleville, "Canon of the New Testament," 391. These comments were made in Eusebius's *Ecclesiastical History* in book 3, chapter 25.
[74] Holmes, "Biblical Canon," 420.
[75] Gregory A. Robbins, "Eusebius' Lexicon of 'Canonicity'," *Studia Patristica* (Berlin: Akademie-Verlag, 1957): 135–136.
[76] Ibid., 136–138.
[77] Ibid., 138–139.
[78] Ibid.

And, of course, Christian martyrs are catalogued as well (e.g., 5.21.5). This catalogue of Eusebius' cataloguing could be continued almost endlessly.[79]

In light of these data, we shouldn't attribute to Eusebius the full-blown concept of canonicity that we hold in our day. On the other hand, it certainly seems that Eusebius accepted a group of OT writings as Scripture, and he also claimed that a group of twenty books (or twenty-two, depending on whether one includes Hebrews and Revelation) were universally accepted by the church in his day as Scripture. Such claims don't include all the notions we bring to our idea of canonicity, but it would be wrong to think that Eusebius's understanding of NT books considered Scripture was totally unlike our idea of an NT canon.

### Athanasius's Festal Letter

As we close this historical section, several more events and facts should be mentioned. One relates to an important *Festal Easter Letter* sent out by Athanasius, bishop of Alexandria, in AD 367. In it, Athanasius listed the twenty-seven books, and only those, in our NT. His letter also included the following instructions:

> These are the sources of salvation, for the thirsty may drink deeply of the words to be found here. In these alone is the doctrine of piety recorded. Let no one add to them or take anything away from them.[80]

As Belleville notes, this letter was significant in a number of respects. It was the first time all twenty-seven NT books were set forth so definitively, i.e., they and they alone are the ones that proclaim the doctrine of godliness. In addition, Revelation is listed as one of the twenty-seven without any wavering, despite the fact that it had been much debated in the East. Then, this was the first time a canonical list explicitly excluded any other than the twenty-seven books of our NT. And, it also clarified the status of works like the *Shepherd of Hermas*. Such books aren't members of the canon, but may be read by those who newly join the church and wish to have some instruction in the word of godliness.[81]

In one sense, this festal letter was an amazing development, because Eusebius's canonical list of only forty-two years earlier didn't name just twenty-seven books for the NT canon and no more. Moreover, given Eusebius's presentation, it is clear that opinions about various books were still fluid, and the discussion of which ones should be included in the NT Scripture was ongoing. So, what changed so dramatically in such a short time so that Athanasius's letter was so emphatic? In a recent very helpful journal article, David Brakke explains that

---

[79] Ibid., 139–140.
[80] Shelly, "Bible as Canon," 9.
[81] Belleville, "Canon of the New Testament," 393.

since the mid-1990s a new fragment of the Coptic text of the *Festal Letter* has been discovered. When this new fragment is added to the letter, it puts the reason for writing the letter in a new light. The new fragment is preserved in the A. S. Pushkin State Fine Arts Museum in Moscow, and was published by Alla Elanskaya in 1994. However, Elanskaya thought the fragment was part of a sermon against the Manichaeans. It wasn't until 2001 that Enzo Lucchesi properly identified it as part of the *Festal Easter Letter*, and published a French translation of it. Since then, translations of it have appeared in several languages.[82]

Prior to discovering this new fragment, Brakke interpreted the purpose of the letter as a response to "two forms of Christian spirituality, authority and social organization that were tradition in Egyptian Christianity, but which Athanasius opposed."[83] The first traditional form was study under the guidance of a learned and inspired teacher. A second form of spirituality "was an apocalyptically oriented mode of piety, found in the traditions that David Frankfurter studied in his book on the *Apocalypse of Elijah* and which I saw continuing into the fourth century in the cult of the martyrs and the use of so-called apocryphal books, both taken up most enthusiastically by the Meletians."[84] In contrast to these forms of spirituality, Athanasius offered an episcopally centered piety that focused on adherence to the clergy and the sacraments, and found revealed truth not in some learned teacher but in a stable canon of Scripture as interpreted by the church.[85]

But, as Brakke explains, this new fragment makes it clear that Athanasius's letter wasn't just focused on the various forms of spirituality and the different social organization and authority that those forms represented. Rather, the new fragment shows that Athanasius was most concerned to refute various heresies. Passages that he quotes or cites from the Bible expose these heresies as impious and heretical. Athanasius names the specific heresies of concern as follows: he wanted to contest the Manichaeans, Marcion, the Montanists, the Arians, and the Melitians (he called them "parasites" of the Arians).[86] Brakke summarizes his revised conclusions about the purpose of the letter as follows:

> Although most scholars remain focused on the lists of books, the greater importance of the letter is that it reveals the role of canon formation in supporting one form of Christian piety and authority and undermining others. Different scriptural practices accompany different modes of authority and spirituality, and we should not take the bounded canon of episcopal orthodoxy as either the inevitable *telos* of early Christian history or the only way

---

[82] David Brakke, "A New Fragment of Athanasius's Thirty-Ninth *Festal Letter*: Heresy, Apocrypha, and the Canon," *Harvard Theological Review* 103 (2010): 47–49.

[83] Ibid., 51.

[84] Ibid.

[85] Ibid., 51–52.

[86] Ibid., 49.

that Christians construed and used sacred writings. The new fragment, how-ever, makes clear that in establishing a defined canon Athanasius sought to undermine not only a general spirituality of free intellectual inquiry and its academic mode of authority, but also the specific false doctrines to which he believed such a spirituality gave rise.[87]

While Athanasius's Letter was a key factor in defining the extent of the canon in the Eastern church, two synods were significant for doing the same in the Western church. They were the Synod of Hippo, which met at Hippo Regius in AD 393, and the Synod of Carthage in 397. The deliberations of both of these synods led to the promulgation of canonical lists that match our twenty-seven-book NT. Two key figures involved in both Synods were Augus-tine and Jerome. It was especially Augustine's argument for "no more and no less" than our twenty-seven-book NT that carried the day. Jerome, too, held to the twenty-seven-book NT, and his translation of the OT and NT into Latin became the "Bible" of the Western church.[88]

With this our historical section concludes, though this doesn't mean that debate about the canon ended after these events. For example, into the fifth century the Syriac version of the NT, the Peshitta, lacks 2 Peter, 2 and 3 John, Jude, and Revelation. These books didn't make it into the Syriac canon until the late sixth century. In contrast, the Ethiopic church recognized the twenty-seven books of our NT but also included *The Shepherd of Hermas*, 1 and 2 *Clement*, and eight books of the *Apostolic Constitutions*.[89] Even in the Western church, discussion continued. One example of this is the apocryphal *Epistle to the Laodiceans*. As late as the tenth century, Alfric, who became Archbishop of Canterbury, listed it among Paul's canonical letters. And the book was so commonly used in Latin manuscripts of the Bible that even in the medieval period, "it passed into several vernacular translations, including the Bohemian Bible as late as 1488."[90]

It is also well known that Luther questioned the canonicity of various NT books such as James, Jude, and Revelation, and the Roman Catholic Church itself didn't finalize a canon for all of Scripture until the Council of Trent in 1546. The Roman Catholic Church affirmed Jerome's fourth-century Latin Vulgate as the official version of the Bible. But, of course, the Catholic Bible and the Protestant Bible differ, most notably in that the Catholic Bible includes the Apocrypha and the Protestant one does not. Even so, by the time of the synods of Hippo and Carthage, and with Athanasius's *Festal Letter*, there was

---

[87] Ibid., 56.
[88] Belleville, "Canon of the New Testament," 393–394.
[89] Sawyer, "Evangelicals and the Canon of the New Testament," 44; and Hoover, "How the Books of the New Testament Were Chosen," 47.
[90] Sawyer, "Evangelicals and the Canon of the New Testament," 44.

a basic consensus in both the Eastern and the Western church on the shape of both Testaments. Moreover, these councils and canonical lists show that the consensus was also that the canon of both Testaments was closed.[91]

## THE QUESTION OF CRITERIA

In discussing OT criteria for canonization, we saw very little, if any, explanation given by the Jews as to why various books became part of the OT canon and others were excluded. As a result, we had to "construct" from Scripture criteria of OT canonicity. As for the NT canon, the situation is somewhat different. In rehearsing the testimony about which books should be included in the NT canon, we cited various authorities who explained their rationale for inclusion or exclusion of particular books. In addition, we can again, from Scripture (the NT in this case), construct criteria of canonicity. The ones we can construct from biblical teaching fit very well those stated by various authorities in early church history. So where should we begin?

We should begin with Scripture itself—in particular, Hebrews 1:1–2. The writer of Hebrews begins his book as follows:

> In the past God spoke to our forefathers through the prophets at many times and in various ways, but in these last days he has spoken to us by his Son, whom he appointed heir of all things, and through whom he made the universe. (Heb. 1:1–2 NIV 1984)

The reference in verse 1 to God speaking to our forefathers through the prophets clearly refers to revelation during the OT era to the people of Israel. This suggests that the author of Hebrews, whoever he was, was a Jew. If not, what group of non-Jews does his mention of "forefathers" in this opening statement refer to? We already saw that God spoke through prophets in the OT era and that being written by a genuinely accredited prophet of God is a mark of a book's canonicity. But the writer of Hebrews says that God spoke through the prophets in various ways. Our study of the doctrine of revelation—especially our study of forms of special revelation—shows this to be true.

Verse 2 doesn't change the subject so much as the time of reference. It might be tempting to see the first phrase of verse 2, "in these last days" (*ep' eschatou ton hemeron*), as referring to the end of the age and events involved in that, but that would be a mistake. The opening phrase of verse 2 continues the sentence begun in verse 1, and seems clearly intended as a contrast to verse 1

[91] For more on Athanasius and later developments related to the canon see Gaffin, "The New Testament: How Do We Know for Sure?," 28; Joseph, "Second-Century Heresy," 40; McDonnell, "Formation of the Canon," 19; Metzger, "Context and Development," 98–99; and Dunbar, "Biblical Canon," 317.

and its phrase "in the past" (*palai*). Thus, the writer is comparing the former days of revelation with the last or latter days of revelation, during which the writer lived.

As opposed to God's revelatory work in the OT, consisting of many different forms of revelation, verse 2 says that in the latter days of revelation, God reveals himself through his Son, Jesus Christ. In verses 3ff., the writer then explains something of the majesty and work of the Son. But we must not miss the implications of verse 2 for the doctrine of Scripture. The writer of Hebrews says that in these last days of God's revealing activity, he is speaking through his Son. In what ways did God speak through his Son, Jesus Christ? First, in his very person as the God-man, Jesus is the highest revelation of God that there is (Col. 2:9; John 1:14, 18, etc.). No revelation can or does supersede him! Second, as God, whatever Jesus said was indeed the word of God. So, his teachings are God's word. Third, Jesus also performed various miracles, and as with OT miracles through the prophets, so Jesus's miracles revealed truth about God's power and might. Moreover, the miracle of Christ's resurrection confirmed everything Jesus claimed about himself and his mission.

How does this relate to canonicity? Since we have defined canonicity in terms of inspiration of a written document, it is very significant. Not, of course, because Jesus wrote various books, because so far as we know, Jesus didn't write any books. But, if whatever qualifies as Scripture is what God has spoken, then the words of Jesus, as God, if written, would be Scripture! And whatever is Scripture—God's word—is canonical, according to our definition of canonicity. But how is this relevant to our subject? It is relevant because even though Jesus didn't write any Scripture, some who heard Jesus teach did write his words. In particular, we have many of his teachings while on earth, recorded in the four Gospels. In addition, there are places in other NT books where the author says he writes what the Lord said or what he received from the Lord (e.g., 1 Cor. 7:10; 11:23ff; Gal. 1:11–12; 1 John 1:1–3, 5). If the words that the various writers record are accurately from Jesus—and, higher critics' protestations aside, there is reason to think those words are authentic—then NT books that contain Jesus's words, contain the words of God. At the very least, those words are the inspired word of God, and so they must be canonical, given our definition of canonicity.

The point I am making about Jesus's words is also relevant to the OT. As we saw in the chapters on inspiration, Jesus viewed the OT as the very words of God. In fact, he quoted from many different books as God's word—I needn't repeat the data; readers can review it in the chapters on inspiration. But then, if Jesus is God, and so whatever he says is God's word, we must look at what he says about the OT, as recorded in the Gospels. What he says is that the OT is God's word, Scripture. If whatever is God's word is also canonical, then we have God's word (the testimony of Jesus in the Gospels) that the OT is also God's word, and so it must also be canonical!

Of course, my line of argument depends on first making the case that the words recorded in the NT as those of Jesus are actually his. Proving that is a task for another book, but biblical scholars, as well as apologists, have made the case for it, and those interested in pursuing that defense should consult those works.[92] Assuming that the case has been amply made, that's not the end of the story. The reason is that, besides the Gospels, most NT books don't say that the material the author presents was received from Jesus. So, perhaps much of the NT is just the pious, religious writings of godly men, but not necessarily inspired, and so we seem to have reached a dead end, if we are looking for words that God has spoken through his Son in these last days of revelation (Heb. 1:2).

Drawing that conclusion, however, would be a mistake. Indeed, once Jesus ascended to heaven, his disciples couldn't hear his teachings as they had before. But that didn't mean that revelation through Jesus ended with his ascension. Before his death, Jesus told his disciples he would leave them, but in John 14, 15, and 16 he also promised to send them the Paraclete, the Holy Spirit. As we saw in our study of inspiration, the purpose of sending the Holy Spirit was in large part to remind the disciples of what Jesus had taught and done. In addition, the Holy Spirit would guide them into all truth (John 16:13). Jesus added that everything that belongs to the Father also belongs to him. He then said that the Holy Spirit would take from what belongs to Jesus and make it known to the disciples (16:15). The Spirit would testify to Jesus's disciples, and they would testify about Jesus (15:26–27).

From these passages, we see that Jesus's teaching didn't stop with his ascension. It continued through the ministry of the Holy Spirit whom Jesus sent from the Father to the disciples. The disciples were then to testify to what they had seen and heard while Jesus was on earth, and to whatever the Holy Spirit revealed to them. Just in case the disciples didn't grasp what he meant, Jesus repeated the command before his ascension (Acts 1:8). The rest of the book of Acts shows that they obeyed. But the further purpose of sending the Spirit was so that, when the disciples would write about Jesus and put into words the further revelation of Jesus through the Spirit, they would get the message right.

Note, then, the implications of Hebrews 1:2 for NT canonicity. In the latter days of revelation, God speaks through his Son, Jesus Christ. But Jesus said that, once he departed, he would send the Spirit. Jesus would continue to speak

---

[92] See my "Reliability of the Gospels," in *Can You Believe It's True? Christian Apologetics in a Modern and Postmodern Era* (Wheaton, IL: Crossway, 2013).

through the Spirit to the disciples, who would then preach what they received and would write what Jesus revealed through the Spirit as they wrote what became the books of the NT. Thus, in John 14–16 Jesus in effect pre-certified the inspiration of the soon-to-be-written NT. But then, books written by the apostles would be God's inspired word, and if so, then, given my definition of canonicity, their books would be canonical.

From this biblical teaching we can say that one criterion for the inspiration of an NT book, and hence for its canonicity, is that it is written by an apostle or someone closely associated with an apostle. From evidence already presented, it is quite clear that apostolicity was a key issue for whether a book was considered Scripture or not. As some scholars have pointed out, the key here is actually twofold. The point of apostolicity isn't just that Jesus commissioned the apostles to be his spokespersons and promised them the Holy Spirit's ministry. It is also that these people had the greatest proximity to Jesus. Given the nature of the historical events upon which the doctrinal and practical teachings of the NT books are built, it is clear why writings by eyewitnesses are so important. If Jesus didn't rise from the dead, then his teachings amount to little. On the other hand, if he did rise from the dead, then his teaching cannot be sloughed off as "good advice if you find it useful." It is the authoritative statement about the human condition, about how to establish (and grow) a relationship with God, about the events of the end of the world and beyond, and about eternal life and eternal punishment. It is ignored only at the extreme peril of anyone who does so!

So, the early church's focus on books written by an apostle or someone closely associated with one is grounded in biblical teaching, and shows abundant common sense. Of course, before NT books were written and widely circulated, members of the church (other than the apostles, who had heard Jesus teach about sending the Spirit) could not have known this teaching.

But then, it might seem that apostolicity is the only criterion that mattered and that should matter to us. That conclusion, however, is wrong for at least two reasons. One is that there seem to be books by apostles that aren't included in the NT, and that never seemed to get serious consideration. As examples, 1 Corinthians 5:9–11 seems to offer evidence of a letter to the Corinthians that was earlier than 1 Corinthians, and Philippians 3:1 appears to suggest the possibility of other letters to the church at Philippi.[93] The second

<hr>

[93] Robert L. Thomas, "Correlation of Revelatory Spiritual Gifts and NT Canonicity," *MSJ* 8 (Spring 1997): 17–18. Here we must be careful, however, not to be confused by some "candidates" for being authored by an apostle. There are books that claim to be authored by a genuine apostle, but they are known to be pseudonymous. For example, Eusebius claims that various heretics wrote Gospels such as the *Gospel of Peter*, the *Gospel of Thomas*, and the *Gospel of Matthias* and attributed them to apostles, and heretics also wrote books that they called *Acts of Andrew* and *Acts of John*, and *Acts* of other apostles (*Ecclesiastical History* 3.35.6). These aren't the writings in view in my discussion or in Robert Thomas's. The information about Eusebius's claims was taken from Lee M. McDonald,

reason is that, in some cases, we don't even know for sure who wrote the book (Hebrews), and in other cases tradition says that the author was an associate of (or wrote under the tutelage of) an apostle (Mark as an associate of Peter, and Luke as an associate of Paul), but even if the traditional view is likely, we can't be absolutely certain. For these reasons, apostolicity, while extremely important, can't be the only criterion for determining inspiration, and hence canonicity of an NT book.[94]

Before leaving biblical teaching, let me mention two other possible criteria of canonicity. A first invokes biblical teaching about NT inspiration. In the chapters on inspiration I offered biblical arguments for the NT's inspiration. The problem with offering inspiration as a criterion for canonicity is that I have defined the canonicity of a book as showing evidence of being the inspired word of God. Of course, this would set up a rather vicious circle in which Scripture is canonical because it is inspired and it is inspired because it says it is inspired. Perhaps some will say that this only shows a deficiency in my definition of canonicity, but I reply that doubters should read again the early part of chapter 10 on the definition of canonicity. I think the definition chosen is the best (for reasons explained), and there is evidence in relation to both the OT and the NT that inspiration was the key in recognizing the books of both Testaments as God's word/Scripture—and hence, by my definition, canonical.[95]

But there is another criterion based on scriptural teaching. Here I am thinking of the doctrine of inerrancy detailed in earlier chapters. Since God knows everything, would not lie, and wouldn't forget anything that would alter the truth of what he says, whatever is his word must be true in all it affirms. But then, a book that affirms things that are false or denies things that are true cannot be a word that God has spoken. Hence, it can't be canonical, because it can't be inspired. So, a second criterion of inspiration (and therefore, of canonicity) is inerrancy. Of course, this can't be a stand-alone criterion, just as apostolicity can't stand alone. That is so, because a book can be inerrant and still not be God's word, and hence not canonical.

The next criteria for NT canonicity aren't explicitly taught in Scripture, but they don't contradict any biblical teaching. These criteria seem to have been used by the early church to determine whether a given book should be considered Scripture or not. The first is that the book must be consistent with the teachings of already established Scripture. This might seem to be identi-

---

"Identifying Scripture and Canon in the Early Church: The Criteria Question," in *The Canon Debate*, ed. Lee M. McDonald and James A. Sanders (Peabody, MA: Hendrickson, 2002), 424.

[94] For more on apostolicity as a criterion of canonicity see Gaffin, "The New Testament as Canon," 168–169; McDonald, "Identifying Scripture and Canon," 424–427; Fisher, "Canon of the New Testament," 75–77; McDonnell, "Formation of the Canon," 9–11; and Roger Nicole, "The Canon of the New Testament," *JETS* 40 (June 1997): 200–201.

[95] For more on inspiration as a criterion of canonicity see Gaffin, "The New Testament as Canon," 169; McDonald, "Identifying Scripture and Canon," 435ff.; and Nicole, "Canon of the New Testament," 202–203.

cal to the criterion of inerrancy, but it isn't exactly the same. A book might make no false affirmations and yet not be about spiritual matters at all. Or it might be internally consistent with itself and yet make claims that contradict what biblical books already in existence say. Similarly, a book considered for canonization before much of the NT was written and circulated might present spiritual claims that don't mesh with what was known by oral tradition as the teachings of Christ and his apostles. It is here that the rule of faith, so emphasized by Irenaeus, comes into play. As he noted, there is a line of teaching that Jesus presented while on earth. He passed it on to his disciples, and they went out and preached the same message. Others heard the message and were saved. When the apostles sat down to write books that told the story of Jesus, or of the spread of the gospel, or when they simply presented their understanding of the basic tenets of the faith, whatever they wrote had to be consistent with apostolic teaching that proclaimed the truth that Jesus himself had taught. So, no matter how many good and inspiring qualities a book might have, if its teachings were heterodox (as determined by comparing it with the OT, any NT books already recognized as Scripture, and with the oral teaching of Jesus and the apostles), it couldn't be considered Scripture.[96]

Some might understand this criterion to mean that any newly written document couldn't be Scripture unless it repeated the contents of other books recognized as Scripture. But that's not the point. Novelty isn't ruled out by this criterion; heresy is. Hence, there are instructions about how things should be done in the local church in books like the Pastoral Epistles that one won't likely find anywhere else in either Testament. That doesn't eliminate the Pastorals as Scripture. Similarly, some things in Revelation are consistent with OT end-time prophecies and with some of Jesus's teaching about the end of the age, but there are also things there that we find nowhere else in Scripture; the novelty of these items doesn't disqualify Revelation as God's word. What *is* ruled out is teaching that directly or even indirectly contradicts teaching in books already widely recognized by God's people as Scripture. In addition, if a book contains material that is factually false, then even if it doesn't contradict any other Scripture, it can't be consistent with Scripture. It can't be orthodox, and of course, this is where the current criterion and the previous one of inerrancy overlap. The main point is that for an NT book to be canonical, its teaching must be consistent with apostolic teaching that stemmed from Jesus and his apostles.

The next criterion seemingly used in the early church was that of a

---

[96] For more on orthodoxy or consistency with apostolic teaching see McDonald, "Identifying Scripture and Canon," 423, 428–430; McDonell, "Formation of the Canon," 11–13; Thomas, "Correlation of Revelatory Spiritual Gifts and NT Canonicity," 25–26; Nicole, "Canon of the New Testament," 201–202; and Hans Dieter Betz, "Is the New Testament Canon the Basis for a Church in Fragments?," in *The Church in Fragments: Towards What Kind of Unity?*, ed. Giuseppe Ruggieri and Miklos Tomka (London: SCM Press, 1997), 37.

document's antiquity. While this might seem to be the same thing as apostolicity, it is not. A document might have been written by someone who was an
eyewitness to the events of Christ's life, or who had talked with people who
were alive when Christ was on earth, and yet the writer wasn't an apostle, nor
were any of the people he talked with about Christ apostles or associates of an
apostle. The basic idea behind this criterion is that those who used it wanted
to ensure that the document was written early enough so that its author could
have witnessed the events of Christ's life, or at least could have talked to people
living during Christ's life or who knew people who were alive (but not apostles)
while Christ was on earth. If the document wasn't written, for example, until
about 150 years after Christ's death, its author probably had no contact with
anyone who had witnessed the events of Christ's life. Given the nature of what,
for example, the Gospels report about Christ's life and teachings, the church
wanted to be sure to accept only documents about such things that rested on
actual eyewitness testimony.

Obviously, this criterion could not have been a key one, for in itself it
wouldn't necessarily be sufficient to guarantee inspiration. A document might
have been written when other NT books were written, but it might contradict
what they said. Surely, that would eliminate it as an inspired document. Or, it
might meet this criterion, contain no factual errors, and contradict nothing already contained in books already recognized as Scripture, yet if it wasn't written by an apostle, an associate of an apostle, or at the very least didn't present
teaching consistent with apostolic doctrine, it wouldn't have been considered
inspired. Suppose, for example, that a book dealing with matters of science or
medicine was written by someone living basically at the time of Jesus: It contains no false assertions (from what we know from our current knowledge of
science and medicine), and it doesn't contradict anything contained in the OT
or NT. In fact, it might be a very fine book on science or medicine, and might
even have been written by someone who knew an apostle, so that its antiquity
would be unquestionable. Still, given the book's subject matter, none of these
other qualities, including antiquity, individually or collectively would be sufficient to warrant concluding that the book was inspired by God. Hence, while
a book's antiquity, if lacking, is a serious blow to its candidacy for a place in
the NT canon, its presence is no guarantee of inspiration and thus canonicity.[97]

Another criterion that seems to have been a factor in determining which
books were considered God's inspired word is the book's use. If a book was
used frequently in public readings of Scripture during worship, if its teachings were deemed authoritative by a wide group of churches, or if there was

---

[97] For more on antiquity as a criterion of inspiration and canonicity see Gaffin, "The New Testament as Canon,"
169; McDonald, "Identifying Scripture and Canon," 423, 430–432; and Thomas, "Correlation of Revelatory Spiritual Gifts and NT Canonicity," 24–25.

evidence that the book was used by many or even most churches, regardless of their locale, the book was more likely to be thought to be God's inspired word. At times this criterion might endanger a book like Revelation from being a part of the canon, because it wasn't widely used in some parts of the church. In other cases, like the *Shepherd of Hermas*, widespread appreciation for and use of the book was a factor in various believers thinking the book was the inspired word of God. These last two examples don't show that use of a book was irrelevant to inspiration and canonicity. Rather they show that use was not a necessary condition of canonicity (otherwise, Revelation would have been omitted), and in itself it wasn't sufficient to render a book accepted. But if a given book met the other criteria, especially ones about apostolic authorship, inerrancy, and orthodoxy, it would likely also meet this criterion.[98]

Two more criteria are worth noting. Roger Nicole lists the first as the witness of the Holy Spirit given corporately to God's people and made manifest by a nearly unanimous acceptance of the NT canon in Christian churches. The point here isn't that none of the NT books has ever had doubters. Nor does this mean that, for example, during the early history of the church (say until AD 250 or so), individual churches knew what other churches "all across Christendom" thought about a given book, and so because others accepted it, they did too. As Nicole rightly notes, the early church probably didn't have access to this criterion. But no one is saying that Scripture teaches this criterion or that it must have been used as a major factor at all times in church history. Nor is anyone trying to take something subjective, namely, the internal witness of the Holy Spirit to individual believers, and turn it into something objective which any onlooker could verify, by simple observation, as having happened.

Instead, this is actually a historical criterion. While it is possible for most believers over the last nearly two thousand years to have believed wrongly that, for example, Matthew, Mark, Luke, and John are inspired, it isn't likely if there has been through the centuries overwhelming acceptance, and little, if any, rejection of these books as the inspired word of God. No passage in Scripture explicitly affirms that the Holy Spirit performs this ministry relative to Scripture, but likewise no Scripture rejects the idea as impossible. There are passages that say the Holy Spirit witnesses to believers' spirits that they are indeed saved (e.g., Rom. 8:16). So, there is such a thing as the internal witness of the Holy Spirit to believers about one thing. Nothing in Scripture makes it impossible for the Holy Spirit to witness to believers about this matter, too. Put another way, if the Holy Spirit has taught generations of believers throughout church history that various books are God's inspired word (and part of the NT), that should

---

[98] For more on use as a criterion see Gaffin, "The New Testament as Canon," 169; McDonald, "Identifying Scripture as Canon," 420, 423, 432–434; and Thomas, "Correlation of Revelatory Spiritual Gifts and NT Canonicity," 26–27.

count for something. It can't overturn failure to meet key criteria like apostolicity, orthodoxy, inerrancy, but it should count for something. If a book meets the main criteria, it would certainly be odd, though I suppose at least possible, if throughout church history few believers had thought it inspired, and/or most believers had been convinced that it wasn't Scripture. So, we should give some weight to this criterion, but it is in itself neither a sufficient nor a necessary condition for a book to be considered inspired and hence canonical.[99]

A final criterion was first proposed by the Reformers, and is still referred to in our day by many who see themselves as part of the Reformed tradition in theology. It relates to the nature and character of the Scriptures themselves. As James Sawyer explains, "this is the Reformers' doctrine of the *autopistie* of the scriptures. Their character was pure and holy, having a beauty, harmony and majesty. The scriptures also breathed piety and devotion to God; they revealed redemption and satisfied the spiritual longing within the soul of man. All these features served to convince that the scriptures were indeed the very Word of God."[100] Typically, this criterion of self-authentication (*autopistis*) is coupled with the internal testimony of the Holy Spirit to the effect that we are indeed reading the very words of God.[101]

Given my sympathy toward and affinity with much of Reformed theology, I am not entirely indisposed to this criterion. However, I would emphasize several important points. The testimony of the church throughout history is significant, as argued above, and the Holy Spirit's testimony to the corporate church is also of great significance. Though I find no verse that says the Holy Spirit witnesses to individual believers that a given biblical book is God's word, I see no impossibility in that idea. I suspect that the Holy Spirit does do this sort of ministry, especially when a believer wonders whether he or she is in fact reading what God has said.

My concern is with the idea that Scripture itself is self-authenticating, *autopistis*. I don't know what verse or verses in Scripture directly teach such a notion, and I'm not certain where to look to find it taught even indirectly. As described by Sawyer, it seems that the qualities described aren't immediately evident in Scripture. That they are present seems to be a subjective judgment that doesn't stand on grounds that couldn't be contested. Proponents of this view often add that the Holy Spirit will testify to the believer that Scripture has these qualities, but then it seems to me that this concept of *autopistis* reduces to the internal testimony of the Holy Spirit to the believer about a passage of the Bible (or much more than just a passage) being God's word. As already said, I

---

[99] For further discussion of this criterion, see Nicole, "Canon of the New Testament," 204–206.

[100] Sawyer, "Evangelicals and the Canon of the New Testament," 48.

[101] See, e.g., how Sawyer joins self-authentication with the testimony of the church and the internal witness of the Holy Spirit. In doing so, Sawyer follows the lead of Charles Briggs in Briggs's *General Introduction to the Study of Holy Scripture*. For details see Sawyer, "Evangelicals and the Canon of the New Testament," 48–51.

find no passage that explicitly teaches this about the Holy Spirit, but I also find nothing that refutes it. But, the testimony of the Holy Spirit and Scripture's self-authentication aren't the same things; they are two separate things that can be said about Scripture.

Part of my concern about the notion of *autopistis* is the lack of biblical evidence teaching it, but another concern is the nature of some parts of Scripture itself. Is it true, for example, that every imprecatory psalm is self-evidently God's word? We saw in the chapter on objections to inerrancy that passages in which God commanded killing large numbers of people raise questions about inerrancy and/or the nature of God, and it also seems that it isn't abundantly clear that such passages are self-evidently inspired. That is, though I think they are God's inspired word, I just don't think such passages match the description of Scripture as *self-authenticatingly* God's word. One also wonders whether the Song of Solomon, read literally and not as an allegory about Christ's and the church's love for each other, qualifies as "pure and holy, breathing piety and devotion to God," to use Sawyer's description.

I suspect that part of the motivation behind the Reformers' promoting this notion was their concern to counter the Roman Catholic claim that only the clergy could truly understand and interpret the Bible. Individual believers alone couldn't tell what is and what is not inspired, nor could they be trusted to interpret Scripture correctly. In contrast, the Reformers rightly argued that one doesn't need a pope or a church to interpret Scripture. And they are certainly not necessary even to identify what is Scripture and what isn't. Genuine believers have the ministry of the Holy Spirit to aid them in understanding what is Scripture and what Scripture means, and in applying it to their lives. In addition, Scripture itself gives evidence of being God's word that no pope, bishop, etc., needs to confirm, and none of these can refute Scripture's own evidence that it is God's word. While I resonate with what the Reformers rejected, that doesn't mean that Scripture teaches or that we should believe in the *autopistis* of Scripture. I am not suggesting that Scripture is just an ordinary book or that it appears upon reading to be nothing special. But holding Scripture to have qualities of no ordinary book isn't the same as saying it is self-authenticating.

In sum, the key criteria of inspiration and thereby canonicity for the NT are apostolicity, inerrancy, and orthodoxy. In addition, several other criteria, while of lesser significance, are also helpful. They are the antiquity of NT books, their use in the early church and in the church through the centuries of church history, and the witness of the Holy Spirit to the corporate church (as well as to individual believers) through the centuries that these twenty-seven books are in fact God's word. I should also say that we should add inerrancy as a criterion for a book written in the OT era to be considered inspired and to have a rightful place in the OT canon. And we should probably also add consistency of doctrine with the rest of the books considered to be part of the OT canon. As noted in discussing this criterion in relation to the NT, it has some overlap with inerrancy, but the two aren't absolutely identical. Certainly, both should be true of any OT book, even as both are true of every NT book. Of course, this doesn't mean that an OT book should match the teaching of Jesus and the apostles in order to be part of the OT canon. Progress of revelation isn't thrown out by this criterion of doctrinal consistency. Rather, the point is that no individual book in the OT canon should contain doctrine that clearly contradicts what other OT books claim is true during the same era of biblical history (i.e., the OT era).

## Is the Canon of Scripture Closed?

Though we have covered many things related to the canon of Scripture, one significant topic still needs to be addressed. The process of recognizing OT and NT books as canonical took some time. Though it ended long ago for both Testaments, there is still some debate about which books belong in the canon, and different segments of Christendom have different Bibles. That doesn't mean that there is no agreement on any books, but only that some books are included in some canons and excluded from others.

Deciding on whose canon is the "correct" one, however, isn't the focus of this section. In our historical sections, we noted that by a certain point in the history of OT and NT canon recognition, the people of Israel, and later of the church, considered the canon of each Testament basically closed. Intertestamental Jews didn't expect more OT books. And there is little historical evidence, if any, that Jews in this period and beyond ever considered any NT books the inspired word of God and hence, in any sense, canonical.

As for the early church, to the extent that apostolicity and the antiquity of a document were deciding factors for whether a book was divinely inspired, once the church was several centuries removed from the life of Jesus and the apostles, it is dubious that clergy or laity expected a new apostle or new books which would qualify as God's word. Both Testaments contain ample divinely inspired material for God's people to study, interpret, and apply, even if God never again revealed anything. Debates among Jews and Christians about which books are inspired didn't focus on new claimants to a spot in either Testament, but instead addressed religious writings already in existence.

Thus, while there was little, if anything, said by either Jewish or Christian authorities about either Testament being closed, it seemed to be the general sentiment (if not consensus) that at some point in history each Testament was in fact closed. While few, if any, arguments were presented that either Testament, or both, was closed so that no more divinely inspired writings were expected, one would also be hard pressed to find an orthodox Jewish scholar from Christ's time onward or an evangelical Christian scholar from the late fifth century AD onward who argued that either canon was still open.

Despite these considerations, in our day some Christians wonder whether the canon of Scripture is closed. Perhaps some wonder even more how we should decide whether a new document, if it were written, is divinely inspired and deserves a place in the canon. Is there a way to show that the canon of Scripture (all of it, both OT and NT) is closed? As we saw in our discussion of revelation, God can still reveal himself in our day, so it makes sense to ask whether any more Scripture might be forthcoming.

It is possible to show that the canon of Scripture is closed, but we must first clarify how to do that, and also reject arguments sometimes used that aren't convincing. As to the former task, there are two distinct matters one might have in mind. *One is how we might discredit any new claimant to a place in the canon.* While this is important, it isn't enough. Even if I can discredit all current candidates vying for a place in the canon, and have a strategy for contesting any other claimant that might be written, that wouldn't conclusively prove that there couldn't be any more Scripture.

There is, thus, a second task that is probably more difficult than the first, but it is even more important, for if it succeeds, it settles once and for all whether there could be any more Scripture forthcoming. *That second task is making a case that conclusively shows that the canon is indeed closed.*

I contend that most arguments for closure of the canon are actually arguments for rejecting any potential new candidate. Being able to refute new candidates is important, but we need an argument that decisively shows that there will be no more Scripture.

Still, I begin with the simpler task, offering arguments to discredit any new claimant to a place in the canon. Suppose a new literary piece claims to be Scripture for the OT canon. For OT canonicity, the key is inspiration as indicated by the book being written by an accredited prophet of God. Tests that a book must pass to be from God are set forth in Deuteronomy 18 and 13. So, to discredit a claim to be a new OT book, one must show that the book has material that doesn't pass the tests of a true prophet. If some book would pass those tests, there is a further test, the test of inerrancy. While the Deuteronomy 18 and 13 tests may seem to include inerrancy, that isn't necessarily so. The test of inerrancy requires anything the new book affirms to match the facts of our world and to be consistent with (i.e., not contradict) anything in already accepted Scripture. For those who think such tests are contained in the Deuteronomy 18 and 13 tests, I won't quibble. The key points are whether the new document speaks the truth, in a correspondence sense; doesn't contradict existing Scripture; and makes no predictions that fail to come true. Deuteronomy 18 and 13 add another test or two. All of these tests taken together are sufficient to discredit any existing claimant to a place in the OT canon, and should also discredit any potential future claimant.

What if the new work claims to be written by an apostle and thus would be added to the NT? I reply that it is dubious that anyone alive today meets the requirements to be an apostle—a point I shall develop in my positive argument for a closed canon—at least not one directly commissioned by Christ and promised the things Jesus promised his disciples in John 14, 15, and 16. Surely, no human alive today was an eyewitness to Christ's life, nor could they know anyone who was. Thus, the issue of antiquity, in the sense of the document being written at a time when the author could have been or could have contacted an eyewitness, is a requirement the new document wouldn't meet. Then, the new document might not be consistent with orthodox doctrine that goes back to Jesus and through his apostles to their preaching and writing. And, the new document might also fail to pass the test of factual accuracy. I know of no existing claimants to a spot in the NT canon that would meet all of these criteria.

These, then, are tests one can use to discredit any new claimant to a place in either Testament's canon. But suppose that, instead of a document written in our day, an archaeologist unearths copies of a document written in the early years of the church, and it claims to be written by one of Jesus's twelve apostles. Suppose in the imagined case, archaeologists find these manuscripts along with manuscripts of books already in our NT. Although this seems purely speculative, at one time there might have been people who speculated about things found at Qumran before anyone discovered the Dead Sea Scrolls. So, this imaginary scenario isn't impossible.

Should this scenario become actual, then we would have to subject it to the tests/criteria for NT canonicity. There is no guarantee that it would pass, but we should say something more. Many documents found at Qumran were copies of books already recognized as OT Scripture. Of course, other documents were found that scholars never thought existed. What is important about those nonbiblical documents is that none of them claimed to be written by an accredited prophet, nor did any claim to be Scripture. There is no evidence that the Qumran community believed those documents were Scripture. Likewise, if someone should find a group of documents written during the first century AD (or copies of such documents), how can we now say that they would contain nothing but copies of NT books we already know of, that were circulating in the first century AD? If there should be books that aren't currently part of the NT canon, how do we know that they would claim to be written by an apostle or claim to be Scripture? If these imaginary books should somehow be confirmed as written by first-century apostles and should claim to be Scripture, then we would need to apply the tests/criteria for NT inspiration and canonicity.

Some will undoubtedly think, but what if such a new book passes all those tests? What should we then think and do with that book? My answer is that the situation imagined is totally hypothetical, and there is no guarantee that what is imagined will ever occur. If it should happen, then we would have to reconsider our criteria for canonicity (and likely also whatever we would say about the doctrine of Scripture's preservation), and decide how to proceed from there. But I must emphasize that we are not now at all in this imaginary situation. What *might* happen *may* also *never* happen, and it is hard to see how a hypothetical scenario, just because it is imaginable as a thought experiment, should overturn what we have already said about NT canonicity.

So, we shouldn't worry that the principles for determining canonicity (already mentioned) should be abandoned or thought to be in jeopardy on the basis of some hypothetical thought experiment. The arguments given above will likely discredit any existing or future candidate for a position in the canon of either Testament. But, of course, that isn't positive proof that the canon is closed. That brings me to my final task, offering a positive argument for closure of the canon.

Some Christians have appealed to Revelation 22:18–19 as "proof" of a closed canon. If someone thinks this is a good argument for the closure of the canon, he or she needs to explain why Daniel 12:8–9 doesn't offer a similar argument. Of course, if it does, then there should be no NT, and that is absurd. So, what is the problem with such arguments? The problem is that they are lifted out of their context in their respective books and used as proof-texts for an issue not under discussion in either text, namely, the closure of the canon of Scripture. While Revelation was likely the last NT book written, that still doesn't mean that the comment in chapter 22 is talking about all of Scripture. Actually, it refers to the book of Revelation itself, even as Daniel 12:8–9 refers to the visions given in the book of Daniel.

So, then, what argument shows that the canon of Scripture is closed? There is a biblical argument for this, but it is inferential in nature and involves several things.[102] The first part of the argument was already mentioned when discussing biblical criteria for NT inspiration and canonicity. It begins with an appeal to Hebrews 1:1–2. These verses compare God's ways of revealing himself

---

[102] This basic line of argument was first suggested to me many years ago by my brother Paul D. Feinberg. The exact articulation and defense of the argument are my own, but the basic strategy and substance of the argument have always seemed to me to offer a valid argument for the closure of the canon.

during the OT era and in the NT era. Verse 2 says that in these last days of God's revealing activities, he is doing that through his Son, Jesus Christ. Jesus revealed God in both his life and his ministry. But Jesus died, rose again, and ascended. Does that mean that God's revelatory activity through Jesus ended? Not at all, because in John 14, 15, and 16 Jesus promised to send his disciples the Holy Spirit. The Holy Spirit would testify to them of the Lord, and would reveal to them the truths of Jesus which are also the things of God the Father (John 16:13–15). To what end? So that they would testify of Jesus, according to his command (John 15:26–27). This they did when they preached, and when they wrote about Jesus and what he revealed to them through the Spirit.

How does this show that the canon of Scripture is closed? It doesn't show this quite yet, so we must add another item, one about the apostles. How long would there be apostles, and if there would be apostles for many years of church history, does Hebrews 1:1–2 mean that Jesus through the Spirit might reveal more Scripture many years after the time of Christ, including in our day? The question of whether there are or even can be apostles in our day is a complicated issue that includes, among other things, the nature of spiritual gifts and whether there are any time limits to when these gifts can operate (1 Cor. 12:4–11; Rom. 12:4–8). This volume isn't the place for that discussion (see the volumes in this series on the Holy Spirit and the church),[103] but even so, we can answer from Scripture about the time of the apostles that Jesus had in mind when he spoke the words of John 14–16. That passage is found in Ephesians 2.

In Ephesians, Paul speaks about the church. In chapter 2 he discusses the difference salvation in Christ makes (vv. 1–10). He then turns to the relation of saved Gentiles to saved Jews. Paul notes that, before the Gentiles came to Christ, they were "excluded from the commonwealth of Israel" and were "strangers to the covenants of promise, having no hope and without God in the world" (v. 12). That all changed when they accepted Christ as Savior (v. 13). Christ not only saves Gentiles as well as Jews; his atoning sacrifice (vv. 14–15) also broke down the barriers that once separated them, and he brings peace as believers (both Jewish and Gentile) relate to one another. Paul adds that Jesus did this to make "one new man" (v. 15), and in this new body to reconcile both Jew and Gentile to one another through the cross, which puts to death all the barriers that the Mosaic law constructed to keep them apart.

As a result, Jews and Gentiles who accept Christ are "fellow citizens" and are members "of God's household" (v. 19). That new household is the church, and if there are any doubts, Paul removes them in verses 20–22. Christ is this new household's chief cornerstone, and the apostles and prophets are its foun-

---

[103] Graham A. Cole, *He Who Gives Life: The Doctrine of the Holy Spirit*, Foundations of Evangelical Theology (Wheaton, IL: Crossway, 2007); Gregg R. Allison, *Sojourners and Strangers: The Doctrine of the Church*, Foundations of Evangelical Theology (Wheaton, IL: Crossway, 2012).

dation. The rest of the building is made out of believers in Christ, Jews and Gentiles, in this current age (vv. 21–22).

In essence, Paul is saying that the church's foundation (with Christ as the cornerstone) is the apostles and prophets. Why not say the prophets (OT) and the apostles (NT)? Because, as many commentators agree,[104] Paul isn't talking about OT prophets, but NT believers in the early church with the gift of prophecy. NT believers had the OT, but before the NT was written, they needed a word from God beyond the OT as they met for worship. God gave some the spiritual gift of prophecy, and through those prophets he gave a new message (i.e., it went beyond the OT) to those believers, relevant to their own time and situation. Even if one believes that the gift of prophecy extends past the apostolic age, it can't be denied that before the NT was written, NT believers with the gift of prophecy were important in building the newly formed church, just as Paul says in verse 20.

What is the point of this for the close of the canon? It is as follows: Paul's claims in verses 13–20, and in 20 in particular, are not just doctrinal points. They are certainly that, i.e., relevant to our understanding of the doctrine of the church. But they also make an important historical point. That point is that, as a matter of historical fact, the church is built on the work of Christ, its chief cornerstone, and on the foundational ministry of the apostles and NT prophets. But if the apostles were involved in the historical foundation of the church (and lest there be doubts, Acts removes them), that historical era is long gone. Does this alone make it impossible for there to be any modern-day apostles in any sense of the term "apostle"? No, but in the sense Paul means in verse 20, there can't be any modern-day apostles who were historically involved in founding the church. And, it is important to note that it was to those apostles alone that Jesus gave the promises found in John 14–16. Nothing is said about those promises being for modern-day (or not so modern, but later than the very early church) apostles, should there be any, or to believers who are not apostles. John 14–16 promised only Jesus's disciples who became the first apostles that they would write inspired Scripture. As Paul says, they were part of the foundation of the church. But the time of laying that foundation is over and gone. I believe this means, among other things, that the spiritual gift of apostles has ended, but even if one thinks that gift lives on, any apostles after the early church era are not part of the founding of the church, nor did Jesus make to them the promises of John 14–16.

Now we must gather together the various strands of this argument. The

---

[104] See, e.g., A. Skevington Wood, *Ephesians*, in *EBC*, ed. Frank E. Gaebelein, vol. 11 (Grand Rapids, MI: Zondervan, 1978), 40–41; Karl Braune, *The Epistle of Paul to the Ephesians*, in *Commentary on the Holy Scriptures*, ed. John Peter Lange, vol. 11 (Grand Rapids, MI: Zondervan, 1969), 98; T. K. Abbott, *A Critical and Exegetical Commentary on the Epistles to the Ephesians and to the Colossians* (Edinburgh: T&T Clark, 1956), 72; and William Hendriksen, *New Testament Commentary: Exposition of Ephesians* (Grand Rapids, MI: Baker, 1972), 142.

argument goes as follows: in these last days of revelation, God is speaking to us through his Son, Jesus Christ (Heb. 1:2). Jesus revealed God while on earth, and he promised to send the Holy Spirit to his disciples after he had departed. The Holy Spirit would remind them of what they had seen and heard from Jesus during his lifetime. The Holy Spirit would also reveal to them things of the Lord that they hadn't seen or heard from Jesus. This would happen so that the apostles would go out and testify about Christ, and so that they would "get the story right" when they did. The apostles testified of Christ both by preaching about him and by writing what he revealed to them through the Holy Spirit. Twenty-seven of the books they wrote became the books of the NT. But these apostles didn't live on indefinitely. As Paul says, they served their function as part of the foundation of the church (Eph. 2:20). But the foundation of the church was laid long ago. The apostles to whom Christ made the promises of John 14–16 are long gone. So, if in these last days of revelation, God is revealing himself through his Son, and his Son reveals himself through the ministry of the Holy Spirit to Jesus's disciples who became the first apostles, and if his apostles were to testify of Jesus (and did) through their preaching and writing, and yet the time of these apostles' ministry was the founding time of the church (and that is long past), then the canon of Scripture is closed. Even if one thinks there are apostles today, they aren't part of the founding of the church, and Christ didn't give them the promises he gave to the disciples before his crucifixion. The Holy Spirit can be active in the lives and ministries of believers today, but there is no evidence that he moves any of them to write more Scripture. God can still reveal himself in our world, and does, but not by means of any forthcoming inspired Scripture.

# THE USEFULNESS
# OF SCRIPTURE

# FIFTEEN

# LIGHT EMBRACED

## The Doctrine of Illumination

This chapter begins the final section of this book, in which I discuss reasons why the Bible is understandable and usable. If the Bible cannot be understood, or if it can be but accomplishes little in the lives of its intended recipients, then God has used a lot of effort to reveal and inspire his word but with very little value to its readers. I intend to show in this final section of the book that Scripture can be understood, and does accomplish God's intended purposes in the lives of those who obey it.

Revelation uncovers God's truth, and inspiration transfers it into writing. But none of that guarantees that its readers will understand and apply it to their lives. God, of course, knows that, and not merely wanting another "publication" (a book of sixty-six books) on his "resume," he needed to do something more if Scripture was to change people's lives. No one can live God's truth if they don't understand it and/or let its teaching govern their lives. That's where the Holy Spirit's ministry of illumination enters the picture.

Because grasping and applying divine revelation is so important, you would think that Christians, especially theologians, would have a lot to say about it. In the terminology of speech act analysis of language, Scripture as a whole and in each verse is divine locution. God wants to perform various illocutionary acts with Scripture—warn, promise, encourage, etc., by what Scripture says. But his illocutionary acts also intend to evoke a response (a perlocution). Unless that perlocutionary act happens,[1] God's ultimate purposes in giving Scripture fail.

---

[1] The terminology in this paragraph comes from speech act analysis of language, most associated with philosophers J. L. Austin and John Searle. It is a theory about oral discourse, not about written texts per se. But since Scripture originated from divine speech in various forms, it is acceptable to apply speech act theory to Scripture. At its core is the contention that oral communication can be analyzed into at least three distinct elements. There is the mere

Given its importance, it is strange that illumination receives so little attention, at least among theologians. Many evangelical systematic theologies barely, if at all, mention it. More often, illumination is discussed by liberal theologians who see revelation as requiring reception, and as a result confuse or conflate revelation with illumination. Evangelical theologians who do discuss illumination seem to think evangelicals universally agree about what it is, and so they discuss it briefly, citing the usual verses to support it.[2]

These attitudes about illumination are wrong, and we can begin to see why when we ask questions about the doctrine. For example, what is actually illumined? Scripture, or the reader's mind? Or is it the interpretive process that needs light? If two students of Scripture are illumined by the Holy Spirit as they read the same passage, will that guarantee that both interpret it identically? If their interpretations differ, does that mean one actually was illumined but not the other, even though both prayed for illumination?

Then, 1 Corinthians 2:14–15 is often cited in this discussion. It says that someone without Christ as Savior ("the natural man") can't understand the things of God, because those truths are spiritually discerned, and the natural man doesn't have the Spirit. In contrast, those who know Christ as Savior ("the spiritual man") have access to the Spirit, and so can understand spiritual truth. Evangelicals know and affirm this. But wait: Don't the gospel of Christ's atonement for our sins and our need to accept him as Savior qualify as "spiritual truths"? But then, if someone without Christ can't understand spiritual truth, and if the gospel is spiritual truth, why witness to her or give her a copy of the Gospel of John to read? Since she doesn't have the Spirit, won't reading John be futile, like trying to make sense of gibberish?

Next, evangelicals typically espouse Scripture's perspicuity. Perspicuity means that Scripture's basic content, especially its message about being saved and living a godly life, is understandable by everyone, regardless of education, exegetical skill, and even spiritual condition. If so, why does anyone need illumination at all? Some passages are difficult, and the Spirit's help would be greatly appreciated, but if Scripture is perspicuous, then for most of it, why does anyone need illumination?

---

act of uttering something, the *locutionary act*. Second, there is the act of "doing x" (warning, promising, informing, etc.) by uttering something, the *illocutionary act*. And third, there is the listener's response, which is called the *perlocutionary act*. Of course, a speaker expects and wants a certain response (perlocution), but listeners don't always respond as hoped.

[2] In some cases, the doctrine gets unusually short shrift. For example, J. Oliver Buswell discusses it briefly amid his treatment of the effectual call to salvation. His point is that illumination isn't equivalent to the effectual call. But he does not then explain what illumination is or how it works, nor does he seem to cover it in the rest of his systematic theology (J. Oliver Buswell, *A Systematic Theology of the Christian Religion*, vol. 2 [Grand Rapids, MI: Zondervan, 1963], 165–166). My point is not to castigate Buswell but rather to note how little coverage this doctrine often receives. See the same minimal coverage in Wayne Grudem's *Systematic Theology: An Introduction to Biblical Doctrine* (Grand Rapids, MI: Zondervan, 1994), 644–645, 1041–1042. Louis Berkhof, *Systematic Theology*, 4th ed. (Grand Rapids, MI: Eerdmans, 1968), doesn't even have a distinct discussion of Scripture, so of course, illumination gets no coverage.

Some may think these questions are ill-formed and unnecessary. After all, "the evangelical consensus" through the centuries has been that illumination is the Spirit's ministry to help readers understand what Scripture means and obey it.[3] Fine, but what does it mean to understand Scripture? Are we talking about interpretation, discerning how the text applies to people in general today, or convicting the reader that the text is relevant to him? Or does "understanding Scripture" involve something quite different?

Even more, is Scripture's meaning what the author wanted to say (illocutionary act), what he intended to say (his illocutionary act) by what he said (his locutionary act), or the response he wanted to evoke (its perlocution)? And if *understanding* what Scripture *means* is about uncovering the author's meaning, does that make training in biblical languages unnecessary, because the Holy Spirit by illumination will transfer to the mind what the text means? If by the Spirit's illumination anyone can grasp the intellectual content of Scripture, why should students pay tuition for courses intended to teach them the biblical languages, exegesis, and theology?

Clearly, this doctrine is more complicated than many think. By some personal stories I can further show the need for careful attention to this doctrine. I was raised in a Christian home and constantly heard (in church especially) illumination mentioned in a certain way. I adopted what seemed to be the concept of illumination commonly held by Christians. Later in my education something happened that raised questions about my understanding of illumination.

How was illumination understood at my church? On the basis of 1 Corinthians 2:14, pastors would repeatedly say that nonbelievers can't understand anything spiritual, so they can't understand Scripture. Believers can, because they have the Holy Spirit to explain it to them. The impression sometimes given was that reading difficult passages might be like reading a foreign language. Though we don't understand what we read, after praying for the Spirit's illumination we read the passages again and can understand them. Exactly how the Holy Spirit does this was never explained, but that he does it was always emphatically affirmed.

Occasionally something else happened that apparently confirmed this view of illumination. On a given Sunday, the pastor would say that he really struggled with preparing his sermon. He had a very difficult week, and couldn't work on his sermon until the end of the week. By Saturday night, he would say, he hadn't written a word of his sermon, so he spent time in prayer, asking God to show him what to preach. After praying for some time, the Lord gave him a message. He then began to preach the sermon he said the Holy Spirit

---

[3] Here see Zuber's "consensus definition" of illumination, gleaned from Calvin, John Owen, Charles Hodge, Lewis S. Chafer, Clark Pinnock, Carl F. H. Henry, Millard Erickson, et al. Zuber presents the definition on page 51 of Kevin Zuber, *What Is Illumination?* (PhD diss., Trinity Evangelical Divinity School, 1996).

had given him. The impression this story gives (and I've heard it from several pastors) is that even when one's mind draws a blank, with prayer for illumination, sometimes the Holy Spirit will transfer a message to our minds when we have to preach but don't know what to say. Of course, the Holy Spirit doesn't do this for unbelievers, because, being unspiritual, they can't understand even one verse of Scripture, let alone a whole message. Why would the Holy Spirit transfer a message to their minds?

This understanding of the Holy Spirit's illumination went unchallenged in my thinking for years. It seemed to square with Scripture, and the Christians I heard talk about illumination said nothing to the contrary. Then, I went to college at a secular university. My brother and sister had gone to the same school some years before I entered, and they advised me to take some history courses from a particular professor whom they thought was outstanding. Of course, in one's first two years of college, most classes meet general education requirements, and he didn't teach any of those, so I planned to take him during my final two years. During my sophomore year, however, I learned that this professor would be leaving soon, so I had to take something from him or I would miss him completely.

Most of his courses were electives for history majors—I majored in English—and I didn't see how I was ready for them. But before he left the university, he did teach a course in Reformation History. Here was something I could understand, and it would be interesting to get a nonbeliever's perspective on the topic. I enrolled in the class.

Of course, I had low expectations, because everything I had been told about the professor said that he wasn't a believer. Holding the view of illumination described above, I was certain that he wouldn't do a good job in describing the theologies of Luther and Calvin, because their theologies involved spiritual truth, and, I had been taught, nonbelievers can't understand such things. But I thought he would be very good at presenting the social, political, economic, etc., circumstances that influenced Luther to do what he did and that convinced ordinary people to pay attention to the Reformers' message.

As the professor described these "secular" influences that led to the Reformation, I enjoyed the lectures immensely! I was absolutely thrilled (though I didn't tell anyone) because I saw God's hand so clearly in history as my professor described the political, etc., situation in Germany in Luther's day. The day finally came when the lecture would be about Luther's theology. I doubted that these lectures would be of any value, because the teacher wasn't a believer, and the subject was "spiritual things." I decided to attend anyway, thinking it would be interesting to hear how badly a nonbelieving "natural man" would warp the doctrinal teaching of Luther and Calvin.

Not long into the first lecture on Luther's theology, I sat in class in total shock. By the end of the lecture, that didn't change. And later, when he lectured on Calvin's theology, I was even more dumbfounded! This man explained the theologies of Luther and Calvin more clearly and understandably than most Christians I had ever met. My first thought was, "how can he, a nonbeliever, know this and explain it so well, including the different nuances between Luther's and Calvin's theologies?" My second thought was that perhaps I was wrong about his being a nonbeliever, a "natural man." Later, I may have even asked my brother and sister if they were sure he wasn't a believer. I mentally marshaled all the evidence I knew and concluded that he couldn't be a believer. But then, the nagging question persisted: as a nonbeliever, he can't know these things, but he does. How is that possible?

Some time later, I began to wonder if the concept of illumination I had been taught was wrong. I couldn't think of any other rational way to explain what I experienced in that history class. But I had little idea of what "a correct view of illumination" might be, in contrast to the view I'd grown up believing. I graduated from college, went to seminary, and later did doctoral work. Eventually, I began teaching. Over all of those years my views on illumination had been changing, and I thought I had figured out the way the doctrine should be understood. When I taught my new understanding, students were at first a bit skeptical. But as I explained the reasoning in support of what I presented, students eventually saw my point.

Some years later, I was privileged to mentor a doctoral dissertation written by Kevin Zuber. The topic was the doctrine of illumination—specifically, he wanted to discover what illumination, as taught in Scripture, actually is. As Kevin worked his exegetical way through various passages on illumination, I saw my understanding of illumination confirmed first, and then expanded a bit. Though this chapter sets forth my own understanding of the doctrine in my own words, it relies heavily on Kevin Zuber's dissertation, *What Is Illumination?*[4]

In what follows, I want first to make some points about illumination that will help readers understand the discussion that follows. Next, I shall offer some definitions and distinctions that will help as we think through this concept. Following Zuber's lead, I'll present what he calls the "consensus definition of illumination" among Christian thinkers in our day. Of course, theologians do much more than define the doctrine; they also cite Scriptures in support of the doctrine. In the latter portion of this chapter, we shall examine these passages and then make a judgment about whether to affirm the "consensus definition" or not. If not, a modified definition will need to be worked out.

---

[4] Zuber, *What Is Illumination?*, 199.

## Preliminary Considerations

### Introductory Points about Illumination

As an introduction, I offer four major points. *First, we must clearly distinguish illumination from revelation and inspiration.* Illumination adds nothing to Scripture's content, nor is it any form of *revelation*. In addition, illumination has nothing to do with the transfer of divine revelation into written form—i.e., it isn't *inspiration*. Instead, illumination helps with understanding revelation, including both natural and special revelation. As a result, illumination relates more to interpreting revelation than to the unveiling and/or inscripturating of revelation. Illumination helps us grasp or understand divine revelation. Of course, what it means to grasp or understand revelation and what it means for divine revelation to have a meaning must be explained, and I shall do so as we proceed.

*Second, what needs to be illumined?* It is tempting to say that Scripture needs to be and is illumined by the Holy Spirit. Of course, we might also think that other forms of divine revelation may need to be illumined, too. Can one grasp, for example, natural revelation's meaning without divine illumination? And, before Scripture was written, did no one need any help in grasping the content of natural and special revelation? That seems highly unlikely.

While the idea that Scripture needs divine illumination is very common among Christians (and probably won't go away anytime soon, if at all), I propose that revelation doesn't actually need illumination. Revelation is divine light unveiled and communicated to humanity. Light doesn't need to be illumined, for it is, by definition, already illumined. If not, how could it be light? No, what needs illumination are the human mind and heart. As we shall see, humans need light for various reasons, but the most obvious is the moral and spiritual darkness of sin that enshrouds our minds and hearts. Whether the content of revelation is the natural universe, God's direct speech to someone, dreams, visions, miracles, the incarnate God-man Jesus Christ, or Scripture, spiritual and moral blindness keep us from understanding what God is saying to us. Without divine light shining in our minds and hearts, revelation's message will likely escape us.

*Third, in light of the above, and in light of scriptural teaching relevant to illumination, we can also say that Scripture is the objective revelation with regard to which human minds are most frequently illumined by the Holy Spirit. Even more fundamentally, our minds are illumined to any spiritual truth,* i.e., any information relevant to understanding divine revelation about God and our relationship to him. Of course, when we think of spiritual truth, we immediately think that the largest deposit of it is in Scripture. However, before Scripture was written, God revealed himself to people in various ways (see the chapters on revelation). And even after Scripture was written and disseminated, God still can and does reveal himself to people in many ways. There is no reason to think humans need no illumination for such revelation whereas they need it for Scripture. Spiritually blind minds and hearts require illumination to understand any spiritual truth, regardless of the form it takes.

Putting together my second and third points, we can say that the Holy Spirit illumines human minds and hearts to understand divine revelation, regardless of its form. *Of course, the need for illumination presupposes that there is darkness that needs to be overcome.* Specifically, what kinds of darkness must the Spirit's light penetrate if humans are to grasp God's revelation? Scripture points us to *four different types of blindness.* First, there is the blindness that falls upon all people as a result of living in a fallen world, having a sin nature, and following the dictates of that sin nature. This kind of blindness besets everyone without a personal relationship by faith with God. Romans 5:12 says that all people inherited Adam's sin and have a sin nature. In Ephesians 4:17–18, Paul urges his readers not to walk according to the lifestyle of the heathen, for they walk in darkness. The darkness results from the sin they commit; that is, Paul isn't talking about physical light or darkness.[5] Likewise, John speaks of the moral condition of the world into which Jesus came as one of spiritual darkness or blindness (John 1:5). In 1 John 1:5–6, the apostle writes that anyone who claims to have a relationship with God and yet disobeys God's commands is a liar and actually lives in darkness (spiritual). In 1 John 2, John repeats this point, specifically focusing on the command to love others. John emphatically states (2:9–11) that anyone who hates his brother lives in spiritual darkness and doesn't know where he is going. In contrast, those who love their brother walk in God's light.

Perhaps we can call this blindness *natural blindness,* as long as we understand that it refers to the sin nature that all of us have from Adam and that we ratify by our acts of sin. A second kind of blindness needing divine illumination can be labeled *Satanic blindness.* While Satan, of course, encourages people to sin and deceives people about God's truth in general, he expends special effort to blind men and women to one central truth. Speaking about the gospel, Paul says that if his gospel is veiled, it is veiled to the perishing (2 Cor. 4:3). He immediately says of them (v. 4),

> in whose case the god of this world has blinded the minds of the unbelieving, that they might not see the light of the gospel of the glory of Christ, who is the image of God.

---

[5] Though he uses different imagery, Paul speaks of a life without Christ as one that is a bondslave to sin (Rom. 6:16–18). Believers are free from sin as their master, and Christ is their new master. Though the imagery of slavery versus freedom differs from that of darkness and light, the concept is the same.

Surely, Paul thinks that "the god of this world" or "age" is Satan. Paul doesn't mean that Satan attacks no other spiritual truth. Rather, his point is that Satan is especially eager to blind people to the truth of the gospel. If he succeeds, then, using Johannine terminology, they will remain "children of the devil" and won't become "children of God" (see 1 John 3 for this distinction).

A third kind of blindness requiring illumination can be called *carnal blindness*. Paul speaks of it in 1 Corinthians 3:1–3, and it is quite important that he does. In chapter 2 Paul distinguishes the "natural man" from the "spiritual man." Only the "spiritual man" can understand spiritual truth (1 Cor. 2:14–15), because that person has the Spirit of God. This might suggest that, once one accepts Christ as personal Savior, God's revelation will always be clear, regardless of whether the believer walks in righteousness or not.

However, Paul shows (at the start of chapter 3) that even people who know God by faith in Christ can live in spiritual darkness. Paul addresses his readers as "brethren," those whom he calls "babes in Christ." Paul uses the terms "brethren" and "in Christ" repeatedly in his writings to refer to those who are saved. However, Paul's message to the Corinthians is not complimentary. He says that he can't address them as spiritual *men* but as *babies*. He can't teach them truths that metaphorically could be called "meat," for they can't "digest" it; he can only give them "milk."

Why is this so? In verse 3ff. Paul explains. They are "carnal" or "fleshly." What does this mean? Paul immediately turns to "exhibit A" of their carnality. In the church at Corinth there were jealousies and strife. Paul mentions (vv. 4–9) the factions in the Corinthian church that had arisen around allegiance to its founder, Paul, and to a significant pastor in the church's history, Apollos. The church at Corinth is God's church, not Paul's or Apollos's. Splitting the church over allegiance to one pastor or another shows their spiritual immaturity and sinfulness.

What does this passage teach about carnal Christians? The carnality of these Corinthians centered on their petty jealousies and strife, and such things are, of course, sin. Presumably, any sin in a believer's life that is unconfessed and is still tolerated evidences carnality.

Hebrews 5 is also relevant here. The writer's aim is to instruct his readers about Jesus, and to tell them that Jesus is a priest of the order of Melchizedek. In verse 11 he adds that he has much more to say but he cannot do so because his readers are dull of hearing. What does he mean? Verses 12–14, in language reminiscent of 1 Corinthians 3:1–2, explain that the Christians addressed should by now have mastered the elementary items of the faith so that they could teach new Christians, but instead, they aren't ready yet for "solid food" but can only handle "milk." The writer doesn't explain what sin or sins have kept them from growing, but it is hard to imagine that their lack of growth in no way relates to sin—even if the sin is merely failing to attend to God's truth and instead leading their lives on their own terms and standards.[6]

What can we conclude from these passages? Initially we can see that, just because someone is saved, that doesn't mean that he or she can't and won't ever sin again. By sinning, a believer doesn't lose salvation, but sin definitely blocks fellowship with God. Just as a son can never cease to be his father's son, and yet he can do things that make his father angry and strain their relationship, so also, once we are saved by faith in Christ, although we can never lose our spiritual "sonship," disobeying God's word angers him and breaks our fellowship with him.

Does sin in a believer's life have any result other than a strained relationship with God? Indeed, it does. Sin is a sign of spiritual immaturity (1 Cor. 3:1–3) and lack of growth. Do such things hamper a believer's ability to grasp the light of God's revealed truth? Of course they do, just as Paul showed how nonbelievers, by rejecting God's truth and falling deeper into sin, had their minds darkened further to spiritual truth (Romans 1).

So, it is possible to be saved and still have unconfessed sin in our lives. Scripture calls that condition carnality. Carnality hinders fellowship with God, and it is hard to imagine that such sin won't hinder our ability to understand spiritual truth. Sin blinds nonbelievers' minds and hearts, and it does the same to believers. Hence, Christians can suffer from *carnal blindness*, and need the Spirit's illumining work in their minds and hearts. But first, the Spirit needs to shine God's light on a believer's mind and heart to move him or her to confess sin and to seek renewed fellowship with God.

A final type of blindness requiring divine illumination can be labeled *Israel's blindness*. Though the people of Israel have possessed the "oracles of God" (Rom. 3:2), through much of their history they have for the most part rejected God's truth. As a result, in Romans 11:25 Paul speaks of a "blindness" (KJV) on Israel. It is a judicial blindness or, if you will, a divine judgment, that God has placed upon the majority of the nation, most specifically because she has rejected Jesus as her Messiah and Savior.

Note, however, two key points in Romans 11:25. This blindness is *partial* and it is *temporary*. Paul says this blindness has fallen on part of the nation, and we must grant that it is the largest part of the nation. But, during the NT era there is still a remnant according to grace, including Paul, who have accepted Jesus as Messiah and Savior (Rom. 11:5). The blindness is also temporary, because Paul says it will last only until "the fullness of the Gentiles has

[6]See here Leon Morris, *Hebrews*, in *EBC*, ed. Frank E. Gaebelein, vol. 12 (Grand Rapids, MI: Zondervan, 1982); B. F. Westcott, *The Epistle to the Hebrews* (Grand Rapids, MI: Eerdmans, 1967); and James Moffatt, *A Critical and Exegetical Commentary of the Epistle to the Hebrews*, ICC (Edinburgh: T&T Clark, 1963).

come in," and then "all Israel" will be saved.[7] Since this blindness is spiritual blindness to the truth about Israel's Messiah, it is most reasonable to assume that the blindness requires the Holy Spirit's illumination to lift it.

This brief discussion of types of spiritual blindness shows that the doctrine of illumination is not only an important theological component of the doctrine of Scripture, but also critically important to everyone's spiritual understanding and growth. For example, the reality of Satanic blindness should help Christians understand why, when they witness to unsaved friends and present the gospel as plainly as possible, their friends may be disinterested, unmoved, or perhaps even robustly opposed to what they hear.

## Definition of Key Terms

Definitions intend to clarify concepts, so defining illumination should do just that. However, the typical way of defining illumination often introduces greater ambiguity than it removes. Roughly, illumination is a ministry of the Holy Spirit whereby he helps people understand or grasp the meaning of divine revelation. Most frequently, the form of revelation in view is Scripture. But what does it mean to "grasp" or "understand" Scripture? Even more fundamentally, what is this "meaning" that illumination helps people grasp? The concepts "understand" and "meaning" in this definition are ambiguous, and to make headway in elucidating the concept of illumination, we must define the various senses of each.

*What Does "Meaning" Mean?*—Several things come to mind here, especially in connection with divine illumination. A most basic sense of "meaning" points to a term's *sense* and *reference*. The sense of a word is its dictionary definition. If you look up the word in a dictionary, you will see various things a term can be used to designate or denote. A word's sense sets forth the characteristics the thing in view must have to qualify as an instance of the item in question. Apart from a term's use in a specific sentence, it *refers* to a broad class of things that have the characteristics stated in the definition, but it doesn't focus on just one specific thing. When a word is used in a sentence, it does refer to something specific. That thing may be an object, an action, a concept, etc., that has the qualities that all other objects, etc., of this sort possess. So, for example, when

---

[7] What the "fullness of the Gentiles" and "all Israel" mean, and when and under what circumstances "all Israel" will be saved, is more properly discussed in ecclesiology and eschatology. My own understanding, though this isn't the place to make the case, is that the fullness of the Gentiles refers to God's program during this current age of calling both Jews and Gentiles from the nations of the world to form his church. The "fullness" will happen when all those whom God plans to include in his church receive Christ. Then, at the end time (after the fullness of the Gentiles, but no one knows exactly how long after), God will turn his attention back to national Israel. He will save the nation as a whole, living at the end time (Rom. 11:25ff.), when he returns to set up his kingdom (Matt. 24:29–31ff.). Of course, this interpretation of Romans 11:25–27 is controversial (as are other interpretations), but these are my answers to the questions raised in this note.

someone mentions Jesus's miracle of turning water into wine, we must know the sense of terms like "miracle," "water," "wine," and of actions such as turning one thing into another. But beyond the sense of these terms, a sentence that uses them refers to a particular event that happened at a specific place and time. There might be other instances of turning water into wine (though we don't know of them), but my sentence *refers* to what Jesus did at a wedding feast in Cana of Galilee.

One determines the sense and reference of a sentence, paragraph, or document by using literal-grammatical-historical hermeneutics to uncover what the author intended to say. In this sense of meaning—let us call it *sense and reference*[1]—understanding the meaning of a passage is understanding the intellectual content the author wanted to communicate when he or she wrote. Put differently, this kind of meaning refers to grasping the author's illocutionary act by means of the locutionary act he performed in the written or oral context in question (i.e., what he *intended* to say by what he said). When the Holy Spirit illumines the reader's mind to a passage's meaning, is the passage's sense and reference[1] in view, or something else?

There is a second sense and reference—call it *sense and reference*[2]—of a passage's meaning. Using principles of exegesis, one uncovers the sense and reference[1] of a number of Scripture passages. Still, the reader doesn't quite grasp what all the passages taken together mean. While reflecting on the various data one knows, all of a sudden (or perhaps less suddenly) "the light goes on" as the interpreter "sees" how all of the passages (and the facts, concepts, etc.) fit together. The sense and reference[2] of Scripture becomes clear.

A biblical example of this is the "opening of the eyes" of Jesus's disciples as he walked with them on the road to Emmaus (Luke 24). The disciples knew various things about the Messiah from the OT. In addition, Jesus had taught them many things. In one sense they "got" what he said, but in another, they "didn't get it." They knew the meaning of various Scripture passages and of various teachings of Jesus, but in a sense, they knew these data in isolation from one another (or at least in enough isolation so that they didn't grasp the full significance of what they knew). As a result, they didn't see these data as identifying Jesus as the Messiah, and as teaching that the Messiah would die and then rise again. As Jesus talked with them, reminding them of things he had said and of OT teachings they knew, they suddenly came to see the data in a new way—that is, the data formed for them a different conceptual gestalt about who Jesus was and about what had happened in recent days. Now they not only knew the sense and reference[1] of various Scripture passages, but they also grasped how all the data fit together, and they realized that they were talking with the risen Christ! They went from being intellectually aware of various distinct data to "getting" what the data pointed to—that is, they moved from understanding the sense and reference[1] of various isolated things to seeing the meaning, the sense and reference[2], of it all. Does the Holy Spirit's illumination of Scripture involve divulging its sense and reference[2]?

There is a third sense in which meaning may refer to sense and reference, though this is seldom discussed in treatments of divine illumination. Suppose that someone wants to formulate a theology of a given topic. Sense and reference[1] and [2] will likely be involved in this process, but even more happens. If a doctrine is correct, it cannot contradict another doctrine that is demonstrably true. While doctrines are not identical, many are interconnected—e.g., what you say about divine sovereign control of the world has significant implications for your understanding of human free will. In fact, a good way to test a doctrinal claim is to see if it generates a contradiction with other doctrines the theologian holds. Here one is determining the meaning of a system of doctrine, or perhaps just of a part of the system. By doing this sort of synthetic work, one is grasping the meaning, i.e., the sense and reference, of a system of truths. Let us call this sort of meaning *sense and reference*[3]. While theologians seldom think the doctrine of illumination is at work at this level of theological formulation, it is worth asking whether divine illumination might help in formulating the "meaning" (sense and reference[3]) of a part of a system (or of a whole system) of doctrine.

From the preceding, we can say that the notion of meaning is ambiguous. Unfortunately, it is even more ambiguous than already suggested. This is so because a text's or an oral statement's meaning may refer to how the claims made *apply* to anyone's situation today. "Meaning" in this sense is not so much about the author's sense and reference, but about the "message" one takes from what was said and applies to one's life. In speech act analysis terminology, this sense of "meaning" has more to do with perlocution than with locution or illocution. Some scholars distinguish this broad sense of meaning from the emphasis on sense and reference by calling the latter sense of "meaning" *meaning*, and the former sense *significance*. Whatever terminology one uses, hopefully the difference between a claim's sense and reference and its application is clear.

Even if the distinction between meaning and application is clear, things become murkier because there are several senses of the application of a sentence's, verse's, etc., meaning. How a concept or teaching impacts another doctrine/concept (theoretical application) or some practical life issue in general is an initial kind of application—let us call it *application*[1]. Even if no one makes the application to a specific life, the principle taught could be applied in the way suggested.

There is a second kind of application—label it *application*[2]. In this case, one asks not just for the implications (theoretical and especially practical) for life in general, but seeks to learn how the principle taught tells *me* to change *my* behavior, philosophy of life, etc. If one uses "meaning" in either sense of application to articulate what illumination is, then when the Holy Spirit illumines my mind to a text's meaning, that means that either he shows me the practical applications in general of the text's truth, or he helps me see how I should personally change in light of what the text teaches. Even if I conclude, on the basis of the passage(s) under study, that I should make a change that no one else needs to make, still that application must be shown to be logically connected to what the text teaches (i.e., "if the text teaches x, then I should do z"). So, for example, if a text, properly interpreted, teaches that one's life should be about helping and serving others, not about accumulating wealth, then perhaps I should seek a new job that meets my basic financial needs while leaving me time to volunteer for community service. That specific application might apply to no one else, but it is a concrete way for me to follow the general principle about a proper view toward wealth and toward serving others.

So far, the different senses of "meaning" as sense and reference and "meaning" as application have focused mostly on objective things. That is, determining the meaning in most of these senses involves analyzing the data of the text, putting the teaching of texts together, and choosing applications that are relevant ways of putting into practice what the text teaches. Anyone who knows the rules of interpretation and of logical implication should be able to discover the "meaning" of the text in any of these senses. Of course, application[2] is more individualistic to a specific person, but even so, it must be an implication of the text. Moreover, even if one discovers an appropriate application for oneself, that doesn't guarantee that the interpreter will commit to live what the text teaches, and actually start doing so.

*What Is the Meaning of "Understand"?*—The key question for our study is whether the Holy Spirit illumines the reader's mind to grasp Scripture's meaning in any of the senses mentioned above. But we must first define what it means to *understand* a text's meaning. Here again there is ambiguity, for there are several senses in which one could understand a text's meaning.

An initial sense deals with grasping the intellectual content of the text. That is, understanding in this sense—call it *understanding*[1] (the verbal form is *understand*[1])—concerns intellectually grasping the sense and reference of a sentence, passage, chapter, book in any and all of the three senses of sense and reference detailed above. This, of course, is a purely intellectual maneuver, and if illumination is needed to understand the content, then to some extent illumination would transfer information to the interpreter's mind that he didn't previously have in mind or understand[1].

A second sense of understanding—label it *understanding²*—correlates with application¹. In this case the reader intellectually grasps how the text's teaching might impact the practical living of life. Such a connection to living one's life is a general one that would be true for anyone, regardless of circumstance or situation. Then, a third sense in which one might grasp the message of a text corresponds to application². That is, this kind of understanding (*understanding³*) involves coming to see how the teaching of a sentence, passage, book, etc., applies specifically to *my* life.

So far, all of these senses of "understand" and "understanding" deal with purely intellectual, cognitive matters. In fact, the second and third senses rest on the first sense of understanding. If not, there is little hope that the practical applications one derives will have anything to do with what the text actually means (for any of meaning¹, meaning², or meaning³). It is, of course, quite possible for someone to understand the text in all three senses of "understanding," and yet refuse to do what understanding³ requires. In fact, if one understands¹ a text's demands and also the consequences for disobeying, one might make a special point to refuse to change one's behavior. Nothing said so far guarantees that knowing application² will result in making any changes in one's life.

If understanding the meaning of a text involves only the items so far defined, then the Holy Spirit's illumining ministry involves only the intellect. It doesn't guarantee behavior change, and thus, nothing defined so far guarantees that revelation will be applied to living. Hence, we need a fourth sense of understanding—*understanding⁴*. To understand⁴ a text means that one commits one's self to obey its teaching—specifically, application², based at least on meaning¹ and meaning².

This fourth sense of understanding involves persuasion, but not persuasion that tries to make an objective case for some truth. Rather it involves becoming subjectively certain that something is correct, and as a result, committing one's life to live what one believes is true. If the Holy Spirit's illumination involves understanding⁴, then certain things follow. The apostle Paul wrote in Romans 8:9 that those in whom the Spirit dwells are in the Spirit. Even more, if someone doesn't have the Spirit of Christ, he doesn't belong to Christ. He or she lives according to the flesh. In 8:13 Paul adds that if you live according to the flesh, you will certainly die, but if you live by the Spirit, you put to death the deeds of the body, and you will live. You are a child of God (v. 14).

Given what Paul says in Romans 8, we can understand better what he says in 1 Corinthians 2:10–16. Verse 10 says that the Holy Spirit has revealed things that eyes have not seen and ears have not heard—the deep things of God. The Holy Spirit can do this, because no one knows a person's mind and heart better than his spirit does, and similarly, no one knows God's mind and heart better than his Spirit, who is the Holy Spirit (v. 11). What Paul says next (v. 12) is crucial: believers have not received the spirit of this world, but the Holy Spirit, so that we might *know* the things given us by God. Now it is clear (if it wasn't already clear from Romans 8) that "the natural man" (v. 14) is the person who doesn't possess God's Spirit; the Spirit doesn't dwell in her and she thus doesn't belong to Christ (Rom. 8:9). She is not saved. In contrast, the "spiritual man" (1 Cor. 2:15) has the Spirit, and so the Spirit dwells in him, and he does belong to Christ (Rom. 8:9).

Do "natural men," without divine enablement, want to obey God's truth? Of course not. That's a major part of Paul's indictment in Romans 1–3 of both Jews and Gentiles. No one is righteous, no one understands, no one even seeks God; not even one person does good (Rom. 3:10–12). All have sinned and come short of God's glory (Rom. 3:23), and the natural man doesn't understand or seek God and his remedy for our condemned estate.

If we use understand[4] when we speak of understanding Scripture, is it any wonder, then, that from what we saw in Romans 3 and 8, the natural man doesn't understand[4] the things of God and they seem foolish to him (1 Cor. 2:14)? This doesn't mean that "understand" in 1 Corinthians 2:14 can only be "understand[4]"—so far we haven't even shown that it should be understood at least in that sense in 1 Corinthians 2:14. All I am now suggesting is that there is this fourth sense of "understand," and if it is in view in 1 Corinthians 2:14–15, it would make sense of what Paul says. It would also help us understand some of what the Holy Spirit's ministry of illumination involves.

In sum, the concepts of meaning and understanding are quite ambiguous. We have defined five different senses of meaning, three that deal with determining the sense and reference of language, and two that deal with applying a text. We also isolated four different senses of understanding, three of which deal with grasping the intellectual content and application of a text and one that deals with moving one's will to obey. As suggested above, sin and not being a believer can result in refusing to understand[4] Scripture. It may also hamper our ability to understand Scripture in the first three senses of "understand," but then, bad hermeneutics or poor application of good hermeneutics may also cause failure to understand Scripture in the first three senses of "understand."

Of course, we want to know whether the Spirit's illumination helps us understand the meaning of revelation. Of all the things that meaning can mean, does the Holy Spirit illumine our minds to grasp intellectually any of them? Of all the things "understand" can mean, does the Holy Spirit illumine our minds and hearts to understand revelation in any of those senses of "understand"? Clearly, defining illumination is complicated, especially because the biblical writers don't explicitly say what sense of "meaning" and "understanding" they have in view.

## DEFINING ILLUMINATION

Before proposing a definition, I should clarify what is not in view in this chapter. First, at issue is not the internal witness or testimony of the Holy Spirit. Calvin seems to have been the theologian who first introduced this notion into Christian theology. He discussed it in several places in the *Institutes*, and he firmly believed that Scripture teaches it.[8] Oddly, however, his discussion in the *Institutes* offers little Scripture support for it. Still, the concept is prevalent in Reformed circles, appearing in the Westminster Confession of Faith (1646), chapter 1, section 5.

According to Calvin, there are two sources of testimony to Scripture's authority and truthfulness. First, there are various external witnesses, arguments, and evidences, so to speak, of Scripture's uniqueness and verity.[9] In addition, the Holy Spirit testifies or witnesses internally to the mind (presumably, this happens for believers, but Calvin isn't clear about whether it could also happen to unbelievers) that Scripture is God's word, fully authoritative, and true. For Calvin, the Spirit's testimony is one aspect of his illumining work. That is how many Calvin scholars understand him,[10] and the reason is evident in the following passage in which illumination and the Spirit's internal witness seem joined together:

> . . . those whom the Holy Spirit has inwardly taught truly rest upon Scripture, and . . . Scripture indeed is self-authenticated; hence, it is not right to subject it to proof and reasoning. And the certainty it deserves with us, it attains by the testimony of the Spirit. For even if it wins reverence for itself by its own majesty, it seriously affects us only when it is sealed upon our hearts through the Spirit. Therefore, illumined by his power, we believe neither by our own nor by anyone else's judgment that Scripture is from God; but above human judgment we affirm with utter certainty (just as if we were gazing upon the majesty of God himself) that it has flowed to us from the very mouth of God by the ministry of men.[11]

In an insightful monograph on the Spirit's internal witness, Bernard Ramm discussed this notion at length. At times the concept under discussion sounds like illumination, especially as Ramm offers biblical support for it.[12] At other times Ramm seems to distinguish the *testimonium* from the Spirit's illumina-

---

[8] John Calvin, *Institutes of the Christian Religion*, ed. John T. McNeill, trans. Ford Lewis Battles (Philadelphia: Westminster, 1967), 78–81 (1.7.4–5).

[9] Ibid., 81–92 (1.8.1–13).

[10] See, e.g., Fred Klooster, "The Role of the Holy Spirit in the Hermeneutic Process: The Relationship of the Spirit's Illumination to Biblical Interpretation," in *Hermeneutics, Inerrancy, and the Bible*, ed. Earl D. Radmacher and Robert D. Preus (Grand Rapids, MI: Zondervan, 1984), 452; and Bernard Ramm's *The Witness of the Spirit* (Grand Rapids, MI: Eerdmans, 1959).

[11] Calvin, *Institutes*, 80 (1.7.5).

[12] Ramm, *Witness of the Spirit*, chapter 4.

tion.[13] If the internal witness of the Spirit is given by divine illumination, we must at least distinguish it from the concept of illumination presented so far in this chapter. This is so because convincing the reader that Scripture is true and from God in no way explains what the text means, nor does it guarantee that the recipient of the witness will apply the text's truth to his or her life. For our purposes, in this chapter, I won't further discuss the Spirit's internal witness to Scripture's truth and authority.

Second, illumination as understood in evangelical theology isn't the concept it once was. As far back as Plato, the idea that enlightenment is necessary to understand anything, not just religious truth, was introduced into Western thought. The first Christian theologian to adopt this belief seems to have been Augustine, relying heavily on Neoplatonism. According to these views, in God's mind are the forms of all things. For humans to know any specific concept or particular instance of a thing, God has to illumine the human mind to know the universal, the form, so as to understand the particular.[14]

During the Middle Ages, an Augustinian version of illumination held sway among many Christian theologians and philosophers. However, once Aristotle was reintroduced into Western thinking, the idea of needing illumination to know nonreligious truth was abandoned.[15]

As for the concept in evangelical theology, Kevin Zuber presents the definition of illumination one finds in many theologians. He offers definitions from Calvin, John Owen, Charles Hodge, L. S. Chafer, Clark Pinnock, Carl F. H. Henry, and Millard Erickson, to name just a few.[16] From these sources, Zuber crystallizes what he labels the consensus definition of illumination:

> Illumination is a work of the Holy Spirit, whereby the hearer or reader of the Word of God, either a believer or an unbeliever, is given understanding of the information contained in it and brought to appropriate its meaning.[17]

Note several things about this definition. First, it seems to limit illumination to Scripture alone. Presumably, illumination won't help anyone understand natural revelation, nor would it be relevant (or needed) when divine revelation other than Scripture is under consideration. But why, for example, should people need illumination when reading the Gospel accounts

---

[13] See ibid., 33–34, 54, and 66, where he seems to distinguish illumination from the testimony of the Spirit. However, through most of the book the two are conflated, and Scriptures often cited for illumination are used as evidences of the *testimonium*.

[14] Gareth B. Matthews, "Knowledge and Illumination," in *The Cambridge Companion to Augustine*, ed. Eleonore Stump and Norman Kretzmann (Cambridge: Cambridge University Press, 2001); Rudolph Allers, "St. Augustine's Doctrine on Illumination," *Franciscan Studies* 12 (March 1952); and Lydia Schumacher, *Divine Illumination: The History and Future of Augustine's Theory of Knowledge* (Chicester, UK: Wiley-Blackwell, 2011).

[15] For further details see R. A. Markus, "Illumination," in *Encyclopedia of Philosophy*, ed. Paul Edwards, vol. 4 (New York: Macmillan, 1967), 129–130.

[16] Zuber, *What Is Illumination?*, 21–44.

[17] Ibid., 51.

of Jesus's teaching, but not need it if they had been present when Jesus gave the teaching?

Second, the consensus definition applies illumination to both believers and nonbelievers. Can a nonbeliever before conversion understand all spiritual truth, not just the gospel? Third, this definition claims that illumination helps the mind grasp the objective intellectual meaning of Scripture in at least the first sense of "meaning." Fourth, presumably, if Scripture's message is to be appropriated by the reader, illumination must also involve "meaning" in the two senses of application. Finally, the definition seems to require the Holy Spirit to be involved in the reader's mind and heart in all four senses of "understand." Otherwise, how could any human move his or her will (and do so freely) to obey what the intellectual content of Scripture demands?

Does Scripture support this concept of illumination and of the Holy Spirit's ministry? In the next section I want to examine carefully the passages most frequently cited in support of illumination.

## BIBLICAL TEACHING ON ILLUMINATION

### Psalm 119

Psalm 119 is about Scripture and about God's law in particular. Key verses are 12, 18, 33, and 108. The psalmist asks the Lord to teach him God's statutes (v. 12), to open his eyes to see wonderful things from God's law (v. 18), to teach him the way of God's statutes so that he can observe them to the end—presumably, the end of the psalmist's life (v. 33)—and to teach him the Lord's ordinances (v. 108). All of this is consistent with the famous verses 9 and 11. In verse 9, the psalmist asks how he can live a pure life, and answers that it can happen by living according to God's word. In verse 11, the psalmist adds that he personally has hidden God's word in his heart to keep from sinning. So, keeping one's way pure involves obeying God's word.

But what part of God's word must be "kept" to avoid sin? The answer is either implicit or explicit in verses 12, 18, 33, and 108. The part of God's word relevant to leading a pure life is God's law, specifically its moral rules (v. 15, its precepts; vv. 16, 33, its statutes; v. 108, its ordinances). As Zuber rightly explains, it would be unthinkable for the psalmist to request what these verses ask, if he didn't know the contents of the Mosaic law. So, he must have had access to it, and thus he wasn't asking God to reveal something he had never heard, read, or known.[18] Likewise, he wasn't asking God to inspire more Scripture; he wanted a deeper understanding of God's precepts, and help in obeying them (v. 33).

---

[18] Ibid., 54–55.

Verse 18 is the one verse in our list from Psalm 119 that doesn't clarify exactly which object(s) need to be understood. The psalmist asks the Lord to show him "wonderful things" (*niphla'oth*) from God's law. He doesn't say what those are, but as Franz Delitzsch explains, the Hebrew term involved "is the expression for everything supernatural and mysterious which is incomprehensible to the ordinary understanding and is left to the perception of faith."[19] Since the psalmist asks for insight into the law he already has, evidently some things are below the surface meaning of the law, and can be understood only with divine enablement. Since the writer doesn't say what those things are, we can't tell whether he refers to some hidden intellectual content that isn't clear to the naked eye, or whether he has something else in mind.

Also noteworthy is the fact that in many verses the psalmist asks the Lord to give him understanding (119:27, 34, 73, 125, 144, 169). The verb involved is *byn*, and its basic meaning is "to understand," "to perceive," or "to discern." In verses 34, 73, 125, 144, and 169 it appears in the Hiphil and has the causative sense of "cause me to understand" or "make me understand."[20] With the exception of verse 169, there is a result or purpose attached to the request for understanding. The psalmist wants to understand in order to "meditate on [God's] wonders" (v. 27), to "observe [God's] law" and "keep it" (v. 34), to "learn [God's] commandments" (v. 73), to "know [God's] testimonies" (v. 125), and to "live" (v. 144). Can these be requests for mere intellectual knowledge of precepts in God's law? Though the reasons given in verses 73 and 125 could be taken to mean that, it would be strange for the psalmist to make such a request, because he already has and intellectually knows God's commands. Even more, the reasons given in verses 27, 34, and 144 for wanting understanding seem to presuppose that the psalmist already knows what the statutes are; he asks God for something other than mere intellectual awareness of data. It is especially clear from verses 34 and 144 that the psalmist sees the understanding he requests, assuming God gives it, as helping him to obey God's law and live. According to verse 144, the psalmist knows that obeying God's commands leads to life; but that was already implicit in verses 9 and 11, so we shouldn't be surprised to read in verse 144 of the goal he hopes to achieve by receiving divine help in understanding. Hence, when he asks for understanding to learn God's commandments (v. 73) and to know God's testimonies (v. 125), he must be thinking of a kind of learning and knowing that are more than acquiring intellectual content he didn't previously know.

What kind of learning and knowing is this? Definitely more than propositional knowledge, cognitive awareness of data. Then, perhaps the psalmist

---

[19] Franz Delitzsch, *The Psalms*, vol. 5 in C. F. Keil and Franz Delitzsch, *Commentary on the Old Testament in Ten Volumes* (repr., Grand Rapids, MI: Eerdmans, 1975), 246, as quoted in Zuber, *What Is Illumination?*, 54.
[20] Zuber, *What Is Illumination?*, 61, 64.

wants experiential knowledge, that is, knowledge by personal experience, not just mere "head knowledge." But what does it mean to know God's law, statutes, ordinances experientially? Does he mean, for example, that he wants to be in a situation where he must tell the truth, but does not do so, and everything turns out horribly, so that then he will understand the importance of truth-telling? While this is possible, he probably already knows that, so he probably isn't requesting a chance to break divine rules so that he can see that they must be kept!

So, what kind of help does he want in relation to God's law? The key seems to be the repeated emphasis, especially in verses 33, 34, and 144, on obeying God's law. In verses 9 and 11, the psalmist shows that the way to avoid sin is to obey God's word, and in verse 11 he even says that he has hidden God's word in his heart in order to avoid sin. This is often understood to mean Scripture memorization, but verse 11 doesn't guarantee that someone who hides God word in his or her heart (by memorizing it or otherwise) will in fact obey it. If it did, why would the psalmist ask God to make him understand God's law so that he can obey it?

Something more than help in memorizing God's precepts must be in view, but what? The psalmist wants understanding so that he can obey, but earlier we saw that "understanding" is ambiguous. It could refer to something intellectual or cognitive, but it might also refer to something volitional. Since the psalmist isn't asking for propositional knowledge, he isn't thinking of understanding in the first sense of "understanding." What about the second sense, grasping how disparate parts of something fit together and what they mean as a whole? This is very unlikely, in part because the rules and precepts of God's law aren't at all hard to understand intellectually. There is no need for a "gestalt" experience where one sees them all at once in a new way and finally "gets it."

What about the third sense of "understand"? Here the psalmist would be asking for help in seeing how a precept applies to him, and for divine conviction that the precept does apply to him. This would require adding no new content to Scripture, but the psalmist would likely see intellectually things he hadn't seen before. But it is highly doubtful that the psalmist needs convincing that God's rules, like the Decalogue and the Leviticus Holiness Code (Leviticus 18 and 20), apply to him. If he didn't know that already, why would he ask for understanding to obey them?

So, the psalmist isn't likely asking for intellectual understanding of any sort. What about the fourth sense of "understanding," the volitional one? This sense refers to the will being moved to obey God's word. In light of his recurring request to understand so that he may obey, this is most likely what the psalmist wants. He understands that merely knowing God's rules guarantees nothing about obeying them. He also must know, because he asks God to "teach" him and to "make him understand" the law, that obedience isn't easy, even though it is necessary (v. 144). In asking God to teach him the law and in wanting to learn it, the psalmist is most likely asking for God's help in obeying it. It's as if the psalmist is saying, "Show me how to obey your law by helping me do so. I want to learn, but can't on my own."

How does this fit with verse 18? Perhaps the "wonderful thing" he wants to be shown is the fullness of life lived by God's empowerment to obey God's law. But perhaps not. Perhaps "law" in this verse doesn't focus narrowly on divine precepts but instead refers to all the Torah's teachings. Some of the Torah isn't easy to understand intellectually, and perhaps the psalmist wants help in gaining intellectual insight into what those things mean (think here of the multiple senses of meaning related to intellectually grasping the sense and reference of a passage). But perhaps not. The verse is sufficiently vague that it is hard to know exactly what sorts of wonderful things the psalmist has in mind, and what he wants God to do when he asks God to open his eyes to those wonderful things.

Despite uncertainty about the request in verse 18, the rest of the verses cited have been explained well enough. The question that remains is whether persuading and enabling a person to obey a divine command qualifies as illumination. Psalm 119 doesn't use the term "illumination" or "illumine," but the concept could be there anyway. However, convicting of sin, persuading to obey God's laws, and enabling the one persuaded to obey all seem to be part of, in NT terminology, the sanctification process. Of course, Psalm 119 relates all of this to the demands of God's word. Does that mean the verses discussed are about illumination? Perhaps so, but we can't conclude that on the basis of this passage alone.

What, then, should we conclude? Only that the psalmist asks God (the Holy Spirit isn't explicitly mentioned in these verses) to help him obey God's ordinances. That is, he wants God's help in applying divine truth to his everyday behavior. This matches what the NT says about the sanctification process and about means that are used to further that process in a believer's life (see, e.g., 1 Pet. 2:1–2). Whether that also qualifies as illumination cannot yet be decided. If other passages teach illumination, and if they match what Psalm 119 requests, then there is warrant for saying that this OT passage teaches something about illumination. But for now, we aren't in a position to make that judgment.

*John 14, 15, and 16*

John 14:26; 15:26–27; and 16:12–15 have often been understood as promising the Holy Spirit's illumining work in believers' lives. If this is correct, in relation to what are they illumined? The common understanding is that the Spirit performs this ministry when believers read Scripture. John 14 says that Jesus promised to ask his Father to send the disciples another paraclete (v. 16)—an advocate, helper, defender.[21] Lest there be doubts about his identity, in verses 17 and 26 Jesus clarifies that he is referring to the Holy Spirit. The same identification is made in 15:26–27, and in 16:7, which introduces the Spirit's ministry on behalf of Christ toward the world (16:8–11) and his ministry to Jesus's disciples (16:13–15).

This raises three crucial questions: (1) what exactly did Jesus promise the Spirit would do for his disciples?; (2) how do these promises apply to believers other than Jesus's twelve disciples?; and (3) in light of answers to the first two questions, do these verses teach anything about the theological doctrine of illumination? I contend that Jesus wasn't promising his disciples illumination of Scripture, but something very different. Hence, these texts don't promise other believers illumination. Such claims are controversial, so how do I defend them?

First, what did Jesus promise his twelve disciples about the Spirit's ministry? When Jesus made these promises, the whole OT was written, and his disciples had access to it. None of the NT was written, and that makes sense, because Jesus made these promises before his death and resurrection. It is hard to see how most NT books we have today could have been written before Jesus's resurrection and ascension.

During his earthly ministry, Jesus taught his disciples many things. He wanted to teach them more, but they weren't ready (16:12). Jesus also told his disciples that he would leave them (this is stated several times in chapter 14 and again in 16:5–7). In the same chapters Jesus promised to send the Spirit, and then in chapters 14, 15, and 16, Jesus described how the Spirit would minister to his disciples once he would come. Jesus said (14:26) that the Spirit would teach (*didaxei*) them all things and remind them of what he had told them. "All things" may refer first to all that Jesus had said, but since the content isn't specifically identified, it may refer more generally to all things they would need to know in their life and ministry after Jesus departed. Could it involve imparting information they didn't already know, or did it only mean helping them grasp how the various things they already knew fit together? Given the unspecific nature of "all things," the question just asked likely presents a false dichotomy. There is reason to think the Spirit's teaching ministry could and would include both. As to reminding them of Jesus's teaching, that makes abundant sense, as Jesus had taught many different things. In light of what Jesus knew would soon happen to him and to them, it isn't hard to imagine that, amid their upcoming shock over his crucifixion, burial, and resur-

---

[21] For a careful discussion of the meaning of this term, see Zuber, *What Is Illumination?*, 151–155. Since my concern is whether these passages teach illumination, I leave to readers the study of the exact meaning of the term "paraclete" in these chapters.

rection, they would be quite confused. The Spirit's ministry of reminding them of Jesus's teaching would be most welcome and needed!

John 15:26–27 mentions another ministry of the Holy Spirit to the disciples. Jesus said the Holy Spirit would bear witness to them. Because he is the Spirit of truth, what he testifies should be believed. In turn, Jesus predicted (v. 27) that the Spirit's witness would lead the disciples themselves to bear witness about Jesus. As Zuber shows, citing various commentators, the idea of bearing witness is that of telling the truth about something.[22] Specifically, the Spirit would testify that what Jesus said is true and that he is who he claimed to be. Hearing this testimony, the disciples would proclaim the same thing about Christ.

In John 16:7–11, Jesus spoke of the Spirit's ministry to the nonbelieving world. Verses 12–15 speak of his ministry to Jesus's disciples. Jesus promised that the Spirit would "guide" them (*odēgēsei*) into all truth (v. 13), "announce" (*anangelei*) or "disclose" things to come (v. 13), and glorify Christ by "disclosing" what he takes (*lēmpsetai*) from Christ (v. 14). In verse 15 Jesus added that all things belonging to the Father also belong to him. So, when the Spirit discloses things from Christ, he would also be disclosing what belongs to the Father. As commentators suggest, Christ is the focus of this truth into which the Spirit would guide the disciples.[23] Carson summarizes these verses by saying that "Jesus Himself is the truth (14:6); now the Spirit of Truth leads the disciples into all the implications of the truth, the revelation, intrinsically bound up with Jesus Christ."[24]

Taken together, these three passages promised the Spirit's ministry to the disciples after Jesus left. The Spirit would teach them, remind them of Jesus's teachings, bear witness to the truth of Jesus and his teachings, glorify Jesus by disclosing the things of Christ, and tell them of things to come. This is how the Spirit would minister to the disciples, but we must ask, *to what end or for what purpose?*

We can identify three goals of the Spirit's promised ministry. The first is that people would understand who Jesus is and what he said. During his life and ministry, Jesus said many things to his disciples. Given their reaction at his crucifixion and even initially after his resurrection, let alone at various points before the final week of his mortal life, the disciples surely didn't fully understand all that Jesus had taught them. That is, they were intellectually confused, at worst, and ignorant, at best, because they heard what Jesus said but didn't understand much of it. If those who lived closest to Jesus during his ministry

---

[22] Ibid., 168–169.

[23] D. A. Carson, *The Gospel according to John* (Grand Rapids, MI: Eerdmans, 1991), 539; cited in Zuber, *What Is Illumination?*, 180.

[24] Carson, *Gospel according to John*, 539–540.

didn't "get" what he taught, what hope is there that those much further removed from Christ would understand him? God could, of course, have directly
revealed to each person all that Christ is and taught, but instead, he chose the
disciples as his "mouthpiece." So, if they didn't grasp what his life and teachings meant, what hope would there be that the rest of humanity would?

Second, Jesus commissioned his disciples to go and preach the gospel. This
would, of course, require telling people about Jesus, and that would require a
proper understanding of Jesus's deeds and words. What the disciples would
say when they preached the gospel had to be correct. If not, a new religious
sect might have been born, but at the very least, the "infant church" would
likely be "stillborn." Lest the disciples forget or misinterpret Jesus's teachings,
he promised the Spirit's ministry to ensure that they would "get them right."

There is a third reason for the Spirit's ministries detailed in these chapters, and I mentioned it when discussing inspiration. When the disciples first
preached about Jesus, they had only their OT and their memories of Jesus's
life and teachings. Many of Jesus's disciples seemed to expect him to return
during their lifetime. Until he did, their OT and their memories would suffice
for telling others about Christ. But time passed, and Jesus didn't return. As
death neared for these disciples, and as some died, it became clear that unless
truth about Jesus's life, ministry, and teachings was recorded, the story of
Jesus could easily be changed from fact to fiction. Moreover, the church began
to grow, and some churches in various places needed instruction beyond the
gospel message from Jesus's disciples. It was definitely time to write down the
truths about Jesus and his teaching. Not all of the first twelve disciples would
write Scripture, but key disciples of Jesus, including the apostle Paul, would
write what became the New Testament. Undoubtedly, if they wrote entirely
just from their memories of Jesus, they would have gotten many things correct.
But what they would write had to be absolutely correct, or how would people
living during Christ's life who didn't know him, and later generations, know
what to believe? Jesus promised the Spirit's aid to his disciples, because some
of them would write books that would be part of the NT, and Jesus wanted
them to "get it right." So, the promise of the Spirit's ministry in John 14, 15,
and 16 also had the purpose of guaranteeing that the soon-to-be-written NT
would be the very word of God and infallibly true.

What do these three purposes of the Spirit's ministry amount to? On the
one hand, they involve revelation, and on the other, they guarantee inspiration
of the soon-to-be written NT. Do they promise the disciples illumination? If
so, it is hard to see how, because what we might call illumination was more
likely revelation to the disciples about Christ's life and ministry. Even if the
revelation would be something God had said before, we saw in the chapters on

revelation that God can reveal information to people that others also have, and that counts as revelation for those who don't possess it. The Spirit's helping the disciples to remember what Jesus said and to "put it together accurately" for the purposes of preaching and writing the NT sounds like revelation to them. Of course, helping the disciples to piece together the details in order to "get the story" right isn't entirely unlike one of the cognitive things the Holy Spirit can do in helping believers grasp Scripture's meaning in the sense of sense and reference[2]. Even so, these passages alone, which don't mention illumination, seem much more relevant to *revelation* (for the purposes of the disciples *knowing* what Jesus taught and *preaching* it) and to *inspiration* (when some of the disciples would write Scripture) than to illumination. Even what Zuber labels the consensus view of illumination doesn't match what we find in these chapters, because the consensus view relates to Scripture, and NT Scripture hadn't been written when Jesus promised the Spirit's ministry to these disciples. So, it is wrong to think Jesus promised the Spirit's illumining ministry when he spoke the words of these passages.

What about our second question—how do these promises apply to other believers/disciples of Jesus? Because 2 Timothy 3:16–17 tells us that all Scripture is God-breathed and profitable for various things, we are inclined to seek a personal application of Scriptures written long ago. And we should, but not just any application is acceptable. Indeed, believers in Christ as personal Savior are his disciples, but disciples of Christ throughout church history aren't on the same footing as those original twelve and others who were eyewitnesses of Jesus's life and were commissioned as his apostles. How do these promises relate to disciples who aren't apostles?

It may be tempting to think they promise that we will remember details of Jesus's life and teachings, but that is unnecessary because those details are already recorded in the NT. The disciples who received these promises had no NT, so it made sense to promise to remind them about Christ so that they would understand who he was and what he taught. We are in a different position; we have the NT, so if we don't remember or are somewhat unsure of what Jesus taught, we can consult the NT.[25]

Perhaps, then, one of the other purposes of the Spirit's promised ministry to the first disciples applies to us? Not really, because neither believers today nor in the future are, or will be, commissioned to write Scripture, so that purpose doesn't apply to us. Of course, many of us will witness about Christ, and some are called to preach, but we have ample source materials for witnessing and preaching, because we have the NT. The disciples who first received these

---

[25] I'm not suggesting that everything in the NT is crystal clear. My point is that many of the Holy Spirit's ministries promised in these chapters were necessary for early disciples because they didn't have a written record of Jesus's life and teachings. Our position is different than theirs.

promises had only the OT and their personal knowledge of Christ. Whatever information they would need for preaching or witnessing we already possess by having the NT. We may need the Spirit to remind us of NT passages relevant to our ministry, but that wasn't so for the disciples who first received these promises of the Spirit's ministry. Beyond that, nothing said yet suggests that "getting help to remind us of NT or OT passages relevant to our witness or preaching" has anything to do with illumination, even if it is something the Holy Spirit can do for us.

All in all, it is very hard to support the idea that what Jesus promised the disciples is something he will also do for us. Are these passages, then, irrelevant to us? Not at all. In these passages Jesus certified the accuracy and inspiration of the soon-to-be-written NT. Thus, when we read any part of the NT, we can be sure that we are reading more than the musings of mere men. We are actually reading God's very words. *That* means that what we read must be completely true, because God wouldn't speak error, nor would he allow the human authors of NT books to include errors in them. As a result, NT books are just as authoritative as OT books, because the Holy Spirit inspired everything in both Testaments.

This, of course, has great practical significance for us today. God hasn't inspired any Scripture beyond the NT. Whatever God says is extremely important; we should be loath to miss any of it, especially things he has said most recently. We must know whether they change any previous teachings (OT), and if they do, what the changes are. These NT passages promise that what the apostles would preach and what some of them would write would present what God wants us to know. The church's judgment throughout its history has been that, beyond the twenty-seven NT books, God hasn't inspired any further written revelation.

Hence, even if these passages in John's Gospel teach nothing about *illumination for the disciples who wrote Scripture or for the rest of us who didn't write it but read it*, they are relevant to people living after the NT was penned. They reassure us that the message the apostles preached would be "supervised" (as indicated in the three passages) by the Holy Spirit's ministry. Hence, we can be certain that the gospel that eventually came to us is accurate, not faulty. As we saw in the chapters on inspiration, most biblical texts that teach inspiration refer specifically to the OT. John 14, 15, and 16 show that the NT is also inspired.

So, contrary to what many Christians think, John 14, 15, and 16 don't actually help us with the doctrine of illumination. Thankfully, however, there is ample scriptural support for the doctrine without imposing it where it doesn't belong.

*Luke 24:13–32, 44–45*

In Luke 24:13–32, 44–45, Luke describes two incidents after Christ's death and resurrection. Both involved Jesus and various disciples. The first involved two disciples, Cleopas and an unnamed disciple. The second involved the two mentioned in verses 13–32, the eleven (presumably the twelve apostles, minus Judas), and those with them (v. 33).

The first happened on the road to Emmaus. As the two walked, they discussed events of recent days. Jesus approached them (v. 15) and walked with them. Verse 16 says they didn't recognize Jesus. Jesus asked them what they were talking about; they stood still, and Luke notes their sadness (v. 17). Cleopas recounted key details of Jesus's life and death (vv. 18–24). His disciples had thought he might be Israel's redeemer—most likely they were thinking in political terms, not about redemption from sin—but Jesus was arrested, tried and convicted, sentenced to death, and then crucified. As they finished the story, they added (v. 21) that it had been three days since these things had happened—they were probably thinking of Jesus's promise to rise from the dead three days after his crucifixion. Perhaps not, but then (vv. 22–24) they told the story of the women going to Jesus's empty tomb on Easter morning, and being told he was alive. Other disciples ran to the tomb and also found it empty, but they didn't see Jesus.

So, Jesus's two companions were quite discouraged and unclear about the meaning of everything that had happened. They knew the main events, but didn't understand the one or more explanatory threads that would tie these events together and let them see what it all meant. They didn't get, so to speak, the "big picture."

In verses 25–27, Luke writes that Jesus began lifting their sadness as he explained what these events meant and how they all fitted together. Beginning with Moses and the prophets—a clear reference to major parts of the OT that these disciples would have known—Jesus explained things related to him and that he had fulfilled. Jesus reminded them that even the OT predicted that the Messiah would die, rise again, and be glorified (v. 26).

None of these three travelers was likely carrying an OT, but all of them knew the OT. When Jesus spoke from Moses and the Prophets, neither disciple asked, "Who is Moses?," or "What are the Prophets?" So, what was Jesus doing? He wasn't giving information they didn't already have; this wasn't an instance of revelation. Rather, Jesus showed them how things that had happened in recent days fit teachings from the OT. They had been focusing on individual events and on Scripture, and couldn't see how those isolated data fit together and made sense of recent events. When Luke writes (v. 27) that Jesus explained (*diermēneusen*) to them things concerning himself, he doesn't mean that Jesus informed them of these passages for the very first time. Rather, Jesus focused on things they knew already; what he told them intellectually connected these Scriptures with what had happened to him.

The three travelers approached their destination, and the two disciples urged Jesus to stay with them that evening. As they had dinner, Luke says (v. 31) that their eyes were opened (*diēnoixthēsan*), and they realized that their companion was Jesus. The verb "were opened" is passive, indicating, as Liefeld suggests, that divine action did this.[26] Not only had Jesus helped them "get it right"—to see the big picture of how recent events fit with OT prophecies—he helped them see that it was Jesus who had done this. Jesus vanished, and they remarked (v. 32) how their hearts had burned within them as Jesus explained the Scriptures to them.

Though the term "illumination" appears nowhere in this narrative, it is hard to see how the imagery of their eyes being opened is anything but that. Now they intellectually grasped the meaning, in the second sense of "meaning" as sense and reference, of facts they already knew. Had they not known Scripture or the events of the previous week, it is dubious that what the narrative describes could have happened.

We should note several things about this instance of illumination. First, this passage doesn't mention the Holy Spirit. He may have been involved in opening their eyes to recognize Jesus or to grasp how all of the facts from the recent week and from the OT fit together, but we aren't told that. Jesus showed them how the Scriptures matched what had happened to the Christ. Something he did or said while breaking bread at the evening meal opened their eyes. So, the focus is on Jesus as the enlightener, not on the Holy Spirit. Jesus, the highest form of divine revelation, is the form of revelation to which their minds were opened.

Second, what Jesus did while walking with his disciples didn't involve transferring intellectual content to their minds that they didn't already know. There was an intellectual element in this instance of illumination, but it involved helping them understand the meaning (in the second sense of "meaning"—putting all the data together to see the "big picture") of things they already knew from personal experiences and from their knowledge of the OT.

Third, there is a sense in which illumination helped them apply the truth they now grasped. Specifically, having grasped the "big picture," their mood turned from depression and sadness to joy and enthusiasm. They returned to Jerusalem and told the eleven disciples what had happened and explained their new understanding of the events of the previous weeks. Of course, once Jesus's disciples understood what had happened, they were ready to

---

live for him and to tell others, though that isn't the focus of this part of the narrative.

So, this instance of illumination relates most to understanding the truth intellectually. Note also that, though these disciples didn't have a Bible as they walked, it was Scripture's *meaning* that Jesus opened their minds to see. Specifically, it was Scripture *in conjunction with* the events of the previous days that Jesus helped them understand. Hence, we can say that, when necessary, divine illumination can help us grasp how the events of our lives fit the teachings of God's word.

Luke adds that the two disciples whose eyes were opened returned to Jerusalem to tell the eleven and those with them. From what they say (recorded in v. 34), it is evident that they really did "get it." As they told what happened on the road to Emmaus, Jesus appeared in their midst (v. 36). They were startled and frightened, thinking they were seeing a ghost, despite what they had just been told (vv. 34–35). Jesus reassured them that he was actually present. To prove that he wasn't a spirit, he showed the disciples his hands and feet and told them to touch him. To further prove he was really there, he ate a piece of broiled fish. According to verse 41, they seemed to understand that Jesus was really risen and standing there with them.

In verses 44–45, we read that Jesus did for these disciples essentially what he had done for the two on the road to Emmaus. He reminded them that he had taught them before his death what the Scriptures said about the Messiah. In this instance, however, he taught them not only from Moses and the Prophets but also from the Psalms, which represents the third major portion of the OT canon. Not only did Jesus connect the various data from OT Scriptures, but verse 45 says he opened their minds to understand the Scriptures, explaining that it was necessary, as Scripture predicted (v. 46), for the Messiah to die and rise again from the dead on the third day for the forgiveness of sins, which they were now to proclaim to all nations (v. 47). The word "opened" in verse 45 is *diēnoixen*, the same word used in verse 31 (in the passive).

As in the first part of this narrative, this seems to be a clear instance of illumination, even though the term is never used. Moreover, what I said about the illumination of Cleopas and his fellow disciple is true here as well. The disciples probably didn't have a copy of the OT with them, but Jesus helped them grasp how data from the OT (prophecies about the Messiah) fit what had happened in the previous weeks and also fit with their realization that Jesus was really standing in their midst. Jesus didn't present any information they didn't already know. He helped them see it in a different way so that they "got" how it fit together and what it all meant.

## 1 Corinthians 2:9–16

First Corinthians 2:9–16, especially verses 14–16, is deemed a key text on illumination. It does affirm some important things, but it also leaves some questions about exactly what the Holy Spirit's illumining accomplishes. I covered this passage in my chapters on revelation and inspiration, so we needn't repeat the teaching's context. A few words of orientation will suffice.

In 1 Corinthians 1–2, Paul compares the wisdom of Greek philosophy with the wisdom found in Christ. Followers of the world's wisdom—represented by the best Greek philosophy of the day—can't understand God's wisdom; it is foolishness to them. But what is foolish to the unsaved is the wisdom of God and is the true path to eternal life and happiness.

In chapter 2, Paul explicitly shows the difference between divine wisdom and the best the world has to offer. Divine wisdom doesn't come from sense perception or rational reflection—the usual paths for attaining human knowledge. It comes from God and is revealed to believers by the Holy Spirit (vv. 9–11). Paul adds that we should expect this, because no one knows his own mind like himself. Similarly, no one knows God's mind as does *God's* Spirit, the Holy Spirit (v. 11). But not only does God's Spirit have access to the divine mind; believers in Christ as Savior also have access to God's thinking through the Holy Spirit (v. 12). When Paul says that believers haven't been given the "spirit of the world," he doesn't mean that believers cannot know secular philosophy in particular or the world's way of thinking in general. He means they can know something that no nonbeliever can know: God's thinking.

Here we must not put words in Paul's "pen." This doesn't mean that, when nonbelievers come in contact with spiritual truth, intellectually they grasp nothing—that it's like a foreign language to them. If Paul meant that, how would that be consistent with all the times and places he preached the gospel and people understood what he said but rejected it? If spiritual truth proclaimed to nonbelievers is mere gibberish, then rejecters shouldn't have such a strong negative reaction to what they can't understand. No, Paul knows that nonbelievers can get the basic "gist" of spiritual truth. The problem is that they think what they've been told is foolishness and so they reject it, sometimes rather vehemently. Such a strong rejection doesn't come from people who hear but understand absolutely nothing.

In verse 13 Paul adds that the Spirit not only revealed truth but also taught him and the other apostles how to express in language the spiritual thoughts revealed to them. This happened so that they would state things correctly when they preached, but we also saw that this ministry of the Spirit related to their writing books that formed the NT.

Verses 14–16 speak of another ministry of the Holy Spirit, one which again shows the difference between the world's philosophies and the genuine wisdom of God. In verses 14 and 15 Paul "introduces" two kinds of people. On the one hand, there are natural men, *psychikos anthrōpos* (literally, "soulish man"), and on the other, there are spiritual men, *pneumatikos anthrōpos* (literally, "spiritual man," though the word *anthrōpos* doesn't appear a second time in these verses). If this discussion only began at verse 13 or 14, we would be hard pressed to explain the difference between these two kinds of people. However, in light of verses 10–12, especially verse 12, we can say that the spiritual man possesses the Spirit of God. The only way to have God's Spirit is to receive him when one accepts Christ as personal Savior. In contrast, the natural man doesn't have the Spirit of God—he isn't saved and lives totally on the basis of mere human wisdom and knowledge.

Paul distinguishes these two types of people in order to show how totally different divine and human wisdom are in all respects. The two kinds of wisdom differ not only in their source and method of transmission; they also differ as to how they can be understood—and as to whether they can be understood at all by those without the "right equipment." This point about needing the "right equipment" says something very important about divine revelation. God not only transmitted truth and superintended its transfer into written form. This alone wouldn't guarantee that his message would be understood and acted upon. To ensure that we would "get the message," God gave us his Spirit.

So, what happens when natural and spiritual men encounter spiritual truth? Paul first (v. 14) addresses the natural man, and says two things about him. First, natural men neither receive nor accept (*dechetai*) spiritual truth, because it is foolishness (*mōria*) to them. Second, natural men can't understand (*ou dynatai gnōnai*) the things of the Spirit, because such truths are spiritually examined and judged (*anakrinetai*). While it is tempting to handle each verb atomistically and so to say that Paul makes four comments about the natural man's intellectual capacities, that would do violence to the sentence structure of each claim. Actually, Paul makes two claims about the natural man and explains why each is true.

Paul first says that the natural man doesn't accept spiritual truth (literally, "things of the Spirit of God"), because he sees it as foolishness. Note that no part of this first point involves inability to grasp anything intellectually. Rather, it assumes that the nonbeliever does *intellectually* understand spiritual truth. Why? For several reasons. First, *dechetai* has nothing to do with intellectual understanding. If it did, this part of the verse would be redundant of the second point Paul makes (*ou dynatai gnōnai*). Instead, it focuses on whether one accepts or rejects what is given.[27] In this case, what is given is spiritual truth. If it were not understood intellectually, we might expect Paul to say that the natural man leaves it alone or overlooks it. In order to reject something, one must first understand it!

This basic intuition seems to be confirmed when Paul explains why the natural man rejects spiritual truth. He does so because it is foolishness to him. Now, something might appear to be foolish because it is incomprehensible gibberish. But if that is Paul's point, then his next point about the natural man's inability to understand is a bit redundant. Why else might something appear to be foolish? Because one understands it intellectually but sees it as so outrageous that it shouldn't be given any credence as true.

While both options might be true, I think that in the context of 1 Corinthians 1 and 2, the latter is more likely. This is so in part because the first notion would likely require that *dechetai* mean "understand intellectually," and as already said, that would make the first claim of verse 14 seem redundant of the second. But, even more significant, Paul has argued in chapters 1 and 2 that preaching of the cross of Christ is foolishness to those who perish (1:18, 23). Why so? Because Jesus is supposed to be both God and man—an apparent logical impossibility. And because Jesus died; if he is truly God, how can he die? Even more, if he died, how could he rise again? And how can dying and rising again pay for other people's sins? None of this makes any rational sense! Though people in the Greco-Roman world of Jesus's day believed in the various gods of the Greco-Roman pantheon, none of those gods or goddesses were ever said to have died and resurrected, nor did anyone think that they paid for the sins of mere mortals. Moreover, many Greek intellectuals were quite skeptical about the existence of the Greek gods, so they likely would have been quite dubious that an apparently mere human could also be God.

Many in our times see the gospel story as just as foolish as it seemed in Paul's day. Given modern anti-supernaturalism, who would take the gospel's claims seriously? Notice, however, that Paul's first claim about the natural man has nothing to do with any inability to understand intellectually the content of spiritual truth!

Paul says something further about natural men. Not only do they reject spiritual truths; they can't understand them. Some might think this is the "smoking gun" that proves that spiritual truth is like gibberish to nonbeliev-

---

[27] According to Kittel's *Theological Dictionary of the New Testament*, *dechomai* can be used in the sense of "to receive." As Kittel explains, "in this sense it is used for the hospitality which was everywhere honoured and regarded as sacred in the ancient world. . . . It is particularly common in this sense in the NT, partly because Jesus and Paul were compelled to rely a good deal on hospitality by their mode of life. . . . The high estimation of hospitality in the NT derives in large measure from a similar high estimation in Judaism. . . . Beyond the special sense of hospitality, δέχομαι denotes the friendly reception which might be accorded a man more generally." See *Theological Dictionary of the New Testament*, ed. Gerhard Kittel, vol. 2 (Grand Rapids, MI: Eerdmans, 1964), 51–52, s.v. δέχομαι.

ers until the Spirit illumines them. We might think this means that they can't even grasp intellectually what spiritual truth is saying. But we should reject that interpretation. Why? Because Paul's explanation of why natural men can't understand spiritual truth doesn't square with the idea that they can't intellectually grasp anything when they hear or read it. Paul says they can't understand spiritual truth because it is spiritually examined and judged (*anakrinetai*). What is "spiritual judgment"? Though Paul uses the adjective here, he most likely means that this judgment is made by means of the Holy Spirit's aid, and natural men don't possess the Holy Spirit.

The verb *anakrinō* is interesting in itself, but also because Paul uses it twice in 2:15. Paul writes that the spiritual man *anakrinei* "all things," but is *anakrinetai* by no man. If *anakrinō* means something different in verse 14 from its meaning in verse 15, it is hard to see how that can be so, especially since the topic is the same—the only difference is that verse 14 is about the nonbeliever while verse 15 is about the believer. So, *anakrinō* most likely means the same thing in both verses. But then how likely is it that it means mere intellectual understanding of the content of some idea(s)? Very unlikely; let me explain why.

Certainly, it makes little sense to say in verse 15 that no one intellectually understands the spiritual man. Hence, it makes even less sense to say that "the spiritual man intellectually understands all things, but is not understood intellectually by anyone." The two parts of verse 15, on this interpretation of *anakrinō*, don't fit together, and hence the sentence makes little sense. Now let's try this meaning of *anakrinō* in verse 14. Verse 14 would mean that "the natural man cannot understand the things of the Spirit, because they are spiritually intellectually understood" (i.e., they are intellectually understood by means of the Holy Spirit's ministry). But if that is so, that seems to contradict Paul's first point in verse 14. How can you reject as foolish something you can't intellectually grasp? That doesn't make sense; what makes sense is that the natural man does grasp *intellectually* the meaning of spiritual truth, but having done so, it seems foolish and so he rejects it. But then the second half of verse 14 can't be talking about mere intellectual understanding of spiritual truth, because the first half of the verse presupposes that the natural man can do that!

What other meaning, then, can we give to *anakrinō*? The meaning implicit in the way I have translated this verb. This is a verb that has the idea of analyzing something or sifting through its various parts so as to make a judgment about it. If this is the meaning of *anakrinō*, then I propose that Paul's second point in verse 14 makes sense and doesn't contradict his first point. Moreover, this understanding of *anakrinō* also makes sense of verse 15. Let me explain.

We have already seen why "he cannot understand it" in verse 14 *doesn't* mean that the natural man can't grasp intellectually the basic content of spiritual truth. But then, in what sense can't he understand spiritual truth? In the sense that, having grasped the basic intellectual content, he (1) can't see that it applies to him, and/or (2) can't get the gist of the whole thing (i.e., what all of it amounts to—think here of the disciples on the Road to Emmaus; they understood in one sense but didn't "get it" in another), and/or (3) can't move his will to embrace the truth with the intent to live it. Which of these three possibilities does Paul have in mind? He doesn't give us enough information to make a judgment. He may have in mind all three, or two, or only one.

What is at least of equal significance is Paul's explanation of why the natural man cannot understand (in one or more of the senses noted above) spiritual truth. It is because such truths are examined/analyzed and judged by means of the Spirit's ministry in one's life, but the natural man doesn't have the Spirit of God. The kind of cognitive activities and volitional activity involved in items (1)–(3) above can be done only when a person examines and decides what to do with spiritual truth and does so by means of the ministry of the Holy Spirit.

Does this understanding of *anakrinō* fit verse 15? Indeed, it does. In contrast to the natural man, Paul says that the man with the Spirit does *anakrinō* all things (clearly, Paul has in mind all "spiritual truth"). He is able to do any and all of (1)–(3) above, though Paul doesn't say in verse 15 which of the three he specifically has in mind. Though the spiritual man examines and judges all spiritual truth, Paul says in verse 15 that no one (presumably, no natural man in particular, but Paul may intend this comment to cover spiritual men as well) examines and judges the spiritual man. Here the meaning of examining and judging is slightly different from the other instances of it in verses 14–15, because examining ideas/truth is not the same thing as examining a person. But surely we shouldn't take this final instance of *anakrinō* in verse 15 to mean "understand intellectually"; such an interpretation makes no sense.

Paul completes his comparison between worldly wisdom and true spiritual wisdom in verse 16. In having the Holy Spirit and his ministry (as described in verses 9–15), believers also have the mind of Christ. Thus, we know what God thinks and can live in accord with it, whereas the most nonbelievers can do is live in accord with mere human wisdom.

What can we learn from this passage about the doctrine of illumination? Though the term illumination isn't used in the passage, Paul speaks about the difference between believers and nonbelievers. Nonbelievers have no access to divine spiritual truth. They can only grasp worldly wisdom, and so spiritual truth seems foolish to them and they reject it. In contrast, believers can understand and accept spiritual truth. This happens as a result of the Holy Spirit's ministry; the contrast in verses 14–15 makes this rather clear, as we have shown.

But what exactly does the Spirit do for believers and not do for nonbelievers? He does not so minister in the lives of nonbelievers that they choose to apply spiritual truth to their life and obey it (option [3] above). This is what Paul means by saying that nonbelievers don't accept (*dechetai*) the things of the Spirit of God. In addition, nonbelievers don't understand the things of the Spirit because they are discerned by the ministry of the Holy Spirit (v. 14). In what sense don't they "understand"? Paul doesn't say explicitly, but it could be any of senses (1)–(3). We already know from the first half of verse 14 that they don't do what option (3) involves. In contrast, spiritual men do examine and judge all spiritual truth. Again, Paul doesn't say exactly what this entails, but it could certainly entail any and all of (1)–(3).

Given these differences between believers and nonbelievers, this passage speaks rather clearly about a ministry that the Holy Spirit performs for believers. Though the term "illumination" is not used, it is hard to see what else this ministry could be. It can't be regeneration and justification, for those things have already happened to spiritual men. Nor do these verses sound exactly like what the NT describes when it speaks of sanctification or glorification. And, it certainly is distinct from revelation and inspiration; if verses 14–16 are just about revelation, then they seem to be redundant of verses 9–12. It is best to say that this passage speaks about the illumining ministry of the Holy Spirit.

But note what this does and doesn't mean. As noted, Paul doesn't specify exactly what the Spirit does. The accepting (*dechomai*) of revelation (v. 14) that the natural man doesn't do is in contrast to the spiritual man's accepting it. Such acceptance is not per se a purely intellectual activity but rather a volitional one. As to the rest of verses 14 and 15, Paul doesn't say whether he has in mind purely intellectual activities or volitional ones, or both. What is crucial, however, is that if Paul is thinking only about intellectual activities, he doesn't mean that the Holy Spirit so moves in the minds of believers who don't intellectually know the contents of spiritual truth that he transfers the unknown spiritual truth into their minds. Illumination as evidenced in this passage does not add to the intellectual content of Scripture. Rather it helps the believer grasp the gist of Scripture, see that it applies to him or her, and/or helps him or her to choose to obey it.

What does this passage mean for nonbelievers and spiritual truth? It doesn't mean they can't read or hear basic spiritual information and intellectually grasp its content. Rather, it means that the Holy Spirit doesn't perform in their lives either of the further intellectual activities or the volitional deed represented by options (1)–(3). How, then, can any nonbeliever hope to understand (in these "deeper" than merely intellectual senses of "understand") spiritual truth, and more fundamentally, how can any nonbeliever ever be saved, if what Paul teaches in 1 Corinthians 2:14–16 is true? For the answer, we must turn to another passage!

### 2 Corinthians 4:4–6

In chapter 3 of 2 Corinthians, Paul addresses the nature of his apostolic ministry. He claims to speak boldly (v. 12), unlike Moses, who spoke with a veil over his face. However, even to this day, when the old covenant is read, the veil still remains in place. But when someone hears the truth and turns to God, the veil is lifted.

In chapter 4 Paul continues the theme of walking in the truth and speaking it plainly. This doesn't mean that everyone who hears the gospel will respond (v. 3). Paul knows that the gospel is still veiled to those who are perishing. In verse 4 he explains why the gospel is veiled, and he places the blame on "the god of this world." This individual can't be any morally good being, divine, angelic, or otherwise, for why would any of them blind the minds of the unbelieving? Paul refers to Satan. According to this verse, Satan blinds unbelievers' minds so that they won't see the gospel of the glory of Christ.

In verse 5, Paul says that he and the other apostles preach the gospel of Christ. Preaching to nonbelievers about morality in general or some aspect of doctrine might have some value, but nonbelievers must first accept Christ before they are ready to hear other spiritual truth.

Can nonbelievers, using only their own intellectual and spiritual abilities, understand the gospel? Paul addresses the noetic condition of sinners, and says that nonbelievers have a problem. To use Paul's terminology in 1 Corinthians 2, they are "natural men." They don't have the Spirit of God, and so aren't saved. Hence, spiritual truth seems to them foolishness. Natural men and women need a total change of spiritual equipment. They need a new nature, and the indwelling Holy Spirit. How can this happen? In 2 Corinthians 4:5, Paul explains how he and others address the veil on nonbelievers' minds: they preach Christ Jesus as Lord.

Why would preaching that message succeed if preached in the face of the opposition envisioned? Because God is a God of light, not of darkness or blindness. In verse 6 Paul links two events that show that only God can dispel darkness. He points first to creation (Gen. 1:3) and the light God called forth from the physical darkness. Second, in a similar way, God dispels the moral and spiritual blindness imposed by Satan on nonbelievers by shining into their hearts the light of the knowledge of God's glory in the face of Christ.

Commentators agree that Paul refers here to his own conversion experience on the road to Damascus. But certainly no such dramatic event must occur to dispel Satanic blindness. Since the key to dispelling it is Christ's light, Paul says (v. 5) that he preaches about Jesus Christ his Lord.

This is the sum and substance of this passage. Does it teach anything about illumination? If so, it is the one place where illumination applies to nonbelievers. But what does this light do? Does it take intellectual content already available but totally unknown to the nonbeliever and transfer it to the nonbeliever's mind? If so, that would be very odd. If 2 Corinthians 4:6 refers to Paul's Damascus Road experience, as many affirm, we can hardly say that Paul was entirely ignorant of information about Jesus of Nazareth and his followers. He knew what the OT said about the Messiah, and he knew what many of his contemporaries believed.

Paul, because of his training and background in Judaism, would have been especially versed in the things said about this Jesus. The Corinthian church wouldn't have had that much knowledge, and nonbelievers at Corinth likely would have known much less than believers. But it is surely doubtful that the city had never heard the gospel at all from anyone. In fact, according to 1 Corinthians 1–2, leaders in Corinth were quite familiar with it, and deemed it foolishness.

So, what actually did nonbelievers at Corinth need, in order to break through the Satanic blindness that kept them from Christ? They needed the light of Christ to shine in their hearts so as to give the "light of the knowledge of the glory of God in the face of Christ" (2 Cor. 4:6). In short, they needed a miniature and less ostentatious "Pauline Damascus Road" experience. No preacher could give them that, nor could they get it as a result of inductive or deductive reasoning. They needed a direct touch from the living God! That is the way to dispel Satan's stranglehold on the nonbeliever's heart, will, and eyes.

Some may reply that this relates to Paul and Corinth, a special case, but it is irrelevant to most nonbelievers who turn to Christ. That may seem so, but we must look closer. Whether a person is a raving atheist, a moderate one, or just a somewhat religious person who doesn't want to get too much "religion," he or she doesn't see the need of a Savior. She may intellectually understand the gospel, and may even grant that many people have held such views and found those beliefs helpful. But ours are different times and places, and nonbelievers today may think those views antiquarian and irrelevant.

If so, what is the problem? Don't they intellectually understand the basic gospel message? Of course they do, but they may not think they are great sinners who need God's forgiveness. Moreover, more learned nonbelievers may be turned off by Christianity's requirement of a blood sacrifice for sin and by its threat of eternal conscious punishment for those who reject Christ. So, they understand the gospel and other elements of Christian truth, but they don't see it as relevant to them, nor do they intend to change their lives to follow Jesus.

If the only way to break through this blindness is the light of Christ shining in their heart, then what should God do? Give them more information to help them understand Christian theology better? Hardly! But then, what? Must the Holy Spirit not somehow persuade nonbelievers that the message they have heard perhaps many times is relevant to them? Mustn't he convince them that the punishment for those who reject Christ will fall on them—forever? And, mustn't he so persuade nonbelievers to trust Christ's provision of redemption that they will ask for forgiveness from sin, and decide to follow Jesus as Savior and Lord? If these things don't happen, won't the Satanic blindness that hinders people from accepting the gospel reign triumphant?

All of the above seem necessary for someone to move spiritually from darkness to light. The question for us is whether what I have described does or doesn't require illumination. This a valid question, since illumination is typically seen as a ministry of the Holy Spirit, but verses 3–6 don't mention him. Of course, those verses neither explicitly nor implicitly exclude his activity altogether. In fact, what I have described above as necessary to break through the spiritual darkness so that the gospel's light may shine in sinners' hearts and draw them to Christ is precisely what the Holy Spirit does.

So, this passage does seem relevant to illumination, but perhaps we shouldn't make that judgment too hastily. After all, in John 16:8–11 Jesus promised to send the Holy Spirit and said that, when the Holy Spirit would come, he would convict the world of sin and righteousness and judgment. Wouldn't that be necessary in cases like the one described in 2 Corinthians 4:4–6? If nonbelievers don't believe they are sinners or deserve punishment, they may be unable to see that the gospel *does* address their needs and that they need to act on it.

What, then, should we conclude about 2 Corinthians 4:3–6? It seems to be the only Scripture we might include in a "list" of illumination passages that speaks about nonbelievers. But is this passage about the "wooing of the Spirit" and the effectual call to salvation for those who are God's elect? Or is it about divine illumination of the resistant, sin-and-Satan-dominated heart of those who refuse to see that the gospel relates to them?

Or, and this is a major "or," is this passage actually about both? That is, does part of the Holy Spirit's wooing of nonbelievers to Christ involve his first helping them to "get" the full thrust of the gospel message, then helping them to see it as relevant to them, and finally persuading them to turn from sin to Christ? While combining all of these elements in the process of bringing someone to Christ may seem odd, this is not the only place theologians do this.

LIGHT EMBRACED: THE DOCTRINE OF ILLUMINATION  □  605

Some have wanted to include God's work of regeneration on the spiritually dead heart of the nonbeliever as part of illumination, for, they claim, only a regenerate sinner can see that the gospel is for him and must be accepted.

On the basis of this passage, I think we learn four things about illumination. First, the focus of this text is God's work in the lives of nonbelievers. Of course, when *believers* harbor unconfessed sin in their lives, they need to confess it and be cleansed, but this passage is about the condition of the lost. Second, this text offers no evidence that God transfers cognitive information to the sinner that he doesn't already know. Rather, its point is that sinners must see how the gospel message fits together, see that it relates to them, and see that they need to act upon it. Third, merely knowing this *intellectually* won't dispel spiritual darkness. Sinners must act upon what they intellectually understand to be the case. Fourth, it isn't entirely clear whether this passage talks about steps the Holy Spirit takes to draw a person to a saving knowledge of Christ or whether instead it is about the illumination of God's word. Thankfully, the kind of illumination required in a nonbeliever's life seems to amount to at least part of what the Holy Spirit does in drawing nonbelievers to Christ. So, perhaps it is best to see that, at least in this one instance, the Holy Spirit's illumining ministry (though not mentioned explicitly in this passage) is part of drawing sinners to Jesus Christ as their personal Savior. Beyond that, the passage allows us to say little else.

## 1 John 2:18–27

In 1 John 2, John details the importance of abiding in Christ. To do so, believers must obey his commands. A key command is the obligation to love brothers and sisters in Christ. John's readers know these things, but they must practice them.

In verses 15–16, John forbids loving the world with its lust of the flesh, lust of the eyes, and its pride of life. These things are passing away and don't come from the Father, who abides forever. Amid this warning, John says that the Christian community is about to be faced with false teachers (John calls them "antichrists"). They will spread their false doctrine, and John's readers must not be fooled by their words. These false teachers will claim to lead genuine believers into depths of spiritual understanding, and to teach them things they couldn't otherwise learn (v. 27). As Glenn W. Barker opines, perhaps the anointing the false teachers promise comes only to some believers, but not to all.[28]

John writes that there are several evidences that the false teachers are false. First, they left the company of believers to whom John wrote (v. 19), and it

---

[28] Glenn W. Barker, *1 John*, in *EBC*, ed. Frank E. Gaebelein, vol. 12 (Grand Rapids, MI: Zondervan, 1981), 327.

wasn't a temporary departure. They left so that it would be clear that they weren't genuine believers in the first place. If they had actually been believers, they would have stayed, but they didn't.

The second evidence that those who left were false teachers was their doctrine. They denied that Jesus is the Messiah (v. 22). John adds that whoever denies the Son also denies the Father. In chapter 4, John returns to this theme and his rhetoric is just as strong. He predicts that there will be, and even were as he wrote this letter, many false prophets. The way to detect them is their denial that Jesus is God incarnate (1 John 4:1–3).

A third evidence of their error is that the false teachers will teach new things that they say are not open to all believers. But John tells true followers of Jesus not to be fooled, because they have heard the truth about Jesus from the beginning (2:24). If John's readers would just remember what they have been taught and abide in it, they would see that the false teachers offer nothing new worth hearing.

A final way John's readers can detect false teaching is mentioned twice (in vv. 20 and 27). It is a special anointing that believers have. One senses that all Christians have it, not just those to whom John wrote. It isn't clear whether God the Father or Christ gives the anointing, but commentators agree that the anointing is the Holy Spirit.[29] John affirms in verse 27 that this anointing abides in believers and teaches them things relevant to the Word of Life, Jesus himself.[30] In fact, the Spirit had already been teaching them, for he had been with these disciples from the moment they first accepted Christ.

John then adds (v. 27) that his believing readers "have no need for anyone to teach you." This is a rather startling claim, one that can be ripped from its context and grossly misinterpreted. Let me first identify several things it can't mean. First, it doesn't mean that there is no reason for believers to listen to spokespersons of God's word. If that were so, John should have stopped writing 1 John! Or, after finishing it, he shouldn't have sent it! Surely, John wasn't suggesting that he intended to stop writing, nor that he wouldn't preach anymore because the Holy Spirit would do all the teaching any believer needs. If that were his message, why write 2 and 3 John and Revelation?

In addition, it is unlikely that John was against corporate Bible study. As in the synagogue, where the elders and scholars pored over Scripture to discover its meaning and application, new Christians wanted to study God's word about Christ. Surely John wasn't rejecting their intellectual enthusiasm! Nor was he forbidding the use of Bible commentaries and other study aids. And he wasn't telling believers not to study biblical languages!

[29] Ibid. 325–327; and B. F. Westcott, *The Epistles of St. John* (Grand Rapids, MI: Eerdmans, 1966), 73–77.
[30] Ibid., 327.

So, what did John mean when he said that believers need only the Holy Spirit's teaching? He was answering what the false teachers said. They claimed that unless believers received a special anointing from God, one they could get only from these false teachers, believers wouldn't understand the deep things of God. The false teachers weren't referring to the Holy Spirit. They meant that only they could give special knowledge, and that they did so for the select few who learned from them.

John answered that no one needs what the false teachers offer, because every believer, from conversion onward, has the anointing that is the Holy Spirit. Whatever deep spiritual truth needs to be taught, the Holy Spirit teaches it, and what he teaches no mere human can teach.

It is in this sense that no one needs a human teacher, Bible commentary, etc. But that is different from the need to grasp intellectually the basic content of Scripture. For that, hard study is required, using the ordinary tools and methods of studying any text, including Scripture.

What, then, does this passage teach about illumination? Though the term "illumination" doesn't appear in it, it allows us to say several things about this doctrine. Because believers, from the moment they are saved, have the Spirit (the anointing), John most likely assumes that the Spirit performs the ministries that other passages say he does. But what does that involve? It doesn't involve revealing new intellectual content that has never been transmitted to anyone before—perhaps the apostles who would write the NT are the lone exception, but chapter 2 of 1 John seems to focus on all believers. Moreover, John is clear (v. 21) that he writes because they already know the truth, not because they need to know some new intellectual content.

What does this anointing teach? John doesn't explicitly say, but we can affirm that it is available to all Christians, not just to a few elite. Does it help believers understand intellectually the cognitive meaning of extremely difficult texts like 1 Peter 3:18–22? Does it help them understand how various strands of Christian teaching fit together so that they grasp the truth as never before (i.e., at last they "get it")? Does it involve getting them to see that the truth they study applies to them and needs to be lived out? Does it involve persuading them to start living the truth? John doesn't answer, so this anointing may involve some of these ministries, or all of them.

Does this passage, then, teach anything about illumination? Probably, but exactly what is uncertain. We can say more about what it excludes than about what it includes. John clarifies that he writes at least in part because among John's readers were people who tried to deceive them doctrinally. They claimed to know and give insights into spiritual truths that no one else could. It is in the sense of *not needing that kind of teacher* that John writes that they need only the Holy Spirit, for only he can teach deep truths no one else can.

What exactly does the Holy Spirit do that no other teacher can do? In the preceding paragraphs I listed various things the Holy Spirit might do, but do those things qualify as illumination? Perhaps, for we have seen similar teaching in passages that seem to address this ministry of the Holy Spirit. Since John intended to warn of false teaching, not to explain exactly what the Holy Spirit does through illumination, perhaps John had all of these cognitive, affective, and volitional ministries in view. We just can't be certain. However, nothing in the passage denies that the Holy Spirit illumines the minds and hearts of believers.

## Theological Summary and Conclusion

Although no passage of Scripture uses the term "illumination," various divine actions described seem to fit the Christian consensus understanding of the concept. Many are intellectual, though the exact cognitive act performed isn't always the same. Other divine activities mentioned are more affective. Not only must someone intellectually grasp what revelation means, but she must also see that it applies to her, not just to others. And, she should have some idea of how it applies.

A further element of illumination is volitional. Whatever the message transmitted in revelation, for it to be fully received the recipient must both understand how it applies to her and respond in obedience. This may involve divine enablement to move her will to do what needs to be done.

The preceding may seem to be all we can say about illumination, but it actually only begins the discussion. In what follows I shall incorporate information from the earlier part of this chapter into a larger understanding and articulation of illumination. To do that, I offer the following nine points.

1. *Illumination is a divine activity performed on the human mind and heart, not on some form of divine revelation.* This is a simple but significant point. Revelation unveils divine light. Why should light need more light? Light doesn't suffer from blindness; the reader/interpreter of revelation does! The various verses that relate to illumination show that either the Lord (Luke 24) or the Holy Spirit (1 Cor. 2:14–16; 1 John 2:20, 27; see also 2 Cor. 4:3–6) gives illumination, but they do so to the human mind and heart in need of understanding. The help given may aid in intellectual grasping of truth, or in applying it. For example, the psalmist (Psalm 19) doesn't ask to understand God's statutes and ordinances. He asks for help in obeying them.

2. *Hence, illumination is neither revelation—communicating new content—nor inspiration—transferring revealed content into written form for oth-*

*ers. It is more about interpreting Scripture aright and applying it.* Repeatedly in this chapter, I have shown that Scripture requires nothing to be added to its *content* for illumination to occur. This means that illumination doesn't involve God somehow transferring to human minds intellectual information that he hasn't already revealed and that is unknown. God won't supernaturally give us this information while our minds remain passive receptors. Hence, divine illumination doesn't remove the need to do the hard intellectual work of exegetically working through texts to grasp intellectually their points. Sadly, busy preachers can't just wait until Saturday night to begin preparing their Sunday sermon, pray earnestly, and then expect the Holy Spirit to transfer from his mind to theirs the content of the next day's sermon!

An implication of this point is that people who don't even know Christ can discover the *meaning*[1] of Scripture. Depending on their knowledge of Scripture's original languages and their exegetical prowess, they may even be better at discerning the *meaning*[1] of a biblical text than are people with little exegetical skill but a long pedigree in the faith. This can also be part of why two spiritually mature Christians, illumined by the same Holy Spirit, can derive different interpretations of a text. When that happens, the cause isn't a defect in the Holy Spirit's ministry, but it can, at least in part, result from the keenness of the human intellectual equipment involved and the exegetical skills of the interpreters.

The case of Philip and the Ethiopian eunuch (Acts 8) illustrates this point. Acts gives the impression that the eunuch wasn't saved, but he was reading Isaiah 53. Did he understand nothing in the passage? Of course not. Otherwise he couldn't have even formulated a question about it and likely wouldn't have understood anything Philip told him.

So, from his knowledge of how to interpret language, the eunuch must have seen that the passage predicted the killing of an innocent person. What was his question? The eunuch understood the passage's sense; he wanted to know its referent, and so he asked, "of whom does the prophet say this?" Had he known more of the OT and/or more about Jesus and his teaching, he might already have known the answer to his question. The Acts passage says nothing about the Holy Spirit transferring information to him. Rather it is about interpreting the text to a point, and then asking Philip for the referent of the prophecy. Once Philip explained how the passage applies to Jesus (vv. 35–36), the eunuch fully "got it" and committed himself to following Christ (as indicated by his being baptized). "Getting" the gist of the passage, seeing its relevance to him, and accepting Christ surely involved the Holy Spirit's ministry. How all of that relates to illumination will be explained as we proceed.

One final word about illumination relating to the human mind rather than to divine revelation: as we saw in our study of Scriptures about illumination, the Holy Spirit often uses Scripture to open the mind of the believer or the nonbeliever, but it is still the human mind that requires illumination. For those who think Scripture is the object of illumination, note the consequences of that view. One is that when Jesus opened the disciples' eyes on the road to Emmaus and later did the same for the other disciples, Scripture wasn't present, so neither incident could have been an instance of illumination. But, as explained when I discussed Luke 24, if what happened didn't at all involve illumination, what should we call it?

A further consequence of holding that Scripture is the object of illumination is that before any of Scripture was written, no one ever received illumination. Does that, however, actually square with what we read about Noah, Abraham, Isaac, Jacob, Moses, Aaron, etc.? All of them lived at least part of their lives before any Scripture was written. In my chapters on revelation, we saw that God revealed himself to them in various ways. But divine revelation to most of them never came in written form, as Scripture. Before Moses began to write Scripture, he had lived a long time, and God had revealed himself to Moses before he wrote any of the Pentateuch.

Think of the implications of these facts. Either illumination of revelation other than Scripture was unnecessary because it was perfectly understandable, so God's revelation to Abraham, Isaac, etc., wasn't illumined to any of them; or, illumination to grasp revelation was needed, but God just didn't give it—it wasn't until Scripture was written that illumination was needed, and at that time the Spirit began to perform that ministry. How absurd are such suppositions! Abraham was told to leave his country and go to a land that God would show him. Moses was told to part the waters of the Red Sea and lead the people of Israel across on dry ground. Abraham was promised a son from his own loins, but after Isaac was born, God told him to sacrifice Isaac as an act of worship. How could any of this have made sense to Abraham, let alone to Isaac? Didn't the Holy Spirit need to minister somehow to Abraham to assure him that it was God demanding this sacrifice, lest, as a deranged man, Abraham would kill his own son?

In sum, first, it is not Scripture that needs illumination; it is the human mind. Second, though in our experience illumination comes mostly in conjunction with written revelation, our minds can be illumined to more kinds of revelation than just Scripture. This likely means that God can illumine nonbelievers' minds to natural revelation, though the longest discourse on natural revelation (Romans 1) shows that no one on their own lives in accord with it. But note that the problem isn't that they don't *intellectually grasp* what natural revelation teaches. According to Romans 1:32, they understand that what they do is wrong and deserves punishment. The problem is that they are so set in their sinful ways that they reject the revelation they have, even though they know that doing so leads to judgment.

3. *To what truths can nonbelievers be illumined?* This is, of course, a difficult question because we haven't clearly articulated what Scripture includes in the illumining work of the Holy Spirit. Even so, two passages offer an initial response to this question. In light of 2 Corinthians 4:3–6, divine light can shine in the minds and hearts of sinners to draw them to Christ. More will be said later about what this entails, but the result is clear.

In contrast, 1 Corinthians 2:14–16 may seem to say that no other spiritual truth is available to nonbelievers. However, we saw through careful exegesis of 2:14 that this doesn't mean nonbelievers can't get a basic grasp of the sense and reference (*meaning*[1]) of a text. They can understand it intellectually well enough to think it foolish and reject it. So, whatever nonbelievers cannot do intellectually with spiritual truth, it involves something deeper than merely missing the basic sense and reference of biblical sentences.

As to the truth of the gospel, nonbelievers can grasp much more than the mere sense and reference of sentences conveying the message. The key question we asked in examining this passage, however, was whether this qualifies as illumination or whether it is, instead, the convicting and persuading ministry of the Holy Spirit to bring a person to salvation in the first place. Though this seems like an either/or, I shall be arguing shortly that it is actually an instance of both/and. That is, regardless of whether the truth embraced is the gospel message or some other spiritual truth, in order to get someone to accept the message affectively and volitionally, illumination is involved in the persuasive ministry of the Holy Spirit. Scripture doesn't lay out the exact dynamics and order of these transactions, but they sound so much alike that it seems hard to say that this is *either* a case of illumination, *or* an example of an effectual call. Why can't we say instead that the effectual call involves illumination of the sort to be explained shortly?

4. *We begin to see the complexity of this doctrine when we recognize the different things the "meaning" of Scripture can mean.* Early in this chapter we noted that illumination typically is defined as the Spirit's opening up of Scripture's meaning to the understanding. However, the terms "understanding" and "meaning" are quite ambiguous. As such, they may involve a variety of activities the Holy Spirit performs, though the deeds aren't identical. In other instances, they don't designate things the Holy Spirit does but instead elucidate the exegete's role in interpreting Scripture.

In analyzing the meaning of "meaning" first, we noted that it can involve divine actions that are intellectual in nature, and it can also refer to deeds that are more affective. As to the former, they relate to determining the sense and reference of what the writer intended to write. The very first of these tasks is performed through the careful work of the exegete, consulting connotative and denotative meanings, learning about background cultures at the time, and paying attention to the syntax and context of sentences. The purpose of this work is to discover what the writer intended to say. This involves the exegete's hard work, and the Holy Spirit does not telepathically (or otherwise) transfer this information to the interpreter's mind.

In addition, we can speak of a passage's meaning in two other senses. Acquiring *meaning*[2] of a text involves the exegete in seeing all the data gathered in a different way than before. He grasps, so to speak, a new conceptual gestalt of what he studies. The data don't change, but rather the framework into which they fit helps him see the passages' teaching in (perhaps) a different way than originally thought. Though this can happen by ordinary human powers (consider the scientist who repeatedly pores over the same data, but suddenly in a stroke of insight sees that they teach a different theory than the reigning one), it is also possible for the Lord or the Holy Spirit to grant this kind of insight into the meaning of biblical data. The two incidents in Luke 24 illustrate this point. Jesus's disciples knew OT predictions about the Messiah. They also were keenly aware of what had happened to Jesus during the preceding week and a half, and they couldn't square those events with what they knew from the OT. As Jesus walked with them toward Emmaus, he helped them "connect the dots," so to speak, of all the data they knew. He explained how the events of recent weeks actually fulfilled OT prophecy—he led them to see things in a different way. Once that happened, they recognized that it was the risen Christ walking with them. In the latter part of Luke 24, the pattern was just the opposite. Jesus first gave tangible evidence to open their eyes to see that he was there in their midst. Then, he reviewed OT teaching about the Messiah and connected it with what they had seen during the years they had served with him in ministry.

Could these disciples have gathered the *meaning*[2] of all of this without any divine aid? Perhaps, but it is rather obvious on these two occasions that the Lord opened their eyes to see who he was and to understand what had happened. It is hard not to see these events as instances of illumination, even though the Holy Spirit didn't do it, and even though the term "illumination" isn't used in the passage.

We also noted a third sense of sense and reference. In this sense, the theologian/exegete moves beyond the meaning of a single passage (or even of a series of passages). He sees how whole sets of doctrines from one area of theology fit another group of doctrines from another part of theology. It isn't clear that this "molding" of a whole system of thought happens to anyone in Scripture, in part because those who grasp the second kind of sense and reference don't often tell us how all the details they came to understand fit together. Even so, this is a cognitive work that can be done by the Spirit, and nothing in Scripture suggests that it can't happen. Indeed, various theologians throughout church history have likely experienced this phenomenon, including the author of this text.

It would be easy to think this just happens when a gifted theologian thinks holistically, and there is an element of truth in that view. However, I can attest that, amid massive amounts of study, whether for a degree thesis, a huge test, or even for writing a sermon, I have experienced that holistic kind of thinking that allows one to link together many different doctrines and passages. Was that the result of a thorough theologian asking questions until the light dawned on how all the data fit together, or did the Holy Spirit do something to quicken my mind and attend it to certain data which, when emphasized, gave me a flash of insight? Perhaps only the Lord can answer that, but it has seemed to me on at least some occasions that the insights produced go well beyond what could be expected, given the information I had and the intellectual maneuvers I made using that information, from normal human intellectual activity.

While I believe this sort of "enlightenment" can be a work the Spirit does in a mind, I see little evidence of it happening in Scripture. Perhaps some of the apocalyptic visions given to prophets that enabled them to see how individual incidents fit into a whole divine plan might be examples, but even here we can't be entirely certain.

We also noted two further meanings of "meaning," and both have to do with applying truth. The first relates more to a person's mind, because it helps the exegete/theologian/layperson see how the doctrine just formed by determining the *meaning*[1], [2], and perhaps [3] might and does impact other doctrines one holds. Here again, this theological maneuver may just be part of a theological *habitus* of mind, or it might be an insight granted by the Holy Spirit by directing the theologian's attention to doctrines that actually have implications for one another, or this maneuver may combine both.

The key thing to note now is that so far all these senses of "meaning" are intellectual in nature, but not in that they add information to someone's mind that was never there before. The idea of a pastor who doesn't know what to preach but prays for illumination and finds himself in possession of a full message just doesn't square with what Scripture teaches. I note also that nothing said so far about different senses of "meaning" would preclude a nonbelieving professor from teaching a theology course and doing it rather well.

So, where is the "rub" between what a believer can and can't do? Here I turn to the final sense of "meaning" that involves asking what the passage(s) say(s) to me specifically about how I should live. In this case, we move from the meaning and application for others in general to what Scripture and a doctrine say to me, and I conclude that they require a change in my life. However, even though this is a more affective aspect of illumination than a purely intellectual one, one can understand the meaning of a group of texts in this sense and still be unchanged. Think, for example, of Jesus's conversation with the rich young ruler who wanted to follow him (Luke 18:18ff.). Jesus told him various things he needed to do, and the young man averred that he had done these things. Jesus then showed him the further application of this teaching: he should sell all his goods and give the proceeds to the poor, and follow Jesus. The text gives no evidence that the young man asked what Jesus meant because his mind couldn't comprehend what Jesus said. He knew full well what Jesus meant and how it applied to him. His problem was neither intellectual nor affective, but volitional. Scripture tells us that he heard Jesus and walked away, changing nothing, because he was a very wealthy man.

Next, we must remind ourselves of the various ways that "understand" or "understanding" can be used of the Holy Spirit's role in a person's mind. We noted that *understanding*[1] relates mostly to the first three senses of "meaning." Thus, it primarily relates to the hard work of exegesis. The Holy Spirit doesn't put into "empty heads" information people never knew or studied before. Indeed, these intellectual activities include works attributable to the Spirit, but they don't cover passages like Psalm 119, 1 Corinthians 2, 2 Corinthians 4, and 1 John 2.

The remaining meanings of "understand" and "understanding" have to do with affective and volitional ministries that only the Holy Spirit can perform. While *understanding*[2] may somewhat overlap the first meaning of "meaning" as application, *understanding*[2] also includes not just how the various doctrines connect, but that they have implications, theoretical *and* practical, for all people. Even more, the third and fourth senses of "understand" move us entirely into the affective and volitional senses of understanding. The third involves the thinker in realizing that a truth is relevant to him or her. As we saw from 2 Corinthians 4, this is critical if the blindness that keeps one from embracing the gospel is to be lifted. Moreover, those false teachers who sought to seduce John's readers by offering them truth they could get nowhere else were wrong, because John's readers already possessed truth that got them to the deep things of God, truth that comes without anything being added by a mere human teacher. All believers need to know for their personal needs is present in the Spirit's teaching, and it has been available for as long as they have known Christ.

As to *understanding*[4], it is volitional. The natural man rejects the things of God (1 Cor. 2:14), because they are foolishness to him. He can intellectually understand spiritual things, but he refuses to change his life so as to obey God's word. He sees biblical teaching as foolishness. Since seeing that it has merit would require admitting that its truth applies to him (so he should change his life by obeying it), he refuses to understand it in the sense of volitionally committing to live what Scripture teaches. The natural man's problem, according to Paul, is that judging the truth aright and applying it can be done only by the Spirit's ministry, and the natural man doesn't have that.

On the other hand, because the spiritual man has the Holy Spirit's ministry, he can understand Scripture in the third and fourth senses presented. That doesn't mean he will always obey what he knows to be true and what he knows he must change, but still, he can understand in the affective and volitional senses of this term. As evidence of the special capacities of the spiritual man, we need only look at the psalmist in Psalm 119. The issue for him was not lack of head knowledge of Scripture's content, nor a failure to take all the commands together and see them in a new way. It wasn't even a matter of seeing that their teaching applied to people in general and to him in particular. All of this he knew and affirmed. So, what exactly did he ask God to do? He wanted from God the kind of help that would keep him on the path of righteousness. He had volitionally decided to follow God, but he knew there would be temptations to disobey God, and so he asked God, in effect, to teach him to obey.

5. *The further role of the Holy Spirit in believers' lives is to keep them from falling into doctrinal heresies.* John speaks of false teachers, and they could have been false in their doctrine, their practice, or in both. Some of John's readers were saying that these teachers got to the depths of spiritual truth in ways that no one else could. Every believer should want this.

In contrast, John wrote that he and other disciples had been with Jesus from the very beginning, and they knew what he said and did. Moreover, Jesus sent his Spirit to all believers, and as the Spirit of God, he would know better than anyone else the deep things of God. Thus, these recent teachers with "the key to spiritual truth" were simply false. Believers already have the Spirit, and he is all the teacher they need.

In this case, the Spirit's activity is primarily cognitive, but he doesn't add new information that believers haven't already heard. Rather the Spirit reminds believers of all they know in Christ and of how it fits together. To what end? One end is to refute the false teachers and to have nothing to do with them. Another goal, should John's readers seek it, would be to see how Scripture and doctrine fit together as a whole, with nothing omitted that any later generation needs to add.

Having said the above, I can say that, while 1 John 2 is relevant to illumination, its teaching doesn't so much define illumination as it intends to safeguard us from false teaching. It should also keep us from asking other people, believers or not, whether they have some new angle on truth. That is unnecessary, for John says that by having the Holy Spirit, we already have all the deep teaching anyone needs.

6. *Despite protests to the contrary, John 14, 15, and 16 aren't about divine illumination, nor is the Spirit's illumination a valid application of these chapters.* In my exegesis of these passages, I offered detailed evidence to support this point, so I needn't repeat it here. Suffice it to say that those who first heard these words were apostles who would preach and then write Scripture. These ministries of the Spirit were necessary, because the disciples had only the OT (none of the NT had been written). Memories of what Jesus said and did would soon fade, so the Spirit's ministry was crucial if stories about Jesus were not to be lost.

But today we are in a very different position. Surely it would help to see all of Scripture fitting together in a holistic form so that we truly "get it" in relation to Jesus, but careful study of Scripture will likely give us that. As to "getting it right" when we preach, again our situation differs from theirs. If we can't remember what Jesus said or did, a good concordance should solve that problem. But most of all, we don't need the ministries mentioned in John 14, 15, and 16 because we won't be writing the NT or any other Scripture.

So, these passages address nothing that has or ever will happen to us. Are they, then, irrelevant to us altogether? Actually, John 14, 15, 16 are more relevant to us than we might think. Their application, however, is not that we can expect the Holy Spirit to do the same things in our lives. Rather, it is that when we pick up the NT, we can rest assured that it is just as authoritative and binding as anything in the OT. Like the OT, it is God's word, and we must learn and obey it. But that also means that God didn't give us just one Testament that presents his answer for humanity and then leave us adrift with no further word (in written form) for approximately the next 2,400 years. The NT is God's most recent written revelation. We should study it in the light of his earlier word, but if the two Testaments seem at times to contradict each other, the reason is likely to be that as revelation progressed, God made some changes that he revealed in the NT.

None of this shows that John 14, 15, and 16 should have a prominent place in biblical support for the doctrine of illumination. But it should encourage us to interpret correctly, and not to seek applications to modern days that could not be implications from things clearly taught in an earlier day. Without John 14, 15, and 16, there still is plenty of biblical grist to "mill" the doctrine of illumination.

7. *Divine illumination is available to the saved on any spiritual topic, and it seems accessible to nonbelievers on topics other than salvation.* So what can happen when nonbelievers read spiritual truth not associated with the gospel? First, if we are talking about understanding intellectually the sense and reference of what is being said, nonbelievers can understand Scripture in that sense. Those who have heard nonbelievers explain complicated Christian doctrinal claims shouldn't be overly surprised. Some nonbelievers may even be able to see the "gist' of a doctrine and even see how parts of theology fit other parts. What 1 Corinthians 2:14 seems to eliminate is the natural person's ability to understand the Scriptures in the affective ways explained and to move his will to obey any of its teachings. The persuasion needed to accomplish such transactions is under the Holy Spirit's control. Are those transactions merely part of his strategy of effectually calling sinners to himself, are they aspects of his illuminative work in nonbelievers' lives, or are the affective and volitional aspects of the Spirit's work merely part of his illumining work necessary to break through Satan's darkness and let the light of Christ's salvation shine in? Scripture doesn't explicitly answer, but I suspect that, given the similarity of the Spirit's illuminative ministries and of his convicting and persuading ministries to bring someone to Christ, all of these ministries are wrapped up in one another.

8. *Finally, what do items 1–7 mean about illumination and the perspicuity of Scripture? If nonbelievers only through illumination can understand the gospel, does that contradict or nullify the doctrine of Scripture's perspicuity/ clarity?* The doctrine of perspicuity says that the basic intellectual content of Scripture is understandable to the average person, regardless of his or her level of education. But this refers to grasping the *meaning*[1] of Scripture's content, regardless of its subject matter. That fits with the main things we saw about illumination and will see in the chapter on perspicuity. Nowhere, including in 1 Corinthians 2:14, does Paul teach that what the nonbeliever can cognitively grasp is something she can accept in the sense of deciding to obey it. Moreover, the doctrine of perspicuity guarantees nothing about whether those who understand Scripture's basic message will *want* to accept and obey it. Nor does perspicuity promise that anyone, in their own ability alone, *can* obey Scripture if they want to do so.

Some may reply that there are affective and volitional elements to understanding Scripture that only the Holy Spirit can bring to pass. That is true, but it doesn't contradict perspicuity, because perspicuity says nothing about the Spirit's enablement in accepting and living out the truth that illumination at its deepest level shows must be lived.

In sum, there is no reason not to hold the concept of illumination espoused

618    □    The Usefulness of Scripture

in this chapter *and* still believe in Scripture's perspicuity. The key is to distinguish between purely cognitive senses of understanding, on the one hand, and affective and volitional senses, on the other. Perspicuity deals with cognitive understanding, not affective and volitional senses of it.

9. *The consensus definition of illumination has some merits, but some rephrasing would help.* According to that definition,

> Illumination is a work of the Holy Spirit, whereby the hearer or reader of the Word of God, either a believer or an unbeliever, is given understanding of the information contained in it and brought to appropriate its meaning.[31]

Several things immediately catch the eye. One is that illumination pertains specifically to the mind's understanding of *Scripture*. While we affirm that, we should add that illumination can also be given to understand any other form of revelation available at any time and place in history.

Second, the definition makes it sound as though what can be done for the believer can be equally done for the nonbeliever. In this chapter, we have seen some challenge to that idea. Even if in some sense true, the consensus definition states it a bit imprecisely.

Third, and most important, though various writers understand the ambiguity latent in words like "understand" and "meaning," they do nothing to remove that ambiguity. Hence, the impression given is that illumination involves two basic things: (1) somehow cognitive information is grasped by the listener/reader, and (2) illumination aids in applying the truth. However, we have seen that there is more than one simple thing involved in intellectually grasping information, and it is just not true that all of them happen whenever anyone is illumined. Moreover, getting someone to appropriate truth isn't a simple one-step task. Like saving repentance and saving faith, appropriation of spiritual truth has several elements, and they don't always come together at the exact same time. So, the consensus definition isn't so much wrong as simplistic. In being simplistic, however, it can easily mislead church parishioners into thinking that Bible reading and hearing is for the unsaved an exercise in listening to gibberish until the Holy Spirit somehow transfers the right information into the reader's/listener's mind. It can also make believers think there is no point in sharing the gospel with nonbelievers, because people won't accept what they don't understand, and nonbelievers don't even intellectually grasp any of the Bible. Anyone who "buys" such nonsense reminds us how crafty Satan can be in keeping us from obeying what God explicitly calls us to do.

Thankfully, when we present the gospel to nonbelievers, and when they read Scripture, they can intellectually understand what they hear and read.

---
[31] Zuber, *What Is Illumination?*, 51.

Understanding in the further senses explained in this chapter is also possible because of the illumining work of the Holy Spirit!

In light of these nine points I propose that we reformulate the definition of illumination as follows:

> Illumination is a work of the Holy Spirit on the minds and hearts of believers and nonbelievers which can accomplish any and all of the following in regard to divine revelation, including Scripture: (1) help them to grasp intellectually the content of the revelation; (2) help them to see how that intellectual content applies to actual situations and circumstances in their lives and in others' lives; and (3) move them to adopt and apply the truth to their own lives.

Our great God has taken great pains to uncover the light of his revelation to those who first received it. But he also wanted other generations to have access to that light, so he took steps to transfer some of it into written form, producing our Bible of sixty-six books. His purpose in doing this was not to give himself more "publications" to list on his resume. Rather, he desperately and truly wants us to "get his message" and to live it. To that end, he also sent his Spirit to teach us. But no one can learn when eyes, ears, mind, and heart are closed. So the Spirit who revealed God's truth and supervised its transmission into written form also illumines human minds and hearts to understand intellectually and to live God's truth!

# SIXTEEN

# CLEAR, UNDERSTANDABLE LIGHT

## The Doctrine of Perspicuity/Clarity

Scripture is also useful because its message is clear. The clarity of Scripture, its perspicuity, has been a significant theme in Protestant evangelicalism as least since the Reformation. Of course, if Scripture is perspicuous, it has always had that quality. But what exactly is perspicuity? Charles Hodge begins his discussion of it with the terse comment that "the Bible is a plain book. It is intelligible by the people."[1] As a result, Hodge adds that people have the right and obligation to read and interpret Scripture for themselves. If they do, their faith will rest on Scripture, not on the church's interpretation.[2] This raises cryptically the historical situation in which this doctrine gained prominence. But more on that later.

Hodge's definition is quite condensed, and we should supplement and clarify this doctrine. But at the outset, the idea of perspicuity seems a bit strange. Many books are clear and understandable, including (hopefully) all current and future volumes in this theology series. Many works of nonfiction and fiction are also clear, but theologians surely wouldn't think the perspicuity of such works has "doctrinal" import, whereas Scripture's clarity is noteworthy theologically. So, what exactly is Scripture's perspicuity and why does it matter?

The very idea of perspicuity is also confusing from another angle, its relation to some other doctrines about Scripture. Most notably, there seems to be some tension when the doctrine of illumination is conjoined to the concept of perspicuity. That is, if perspicuity means, as some have defined it, that Scripture is understandable to any person of even average intelligence, then why does any

---

[1] Charles Hodge, *Systematic Theology*, vol. 1 (London: James Clarke, 1960), 183.
[2] Ibid.

Scripture need divine illumination? On the other hand, given divine illumination, couldn't Scripture be very unclear and yet serve God's purposes so long as the Spirit enlightens the mind of the reader?

And perhaps even more troublesome, how do we account for Scripture's clarity when Scripture itself says that it is impossible for the natural man (the one who doesn't know Christ as Savior) to understand the things of God (1 Cor. 2:13–14)? In addition, though many Christians would argue that the gospel message in Scripture is clear and easy to understand (apparently supporting its perspicuity), Scripture itself affirms that Satan works especially hard to blind human minds to the message of the gospel (2 Cor. 4:3–4). Sadly, we know that Satan is quite successful in those efforts. And, if Scripture is as clear as perspicuity suggests, why don't Satan and his minions who clearly know Scripture seem to understand it?[3]

How should we proceed? In this chapter I propose to do several things. First, I shall offer a brief, working definition of perspicuity. That will be followed by a discussion of views within the evangelical Protestant tradition about this concept. Of course, the key for evangelical theology is what Scripture teaches about it. So our discussion will turn next to Scripture. While perspicuity per se is nowhere addressed in Scripture, Scripture is not irrelevant to this doctrine.

After discussing Scriptures relevant to our topic, we shall then look at other conceptual arguments in favor of the doctrine. Of course, we must answer objections to the doctrine, so that will be our penultimate task in this chapter. The chapter will conclude with a more precise articulation of this concept as Scripture, theology, and reason support it. I do believe that Scripture is perspicuous, and that a variety of evidence, biblical and otherwise, supports this. But first, let us turn to a basic definition of this concept.

## AN INITIAL WORKING DEFINITION OF PERSPICUITY

While there is nothing incorrect about Hodge's definition, we can say more. However, it would be wisest to offer our most thorough explanation of this concept after we present biblical and theological evidence to support it.

For now, a working definition is sufficient to get started. In general, to say that something is perspicuous means that it is clear and easy to understand. Hence, Scripture's perspicuity is often referred to as its clarity. But what is it about Scripture that is easy to understand? Certainly, passages like 1 Peter

---

[3] From the temptations of Jesus, we know that Satan knows Scripture, for he uses it to tempt Christ to sin. Jesus refutes Satan by quoting Scripture, and Satan seems to understand what Jesus said. In fact, when Jesus quoted Scripture, Satan immediately dropped his current temptation and turned to another. So, no one should think Satan's problem is lack of biblical knowledge and that we could "reform" him if he would just take some sound Bible courses. Satan already knows the content of such courses, even better than human teachers do.

3:18–22 aren't easy to understand, even for those who know Greek, theology, and the basic argument of 1 Peter. Passages about end-time events generate debates over their meaning and even about whether they have been fulfilled or are yet to be fulfilled. In addition, Jesus told his disciples that he taught in parables so that they would understand "the mysteries of the kingdom of heaven," while those who opposed and rejected Jesus would not understand. They heard his words, but they didn't understand. In fact, they were determined to oppose Jesus, so they deliberately chose to misunderstand him and interpret his words in ways that would support their unbelief. Given the condition of their minds and hearts, Jesus accommodated their determination to reject him by teaching in parables that they wouldn't understand because of the hardness of their hearts (Matt. 13:11–15).

What, then, does it mean to say that Scripture is clear, understandable, perspicuous? The basic idea is that Scripture's message and meaning are understandable to even the most unlearned persons without the aid of teaching or instruction from those who have studied it. Of course, this definition is too broad, for it covers everything Scripture addresses, and some things in Scripture are not easy to understand. Hence, perspicuity, as held by evangelical theologians, is usually said to apply to the basic message of salvation that Scripture presents; that basic message can be understood without instruction and aid from those who have studied Scripture in more depth.[4]

As one writer notes, perspicuity is a basic governing assumption of any Bible society that believes "that you can leave a copy of the Bible in a hotel or motel room or a colporteur can take it into the most remote regions and simply leave it without comment, and it can do its salvific work."[5] Of course, this doesn't mean that without attending to what the text is saying, one can and will understand Scripture simply by allowing one's eyes to pass over the written text on the pages of Scripture. Nor does Scripture's perspicuity negate the Holy Spirit's ministry of illumining and applying Scripture to the minds and hearts of its readers.

Clearly, perspicuity has implications for a number of bibliological doctrines, let alone how one should read Scripture and how one comes to understand it. But what exactly does it mean to understand Scripture? I covered this in some detail in chapter 15, so let me just remind readers of a few key points.

---

[4] Walter C. Kaiser Jr. and Moises Silva, *An Introduction to Biblical Hermeneutics: The Search for Meaning* (Grand Rapids, MI: Zondervan, 1994), 19, as quoted in Jesse Acuff, "The Analogy of Faith as It Pertains to Tradition, Interpretation, and the Perspicuity of Scripture," *A Journal from the Radical Reformation* 14 (Fall 2007): 26. For other similar definitions see Hodge, *Systematic Theology*, vol. 1, 183; Robert T. Sandin, "The Clarity of Scripture," in *The Living and Active Word of God: Studies in Honor of Samuel J. Schultz*, ed. Morris Inch and Ronald Youngblood (Winona Lake, IN: Eisenbrauns, 1983), 243–244; James Patrick Callahan, *The Clarity of Scripture: History, Theology, and Contemporary Literary Studies* (Downers Grove, IL: InterVarsity Press, 2001); and Wayne Grudem, *Systematic Theology: An Introduction to Biblical Doctrine* (Grand Rapids, MI: Zondervan, 1994), 108.
[5] Fred B. Craddock, "The Bible in the Pulpit of the Christian Church: The Forrest F. Reed Lectures, 1981," *Impact* (Special Issue, 1982): 4.

There are different senses in which one might understand a written text, especially Scripture. Let me introduce a helpful distinction often used in soteriology when elucidating concepts like faith and repentance. Having faith or believing in something or someone may take various forms. It may be nothing more than being intellectually aware of the truth or falsity of a belief.

Faith may also involve a belief that this information has implications for the person who knows it. Someone who only intellectually believes that Christ died for sin, may understand that to mean just that God has revealed his rules for human conduct, and humans have broken those rules. With disobedience comes guilt and punishment. Knowing this, Christ came to earth and died to pay the penalty for all the sins of the human race. As a result, those who accept Christ's payment for their sin will be saved from sin, spend eternity with God, and experience a more abundant life now while on earth.

Believing this in an intellectual sense alone won't save anyone from sin. But someone who believes intellectually in God's plan of salvation may also agree that she has personally broken God's law and deserves punishment. As a result, she sees that she needs to be saved, and also that Christ would save her if she asked him to be her Savior. But faith of this second kind won't actually save her either.

Something more is needed for someone to have saving faith. That third element is a volitional one. The person who believes that Christ would save her, must actually exercise her will to accept Christ as Savior. Only with this third element of faith will she actually be saved.

Similarly, I propose that there are three senses in which one can *understand* God's word. The first is purely intellectual and involves merely grasping the linguistic meaning of a given passage. This is possible by knowing the language's vocabulary and its grammatical rules. A second sense of understanding includes grasping that what the Bible teaches/affirms is more than intellectual concepts and rules of conduct; it also involves seeing that the truths are relevant to the way people live and what they think. They apply to the one reading them.

Of course, it is possible to understand all of this, and yet the reader may fail to act on it. If that happens, there is, then, a significant sense in which the reader hasn't understood what the text means. Hence, third, as with saving faith, the fullest sense of understanding a written text involves choosing to obey what the text demands. Without that, then in a most significant sense the reader didn't "get it" when reading the text.

How do these senses of understanding relate to perspicuity? Hopefully, readers will see that we must do more than merely grasp intellectually whether Scripture teaches that it is understandable to anyone of at least average intelligence when it speaks about salvation. In addition, Scripture's message of salvation being perspicuous means that readers will actually obey it and accept Christ as Savior.

If perspicuity involves all three levels of understanding, then most people who have ever lived haven't found Scripture to be perspicuous, because they haven't applied its message to their own life. In addition, we can say in light of what we learned in discussing illumination that no one can understand Scripture in the volitional sense without the Holy Spirit's ministry and aid. If so, then in that sense, Scripture alone, unaided by the Holy Spirit, is not perspicuous. In fact, we might reasonably wonder if Scripture is clear in any of the three senses of clarity without the ministry of the Holy Spirit.

As we shall see, evangelicals, especially at the time of the Reformation, have made a special point to affirm Scripture's perspicuity. Of course, there is evidence that throughout church history the belief has been held, but its importance came to the fore in Reformation-era debates over who could and who was fit to interpret Scripture. But first we must see what Scripture itself teaches about this topic.

## SCRIPTURE ON PERSPICUITY

While no passage discusses Scripture's clarity as a theological topic per se, the Bible is still helpful in understanding this doctrine.[6] No one has done a more thorough analysis of scriptural teaching relevant to this doctrine than Gregg Allison in his doctoral dissertation. In what follows, I rely heavily on his work.[7]

For sake of clarity, I have divided our discussion of biblical teaching into three categories: (1) passages that say that understanding Scripture isn't hard or that amount to saying that it is clear; (2) passages that imply that Scripture is perspicuous; and (3) passages that suggest that Scripture contains things that are difficult to understand. As readers may suspect from these categories, we will have to draw inferences from what many passages affirm to the doctrine of perspicuity. That doesn't nullify the doctrine, as long as the inferences are warranted.

---

[6] Wayne Grudem's *Systematic Theology* and Charles Hodge's *Systematic Theology* are two of the few that even cover the doctrine, but even so, coverage is limited. Hodge covers it in volume 1 (183–187), and explains that perspicuity involves the right of judgment about any passage's meaning. This underscores the Reformation contention that no one needs a pope or a priest to understand Scripture, for it is clear enough for anyone to understand its basic message. Grudem treats the doctrine on his pages 105–111, offering much biblical support and some practical implications of the doctrine.
[7] Gregg Allison, "The Protestant Doctrine of the Perspicuity of Scripture: A Reformulation on the Basis of Biblical Teaching," vols. 1 and 2 (PhD diss., Trinity Evangelical Divinity School, 1995). In addition to Allison's dissertation and Grudem's *Systematic Theology*, I have found helpful the discussions of biblical teaching on this doctrine in the following: David Kuske, "What in Scripture Is Universally Applicable and What Is Historically Conditioned?," *Wisconsin Lutheran Quarterly* 91 (Spring 1994): 94–95; Paul Brewster, "The Perspicuity of Scripture," *Faith and Mission* 22 (Spring 2005): 17–18; Larry D. Pettegrew, "The Perspicuity of Scripture," *MSJ* 15 (Fall 2004): 211–212; C. George Fry, "The Doctrine of the Word in Orthodox Lutheranism," *CTQ* 42 (January 1979): 36–37; and John MacArthur, "Perspicuity of Scripture: The Emergent Approach," *MSJ* 17 (Fall 2006): 154–157.

*Passages Affirming Scripture's Clarity or that*
*Scripture Is Not Hard to Understand*

This group consists of seven passages, and I shall discuss them in their canonical order. The first is Deuteronomy 29:29. This passage actually belongs in the second group of passages—passages that imply perspicuity—but I discuss it here because it sets the framework for Deuteronomy 30:11–14, a passage that does affirm Scripture's clarity by showing that it isn't hard to understand.

In the majority of chapter 29, Moses pleads with his people to obey the Lord and the demands of the covenant. If they do, there will be great blessing (29:9–15), while disaster awaits if they disobey (29:16–28). In verse 29, Moses distinguishes between secret things that God has *not* revealed, and revealed things. The revealed things belonged to Israel at that time and to all future generations. Moses adds that they possess the revealed things so "that we may do all the words of this law" (ESV).

To what does Moses refer when he speaks of the revealed things, and where might one find them? We need look no further than Deuteronomy 29:29 itself. In chapter 29 Moses speaks about God's covenant with Israel, reminding the people of its curses and blessings, and pleading with them to obey. But where would this generation of Israelites find the details and demands of the covenant? Certainly, Moses taught about that, but they would also know from what Moses wrote about their history in Egypt, the exodus, God's commands given at Mount Sinai, and all other instructions God revealed and Moses wrote in the Pentateuch.

Verse 29 adds that God gave the revealed things so that they might obey all the words of this law. Undoubtedly, when Moses wrote verse 29, many Israelites didn't know how to read or write. Likewise, although some probably were literate, there were no facilities to make Xerox copies of the revealed things Moses had written down. Hence, it is likely that the only way most Israelites in Moses's day had any access to this information was through oral teaching by Moses (and perhaps by other Israelite leaders).

Understanding "the words of this law" could be challenging even for people who could read and who possessed a copy of the law. It is even harder if one's only access is through oral transmission. However—and this is crucial for the doctrine of perspicuity—it would be impossible for anyone to understand such teaching if it were opaque or even only somewhat understandable in various ways that were mutually contradictory. Of course, understanding the law doesn't guarantee obeying it, but how can people be justly held accountable for failing to obey what they don't know or can't understand?

It should be clear that what Moses said in chapter 29 (and in the Pentateuch more generally) must have been understandable to the people of Israel.

What Moses wrote in Deuteronomy 29:29 affirms that they did understand. If not, it makes little sense to say that there are *revealed* things from God in his law? Calling this information *revealed* and holding Israel accountable for obeying or disobeying it makes sense only if the instruction is understandable.

What sort of understanding is in view here? Certainly, both intellectual grasping of the law's content with its various demands and a recognition that the law requires not just assent but action. Of course, God hoped his people would understand in the third sense of obeying his commands, but Deuteronomy 29:29 makes no guarantees that they would. So, this verse assumes that the people of Israel will understand, in at least the first two senses of understanding, the law and the need to obey it.

Can this verse be used to support the perspicuity of more than the Pentateuch? I believe so, but only by an inferential argument. Deuteronomy 29:29 affirms that there are things God has revealed and that he expects people to obey them. Disobedience leads to punishment. From this, it doesn't stretch credulity to say that this verse teaches that *there are things God has revealed, and those who receive the revelation are held accountable for what they do with it.* But, as seen in my chapters on revelation and inspiration, all Scripture is God's revelation. There are many things God knows that he hasn't told us—they are his secret things. But God *has* revealed many things in various forms, including Scripture. Of course, if the demands of Scripture were incomprehensible, it wouldn't be fair to judge us for failing to obey it. Our study of revelation and inspiration showed that God does hold people accountable for what they do with all of Scripture. The only way for that to be just is if what it reveals is clear and understandable.

*Deuteronomy 30:11–14*—Chapter 30 begins with a plea to obey the covenant God made with Israel. Moses then enumerates all the blessings God will heap upon Israel if she repents of her sin and obeys his commands. Having heard about the wonderful blessings God promises to those who obey his word, many might wonder if Moses (and God) aren't setting forth an enticing but impossible goal to achieve. After all, how could people even *know* everything that God commands, let alone obey it? In verses 11–14 Moses addresses whether it is possible to know what God requires.

In verses 11–13 Moses says that what God commands isn't hard to obey ("not too difficult for you"), because it is understandable.[8] Moreover, God hasn't hidden his commands, nor has he put them somewhere far away from his people's everyday lives (v. 11). If they were, someone might need to travel afar to find them, acquire the commands, and bring them back to the people

---

[8] Allison, "Protestant Doctrine of the Perspicuity of Scripture," 1:175–176.

so that they could obey (vv. 12–13). No such effort is necessary, for God's word is already well known to them. It is in their mouth and their heart (v. 14). How can this be so? Undoubtedly, it was true because God's demands were taught in the family (see Deut. 6:6; 11:18), because they were part of a covenant that was to be regularly read before the entire assembled people of Israel (see Deut. 31:10–13), because it was likely also memorized and meditated upon with a view to obeying it (Deut. 6:6; 11:18), and because once Moses wrote the Pentateuch, it would be available in that form.[9]

This passage's point, then, is that God's commands in his law are clear and understandable, and they aren't difficult to obey. They are understandable intellectually and are known by all to require obedience. God also wanted his people to understand in the sense of volitionally obeying, but of course there were no guarantees that they would obey. Of course, while this passage applies to the whole Mosaic law (the Pentateuch), we cannot say it is about the parts of the OT not yet written. Thankfully, however, passages in other parts of the OT and NT say that those portions of Scripture are also clear.

*Psalm 119:105*—Our next two passages are both found in Psalm 119. The first is the very familiar and well-loved verse 105, "Thy word is a lamp to my feet, and a light to my path." Scripture, of course, is not a literal light or lamp, but just as a literal light shows where an actual path is so that one knows where to step safely, so Scripture describes actions that are morally right. If one follows that "light," one will obey Scripture and do what God commands. This will ensure "arriving" at the places in life where God wants us to go, and being morally and spiritually safe each step along the way.

For Scripture to play this role in our lives requires all three levels of understanding. We can't obey what we don't understand intellectually. So, God's word and its demands must be clear enough for anyone to understand. One must also understand that without obedience, one will lose one's way. Of course, for Scripture actually to guide our feet along life's journey, we must choose to obey its commands. But regardless of what one does with Scripture, the psalmist affirms that Scripture is clear enough in itself to serve us in all of these senses of understanding.

*Psalm 119:130*—Verse 130 of Psalm 119 also uses the metaphor of light, but it more literally explains the role Scripture plays. The psalmist says of God's words that the "unfolding" of them gives light. As various commentators suggest, the term "unfolding" evokes the notion of unrolling a scroll of God's word. This, of course, allows the scroll to be read. So, the basic idea is that,

---

[9] Ibid., 1:178–179.

whenever someone opens God's word and begins to read it, there is an un-folding or disclosure of God's word.[10] Doing this, the psalmist affirms, brings light. Here the idea is the same as in verse 105, giving guidance and showing the right way to live.

The next part of the verse tells the results (at least the intended ones) of unfolding Scripture's light: "it gives understanding to the simple." Though there is some debate over who the "simple" are, it is best not to overcomplicate the psalmist's point. What he most likely has in mind refers to those who are young and inexperienced and lack insight for living. They lack discernment and tend to be easily fooled.[11] Though we might think this refers only to children, it seems instead to point to anyone lacking experience and insight, regardless of how old they are.

Does this mean that Scripture is of little help for those who are more ma-ture, emotionally and spiritually? Certainly not. Rather, the psalmist's point is that even the most naïve and immature will find guidance for living whenever they encounter God's word. Of course, it will serve the same function for those who are more mature. But, the fact that the psalmist speaks of the simple shows, in effect, that Scripture is understandable to all people, even the most naïve and inexperienced. Surely this involves both intellectual understanding as well as awareness that Scripture's message is relevant the reader. The guid-ance it gives should also encourage everyone to obey it, but the verse doesn't guarantee that this third and fullest sense of understanding will happen.

Do these two verses from Psalm 119 apply to all of Scripture or to just a part of it? In neither verse does the psalmist limit the amount of God's word in view. Surely, he believed that what he wrote is true of God's word in any form, but his focus in this psalm is God's word recorded in Scripture. There is no reason to think he would restrict this only to his own psalms; surely he has in view whatever Scripture had been written up to that time. Even more, whatever qualifies as Scripture has these characteristics, so it is appropriate to *apply* the teaching of these verses to the whole canon of Scripture.

*Proverbs 6:20–24*—This is another OT passage that teaches that what God commands is clear and easy to understand. The writer instructs a young man to follow his parents' commands. While this might refer only to general rules for successful living, in the context of Proverbs it more likely means com-mands taken from God's word and taught to children in the home. These commands, if followed, will keep the son from various evils, especially the temptations of an evil woman (v. 24).

---

[10] Ibid., 1:243–245.
[11] Ibid., 1:246.

Lest anyone think these commands are hard to follow, because they are unclear, the writer affirms (v. 23) that the commandment is a "lamp" and the law is "light." He adds that the reproofs of instruction are the "way of life." This is the same kind of metaphor used in Psalm 119. Commands are referred to as a lamp and a light. What can that mean other than that the godly instruction of the young man's parents makes clear a life path that will lead him in the ways of righteousness and will keep him from evil? But if the commands and law of his parents can produce such results, they must not be difficult to understand. The son is told to bind the commands on his heart and tie them to his neck (Prov. 6:21). Surely, this means that he must internalize them so that they become an integral part of his way of thinking and acting. Such intimate knowledge requires the commands to be understandable.

Where did these commands come from? His parents gave him the commands, but where did they get them? Most likely from the word of God, Scripture. Certainly the one command most specifically mentioned (v. 24) is part of Scripture. So, most likely the writer recommends these commands because he knows they come from God's word.[12] Presumably, he has seen the result when the commands are followed and when they are disobeyed. His advice to the young is not merely theoretical, for he knows by experience the value of obeying the commands.

*1 Corinthians 2:14–15*—Our next passages are from the NT. The first is 1 Corinthians 2:14–15. We have already discussed this passage several times in this book, but it is also relevant to the doctrine of perspicuity. As we saw when discussing revelation, the focus of 1 Corinthians 2:9–12 is God's revelation, and in the chapters on inspiration, we saw that verse 13 is about that doctrine. Verses 14–15 relate to illumination, but they also have something to say about Scripture's clarity. In sum, these verses teach that those without a saving relation to God—"natural men"—cannot understand the things of the Spirit of God. Since the Spirit superintended the writing of Scripture, verse 14 means that nonbelievers can't understand Scripture. It is foolishness to them, and they can't know it, because it is "spiritually discerned," and "natural men" don't have the Spirit. On the other hand, verse 15 affirms that those who are saved—the "spiritual"—can understand all things. Surely, Paul includes in "all things" spiritual truths, including those found in Scripture.

So, these verses teach that, in general, Scripture is unclear to those who don't know Christ as Savior, and clear to those who do. What does this mean? Are the unsaved unable even to grasp intellectually what Scripture says? Perhaps in some cases that is true, but the stories I shared at the start of my chapter

[12] Fry, "Doctrine of the Word in Orthodox Lutheranism," 37.

on illumination—about nonbelievers who know the content of Scripture and some key doctrines even better than many who know Christ as Savior—suggest otherwise. So, verse 14 may mean that *some* nonbelievers are unable to intellectually grasp the meaning of Scripture. In addition, others may understand Scripture's points but fail to see that they are relevant to them. Furthermore, *all* nonbelievers, by definition, have chosen not to act on what Scripture requires in order to have a relationship with God. Whatever the reason, no nonbeliever has chosen to accept Scripture's message. If they had so chosen, they would be saved.

Given the overall context of 1 Corinthians 2 and the distinction between the unsaved and saved in verses 9–15, Paul's main point is that nonbelievers don't understand things of the Spirit, including Scripture, in that they don't decide to accept them and live in accord with them. Maybe they know the intellectual points Scripture makes, and they might even acknowledge that Scripture's message is relevant to them, but they refuse to submit to what God's word requires.

On the other hand, the understanding that involves volitional acceptance of God's word is possible for those who know Christ, "the spiritual." They have the necessary "equipment" for fully grasping what Scripture teaches; they have the Holy Spirit indwelling them. However, Paul doesn't say that everyone who knows Christ as Savior will in fact accept Scripture in the third sense of understanding. In fact, in 1 Corinthians 3 Paul begins to address some of the problems at the church of Corinth, and one is that they are carnal. That is, they are saved, but they aren't growing and in some ways they are living like the unsaved. As a result, Paul says he couldn't teach them the more substantial things of the faith ("meat" or "solid food"), but had to settle for simpler, less substantial ("milk") truths, instead. What was their problem? Weren't they intelligent enough to learn more complex truths? From what Paul says in chapter 3, that doesn't seem to have been the problem. Rather, the problem apparently was that sin had gotten in the way of their growing in Christ. Perhaps they didn't even understand God's word in the second sense of seeing its relevance to them, but it is certain that they didn't understand it to the point of internalizing and living it.

As one reads the rest of 1 Corinthians, one sees that Paul had to address a variety of sinful attitudes and actions that were hindering the Corinthian believers' growth. The overall message in 1 Corinthians, with regards to perspicuity, is that Scripture is clear and understandable, if you have the "right equipment," i.e., the indwelling Holy Spirit. But its point will be missed if you don't have the Spirit; and believers who are carnal can also misunderstand Scripture and fail to apply it (1 Cor. 3:1).

*2 Peter 1:19*—This is a crucial verse for inspiration, but it also seems relevant to perspicuity. Peter's teaching rests on eyewitness testimony, but also on something even more certain, a "more sure" word of prophecy: Scripture (v. 19).

Peter adds that his readers should pay attention to this more sure word, as they would to a light shining in a dark place. Metaphorically, then, Peter is saying that Scripture is a light shining in a dark place. Light makes things clear as it dispels the darkness. It shows the way to go so that one can arrive safely at an intended destination without losing one's way. How could this be true, if Scripture were unclear?

Of course, the kind of understanding most fundamentally in view in this passage is intellectual knowledge about who Jesus is and what he did. But that knowledge isn't an end in itself. Remember that Peter begins this epistle with a plea for readers to live godly lives. The need to do so stems from the truthfulness of the whole "Christian story." It can be believed at least in part because it can be understood, though that fact alone doesn't guarantee that it will be applied in the lives of those who understand it.

### Passages Implying and thus Requiring Scripture's Clarity

Many passages fit this category, but we can't discuss them all in depth. However, we can at least say a word about many of them. A good place to start is Deuteronomy 6:4–7.

*Deuteronomy 6:4–7*—Israel is told to reflect on the fact that there is only one God, Yahweh. She is to love him with every fiber of her being (vv. 4–5). Moses then says that the words he commands the people are to be in their hearts. Even more, they must teach them to their children. These words should always be on their minds, regardless of what they are doing (vv. 6–7). Of course, Moses was referring to the words of the Pentateuch, words of Scripture. If parents are to teach them even to their children, Scripture must be clear enough for a child to understand. The description of when this should be done (v. 7) shows that more than just having children memorize verses is necessary. Everyone knows that something can be memorized without being understood. And, if the only goal is Scripture memorization, it wouldn't take all day for that, nor would it be necessary to talk about Scripture when sitting, walking, etc. So, the internalizing of God's word in view requires it to be discussed, meditated upon, and analyzed for how it should impact daily living. None of that can happen unless Scripture is understandable even to a child.

Many Jews through the centuries have taken this passage to apply to whatever part of the OT was written when they were alive. This doesn't mean that every portion of Scripture is equally clear, but it means that Scripture's central teachings are accessible, even to children, so children should start learning them during their childhood, not later. At the very least, this requires every Jew to understand the law intellectually. It also means that they should be able to understand that the law applies to them, not just to others. God also wants everyone to obey his commands, although there are no guarantees that this will happen. But constant repetition of and reflection upon God's demands is a first step in internalizing what God requires.

*Deuteronomy 31:9–13*—The message of Deuteronomy 31:9–13 is like that of Deuteronomy 6:4–7, although Moses here is writing not about daily life in general but about what should happen at the end of every seven-year period. The people of Israel are to celebrate the Feast of Tabernacles. As part of this feast, the people are to meet corporately and listen to the reading of the law. This requirement includes not only adult men, but women, children, and any strangers in their city. The purpose of this public reading is that those present may hear, learn to fear the Lord, and learn to obey all the words of the law. Gathering all the people together once every seven years wouldn't be difficult, but it would be impossible for those present to do the other things (learning and obeying) if they couldn't understand what was read to them.

Of course, the initial intent of this ceremony was for the people intellectually to know God's requirements. Hopefully, the public reading of God's law and the example of older family members and friends who obey the law would teach everyone the details of God's commands, and move them to obey. If nothing else, they should learn that judgment will fall if God's law is ignored or deliberately disobeyed. None of this seems likely if Scripture's teachings are unclear and difficult to understand.

*Psalm 19:7–8*—Another passage that implies Scripture's clarity is Psalm 19:7–8. In verse 7 the psalmist writes that God's law "converts" the soul (cf. KJV). He adds that the Lord's testimony makes wise the simple. However, if God's law is unclear, it can confuse, and won't likely convert the soul. And, if the Lord's testimony is opaque, the simple won't learn much of anything to help them live wisely. The psalmist next adds that the Lord's statutes rejoice the heart and enlighten the eyes (v. 8). How could one rejoice over what one doesn't comprehend? The latter portion of this verse again uses the metaphor of God's word as light. As in other instances, this requires clarity; otherwise confusion, not enlightenment, will result from hearing or reading God's commands.

Though these verses don't explicitly say that God's word is clear, they seem to imply just that. Of course, the psalmist would think we can find the Lord's law, his testimony, statutes, and commandments in the words of written Scripture available during his lifetime. Can this passage *apply* to the rest of Scripture yet to be written? There is no reason to think the psalmist would say no, for these verses are general enough to show that the psalmist must have believed that whatever is God's law, testimony, or commandment can accomplish the things ascribed to it in these verses.

The NT has many passages whose teaching also implies Scripture's clarity. For example, think of many of Paul's epistles. In their first verses, Paul's salutation shows that these letters are for all the members of the church or churches in the cities or regions addressed (1 Cor. 1:2; 2 Cor. 1:1; Gal. 1:2; Eph. 1:1; Col. 1:1–2; 1 Thess. 1:1; 2 Thess. 1:1). In one case, the church at Philippi, Paul even mentions the elders and deacons in addition to all the other believers at Philippi. That salutation clearly shows that Paul's letter wasn't just for the learned and the leaders, but for all believers in that city. The same effect is achieved in other books that Paul addresses to the Christians in each church.

Similarly, James (1:1) addresses the "twelve tribes who are dispersed abroad," and Peter writes to "sojourners" scattered throughout various parts of Asia Minor (1 Pet. 1:1) and to those who "have obtained like precious faith with us through the righteousness of God and our Saviour, Jesus Christ" (2 Pet. 1:1 KJV). John begins the book of Revelation with letters or messages to seven churches in Asia Minor (Revelation 2–3), obviously intending all the members of those churches to hear what he says. But then, after he ends those messages, he doesn't begin chapter 4 by saying that the rest of the book is only for the intellectually elite. Like the letters to the seven churches, the rest of Revelation is for all believers. See also Jude 1.

Those included in the salutations to these books wouldn't just be the leaders, or the educated, or the spiritually mature in those churches. These epistles are addressed to every member of the church, and their contents were relevant not only to the learned but also to the unlearned and to believers at all stages of spiritual maturity. Of course, some passages in each book are hard to understand. But if the vast majority of these books' contents were opaque, even to the most mature and learned, there would be no point in addressing them to the whole church. That they are addressed to every believer in these churches *implies* that anyone could understand what the apostles wrote. Though we live nearly two thousand years after these epistles were first written, we also can affirm that their basic message isn't impossible to understand. Most of these letters were written in a straightforward, easy to understand style, and their content is accessible.

The facts just rehearsed imply that all recipients can intellectually grasp these letters' message. The apostles who authored the books rather pointedly raised problems in the churches to which they wrote, and their instructions and encouragement were straightforward and easy to understand. Sometimes the author even knew specific people in the church who were the source of problems, and addressed them directly (e.g., Phil. 4:2). Other than knowing that Euodia and Syntyche were prominent in the church at Philippi, for example, we know little about how educated, intelligent, etc., they were, but Paul had no doubt that they (and other believers at Philippi) would understand his message that there must be unity of mind, will, and love, and humility and helpfulness toward every believer in that church (Phil. 2:2–4), regardless of each member's position and role. Such thoughts are high and noble, but they would matter little if Paul's letter was so opaque that even "scholars" in that church would disagree about his message.

Paul surely believed that those addressed in these letters would understand that his message applied to them. Would they act on what he said or not? Paul hoped they would, and given the kind of reception he had received, for example, in person at Thessalonica (see 1 Thess. 1:5–10), he undoubtedly believed his letters would also receive a positive reception. We don't know whether that happened, but understanding to the point of internalizing these letters' messages was certainly the goal of both their divine and human authors!

*Matthew 28:18–20*—The Great Commission passage, Matthew 28:18–20 (par. Mark 16:15) is one of our Lord's best-known commands. Most of us, however, think only of its commands to bring the gospel, to all nations and to baptize those who believe. But what is the gospel, and how do we know it? During Jesus's life on earth, if someone wanted to hear the gospel, he could find out where Jesus would be preaching and hear him. After Christ's death, resurrection, and ascension, for many years people could have heard the gospel by listening to one of Jesus's disciples. But anyone living more than a century or so after Christ's ascension couldn't attend a meeting where any of these people would be preaching.

So how would people living after the time of Christ and his apostles know the gospel message? They could learn it from NT Scripture. But if preachers over the last two millennia present a gospel (found in Scripture) that is unclear, how can they expect anyone to be saved? Thankfully, the gospel is clearly articulated in many NT passages, and if those who preach it simply expound Scripture, their message will be clear. Not all who hear will be saved, but not because the gospel is too hard to understand and/or communicate. Thankfully, the gospel and the Scriptures that expound it are clear about what the gospel is and what it requires. Jesus didn't leave his disciples a hopelessly difficult task!

Sadly, believers often overlook or minimize one part of the Great Commission. Jesus not only commanded his disciples to spread the gospel to the whole world (Matt. 28:19). He also ordered them to teach the nations "to observe all that I commanded you" (28:20). Thus, the Great Commission isn't just about presenting the gospel and leading people to Christ as Savior. It includes teaching *all that Christ has commanded*! Where do we learn what that is? At the very least, we find Jesus's teachings in the Gospels. In addition, as we saw when discussing inspiration, Jesus promised to send the Holy Spirit to teach his disciples and remind them of what Jesus had said and done (John 16). To what end? Not just to minister to the disciples, but to aid them, so that when they preached *and penned the soon-to-be-written* NT, they would "get it right!"

But what would be the point of presenting Jesus's teachings to people all over the world, if understanding them requires special training? The only way to teach worldwide what Jesus commanded is to teach Scripture. And, that teaching can be successful only if Scripture is clear and easy enough to understand for everyone. So, the Great Commission assumes that God's word can be understood intellectually and used by the Holy Spirit to draw men, women, and children to a saving knowledge of Christ.

*Matthew 24:15*—Matthew 24:15 is part of the Olivet Discourse. Jesus's disciples drew his attention to the Jewish temple. Jesus said that not one stone of it would fail to be thrown down (vv. 1–2). The disciples were undoubtedly shocked, and as Jesus sat on the Mount of Olives, they came and asked him three questions: (1) when will these things (destruction of the temple) happen? (2) what will be the sign of your coming? And (3) what will be the sign of the end of the age (Matt. 24:3)? Jesus's response, recorded in Matthew 24–25, is known as the Olivet Discourse. In 24:4–14, Jesus detailed various events that will happen as a prelude to the end of the age. Elaborating on those events, he added in verse 15 that when his disciples would see the abomination of desolation, of which Daniel the prophet spoke, standing in the holy place, then they should flee to the mountains (v. 16).

Verse 15, however, also includes the words "let the reader understand." It isn't clear whether these words come from Jesus's mouth or Matthew's pen, but their intent is clear: let the reader understand that the predicted abomination of desolation is the one about which Daniel wrote. Daniel mentioned the abomination of desolation in three distinct passages: Daniel 9:27; 11:31; and 12:11.

Though the fulfillment of each passage is debated, 11:31 is part of a lengthy passage that runs from (at least) Daniel 11:21–35 and is usually taken to refer to Antiochus Epiphanes and his desecration of the temple. However, Antiochus (175–164 BC) did these things approximately two hundred years before Jesus spoke these words (or if they are Matthew's insertion, then Matthew wrote them more than two hundred years after Antiochus desecrated the temple).

Why does this matter? Because Jesus was asked about *future* events. Jesus's answer in Matthew 24:4ff. doesn't talk about the past; he addressed questions his disciples asked about the future. Hence, if Jesus's comment about the abomination of desolation refers to Daniel 11:21–35 and Antiochus, it can't answer the disciples' questions about events future to them and to Jesus on that occasion.

So, the reference to Daniel can't be to Daniel 11:21–35. Can it refer to Daniel 9:27 and/or 12:11? Would events predicted in those passages be future from when Jesus spoke the words of Matthew 24:15? Indeed, they would be. Daniel 9:27 is the prophecy of Daniel's Seventieth Week, and I believe 12:11 also refers to events that will happen in that seventieth week and beyond. Of course, we must ask when the seventieth week occurred. Some think it occurred several decades after Jesus's death and resurrection and included the destruction of Jerusalem in AD 70.[13] In my understanding of both Daniel's Seventieth Week and Jesus's reference in Matthew 24:15 to Daniel's prophecy, Jesus spoke about events not only future to his time, but future even to our day.

Regardless of one's interpretation of Matthew 24:15 (and of the Daniel passages), the clear reference to the abomination of desolation, plus the comment that the reference to Daniel is there so that the reader may understand, show something very important about the nature of Scripture. Even in passages that many would say are open to great misunderstanding and misinterpretation, namely, prophetic Scriptures, the biblical author wants the reader to understand. That doesn't sound like a book written to hide the meaning of God's revelation, but rather one that intentionally includes clues to help readers grasp what Jesus means. That alone doesn't prove that all Scripture is clear, but it is consistent with other passages that require and imply it. Why would Jesus include this clear reference to Daniel if not to help his audience understand?

*John 5:39*—In John 5:30ff. Jesus offered evidence of the truth of his teachings and of who he claimed to be. He then encouraged his audience to search the Scriptures, for they believed that in them they would find information which, if

---

[13] In support of this view, many would cite Luke's version of the Olivet Discourse, as recorded in Luke 21:5–14. This is often linked with verses 20–24 of Luke 21, which do predict the destruction of Jerusalem that happened in AD 70. However, I disagree with this understanding of Matthew 24:15ff. The things predicted in Matthew 24:4–14 did not happen prior to the AD 70 attack on Jerusalem, and by the time we get to Matthew 24:29–31, also part of Jesus's answer to his disciples three questions, we are certainly not looking at AD 70. Matthew 24:29–31, with its prediction of the return of Christ (second advent) and the gathering of the elect, followed in chapter 25:31ff. with a prediction of the establishment of Christ's kingdom and the judgment of the nations, has not happened yet and is still future even from our perspective. Luke's version of the Olivet Discourse does include Christ's prediction of his return (21:27), but Luke links this very briefly to Jesus's answer about the signs of the end of the age (21:25–26). Matthew's account of the Discourse includes more details. Matthew included more of Jesus's answer to the questions about signs of his coming and of the end of the age (Matt. 24:4–31). So Luke's account of the Olivet Discourse moves immediately from Jesus's prediction of the soon-to-happen sack of Jerusalem and destruction of the temple in AD 70 (21:20–24) to the end of the tribulation and the second advent of Christ (21:25–28). Given biblical inerrancy, we must believe that Jesus spoke of all of these events recorded by both Matthew and Luke, though each apostle's account of the Olivet Discourse has its own nuances. Of course, the interpretation of the Olivet Discourse just offered is debated by biblical scholars, as are other interpretations. For our purposes in this volume, it isn't necessary to present arguments and evidences for and against each understanding. That falls within the range of topics covered in the Foundations of Evangelical Theology volume on eschatology.

followed, would give them eternal life. Jesus didn't deny that Scripture contains such information. Rather, he affirmed that Scriptures that teach about attaining eternal life testify that he is who he claimed to be.

This passage is significant for at least three reasons. First, if one wants to know how to attain eternal life, one should search the Scriptures. What will one find? That Scripture teaches that knowing Jesus as Savior is the way to live forever. That is the second thing we should note about this passage. Of course, this specific verse doesn't say what it is about Jesus that makes him the way to eternal life, but throughout John's Gospel, John includes ample amounts of Jesus's teachings that clarify exactly how there is eternal life in Jesus, and how anyone can attain it.

Third, in this verse, Jesus seems to take for granted that anyone who searches Scripture can reach the conclusions he has just mentioned (Scripture reveals how to attain eternal life, and Jesus is the way). Jesus didn't say that one needs an apostle, a good hermeneutics text, or anyone or anything else in order to find the answer. Why not? Evidently, Jesus thought the answer to such important questions is clear to anyone who opens Scripture and just reads. Or if one can't read, one can still understand if someone else reads it to him.

It is hard to see how what Jesus said doesn't assume that Scripture is clear and understandable on these matters!

*Romans 4:1–25; 15:4; and 1 Corinthians 10:1–11*—Our next three passages (Rom. 4:1–25 [esp. vv. 23–25], Rom. 15:4, and 1 Cor. 10:1–11) all have a common element, although at first one might not think so. Romans 4 recounts various events in Abraham's life, and Paul says that Abraham's trust in God in those circumstances was counted unto him for righteousness. In Romans 15:4, Paul offers a summary comment on the various themes expounded in the book. And in 1 Corinthians 10:1–11, Paul presents various things that happened to the children of Israel during their wilderness wandering.

In each case, Paul says that these things happened as examples for believers and were written so that we might believe and obey the point(s) under discussion. In Romans 4:23–25, Paul concludes his exposition on Abraham and justification by faith with such a comment. In chapter 15, having just ended a discussion on Christian liberty, Paul points to things written in earlier times, and says that they were written for our learning so that we might find comfort and encouragement from the Scriptures. In other words, Paul connects "things written in earlier times" with the encouragement one can get from the Scriptures. The best way to understand this is to see that the phrase "things written in earlier times" refers to Scripture—undoubtedly, the OT.

In 1 Corinthians 10:1–11, Paul writes about Israel in the wilderness, and he mentions that they "passed through the sea" (a reference to deliverance through the Red Sea), were "under the cloud," were "baptized into Moses in the cloud and in the sea," and "ate the same spiritual food" and drank from the spiritual rock that followed them, which rock was Christ. Even so, God wasn't pleased with many of them, and they died in the wilderness. In verse 6 Paul tells readers that these things were examples for believers at Corinth that they should not lust after evil things. Paul details in verses 7–10 other divine commands, some of which were disobeyed by some Jews in the wilderness and resulted in their punishment. In verse 11 Paul repeats that these things happened as examples and are a warning to the Corinthians. By extension, anyone who reads these verses should also be warned not to follow the path of sin that many in Israel followed.

So, the common thread in these passages is that they present examples for the Roman and Corinthian churches, and for anyone else who reads them. But these events and the NT accounts of them serve as examples only if those who read them can understand what they read. Paul assumed that his recounting of these stories was easy enough to understand so that Roman and Corinthian Christians could grasp them and the stories could accomplish their intended goal. Though none of these passages asserts the clarity of Paul's inspired commentary, the fact that Paul says that he recounts these events as examples for his readers' sake, assumes that what he wrote is understandable to any who would read them.

Here I must add that the level of understanding expected must be more than mere intellectual awareness. Saying that these things were written "for our sake also, to whom it will be reckoned, as those who believe in Him who raised Jesus" (Rom. 4:23–24), that they were written "for our instruction, that through perseverance and the encouragement of the Scriptures we might have hope" (Rom. 15:4), and that they "were written for our instruction" (1 Cor. 10:11) clearly means more than that the lessons taught are relevant to us. Indeed, Paul expected that believers would see the need to apply the lessons the examples teach and to avoid repeating the same mistakes. That would be impossible if the OT stories Paul recounts, or his instruction based on them, were opaque and understandable only to experts in biblical and theological studies.

*Ephesians 6:4*—Another passage that implies perspicuity is Ephesians 6:4. Paul begins Ephesians 6 with a list of moral rules. In verse 4 he instructs parents not to make their children angry by what they say or do, but rather to raise them in the "discipline and instruction" of the Lord. But what should parents teach their children, to give them a godly upbringing? Surely Paul's answer echoes Deuteronomy 6:1–9, even though Paul makes the point more briefly. In order to raise children in the discipline and instruction of the Lord, the best tool available is Scripture. Fathers should teach their children Scripture with its commands and promises.

But how can this succeed if Scripture's commands are either too hard to understand or too difficult to obey? For fathers to understand the command in Ephesians 6:4, that verse must be clear, and what it commands also requires that both fathers and their children can understand Scripture's demands. Hence, this verse assumes Scripture's perspicuity, and the kind of clarity envisioned isn't mere intellectual understanding. Fathers are to teach Scripture's commands not only so that their children understand that the commands apply to them, but also so that they obey them.

*Colossians 3:16*—In Colossians 3:16 Paul exhorts the Colossians to let the "word of Christ" dwell in them "richly." As Allison explains, when Paul wrote Colossians, the "word of Christ"

> would have consisted of the basic kerygma, or foundational message of the death and resurrection of Jesus Christ; the growing body of apostolic teaching transmitted both orally and, ever more so, in written form (cf. Col 4:16); and certainly would not have excluded the Old Testament which constituted the canonical Scriptures of the early church and thus was the authoritative document for understanding the person and work of Christ.[14]

What should the Colossian believers do with this word so that it would dwell richly among them? They were to tell it to one another by teaching and singing. As Allison suggests, these psalms, hymns, and spiritual songs most likely included traditional OT psalms and hymns as well as compositions written more recently which presented and extolled the great truths of the new Christian faith.[15] To say that these words were to dwell among them *richly* suggests that teaching and singing the truths of the faith were to be the mainstays of the Colossians' life and worship!

Where would Paul have thought one could find the word of Christ? Undoubtedly, he thought of OT Scriptures that looked forward to Christ. But apostolic teaching also repeats the words and deeds of Christ. The latter would include written documents like the letter to Colossae and his letters to other churches. It would also include writings of other apostles. Some of these would ultimately become NT books, but surely the apostles also wrote letters to individuals and groups of believers that also contained the word of Christ. Perhaps Paul knew that the Colossians were familiar with such letters, but even if not, plenty of information about Christ was available in oral and written form.

---

[14] Allison, "Protestant Doctrine of the Perspicuity of Scripture," 2:370.
[15] Ibid., 2:374.

As to Christ's word in written form, Paul assumed that it was clear and understandable. He never says it is hard to understand or that they will need an interpreter to grasp it. Teaching in its various forms and singing the word of Christ are possible, because that word is clear. Certainly, Paul assumed intellectual clarity, but he likely also believed that the Colossians would want to teach and sing Christ's words because they had personally found them to be true and life-changing. If so, that requires a deeper understanding than merely grasping the intellectual content of what Jesus said and taught.

*1 Timothy 4:13*—The final passages in this category all appear in Paul's letters to Timothy. In 1 Timothy 4:13, Paul told Timothy to give attention to reading, exhortation, and doctrine until Paul arrived. Reading of what? Exhortation based on what? Doctrine constructed from what? Undoubtedly, Paul assumed that Timothy would know the source material for these activities, and Timothy surely did. The source material was Scripture, and also apostolic teaching, including Jesus's teachings, that Timothy would have learned from Paul, even if from no one else.

Paul didn't tell Timothy to understand the content of what he would read, preach, and study according to Paul's (or someone else's) interpretation. Nor did Paul tell Timothy to wait until Paul arrived so that he could help Timothy grasp the meaning of these teachings. While Paul had surely previously taught Timothy many things, nothing in this verse suggests that Timothy should focus only on what he had learned from Paul. Paul's instructions were general enough so that, in obeying them, Timothy was free to consult any Scripture and oral teaching he had heard.

Some may say that this open-ended instruction to Timothy made sense because Timothy was one of Paul's "star pupils"; we aren't that knowledgeable, so this instruction couldn't apply to us. But Paul doesn't give even the slightest hint that what he told Timothy to do can't be done by other Christians, regardless of how learned or biblically literate they are. Paul just advised Timothy to give himself to the tasks mentioned in this verse. The best explanation of why Paul gave Timothy that assignment is that he believed that Scripture, the source for Timothy's study, is understandable even without an apostle to guide him as he interpreted it.

It is also true that for Timothy to do what Paul commanded would require more than just getting a cursory intellectual knowledge of Scripture. Of course, one can read Scripture incorrectly, exhort people to do things Scripture doesn't require, and formulate heresy rather than orthodox doctrine. But Paul didn't seem worried that any of that would happen. Surely he had great confidence in Timothy, but he also knew that God's word is clear!

*2 Timothy 3:15–4:2*—A final passage in this category is the familiar passage 2 Timothy 3:15–4:2. In chapter 3, Paul wrote that perilous times will come on the world in the last days. All sorts of immorality and doctrinal error will be the order of the day. Timothy should guard against being entrapped by any of it, and Paul added that Timothy had two safeguards to keep him from wrong-doing and wrong thinking. He had the godly example and teaching of other Christians like his grandmother Lois, his mother Eunice, and Paul himself. Timothy's second weapon for resisting the evil of the last days was Scripture.

Paul says several things about Scripture, and once we understand them, we can see that they imply perspicuity. The first is that (v. 15) from childhood Timothy had known the Scriptures, which show readers how to be right with God (how to be saved). Some of us were also taught Scripture from our earliest childhood. We learned the gospel and at a very young age accepted Christ. Of course, we learned about Jesus through the NT. Timothy grew up when only the OT had been written. Even so, Timothy had been taught it, and through that teaching likely came to know God as Savior.

This is a biographical fact about Timothy, but it is much more. Scripture must be clear and understandable enough for even a child to grasp what it says about forming a saving relationship with God. Undoubtedly, Timothy's mother and grandmother spoke of these things, but if such biblical truths were opaque, Timothy wouldn't likely have understood them. The fact is that even OT Scripture presents the gospel clearly enough for someone to read it, accept it, and be saved.

In verse 16, Paul explains that Scripture is such a potent safeguard because it is the very word of God. As such, it is useful for doctrine, reproof, correction, and instruction in righteousness. That is, Scripture teaches things that lead us to understand God, ourselves, and our relation to him—we express these truths in doctrinal claims. Scripture also scolds those who disobey its precepts; but even more, positively, it shows us how God wants us to live. And it also teaches what is righteous, what is not, and most importantly, how to be right before God.

As one thinks of these various uses of Scripture, one might think Scripture was written as a theology text or a how-to manual for daily living. Scripture isn't written as either of these things, and yet Paul didn't add, "and this is why we need Bible scholars and systematic theologians." Paul, of course, had no complaint with such people—he was himself one of the best Bible scholars and theologians of all time. Rather, his point was that anyone, regardless of training and expertise, can use Scripture for these purposes. How could that happen if Scripture were opaque, and if implications of its teachings were impossible to infer? The various things Paul says that *anyone* can do with Scripture imply that Scripture is understandable enough for anyone to read and use in the ways mentioned.

How understandable is Scripture? Only intellectually, as information? Or in a deeper way? Verse 17 answers that Scripture can be understood so as to prepare anyone to obey God's commands and actually follow them. If not, how could someone by knowing Scripture be completely "equipped for every good work"? Obviously, the Holy Spirit must move the minds and wills of readers so that they will choose to do the good works for which they are prepared, but that does not contradict what Paul teaches about Scripture preparing us for such obedience.

Note also that Paul says (v. 16) that *all* of Scripture is God's word and valuable for the uses Paul details. As we saw when discussing inspiration, this includes the whole OT, which was available in Paul's and Timothy's day, and the soon-to-be-written NT, much of which was not yet available when Paul wrote this letter. Don't overlook the significance of this point. We are inclined to think that Jesus's teachings and Paul's and Peter's, etc., letters can be used for these purposes. But how do the genealogies of Jesus in the Gospels serve these purposes? And how are the "who begats" of the Pentateuch and the various details in OT historical books usable for these ends? Paul doesn't explain, and of course, his point is about Scripture in general. But even so, "all" is all-inclusive! Though it may be hard to see how some passages can be used for the purposes Paul details in this passage, that doesn't mean they cannot be so used. Biblical inerrancy requires that Paul is right, even if we can't currently explain how every Scripture can serve the purposes Paul lists.

Given Scripture's nature and its uses, Paul next charges Timothy (and by extension, all preachers) to preach Scripture (2 Tim. 4:1–2). Because Scripture is alive and gives life (animation), as is evident from its uses (3:16–17), why would any preacher preach anything else? Only a fool would preach lifeless material in an attempt to grow believers and introduce nonbelievers to a saving relationship with Christ. Scripture must be the foundation of and provide the content of our sermons, and those sermons must both teach Scripture's truths and show listeners how those truths apply to their lives!

How can any of these things happen if Scripture is unclear and hard to understand? It can't! What Paul says requires that even the unlearned and biblically ignorant can understand *what* God's word teaches and *how* to apply it to life so as to produce men, women, and children who are people of God, completely prepared for all good works![16]

---

[16] In addition to Scriptures that *teach* the clarity of God's word, other Scriptures recount incidents when Scripture was read, and its hearers understood it immediately. Some of those passages illustrate Scripture's perspicuity. In others, it isn't entirely clear whether the incident illustrates perspicuity. Consider the following narratives: Nehemiah 8, Acts 8:31–38, and Acts 17:10–12. Nehemiah 8 presents two incidents which seem to illustrate Scripture's clarity. The first is covered in verses 1–12, and the second is recounted beginning in verse 13. In both instances,

### Passages Limiting the Clarity of Some Scripture

In spite of the preceding discussion, some Scriptures appear to limit Scripture's clarity by offering reasons why it is hard to understand Scripture. What are these exceptions, and do they contradict and even nullify the passages that affirm Scripture's clarity? My contention is that the passages to be discussed place some limitations on biblical clarity, but they don't completely remove it. The passages are Matthew 13:10ff; Romans 6:19; 1 Corinthians 2:14–15; 2 Corinthians 4:3–4; and 2 Peter 3:15–16. Let's address them in their NT canonical order.

In Matthew 13, Matthew says that Jesus spoke many things in parables to the multitudes. His first parable was the parable of the seeds and the soils. Matthew 13:3–9 records the parable, and verses 18–23 give Jesus's explanation of it. Why not give the explanation beginning in verse 10? Because Jesus's disciples asked (v. 10) why he spoke to the crowd in parables, and in verses 11–17 we find Jesus's answer.

Jesus's explanation of why he spoke in parables amounts to saying that his disciples should understand the mysteries of the kingdom, but God doesn't want those who reject Jesus to know this information. Rejecters' eyes and ears are closed to the truth, and their hearts are hardened against it (v. 15). This has happened so that they won't understand Jesus's teaching, for if they did, they might be converted. But they don't want to be converted, and so in effect, Jesus says they will get what they want. He will teach in parables that they can't understand, and so they won't be saved.

In contrast, Jesus's disciples, who willingly accepted his teaching, will understand his parables and the mysteries of the kingdom they contain (vv. 11–12). To ensure that his disciples understand the parable of the seeds and soils, Jesus then explains its meaning (vv. 18–23).

---

the audience understood Scripture to the point of celebrating and obeying it. Scripture's clarity also seems to be illustrated in the two incidents cited from Acts. However, neither passage says exactly how much prior knowledge those who grasped Scripture's meaning had. So, these passages may illustrate biblical perspicuity, but I leave it to readers to decide. The first is Acts 8:26–38, the story of Philip and the Ethiopian eunuch. The second is about the Bereans, recorded in Acts 17:10–12. As to the first, the impression given (and usually taken by Bible expositors) is that the Ethiopian had a copy of Isaiah and little else. He read and understood Isaiah 53's predictions, but didn't know who fulfilled them. If he understood the *what* of Isaiah 53 without training in interpreting literature or access to commentaries, then this passage shows the clarity of Scripture, even of prophecies. But he may have had prior training in Scripture. Since we don't know what prior training or knowledge of Scripture he had, we can't say with certainty that this passage illustrates Scripture's clarity. As for Acts 17:10–12 and the Bereans, this incident is usually taken to show that anyone can read Scripture and test ideas in light of its teaching. In this case, the Berean *Jews* found Paul and Silas's preaching consistent with their reading of the OT. Verse 12 adds that many *Greek* men and women also believed. We are not told, however, whether they believed because they found the preaching to match the OT, or because the preaching itself was too compelling to resist. Of course, it is unlikely that the Berean Gentiles had much, if any, prior knowledge of Scripture—though we aren't told this for sure. So, does this passage illustrate perspicuity? If the Berean Jews were basically ignorant of OT Scriptures and then studied them with Paul and Silas's preaching in mind, then this incident likely illustrates Scripture's clarity. But if they found Paul and Silas's preaching convincing at least in part because they knew the OT well, then their response probably doesn't illustrate Scripture's clarity. As for the Berean Gentiles, Luke doesn't say whether they had any prior knowledge of Scripture before Paul and Silas came to town. It is quite natural to assume that these Gentiles would have been biblically illiterate, but we can't be absolutely certain. After all, the Ethiopian eunuch was a Gentile, and he knew a lot about Isaiah 53 anyway. Berean Gentiles may have previously learned more about the OT than we might suspect. We just aren't told.

It is quite interesting that this whole conversation begins with this particular parable, because it is about how various people respond to the word of God. The four different soils in the parable represent four different kinds of heart. Each differs in its receptivity to spiritual truth, and accordingly, either rejects or accepts the truth. Some hear the truth and don't understand it, because the wicked one catches the seed sown "by the wayside," and it brings forth nothing. Others receive the truth and initially rejoice over it, but it doesn't take root in their heart, and when trouble and persecution arise, their devotion to the truth falters and dies (v. 21). Yet others hear the word amid "thorns." The thorns represent the cares of this age and its temptations. These things choke off the seed (the word), and no fruit is produced (v. 22). A fourth group, however, represented as good ground, hears, understands, and receives the word, and bears fruit (v. 23).

So, both this incident and the parable Jesus presents teach the same thing. Not everyone who hears God's word understands and accepts it. What is the problem? Are parables too hard to understand? Not at all. The problem, as the parable so aptly teaches, is the spiritual condition of the listener's heart. In the parable, the seed sown on all four soils is exactly the same—it is the word of God. Any problem in understanding has nothing to do with the seed; everything goes well or poorly depending on the condition of the soil.

In essence, this is also the point of Jesus's teaching in parables. Jesus didn't say parables are impossible or even hard to understand. And why should he, for his disciples understood him, especially when he explained each parable's meaning? Jesus used parables because they hide truth from those who refuse to accept God's truth, regardless of the form in which it comes.

So, this passage doesn't deny *Scripture's* clarity. The difference in reception depends not on the seed (Scripture), but on the condition of the soil. God's word is clear in itself. It becomes unclear only when those who hear it refuse to understand, accept, and obey it. Rather than contradicting biblical perspicuity, this parable affirms it.

Romans 6:19a may also seem to contradict biblical clarity. In the first chapters of Romans, Paul shows that everyone has some revelation of God, but has rejected it. Thus, humanity stands guilty before God, and cannot correct their lost condition. The only hope for a right standing before God is justification by faith in Christ. When anyone trusts Christ as Savior, there is peace with God, and all the other blessings of salvation accrue to him or her as well (Romans 5).

In Romans 6 Paul likens the spiritual condition of humans without Christ to the institution of slavery. Before one accepts Christ, one is enslaved to sin. After salvation, one is enslaved to Christ. Using slavery as a literary figure to present the spiritual condition of the lost is a powerful way for Paul to illustrate his theological point. Paul's readers were quite familiar with slavery, and they knew that slaves must serve their master.

Of course, Paul, so to speak, "stretches" the imagery when he applies it to one's relation to Christ. The lost are enslaved to sin, and that bondage is in no way pleasant! Bondage to Christ, in contrast, gives liberation from sin, so it is a good thing, not bad! Using slavery and freedom to illustrate the different states of the saved and the unsaved wonderfully helps Paul make his point about the difference salvation makes in one's ability to handle sin.

But Paul knows that some might wonder why he used slavery to explain such important spiritual truths. In verse 19a, Paul explains that using slavery is "speaking in human terms." That is, it speaks in a way that the recipients of his letter would fully understand, because they know what slavery is. Paul adds that he speaks this way "because of the weakness of your flesh." What does this mean? Does the term "flesh" refer to our sinful human nature (as Paul sometimes uses it)? If so, then, was Paul assuming that the Roman Christians were carnal believers? If not, that is, if they were living godly lives, then why use this imagery?

These are significant questions which impact the interpretation of this text. Commentators differ on the meaning of what Paul says.[17] Some think that Paul speaks of the fallibility of human understanding due to our sinful human nature. Even a redeemed person who obeys the Lord cannot completely escape the old sin nature. Others think Paul isn't complaining about our moral status but rather speaks of our human finitude, which makes it difficult at times to understand concepts, especially abstract theological ones.

It is difficult to decide between these two options. Perhaps the best solution is that Paul has both types of finitude (moral and intellectual) in view. If moral finitude is at all in view, however, Paul doesn't intend to accuse Roman believers of being disobedient to God's word. Rather, he just means that in our unglorified state, all believers struggle with sin to one extent or another. Because of living in a fallen world with its temptations that can and do attract believers, sometimes the fact that we aren't glorified yet makes it harder to understand spiritual truth than it will be when we are glorified and totally removed from sin's presence and power. Moreover, by being saved we don't attain omniscience or even add points to our IQ score. Even intellectually brilliant people aren't omniscient and don't understand everything. It isn't a sin to be less than omniscient; it is just a part of being human.

In sum, if one thinks Paul here combines both types of finitude, then he is

---

[17] Here Allison offers a thorough and helpful presentation of the different exegetical issues and options ("Protestant Doctrine of the Perspicuity of Scripture," 2:291–298). Allison cites various commentaries, and especially helpful are those by Cranfield and Moo on Romans. Those are Douglas J. Moo, *Romans 1–8*, Wycliffe Exegetical Commentary, gen. ed. Kenneth Barker (Chicago: Moody, 1991); and C. E. B. Cranfield, *A Critical and Exegetical Commentary on the Epistle to the Romans* (Edinburgh: T&T Clark, 1982).

saying that he wants his readers to understand his theological points but that, in light of our moral and intellectual finitude, we might have some trouble grasping his point. For the sake of those who do, Paul says he used the imagery of slavery to make this crucial theological point. Even those who can understand Paul's point without the reference to slavery can appreciate that using this imagery makes his point quite vivid!

What does this verse tell us about Scripture's clarity? First, Paul's explanation of why he used the imagery of slavery has nothing to do with Scripture's clarity or lack of it. It totally focuses on the nature of what it means to be a nonglorified human—even a saved one. Thus, Paul's comment doesn't nullify the clarity of Scripture.

But, second, because Paul is quite familiar with human abilities to understand abstract concepts, he makes his theological point using an analogy his readers can easily grasp. That analogy, and Paul's use of it, became part of Scripture because Romans 6 is part of a book inspired by God. Paul's use of this imagery shows his desire for his writing to be clear, and I believe most, if not all, readers would say that Paul's reference to slavery helps clarify his point. So, this text doesn't teach perspicuity as its main theme, but it illustrates how much at least one biblical author, Paul, wanted to be as clear as possible in what he wrote. Elsewhere in his writings Paul helps readers understand what he writes by including various figures of speech such as allegories (Gal. 4:21–31), quotes from OT Scriptures, and other literary devices to enhance clarity. We can also affirm that Paul isn't the only biblical writer who does this. Other writers use a variety of literary devices to communicate truth understandably.[18] And, of course, this is true of Jesus's own teachings. He taught some abstract and difficult concepts but invariably used imagery taken from daily life to make those points. His listeners, even those who rejected him and his teaching, understood quite well what he said and meant!

Our next passage, 1 Corinthians 2:14–15, has already been discussed, so I can be brief. This passage teaches Scripture's clarity to the "spiritual" man. It also teaches that Scripture is unclear to the "natural," unsaved person. Is the problem Scripture? Not at all! The problem is the spiritual condition of the reader's heart and mind. Paul shows that those who don't understand Scripture lack a key piece of "equipment" for grasping its meaning. The Holy Spirit doesn't dwell within them, and they don't seek his guidance to understand Scripture.

As also noted in this chapter, being saved gives believers a clear advantage in understanding Scripture, but it doesn't guarantee that they will do so. Saved

---

[18] For more on this point see Allison, "Protestant Doctrine of the Perspicuity of Scripture," 2:299. As he explains, one of the wonderful facts about this imagery is that it seems timeless. Nearly two thousand years since Paul wrote Romans, readers still understand his literary images (see ibid., 300–301).

but carnal Christians may grasp no more of Scripture's meaning than do the unsaved, or they may fail to understand Scripture's more complex concepts (see 1 Cor. 3:1–3), and they may not be inclined to apply spiritual truth to their own lives. Thankfully, sin's hindrance to the believer's understanding can be derailed when the believer repents of sin and commits to studying God's word.

Two more Scriptures deserve our attention. The first is 2 Corinthians 4:3–4. Paul says (v. 3) that he knows that not everyone understands the gospel he preaches. Those who don't understand don't know Christ. In verse 4 Paul explains why they don't understand the gospel. It is *not* because his message was inherently opaque—this is important, because the gospel Paul preached is the same one he and other NT authors wrote about. The reason that some reject the gospel is that Satan ("the god of this age") has blinded their minds to it. Satan does this because, if he doesn't, the "glorious gospel of Christ" might be clear to them and draw them to accept Christ.

This is a very significant verse for perspicuity. The reason is that theologians typically define perspicuity as Scripture's ability to be understood by anyone of ordinary intelligence *so that they know how to be saved*. But Paul knows that many people don't understand what Scripture says about how to be saved to the point of being volitionally moved to accept its truth and be saved!

Second Corinthians 4:4 explains why many don't understand it. Now Paul isn't likely talking only about mere intellectual understanding of the gospel. Perhaps some nonbelievers do have that problem. But Paul is talking about a deeper level of understanding, one that moves a person to accept Christ. It is that kind of understanding that Satan most opposes, and he does so successfully quite often. The problem for rejecters isn't that their IQ is too low to "get" the gospel. The problem is that Satan and his cohorts work overtime to distract and dissuade hearers of the gospel from accepting it. The only remedy is for God's light to shine into the nonbeliever's heart so that he yields to its demands.

A final passage that might at first seem to contradict biblical perspicuity is 2 Peter 3:15–16. As Peter concludes his letter, he encourages his readers to know that God's withholding judgment on the ungodly stems from God's desire for more people to be saved. Peter then affirms that Paul has also written the same thing.

In verse 16 Peter says that Paul's epistles contain some things that are hard to understand. Does this comment refute the doctrine of perspicuity, at least as it relates to Paul's letters? Not at all, for two reasons. First, perspicuity doesn't mean that every topic in Scripture is set forth with perfect clarity. Rather, perspicuity is a quality of Scripture *in general* whereby anyone of even average intelligence can understand what it says about *how to be saved and lead a life pleasing to God.*

Of course, Scripture addresses more than the topics just noted. Peter's comment about some things in Paul's epistles being hard to understand doesn't identify those things to be what Paul says about how to be saved and live a god-pleasing life. It isn't hard to understand what Paul says about those topics, and I am not alone in that assessment. Paul also covers more difficult topics, but they aren't about how to be saved and live a godly life! So, we can agree with Peter's assessment of Paul's writings without jeopardizing the perspicuity of Paul's work.

Second, Peter's comments don't negate the perspicuity of Paul's writings because Peter adds that things in Paul's writings that are hard to understand are that way because "the untaught and unstable "distort" those things, as they do also "the rest of the Scriptures." What does that mean? It means that at least one reason Paul's writings seem hard to understand to some is that they twist or distort what he says so as to misunderstand his teaching. In doing that, they actually increase the likelihood that God will judge them, because what they do is just another way of rejecting God's word!

To whom does the phrase "untaught and unstable" refer? Commentators debate this, but we shouldn't automatically assume that it refers only to non-believers. As various commentators note, this could refer to believers new to the faith who haven't yet been taught and/or haven't studied the truths of the faith very deeply. Such people especially might be open to being deceived by the mockers and scoffers Peter mentions at the start of chapter 3.

Regardless of whether Peter has those skeptics in view, it is true that young Christians are often very eager to get into Scripture and learn what it says. They don't always accurately assess their own interpretive abilities or their level of knowledge of spiritual things. Nor do they realize that some things in Scripture are very hard to understand. They begin to read Scripture, thinking they are fully equipped to understand everything, but they are wrong. They come to conclusions about Scripture's teachings and demands that are incorrect, but thinking they must obey, they follow these misunderstandings. Rather than obeying God and his word, they unwittingly fall into sin.

This interpretation of "the untaught and unstable" is a charitable assessment of them and their motives. But it isn't the only possible understanding of who these people are. Perhaps "the untaught and unstable" have more sinister motives as they read Scripture. I leave to readers a decision about who these people are and why they misunderstand Scripture.[19] I do so because we don't have to solve this problem in order to understand the point I want to make about perspicuity.

---

[19] In addition to many helpful commentaries, I strongly encourage the reading of Allison's most helpful discussion of this passage. See Allison, "Protestant Doctrine of the Perspicuity of Scripture," 2:500–514.

What is my point? It is that Peter isn't saying that failure to understand Scripture is Scripture's fault. Rather, he affirms that it happens because untaught and unstable interpreters misinterpret and distort Scripture. That's a problem with Scripture's interpreters, not with its clarity!

Does this mean Peter is saying that everything in Scripture is clear? No, Peter affirms that some things are hard to understand. But *hard* to understand isn't *impossible*, and Peter doesn't identify the difficult things as passages about how to be saved and live a godly life. So, Peter's comment doesn't refute what Scripture teaches about its clarity.

*In sum, our discussion of the various biblical passages relevant to perspicuity has shown that Scripture affirms this characteristic of itself. It also shows that not everything in Scripture is equally clear, but the basic biblical message of how to establish a relationship with God and maintain it is clear.* Even so, how exactly should we formulate the doctrine of biblical perspicuity? Before addressing that, let me turn to a brief historical discussion about perspicuity.

## HISTORICAL CONCERN FOR PERSPICUITY

Is perspicuity a doctrine the church has held throughout its existence? Indeed, it has, but it hasn't always been stressed. A comprehensive historical study is beyond the scope of this work, but a few points from the start of church history through the Reformation era are worth noting.

In the early church, after the NT was completed, there were some interpretive disagreements. Thus, regardless of Scripture's clarity, Christians didn't all agree on what it means. For example, there were early church controversies over Marcion's views about the OT, and there were Gnostic teachers who argued that Scripture supported their dualistic theories. To counter this, Irenaeus (120–200 AD) proposed that the church adopt a "rule of faith" to serve as a norm for assessing the accuracy of biblical interpretation. This resulted in the main doctrines contained in early church creeds becoming the standards by which interpretation of Scripture would be judged.[20] Of course, to the extent that these doctrines were based on Scripture, the rule of faith assumed that Scripture is clear; otherwise, the rule of faith itself would need proof that it was the proper understanding of Scripture.

One might think that adopting the rule of faith would result in uniform interpretation of Scripture, especially if Scripture is clear. However, unity in interpretation was not the result, for two different schools of interpreting Scripture arose, an Alexandrian school and an Antiochene one. Key figures in the Alexandrian tradition were Clement of Alexander and Origen.

While interpreters in the Alexandrian tradition believed that one could

[20] Paul Brewster, "The Perspicuity of Scripture," *Faith and Mission* 22 (Spring 2005): 19.

distill a clear message from Scripture, they also held that Scripture contained various layers of meaning. By Origen's time, exegetes were accustomed to looking not only for Scripture's literal sense but also for its moral and allegorical senses. These senses were arranged in hierarchical order, so that the literal sense was the starting point and the allegorical sense was the deepest and most prized level of meaning.[21]

Regardless of one's opinion of such interpretation (one definitely rejected by the Reformation), belief in multiple senses of meaning goes hand in hand with a belief that Scripture's meaning is not in fact clear. Of course, for many, a text's literal meaning might be rather clear, but ascertaining that level of meaning was only the beginning of the interpretive process.

How did biblical interpretation and Scripture's clarity fare at the hands of Antiochene interpretation? Actually, in the early church the Antiochene approach was much more amenable to the notion of biblical clarity, because it used the literal-historical approach to interpretation. It looked for the plain, literal meaning of the text, not some higher, allegorical level of meaning.[22]

Though these two approaches (Alexandrian and Antiochene) might seem radically different, that isn't necessarily so. Both began with the literal sense of Scripture, but the Alexandrians thought that sense alone was sometimes inadequate. Hence, they looked for hidden allegorical meanings. The Antiochenes emphasized a text's literal sense, but also believed that many texts required a fuller sense. Rather than turning to allegorical interpretations, however, Antiochenes sought a fuller sense through a referential typological approach. This approach took the literal sense as fundamental and primary, but argued that some texts point beyond themselves typologically to an important spiritual truth.[23]

Despite such differences, these two approaches weren't as radically distinct as might appear. Alexandrians never rejected the idea that there was a historical sense; in fact they began interpretation by uncovering the historical meaning. Antiochenes never denied that texts had a spiritual meaning. As some have argued, the "point of departure between the groups was the control that the historical sense exercised over the interpretive process."[24]

Over time, the Antiochene approach's influence waned, but the notion that interpretation should at the very least begin with the literal sense didn't go away. Even the belief in a fourfold sense of Scripture, the dominant view from Augustine to the Reformation, didn't eliminate the literal sense entirely, for the literal sense was seen as the foundation for all other senses. With this

---

[21] Ibid., 20.
[22] Ibid., 21.
[23] Ibid. Brewster quotes Diodore's explanation of how this typological method works. See Brewster, "Perspicuity of Scripture," 21–22.
[24] Ibid., 22.

emphasis on Scripture having multiple senses, it is clear why it was widely believed that the masses were not capable of interpreting Scripture on their own. This was especially so because so few people in society could even read, and so interpreting Scripture (or any other written text) according to one method or another was unthinkable.

But different approaches to interpretation don't actually say whether Scripture is or isn't clear. If it is, various methods of interpretation can't remove that clarity from the text. They can only make understanding far more complicated than one might expect. When church history moved into the Reformation era, however, the perspicuity of Scripture became a very significant issue.

Though most Reformers had something to say about Scripture's perspicuity, no interchange was quite so famous as the one between Luther and Erasmus. As James Callahan explains,

> Rome advocated Scripture's obscurity and the necessity of Church hierarchy as interpreter. Trent charged that it was the role of 'holy mother Church . . . to judge of the true sense and interpretation of the holy Scriptures.' But this was only another way of asserting the authority of the Church over Scripture. By contrast, Protestants opted for fusion of hermeneutic authority and Scriptural authority. For example, viewing perspicuity as a quality of or inherent in the nature of Scripture itself might lessen the interpretative tangles addressed by Rome's claims against Protestantism. . . . While perspicuity was the Protestant counterclaim to the charge of Scripture's obscurity—an assertion with a connotation of objectivity—the subjectivity and limits of Scripture's clarity were projected upon the interpreter to explain various interpretative discrepancies.[25]

The key exchanges between Luther and Erasmus came in the latter's *Discussion Concerning Free Will*, published in 1524. Luther responded a year later in his *The Bondage of the Will*. Erasmus argued that God didn't intend us to delve into some things in Scripture. If we try to do so anyway, things become darker. Ultimately, we must just admit the "unsearchable majesty of the divine wisdom, and the weakness of the human mind."[26] Amplifying this point, Erasmus claimed that some things about God in Scripture are to be contemplated in mystic silence. And, many commentators have guessed about the meaning of various biblical passages, but no one has completely removed their obscurity. Unsolved matters include the distinction between the divine persons, the hypostatic union of Christ's two natures, and the unforgivable sin. On the other hand, God has made some things in Scripture quite clear and evident, and these

---

[25] James Callahan, "*Claritas Scripturae*: The Role of Perspicuity in Protestant Hermeneutics," *JETS* 39 (September 1996): 355–356.

[26] Brewster, "Perspicuity of Scripture," 23, quoting Erasmus. All of this is found in *Luther and Erasmus: Free Will and Salvation*, LCC, ed. E. G. Rupp et al. vol. 17 (Philadelphia: Westminster, 1969), 38.

are precepts for the good life. Everyone should learn them, but obscure matters should be committed to God. Obscure parts of Scripture should be worshiped, but not discussed, for they are insoluble, anyway.[27]

Of course, since most people didn't know how to read, the only real way to learn much about any Scripture, clear or obscure, was through religious instruction. And, the source of that teaching was the church. In effect, Erasmus and the Roman Catholic Church were saying that there are obscurities in Scripture that are hard to understand even for learned members of the clergy, and therefore, for most people, there is little hope of understanding even the simpler things without the church's aid. Of course, this in effect withheld Scripture from direct reading, study, and interpretation by most common people. It also meant that the church could construct doctrines that favored its own power and flourishing, and if such doctrines, based on Scripture interpretations the church sanctioned, were questioned, the church could always say that those who rejected its doctrines and interpretations simply weren't in a position to do so. For one thing, Scripture contains obscurities. In addition, who would be better trained to know how to understand Scripture than the clergy?

Luther agreed that many things about God himself are hidden, but insisted that God and Scripture are two separate things. Scripture, according to Luther, is not unclear, and those who say it is "have never cited a single item to prove their crazy view; nor can they."[28] This sounds like a "cannon blast" aimed in general at what Erasmus had said, but Luther also addressed more directly Erasmus's claims about the Trinity, the hypostatic union of Christ, and the unforgivable sin. He agreed that there are those ("godless Sophists," he labeled them) who have never "solved" such problems, but that doesn't mean Scripture is at fault. "Scripture makes the straightforward affirmation that the Trinity, the Incarnation and the unpardonable sin are facts. There is nothing ambiguous or obscure about that. You imagine that Scripture tells us *how* they are what they are; but it does not, nor need we know."[29]

While this implies that Scripture is clear, it doesn't explicitly affirm it. That is understandable, since Luther's intent was to refute Erasmus's claims. However, Luther did state positively what he thought about Scripture's clarity, and in doing so, he introduced a distinction between Scripture's external and internal perspicuity. He wrote,

> In a word: The perspicuity of Scripture is twofold, just as there is a double lack of light. The first is external, and relates to the ministry of the Word; the second concerns the knowledge of the heart. If you speak of *internal* perspicuity, the truth is that nobody who has not the Spirit of God sees a jot

---

[27] Ibid., 24–25. This material is taken from Rupp et al., *Luther and Erasmus*, 39–40.
[28] Luther, *Bondage of the Will*, 71, quoted in Brewster, "Perspicuity of Scripture," 24.
[29] Luther, *Bondage of the Will*, 73, quoted in Brewster, "Perspicuity of Scripture," 24.

of what is in the Scriptures. . . . If, on the other hand, you speak of *external* perspicuity, the position is that nothing whatever is left obscure or ambiguous, but all that is in the Scripture is through the Word brought forth into the clearest light and proclaimed to the whole world.[30]

Essentially, Luther's distinction between external and internal perspicuity is tantamount to the difference between mere intellectual understanding of Scripture and understanding that sees how Scripture applies to oneself and then chooses to obey it. Throughout his writings, Luther affirmed Scripture's clarity. However, he did grant that some things in Scripture are hard to understand, but the reason isn't Scripture's fault. The problem stems from our own linguistic and grammatical ignorance. It may also stem from the fact that we look at an obscure passage in isolation from the rest of Scripture. If that happens, Luther claimed, then God has made the point clear in other passages. As Brewster states, "This principle was codified as one of the key hermeneutical presuppositions of the Reformation in the phrase *Scriptura sui ipsius interpres.*"[31]

Of course, it would be easy to read Luther here and assume that he claims that everyone reading Scripture for himself will conclude the same thing about each passage's meaning. But Luther knew better than that. While some scholars like John Eck said that, in cases of disputed interpretation, the Roman Catholic Church would decide the proper interpretation, Luther, as expected, disagreed. He argued that in such cases there was need for a second test, one he called the principle of "external judgment." This principle was to be used to judge the doctrines and the spirits of men as they interact with the text. The purpose was to determine what would be for the benefit and salvation of others. In effect, this principle meant that exegetical study should continue. As Brewster explains, this idea eventually found expression in the Protestant principle of the analogy of faith. According to that principle, it is wrong to take an isolated biblical passage and form it into a doctrine that contradicts the whole tenor of biblical revelation. Rather, after working on all passages relevant to a topic, one should bring together their teaching "in such a way as to show the proportionality and total sum of the teaching of Scripture on that aspect of doctrine or discipline."[32]

Luther wasn't the only Reformer to emphasize biblical perspicuity. Calvin, Zwingli, and others of that era held it. And Post-Reformation Protestant theologians also stressed this doctrine, arguing that perspicuity, "as a quality of Scripture, was implied by the nature of Scripture's authority."[33]

---

[30] Luther, *Bondage of the Will*, 73–74, quoted in Brewster, "Perspicuity of Scripture," 24.
[31] Brewster, "Perspicuity of Scripture," 26.
[32] Ibid., 27. Here Brewster quotes from Walter C. Kaiser Jr., "Evangelical Hermeneutics: Restatement, Advance, or Retreat from the Reformation?," *CTQ* 46 (1982): 173.
[33] Callahan, "*Claritas Scripturae*," 257.

As might be expected, Roman Catholics, even after the Reformation, raised various objections to the doctrine. For example, the case of Philip and the Ethiopian eunuch, who didn't understand what he was reading; Paul's comment in 1 Corinthians 13:12 that we see through a glass dimly; and Peter's comment that things in Paul's writings are hard to understand were all used as arguments against perspicuity. The situation of the Ethiopian has already been explained, and as we saw, the eunuch understood quite well what Isaiah predicted. He just wanted to know who fulfilled the prophecy. Hence, we can't say he understood nothing that he read. And, Peter didn't say that everything in Paul's writings is hard to understand, but he did say that a lot of the ambiguity comes from interpreters deliberately twisting Paul's words. As for Paul's comment about seeing through a glass dimly, thinkers such as Turretin responded that the verse only speaks of the "relative obscurity of our present, earthly knowledge of God as compared to the fullness which we will enjoy in the eschaton."[34]

In addition, some have asked why commentaries on Scripture are written, if it is supposed to be so clear. In answer, thinkers such as Quenstedt noted that not every passage of Scripture is clear, and commentaries help with those that aren't. In addition, commentaries allow their authors to explain how to apply clear Scriptures. And commentaries help those who are uneducated and have little training in interpretation.[35] None of these things, however, refutes biblical teaching in support of perspicuity.

After the Reformation era, biblical perspicuity has continued to be an important principle in Protestant circles. As for Roman Catholic thinking, for a very long time it has embraced the view that Scripture has multiple senses and that the Roman Catholic Magisterium has the sole right to judge what the meaning of Scripture is.[36] Post–Vatican II, the Catholic Church has encouraged Catholics to read and study Scripture,[37] but that doesn't sanction adopting an interpretation that counters the Roman Catholic Magisterium's understanding. The key question, of course, isn't whether one's church or denomination teaches the perspicuity of Scripture, but whether Scripture itself teaches it. And, as shown in my biblical discussion in this chapter, there is ample evidence for the doctrine. Of course, large segments of the church have held the doctrine, but it came into prominence and contention during the Reformation. That is so because of the way the Roman Catholic Church maintained that

---

[34] Allison, "Protestant Doctrine of the Perspicuity of Scripture," 1:157, citing a statement from Francis Turretin, *Institutes of Elenctic Theology*, vol. 1, ed. James T. Dennison Jr., trans. George M. Giger (Phillipsburg, NJ: Presbyterian & Reformed, 1992), 146, 20.
[35] Allison, "Protestant Doctrine of the Perspicuity of Scripture," 1:158–159.
[36] For an explanation of these four senses of Scripture, see Gregg R. Allison, *Roman Catholic Theology and Practice* (Wheaton, IL: Crossway, 2014), 81, 108. The four senses are the literal, the allegorical, the moral, and the anagogical.
[37] Ibid., 99.

Scripture's obscurity makes it necessary for only the specially trained, namely, Roman Catholic clergy, to interpret and explain it to the masses.[38]

## What Does Biblical Perspicuity Mean, and Should It Be Held?

Having discussed various Scriptures that are relevant to our topic, we can answer the questions posed in this section's title. Let me address the second question first. From our study of relevant biblical data we can say that we should hold the doctrine of biblical perspicuity. Let me explain.

First, there are various forms of special revelation, but perspicuity specifically relates to whether Scripture is understandable. Perspicuity isn't normally applied to other forms of special revelation, and it isn't clear what it would mean if applied, for example, to miracles.

So, how should we define biblical perspicuity? Here I note that Scriptures that teach it don't say that every passage in Scripture is clear intellectually. Some Scriptures speak in general about Scripture's clarity, and that isn't falsified by difficult texts whose meaning and reference are obscure.

Before going any further, however, I note that perspicuity deals with humans' ability to understand Scripture. The concept of understanding is, in philosophical discussions, ambiguous, and that is also true in ordinary language usage. In fact, at the outset of this chapter I noted three levels of/kinds of understanding: (1) intellectual awareness of some truth; (2) awareness of how a set of facts fits together and presents a whole perspective on a topic; and (3) volitional commitment to and application in one's life of what one has understood in the previous two senses. Because of these different senses of understanding, when we examined Scripture, we had to clarify for each passage the kind of understanding it teaches.

So, however we define Scripture's perspicuity, we should incorporate these insights about different levels of/kinds of understanding. But perhaps the best way forward is to offer a basic definition of biblical perspicuity, and Gregg Allison's is as good as any. He defines it as follows:

> The clarity of Scripture means that it was written in such a way that ordinary human beings, possessing the normal acquired ability to understand written and/or oral communication, can read Scripture with understanding or, if they are unable to read, can hear Scripture read and comprehend it. Men and women, young and old, urbanites and desert nomads, seminary-trained and uneducated can read and understand the Bible.[39]

---

[38] For further discussion of the history of this doctrine see Erling T. Teigen, "The Clarity of Scripture and Hermeneutical Principles in the Lutheran Confessions," *CTQ* 46 (April–July 1982); Priscilla Hayden-Roy, "Hermeneutica gloriae vs. Hermeneutica cruces: Sebastian Franck and Martin Luther on the Clarity of Scripture," *Archive for Reformation History* 81 (1990); Beverly J. Stratton, "Here We Stand: Lutheran and Feminist Issues in Biblical Interpretation," *Currents in Theology and Mission* 24 (1997); Larry D. Pettegrew, "The Perspicuity of Scripture," *MSJ* 15 (Fall 2004): 217–225; and Keith D. Stanglin, "The Rise and Fall of Biblical Perspicuity: Remonstrants and the Transition toward Modern Exegesis," *Church History* 83 (March 2014).
[39] Allison, *Roman Catholic Theology and Practice*, 96–97.

This definition accurately summarizes what Scripture teaches about its own clarity. It also correctly represents the majority position of believers before the Reformation and the view held at least by Protestants since the Reformation.

I would only add two things to this definition. The first is my point about different senses of understanding. The definition is true of intellectual understanding, and also true in that humans can grasp that what Scripture demands applies to them. The *definition* doesn't guarantee that anyone, even the saved, will understand Scripture in the sense of volitionally choosing to obey its demands. *Scripture makes no such guarantees.* And, some Scriptures claim that some biblical passages are hard to understand, but passages that say this invariably blame the problem on the sinfulness of those who read Scripture, understand its intellectual content, and refuse to obey. None of those texts says that Scripture in itself is impossible to understand either intellectually or in the sense that it applies to the one who reads it.

My second point is that neither the definition says, nor would I say, that every passage in Scripture, regardless of topic, is perfectly clear. In some passages there are textual questions that still remain about what the original text exactly said. Moreover, some passages refer to currently obscure events and personages, even if they were known to those who first read them. The point of biblical perspicuity is that Scripture's main themes and requirements (including its requirements for salvation) are understandable intellectually, and that when the passages involved apply to readers at any time in history, ordinary humans can grasp that this is so. Hence, on judgment day no one will be justified in God's eyes by saying that they would have believed in God and obeyed Scripture's demands if only Scripture were clear about those matters. Scripture is clear enough!

Finally, I must address one last item. In light of biblical perspicuity, is divine illumination necessary to understand Scripture? That is, even if Scripture were tortuously difficult to understand, couldn't the Holy Spirit "save the day" by illumining its meaning to readers? These questions suggest that either divine illumination is unnecessary because of perspicuity or that perspicuity is unnecessary because the Holy Spirit can shed light on Scripture's meaning.

So, we must harmonize these two doctrines, and in what follows, I want to show how. First, the key for both doctrines is that there are various senses in which a person can understand a written text or a spoken discourse. These different senses of understanding correspond to different things that illumination might cover, and therein lies the answer to our questions about harmonizing illumination and perspicuity. Illumination enables the person receiving it to understand Scripture, but we must remember what that means. Just as with perspicuity, we must ask whether someone is blinded to the basic intellectual content of Scripture and whether divine illumination might help him or her to understand that content. There is also a question about whether biblical content, understood intellectually, needs illumination in order for the reader and listener to see that this information applies to him or her personally. And finally, someone who grasps Scripture's intellectual content and realizes that its teaching applies to him still cannot, without the Holy Spirit's aid, choose to obey the truth he knows.

As we saw in the chapter on illumination, the Spirit's light may at times help a person to grasp a passage's intellectual content. But that isn't always so, nor is it always necessary. In fact, at the stage of "intellectual grasping," the Spirit's main activity may be little more than to draw the reader's or listener's attention to key words, phrases, or verses in a particular text. Having pointed the reader in that direction, the reader can often grasp intellectually what Scripture says.

While the Spirit's illumination isn't always needed to grasp a text's basic intellectual content, it is often necessary for the reader to understand that what he has just read and understood intellectually applies to him. For example, it isn't just other people, at other times in history, who are sinners and need a savior. Everyone alive today, including myself, is a sinner and needs a savior. And, I must choose to accept Christ's sacrifice on my behalf for me personally to be saved.

But illumination, if needed to inform someone of the human predicament and the divine solution, and illumination by the Spirit to help them see that all of these things are true for them, not just for others, isn't enough to save. In fact, as 1 Corinthians 2 teaches, those without Christ and the Holy Spirit ("natural men") can't "understand" Scripture to the point that they would choose on their own to accept its message and obey it. Only believers, by the Holy Spirit's enablement, can understand Scripture in the sense of choosing to obey it. The Bible's perspicuity doesn't guarantee that anyone will choose to bow the knee, the head, the heart to Scripture's teaching and live out its truth.

From the preceding discussion, we can now see how divine illumination and biblical perspicuity fit together. And, no one should doubt that both need to be true of Scripture. Let me summarize what we should conclude. First, we can say that biblical perspicuity requires that the basic themes and message of Scripture are *not difficult to identify and grasp intellectually*. This is especially so for what Scripture teaches about humans' lost condition and God's remedy. But it is also true for many other biblical themes. Biblical perspicuity doesn't mean that every sentence in Scripture is easy to grasp intellectually, but sentences that present Scripture's main themes can be understood intellectually. How does divine illumination play a role at this stage in the process of understanding Scripture? As we saw in the chapter on illumination, illumination doesn't turn texts which seem intellectually like "gibberish" into clear language. Perspicuity makes it unnecessary to do so, for perspicuity means that very few, if any, biblical texts will appear to be *intellectual* gibberish. Illumination may help the interpreter to attend to certain key aspects of a text which are necessary to grasp its intellectual content. But in any given instance that may be unnecessary.

What about the second level of understanding, seeing that what a text teaches applies to the reader himself or herself? Our discussion of perspicuity has shown that for key themes relating to our spiritual need and God's remedy, Scripture is clear that these truths apply to each human being. But can every reader "get" this point? The answer seems to be yes and no. As we saw in discussing perspicuity, passages about our sinful condition and God's glorious remedy may require the Holy Spirit's light in order for the reader/hearer to understand that this material pertains to him. But, in some cases, just understanding the intellectual content of such passages may be enough for the reader to grasp that the text is relevant to him. The exact relation between divine illumination and this second level of understanding isn't always clear in any given instance. A specific Scripture's point may be quite clear, and for some people to grasp that the text's point applies to them may require little divine illumination. For others, without the Spirit's illumination, they may intellectually grasp the message of a passage but think it doesn't apply to them. In any given instance, perhaps only God knows exactly how Scripture's perspicuity and the Spirit's light intertwine.

When it comes to the third level of understanding ("getting" a text's point to the extent that one decides to obey what one reads or hears), this chapter's study of scriptural teaching shows that this level of understanding any text and biblical theme is neither guaranteed nor automatic. In fact, for inveterate sinners, a clear biblical statement of the gospel may matter little, if at all. That is, whether or not the reader thinks the teaching applies to him, there is no way that he will ever bow the heart and mind to choose to obey what Scripture teaches. So, then, if the Bible is perspicuous but that clarity does not guarantee that anyone will understand Scripture in the sense of choosing to obey it, how does anyone get saved, grow in their relation to the Lord, etc.? This is where the Spirit's illumination is crucial. Without the Spirit's light to enable and move the will of the reader/hearer of Scripture, this kind of understanding will never occur! In fact, it can't occur (see 1 Cor. 2:14ff.)!

*In sum, the Holy Spirit's illumination of Scripture and Scripture's clarity do not contradict each other; they complement each other!* At the level of understanding the intellectual content of a text, this can happen because Scripture is clear. The Holy Spirit's inspiration moved the biblical writers to pen books whose main topics and contents are clear. Inspiration extends to the very words of Scripture, so it is reasonable to believe that if a particular sentence were intellectually unclear, the Holy Spirit would have moved the writer to choose wording that is intellectually clear!

As to the second level of understanding (seeing that a text's message applies to the one reading/hearing it), the Spirit's illumination and Scripture's clarity again complement each other. How much illumination is required for a reader to understand that a text applies to him or her is not always clear or predictable. A text's relevance to the reader may be very clear, and yet without divine illumination the reader may not think the text relevant to him or her at all. Or a text's message as written may be so clear that in understanding the message of the text at all, the reader sees that it applies to him. In such a case, little divine illumination may be required for the reader/hearer to understand that point. The best we can say is that divine illumination and biblical perspicuity probably complement each other when it comes to this second level of understanding Scripture, even if only God knows exactly how the two work together in specific instances.

Finally, as for the third level of understanding a text (endorsing and internalizing it by choosing to live what it teaches), the Holy Spirit's illumination is required for believers and nonbelievers alike. Biblical teaching on perspicuity doesn't guarantee that anyone will understand Scripture in this third sense. In fact, without the Spirit's light to move the reader's/listener's will, any biblical text in view will be unclear. That is, without the Spirit's action, the reader not only won't obey what he or she reads; she may not even fully grasp the intellectual content of the text and/or see that it applies to her.

My undergraduate professor, who could explain the theologies of Luther and Calvin better than many who know Christ as Savior, didn't thereby show that he was saved. He illustrated biblical perspicuity—at least the first level of intellectually understanding biblical and theological truth. But, if he wasn't in fact saved, he also showed that there is more to understanding Scripture than what merely meets the eye and ear! Thankfully, it is possible for the word to come with the Spirit! Illumination and perspicuity aren't in conflict; they complement each other! Our God of light hasn't given the light of biblical revelation without the Spirit also providing his special light so that any reader can understand what Scripture requires and be moved and enabled to do it! Disobeying God's word can't be excused by claiming ignorance of its content! Pray for the Spirit's enablement to obey what God has clearly revealed in his word!

# SEVENTEEN

# LIVING, POWERFUL LIGHT

## The Animation of Scripture

Scripture is God's inspired word. Since God is omniscient, he knows what is true and what is false. As morally perfect, he cannot lie, and so we expect him to tell the truth. Scripture confirms that its every assertion is true. Moreover, Scripture's meaning is clear and understandable on the essentials of the faith. And, the Holy Spirit stands ready to open minds and hearts of Scripture's readers to understand intellectually and apply the truths of Scripture so that they will live them out.

All of these things are possible, but what if Scripture's teachings were interesting but not life-changing? Internalizing them wouldn't alter anyone's life much, if at all. But Scripture is the word of a God who is supremely authoritative, knows everything, and speaks only the truth. Hence, we would expect his words to have great power, and they do! Many have thought they could ignore or reject God's word with little consequence. But sooner or later everyone learns that we must live in accord with the truth, regardless of whether we want to or not. Truth, enforced by an almighty God, must be embraced, or we must sooner or later own up to the consequences.

Evangelical theologians have affirmed that Scripture is powerful, and it isn't hard to find biblical support for this. In fact, it is so much the underlying assumption of evangelical theology, that it is often taken for granted and not even discussed in many theological treatments of Scripture.[1] Still, we should understand this quality of Scripture and see what Scripture says about it. It is my contention that a proper understanding of Scripture's power, along with

---

[1] Here it is interesting to consult various standard evangelical systematic theologies. One finds few that even discuss the subject, though clearly none denies it.

knowledge of what that power can do, should lead Christians to make reading and obeying it a central part of their lives. And, if Scripture is so powerful, then proclaiming it is essential to sustaining and nurturing spiritual growth and health. Thus, it must be the focus of pulpit ministry, Sunday school lessons, and personal study.

When theologians discuss Scripture's power, they often label it Scripture's *animation*. We should begin with a definition. Scripture's animation refers to that "inimitable element of vitality or life which obtains in the Bible as in no other book."[2] More specifically, animation speaks of the power of God's word to accomplish God's purposes in people's lives.

Attributing this quality to Scripture doesn't mean that no other literature influences thinking and behavior. Not only have other religions' sacred books exerted great power over those who follow their teachings, but nonreligious books have also been quite influential. Think, for example, of the Koran and the Bhagavad Gita, but also of works like *The Communist Manifesto*. And, of course, many people have found moving and meaningful various literary works of fiction (novels, poems, plays, e.g.). Despite the significance of all those works, however, none of them has the power inherent in Scripture to transform relationships with the true and living God (the one revealed so clearly in Scripture), with other people, and with oneself. Nor can obeying those other works dramatically alter one's eternal destiny.

Of course, affirming Scripture's animation doesn't mean that it can serve as a "textbook" for every discipline of study and every imaginable activity. It won't teach you much, if anything, about mathematics and logic; and you won't find it to be of much help in many of the natural and physical sciences. It can help in many of the disciplines that fall under the rubric of the humanities, but even so, there is also ample reason to pursue many other sources when studying those fields of learning.

But when it comes to topics that are Scripture's main foci, one finds more than just interesting information. Scripture tells us who God is and what he is like; it tells us about who we are; and it tells us what God expects of us and how to relate to him. It also presents the results if we obey God according to his rules, and it shows vividly and clearly the consequences if we try to win his favor in our own way or if we decide to fight or ignore him altogether. Scripture also reveals something of God's past dealings with humans, and it sets forth God's basic plans for the future. And, of course, in Scripture we learn more about Jesus, the most important person in human history, than we can learn from any other source.

Before presenting what Scripture teaches about its animation, we should

---

[2] Lewis S. Chafer, *Systematic Theology*, vol. 1 (1947; repr., Dallas: Dallas Seminary Press, 1974), 120.

clarify what is and is not the focus of this concept. When speaking of the power of God's word, one might be addressing any of three distinct topics. First, *God's spoken word* has power. When God speaks, regardless of the topic, regardless of whether we know exactly what he said, and regardless of whether his exact words are recorded anywhere, there is great power in what he says. There are various examples of this in Scripture, but as clear as any are the words God spoke at creation. Throughout Genesis 1 we read the words, "Let there be . . . and it was so." The results of God's repeated "Let there be . . . " are the creation of the universe, culminating with God's "Let Us make man in Our image . . . " (Gen. 1:26).

Other examples of the power of God's spoken word are evident throughout Scripture. Think of what happened when our Lord Jesus Christ said, "Lazarus, come forth" (John 11:43). Lazarus, the brother of Mary and Martha, had been dead for four days (11:17, 39). In response to Jesus's command, Lazarus rose from the dead.[3]

When God speaks, things happen. A second powerful divine word is *God's incarnate Word, Jesus Christ.* I offered above an example of Jesus's power, and there are many other examples. The power of Jesus's word was amply revealed to Paul on the road to Damascus (Acts 9), transforming him from a chief persecutor of Christ's followers to the person who as much as any human being was responsible for the early spread of the gospel throughout the Roman world. During Jesus's life on earth, on many occasions recorded in the Gospels, Jesus used the awesome power at his disposal to perform miracles, and there is also great power in his teachings. For example, even many who have little use for religion and Christianity in particular have to agree that Jesus's Sermon on the Mount sets a standard of moral conduct that has no equal. If its various precepts were obeyed, our world would be a much more congenial place in which to live.

Occasionally, Jesus spoke of his power. I mention two noteworthy instances of this: After his resurrection, Jesus commanded his disciples to go and teach all nations to observe all that he had commanded and to baptize those who believed. But Jesus began this command by saying, "All power is given unto me in heaven and in earth" (Matt. 28:18 KJV). The task he was about to give his disciples wouldn't be easy, but they could at least rest in the fact that the one giving the "assignment" possessed all the necessary power to enable them to fulfill it.

Some might respond that, of course, after his resurrection and glorification Jesus had tremendous power, but what about his power before he died? Even a hasty reading of any of the Gospels should convince anyone that Jesus's miracles

---

[3] As some popular preachers have said, it is a good thing that Jesus prefaced his command by naming Lazarus specifically. Otherwise, everyone in the whole graveyard might well have risen from the dead!

displayed great power. But even more, what Jesus had to say about his power over his own life and death is most instructive. On one occasion Jesus told his disciples that he is the Good Shepherd who lays down his life for the sheep. Before he finished that discourse, he affirmed that no one could take his life from him. Rather, he would lay it down himself. He would do so because he has power to lay down his life and power "to take it up again" (to resurrect it) (John 10:14–18).

While a mere mortal might in a fit of extreme hubris make such a claim, no mere mortal could actually deliver on that boast. Jesus, of course, is no mere mortal. The incarnate Word of God has immeasurable power. There is a third sense, however, in which we can speak of the power of God's word. In this case, the *power of God's written word, Scripture*, is in view. As already stated, if Scripture is what God said and thus is totally true, we should expect it to have great power. Scripture, of course, isn't everything God knows, but that in no way limits its truthfulness and certainly not its power. Had God inspired a book that contained everything he knows, it would take any human multiple lifetimes just to read it, let alone even to begin to understand it. Given our lack of understanding and, at times, our laziness and reluctance to devote time to reading any book, it is good that God didn't inspire a book that contains all he knows. Nonetheless, one could devote "many lifetimes" to the study of Scripture without fully understanding all it teaches. But however long one studies Scripture and however much of it one grasps, Scripture never loses its inherent power!

In this current chapter, it is the power of God's written word, Scripture, that is in view. In what follows, I shall offer various biblical supports for this doctrine. As we shall see, there is not much direct biblical teaching on this doctrine, but there is biblical basis for it.

## BIBLICAL TEACHING ON SCRIPTURE'S ANIMATION

Not many biblical passages directly address Scripture's power. That may be surprising, but it shouldn't be. Biblical writers certainly seemed convinced that what they wrote came from God; instances are legion where they report that the Lord spoke to them or revealed something to them, things which often they wrote down for everyone to read. And there is ample evidence that the writers of Scripture believed that God possesses all the powers that a being of his sort can possess.[4] It is reasonable, then, to think that they believed that everything God does and says has great power. After all, biblical authors surely knew that, in general, words can be powerful. They could easily have drawn such conclusions from responses to their own preaching and writing (Scripture or other-

---

[4] For any who doubt this point, see my discussion of divine omnipotence in *No One Like Him: The Doctrine of God*, Foundations of Evangelical Theology (Wheaton, IL: Crossway, 2001). Clearly, the biblical writers believed God to be omnipotent!

wise). And, they could see that human words, even those of nonbelievers, can also have great power to change people's thinking and actions. If words of a mere human can be powerful, how much more powerful the words of almighty God, however and whenever delivered, would be!

For the reasons just explained, it shouldn't surprise us that the writers of Scripture don't address the topic of animation in great detail. They don't, at least in part, because they must have just assumed this truth about Scripture, because they would believe that if God said anything, it would be of utmost significance and should not be ignored. Moreover, most biblical authors would have had access to some (perhaps even to much) of the Scripture already written before and even during their lifetime. Undoubtedly, they would have read it, and it would have impacted their own life and ministry. Knowing experientially of the power of God's word in their own life, they would naturally expect it to have the same power for anyone who would read it.

So, biblical writers likely fully believed in Scripture's animation, even if they didn't write much about it. But this doesn't mean that the only task for the theologian is to define the doctrine and reassure readers (as I have done) that biblical authors held it. In fact, we can and should say much more from Scripture in support of this doctrine. There are passages in which biblical authors relate what Scripture has accomplished or can do in someone's life when obeyed. How could such claims be true if Scripture is powerless?

What, then, does Scripture teach that is relevant to this doctrine? I begin with a passage that is probably the closest thing in Scripture to a clear affirmation of Scripture's animation. That passage is Hebrews 4:12, but sadly this verse is often ripped from its context and used as a "proof-text" to teach the doctrine. It is more intellectually honest and, I think, theologically rich, to understand the verse within its context. After examining this passage, I shall look at other Scriptures that speak about Scripture's nature and how it can be used. Granting the truth of these texts, the only reasonable conclusion is that Scripture is powerful. Our discussion will turn, finally, to what Scripture further says about the Bible's power on the saved and on the unsaved.[5]

## Hebrews 4:12

The author of this text doesn't appear to be discussing the nature of Scripture in the chapters that precede and follow it. Nonetheless, he writes about the word of God (*ho logos tou theou*):

---

[5] Of course, many people could offer a personal testimony of Scripture's impact on their life. But appeal to personal testimonies isn't the way for evangelicals to formulate doctrine. If it were, then one would have to include the testimony of those who find Scripture useless, boring, and ineffectual. But such claims say nothing about what Scripture teaches about itself, nor would it make sense to believe that personal testimonies are the governing data for formulating this doctrine. Likewise, personal testimonies about Scripture's positive influence can't be the basis of this doctrine.

> For the word of God is quick, and powerful, and sharper than any two-edged sword, piercing even to the dividing asunder of soul and spirit, and of the joints and marrow, and is a discerner of the thoughts and intents of the heart. (KJV)

Before we discuss this verse's relevance to animation, we should explain its context.

*The Context of Hebrews 4:12*—The book of Hebrews begins by extolling Christ as superior to any and every created being. In chapter 3, Jesus is compared to Moses. While Moses was faithful to God, he lived as a servant to God. In contrast, Christ is not a mere servant in God's house, but a Son. The writer then identifies Christ's "house" as believers, and adds that they are "Christ's house" so long as they continue to be faithful to the Lord (3:6). Having made the point that those who belong to Christ must remain true to him, the writer then adjures his readers to hear and obey the Holy Spirit without hardening their hearts.

After offering this warning, the writer shows that there is good reason for heeding it by reminding his readers of what happened to Israel in the wilderness (3:7–19). God gave them promises and commands; he also gave them a leader, Moses, who was prepared to lead them to the Promised Land. Things went well until spies were sent to scout the land in preparation for Israel to enter and conquer it. Sadly, most of the spies were overcome with fear about the difficulty of driving out the land's inhabitants. They reported that the land was definitely worth possessing, but its inhabitants were too mighty to vanquish. If Israel tried to take the land, its inhabitants would utterly destroy them (Numbers 13–14).

The Lord was furious with his people, and understandably so! He had miraculously freed them from their Egyptian overlords, and had protected them all the way through the Sinai Peninsula. Moreover, he had promised to give them a great new land where they could flourish and live in peace. Finally, they had arrived at Kadesh-barnea, and Moses sent spies on a reconnaissance mission. All of the spies except Joshua and Caleb returned and gave an evil report about the land. Rather than trusting the Lord because of all he had already done for them, the people of Israel rebelled. Their unwillingness to obey God's command to go in and possess the land even moved them to exclaim that it would have been better if they had never left Egypt! Even more, they started to make plans to appoint a captain to lead them back to Egypt (Num. 14:3–4)! Moses and Aaron were totally shocked, and God was furious, threatening once and for all to destroy this ungrateful and unbelieving multitude. Had Moses and Aaron not intervened for the people, God would have done just that. But God relented, deciding that, while he wouldn't destroy them, the rebellious nation would be condemned to wander for forty years in the wilderness. That would be long enough for the disbelieving multitude to die, and only then could their children and grandchildren enter the land and receive the peace and rest God had promised.

In Hebrews 3:7–19 the author briefly but powerfully reminds readers that, just because one is numbered among the people of God, that doesn't mean that obeying God is optional. The people of Israel who came out of Egyptian bondage were God's chosen people. God had promised them great blessings, and all they needed to do was to listen to and obey what God commanded. And they did, to a point, but at the crucial point, when they were just about to receive the fulfillment of what God had promised, they lost heart and were ready to return to Egypt. If those who had seen God do so much for them could at the crucial moment lose heart and stop believing God's word, who are we to think that such disobedience is impossible for us? The generation that followed God's voice to a point, but then turned away at the crucial moment, was condemned to wander in the wilderness for forty years. They never entered the Promised Land and never received the rest that God had promised them.

It is crucial to note that the author emphatically makes this point in two ways. The first and most obvious is his blatant statement in Hebrews 3:7–19 of what Israel did in the wilderness, and his warning that his readers must not do the same.

But someone might say, "That's only the writer's opinion, and nothing more." Such a supposition is demonstrably false, however, because the writer makes these points secondly by alluding to, paraphrasing, and quoting Psalm 95:8–11 (in Heb. 3:7–19). In other words, the warning in Hebrews 3:7–19 is not just that of the writer of Hebrews. It is Scripture's warning as well!

The same theme and points are made at the start of chapter 4, with verse 7 again quoting Psalm 95:7–8. What is the point, however, of alluding to and even quoting from Psalm 95 in Hebrews 3:7–19 and then again at the start of Hebrews 4? That is, even if the warnings are from Scripture, so what? Can't one hide unbelief, fake obedience, and be fine with God? No, one cannot do that; you cannot hide from God or from Scripture! Why? Because of what Scripture is and what it can do (Heb. 4:12)!

So, receiving God's rest isn't automatic; it requires continual obedience to God's word. Hearing and knowing God's word is of no profit unless those who hear it have faith to obey it (4:2). Those who do believe and obey will enter God's rest (4:3–11).

Why, though, is it so important to follow God's word? The author answers in verses 12 and following. The first reason for following God's word is the nature of God's word itself. You may be able to act outwardly like you are following God, and you may fool others. You may even convince yourself that you are God's obedient servant. But the word of God is of such a nature that it cannot be fooled. If our "religious devotion" is phony, God and his word will detect that![6]

*Hebrews 4:12 and the Animation of Scripture*—In the verses preceding verse 12, the author exhorted his readers to listen to and obey whatever God says. Compliance to God's word must not be merely external, for if it is, God won't be fooled. Two reasons are offered. The first is the nature of the God's word itself (v. 12), and the second (v. 13) is God's omniscience. As a result of the latter, it is impossible to feign obedience when one's heart is impure.

In verse 12 the author makes the point more clearly set forth in verse 13, but he does so by telling his readers of the power of God's word. Israel in the wilderness heard the word of the Lord, and at times the people obeyed. At other times they disobeyed, sometimes rather blatantly (as with their refusal to enter the land and their desire to return to Egypt), and other times more tacitly. Disobeying God's word, regardless of who one is and what the situation, is foolish and leads to disastrous consequences. That is so because of the nature of the word and what it can do. No secret sinful motives, plans, and deeds can be hidden from it. But why is this so? Verse 12 explains that it is the nature of God's word that makes it inescapable.

An initial question about verse 12 is whether *logos tou theou* refers to the incarnate Word, Jesus; to whatever word God speaks to humankind; or to Scripture. As many commentators note, the general consensus of the early church fathers seems to have been that the phrase refers to Christ.[7] Though this is possible, especially because in verse 14 the writer moves the discussion to the high priestly work of Christ, it isn't likely. The discussion in chapter 3 and especially 4 focuses on connecting God's rest with obedience to and faith in his word. The *word* repeatedly referred to, as the writer reminds readers of notorious occasions when God's people disobeyed his word, isn't the incarnate Word, Christ. Rather it is, in general, God's word of promise of rest to his people Israel at one time or another in their history to which the writer of Hebrews refers; and, as noted above, it is Scripture (Psalm 95) to which the writer

---

[6] In summarizing the teaching of Hebrews 3–4, I found most helpful the following commentaries: John Calvin, *Commentaries on the Epistle of Paul the Apostle to the Hebrews*, Calvin's Commentaries (Grand Rapids, MI: Eerdmans, 1948); James Barmby, *Hebrews*, in *The Pulpit Commentary*, ed. H. D. M. Spence and Joseph S. Exell, vol. 21 (Grand Rapids, MI: Eerdmans, 1950); James Moffatt, *A Critical and Exegetical Commentary on the Epistle to the Hebrews*, ICC (Edinburgh: T&T Clark, 1963); B. F. Westcott, *Epistle to the Hebrews* (Grand Rapids, MI: Eerdmans, 1967); F. F. Bruce, *The Epistle to the Hebrews*, in New International Commentary on the New Testament, ed. F. F. Bruce (Grand Rapids, MI: Eerdmans, 1972 printing); Leon Morris, *Hebrews*, in *EBC*, ed. Frank E. Gaebelein, vol. 12 (Grand Rapids, MI: Zondervan, 1982); and Adolph Saphir, *The Epistle to the Hebrews: An Exposition*, 6th American ed., vol. 1 (Grand Rapids, MI: Zondervan, n.d.).
[7] See, e.g., this point in Westcott, *Epistle to the Hebrews*, 101; Barmby, *Hebrews*, 110; and Calvin, *Commentaries on the Epistle of Paul the Apostle to the Hebrews*, 100, footnote.

of Hebrews specifically and repeatedly refers in Hebrews 3 and 4. Of course, in the writer's own day, God's revelatory word had come most clearly through his Son, Jesus Christ, but in the context of Hebrews 3 and 4 the point is the need to trust and obey God's word, which in the writer's time (and thereafter) centers on Christ and his priestly work for us. But the point of emphasis is still the need to obey whatever God says, including what he has revealed about Christ. Anyway, if the phrase is a reference to Christ, what does it mean to say that Christ is sharper than any two-edged sword? Clearly, the characteristics attributed in this verse to God's word are intended to communicate something. As some have suggested, the verse seems to personify the word of God, but if the reference is to Christ, we don't have a personification, but a literal reference to him. So, I repeat, if the verse refers to Christ, what does it mean to say that he is "sharper than any two-edged sword"? And what is the point of saying that he can divide asunder soul and spirit, joints and marrow? If that phrase is taken literally, it is likely true of Christ, but again, what does it say about him that is relevant to the overall theme of chapters 3–4? So, while *logos tou theou* could refer to Christ, it is more likely here that it does not.[8]

Is the reference to *ho logos tou theou*, then, a reference to Scripture? Probably so, because of what we saw about the context of Hebrews 3 and 4 and the repeated references to Psalm 95. Of course, some commentators think the reference is to anything the Lord has revealed. The author of Hebrews uses incidents of Israel's disobedience (referred to in Hebrews 3 and 4) as a way to warn his readers not to reject what God has said. Moreover, as various commentators suggest, the word of God that the writer of Hebrews most encourages his readers to obey is the word about salvation being available in Christ and about the need to trust and follow him with one's whole being. Before the NT was written, this was the word of God that was preached to many unsaved people, who turned from their sinful way of life to follow Christ. And the author's point is that one must follow wholeheartedly whatever God says and in whatever form it is received; otherwise we won't enter into God's rest.

Still, in light of my preceding discussion, the emphasis on Scripture in Hebrews 3 and 4, and the repeated allusions to and quotes of Psalm 95 (and of the incidents recorded in Numbers), I think that Hebrews 4:12 is a statement about the nature of Scripture. What the writer says probably also applies to other words that God says, but this verse certainly emphasizes the power of Scripture, and we are not wrong in using it to support that doctrine.

What, then, does this verse say about Scripture's nature? The overall thought of the verse emphasizes Scripture's power, especially its ability to

---

[8] Saphir argues that in the book of Hebrews, the Son of God is never referred to as "Word"; see his *Epistle to the Hebrews*, vol. 1, 234.

probe one's mind and heart. The author personifies the word of God and at-tributes to it characteristics that a human person might have. He says that the word is alive (*zōn*), and as a result, it can function in ways that something dead could not. He adds that it is also powerful (*energēs*). This means more than that God's word has the potential to act and accomplish things; it suggests that it actually does so.

Next, the author says that God's word is sharper than any two-edged sword. Here one is reminded of Ephesians 6, where Paul describes the Christian's "armor" for fighting spiritual battles. Included in that armor is the "sword of the Spirit, which is the word of God" (Eph. 6:17). Hence, referring to Scripture in such terms isn't unusual, but the writer of Hebrews elaborates on the idea of God's word as a sword. He writes that it is sharper than any two-edged sword. Typically, a sword used in a military battle might have only one sharp edge, so referring to Scripture as a double-edged sword emphasizes its power to cut. But Scripture is a sword that cuts like no other, for it can probe and dissect the internal aspects of one's mind and thought life.

The power of God's word is so great that it can even "[pierce] . . . to the dividing asunder of soul and spirit, and of the joints and marrow." The first pair of things divided refers to the immaterial part of human nature, and the latter two denote the physical human body. It is important, however, not to mis-read this. One way to misunderstand these phrases is to think that the writer says Scripture is so powerful that it is even able to divide a soul from a spirit and joints from marrow. While such ability would suggest a certain degree of power, it isn't at all clear what Scripture would accomplish by doing this, and so it is unclear that such power attributes any desirable quality to Scripture. But each of the four terms (soul, spirit, joints, and marrow) in the Greek text are in the genitive case. If we take these genitives as *objective* genitives, then we arrive at the meaning just described, a thought that doesn't make much sense.

On the other hand, we can see these genitives as *subjective* genitives, and that is the better way to understand them. As subjective genitives, each term speaks of something which is itself "divided asunder." In other words, God's word is so powerful that it is able to penetrate to the very core of one's soul, the very center of one's spirit, etc. That is a kind of power that makes much more sense to attribute to Scripture, and it also fits the rest of the verse. It is because Scripture can penetrate to the very core of our soul that it can judge exactly what we are thinking, including not only our thoughts but also the intentions behind them. And, of course, it can uncover what is at the heart of our inten-tions. Because Scripture can probe to the core of our spirit and our bodies, nothing of who we actually are and of what we are thinking in our innermost being can escape the power of Scripture.

As a result of this power, God's word can expose what we are actually planning to do. If we outwardly promise to obey God and even overtly go through the motions of doing so, that won't fool God. God knows what we really think, for nothing is hidden from the eyes of God (4:13). If our outward compliance is merely a "phony" cover for an inwardly stubborn and disobedient heart, God and his word will detect that. Just as God knew the condition of the hearts of the Jews as they came to the Promised Land, and even as it was only a matter of time until their unbelief issued in blatant rejection of God's command to go in and possess the land, God knows what we are really thinking. When our actions match the evil intentions of our heart, God is in no way surprised.

While Hebrews 4:12 clearly teaches the power of God's word, it doesn't tell us the whole story of what Scripture can do. In fact, if one reads only this verse, one might be frightened and repelled from going near God's word. Why? Because the only function of Scripture emphasized in this verse is a negative, judgmental one. The message is that we need to be genuine in our devotion and obedience to God's word, because if we aren't, we can't hide from God's word and what it says about such disobedience. While it is significant that Scripture can do this, is there nothing else? Can't it also comfort the grieving, encourage the downhearted, teach the unlearned? Indeed, Scripture has power to do all of these things and more, but other Scriptures speak of such capacities. Hebrews 4:12 makes the general point that Scripture has life and accomplishes its intended purposes. The writer gives only one example of what it can do, something quite appropriate for the context of chapters 3–4. But nowhere in this verse does he say that Scripture can accomplish nothing else. In fact, because Scripture is living and active, we should expect it to do many things, and other Scriptures confirm that it does.

### Further Biblical Teaching on Scripture's Power

Other passages speak of Scripture's power, and I note some of the more significant ones. One such passage is 2 Timothy 3:16–17. Normally, this passage is emphasized for what it teaches about inspiration, but it is also relevant to the doctrine of animation. Paul says that Scripture is profitable, exactly what we would expect of words issuing from God's mouth. Specifically, Paul says Scripture is useful for doctrine, reproof, correction, and instruction in righteousness. Hence, we can use it to form a correct theology of God and his relation to the created universe. When we disobey God's commands (also contained in Scripture), Scripture tells us that we have erred, and sometimes it explains why what we have done is sinful. And when our thoughts about God and his demands on our lives are wrong, Scripture can point out the need to change our thinking.

But Scripture does more than just that. It shows us how to correct our wrong deeds and thoughts. Even more, it clearly sets forth God's demands for a life that obeys his commands and pleases him.

If Scripture can accomplish all of these things in the lives of those who read and obey it, it is indeed a valuable resource of information. But as valuable as all of Scripture's information is, Paul adds that God has given us Scripture to teach us doctrine, etc., for the ultimate purpose that those who know and obey Scripture will be prepared for every good work (v. 17). Hence, Scripture isn't just information for the sake of increasing our knowledge (or even so that we can pass a theology or Bible exam). God wants this knowledge, based on what Scripture demands, to be our blueprint for a God-honoring and pleasing life. Paul isn't saying that nothing else might be useful instruction for living successfully. His point is that God gave Scripture so that we could know how to live and be fully prepared to live in ways that please God. We should be thankful that we don't have to go through life wondering what God expects of us. Scripture tells us what God wants, and how to establish and maintain a positive relationship with him. Most importantly, Scripture does these things by introducing us to Jesus, the one who died for our sins and who wants to be our Savior!

Several other passages speak of Scripture's power in general and are worthy of note. Psalm 119 is a great psalm about the word of God. It speaks of many valuable things God's word can do, and I could easily present the whole psalm as teaching the power of God's word. However, I shall limit my comments to three verses. In verse 93 the psalmist affirms that God's precepts are life. The thought, of course, is that the one who follows God's laws will prosper both naturally and spiritually. In contrast, those who don't obey can expect a difficult life, and even if they should live their life in relative ease and comfort, in light of biblical teaching about eternity we can say that those who reject God's precepts won't have a pleasant eternity. If God's precepts, and our obedience or disobedience to them, can have such an effect on our time on earth and thereafter, they must possess significant power. But where can one find such precepts? They are detailed in the pages of Scripture.

Then, in Psalm 119:142 the psalmist writes that God's law is truth. Of course, the emphasis isn't just on the law's precepts and requirements but rather on the law as anything that God teaches. We know that God's law in both the broader and narrower sense is contained in Scripture. In our discussion of biblical inerrancy we saw many passages that affirm the truth of all of God's word. My reason for raising this verse and point now is that truth is powerful. We may not like truth, and we may even fight against it in an effort to defy it. But truth cannot be denied or overturned. Whatever is true of our world sets the rules and regulations by which we must govern our lives or else expect failure and even disaster.

The psalmist also speaks of the ability of God's word to guide our path along life's way. As he says (119:105), God's word is a lamp to our feet and a light to our path. Such light shows us where it is safe to walk, and where it is unsafe. This verse is just another way of emphasizing the point already made in verse 93 that God's word gives life. If Scripture can do all of these things for those who obey it, then surely it is a powerful book.

How sad it is that so many people think they can live a successful, prosperous, and happy life by following their own personal philosophies and wishes without giving much or even any heed to God and his word! Many would say that the key to life is love, or having enough money to buy the things that they think make life comfortable and happy. And even those who know Christ as Savior can attest that these things can help in having a successful and happy life. However, Jesus put this whole matter in proper perspective when he answered Satan's temptation to turn stones into bread. He told Satan that man doesn't live just by bread alone; instead, life ultimately depends upon and should be lived in accordance with every word that comes from God's mouth (Matt. 4:4). At the time Jesus said this, none of the NT was written, but the OT was complete, and Jesus would surely have known that more Scripture (the NT) was forthcoming. While Jesus knew that sometimes God speaks in dreams, visions, and even in direct speech, such instances of divine revelation don't come to everyone. However, anyone can learn about God and his demands by reading Scripture. It is God's word, and it is written for everyone. If following Scripture produces life, especially a spiritual life pleasing to God, it is indeed a powerful word!

In addition to these more general comments about the power of God's word, various Scriptures show us specific things that Scripture can accomplish. We can divide these things into the power of God's word on the unsaved, and its power on believers.

*Power of the Word on the Unsaved*—God's word can have one of two effects on those who don't know Christ. How it relates to them depends on whether they choose to obey its teachings or reject them. In particular, what one decides to do with Christ, who is so clearly revealed in the pages of Scripture, determines not only the course of one's life here on earth but also one's eternity.

Hopefully, those who don't know Christ will hear God's word and accept Christ as personal Savior. Scripture clearly teaches that it is the instrument of salvation. In Romans 10 Paul writes that all people need to accept Christ. But he then asks how they can do so if they have never heard of Christ. Obviously, they can't, so those who know Christ must tell those who don't know him.

When they hear, hopefully they will accept him in faith. Paul then (10:17) summarizes the whole process of evangelizing the lost by writing that "faith comes from hearing, and hearing by the word of Christ." Of course, Paul has in mind Scripture. If we are at all unsure of that, doubts should be removed when we read what Paul says about Scripture in 2 Timothy 3:15. He writes that the holy Scriptures can make one wise unto salvation through faith in Christ. Timothy is especially blessed, because from the time of his childhood onward he has had access to these Scriptures. Though Paul would be thinking most specifically of the OT, it is safe to say that he would make the same comment about anyone who has access to both the OT and NT as well.

Peter and James are very specific about the role of God's word in saving the lost. Peter writes (1 Pet. 1:23) to believers that they have been born again by the word of God, which lives and abides forever. James says that, of his own will, God "begot us" with "the word of truth" (James 1:18), and he intended that we should be "a kind of firstfruits of his creatures" (KJV). In light of God's intentions, James exhorts his readers to pursue a life of godliness. That life involves continuing to receive God's word, "which is able to save your souls" (1:21). It is no stretch to think that in these verses Peter and James are thinking of God's word as contained in Scripture. For them, that would refer most certainly to the OT, but they would surely say the same of the NT, including their own books.

There is a second possible impact of God's word upon those who don't know Christ. Sadly, most people who hear the word don't trust Christ. When they reject him, they reject both God and his word. Scripture is clear enough about the results of rejecting God's word. On one occasion recorded in John's Gospel, Jesus said that those who hear him and reject him and his words will be judged by his words in the last day (John 12:47–48). Jesus's message was about our need for salvation and about God's provision of him and his atoning death to pay for our sins. Those who reject him and his work on Calvary also reject his teaching about how to be saved. Where does one find Jesus's words and revelation of the salvation he offers? In Scripture, of course. Thus, we can say that those who read what Scripture says about how to be saved and reject it will pay the penalty for doing so, and that is also clearly revealed in Scripture.

In writing to the Corinthian church, the apostle Paul made a similar statement. He wrote that the words he preached (everywhere, not just in Corinth) were a sweet savor of Christ. The words Paul preached everywhere contained the gospel and emphasized the need of every hearer to accept his words and the Savior of whom they speak. Of course, some received his words gladly, while others rejected them. Paul says that his words were the "savour of life" to those who accepted them and the "savour of death" to those who rejected them

(2 Cor. 2:14–16 KJV). Though Paul doesn't explain how his words function as the "savour of death," he doesn't need to. The point is the same as the one Jesus made. Those who accept the message and the Savior of whom it speaks will have life. Those who reject the message will be punished for not heeding the gospel. Where can we find these words that Paul preached and taught? The substance of what Paul taught is contained not only in the NT books he wrote but also in the rest of the NT, which presents the same gospel that Paul preached so tirelessly and so well.

Clearly, how people respond to the gospel is quite important. What is at stake is ultimately whether one will go through life with a positive relationship with our God and creator or not; and of even further significance, how one responds will determine where and how one spends eternity. Words that have such a profound impact on one's life and destiny possess great power! None dare take them lightly!

*Power of the Word on the Saved*—The power of God's word is also evident in the lives of those who know Christ. Those who have Christ as personal Savior were born again of the word of God (1 Pet. 1:23). However, God doesn't want members of his family to remain in spiritual infancy; they need to grow in their faith. Peter again is very clear about the divinely appointed means for growing believers: it is God's word (1 Pet. 2:2).

When Peter speaks of this function of God's word, he makes it clear that a casual and occasional glance at Scripture won't do. Rather, Peter likens Scripture to the mother's milk that an infant newly born through natural reproduction craves. When a baby is first born, he or she can't digest any other food. One might think that a baby would at some time get tired of the mother's milk; it is always the same food, with no variety. Babies are hungry quite frequently, and even though their mother's milk is always the only thing on the menu, babies never tire of it. No baby has ever been heard to complain about Mom serving "leftovers"! Babies drink with abandon, as though tasting something new each time.

Peter tells his readers to long for God's word with the same kind of enthusiasm and with a commitment to "nurse" frequently on it. Just as the newborn is totally dependent on its mother's milk, and couldn't survive without it, so Christians desperately need the milk of God's word. It gave them life in the first place, and it is the only food there is for spiritual growth. What Peter says in the first verses of chapter 2 doesn't just describe how spiritual growth comes about. It is a direct command to those born again to grow in their relationship with God; and as always, when God gives a command, he provides the resources to do what he requires. Scripture is the God-appointed means for spiritual growth. It is a rich banquet with great variety, and all of it is useful in furthering our spiritual growth and maturity.[9]

As believers feast on God's word, learn it, and internalize it, they should become increasingly less enamored with sin and its temptations, and more determined to live a godly life. When that happens, they become increasingly sanctified, i.e., set apart from sin unto God and righteousness. Scripture affirms repeatedly that the means for this sanctification is God's word. In his High Priestly Prayer, Jesus asked his Father to sanctify his disciples, and he specifically requested that this would happen through the word of God (John 17:17–19). Jesus would have believed that God's word is found in Scripture in particular. That included the already written OT and the soon-to-be-written NT.

In Ephesians, the apostle Paul wrote about the church. In chapter 5 he likened the relation of Christ to his church to that of a husband to his wife. In verse 25, Paul instructed husbands to love their wives as Christ loves the church and gave himself for it. In verse 26, he added that Christ gave himself so that he might sanctify and cleanse the church with the washing of the water by the word. He did this so that someday he might present it to himself as a bride without any spot or blemish, a glorious church. In this passage, then, Paul likens the sanctification process to washing the taint of sin out of believers' lives. The cleansing agent ("God's detergent," we might say) is his word. As believers read and obey it, their actions become more Christlike and less like Satan and the world. That's how God's word serves as a cleansing agent to promote our sanctification.

Of course, this doesn't mean that in this life we can completely remove ourselves from sin and its influences. As Paul says in Romans 7, when we were saved we received a new nature that moves us to please God. Unfortunately, that didn't get rid of our old sin nature that pushes us to disobey God. Hence, through the rest of our lives on earth Christians are engaged in a battle to follow the dictates of our new nature and to reject the sinful desires of our old nature. Thankfully, as we are sanctified, we affirm desires of the old nature less and less. But the fight between the two natures continues for the rest of our life. Thankfully, God's word also teaches that, when believers sin, we can confess and be cleansed again and move on in our walk with God (1 John 1:6–10). As Scripture presents our situation, all of this can happen with God's word as the instrument the Holy Spirit uses to promote our sanctification.

---

[9] The author of Hebrews uses a different metaphor for spiritual food. He chides his readers for their apparent satisfaction with their lack of growth. By now they should be accustomed to more substantial spiritual food—meat—but they are content to drink only milk. This may seem to contradict what Peter says about God's word as milk, but the two writers use different metaphors and make two different points. Peter's point is that baby Christians need to grow, and God's word is the food to help them do so. The writer of Hebrews exhorts his readers to remove their spiritual lethargy and grow in Christ. Since they have been Christians for a while, they should be further along in their faith and relationship with God, but they aren't. Hence, the writer must write of elementary matters of the faith; they aren't ready for more complicated truths. Hebrews 5:11–14 and 1 Peter 2:2, then, don't contradict each other.

What Scripture says about its role in believers' growth, maturity, and sanctification fits exactly what it says we should do with Scripture. In a well-known, loved, and oft-quoted passage, the psalmist asks, "wherewithal shall a young man cleanse his way?" The answer is, "by taking heed thereto according to thy word" (KJV), that is, by taking heed to Scripture. Since this is how one cleanses one's way, the psalmist adds that he has hidden God's word in his heart (he has memorized it, meditated on it, and internalized it, no doubt) so that he might not sin against God (Ps. 119:9, 11). This is a wise path for young and old believers alike!

But how does knowing God's word keep us from sin? Presumably in the same way Jesus used it to conquer Satan's temptations. With each new temptation, Jesus responded by quoting Scripture (see Matt. 4:1–11). It's as if Jesus said, "Satan, I've heard what you think. Now listen to what God says. I'll obey him!" For us as well, when temptation entices us, we should respond by remembering that Scripture forbids what the temptation offers, and then we should choose to follow Scripture, not the temptation. Of course, we can't do this if we don't know what God's word says. Hence, each believer should be eager to "ingest" as much of God's word as quickly as possible. The more we internalize it, the better prepared we will be to fight temptation. Satan won't "courteously" withhold temptations until we've had more time to learn more of God's word. He attacks whenever and however he can. But we can win this battle if we possess "the sword of the Spirit, which is the word of God" (Eph. 6:17). There is no time like the present to work on learning what our "sword" teaches and to get it ready for battle!

## APPLICATIONS AND CONCLUSIONS

From our discussion in this chapter, it should be clear that Scripture is no ordinary book. It contains words that give life and prosperity to those who follow it. Those who reject it do so at their own risk and to their own peril. As Scripture says, "It is a fearful thing to fall into the hands of the living God" (Heb. 10:31 KJV)—all the more so, if we have ignored and/or rejected his word!

Undoubtedly, many think the Bible has no such power. Perhaps they have even read some of it and found it to be boring and irrelevant to their everyday life and to the big issues of life that we all face. That isn't Scripture's fault; it is a result of the callousness and indifference of many human hearts to God and his word.

But we must say more than this, for even believers have experienced times when they have read Scripture or listened to an expository sermon, and it had little or no impact on them. That can happen because we read or hear Scripture with a cold heart. But that isn't the whole story. I must emphasize the critically important ministry of the Holy Spirit in conjunction with Scripture. As we saw in discussing illumination, God's revelation isn't accessible to the natural man on his own; only the spiritual man can grasp its message and significance (1 Cor. 2:14ff.). But even the spiritual man will get nothing out of Scripture without the Holy Spirit's ministry to illumine his mind and move his will to obey.

Likewise, when God's word is preached and taught to the unbelieving, they can't hear it and on their own turn to Christ. Only as the Holy Spirit takes Scripture's truth and convicts of sin, convinces the sinner to turn to Christ, and then moves and enables the sinner's will to choose Christ does Scripture's power to produce new spiritually born babes become evident. So, indeed, God's word has great power, but it is impotent to accomplish anything without it being read and attended to, and without the Spirit's work in a person's life as he uses the word to draw people to Christ and to grow believers spiritually. Thus, the theme of Scripture's power must include teaching about both word *and* Spirit. Without the Spirit's ministry in the lives of the readers and hearers of Scripture, the power of God's word will remain dormant. It is still there in Scripture; we just need to let it loose by yielding to the Spirit, who uses it in lives to accomplish things no mere human could ever do!

The practical implications of Scripture's animation should be obvious, but sometimes even the self-evident should be spoken. God's word has power like no other words ever spoken. Thus, it should be the focus of our study and of our everyday living. Whatever we are called to do, and whatever challenges confront us, our first response should always be to ask what Scripture says about the subject and the deeds in question. Needless to say, that can't happen if we don't read and ponder Scripture. Sadly, even Christians committed to verbal plenary inspiration, the full inerrancy of Scripture, and the power of God's word find little time in the course of a week to read even a little of it. Believers know the message of Psalm 1 as it compares the happy and blessed man with the man who is unhappy and heading for disaster. The key to both is what they do with Scripture. The happy man grounds his life in God's word. He does not merely take a "small taste" of it for a half-hour each Sunday morning when his pastor preaches. He meditates on God's word both day and night. As a result, when the storms of life confront him, he survives and even flourishes. The unhappy man, whose life is grounded in pleasure, money-making, self-aggrandizement and/or any of the many philosophies that leave out God and his word, is not ready for life's challenges. At some time in his life there will likely be disaster and ruin, and even if not in this life, he is headed for a horrific eternity.

Evangelicals know the message and meaning of this psalm, and yet we all too often find relatively little time for God's word in the course of a week. But Scripture is our life source, our spiritual food. You wouldn't limit yourself to just one regular meal a week. If you did, you would eventually starve. Why, then, can't we see that there will be dire consequences if we limit our intake of God's word to once or twice a week—and some weeks to nothing?

There is another implication and application of Scripture's power. While there are many reasons that someone might go into ministry, the right reason is, as Peter instructs, to "shepherd the flock of God among you" (1 Pet. 5:2). You don't have to be a shepherd to know that an essential duty of a shepherd is to feed his sheep. No matter what else a shepherd does for his sheep, if the sheep starve, the shepherd fails. Sheep must be well-fed, and it is the minister's, the preacher's, job to ensure that they are.

So, what should the preacher preach? Should he fill his sermons with the latest news about current events, or emphasize key themes in popular culture? Those who preach should remember that ministry is all about tending the sheep, and that involves, for human "sheep," saying and doing things that will motivate them to live more and more like Christ! If so, what kinds of sermons will most likely accomplish those goals?

The answer should be crystal clear, and preachers must never forget it: the only message that can change lives is one based on what God has revealed. That means we must preach the word! After Paul told Timothy that Scripture is inspired of God, he listed all the positive things that can be accomplished by and through Scripture (2 Tim. 3:16–17). Because chapter 3 ends at verse 17, many, unfortunately, don't read beyond that verse, but we must. In the very next verses (2 Tim. 4:1–2), Paul says that in light of what he has just written about Scripture's nature and intended use, Timothy must preach the word! Not just occasionally, and not just when the audience feels like hearing it. Timothy must preach it "in season and out of season." He must use it to "reprove, rebuke, exhort, with great patience and instruction."

Preaching God's word in the power of the Holy Spirit is the only thing that makes sense! God has promised that his word won't return to him void (Isa. 55:11; Matt. 5:18). It will fulfill its intended purposes! The preacher's task is not to entertain and/or amuse his audience. It is to present a banquet of spiritual food that the Holy Spirit can use to accomplish things in our lives that are for our best benefit and that bring the most glory to God. If you want truth that can change lives, preach the word! Why would anyone preach anything else?

# EIGHTEEN

# LIGHT ENOUGH

## The Sufficiency of Scripture

Among the so-called attributes of Scripture (necessity, inspiration, authority, etc.) is Scripture's sufficiency. Some may think that theologians began to make this point only during the Reformation era. Indeed, Scripture's sufficiency was a very important point for the Reformers and post-Reformation thinkers, but this attribute was emphasized long before that era. Of course, in answer to the Roman Catholic Church, which gave equal weight to church councils, papal pronouncements, and other traditions plus Scripture, the Reformers argued that Scripture alone is sufficient for both doctrine and practice.

But what exactly does this mean? Is there nothing more to say than what the Reformers said? Does this doctrine address only one question? I contend that it raises a variety of issues. Let me mention a few to get the discussion going. First, was Scripture sufficient before the canon closed? If so, why did God reveal and inspire more books? If not, was it basically unusable until all of Scripture was written?

Then, as we have seen, Jesus had a very high regard for Scripture (the OT, in his day), and yet he told his disciples that he had much more to teach them than they could learn while he was with them. He promised to send the Holy Spirit, and in the chapters on inspiration we saw that this was a promise of the inspiration of the soon-to-be-written NT. In making this promise, was Jesus at least implying that the OT alone wasn't sufficient? And once NT books started to be written, until all were penned was Scripture insufficient?

The questions suggest a further question about canonicity. Does Scripture's sufficiency logically entail that Scripture's canon is closed? Or, alternately, did Scripture become sufficient only when the church concluded that the canon was closed and no more Scripture was forthcoming? Even more, is Scripture's sufficiency an argument for the canon's closure? These questions aren't often asked, but they are relevant to how we should understand this doctrine.

Of course, there are more fundamental questions about this doctrine. No one thinks Scripture's sufficiency means it teaches how to drive a car, ride a bicycle, cook a multicourse dinner, or solve calculus problems. Scripture's sufficiency refers to the topics it addresses. But even so, does Scripture's sufficiency, along with the Holy Spirit's illumination, mean that Bible teachers are unnecessary, as are commentaries and theologies? If such learning aids do have a proper role, is it only to repeat what Scripture itself says—perhaps using only Scripture's very words?

And, what about Scripture's sufficiency and our understanding of it? Does Scripture's sufficiency mean that what it teaches is patently clear to everyone who reads it? Are both Scripture's teaching and its proper interpretation contained within the pages of holy writ? If not, or if there are passages that are difficult to understand—and some whose meaning still befuddles Bible scholars—does that mean that, after all, Scripture isn't sufficient to present the teachings that God revealed in it? In contrast, if Scripture's meaning is clear to everyone, why then do so many Christians, even evangelicals, disagree about its doctrinal teachings? It would be easy to attribute such differences in understanding to some spiritual lapse by those who disagree with the majority, but couldn't godly, well-trained students of Scripture still understand passages and doctrines in ways that many others think incorrect? If so, does that mean that Scripture isn't sufficient after all?

One final set of questions should also be raised. If Scripture is sufficient, is there nothing more to say about a topic than what Scripture says? This might be so because Scripture covers the topic exhaustively. Or it might be that Scripture doesn't say everything about a topic but Scripture's sufficiency means that we shouldn't seek information outside of Scripture or say more than Scripture does. Some theologians have written systematic theologies with a mind-set to include nothing that isn't in Scripture itself. Information not in Scripture could be wrong—even if we think not—while Scripture couldn't be wrong. Hence, some think it unwise to incorporate in our thinking, preaching, and theologizing anything not taught in Scripture.

Clearly, this doctrine raises many different issues, including some very troublesome ones about biblical and theological studies. That is sad, because it was never formulated with such intent. It was most notably proclaimed at a time in church history when the Catholic Church's stranglehold on biblical and theological teaching and interpretation was increasingly silencing Scripture's own voice, in effect negating the spiritual food souls desperately needed.

However, Scripture's sufficiency shouldn't be a theological or ecclesiastical battleground; it should be an encouragement to anyone who needs to hear a word from God. But before we can affirm it, we must clarify its meaning. And, we must ask whether the doctrine is taught in Scripture either explicitly or even inferentially.

## Defining the Doctrine of Scripture's Sufficiency

### The Problem in Defining Scripture's Sufficiency

While this doctrine isn't as complicated as some, it still needs to be defined carefully. As already noted, the doctrine was articulated even before the Reformation era. However, it isn't clear whether Christian thinkers even thought about the concept before the church agreed that the canon of Scripture was closed. Of course, once the consensus was that no more Scripture was forthcoming, it made sense to ask if inscripturated revelation is enough.

From our perspective, it would be easy to say that there is sufficient written divine revelation. But exactly what does that mean, and did Scripture become sufficient only once the last book of the Bible was written? Would it have been wrong, for example, for an OT saint living about 1000 BC, when many OT books were yet to be written, to have thought that the Scripture available was sufficient? What about during the life of Christ, when the whole OT was available but no NT book was written? Must we so qualify the notion of Scripture's sufficiency to fit the amount of written revelation available at various points in history, that the doctrine actually becomes vacuous? If so, then the doctrine seemingly could be dropped with little damage to the Christian faith in general and to the doctrine of Scripture in particular.

Questions can also be raised about Scripture's contents. Can Scripture be sufficient even though doctrines like the Trinity and the hypostatic union of Christ are nowhere stated explicitly as they would be in a doctrinal treatment of God or Christ? And Scripture speaks of heaven and hell, but there are many questions we might wish to ask about them whose answers are nowhere found in Scripture. The same is true of Satan, angels, demons, and many other topics. Can Scripture be sufficient when such subjects are covered in only a partial way? What is it about Scripture that makes it sufficient?

There are also questions about Scripture's effect. Is Scripture sufficient to guarantee that those who accept what it says about salvation will no longer fear that their relation to God is in trouble? Is there sufficient information to assure believers that they can't lose their salvation, or does biblical revelation only teach that we must persevere in the faith, because if we don't, we will lose our salvation? And in light of Scripture's sufficiency, can anyone find in it the answer to emotional and psychological problems? If not, is Scripture insufficient for use by Christian counselors?

## An Initial Working Definition

The foregoing questions help to clarify what the sufficiency of Scripture is about. Various definitions of Scripture's sufficiency have been offered, and I think the elements emphasized in Wayne Grudem's definition make it a good working definition as a point of departure. Grudem says that Scripture's sufficiency means *that Scripture contained all the words of God he intended his people to have at each stage of redemptive history, and that it now contains everything we need God to tell us for salvation, for trusting him perfectly, and for obeying him perfectly.*[1]

One of the strongest points about this definition is that it allows us to say that, though we must believe in the progress of revelation (God didn't say everything he wanted to at once, but did so incrementally), at any point during Scripture's composition, it would have been correct to say that the books already written had the characteristic of sufficiency. This is so because Scripture's sufficiency shouldn't be thought of as a quantitative attribute, but rather as a qualitative one. That is, the sufficiency of Scripture doesn't depend on how much of it is written, how long the books are, or any other such quantitative notion. Rather it is about the nature of Scripture's contents. Does Scripture teach us what we must know about God, about ourselves, and about how to initiate and nurture a saving relationship with God? Put differently, does Scripture present how to be saved and live a life pleasing to God? The answer is yes, regardless of whether one lived when only a few OT books were written, or when the OT was finished but no NT had been written, or when all sixty-six books were done.

Second, according to this definition, Scripture's sufficiency has to do with the most fundamental soteriological issues of all, namely, how to be saved and how to live out that salvation before God and humankind. This doesn't mean that Scripture is a "wasteland" for information about other doctrines. Scripture doesn't reveal everything about God's nature and attributes, for example, but it says more than enough for us to fashion a biblical portrait of God. The same is true for many other doctrines, such as the two natures of Christ, the concept of sin, the nature of the church, Christ's second coming, and the kingdom of God.

All of that information is needed to construct a biblical worldview. But without denying any of it, theologians have formulated the doctrine of Scripture's sufficiency so as to focus on how humans can establish and maintain a saving relation with God. I wouldn't say that this is the only theological topic

---

[1] Wayne Grudem, *Systematic Theology: An Introduction to Biblical Doctrine* (Grand Rapids, MI: Zondervan, 1994), 127 (italics are Grudem's).

that matters—all doctrines based on Scripture are important—but if humans don't get these issues right, the consequences are both devastating and unending. We can also add that at least part of why the emphasis of this doctrine (at least since the Reformation) has been on salvation is that by the Reformation era, the Roman Catholic Church was blatantly and emphatically insisting that more than what Scripture teaches is necessary to be saved.

Grudem's definition reflects what Christians have historically held. At root, the concept's most fundamental idea is that God's word, comprised of the sixty-six books of the Bible, is sufficient to tell humans at any time and place how to establish a saving relationship with God and how then to live a life that pleases Him.[2] For a more extensive definition of this doctrine, the *Belgic Confession* of 1561 is a good example, but its substance is the same as Grudem's. Article 7 of the *Belgic Confession* is entitled "The Sufficiency of the Holy Scriptures to be the Only Rule of Faith." It says,

> We believe that these Holy Scriptures fully contain the will of God, and that whatsoever man ought to believe unto salvation, is sufficiently taught therein. For since the whole manner of worship which God requires of us is written in them at large, it is unlawful for any one, though an Apostle, to teach otherwise than we are now taught in the Holy Scriptures: *nay, though it were an angel from heaven*, as the Apostle Paul saith. For since it is forbidden *to add unto or take away anything from the Word of God*, it doth thereby evidently appear that the doctrine thereof is most perfect and complete in all respects. Neither may we compare any writings of men, though ever so holy, with those divine Scriptures; nor ought we to compare custom, or the great multitude, or antiquity, or succession of times or persons, or councils, decrees, or statutes, with the truth of God, for the truth is above all; for all men are of themselves liars, and more vain than vanity itself. Therefore we reject with all our hearts whatsoever doth not agree with this infallible rule, which the Apostles have taught us, saying, *Try the spirits whether they are of God*; likewise, *If there comes any unto you, and bring not this doctrine, receive him not into your house.*[3]

## EXPLAINING THE CONCEPT AND ITS IMPLICATIONS

Though the definition above is clear, several items fill out the concept more fully. We can divide these points into what the definition doesn't mean and what it does mean.

---

[2] This seems to be the substance of definitions found in essays like the following: Peter Adam, "The Preacher and the Sufficient Word," in John Stott, J. I. Packer, D. A. Carson, Frank J. Retief, et al., *When God's Voice Is Heard: The Power of Preaching* (Downers Grove, IL: InterVarsity Press, 1995), 29; Timothy Ward, "The Diversity and Sufficiency of Scripture," in *The Trustworthiness of God: Perspectives on the Nature of Scripture*, ed. Paul Helm and Carl R. Trueman (Grand Rapids, MI: Eerdmans, 2002), 193; and Dennis Jowers, "The Sufficiency of Scripture and the Biblical Canon," *TJ* 30 (2009): 49.

[3] Quoted in Philip Schaff, *The Creeds of Christendom with a History and Critical Notes*, 6th ed., vol. 3, *The Evangelical Protestant Creeds with Translations* (1931; repr., Grand Rapids, MI: Baker, 1983), 387–389, quoted in Nelson D. Kloosterman, "The 'Redemptive-Movement Hermeneutic' and the Sufficiency of Scripture in Light of the History of Dogma," *MAJT* 17 (2006): 194.

## What Sufficiency Doesn't Mean

*Enough, but Not Exhaustive*—Scripture's sufficiency doesn't mean its coverage is exhaustive. Of course, coverage could be exhaustive and also sufficient, but that isn't so for Scripture. Scripture as sufficient but not exhaustive means at least two different things. First, Scripture's sufficiency doesn't mean it covers every possible theological topic. But it does cover what humans need in order to be saved and live a life pleasing to the Lord. And it covers many other doctrines as well.

Second, even the topics Scripture does address, including those about our salvation and God's expectations for our behavior, don't say everything that could be said. For example, Scripture doesn't raise every possible interpersonal disagreement two people might have and then explain how to resolve them. As another example, it doesn't present a lengthy treatise on how and why God's justification of guilty sinners on the basis of Christ's sacrifice not only meets the requirements of justice from a human perspective, but also explain how God himself can be just in justifying sinners. That doesn't mean that Scripture says nothing relevant to these matters, for it does reveal basic principles that are useful in resolving disagreements and in offering a full-blown theological explanation of how God's method of salvation meets all requirements of justice.

Just as I don't need to know every single traffic law in a given country or state in order to pass the exam to get a driver's license, so it isn't necessary to know everything about the doctrines revealed in Scripture in order to understand God's requirements and to construct, if I so choose, a system of theology based on Scripture. It is also worth noting that, in saying that Scripture is sufficient, no one intends to say that Scripture is everything God knows. As omniscient, God knows everything that can be known, and thus, he knows everything there is to know about the subjects discussed in Scripture, and about subjects not discussed in Scripture. The key is that God has given us enough information, even if not exhaustive, about how to be saved and live a godly life, so that if we refuse to obey, we can't be excused on the grounds that God failed to explain the rules and expectations.

*No Further Revelation Needed to Know How to Be Saved*—Scripture's sufficiency also means that there are no supplementary revelations of the Spirit or decisions by church councils or practices arising from tradition that are necessary in order to understand God's plan of salvation and instructions for godly living. None of these other sources of information is inspired of God, nor do they deserve a place in Scripture. Material from such sources may help interpret Scripture and/or suggest helpful ways of applying Scripture, but those other sources don't "set the rules" for salvation and godly living, and they aren't binding on Christians, for they aren't God's word. Even if those supplementary materials never existed, the people of God would be adequately informed and equipped by Scripture to know and meet God's requirements.

*Not Everything Jesus, the Prophets, and the Apostles Taught*—Scripture's sufficiency also doesn't mean that it contains everything spoken by OT prophets, Christ, and the apostles. In fact, John 20:30 says that there were things Jesus taught and did that the Holy Spirit didn't inspire the NT writers to include in their books. This should disturb no one, for given divine superintendence of the writing of Scripture, we can safely say that every one of Christ's teachings and deeds that God wanted in Scripture is there.

*Not a Manual for Organizing and Running a Local Church*—Then, Scripture's sufficiency doesn't mean it describes all the practices and regulations required by a local church for its organization. While Scripture speaks of various church officers and their duties, and gives general descriptions of what often happened in actual worship services in local churches, none of that describes everything a given church (or set of churches) did in organizing and running its local assembly. Given the tendency of many people to turn descriptions into prescriptions, it is good that we don't have an exhaustive list of these things. If we did, no doubt some Christians and churches would try to absolutize such procedures and practices as requirements for all churches.

*Not Equivalent to a Full Systematic Theology or Commentary on Christian Doctrines*—Next, we can also say that even though Scripture is sufficient, it doesn't contain every doctrine stated fully as a systematic theology might. This doesn't mean that evangelical systematic theology is nonbiblical or that it has no roots in Scripture. Rather, it means that we don't find anywhere in Scripture a full statement and explanation of doctrines like the Trinity or the hypostatic union of Christ as one might find them explained in a theological treatise. Of course, all the data from which to construct such doctrines are present in Scripture. Thus, as long as theologians and Bible scholars base their doctrines on what Scripture teaches, doctrines like the Trinity are warranted, even if they aren't explicitly stated in the pages of Holy Writ.

In light of this last point, Scripture is sufficient, and yet it leaves room for doctrine to grow. This is so because sufficiency doesn't require doctrines to appear in Scripture in the very words in which they would later be stated, and it doesn't teach that we shouldn't draw out other doctrines that are entailed by doctrines explicitly covered in Scripture.

This must not be misunderstood. It doesn't mean that theologians can construct any doctrine whatsoever and claim biblical data as its source, even though Scripture says nothing even vaguely relevant to the newly constructed doctrine. Any acceptable doctrine must be grounded in Scripture's teachings. Scripture's sufficiency doesn't require that doctrines formed after the canon's close (like the Trinity and hypostatic union) must be stated in Scripture as they would be later. It only requires sufficient biblical data to support the doctrine in question, regardless of when in church history and how it was constructed.

### What Sufficiency Does Include

Several points help to explain what sufficiency includes.

*Enough to Be Saved and Live a Godly Life*—Scripture's sufficiency means that the Bible teaches all doctrines that God wanted to reveal and that we need to know. This especially includes information about how to be saved and live a life pleasing to God. Scripture also contains all the moral precepts we need to know and are required to obey. And, it speaks of the blessings we receive if we obey, and of punishments we must endure if we disobey.[4]

God could have created human life and then left us to "stumble in the dark" over whether he exists, and if so, what he requires of us. But God did more. He gave humankind the guidebook/rule book/manual for using the "equipment" (mental and physical) he gave us. While the manual doesn't cover every area of life, it explains quite clearly everything we need to know about establishing and maintaining a positive relationship with God.

*The Sole and Final Norm for Faith and Practice*—Scripture's sufficiency means even more. As Timothy Ward explains, Scripture's sufficiency, as understood in the Reformation era, means that Scripture is the sole and final norm for all matters of faith and practice. That is, it is the *norma normans non normata* ("the norming norm that is not itself normed").[5] This means that Scripture is the highest rule and teaching of what we must believe and of how we are to relate to God. While other sources for biblical and theological study are to be judged by Scripture for their accuracy and worthiness for inclusion in biblical and systematic theology (or in any other area of biblical studies), Scripture is the only judge of its own accuracy and authority. In earlier chapters we saw that Scripture teaches that it is God's inspired and inerrant word. It also affirms that it is supremely authoritative. Scriptural teaching determines what is true in moral and spiritual matters. There is no other source to which we may appeal for a second and more decisive opinion. While Scripture and its teach-

---

[4] Kloosterman, "'Redemptive-Movement Hermeneutic'," 195; Adam, "Preacher and the Sufficient Word," 29; and Jowers, "Sufficiency of Scripture and the Biblical Canon," 49, make these various points, though more briefly than I have. The development of these points is my own.

[5] Ward, "Diversity and Sufficiency of Scripture," 193.

ing are the tool for assessing the worth of everything else, nothing else judges Scripture's value and authority. That is what it means to be the "norming norm that is normed by nothing else"!

*Enough without Negating the Value of Aids in Interpreting and Applying Its Teaching*—Does Scripture's sufficiency entail that teachers, commentaries, theologies, etc., are unnecessary and useless? In light of Scripture's sufficiency, do we need any of them to understand God's will and wishes for our life? I answer the latter question affirmatively, but I must explain how Scripture can be sufficient and yet warrant these other aids to understanding. Initially, I note that Scripture is written revelation from God. Explanations of what biblical revelation means and guidelines for applying its teaching aren't normally included in Scripture. Of course, sometimes a biblical author records a vision from the Lord that is filled with symbolism and figurative language, and he also includes its interpretation (e.g., Ezek. 37:1–14; Daniel 7; Revelation 17). But—and this is a key point—none of these passages contains an explanation of how we should interpret and apply the interpretation itself. We, the readers, must still interpret the biblical author's explanation of his own writing.

What do these foregoing comments mean? Do they suggest that Scripture is impossible to interpret, even if the author records, for example, a vision and then explains its meaning? Or does it mean that the only hope for understanding such passages is the illumining ministry of the Holy Spirit? We must respond negatively to all of these questions. Scripture isn't impossible to interpret or understand (see my chapter on perspicuity for reassurance on that point); if it were, in what sense would it qualify as *revelation*? Moreover, it is advisable to seek the Holy Spirit's illumining ministry when reading Scripture, but that ministry doesn't involve transferring the intellectual content of a passage, which the reader couldn't at all grasp, to the reader's mind so that he or she can thereafter understand what Scripture means. Rather, illumination predominantly involves the Holy Spirit's ministries of convicting us that what we are reading applies to us, showing us how it applies, and especially moving our mind and heart to apply the truth in our life.

But how do we understand what the Bible is actually saying, so that the Holy Spirit has some "content" to apply in our lives? We understand Scripture through careful exegesis, using rules of interpretation that we have learned from our understanding of ordinary language. We also get help in grasping the writer's message from teachers who have already studied the text in more depth and can draw our attention to key elements in the text and explain what they mean. We may also glean information from commentaries, from theological works which discuss doctrines raised in passages we are studying, and from various works in Bible background fields of study like ancient Near Eastern literature, archaeology, etc. None of these is Scripture, nor are teachers' explanations equal to Scripture. All of these "study helps" are humanly produced and fallible to some extent, but that doesn't mean they are of no help when we want help in understanding Scripture.

So, espousing Scripture as sufficient to present God's message doesn't rule out the need for or usefulness of the various study aids mentioned, for Scripture must still be interpreted, understood, and applied. It doesn't interpret and apply itself all by itself. The Holy Spirit stands ready to help us in these matters, but he seldom works in a total intellectual vacuum, filling our minds with content that was never there in the first place. Rather, he takes the content we have learned through careful exegesis and from the instruction available from teachers and teaching aids such as commentaries, and he shows us that what we read applies to us, and then he moves our heart and mind to commit to living out what we understand Scripture to teach.

Despite what I have said, some will disagree, because it appears to contradict 1 John 2:27. John speaks of an anointing that each believer has. That anointing is the Holy Spirit himself, but then John says something that appears to contradict what I have said about the need for and usefulness of teachers and various teaching aids. John writes, "But the anointing that you received from him abides in you, and you have no need that anyone should teach you. But as his anointing teaches you about everything, and is true, and is no lie—just as it has taught you, abide in him" (ESV).

While this may seem to teach the sufficiency of Scripture itself, so that we don't need any human teachers, it actually doesn't. The passage actually teaches *the sufficiency of the Holy Spirit as our* teacher, but this requires explanation. Readers may be thinking, if the Holy Spirit is sufficient to teach us Scripture, why do we need human teachers, commentaries, etc.? Indeed, why do we even need to read Scripture at all—can't the Holy Spirit just "zap" the contents of Scripture into our minds?

Though the questions just posed imagine the absurd, sadly, some think that 1 John 2:27 implies that human teachers, etc., are unnecessary, because as we read Scripture (often mindlessly), or even if we don't read the Bible at all, the Holy Spirit can and will mysteriously and miraculously transfer Scripture's contents to our minds. First John 2:27 supports such notions, or so they think.

Don't believe that! John isn't in this passage rejecting all human teaching. He is warning his readers against being seduced by the errors of false teachers. These false teachers had mingled with others in the Christian community and appeared to be genuine believers. But that lasted only for a time, and then they left the community, and their apostasy became clear. Even so, these false teachers claimed that they had unusually deep insights into spiritual truth; without them and their teaching (they claimed), genuine believers could go only so far in the faith and attain only a relatively superficial knowledge of the things of the Lord.

John instructs his readers to reject the teachings of such apostates. They claim that they can lead believers into the depths of knowledge, but they can't do so. They only mislead and confuse, so no one should follow them or their teachings. Anyway, there is no need to follow them, because each believer has the Holy Spirit and his ministry in his or her life. He is the only one who can lead anyone into the depths of spiritual truth, and those who know Christ as Savior already possess the Holy Spirit, because he indwells them.

What John wrote in this letter applies to all other believers as well! John didn't reject all human teachers as worthless and urge his readers merely to cling to the Holy Spirit, who would unpack the deep things of God and lead them into the depths of spiritual truth. Rather, he warned readers that the kind of knowledge and understanding of spiritual truth that false teachers offer is a sham. What they promise can be divulged only by the Holy Spirit. It is in that sense that John means that his readers don't need any human teachers![6]

A sufficient Scripture still needs to be interpreted and applied. Human teachers, commentaries, etc., can help with that. Only the Holy Spirit can move our wills to accept God's truth and live it, but we must first know and learn what God wants of us. The latter activities require our own study and even learning from human instructors. The former ones (accepting and living God's truth) result from the Holy Spirit's ministry in our lives, but the Holy Spirit doesn't work with an intellectual/content vacuum in our minds. So, despite Scripture's sufficiency, there is ample reason to teach and learn God's word and to write commentaries and other books that help people understand Scripture. Of course, these "learning helps" are not additions to Scripture. The sixty-six books composed by the divinely moved writers, while not everything God knows about the topics covered, are sufficient to communicate everything God wanted to say on the topics addressed.

## DOES SCRIPTURE TEACH ITS OWN SUFFICIENCY?

Just as Scripture nowhere formally defines sufficiency, no passage explicitly raises the question of whether Scripture is sufficient and answers it. But this must not be misunderstood. Scripture does say many things about itself and

---

[6] Note also that John says nothing about *how* the Holy Spirit leads believers into deeper levels of the truth. Certainly, he doesn't hint that the Holy Spirit will miraculously transfer biblical content, along with its meaning, into the empty minds of believers or unbelievers. If John had suggested that, he apparently would have contradicted other Scriptures that speak of the need to study God's word (2 Tim. 2:15). And he would have contradicted even the passage where Jesus spoke of searching the Scriptures (John 5:39). He would also have contradicted Psalm 1, which says the prosperous person meditates in God's law (Scripture) day and night. First John 2:27 contradicts none of these Scriptures!

other topics, and those teachings have implications for the doctrine of sufficiency. I believe they provide biblical warrant for this doctrine, even if they
don't explicitly define and affirm it. So, we can answer the question raised in
the subtitle above affirmatively, as long as we realize that something might be
taught indirectly from something else Scripture teaches or as an implication of
what Scripture clearly says. These points will become clear as I present passages
of Scripture relevant to Scripture's sufficiency.

First, there are verses that show that Scripture sufficiently explains how humans can enter a saving relation with God. An initial passage, 2 Timothy 3:15,
is usually thought of as part of an overall text that teaches inspiration. But as
also noted, 2 Timothy 3's context also teaches inerrancy. In addition, verse 15
is relevant to Scripture's sufficiency. In 2 Timothy 3 Paul warns Timothy of the
perils of the last days. He then admonishes Timothy to hold fast to the truth
he had learned. Timothy should do this because of those who taught him the
Scriptures (his grandmother Lois, his mother Eunice, and Paul himself). Their
lives are a testament to how to live out biblical truth, and they also show that
it is possible to live a godly life in spite of the pressure to do evil in the troublesome last days.

Paul offered a second reason for Timothy to continue in the truth. Not
only does he have godly examples (3:14), but he also has Scripture. Why is that
a safeguard against the evils of the last days? There are several reasons. The
first is that Scripture is (v. 15) "able to make you wise for salvation through
faith in Christ Jesus" (ESV). In verses 16–17, to which we shall return shortly,
Paul speaks about Scripture's nature, and in so doing explains why it is such a
valuable safeguard against the evils of the last days.

But we must not move too quickly from verse 15 to 16 and 17. What Paul
says in verse 15 is actually quite remarkable. Paul says that the Scriptures are
able to make humans wise unto salvation. What Scriptures would have been
available to Timothy from his childhood? Most of the Scripture he would have
known would be the OT. When Paul wrote 2 Timothy, some NT books had
been written, but not all. For example, all Johannine literature was composed
after Paul wrote 2 Timothy.

Despite how many NT books were written before 2 Timothy, it is dubious as to how much they had circulated in early Christian communities that
received the gospel and turned to Christ. During his childhood, Timothy and
his family might have had little or no access to any of the NT. During his adult
years, we have no way of knowing which NT books (other than 1 Timothy)
Timothy would have seen before Paul wrote 2 Timothy.

Perhaps readers agree, but wonder what difference it makes? The answer is
that, even though Paul would have known that most of the Scripture Timothy

had seen (and most, if not all, the Scripture to which he referred in 2 Tim. 3:15) was the OT, that didn't stop Paul from saying that Timothy would have known the Scriptures from childhood, Scriptures that can make a person wise unto salvation *through faith in Jesus Christ*. In effect, Paul is saying that even the OT is sufficient to point people to Jesus as God's way to salvation! So, anyone who claims that OT saints, or those relying only on the OT, couldn't be saved, contradicts 2 Timothy 3:15!

It should go without saying, though it is worth noting anyway, that if the OT is sufficient to make people wise unto salvation through faith in Christ, then surely the NT is no less sufficient for this! The NT not only clearly teaches that salvation must be purchased with the blood of a sacrificed lamb, but also that the "lamb" who made the all-sufficient sacrifice for sin is God's sacrificial lamb, Jesus of Nazareth, who is the Messiah/Christ.

Anyone who wonders whether Scripture presents enough information about how to be saved has the answer in 2 Timothy 3:15. And many more passages teach it, too. Let me mention just a few. In James 1:18, James writes that God "brought forth" believers, i.e., he gave them salvation (the new birth) "by the word of truth." To what does the "word of truth" refer? Undoubtedly James had in mind Scripture. James and his readers would know that, though there is truth elsewhere, Scripture is the most notable repository of truth. It is certainly the deposit of truth that God most frequently uses to give new birth to those who believe it. James would likely have been thinking about the OT when he wrote his epistle, but he would surely say the same thing about extant NT revelation, let alone NT books yet to be written.

Similarly, Peter wrote 1 Peter to encourage Christians who were experiencing much suffering and persecution. He began by reminding them that though they were aliens and sojourners in this world, they were God's elect. As aliens and strangers, they had little standing in the Roman Empire, but they were important where it really matters; they were God's chosen ones. In the rest of chapter 1, Peter discussed various aspects and implications of that salvation. In verse 22, he urged them to love other believers. What is most interesting is Peter's basis for making this command. He writes,

> [22] Seeing ye have purified your souls in obeying the truth through the Spirit unto unfeigned love of the brethren, see that ye love one another with a pure heart fervently: [23] Being born again, not of corruptible seed, but of incorruptible, by the word of God, which liveth and abideth forever. (KJV)

Note two things from these verses. Peter said his readers had "purified [their] souls in obeying the truth." He added that they were "born again" by an "incorruptible seed," namely, "the word of God." Where would Peter think truth that purifies the soul could be found, and to what word of God did he likely refer in verse 23? Undoubtedly, he would first be thinking of the gospel (see also v. 25). Second, given what else he says about the word of God (vv. 23–25), Peter was also probably thinking of Scripture more generally, the OT in particular. This is so because he quoted Isaiah 40:6–8 and used it to make a point about God's enduring word in general. That thought seems to broaden his reference beyond the specific words of the gospel, and what he says is also true of the NT.

While Peter didn't explain how God's word works to bring salvation to those who believe it, he didn't need to in order to affirm that he was saying that Scripture tells what anyone needs to know and do in order to be saved. This is also true of so many other passages about salvation. For example, in Romans 4 Paul meticulously explains, by referencing Abraham especially, that salvation is not by works, but by faith. By the end of chapter 4 Paul explains that the biblical stories about Abraham's imputed righteousness weren't written just for Abraham. They were also written for our sake, so that we, too, would understand that righteousness is imputed to our account by our faith in Christ, not by works (Rom. 4:23–25). Just in case readers wouldn't completely grasp what Romans 4 teaches about how to be saved, Paul began chapter 5 by writing, "Therefore, having been justified by faith, we have peace with God through our Lord Jesus Christ." In the rest of chapter 5 Paul explained more fully the justification believers have. It's as if Paul is saying—"just in case you didn't understand what I was saying in chapter 4 about how to be saved, let me summarize it in a brief statement—'therefore, having been justified by faith'." That's the point; justification comes not by works but by faith. Anyone reading Abraham's story in the book of Genesis can easily come to the same conclusion. Abraham believed God, and it was counted unto him for righteousness; the same is true for us (Rom. 4:3, 23–24). Paul didn't misread Abraham's story, nor should we.

Paul clarified the path to salvation again in great detail to believers in Galatia. Salvation isn't attained by faith plus works. It is won by faith alone. And we find repeatedly in the Gospels a clear statement of what one must do to be saved. Think, for example, of Jesus's conversation with Nicodemus (John 3). Nicodemus flattered Jesus about his teaching and miracles. Jesus knew, however, what was most on his mind, and so he said that unless a person is born again, he cannot see the kingdom of God. Nicodemus was puzzled, so Jesus clearly explained what he meant. He presented God's method of salvation, culminating in that great verse, John 3:16.

The apostle John also wrote in 1 John 5:11–12,

> And this is the testimony, that God gave us eternal life, and this life is in his Son. Whoever has the Son has life; whoever does not have the Son of God does not have life. (ESV)

Could God's method of salvation be any clearer? If you have the Son, you have life; if you don't have the Son, you don't have life. How do you get the Son? John 3:16 has the answer: God gave his only Son so that whoever believes in him shall not perish, but have everlasting life! Or as Paul and Silas answered the Philippian jailer's question about how to be saved, "Believe in the Lord Jesus, and you shall be saved, you and your household" (Acts 16:31).

Is Scripture sufficient to explain the way of salvation? Absolutely! Both the OT and the NT teach that salvation is by grace through faith. What about requirements for living a life that is pleasing to God? Does Scripture present that? Absolutely yes! Let's return to 2 Timothy 3, and examine closely verses 16–17. The first phrase of verse 16 is rightly emphasized for what it teaches about Scripture's inspiration. But Paul also says that Scripture is profitable (*ōphelimos*). The Greek word can be translated "useful," "beneficial," "helpful," or "advantageous." Now, something could be beneficial and helpful for doing a task even if it isn't entirely sufficient for what needs to be done. Is Paul saying that Scripture will help you some, but you will need something more? The answer lies in our text. Note first that Paul mentions the things for which Scripture is helpful. It is beneficial for "doctrine, for reproof, for correction, for instruction in righteousness." So, Scripture helps anyone to know what is correct to think about God, ourselves, and our relations to everyone and everything in creation. If our actions displease God and break his rules, Scripture shows that, and reproves our behavior. But it doesn't just accuse us of wrongdoing, it also tells us how to change our behavior so as to obey God's commands. Scripture not only helps in particular instances, but more generally it also presents God's standards for righteous living and reveals how to meet those standards.

Does Scripture show us accurately and conclusively what God demands? The answer is a resounding yes. How can we know? Because verse 17 shows the result when Scripture is read, understood, and obeyed. What God intended when he gave Scripture is "that the man of God may be perfect (*artios*, "proficient, i.e., able to meet all demands"[7]) thoroughly furnished (*exērtismenos*, from *exartizō*, "to equip" or "to furnish") unto all good works" (KJV).

From what 2 Timothy 3:17 says about the results when Scripture is followed, we can say unequivocally that Scripture is totally sufficient for godly living. If reading, studying, and obeying Scripture prepares people to meet all demands, i.e., to be fully equipped for all good works, how could it not be sufficient to communicate what God requires to please him each day? As already noted, when Paul wrote this verse, he would most specifically have been thinking about the OT. But since, as we noted when studying inspiration, this

---

[7] William F. Arndt and F. Wilbur Gingrich, in *A Greek-English Lexicon of the New Testament and Other Early Christian Literature* (Chicago: University of Chicago Press, 1965), 110.

passage can rightly be applied to the NT, what Paul says is true of the whole Bible. Of course, to know God's requirements we must read and study Scripture, and if we do, we can know what God expects. Scripture sufficiently shows the path to what God considers *all* good works!

Other Scripture passages also teach that God's word is sufficient to show God's demands for godly living. For example, in 2 Peter 1:3, Peter wrote that the Lord has given us all things relevant to life and godliness. In the following verses, Peter enumerated various Christian virtues that believers should develop (vv. 4–10), especially because we have been given wonderful promises so that we might be partakers of the divine nature (1:4).[8]

The OT has similar thoughts about the sufficiency of God's word for both salvation and life's various circumstances. Psalm 19:7–14 is an especially rich passage on these topics. The psalmist speaks of the law of the Lord, and as he often does, he refers to God's instruction more generally, not just to God's precepts. This instruction is, of course, available in Scripture. In verse 7, he says that God's law is "perfect" or complete, meaning that it can cover any spiritual needs in our life. It "converts" the soul (KJV), though the idea isn't so much being saved as it is that of restoring or refreshing the soul, and "soul" is used here as metonymy for the whole person. In addition, verse 7 says that God's word "[makes] wise the simple." The thought is that Scripture makes those who are undiscerning, naïve, and even gullible skilled in the art of godly living.

In verse 8, the psalmist addresses the precepts recorded in God's word. They are "right" because they show the way to a life that pleases God and blesses those who follow them. They are also called pure, and the point is their clarity. In verse 9, the writer adds that God's ordinances or judgments are "true" and "righteous altogether." In the verses that follow, the psalmist speaks of the benefits of following God's word, and then asks the Lord to keep him from falling into sin.[9]

Psalm 119 is another great psalm that speaks of the many things Scripture can do in one's life. For example, the psalm says (v. 1) that those who walk in the Lord's law are undefiled or blameless. As Grudem notes, the psalmist claims that "all that God requires of us is recorded in his written Word: simply to do all that the Bible commands us is to be blameless in God's sight."[10] In addition, the psalmist writes that when he is afflicted, he finds "comfort" in Scripture and is "revived" by it (v. 50). Scripture also guides those who need counsel (v. 105). And Scripture won't mislead, for it is true (v. 160). Moreover, it would be useful not only to those who first read it after the psalmist penned these words, but also to

---

[8] Wayne A. Mack, "The Sufficiency of Scripture in Counseling," *MSJ* 9 (Spring 1998): 80–81, makes these points.
[9] My description of the teaching of this passage was greatly helped by John MacArthur's discussion of it in his "The Sufficiency of Scripture," *MSJ* 15 (Fall 2004): 167–174.
[10] Grudem, *Systematic Theology*, 128.

later generations, for it is true and its ordinances will last forever (v. 160). This makes abundant sense, for though times, knowledge, and technology, for example, change, human nature and God's standards are constant. What Joshua in his day told Israel about the Scripture God had given through Moses is true today for all of God's word: "This Book of the Law shall not depart from your mouth, but you shall meditate on it day and night, so that you may be careful to do according to all that is written in it. For then you will make your way prosperous, and then you will have good success" (Josh. 1:8 ESV).

If Scripture can do these different things in the lives of those who read and obey it, perhaps we need even more words from God so as to be more successful. Though we might think so, Scripture is clear that what we already have is sufficient. Various passages like Deuteronomy 4:2; 12:32, Proverbs 30:5–6, and Revelation 22:18–19 instruct readers to neither add to nor take away from the Scripture God has given. Of course, these verses refer initially to a very small portion of God's word (referred to in the texts listed), but it isn't inappropriate to apply these passages to Scripture more generally. This is so especially if one agrees that the canon of Scripture is closed.

The passages discussed in this section aren't exhaustive. Rather the point is to see whether Scripture teaches its own sufficiency. The texts discussed show ample biblical support for concluding that Scripture is sufficient to teach us how to be saved and to lead a life pleasing to God. What other books teach about pleasing God and living a life that glorifies him may be helpful, but there is no substitute for the Bible!

## IS THIS DOCTRINE A RECENT INVENTION?

In systematic theologies and in individual volumes on the doctrine of Scripture, the doctrine of Scripture's sufficiency isn't always discussed. Hence, some may wonder whether the church has always espoused it, or whether it is something only recently held. The Reformers eagerly affirmed it, but of course, that was to make a point that no one needs the decisions of church councils, papal pronouncements, or knowledge of what Christians have traditionally believed in order to know how to be saved and lead a godly life.

In the early church it was the consensus that Scripture is sufficient for knowing how to establish a saving relationship with God and to live a life pleasing to him. This isn't surprising, for Scripture itself makes this point. As explained above, speaking specifically of the OT, the apostle Paul wrote that the Scriptures can make one "wise unto salvation" through faith in Jesus Christ (2 Tim. 3:15 KJV).[11] In the next verses, Paul explains what is so special

---

[11] Gregg R. Allison, *Historical Theology: An Introduction to Christian Doctrine* (Grand Rapids, MI: Zondervan, 2011), 143, makes the point that Scripture itself states its own sufficiency.

about Scripture, namely, its divine origin, and adds that it is also profitable for accomplishing all of the ministries mentioned in verses 16–17.

Though Paul refers specifically to the OT, we have seen that he would likely agree that what he said also applies to the NT. This passage, plus the others discussed in the previous section, shows that the idea of Scripture's sufficiency is at least as old as Scripture itself. It is not a recent invention.

Early church fathers agreed that Scripture is sufficient. In his *Treatise against Hermogenes*, Tertullian said of God's word, "I revere the fullness of His Scripture."[12] And Vincent of Lerins added that "the canon of Scripture is complete, and sufficient of itself for everything, and more than sufficient."[13] As a result, Scripture was deemed the only proper source for doctrine. In the words of Cyril of Jerusalem, "For concerning the divine and holy mysteries of the faith, not even a casual statement must be delivered without the Holy Scriptures. . . . For this salvation which we believe depends not on ingenious reasoning, but on demonstration of the Holy Scriptures."[14]

Of course, this meant for the church fathers that whatever doesn't conform to Scripture is heresy and must be rejected.[15] As Allison explains, there was another development in the early church related to Scripture's sufficiency. Three other sources were appealed to for Christian belief and practice. Allison writes,

> These were (1) apostolic tradition, the testimony of the apostles as it was handed down in the proclamation and teaching of the early churches (1 Cor. 11:23; 2 Thess. 2:15; 3:6); (2) the canon of truth, or the rule of faith, a summary of the growing doctrinal understanding of the early church; and (3) church authority, especially the practice of appealing to the church fathers in support of theological positions.[16]

While each of these proved useful in fighting various heresies in the early church, at that time in history none of the three was deemed more important than Scripture. Nor did these sources suggest to early church believers that Scripture was not sufficient.

During the early part of the Middle Ages, there continued to be a consensus that Scripture is sufficient. Noteworthy is Duns Scotus's rejection of arguments against Scripture's sufficiency. While some might point to the progressive nature of revelation as evidence that only when Scripture was complete could it be sufficient, Scotus disagreed. Others might think Scripture insufficient because it contains superfluous ceremonies and historical accounts. Moreover,

---

[12] Tertullian, *Treatise against Hermogenes*, 22, in ANF 3:490, quoted in Allison, *Historical Theology*, 143.
[13] Vincent of Lerins, *Commonitory*, 2.5, in NPNF² 11:132, quoted in Allison, *Historical Theology*, 143.
[14] Cyril of Jerusalem, *Catechetical Lectures*, 4.17, in NPNF² 7:22, quoted in Allison, *Historical Theology*, 144.
[15] Here see Clement of Alexandria, *Stromata*, 7.16, in ANF 2:553–554; and Athanasius, *Against the Heathen*, 1, NPNF² 4:4; both quoted in Allison, *Historical Theology*, 144.
[16] Allison, *Historical Theology*, 145.

Scripture doesn't comment on every activity as to its sinfulness or correctness. In response, Allison writes,

> Responding to these objections, Scotus affirmed Scripture's sufficiency, citing Augustine's belief that canonical Scripture is supremely authoritative in "those things of which we must not be ignorant, but which we cannot know of ourselves." For Scotus, then, "sufficient holy Scripture contains the doctrine necessary for Christian pilgrims." Aquinas concurred: "The truth of faith is sufficiently explicit in the teaching of Christ and the apostles."[17]

Given the importance of topics addressed by Scripture, and Scripture's sufficiency on those topics, it was clear that Scripture should be read and studied. Of course, there was still a question about what sort of reading and interpretation of Scripture would be permissible. The main view in the medieval church was that Scripture should be understood within the bounds of the church's historical interpretation. This, of course, would safeguard against heresy, so long as traditional interpretations were accurate, but it didn't leave much room for doctrinal discovery and development. Nonetheless, as Allison observes, at least in the earlier part of the Middle Ages, the church "closely correlated Scripture and the historical interpretation of the church, and (2) it clearly acknowledged the supreme authority of the former in relation to the latter."[18]

Though later in the Middle Ages there would be a disagreement as to whether church tradition and interpretation was superior to Scripture itself, in the early Middle Ages church divines saw Scripture alone as sufficient. In comparing the value of Scripture and the writings of the church fathers, Hugo of St. Victor wrote,

> All divine Scripture is contained in the two Testaments, the Old and the New. Each Testament is divided into three parts: The Old contains the Law, the Prophets, the Historians. The New contains the Gospels, the Apostles, the Fathers. . . . In the last category [i.e., the Fathers] the first place belongs to the decretals which are called canonical, that is, regular. Then there comes the writings of the holy fathers—Jerome, Augustine, Ambrose, Gregory, Isidore, Origen, Bede and the other doctors; these are innumerable. Patristic writings, however, are not counted in the text of the divine Scriptures.[19]

Sadly, in the latter part of the Middle Ages, Scripture's sufficiency came under attack. In particular, the Roman Catholic Church elevated the

---

[17] Ibid., 148. Allison presents quotes from Duns Scotus's *Ordinatio*, prologue, 2, q. 1, n. 95–97 and 98. He also quotes from Aquinas's *Summa Theologica*, 2nd pt. of pt. 2, q. 1, art. 10.
[18] Allison, *Historical Theology*, 149.
[19] Hugo of St. Victor, *De Scriptura et Scriptoribus Sacris*, in George H. Tavard, *Holy Writ or Holy Church: The Crisis of the Protestant Reformation* (London: Burns & Oates, 1959), 16, quoted in Allison, *Historical Theology*, 149–150.

importance of church tradition. This tradition was supposed to be "the unwritten teaching of Christ that was communicated orally from him to his disciples, and from them to their successors, the bishops."[20] Of course, because
it was unwritten, no one could prove that Christ had taught such things, but
if the church said these teachings came from Christ through his apostles,
what layperson (or clergy) would challenge the church on that point?

Even so, this wouldn't have had to result in problems if Scripture had
remained the final and authoritative judge of doctrine and practice. Unfortunately, Scripture became one authority among others, and those others didn't
always agree with Scripture's teachings. Quoting Thomas Netter Waldensis's
opinion of the relation of Scripture to church tradition, Allison explains the
ultimate result:

> "Such is the dignity of the apostolic traditions which did not transmit in the
> Scriptures, that the same veneration and the same fervent faith is due to them
> as to the written ones. . . . If therefore, once we have studied the Scriptures,
> we see what the church universally accepts, either in the popular tradition or
> in the common agreement of the fathers, we must consider it as a full defini-
> tion of faith as though it were found in the Scriptures." So the church in the
> latter part of the Middle Ages affirmed in a novel way the reality of church
> tradition derived from unwritten apostolic sources and even of postapostolic
> divine revelation. To these were added the teaching of general church councils
> (e.g., the Council of Nicea, AD 325).[21]

Though the Reformation was concerned with various theological issues,
one key question was this issue of Scripture versus tradition. For evangelicals
today, it undoubtedly seems odd (or at least it should) that a minister would
get himself in trouble by preferring what Scripture teaches as opposed to the
dictates of church tradition. Nonetheless, that was exactly one of the main
issues at stake in the Reformers' challenge of the Roman Catholic Church.
Quotes from the Reformers in support of Scripture's sufficiency are legion, and
we cannot present them all. However, some from Luther and Calvin make the
Reformers' position clear, and also help to explain part of their dissatisfaction
with the church.

For example, Luther's controversy with the Roman Catholic Church
stemmed in part from his protest over the Church's selling of indulgences,
which the Church claimed removed one's sins. It is hard to believe that anyone
could think that practice would satisfy God's demands for justice, but the pope
had decreed that it was so. In response, Luther said,

---

[20] Allison, *Historical Theology*, 150.
[21] Ibid., 150–151. Allison quotes from Thomas Netter Waldensis, *Doctrinale Antiquatum Fidei Catholicae Eccle-siae*, chapter 23, as quoted in George H. Tavard, *Holy Writ or Holy Church: The Crisis of the Protestant Reforma-tion* (London: Burns & Oates, 1959), 58.

> A simple layman armed with Scripture is to be believed above a pope or a council without it. As for the pope's decree on indulgences, I say that neither the Church nor the pope can establish articles of faith. These must come from Scripture. For the sake of Scripture, we should reject pope and councils.[22]

As Allison rightly explains, Luther's commitment to the sufficiency of Scripture didn't mean that he was an iconoclast of the church's consensus views on doctrines and practice. Certainly, Luther didn't deny that the Holy Spirit had taught other generations of Christians, and he believed that what they had said about various doctrines taught in Scripture mattered. But the dictates of Christian clerics and/or laypersons couldn't overturn clear biblical requirements. As an example of what Luther and his church saw as the correct balance between Scripture and the consensus views of earlier Christians, the *Formula of Concord* affirms,

> Inasmuch as immediately after the times of the apostles—indeed, even while they were yet alive—false teachers and heretics arose, against whom in the early church symbols were composed, that is to say, brief and explicit confessions, which contained the unanimous consent of the catholic Christian faith, and the confession of the orthodox and true church (such as the *Apostles'*, the *Nicene*, and the *Athanasian Creeds*). We publicly profess that we embrace them, and reject all heresies and all dogmas that have ever been brought into the church of God contrary to their decision.[23]

Perhaps Luther's most famous statement is what he said to the Catholic Church officials at the Diet of Worms when asked to recant his books and their teachings. Luther replied,

> Since then Your Majesty and your lordships desire a simple reply, I will answer without horns and without teeth. Unless I am convicted by Scripture and plain reason—I do not accept the authority of popes and councils, for they have contradicted each other—my conscience is captive to the Word of God. I cannot and I will not recant anything, for to go against conscience is neither right nor safe. God help me. Amen.[24]

Quite clearly, Luther's allegiance was to Scripture. That was so because he thought it to be God's authoritative word, and as such it could never be overturned by the words and decisions of mere humans, regardless of how holy and knowledgeable they might be. But Luther also chose Scripture because he saw it as sufficient to decide the doctrinal disputes in which he was embroiled.

---

[22] The Leipzig Debate (July 1519), quoted in Allison, *Historical Theology*, 151.

[23] *Formula of Concord*, Epitome 1, "Of the Compendious Rule and Norm," in Philip Schaff, *Creeds of Christendom*, 3 vols. (New York: Harper, 1877–1905), 3:93–94, quoted in Allison, *Historical Theology*, 152.

[24] Martin Luther at the Diet of Worms (April, 1521), quoted in Roland H. Bainton, *Here I Stand: A Life of Luther* (New York: Mentor, 17th printing), 144.

Clear biblical teaching doesn't need popes' and councils' opinions to confirm it. Scripture is enough.

Calvin agreed with Luther. In a brief comment in his *Institutes*, Calvin wrote that "Scripture is the school of the Holy Spirit. Just as nothing is omitted that is both necessary and useful to know, so nothing is taught except what is expedient to know."[25] As is evident from Calvin's linking Scripture with the Holy Spirit in this quote, he thought that the right combination for understanding God's truth is both word and Spirit. In fact, in a comment on John 16:13, Calvin claimed that to deny Scripture's sufficiency was in effect to reject the Spirit, and of course, to do that would be blasphemy. In his explanation of John 16:13, Calvin wrote,

> The very *Spirit* had *led them* [the apostles] *into all truth,* when they committed to writing the substance of their doctrine. Whoever imagines that anything must be added to their doctrine, as if it were imperfect and but half-finished, not only accuses the apostles of dishonesty, but blasphemes against *the Spirit*. If the doctrine which they committed to writing had proceeded from mere learners or persons imperfectly taught, an addition to it would not have been superfluous; but now that their writings may be regarded as perpetual records of the revelation which was promised and given to them, nothing can be added to them without doing grievous injury to the Holy Spirit.[26]

Allison aptly summarizes Calvin's views on Scripture's sufficiency by quoting from Calvin's commentaries on Psalm 19 and 2 Timothy 3 as follows:

> For Calvin, the sufficiency of Scripture was confirmed by David's rule for living rightly (Ps. 19): "the law of God alone is perfectly sufficient for this purpose. . . . As soon as people depart from it, they are liable to fall into numerous errors and sins." Calvin pointed to Paul's description of a fully formed Christian (2 Tim. 3:15–17) in support: "Paul asserts absolutely, that the Scripture is sufficient for perfection. Accordingly, he who is not satisfied with Scripture desires to be wiser than is either proper or desirable."[27]

In response to these Reformers' views, the Roman Catholic Church adamantly demanded that Scripture plus other items are sufficient for doctrine and practice. In fact, at the Council of Trent, Protestants were condemned for espousing both Scripture's necessity and its sufficiency. Writing on behalf of the Catholic tradition, Robert Bellarmine claimed that Scripture, plus divine

---

[25] John Calvin, *Institutes of the Christian Religion*, ed. John T. McNeill, trans. Ford Lewis Battles (Philadelphia: Westminster, 1967), 924 (3.21.3).

[26] John Calvin, *Commentary on the Gospel according to John*, vol. 2, trans. William Pringle (Grand Rapids, MI: Eerdmans, 1949), 143, quoted in Allison, *Historical Theology*, 153.

[27] The quotes are taken from two of Calvin's commentaries: *Commentary upon the Book of Psalms*, I, 325; and his *Commentaries on the Epistles to Timothy, Titus, and Philemon*, 250–251. All of the cited quote comes from Allison, *Historical Theology*, 154–155.

and apostolic traditions, are necessary for doctrine and life. The reason is that Scripture doesn't contain the materials in these other traditions, and so must be supplemented by them. More specifically, Bellarmine argued that the sources of theological truth are "revelation contained in holy Scripture or in the tradition of the apostles or in the holy doctors, or reason reaching a firm conclusion from theological principles."[28]

Post-Reformation Protestant thinkers continued to espouse Scripture's sufficiency. As an example, John Owen's comments on sufficiency are instructive. He wrote,

> The Holy Spirit of God has prepared and disposed of the Scripture so as it might be a most sufficient and absolutely perfect way and means of communicating unto our minds that saving knowledge of God and his will that is needed which we may live unto him, and come unto the enjoyment of him in his glory.[29]

Later in the same treatise, Owen wrote specifically about what Scripture could actually accomplish, showing thereby its sufficiency to produce what God intends it to do. Scripture is

> sufficient with respect to the end of the revelation itself . . . sufficient unto the end for which it is designed—that is, sufficient to generate, cherish, increase, and preserve faith, and love, and reverence, with holy obedience, in them, in such a way and manner as will assuredly bring them unto the end of all supernatural revelation in the enjoyment of God.[30]

In the modern era, Protestant thinking has generally affirmed and espoused Scripture's sufficiency. This can be seen in the works of theologians like Charles Hodge, John Murray, Millard Erickson, and Wayne Grudem.[31] This doesn't mean, however, that Scripture's sufficiency hasn't come under any question, for it has, even if indirectly. For example, one issue debated among evangelicals is whether divine revelation of any kind has ceased. If not, then would any supplementary revelation mean that our current Scriptures aren't enough for formulating doctrine and understanding God's expectations in regard to practice?

Though such questions are especially acute among various charismatics

[28] Robert Bellarmine, *De Auctoritate Papae et Concilii* (1511), in George H. Tavard, *Holy Writ or Holy Church: The Crisis of the Protestant Reformation* (London: Burns & Oates, 1959), 115, quoted in Allison, *Historical Theology*, 157.
[29] John Owen, *The Causes, Ways, and Means of Understanding the Mind of God as Revealed in His Word, with Assurance Therein* (London, 1687), chapter 6, in *The Works of John Owen*, ed. William H. Goold, 16 vols. (Edinburgh: Banner of Truth Trust, 1967), 4:187, quoted in Allison, *Historical Theology*, 157.
[30] Ibid., 4:196, quoted in Allison, *Historical Theology*, 157.
[31] See, e.g., John Murray, "The Finality and Sufficiency of Scripture," in *Collected Writings* (Carlisle, PA: Banner of Truth Trust, 1976); Charles Hodge, *Systematic Theology*, vol. 1 (London: James Clark, 1960); Millard Erickson, *Christian Theology*, 2nd ed. (Grand Rapids, MI: Baker, 2000 printing); and Grudem, *Systematic Theology*.

who believe that, for example, the gift of prophecy is operative today, it is also a question that can be raised by noncharismatics who believe that God can and does reveal himself today. If he does, should we view the new revelation as necessary, because scriptural revelation isn't sufficient to tell us all God wants us to know? Typically, those who believe that revelation occurs today would still subscribe to Scripture's sufficiency, though it isn't always clear as to how these two ideas (current revelation and Scripture's sufficiency) fit together.

Similarly, there are differences of opinion about how Scripture's sufficiency applies to ministries like counseling, church planting, and church administration. Gregg Allison explains the nub of the disagreement as follows:

> . . . the last part of the twentieth century into the twenty-first century witnessed an ever-widening divide between evangelicals over the issue of counseling, church planting and church growth, church leadership and administration, even preaching. At the core of this debate were different notions and applications of the sufficiency of Scripture. Although the spectrum is broad and many practitioners defy easy categorization, a general division has grown and continues to grow between integrationists on the one hand and strict biblicists on the other hand. In the first camp are included Christians who seek to integrate biblical instruction about human beings, the church, leadership, preaching, and the like with the best insights of secular psychology, sociology and demographic studies, business theories, secular leadership principles, communication techniques, and much more. In the second group are Christians who insist that Scripture's sufficiency rules out any integration of biblical truth with humanly derived knowledge.[32]

Such debates are quite divisive, pitting evangelicals equally committed to Scripture's full inspiration, inerrancy, and authority against one another. A proper understanding of the Bible's sufficiency would, I believe, help, although it is not likely to resolve the entire debate. Put simply, Scripture's sufficiency means that it gives the needed information for anyone to be saved and lead a life pleasing to God. The doctrine says nothing about whether Scripture is sufficient to guide us in everything involved in church planting, church administration, counseling the mentally and emotionally troubled, and sermon preparation and delivery. Scripture may offer some help for each of these activities, but the doctrine of sufficiency doesn't mean that Scripture covers everything that these ministries require.

## IMPLICATIONS OF SCRIPTURE'S SUFFICIENCY

Because Scripture is sufficient, many implications for both doctrine and practice follow. I want to present what I think are the major ones. The first and most

---

[32] Allison, *Historical Theology*, 161.

obvious implication is that because of Scripture's sufficiency, we must make it the focus of both our preaching and our teaching. It is not by accident that, after Paul presents his concerns about the evil of the last days and then tells Timothy to stand fast, etc. (2 Tim. 3:1–17), he next (4:1ff.) exhorts Timothy to preach God's word. He must do this diligently and regardless of whether people are inclined to hear it or not. He should use it to "reprove, rebuke, exhort with great patience and instruction." It would be perhaps helpful but ultimately inadequate to do this if Scripture contained some of what we need to hear, but didn't give God's answers to life's most pressing and perplexing problems. The fact that Paul exhorts Timothy to preach the word, not something else, shows that he believed that Scripture contains whatever believers need to please God and address the problems and challenges they confront every day.

Some might respond that, of course Paul would say this, because what else did he know beyond Scripture? Readers will immediately recognize the error of this response, however, because they know that Paul was a brilliant thinker who had been very well educated. His knowledge of, for example, the writings of various pagan poets (as seen in Acts 17) is evidence of that. Moreover, he couldn't have held his own during his ministry throughout the Greco-Roman world if he was merely a religious zealot with a full heart and empty head. Reading of his missionary journeys (as recorded in Acts), we see that his intellect and knowledge were significant in every circumstance he faced.[33] Though his message always emphasized Christ and his work on Calvary, that wasn't because he knew nothing else.

It is also noteworthy that Paul urged Timothy to preach the word, even though at the time he wrote 2 Timothy, "the word" was mainly the OT. If his exhortation was correct when only the OT was complete, how much more should we, who have so much more Scripture than Paul and Timothy had, heed Paul's exhortation!

Preaching the word is also mandated because, as we saw in the chapter on animation, Scripture as sufficient has great power. In fact, that is an aspect of its sufficiency. If it had only minimal power to turn lives toward God, we might need to preach and teach Scripture plus something else. But nothing else has Scripture's power, and it is abundantly clear from changed lives through the centuries because of Scripture's impact that Scripture has power enough! Whether one is in ministry or not, if the goal is transforming lives, including one's own, nothing can do what Scripture can! It is sufficient to change lives, so preach and teach it! Preaching and teaching something else may attract a crowd for a time, but the result will likely be that people will go away spiritually

---

[33] For example, in Acts 17 we read of Paul preaching to the Athenians. What Luke records shows that Paul knew the works of various pagan poets with whom his audience would have been familiar.

starved, or at the very least quite unsatisfied. The word of God, proclaimed with creativity and enthusiasm, won't put people to sleep; it will meet their deepest needs and nurture their souls. Most importantly, it will give them accurate information about God and how to have a healthy relationship with him. What could possibly be more important than to be on the best of terms with one's creator, judge, and Lord? Scripture can accomplish all of that because its power is sufficient![34]

This first point leads immediately to a second: Scripture's sufficiency is most seen when it is joined with another "minister" to our souls, the Holy Spirit. It is, of course, possible to read Scripture and hear it preached, and get nothing from it.[35] But this isn't Scripture's fault, nor that of the Holy Spirit who inspired it. Rather, this can happen because our hearts are so hard that we refuse to hear Scripture or, having heard it, we refuse to obey. In other words, Scripture isn't some "lucky charm" or talisman which, by merely possessing a copy or even reading it, brings good things to us. The power and sufficiency of Scripture will be of no effect without the Holy Spirit's ministry to open our eyes to Scripture's truth and apply it to our lives.

Here Calvin, speaking of Scripture's sufficiency, makes this point well, about the ministry of both word and Spirit:

> Persons who, abandoning the Scripture, imagine to themselves some other way of approaching to God, must be considered as not so much misled by error as actuated by frenzy. For there have lately arisen some unsteady men, who, haughtily pretending to be taught by the Spirit, reject all reading themselves, and deride the simplicity of those who still attend to (what they style) the dead and killing letter. . . . How diabolical . . . is that madness which pretends that the use of the Scripture is only transient and temporary! . . .
>
> The office of the Spirit, . . . which is promised to us, is not to feign new and unheard of revelations, or to coin a new system of doctrine, which would seduce us from the received doctrine of the Gospel, but to seal to our minds the same doctrine which the Gospel delivers.
>
> Hence we readily understand that it is incumbent on us diligently to read and attend to the Scripture, if we would receive any advantage or satisfaction from the Spirit of God. . . . He is the author of the Scriptures; he cannot be mutable and inconsistent with himself. . . . For the Lord hath established a kind of mutual connection between the certainty of his word and of his Spirit.

---

[34] See Adam, "Preacher and the Sufficient Word," 39, for the basic point I am making. Both of us develop the idea in our own way, but the fundamental point is the same.

[35] How well I remember in my undergraduate years taking an English course in the Bible as literature. The basic assignment was to read the Bible. One day, not too far into the course, before the class started, I overheard a conversation between two other students in the class. One said, "Well, I always wondered whether the Bible was of any use. Now I know it has a use. As I was reading it, it put me to sleep." I thought to myself, "Oh, she must have been reading somewhere in the OT with all the 'who-begat' lists. Those parts certainly aren't the most exciting." But later, I realized that she might have been reading some very exciting parts of Scripture and still had that reaction. I reflected on what I'd been taught in church about the natural man not being able to understand the things of God. I doubted that these students I'd overheard were believers, and so I just thought that what they said was to be expected from those who are spiritually blind.

. . . God did not publish his word to mankind for the sake of momentary ostentation, with a design to destroy or annul it immediately on the advent of the Spirit; but he afterwards sent the same Spirit, by whose agency he had dispensed his word, to complete his work by an efficacious confirmation of that word. . . . A very different sobriety becomes the children of God; who, while they are sensible that, exclusively of the Spirit of God, they are utterly destitute of the light of truth, yet are not ignorant that the word is the instrument, by which the Lord dispenses to believers the illumination of his Spirit. For they know no other Spirit than that who dwelt in and spake by the apostles; by whose oracles they are continually called to the hearing of the word.[36]

A further implication of Scripture's sufficiency follows from things already noted. Scripture is powerful and sufficient to meet our spiritual needs, but it will do nothing for us if we don't read it, meditate on it, grasp how its teachings apply to us, and then consciously decide to obey it. Many of us have lived most or all of our life in places where there was easy access to Scripture. In fact, at various times we may have owned multiple copies of Scripture, each a different translation. Because of the easy access to Scripture, we can take it for granted that Scripture will always be available whenever we need it. And because of this, we may put off its study for some other more convenient time in our life. In fact, even some believers, when they confront difficult challenges and problems, may think that they can always, as a last resort, see what Scripture has to say. But first, they want to explore what some current thinker or other philosophy has to say that might "answer" their current situation.

This is a dangerous practice for believer and nonbeliever alike. One can always find a new fad or novel approach to problems. I don't want to suggest that creative thinking and new slants on old problems are useless. But if the new way of thinking and/or acting is so valuable, why has no one ever thought of it before? And, if it is really what we most need, surely God, who knows everything, would know that we need this novel approach. As a good God, why would he withhold this information? The truth is that our totally beneficent creator and preserver of all life knows exactly what we need to know. And, he has already revealed it—perhaps in natural revelation, but definitely in special revelation. Of course, Scripture isn't everything God knows, nor is it a textbook for solving every possible problem in every field of study and area of life. But the topics it addresses are relevant to everyone, for they deal with God's nature and actions, human nature and its limitations, divine expectations of humans, and divine answers to life's most significant problems. Times and cultures change, but Scripture handles topics that are relevant to people of all times and cultures.

---

[36] Calvin, *Institutes*, 1.9.1–3, in Hugh T. Kerr, ed., *A Compend of the Institutes of the Christian Religion by John Calvin* (Philadelphia: Westminster, 1964), 17–19.

Undoubtedly, some skeptics think Scripture is irrelevant to modern times and contemporary humans. Perhaps some of them have even read some Scripture and reached this conclusion. But giving Scripture only a cursory reading, or reading it with a resistant frame of mind won't likely result in finding answers to our problems. Is the problem with Scripture? Not at all, for if we read anything that intends to answer our problems with such a negative attitude, we won't likely find other answers useful either. Scripture will do you little good if you read little of it, read it with a disengaged mind, read it with a resistant and skeptical attitude, or read it thinking that Scripture must solve your problems immediately or it is useless.

A much better strategy for reading Scripture appears in Psalm 1. As the psalmist describes the blessed, happy man, he says that he is someone who doesn't follow the world's way of thinking and doing things (v. 1). Rather, his "delight is in the law of the LORD; and in His law he meditates day and night" (v. 2). You can't delight in what you don't know and haven't read. The verse doesn't say that the happy man memorizes Scripture, but that isn't ruled out. However, memorizing without understanding and meditating on God's word won't produce the desired results either. So how does one meditate on Scripture? It seems hard to do this without taking care first to interpret and understand exactly what Scripture means by what it says. But once we grasp what the text means, we must ask how it applies to us. Discerning Scripture's meaning and its significance for us may require a good bit of our time and thought. That is more than acceptable; meditating on God's word will allow you to let God speak through it to you. No one can predict how long it may take for the Spirit to minister the word to you, so be patient. Honest searching of the Scriptures with a willingness to obey whatever it teaches will sooner or later, or both, yield a positive result!

None of this means that we should ignore our daily routines and responsibilities, isolate ourselves from others, and sit quietly and meditate. Indeed, we should set aside some time each week, even each day, for reflecting on God's word, but that will still leave us plenty of time to attend to our daily duties. Constantly letting Scripture inform our life and our decisions means that we need to cultivate the habit of asking, with each new problem and decision we face in any area of life, what does Scripture say about this matter? And, when we think we have a resolution to the issue before us, we should ask whether our solution violates anything Scripture either implicitly or explicitly teaches. Cultivating the habit of viewing every problem (and every answer) in the light of what Scripture teaches means that at multiple points in every day, we should and will evaluate our ideas and actions in light of what Scripture teaches. Some would say that doing that isn't the same as meditating on God's word day and night. Perhaps not, but at the very least it takes God's word with utmost seriousness, and it warns us to evaluate every problem and every answer in light of what Scripture teaches. Of course, if one asks what Scripture says about a problem, and then rejects Scripture's word summarily, that is little better than not consulting Scripture at all. What I am suggesting requires first a decision to submit to the final and decisive authority of God's word, regardless of what it requires in any situation. Without that decision, merely reading (and even memorizing) Scripture may be of little use.

So, whether we turn to Scripture first or last, or both, when confronting a challenge, we must ask what Scripture says about whatever we face. If we actually believe that Scripture is sufficient, not invoking it and seeking seriously what it says means that in practice we live as though it isn't sufficient (perhaps not even relevant)—or at least not sufficient enough. When we face a difficult challenge and finally arrive at a solution, before implementing it, we should ask whether it contradicts anything Scripture teaches. And we should evaluate any solution with rigor; just because you may be personally fond of the solution you've come up with, that doesn't give the right to dismiss any objections after only minimal consideration. Be as rigorous in your evaluation as you would be with an answer you don't like very much. Be certain that Scripture doesn't contradict what you are planning to do! It isn't just our sermons, our commentaries, and our theologies that must be grounded in Scripture if we want to reflect our belief that Scripture is sufficient; our lives, including our daily way of confronting any problem, any responsibility or duty, and any decision, must show that we believe Scripture is sufficient!

Let me mention another doctrine that fits with Scripture's sufficiency. Part of the reason that Scripture is sufficient is its truthfulness. That is, biblical inerrancy isn't just a theological idea that scholars debate which has little relevance to everyday life. Biblical inerrancy is immensely practical, and that is so because if Scripture doesn't tell us the truth, it can't be sufficient for the topics it addresses. While it can be a pleasant diversion to dream of and wish for all sorts of things, each of us must live in the real world. Sooner or later, our fantasies will prove insufficient to address life's most significant problems. We don't need wishful thinking to guide us along life's way. We need truth—truth about doctrines we should hold; truth about whether our proposed course of action is forbidden, required by God, or allowed because God has not forbidden it; truth about the consequences of actions we take and decisions we make; and truth about what happens after life on this earth in a natural body ends!

If Scripture answers these questions—and it does—we must listen carefully, and obey what it teaches and requires. Sooner or later you will bow the knee to what Scripture teaches. Given its truth, you can reject it, ignore it, and try to get around it, but you will ultimately have to yield to what it says! That's the nature of truth; it can't be ignored and avoided forever. Why not yield to Scripture sooner, rather than later, because it is true, and because it tells you truthfully the answer to your problems! If Scripture were inerrant but insufficient, then it would leave us wishing and asking for more. But when it comes to life's most significant and important issues, Scripture presents truthfully exactly what we need to know and do to meet those needs. What a wonderful reassurance to know that God knows the answers to life's most important questions and he has revealed enough in his word for us to get the right answers! Without inerrancy, Scripture wouldn't be sufficient to meet our needs. Without sufficiency, inerrancy wouldn't be so significant—we would be teased and tantalized with the possibility of answers to our problems, but an insufficient Bible would leave us wanting. Thankfully, Scripture tells us the truth, and it tells us sufficient truth to meet our most important needs and to foster well the most important relationship anyone can have, the relationship with our creator!

Then, Scripture is sufficient, but we must not misunderstand this. Scripture is sufficient for the topics it addresses, but it doesn't address everything we might wish to know.[37] For example, it doesn't say that even as there are three members of the Trinity with different roles and responsibilities, we must pattern our human institutions after the way the members of the Trinity relate to one another. Don't misunderstand this. I'm not suggesting that it would be wrong to pattern our church, our home, our work environment after the way the various members of the Trinity relate to one another. My point is that Scripture itself *does not require* this, *nor does it forbid it*. Implementing such a structure in our institutions (in order to pattern the organizational structure of our institution after God's internal relations within the Trinity) won't guarantee that we will produce a well-functioning, God-pleasing organization. Patterns aren't necessarily prescriptions; thinking they are when Scripture neither explicitly nor implicitly makes such requirements uses Scripture in ways it never intended.

Sadly, there are Christians who so badly want Scripture to say something about everything in the church, home, etc., that they force it to address issues it actually leaves open. Even worse, they are sufficiently adamant about such things that they believe that unless others see things their way, those others are actually violating Scripture! The result can often be broken fellowship over things about which Scripture doesn't offer instruction and leaves room for believers to choose between several options. There are topics that Scripture

---

[37] Grudem, *Systematic Theology*, 134, makes the point that, if Scripture doesn't give us a requirement in a given area, then we are free to choose the option that seems best, practically speaking.

doesn't actually address, and yet some are certain that Scripture says something about them (or at least that Scripture teaches something that "can inform" our thinking), and so they decide that those who disagree with them (on either a practical or a doctrinal issue) reject Scripture's authority and sufficiency. Whatever Scripture actually teaches or even implies must be obeyed, but it doesn't teach something on every topic!

What I have been saying about many of these implications of Scripture's sufficiency raises the matter of Scripture's proper interpretation and application. Scripture is sufficient, but that doesn't mean that either its meaning or its application will always be clear! Here we can't present a full-blown discussion of hermeneutics, but I must at least mention several items. A critical point in interpreting Scripture is to decide which parts of it apply today. For example, are we bound to the Mosaic law as detailed in the OT, or are we required only to obey what is often referred to as the Law of Christ as found in the NT? This isn't an easy issue, and proponents of opposing positions aren't always consistent in how they interpret and whether they think OT law applies today.[38] Let me offer an example or two that will illustrate the problem.

Those who see more discontinuity between the OT and NT would typically say that we are not under the Mosaic law, and hence aren't bound to obey its demands. Nonetheless, it isn't unusual for some proponents of this position to say that at least nine of the Ten Commandments apply today. And, some Christians of this theological persuasion also think there is some value, if not a requirement, in fasting, given the fact that periods of fasting were required at some times under Mosaic law. But perhaps most troublesome in the local church is when Christians of both the discontinuity and continuity positions believe that Christians are duty-bound to tithe. In fact, I have known of instances where people in a local church who had access to giving records have said that some members of the church are breaking scriptural demands about tithing, because they clearly don't give a tenth of their income to the church.

This must not be misunderstood. I am not saying that fasting is a useless, unnecessary, and/or unhelpful practice. Nor am I saying that Christians shouldn't give money to the Lord's work. My point is a theological one that relates to how the Testaments of Scripture relate to one another. If you believe there is more discontinuity between the Testaments than continuity and that as a result, NT people are not under Mosaic law, then don't interpret OT Mosaic

---

[38] Elsewhere I have discussed this issue in some detail. See my "Systems of Discontinuity," in John S. Feinberg, ed. *Continuity and Discontinuity: Essays in Honor of S. Lewis Johnson* (Westchester, IL: Crossway, 1988), and to get a further grasp on the complexity of how the Testaments relate, read all the essays in that book. In addition, I have addressed the question of continuity and discontinuity as it relates to how to use the Bible (the OT in particular) in Christian ethics. See John S. Feinberg and Paul D. Feinberg, *Ethics for a Brave New World*, 2nd ed. (Wheaton, IL: Crossway, 2010), chapter 1, on moral decision making.

requirements as though they apply to people today, and don't "read these requirements" into the NT where they aren't stated.

Just as there is ambiguity and lack of clarity in the discontinuity camp on the relation of the Testaments, the same is true in the continuity camp. Proponents of more continuity than discontinuity typically argue that the OT Mosaic law is at least in some respects in force in the NT era. Hence, they believe that Christians not only should give to the Lord's work, but think that at least 10 percent of one's income is *required*. However, the Mosaic law also requires home owners to build a parapet around their roof so that when they entertain guests, the parapet will keep them from falling off. It would be very difficult to find a continuity proponent who thinks this requirement applies today. But why, if one part of the Mosaic code applies, doesn't other legislation in the code apply? Certainly, if the NT cancels a precept from the Mosaic law, then it doesn't apply, but the NT says nothing about the parapet rule, just as it doesn't repeat the requirement of giving a tithe (a tenth) of one's income to the Lord. Still, many continuity proponents think there is a tithing rule in force (and perhaps also think fasting in some instances is required), but they don't have houses with flat roofs and don't think the Mosaic rule about parapets would apply if their roofs were flat. How can this be a consistent way to interpret Scripture?

As another example, as they look at pre-Mosaic legislation in Genesis 9, some in both the continuity and discontinuity camps believe they see warrant in verse 6 for capital punishment. Yet Genesis 9:4 seems clearly to prohibit practices like eating a rare steak. How often have either continuity or discontinuity proponents ordered well-done steaks to avoid disobeying this command? Probably, Genesis 9:4 is the last thing on our minds when we place an order at a restaurant.

What is the point of this example from Genesis 9? For continuity proponents, why is it only the Mosaic law that somehow applies today? Why not also pre-Mosaic commands? If you are continuity-oriented and pro–capital punishment, why do you think Genesis 9:6 applies today, but not Genesis 9:4? On the discontinuity side, if humans today are bound only by the Law of Christ as revealed in the NT, then how can tithing (from the Mosaic law) and capital punishment from both the Mosaic and pre-Mosaic legislation be binding (Lev. 27:30–32; Deut. 14:22; and Gen. 9:6) today? Wouldn't a discontinuity proponent need to find NT warrant for thinking these OT regulations are still in force—or at least that the Law of Christ in some way repeats them, in order for them still to be in force?

There are, of course, other examples of how theological confusion can arise when plotting one's views on how teachings in the OT relate to NT teaching. I raise these points not to confuse readers, nor do I intend here to solve the problems mentioned. I have addressed some of them in some detail in *Ethics for a Brave New World*, and, along with other scholars, in *Continuity and Discontinuity*. I have raised the issues in the previous paragraphs to illustrate the point that even though Scripture is sufficient, answers to the issues raised aren't self-evident in Scripture and aren't always easy to deduce and support convincingly. To address these questions appropriately requires knowledge of the rules for interpreting any kind of literature, and also awareness of the biblical narrative's general flow from Testament to Testament. In addition, they require skills developed over years of applying hermeneutical principles to interpret texts, and skills for moving from biblical interpretation to theological formulation.

Having read these last paragraphs, many may think proper interpretation and application are impossible, and so no matter how one tries to "get it right" when interpreting Scripture, failure is inevitable. While this is an understandable reaction, it isn't necessary. Any Bible student, despite education and level of knowledge, can interpret Scripture and "get it right." I raised the above difficult issues not to discourage readers but to alert them that all interpreters need to check very carefully their interpretation and application of specific Scriptures with what they know about Scripture's teaching as a whole. Given Scripture's general clarity, there is good reason to believe that the more we study Scripture, the more we will understand how to make sense of its more difficult passages and the issues they raise.

Even so, readers may be discouraged. After all, you may be thinking, it would be nice to answer all these biblical and theological questions, but God has called me to a different vocation. Your hope when you read and study Scripture is just to be able to understand what it says about having a saving relationship with God, and to know what God requires in order to live a life pleasing to him. If interpreting and applying Scripture is as hard as the questions raised in the last few paragraphs suggest, then what hope do Christians who aren't theologians and Bible scholars have of understanding and answering these most fundamental things?

I appreciate the concerns, and there is good news! Scripture's sufficiency doesn't guarantee that you will find easy, uncontroversial answers for every item it addresses. But it does guarantee that God has clearly in both Testaments told people of every era who possessed any Scripture what they must do to establish and maintain a saving relation with him. Salvation has always been by God's grace through our faith, and the most basic rules for godly living are revealed in both Testaments. Our growing familiarity with Scripture as a result of reading, studying, meditating on, and obeying it, will only enhance our certainty about God's answers to these most fundamental issues.

Thank God that Scripture isn't written like an abstract textbook in complicated mathematics or science that only a few highly intelligent and knowledgeable could understand! Scripture is sufficient in part because it is clear and true, and because it requires us only to know and obey what God has said in it. We needn't search other sources or opinions to answer these most basic and crucial questions. Scripture is sufficient!

# NINETEEN

# ENDURING LIGHT

## The Preservation of Scripture

God knows, has always known, and will always know every word of Scripture. In fact, he knows it all in every existing and possible language. So, in those senses, Scripture can never be lost. But is that what theologians mean when they talk about the doctrine of Scripture's preservation? Not at all.

Then, perhaps theologians have in mind the story of how God has providentially safeguarded enough manuscripts of biblical books so that Bible scholars and theologians can reconstruct the equivalent of the original texts written by the biblical authors. But the story of how through the centuries Scripture has been preserved is not what this doctrine is about.

What, then, is this doctrine, and is there biblical and theological warrant for it? Put simply, this doctrine addresses whether Scripture teaches that the Bible will be preserved in written language that will be available to humans until the end of world history on the current earth and under the current heavens. Whether or not there will be copies of the Bible in the new heavens and the new earth is not normally the focus of this doctrine, but one could ask that question as well. Moreover, this doctrine is not about whether Scripture will be available in any specific language, but only whether it will exist in some written language.

While these may seem easy questions to answer, things aren't as easy as they seem. This is so in part because no biblical text directly addresses this topic in any significant length, and only a very few passages even indirectly seem relevant to it. In addition to those few biblical texts, some logical arguments support this doctrine. I call them logical, because I mean that if other bibliological doctrines are true, logic demands that there must be a doctrine of preservation—at least various evangelical theologians have thought so.

So, how should we proceed? No doubt many would look at the history of the transmission of Scripture's text and exclaim that surely God has providentially ensured that this book's contents have not been lost. Preservation of Scripture's original text can easily be confirmed by textual critics, and for many Christians that is enough. But of course, Scripture's existence through the centuries since it was finished doesn't guarantee its continued existence into the distant future. In our age of computers it may be hard to imagine that anyone could ever get rid of any written document, but it isn't unthinkable that there will be attempts in the future (near and distant) to expunge the words of Scripture entirely. If God hasn't promised to preserve his word, it isn't impossible that this should happen.

In this chapter, I shall argue that there is biblical and theological warrant for holding the doctrine of Scripture's preservation. Thus, evangelicals should hold it. To support this doctrine, theologians don't need to present all the manuscript evidence supporting claims that we know what the various biblical authors originally wrote, unless, of course, someone thinks that even today we don't know what was in the original.[1] Similarly, we need not set forth the history of the transmission of a biblical book's text, and while it is of interest to canonicity to know why the church recognized a religious text as part of Scripture's canon, that information won't teach much about the doctrine of preservation. These topics have a proper place in biblical and theological studies, but they aren't typically the focus of the doctrine of preservation.

In this chapter, I shall offer evidence to support this doctrine. But first, I must clarify what this doctrine does and does not affirm.

## DEFINING THE DOCTRINE OF PRESERVATION

Few, if any, evangelical scholars would deny that Scripture has been preserved, and many nonevangelicals would agree that the biblical books as we have them have been essentially preserved as first written. So, what is the theological issue that Scripture's preservation raises?

Most specifically, the question is whether or not *in Scripture* God promises to preserve Scripture. Does Scripture teach/affirm that God will preserve the Bible, his word? Clearly, the key here isn't the historical, empirically testable claim that Scripture has been preserved. Rather it is that Scripture requires God to preserve it, and to do so in its purity. By purity I don't mean that we must know exactly every single word of Scripture as it was penned by the biblical

---

[1] Though such information is unnecessary in a systematic theology, it would be relevant in a commentary, especially where texts or parts of them are in doubt, and it would be relevant in an apologetic treatment of Scripture. As for the latter, in showing that a biblical book's teachings are reliable, a first step would be to establish that we know exactly what the author wrote. As an example, see my handling of the reliability of the Gospels in *Can You Believe It's True? Christian Apologetics in a Modern/Postmodern World* (Wheaton, IL: Crossway, 2013), chapter 11.

authors. Rather, the requirement is that the biblical texts we have accurately reflect what was originally written, and that our inability to determine in some cases the exact words of the original (because textual variants leave textual critics in doubt about the exact wording of the original text) doesn't change any doctrine the passage teaches.

In sum, then, the doctrine of Scripture's preservation affirms that *God has promised in Scripture to preserve his word in essential purity so that the Scriptures will not perish*. Note that this says nothing about a particular version of Scripture being the one that best represents the original. Presumably, there could be various versions and translations that fit the requirements of this doctrine.

Note also that this says nothing about *how* God will preserve Scripture. He could do so by miraculous intervention, but given what we know of the Bible's actual transmission, it is better to understand him as doing this through providential control of secondary means, especially the actions of ordinary human beings. This doesn't prevent him from using miracles in the future to preserve his word, but only notes how he has preserved his word in the past and that he may likely use similar means in the future.

Nor does my definition require that everyone at every time in history have access to Scripture. Throughout most of the Bible's existence, most people haven't known how to read. Many who have known how to read haven't owned or even seen a copy of the Bible. Missionaries report that even in our day, they occasionally run into people living in a remote part of the world who have never even heard of Scripture. So, we can believe in Scripture's preservation even if Scripture isn't accessible to everyone.

Finally, this definition says nothing about *how long* God will preserve his word. Of course, evangelicals assume that God's word will be preserved indefinitely into the future. This doesn't mean that every part of it will always apply in the future, even as some parts of the OT (like the sacrificial system) don't apply in our day. But Scripture in its entirety will continue to exist in some form (in printed book form, in digital format, etc.) indefinitely into the future.[2]

## Biblical Support for the Doctrine of Preservation

So, what is the biblical case for preservation? I wish I could point to even one Scripture that explicitly says Scripture is eternal in the sense that once a book

---

[2] In articulating the various elements of this doctrine, I found quite helpful the following works: William W. Combs, "The Preservation of Scripture," *Detroit Baptist Seminary Journal* 5 (Fall 2000): 6–12; Daniel B. Wallace, "Inspiration, Preservation, and New Testament Textual Criticism," *GTJ* 12 (1992): 41–43; James Borland, "The Preservation of the New Testament Text: A Common Sense Approach," *MSJ* 10 (Spring 1999): 43–47; and Jon Rehurek, "Preservation of the Bible: Providential or Miraculous? The Bible View," *MSJ* 19 (Spring 2008): 72–74.

of Scripture was written, it was destined to last forever. Sadly, there is no such verse. The Greek word *graphē*, used in 2 Timothy 3:16 to refer to Scripture, nowhere appears in an NT verse that says Scripture will last forever. Likewise, in the OT there seems to be no technical Hebrew term for Scripture, so it shouldn't surprise us that we will look in vain for an OT verse that says Scripture, once given, will never pass away.

Perhaps some readers will be troubled by what I've just said, because in this book I have discussed many Scriptures that teach something about Scripture. Moreover, the phrase "the word of the Lord" shows up frequently in the pages of Scripture. How, then, is it possible that no verse says Scripture will never go out of existence?

Here I encourage readers to reread carefully what the first paragraph of this section says. I'm not saying there is *no biblical support* for the doctrine of preservation. Rather, I am saying there is *no biblical passage that clearly refers to Scripture as a whole* (by using either the Greek word *graphē* or a Hebrew term that stands for Scripture) *and affirms that Scripture will endure forever.*

As for the phrase "the word of the Lord," indeed, it is used in Scripture. But it is ambiguous, for the phrase as used in Christian parlance may refer at the very least to any of the following: (1) Scripture (as a whole or part of it); (2) the body of truth which made up the apostles' gospel; (3) the gospel message itself; (4) a discourse on some topic of God's choosing which is recorded in a chapter/s of a particular biblical book or in several books, and was intended either for a particular group or for groups of people living at various times and places after the specific "word of the Lord" was given; or (5) something specific God said to one individual on a given occasion, which thing is not necessarily an instruction and/or demand for anyone else and which the biblical writer didn't record (i.e., he recorded the fact that God's word came to him, but he didn't then write what God said to him).[3] Given this ambiguity in the phrase "the word of the Lord," we need to examine verses where it appears and is typically thought to teach Scripture's preservation and ask whether the phrase is used in the verse in question in sense (1), i.e., as a clear reference to Scripture.

But what verses in particular are under discussion for this doctrine? The verses that theologians and Bible scholars typically use in support of this doctrine are Psalm 12:6–7; 119:89, 152 and 160; Isaiah 40:8; Matthew 5:17–18; 24:35; Luke 16:17; John 10:35; and 1 Peter 1:23–25. In what follows, I shall examine each verse in its context and then ask whether it either directly or indirectly teaches that Scripture will last forever.

---

[3] See Combs, "Preservation of Scripture," 12–14, for a fine explanation of the various biblical uses of the phrase "the word of God."

*Psalm 12:6–7*

If these two verses are completely isolated from the context of Psalm 12, they may seem unequivocally to say that the Lord will preserve Scripture forever. They read,

> The words of the LORD are pure words;
> As silver tried in a furnace on the earth, refined seven times.
> Thou, O LORD, wilt keep them;
> Thou wilt preserve him from this generation forever.

However, we must understand the force of these verses in Psalm 12. The psalmist laments the fact that godly people are on the wane, while the wicked and those who use speech to boast and enhance their own position in society are on the rise. As also might be expected, the wicked oppress the poor and the needy (v. 5). Before verse 5 ends, the psalmist records what God says to those scoundrels and to their victims. God says, "I will arise . . . ; I will set him in the safety for which he longs."

It is in this context, then, that the psalmist in verse 6 speaks about God's words. Unlike the wicked, whose words can't be depended on, God's words are different. Using the metaphor of refined metal, the psalmist says that God's words have been put to the test and have passed. They are as pure and dependable as metal refined and purified through the smelting process.

But why make this point in this verse? And does it refer to Scripture or even to one biblical book? The words in question are ones the psalmist has attributed to God (in verse 5). They promise the safety of the oppressed and the punishment of their oppressors. Since the wicked say all sorts of things they don't intend to fulfill, perhaps God's promises (v. 5) can't be trusted either. In verse 6 the psalmist contrasts God's words of promise with the words of evil flatterers and the powerful (vv. 1–4). What he has said in verse 5 is dependable. God will surely do what he has promised!

In verse 7, the psalmist adds that the Lord will keep *them*; he will "preserve *him* from this generation forever." As Delitzsch notes, the sentence in verse 7 (Hb. 8) contains two suffixes on the verbs in the sentence. The first is *em* ("Thou . . . wilt keep *them*") and the second is *ennu* ("Thou wilt preserve *him*").[4] The key question, of course, is to what these suffixes refer. They could refer to "the words of the LORD" in verse 6, but if so, it is hard to understand why the plural suffix ("them") wouldn't be used in both instances and what "him" means as a reference to the words of the Lord. The other, and clearly more preferable option, is that the pronouns designated by these suffixes refer to the poor and oppressed. As Delitzsch suggests, *em* refers to the poor and

---

[4] Franz Delitzsch, *Biblical Commentary on the Psalms*, vol. 1 (repr., Grand Rapids, MI: Eerdmans, 1968), 197.

oppressed (referred to in verse 5), and *ennu* refers to the person who longs for the deliverance mentioned in God's utterance (in verse 5).[5]

The result of these considerations is that, even though verses 6–7, isolated from the rest of the psalm, seem "potentially" to comment about Scripture, in the context of the whole psalm, verse 7 isn't about Scripture at all. It is the psalmist's affirmation that the Lord will indeed protect the poor and afflicted, just as he promised (as recorded in verse 6). The only thing this psalm teaches about God's words are their purity and dependability, i.e., that they can be trusted. But that has more to do with inerrancy and its implications than with the preservation of Scripture. Hence, this passage neither affirms nor denies Scripture's preservation, because that topic isn't under consideration in this psalm.[6]

### Psalm 119:89

Psalm 119 is the longest psalm. In it the author touches on many subjects, but a major emphasis to which he periodically returns is the word of God. In this section of the psalm (vv. 89–96), the writer recounts a series of things that have helped him survive not only the different challenges of life but also the opposition of his enemies. The overall emphasis of this section is on things that are stable and dependable. In fact, the psalmist emphasizes three things that have this attribute. The first is God's law (v. 89), and after mentioning two other dependable things, the rest of this section of the psalm (vv. 92–96) focuses on God's law. The psalmist affirms that God's precepts have helped him make it through difficult times in his life. A second unwavering thing is God's faithfulness (v. 90). Evidence that God is dependable is the fact that his goodness and preservation have been extended to all generations. While the psalmist could next give a lengthy list of ways in which God has been faithful to all people, he mentions only one: God has created and sustained the earth in existence (vv. 90–91). That is the third thing that anyone can rely on. Of course, the key to all of this is God and his faithfulness. The stability of God's law and of the universe stems from God himself, who is totally reliable in everything.

In the context of this part of the psalm, it is probably best to see the references to God's law and precepts as intending to invoke the whole of God's word that would have been available to the psalmist when he wrote this psalm. That is, he had more in view than just God's rules and commands. That is so because of how this part of the psalm begins, and also because the section as a whole speaks of things that are dependable and can be counted on. More

---

[5] Ibid.
[6] See also Combs, "Preservation of Scripture," 14–15, and Rehurek, "Preservation of the Bible," 81–85, for a similar understanding of this passage.

than just God's precepts are reliable. Whatever he says is dependable. In fact, because God's law is reliable, it was possible for the psalmist to find comfort and encouragement in God's word. In verses 92–96 he affirms that God's law has been his delight and source of strength. Without it, he surely would have perished because of his afflictions and because of the wicked who oppose him.

One further preliminary item should be mentioned. Does this verse refer to Scripture? I think so. The main reason is that the whole of Psalm 119 has God's word as its focus. Though the writer never uses a special Hebrew term for Scripture, all the references to "the word of God," "thy word," etc., in this psalm have Scripture in mind. Of course, when this psalm was written, only part of the OT had been written, and none of the NT existed. Still, if one thinks that the other books traditionally considered canonical qualify as Scripture, then there is no reason to think this verse wouldn't apply to the whole OT and NT. It wouldn't make sense for some of God's words considered Scripture to be settled in heaven, while other divine words also considered Scripture are not.

So, while the writer might think that what he says in this verse includes things God has said which aren't Scripture, at the very least he must have in mind the words of Scripture. As to verse 89, it is a general comment about God's word. That word, of course, contains precepts, but much more. The psalmist writes, "Forever, O LORD, Thy word is settled in heaven." Both the word "forever" and the phrase "settled in heaven" affirm stability and permanence. Heaven isn't subject to the changes that the rest of the universe experiences. As noted, the theme of dependability is at the heart of this section of the psalm.

But the key question for our discussion is whether verse 89 affirms and/or even supports the doctrine of Scripture's preservation. I maintain that if it does, it does so only very indirectly. Let me explain. The first question we must ask is whether the psalmist has in mind Scripture when he speaks of God's word, God's law, God's precepts, and God's testimonies (v. 95, 'ēdôteykā in the sense of laws as divine testimonies or solemn charges[7]). Though one might suspect that he thinks only of the moral rules knowable through natural revelation, the subject is clearly Scripture. Natural revelation doesn't contain words, nor is it "settled in heaven" (v. 89). Moreover, with what the psalmist says about relying on God's precepts and commands, it is unlikely that he is thinking only of natural revelation. And, the rest of the psalm is about Scripture, so if this portion is only about natural revelation, we need more evidence of that than is available in verses 89–96.

But then, is the psalmist thinking of all of Scripture as he writes these

[7] See Francis Brown, S. R. Driver, and Charles A. Briggs, eds., *A Hebrew and English Lexicon of the Old Testament* (London: Oxford, 1966), 730. A special word of thanks is due to my colleague Richard Averbeck for his help with transliteration of this Hebrew word.

verses? Actually, this question isn't as easy to answer as it might seem. For at the time Psalms was written, not all of the OT had been written. And we don't know how much of the OT the author of this psalm knew. But with the repeated emphasis on God's precepts and laws, it is reasonable to believe that he knew at least the books of Moses, containing the law of Moses. Of course, as already noted, it is more than likely that his reference to God's law includes more than just rules covering one area of life or another. And we must remember that verses 89–96 are part of a lengthy psalm whose focus is the whole of Scripture. Though the psalmist certainly knew other parts of the OT that had been written by the time he wrote, the point of this section of chapter 119 needn't require him to know of every OT book available when he wrote this psalm.

Hence, we can't say with certainty that he refers to all of OT Scripture. On the other hand, it seems unlikely that he isn't thinking of *any* OT Scripture at all. So, while we might immediately wish to apply this verse more broadly to all of Scripture (OT and NT), we should move slowly, for the verse doesn't explicitly mention all of Scripture, even though it is undoubtedly true that all of Scripture is forever settled in heaven.

But even if one grants that this verse's teaching can be applied to all of Scripture, that doesn't tell us whether or not verse 89 supports the doctrine of Scripture's preservation. I think it is best to conclude that if it does, it does so only very indirectly. Let me explain.

Verse 89 speaks of what is the case in heaven. This doesn't mean that there exists in heaven an archetypal copy of Scripture. Since the major point of this part of the psalm is the dependability of God's word, it is hard to see how affirming an archetypal copy of Scripture in heaven makes that point. The point, instead, is, as Delitzsch explains, that God's word has the qualities of heaven. One of heaven's key features is its stability, i.e., things in heaven have permanence and are unchanging, especially in comparison to the transience of the rest of God's created universe.[8]

Lest we think that attributing permanence to God's word can't be supported by saying it is "established in heaven," the psalmist in verse 89 adds that God's word is settled in heaven *forever*. Though the use of "forever" might be hyperbole to emphasize stability and permanence, there is no reason to think that we shouldn't take "forever" literally. Why wouldn't God's word continue to exist in heaven? Since God will always exist, and since there is no evidence that his place of abode will go out of existence, there is no reason for us to understand what the psalmist says about God's word as not literally true. Of course, the writer doesn't say in what form God's word will be present (in

---

[8] Delitzsch, *Biblical Commentary on the Psalms*, 254.

written form, in the memories of those in heaven, or whatever), but that isn't his point.

So far, this discussion seems encouraging for the doctrine of Scripture's preservation. However, we are wrong if we think this verse directly teaches that doctrine. The doctrine refers to the continued existence of God's word *on earth* so that it is and will be available to nonglorified humans living on earth. Unfortunately, the verse before us now neither affirms nor denies the permanence and availability of Scripture for humans living on earth. We might think that if all of God's word exists forever in heaven, surely he would make it available to earth's inhabitants as well. But we do know that even the whole OT wasn't available at all times during the OT era. Until the first OT book was written, many people had lived and died without any Scripture being available to anyone. Even after OT books began to be written, most people alive had no access to them. Even many who did have access to them couldn't read, so unless someone read or quoted Scripture to them, they wouldn't have known much about its contents. This, of course, doesn't mean that God had no way of communicating with humans and never did so before he began to reveal Scripture. As we saw in discussing the doctrine of revelation, there are many forms of divine revelation, and there is good reason to think that some other than Scripture were available to humans before any Scripture was written.

From the preceding, it should be clear that whether or not Scripture is and will be available to all present and future people has nothing to do with whether Psalm 119:89 is true or not. Put differently, the author of this verse doesn't actually address the issue that the doctrine of preservation is about, namely, the continued availability of Scripture to nonglorified humans. The psalmist affirms that God's word is forever settled in heaven, though in referring to "God's word" he surely wasn't thinking of all sixty-six books of our Bible. He likely meant at least some of the books available when he lived, but we don't know how much Scripture he knew.

Should we understand this verse to refer only to God's words found in Scripture? Mightn't it also mean that whatever God has spoken (whether it has or hasn't been transferred to writing) is also present in heaven? Thankfully, nothing of doctrinal significance hinges on how we answer this question. This is so because, if words God has spoken that aren't part of Scripture are also settled in heaven, how would most people know what they are? And if we don't know what they are, how can they be part of our doctrinal understanding? If they do contain points we should include in our theology, surely God would have revealed those words to us.

In light of these considerations, it is safe to say that, especially given that all of Psalm 119 is about Scripture, the psalmist is thinking only of God's words found in Scripture. Of course, the psalmist is just thinking of some Scriptures that he has found encouraging and helpful, but his statement in verse 89 is so general that he surely refers to all of Scripture, not just to passages that had helped him by the time he wrote this psalm. But it doesn't seem wrong to think that this verse can and should *apply* to all Scripture we possess, even though the author would only have thought of Scripture available when he lived.

So, does this verse teach something helpful to the doctrine of Scripture's preservation? Perhaps, but certainly not as much as some may think. The verse teaches the permanent availability of God's word, but it says this is true in heaven. It doesn't say how much of God's word is and will be available to humans on earth, nor does it say how long Scripture will be available to humans *on earth in nonglorified bodies.*

We know, because of the history of the preservation of both the OT and NT, that Scripture has lasted many centuries since its writing was completed. We hope and assume that it will last far into the future. But we have such assumptions at least in part because we know that current technology can protect and preserve written texts, and because we probably assume that people living during the millennial kingdom age will have access to Scripture. Will Scripture as we know it be present in the new heavens and the new earth? Probably, we are inclined to answer, but we must admit that this verse doesn't say anything about how long God's word will be available *on earth.* Since the doctrine of Scripture's preservation is primarily, if not exclusively, about the continued availability of God's word to people on earth, Psalm 119:89 doesn't offer much help in supporting the doctrine.[9]

*Psalm 119:152*

Psalm 119:152 comes at the end of one of the eight-verse sections of the psalm (vv. 145–152). The psalmist says that he cried out to the Lord to preserve him from his enemies, harm, and danger. He adds that if God does preserve him, he can then continue to meditate on God's word. In contrast, he writes that his enemies who draw near to harm him are far from God's law (v. 150). This, of course, means that their lives are not governed by God's law, not that they know nothing of it at all.

As this part of the psalm ends, the psalmist reassures himself that God, too, is near, and all of his commandments are true. In verse 152, he adds that God's testimonies (ʿēdôteykā again, the same Hebrew word used in verse 95) have been founded forever, and he affirms that he knows this is true. The Hebrew verb translated "founded" is yāsad, and it means "to establish" or "to fix." So the

---

[9] For further discussion of this passage see Combs, "Preservation of Scripture," 15–17; Wallace, "Inspiration, Preservation, and New Testament Textual Criticism," 42; and Rehurek, "Preservation of the Bible," 79–80.

overall thought of verses 149–152 seems to be something like the following: the psalmist needs God's protection from his enemies and he relies on God's justice to do what is right by him and his enemies. Though his enemies do evil things, and he senses that they are planning to harm him, he takes refuge in God's nearness and in the truth of God's commandments. Why would God's commands be a source of encouragement? Because they also present God's punishments for those who disobey. Of course, someone might ask why that matters if God's law with its commands, blessings, and punishments is merely a passing thing. Verse 152 gives the answer: God's laws, and what pertains to them, were founded by God himself with the intent that they would last forever.

In light of these truths, the psalmist takes comfort and gains strength to go on living in accord with God's laws, despite the wicked people who want to destroy him. For the purpose of our discussion on preservation, we must ask whether and how verse 152 relates to the doctrine of preservation. I believe it does, and that in its context it is one of the clearer statements to that effect. Let me explain.

First, I note that the psalmist focuses on God's laws and commands. As in the earlier parts of the psalm when such language is used, it is best to take these comments as referring to more than just God's rules and regulations. Of course, the psalmist intends to invoke those rules, but he is most likely thinking of anything God reveals.

Second, we must ask how the writer would know of God's commands with their promises of blessings and punishments. Undoubtedly, he could and did learn of some of those rules from natural revelation, but surely that isn't this psalm's focus as a whole, or even of this part of it. In order for the writer to meditate on God's word (v. 148) and to keep God's statutes (vv. 145–156), he needs access to more of divine revelation than is available in natural revelation through the human conscience.

The answer to where he gets this knowledge that makes the most sense is that he gets it from God's written word. Given the references in this part of the psalm to God's laws, statutes, and testimonies, it is safe to say that at the very least the psalmist has in mind the Torah. Perhaps that is all he has in mind, so we should comment on whether this passage can teach something about all of Scripture, but before we address that issue, we should expound more fully what verse 152 says.

Verse 152 states that God has established his word forever. Hence, if this verse can apply to all of Scripture, it surely seems relevant to the doctrine of preservation. But verse 89 (discussed above) also speaks of God's word lasting forever, and we concluded that it isn't as helpful as some think. So, perhaps we should conclude the same thing for verse 152.

It would, however, be unwise to draw the same conclusion about verse 152 as we did for verse 89, because there are significant differences between the two verses. The earlier passage emphasizes things that are stable and permanent. Verse 152 sounds a similar note, but it is in a context where the thought is God's preservation of his servant from the wicked who would harm him and God's punishment of the psalmist's wicked enemies. A more important difference, however, is that verse 89 talks about God's word in *heaven*, whereas verse 152 doesn't say where God's testimonies have been founded. If they are available only in heaven, then how would the psalmist know them, meditate on them, and rely on them? Thus, the thought must be that God's word in written form must be and is founded and available everywhere forever. So, this verse seems rather clearly to teach ideas that are part of the doctrine of preservation.

We should, however, tie up a few loose ends. When the psalmist writes that God has founded his testimonies to last forever, is that hyperbole? It could be, if God's word won't be available in the eternal state, but we don't know whether Scripture will or will not be present there. It is dubious that the inhabitants of the eternal state will have complete amnesia with respect to the contents of Scripture, but that alone doesn't mean there will be Bibles in the eternal state in the form(s) in which we now have them. On the other hand, nothing in this passage or elsewhere in Scripture prohibits possession of God's written word for all eternity.

Regardless of readers' thoughts about Scripture's availability in the new heavens and new earth, if this verse is hyperbole, what does it literally mean? Would it allow for the Bible to cease to exist in a few hundred or even a few thousand years after it was written? Of course not! The point of the verse is the permanence of God's word. Whether or not that means there will be Bibles as we know them in the eternal state, it is safe to infer from this verse that God's word will be preserved.

A further reason to think this verse is relevant to our doctrine is what it says about who will do the preserving. If it were left to mere humans, who knows how widely the Bible would be available or whether there would be a time when no one possessed God's word? But the psalmist is clear that it is *God* who has founded his testimonies forever. While it is true that this verse says nothing about how God will preserve his word, that in no way refutes the psalmist's claim that God *has* founded his word forever.

A final question about this verse is whether it can apply to all of Scripture. Above, I suggested that it must at least apply to the Torah, for that is the most likely source of the commands and laws the author references. But, I think that, even if the psalmist had in mind only a portion of the OT, it isn't wrong to *apply* this verse's teaching to the rest of Scripture. As noted, Psalm 119 is about all of Scripture, not just about passages that set forth God's rules and punishments. What the psalmist is talking about are words that God has spoken, which human beings are aware of because they have been recorded in written form and preserved. As a result, I argued that it isn't a mistake to infer that what this passage says about God's commands and laws is also true of the Torah. Why should we have such confidence in these written words? Because they are God's, and because he has founded them forever (v. 152) so that many people (besides those who first received them) can know them and benefit from them.

So, it is safe to say that the psalmist greatly reveres these words because they come from God, and he knows from personal experience how encouraging, instructive, and comforting they can be (see what he says in the whole of Psalm 119 about God's word). From this line of reasoning it seems that we have a right to conclude that anything that actually qualifies as God's word in written form would have the same qualities as do the parts of Scripture to which the psalmist most specifically refers. Would that include the rest of the OT, not just the Torah? And would it apply to the NT? Certainly! What possible argument could there be that would refute the idea that words from God in written form are Scripture and that God has founded Scripture forever?

This must not be misunderstood. I am not arguing that Psalm 119:152 explicitly affirms that all of Scripture will be preserved forever. Rather I am saying that it is warranted, given the context of this psalm and of verses 145–152 in particular, to apply the teaching of verse 152 to the rest of God's written words, i.e., to all of Scripture. So it seems that even though this verse teaches the preservation of Scripture somewhat indirectly, those who reference it as support for that doctrine are right in doing so![10]

## Psalm 119:160

This text is in the section of Psalm 119 immediately following verse 152. The message of this section is much the same as that of the preceding one (vv. 145–152). The psalmist has enemies and afflictions, and his enemies don't obey God's word (v. 158). This grieves the psalmist, and he reminds God that, in contrast to the wicked, he loves God's precepts (v. 159). In view of these things, the psalmist requests God's deliverance from his foes and afflictions (vv. 153–154). What he asks isn't something unthinkable, because in verse 154 he asks God to plead his cause and deliver him. And he adds a request for God to revive him according to God's word.

As a result, there is a heavy emphasis in verses 153–160 on God's word,

---

[10] For further discussion of this verse as it relates to the preservation of Scripture, see Combs, "Preservation of Scripture," 17–18; and Rehurek, "Preservation of the Bible," 87–89.

the psalmist's reliance upon and love for it, and on the fact that his enemies reject God's word. Why should the psalmist place such emphasis on God's word? Why would it be a source of strength and encouragement in his times of trouble? The answer comes in verse 160, where he writes about the nature of God's word. Two of its characteristics are his focus.

The first is the truthfulness of God's word. Why should this matter in his current circumstances, and why should it be relevant to his request for deliverance? The truth of God's word matters greatly, for in it the psalmist has learned about God's laws, about the punishment that awaits those who disobey and even ignore it, and about God's blessing and protection of those who love and obey it. If God's word were not true, what hope would there be for the psalmist in his circumstances? There would be little if any hope, and hence all of his pleas for help in the preceding verses would result in nothing.

But God's word is true and its promises are reliable. Hence, it makes sense for the psalmist to plead for God's deliverance, for his pleas are based on the truth of God's word. Even so, a skeptic might say that God's word may have been dependable in the past, but who knows whether it will even exist in the future? And, if it does continue to exist, how long will it last? All God's promises are of little worth if his word is overturned and annulled in the future.

Thankfully, any believer in need has nothing to worry about, because each of God's righteous ordinances will last forever. Interestingly, as some have noted, in this verse (v. 160), the first half speaks of God's word in toto (it is all true), while the second half focuses on each individual portion of God's ordinances.[11] The net result is that all of God's word is both true and lasts forever.

Having said the above, we must again face the questions raised in handling the previous verses in this psalm. To what do the phrases "word of God," "thy law," "thy statutes," "thy ordinances [or judgments]" refer? And how would the psalmist know anything about the various laws, statutes, and ordinances of God? Undoubtedly, the phrases refer to the Scriptures the psalmist knew. The fact that they existed and were accessible to some extent to him explains how he would know of these rules and precepts. As noted in discussing verse 152, the most likely candidate is the Torah, but the psalmist might also have in mind other parts of the OT that had been written and were known to him when he wrote Psalm 119.

Would the comments in this part of the psalm (vv. 153–160), especially those in verse 160, refer to nothing but laws/rules and punishments for breaking the rules? As explained when addressing other verses in this psalm, the

---

[11] See, e.g., George J. Zemek, *The Word of God in the Child of God: Exegetical, Theological, and Homiletical Reflections from the 119th Psalm* (Mango, FL: self-published, 1998): 332, as quoted in Rehurek, "Preservation of the Bible," 89.

author was most likely thinking of all the words and teachings of the biblical books to which he had access when he wrote verse 160. Even so, can we apply these comments to the part of the OT that had not been written and to the NT, which would be written much later? Again, we must answer affirmatively, because the psalmist's comments in this part of the psalm, including those in verse 160, are about anything that qualifies as God's word, especially the words put in writing to form the basic biblical books. That is, if a written document proves to be "the product of God's breath" (*theopneustos*; 2 Tim. 3:16), it must also have the characteristics mentioned in Psalm 119:160. It is true, and it lasts forever.

The only remaining questions of any import are how this preservation will occur, and who will preserve God's word. The psalmist doesn't give an explicit answer. God could do something unilaterally without any human help. Or God could use secondary means to preserve his word. In particular, to preserve his word God could use the actions of translators, copiers, and those who guard the safety of the manuscripts so that they are neither lost nor destroyed. Or, humans, on their own initiative and by their actions alone without any divine help, could preserve God's word. While this third option is logically possible (that is, the very idea itself doesn't contain a contradiction), it removes God's actions from the picture. However, we know that God revealed his word and moved the writers to write what he wanted. Why would he then abandon this "project" and leave the preservation entirely to his word's human recipients? That makes little sense. Likewise, while it is possible that humans on their own might preserve Scripture, when you consider all the centuries that Scripture has existed and will exist into the future, it is unrealistic to think that humans alone could succeed in preserving God's word for so long a time.

No, the best answer to how God's word will be preserved relies predominantly on God. Given what we know of the history of the writing, copying, and transmission of Scripture, the best answer to how God has preserved his word is through the deeds of his human creatures. But Psalm 119:160 doesn't give us the "how" of preservation. It certainly does assure us, however, *that* God's word will be preserved. This verse is biblical affirmation of the doctrine of preservation.[12]

## Isaiah 40:8

Throughout the first thirty-nine chapters of Isaiah, there is much talk of gloom and doom and judgment. Some of it is predicted for Israel's enemies, but much of it is in store for Israel herself. Beginning with chapter 40, we find a difference

---

[12] For further discussion of this verse see Combs, "Preservation of Scripture," 18–19; and Rehurek, "Preservation of the Bible," 89–90.

in tone and emphasis. Of course, the rest of the book still speaks of God's judgment on sin and the need to live according to God's law in order to experience his blessing, but the general tone is more one of comfort and consolation than in chapters 1–39.

Chapter 40 contains many very well-known verses. Some are famous, at least in part, by being used in the early portions of Handel's *Messiah*. The early verses of chapter 40 contain predictions of events fulfilled at Christ's first advent (e.g., vv. 3ff. foreshadow the coming of John the Baptist), but the chapter also has prophecies that can be fulfilled only at Christ's second advent (e.g., vv. 2, 9–11).

In the midst of this passage we find verses 6–8. They speak of the transient nature of human life. Isaiah likens human beings to the grass and flowers of the field. Everyone knows that, no matter how beautiful flowers are in full bloom, the bloom will soon die and fade away. And, the grass of the field will stay green and flourish for only so long. Verse 7 makes explicit the comparison between humans and plant life. In a short amount of time, grass withers and flowers fade. Isaiah then bluntly affirms the metaphor which compares humans to vegetation; he says, "surely the people are grass." The underlying theme is that, in comparison to God, these things are temporary and transient and have little power to resist the withering processes of time.

In verse 8, Isaiah expands on his basic theme, but he adds another item to the discussion and the comparison. The point about the difference between human life and earthly vegetation in comparison to God is expanded to include the words of God. Grass withers and the bloom of flowers fades away, but God's word is permanent. As Isaiah says in verse 8, "The grass withers, the flower fades, but the word of our God stands forever." The verb translated "stand" is *yākum*, and it can have the sense of being "fixed," "confirmed," "established," "enduring," and "be fulfilled."[13]

Though some claim that the verb in verse 8 should be translated "be fulfilled," as we understand someone's word being fulfilled,[14] I am not sure that translation alone makes Isaiah's point. That is, we normally think of a prophecy or prediction of the future as coming to fulfillment. Fulfillment means that

---

[13] Brown, Driver, and Briggs (*Hebrew and English Lexicon of the Old Testament*, p. 878) claim that in this particular verse, the verb has the sense of "being fulfilled."

[14] Here Combs, "Preservation of Scripture," 19, explains that some see this passage as parallel to Isaiah 46:10. In both verses, many commentators think the point of saying that "the word of our God stands forever" is that it will be fulfilled. That seems to be the most likely meaning in Isaiah 46:10, but that doesn't mean it must have the same sense in Isaiah 40. Even Combs grants that most commentators understand the point here to be permanence. So if, e.g., God makes a promise, it will be fulfilled. It can't be forgotten or annulled by time's passage. See, e.g., the following commentaries: Edward J. Young, *The Book of Isaiah*, 3 vols. (Grand Rapids, MI: Eerdmans, 1965, 1969, 1972); John N. Oswalt, *The Book of Isaiah*, 2 vols., New International Commentary on the Old Testament (Grand Rapids, MI: Eerdmans, 1986, 1998); Barry G. Webb, *The Message of Isaiah*, The Bible Speaks Today (Downers Grove, IL: InterVarsity Press, 1996); George A. F. Knight, *Isaiah 40–55*, 2nd ed., International Theological Commentary (Grand Rapids, MI: Eerdmans, 1984); and R. N. Whybray, *Isaiah 40–66*, New Century Bible Commentary (Grand Rapids, MI: Eerdmans, 1975).

the prophecy is true. Those who believe that a prophecy is true can either adjust their life to fit what will happen or try to fight what will occur. Regardless of one's response, the prophecy will come true.

But saying that a prophecy will be fulfilled doesn't inherently include the notion of permanence. After the prophecy is fulfilled, history moves on, and the fulfilled prophecy may no longer even apply as life and history change.

So, what should we say about the meaning of *yākum* in verse 8? While it could mean only "be fulfilled," I don't see that translation as capturing everything Isaiah wanted to say. We must remember that Isaiah is comparing and contrasting things in the natural order (flowers and grass) with God's word. That being so, what does it mean to compare these things if the verse means that God's word will be fulfilled? That is, what does it mean, by contrast in relation to grass and flowers, to suggest that they will go "unfulfilled"? Such a notion makes little sense and seems to destroy the metaphor used in these verses, especially since the point of verses 6–8 is the impermanence of created things versus the enduring existence of God and his word.

In addition, if the sense is *not at all* permanence and endurance, why is the word "forever" (*lᵉ'olām*) needed, and what could it possibly mean to say that God's word will be "fulfilled forever"? In sum, the sense that seems to make the point of contrast best and hence, seems to be what Isaiah has in mind, is that God's word endures forever. Grass, flowers, and even humans are present on earth for a relatively short time, but God and his word last forever.

If this is the meaning of verse 8, how do verses 6–8 fit the theme of Isaiah 40? Actually, they fit quite well. God through Isaiah turns from speaking about judgment and doom to comfort and consolation. Is this change of message dependable or not? That is, will God actually bring to an end his destruction and judgment on Israel through her enemies, or does Isaiah merely write words with nice thoughts that can't be counted on? Can God's promises be trusted, or are they no more dependable than the temporary nature of things in creation?

Verses 6–8 answer that, while vegetation and human life itself last only so long, God exists forever, and what he says will be done. No one can overturn what God promises to do. Whatever he promises will come to pass. Hence, in this verse, "stands" certainly contains the idea of fulfillment, but for the metaphor in verses 6–8 to work, God's word must endure, not just in the sense that what it promises must come to pass, but also that unlike grass, flowers, and humans, it will never fade away. No matter how long it takes to fulfill a promise or prophecy, God will do it, and once the promise is fulfilled, God won't undo the fulfillment. Isaiah's message of comfort is genuine grounds for encouragement. God and his word can be trusted!

The preceding discussion seems the best way to understand Isaiah 40:8. What, however, does the interpretation offered teach about Scripture's preservation? Though this verse is often cited to support preservation, I think we must be careful not to see too much in it. Let me explain. First, Isaiah doesn't say *Scripture* will stand forever, but rather that God's word will. Since the Scripture (in the book of Isaiah) that promises the blessings to Israel was under construction in chapter 40 and following, as Isaiah wrote verse 8, most of the rest of the book wasn't written. As Isaiah wrote chapter 40, did he understand himself to be writing Scripture? Perhaps, but perhaps not. He surely saw himself as passing on words that God told him to write, but whether he understood that (at the time he wrote) to mean that he was writing Scripture is unclear. Hence, we must not force Isaiah into making a direct statement in this verse about Scripture.

Of course, some may respond that whether or not Isaiah knew he was writing Scripture as he penned this verse, we know that he was. Indeed, that is true, but that shows only that if this verse can be *applied* to Scripture, it is we, the readers, who make that application. That is not the same as saying that in this verse Isaiah *teaches* or *affirms* something about Scripture.

Even so, some may reply, "but where would Isaiah think one could find God's words? Wouldn't he think the place to find them is in Scripture?" Surely, Isaiah would agree with that sentiment, but that doesn't prove that he would think Scripture is the only place to find God's word. In his own experience, God sometimes spoke to him, and what God said didn't always become part of Scripture (this, of course, assumes that Isaiah saw the book he was writing as Scripture; he probably did, but we can't be sure). So, in speaking of the "word of God," Isaiah wouldn't necessarily think only of Scripture. But even if he did think of Scripture, his point in verses 6–8 isn't about the nature of Scripture (and surely not about the doctrine of preservation). It is that, contrary to everything else in the created universe, you can rely on whatever God says!

Something else should give us pause about the degree to which this verse teaches the doctrine of preservation. The verse says God's word endures forever. What makes that so, and in particular, who sees to it that this happens? The natural response is that God will see that his word is fulfilled and isn't lost in the ravages of time. Probably that is what Isaiah would say if asked this question. But Isaiah doesn't explicitly say that God will preserve his word, and the idea that God will providentially preserve Scripture seems somewhat distant from the point of verses 6–8, and 8 in particular. Why does this matter? Because the doctrine of Scripture's preservation clearly affirms that it is God who preserves his word.

This must not be misunderstood. I am not saying that what I said in the previous paragraph negates the doctrine of preservation or even means that Isaiah wouldn't affirm it. It only makes a claim about what Isaiah 40:8 actually says, and about whether we as theologians and exegetes have a right to say that this verse *teaches* that doctrine. From what the verse *does say*, it is reasonable to *infer* that God's word is permanent and enduring and that *it is most likely God* who has and will ensure that his word (Scripture) isn't lost. But that's not the same thing as saying that this verse (or Isaiah) *explicitly* teaches the doctrine of preservation.

So, what should we conclude this verse says about the doctrine of Scripture's preservation? We can say that it teaches things relevant to the doctrine, and that nothing in the verse negates the doctrine. But we don't have a right to say that it *directly* affirms the doctrine. Should a discussion of this doctrine include this verse? I hope that from reading my discussion of this passage readers will agree that it should be included. Even more, if one takes what the verse says, adds that Scripture is a place where God's word can be found (other passages and other bibliological doctrines like revelation and inspiration teach this), and also affirms that God preserves his word through various means, then we can use this verse in making a case for Scripture's preservation. To assert, however, that this verse clearly and explicitly claims more about *Scripture* than what I have just suggested sees more in the passage than we can prove is there.[15]

## Matthew 5:17–18

This passage is frequently cited in support of the doctrine of preservation. Interestingly, it is also a key passage at the heart of the debate over whether the Mosaic law still applies in NT times, and if so, how much and which parts of it apply. The context of these verses helps to determine what is its major emphasis.

Matthew 5–7 contains Jesus's Sermon on the Mount. Jesus begins this sermon with the Beatitudes (5:1–12), and then tells his audience that they are the salt and light of the earth. He encourages them to function as salt and light, lest their presence in the world become essentially irrelevant (5:13–16). Next Jesus comments about the law and his fulfillment of it, and adds in verse 18 that "till heaven and earth pass, one jot or one tittle shall in no wise pass from the law, till all be fulfilled" (KJV). It is important that Jesus says this, for beginning in verse 21 and running at least to the end of chapter 5, Jesus mentions various laws from the Mosaic code and gives them a deeper meaning. That is, he shows that in order to fulfill the law, one needs more than just external conformity to it. What Jesus says about these laws is "radical enough" that his listeners

---

[15] For more on this passage, see also Combs, "Preservation of Scripture," 19–20; and Rehurek, "Preservation of the Bible," 83–85.

might think he is cancelling the law altogether. Hence, it is a good thing that he clarifies (vv. 17–18) that he doesn't intend to abolish the law but to fulfill it, and that everything in it will be fulfilled, without exception.

Readers should easily see why this passage is so important in making the case for the ongoing continuity of the Mosaic law in the NT era. Discontinuity proponents, on the other hand, can't ignore this passage either. They must explain how to uphold its truth even though they believe the Mosaic code isn't in force in the NT era. That is a very important issue, but not our focus here.[16] However, it is crucial to keep it in mind as we ask whether or not this statement by Jesus intends to teach the preservation of any of Scripture. The verse's main purpose is to comment on the continuing validity of the Mosaic law as a prelude to what Jesus will say about the Mosaic code, as recorded in the upcoming chapters of Matthew.

In verse 17, Jesus references two of the three major parts of the OT, the Law and the Prophets. He doesn't mention the third part, the Writings, but in light of what he does say, it is dubious that he intends to exclude it from his point. His point is that, as verse 17 says, he didn't come to abolish but to fulfill the OT. There are, of course, messianic psalms and other parts of the Writings that point forward to someone, and Jesus is the one who most likely fulfills those passages. As various commentators note, *plēroō* ("fulfill") is best understood here to mean "bring to completion."[17] Jesus is the one to whom the OT has been pointing all along. Of course, prior to Christ's life, death, and resurrection, anyone reading OT messianic prophecies would likely have expected the Messiah to come once and to fulfill all of those prophecies at his coming. It was only after he came the first time and was rejected that it began to be clear that at his first advent Christ would fulfill some OT prophecies, but not all. A second advent becomes necessary, not just because Jesus promised his disciples that he would come again, but because there are still various OT prophecies about the Messiah that must be fulfilled. Verse 17 guarantees that everything predicted will be fulfilled—Jesus doesn't explain the how and when of each prophecy's fulfillment; his point is to affirm the law's ongoing validity.

But if all OT promises and prophecies about the Messiah must be fulfilled, that has implications for the Scriptures that contain them. Can passages already fulfilled be ignored and/or discarded? As to those not yet fulfilled, how will anyone know what they are if the OT is lost or entirely cancelled? This is the point where Jesus's words in verse 18 come into play. Not just OT messianic

---

[16] For those interested in pursuing this debate, let me offer two items of bibliography to get started. First, see the articles on the Mosaic law by Knox Chamblin and Douglas J. Moo in *Continuity and Discontinuity: Essays in Honor of S. Lewis Johnson*, ed. John S. Feinberg (Westchester, IL: Crossway, 1988); and see the discussion of how the OT law relates to the NT era in John S. Feinberg and Paul D. Feinberg, *Ethics for a Brave New World*, 2nd ed. (Wheaton, IL: Crossway, 2010), chapter 1.

[17] Douglas J. Moo, "The Law of Moses or the Law of Christ," in Feinberg, *Continuity and Discontinuity*.

passages, but all of the OT is in view (here, as commentators suggest, it is best to see Jesus's reference to the "law" as referring to the whole OT as law, for why would Jesus make verse 18's claim only about precepts and rules of the Mosaic code, and nothing else?).

Jesus's comment about the OT can be taken as both a prediction and a promise. We should note several things about it, and then we can determine whether and what this passage offers in support of the doctrine of preservation. First, I note that all of the OT is in view, but Jesus makes this point by including in his promise even the most minute details of the OT. That is, his promise applies not just to the OT in general, but even to the smallest letter of the Hebrew alphabet (yod) and to parts that are made by "the least stroke of a pen" (tittle). While some may see Jesus as exaggerating to make his point, even so that doesn't change his point. Jesus clarifies that what he is saying covers everything in the OT from the most significant to the very smallest of details. Nothing is left out!

Second, Jesus promises the fulfillment of it all. Again, since Jesus makes a general comment about the whole OT, we shouldn't limit this remark just to the parts that are predictions. Jesus's comment is sufficiently universal in scope that his audience should understand that he doesn't want them to think they should parse out the parts of the OT that will be fulfilled and those that won't be, and apply his claim only to passages that are predictions and will be fulfilled.

Third, Jesus tells how long the OT will be in force. Actually, he says two things about that. On the one hand, he says it will be in force until heaven and earth pass away, and on the other, it will last until it is all fulfilled. We must not misread this. To read it as though Jesus intends to make a precise statement about the exact moment when Scripture will no longer be in force reverses the force of the verse. That is, Jesus's point is the ongoing validity, fulfillment, and authority of the OT, not the ending of those things. From other Scriptures (e.g., 2 Pet. 3:10–12) we know that eventually God will destroy the current heavens and earth and create a new heaven and earth (see Revelation 21–22); surely Jesus doesn't mean that the OT will last until the eternal state, and then it will be lost or ignored. Nor does he say anything about whether all of it will apply in the same way at all times—Jesus certainly knew that his sacrifice for sin would cancel the need to continue the Mosaic system of blood sacrifices, a point which Hebrews quite clearly affirms. Nor should we take this statement to say anything about how well and accurately copyists will copy the various parts of Scripture. That is, Jesus isn't saying that no copy will ever omit even the smallest letter or stroke of a pen that was in the original. Even a cursory perusal of the various manuscripts we have just of the NT should convince anyone that copyists have misspelled, omitted, or even added words in various copies, so if Jesus intends to predict perfection in the copies, he is wrong. And, of course, to think that is to think the absurd!

So, what is Jesus's point? Here the context helps, for as always, whatever we say about a verse's meaning cannot contradict the verse's context. The context is that Jesus is going to offer a deeper understanding of various commands in the Mosaic code than anyone had previously heard. Some may think he actually threw out the law, but Jesus had no intention of abolishing it; he came to fulfill it (v. 17), and all of it will in fact be fulfilled (v. 18).

As some correctly note, one implication of Jesus's statement is that the OT will have ongoing authority.[18] If it doesn't, what difference would it make whether it is all fulfilled or not? So then, what is this passage's point? The main point is that Jesus came to fulfill the OT and will fulfill it all, no matter how long it takes. Anyone who thinks he is an iconoclast, intent on introducing a new era of lawlessness, totally misunderstands what he says in the Sermon about the various commands of the law. Saying that heaven and earth will pass away before any of the law goes unfulfilled doesn't mean either that the law will be preserved until the eternal state or that there will be a time when it will be lost because it is no longer needed. It is a hyperbolic way of Jesus making the point that he is totally determined to fulfill every single part of the OT. What he will do with the commands of the law doesn't show disregard and disrespect for them, but utmost concern—Jesus wants everyone to understand the most fundamental issues involved in each command and to obey what each one at its deepest level is about.

With this understanding of the passage, it should be clear that it isn't first and foremost about Scripture's preservation. Rather, it is about Jesus's respect for the law/OT and his determination to fulfill it all. Derivatively, if the law/OT is in force at least as long as it takes to fulfill it, that must mean its authority will remain. Is the notion of Scripture's preservation also included in this verse? I think it is best to say that from this verse it is acceptable *to infer* that the OT will continue to exist. For even if Jesus will fulfill it all, how could it have authority if no one knows what it says? That is, what the verse teaches seems to *imply* that the OT will be around for a long while—at least as long as it takes to fulfill it. But that isn't the same as saying the verse *directly* or even *indirectly* intends to teach Scripture's preservation. The OT's preservation is a logical concomitant of what the verse does teach.

One final question is whether this passage can apply to the NT. As spoken from the mouth of Jesus, it doesn't, because none of the NT existed during his lifetime. But if there is reason to think that the NT is God's word, so that

---

[18] Combs, "Preservation of Scripture," 23.

there is a sense in which it is also binding on humanity (it is law, in that sense), and that Jesus can and will fulfill what it promises and predicts, then there is reason to think the NT's preservation is a logical concomitant of what this verse teaches.

So, in sum, I think this verse offers some support for the doctrine of Scripture's preservation, even though that doctrine is by no means the focus of what Jesus says. This verse has probably been seen as offering more direct support for the doctrine than it actually has. What I have just said, however, doesn't mean that the verse is unusable in building a case for Scripture's preservation. It confirms what is more directly taught elsewhere in Scripture.

## Matthew 24:35

Matthew 24:35 comes from Jesus's mouth, and it is part of his Olivet Discourse recorded in Matthew 24–25. As Matthew 24 opens, Jesus's disciples drew his attention to the beautiful buildings of the temple. Jesus replied that all of those buildings would be destroyed (24:1–2). This troubled the disciples greatly, and so as they sat with Jesus on the Mount of Olives, they asked him three questions (24:3): (1) when will these things happen? (2) what will be the sign of your coming? and (3) what will be the sign of the end of the age? Jesus had previously told them on a number of occasions that he would leave them, but that he would also return for them. They also knew OT prophecies about the end of the age. They used this occasion to ask Jesus about all three of these matters. In the rest of chapters 24–25, Jesus answered their questions. Each of the Synoptic Gospels contains a version of the Olivet Discourse. Matthew's focuses mainly on Jesus's answers to the second and third question.

In 24:4–28, Jesus details various events that will be signs that the end of the age is upon the world and that Christ will soon return. Verses 29–31 then predict his return to earth and the gathering of the elect. Immediately after Jesus answers their questions about the signs of his coming and the end of the age, he tells them the parable of the fig tree (24:32–35). Verses 32–33 are the parabolic story and verses 34–35 are the moral to be drawn from the parable.

The parable's point is that the farmer looks for certain signs in relation to the development and fruit-bearing of the fig tree. When he sees them, he knows harvest time is near. In the same way, Jesus tells his disciples to look for the signs detailed in verses 4–31; they are the events which, when they happen, will signal the end of the age and the return of the Lord. In verse 34, he says that the generation that sees these signs won't pass away until everything predicted in verses 4–31 is fulfilled.

Immediately following verse 34 Jesus says, "Heaven and earth shall pass away, but my words shall not pass away" (v. 35 KJV). Jesus then emphasizes the need to be ready for the events detailed in these chapters. He especially warns that there is a need to be ready so as not to be caught unaware. The rest of chapter 25 details a judgment after Christ's return in preparation for the kingdom that begins after the judgment.[19]

Given the context of verse 35, does it actually address our doctrine of preservation? Some think it does, while others disagree. What is a bit discouraging is that many who disagree do so without any comment about the context in which the verse appears. As a result, they think the verse is relevant to our issue but then argue that it doesn't teach Scripture's preservation. This is so, we are told, because Jesus speaks only of his oral words, and only some of all of his oral teachings appear in Scripture. Hence, what he says about his words not passing away until all are fulfilled can't include everything Jesus taught, let alone the whole of the NT. Surely this verse includes hyperbole, as is the case in Matthew 5:18.[20] It really isn't about written revelation, or so we are told.

Sadly, such debates about whether or not this verse supports Scripture's preservation are off the mark, most fundamentally because they don't understand the verse in the context of the parable of the fig tree and the Olivet Discourse. When one properly sets the verse in the context of chapters 24 and 25, Jesus's meaning becomes clear. In verse 34 Jesus says, "This generation shall not pass, till all these things be fulfilled" (KJV). What things? All the things he has detailed in 24:4–31! After all, what has he been talking about in chapter 24? What *generation* is in view? The one that sees all the things happen that Jesus has described, but currently we don't know which generation that will be, nor the date when these things will happen.

Now we are ready for verse 35. Lest anyone think Jesus is wrong in what he says in verse 34—and that would mean he is wrong about everything he describes in verses 4–31 (the "these things" referred to in verse 34)—Jesus adds that heaven and earth will pass away, but his words won't pass away. That is, they will be fulfilled! But in verse 35, *which* words does Jesus have in mind? All those already spoken in Matthew 24 and those yet to be said in the rest of the Olivet Discourse!

So, in light of this explanation, is 24:35 a guarantee of the preservation of Jesus's words of Scripture? Of course not! Is it a guarantee of the preservation of all of his teachings? Again, of course not! Is it a guarantee of the preserva-

---

[19] Undoubtedly, not everyone will interpret Matthew 24–25 as I have. My purpose in describing its contents is not to initiate a debate over end-time events. Rather, it is to describe in general the contents of these chapters and to insist that we must not lift 24:35 out of chapters 24–25 and try to use it to support any doctrine we choose. We must understand it in its context. When we do, it is dubious that Jesus intends to say anything in this verse about the doctrine of Scripture's preservation.

[20] Combs, "Preservation of Scripture," 24–25, offers such objections, but others also do (Rehurek, "Preservation of the Bible," 78) and cite other commentators who use the verse to say something about the preservation of Scripture, or who deny that it does. Note the commentators and theologians quoted and cited in Combs, "Preservation of Scripture," 24–25, who think this verse either does support Scripture's preservation or doesn't.

tion of all (OT and NT) or even of part of Scripture? Absolutely not! Then what is Jesus guaranteeing? He guarantees that the events he has described as happening before the end of the age and his return and the things that will happen after his return (detailed in chapter 25) are most certainly going to happen.

What does this teach about the preservation of *Scripture*? Absolutely nothing! But, some will reply, the Olivet Discourse is part of Scripture, and we still have it today, so doesn't that mean Jesus in 24:35 teaches the preservation of at least part of Scripture (the Olivet Discourse)? Again, no! What Jesus certifies as firmly fixed and guaranteed to happen are all the events he has described in verses 4–31, and those he will describe in the rest of the Olivet Discourse. I am immensely thankful that God has seen fit to preserve this part of the Gospel of Matthew (as well as the rest of Scripture), but that in no way means that Matthew 24:35 teaches the preservation of all Scripture!

### Luke 16:17

This passage actually makes the same basic point as does Matthew 5:18 (though not in the very same words), but the contexts are quite different. As with Matthew 5:17–18, however, the focus of this verse isn't some point about the preservation of Scripture. Matthew 5 is part of the Sermon on the Mount given to Jesus's disciples. Luke 16 begins with a parable Jesus teaches his disciples about using money shrewdly so that if and when one's master "fires" him, the servant will find that his masters' former debtors will be sympathetic to him and his plight. This is followed by comments to the effect that those who are faithful in little will be faithful in much, and in the same way those who are unjust in some small issue will be unjust in bigger ones. A person's characteristics will lead him to act in the same way, regardless of the issue involved (v. 10), and he can expect the same kind of response from others when he acts in this way, regardless of the specific issue involved (vv. 11–12). This is followed by the claim that one can't serve both God and money (v. 13).

Luke then writes that the Pharisees who were covetous heard Jesus say these things about money, and they derided him (v. 14). Jesus rebuked them for their habit of justifying themselves in the eyes of men, even though they were evil in God's estimation (v. 15). In verse 16 Jesus makes a comment about the times of the Law and the Prophets until John. He adds that since that time, the kingdom of God is preached and everyone is trying to get into it. This is followed by Jesus's comment in verse 17 that it is easier for heaven and earth to pass away than for even the smallest part of the law to fail to be fulfilled, and then in verse 18 Luke includes a cryptic statement of Jesus's teaching on divorce and remarriage, and the rest of the chapter tells the story of the rich man and Lazarus. How all of these disparate parts of chapter 16 fit together is a puzzle with which commentators continue to wrestle. We don't need to solve that, however, in order to understand Jesus's basic point in verse 17.

Verse 17 doesn't actually say anything about how long Scripture will last, nor does it directly say anything about whether God will or will not preserve his word. Rather, it imagines something catastrophic, the destruction of heaven and earth, and affirms that it would be easier for that to happen than for even the smallest part of Scripture ("the Law") to "come to an end," that is, to "cease to be valid" (*pesein*, from *piptō*). Of course, for heaven and earth to be destroyed presumably would take a certain amount of time—at least, who would not think so? Because we reason that it would take time for heaven and earth to be destroyed, it is understandable that we should think that what the rest of the verse speaks about would take a long time, too—hence preservation (which would take time) of Scripture. But why should we think that the point of the analogy is about time or that Jesus is making a temporal point? It seems that, most fundamentally, the point of the analogy is that Jesus is comparing things that in common parlance would be deemed impossible to happen. No one expects the created universe to collapse at any moment; if we think about this at all, we aren't usually thinking in scientific terms.

The point is that the universe continuing to exist is a stable, foundational notion for us; without presupposing its continued existence, we can't say much of anything that makes sense, since what we would say presupposes its existence. Similarly, the truthfulness of Scripture is the same kind of presupposition, but it is even more secure than our presuppositions about the continued existence of the universe. The universe might cease to exist—though there is no reason to worry that this will happen anytime soon—but the truthfulness of Scripture is even more certain than the universe's continued existence. There is no imaginable circumstance in which Scripture could be wrong. What it says is more certainly true and unassailable than even the most fundamental truths about the created universe that we take for granted every day of our lives! Jesus's point is that it is impossible for Scripture to be invalid, untrue, and/or no longer applicable and useful.

What does this mean, however, for the doctrine of Scripture's preservation? Some principle(s) could be accurate and applicable even if people are ignorant of them. People might be ignorant of them because no one has yet discovered them, or perhaps because they were once known but for some reason fell out of use and were taught to no one. What is my point? My point is that, even if Scripture can't ever be invalid, that doesn't mean that everyone or even anyone will know its contents. Everything taught in Scripture was true before any of it was revealed. In a similar way, at some point in the future every copy of Scripture in any and every language might be destroyed and enough time might pass so that no one knew or remembered any of Scripture's contents (I have doubts that this would happen, but I'm entertaining this possibility to make a point). The contents of Scripture would still be just as true as they have always been and as we know them to be today. That alone doesn't guarantee that any actual copies of Scripture will exist indefinitely into the future. That is, the point of this verse isn't about whether, how, or how long copies of Scripture will exist. The point is the inerrancy (truth) and continued validity of Scripture.

But, one might respond, how can something be valid if no one knows it, and if no one knows it because they have no access to it? It can be valid in the same way that various scientific truths were valid before anyone made discoveries that taught those truths to humankind. That is, just as the law of gravity obtained in our universe before anyone named, explained, or proved the facts that led humans to understand this "law," the teachings of Scripture, properly interpreted, were always true even before any of it was revealed to anyone, transmitted to others beyond those who first received it, or interpreted and understood correctly by anyone. Something can be true even if no one knows it. But if no one knows it, it is hard to think of "preserving" this truth in the sense involved in the doctrine of preservation.

So, what does the preceding discussion amount to? Does it mean that Jesus didn't believe in the preservation of Scripture, or that he *did* believe in it but that wasn't his point in this verse? Certainly, Jesus believed that Scripture would never cease to exist, and as the divine Son of God, he would know that it would be preserved. What is at issue here is what exactly Jesus is saying in Luke 16:17. What is clearly in view there is Scripture's truthfulness and ongoing validity. That could be true even if no one had any access to it. We may infer that this would make little practical difference if no one knew the contents of Scripture, and that is probably true. What this inferred result does not mean is that Jesus was guaranteeing the continued existence of copies of Scripture. Of course, he knew that Scripture would never cease to exist, but that doesn't mean that he was making that point in this verse.

In sum, there may be inferences upon inferences that stem from this verse which amount to the notion that Scripture won't go out of existence, but that isn't its fundamental point. Nor is an inference to Scripture's preservation easy to certify from what this verse actually teaches. Jesus may have had the preservation of Scripture on his mind when he made this point, but that doesn't mean the words of this verse affirm that doctrine.

### John 10:35

This familiar passage is appealed to in discussions of inerrancy and authority, but it isn't normally cited as support for the doctrine of Scripture's preservation. Nonetheless, some might think it does offer credibility to that doctrine.[21] The key phrase is, "and the Scripture cannot be broken," and those who cite it take it to mean that Scripture can't be broken up, dissolved, or cease to exist. Hence, it must be permanent, and if so, then it must be preserved.

Despite such sentiments, we have seen the actual meaning of this phrase in our discussions of inerrancy and authority. Jesus was accused of blasphemy for calling himself God. To meet the charge, Jesus cited a passage from Psalm 82:6 in which mere mortals are referred to as gods. They received that designation because they served as judges in Israel who were supposed to render justice on behalf of God. Because of their position, they were called gods, even though they were mere men, and evil ones at that. Jesus then says that if such evil individuals were called gods, how can there be a problem when he does what is right and refers to himself as the son of God! Lest his enemies respond that there is no Scripture that teaches what Jesus has said, or that Scripture is just wrong, Jesus adds the clinching argument when he says, "and the Scripture cannot be broken." In other words, Jesus is saying, "You know I'm right, because Scripture says what I claim, and Scripture can't be wrong." Whatever it says cannot be "broken" in the sense of being refuted.

Hopefully, any reader can see how Jesus's use of this comment refutes his enemies' charge of blasphemy. It is not clear, on the other hand, how saying that Scripture can't cease to exist is even relevant to the point Jesus made. Scripture could continue to exist forever, but that alone wouldn't support Jesus's argument that Scripture called evil human judges "gods" without committing blasphemy, so he is not blaspheming when he, who does good, calls himself God. Jesus's defense hinges not on the existence of Scripture but on the truthfulness of what it says in Psalm 82! Hence, "and the Scripture cannot be broken" has nothing to do with Scripture's preservation, and everything to do with Scripture's truth and authority! That's why Jesus appeals to it in order to defend himself against the charge of blasphemy.

*1 Peter 1:23–25*

While these verses contain a quote of Isaiah 40:6b–8,[22] the contexts of Isaiah 40 and 1 Peter 1 are quite different. Thus, we can't assume that the identical parts of these passages function identically in each context. The context of Isaiah 40 is one of threatened and impending judgment for sin upon the ungodly in Israel and upon Israel's ungodly neighbors. Isaiah 40 begins a section of the

---

[21] For example, one finds such sentiments in D. A. Waite, *Defending the King James Bible* (Collingswood, NJ: Bible for Today Press, 1992), 13; and Donald L. Brake, "The Doctrine of the Preservation of the Scriptures" (ThM thesis, Dallas Theological Seminary, 1970), 14, cited in Combs, "Preservation of Scripture," 23.
[22] Rehurek, "Preservation of the Bible," 85.

book that promises restoration and blessing to Israel if she will return to her God. Verses 6–8 of Isaiah 40 function to show Israel that God's promises are dependable; his word can be trusted, because God won't let it be rendered null and void, and he will bring to pass what he has promised. So, Israel should be comforted, but she should also be motivated to turn from her wicked ways so as to experience God's full blessings for her.

The context of 1 Peter is quite different. Peter wrote to saints suffering for their faith in Christ. His task wasn't to call them to repentance in order to avoid further judgment. Rather, his goal was to encourage and comfort them in the face of persecution, and to instruct them on how to handle present and future persecution.

Peter begins this epistle by reminding his readers of their salvation and by discussing the results of their being saved. We might think that a basically theological discussion of salvation is an odd way to comfort people suffering for their faith, but it actually makes quite a bit of sense. It's as if Peter is saying, "I know you are facing difficult trials, and unfortunately they are not at an end. In this world you undoubtedly feel disenfranchised and alone. Even though those who are of the world have little respect for you and so they marginalize and persecute you, things aren't quite what they seem. Things could be worse. At least Christ is your Savior; you matter very much to him, he hasn't forgotten you, and he knows what you are facing. As his people, you have an everlasting inheritance reserved in heaven, and nothing can take that away. Take heart in your salvation and all it involves" (1 Pet. 1:1–13).

After these introductory comments, Peter offers instructions on how believers should live. They should live holy lives (vv. 14–17), and pass their time on earth in reverence and fear of God (vv. 18–21). This should be their attitude because, among other reasons, their salvation cost God immeasurably and is worth more than any this-worldly possession (vv. 18–19 especially). Specifically, believers should be characterized by love of other believers in Christ (v. 22).

Peter then explains (vv. 23–26) that they were not redeemed or born again spiritually by anything that can decay and wear out. The "seed" planted in their hearts which bore fruit in bringing them to Christ is God's word. Peter then describes the nature of that word in verses 23b–25. It is alive, and it remains (v. 23b). Some translations add the word "forever" to verse 23b, and so they can be read as implying that God's word will last/be preserved forever (see more on this point below). This is in contrast to what we as human beings are. Like grass and other vegetation, we flourish for a time, and then die. We are temporary, not permanent. This was Isaiah's exact point (in Isaiah 40:6–8), using the same metaphor, as he compared human flesh and vegetation to God's word.

First Peter 1:25 reaffirms that God's word is quite different; it won't perish, for it is permanent. This sounds like Isaiah 40:8, but Peter adds something Isaiah omits. Peter adds that "this is the word which by the gospel is preached unto you" (KJV). Here Peter narrows the reference of "the word of God" to the specific gospel message Peter's readers had heard and accepted. This seems to negate the idea that "the word of God" in these passages refers to Scripture—either the OT and/or the parts of the NT that had been written when Peter wrote 1 Peter. D. Edmond Hiebert writes,

> "But" (*de*) adds the contrasting fact of the abiding nature of God's word, "but the word of the Lord stands forever" (v. 25a). The term rendered "the word" (*to rhema*) is not the same term rendered "the word" (logou) in v. 23. *To rhema* is the term used in the Septuagint. The same transition occurs in Peter's sermon in Acts 10:36-37. *To rhema* is more concrete and denotes that which is spoken—the utterance itself. *Logos* is more comprehensive and includes the thought as well as its expression. The term *rhema*, "utterance" or "message," pointedly designates the message spoken by the mouth of God; it is the divine revelation made known in the Christian gospel (cf. Heb 1:1-2). The repetition of the term in the next phrase identifies that divine utterance with the gospel proclaimed to the readers. It is indeed "the word of the Lord."[23]

In light of the flow of Peter's thought in 1 Peter 1, in light of his comments on how his readers came to know the Lord, and especially because Peter adds to his comments about God's word enduring forever that this word is the gospel message preached to them, it seems natural to limit the references in 1 Peter 1:23–25 to "the word of God" to the gospel message alone. That is, it seems most accurate to understand Peter as affirming that the gospel message—which, when his readers heard, they accepted—is the specific word of God in view, not Scripture in whole or in part.

If so, then we must ask whether this passage is at all relevant to the doctrine of Scripture's preservation. I think it is relevant, but several points must be emphasized. First, though some might think this passage contains two references to Scripture's enduring nature (one in v. 23 and a second in verse 25), that isn't actually so. This mistake probably stems in part from some translations that end verse 23 with the words "by the word of God, which liveth and abideth forever" (KJV). The error in this translation is that the Greek text doesn't include the words for "forever" (*eis ton aiōna*). This point is significant, because verse 23 can be understood as a comment about God's word in general as the source of believers' experiencing the new birth, rather than as a reference to the specific gospel message that one believes

---

[23] D. Edmond Hiebert, *1 Peter* (Winona Lake, IN: BMH, 1984): 117, as quoted in Rehurek, "Preservation of the Bible," 86–87.

unto salvation. If verse 23 is a general comment about God's word, we might be inclined to see it even as a reference to Scripture. If verse 23 contained the words "forever," then this verse would seem to be a blanket affirmation that God's word as a whole, i.e., Scripture, lives and abides forever. Wouldn't that claim in substance amount to the idea that Scripture will be preserved? It seems so.

The problem with this line of thought is that verse 23, the more general comment about God's word, doesn't contain the words meaning "forever." So, God's word could be living and abiding, but nothing in the verse would promise that it would abide forever. To affirm that this verse asserts the basic notion of the doctrine of Scripture's preservation would seem to require the Greek text to include the Greek words for "forever."

On the other hand, *eis ton aiōna* ("forever") does appear in the Greek text of verse 25, which says that "the word of the Lord" endures. If the verse ended with "the word of the Lord endures forever," then we would be in much the same situation we found in Isaiah 40:8. But 1 Peter 1:25 adds another sentence: "and this is the word which was preached [*euangelisthen*—not just any preached word, but the gospel message] to you." The effect of this added sentence is to take verse 25's apparently general comment about God's word and focus it specifically on the gospel message. So, there is ample reason to question whether verse 25 teaches or even supports the notion that *all* of Scripture will be preserved forever—the doctrine of preservation.

Readers may be a bit dismayed, because it now seems that we can't use this passage to support the doctrine of preservation. But we shouldn't abandon this passage as unhelpful to the doctrine. Why? Let me explain.

First, the last phrase of verse 23 seems to be a relative clause which describes the word of God in general, by which Peter's readers have specifically been born again. Even though the relative clause in question in verse 23 doesn't say the word of God lives and abides *forever*, it does say that it lives and abides or remains. Though the verse doesn't say how long God's word will remain, nothing in the verse precludes the notion that it will abide indefinitely or even forever. So, even if verse 23 doesn't explicitly assert Scripture's existence forever, it says nothing that negates such a notion, and if other Scriptures teach that Scripture will last forever, those verses don't in any way contradict verse 23. So, Peter might have been thinking that Scripture as God's word would abide forever; this verse alone just doesn't say that.

Second, verse 25 does link the word of God with existing forever. If the verse said no more, we would take the verse as clear support for the key idea in the doctrine of preservation (the notion that Scripture won't perish). But in his next sentence, Peter identifies the word of God as the gospel message preached to his readers. So, this verse doesn't seem to be a comment on the whole of Scripture, but we shouldn't be too quick to end the discussion and assume that this passage is irrelevant to our subject.

We should examine further this gospel message that was preached to Peter's readers. Of course, Peter believed that the message came to his readers through preaching. But preaching of what? Only memories of people who knew Jesus, or stories about Jesus that had been passed around through oral presentation alone? It is unlikely that those things would be the only sources for sermons. Wouldn't at least some sermons, including evangelistic ones, incorporate various OT Scriptures? If the preachers in view had access to any NT books written by the time they did their preaching, wouldn't at least some of them refer to those books?

Readers may wonder why I ask such questions. The answer is that there was plenty of material from the OT and from available NT books at the time 1 Peter was written that Peter's audience might have known and that Peter himself would likely have known. Would those books available have been at all relevant to the message Peter and others preached? Indeed they would be—it is certainly possible to preach the gospel from the OT! So, even if we limit the scope of the Scripture to which 1 Peter 1:25 refers just to things relevant to the gospel, there is still a lot of Scripture that 1:25 would include. And, since 1:25 says that God's word remains forever, Peter would be affirming that the Scripture this verse refers to exists forever.

What I have just said means that 1 Peter 1:25 doesn't straightforwardly assert the permanence of all Scripture, but taking into consideration all that the gospel message covers and entails, Peter most likely refers (even if somewhat indirectly) to more Scripture than we might think. And, given what Peter says about Scripture as inspired (2 Pet. 1:19), if we could ask him if he thinks that parts of God's word which aren't about the gospel message also abide forever, he would surely answer affirmatively. The only real question remaining is whether Peter would at all equate God's "word" (as he uses it in 1 Pet. 1:25) with Scripture. Though there is room for doubt that he would, it isn't unreasonable, given what we find in his two epistles (esp. 2 Peter) about Scripture, to think he would make that equation.

So, in sum, what should we conclude about 1 Peter 1:23–25 and the doctrine of Scripture's preservation? Are we on no firmer conceptual ground than we are with Isaiah 40:8? In reply, I believe that even Isaiah 40:8 is useful for this doctrine, though one must add other biblical truths in order to produce at all an inferential argument that would succeed in support of preservation. As to 1 Peter 1, given the preceding discussion of the text, I think we still need to structure an inferential argument from it and other things we know about

Scripture. But because of things Peter says which aren't in Isaiah 40, and because of what we know about Peter's experiences and his general knowledge and circumstances when he wrote this book, I think the inferential argument isn't as hard to construct as it is for Isaiah 40. So, I think 1 Peter 1:23–25 does support this doctrine, even if a bit more indirectly than we might wish.

### Summary of Biblical Teaching on Preservation

From the preceding, readers may be a bit discouraged, because some verses typically used to support this doctrine aren't actually about it at all. However, a doctrine can be confirmed even by one verse that clearly teaches it; it need not be supported by multiple verses.

As for biblical support for this doctrine, we can initially say without hesitation that no verse refutes it. But our study of passages often cited in its support allows us to say more. Some verses seem clearly applicable to Scripture's preservation. In addition, other verses, even if not directly or mainly about this doctrine, also support it, even if only somewhat indirectly. And, some verses occasionally invoked really aren't about this doctrine.

Probably the strongest biblical support for this doctrine is found in Psalm 119, and verse 152 is most relevant. This verse refers to God's word in written form, and it can be applied to all Scripture, not just to this psalm or even just to the parts of the OT the psalmist would have known. It affirms that God has founded his word everywhere (heaven and earth) forever. Thus, the underlying thought is God's word being permanently available. Verse 160 of Psalm 119 adds a further encouraging note. The psalmist says that God's word lasts forever, and it is true. This makes sense since truth is always truth. For God's word to last forever, it must somehow be preserved. Verse 160 doesn't say who is responsible for preserving God's word, but in this psalm's context, including verse 152, surely the psalmist means that God will see to it.

Isaiah 40:8 is also significant for our doctrine. Though this verse most directly reassures the people of Israel that the comfort God offers is genuine—i.e., if they obey him, he will truly comfort them in their current circumstances—Isaiah also comments about God's word in general. God's words of comfort and his promises are significant, because his word cannot be overturned, and it lasts forever. Thus, there is genuine reason for them to be encouraged. We noted in discussing this verse that it also *applies* to all of God's word and to all people, regardless of their situation. Being applicable isn't the same as explicitly affirming something, but I also explained why this verse does offer some support for the concept of preservation. In addition, 1 Peter 1:23–25, which quotes Isaiah 40:8, also lends support to this doctrine, even if only indirectly.

Interestingly, verses often used as foundational for this doctrine, like Matthew 5:17–18 (par. Luke 16:17), aren't quite as relevant to it as some think. Jesus's main point is that he intends to fulfill everything the OT predicts and promises about him, no matter how long it takes. As we saw, this doesn't say that Scripture itself will be preserved indefinitely. But, what Jesus says is not totally irrelevant to this doctrine. Preservation of the OT is at the very least a logical concomitant of Jesus's promise not to abolish but to fulfill it.

For reasons presented in discussing verses often cited to support this doctrine, the verses mentioned above are key ones relevant to this doctrine. Other verses discussed don't deny Scripture's preservation; they just don't teach it. For example, Psalm 119:89 speaks of the permanent availability of God's word, but it clearly says this is in heaven. It makes no comment about Scripture's accessibility on earth. Since the doctrine of preservation is most directly about the latter, Psalm 119:89 doesn't actually offer the kind of support some have thought.

But, the final question of import about biblical support for this doctrine is whether verses taken to affirm it are enough grounds for holding it. Here the answer is affirmative, but not because there is a certain number of verses that teach it that is required in order to say Scripture proclaims the doctrine. The number of verses supporting a doctrine is never the key; the content of the verses is what matters. Even a few verses that clearly present a concept are reason enough to include it in our theology and believe in its truth. Though we might wish there were more verses that teach this doctrine, the verses noted above are clear and relevant enough to warrant believing it.

## OTHER ARGUMENTS FOR PRESERVATION

In addition to the biblical evidence already presented, two other arguments have been offered in favor of Scripture's preservation. Unfortunately, some have used one or the other to affirm that only one version of the Bible (King James Version/Textus Receptus [KJV/TR]) is actually Scripture and the word of God; any other version—or at least any other version based on manuscripts and texts not behind the Textus Receptus—isn't Scripture. Those interested in the particular debate about the KJV and the TR are welcome to pursue it in the plenitude of literature devoted to this debate.[24] That debate needn't concern us here.

Above I noted that it is *unfortunate* that arguments to be discussed in this

---

[24] See, e.g., Wallace ("Inspiration, Preservation, and New Testament Textual Criticism"), and Combs ("Preservation of Scripture"), whose articles interact with the KJV/TR debate extensively. For an even more thorough discussion of the debate, see D. A. Carson, *The King James Version Debate: A Plea for Realism* (Grand Rapids, MI: Baker, 1979). None of these writers is in the KJV-only camp, but each offers a fair presentation of that viewpoint, as well as significant critique of it. But these are just a few of very many writings on this topic.

section have been used in the KJV/TR debate. That is so, not because those arguments are inextricably tied to the KJV/TR debate. It is so, instead, because there is a form in which these arguments can be and should be presented that avoids embroiling oneself in the KJV/TR debate. When we look at the simple arguments, apart from considerations of whether they require a certain version or translation, I think they help in supporting this doctrine.

The first argument is that preservation is a logical corollary to the doctrine of inspiration. In other words, if God inspired the writing of Scripture, he surely wouldn't have done so (nor would he have put the writers of Scripture through whatever they had to do to write their book) if, after inspiring Scripture, God left to chance what would happen to these books. If God had done that, it is probable that over hundreds and thousands of years at least some of it would have been lost.

William Combs is one who presents this argument, and he begins discussing it by quoting Webster's Dictionary's definition of the word "corollary." Next, Combs writes, "Thus to say that preservation is the corollary of inspiration means that preservation is a doctrine that can be 'inferred immediately' from the 'proved proposition' of inspiration; preservation 'naturally follows' or 'parallels' inspiration."[25]

While I understand fully the argument that Combs presents, I am concerned that we take care in how we state it. Specifically, we must be sure that we don't give the impression that inspiration *logically entails* preservation. Logical entailment is a philosophical notion that in this case would mean that if the first item, inspiration, is true/held, then the second must be true because inspiration necessitates (in the strong philosophical sense that you can't have one without the other) preservation. That is simply not so. In my discussion of the doctrine of inspiration, I explained the concept and the biblical teaching in support of it. Nowhere in those chapters did we see that writing which is the product of God's breath of necessity (almost automatically, one is inclined to say) will be preserved. It certainly makes sense for God to ensure that what he has inspired won't be lost, but it doesn't require it. One of the reasons is that there are surely things which were applicable to the person/people and time that first received them, but are no longer applicable after a certain amount of time passes. So long as such material is available to those to whom it applies, once it no longer applies, there is no absolute necessity for its continued existence at all.

To illustrate this point further, I note that while some passages that teach preservation speak about Scripture being preserved forever, that doesn't clarify whether there will be copies of Scripture in the new heavens and new earth.

---

[25] Combs, "Preservation of Scripture," 27.

Though it is unlikely that everyone in that state will forget everything Scripture says, that doesn't prove that copies of the Bible will be there. In truth, conditions in the eternal state will likely be so unlike present conditions that we can't really imagine exactly what we will know and how we will know it—perhaps there will be no need for Bibles, for everyone in a glorified state will know intuitively every word of Scripture. All of this is speculative, but I offer it only to say that while Scripture teaches preservation of God's word forever, it doesn't explain precisely how Scripture will be preserved at various times in history, nor does it say whether there will be Bibles (and if so, in what form—paper, digital, or something else) in eternity. Hence, it is possible that even though we should hold this doctrine, we can't explain exactly what this means about having Bibles in the eternal state. I present these points most fundamentally to illustrate my point that, just because Scripture is inspired, that doesn't mean that its preservation is logically required (in the strong philosophical sense of logical entailment).

Having said the preceding, some may think, then, that there is no argument to be made for preservation on the basis of inspiration. However, it would be wrong to draw that conclusion. There is still an argument that incorporates the doctrine of inspiration. But, instead of talking of logical corollaries and logical entailment, we should talk about probabilities. That is, in light of both divine revelation and inspiration, it is highly probable that God would preserve his word. In fact, the probability is so high that while it is imaginable (i.e., the very idea of not preserving Scripture doesn't contain a contradiction) that God would not preserve his word, it is so likely that he would, that it makes little sense to doubt that he would.

Such a probability assessment is warranted, but I can't simply say so; I must explain why. I begin by noting that God didn't need to create anything in order to be who he is. Creating a world was a fitting thing for God to do, but it wouldn't at all have been wrong for him to create nothing. In fact, God has existed forever, and our universe, while old, certainly isn't as old as God. So, for a long time in God's life there was no universe, and that in no way diminished his grandeur and glory. Hence, he didn't need to create a universe in order to enhance his worth.

Still, God decided to create. But the universe he created didn't have to contain creatures at all like humans with their abilities to understand concepts of various kinds. Nonetheless, God did create humans with their intellectual abilities. Having created them, God wasn't obligated to communicate with them. Communicating with them in no way enhanced his value, and failing to do so wouldn't have diminished his worth at all. Still, God knew that humans are finite in intelligence and wouldn't automatically know how to live in the world he created without endangering themselves and others. In addition, he wanted a relationship with his human creatures, but sin blocks that relationship. Without knowing what actions are right or wrong and without knowing the penalties for breaking moral rules and the blessings for obeying, humans might engage in various actions which God would know were immoral and also detrimental to their well-being.

So, God lovingly revealed his own existence and something of his rules for proper conduct. He did this through the various forms of natural revelation, but also through direct communication. Genesis 1–3 presents certain rules God gave his first human creatures. Sadly, they broke those rules; sin and its negative consequences entered human history. God could have "thrown up his hands in disgust" and refused to say anything more; he could have left us with sin's consequences and done nothing to remedy the problem. But God didn't do that. Before any Scripture was written, God communicated to humans in various ways. We know this happened because so much of the early chapters of Genesis describes times and events before any Scripture was given, and shows that God communicated with various people in different ways during those times.

Sadly, God's various revelations were not successful in getting humans to correct their ways and obey even the most basic moral norms. In fact, at one point in history humans were so evil that God decided to destroy everyone and every living thing except those that entered Noah's ark. After the flood, humans began to multiply in large numbers again. God communicated with them through various forms of revelation other than Scripture—Genesis's account of history after the flood but before any Scripture was written shows this.

Despite God's revealing his rules and his remedy for sin when humans disobey, humans continued to sin and to bear sin's consequences. Whether or not this motivated God to communicate in a way that would be more accessible to more people than just a few and that would be more understandable than natural revelation, God decided to reveal himself in a written form. He chose specific servants to receive his revelation and transfer it to writing. Those words contained information about God himself and also presented, among other things, his requirements for maintaining a positive relationship with him, and the punishments for breaking his commands. He also revealed how humans could have their sins forgiven and continue living in harmony with God. God wasn't obligated to do any of this, but out of love and concern for us he revealed his word and superintended its transfer into writing. Though large portions of God's word were addressed to his people Israel, OT books were intended not just for those who first received them, not just for the generation of Israelites alive when OT Scriptures were revealed, and not just for the people of Israel in general. In addition, NT books were clearly intended for people of all races and nationalities, living at times long after the books were first written.

Even so, most people who have ever lived haven't known how to read. Those who could would have to teach those who couldn't about God's word and its demands. In addition, since all humans of all times are sinners and need God's remedy, there would have to be a way for people who couldn't read to learn of God's provision of salvation. Of course, they could be told of God's remedy by those who could read, but literate people can't pass on what they don't know. There had to be some way to learn of God's plan of salvation.

How could that happen? Perhaps God would just tell someone the remedy, and he could pass it on. Or perhaps God could reveal his answer to sin directly to everyone who ever lived. Undoubtedly, God has always been able to do just that, and to do so in a nonwritten form. But what if God's revelation were rejected or simply set aside and in time forgotten? God could, of course, give the same information in nonwritten form repeatedly to each living person until she or he either accepted God's remedy for sin or so totally rejected it that it would be fruitless for God to present salvation's plan again. God, of course, wasn't obligated to tell anyone anything (in writing or otherwise), but if he decided to reveal his answer to sin and his expectations of how to live a God-pleasing life, doing so by repeatedly speaking the same message directly to everyone who ever lives seems to be a rather inefficient way to do it. Why use a method of communicating that keeps you constantly busy repeating the same rules and regulations to everyone?

Of course, God could have done exactly what I just described. Deciding not to do that creates no "stain" on God, for God has no obligation to provide a remedy for our sin or to tell us by any method his solution. Still, for whatever reason(s), God decided to communicate with humankind in a written form. In those written pieces of revelation, God told us about himself, about angelic, demonic, and satanic beings, about ourselves, and about other creatures in his universe. God knew that Jesus, his answer to our sin problem, wouldn't be alive in a nonglorified human state at all times in history, but since their salvation depends on Christ's work, humans would need to have as much information as possible about Jesus and the salvation he provides. God could have transmitted that information to each person repeatedly by means of special revelation other than Scripture, but he decided to transmit it in written form, and so at various times in history, the Holy Spirit moved specially prepared humans to pen the books that became parts of Scripture.

Having taken all of these steps to give humans information about himself, themselves, and the way to a right relation with God, how likely is it that, once that information was transferred into written form, God would let it be lost? Of course, God wasn't obligated to preserve his word any more than he was obligated to give it in the first place. But, having revealed it and having inspired writers to compose the books of Scripture, how likely is it that God would allow these writings to be lost? Would God want these books to be available only to the people who first received them, but not to later generations and other people groups? Is it likely that he would reveal truth to a limited number of people living only a short time, and then just leave everyone else in the dark about himself, their need for salvation, and his provision for it?

Some may answer that God did just that, at least with the OT. And, when NT books were first written, they were delivered to a very limited number of people. In response, this is true, but it is also true that God always intended Israel to be "a light unto the Gentiles," and Jesus told his disciples to go into all the world and preach the gospel. Surely, the books of both Testaments were intended for more people than just those who first received them. In other words, though the various OT and NT books may have been *addressed to* a very small set of people, their message about how to get right with God and about how to please him is about everybody, and is intended for more than just the first recipients. As Combs rightly explains, Paul told the Romans that "whatever was written in earlier times was written for our instruction, that through perseverance and the encouragement of the Scriptures we might have hope" (Rom. 15:4). And as Paul told Corinthian believers, OT Scriptures about Israel's failure to obey and follow God "happened to them as an example, and they were written for our instruction, upon whom the ends of the ages have come" (1 Cor. 10:11). "If the Old Testament Scriptures ('these things') were 'written,' that is, inspired for the purpose of instructing future believers ('our instruction'), that purpose demands their preservation."[26]

It is hard to fault Combs's argument. Put differently, because God wasn't obligated to reveal any Scripture but did, anyway, and because what was written wasn't just for those who first received it, how likely is it that, having revealed so much truth about himself and us in Scripture, God wouldn't take steps to see that all generations from all nations who would live after the books were first written would also have the possibility of accessing that information? This must not be misunderstood. I am not suggesting that it is unlikely that no one living during and after the times when the books of Scripture were composed would be ignorant of its contents. Rather, my point is that it is just highly unlikely (for the reasons mentioned) that while

---

[26] Ibid., 28. See his whole discussion on the relation of inspiration to preservation, as contained on 27–29. Though his talk of logical corollaries may, as I explained, be unwarranted, his argument about the connection between inspiration and preservation is quite helpful.

Scripture was being written and after it was completed, there would be no possible way for most people on earth to access it. It is hard to see how God could justly hold people accountable for failing to obey truth that they had no possible way of knowing.

Humans without any Scripture still have natural revelation, and they are accountable for disobeying it. Paul is very clear on that point (Rom. 1:20). While God wasn't obligated to give anyone even natural revelation, he also wasn't required to give anyone any form of special revelation. But God did give various forms of special revelation, including Scripture. Why would he give, in written form, information which every human being needs, and then make it impossible for anyone to know it by letting it go out of existence, by doing nothing to ensure that it would at least remain in some people's memories, or by doing nothing to guarantee that people could access this information in at least some way(s) if they wanted it? If everyone needs this information, and no one has a "right" to get it, but you give it to some, why would you not give it to others, especially if they will be held accountable for what it teaches? Not to preserve Scripture, so that there isn't even a chance for people without it to receive it in some way or form, makes little sense. It makes more sense to believe either that God would give it to no one, or that he would preserve it so that anyone living after each book of Scripture was composed could have some access to it.

Does this line of argument mean that we can say that, by inspiring Scripture, God obligated himself to preserve it? The answer is that, while inspiration doesn't *obligate* God or logically require him to preserve Scripture, from what we know of God, of mankind's need, and of Scripture's content, it is most likely (well beyond 50 percent probable) that God, having given Scripture, would also preserve his word.

In truth, this line of argument is not just an argument from inspiration to preservation. Rather, it is an argument from God's character, his revelation and inspiration of Scripture, and humanity's need of the information contained in Scripture to the *likelihood* or *probability* of Scripture's preservation. Since it makes sense to believe what is most probable and reject the improbable, it makes sense to believe that a revealed and inspired text will also be a preserved one.

There is another argument for preservation worth noting. Combs claims that there is a second *corollary*, from Scripture's authority to its preservation. Though we should be careful about how we use the term "corollary," Combs's basic point is hard to contest. As argued in my chapter 9, Scripture is authoritative. This is so because it is the word of God (the supreme ruler of the universe who has a right to require his creatures to obey whatever he chooses), and because it is inerrant. Truth is always authoritative.[27]

Scripture's authority comes at least in part from its inspiration. There is no evidence that its authority applied only to those who first received it. Its authority applies to everyone at all times after Scripture comes into existence. Of course, Scripture can't have any authority if it isn't preserved, even as it couldn't be used to judge human actions before any of it was given.

Moreover, we must remember what 2 Timothy 3:16–17 says about the purposes for which Scripture was given. Paul says that Scripture is profitable for "doctrine, for reproof, for correction, for instruction in righteousness, that the man of God may be perfect, thoroughly furnished unto all good works" (KJV). That is, God's ultimate goal in giving Scripture is for humans to be prepared to do all good works. These verses don't say that there are multiple ways to prepare oneself to do good works which God would find pleasing. Rather, the reading of, study of, and whatever else it takes to master *and* obey Scripture is the God-appointed means to prepare ourselves for and to do all good works. Scripture is the *authoritative manual* for what humans need to know and do to fulfill God's purposes for them in the world. Of course, people can't do what God wants if they don't know what he requires. Thus, Scripture can be the authoritative guide on how to relate properly to God only if it is preserved in existence. Hence, it is most likely that, given Scripture's binding and ongoing authority, God would ensure that Scripture doesn't cease to exist.[28] This doesn't say which translation(s) will be preserved, or that everyone living during and after the times when Scripture was given will personally possess (and be able to read) a copy of God's word. It only means that versions and translations that represent what God inspired the biblical writers to write will continue to exist. Because of that ongoing existence, it is and will be possible for people to know what God's word says, even if some people have little or no access to an actual copy of Scripture in their language, and even if some people can't read. In order to uphold the doctrine of Scripture's preservation, it isn't necessary for everyone alive during and after Scripture's composition to know how to read. It is only necessary that the Bible continues to exist.

## SUMMARY AND CONCLUSION

In this chapter we have explained what the doctrine of Scripture's preservation does and doesn't mean. We have also investigated its biblical grounding. Our study of Scriptures traditionally cited in support of preservation resulted in

---

[27] For a fuller explanation and argument to this effect, readers can consult the chapters in this book on Scripture's inerrancy and authority.

[28] I am indebted to Combs for the main ideas contained in this argument (presented in Combs, "Preservation of Scripture," 29–30). The particular wording, explanation, and defense of the argument are my own.

a mixed assessment. Some passages studied don't actually teach the concept, but several passages, when properly interpreted in their biblical contexts, do support the doctrine.

In addition, I presented two conceptual arguments which lend further support. The first moves from God's character, humanity's need, and Scripture's revelation and inspiration to the likelihood that God would preserve what the biblical authors wrote. The second argument appeals to Scripture's ongoing authority over what humans must know and do in order to live lives pleasing to God. From God's requirements and from his own statement (through Paul in 2 Tim. 3:16–17) of the roles he wants Scripture to play in helping humans meet those requirements, we can conclude that God will most likely preserve his word.

Readers will note that my case for preservation doesn't rest on the *fact* that Scripture has been preserved so that we have it today. The story of how that happened is both interesting and encouraging. Evangelicals versed in textual criticism can and have given its details. I haven't based support of the doctrine on such historical facts, because if that were its only basis, its continued existence into the present might be seen by nonbelievers (and perhaps even by some believers) as a set of happy and lucky coincidences that have kept this book in existence. Of course, if things happen by "luck," at some point luck can run out. So, if Scripture exists and has been preserved by chance and good fortune, that alone won't guarantee its future existence. In this chapter, I have argued that there are both biblical and theological grounds for believing that God will preserve his written word. Those arguments can and do assure believers that Scripture won't cease to exist.

Scripture is a treasure! Some treasures should be put on display and admired from a distance. We may hope other treasures won't be lost, but we realize that some may perish. Scripture is a treasure not merely to own, but to read and internalize, because it tells us how to establish and nurture a relationship with God. And, it nourishes the soul along life's journey. It is a sad and even dangerous thing to be hungry and have no access to food. We need food for our physical bodies, and we also need food for our souls! Because God has preserved and will continue to preserve his soul-nourishing word, we need never worry that our source of spiritual food will ever run out! And for that, everyone should be most grateful to God!

# CONCLUSION

# TWENTY

# LIGHT IN A DARK PLACE

## Does It Make a Difference?

Over many centuries, using various ways and many different human instruments, God gave his holy word to the human race. In the chapters of this book we have seen what Scripture, theology, and reason teach about Scripture. God so superintended the human writers of Scripture that they wrote exactly what he wanted. The result is a book that gives us God's authoritative, inerrant instructions and answers to life's most basic and important questions. It is a book that is sufficient to answer our spiritual needs and to point us in the direction of our creator and Savior. And, Scripture affirms its power to accomplish all of these things and more in the lives of those who obey it.

But all of this is in a sense theory. If the various bibliological doctrines I have presented in this book merely describe what people have thought Scripture to be and what Scripture itself claims to be, then Scripture may actually be of little practical value to people in real life. On the other hand, if the truths of God's word can be lived with the results Scripture promises to those who follow its teaching, then no right thinking person should ignore Scripture or relegate it to an inconsequential role in their thought and action. So, before we end this study of the doctrine of Scripture we should ask whether Scripture actually is and can be a light for both the light and dark places of our lives. Undoubtedly, God wanted Scripture to be light in everyone's life. For those who ignore or reject it, it can only ensure their ultimate judgment for failing to follow the light it sheds on our way. But for those who by God's grace and enablement live a life obedient to its teaching, does Scripture actually make a difference—other than keeping us from God's judgment—if we obey it?

Throughout the centuries that God's word has been available, many have followed its teachings, and have claimed that doing so has made a difference in their lives. It is hard to imagine, for example, what the lives of Christ's apostles, including Paul, would have been like without their knowing and obeying Scripture. And what about saints throughout church history? How can we possibly imagine what the lives of saints like Augustine, Anselm, Aquinas, Luther, Calvin, Jonathan Edwards, John and Charles Wesley, and so many others would have been without Scripture? Of course, these are all "heroes of the faith," and we would expect Scripture to matter in their lives in special ways. What about ordinary Christians living in the twenty-first century AD? Can Scripture be and is it a light in their lives?

I want to affirm most emphatically and unequivocally that Scripture not only can be but is a light in all the places of our lives! But I must do more than just say this. Without proof, my claim may be dismissed as a mere pious thought divorced from the reality of actual life events and circumstances. So what is my "evidence," my "proof," that Scripture is a light for every place in our lives? While I might offer some biblical, theological, and/or philosophical "evidence," that would only present more "theory" about what the Bible can do in our lives. What is needed is evidence from actual life that Scripture makes the difference it says it can. Of course, I am most familiar with my own life history, and so it is only natural to appeal to my own story. In fact, the most powerful "proof" for anyone that Scripture is all it claims to be is how Scripture has impacted their own life. I do not intend to rehearse my whole life history; that would be unnecessary to make the point. Instead, I want to focus on three things (some of them are major events in my personal history) that show the role Scripture has played in my life. I don't offer this as "proof" (theological or philosophical) of the various doctrines presented in this book, but rather as a personal testimony. If Scripture actually is what it says it is, life impacted by and lived in accord with Scripture should be different than it would have been without Scripture. That has certainly been my experience.

I begin with my childhood and upbringing. Both my father and mother, Charles and Anne Feinberg, were born and raised in very strict Orthodox Jewish homes. The Bible (the OT for them) was not merely revered, but their lives were governed daily by what Scripture requires. As a child, my father went to two schools every day, public school and Hebrew school. The result in part was that at a relatively young age he began to acquire what would become a truly phenomenal knowledge of Scripture. In fact, for some thirteen years in his early life he planned to become a rabbi, and his study of Scripture was at the heart of his training. During his university years at the University of Pittsburgh, he saw and was shocked at how little other Jews cared about following the demands of biblical law. The Lord used this and many other things eventually to bring him to embrace Christ as the Jewish Messiah and his own personal Savior.

My mother was born in Kovel, Ukraine, several years before the Bolshevik Revolution swept across Russia. As Jewish peasants, her family experienced significant persecution, and decided to leave Russia for the United States. Her father came to the States first, and eventually settled in Chicago. Some seven years later, in 1921, the rest of the family came to America, entering through Ellis Island. While living on the south side of Chicago, my mother came in contact with a missionary to the Jews. Eventually, my mother came to see that Jesus is Israel's Messiah, and she accepted him as her Lord and Savior.

A few years later, despite protests of her family about her new-found faith, my mother became a student at Moody Bible Institute. At that same time, my father was a student at Dallas Seminary, preparing for ministry. On one occasion he had a speaking engagement in Michigan. In those days the most reliable means of travel was by car, so my father and a friend drove from Dallas to Michigan. On the day before arriving in Michigan, they came to Chicago. Friends at Moody told them about a social event to be held for Moody students, and invited them to attend. It was there that my father and mother met. Shortly after that, they were engaged, and then married in 1935.

In 1946, I was born, the third and youngest child in my family. From my earliest years, my parents taught me Scripture, and emphasized that Scripture is God's word. The message delivered was loud and clear: on any issue or activity, what we are required to think and to do must follow biblical teaching. Anything that contradicts Scripture or doesn't fit with biblical teaching was forbidden. When my brother, sister, or I asked my parents if we could do one thing or another, the answer always depended on whether the proposed activity did or didn't violate biblical teaching. When Mom or Dad said no, we would often ask why. Often the answer was that the proposed activity just wasn't something Christians do, but my parents said more, especially if we asked, "Why?" Invariably, my parents would quote a Scripture and/or explain a biblical teaching that ruled out the proposed activity. On rare occasions, we would ask, "But why do we have to do what Scripture says?" They answered, "Because it is God's word." If we wondered why that was the determining factor, we were told that God is the supreme authority, and no one can debate or contest God and win. Whatever God commands must be done!

Though I didn't like being told that I couldn't do what I wanted to do, before long I learned that it makes no sense to contest God about right and wrong or anything else. Even worse than disobeying Mom and Dad was disobeying God. So, it made abundant sense to find out what God required and obey. To ensure that we would know what God expected, my parents did three things in particular. One was to explain why we could or couldn't do what we proposed to do by telling us what Scripture allowed in the matter. Second, my parents expected us to memorize Scripture. At that time, part of Sunday school for children involved memorizing various Scriptures. That underscored the importance of what my parents expected us to do, but even if Scripture memory wasn't required in Sunday school, Mom and Dad demanded it. I can't remember how many Scripture verses my parents made me memorize (at the time it seemed like an "infinite" number), but throughout my life that exercise of memorizing Scripture has served me very well.

There was a third thing my parents did that daily underscored the importance of Scripture in everything we do. No matter how busy anyone in the family was, all of us were expected to be together for breakfast. This was a time for a hearty meal, conversation about the events of the upcoming day, and something else. At some point during the meal, Mom would get her Bible and read a portion of it for that morning. We were expected to listen quietly and reverently, and we knew that no matter how busy we might be, we could not leave before this part of the meal ended. If we had questions about what was read, we might voice them, and Mom and Dad would be sure that, before the day ended, we received answers. After Mom read Scripture, Dad led the family in prayer, praying for each member of the family and about the events of the day. This had been their procedure every day of their marriage before I came along, and it was their practice for the rest of their lives.

Clearly, Scripture was the foundation of our home and of my upbringing. But what I have said so far is only part of the picture. My dad was a prominent biblical scholar and educator. In addition, he had a very active pulpit ministry, being much in demand. He was the founding dean of a theological seminary, and taught a full load of classes each day. In addition to his teaching and preaching ministries, Dad had an active writing ministry, and most weeks, he spent time in a recording studio taping various programs that were on the radio each week. I have never known anyone so busy as my father, and I am still amazed at how much he accomplished for the Lord in his lifetime!

Given what I have described, you may be wondering how my father ever completed anything. Discipline is the answer. I have never known anyone so disciplined as he. But you may also be thinking that, with all those responsibilities, there must have been little time for his own personal devotional life. And that brings me to what in many ways is the most amazing thing of all about my father. No matter what the responsibilities for the day or how busy he was, Dad always made time for reading his Bible, devotionally, not as part of any academic or scholarly endeavor. This was true regardless of whether he was in town or any other place all over the world.

While this in itself is quite impressive, it doesn't actually explain how unusual his practice was. For my father didn't read just a few verses or even a chapter or two each day. Rather, it was his habit each day to read ten *pages* in the OT and five *pages* in the NT. Dad had seen a Bible reading plan that showed that if one reads the aforementioned number of pages each day, one would read through the whole Bible four times every year! As a result of following this strategy, during his lifetime my father read through the whole Bible well over one hundred times.

Watching our father read his Bible daily left an indelible mark on my siblings and me. While none of us has copied his exact practice for Bible reading, the underlying message of what we witnessed escaped none of us. The busiest person we ever knew always made time for a significant amount of Bible reading each and every day of his life! With what I have described in these last few pages, I'm sure that you can see that it is hard to imagine how my parents could have communicated any more clearly and constantly that Scripture is the foundation of every aspect of life! As a result, throughout my life (and I'm sure this was true of my brother and is true for my sister), regardless of what I am asked to do or of what I am thinking of doing, one of my very first thoughts (if not my first) is to ask what Scripture would say about the matter before me. It is a "habit" that was ingrained in me from the very beginning of my life, and it is an excellent one!

What I have described above tells you much about my family and my upbringing. But, still, the question remains whether Scripture and my knowledge of it made any difference at key times of crisis in my life. In answer I want to turn to two moments of crisis where Scripture played a crucial role in my life. The first centers around my college years. Though I had grown up going to a Christian church and had been in church regularly for all of my life, as is the case with others raised in a Christian home, my faith in Christ and Christianity was not often challenged. As the son of a minister, there were certain expectations about my thinking and behavior from other believers. Expectations were even higher, given the prominence of my dad as a theological educator and minister. My parents had early in my life emphasized that how my siblings and I acted would make a difference in my dad's ministry. These were the days when evangelicals expected children of full-time Christian ministers to be "perfect," and if they weren't, that was often taken as a sign that their parents hadn't done as good a job in raising them in "the nurture and admonition of the Lord" as they should have. What the children thought and did, if not consistent with biblical teaching, could be harmful to their parents' ministry.

So, it was very clear that my siblings and I had a specific role to play in our family, related to my dad's ministry, even though we weren't personally involved in ministry at the time. And I played that expected role for many years. Toward the end of high school and during the first few years of college, I became increasingly uncomfortable with "playing the expected role." I had no doubts about my salvation, but I also knew I wasn't experiencing much of the joy, victory over various sins and temptations, and growth in my relation to the Lord that Scripture and other believers said should happen in a Christian's life. At the root of my spiritual problems was the matter of who would control my life, me or the Lord. I knew what was supposed to happen, and so time and again, I would make a commitment to let the Lord rule in my life. But repeatedly, I failed to keep that commitment, and fell into guilt and frustration. This struggle went on for many years. Outwardly, I spoke and acted as other Christians expected, but inwardly there was a war raging over who would control my life. It wasn't long before I became extremely uncomfortable with playing the role of a dutiful Christian, and that only made my spiritual problems more intense.

If that wasn't bad enough, something further was troubling me. Very early in life I sensed God calling me into full-time ministry, and so that had always been my plan. But as the years passed and I was getting closer to the time when I would graduate from college and enroll in seminary, I just couldn't see how that could happen. I hadn't abandoned my beliefs, and I still believed that God had called me to serve him. I just couldn't see how someone in my spiritual condition would have anything of value to say either from the pulpit or a lectern, and I knew that I could never get away with "faking" a vibrant, growing relationship with the Lord. How could I counsel others about growing in the Lord and properly relating to him, when that wasn't happening in my own life? As this war about who would control my life dragged on, I seriously considered that perhaps I would have to abandon the idea of ministry and pursue a career of teaching English and English literature (my undergraduate major). I didn't find that option tremendously exciting, but in my then current spiritual state, little seemed attractive as I contemplated the future.

While some might think all of this happened because I attended a secular university and "lost my faith," as many Christian young people do, that wasn't what was happening. Though I was at a secular university, I was a member of a Christian fraternity. The fraternity wasn't just Christian in name only; one could not be a member if he wasn't a born again Christian! During the years I lived in the fraternity, I saw other members, also raised in Christian homes, going through a time of spiritual struggle. In fact, I saw some of them stop going to church and stop professing a commitment to Christ. It appeared that they had left the faith, and to this day, I don't know whether many of these men returned to walk with the Lord. It is understandable that in these circumstances, a young person might turn away from the Lord. And, the courses we were taking at school weren't helping. Every class was taught from either an agnostic or an atheistic stance. While I didn't have any classes where the professor went out of his or her way to attack Christianity, it was clear that many things being taught, if true, didn't fit the Christian worldview.

In that setting, the situation was "ripe" for a Christian young man or woman to reject Christianity as false (at worst) or ineffectual and irrelevant (at best). Some of my Christian friends did just that. From what I've said about my spiritual struggles, it would be easy for readers to conclude that I became one of those "casualties," but I didn't. Why? Because of my knowledge of Scripture and my belief in its truthfulness. Let me explain.

As I was growing up, I was privileged to hear my dad preach many times. It seemed that he had messages on just about every biblical book and topic. A special interest and area of expertise for my father was biblical prophecy. I heard him preach on many prophecies about the first advent and the second advent of Christ. I can remember that the first few times I heard him preach on prophecy, I was amazed, but a bit skeptical. I thought that the prophecies expounded could probably be passed off as "lucky guesses." After all, anyone with a good knowledge of the present and a general knowledge of human nature and of conditions in the society of his day could probably guess what might happen a few months or even a few years down the road.

But the prophetic passages my father explained made predictions of things that would happen hundreds of years after the prophecy was given. And this was so not just for a few prophecies, but for each new prophecy we studied. What especially amazed me was how detailed some of the predictions are (especially in books like Daniel, for example) and that those prophecies were fulfilled not just in general but in every detail of the prophecy! It didn't seem to matter which biblical book the prophecy came from; the prophecy was detailed and it had, in many cases, come true in toto, despite the fact that the prophet had predicted something far in the future from his own day.

As I heard my father present these messages, I was thrilled, but also a little bit shocked. Though I had lived only a short while, I had never met or heard of any mere human who could predict the future in such detail and accuracy. I remember coming to the conclusion very early in life that any book that could predict so many future events so accurately and with so much detail is no ordinary book. This could only have happened if Scripture truly is the word of God. That meant also that Christianity, which is built upon the foundation of Scripture, must have something very special going for it. It must be true, and whatever it teaches must be taken very seriously!

Because of my grounding in the word of God, especially my knowledge of biblical prophecy, limited though it was, when I experienced spiritual problems during my college years, I knew that the problem wasn't with Christianity. The problem was me and my relation to the Lord. Other young Christian friends turned away from God, but that never seemed to be an acceptable option for me. How could a book that predicts accurately so many events so far in advance be just another religious book? Because of what I had been taught about Scripture and its contents, I had adopted a very specific posture as I went through my college days. I had heard so many Christians at my church speak about young people going to college and losing their faith, and I was determined that wouldn't happen to me. I knew I would have many nonbelievers for professors, and some of them might even make a point of "bashing" Scripture and Christianity. To defend against the attacks I would undoubtedly hear, I thought it wisest to adopt the following posture toward whatever I heard in the classroom: I should be skeptical about everything my professors said, and I should ask about whatever they taught, "Does it square with Scripture?" If not, I would reject it as false. I could learn it and repeat it on a test, but that didn't mean I had to believe it! If my professors' lectures either affirmed Scripture or were neutral to it, then, given the credibility of their support for their views, I would believe it.

I mention this strategy for my undergrad studies, because I'm sure you can see that it mirrors exactly the attitude expressed toward Scripture in my home as I was growing up. My parents' desire that their children would see that everything has to be judged in the light of Scripture, because Scripture is God's word and God can't be wrong about anything, was fulfilled in my case. Because of those beliefs, during my university years I wasn't really challenged on intellectual grounds to desert the faith. Despite my spiritual struggles, I always thought Christianity and the Bible are true and make sense.

And yet, despite these beliefs about Scripture, I still struggled with my faith in the ways already described. I can say without any hesitation, however, that it was the light of God's word, especially my belief that any book and religion that could predict the distant future with such detail and accuracy must be true, that kept me from abandoning my faith. Rather than seeing Christianity as the problem, I clearly saw that I was the problem. The struggle wasn't about the Bible's truth or authority; it was about whether I would yield my will to God's control in my life.

So, I can say without a doubt that during my spiritual struggles in my university years, Scripture proved very much to be a light in the midst of the darkness of the issues with which I was wrestling. But, I should tell you how this episode ended, for Scripture was instrumental in helping me to overcome the spiritual problems I was undergoing.

The "war" for control of my life went on for most of my undergraduate years. I knew I needed to commit my will to God's leading, but I had made many commitments before and had failed to keep every one of them. Finally, I decided to talk with my father about what was going on. I figured that if any person would know the answer, he would. But I was somewhat hesitant to do so. As far as I knew, none of my siblings nor I had ever had problems with our faith before, and I wasn't sure how Dad would react when he heard what I had to say.

When I finally talked with my dad, I didn't hear one word of condemnation or rebuke in response. Instead, he said that he and my mom had sensed that something was wrong, but they didn't want to say anything unless I brought it up. In the meantime, they had just prayed for me that whatever the problem was, it would be resolved before long. I told my dad about my desire to make a genuine commitment to let God be Lord of my life, but my fear that I couldn't keep the commitment made it hard to yield. I was tired of playing the role of a committed Christian but not actually being one.

I don't remember everything my dad said, but what he said was very helpful. As the conversation ended, Dad made a suggestion. He said that since I had concerns about not experiencing the joy of being saved, I might find it helpful to read the book of Philippians, since it emphasizes joy and rejoicing as a Christian.

Encouraged by my conversation with my dad, I decided to do what he suggested. I am sure he knew what I would soon find, but I don't think either of us could have predicted my reaction. I know I couldn't have. Philippians 1 begins with Paul's expression of thankfulness and commendation for the Christian walk and testimony of the believers in the Philippian church. Philippians 1:6 hit me like an avalanche. Paul wrote about the believers at Philippi,

> being confident of this, that he who began a good work in you will carry it on to completion until the day of Christ Jesus. (NIV 1984)

Here was the answer to my struggles. I was tired of playing a role, and I wanted a genuinely committed walk with the Lord. But I didn't see how I could make a commitment to yield to the Lord's control of my life and keep that commitment. The good news of Philippians 1:6 is that I don't have to do this alone. God is just as concerned about me keeping my commitment to him as I am. Even more, he will be at work within me to enable me to live the life he wants me to live. Will my life be one of unbroken spiritual advance? Not likely, but the ultimate goal will be achieved. That is so because the one who began the work in me, i.e., God, will so work in me as to bring the work to successful conclusion at the day of Christ. This doesn't mean I can live as I please, because

God will fix up whatever mess I make. No, I need to obey his word, but I can be sure that God will always be there to help me do so and to be and do whatever he calls me to do in my life. On the basis of that ray of light from Scripture, I yielded my life fully to the Lord, and the struggle for control over my life that had gone on so long ended. I don't know how this would have ended without the light of God's word. I went to a major secular university, took many of the courses that are notorious for destroying the faith of young Christians, and graduated with my faith intact and my life ready to enter seminary to prepare for ministry. Does Scripture's light matter in the dark moments of our lives? Indeed, it does!

There is another moment of darkness in my life when Scripture proved to be of critical importance. It has to do with my wife, Patricia, and our family, and it is something that I must deal with for the rest of my life. Throughout my life, for a variety of reasons, I have always been fascinated by the problem of evil, the issue of how an all-loving and all-powerful God could allow evil to happen in the lives of his human creatures, especially those whose basic pattern of life is to obey Scripture and follow him. During my educational journey, I thought about this problem on many occasions. I even wrote my doctoral dissertation at the University of Chicago on the problem of evil. If anyone was prepared to deal with genuine tragedy, you would think that I would be that person.

During my student days I met and later married my wife, Patricia. I had been told that her mother had been institutionalized some five years before my wife and I met, and I was told that it was because of mental problems. As Pat and I became serious about marriage, we consulted some psychologists about whether she could in some way "inherit" her mother's problems. We were assured that if there were to be any problems, they already would have been evident. Since she was a normal and healthy person, we were told that there was nothing to worry about.

Given that assurance, you can imagine how shocked we were when on November 4, 1987, some fifteen years after we married, my wife was diagnosed with Huntington's Disease, the disease her mother had. Huntington's Disease causes the premature deterioration of part of the brain; brain cells just drop out. The result is a variety of physical, mental, and psychological problems. Currently, there is no known cure, though researchers continue to search for answers. Over time the disease takes its toll, eventually taking the life of the person who has it. As devastating as this news is, the situation is even worse. Huntington's is a genetically controlled disease, governed by a dominant gene. That means that if one parent has the disease, there is a 50 percent chance that each child will get the disease. My wife's mother had the disease, but her father didn't. Still, she got the disease. At the time my wife was diagnosed, we already had children, three sons.

I can well remember how, after receiving this news, our situation seemed so helpless and hopeless. All of the study and reflection about God and evil offered me little comfort. Of course, I knew that bad things sometimes happen to good people, but even so, this was a tragedy that far exceeded my worst fears. I remember thinking that I am a teacher of theology, and yet I was not sure I could continue to teach. With what had happened, I wasn't certain that I actually knew anything about God and his providential dealings in our world.

Over the ensuing months and years God has brought into my life many people who care about us, and he has brought to my attention various biblical truths which, even if they have not removed all the pain, anguish, and uncertainty about the future, have made it possible for me to care for my wife and continue to minister. Elsewhere I have written at some length about our experiences and what the Lord has taught me through them. I would encourage readers to read that material, and I hope that if you are suffering or ministering to the afflicted, you will find what I have written helpful![1] Most of the things that have been helpful to me are scriptural truths.

Over the years of dealing with this disease, I have repeatedly found comfort and encouragement in the pages of Scripture. As you can imagine, the book of Job is significant, but so are other Scriptures. Of special help is 1 Peter, written to suffering saints. His theme is not just that the righteous will suffer. It is suffering and glory—that is, though in this life those who take a stand for Christ can expect persecution and affliction, there will someday be great glory and blessing! But even more than this promise of future blessing, for our present experience and for the rest of our lives, it is encouraging to know that God is fully aware of what is happening to me and my family *and he cares* (1 Pet. 5:7). God's care and concern are not just theories. I have repeated evidences in my family's lives that he does care. Though some might be dubious about that, my reply is that in a fallen world it is amazing that anything ever goes right! Despite how bad our situation is, I can always think of ways it could be much worse! The fact that it isn't is evidence of God's grace, care, and concern! How do I know this to be so? The Bible teaches me about God's grace and concern. It also tells me that God will never leave nor forsake his children (Heb. 13:5–6; see also Deut. 31:6). And he won't give us burdens that he knows we can't bear!

Though I could recount other times in my life when Scripture has been light—sometimes the only light available—I think the message is clear. For me

---

[1] For those suffering with tragedy and those ministering to them, see my *When There Are No Easy Answers: Thinking Differently about God, Evil, and Suffering* (Grand Rapids, MI: Kregel, 2016). For those interested in a thorough treatment of the academic and intellectual problems of evil, see my *The Many Faces of Evil: Theological Systems and the Problems of Evil* (Wheaton, IL: Crossway, 2004).

the doctrine of Scripture is not just an academic interest and a subject to teach students. It has been and continues to be an ever-present, unrelenting source of light and life along the path of my life. I am confident that many readers could testify to the same in their lives. Scripture is all the things I have described it to be in the preceding chapters of this book, and yes, that matters immensely!

A story is told about Karl Barth, one of the preeminent theologians of the twentieth century. On one occasion, someone asked him if he could summarize his whole life's work in theology in a sentence. Barth replied, "Yes, I can. In the words of a song I learned at my mother's knee:

> 'Jesus loves me, this I know,
> For the Bible tells me so'."[2]

I think Barth got it right! These lines from a song that many of us learned as children are an apt way to conclude this volume on Scripture! After all, what could be more important to our well-being both now and forever than the assurance that Jesus loves us, not just collectively, but each of us individually! But don't miss the key point. We don't just hope, wish, and believe that this is true. We *know* it! How? *Because the Bible tells us so!* Scripture teaches it, and that settles it! Scripture is light for all of the places of our life—the dark ones, the light ones, and everything in between. It is that because it points us to and instructs us about God and his love. And nothing could be more important than that, for there is no one like him! The Bible tells us so!

---

[2] Taken from "Did Karl Barth Really Say 'Jesus Loves Me, This I Know . . . ?'" This information was found at the following website: http://www.patheos.com/blogs/rogereolson/2013/01/did-karl-barth-really-say-jesus-loves-me-this-i-know/. Accessed on June 24, 2016.

*the*

# FOUNDATIONS
# OF EVANGELICAL
# THEOLOGY

*series*

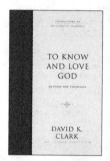

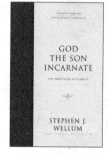
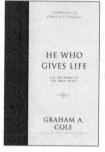
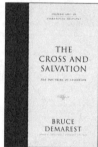
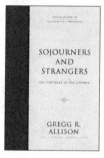

## EDITED BY JOHN S. FEINBERG

The Foundations of Evangelical Theology series incorporates the best exegetical research, historical theology, and philosophy to produce an up-to-date systematic theology with contemporary application—ideal for both students and teachers of theology.

Visit crossway.org for more information.